This is a standard work of reference for the study of the religious history of western Christianity in the later Middle Ages which, since its original publication in French in 1981, has come to be regarded as one of the greatest of recent contributions to medieval studies.

Hagiographical texts and reports of the processes of canonization – a mode of investigation into saints' lives and their miracles implemented by the popes from the end of the twelfth century – are here used for the first time as major source materials. The book illuminates the main features of the medieval religious mind, and highlights the popes' attempts to gain firmer control over the wide variety of expressions of faith towards the saints in order to promote a higher pattern of devotion and moral behaviour among Christians. The importance of this papal programme is emphasized, as is its partial failure – owing to the opposition of a section of the clergy and laity which remained attached firmly to traditional models of Christian sainthood, embodied by martyrs, pilgrims, hermits and other healer saints. The book also refers throughout to the iconography of the period, and contains many images which illustrate the growing importance of saints in western art at the end of the Middle Ages.

SAINTHOOD IN THE LATER MIDDLE AGES

SAINTHOOD
IN THE
LATER
MIDDLE AGES

ANDRÉ VAUCHEZ

TRANSLATED BY JEAN BIRRELL

CAMBRIDGE
UNIVERSITY PRESS

Published by the Press Syndicate of the University of Cambridge
The Pitt Building, Trumpington Street, Cambridge CB2 1RP
40 West 20th Street, New York, NY 10011-4211, USA
10 Stamford Road, Oakleigh, Melbourne 3166, Australia

Originally published in French as *La sainteté en Occident aux derniers siècles du Moyen Age*
by Ecole française de Rome 1988
and © Ecole française de Rome 1988
First published in English by Cambridge University Press 1997 as *Sainthood in the later
Middle Ages*
English translation © Cambridge University Press 1997

Printed in Great Britain at the University Press, Cambridge

Library of Congress cataloguing in publication data
Vauchez, André.
[Sainteté en Occident aux derniers siècles du Moyen Age.] English translation:
Sainthood in the later Middle Ages/André Vauchez: translated by
Jean Birrell.
p. cm.
Includes bibliographical references and index.
ISBN 0 521 44559 0
1. Canonization. 2. Christian saints – Cult – Europe. 3. Europe –
Religious life and customs. I. Title.
BX2330.V3813 1996
235′.2′0902–dc20 96-6461 CIP
ISBN 0521 44559 0 hardback

CONTENTS

⌘⌘⌘

PLATES

തരംഗം

MAPS

⋘⋙

TABLES

രാരാരാ

FOREWORD BY RICHARD KIECKHEFER

cↄcↄcↄ

The reputation of this book in the English-speaking scholarly world precedes its arrival in this English translation. Indeed, it was being discussed widely even before its original publication in French in 1981. Having myself first perused the typescript in the library of the Sorbonne, I was eager to meet its author when I revisited Europe in the early 1980s. Complications nearly prevented the meeting, but a few days before my departure for home I received a letter from him that had been forwarded from one spot to another along my itinerary before finally catching up with me; from it I learned that he could be found at a vacation chalet in the Swiss Alps. A succession of trains, each smaller than the last, took me to the mountainside where he and I strolled through an Alpine forest as we discussed medieval saints. He told me of having been discouraged at first from studying this subject because it was deemed insufficiently serious. Its recognition in recent years as an important topic of inquiry is in no small part his doing, even if František Graus and others preceded him with similarly magisterial studies of medieval sainthood. Rarely has research on saints and their cults attained Vauchez's combination of breadth and depth, his grasp of both the forest and the trees, his mastery of particulars and his confidence in showing their place in the landscape. The setting for my first encounter with him, then, has always struck me as symbolically fitting.

From his other books, two of which are already available in English, Vauchez's interest in the history of the laity is well known. The present book also deals with this theme, and indeed has as its central explicit focus the relationship between curial and lay perceptions of sainthood. While his analysis of this connection does not reduce to any simple formula, the very complexity of the argument is worth highlighting. On the one hand he shows that in the century and a half after 1260 the popular veneration of saints, especially of local heroes and victims of unjust killing, increasingly came into conflict with curial reluctance to approve large numbers of cults. Vauchez knows fully the difficulty of interpreting the records of canonization, yet he finds in them evidence not only of clerical stereotyping but also of tension between the witnesses and the interrogators, and of lay resistance to the grid some clerics sought to impose. Canonization of saints could thus be a site of cultural confrontation, and this is one main concern of the book. But Vauchez goes beyond this level to find respects in which lay and clerical mentality converged. If opinions divided on the identification of specific saints, there was broad consensus which, in the fourteenth century, increasingly perceived even the living and recently deceased saint as a heroic and legendary figure, cast in the mould of the Golden Legend. Underlying the political and cultural divisions in late medieval Christendom were elements of a common mentality.

On a still more fundamental level, Vauchez's book serves as a model for the role of generalization in history, a matter that has become something of a historiographic battleground in the years since 1981. Aviad M. Kleinberg's *Prophets in their own country: living saints and the making of sainthood in the later Middle Ages* (University of Chicago Press, 1992) represents an approach to the study of late medieval saints fundamentally different from that of Vauchez. Kleinberg's book, itself a highly accomplished exercise in microanalysis, shows how social and cultural factors determined which individuals became recognized as saints, but Kleinberg deliberately eschews generalization. From his perspective, a more classical analysis such as Vauchez's reduces the individual saints to the types that they exemplify. The risk of such reduction is indeed a hazard in any generalization, but the conceptual categories established within the historical culture are themselves central matter for historical examination, and this is the main concern of a historian such as Vauchez. The point is not so much to create an interpretive grid that can make sense of the individual saints, but to discern the grids created, diffused, adapted and contested within the complex society of the late Middle Ages. This book is richly informative precisely in its nuanced articulation of those types of saint and saint-manqué – the voluntary poor, the visionaries and ecstatic prophetesses, the 'false martyrs' – that would have governed much late medieval thinking about the sorts of people likely to be recognized as saints. Kleinberg's close attention to local specificities may help explain why a spark does or does not catch fire. Vauchez's greater interest is in whether the fire then spreads, and to answer that question we must know something about the interplay of specific cases and general processes.

To state the point differently, the particular cases Vauchez studies are scarcely mere illustrations of a general argument, nor are his analyses simply abstractions from the data; rather, the analysis seeks to bring to life the tension between the multiple interpretive categories available in the late Middle Ages and the individuals who, while irreducibly unique, were nonetheless seen as playing roles in the drama of late medieval culture that were largely predefined. Neither Catherine of Siena nor Joan of Arc can be reduced to the roles they were made to play, but Catherine would never have been canonized were it not for the interest of Dominican reformers in promoting a saint with her profile, and both the allies and the judges of Joan did their best to fit her into categories that struck them as apt. The success of this book at unfolding this complex relationship is a main reason why it was arousing such excitement among those who knew it or knew of it, even before it was in print. The relevance of Vauchez's work to this central historiographic issue should itself be a strong inducement to careful reading of his tome.

PREFACE TO THE ENGLISH EDITION

ℛℛℛ

It makes me very happy that this book, which has had so far three editions in French and one in Italian, will now become available to a new public through its translation into English. My heartfelt thanks go to those who have worked for its publication: to the Cambridge University Press, and specifically to Mr William Davies, to Miss Jean Birrell, a translator always as precise in her translating as she is accurate and – last but not least – to my colleague and dear friend Richard Kieckhefer who has gone out of his way to help complete a project he was the first to initiate. I am also grateful to the *Direction du Livre* of the French *Ministère de la Culture* which, by subsidizing this translation into English has brought about its realization.

Another cause for satisfaction is the fact that the book has, from the beginning, met with special success in English-speaking countries. One of the first significant reviews ever published came out in the *Journal of Ecclesiastical History*, under the signature of Peter Linehan, and others, just as laudatory on the whole, followed in a number of scientific periodicals in the US. While at Oxford (All Souls, 1986) and Princeton (Institute for Advanced Study, 1991) I had the opportunity to find out how widely known the book was in academic circles. Several highly qualified specialists have assured me that it has – together with others dealing with the same topics, which came out later – contributed to a large extent to the impressive development in English-speaking countries of the study of medieval hagiography and sainthood.

As this book has now reached the status of a classic, I have not felt that it needed a revision either in its contents or in its bibliography finishing with 1987. As a matter of fact I could not possibly include in my own text the new scholarship deriving from works published since then, as the field is now teeming with them, and as this would have compelled me to rewrite the whole book, a task I was in no position to launch into. To be sure, recent studies may have in places called in question the accuracy of my own analysis or conclusions. Far from deploring it, I find in this confirmation of my work, whose aim was not to achieve a complete and final synthesis of the history of medieval sainthood, but rather to explore the field by means of a then original "problématique" as well as sources till then rather neglected by historians. As a result, the text of the English version is that of the 1988 French version including corrections of the few minor errors I had previously overlooked.

André VAUCHEZ

PUBLISHER'S NOTE: this translation could not have been undertaken without the generous and much appreciated financial assistance of the Ministère français de la culture et de la communication.

ABBREVIATIONS

cococo

AA.SS.	*Acta sanctorum quotquot toto orbe coluntur*, published by the Bollandists, 3rd edition, *Ianuarii 1–Novembris 1*, Paris, 1863–87
AFH	*Archivum Franciscanum historicum*
AFP	*Archivum Fratrum Praedicatorum*
ALMA	*Archivum Latinitatis Medii Aevi (Bulletin du Cange)*
Anal. Boll.	*Analecta Bollandiana*
Ann. Cist.	*Cisterciensium seu verius ecclesiasticorum annalium a condito Cistercio tomi III*, 4 vols., Lyons, 1642–9
Ann. eccl.	*Annales ecclesiastici ab anno MCXCVIII, ubi desinit Baronius, auctore Odorico Raynaldo*, 15 vols., Lucca, 1747–56
ASV	Archivio Segreto Vaticano
Auvray	*Les registres de Grégoire IX (1227–1241)*, ed. L. Auvray, Paris, 1890–1955 (= *BEFAR*, 2nd ser., 9)
BECh.	*Bibliothèque de l'Ecole des chartes*
BEFAR	*Bibliothèque des Ecoles françaises d'Athènes et de Rome*
Berger	*Les registres d'Innocent IV (1243–1254)*, ed. E. Berger, Paris, 1884–1921 (= *BEFAR*, 2nd ser., 1)
BHL	*Bibliotheca hagiographica latina antiquae et mediae aetatis*, 2 vols., Brussels, 1898–1901, and supplementary vol., Brussels, 1987
BISIME	*Bullettino dell'Istituto storico italiano per il medio evo e Archivio Muratoriano*
BL	British Library
BN	Bibliothèque Nationale (de Paris)
BS	*Bibliotheca sanctorum*, under the direction of F. Caraffa, 12 vols., Rome, 1961–9

Bull. Franc.	*Bullarium Franciscanum*, ed. J. Sbaraglia and C. Eubel, 7 vols., Rome, 1759–1904
Bull. OP	*Bullarium ordinis FF. Praedicatorum*, ed. T. Ripolli, 8 vols., Rome, 1729–40
CRAI	*Académie des inscriptions et belles-lettres, Comptes-rendus des séances*
DTC	*Dictionnaire de théologie catholique*, ed. A. Vacant and E. Mangenot, 15 vols., Paris, 1900–72
Kaftal 1	Kaftal, G., *Iconography of the saints in Tuscan painting*, Florence, 1952
Kaftal 2	Kaftal, G., *Iconography of the saints in central and southern Italian schools of painting*, Florence, 1965
Kaftal 3	Kaftal, G., *Iconography of the saints in the painting of north east Italy*, Florence, 1978
LThK	*Lexicon für Theologie und Kirche*, ed. J. Höfer and K. Rahner, 10 vols., Freiburg im Breisgau, 1957–67
Mansi	Mansi, J. D., *Sacrorum conciliorum nova et amplissima collectio*, 53 vols., Paris, 1901–27
MEFR	*Mélanges de l'Ecole française de Rome*
MGH	*Monumenta Germaniae historica*
AA	–*Auctores antiquissimi*
Ep.	–*Epistolae*
SRG	–*Scriptores rerum Germanicarum*
SRM	–*Scriptores rerum Merovingicarum*
SS	–*Scriptores* in folio
MIOG	*Mittellungen des Instituts für Oesterreichische Geschichtsforschung*
MOPH	*Monumenta ordinis Praedicatorum historica*, ed. B. M. Reichert *et al.*, 25 vols., Rome and Paris, 1896–1966
OCarm	Order of Carmelites
OCist	Order of Cistercians
OFM	Order of Friars Minor
OHSA	Order of Hermits of St Augustine
OP	Order of Friars Preacher
OSB	Order of St Benedict
OSM	Order of Servites of Mary
PC	*Process of canonization*
PL	*Patrologia Latina*, ed. J. P. Migne, 217 vols., Paris, 1844–64

Potthast	Potthast, A., *Regesta Pontificum Romanorum inde ab anno 1198 ad annum 1304*, 2 vols., Berlin, 1873–5
Pressutti	*Regesta Honorii papae III*, ed. P. Pressutti, 2 vols., Rome, 1888–95
QFIAB	*Quellen und Forschungen aus italienischen Archiven und Bibliotheken*
RHE	*Revue d'histoire ecclésiastique*
RHEF	*Revue d'histoire de l'Eglise de France*
RIS²	*Rerum Italicarum scriptores*, new edn, Città di Castello and Bologna, 1900–
RSCI	*Rivista di storia della Chiesa in Italia*

INTRODUCTION

෴෴෴

In 1929, reviewing the Bollandist H. Delehaye's famous *Sanctus: essai sur le culte des saints dans l'Antiquité*, Marc Bloch wrote: 'Essentially, this is a contribution to that history of sanctity within the Church which, if ever it finds an author brave enough to attempt it, and sufficient of a scholar and psychologist to complete it, will be a book almost without equal in the insights it will offer into the human mind.'[1] The hope expressed so many years ago by the founder of *Annales* has not materialized in the form he expected, which is perhaps hardly surprising. Which historian could be acquainted with the thousands of Saints' Lives written between the fourth and the fifteenth centuries, or master the massive documentation contained in the sixty-seven volumes of the *Acta sanctorum*, not to speak of those unpublished? But the call put out by the author of *Les rois thaumaturges*, himself, in his time, an editor of hagiographical texts, did not go unheard; the pioneering works of R. Folz on the liturgical cult of Charlemagne and, more recently, of F. Graus, K. Bosl, F. Prinz and J.-C. Poulain on the saints of the Merovingian and Carolingian periods have made it possible to bring within the 'territory of the historian' the *terra incognita* which the history of sanctity has long represented, by revealing the relations between the ideal models offered by the clergy, contemporary mentalities, and social and political structures.

These works all, however, concern the early Middle Ages; none deals with the period between 1200 and 1500, which marked the apogee of the diffusion and popularity of the cult of the saints in the West. To have extended them on the same basis into the last three centuries of the Middle Ages would hardly have been practicable for one historian; for this period, the number of liturgical offices and hagiographical texts is huge, and their

---

[1] M. Bloch, *Revue de synthèse*, 47 (1929), p. 89.

analysis could only be undertaken by a team, something specialists still hope for.[2] I have, accordingly, preferred a different approach, in the hope of making, in my turn, a modest contribution to that history of value systems which has, for some years now, been attracting increasing interest. Without neglecting the Saints' Lives, which are a source of much valuable information, I have chosen to rely primarily on another type of source: the processes of canonization held between 1185 and 1431 on the orders, or with the consent, of the papacy.[3] These documents have long enjoyed a bad press. The Bollandists themselves, when acquainted with them, saw them as little more than a jumble of stereotyped declarations. As a result, they were content to reproduce extracts in fragmentary form, anxious not to exhaust the patience of their readers.[4] Since the nineteenth century, scholars have gone some way to fill this gap by publishing a number of processes in full; but many, and not the least important, remain unpublished. In all, some four hundred survive for the period under consideration. They are very uneven in importance; some enquiries from the early thirteenth century take up only a few pages; those held after 1260 all involved scores, even hundreds, of witnesses, whose depositions fill large volumes.

If medieval canonization processes have been neglected, it is because they had so little to offer to positivist history, since most of the facts that could be gleaned from them were already known from other sources. Research carried out from this perspective has little, in general, to add to what is already known about saints from their legends.[5] In fact, the depositions of the witnesses tell us less about the lives of the servants of God

---

[2] See, in particular, J. Leclercq's review of B. de Gaiffier, *Etudes critiques d'hagiographie et d'iconologie* (Brussels, 1967) in *Studi Medievali*, n.s., 9 (1968), p. 240: 'Who, in this "second twentieth century", will create the laboratory of historical psychology for which three hundred and fifty years of the Bollandists' scholarship have prepared the raw material?'

[3] For a detailed list, see below, pp. 540–8.

[4] The extreme case is the canonization process of Peter of Luxembourg (d. 1387); the text was literally pulled to pieces and put back together in a new order before it was published (*AA.SS.* Iul. I, pp. 446–90). Some others were hardly better treated, at least in the pre-nineteenth-century volumes.

[5] On the other hand, some canonization processes can be of exceptional interest for social and political history, since they make it possible to observe a very specific group: people who had been connected with the saints while they were alive and tried to gain approval for their cult. See the remarkable study by Arnold Esch of the witnesses who appeared before the enquiries made in Rome between 1440 and 1453 into the sanctity of St Francesca Romana (d. 1440) ('Die Zeugenaussagen im Heiligsprechungsverfahren für S. Francesca Romana als Quelle zur Sozialgeschichte Roms im frühen Quattrocento', *QFIAB*, 53 (1973), pp. 93–151.

than about how their contemporaries remembered them, that is, in the last analysis, about their conception of sanctity. This is precisely what makes them precious to the historians of today, more alive to the importance of mental representations and ideologies. The interest shown in canonization processes is part of a wider movement which has, for some years now, appreciated a type of source long neglected, or seen only as a source of factual information, that is, inquisitions. Whether their aim was fiscal or political, or whether they concerned the assertion of certain rights on the part of the temporal power or the repression of deviant beliefs, one always finds there – if one asks the right questions – something more than the raw facts they contain: they provide, at first hand, both concrete and suggestive information about conceptions of time and space, forms and expansion of the individual and collective memory, and the 'consciousness of self' of the group to which the individuals interrogated belonged.[6] For proof, I need simply mention – to quote only the most recent works which are closest to my subject – the use made of records of the Inquisition by E. Le Roy Ladurie in France, and E. Dupré Theseider and G. G. Merlo in Italy. Whilst their studies have certainly enriched our knowledge of dissident religious beliefs, they have above all made it possible to observe, in their concrete reality, the ways of life and thought of the inhabitants of the valleys of Ariège or Piedmont and the artisans of Bologna.[7] Canonization processes are simply a specific application in the case of the saints of the procedure of *inquisitio* as we see it develop in every sphere during the course of the thirteenth century.

The increasing popularity of this type of document derives also from the fact that they describe a confrontation, sometimes peaceful, sometimes conflictual, between the culture of the dominant strata, to which those who ordered and those who carried out the enquiry belonged, and that of the subordinate classes, which provided many of the witnesses. Such encounters were infrequent in medieval society, so that evidence concerning them is all the more valuable. Through canonization processes, we are able to see what individuals who belonged to very diverse social and cultural milieux thought about a person they had known or heard talked

---

[6] See, for example, B. Guenée, 'L'Enquête historique ordonnée par Edouard Ier, roi d'Angleterre en 1291', *CRAI* (1975), pp. 572–84.

[7] E. Le Roy Ladurie, *Montaillou, village occitan de 1294 à 1324* (Paris, 1975), trans. Barbara Bray as *Montaillou: Cathars and Catholics in a French village, 1294–1324* (London, 1978); E. Dupré Theseider, 'L'eresia a Bologna nei tempi di Dante', in *Studi storici in onore di G. Volpe*, I (Florence, 1957), pp. 381–444; G. Merlo, *Eretici e inquisitori nella società piemontese del Trecento* (Turin, 1977).

about, and what idea they had formed of Christian perfection or human success.

However, the value of the depositions recorded during the processes has been questioned, by emphasizing their lack of spontaneity: the witnesses, chosen for the most part by the promoters of the cause, could not express themselves freely; their declarations were oriented and channelled by a questionnaire drawn up in advance by the promoters or, exceptionally, by those conducting the enquiry, that is, in all cases, by the clergy.[8] The *articuli interrogatorii*, whose principal function was to make a person venerated locally fit a model of sanctity approved by the church, came between the memory left by the saint and those who evoked it.[9] From this perspective, all that the commissioners appointed by the papacy sought from the witnesses was 'that they confirm from their historical memory a legend in the process of formation'.[10] Even if we accept that this is the case, the processes of canonization remain of great interest, since they allow us to see in operation the transformation of the life of a man or woman into the Life of a saint. Indeed, it is fascinating to trace in detail the attempts of the authors of the schema on which the interrogation was based to tone down some features of their subject's behaviour and emphasize others. When we are well informed about saints from other sources, accordingly, we are able to assess the extent of the reorientations or modifications imposed on their personality and actions. This is something I will try to do below, when studying the image that the organizers of the processes sought to project of, say, a bishop or monk, in the hope of obtaining his canonization.

But it is my view that the enquiries *in partibus* allow us to observe far more than the avatars of an official model. In the first place, the stereotyped character and conformism of the depositions have been much exaggerated. Many thirteenth- and even fourteenth-century processes entirely lack *articuli interrogatorii*; this allowed the witnesses to testify with more spontaneity than in the case of the process of St Louis of Anjou, main source of the unfavourable opinion referred to above.[11] Further, it is mis-

---

[8] See, in particular, J. Paul, 'Témoignage historique et hagiographique dans le procès de canonisation de Louis d'Anjou', *Provence historique*, 93–4 (1973), pp. 305–17.

[9] For the appearance and role of the *articuli interrogatorii* in canonization processes, see below p. 49.

[10] Paul, 'Témoignage historique', p. 310.

[11] This is true of all processes prior to 1260 with the exception of that of St Dominic. They sometimes even include statements in direct speech. In the fourteenth century, there were still some enquiries without articles, for example that of St Thomas Aquinas held in

taken to see the medieval clergy as constituting a coherent and homo-geneous block. As we shall see below, the most sceptical witnesses with regard to the sanctity of St Thomas Cantilupe of Hereford (d. 1282) were a group of Franciscans who openly questioned the reality of his miracles.[12] The same could be said of the process of the nun Clare of Montefalco (d. 1308), during which a Friar Minor who had been her confessor denounced as a fraud the alleged discovery of the instruments of the Passion in the saint's heart.[13] Even when a schema to guide the witnesses existed, it was still possible for them to reject it. This happened, for example, at the process of Delphine of Sabran (d. 1360), where the promoters of the cause emphasized, in a way which seemed excessive to some witnesses, the most extraordinary aspects of her life and quoted miracles which they had to accept could not be proved.[14]

Finally, in the many cases where a list of questions was actually used, and where the witnesses kept to it, one can observe discrepancies between questions and answers. Some questions put by the commissioners, for example, were clearly not understood by the witnesses. Even more inter-esting, one can see, through the examples offered by the laity to illustrate a particular virtue of a saint, that words did not always have the same meaning for them as for their interrogaters.[15] All the time, impressions or judgements filter through which express a vision of things which can only partly be reconciled with that of the 'great minds', and which was expressed in a quite different way. Lastly, significant divergences of appreciation can appear between the depositions of the witnesses, even when they were answering the same questions. Despite the impression of monotony produced by the employment of a standard formulary and the unremitting ponderousness of notarial style, medieval processes of canon-ization offer to anyone who sets out to 'decode' them the possibility of

---

Naples in 1319, and that held in Angers in 1371 concerning the virtues and miracles of Charles of Blois (d. 1364).

[12] See Appendix 2.

[13] PC Clare of Montefalco, ASV, Riti, Proc. 2929, fols. 877v–881.

[14] At the canonization process of Delphine of Sabran (1363), no witness vouched for seven of the ninety-one articles produced by the procurator of the cause (nos. 59, 63, 80, 81 and 82). The accuracy of articles 12 and 25 was challenged, in particular by witnesses 5 and 7.

[15] Questioned by the commissioners about the persecutions which, according to the pro-moters of the cause, St Thomas Cantilupe had suffered during his lifetime, his barber candidly replied that he knew nothing about them 'nisi . . . quod viderat eum bene viginti vicibus infirmum infirmitatibus brevibus et recipiebat medicinas et curabatur' – hardly the reply the bishop's entourage had expected! (PC Thomas of Hereford, MS Vat. lat. 4015, fol. 26v).

identifying representations of sanctity which often only imperfectly coincide.

This is the aim of my book. I have not attempted to give an overall view of the cult of the saints at the end of the Middle Ages. An enterprise so ambitious could only successfully be attempted in the context of a regional, if not local, study, and would involve research into liturgical offices, church dedications, pilgrimages, processions etc. Nor will I deal with the Marian cult or the devotions solidly established for centuries. I have deliberately chosen to look only at the *novi sancti* whose cult appeared and grew in the West between the end of the twelfth and the beginning of the fifteenth centuries. This plan has a twofold justification. The first is the remarkable increase in the number of recent saints who were venerated by the faithful; in some regions, the pressure of a public opinion which was very receptive to 'modern' forms of sanctity gave rise to a large number of new intercessors. This enrichment and rejuvenation of the sanctoral has never been systematically studied. In my view, it deserves to be, since it marks a turning-point in the religious life of western Christendom, and since it had considerable repercussions at the level of piety, hagiography and iconography. But this is not all. If I have concentrated exclusively on these late-comers, it is above all because the investigations into their life and miracles by the ecclesiastical authorities allow us to get back to the sources of the perception of sainthood and identify the signs by which the people of that age – whoever they were – recognized the *viri Dei*.

Once the decision in favour of recent saints and canonization processes was taken, the chronological and geographical spread of the study more or less decided itself. Given that the first enquiries ordered by the papacy date to the last decades of the twelfth century, it was logical to start my study then, after retracing the main stages in the development of the cult of the saints during the preceding thousand years. The end date was less easy to determine since the procedure, stabilized by the last decades of the thirteenth century, continued relatively unchanged. It did not, however, seem possible to go as far as the Reformation. At the level of sources, there is another rupture which, though less visible, is no less significant: between 1418 and 1445, to my knowledge, the papacy neither ordered a single new enquiry nor completed a single canonization process. When the 'saint factory' resumed, with the glorification of St Bernardino of Siena, the climate had changed. The processes of the second half of the fifteenth century were increasingly closely controlled by the Curia and the role of the witnesses tended to be restricted to approval of the schema put to them. A few soundings have overwhelmingly suggested that the only original material to be gleaned concerns the expansion and manifestations of the devotion. Since my aim is to study representations of sanctity, it made sense to stop with the end of the pontificate of Martin V, after which the Roman Church resumed control of the cult of saints and gradually imposed a new discipline which paid much less heed to popular conceptions.

Canonization processes have another characteristic which has both advantages and disadvantages for the historian. Their geographical spread puts us at the level of Christendom as a whole, from Sweden to Italy and from Ireland to Hungary. This spatial dispersal has the merit of giving us the perspective of the medieval papacy, called on to pronounce as final arbiter on servants of God who had originated in very different countries; it also makes it possible to distinguish large cultural and religious areas within which homogeneous representations of sainthood prevailed. The other side of the coin is the consequent need to define on every occasion, at least in outline, the political context within which the process took place, the social structures of the region or town, the original features of its ecclesiastical organization etc. I make no claims to know everything about all these milieux, and I have no doubt neglected some factual information the documents provide. But any other method would have been impractical; the small number of processes which survive made it impossible to select or use only those concerning the countries with whose history I am more familiar, such as Italy and France; in any case, for a juxtaposition of monographs it would have been necessary to print and quote many unpublished documents, which would rapidly have exhausted the patience of the most favourably disposed reader. I should add, as a final justification of my approach, that my aim has been not to recreate, in its objective reality, the existence and personality of the various saints of that period, but to study the feelings inspired in contemporaries by the spectacle of their life and miracles.

In the happy formulation of S. Bonnet, 'a saint is first an extraordinary man inhabited by God. He is also a response to the spiritual needs of a generation. And he is a man who is the eminent illustration of the ideas of sanctity which are held by the Christians of a particular period.'[16] The first aspect hardly lends itself to historical study; as the individual experi-

---

[16] S. Bonnet, *Saint-Rouin, histoire de l'ermitage et du pèlerinage* (Paris, 1956), p. 75.

ence lived by a man or a woman in search of perfection, Christian sanctity is, in its very essence, timeless and unchanging.[17] Its profound nature therefore necessarily escapes an analysis which makes no claim to penetrate the secret of consciences. The two last aspects, however, are central to my concerns, since my purpose is to identify the various reasons as a result of which Christians of the last three centuries of the Middle Ages, in the West, accorded the title of saint to some of their contemporaries. This problematic will operate at three different levels; first, I will seek to show the action of the institutions and groups which, within the Church and contemporary society, were called on to pronounce on the sanctity of the servants of God and take the initiative in according them a cult: the papacy, obviously, whose role with regard to discipline and control significantly increased between the end of the twelfth and the beginning of the fifteenth centuries, but also the religious orders, the secular clergy and, lastly, the simple faithful, without whose support no devotion could spread. Once the modalities and levels of intervention of these various actors have been defined, I will try to establish a typology of sainthood which reveals the close links existing between the models then in favour, the political and social structures within which they developed, and the religious aspirations of the age. Lastly, by comparing the enquiries *in partibus* with the documents drawn up in curial circles on the basis of the declarations of witnesses, I will ask to what extent the representations which emerge from these two types of sources are similar, and if it is possible to speak, in this regard, of a mental attitude common to all the people of the age. So the history of the Church and that of spirituality lead to a wider enquiry concerning what Georges Duby has called 'the role of ideas in the development of human societies'.[18]

---

[17] A. J. Festugière, *La sainteté* (Paris, 1942), especially p. 107: 'every holy life is summed up in this: the gradual victory within an individual of the saint over the non-saint, until nothing of the carnal man remains . . . every saint's life offers the spectacle of a dispossession of self, I mean of the natural being, and of the divine taking possession'.

[18] G. Duby, 'Histoire sociale et idéologie des sociétées' in *Faire de l'histoire*, I: *Nouveaux problèmes*, ed. J. Le Goff and P. Nora (Paris, 1974), p. 168.

BOOK I

THE CHURCH AND THE CULT OF THE SAINTS IN THE MEDIEVAL WEST

PART I

CONTROL OF THE CULT OF THE SAINTS FROM ITS ORIGINS TO THE THIRTEENTH CENTURY

☙☙☙

Among the prerogatives which the Supreme Pontiff today enjoys within the Catholic Church, the right to canonize saints is one of the least disputed. Who, indeed, if not the pope could, as judge of last resort, passing definitive sentence, decree that a cult should be accorded to a servant of God? But it is only relatively recently that canonization has been within the exclusive remit of the bishop of Rome, and it was a long time before the very idea of control of the cult of the saints by an authority external to the local church was accepted.[1] It is not part of my purpose to trace in detail the historical process which resulted in the Holy See being invested with a regulatory power so great that, after Urban VIII's decrees of 1625 and 1634, the sanctity of a servant of God could only be approved by the Church if he or she had never been the object of a public cult.[2] But it might be useful briefly to recall the principal stages, since the changes experienced in this sphere over the centuries reflected new attitudes towards sanctity.

---

[1] Chief among the many general studies of the history of canonization are: T. Ortolan, *Canonisation des saints dans l'Eglise romaine*, in *DTC*, II, 2 (Paris, 1932), cc. 1626–59; E. W. Kemp, *Canonization and authority in the western Church* (Oxford, 1948); Benedict XIV (Prosper Lambertini), *De servorum Dei beatificatione et beatorum canonizatione*, 2 vols. (Prato, 1839); C. De Clercq, 'L'établissement progressif de la procédure de canonisation', *Revue de l'Université Laval*, 2 (1948), pp. 473–85, 672–82; D. J. Blaher, *The ordinary processes in causes of beatification and canonization* (Washington, 1949).

[2] Except, obviously in the case of long-dead saints, in which case the cult *ab immemorabili* applied. For the procedure actually followed here, see R. Naz, sv Causes de béatification et de canonisation, in *Dictionnaire de droit canonique*, III (Paris, 1942), cc. 10–37; P. Delooz, *Sociologie et canonisations* (Liège and The Hague, 1969), pp. 41–103.

CHAPTER 1

LATE ANTIQUITY AND THE EARLY MIDDLE AGES: 'VOX POPULI' AND EPISCOPAL POWER (THIRD TO TENTH CENTURIES)

ജ ഇ ഇ

During the first centuries of Christianity, the only saints venerated by the Church, if we except the Virgin, John the Baptist and the Apostles, were the martyrs. Christian communities very soon felt the desire to honour their memory and seek their intercession.[1] These martyrs were not canonized, in the juridical sense of the term, any more than the majority of the saints of the first millennium. Their sanctity, publicly demonstrated by their death and perseverance in the faith, was soon recognized and proclaimed by the churches to which they belonged: *vox populi, vox Dei*. No hierarchical intervention was necessary to ratify what was public knowledge, or even to have the new elect inscribed in the martyrologies which, from the third century, Christian communities were beginning to compile and update. At this period, the fact of awarding the title of saint to a deceased person was the spontaneous act of a local church.[2] With the end of the persecutions, the liturgical cult of the martyrs experienced a rapid growth. There then began the process of exhuming their remains and transferring them to worthier and safer tombs than those of the cemeteries in which they had originally been laid.[3] These ceremonies had no special

---

[1] For the cult of the saints in Christian Antiquity, the essential works of reference remain: H. Delehaye, *Sanctus: essai sur le culte des saints dans l'Antiquité* (Brussels, 1927); Delehaye, *Les origines du culte des martyrs* (2nd edn, Brussels, 1933). See also W. Rordorf, 'Aux origines du culte des martyrs', *Irenikon*, 46 (1972), pp. 315–31.

[2] Examples listed in H. Leclercq, sv Saint in *Dictionnaire d'archéologie chrétienne et de liturgie*, XV (Paris, 1949), cc. 373–462.

[3] For more detail, see the magisterial synthesis of C. Pietri, *Roma Christiana: recherches sur l'Eglise de Rome, son organisation, sa politique, son idéologie de Miltiade à Sixte III (311–440)*, 2 vols. (Rome, 1976), pp. 121–6, 595–624. See also R. Pfister, sv Kultus, in *Paulys Realencyclopädie der classischen Altertumswissenschaft*, XI (Stuttgart, 1922), cc. 2106–92; P. Séjourne, sv Saints (culte des), in *DTC*, XIV, 1 (Paris, 1939), cc. 870–979; E. Lucius, *Les origines du culte des saints dans l'Eglise chrétienne* (Paris, 1908); B. de Gaiffier, 'Réflexions sur les origines du culte des martyrs', in *Etudes critiques d'hagiographie et d'iconologie* (Brussels, 1967), pp. 7–30.

13

significance on the disciplinary plane; they were simply demonstrations of veneration towards a servant of God whose memory was honoured by the local Christian community.

As the cult of the martyrs grew, the bishops began to play an increasingly active role within it. Responsible for the liturgy, they organized the regular celebration of the feasts of the saints, whose memory was commemorated on the anniversary of their death. Under their control, and sometimes on their initiative, Acts describing the circumstances of their martyrdom were compiled.[4] These texts were transmitted from church to church and, in the fourth century, the worship of certain saints began to spread far beyond their original communities. By 354, according to the *Depositio martyrum*, African martyrs such as Perpetua, Felicity and Cyprian were venerated in Rome; later, the cult of the famous Roman martyr St Lawrence spread throughout the West. So did that of St Martin, soon known beyond the frontiers of Gaul.[5] In consequence, the risks of error or abuse greatly increased. This caused some unease, for example to the priest Vigilantius in Aquitaine, who was taken to task in 404 by the irascible St Jerome for having cast doubt on the authenticity of various martyrs.[6] In Africa, the Catholic hierarchy had to ensure that this title was not given to the Donatists it had condemned as schismatics. In 401, a decree of the Council of Carthage established that every bishop was responsible for overseeing within his diocese the manifestations of the cult of saints.[7] But no text said that bishops had to institute it. Their role was to combat deviations, not canonize in the modern sense of the term. In this regard, the initiative still belonged to the *populus Christianus* as a whole.

At the same time, however, the question of sanctity began to be posed

---

[4] See P. Jounel, 'Le culte des saints', in A. Martimort, *L'Eglise en prière: introduction à la liturgie* (Paris, 1961), pp. 766–85; H. Vorgrimler, sv Heiligenverehrung, in *Lexicon für Theologie und Kirche*, V (Fribourg, 1960), cc. 104–6. Also useful is the excellent bibliography in S. Boesch Gajano, *Agiografia altomedioevale* (Bologna, 1976), pp. 259–300, especially pp. 274–5 on the Acts of the martyrs; and the recent synthesis by A. Amore, 'Culto e canonizzazione dei Santi nell'antichità cristiana', *Antonianum*, 52 (1977), pp. 38–80.

[5] For the spread of the cult of St Martin in the West, see J. Van den Bosch, *Capa, basilica, monasterium, et le culte de saint Martin de Tours: étude lexicologique et sémasiologique* (Nimwegen, 1959); E. Ewig, 'Der Martinskult im Frühmittelalter', in *Archiv für Mittelrheinische Kirchengeschichte*, 14 (1962), pp. 11ff; C. Garcia Rodriguez, *El culto de los santos en la España romana y visigoda* (Madrid, 1966).

[6] St Jerome, *Contra vigilantium*, PL, 23, 339–52.

[7] P. Monceaux, 'Les martyrs donatistes. Culte et relations', *Revue de l'histoire des religions*, 68 (1913), pp. 146–92, 310–44.

in new terms. As long as those who aroused the veneration of clergy and laity were martyrs, their constancy under persecution was enough to attest to their perfection. To have confessed Christ without faltering even to the point of death was the sole criterion for sanctity recognized by the Church. But, with the reign of Constantine, Christians finally emerged from clandestinity and, thanks to imperial tolerance, began to participate in the society of the late empire. This development had repercussions for the spiritual climate; the age of the martyrs was succeeded by the age of the confessors.[8] Admittedly, the classical opposition between these categories of saints should not conceal the continuity between them, since, in both cases, it was the confession of faith which was crucial. But the fact that, in the case of the confessors, it was not generally accompanied by the shedding of blood led to an enlargement of the notion of sanctity, of which the great Doctors of the Church were the first beneficiaries. The battles that some of them had had to fight in the fourth and fifth centuries against heretics, schismatics and certain emperors who were Arian or hostile to the Church won them the right to be put on the same plane as the pre-Constantine martyrs, even though they had rarely paid with their life for their attachment to orthodoxy.[9] Sometimes in their lifetime, but more often after their death, prelates such as SS Athanasius (d. 373), John Chrysostom (d. 407) and Augustine (d. 430) became the object of a strong devotion. The term *confessor* was eventually applied to all those who deserved to be venerated by the faithful as a result of the pain they had suffered, or inflicted on themselves, for the love of Christ. This was the case with some bishops such as St Martin in Gaul, but also with monks and recluses such as SS Antony and Hilarion in Egypt, or women dedicated to God such as St Radegund, who were presented by their biographers as martyrs of asceticism.[10] In the fifth century, this very wide interpretation of the word confessor was eventually accepted, as we see from the writings of Sulpitius Severus and Gregory of Tours. In future, all forms and experiences of religious life could give rise to a *fama sanctitatis*.

---

[8] For the appearance and changing significance of the term confessor, see P. de Labriolle, 'Martyr et confesseur', *Bulletin d'ancienne littérature et d'archéologie chrétienne*, 1 (1911), pp. 50–4; Delehaye, *Sanctus*, pp. 74–121.

[9] B. Botte, 'Confessor', *ALMA*, 16 (1942), pp. 137–48; A. Bugnini, 'Confessor', *Ephemerides liturgicae*, 60 (1946), pp. 169–70.

[10] L. Bouyer, *La vie de Saint Antoine: essai sur la spiritualité du monachisme primitif* (Saint-Wandrille, 1950); J. C. Guy, ed., *Paroles des anciens: apophtegmes des Pères du désert* (Paris, 1976); E. Delaruelle, *Sainte Radegonde, son type de sainteté et la chrétienté de son temps*, in *Etudes mérovingiennes* (Paris, 1953), pp. 65–74.

Another phenomenon contributed to the increase in the number of saints at the end of Antiquity and in the first medieval centuries. Until the fourth century, the cult of the martyrs had been only a minor devotion, which seems to have played a far less important role in Christian piety than eucharistic celebrations or the practice of prayer. Its relative importance increased as soon as Christianization spread from the towns into the countryside and to Germanic peoples who were totally unfamilar with the religious traditions and cultural values of the 'Spätantike'. Incapable of understanding dogmas and theological discourse, the *pagani* and the barbarians preferred within Christianity the most obvious manifestations of the power of their new God, which they primarily experienced through military victories and miracles.[11] They also showed great enthusiasm for relics, which they saw as effective amulets and talismans. The frequency of the 'discoveries' of saints' bodies by the clergy from the end of the fourth century clearly corresponds to an attempt on the part of the ecclesiastical hierarchy to orient popular devotion towards more authentic cults than those it spontaneously adopted. The example was set in Milan by St Ambrose who, in 383, exhumed the remains of SS Gervasius and Protasius. He was rapidly copied and, more or less everywhere in the West, the search was on for the remains of the martyrs of the period of the persecutions or the first evangelization. Gregory of Tours describes many finds of this type, such as that of the body of St Benignus in Dijon at the beginning of the sixth century, by Bishop Gregory of Langres.[12] The clergy had other reasons for this attitude, such as the rivalry which developed between sanctuaries and the desire to possess relics of unimpeachable authenticity. This feeling is very clear in the *De laude sanctorum* of Victrit-

---

[11] For the increased importance of the cult of the saints in the religious life of the Merovingian period, see A. Marignan, *Etudes sur la civilisation française*, II: *Le culte des saints sous les Mérovingiens* (Paris, 1899); F. Graus, *Volk, Herrscher und Heiliger im Reich der Merowinger: studien zur Hagiographie der Merowingerzeit* (Prague, 1965); H. Fichtenau, 'Zum Reliquienwesen im Früheren Mittelalter', *MIOG*, 60 (1952), pp. 60–89. See also S. Boesch Gajano, 'Il santo nella visione storiografica di Gregorio di Tours', in *Gregorio di Tours (Todi, 1971)* (Todi, 1977), pp. 29–91; B. Kötting, *Der frühchristliche Reliquienkult und die Bestattung im Kirchengebäude* (Cologne, 1965); J. McCulloch, 'The cult of relics in the letters and dialogues of Pope Gregory the Great: a lexicographic study', *Traditio*, 22 (1976), pp. 145–84.

[12] Gregory of Tours, *In gloria martyrum*, 50. In *c.*535, Acts which were perhaps those of a Greek martyr (Benignos, Menignos?) from the Hellespont region were brought to the bishop of Langres; these sufficed until about 560, when Acts were composed which made St Benignus into a disciple of St Polycarp, who had evangelized the regions of Dijon, Langres and Autun.

ius of Rouen who, when he wrote his famous treatise, had just received some relics from St Ambrose for his new basilica.[13]

The success of the cult accorded to saints who were already old did not prevent the appearance of new devotions concerning people who were nearer in time and space. The disintegration of the Roman empire was followed by an increase in the regional, if not local, character of sanctity, the principal beneficiaries of which were the bishops. This development reflects a specific historical and social reality which made the bishops, in most regions of the West, the supreme *defensores civitatis* between the fifth and the eighth centuries. The role played by a St Leo in Rome or a St Avit in Orléans is a well-established fact, repeated elsewhere in comparable circumstances. Later, especially in the Merovingian kingdoms, the prelates alone were capable of standing up to a monarchy inclined to abuse its strength and impose excessive taxes on its new subjects. As A. Orselli has shown for Italy, the patronage of the bishop over the urban community appeared as the logical extension of the *patrocinium* he had exercised over it in his lifetime. It was a relationship of a juridical nature, based on the idea that Christians living in this world, not yet having obtained all their rights, were placed under the tutelage of the inhabitants of the City of God and more particularly the former bishops of their diocese who had distinguished themselves in the performance of their duties. Having protected the faithful in adversity, they continued to do so after death, assisting them, when the time came, to obtain celestial citizenship.[14] So a link was established at this period between the towns of the West and certain saintly prelates, which soon acquired a collective and permanent dimension.

One final factor contributed, during the early Middle Ages, to an often disturbing increase in the number of saints venerated by local churches. This was the generous use made of the word *sanctus*. In pagan Antiquity, this title was automatically accorded to all those who exercised the priesthood and were, as a result, in close contact with the supernatural world. The Church quite naturally adopted this terminology and, in many regions of the West, up to the seventh century, all the prelates who had been heads of the local Church were recorded in episcopal lists with the adjective *sanctus* before their name. When these records were compiled, the

---

[13] *PL*, 20, cc. 443–58.
[14] A. M. Orselli, *L'idea e il culto del santo patrono cittadino nella letteratura cristiana* (Bologna, 1965). See also plate 1.

use of this term did not imply a value judgement on the person of the dead bishop. It was simply a functional epithet, conferring a sort of honour which was refused only to those who had showed themselves truly unworthy of it.[15] But, from the middle of the sixth century in Rome and from the seventh century elsewhere in the West, the meaning attached to the word *sanctus* changed, and it was increasingly used to indicate those whose names appeared in the martyrologies, and whose cult was therefore recognized by the Church.[16] As a result, when, at this same period, general martyrologies, that is hagiographical compilations which brought together the martyrologies and liturgical calenders of many churches, were beginning to be compiled, their authors, in particular Bede, Florus, Ado and Usuard, to quote only the most famous, had great difficulty in allowing for this and distinguishing the true 'saints', in the modern sense of the word, from those who had received this title *ex officio*.[17]

As a result, many prelates were now venerated without their merits having been controlled by the ecclesiastical hierarchy. The same was true of monks, though in a slightly different context. In monasteries, which were then true 'nurseries of saints', the abbots often took the initiative in establishing a cult to the remains of certain members of the community whose memory was particularly revered. Secular prelates were sometimes associated with these ceremonies, but their presence seems to have been sought only in order to give greater impact to the celebration.[18] The promoters of these cults compiled written collections of *Miracula* and a Life or *Passio* to enhance the credibility of their heroes. These, however, were very different from the Acts of the martyrs of the first centuries.[19] Whilst

---

[15] Delehaye, *Sanctus*, pp. 1–73. For the resulting sanctity 'inflation', see H. F. Muller, *L'époque mérovingienne: essai de synthèse de philologie et d'histoire* (New York, 1945), especially pp. 82–3 which give some figures for Gaul: 54 saints, 52 of them bishops, in the fourth century; 175 saints, including 123 bishops and 8 abbots, in the fifth century; 293 saints, including 148 bishops, 45 abbots and 8 abbesses, in the sixth century. For functional sainthood in the early Middle Ages, see J. Van der Lof, 'Grégoire de Tours et la magie blanche', *Numen*, 21 (1974), pp. 228–37.

[16] For this semantic change, especially with regard to popes, see J. Löw, 'Bemerkungen zu den Selig- und Heiligsprechungen', *Theologisch-praktische Quartalschrift*, 103 (1955), pp. 89–102.

[17] Delehaye, *Sanctus*, pp. 132–5; R. Aigrain, *L'hagiographies, ses sources, ses méthodes, son histoire* (Paris, 1953), especially pp. 50–68.

[18] See the examples discussed by Kemp, *Canonization and authority*, pp. 30ff; R. Baix, 'Saint Hubert, sa mort, sa canonisation, ses reliques', in *Mélanges Fr. Rousseaux* (Brussels, 1958), pp. 71–80. This was a translation carried out in the eighth century without the participation of a bishop.

[19] H. Delehaye, *Les Passions des martyrs et les genres littéraires* (2nd edn, Brussels, 1966); Delehaye, *Etudes sur le légendier romain: les saints de novembre et décembre* (Brussels, 1936), pp. 14–41.

the latter are presented as simple accounts of the process of and sufferings inflicted on a servant of God, the hagiographical compositions of the Merovingian period were veritable romances. They were often discovered 'by chance', either in the sarcophagus itself in the case of the relics, or in a distant country, usually Italy, in the case of a recent saint. The originality of these *Vitae* is extremely limited, their authors for the most part confining themselves to pillaging ancient texts and piling up stereotyped claims. Their aim, in fact, was to associate their subject with a type of sanctity in favour, not to illumine their personality or history.[20]

It was inevitable that the anarchic proliferation of cults would, in the long run, cause problems. The ecclesiastical hierarchy seems not, at first, to have realized this, or at least to have lacked the means to impose a modicum of discipline. In some regions, certainly, we see bishops intervening to end abuses; St Martin himself set an example by overturning the altar of a 'martyr' venerated near Tours, which actually contained the remains of a brigand.[21] But such an attitude remained exceptional and it was more a sign of clerical suspicion of possible pagan survivals than a conscious desire to control the cult of relics. In the Carolingian period, in contrast, in this as in other spheres, we see a reaction against the laxity which had characterized the preceding centuries. The excesses which had arisen attracted the attention of a clergy which was probably better trained and was certainly more conscious of its duties. The sovereigns lent their authority to this reimposition of order, which aimed to restore all its dignity to Christian worship. In practice, this meant, from the end of the eighth century, a strengthening of episcopal control which was expressed in a series of instructions included in various capitularies of Charlemagne and Louis the Pious. These texts expressly forbade the veneration of new relics without the agreement of the ordinary, and reserved to the prince or to an assembly of bishops the right to decree the translation of saints' bodies.[22] The importance of this ceremony was

---

[20] L. Van der Essen, *Etude critique et littéraire des Vitae des saints mérovingiens de l'ancienne Belgique* (Louvain and Paris, 1907); Graus, *Volk, Herrscher und Heiliger*, pp. 60–139. For hagiography from the end of Antiquity to the Middle Ages, see S. Clasen, 'Das Heiligkeitsideal im Wandel der Zeiten. Ein Literaturbericht über Heiligenleben des Altertums und des Mittelalters', *Wissenschaft und Weisheit*, 23 (1970), pp. 46–64, 132–64.

[21] Sulpitius Severus, *Vie de saint Martin*, ed. J. Fontaine, I (Paris and Lyons, 1967), pp. 277–8. For interventions by Gregory of Tours, see Boesch Gajano, 'Il santo nella visione storigrafica', pp. 83–5.

[22] See *MGH. Capitularia regum Francorum*, I, p. 56, no. 42, p. 223, no. 25; *Concilia aevi Karolini*, II, p. 157. See also C. De Clercq, *La législation religieuse franque de Clovis à Charlemagne* (Louvain and Paris, 1936); K. L. Mikoletzky, 'Sinn und Art der Heiligung im frühen Mittelalter', *MIOG*, 13 (1949), pp. 83–122.

accordingly enhanced; it consisted no longer of a simple transfer performed on the initiative of a local community, but of an official recognition
of the sanctity of a deceased person, along with an authorization of the
cult. To be valid, this rite had to be performed under the control of the
ecclesiastical hierarchy and in the presence of at least one bishop. In future
and for many centuries to come, the exhumation of the relics of a saint by
the local ordinary, who laid them in a more dignified sepulchre (elevatio),
constituted a liturgical act sufficient to guarantee in the name of the church
the legitimacy of the cult they would be accorded.[23] Its importance is
shown by the fact that, up to the thirteenth century at least, the feast of
the new saints was celebrated on the anniversary of their solemn translation. As far as possible, this day was made to coincide with the date of
their death, their dies natalis. When the two dates competed, it was often
the commemoration of the translation which assumed greater importance.

These disciplinary measures should also be related to the growing fascination of relics for the clergy and the faithful. Even in Rome, from the
eighth century, the juridical decrees which forbade the violation of tombs
and the dismemberment of the remains of the deceased ceased to be
respected.[24] Large numbers of 'holy bodies' were exhumed in the Cata-
combs and divided into innumerable fragments destined to enrich the
altars and treasuries of regions of Christendom which were less well provided with martyrs and confessors.[25] After 800, many transalpine abbots
and bishops who wished to raise the religious level of the cult of the saints
by providing authentic – or allegedly authentic – relics for the veneration
of their flocks, hastened to Rome to procure them. But other than purely
pastoral motives were involved, and many clergy saw the possession of
precious relics primarily as an opportunity to increase the prestige and
revenues of their church.[26]

---

[23] Kemp, Canonization and authority, pp. 75ff. See also A. Amore, 'La canonizzazione vescovile', Antonianum, 52 (1977), pp. 231–66.
[24] N. Hermann-Masquard's Les reliques des saints: formation coutumière d'un droit (Paris,
1975), though disappointing in many regards, remains the only general study of the history
of the cult of relics in the Middle Ages. See also P. Jounel, Le culte des saints dans les
basiliques du Latran et du Vatican au XIIe siècle (Rome, 1977).
[25] For greater detail, see W. Hotzelt, 'Translationen von Märtyrer-Reliquien aus Rom nach
Bayern im 8.Jahrhundert', Studien und Mitteilungen zur Geschichte des Benediktiner Ordens,
53 (1935), pp. 286ff. See also M. Forster, Zur Geschichte des Reliquienkultus im Alten
England (Munich, 1943); P. Riché, 'Translations de reliques à l'époque carolingienne.
Histoire des reliques de Saint Malo', Le Moyen Age, 82 (1976), pp. 201–18.
[26] J. Guiraud, 'Le commerce des reliques au commencement du IXe siècle', in Mélanges G.
B. De Rossi (Rome, 1892), pp. 73–95; E. Dupré Theseider, 'La grande rapina dei corpi
santi dall'Italia al tempo di Ottone I°', in Festschrift P. E. Schramm, I (Wiesbaden, 1964),
pp. 420–32.

The rules established by the Carolingian councils were far from being universally applied. Bishops were often content to give oral or written permission for the translation of saints' bodies without their own presence.[27] Nevertheless, in certain regions of the empire, in particular in Germany, it became increasingly common in the ninth century for prelates asked to perform a translation of relics to consult first the diocesan or provincial synod, or even a national council, and involve other bishops in the ceremony. This quest for a superior authority capable of dispelling any doubts about sanctity ultimately brought the clergy face to face with the pope.

[27] In 823, Fulrad, abbot of Lobbes, arranged for the *elevatio* of the body of his predecessor St Ursmer (d. 713) 'on the orders and with the permission of he who was then bishop of Cambrai'; Folcuin, *Gesta abbatum Lobensium, MGH.SS.*, IV, p. 60.

CHAPTER 2

TOWARDS PAPAL RESERVATION OF THE RIGHT OF CANONIZATION (ELEVENTH TO THIRTEENTH CENTURIES)

෫෨෫෨෫෨

It is customary to date the beginning of pontifical canonization to 993. It was in that year that Bishop Ulric of Augsburg (d. 973) was proclaimed a saint in Rome by John XV. For the first time, it seems, the papacy intervened outside Italy in connection with the cult of the saints. The significance of this event should not, however, be exaggerated and it needs to be seen in its historical context.[1] Liutulf, bishop of Augsburg, presented the Roman synod, meeting at Lateran, with a book containing the life and miracles of his predecessor, St Ulric. It was favourably received, and the pope drew up a bull – the first known bull of canonization – decreeing that the memory of the bishop should be solemnly venerated. It was sent to the archbishops, bishops and abbots of France and Germany. Contrary to what has since been believed, this canonization did not, strictly speaking, constitute a juridical innovation, and the bishop of Augsburg had never intended his action to lead to new measures of control. But the papacy was adroit enough to seize this opportunity to assert its authority within the western Church. It was not, however, until the beginning of the eleventh century that the term *canonizare* appeared, in a letter from Benedict VIII to the count of Mantua, in which he ratified the cult of St Simeon of Padolirone, a hermit who had died in 1016, and it was only rarely used before the mid-twelfth century.[2]

With the Gregorian Reform, the growth of papal prestige within the Church and within western Christendom led to an increase in the number

---

[1] There is an excellent analysis of this episode in Kemp, *Canonization and authority*, pp. 57–8.

[2] *Ibid.*, p. 58. For the canonizations performed by popes at the beginning of the eleventh century, see A. Heintz, 'Der Heilige Simeon von Trier, seine Kanonisation und seine Reliquien', in *Festschrift Alois Thomas* (Trier, 1967), pp. 163–73.

of its interventions in the sphere of the cult of the saints. Leo IX and his successors were several times appealed to by isolated bishops or the bishops of a particular region who wanted them to ratify their initiatives.[3] But there was no question of an obligation of a judicial order. The clearest proof of this is that most translations at this period were performed by secular or regular prelates, without papal authorization having been requested. The approval of the Holy See was sought only in order to confer extra lustre on certain cults.

Things changed with the pontificate of Gregory VII (1073–85), whose personal role in the growth of control of the cult of the saints has been seen in different and not always reconcilable ways. The decisions taken by the Lateran synod of 1078 regarding the celebration of the feast of the saint-popes in the Roman basilicas, the pontiff's insistence on the sanctity of many of his predecessors in the famous letter to Hermann of Metz and, above all, the formula of the *Dictatus papae*, 23: *Romanus pontifex indubitanter efficitur sanctus* certainly all contributed to exalt the sanctity of the bishop of Rome. However, it is arguable whether it follows, as K. Hofmann has claimed, that Gregory VII wished to attribute a hereditary sainthood ('Erbheiligkeit') of a personal order to the successors of Peter.[4] W. Ullmann has justly emphasized that the claim contained in the *Dictatus papae* only summarized, with extreme concision, traditional conceptions to the effect that the Supreme Pontiff enjoyed a functional sainthood independent of his own merits, to the extent that, as heir to the powers of Peter, he exercised an authority both terrestrial and celestial.[5] This does not imply that all deceased popes should be the object of a liturgical cult, and in fact, as D. Lindner has noted, Gratian and his later commentators were hostile to the very idea of a sanctity of function or the hereditary transmission of the merits of Peter to his successors.[6] Many canonists of the late twelfth and early thirteenth centuries spoke of the *sanctitas* of the Roman pontiff, but a careful examination of the texts shows that they

---

[3] These cases are discussed in great detail, though without generalization, in C. H. Brakel, 'Die vom Reformpapsttum geförderten Heiligenkulte', *Studi Gregoriani*, 9 (1972), pp. 240–311. See also H. Paulhart, 'Zur Heiligsprechung der Kaiserin Adelheid', *MIOG*, 64 (1956), pp. 55–67 (canonization by Urban II in 1097).

[4] K. Hofmann, *Der Dictatus papae* (Paderborn, 1933), pp. 63–73.

[5] W. Ullmann, 'Romanus pontifex indubitanter efficitur sanctus. Dictatus papae 23 in retrospect and prospect', *Studi Gregoriani*, 6 (1961), pp. 229–64.

[6] D. Lindner, 'Die sogennante Erbheiligkeit des Papstes in der Kanonistik des Mittelalters', *Zeitschrift der Savigny-Stiftung für Rechtgeschichte, Kan. Abteilung*, 84 (1967), pp. 15–26.

meant simply that he should be credited, until proved to the contrary, with an exceptional moral integrity and religious piety.[7]

However, the fact of recognizing in the bishop of Rome a *divina potestas*, and of exalting his power within the Church, inevitably helped to make him the sole authority qualified to pronounce in the last resort on the sanctity of the servants of God. By the end of the eleventh century, it was believed in some ecclesiastical circles that there existed a decree forbidding *ne quis sine apostolica auctoritate canonizaretur*. Even if this belief had no real juridical foundation, it is significant that it was so widespread. Nevertheless, it was more than a century before these claims in principle took concrete form in canonical norms. In the history of the control of the cult of the saints, the twelfth century was a period of transition.[8] Pontifical canonization was increasingly frequently sought, without the translation of saints' bodies by bishops ceasing. It is difficult to trace in detail a change which happened at different rates according to pontificates and countries. But one can safely claim that, from the pontificate of Eugenius III (1145–53), the papacy felt sufficiently sure of its rights to pronounce canonizations outside a council or synod, by virtue of the sole authority of the Roman Church, competent to speak and act in the name of the universal Church.[9] Consultation with the bishops was replaced by consultation with a limited number of cardinals who, from the end of the twelfth century and throughout the Middle Ages, were to play a crucial role as papal counsellors in the canonization procedure.

During the second half of the twelfth century, papal canonization began to compete with episcopal translation and then to surpass it. From this period, requests for the canonization of saints who had already been the object of a solemn translation by one or more bishops poured into the Holy See, either because doubt was felt as to the canonical value of this liturgical act, or because the promoters of the cult wanted to give it extra lustre by having it approved by the pope.[10] For its part, the papacy seems

---

[7] In his Commentary on the *Decretum* (vv. 1157–9) (ed. H. Singer (Paderborn, 1902), p. 93), Rufinus says, bluntly: 'non loca sed vita et mores sanctum faciunt sacerdotem'.

[8] M. Schwartz, 'Die Heiligsprechung im 12 Jahrhundert', *Archiv für Kulturgeschichte*, 39 (1957), pp. 43–62.

[9] Eugenius III canonized the emperor Henry II (d. 1024) in 1152; see R. Klauser, *Der Heinrichs- und Kunegundenkult im mittelalterlichen Bistum Bamberg* (Bamberg, 1957), also *Anal. Boll.*, 76 (1958), pp. 262–4.

[10] The canonizations of the first half of the twelfth century are studied in detail in L. Hertling, 'Materiali per la storia del processo di canonizzazione', *Gregorianum*, 16 (1935), pp. 170–95, especially pp. 177–85. See also R. Klauser, 'Zur Entwicklung des Heiligsprechungsverfahrens bis zum 13. Jahrhundert', *Zeitschrift der Savigny-Stiftung für Rechtgeschichte, Kan. Abteilung*, 40 (1954), pp. 85–101.

for a long time to have been content with this confirmatory function, leaving a particular bishop or legate the power to pronounce on the sanctity of the candidate.[11] Things took a more juridical turn with Alexander III, during whose pontificate twelve canonization causes were introduced and five completed.[12] No previous pope had been so active in this field. But this trend was not maintained under the reigns – admittedly much shorter – of his successors, Clement III and Celestine III, who pronounced, respectively, three and five canonizations.[13]

At this point, a text which was to become the *locus classicus* of the canonists with regard to the control of the cult of the saints was produced, that is, the letter *Aeterna et incommutabilis*, sent by Alexander III to King Kol of Sweden in 1171 or 1172.[14] It contains a paragraph, beginning with the word *Audivimus*, in which the pope prohibited a cult in the case of a man who had died in a drunken state (this was a reference to King Eric – St Eric to the Swedes – who had been killed by his successor, the recipient of the letter), 'since, even if prodigies and miracles were produced through his intermediary, you would not be permitted to venerate him publicly as a saint without the authorization of the Roman Church'. It was long believed that this text constituted the first solemn assertion of the exclusive right of the Roman pontiff to canonize saints.[15] S. Kuttner, in an important article, tried to show that this was not the case, arguing from the silence of the canonical texts on this issue before 1234, the date when the brief *Audivimus* was inserted in the Decretals.[16] Others have pushed the argu-

---

[11] J. Petersohn has emphasized the importance of the *canonizatio in forma commissoria* in papal acts concerning the control of the cult of saints, especially 1160–80. In the second half of the twelfth century, five canonizations were delegated by a pope, whilst twelve were pronounced directly; to which should be added that of Charlemagne, pronounced by Frederick Barbarossa, as delegate of the anti-pope Paschal III, in 1165: J. Petersohn, 'Die päpstliche Kanonisationsdelegation des 11. und 12. Jahrhunderts und die Heiligsprechung Karls des Grossen', in *Proceedings of the fourth international congress of medieval canon law (Toronto, 1972)* (Vatican City, 1976), pp. 163–206. The transitory nature of this type of delegation is shown by the case of St Rosendo de Dumio, in Spain, canonized in 1172 by the papal legate Hyacinth Bobo, who, when he became pope (Celestine III), felt it desirable to canonize him again: Y. Garcia y Garcia, 'A propos de la canonisation des saints au XIIe siècle', *Revue de droit canonique*, 17 (1968), pp. 3–15.

[12] E. W. Kemp, 'Pope Alexander III and the canonization of the saints', *Transactions of the Royal Historical Society*, 4th ser., 27 (1945), pp. 13–28. The anti-popes were no less active; see R. Folz, 'La Chancellerie de Frédéric Ier et la canonisation de Charlemagne', *Le Moyen Age*, 70 (1964), pp. 13–31.

[13] For Celestine III, see P. Zerbi, *Papato, Impero e respublica christiana dal 1187 al 1198* (Milan, 1955), p. 78.

[14] The full text is in *PL*, 200, cc. 1259–61.

[15] In particular by Benedict XIV, *De servorum Dei beatificatione*, L. I, c. XI, 9.

[16] S. Kuttner, 'La réserve papale du droit de canonisation', *Revue historique de droit français et étranger*, 4th ser., 18 (1938), pp. 172–228.

ment further, emphasizing that the late twelfth- and early thirteenth-century popes never clearly specified, in the bulls of canonization they promulgated, that their right to canonize was exclusive of that of the bishops.[17] But E. W. Kemp, by relocating the document within the context both of all Alexander III's interventions in canonization and of contemporary Swedish affairs, has defined its significance and importance more satisfactorily; it was, he says, neither a specific instance concerning a recently converted people, as argued by Kuttner, nor a new juridical rule introduced at this date and valid for the whole of the Church, as has been claimed by Roman and ultramontane canonists, following Benedict XIV.[18] Rather, the words of the pontiff expressed 'what Alexander III believed to be the law, possibly unwritten, but still the law in force . . . many years before it was canonically defined by a text, the existence of pontifical reservation is assumed in his acts by a great pope who was also a great legist'.[19]

We can therefore summarize the position with regard to control of the cult of the saints in 1170 by saying that, without the ancient right having been abolished (that is, episcopal translation accepted as giving definitive approval), 'it was widely believed that the pope ought to be consulted and that it was for him to exercise a degree of control over canonizations'.[20] It is not impossible, however, that Alexander III took advantage of the fact that he was addressing the sovereign of a recently converted people, poorly informed about ecclesiastical traditions, to phrase his reminder of the prerogatives of the Holy See with particular clarity, as Benedict VIII had done in 1039 with regard to the duke of Bohemia, on the occasion of the theft of the relics of St Adalbert.[21] In any case, we should not confuse the

---

[17] Especially J. Schlafke, *De competentia in causis sanctorum decernendi a primis post Christum natum saeculis usque ad annum 1234* (Rome, 1961); Schlafke, 'Das Recht der Bischöfe in causis sanctorum bis zum Jahre 1234', in *Kirche und ihre Amter und Stände, Festschrift Kard. Frings* (Cologne, 1960), pp. 417–33.

[18] Kemp, *Canonization and authority*, pp. 99–104. The belief that Alexander III introduced pontifical reservation of the right of canonization was already current in the Middle Ages, as we see from a passage in the early fourteenth-century *Chronica minor auctore minorita Erphordiensi* (ed. O. Holder-Egger, in *MGH. SS.*, XXIV (Hanover, 1879), p. 193): 'Hic papa [Alexander III] constituit ut nullus sanctus novus in veneracione habeatur nisi ex auctoritate apostolica et nisi sit canonizatus a papa. Tamen antea quelibet dyocesis suum sanctum sollemniter canonizavit. Exemplum de sanctis scilicet Martino, Ambrosio, Burchardo, Wigberto, Severo, Augustino et aliis.'

[19] P. Grosjean, *Anal. Boll.*, 63 (1945), pp. 273–5 (review of Kemp, 'Pope Alexander III').

[20] *Ibid.*, p. 275.

[21] For the Swedish context, see S. Tunberg, 'Erik den helige, Sveriges helgenkonung', *Fornvännen*, 36 (1941), pp. 257–78 (reviewed by P. Grosjean, *Anal. Boll.*, 60 (1942), pp. 268–9); E. Carlsson, *Translacio archiepiscoporum, Eriklegendens Historicitet* (Uppsala,

issue by approaching the problem in too theoretical a fashion. For the papacy, the cult of the saints remained, and would long remain, a marginal issue, essentially regulated by custom. The long silence of the juridical sources on this subject is hardly surprising. At the end of the twelfth century, it was enough for the Holy See that its prerogatives were recognized and that there were no outstanding excesses or abuses, such as would have been constituted by the cult of a man who had died in a drunken stupor. When not officially requested to intervene, the pope was wary of claiming to regulate or even control local cults.[22] There was no need to abolish customs in force; clergy and laity were well aware that the validity of a cult not ratified by the Holy See would always be open to question. It was they who were the chief architects of the strengthening of pontifical prerogatives, by increasingly seeking the intervention of the pope in the causes of the saints they held dear.[23]

On the legal plane, no new text appeared in the late twelfth or early thirteenth centuries until the Fourth Lateran Council, to which we will return. However, a number of solemn declarations by Innocent III confirm that the papacy was by then confident it possessed the privilege of canonizing saints. The bull of canonization of St Cunegund in 1200 contains two important passages which are relevant here; the first concerns pontifical reservation, which is clearly asserted: 'since this sublime judgement belongs solely to He who is the successor of St Peter and the Vicar of Jesus Christ'; the second, for the first time, explicitly relates the power of the pope to canonize saints to his *plenitudo potestatis*.[24] It is also interest-

1944). At the instigation of the Polish bishops, Benedict VIII intervened to condemn the theft of the relics of St Adalbert, taken from Gniezno to Prague by the Duke of Bohemia; in a reproachful letter to the duke, he said 'quod nulli liceat sine nostra permissione de loco ad locum sacrum transferre corpus, testantur canones, prohibent patrum decreta': *Cosmae Pragensis Chronica Boemorum*, in *MGH. SRG.*, n.s., II, p. 92. At the beginning of the eleventh century, this claim is out of line with what we know about control of the cult of the saints from other sources.

[22] This is made plain by the glosses of Huguccio on Gratian's *Decretum*, where the famous canonist recognizes the considerable autonomy of the metropolitan to institute new feasts in his province; see Hermann-Masquard, *Les reliques des saints*, p. 99.

[23] The case of St Wulfstan (d. 1095) is particularly significant. Bishop John of Worcester, who had translated his relics, in September 1198, without solemnity or authorization, died soon after. His death was interpreted as a heavenly punishment, and his successor, Bishop Mauger, had the saint's body restored to its tomb. He then asked Innocent III to canonize him, which was done on 21 April 1203, after proper procedures. As the generosity of the faithful made it possible to rebuild the choir of Worcester cathedral, damaged by fire in 1202, the translation may have taken place on 7 June 1218; see R. R. Darlington, *The Vita Wulfstani of William of Malmesbury* (London, 1928), pp. xlvii–xlviii.

[24] Ed. J. Petersohn, 'Die Litterae Papst Innocenz III zur Heiligsprechung des Kaiserin Kunigunde (1200)', *Jahrbuch für fränkische Landesforschung*, 37 (1977), pp. 1–25. Peter-

ing to note that it was during the pontificate of Innocent III that the brief *Audivimus* began to be inserted in private collections of Decretals, especially in England (*Sangermanensis, Abrincensis, Bodleiana*, collections of Master Alan, around 1206, and of John of Wales around 1210). In two of these, the passage in question is preceded by the following gloss: 'The approval of the Roman pontiff is necessary before anyone can be deemed a saint.'[25]

It is not without relevance that the majority of these juridical collections are of Anglo-Norman origin, since it was in England that awareness of pontifical prerogatives in this sphere seems to have been most marked. In other regions of Christendom, in contrast, they were still, at this period, ignored. The extreme case is that of Iceland, where the local episcopate and the Althing – the assembly of the people – instituted the public cult of the bishops Perlakr Perhallsson (d. 1193) in 1199 and Jon Ogmundsson (d. 1121) in 1201.[26] Most other countries fell between these two extremes. Even in Italy, there were still many instances of translations of saints' bodies by bishops, though their precise significance is not always clear. For example, towards the end of the pontificate of Innocent III, the bishop of Anagni, surrounded by many Campanian bishops, performed the translation of the relics of St Peter of Trevi (d. 1052). But this ceremony, celebrated in 1216 under the eyes of the pope, could hardly have had the same effect as a pontifical canonization. Although the documentation for this affair is obscure, it seems rather to have been simply confirmation of a local cult.[27] The same conclusion can be drawn from the vicissitudes of the cult of St John of Gualdo (d. 1170). An enquiry had been opened in 1218 into the sanctity of this person, whose remains lay in the abbey of Santa Maria of Gualdo Mazocca, in the province of Benevento. For reasons which are not clear, the process decreed by Honorius III came to nothing,

---

sohn emphasizes that the phrase in question (*cum hoc sublime judicium*) belongs to the *narratio*, that is to the part of the bull which repeated the text of the *petitio* of the postulants; it cannot therefore be assumed that it expresses the official doctrine of the Roman Church, or even the personal opinion of Pope Innocent III. Whilst this reasoning is soundly based at the diplomatic level, it nevertheless seems to me excessively formalistic. It is highly unlikely that the pope would have adopted the arguments of the postulators unless he agreed with them.

[25] Kemp, *Canonization and authority*, p. 102.

[26] See the sources and works quoted by S. Kuttner, 'St. Jón of Holar. Canon Law and Hagiography', *Analecta Cracoviensia*, 7 (1975), pp. 367–75, especially p. 369; also H. Bekker-Nielson, 'A note on two Icelandic saints', *The Germanic Review*, 36 (1971), pp. 108–9. Perlakr Perhallsson is sometimes called Thorlakr Thorallsson. See plate 18.

[27] *AA.SS.*, Aug. VI, pp. 645–6; F. Caraffa, sv Pietro, eremita, in *BS*, X (Rome, 1968), pp. 735–7.

and the monks lost hope of seeing their founding saint canonized by the pope.[28] They then applied to the archbishop of Benevento, who gave them a favourable reception and delegated the bishops of Vultuaria, Dragonara and Montecorvino to act for him. They proceeded to the solemn translation of the relics which they placed in a new altar, after detaching a few fragments for themselves and their churches.[29] Did this amount to a canonization? It is difficult to argue that it did, since the bishop only intervened after the failure of attempts to win papal approval for John of Gualdo. The archbishop of Benevento seems to have had no scruples about ordering the translation, though he must have been aware that the pope was not favourably inclined towards this cause. Perhaps he believed, when he organized the ceremony, that he was simply authorizing a local cult, valid for the abbey, or at most the ecclesiastical province of Benevento, which did not exceed his competence.

On the juridical plane, the situation became clearer after the Fourth Lateran Council, canon 62 of which, repeating a decree of the synod of Mainz of 813, already inserted in the *Decretum* of Gratian, prohibited the veneration of relics *de novo inventas* without the authorization of the *princeps*.[30] In the Carolingian document, this word obviously referred to the emperor. By the thirteenth century, it could mean only the pope. It is true that this text did not refer directly to the right of canonization. But, as N. Hermann-Masquard has justly remarked, 'it is clear that if the pope reserved the right to approve the cult of newly discovered relics, he with more reason reserved the right to authorize the veneration of the relics of as yet uncanonized servants of God'.[31]

An episode which occurred in England a few years after the meeting of the Council confirms this impression. In 1223, Honorius III received a request from the abbot and convent of Dorchester to authorize the translation of the remains of St Birinus, one of the architects of the conversion of the Saxons. He answered by instructing the archbishop of Canterbury, in association with the archdeacon and official of Dorchester, to carry out

---

[28] The material relating to St John of Gualdo and his canonization has been collected by A. Casamassa, 'Per una nota marginale del Cod. Vat. lat. 5949', in *Miscellanea Historica P. L. Oliger . . . oblata* (Rome, 1945), pp. 201–26.

[29] *Ibid.*, pp. 223ff.

[30] J.-D. Mansi, *Sacrorum conciliorum nova et amplissima collectio*, XXII, c. 30. The canon *Cum ex eo* was primarily directed against the abuses of collectors who extorted money from the faithful by showing them false relics in return for the promise of indulgences; see R. Foreville, *Latran I, II, III et Latran IV* (Paris, 1965), pp. 377–8.

[31] Herrmann-Masquard, *Les reliques des saints*, p. 101.

an enquiry into the miracles which had occurred at the saint's tomb, and then, if it seemed appropriate, proceed to the translation, 'since his name appears in the catalogue of saints'.[32] This was only a standard clause, since the name of St Birinus did not appear in the Roman martyrology and the 'catalogue of saints' referred to in bulls of canonization had no real existence. But the formula is interesting as an illustration of the pope's desire to make the translation appear simply as the liturgical extension of an assumed canonization, pronounced by the pope.[33]

But even if, in detail, doubts persist as to the degree to which some bishops were aware of pontifical reservation, the general trend in the development of the cult of the saints during the first third of the thirteenth century is clear.[34] Papal canonization far outclassed episcopal translation, which lost its decisive and definitive character. After 1234, the date of the insertion of the brief *Audivimus* in the Decretals of Gregory IX, the period of juridical uncertainty and imprecision which had characterized the preceding decades was finally over.[35] Pontifical reservation of the right to canonize saints was included in the legislation of the Church and the excuse of ignorance was no longer acceptable, knowledge of the rules being accessible to all.

It was not long before the new decretal was glossed by the canonists, who spelled out its meaning and implications. Innocent IV, in his commentary on *Audivimus*, defined canonization in the following terms: 'To

---

[32] Honorius III, *Ex parte dilectorum*, 9.III.1224, ed. P. Pressutti, *Regesta Honorii papae III* (Rome, 1888–95), no. 4847.

[33] When asked by the bishop of Passau, in 1224, to canonize St Colman (d. 1012), a 'martyred' monk whose body was venerated at Melk, and whose cult was widespread in Lower Austria, Innocent IV authorized the celebration of the feast 'si beatus Colomannus martyr canonizatus per Apostolicam Sedem existit': Innocent IV, *Cum sicut ex*, 10.V.1244, ed. *AA.SS.*, Oct. VII, pp. 355–7. 'Who, if not the pope, would know if Colman had been canonized?' is the least objection which occurs to the modern reader; but other documents of this period show that the Holy See was aware of gaps in its archives!

[34] The last known cases of episcopal canonization date from *c.*1230: in 1229, the provincial synod of Nidaros, in Norway, proclaimed the former archbishop Eystein Erlendsson (d. 1188) a saint. But this initiative is probably to be explained by local ignorance of new trends, as, in 1240, the Norwegian episcopate approached the papacy in order to get proper canonization procedures started; see T. Lundén, sv Kanonisering, in *Kulturhistorisk Lexikon for Nordisk Middelalder*, VII (Copenhagen, 1963), c. 217. In 1236, Bishop Rudiger of Passau canonized, on his own authority and without authorization, Abbot Bertold of Garsten (d. 1142). But he was a prelate who supported Frederick II, who carried his hostility to the papacy to the point where he was deposed by Innocent IV in 1250. For this episcopal canonization, see *Sacra rituum congregatio, sectio historica, positio de Bertoldo* (Vatican City, 1964), pp. 144–54; also J. Lenzenweger, *Berthold, Abt von Garsten* (Graz, 1958), who gives the text of the bull (pp. 283–4).

[35] Decretals of Gregory IX, L. III, vol. XLV, c. 1, *de reliquiis et veneratione sanctorum.*

canonize is to decide, correctly and canonically, that a saint should be honoured as such, that is that he should be accorded a solemn cult as for other saints of the same category; so that if he is a confessor, the office of a confessor should be celebrated for him, if he is a martyr the office of the martyrs, and so on.'[36] It is interesting to note that to Sinibaldo Fieschi, canonization was essentially defined by the grant of a liturgical office and an authorization of public cult, since this view, which was shared by the clergy of his day, would have important repercussions on the disciplinary plane. For him, it is clear, 'only the pope can canonize the saints'.[37] Reservation of this right was justified by the argument of universality; the Supreme Pontiff alone was competent in this domain, because his decisions constrained the whole of the Church. Another eminent canonist of this period, Henricus de Segusio (*Hostiensis*), in the various commentaries on the Decretals he composed between 1250 and 1270, offered several arguments in favour of papal reservation.[38] Three of them are theological: canonization can be compared with the *causae maiores*, traditionally reserved to the pope. Further, miracles are a matter of faith, and everything to do with faith came within the province of the pope. Lastly, it was for the pope to interpret the Scriptures: *a fortiori* the sanctity which, in human eyes, was always doubtful. His two final arguments were more concrete; one was fear of the *simplicitas* of many bishops, the second the danger of the depreciation of sanctity which would inevitably follow an ill-considered proliferation in the number of saints.[39]

From this reservation, now solidly founded in law, some commentators of the Decretals concluded that bishops retained only the facility of introducing in their dioceses cults approved by Rome.[40] *Hostiensis* goes furthest in the support of papal prerogatives, since he thought it was forbidden to venerate publicly a saint who had not been recognized as such by the Holy See, in which he was well in advance of the current practice of his day.[41]

[36] Innocent IV, *In quinque libros Decretalium commentaria* (Venice ed. of 1578), p. 188.
[37] *Ibid.* For the commentaries of the canonists, see Kemp, *Canonization and authority*, pp. 107–10.
[38] Henricus de Segusio (*Hostiensis*), *Summa aurea* (ed. Lyons, 1568), pp. 276–7.
[39] Henricus de Segusio (*Hostiensis*), *In tertium Decretalium librum commentaria* (Venice edn of 1581), p. 173: 'ne contingeret populum decipi per multorum episcoporum simplicitatem'.
[40] Innocent IV, *In quinque libros Decretalium commentaria*, p. 188: 'nec valet si dicas quod saltem cuique [episcopo] debet esse licitum quod in sua diocesi faciat, quia oratio eis [= sanctis] facta debet esse communis'.
[41] Henricus de Segusio, *Summa aurea*, p. 276: 'Quod publice non veneretur aliquis tanquam sanctus quosque sit per papam approbatus.' The canonists of the period were not, how-

To what extent did these clear-cut claims correspond to reality, and what influence did they exert in practice on control of the cult of the saints? Admittedly, after 1234, episcopal canonizations disappear and the movement which drove many religious communities to seek the canonization of saints long dead and venerated continued to gain ground. But despite claims by Gregory IX, who, after the events at Assisi in 1230 on the occasion of the translation of the relics of St Francis, claimed for the pope the exclusive right to authorize the transfer of saints' bodies, one does not get the impression that the Roman Church was particularly concerned to make these claims effective.[42] Until the sixteenth century, much to the chagrin of the canonists most attached to pontifical prerogatives, bishops continued to proceed on their own initiative to translations *in loco decentiori*.[43] For a long time to come, ordinary people tended to confuse translation and canonization, even to attach greater importance to the former than to the latter.[44] In the end, the Holy See adapted to this situation and, as we shall see below, soon renounced control over all the cults accorded to the servants of God. Henricus de Segusio wrote, around 1270, with regard to the cult of the saints, that 'he whom the pope approves is approved and he of whom he disapproves is disapproved'.[45] But during the last centuries of the Middle Ages, the majority of new cults which emerged in western Christendom were neither approved nor disapproved of by the supreme authority, and developed locally with complete freedom. This fact does not detract from the absolute character of papal reservation on the juridical plane, but it makes it possible to define the place of canonization in the hierarchy of honours accorded to the servants of God. It was, in fact, the highest consecration, reserved to a tiny number of saints judged worthy of it by the Roman Church, having successfully passed the tests of a veritable trial.[46]

---

ever, unanimous on this point, as is shown by Vincentius Hispanus, who comments: 'argumentum potest episcopus canonisare sanctos, quod concedo in sua diocesi tantum': *De consecratione*, Dist. III, c. 1, quoted by Kemp, *Canonization and authority*, p. 110. This short passage made Vincentius Hispanus the favourite target of the glossators who favoured a maximalist interpretation of pontifical reservation.

[42] Gregory IX, *Speravimus hactenus*, 16.VI.1230, ed. *Bull. Franc.*, I, p. 66.

[43] For the canonists, see Hermann-Masquard, *Les reliques des saints*, pp. 187–9, and, for particular cases, pp. 91–4 below.

[44] See the examples analysed by O. Reber, *Die Gestaltung des Kultes weiblicher Heiliger im Spätmittelalter* (Hersbruck, 1963), especially pp. 78–80.

[45] Henricus of Segusio, *Summa aurea*, p. 279.

[46] See plate 3.

CHAPTER 3

THE PROCESS OF CANONIZATION FROM ITS ORIGINS TO ITS CLASSICAL FORM
(c.1200 to c.1270)

☙☙☙

Papal reservation of the right of canonization did not only enhance the prestige of the Holy See. It gave it the right to examine the nature and content of the devotions it was asked to approve. The papacy's new involvement in the cult of the saints was accompanied, throughout the twelfth and early thirteenth centuries, by the development of forms of control which led eventually to the process of canonization.[1] Once again, it is difficult to give precise dates or even fix a *terminus a quo*. By the eleventh century, the need for an enquiry into the miracles performed by the servants of God was several times asserted in pontifical documents. When asked by Benedict, abbot of Sainte-Croix of Quimperlé, to canonize his predecessor, St Gurlo (d. 1057), Urban II replied that this distinction could not be granted without a minimum of guarantees, in particular an investigation of the prodigies attributed to him.[2] These requirements were repeated and extended by his successors. When, in 1120, Calixtus II visited Cluny, the abbot and monks asked him to canonize St Hugh, and read him texts describing his life and miracles. But the pontiff was not satisfied and demanded that authentic witnesses should appear and testify publicly before him, which was done.[3]

---

[1] For the history of the canonization process in the Middle Ages, see L. Hertling, 'Materiali per la storia'; M. Toynbee, *S. Louis of Toulouse and the process of canonization in the fourteenth century* (Manchester, 1929). A heavily juridical and ultramontane approach detracts from the historical value of F. Gagna, *De processu canonizationis a primis Ecclesiae saeculis usque ad codicem Iuris canonici* (Rome, 1940). Processes edited are listed in L. Hertling, sv Canonisation, in *Dictionnaire de spiritualité*, II (Paris, 1953), cc. 79–81. All these works are based exclusively on published texts, though many important enquiries are unpublished.

[2] Mabillon, *AA.SS. OSB*, IX, p. 109; Toynbee, *S. Louis of Toulouse*, p. 137.

[3] The bull of canonization of St Hugh is in G. Fontanini, *Codex constitutionum quas summi pontifices ediderunt in solemni canonisatione sanctorum a Johanne XV ad Benedictum XIII* (Rome, 1729), n. 8; Hertling, 'Materiali per la storia', p. 188.

Admittedly, we should not exaggerate the rigour of this procedure. In the twelfth century, the popes usually entrusted to bishops or papal legates the task of conducting these enquiries, which consisted simply of reading a *Vita* of the candidate and hearing several witnesses to his miracles.[4]

Nevertheless, by the beginning of the twelfth century, at Rome itself and in Latium, a procedure had been established which, as P. Toubert has argued, 'already looks like the fairly clear beginnings of a canonization process'.[5] In the hagiographical writings of this region, the principal marks of sanctity were the prophetic gift *in articulis mortis*, death in an odour of sanctity and thaumaturgic power. The latter was essential, but its use was fairly controlled. The collections of *miracula* of the saint-bishops of Latium reveal a certain reserve and desire for quality. Only a small number of miracles were retained, generally attested by eye-witnesses: 'the marvellous and the prodigious were avoided as far as was possible in the case in point'.[6] This desire for restraint in the sphere of the miraculous originated in a frame of mind similar to that visible at the same period in a work such as the *De pignoribus sanctorum* of Guibert of Nogent.[7]

The desire of the Holy See to impose a degree of control on the cult of the saints was accompanied by critical demands which were soon greatly feared. When, around 1165, Geoffrey of Auxerre was asked to send his Life of St Bernard to the Curia in support of the latter's canonization, he deleted the names of the witnesses who were still living so that the authenticity of the miraculous events he related could not be verified![8] But here, too, the risk of anachronism in the use of the notion of 'critical' is obvious. As A. Bredero has shown with reference to the canonization of St Bernard, the requirement to include a *Vita* in due form in support of a request was not only because Rome wished to be fully informed before pronouncing on the sanctity of a servant of God; the aim was rather to judge if the *Vita* was suitable to support the pastoral intent which lay behind every canonization, and 'to ensure that the life of the saints was told in a manner

---

[4] See the case of St Rosendo in Spain, studied by Garcia y Garcia, 'A propos de la canonisation des saints', p. 29.

[5] P. Toubert, *Les structures du Latium médiéval: le Latium méridional et la Sabine du IXe à la fin du XIIe siècle*, 2 vols. (Rome, 1973), pp. 823–9.

[6] *Ibid.*, p. 824.

[7] Guibert of Nogent, *De pignoribus sanctorum*, in *PL*, 156, cc. 607–79. For this work, see K. Guth, *Guibert von Nogent und die Hochmittelalterliche Kritik an der Reliquienverehrung* (Ottobeuren, 1970); C. Morris, 'A critique of popular religion: Guibert de Nogent on the miracles of the saints', in *Popular belief and practice* (Cambridge, 1972), pp. 55–60.

[8] A. Bredero, 'La canonisation de Saint Bernard et sa "Vita" sous un nouvel aspect', *Cîteaux, Commentaria Cisterciensia*, 25 (1974), pp. 185–98.

likely to promote imitation of their virtues, and not marred by extravagant and unedifying tales'.[9] The same was true of the miracles *post mortem*; the postulators tended to collect as many as possible in a *Liber miraculorum* which was often of greater literary than juridical interest. Even when witnesses had been heard, their evidence was not directly reported, but used to fill out a story shaped by a cleric, who adorned their unpolished depositions with the flowers of hagiographical rhetoric.

In the last decades of the twelfth century, the Roman Curia tried to check this tumultuous flow by suggesting that only the least questionable prodigies should be retained.[10] We can appreciate the progress achieved by looking at the acts of the oldest canonization process to have survived, that of St Galgano (d. 1181), held at Montesiepi, in Tuscany, 4–7 August 1185. The enquiry into the saint-hermit was conducted by the cardinal-bishop of Sabina, Conrad of Wittelsbach, assisted by two other pontifical commissioners. Twenty sworn witnesses appeared before them, after declaring that they testified in all sincerity and without having been suborned. They included Galgano's mother and hermits who had lived with him. Their statements were then transcribed in reported speech. With only two exceptions, they concerned the miracles performed by the saint, either during his lifetime or after his death.[11] The procedure remained fairly basic and few questions were put to the witnesses as to the circumstances surrounding the wonders to whose reality they attested. In spite of these imperfections, we can say that in Italy, by the last quarter of the twelfth century, the basic features of what would in the thirteenth century become the process of canonization were already in existence. This precocity is easily explained by the presence of the Curia in this region and, above all, by the diffusion there of the notarial act with the force of a public instrument. It remained to give the investigation a more precise juridical form and to disseminate the new model throughout Christendom.

---

[9] A. Bredero, *Etudes sur la 'Vita prima' de Saint Bernard* (Rome, 1960), p. 98.

[10] See, for example, the letter from the cleric Vital to the archbishop of Auch after his abortive journey to Rome to obtain the canonization of St Bertrand of Comminges (between 1161 and 1170), ed. M. J. Contrasty, *Revue historique de Toulouse*, 30 (1943), p. 100. E. Delaruelle and C. Higounet, in 'Réformes prégrégoriennes en Comminges et canonisation de S. Bertrand', *Annales du Midi*, 61 (1948), pp. 152–7, show that St Bertrand (d. 1123) was not canonized between 1165 and 1170, as Kemp believed, but after 1218, if at all.

[11] For this process, see F. Schneider, 'Der Einsiedler Galgan von Chiusdino und die Anfänge von San Galgano' (d. 1181), *QFIAB*, 17 (1914–24), pp. 71–7. Curiously, this important document seems to have escaped the attention of all later historians of the process of canonization.

This was the role of Innocent III, whose pontificate marked a decisive turning-point in the history of attitudes to the supernatural.[12]

The fundamental problem faced by the papacy in its desire to reserve the examination of the causes of the servants of God, was that of the proofs of sanctity. For the postulators, this was something evident which had no need of proof. In the case of the first canonization he made, that of St Homobonus of Cremona in 1199, Innocent III reacted against this approach, which his predecessors, primarily anxious to assert their prerogatives at the expense of the bishops, had seen no reason to criticize. In the bull of canonization of St Homobonus, Innocent expressed his desire to subject sanctity itself to careful scrutiny:

> Although, according to the testimony of Truth, only final perseverance is required for a soul to achieve sanctity in the Church triumphant, since 'he who stands firm to the end will be saved', nevertheless, in the Church militant, two things are required before someone can be regarded as a saint: virtue of morals and truth of signs, that is, works of piety in life and evidence of miracles after death.[13]

The fact that the life of a saint, that is, his faith and his works, should be put by the pope on an equal footing with miracles, may seem banal. It represented, nevertheless, a decisive choice on the part of the Roman Church, given that, for the vast majority of the contemporaries of Innocent III, sainthood was defined essentially, if not exclusively, as a collection of supernatural powers, chief of which was healing the sick; we will see below how difficult it was for the papacy to impose the idea that virtues were as important as miracles.

In other respects, however, Innocent III preserved the popular roots of Christian sanctity by affirming, in the same bull, that 'merits without miracles or miracles without merits are insufficient evidence of sainthood, when Satan turns himself into an angel of light and there are some who seek, by their works, human glory'.[14] In adopting this position, the pontiff distanced himself from the rigorist attitude which had prevailed, for

---

[12] For this aspect of the pontificate of Innocent III, see M. Maccarrone, 'Riforma e sviluppo della vita religiosa con Innocenzo III', *RSCI*, 16 (1962), pp. 29–62; J. Baldwin, 'The intellectual preparation for the canon of 1215 against the ordeals', *Speculum*, 36 (1961), pp. 613–36. For the early use of notaries in Rome and Latium, see P. Toubert, 'Techniques notariales et société aux XIIe–XIIIe siècles: les origines du minutier romain', in *Economies et sociétés au Moyen Age: mélanges offerts à Edouard Perroy* (Paris, 1973), pp. 297–308.

[13] The bull of canonization (12 January 1199) is ed. O. Hageneder and A. Haidacher, *Das Register Innocenz' III*, I (Graz and Cologne, 1964), pp. 761–4.

[14] *Ibid.*, p. 762.

example, among certain Cluniac hagiographers, for whom miracles, which had abounded in the early Church, were on the way out and could no longer be regarded as a criterion of sainthood.[15] To Innocent III, on the contrary, they were signs which were indispensable before a Christian could be proclaimed saint by the Church, their function being to confirm both their divine election and their popularity among the faithful. True to his views, Innocent III did not canonize Peter of Castelnau, the Cistercian legate murdered on 16 February 1208 by the supporters of the count of Toulouse, even though, in the four solemn bulls in which he announced his death to Christendom, he several times described him as a martyr. The 'lack of belief' of the inhabitants of Languedoc made it impossible for miracles to occur at his tomb.[16] The Roman Church thus recognized, with Innocent III, that it could only proclaim as a saint a man or a woman who had been indicated as such by the *vox populi*, but it claimed the right to submit this belief to an examination which, significantly, took the form of a judicial procedure. The process of canonization would now be the main arena for the confrontation between the requests of the faithful and of local churches and the requirements of the papacy.

The chief problem the Church faced was that of evaluating the miracles; Innocent III, in the bulls of canonization he promulgated, emphasized that 'Pharaoh's magicians performed marvels in times past and Antichrist will work wonders to lead into error the elect themselves', thereby putting the accent on the ambiguity of supernatural phenomena, for which a diabolical origin was not excluded.[17] Accordingly, the early thirteenth-century popes were primarily concerned to improve the conditions of the enquiry by requiring greater rigour in examining witnesses. This is already visible in the canonization process of St Homobonus in 1199, when the pontiff himself interrogated, in the Curia, a delegation which had travelled specially from Cremona under the direction of Bishop Sicard, the promoter of the cause and biographer of the merchant saint.[18] The principal

---

[15] See, for example, Odo of Cluny, *Sermo de S. Benedicto, PL,* 133, c. 722.

[16] The text of these bulls is *AA.SS.,* Mar. I, pp. 411–15. The absence of miracles is made very clear: 'qui profecto cum ob fidem et pacem quibus nulla est prorsus causa laudabilior ad martyrium sanguinem suum fuderit, claris iam, ut credimus, miraculis coruscasset nisi hoc horum incredulitas impediret' (p. 414). See also P. Delooz, 'Note sur les canonisations occitanes à l'époque de la croisade des Albigeois', *Annales de l'Institut d'etudes occitanes,* 4th ser., 1 (1965), pp. 106–12, especially p. 109.

[17] Bull of St Homobonus, ed. Hageneder and Haidacher, p. 762.

[18] *Ibid.*: 'Sane veniens ad presentiam nostram venerabilis frater noster Sicardus episcopus vester multis viris religiosis et aliis honestis personis de sua diocesi comitatus.' Bishop Sicard of Cremona's Life of St Homobonus, entitled *Acta et obitus S. Homoboni,* has sadly

witness was the priest Osbert, who had been the saint's confessor for twenty years, and the miracles were corroborated by a collective oath on behalf of the whole group.[19]

The process which best demonstrates Innocent III's desire to innovate, however, was probably that of St Gilbert of Sempringham (d. 1198), which was studied some years ago by R. Foreville.[20] The procedure followed in this case deserves to be examined in detail. In response to petitions from the Gilbertine order, with the support of the king of England and the English episcopate, the pope charged the latter, in 1200, with the task of investigating the life and miracles of the founder of Sempringham. This was a very general mandate, which left considerable latitude to the executants.[21] The archbishop of Canterbury proceeded by entrusting to three abbots of his province, assisted by three priors, the task of collecting the depositions of the witnesses at the saint's tomb.[22] When the dossier was taken to Rome, the response, against all expectations, was negative, and Innocent III, by the bull *Licet apostolica sedes* (summer of 1201), ordered the investigation to be repeated on a new basis. First, the enquiry was entrusted to four commissioners specially nominated by the Holy See and acting by virtue of a papal mandate. They were ecclesiastics of high rank: the archbishop of Canterbury, the bishop of Ely and two abbots.[23] The incident is significant; in future, the papacy was no longer content to ratify the initiatives of the local hierarchy; it aimed to control the procedure from start to finish and confer enhanced solemnity on the enquiry. The bull contains a second important innovation; the depositions of the sworn witnesses must be recorded accurately and forwarded as they stood, whereas the first commission, as had hitherto been customary, had been content to forward a brief report synthesizing the evidence.[24] The require-

been lost. There are echoes, however, in the 1199 bull of canonization; see E. Brocchini, *Sicardo di Cremona e la sua opera letteraria* (Cremona, 1958), especially pp. 103–4.

[19] Bull of St Homobonus, ed. Hageneder and Haidacher, p. 764: 'per testimonium dilecti filii Osberti presbyteri sancti Egidii Cremonensis . . . qui patrinus eius existens, per XX annos et amplius confessionem eius sepe receperat'.

[20] R. Foreville, 'Un procès de canonisation à l'aube du XIIIe siècle (1201–1202): le Livre de Saint Gilbert de Sempringham', (thèse complémentaire, Paris, 1943).

[21] 'Ex parte domini pape injungimus ut cum omni devotione et promta voluntate eorum inquisitioni intendatis' (Letter from Philip, apostolic notary, to the English bishops): *ibid.*, p. 9.

[22] Letter from Hubert Walter, archbishop of Canterbury, to the abbots of Swineshead, Bourne and Croxton: *ibid.*, p. 10.

[23] *Ibid.*, pp. 27–8. If one of the bishops was unable to attend, the enquiry could continue as long as the other three were present in person.

[24] 'Non solum per testimonia sed per testes, per famam quoque vulgatam et scripturam auctenticam, de virtute morum et virtute signorum, operibus videlicet et miraculis, certitudinem inquiratis': *ibid.*, p. 28, see also the discussion in pp. xxxv–xxxix.

ment for direct evidential proof was accompanied by other detailed measures, all of which were designed to give greater solemnity: the enquiry
must be preceded by three days of fasting and prayer, as was customary
before important ceremonies such as councils; the witnesses should come
from all social categories with none debarred; if they were of age and had
sworn an oath, their testimony was acceptable.[25] Some were even summoned to appear in the Curia.[26] Lastly, the scope of the enquiry was
enlarged; the commissioners were not only to record depositions concerning the life and miracles; they were also to enquire into the reputation
enjoyed locally by the saint and collect any documents written about him,
if there were any which were authentic.[27] The process was repeated according to these new instructions, and St Gilbert was canonized on 11 January
1202.[28] In the same year, an identical procedure was followed for the
canonization of St Wulfstan, former bishop of Worcester (d. 1095).[29] It is
not irrelevant that the two first causes where the rules defined by Innocent
III were applied concerned English saints. The highly developed awareness of and respect for pontifical prerogatives found in England, and the
high cultural level and efficient organization of its solidly structured epi-
sopate, made it particularly receptive to the extension to the whole of
Christendom of more rigorous requirements with regard to the control of
sanctity.[30]

   The significance of the innovations introduced by Innocent III should
not, however, be exaggerated. The rules he laid down for the collection of
evidence were not altogether new. Innocent simply gave a more coherent
formulation and wider diffusion to investigatory principles which were for
the most part already practised in Italy at the end of the twelfth century.
Further, if he should be credited with emphasizing more clearly than any

[25] Innocent III, *Cum secundum evangelicam* (bull of canonization of St Gilbert), 30 January 1202, *ibid.*, p. 34: 'secundum mandati nostri tenorem, testes iuratos, tam religiosos quam saeculares, tam clericos quam laicos, tam viros quam mulieres, examinare diligentius procurastis'.
[26] 'Ad maiorem vero cautelam, quinque de fratribus ordinis memorati ad nostram presentiam accidentes examinare fecimus sub iuratoria cautione': *ibid.*, p. 35.
[27] See the passage quoted in note 24 above.
[28] The full text of the bull is *ibid.*, pp. 32–6.
[29] St Wulfstan was canonized by Innocent III on 21 April 1203. The bull is Fontanini, *Codex constitutionum*, pp. 40–1. The promoters of the cause had sent the Holy See 'scriptu-ram quoque authenticam de vita ipsius ante centum annos anglicana lingua conscriptam': *ibid.*, p. 40.
[30] For the English episcopate and its cohesion in the thirteenth century, see J. R. H. Moorman, *Church life in England in the thirteenth century* (Cambridge, 1945); F. Powicke and C. Cheney, *Councils and synods relative to the English Church*, 2 vols. (Cambridge, 1964); D. Knowles, 'The English bishops, 1070–1532', in *Medieval studies presented to Aubrey Gwynn, SJ*, II (Dublin, 1961), pp. 283–96.

of his predecessors the importance of the virtues in the appraisal of sanctity, he was content, in the case of St Gilbert, with a *Vita* of the traditional
type, without seeking the depositions of the witnesses, even though these
had been collected by the investigators.[31] We should therefore qualify
Foreville's claim that, after Innocent III, 'the action was comparable to a
veritable trial'.[32] It is true, however, that, under his influence, the investigations of sainthood became both more complex and more juridically
rigorous.

How, in practice, did a canonization process happen? We can see, from
the requests presented to Innocent III and Honorius III, that, as a general
rule, the initiative came from the ordinary of wherever the saint had died
or from the metropolitan.[33] However, we should distinguish between the
original initiative and the support it later received. The papacy would not
embark on an enquiry unless the requests were supported by a sufficient
number of petitions from influential persons and local authorities, both
lay and ecclesiastical. Sometimes, the support extended to a whole
country, for example in England, where, by the beginning of the thirteenth century, the episcopate united round national saints. In the collections of petitions gathered in support of the canonization of St Gilbert of
Sempringham in 1200, and of St Hugh of Lincoln in 1218, letters from
the king and several high lay dignitaries of the kingdom rubbed shoulders
with those from the two archbishops, almost all the bishops and also many
abbots and priors.[34] To judge from the tenor of these documents, it seems
that a sort of encyclical providing a model had been circulating among
interested parties, who had conformed to it more or less faithfully.

In some cases, there were even 'pressure groups' which transcended
national boundaries; the canonization by Honorius III of St Lawrence
O'Toole, in 1225, had been requested by the regular canons of Sainte-Marie
of Eu, in Normandy, where his body lay, the prior of Saint-Victor in Paris,

---

[31] Shown by Archbishop Hubert Walter's report of the enquiry he and two other prelates
had made during the summer of 1201: Foreville, 'Un procès de canonisation', pp. 30–2.

[32] *Ibid.*, p. xxiv.

[33] The canonization of St William (d. 1203), a French Victorin who became abbot of Aebelholt (Denmark), was requested by the archbishop of Lund, but the enquiry was entrusted
to the ordinary, the bishop of Roskilde: Honorius III, *Sacrosancta ecclesia* (21.I.1224),
ed. Fontanini, *Codex constitutionum*, pp. 53–4. Similarly, that of St Bertrand of Comminges was requested by the archbishop of Auch, metropolitan of Saint-Bertrand de
Comminges, where his body lay: Honorius III, *Venerabilis frater noster* (26.XI.1218), ed.
A. Manrique, *Ann. Cist.*, IV (Lyons, 1649), p. 173.

[34] For St Gilbert, see Foreville, 'Un procès de canonisation', pp. 15–26; for St Hugh,
see H. Farmer, 'The canonization of St Hugh of Lincoln', *Lincolnshire Architectural and
Archaeological Society, Reports and Papers*, 6 (1956), pp. 86–117.

the archbishop of Rouen and the whole Irish episcopate.[35] After 1230, the civil powers played an increasingly important role in these actions, in particular in Italy, where the communal authorities themselves applied to the Holy See to request the canonization of saints who had died in or near their city, as, for example, in the case of Padua in 1231, on behalf of St Antony, and Orvieto in 1240, for Ambrose of Massa.[36] In France at this period, we still see lords who were not of particularly high rank soliciting the pope to the same end.[37] By this period, however, the canonization process was tending to become an affair of state, in which the monarchy and bishops of a country joined forces. These displays of 'sacred union' around the causes of saints became the rule after 1260, and, all over Christendom, we see kings act as postulators alongside primates.[38] In practice, the requests almost always had to be repeated several times and it needed great perseverance and continuity to achieve the desired result. Only sovereigns and bishops with access to a network of representatives in and around the Holy See were in a position to sustain such efforts.[39]

[35] M. V. Ronan, 'S. Laurentius' original testimonies for canonization', *Irish Ecclesiastical Record*, I (1926), pp. 337–64; II (1926), pp. 246–56, 467–80. The secular prelates often sought the support of the religious orders, as for example in the case of the canonization process of the Cistercian abbot Hugh of Bonnevaux (d. 1194), requested by the archbishop of Vienne and the abbot of Cîteaux in 1220: J. M. Canivez, ed., *Statuta capitolorum generalium ordinis Cisterciensis*, I (Louvain, 1933), p. 526.

[36] For St Antony of Padua, see the bull of Gregory IX, *Litteras quas per* (30.V.1232), announcing the canonization to the podesta and people of Padua, who had requested it (Fontanini, *Codex constitutionum*, pp. 66–7). It gives the names of the *nuncii* sent by the Commune to the Holy See. For Ambrose of Massa (d. 1240), see Gregory IX, *Dei sapientia* (8.VI.1240), ed. *Bull. Franc.*, I, p. 280.

[37] In 1244, Raoul, lord of Fougères, wrote to Innocent IV to ask him to inscribe in the catalogue of saints Vital of Savigny (d. 1122) and his companions, the translation of whose relics had been authorized by the General Chapter of the Cistercian Order in 1243. The text is in C. Auvry and A. Laveille, *Histoire de la congrégation de Savigny*, III (Paris, 1898), pp. 359–61.

[38] This had not always been the case. We know, for example, that Henry III did everything in his power to prevent the canonization of St Edmund of Canterbury (d. 1240), whose cause was supported by St Louis: C. H. Lawrence, *St Edmund of Abingdon: a study in hagiography and history* (Oxford, 1960), pp. 18, 170–82. But collaboration between episcopate and monarchy was more common. In 1232, Andrew II of Hungary approached Gregory IX to request the canonization of the former archbishop of Esztergom, Luke Banffy (d. 1179): Gregory IX, *Licet quicquid laudis* (17.II.1233), ed. L. Auvray, *Les registres de Grégoire IX (1227–1235)* (Paris, 1890–6), no. 1098; in 1240, King Haakon Haakonsson of Norway and Archbishop Sigurd of Nidaros and his suffragans jointly requested the canonization of Eystein Erlendsson (d. 1188), a former archbishop of Nidaros: C. Thouzellier, 'Un dépôt de l'archevêque de Nidaros à Sainte-Sabine', *AFP*, 21 (1951), pp. 296–7.

[39] For the importance and role of the procurators maintained at great cost at the Curia by some English bishops and chapters, see R. Brentano, *Two churches: England and Italy in the thirteenth century* (Princeton, 1968), pp. 38–48.

To inform the pope and cardinals about the saints they were being asked to canonize, the postulators soon found it advisable to make preliminary enquiries on their own initiative, and attach the results to their petition. Mentioned once under the pontificate of Honorius III, this practice became general after 1230.[40] These diocesan informative processes were designed not so much to inform the Holy See about the merits of a servant of God as to convince him that they enjoyed a local reputation for sanctity (*fama sanctitatis*) sufficient for the cause to be noticed by the Roman Church. The preliminary enquiry needed also to show that many miracles had occurred at the saint's tomb, though it was not necessary for the applicants to prove their reality, since that would be the purpose of the canonization process properly speaking.[41] If the results of the preliminary enquiry were deemed satisfactory, it only remained for the pope to send the prelates charged with the investigation letters remissory, whose stereo-

---

[40] The first known case is that of the process of Stephen of Châtillon, bishop of Die (d. 1208). This former Carthusian had left a great reputation for sanctity in his diocese and Honorius III was asked to canonize him in 1222 by the bishop of Die. By the bull *Etsi non immerito* of 24 October 1222 (Pressutti, 4135), the pope asked the cardinal-bishop of Porto, then legate in Languedoc, to investigate the merits and miracles of this saint. It is not known if he was able to fulfil his mission, but in 1231 the archbishop of Vienne and his suffragans renewed the request and sent the acts of an enquiry made by the bishop of Die in his diocese into the miracles of his illustrious predecessor to Gregory IX (*AA.SS.* Sept. III, pp. 194–200). Essentially the same procedure was followed in most processes of this period. In the case of St Elizabeth of Hungary (d. 1231), Archbishop Siegfried of Mainz went to Marburg in 1232, where Conrad of Marburg, who had been the saint's director of conscience, produced several witnesses who attested to fifty-nine miracles. The prelate approved their depositions, which were forwarded to the pope with a brief biography, the *Summa vitae*, compiled by Conrad; see H. Knies, 'Miracula sanctae Elizabeth, Bemerkungen zu den Kanonisationsakten der Heiligen Landgräfin', in *Universitas, Festschrift A. Stohr*, II (Mainz, 1960), pp. 78–88. In the case of St Edmund of Abingdon (d. 1240), a preliminary enquiry *de fama* was carried out at the abbey of Pontigny, where his body lay, by the ordinary, Bernard of Sully, bishop of Auxerre; the text is in E. Martène and U. Durand, *Thesaurus novus anecdotorum*, III (Paris, 1717), c. 1837.

[41] This point was made in the fourteenth century by the canonist Joannes Andreae in his treatise *In tertium Decretalium librum Novella Commentaria* (Venice edn of 1581, p. 230): 'Consuevit . . . Romanus Pontifex . . . personis honestis et incorruptibilibus committere ut inquirant de fama et devotione populi, de miraculis et aliis que eidem sunt nuncianda, in genere non in specie et quo ad famam, non quo ad veritatem.' From the late thirteenth century, the scrutiny of these diocesan processes was entrusted to a commission of three cardinals, as we see from the petition addressed in 1298 to Boniface VIII by the Dominicans of Barcelona seeking the canonization of St Raymond of Peñafort, which refers to the creation of a commission of this type by Martin IV in 1282: J. Ruis Serra, *Sancti Raymundi de Penyafort opera omnia*, III: *Diplomatario* (Barcelona, 1954), pp. 190–1. As we see from the diocesan process of St Raymond, held in Barcelona in 1279 and begun again in 1318, the inquisitor was a delegate of the local bishop and the depositions were recorded by a notary: MS Vat. lat. 6059, fols. 40–9 (1279); Rius Serra, *Sancti Raymundi*, pp. 207–63 (1318).

typed form is clear evidence that they had become a matter of routine for the pontifical chancery.[42]

The enquiry properly speaking, called in contemporary texts the *processus* or *informatio in partibus*, was entrusted to three commissioners, who included, in principle, at least one bishop. Their mandate was precisely defined in a papal bull; they were to enquire into the life and miracles of the candidate and send the evidence they collected to the pope, together with a report on the form of the process. In the early thirteenth century, it was still sometimes the case that the local bishop served on the commission. Benedict XIV, in his monumental treatise on canonization, believed that this happened only once at this period, misled by the fact that the practice later disappeared.[43] However, during the pontificate of Honorius III alone, we know of three processes in which the local ordinary was one of the commissioners.[44] The practice of excluding him, to give the investigation greater objectivity, did not become usual until the last decades of the thirteenth century.[45]

In general, only a few months elapsed between the receipt of the bull and the effective opening of the process, since the applicants wanted to take advantage of the pope's goodwill without losing time. A change of

---

[42] For bulls directing a canonization process, the pontifical chancery employed various incipits: under Honorius III, that for St William of Aebelholt (25 May 1218) began with the words *Licet angelus Sathane* (Pressutti, 1386); a few days later, the bull for John of Gualdo began *Ineffabilis sapientia Dei* (3 June 1218, Pressutti, 1405). But after a few different initial phrases, the second text followed the first; later bulls, in the cases of Maurice of Carnoët and St Lawrence O'Toole, dated respectively 4 and 5 December 1224, are identical, including the incipit (Honorius III, *Etsi frigescente* (Pressutti, 5197 and 5205)). See plate 4.

[43] Benedict XIV, *De servorum Dei beatificatione*, II, c. III, p. 19.

[44] The enquiry concerning Hugh of Bonnevaux (1221) was entrusted to the archbishop of Vienne, who was the ordinary, and the bishop of Grenoble; that for St Lawrence O'Toole (1224), to the archbishop of Rouen and two canons of the same diocese (his body lay at Eu); in the case of William of Aebelholt (1218), the bishop of Roskilde, the local ordinary, was the second commissioner.

[45] As late as 1240, the enquiry into the life and miracles of Ambrose of Massa was entrusted to the bishop of Orvieto; in 1252, that for Simon of Collazzone was made by the bishop of Spoleto. Even when it was not the local bishop who was entrusted with the enquiry, it was often, in the thirteenth century, regulars of the diocese. In 1240, the abbot of Saint-Martin of Turano and the warden of the Friars Minor of Avezzano collected evidence of the sanctity of Odo of Novara (d. 1200, buried at Tagliacozzo); in 1252, the priors of the Dominicans and of San Sisto of Viterbo did the same for Rose of Viterbo (d. 1251). This practice was not confined to Italy; in Norway, in 1251, the Cistercian abbot of Tuttero, the Benedictine prior of Nidarholm and the prior of the Dominicans of Nidaros investigated the sanctity of Eystein Erlendsson, former archbishop of Nidaros (d. 1188). But, after 1276, commissions of enquiry included at least one bishop and only very exceptionally the ordinary of the place where the saint was buried.

pope meant a suspension which risked being definitive if the commission was not confirmed in its functions by the new pope.[46] The enquiry was usually held wherever the saint was buried and the miracles which had given rise to the cult had been performed.[47] But, as interest in the life of the servants of God developed, the process increasingly took place wherever they had lived for any length of time.[48] In the fourteenth century, the enquiry into the miracles sometimes spread to several countries, as the link between the saint's tomb and the prodigies he or she had worked became looser.[49] The duration of the investigation varied, but as a general

[46] According to a Swedish account from the late fourteenth century, the procurator of the convent of Vadstena, 'Magnus Petri', who had travelled to Rome in 1390 to seek the canonization of St Bridget, arrived to learn that 'papam Urbanum vita excessisse et Bonifacium postea sine dilatione in pontificem electum. Qua de re statusque mutatione multum solicitus necnon afflictus, Dominus Magnus animo inquieto fluctuare incepit, dubitando scilicet ne forte suum canonisationis negotium sinistrum sortiretur progressum': K. H. Karlsson, *Lars Romares Berättelse om den heligi Birgittas Kanonisering* (Stockholm, 1901), pp. 3–4.

[47] See the report sent to Honorius III by the commissioners after the process of St Hugh, bishop of Lincoln (d. 1200), held in Lincoln Cathedral in 1219: 'Venientes autem ad ecclesiam memoratam die prefixo cum episcopo et canonicis eiusdem ecclesie, multos viros religiosos diversorum ordinum invenimus congregatorum aliorum clericorum necnon et laicorum multitudinem copiosam ut ascertio plurium fidem faceret certiorem super hiis de quibus oportebat inquiri': Farmer, 'Canonization of St Hugh of Lincoln', p. 92.

[48] The oldest canonization process held in more than one place is that of the bishop of Vicenza, John Cacciafronte (d. 1183). By the bull *Divine dispensatio*, 5 April 1223 (Pressutti, 423), Honorius III entrusted it to Bishop Jordan of Padua, Joachim, prior of Santa Maria of Vanzo and Brother Albert, prior of the Santo Spirito of Verona; but as the saint had for many years been abbot of San Lorenzo of Cremona, the commission delegated power, in the form of letters rogatory, to Homobonus, bishop of Cremona, who took depositions concerning the candidate's life in Cremona. The whole dossier, from Cremona and Vicenza, is published in A. Schiavo, *Della vita e dei tempi del B. Giovanni Cacciafronte* (Vicenza, 1866), pp. 239–68 (I refer always to this edition in preference to the better-known but very defective edition of F. Dondi dell'Orologio in *Dissertazione sopra l'istoria ecclesiastica di Padova*, VIII (Padua, 1808), pp. 35–41). In the case of St Dominic, after a preliminary enquiry in Bologna, 6–19 August 1233, the commissioners appointed by Gregory IX charged sub-commissioners residing in Toulouse to collect information about the saint's acts and miracles in Languedoc. The latter did not examine the witnesses themselves, but got some Friars Preacher to visit the places where the founder of their order had lived. They synthesized these partial reports and sent them to the commission in Bologna: M. H. Vicaire, *Histoire de Saint Dominique*, II (Paris, 1957), pp. 334–63; V. J. Koudelka, 'Les dépositions des témoins au procès de canonisation de S. Dominique', *AFP*, 42 (1972), pp. 47–67. Sometimes, popes preferred to order two enquiries when a candidate had lived in different countries, as in the case of St Edmund of Abingdon, archbishop of Canterbury, who died in 1240 at Pontigny: Innocent IV, *Cum dilecti filii* to the bishops of London and Lincoln, and *Gaudet pia mater* to the archbishop of Armagh, the bishop of Senlis and the dean of Paris, both dated 23 April 1244, in Martène and Durand, *Thesaurus*, III, c. 1902.

[49] The extreme case is probably that of St Bridget of Sweden (d. 1373); enquiries were held in Sweden, Spoleto, Naples and Rome 1376–80. All these texts are in I. Collijn, *Acta et processus canonizacionis beate Birgitte* (Uppsala, 1924–31).

rule, they grew longer between the thirteenth and the fifteenth centuries.[50]

The commissioners were accompanied by large retinues, consisting usually of regulars, mostly Mendicants, who assisted them in their duties and assured the legality of the procedure.[51] They sometimes included interpreters, who translated the questions posed in Latin by the commissioners into the vernacular, and the replies of the witnesses into Latin when, as was frequently the case, they were *illiterati*.[52] Notaries began to appear in Italy by the 1220s, a little later elsewhere. Their role was to put the depositions *in formam publicam* and make several copies of the whole enquiry, to which the commissioners put their seals.[53] One copy was sent to the pope or placed at his disposal;[54] the other, or others, remained in the hands of the postulators. All were authenticated by the particular *signum* of each notary and bore subscriptions which gave their names. The notaries played no direct part in the process, but their role was nevertheless considerable inasmuch as their presence, by conferring on its acts

---

[50] For the gradual increase in the length of the enquiries, see below, pp. 62–4.

[51] In fact, the popes of the first half of the thirteenth century required the commissioners to surround themselves with collaborators. The formula *ascitis vobis viris religiosis et deum timentibus* appears in most letters remissory issued by Gregory IX and Innocent IV. It later disappeared, being taken for granted. These popes seem to have favoured Mendicant involvement as they lifted the prohibition on their participation in a judgement by employing the following formula: 'non obstante Sedis Apostolicae indulgentia qua dicitur ordini tuo prius esse concessum ut dicti ordinis fratres non possint inviti cognoscere de causis seu intromittere se de negotiis ab ipsa Sede committendis eisdem': Alexander IV, *Significarunt nobis*, 13.XII.1255, in Raynaldi, *Ann. eccl.*, II, p. 528.

[52] This was the case, for example, in the canonization process of St Thomas Cantilupe (d. 1282), at Hereford in 1307. Two Dominicans translated into Latin the evidence of witnesses to the miracles, who spoke in English. This process is particularly interesting from the linguistic point of view: most of the clergy testified in Latin, the members of the lay aristocracy in French, the people *in vulgari anglico*: *PC Thomas of Hereford*, MS Vat. lat. 4015, *passim*.

[53] To quote only one example, the acts of the process of St Dominic (Bologna, 1233) end as follows: 'Aldebrand, son of the late Thibaud, notary by imperial authority, by mandate of the lords . . . delegated by the lord pope Gregory IX, collected, drew up and wrote these depositions in official form': *PC Dominic*, ed. and trans. M. H. Vicaire, *Saint Dominique, la vie apostolique* (Paris, 1965), p. 75. The spread throughout Christendom of this typically Italian practice was not without its problems, especially in countries where notaries did not have the power to authenticate acts. This was the case in Sweden, as is shown by a letter from Bishop Nicholas of Linköping to Gregory XI in 1377, in which he explains why the inquisitors charged with the diocesan process regarding the miracles of St Bridget had put their seals on it: *PC Bridget*, p. 179. This must have been serious, since in his deposition to the Rome process in 1380, Alfonso of Jaen returned to the point and explained to the commissioners, all Italians, that 'in partibus illis, non est consuetudo notariorum nec testium sed instrumenta munita sigillis episcoporum vel nobilium reputantur auctentica et faciunt plenam fidem': *ibid.*, p. 393.

[54] For the circumstances in which the acts of enquiries were transmitted to the pope, see below, pp. 68–9.

the value of a public instrument, emphasized the juridical nature of the investigation.

The notaries were, of course, in the service of the commissioners. At the same period, that is, from the second third of the thirteenth century, the applicants, too, improved their organization, by the use of 'procurators'. Their job was to coordinate the activities designed to procure the opening of the process, assemble the witnesses at the given place and time, and produce them before the investigators.[55] Above all, after 1230, it was the procurator of the cause who drew up the *articuli interrogatorii* or *capitula generalia*, that is, the schema of the interrogation on which the depositions would later be based.[56]

Among the many processes of canonization held in the thirteenth century, it is possible to distinguish several principal types. The first is that of the old saints, long dead and venerated. In this case, the examination of the witnesses could relate only to the miracles. But to compensate for the lack of direct evidence for the life of the saint, there was recourse to written sources, and the postulators produced documents from the archives and ancient texts. The 'dossier' on St Osmund (d. 1099), for example, who was the subject of an enquiry in 1228, comprised, in addition to the depositions of twenty-nine witnesses concerning nineteen miracles performed at his tomb, the text of the *Consuetudines Saresbiriensis ecclesiae* and the *Ordinaciones* drawn up by the prelate, the foundation charter of Salisbury cathedral and extracts from a contemporary chronicle in which his role was mentioned. The commissioners also investigated his *fama* and the spread of his cult.[57]

---

[55] The procurator begins to be distinguished from the postulator from the second third of the thirteenth century: A. Mitri, *De figura iuridica Postulatoris in causis beatificationis et canonizationis* (Rome, 1962). The first person of this type known to us is the Dominican Philip of Verceil, 'named procurator by brother Ventura, prior of the convent and church of Saint Nicolas, of the order of Friars Preacher at Bologna, and by the chapter of the same church gathered according to custom at the sound of the bell in the chapter house': Vicaire, *Saint Dominique*, p. 35. His role was to see that the canonization process, held in Bologna in August 1233, proceeded properly. But it is not until 1265, and the process of Philip of Bourges, that we find true procurators, appointed in letters of attorney issued by the chapter of Bourges under the name of *procuratores, promotores et prosecutores*, which nicely defines the various aspects of their mandate: *PC Philip of Bourges*, MS Vat. lat. 4019, f. 5.

[56] See below, p. 49 and plate 5.

[57] The dossier is ed. A. R. Malden, *The canonization of S. Osmund* (Salisbury, 1901), pp. 32–54. Similarly, in the canonization process of St Stanislas (d. 1079), Innocent IV, having asked for more information after a preliminary enquiry made in 1250 by Polish prelates, instructed his legate in eastern Europe, the Franciscan James of Velletri, to look personally at the historical texts dealing with the martyred bishop, in particular the Book of the Chronicles of the chapter of Cracow, the Annals of Poland and the epitaph on his tomb.

Though for different reasons, the enquiry into the life was also reduced to its simplest expression in the case of very recent saints who were known personally to the pope, such as SS Francis of Assisi and Antony of Padua.[58] This procedure did not, however, become general. On the contrary, in the case of SS Dominic (1233) and Clare (1253), both of whom had been closely connected with the popes who canonized them, an official enquiry into their life and merits was carried out in the normal way by a specially appointed commission.[59]

With these few exceptions, notable though they are, the canonization processes of this period were all characterized by a twofold investigation into the life and the miracles. In the oldest, the time spent at the enquiry on the life was still limited; a few witnesses were questioned on this aspect, whereas several dozen testified concerning the miracles worked by the saint after death.[60] But, if unevenly, the importance attached to the virtues and the reputation of the candidates tended to grow during the thirteenth century.[61] This was not only because a high proportion of the saints then canonized had only very recently died when the process of collecting information about them began. In many investigations made in Italy

---

He also asked him to see, in the absence of eyewitnesses, 'illos duos centenarios, si superstites fuerint, de quibus est mentio in actis, qui dicuntur de aliquibus accepisse, vel eorumdem alterum, quod sanctum noverunt eumdem et de ipsius clara et honesta conversatione dum viveret audiverunt, inquisiturus ab eis an ita sit': Innocent IV, *Licet olim venerabilis*, 26.V.1252, ed. in *Bull. Franc.*, I, p. 610.

[58] M. Bihl, 'De canonizatione S. Francisci', *AFH*, 21 (1928), pp. 468–514, who also examines the circumstances of the canonizations of all St Francis' saintly contemporaries.

[59] For St Dominic, see above, p. 44. Innocent IV would have liked the office of the Virgins, rather than that of the Dead, to be celebrated at the funeral of St Clare of Assisi (d. 1253), but was prevented by the cardinals who pointed out that she could not be considered a saint if she had not been canonized according to the rules. A process was therefore held at Assisi 24–9 November 1253. There survives only an Italian translation of the acts, dating from the fifteenth century, which is ed. Z. Lazzeri, 'Il processo di canonizzazione di S. Chiara d'Assisi', *AFH*, 13 (1920), pp. 439–93.

[60] In the process of the hermit Odo of Novara (d. 1200) at Tagliacozzo in 1240, only six out of 106 witnesses testified to his life and merits; see the edition in *Anal. Boll.*, I (1882), pp. 323–53. In the process of Ambrose of Massa (d. 1240) in Orvieto in 1240, nine witnesses testified concerning his life, some 140 concerning his miracles: *AA.SS.* Nov. IV, pp. 571–608; L. Fumi, 'Processi della canonizzazione del B. Ambrogio da Massa dei Minori', *Miscell. Franc.*, I (1886), pp. 77–80, 129–36. For the distribution of witnesses in different processes, see table 33.

[61] One can assess the extent of the change by comparing the processes 1230–40, where the number of witnesses *de vita* was generally fairly small (except in the case of St Dominic), with enquiries such as that in 1265–6 regarding the sanctity of Philip of Bourges and that in 1276 for St Margaret of Hungary, where the enquiry into the life reached a length which was rarely if ever surpassed: *PC Philip of Bourges*, MS Vat. lat. 4019, fols. 28–49v; *PC Margaret of Hungary*, ed. G. Fraknoi in *Monumenta Romana Episcopatus Vesprimiensis*, I (Budapest, 1896), pp. 163–383.

before 1260 regarding people who had died some decades earlier, the evidence about their life and merits bulked large. This was the case, for example, with the process of John Cacciafronte, a bishop of Vicenza assassinated in 1183, which was held in Vicenza and Cremona in 1223–4. Although the enquiry took place forty years after his death, the depositions regarding his life were already sufficiently important to anticipate the classic form of the process.[62] Furthermore, in the best conducted investigations, one can clearly distinguish the miracles performed after the death of the saint from those performed while the saint was still alive. The latter were examined in the context of the enquiry into the life. This was not simply a presentational change; the new obligation on postulators to prove that 'their' saint had also performed miracles during his or her earthly life tended to loosen the link between sainthood and the supernatural occurrences around tombs, and to present them as the prolongation of a virtuous existence.[63]

The results were uneven. In a process such as that for Hildegard of Bingen (1233–43), so much emphasis was put on the miracles performed by the saint during her lifetime that the depositions, which are in any case recorded in a muddled way, give us a less than clear picture of the great visionary.[64] One single witness – a cleric – made a clearly structured statement in which he referred successively to her life, her behaviour, her virtues, the extraordinary phenomena which happened around her and,

---

[62] At the enquiry in Cremona 7–9 November 1223, all sixteen witnesses testified regarding both the life and miracles of the holy bishop; in Vicenza, in January 1224, four witnesses testified to the life and nineteen to the miracles: *PC John Cacciafronte.*

[63] The distinction between the enquiry into the life and that into the miracles was already clear, in principle, at the beginning of the thirteenth century, as we see from the bull of canonization (1218) of St William of Bourges (d. 1203): 'de illius conversatione et vita, ac deinde de miraculis inquisitionem facientes': Fontanini, *Codex constitutionum*, p. 50. In the process of St Hugh of Lincoln (1219), the miracles were classified according to the period when they were performed: of the thirty-six retained by the commissioners, five were miracles *in vita*, two were *post mortem ante sepulturam* and twenty-nine were *post sepulturam*: *PC Hugh of Lincoln*, pp. 97–104. In later processes, only miracles *in vita*, which were examined in the context of the investigation into the life, and miracles *post mortem*, the proper subject of the enquiry into the miracles, were distinguished. The papacy regarded the former as very important; Honorius III explicitly refused to canonize Robert of Molesme (d. 1111), despite the insistent requests of the Cistercian order, because the inquisitors had neglected the miracles *in vita*: Honorius III, *Cum olim nobis*, 8.I.1222 (Pressutti, 3701), ed. P. Labbé, *Novae bibliothecae manuscriptorum librorum*, I (Paris, 1651), p. 650.

[64] P. Bruder, 'Acta inquisitionis de virtutibus et miraculis S. Hildegardis', *Anal. Boll.*, 2 (1883), pp. 118–29; this confusion was denounced by Innocent IV in the bull *Supplicantibus olim*, 24.XI.1243, in which he ordered the enquiry to be begun again: ed. S. A. Würdtwein, *Nova subsidia diplomatica*, XI (Heidelberg, 1781), p. 34.

lastly, to her writings and their fame. L. Hertling has argued that this deposition must be the result of the first known example of *articuli interrogatorii*.[65] Though this is arguable, in that it extrapolates from a special case, it is undeniable that, at the end of the first third of the thirteenth century, there was an attempt to direct the flow of the evidence.

The canonization process of St Dominic, held at Bologna and around Toulouse, also dates from 1233. To assist the investigation, the procurator of the cause, the Dominican Philip of Verceil, drew up a list of articles intended to cover all the elements which characterized the sanctity of the founder of the order of Preachers.[66] The role of these 'capitularies' was primarily to prevent idle chatter and orient the depositions of the witnesses towards the essential points. But, in so doing, they also assembled the elements of a brief biography of the saint in order to bring out the original aspects of his personality. In the case of St Dominic, it remained simply a list of virtues illustrated by a few concrete episodes from his life. With the process of Philip of Bourges (1265–6), which is the first to display the classic form destined to last to the end of the Middle Ages, the biographical aspect was even more marked, with a more or less harmonious fusion operating between the story of a saintly life, from childhood to death, and the catalogue of virtues appropriate to each of the ages and states through which the saint had passed.[67] So, where there was a canonization, there was a *Vita per Curiam approbata* which could be used to create liturgical offices and serve as a basis for later hagiographical compositions.

As the importance of the life of the saints increased within the processes of canonization, major advances were also being made in the investigation of the miracles. In the first thirteenth-century process to have survived complete, that of Gilbert of Sempringham (1202), the commissioners retained thirty miracles, classed by medical category (*de frenesi*, *de oculo maculoso* etc.), and each attested by several witnesses (between two and five per miracle), whose names were recorded with a note of where they had lived.[68] But the weak point of these enquiries was the imprecision of the depositions, which mostly consisted simply of approval of the schema

---

[65] The deposition was that of Bruno, *Custos S. Petri in Argentina et presbyter*: Bruder, *PC Hildegard*, pp. 124–5; Hertling, 'Materiali per la storia', p. 193.

[66] The list has been reconstituted by Vicaire (*Saint Dominique*, p. 25); see also below, pp. 506–7.

[67] The conception of sanctity expressed in the *articuli interrogatori* will be discussed later (see pp. 505ff); I refer here only to procedure. For the material presentation of the depositions, see plate 6.

[68] Foreville, *PC Gilbert of Sempringham*, p. 16.

proposed by the promoters of the cause. An important step forward was taken during the pontificate of Gregory IX, when the letters remissory ordering the enquiry began to be accompanied by a *forma interrogatorii*, that is, a stereotyped formulary for the use of the commissioners responsible for the inquiry. The aim was to gather as much information as possible about the circumstances in which the miracles had occurred.[69] The questions posed were primarily intended to eliminate all possibility of fraud and detect superstitious practices, in particular any use of incantatory formulas (*quibus verbis interpositis?*). Those concerning the duration and date of the sickness and its cure were particularly numerous and detailed.[70] From the perspective of the pontifical questionnaire, there was no miracle unless an individual was permanently cured of an obvious disease from which he had suffered for a long time. As long as we do not give these words the very precise meaning they have today, we may speak of a sort of medico-legal enquiry.[71] To complete these precautions, in the thirteenth century, the popes several times asked that the beneficiaries of miracles should be produced at the Curia and subjected to direct examination.[72] But this requirement seems not to have persisted beyond 1262, since no trace of it survives after that date in the records of the enquiries or bulls of canonization. It presented very great practical problems for the postulators, who had to persuade more or less recalcitrant witnesses to leave their homes and travel to Rome.[73]

[69] The *forma* appears for the first time, to my knowledge, at the end of a bull ordering the canonization process of St Elizabeth of Thuringia: Gregory IX, *Ut caeci viam*, 13.X.1232, ed. *Bull. Franc.*, I, pp. 85–6.

[70] The text of the *forma*, which was repeated *ne varietur* throughout our period, is as follows: 'Testes legitimos quos super vita et miraculis recolende memorie . . . debetis recipere, prius prestito iuramento, diligenter examinare curetis et de omnibus quae dixerint interrogetis eosdem: quomodo sciunt? Quo tempore? Quo mense? Quo die? Quibus presentibus? Quo loco? Ad cuius invocationem et quibus verbis interpositis? Et de nominibus illorum circa quos miracula esse facta dicuntur; et si antea eos cognoscebant? Et quot diebus ante eos viderint infirmos? Et quanto tempore fuerint infirmi? Et quanto tempore visi sunt sani? Et de quo loco sunt oriundi? Et interrogentur de omnibus circumstanciis diligenter, et circa singula capitula fiant questiones predicte et fiat series testimonii: et verba testium prout seriose ac diffuse prolata fuerint, fideliter redigantur in scriptis.'

[71] The question is discussed, though unfortunately very briefly for the Middle Ages, in F. Antonelli, *De inquisitione medico-legali supra miraculis in causis beatificationis et canonizationis* (Rome, 1962).

[72] This procedure was still often employed in the middle of the thirteenth century; see Innocent IV, *Gaudet pia mater*, 23.IV.1244: 'quatuor aut tres duos ad minus, in quibus evidentiora miracula per ipsius archiepiscopi [St Edmund] merita fuit Dominus operatus, ad rei certitudinem pleniorem, ad nostram presentiam transmittatis'; Martène and Durand, *Thesaurus*, III, cc. 1841–2; bull of canonization of St William Pinchon, bishop of Saint-Brieuc (d. 1234), in 1247, ed. Fontanini, *Codex constitutionum*, p. 81.

[73] When the archdeacon of Canterbury tried to persuade some English peasants, miraculously cured by St Edmund, to accompany him to the Curia, he nearly sparked off a

The rapid development of the canonization process during the first third of the thirteenth century is a phenomenon of interest to more than just historians of canon law. The emergence among the ruling circles of the Church of a cautious, if not critical, attitude towards spontaneous manifestations of popular fervour also marks an important turning-point in the history of mentalities, in that it implies a new demarcation of the religious field. In fact, though the procedure did not yet involve a Devil's advocate, and though the requirements of the investigators do not seem very rigorous compared with those of today, the simple fact of having recourse to law – the critical discipline of the period – in order to distinguish the true from the false in this sphere in itself constitutes a major innovation. The best proof of this is the difficulty experienced by the postulators in adapting to the procedures which the Holy See was attempting to impose. Of the forty-eight enquiries ordered by Rome between 1199 and 1276 with the canonization of a saint in mind, twenty-five, that is, over half, were never completed at the time (see table 1). More significant still is the number which the Holy See ordered to be done again, because the acts, as they had been transmitted, did not meet the new norms. This was the case in eighteen out of the forty-eight cases (see table 2).

What was it that the applicants found so difficult and how can we explain the high failure rate? Perhaps paradoxically to our eyes, many of the objections made by the Holy See to investigations *in partibus* concerned the way in which evidence had been taken and recorded. In fact, in many cases, the witnesses had not been questioned singly (*singillatim*) or, at least, their depositions had not been taken down literally (*verbatim*) but merged into an impersonal report drawn up later by the commissioners.[74] Honorius III several times attacked this practice; the reproachful letter he sent to the Breton prelates on the subject of the enquiry into the miracles of St Maurice of Carnoët, which he thought had been badly conducted, even passed into the Decretals of Gregory IX under the title *Venerabili*,

---

revolt; see the letter from Stephen Langton to the English Cistercian cardinal, John Tolet, in Martène and Durand, *Thesaurus*, III, c. 1914.

[74] Honorius III rejected the first enquiry into the sanctity of St William of York (d. 1154) 'cum in ea nequaquam dicta testium sint expressa': *Etsi non immerito*, 11.IV.1224 (Pressutti, 4935), ed. in part in Raynaldi, *Ann. eccl., ad an. 1224*, XLVII. In the process of St Hildegard at Bingen in 1233, we find expressions such as 'quaerentibus nobi a conventu', or 'quod sanior pars conventus iurata protestatur', which provoked papal disapproval: Innocent IV, *Supplicantibus olim*, 24.XI.1243, ed. in Würdtwein, *Nova subsidia diplomatica*, IX, p. 34. It was still necessary for Innocent V to remind the Hungarian bishops of this requirement in 1276, after they had investigated the sainthood of St Margaret and sent only a very confused account: *Dudum ex parte*, 14.V.1276, ed. Fraknoi, *Monumenta Romana*, pp. 160–1.

Table 1 *Enquiries ordered by the papacy which did not result in a canonization (1198–1276)*

Saint	Date of the enquiry
Caradoc (d. 1124)	1200[a]
Bertrand of Comminges (d. 1125)	c.1218 (?)
John of Gualdo (d. 1170)	1221
Robert of Molesme (d. 1111)	1221
Hugh of Bonnevaux (d. 1194)	1223
John Cacciafronte (d. 1183)	1223–4
Maurice of Carnoët (d. 1191)	1225
Rainerius of Furcona (d. 1077)	c.1225 (?)
Osmund of Salisbury (d. 1099)	1228[b]
Luke Banffy (d. 1179)	1232–3
Stephen of Die (d. 1208)	c.1233[c]
Hildegard of Bingen (d. 1179)	1233
Benvenuto of Gubbio (d. c.1232)	1236
John of Montmirail (d. 1217)	c.1236
Bruno of Wurzburg (d. 1045)	between 1238 and 1247
Odo of Novara (d. 1200)	1240
Ambrose of Massa (d. 1240)	1240–1
Lawrence Loricatus (d. 1243)	1244
Eystein Erlendsson (d. 1189)	between 1251 and 1254
John Bonus (d. 1249)	1251–4
Simon of Collazzone (d. 1250)	1252
Rose of Viterbo (d. 1251)	1252
Nicholas of Denmark (d. 1180)	1254 or 1255
Philip of Bourges (d. 1261)	1265–6
Margaret of Hungary (d. 1270)	1272[d]

Notes:

[a] The enquiry, ordered by Innocent III on 8 May 1200, was never held, the two commissioners appointed having destroyed the pontifical bull in order not to have to carry it out, if we are to believe Giraldus Cambrensis (*Giraldus Cambrensis, De invectionibus*, III, 7, in *Geraldi Cambrensis Opera*, III, ed. J. S. Brewer (London, 1863), pp. 64–5, with the text of the bull).

[b] St Osmund was finally canonized in 1457 by Calixtus III. But the enquiry held in the thirteenth century can be regarded as having failed.

[c] First enquiry in 1223 (?).

[d] Canonized by Pius XII in 1943.

and was later glossed by all the commentators of the period.[75] He drew attention to the faults referred to above and emphasized that this manner of proceeding made it impossible to get a clear idea of the circumstances in which the alleged miracles had taken place.[76] Several times, the Holy

[75] Honorius III, *Venerabili fratre*, 1.IX.1225, ed. A. Manrique, *Ann. Cist.*, 4, p. 242. The text appears in the Decretals, C. 52, X, 11, 20, *De test. et attest.*

[76] *Ibid.*: 'Idem episcopus et abbas quamdam nobis paginam transmiserunt . . . in qua multum quidem et magna miracula continentur . . . quae licet probata per testes juratos et nominatos in ipsa pagina minuantur, non tamen apparet per paginam sepedictam quod

Table 2 *Enquiries deemed inadequate by the pope and repeated at his request (1198–1276)*

Saint	Date of papal bull criticizing the earlier enquiry	Canonization (in the Middle Ages)
Gilbert of Sempringham	1201	yes
Robert of Molesme	1222	no[a]
William of York	1224	yes
Maurice of Carnoët	1225	no
Stephen of Die	1233	no
Luke Banffy	1233	no
Hildegard of Bingen	1243	no
Edmund of Abingdon	1245	yes
Margaret of Scotland	1246	yes
Bruno of Wurzburg	1247	no
Ambrose of Massa	1250	no
Stanislas	1251	yes
Simon of Collazzone[b]	1252	no
John Bonus	1253	no
Eystein Erlendsson	1255	no
Nicholas of Denmark	1255	no
Hedwig of Silesia	1263	yes
Margaret of Hungary	1276	no

Notes:
[a] Honorius III granted the monks of Molesme the right to venerate St Robert *tamquam sanctum in vestra ecclesia*, which was tantamount to a polite refusal of canonization (*Cum olim nobis*, 8.I.1222, ed. Labbé, pp. 649–50). In the same bull, he criticized the inadequacies of the process held in 1221 by the bishops of Langres and Valence.
[b] Innocent IV authorized the commissioners to delegate their powers to some regulars charged with conducting the enquiry outside Spoleto. This was an indirect way of criticizing its inadequacy (Innocent IV, *Litteras nostras*, 10.VII.1252, ed. *Bull. Franc.*, I, p. 619).

See reproached the investigators for failing to hear witnesses directly, or for neglecting the biographical facts and written documents which, in the case of a long-dead saint, would have made it easier to assess their actions and the impression made on contemporaries.[77] In fact, these rejections, though they appear to apply exclusively to questions of form, attack an insufficiently critical, or too exclusively thaumaturgical, conception of

ipsos testes examinaverunt singillatim et quod eos super hiis de quibus sunt testificati ac circumstanciis cum ea interrogaverunt diligentia quae solet et debet in testium receptione adhiberi.'
[77] Gregory IX demanded that the sainthood of Stephen of Die (d. 1208) should be shown 'non solum per testes sed per famam etiam et scripturas authenticas': *Patri luminum*, 16.XII.1233, ed. in *Gallia Christiana*, XVI, instr., p. 213. The same formula appears in the same year in the bull ordering a repeat of the process of the Hungarian archbishop, Luke Banffy (d. 1179): *Licet quicquid*, 17.2.1233 (Auvray, 1098).

sainthood; many enquiries had to be repeated because the papacy judged insufficient attention had been paid to the saint's life.[78]

But miracles caused still other objections; the commissioners often forgot to ask for information about those that the saints had performed during their lifetime, or conversely, in the case of the great healers, they failed to enquire into the prodigies which had occurred after their death through their intercession.[79] The number of miracles attested was sometimes deemed excessive. Innocent IV ordered that the enquiry into St Edmund of Canterbury, held in France in 1244, should be done again *omissa miraculorum multitudine*, and reminded the commissioners that it was better to collect detailed and unarguable evidence about four or five miracles than list a large number that were insufficiently proved.[80] It remained difficult to put this advice into practice, so persistent was the conviction that a superabundance of miracles was the most obvious proof of the sanctity of a servant of God.

After 1250, pontifical bulls ordering enquiries into the life and miracles of saints to be repeated became rarer. In spite of a few isolated cases which concerned outlying regions of Christendom (Scandinavia, Hungary), the demands of the papacy with regard to evidence, and even its conception of a sainthood focussed more on the virtues than the prodigies, seem to have been assimilated by the clergy.[81] But the process of canonization did not, for all that, become easier, because, at this period, its centre of gravity shifted. If the popes of the second half of the thirteenth century referred only exceptionally to errors of form in the processes, it was also because

---

[78] Innocent IV ordered a repeat of the enquiry into Bruno of Wurzburg (d. 1045), as he thought it should deal as thoroughly with his life as with his merits: *Dudum venerabili*, 5.XI.1247, ed. E. Berger, *Les registres d'Innocent IV*, no. 3414. In 1253, he ordered a supplementary enquiry into the faith, that is, essentially, the orthodoxy, of John Bonus (d. 1249), a former jongleur who became a hermit and founder of the congregation of the 'Zamboniti'; the bull has been lost, but the acts of the new process, which took place at Mantua and Cesena, November 1253 to January 1254, are ed. *AA.SS.* Oct. IX, pp. 771–885.

[79] Alexander IV ordered the enquiry into the miracles of Nicholas of Denmark (d. 1180) to be repeated, because they had been neglected by the commissioners: *Significarunt nobis*, 13.XII.1255, ed. in Raynaldi, *Ann. eccl., ad an. 1255*, p. 528.

[80] Innocent IV, *Attendentes quod*, April or May 1245, ed. Martène and Durand, *Thesaurus*, III, c. 1844 (Potthast, 1645).

[81] See table 2. In the fourteenth century, however, the papacy occasionally still demanded additional information after a first enquiry *in partibus*, for example in the case of St Thomas Aquinas (d. 1274). John XXII in 1321 charged the bishops of Anagni and Terracina along with a curialist to investigate the miracles performed at Fossanova; the process held in 1319 in Naples was insufficiently informative on this point: *Cum secundum evangelicam*, 1.VI.1321, ed. G. Mollat, *Lettres communes de Jean XXII (1316–1334)*, IV (Paris, 1906), no. 13561.

the investigation *in partibus*, which had been the crucial stage in the procedure at the time of Innocent III and Honorius III, lost ground in favour of the curial stage. The commissioners delegated by the Holy See were now, in effect, required not so much to judge as to investigate in a way which assured the validity of the evidence. To the extent that the process came increasingly to resemble a real trial, the examination of the depositions by the pope and cardinals became all-important.

Once the local enquiry had been completed, the commissioners put the acts at the disposal of the pope. He entrusted them to one or more cardinals, usually three from the mid-thirteenth century, who broke the seals after identifying them and proceeded to examine the dossier.[82] In the first third of the thirteenth century, this examination seems to have been fairly cursory, since it rarely took more than a few days.[83] Later, it lasted much longer, often taking several years. First, the cardinals' chaplains made a close study of the text of the enquiry, and extracted the substance under headings, under which they arranged the supporting evidence. The cardinals themselves then examined the documents and prepared a report or *relatio* for the pope and their colleagues.[84] It was at this stage that reservations or doubts about the sanctity of a candidate were expressed, and one understands the unease felt by contemporaries at the arrival of a stage when the risks of the process failing or getting bogged down were considerable.[85]

When the commission had finished its work, the pope summoned the cardinals in secret consistory. A report or *summarium* was read by those charged with the affair, and all the members of the Sacred College who were present gave their opinion. Then, at a second consistory, the Supreme Pontiff consulted those bishops and archbishops who were

---

[82] The role of the cardinals in the scrutiny of canonization files is attested by the twelfth century; it continued to grow in the thirteenth, as we see, for example, from the letter sent by the bishop and dean of Lincoln to the Sacred College in 1219 in the hope of persuading them to advance the cause of St Hugh, whose enquiry *in partibus* had just been completed. We know from the bull of canonization that it was examined by the cardinal-bishop of Sabina: Farmer, 'Canonization of St Hugh of Lincoln', pp. 114–16.

[83] The acts of the process of St Lawrence O'Toole were sent by Honorius III on 28 October 1225 to the cardinal-bishop of Tusculum. He reported in consistory 4 December, and the canonization was pronounced the following day by the pope: G. Bessin, *Concilia Rotomagensis provinciae*, II (Rouen, 1717), p. 47.

[84] All these operations are clearly described for the first time in the canonization process of Philip of Bourges, 1265–6. Reports from the years 1266–70 make it possible to trace in detail the vicissitudes of the curial phase of the process (MS Vat. lat., 4019, fols. 1–11v); see also plate 7.

[85] For the fears generally inspired by the scrutiny of canonization processes by the cardinals, renowned for their scepticism, see below, pp. 481–2.

present at the Curia and pronounced his sentence.[86] In some ways, this procedure recalls the not too distant time when canonizations had only been pronounced on the occasion of a council or synod. But the resemblance should not be pushed too far, since, by this period, the assent of prelates of inferior rank seems to have been required only as a matter of form;[87] the role of the cardinals and the pope was supreme. The pope then moved to a larger room where a third consistory, specially summoned, was held, this time in public, where he announced his intention of inscribing a servant of God in the catalogue of saints.[88] The liturgical ceremony followed, usually a few days later, after which the news was notified to the clergy and the faithful by one or more solemn bulls.[89] These consisted of a report on the circumstances of the process, a rehearsal of pontifical prerogatives in the sphere of canonization, a flowery eulogy of the virtues of the new saint and a list of the miracles. The pope announced his decision to canonize and communicated the text of three prayers (collect, secret, postcommunion) which would be those of the new saint. Lastly, he instructed the bishop or archbishop of the diocese which held the relics of the saint to celebrate his festival with solemnity.[90]

---

[86] An intervention by Frederick Visconti, archbishop of Pisa, at the consistory gathered to pronounce on the canonization of St Clare of Assisi in 1253 gives us an impression of how things happened: Z. Lazzeri, 'Consilium Friderici Vicecomitis Archiepiscopi Pisani', *AFH*, 11 (1918), pp. 276–9; see also plate 8.

[87] The usual formula from the mid-thirteenth century is: 'de fratrum nostrorum et prelatorum omnium apud sedem apostolicam existentium unanimi consilio et concordi consensu, auctoritate beatorum apostolorum Petri et Pauli . . . eum sanctorum catalogo duximus adscribendum'. John XXII modified this significantly and, in many bulls of canonization promulgated during his pontificate, we find: 'ad requisitionem instantem et supplicationem humilem et devotam praelatorum multorum apud sedem apostolicam existentium, de dictorum fratrum nostrorum concilio et assensu': Fontanini, *Codex constitutionum*, p. 134. But Clement VI, in the bull of canonization of St Yves (1347), reverted to the old formula: A. de La Borderie, *Monuments originaux de l'histoire de saint Yves* (Saint-Brieuc, 1887), p. 485. For the significance of the changes, see A. P. Frutaz, 'Auctoritate . . . beatorum Petri et Pauli. Saggio sulle formule di canonizzazione', *Antonianum*, 47 (1967), pp. 435–501.

[88] The last stages of the procedure are described in detail in the ceremonials of the early fourteenth century; see L. H. Labande, 'Le Cérémonial romain de Jacques Cajétan', *BECh*, 54 (1893), pp. 45–74; B. Schimmelpfennig, *Die Zeremonienbücher der römischen Kirche im Mittelalter* (Tubingen, 1973), pp. 164–74.

[89] For the liturgy of canonization in the Middle Ages, see the fine study by T. Klauser, 'Die Liturgie der Heiligsprechung', in *Heilige Uberlieferung, Festschrift I. Herwegen* (Münster, 1938), pp. 212–33.

[90] See, for example, the end of the bull of canonization of St Gilbert of Sempringham (1201): 'faciens festivitatem ipsius per tua provincia [sic] sollemniter celebrari': Foreville, 'Un procès de canonisation', p. 35. The bull of canonization strictly speaking was generally followed by another bull, in which the pope asked the local ordinary to proceed to the

So, from a typically 'Gregorian' perspective, the need for control and the desire for greater authenticity led, in the sphere of the cult of the saints, as elsewhere, to a concentration of decision-making powers in the hands of the Roman Church. The process speeded up during the thirteenth century, but it was already present in embryo in Innocent III's efforts to impose a form of enquiry which reflected the desire of the papacy to control the procedure from start to finish and impose its own conception of sainthood.

translation of the relics of the saint: Fontanini, *Codex constitutionum, passim*. Lastly, from the time of Gregory IX, a third bull was promulgated in many cases, to announce the news to *universis Christi fidelibus*, so as to mark the universal significance of the pontifical sentence.

PART II

THE CHURCH AND THE CONTROL OF SAINTHOOD IN THE LATER MIDDLE AGES (*c*.1270 to *c*.1430)

෨෨෨

CHAPTER 4

THE EVOLUTION OF THE ROLE OF CANONIZATION: FROM CONTROL TO SELECTION

ೞೞೞ

A quick glance at the figures reveals the difference between the thirteenth century and later with regard to canonizations: forty-nine processes were decreed by the papacy between 1198 and 1304, compared with twenty-two between 1305 and 1431;[1] the figures are comparable for canonizations pronounced: twenty-four in the thirteenth century, eleven in the fourteenth and early fifteenth centuries. But a comparison between centuries is not necessarily the most helpful. In table 3, therefore, I have given the figures for four quite distinct chronological periods, each of which has its own characteristics.

Table 3 at once suggests certain conclusions. An initial period of intense activity was followed by a period of relative inaction which lasted until the pontificate of Clement V; numbers then picked up slightly, though they never again reached the high levels of the years 1198–1268. In fact, when we compare this period with that of the Avignon papacy (1305–78), which was of roughly the same length, we see that both processes (twelve, as compared with forty-seven) and canonizations (six compared with

Table 3 *Processes and canonizations between 1198 and 1431*

Periods	Processes decreed by the papacy	Canonizations pronounced
1198–1268 (71 years)	47	23
1269–1304 (35 years)	2	1
1305–1378 (75 years)	12	6
1379–1431 (52 years)[a]	10	5

Note:
[a] Including all rival obediences during the period of the Great Schism.

[1] See the complete list of canonization processes below, pp. 252–5.

twenty-three) were almost four times less numerous in the fourteenth than in the thirteenth century. The figures rose slightly with the Great Schism, but we should remember that the figures in table 3 include all causes promoted by the rival obediences and by the Council of Constance. Table 3 confirms that the 1260s marked a turning-point in the history of canonization. We need next to analyse this phenomenon more closely to appreciate fully its significance and impact.

One reason for the sharp drop in the number of canonizations made after 1268 was simply the increasing length of the procedure. In 1254, the enquiry at Assisi into the sanctity of St Clare was completed in six days;[2] in 1276, the process of St Margaret of Hungary lasted nearly three months, even though it was confined to one place and was not interrupted.[3] In 1307, that of St Thomas Cantilupe stopped after four months, at the request of the commissioners, on orders from the pope; hundreds of miracles had to be recorded in haste during the final days and the records show all the signs of time running out.[4] In the second half of the fourteenth and the early fifteenth centuries, some enquiries in partibus dragged on for several years, because the bishops responsible for them could not leave their dioceses for any length of time. The process of Dorothy of Montau, held at Marienwerder, in eastern Prussia, consisted of four sessions, each lasting several months, spread over three years (1404–6).[5]

The principal reason for the greater length of the procedure, however, was the increasing length of the curial stage: the receipt of the documents in the Curia, their authentication, which was sometimes contested, the meticulous examination and rubrication of the acts of the enquiry by the chaplains of the cardinals appointed by the pope to act in the matter, and the compilation of their report, all took years, even decades. Without there necessarily being a conscious desire to stall the proceedings, a dossier, however well prepared, could be blocked at various points before it

---

[2] 24–29 November 1253: *PC Clare of Assisi*, p. 405.

[3] 23 July–20 October 1276: *PC Margaret of Hungary*, pp. 383–4.

[4] *AA.SS.* Oct. I, pp. 592–6. The day before the day fixed for the process to end, the procurator presented the commissioners with a list of 304 miracles which he offered to prove in writing, as he was no longer able to do so by oral testimony.

[5] The sessions were: 24–27 June 1404, 13 October–6 November 1404, 30 April–7 May 1405 and 6–10 February 1406; see *Gedanen. beatificationis et canonizationis servae Dei Dorotheae Montoviensis . . . Positio super cultu* (Vatican City, 1971), p. 261. The length was, of course, related to the number of witnesses whose depositions were heard during the process: 110 at that of St Margaret of Hungary, 205 at that of St Thomas Cantilupe, 257 at that of Dorothy of Montau.

reached the final stage.[6] Indeed, it only needed one of the three cardinals responsible – a deacon, a priest and a bishop – to be summoned to other duties, or to die, for there to be a hiatus of several months in the examination of the documents. More serious still was the death of the pope who had ordered the process or its repetition, especially if it happened before the investigation was complete, as it was then necessary for the commission to be confirmed in its duties by his successor, which involved new delays. The series of very short or very turbulent pontificates which marked the years 1268–1304 must have contributed to the inertia of the Holy See during this period, if we except the canonization of St Louis.[7]

---

[6] Thanks to the documents preserved in MS Vat. lat. 4019–21, we can trace in detail, from 1262 to 1331, the vicissitudes of a process which originally appeared extremely promising, that of the archbishop of Bourges, Philip Berruyer (d. 1261). A first commission of enquiry was set up in 1262 by Urban IV, consisting of the bishops of Chartres and Nevers and the prior of the Dominicans in Paris. After Urban's death, his successor, Clement IV, renewed the commission's mandate in 1265. The enquiry *in partibus* then proceeded smoothly in Bourges, Beaugency and Orléans from November 1265 to July 1266, culminating in a document which was, for its time, a model of the genre, and which was sent to the pope in August 1266. In September 1267, Clement IV asked Cardinal Eudes of Châteauroux, bishop of Tusculum, to examine the acts, with the aid of two fellow cardinals and numerous chaplains. But the pope's death and the various crises which followed – from the conclave of Viterbo to the assault at Anagni – brought the proceedings to a halt, and it was not until the reign of Clement V that they were reactivated. But the dossier from the 1265–6 process had gone astray, and the affair again stalled. At the request of the archbishop and clergy of Bourges, John XXII organized a thorough search and the sealed chest containing the original documents was eventually found – at Viterbo – and taken to Avignon (John XXII, *Lettres communes*, nos. 18624, 18626, 43842–4). Late in 1329, John instructed a commission of three cardinals to examine the documents, and they also investigated the miracles which had occurred since 1266. They presented a first report in consistory in June 1330, but it seems not to have persuaded the pope, since they were again working on the dossier in January 1331, which is when MS Vat. lat. 4019 was compiled. We can follow later developments, at least in outline, thanks to a bull of Urban V which summarized the history of the cause up to 1364 (Urban V, *Lettres communes*, ed. M. and A. M. Hayez, no. 11140 (17 June 1364), III, 2 (Rome, 1977), pp. 401–2). From this we learn that Clement VI, at the request of the clergy of Berry and the king of France, appointed a new commission of cardinals, which, after an initial delay caused by the death of one of its members, went on to produce a very favourable report which was presented to the pope in public consistory. But Clement VI died before making a definitive pronouncement. Both Innocent VI and Urban V resumed the examination of the acts, but neither was able to reach a decision before his death. After 1364, we lose track of the cause, but it may well have fallen victim to further delays. Finally, by extreme ill luck, when the Bollandists turned their attention to Philip of Bourges, finding nothing precise about him, they classed him among the *praetermissi* (*AA.SS.* Ian. I, p. 565). So a saint who had preoccupied the papacy for more than a century, and in whom at least seven popes had taken a close interest, remained almost totally unknown until our day! This was, it is true, an extreme case, but there were few medieval canonization processes whose progress was never disrupted, if not halted, by chance events.

[7] The progress of the process of St Louis is entirely typical to the extent that it was subject to most of the difficulties mentioned. In late 1283 or early 1284, Martin IV appointed three cardinals, including Giordano Orsini, to examine the reports of the enquiries held

A minimum of continuity was necessary for affairs so delicate to be brought to a successful conclusion. The delay between the petition – or postulancy – on behalf of a saint and his or her canonization, which averaged two years at the time of Innocent III and Gregory IX, had stretched to ten years at the end of the thirteenth century, twenty at the beginning of the fourteenth, and over thirty by the time of the Avignon papacy.

This meant that, after 1250, it was practically impossible for a process to be successfully completed during the reign of the pope who had ordered it, which had been the norm during the first half of the thirteenth century.[8] The situation worsened during the fourteenth century: two out of three canonizations performed by John XXII concerned saints for whom enquiries had started under Clement V and of the seven processes he decreed himself, only one resulted in a canonization during his pontificate: that of St Thomas Aquinas (1318–21), the brevity of which recalls the rapid success of the founders of the Mendicant orders. One of these causes, that of St Yves, was successfully concluded under Clement VI, in 1347. The others were never completed, at least in the Middle Ages.[9]

The growing complexity of the canonization procedure and consequent delays led to a considerable increase in the costs which had to be borne by the postulators. Unfortunately, we have no global figure before the mid-fourteenth century, but the fragmentary indications which survive for the earlier period are highly suggestive. We know from English documents from the years 1310–30 that the costs associated with the postulancy and the opening of the cause were in themselves very heavy.[10] But those which followed the start of the process were heavier still; it was necessary

---

at Saint-Denis in 1282–3. Martin having died soon after, they made a first and only partial report to his successor, Honorius IV, whose early death then halted proceedings. In 1288, all three cardinals appointed by Martin IV being dead, Nicholas IV appointed three others: Benedict Caetani, Bernard of Languisel and Latino Malabranca-Orsini. It took ten more years before, under Boniface VIII, the process reached the desired conclusion; see Boniface VIII, sermon prior to the canonization of St Louis (6.VIII.1297), ed. Raynaldi, *Ann. eccl., ad an. 1297*, §LIX, pp. 243–4.

[8] Both Innocent III and Honorius III had themselves ordered the enquiry into the life and miracles of almost all the saints they canonized.

[9] St Clare of Montefalco, for whom John XXII had ordered an informative process, held in 1318–19, was canonized by Leo XIII in 1881.

[10] In 1327, the bishop of Bath and Wells, who wanted to have a canonization process started for his predecessor, William March, decided to levy a tenth on the revenues of the ecclesiastical benefices in his diocese to finance the proceedings. This measure was repeated in 1328 and action taken against defaulters: E. Hobhouse, *Calendar of the register of John de Drokensford, Bishop of Wells and Bath* (Bath, 1887), pp. 273–4, 297.

for the commissioners to be maintained throughout their stay,[11] and to pay the expenses of the witnesses summoned to appear and also the fees of the notaries who drew up and copied the documents recording the depositions.[12] The subsequent curial stage was equally expensive, since it was necessary to pay the procurators instructed to pursue the case, and make many presents and give favours to influential people,[13] to prevent the dossier from getting bogged down.[14] Lastly, if the case was won, the postulators or their representatives had to bear the cost of the banquets and festivities which followed the liturgical ceremony.[15] None of this came cheap. The cost of the final phase of the canonization process of St Yves

[11] At the process of Charles of Blois in 1371 at Angers, the commissioners threatened to suspend the enquiry if their wages were not paid, according to a letter from Louis of Anjou to his 'accountants' in Angers: P. Hay du Chastelet, *Histoire de Bertrand du Guesclin* (Paris, 1666), p. 306.

[12] In 1299, a Florentine notary received 200 *livres tournois* for his work during the process of St Louis, at Saint-Denis and in the Curia: C. Du Cange, *L'histoire de S. Louis par Jean de Joinville* (Paris, 1668), p. 120.

[13] From the end of the thirteenth century, those who wanted a process started were obliged to employ special procurators. In 1327, when the dean and chapter of Lincoln decided to take steps to obtain the canonization of their former bishop, John of Dalderby (d. 1320), at whose tomb many miracles had occurred, they made a contract with a famous canonist, John of Athon. He, in recognition of future services, was promised an annual pension of 100s, payable in two instalments at Lincoln, until he was provided with a benefice in the diocese. The canons also provided him with a letter of procuratory including a substitution clause (he could find a replacement if need be) and a deed authorizing him to borrow up to £24 from merchants. John of Athon having failed in his task, the chapter appointed a new procurator, a certain John of Haugh, with whom they made an even more detailed contract: he had the right to 3s a day while travelling, 5s a week during his stay in Avignon, and reimbursement of his expenses in removing and while in the Curia while working on the cause: E. G. Cole, 'Proceedings relative to the canonization of John Dalderby, Bishop of Lincoln', *Associated Architectural Societies' Reports and Papers*, 34 (1916), pp. 243–76. For the psychology of these special procurators and their activities, see the interesting correspondence between the Magistrate of Nuremberg and his representative at the papal court, Martin Konhofer, who, in 1425, obtained the canonization of St Sebald, patron of the town, in M. Weigel, 'Dr. Martin Konhofer, Ein Beitrag zur Kirchengeschichte Nürnbergs', *Mitteilungen des Vereins für Geschichte der Stadt Nürnberg*, 29 (1928), pp. 171–297, especially pp. 270–4.

[14] In 1320, a few months before the canonization of St Thomas Cantilupe, the bishop of Hereford, Adam of Orleton, guaranteed annual pensions to those cardinals who worked for the success of the cause (A. T. Bannister, ed., *Registrum Ade de Orleton (1317–1327)* (London, 1908), pp. 120–1). It was also necessary to make a copy of the acts of the enquiry for each cardinal. At the process of St Bridget of Sweden, the procurator 'Magnus Petri triginta scriptores expeditioris calami conduxit qui duodecim libros attestacionum descripsere eosque compactatura ita nobili compingi fecerat ut quilibet eorum viginti pretio ducatis constiterit': ed. Karlsson, *Lars Romares*, p. 5.

[15] After the canonization of St Bridget, Boniface IX was the guest of the Swedish procurator, 'Magnus Petrus', who entertained him lavishly. The details of the menu with the price of the provisions are in Karlsson, *Lars Romares*, pp. 9–12.

(1346–7), wholly paid for by the duke of Brittany, Charles of Blois, was estimated by contemporaries at 3,000 florins;[16] that of St Bridget of Sweden (1375–91) came to 5,000 ducats.[17] In 1429, the envoys of the town of Nuremberg had to pay 5,000 florins to obtain the bull of canonization of St Sebald.[18]

These were sums beyond most people's pockets, even if the Holy See sometimes tried to take account of the economic situation of the applicants.[19] By the mid-thirteenth century, however, many religious communities and local churches had realized that there was little point in seeking to have canonization proceedings started, as these might well cost more than they could afford.[20] In the last analysis, only influential groups

[16] See the deposition of the clerk William Andrew at the canonization process of Charles of Blois in *Monuments du procès de canonisation du Bienheureux Charles de Blois*, ed. A. de Serent (Saint-Brieuc, 1921), p. 93.

[17] This is the figure suggested by Y. Brilioth, *Svenska Kyrkans Historia*, I (Uppsala, 1941), pp. 294ff.

[18] According to a letter from the procurator, Martin Konhofer, dated 31 March 1425 (Weigel, 'Dr. Martin Konhofer'). To this must be added the costs of Konhofer's mission which came to 1388 florins, paid for by the municipality, while the costs of the bull were met by the fabric of the church of St Sebald in Nuremberg. It is possible that the procedure became slightly less costly at the end of the fifteenth century, as the *Ordo canonizationis sanctorum* drawn up in England *c*.1494 estimated the cost of a canonization at 869 ducats (Wilkins, *Concilia*, III, p. 639). But this seems to refer only to the expenses of the curial phase. We know that the final stage of the process of St Osmund (1442–57) cost the diocese of Salisbury some £713, which was largely met through borrowing: Malden, *The canonization of St Osmund*, p. xxxii.

[19] In 1318, a bull of John XXII forbade the inquisitors charged with the canonization process of Clare of Montefalco (d. 1308) to ask more than two gold florins per day per person from the sisters of the saint's convent at Montefalco, in view of their extreme poverty (John XXII, *Dudum vobis*, 22.III.1318, ed. *Bull. Franc.*, V, p. 147). The financial difficulties of the convent as a result of the process are confirmed by notarial acts recording donations of houses and lands made by local people in favour of Berenger of Saint-Affrique, promoter of the cause, who had lent the sisters some of the necessary money *de sui pecunia*. These documents are published in S. Nessi, 'I processi per la canonizzazione di Santa Chiara da Montefalco', *Bollettino della Società Umbra di storia patria*, 65 (1968), pp. 139–43.

[20] As early as 1247, archbishop Albert of Armagh, who had played a key role in the canonization of St Edmund of Canterbury, passed on stories to the effect that this saint 'si pauper et humilis fuisset in saeculo, quamvis miraculis coruscaret in caelo, tamen memoria eius in oblivione operta in perpetuum delitesceret in sepulcro' (*Prologus in historiam canonizationis et translationis S. Edmundi*, ed. Martène and Durand, *Thesaurus*, III, c. 1832). There is ample evidence for the financial and other problems posed to towns of middling size by a request for canonization. Most typical is perhaps that of Osimo, in the Marches, where the Council asked the nobles in 1284 to go as ambassadors to the Curia, at their own cost, to seek the canonization of Bishop Benvenuto Scotivoli (d. 1282), so that the commune would not have to sell a house or levy a special tax (F. Vecchietti, *Memorie istorico-critiche di Osimo* (Rome, 1782), pp. 103–10). In 1318, the commune of Cortona made a huge financial effort to send the rector of St Basil to Avignon to ask for the canonization of Margaret of Cortona (d. 1297), or, at least, more generous indulgences than those so far granted by the bishops of the region: G. Mancini, *Cortona nel Medio Evo* (Cortona, 1897), p. 177.

such as religious orders or reigning dynasties were wealthy enough or in a position to exert sufficient pressure to embark on such a risky venture.[21]

This was not, however, the chief problem; if canonizations and preliminary enquiries were fewer after 1268, it was primarily because of a change in the attitude of the Roman Church. In fact, in the first third of the thirteenth century, as we have seen, the Holy See usually gave a favourable reception to requests for enquiries, even when they concerned persons whose reputation for sanctity did not extend beyond an abbey or diocese. At most, it obliged the postulators to repeat their request once or twice, at intervals of a few years, to ensure that the devotion to the saints in question was more than just a flash in the pan.[22] Admittedly, the fact of decreeing an informative process did not imply papal commitment, even tacit, to the success of the cause. But to get a procedure under way which might one day result in a canonization was within the reach of all.

[21] In 1311, King Robert of Naples gave 400 gold florins to the Franciscan William of Saint-Marcel, his procurator at the Curia, 'pro expeditione inquisicionis facte de miraculis clare memorie domini Ludovici episcopi Tolosani fratris nostri' (*Reg. Ang.* 1310, C. no 195, fol. 112 t), whilst, in 1316, the *clavaire* of Apt reimbursed the seneschal of Provence 200 livres spent on behalf of the king in the same affair (M. H. Laurent, *Le culte de S. Louis d'Anjou à Marseille au XIVe siècle* (Rome, 1954), p. 40). The great religious orders resorted to taxing the provinces to pay for the costs of the canonization processes of their members. See the decision of the general chapter of the Dominicans meeting at Rouen in 1320: 'Cum de canonizatione fratris Thome de Aquino bona spes habeatur, volumus et iniungimus prioribus provincialibus quod tot florenos ad sequens capitulum generale mittere teneantur quot fratrum conventus in suis provinciis habeantur, quem florenorum numerum per conventum suarum provinciarum condividant secundum quod eis videbitur expedire': *Acta capitulorum generalium ordinis Fratrum Praedicatorum*, ed. B. M. Reichert, II (Rome, 1899), p. 123. Similar measures were taken by the general chapter of the Carmelites in 1375 to cover the costs of the proceedings for Albert of Trapani (d. 1307): G. Wessels, ed. *Acta capitulorum generalium ordinis Fratrum B. Virginis de Monte Carmelo, 1318–1593*, I (Rome, 1912), p. 76.

[22] One need only look at the list of processes ordered by Innocent III, Honorius III and Gregory IX. The need to repeat requests several times before an enquiry was granted is evident by the early thirteenth century: in the case of William of Donjeon, a Cistercian who became archbishop of Bourges (d. 1209), a first request for an enquiry was rejected by Innocent III in 1210 (*Ex tenore literarum*, 28.XII.1210, Potthast 4154); when they tried again in 1212, the pope said they still had to wait (*Literas quas pro*, 27.V.1212, Potthast 4505); at the third time of asking, at the Fourth Lateran Council, by the archbishop of Bourges and the prior of the order of Grandmont, Honorius III granted an enquiry, 17.I.1217 (*Venerabilis frater*, ed. *Bull. Rom.*, III, p. 311). For St William, see S. Steffen, 'Der Heilige Wilhelm von Bourges', *Cistercienser Chronik*, 19 (1907), pp. 74–82. In the fourteenth century, the Holy See put even greater emphasis on the need to move slowly. When Thomas of Lancaster pressed the pope to canonize the archbishop of Canterbury, Robert Winchelsea (d. 1313), John XXII firmly replied: 'Scire te volumus quod Romana mater Ecclesia non consuevit super tanta causa praesertim praecipitanter aliquid agere, quinpotius tale negotium sollempni indagine ponderare': John XXII, *Porro circa id*, 26.XII.1318, in *Literae Cantuarienses*, ed. J. Brigstocke-Sheppard (London, 1888), p. 400 (Rolls Series, 85).

This accommodating policy made it possible for the papacy to eliminate episcopal canonization, first in practice, then in law, and impose respect for its own prerogatives, without offending local susceptibilities. Once this had been achieved, around 1230–40, it looks as if the popes sought to check the demand in order not to depreciate the supreme honour of canonization by granting it too frequently. To this end, they resorted to devious measures. During the pontificates of Innocent III and Honorius III, and at the beginning of that of Gregory IX, it was always specified in the bulls ordering the opening of an enquiry that the acts of the process should be sent to the Holy See as soon as it had been completed.[23] After 1232, this clause disappeared, and popes often instructed the postulators to hold on to the report of the enquiry until they received further instructions.[24] In the absence of any explanation of these changes in contemporary documents, we are reduced to informed guesses, the most convincing of which is that, in order not to offend a public which was passionately attached to the cause of the new saints, the popes continued freely to grant letters remissory (fourteen during the pontificate of Gregory IX alone), since the opening of an enquiry satisfied the pride of the postulators and their agents. By authorizing the process but forbidding the acts to be forwarded without specific instructions, the popes allowed themselves the possibility of postponing a decision they did not want to have to take.[25]

Once the conflict with Frederick II was over, the Holy See felt less need to be tactful in its handling of the bishops and communes who asked for the canonization of a person regarded locally as a saint. In 1252, for example, in the space of a few months, Innocent IV ordered two investigations, one for the Dominican preacher Peter of Verona, St Peter the Martyr, murdered earlier that year near Milan by heretics, the other for the lay penitent, Rose of Viterbo (d. 1251). In the former case, the

---

[23] The formula was generally as follows: 'quod inveneritis nobis sub sigillis vestris fideliter exponentes et predictos libros nobis sub sigillis eisdem per fidelem nuntium destinantes': Gregory IX, *Mirabilis Deus*, 27.I.1228, in *PC Hildegard*, pp. 118–19.

[24] For example, for the process of Odo of Novara (d. 1200), held in 1240 at Tagliacozzo: 'et quae inveneritis fideliter in scriptis redigentes authenticis sub sigillis vestris apud aliquem religiosum locum eadem deponatis, ad Sedem Apostolicam nullatenus transmissuri, nisi super hoc a nobis mandatum receperitis speciale': Gregory IX, *Ad audientiam nostram*, 10.XII.1239, ed. *Anal. Boll.*, 1 (1882), p. 325.

[25] The Holy See's concern for the reactions of petitioners in the first half of the thirteenth century is revealed in a letter from Innocent IV to the podesta and commune of Orvieto announcing, very gently, that the enquiry made in 1240 into the sanctity of the Franciscan Ambrose of Massa (d. 1240) must be done again. In conclusion, the pope in effect asked them to continue to feel well disposed towards him in spite of this setback: Innocent IV, *Grata nobis admodum*, 2.XII.1250, ed. *Bull. Franc.*, I, p. 562.

1 The saint-bishop as protector of the city (Taddeo di Bartolo, *c.*1400,
Museo Civico, San Gimignano)

2 An episcopal translation: translation of the relics of St Magnus by a bishop of Anagni (fresco, early thirteenth century, cathedral crypt, Anagni)

3 The canonization of St Francis of Assisi by Gregory IX (Assisi, 1228)
(school of Giotto, *c*.1300, lower basilica of St Francis of Assisi)

4 Urban IV: bull *Ut corda fidelium* (30.VII.1262), ordaining the opening of the process of canonization of Philip Berruyer, archbishop of Bourges (d. 1261) (MS Vat. lat. 4019, fol. 4)

ad pbandum miracula mdueendi, contingit tempus circa cor expunuato
ur i ueniu expendi. et menbranas i utilit occupari.

¶ Primus articulus est de fide vita moribz i comisatione dm dm Thome.
i circunstancis ptinentib; ad predicta. · Sup quo mirogent pmo
dicti testes vnde i a quibz i qualibz penitibz deus dm Thom trarit
origmem i vbi fuit baptizat? i vbi m puericia adolescencia nuetute
i senectute sua i cum quibz i qualiter suersat? i qualit moribz teperat?

¶ Item sedo mirogentur quibz studus i exercias idem dm Thom manapi
uit se anteqm eet assuptus ad Epatum i que i qualia officia m dm
Epatum i quem statum huit i qualit m eis se gessit.

¶ Item trio mirogent de fide ipius dm Thom p dilectionem opinte. i de
vita ipius i de vite excellencia salice sit qd virtutes sue opationes
virtutu habuit m excellencia precipuas i quanto tempore m eis pse
uauerit i si dicas excellencias i operationes virtutu lelut singulariter
siue notabilit vltra modu Ordinem seu comisationem alioz q erat
m confunlib statu vl gradu cum eo.

¶ Item iiij mirogent qualt m epatu rexit seipm et Ecliam atq; plebe
s comissam et si diligent misistebat circa gubernatione visitationem i
correctione subditoz i circa pdicationes officiu i officia celebrationes.
i alia spiritualit i temporalit officio Epali m conubencia i qualem igressit
m eo habuerit.

¶ Item quito mirogent si erat naturalit clisciet? i prudens humilis mi
tis i mansuetus paciens et benignus sobri pudic? i cast? si m oratione
deuotione i contemplatione seu meditatione sedulus si iustus timens
deum i misericors i pacificus fit i quales psecutiones ut aduisitates pns
sus fuit m vita sua i ipse qui cuisam.

¶ Item vi mirogent quot annoz erat quado migrauit ad dns i vbia glit
finiuit hanc vitam i si receptis Ecliasticis sacramentis i v corp eucarisat.

¶ Sedus articulus est de fama i com uoce i opinione sup q mirogent
pmo testes vtru sit fama publica i comis vox i opinio siue credulitas
gentiu qd deus dm Thom sit sais.

¶ Item sedo si deponant de pdictis mirogent quomodo hec sciunt i vbi est
de pmissis dica fama pub i comis vox i opinio i a quo tempore circa sa
uerut vl audiuint dica esse deam fama voce i communem opinione.

5 *Articuli interrogatorii*: process of canonization of St Thomas Cantilupe, bishop of Hereford (d. 1282) (1307) (MS Vat. lat. 4015, fol. 4)

...min tredeaun ⁊ faciebat dari magnam elemosinam ad portam suam.
⁊ ⁊ viatorib; quando equitabat p patriam et dabat ⁊ libenter ad refec
tionem ponam ⁊ viax quando requirebat feat etiam cancellos de no
uo in ecclesiis suis de Coleby Lincs ⁊ Wyntingham Ebor dioc ⁊ fa
ciebat ante quam erat Episcopus aulas, cameras Grangeas ⁊ alias domos
necessarias fieri de nouo ⁊ etiam iam factas reedificari Dixit etiam
quod in pochijs suis inducbat aliquos pauperes, s; nescit quot ipe tamen
testis erut pannum ⁊ aliquando simul ultra centum ulnas ad dand
dans pauperib; postquam dictus dominus Thomas fuit Episcopus.

¶ Item dixit quod quando declinabat ad ecclesias suas pusquam erat Episcopus insi
tabat pochianos suos ⁊ firmos ⁊ faciebat bladum pauperib; pochia
nis suis ministrari: juris tamen qb; ministrabat dan bladum
⁊ que visitabant dixit se no recordari ⁊ de anno mense ⁊ die.

¶ Item reddit quod erat pacificus juciog; quorum hoc fat dixit quod
ex eo quia non stendebat cum aliquib; nisi eos castigando uel p
iurib; sue ecclesie litigando cum eis si tamen discordes ad concordiam
⁊ pacem reuocaret dixit se non recordari.

¶ Item respondit quod postquam fuit Episcopus non hunt pacem nec
tranquillitate s; ppt iura ecclesie sue defendenda ⁊ recupanda ha
buit lites de quib; deposuit sup.

¶ Item reddit quod habuit infirmitates corpales multas ⁊ arduas.
⁊ firquenter habat torsiones in ventre.

¶ Item ad sextum interrog; respondit quod credebat ipm fuisse sexage
narium uel ult tempe obitus sui ⁊ audiuit dici quod obiit in Curia Rom.
⁊ quod ei ossa fuiant apportata in Angl ad Ecclesiam Heref.

¶ Item ad septim articulu de fama reddit fama publica ⁊ comm
wocem ⁊ comm opinione ⁊ credulitate gencium ee ⁊ fuisse in Angl
Scotia ⁊ Wallia a decem ⁊ octo annis ait quod dictus dominus Thomas
est sanctus Interrog; quoniam hoc fat dixit quod audiunt pdictam a mille ⁊
ultra ⁊ gentes recurrunt ⁊ pegnant ad eum sicut ad sanctum Interrog;
quid vocat famam piu ⁊ vocem comm dixit quod illud quod gentes
coit ⁊ piu dicunt comm aute opinione vocat illud quod gentes coit
credunt Interrog; quoniam fat quod gentes coit credunt ipm ee sanctum
reddit quod ex eo quia gentes ita dicunt ⁊ ad ipsum ut sanctum

6 The interrogation of a witness: process of canonization of St Thomas Cantilupe,
bishop of Hereford (1307) (MS Vat. lat. 4015, fol. 39)

7 The rubrication of the process of canonization of St Elzear (1363)
(MS Vat. lat. 4018, fol. 12)

8 The *Summarium* of the process of canonization of Philip Berruyer, archbishop of Bourges (*c*.1331) (MS Vat. lat. 4021, fol. 3)

pope asked for the acts to be sent to him as soon as the enquiry was completed; in Rose's case, in contrast, he formally forbade them to be sent until they were asked for.[26] This differential treatment confirms that the purpose of the final clause concerning the destination of the acts was, indeed, to allow discrimination between the causes of the saints. In fact, Peter of Verona was canonized a few months later, whilst Rose of Viterbo never received this honour, at least in the Middle Ages.

The mid-thirteenth-century popes also stepped up their requirements with regard to the saints' *fama*, that is their popularity and the extent of the cult they were accorded. On three occasions before 1260, the Holy See had replied to requests concerning persons whose reputations seemed too localized by offering simple authorizations of local cult, which was equivalent to an outright rejection, since such an authorization was not, in practice, essential.[27] In a few very similar cases, the enquiry was given a second chance, when the pope, by a special bull, extended the mandate of the commissioners to other regions than those in which they had operated, by means of letters rogatory, which allowed the applicants further to flesh out their dossier.[28] In the case of saints from countries on the margins of Christendom, such as Scandinavia, Poland and Hungary, the problem was posed in slightly different terms. In Roman eyes, it was *a*

---

[26] For St Peter the Martyr, see Innocent IV, *Iudicium ecclesiae*, 31.VIII.1252, ed. *Bull. OP*, I, p. 216; for Rose of Viterbo, *ibid.*, *Sic in sanctis*, 25.XI.1252, ed. in *Bull. OP*, I, p. 218. The latter ends: 'et ipsorum dicta fideliter in scriptis redacta . . . in diversis locis caute servanda exponere studeatis, donec predictis Electo, clero, consilio et populo nobis supplicantibus vel motu proprio ea viderimus requirenda'.

[27] The first known example is that of William of Malavalle (d. 1157): when, in 1202, the bishop of Grosseto asked him to canonize this Tuscan hermit, Innocent III confined himself to confirming the permission to accord him a cult within the diocese already granted by Alexander III: *Ex literis fraternitas*, 8.V.1202, ed. Fontanini, *Codex constitutionum*, p. 644. The second is that of Robert of Molesme (d. 1110): the enquiry ordered by Honorius III having produced disappointing results, the pope allowed the monks of Molesme to venerate him as a saint in their church: *Cum olim nobis*, 8.I.1222, in Labbé, *Novae bibliothecae manuscriptorum librorum*, I, pp. 649–50. Lastly, in 1257, Alexander IV authorized the bishop of Orvieto to translate the remains of Ambrose of Massa (d. 1240), even though the enquiries into his sanctity had not been conclusive: *Intelleximus corpus*, 14.VI.1257, ed. *AA.SS.* Nov. IV, p. 567. In the fourteenth century, there were a few other cases where translation was authorized, but they generally concerned old saints: for example, by Clement V for St Bertrand of Comminges (d. 1123) (*Celestis Ierusalem*, 16.I.1309, ed. L. Tosti, *Registrum Clementis Papae V* (Rome, 1885), no. 3994) and by Clement VI for St Robert of La Chaise-Dieu (d. 1067) (*Laudabilis et longaevae*, 16.XI.1351, ed. Fontanini, *Codex constitutionum*, pp. 145–6); see also J. Van der Straeten, 'Robert de la Chaise-Dieu, sa canonisation', *Anal. Boll.*, 82 (1964), pp. 37–56.

[28] This was the case with Ambrose of Massa and Simon of Collazzone (d. 1252), both Franciscans whose reputation for sanctity had remained purely local; for the former, see Innocent IV, *Literas nostras*, 24.III.1252, ed. *Bull. Franc.*, I, p. 599, for the latter; Innocent IV, *Literas nostras*, 10.VII.1252, ed. *Bull. Franc.*, I, p. 619.

priori doubtful whether the servants of God venerated in these distant regions deserved to accede to the honour of canonization. For this to happen, the pope had to be firmly persuaded that the cult was deep rooted and extended to the whole of a country.[29] Many processes failed, at this period, as a result of a fault called, in pontifical bulls, *defectus solemnitatis*. This very general criticism could apply to different aspects; it referred sometimes to the excessively restricted spatial area of the enquiry, or the poor quality of the evidence,[30] sometimes to the fact that the canonization had been requested by people of insufficiently elevated rank in the name of a community which was too small.[31] The result was always the same, that is, the request or enquiry was rejected.

Finally, and above all, the Holy See rejected outright a growing number of requests from all over Christendom. This is clear from table 4, which includes the names of all the saints for whom canonization is known to have been requested in vain between 1198 and 1431.

---

[29] This is apparent from the process of St Stanislas (d. 1079); the enquiry into his sanctity made in 1250 left the Curia perplexed, 'nonnullis cardinalibus propter vetustatem et longinquitatem temporis de veritate tam martyrii quam miraculorum haesitantibus, maioraque et lucidiora experimenta sanctitatis B. Stanislai deposcentibus': *Vita maior* (= *BHL* 7841), ed. *AA.SS.* Maii II, p. 254. So Innocent IV instructed his legate in Poland, James of Velletri, to verify locally the popularity and diffusion of the cult: 'Inquiras insuper utrum Cracoviensis diocesis Paganis et Ruthenis schismaticis sit confinis ut per hoc [= the canonization] ex ipsorum confinio lucrum provenire valeat animarum': Innocent IV, *Licet olim venerabilis*, 26.V.1252, ed. *Bull. Franc.*, I, p. 610. The results of the enquiry must have been positive, as St Stanislas was canonized on 17.IX.1253. Usually, however, the causes of saints from peripheral countries tended to stall, as we see in the case of the archbishop of Nidaros, Eystein Erlendsson (d. 1188): his process was started by Gregory IX, who entrusted the enquiry to three Norwegian regulars (*Ut corda fidelium*, 20.IV.1241, ed. C. Lange, *Diplomatarium Norvegicum* (Oslo, 1849–1903), I, 1, p. 18); their commission was renewed by Innocent IV (*Ut corda fidelium*, 14.X.1246, ed. Lange, *Diplomatarium Norvegicum*, VI, 1, p. 12); one of them having died, the pope added the bishop of Bergen (*Sicut suis nobis*, 5.I.1251, *ibid.*, p. 23). The enquiry took place between 1251 and 1254, but Alexander IV ordered it to be repeated because it was faulty (*Venerabilis frater noster*, 5.IV.1255, *ibid.*, p. 28). Finally, Clement IV authorized a resumption of the process on condition that the *fama* was sufficient (*Insinuantibus venerabili fratre*, 26.IX.1268, ed. Raynaldi, *Ann. eccl., ad an. 1268*, §48, p. 250). We do not know whether the extra information was forthcoming and it looks as if things went no further.

[30] This was the case in the process of Ambrose of Massa: Innocent IV, *Grata nobis admodum*, 2.XII.1250, ed. *Bull. Franc.*, I, pp. 561–2: 'quantalibet nempe ipsorum testium dicta privata credulitatis fide nitantur, tamen ob solemnitatis in quibusdam ommissae defectum, illam auctoritatem plenarie non preferunt publice notionis'.

[31] In 1264, the acts of the diocesan process regarding the miracles of Thomas Hélye, curé of Biville, in the Cotentin (d. 1257), were taken to Rome by two simple priests from the diocese. According to the author of the saint's *Vita* (= *BHL* 8252–3), this so annoyed Clement V that he demanded extra information: 'propter defectum solemnitatis nuntiorum, remisit papa episcopo prefato inquisitionem super miraculis' (*AA.SS.* Oct. VIII, p. 615).

Table 4, which makes no claim to be comprehensive, since it is likely that many requests not resulting in a process have left no trace, suggests a number of conclusions. The first concerns the growing importance, from the 1260s, of *a priori* selection. Whereas previously, the majority of requests resulted in at least the opening of an enquiry, the barrier now, it was increasingly clear, came down at the point of postulancy.[32] This new attitude on the part of the Holy See meant the failure of many causes concerning persons who, though doubtless very worthy, were known in too restricted an area. In northern and central Italy at this period, for example, communes made many fruitless attempts to obtain papal ratification for cults which had not spread beyond the frontiers of a city and its *contado*.[33] It seems also that candidates who were too similar harmed each other's chances; this was the case with the English bishops, in spite of the highly organized pressure group constituted by the English episcopate, with royal support. After the canonizations of St Richard of Wich, bishop of Chichester (d. 1256), in 1262 and St Thomas Cantilupe, bishop of Hereford (d. 1282), in 1320, the papacy seems to have been reluctant to confer the supreme honour on a number of British prelates who enjoyed a reputation for sanctity within their country.[34]

On the other hand, the Roman Church did not hesitate to intervene on

---

[32] The only known case of an explicit refusal to start canonization proceedings before 1244 is that of Innocent III in the case of Peter Parenzo, podesta of Orvieto, murdered in 1199 by 'heretics'. But the case was dubious because he had behaved in an equally repressive manner to all his political adversaries: V. Natalini, *S. Pietro Parenzo* (Rome, 1936); M. Maccarrone, *Studi su Innocenzo III* (Padua, 1972). This did not stop him from being venerated as a saint locally; his *Vita*, which presents him as a martyr, was included by the mid-thirteenth century in the lectionary of Orvieto cathedral. It is likely that the popes received other requests for canonization at this period, of which no trace has survived.

[33] For example, in the case of 'St' Bevignate of Perugia: from 1260, the commune tried almost every year for half a century to gain approval for the cult of this mysterious person, probably a local hermit or penitent of the late twelfth or early thirteenth century: L. Kern, 'Saint Bevignate de Pérouse', in *Studien aus dem Gebiete von Kirche und Kultur, Festschrift G. Schrörer* (Paderborn, 1930), pp. 39-53. At the same time, the commune of Padua was supporting the cause of Antony Peregrinus (d. 1267), Treviso that of the monk Parisio (d. 1267), Osimo that of its bishop Benvenuto (d. 1282) etc.

[34] Robert Grosseteste (d. 1253), whose canonization was vainly sought in 1260, 1285, 1289 and 1307, is a special case. The true reasons for his rejection have never been fully explained, but it seems likely that the illustrious bishop of Lincoln fell victim to his virulent anticurialism, and that the harsh words he had uttered against Innocent IV and the abuses of papal fiscality were held against him; see E. G. Cole, 'Proceedings relative to the canonization of Robert Grosseteste, Bishop of Lincoln', in *Associated Architectural Societies' Reports and Papers*, 33 (1915), pp. 1–34; E. W. Kemp, 'The attempted canonization of Robert Grosseteste', in D. A. Callus, *Robert Grosseteste* (Oxford, 1955), app. 2, pp. 241–6. For Richard of Wich, see E. F. Jacob, 'St Richard of Chichester', *Journal of Ecclesiastical History*, 7 (1956), pp. 174–88.

Table 4 *Requests for canonization submitted to the Holy See but not followed by a process (1198–1431)*

Date of request	Saint	Category	Applicants
1244	Vitalis of Mortain, Geoffrey and William Niobé, founders of Savigny (twelfth century)	monks	Raoul, lord of Fougères
1254	1. Robert Grosseteste, bishop of Lincoln (d. 1253)	bishop	Bishop and chapter of Lincoln
1260	Bevignate of Perugia (twelfth century?)	laity	Commune and bishop of Perugia
1260–74	Thomas Hélye of Biville (d. 1257)	priest	Bishop of Coutances
1267	Antony Peregrinus (d. 1267)	laity	Commune of Padua
1268	Parisio of Treviso (d. 1267)	monk	Commune and bishop of Treviso
1275	Jutta of Sangerhausen	laity	Teutonic knights
1279	1. Raymond of Peñafort (d. 1275)	OM	King of Aragon and town of Barcelona
1280–1	Olaguer, bishop of Barcelona (d. 1137)	bishop	ditto
1284	Benvenuto of Osimo (d. 1282)	bishop	Commune of Osimo
1285–9	2. Robert Grosseteste	bishop	Bishop and chapter of Lincoln
1288–98	Ambrose Sansedoni (d. 1286)	OM	Dominicans and commune of Siena
1296–8	2. Raymond of Peñafort	OM	King of Aragon and town of Barcelona
1306	Margaret of Hungary (d. 1270)	OM	King of Hungary and Dominican order
1307	3. Robert Grosseteste	bishop	Bishop and chapter of Lincoln
1316–17	Henry of Bolzano (d. 1315)	laity	Commune and bishop of Treviso
1316–17	2. Parisio of Treviso	monk	ditto
1317–18	3. Raymond of Peñafort	OM	King of Aragon and town of Barcelona
1318	Margaret of Cortona (d. 1297)	laity	Commune of Cortona
1318–20	1. Robert Winchelsea (d. 1313)	bishop	Thomas of Lancaster and archbishop of Canterbury
1321	Franciscan martyrs of Ceuta (d. 1227)	OM	King of Aragon
1325	Augustine of Trau (d. 1323)	bishop and OM	Duke of Calabria
1325	1. William March (d. 1302)	bishop	Bishop and chapter of Wells
1326–8	2. Robert Winchelsea	bishop	Archbishop of Canterbury
1326–30	Burchard of Magdeburg (d. 1325)	bishop	Archbishop and municipality of Magdeburg

Table 4 *cont.*

Date of request	Saint	Category	Applicants
1327–31	John of Dalderby (d. 1320)	bishop	Bishop and chapter of Lincoln
1327–31	Thomas of Lancaster (d. 1322)	laity	King of England
1328	Agnes of Prague (d. 1282)	OM	Queen of Bohemia and Poland
1329	2. William March	bishop	Bishop and chapter of Wells
1346	Joachim of Fiore (d. 1202)	monk	General chapter of order of Fiore
1349–51	4. Raymond of Peñafort	OM	King of Aragon and town of Barcelona
1360	Martyrs of Sandomierz (d. 1260)	OM	King of Poland
1366	Peter Thomas (d. 1366)	OM	King of Cyprus
1375	Albert of Trapani (d. 1275)	OM	General chapter of Carmelites
1386	1. Edward II (d. 1327)	laity	King of England
1392–8	2. ditto	laity	ditto
1415	Joan-Marie of Maillé (d. 1414)	laity	Earl of La Marche
1426–9	Werner of Oberwesel (d. 1287)	laity	Palatine count of the Rhine

Note:
OM: member of a Mendicant order (Friars Minor, Preachers, Hermits of St Augustine and Carmelites).

behalf of the cult of certain saints it wished to offer as models to the faithful, when it believed them to be particularly appropriate to the needs of the age.[35] In such cases, the normal rules of procedure were often set aside and canonization occurred with hardly any delay. This was the case with the founders of the first Mendicant orders, SS Francis, Dominic, Antony of Padua and, to a lesser extent, St Clare.[36] Further, the popes

[35] The decisive role of the papacy in the canonization of St Francis is well known; it is equally evident in the case of St Dominic, as is shown by the letter from Gregory IX to the bishop of Bologna inviting him to send him a request to this effect, quoted by Benedict XIV, *De servorum Dei beatificatione*, L. I, c. 15, §5.

[36] Gregory IX thought it would be pointless to order an enquiry into the merits of St Francis, 'cum gloriose vite ipsius insignia ex multa familiaritate quam nobiscum habuit in minori officio constitutis plene cognita nobis essent' (*Mira circa nos*, 19.VII.1228, ed. Fontanini, *Codex constitutionum*, p. 62); he was therefore content to record several depositions concerning his miracles (Bihl, 'De canonizatione S. Francisci'). Later, *c.*1237, on the orders of the pope or Brother Elias, there was an enquiry among the eyewitnesses of the stigmata, in order to confirm, against his detractors, the reality of this phenomenon (M. Bihl, 'De quodam elencho Assisiano testium oculatorum S. Francisci stigmatum', *AFH*, 19 (1926), pp. 931–6), but this was unrelated to the canonization which had been pronounced long before.

continued actively to urge national episcopates to promote the veneration of these saints in their respective countries and make their cult more attractive to the faithful by promising generous indulgences to those who devoutly celebrated their festival.[37]

In the second third of the thirteenth century, a relative equilibrium was established between the two functions of the processes: the control of requests from local churches and the encouragement of cults which the Holy See favoured. From the years 1268–70, however, Rome turned a deaf ear to requests from all directions and adopted a negative attitude which contrasted with its previous policy. The canonization process, with its innumerable stages, which took ever longer, became a blocking mechanism. Many requests were rejected at the stage of postulancy. Those which successfully negotiated this barrier got lost in the meanderings of a procedure which seems to have been deliberately designed to slow things down and protect the pope from having to make a decision.

The selective nature of the process became even more marked in the early fourteenth century, especially during the pontificate of John XXII, who made a personal contribution to the development of canonization in the Middle Ages.[38] Though he made three canonizations (SS Louis of Anjou, Thomas Cantilupe and Thomas Aquinas), and started four enquiries which were still in progress at the time of his death (concerning St Clare of Montefalco, Gregory X, SS Nicholas of Tolentino and Yves), he also refused to act on fourteen requests made to him. His long pontificate (1316–34) marked a decisive stage in the widening of the gulf which had begun to appear at the end of the thirteenth century between the sainthood

[37] There were no fewer than nine pontifical bulls on behalf of the cult of St Francis between 1237 and 1291. They are listed and analysed in A. Vauchez, 'Les stigmates de S. François et leurs détracteurs aux derniers siècles du Moyen Age', *MEFR*, 80 (1968), pp. 601–4. The introduction of the feast of the newly canonized St Peter Martyr was urged in five bulls sent by the successors of Innocent IV to all prelates of Christendom (*Bull. OP*, I, pp. 271–85, 403, 420, 473). That of St Dominic was similarly recommended by Alexander IV (*Deum in sanctis*, 21.I.1255, *ibid.*, p. 268). The level of the indulgences granted by popes on the occasion of canonizations grew steadily between the early thirteenth and the early fourteenth centuries, but there were significant variations. Gregory IX granted forty days' indulgences for the canonization of St Virgil of Salzburg (d. 784) in 1233 (*Sicut phialae aureae*, 27.XI.1233, ed. Fontanini, *Codex constitutionum*, pp. 68–9), but a year and forty days to pilgrims to the tomb of St Elizabeth of Thuringia (d. 1231) at Marburg (*Gloriosus in maiestate*, 27.V.1235, *ibid.*, p. 75). Even more than the quantitative increase in indulgences, which was a general phenomenon in the later Middle Ages, these variations between canonizations would repay study.

[38] For the acts and historical role of John XXII, see R. Manselli, 'Un papa in un'eta di contradizione: Giovanni XXII', *Studi Romani*, 22 (1974), pp. 444–56, with full bibliography.

approved by the Roman Church and that recognized by the local churches and faithful.[39] Subsequently, the rejection of requests became rarer. This is hardly surprising given that the majority of postulators chose not to embark on a procedure whose outcome was increasingly problematic.[40] Admittedly, the Avignon papacy still occasionally canonized saints whose memories they believed it would be useful to exalt. But their interventions seem to owe as much to opportunism as to the real sanctity of the persons in question. The favour with which John XXII regarded the Dominicans certainly facilitated the canonization of St Thomas Aquinas in 1323, which was accompanied by a ringing eulogy of their order.[41] In contrast, the Franciscans, generally out of favour at this period, failed to obtain the canonization of the martyrs of Ceuta (d. 1227), requested in their name by the king of Aragon.[42] At the end of the century, the Mendicant orders joined forces to prevent the glorification of one of their principal enemies, Richard Fitzralph, archbishop of Armagh (d. 1360), who enjoyed a great reputation for sanctity in England and Ireland.[43] In the fifteenth century,

---

[39] This is, of course, only one aspect of the much larger phenomenon of the triumph of pontifical centralization in the western Church; see F. Heiler, *Altkirchliche Autonomie und Päpstlicher Zentralismus* (Munich, 1941).

[40] According to the Chronicle of the abbey of Aduard, in the Low Countries, abbot Frederick XV (1329–50) visited Avignon between 1330 and 1340, 'pro canonizatione S. Ricardi nostri [Richard of Aduard, d. 1200] et S. Emmanuelis [?] . . . sed nimietatem expensarum veritus infecto negotio rediit': ed. in *Bijdraegen en Mededeelinges v.g. Hist Genotschap*, XXIII (Utrecht, 1902), p. 56.

[41] It seems to be established that, *c.*1317, John XXII offered, as a mark of his esteem, to canonize a member of the Dominican order. At least this is claimed by Pierre Gui in an interesting addition to the life of brother Martin Donadieu of Carcassonne, OP (d.1299), written by his brother, Bernard Gui (ed. T. Kaeppeli, *AFP*, 26 (1956), p. 288). The order proposed Thomas Aquinas. For the theological and political context of his canonization, see L. Gerulaitis, 'The canonization of St Thomas Aquinas', *Vivarium*, 5 (1967), pp. 25–46; A. Walz, 'Papst Johannes XXII und Thomas von Aquin. Zur Geschichte der Heiligsprechen des Aquinaten', in *St Thomas Aquinas, 1274–1974, commemorative studies*, I (Toronto, 1974), pp. 29–47.

[42] See the letter from James II of Aragon (12.VII.1321) in H. Finke, *Acta Aragonensia*, II (Berlin, 1908), p. 754.

[43] An enquiry into Richard's sanctity and cult was ordered, at a date unknown, by Urban VI. We know of the Mendicant intervention from the English chronicler Ralph Higden: 'eodemque anno [=1385] Hibernienses satis solliciti fuerunt in curia papae pro canonizatione magistri Ricardi filii Radulphi Archiepiscopi ecclesiae Armachanae, contra quos viriliter steterunt fratres mendicantes et impediverunt in quantum potuerunt': *Polychronicon Radulphi Higden Monachi Cestrensis*, ed. R. Lumby, IX (London, 1886), p. 79 (Rolls Series, 41). Initially, they could not prevent Boniface IX from relaunching the investigation by extending it to England, where the Irish prelate had spent part of his life: *Oraculo digne laudis*, 27.I.1399, in W. H. Bliss and J. A. Twemlow, *Calendar of entries in the Papal Registers relating to Great Britain and Ireland, Papal letters*, V (London, 1905), p. 245; but they were probably responsible for the ultimate failure of the cause, about which no more is heard. For the polemic between Richard Fitzralph and the Mendicants, see K. Walsh, 'Archbishop Fitzralph and the Friars at the Papal Court in Avignon',

the Friars fared even better and, after 1431, enjoyed a quasi-monopoly of canonizations, much to the displeasure of the seculars.[44]

It is hardly surprising that, within the Church, as in any other society, pressure groups clashed with each other or that their influence, varying according to period and circumstances, had repercussions for the fate of some processes. In fact, every canonization inevitably had theological implications. For example, the favour shown by John XXII to the Dominican order when he canonized St Thomas Aquinas can only be understood by reference to the very flexible positions adopted by the Preachers towards the problem of Christ's poverty, a cause which the Minors had made their own.[45] Similarly, it is highly likely that the failure of the causes of saints such as Margaret of Cortona (d. 1297), Angela of Foligno (d. 1309), Clare of Montefalco (d. 1380) and Delphine of Sabran (d. 1360) is to be explained by their sympathy – real or supposed – with certain views of the Spirituals regarding the practice of the Franciscan rule and the question of poverty. All four women, in fact, had some connection with Ubertin of Casale.[46] We know that he was on good terms with Margaret and that he echoed the approval given by cardinal Napoleon Orsini to the *Revelations* of Angela of Foligno in 1309.[47] Later that year, he was present, with cardinals James Colonna and Napoleon Orsini, when the instruments of the Passion found in the heart of Clare of Montefalco were recognized, and was, on that occasion, miraculously cured of a hernia.[48] Lastly, he

---

Traditio, 31 (1975), pp. 223–45. The canonization process has disappeared but we know it existed, as Wadding was able to consult it in the Vatican: A. Gwynn, *Father L. Wadding commemorative volume* (Dublin, 1957), p. 275.

[44] Not without bitterness, the cardinal of Valence, Alfonso Borgia, the future Calixtus III, said to the bishop of Salisbury's procurator, when he complained, *c.*1452, that the cause of St Osmund had been in abeyance since 1228: 'Si iste Osmundus fuisset de ordine Mendicantium, canonizatus fuisset diu ante haec tempora, sed quia portavit habitum nostrum, tangendo rochettum suum, ideo diferre debet, quod nobis dedecus est': Letter of Simon Houchyns, ed. in Malden, *The canonization of St Osmund*, p. 144. The only saints canonized after 1430 were SS Nicholas of Tolentino (1446), an Austin friar, Bernardino of Siena (1450), the martyrs of Morocco (1481) and Bonaventure (1482), all Franciscans, SS Vincent Ferrer (1455) and Catherine of Siena (1461), both Dominicans, and St Albert of Trapani (1457), a Carmelite. The only secular cleric was St Osmund (d. 1228), finally canonized by Calixtus III in 1457; the only layman was the duke of Austria, Leopold III (d. 1136), canonized in 1485 by Innocent VIII.

[45] For the theological context of this canonization, see below, pp. 394–5.

[46] The fullest study of St Ubertin remains that of F. Callaey, *L'idéalisme franciscain au XIVe siècle: étude sur Ubertin de Casale* (Louvain, 1911); see also C. T. Davis, 'Le pape Jean XXII et les Spirituels: Ubertin de Casale', in *Franciscains d'Oc: les Spirituels, ca. 1280–1324* (Toulouse, 1975), pp. 263–83.

[47] J. Ferré, 'Les principales dates de la vie d'Angèle de Foligno', *Revue d'histoire franciscaine*, 2 (1925), p. 33.

[48] Nessi, 'I processi per la canonizzazione de Santa Chiara', p. 105.

makes an appearance in the canonization process of Delphine, where we learn from one witness that he helped the recluse of Apt to emerge from a period of spiritual aridity.[49] The presence of the author of the *Arbor vitae* in the life of these four women or their posthumous fates was no doubt not the direct cause of the failure of the efforts to have them canonized. But it shows how they all shared ideas which it was hardly opportune to extol at the time of the revolt of the Fratricelli against 'the great whore of Babylon', even if none of these women could seriously be suspected of heresy or disobedience to the ecclesiastical hierarchy.[50]

Newer, and probably of greater long-term significance, was the fact that, in the fourteenth century, the notion of opportuneness was understood in an increasingly down-to-earth manner and, in many cases, considerations of a political nature influenced papal decisions. As early as the thirteenth century, some canonizations were made in circumstances in which the relations between the pope and a particular country or sovereign played a far from negligible role.[51] During the Avignon papacy, these factors became supreme. To justify this claim, we need to look in detail at the persons who were the subject of canonization proceedings at this period, and ask why their cause succeeded or failed, in so far as we can know or guess from the documentation at our disposal.

Political factors played a crucial role in the canonization of St Peter of Morrone (Celestine V, died 1296, process 1306, canonized 1313). It is well known that Philip the Fair repeatedly demanded that he be inscribed in the catalogue of saints, and that Clement V and the Council of Vienne only agreed so as to avoid having to pronounce the *damnatio memoriae* of Boniface VIII which the king of France was also requesting.[52]

---

[49] *PC Delphine*, MS Aix-en-Provence, Bibliothèque Méjanes, no. 355, fol. 81 (7th witness).

[50] A. Vauchez, 'La place de la pauvreté dans les documents hagiographiques à l'époque des Spirituels', in *Chi erano gli Spirituali? Atti del IIIo convegno della società internazionale di studi francescani (Assisi, 16–18 ottobre 1975)* (Assisi, 1976), pp. 127–43.

[51] During the negotiations preceding the treaty of San Germano, in 1230, Archbishop Eberhard of Salzburg told Gregory IX about the miracles performed by his distant predecessor St Virgil (d. 780) and obtained the process which resulted in his canonization in 1233. It may well be that the temporary *rapprochement* between the papacy and Frederick II was not irrelevant to these decisions (Gregory IX, *Gratias agimus*, 11.XI.1230, ed. Raynaldi, *Ann. eccl., ad an. 1230*, 26). It would be interesting to study papal policy with regard to canonizations in the Germanic and Slav countries in the thirteenth century as a function of relations between the Holy See and the Empire.

[52] See G. Lizerand, *Clément V et Philippe le Bel* (Paris, 1910), pp. 211–13; C. Borromeo, 'Avignone e la canonizzazione di Pier Celestino' in *Celestino V e il VIIo centenario della sua incoronazione* (L'Aquila, 1894), pp. 267–300. The French king wanted Celestine V to be canonized as pope and martyr, not as confessor; in the end he had to abandon this demand.

St Thomas Cantilupe (bishop of Hereford, died 1287, process 1307, canonized 1320) was the only Englishman whose sainthood was recognized by the Avignon papacy. His canonization was several times requested by the English bishops and by both Edward I and Edward II. The situation was delicate, as the bishop of Hereford had died whilst excommunicated by his metropolitan, the archbishop of Canterbury, John Peckham, with whom he had for many years been in open conflict.[53] It was necessary for there to be a first process to establish that the excommunication was null before the enquiry into his life and miracles could proceed.[54] Further, during the debate, several witnesses expressed grave doubts about the bishop's sanctity, something which was extremely rare in processes at this period.[55] This was, clearly, a questionable case, and its ultimate success can only be explained by the popularity of his cult in England and, above all, political pressure.[56]

The cause of Louis of Anjou, also called of Toulouse or of Marseilles (died 1297, process 1308, canonization 1317), was one of many supported by the house of Anjou, which was the major beneficiary of the canonizations pronounced by the Avignon papacy. In this case, the intervention of the Angevins of Naples – first Charles II, then King Robert – is not in doubt. It was not the Franciscan order, despite their interest in this illustrious recruit, which took the initiative, but his father and later his brother.[57] E. Bertaux has shown how successfully the latter exploited the canonization of his elder brother in furtherance of his dynastic policy.[58] This

---

[53] See T. F. Tout, sv Canteloupe (Thomas of), in *Dictionary of national biography*, III (London, 1908), pp. 900–4; A. B. Emden, sv, in *Biographical register of the University of Oxford*, vol. II (1958).

[54] The text is in MS Vat. lat. 4016.

[55] *PC Thomas Cantilupe*, MS Vat. lat. 4015, fols. 45v–48v. It was four Franciscans who challenged the reality of the miracles; for a fuller discussion, see below, pp. 580–3.

[56] Edward I's first intervention on behalf of St Thomas Cantilupe with Clement V and the cardinals was 2 December 1306 (Rymer, *Foedera*, I, part 4 (London, 1745) pp. 43, 51). On 7 August 1307 (not 1320, as appears in error in the edition quoted), Edward II congratulated the pope on the conduct of William Durand, bishop of Mende and the pope's personal envoy, during the enquiry (*ibid.*, II, part 2, p. 6) and strongly pressed the cause. He approached the Holy See again in December 1307, September 1309, January and May 1318 and January 1319 (*ibid.*, II, part 1, pp. 14, 145, 151, 168, III, p. 39). After the canonization, he warmly thanked John XXII (*ibid.*, II, part 2, p. 179) (26 June 1320, not 1319). The success of the pilgrimage to Hereford is well documented by the end of the thirteenth century: A. T. Bannister, *The cathedral church at Hereford* (London, 1924); R. C. Finucane, *Miracles and pilgrims: popular beliefs in medieval England* (London, 1977), pp. 173–88.

[57] E. Pasztor, *Per la storia di San Ludovico d'Angio (1274–1297)* (Rome, 1955), pp. 25–6.

[58] E. Bertaux, 'Les saints Louis dans l'art italien', *Revue des deux mondes*, 158 (1900), pp. 616–44; B. Kleinschmidt, 'St Ludwig von Toulouse in der Kunst', *AFH*, 2 (1909), pp. 197–215; Toynbee, *St Louis of Toulouse*, pp. 212–28.

propaganda exercise won papal favour, though it was hardly in its interests to inscribe in the catalogue of saints, just when the internal crisis within the Franciscan order was at its height, someone who was much influenced by Olivi, and closer to the Spirituals than to the Conventuals.[59]

This emerged during the process, when the rigorists took the opportunity to reaffirm their views on the *usus pauper* and ascetic life-style which ought to be adopted by bishops from the Franciscan order. In the bull of canonization, John XXII was careful not to dwell on these controversial issues and confined himself to a conventional eulogy, passing over in silence the most original – but also the most 'explosive' – aspects of the sanctity of the young prince.[60]

The success of the next cause, that of St Thomas Aquinas (died 1274, process 1319–21, canonized 1323) was essentially for doctrinal and religious reasons, as noted above.[61] But the political aspects of this canonization should not, for all that, be overlooked. The initiative came, in 1317, from the Dominican province of Sicily, soon supported by King Robert. At the process, held in 1319 in Naples, the Logothete Bartholomew of Capua, a high officer of the Angevin monarchy, was one of the principal witnesses, and the presence of Robert of Anjou in Avignon on the day of the canonization, not to speak of his contribution to the cost, is sufficient evidence of his close personal interest in the affair.[62]

During the following decades, all the other saints for whom canonization processes were started were linked more or less closely to the royal houses of Anjou or France.[63] The canonization of St Yves was requested

---

[59] See 'L'épître aux fils de Charles II de Naples, en l'an 1295', trans. M. H. Vicaire, in *Franciscains d'Oc*, pp. 127–38; R. Manselli, 'L'idéal du Spirituel selon Pierre Jean-Olivi', *ibid.*, pp. 99–126.

[60] Pasztor, *Per la storia*, pp. 28, 35–47.

[61] See above, notes 41 and 45.

[62] The canonization of St Thomas was requested from John XXII by Queen Marie, widow of Charles II, her sons Robert, Philip and John, the counts and barons of the kingdom of Sicily and the town and university of Naples. On the day of the canonization, at Avignon 18 July 1323, King Robert preached a veritable sermon in honour of the new saint. When the representatives of the Dominican order thanked him for his assistance, the sovereign replied: 'Nos ita efficaciter laboravimus et laborasse voluimus quos cum volumus aliquid pro persona nostra a sanctissimo patre, significamus ei per cedulam, et pro isto sancto libenter quando opportuit accessimus personaliter ad beatitudinem suam': anonymous account of the canonization of St Thomas, probably the work of Bernard Gui, ed. P. Mandonnet, 'La canonisation de Saint Thomas d'Aquin, 1317–1323', in *Mélanges Thomistes* (Le Saulchoir, 1923), p. 37. Even if there is an element of boasting in these words, they nevertheless correspond to a reality.

[63] For the close links between the Avignon papacy and the French monarchy, see F. Bock, 'Kaisertum, Kurie und Nationalstaat im Beginn des 14. Jahrhunderts', *Römische Quartalschrift*, 44 (1936), pp. 105–22, 169–220; G. Tabacco, *La casa di Francia nell'azione politica di papa Giovanni XXII* (Rome, 1953).

from John XXII by John III, duke of Brittany, but he had sought the support of Philip VI. After the enquiry *in partibus* in 1330, the cause faltered. It was taken up again by Clement VI at the request of Charles of Blois, the new duke of Brittany, who was closely related to the kings of France and the Angevins.[64] The latter probably played an important role in the processes of St Elzear of Sabran, count of Ariano and collaborator of King Robert, and his virginal wife, Delphine, who had divided their time between Provence and southern Italy. St Elzear was canonized in 1369 by Urban V, who was also his godson.[65] In the case of Charles of Blois (died 1364, process 1371), political factors were even more obvious. It was hoped that recognition of the sanctity of the deceased duke, father-in-law of Louis of Anjou and leader of the French party in Brittany, would drive home the point that his successor, John IV de Montfort, who was supported by the English, was a usurper.[66] John was well aware of this and did everything in his power to stop the enquiry from starting or proceeding.[67] Lastly, the causes of Urban V (d. 1370) and Peter of Luxembourg (d. 1387) were both sponsored, after the Schism, by the Valois.[68]

[64] Y. Ricaud, *VIe centenaire de la canonisation de Saint Yves (Avignon, 19 mai 1347 – Tréguier, 19 mai 1947): histoire de la canonisation* (1947); B. Pocquet du Haut-Jussé, *Les papes et les ducs de Bretagne: essai sur les rapports du Saint-Siège avec un Etat*, I (Paris, 1928), pp. 290ff. We know that Charles of Blois was a devotee of St Louis of Anjou: 'dum erat comes Penthevri, fecit fieri in dicta ecclesia fratrum minorum de Guingampo unum altare ad honorem B. Ludovici de Marsilia, de cuius genere erat dictus dominus comes': *PC Charles of Blois*, p. 54.

[65] The canonization of St Elzear was requested by the Franciscan Francis de Meyronnes who was very close to King Robert of Naples and enjoyed the favour of John XXII (C. Langlois in *Histoire littéraire de la France*, 36 (1927), p. 308). The memoir (*Libellus supplex*) he compiled to this end was presented to the pope by the archbishop of Apt, Raymond Bot, 3 May 1327 (ed. *AA.SS.* Sept., pp. 557–9). In 1351, the Estates of Provence decided to present a new petition to Clement VI, which was followed by the opening of the process held at Apt 11 December 1351 to 3 February 1352. For these two and their cult, see J. Cambell, *Vie occitanes de Saint Auzias et de Sainte Dauphine* (Rome, 1963), pp. 32–7.

[66] For the political aspects of the canonization process of Charles of Blois, see Pocquet du Haut-Jussé, *Les papes et les ducs de Bretagne*, I, pp. 357–61; H. Martin, *Les ordres mendiants en Bretagne (v. 1230–v. 1530)* (Rennes and Paris, 1975), p. 409.

[67] A. Vauchez, 'Canonisation et politique au XIVe siècle. Documents inédits des Archives du Vatican relatifs au procès de canonisation de Charles de Blois, duc de Bretagne (d. 1364)', in *Miscellanea in onore di Mgr M. Giusti*, II (Vatican City, 1978), pp. 381–404.

[68] The canonization of Urban V (d. 1370) was requested from Clement VII by Queen Joan of Naples, Charles V, Charles VI, Louis of Anjou and many French and Provençal prelates (Clement VII, *Pridem in consistorio*, 17.IV.1381, ed. Raynaldi, *Ann. eccl.*, VII, p. 445). That of Peter of Luxembourg was sought by Peter of Ailly, in the name of Charles VI and of the church and university of Paris on 16 June 1389 (*AA.SS.* Iul. I, pp. 535–6). That certain statesmen had a conscious policy with regard to canonizations is confirmed by a passage in the will of Louis I of Anjou (25 September 1383): 'Item diligemment et de tout notre pouvoir, nour poursuivrons a despens les canonizacions de sainte mémoire le pape Urbain Ve, de Messire Charles jadis duc de Bretaigne, père de la reyne notre

To sum up, of all the canonization processes decreed by the papacy between 1305 and 1378, only three, in the current state of documentation, were not closely connected with what might be called the Franco-Angevin 'lobby': those of SS Thomas Aquinas (d. 1282) and Clare of Montefalco (died 1308, process 1318–19, but not canonized until 1881) and Gregory X (d. 1276; the process decreed in 1323 was never completed). So, that of St Thomas was the only one to be successfully completed at the time.[69] In other words, the nepotism and favouritism which has long and justifiably been held against the Avignon popes extended even to their choice of saints.

This impression is confirmed if we look at the requests for canonization which were rejected at this period, in particular by John XXII. One cannot but be struck by the fact that none of the causes sponsored by the kings of Aragon between the late thirteenth and the mid-fourteenth centuries got past, at best, the stage of the diocesan informative process. The most striking example is that of St Raymond of Peñafort, whose dossier was excellent and who also enjoyed the support of the Dominican order.[70] After a first failure in 1279, his cause failed again in 1296–8 and 1317–18. The same fate awaited the attempts of the kings of Aragon to obtain the canonization of St Olaguer, former bishop of Barcelona (d. 1137), in 1280–1, and the Franciscan martyrs of Ceuta (d. 1227) in 1321.[71] All their efforts were in vain, as were those of the English episcopate and monarchy on behalf of Robert Grosseteste (d. 1253) in 1307, Robert Winchelsea (d. 1313) in 1318–20, John of Dalderby (d. 1320) in 1328–9 and William March (d. 1302) in 1329, not to speak of Thomas of Lancaster (d. 1322) in 1327–31.[72] Discouraged by all these rejections, which, under John

---

compaigne, et celle de la femme saint Elizart comte d'Arian': ed. Martène and Durand, *Thesaurus novus anecdotarum*, I, c. 1606.

[69] But, having stalled after the enquiry of 1307, the cause of St Thomas Cantilupe was revived after an intervention by Philip the Fair at the Council of Vienne: Rymer, *Foedera*, II, 1, p. 179, III, pp. 77, 347–8.

[70] The medieval documents relating to this cause have been published by J. Ruis Serra, *Sancti Raymundi*, pp. 185–96. See also H. Finke, *Acta Aragonensia*, II, pp. 901–4.

[71] The petitions of Peter I and the town of Barcelona on behalf of St Olaguer are ed. *AA.SS.* Mar. I, pp. 494–6; those of James II for the martyrs of Ceuta are in Finke, *Acta Aragonensia*, II, p. 754 (12.VII.1321).

[72] For Robert Grosseteste, see Cole, 'Proceedings relative to the canonization of Robert Grosseteste'. For Robert Winchelsea, see *Literae Cantuarienses*, III, pp. 398–402; Wilkins, *Concilia*, II, pp. 486–91, III, p. 491; Rymer, *Foedera*, II, 2, p. 183. For John of Dalderby, see Cole, 'Proceedings relative to the canonization of John of Dalderby'. For William March, bishop of Wells, see Rymer, *Foedera*, II, 3, p. 21, IV, p. 375. Edward III wrote to John XXII in 1327, 1330 and 1331 asking him to canonize Thomas of Lancaster (*ibid.*, II, 2, p. 181, III, pp. 39, 61).

XXII, began to look systematic, the English and the Aragonese gave up trying, except for a last and still unsuccessful request on behalf of Raymond of Peñafort in 1349–51, preferring not to make any new requests, but await better times.

In the last analysis, it is difficult to deny that the criteria of 'opportunism' in the sphere of canonization changed perceptibly between the thirteenth and the fourteenth centuries. Whereas the pastoral dimension was always predominant before 1270, after that date the papacy only followed up requests concerning saints recommended by reigning dynasties or orders which gave unreserved support to the Holy See in political and religious matters. This development combined with the changes we have already noted to the procedural and financial aspects of canonization: in practice, only rich and powerful institutions now possessed the means to introduce and carry to fruition the cause of a saint. But among the latter, there was discrimination in favour of those closest to the Curia or with the greatest influence. This is not to say that fourteenth-century popes canonized or considered canonizing unworthy persons. However, among those who had a claim to this honour – of whom there were many – choices were made which often appeared questionable to contemporaries, in that they smacked of partiality.[73]

Far from lessening, this trend was accentuated with the Great Schism of 1378, when each obedience was anxious to prove the justice of its cause by showing that it counted authentic saints among its ranks. This probably explains the rapid canonization – much disputed at the time – of St Bridget of Sweden by the Roman papacy and the starting of proceedings for Peter of Luxembourg (d. 1387) at Avignon in 1390.[74] Having become very

---

[73] To quote only one example, the three authors (all Dominicans) of the *Vita* of Ambrose Sansedoni (d. 1287), the illustrious Sienese preacher (= *BHL* 382), did not hesitate to attack Boniface VIII in the epilogue for having refused him a canonization process (*AA.SS.* Mar. III, p. 200): 'Huic successit Bonifacius VIII homo factiosus qui Gibellinam factionem miro modo persequens, cum a fratribus ordinis et a propinquis B. Ambrosii rogaretur ut eum sanctorum catalogo adscriberet, hoc recusavit pro eo solum quia eius propinqui ex factione gibellina erant.'

[74] In principle, objectors could testify at canonization processes, and were even invited to do so, as in the case of St Bridget. In fact, the commissioners put up a notice declaring: 'Universis sit notum dominum papam intentionis esse canonizandi B. Birgittam et per Dei gratis concernentem rei seriem ad finem perducendi; eapropter si quis fuerit qui qualibuscumque rationibus vel probationibus disputare aut canonizationem hanc quoquo modo impedire intenderet, comparendum illi esse': Karlsson, *Laurentius Romanus*, p. 5. Two opponents turned up on the day, but the cardinal in charge of the enquiry said to the first 'melius et utilius sibi fuisse . . . incessisse per vias et compita et comedisse stramina ad instar bovis et asini quam tractasse et disputasse de rebus super intellectum et scientiam suam constitutis' and had him ejected from the room; the second, a Benedictine monk,

dependent on their respective supporters, the two Curias were compelled to lend a more receptive ear to their demands. So the English and Irish churches, for long shabbily treated by the Avignon popes, won from Urban VI and his successors the opening of proceedings in the cases of Thomas de la Hale (killed during a French raid on Dover in 1295 and venerated locally as a martyr) in 1380 and of the archbishop of Armagh, Richard Fitzralph (d. 1360) in 1399, followed by the canonization of the regular canon John of Bridlington (d. 1379) in 1401.[75]

Some years later, thanks to the Council of Constance, those countries whose saints had failed to win favour with the papacy in the fourteenth century sought to take their revenge. In 1417, the Swedish Church was simultaneously granted the opening of proceedings in three cases: those of Ingrid of Skänninge (d. 1282) and bishops Brynulph of Skara (d. 1317) and Nicholas of Linköping (d. 1391), whilst the Teutonic order tried to have the sainthood of Dorothy of Montau recognized in 1410.[76] Lastly, in 1429, the town of Nuremberg extracted from Martin V the canonization of its patron saint St Sebald, an obscure person who had lived in the eleventh century, and who would, at other times, scarcely have aspired

preferred to slip away and the lampoon he had sent the cardinal, which contained objections to the canonization, was rapidly torn up (*ibid.*, pp. 6–7). A similar approach was found in the opposing camp, as we see from the prologue to the *Vita antiquissima* of Peter of Luxembourg, drawn up at the time of the canonization process: 'Crede igitur, Bartholomista [= a partisan of Bartholomew Prignano, Urban VI] Domino Clementi tamquam Romano Pontifici, Vicario Christi et Petri unico successori, sub cuius triumpho tam gloriosa refulgent miracula sancta . . . quis vero aestimaret Cardinalem hunc beatissimum tot praefulgidis atque stupendis coruscare miraculis si schismatico pontifici adhaesisset, qui etiam schismaticus extitisset?': *AA.SS.* Iul. I, p. 437.

75 For Thomas de la Hale, see Urban VI, *Grandis nobis adest*, 20.XII.1380, ed. Wilkins, *Concilia*, III, pp. 174–5. The opening of an enquiry concerning Richard Fitzralph by Urban VI (*c.*1385) is revealed by a bull of Boniface IX: *Oraculo digne laudis*, 27.I.1399 (W. H. Bliss, *Calendar of papal letters*, II, p. 245). The same pope ordered an enquiry into the life and miracles of the regular canon John of Bridlington: *Quia saepe*, 16.II.1391 (Bliss, *Calendar*, II, pp. 378–9). In 1400, Henry IV sent Canon John of Gisburn to Rome to request his canonization (Rymer, *Foedera*, VIII, pp. 161–2), which was pronounced 24 September 1401 (Boniface IX, *De summis caelorum*, ed. J. S. Purvis, *St John of Bridlington* (Bridlington, 1924), pp. 31–7). For John and his cult, see P. Grosjean, 'De S. Iohanne Bridlingtoniensi collectanea', *Anal. Boll.*, 53 (1935), pp. 101–29.

76 For the activities of the Swedish clergy on behalf of these three saints, see T. Lunden, *Sankt Nikolaus av Linköping Kanonisationsprocess* (Stockholm, 1963), especially pp. 23–6; H. Schuck, *Ecclesia Lincopensis* (Stockholm, 1959); J. Gallen, 'Les causes de Ste Ingrid et des saints suédois au temps de la réforme', *AFP*, 7 (1937), pp. 5–40. The triple process was ordered by the Council of Constance (*Felix prorsus*, 27.IV.1416, ed. Lunden, *Sankt Nikolaus*, pp. 45–50). The commissioners were confirmed in office by Martin V on 7 May 1418 (*Svenskt Diplomatarium*, III, 2473). The process of Dorothy of Montau was ordered by Boniface IX on 17 May 1404 (*Dudum pro parte*, ed. in *Gedanen. beatificationis*, pp. 252–5).

to such an honour.[77] This new laxity was the paradoxical consequence of the restrictive and partisan policy of the Avignon papacy prior to the Schism. A long period of blockage in the 'saint factory' was followed by a period of relative easing as a result of the weakening of authority within the Church. But, ultimately, it no longer much mattered, since clergy and faithful, at the level of their monastery or diocese or town, had grown accustomed to the idea of expecting nothing from the centre in the sphere of the cult of the saints.

It is difficult to date this change of attitude at all precisely. It took all the longer to happen in that there was apparently no change to the rules controlling canonization. So, between 1260 and 1330, many local communities and churches spent heavily – in every sense of the term – to win approval of their new saints from the Holy See. In the long run, the repeated failure of these requests produced weariness and discouragement. Some, frustrated in their legitimate hopes, engaged in recriminations. The majority, sensing that times had changed, made their own arrangements to venerate the intercessors that the popes persisted in ignoring. Ultimately, this process resulted in the creation of two levels in the cult of the saints: on the one hand, a small number of canonized saints who were officially permitted a public cult; on the other, a multitude of local devotions developing outside the control of the Roman Church.

---

[77] Martin V, *Sane pro parte*, ed. *AA.SS.* Aug. III, pp. 762–4. For the circumstances of this canonization, see Weigel, 'Dr. Martin Konhofer'; A. Borst, 'Die Sebaldlegenden', pp. 19–178.

CHAPTER 5

'SANCTI' AND 'BEATI'

❧❧❧

Until the middle of the thirteenth century, no distinction was made between saints in everyday terminology. They were all described indifferently as either *sanctus* or *beatus*, in hagiographical texts and in liturgy.[1] The developments in procedure of the first decades of the century seem not to have had any immediate repercussions on vocabulary, and the clear distinctions established by the jurists between canonized saints, for whom the honour of a cult was reserved, and the rest, passed only slowly into the public domain. When they were not purely and simply ignored, people generally failed to draw the concrete conclusions they implied with regard to control.[2] However, the growing success of the cults accorded to saints who had not been recognized as such by the Roman Church provoked a hostile reaction on the part of certain clerics, who began to demand that the existing legislation be enforced.

The earliest and clearest evidence of this is provided by the Franciscan chronicler Salimbene. Describing events between 1270 and 1280 in many villages in Lombardy and Romagna, he strongly criticized the local secular clergy, who were guilty, in his eyes, of having encouraged the growth of the cult of such dubious saints as Antony Peregrinus (d. 1267) in Padua,

---

[1] Previously, the words *sanctus* and *beatus* were simply honorific titles conferred by a group of Christians on someone who, in their eyes, had lived a saintly life. See St Augustine, *De civitate Dei*, XI, 12 (*Corpus Christianorum*, Turnhout, 1955, p. 333): 'Cum hodie non imprudenter beatos vocamus quos videmus juste ac pie cum spe futurae immortalitatis hanc vitam ducere sine crimine vastante conscientiam, facile impetrantes peccatis huius infirmitatis divinam misericordiam.' See also Du Cange, *Glossarium*, sv Beatus, and *Mittellateinisches Wörterbuch bis zum Ausehenden 13. Jahrhundert*, I (Munich, 1966), cc. 1401–4. At the beginning of the thirteenth century, the terminology was still very fluid; St Gilbert of Sempringham was described as *dominus* and *pius pater* in texts prior to his canonization (1202), and *beatus* after: Foreville, 'Un procès de canonisation', pp. 9–41.
[2] Kemp, *Canonization and authority*, especially chapter 6; G. Garampi, *Memoria . . . della Beata Chiara da Rimini* (Rome, 1755), pp. 427–36.

Albert of Villa d'Ogna (d. 1279) in Cremona, Parma and Reggio, and Armanno Pungilupo (d. 1269) in Ferrara.[3] Salimbene fiercely attacked the bishops who tolerated such abuses, or even encouraged them, by processing with their clergy to welcome the relics of such persons as they were carried from town to town by enthusiastic crowds. He spoke in dismissive terms of the popular devotion which was expressed in the many paintings depicting such saints on the walls of public buildings and churches. 'All this', he said, 'is done in contempt of the rule that no new relic should be venerated without the authorization of the Roman church.'[4] For Salimbene, only the greed of the prelates, the troubled political situation in the communes of Emilia, and, above all, the desire of the secular clergy to compete with the Mendicants, could explain this collective folly.[5] In his diatribe against those of his compatriots who had been led astray by these bad shepherds, Salimbene even claimed that there should be no pictorial representation of a person with the attributes of a saint unless he had been canonized by the pope.[6] It is difficult to follow him here, in the absence of a specific text on the question in contemporary canon law. The facts contradict his claims, since innumerable frescoes and paintings from the thirteenth, fourteenth and fifteenth centuries portraying saints who had never been canonized have survived to this day.[7] Both clergy and faithful believed that the image was within the realm of private devotion, not public worship.[8]

[3] Salimbene, *Cronica*, ed. G. Scalia, II (Bari, 1966), pp. 733–6. For Armanno Pungilupo and the vicissitudes of his cult, see A. Benati, 'Armanno Pungilupo nella storia ferrerese del 1200', *Analecta Pomposiana*, 2 (1966), pp. 85–123. In 1301, his body was finally exhumed by the Inquisition and burned.

[4] Salimbene, *Cronica*, pp. 733–4.

[5] *Ibid.*, p. 735.

[6] 'Quod [the paintings with likenesses of these persons] contra statuta ecclesiae expresse cognoscatur esse, quia reliquiae alicuius in reverentia haberi non debent nisi prius a Romana ecclesia approbentur et sanctorum cathalogo ascribantur nec etiam aliquis ymago ad modum sancti alicubi debet depingi, nisi prius ab ecclesia eius canonicatio divulgetur': *ibid.*, p. 733. He was probably referring to the passage in the Decretals of Gregory IX, L. III, 46, 1–2, commenting on canon 62 of the Fourth Lateran Council (*Cum ex eo*).

[7] One need only glance at the invaluable lists compiled by G. Kaftal, *Saints in Italian art: iconography of the saints in Tuscan painting* (Florence, 1952) (hereafter Kaftal 1); *Saints in Italian art: iconography of the saints in central and south Italian schools of painting* (Florence, 1965) (hereafter Kaftal 2); *Iconography of the saints in the painting of north east Italy* (Florence, 1978) (hereafter Kaftal 3).

[8] This emerges clearly from the statements of witnesses at canonization processes. For example, at that of Charles of Blois (1371), a woman whose child had been miraculously saved by his intercession 'promisit quod si contingeret ipsum Dominum Carolum canonizari, quod ipsa quam cicius unam capellam fundaret ad honorem dicti Domini Caroli. Et dicit etiam quod dicta mater fecit fieri unam ymaginem in honore dicti Domini Caroli et dictam ymaginem supra quendam equum ad modum ymaginis Sancti Georgii fecit poni

In the fourteenth century, the situation began slowly to change, in the spheres of both vocabulary and iconography. In a painting in the sacristy of Santa Maria Novella in Florence, executed shortly after 1336, the artist implied a distinction between saints, according to whether they had or had not been canonized by the papacy.[9] But it was not until the pictorial cycle of another Dominican church, San Nicolò of Treviso, around 1352, that some saints were given a halo, whilst others were represented simply with rays around the head.[10] At this period, the distinction between *sancti* and *beati* became effective, in that these terms acquired a precise meaning they had not previously possessed in ordinary language; the former indicated the saints who had been canonized by the Roman Church, the latter those about whom no pronouncement had been made.[11]

in dicta abbatia coram ymagine Beate Marie Virginis': *PC Charles of Blois*, p. 242. To build a chapel in honour of an uncanonized saint was then regarded as an illicit act, but to offer a church a statue or picture representing one presented no problems. However, in early fifteenth-century Venice, there were those who thought it was wrong of the Dominicans to have had a likeness of Catherine of Siena painted in San Zanipolo, 'que etiam in pluribus locis depingitur et multis videtur quos non sit bene factum, non secundum ordinancias sacrosanctae Romanae ecclesiae, ex quo ipsa nondum est canonizata': *PC Catherine of Siena*, ed. M. H. Laurent, *Il processo Castellano* (Milan, 1942), p. 3. Similarly, one of the accusations levelled against Joan of Arc was that she had caused her own likeness to be put on medals and in churches, thus usurping the prerogatives of saints recognized by the Church: *Procès de condamnation de Jeanne d'Arc (1430)*, art. LII, ed. P. Tisset and Y. Lanhers, II (Paris, 1970), pp. 220–1.

[9] In fact, the painter known as the 'Master of Dominican Effigies' represented several groups of saints: the first consisted of SS Dominic, Thomas Aquinas and Peter Martyr, all of whom were canonized and had a halo. The second group consisted of Ambrose Sansedoni, Augustine Gazotti, Benedict XI, Raymond of Peñafort, Jordan of Saxony, Margaret of Hungary and Vanna of Orvieto; none had been canonized at the time, but their names are nevertheless preceded by the word *sanctus* and their heads surrounded by a halo. The third group comprised Lawrence of Spain, Dominic of Spain, Yves, John of Vicenza, John of Salerno, James of Forli and Maurice of Hungary; they are described as *beatus* and also have a halo; they were persons of lesser importance, whose reputation for sanctity was less solidly established. Kaftal speaks of 'the first use of the word *beatus* in a technical sense' (Kaftal 1, p. xxx). This is not quite accurate, as the persons in the second group were called *sancti* though none had been canonized, and as all these 'saints' were given a similar halo. But it is interesting to note that the Dominicans were the first to try to express at the level of iconographical representation the canonical distinctions the papacy was trying to impose. See plates 9 and 10.

[10] The whole cycle of the Dominican saints and blesseds (the work of Thomas of Modena) is reproduced in J. J. Berthier, *Le chapitre de S. Nicolò de Trévise* (Rome, 1912). When Fra Angelico portrayed the chief glories of the Dominican order in the chapter house of San Marco and in the triptych of the high altar of San Dominico in Florence (1428–35), he clearly distinguished the order's three canonized saints, represented with halos, from the rest, who were described as *beati*, and whose heads were surrounded by rays: S. Orlandi, *Beato Angelico, monografia storica della vita e delle opere* (Florence, 1964); see plates 11 and 12.

[11] We can be a little more precise about the chronology: in a sermon preached at Pisa between 1253 and 1256, Archbishop Frederick Visconti deplored the fact that his predecessors had

We should not, however, exaggerate the inflexibility of this line of demarcation, as the artists and their patrons helped to ensure that it remained fairly fluid in practice. Contemporary texts and iconographical documents still visible today make it possible to trace shifts from one category to another; a person initially represented as 'blessed' eventually became a 'saint', with the aid of a few brushstrokes.[12] The role of these 'canonizations by the image' was considerable in that they helped to entrench devotions. In fact, by this means, the cult of many *beati* who had not received the support of the ecclesiastical authorities acquired a quasi-official existence.[13]

What was the attitude of the Holy See towards practices which were so clearly contrary to its prerogatives and canonical rules? On the whole, the

neglected to have canonized several recent Pisan saints, namely Rainerius (d. 1160), Ubaldesca (d. 1206), Bona (d. 1207) and Dominic Vernagalli (d. 1219): 'sanctos nostros, quos prediximus, non curaverunt facere per Romanam Ecclesiam canonizari, id est sanctorum cathalogo adscribi, ut sic possent a nobis publice venerari': *Cod. Laurent., Plut.* XXXIII, 1, sermon 87. In 1292, the holy bishop Benvenuto of Osimo (d. 1282) was called both *beatus* and *sanctus* in a letter written about his miracles by cardinal Berard of Palestrina: Vecchietti, *Memorie istorico-critiche di Osimo*, pp. 109–10. In 1330, the Franciscan Benvenuto of Recanati (d. 1289) was called *sanctus* in a bull of indulgences sent from Avignon by twenty-one bishops in favour of the church of St Francis of Recanati: *PC* (Rome, 1796), Paris, *BN*, H. 741, *Summarium*, pp. 15–16. In 1366, on the other hand, Philip of Mézières, in his *Vie de S. Pierre Thomas*, records as follows the terms of a petition sent by King Peter I of Cyprus to Pope Urban V on the subject of Peter's canonization: 'Verum quia nullum nisi decreto canonico vel apostolica dispositione praecedente praedicari vel sanctum appellari, quamvis reputari sive pie beatum nuncupari permissum est': J. Smet, *The life of St Peter Thomas by Philippe de Mézières* (Rome, 1954), p. 186. The turning-point, at the level of vocabulary, is thus situated in the mid-fourteenth century. Nevertheless, fluidity long persisted at the level of ordinary speech, as is shown by the following passage from a will of 1428, where a craftsman of Mantua makes a bequest to the church of the Servites, on condition that the brothers celebrate two masses every year 'ad altare sancti Pelegrini sive beati Pelegrini'; this was B. Pelegrino Laziosi, Servite of Forli (d. 1345), not then canonized: *PC* (Forli, 1697–8), *ASV, Riti*, Proc. 828, fols. 623–6v.

[12] See the deposition of brother Thomas of Siena at the process of St Catherine of Siena (Venice, 1411–16): 'Ego semper percepi figuram sive ymaginem dicte virginis depictam fuisse cum radiis sive cum diademate radioso circa caput quemadmodum persone beate nondum canonizate depingi consueverunt, licet viderim de aliis pluribus nondum canonizatis cum diademate rotundo depictis, prout de canonizatis fieri consuevit': *PC Catherine of Siena*, ed. Laurent, p. 28.

[13] The Florentine humanist Franco Sacchetti deplored this development in a letter to Giacomo Count of Perugia '*sopra le depinture de' Beati*' (1392–5): 'E chi n'assicura che non siano assai che dubitino che gli altri santi non principiassono in questa forma che li raggi da capo e 'l beato a piedi, in ispazzio di tempo gli raggi si siano conversi in diadema e 'l beato in santo?' In support of this claim, he cited many 'blesseds', including Gerard of Villamagna and Umiliana of Cerchi, 'che dal Beato son venuti al santo': *Opere*, ed. A. Borlenghi, I (Milan, 1957), p. 1115. See plate 13.

popes of this period seem only to have been interested when trouble or scandal erupted. For example, Boniface VIII intervened in 1300, at the request of the inquisitors of Romagna, to put a stop to the cult accorded to Armanno Pungilupo (d. 1269) in Ferrara cathedral. There were serious doubts as to the latter's orthodoxy and a series of enquiries conducted by the Mendicants established that he had very probably been an eminent member of a Cathar sect.[14] The same pope, alerted by the Inquisition, also took action against the devotees of a certain Guglielma Boema, who had acquired a great reputation for sanctity in Milan and its surroundings, and whose image was venerated in many churches in the region.[15]

In the fourteenth century, on the other hand, it was primarily the abuses of the Mendicants which attracted papal attention. In 1368, for example, Urban V condemned the cult accorded to the duke of Brittany, Charles of Blois (d. 1374), in the church of the Cordeliers in Dinan, where there was an image of the deceased duke which had begun to bleed when his adversary and successor, John IV de Montfort, tried to have it removed. In this case, however, the political implications were obvious and the pope intervened at the express request of John IV. It is by no means certain that his bull was sent, and, in any case, Urban's hostility was shortlived, since in 1369 he set up an enquiry into the life and miracles of Charles of Blois.[16]

More interesting, in its precision and in the circumstances in which it originated, is the bull *Molesta significatio*, which the same pope sent to the archbishop of Ravenna on 1 September 1368; in it, he criticized in the strongest possible terms the Dominicans and Augustinians of Romagna for according a public cult to two monks who had died after being struck by lightning, and who were popularly venerated as martyrs: 'non sanctos, cum sit eis sub tali vocabulo a jure prohibitum, sed beatos publice in plateis et eorum ecclesiis, in predicationibus et aliis astruere moliantur'. This is an important text not only because it implies the existence of a clear distinction between the saints and the blesseds, but because it implies

[14] Benati, 'Armanno Pungilupo'; the whole dossier is ed. Muratori, *Antiquitates Italiae Medii Aevi*, V, *Diss.*, LXI, pp. 81–152. The brief of Boniface VIII (20.VIII.1300) is ed. A. Frizzi, *Memorie per la storia di Ferrara*, III (2nd ed., Ferrara, 1850), pp. 225–9.

[15] G. Tocco, 'Guglielma Boema e i Guglielmiti', in *Atti della R. Accademia dei Lincei, Memorie* (1900), 5th ser., 8, pp. 3–22.

[16] Urban V, *Molesta significatio* (15.IX.1368), to the bishops and clergy of Brittany, ed. Raynaldi, *Ann. eccl., ad an. 1368*, p. 164. See also Pocquet du Haut-Jussé, *Les papes et les ducs de Bretagne*, I, p. 359.

that the *beati* could not be venerated without the authorization of the local bishop, in this case the archbishop of Ravenna.[17] Tending in the same direction, though in a rather different context, was Gregory XI's letter to the bishops of Sicily, asking them to oppose the devotion being accorded to the remains of several heretical Fratricelli recently burned by the Inquisition.[18]

Overall, the number of such interventions was not large, and it seems clear that, in the fourteenth century, not much was done by the Roman Church to control the cult of uncanonized saints, the Avignon popes showing little interest in this aspect of religious life.[19] After the Great Schism, the various obediences were generous in granting indulgences to local sanctuaries. It would be mistaken, however, to see this as the consequence of a desire to reassert control over popular devotions. It was simply that the diminished prestige of the Holy See made it more dependent on its supporters and obliged it to take more notice of popular demands. Thanks to this crisis, which lasted nearly half a century, many recent saints emerged from the obscurity, even clandestinity, in which they had previously been shrouded.[20]

---

[17] Urban V, *Molesta significatio* (1.IX.1368), to the archbishop of Ravenna and his suffragans, ed. Raynaldi, *Ann. eccl., ad an. 1368*, p. 165.

[18] Gregory XI, *Molesta significatio* (12.IX.1372), to the bishops and prelates of Sicily, ed. *Bull. Franc.*, VI, no. 1218, p. 487. The cult accorded to Olivi had already been condemned at the time of Clement V. See Raymond of Fronsac's treatise against the Spirituals of Provence and the reply of Angelo Clareno, ed. F. Ehrle, 'Zur Vorgeschichte des Conzils von Vienne', *Archiv für Litteratur und Kirchengeschichte des Mittelalters*, III (1887), pp. 17, 442–7.

[19] It was often governments that asked for a particular cult to be prohibited, as in the cases of Charles of Blois (see note 16) and Thomas of Lancaster: in 1323, Edward II asked the bishop of London to stop the public cult of Thomas in St Paul's Cathedral: Rymer, *Foedera*, III, p. 1033.

[20] In the thirteenth century, a few papal bulls granted indulgences to churches which held the remains of recently deceased but uncanonized saints: for example, Innocent IV to all who visited the convent of St Peter of Mileto, in the diocese of Rieti, for certain feasts and the anniversary of 'St Philippa', that is, the Clare Philippa Mareri (d. 1236), whose body lay there (Innocent IV, *Licet is de*, 27.VI.1248, ed. *Bull. Franc.*, I, pp. 520–1), and Boniface VIII (1295) for the martyrs of Sandomierz, a group of forty-nine Polish Dominicans killed by the Tartars in 1259; the church of Sandomierz received a special indulgence by the bull *Venientes ad nos*, 11.XI.1295 (ed. *Bull. OP*, II, p. 45). But the practice remained exceptional until the time of the Great Schism. After 1378, the Roman obedience, in particular Boniface IX, showered indulgences on those regions of Christendom which remained loyal, sometimes for saints long venerated, such as Bishop Roger Niger of London (d. 1241) (see W. H. Bliss and J. A. Twemlow, *Calendar of entries in the Papal Registers relating to Great Britain and Ireland, Papal letters*, IV: *A.D. 1362–1404* (London, 1902), p. 399), sometimes for more recent persons whose feast was already celebrated in some Italian towns, such as Peter Crisci (d. 1323) at Foligno (Bull *Licet is de*, 11.V.1391, ed. *Anal. Boll.*, 8 (1889), pp. 363–4), James Bianconi, OP (d. 1301) at Bevagna (*AA.SS.*

In general, control of the cult of the saints remained a matter for the bishops. It had, after all, been one of their traditional functions to *relevare corpora sanctorum*, that is, accord relics the honour due to them.[21] In fact, prelates frequently intervened as soon as miracles began to be attributed to a person who had died in an odour of sanctity within their diocese.[22] They played an important role in the birth of cults, for example by forbidding the body of the deceased to be buried in the ground and having it laid in a tomb of stone.[23] It was also the bishop who authorized the compilation of a *Liber miraculorum*, in which a notary or clerk, employed specially for the purpose, entered, on a daily basis, the miraculous cures which occurred.[24] Lastly, they were able to orient the devotion

Aug. IV, p. 720) and Margaret of San Severino (d. 1395) (*AA.SS.* Aug. II, p. 119). In all cases, the grant of indulgences was indirect ratification of a pre-existing local cult.

[21] It was one of the specific duties of a bishop: see *PC Philip of Bourges*, fol. 362: 'consecrando ecclesias, confirmando, predicando, benedicendo cymeteria, relevando corpora sanctorum et omnia alia quae ad officium pastoris pertinent.' As Carolus-Barré has justly observed ('Saint Louis et la translation des corps saints', *Etudes d'histoire du droit dédiées à G. Le Bras*, II (Paris, 1965), p. 1098), we should distinguish the *relevatio* or *elevatio corporis*, that is, exhuming a saint's body from its tomb to place it above ground or in a reliquary, from the *translatio*, a transfer of relics from an old to a new reliquary or from the old place of worship to a new church or chapel. In practice, however, the terminology used by contemporary authors was far from clear and it is not always possible to specify the nature of the ceremony performed.

[22] When, after her death, her fellow-nuns claimed to have found the instruments of the Passion in the heart of Clare of Montefalco, the vicar-general of the bishop of Spoleto, Berenger of Saint-Affrique, hastened to Montefalco, 'accensus indignatione et suspicatus quod malitiose esset facta . . . proposito quod contra sorores processisset quanto severius potuisset' (*PC Clare of Montefalco* (1318), *ASV, Riti*, Proc. 2929, fol. 95). Other evidence from fourteenth-century processes shows the fear of intervention from on high if a cult not authorized by the bishop was accorded to a saint. At the process of Charles of Blois (1371), a witness from Angers said he had advised his wife to avoid any external show of devotion to the dead duke, 'quia per hoc possemus multum dampnificari et per officialem reprehendi' (*PC Charles of Blois*, p. 230). However, what the bishops really feared seems to have been the disapproval of the Holy See: *PC Delphine*, fols. 27v–28.

[23] As in the case of Agostino Novello, OHSA (d. 1309), at Siena (*Liber vitas fratrum*, ed. R. Arbesman and W. Hümpfner (New York, 1943), p. 153): 'Claruit autem iste venerabilis pater multis miraculis post mortem suam. Unde dominus episcopus Senarum venerandum corpus non permisit in terra sepeliri, sed potius in quadam tumba decente reponi ipsum fecit et in ecclesia fratrum honorifice collocari.' Some texts seem to imply that episcopal authorization was necessary to erect an altar in honour of a new saint inside a cathedral, as at Siena, *c.*1374, when the townspeople wanted to build 'altare cum ymagine et figura praefati Domini Urbani' (d. 1370): *PC Urban V*, 54th miracle, in J. H. Albanès and U. Chevalier, *Actes anciens et documents concernant le Bienheureux Urbain V*, I (Paris, 1897), p. 461.

[24] Three examples of many: for the preacher Ambrose Sansedoni (d. 1286), at the request of the Dominicans of Siena, Rinaldo, Bishop of Siena, 29 May 1287, granted 'licentiam scribendi et faciendi publicare quae Deus per merita supradicti beati fratris quotidie operatur' (*AA.SS.* Mar. III, p. 200); the miracles of B. Simon of Todi (d. 1322) were collected at Bologna in 1322–3 by the Hermits of St Augustine, to whom he had belonged, with the permission of the vicar-general of Bishop Hubert of Bologna (*AA.SS.* Apr. II,

now real:ff

of the faithful towards the cult of certain saints by granting indulgences to those who made a pilgrimage to the church or chapel where their relics lay.[25] In the later Middle Ages, the bishops do not appear to have attempted to limit or exercise strict control over new devotions;[26] either they followed in the wake of the surges of enthusiasm which, especially in Mediterranean regions, often accompanied the death of a servant of

pp. 816–28); at Forli, 1399, Bishop Scarpetta of Ordelaffi authorized the Friars Preacher of Forli 'omni debita diligentia legaliter exemplare miracula et gesta beati fratris Marcolini de Forlivio' (PC Marcolino (Forli, 1624–5), ASV, Riti, Proc. 772, fol. 21).

[25] For example, on 30 March 1274, Bishop Bernard of Siena granted one year of indulgences to all attending the Dominican church on the feast of B. Andrew Gallerani (d. 1251), 'cuius corpus apud ipsam fratrum ecclesiam requiescit': AA.SS. Mar. III, p. 50. The cult of St Margaret of Cortona (d. 1297) started in a similar fashion (see the bulls of Bishop Peter of Chiusi (1297) and Bishop Ildibrandino of Arezzo (1308), ed. L. da Palago, Antica leggenda . . . di S. Margherita da Cortona (Lucca, 1793), pp. 162ff). At Pesaro, in 1393, Bishop Francis granted indulgences to the confraternity of St Mary of the Annunciation, founded by BB Michelina and Cecco, on the occasion of the masses celebrated in honour of the Virgin and for the anniversary of these beati: PC Michelina of Pesaro (Pesaro, 1733), ASV, Riti, Proc. 2264, fols. 463v–464v. The case of B. Francis of Fabriano was similar (Bull of indulgences of Bishop Nuccio of Camerino, 17 June 1398: PC Francis of Fabriano, ASV, Riti, Proc. 699, fols. 118v–119) as were those of BB Silvester Guzzolini (d. 1276) and John of the Staff (d. 1290), respectively founder and first prior of the Silvestrin order; for the former, indulgences were granted in 1285 by Bishop Rambotto of Camerino to those visiting his tomb at Monte Fano (A. Bolzonetti, Il Monte Fano e un grande anacoreta (Rome, 1906), pp. 74–5), renewed in 1365 by his successor Mark, confirmed later the same year by eighteen archbishops and bishops who were at Avignon (C. S. Franceschini, Vita di S. Silvestro abbate (Iesi, 1772), L. III, c. XV); for the latter, bull of indulgences of three bishops of the Marches in favour of the altar dedicated to him in the church of St Benedict of Castellare at Fabriano (PC John of the Staff (Fabriano, 1758), ASV, Riti, Proc. 698, fols. 130–131v). Such acts were not confined to Italy: in January 1284, the bishop of Worcester promised forty days' indulgences to those making a pilgrimage to the tomb of St Thomas of Hereford (d. 1282), who was canonized only in 1320. Most English bishops made a similar grant over the next few months: W. Capes, Charters and records of Hereford Cathedral (Hereford, 1908), pp. 153ff. The same happened for Robert Grosseteste, John of Dalderby, Robert Winchelsea and other fourteenth-century English bishops venerated as saints in England. In the Rhineland, the cult of the young Werner (d. 1287), regarded as a martyr murdered by the Jews, was encouraged on numerous occasions between 1289 and 1320 by the grant of indulgences by local bishops and archbishops, granted to the chapel of St Cunibert, where his body lay. Further indulgences between 1426 and 1430, issued by cardinal-legates, archbishops and bishops, referred to capellam sancti Wernheri in Bacheraco: AA.SS. Apr. II, pp. 714–34.

[26] Thirteenth- and fourteenth-century diocesan and provincial synods often took action against itinerant collectors who extracted money from credulous faithful by showing them false relics, but their frequent repetition suggests their futility: J. Hartzheim, Concilia Germaniae (Cologne, 1769), III, pp. 600, 612, IV, p. 145, for the provinces of Mainz and Trier. It is unlikely that these were recent saints. In some regions, measures had to be taken against the cult accorded to bodies exhumed by the faithful and then venerated, probably because they had been found in a good state of preservation. See, for example, the acts of the synod held by Simon of Caraman at Poitiers in 1387, which forbade 'corpora mortuorum de novo reperta, adorare et ipsa corpora pro sanctis venerari': L. Bouchel, Decretorum Ecclesiae Gallicanae . . . Libri VII (Paris, 1609), IV, c. VIII, pp. 572–3.

God, or they themselves originated the new cults, especially in the countries of north-west Europe, where many prelates strove to promote veneration of the memory of their predecessors or saints they held dear.[27] Everything we know about their role here justifies the scepticism of
contemporary canonists with regard to their ability to make the norms of
ecclesiastical discipline prevail.[28] Too weak to resist the pressure of the
faithful or the monks, and too closely interested in the benefits which
would accrue to their church from the growth of a new pilgrimage, thir-
teenth- and fourteenth-century prelates, though they never contested the
principle of pontifical reservation of the right of canonization, seem to
have done little to stem the growing tide of devotions.[29]

[27] The collective letters of indulgence issued on behalf of uncanonized saints by bishops
resident in or visiting the Curia deserve separate treatment. For the promoters of the cult,
they amounted to quasi-official support, in the absence of a papal decision, which was in
any case unlikely. In June 1318, twelve bishops at Avignon issued a bull of indulgences
in favour of the church of St Basil, Cortona, 'in qua ecclesia bone ac reverende memorie
Beate Margarite iacet et existit corpus tumulatum' (L. da Pelago, *Antica leggenda, Registro*,
no. XII, p. 167). In 1324, twelve bishops at Avignon issued a collective letter granting
indulgences to those visiting the monastery of St Rupert of Bingen on certain occasions,
including the festival of St Hildegard (*Anal. Boll.*, 2 (1883), p. 129). In 1330, twenty-one
bishops at Avignon granted indulgences in favour of the church of St Francis of Recanati,
where the memory of *sancti Benvenuti de dicta terra* was venerated (*PC Benvenuto*
(Recanati, 1696), Paris, BN, H. 741, fol. A,1). Cardinals also used this procedure. On 6
September 1306, Napoleon Orsini granted 100 days' indulgences to those visiting the
Franciscan church of Borgo Sepolcro, where an altar had recently been erected by the
commune in honour of B. Rainerius of Borgo San Sepolcro (d. 1304): L. Kern, 'Le
Bienheureux Rainier de Borgo San Sepolcro de l'ordre des Frères Mineurs', *Revue d'histoire franciscaine*, 7 (1930), p. 244.
[28] See above, p. 31.
[29] The practice of translation of holy bodies by bishops continued well into the fourteenth
century: 1311, translation of the remains of B. Umiltà of Faenza (d. 1310), abbess of the
Vallombrosian abbey of San Giovanni in Florence, by Bishop Antonio Orso; 1317, collective letters of indulgence issued from Avignon by twenty-one bishops in favour of those
who visited her tomb (*AA.SS.* Maii V, pp. 204–12). In 1320, during a pastoral visit to
Polizzi (Sicily), the bishop of Cefalù, James of Narni, under pressure from the local clergy
and people, was obliged to exhume the remains of the Franciscan Gandolph of Binasco
(d. 1260), and transfer them to beneath the high altar of the town's principal church. After
this ceremony, he arranged for the miracles attributed to B. Gandolph to be recorded, and
instituted a feast of the translation which was added to that of the *dies natalis* (*AA.SS.*
Sept. V, pp. 709–10). In Barcelona, in 1380, the bishop and King Peter of Aragon
transferred with great pomp the remains of the nun Mary of Cervellon (d. 1290), called
'del socos' (*de subsidio*), 'ab arca antiqua in qua integra iacebat in alteram . . . apprime
compositam regiis sumptibus structam'. But the relics objected to being moved and the
body was eventually returned to the old *arca*, in the sacristy of the Mercedarian convent
in Barcelona (*PC Mary of Cervellon* (Rome, 1691), Paris, BN, H. 1246, Summarium, n.
14, p. 43: letter from the General of the Order of Mercy to the commanders of the houses
in Catalonia, 31 July 1380). Perhaps this strange incident was provoked by unease at the
excessive solemnity of a ceremony which had not been authorized by the pope, or by a
denunciation by the Order of Mercy. In general, however, late medieval bishops seem
not to have worried unduly about their right to authorize a local cult. Some prelates even

Is this to say that the situation was one of total anarchy? It is very difficult to give a global answer to this question, as the situation varied so much from one country and period to another. In northern Europe at the beginning of the fifteenth century, it was generally believed that it was forbidden to proceed to the solemn translation of the remains of a saint who had not been canonized by the pope.[30] In Germany at this period, we see parish priests distance themselves from certain devotions which had not been approved by the Roman Church, while sharing the convictions of their flocks as to the sanctity of the *beati* in question.[31] In the Mediterranean countries, on the other hand, the canonical rules in force seem hardly to have been respected before the Counter-Reformation.[32] We should also distinguish between the seculars and the regulars. The religious orders and above all the Mendicants had, as we have seen, a particularly active policy in the sphere of the cult of the saints, and often showed scant regard for the official rules. In the fourteenth and fifteenth centuries, innumerable witnesses denounced the abuses of the Dominicans and Franciscans, who, in some regions, promoted the cult of their saints without seeking any authorization.[33]

oriented devotion towards new saints by encouraging the faithful to dedicate themselves to them: the bishop of Saint-Pol-de-Léon, William Villesauxe, in 1329, advised a peasant to dedicate his daughter, who had gone mad, to St Yves (canonized in 1347) and take her to the saint's tomb at Tréguier (*PC Yves*, p. 178).

[30] See, for example, the deposition of the priest Haakon Albertson at the canonization process of Nicholas of Linköping (1417): *PC*, p. 328.

[31] The priest Johannes Provisoris, declared in 1428, with regard to the cult of Werner of Bacharach (d. 1287), 'martyred' by the Jews: 'Licet progenitores sui et ceteri omnes populi quos noverit colant eum pro tali, ipse tamen et alii presbyteri non colunt eum manifeste. Et hoc credit provenire ex eo quod pastores Bacheracenses semper fuerint litterati viri, curtisani et, ut plurimum, doctores, qui hoc non fecerunt': *PC Werner, AA.SS.* Apr. III, p. 722.

[32] This was still claimed in 1442 by St Antonin of Florence, in a work in the vernacular intended for the lower clergy: 'Le feste di quelli santi che non sono canonizzati, dato che la terra ne faci festa grande come à Siena del beato Ambrosio nostro e della beata Margherita del Terz'Ordine a Cortona, nessuno e obbligato a guardarle, ne di tali santi si debbe fare alcuno uffizio o messa propria': St. Antonino, *Curam illius habe* (Florence edn of 1565), p. 38. Similarly, the German Dominican Johannes Meyer, in his *Liber de viris illustribus ordinis Praedicatorum*, written 1466 (ed. P. von Loë (Leipzig, 1918), p. 71): 'tam supradicte beate Vanne quam huius beate Marguerethe in suis civitatibus a suis compatriotis, quamvis canonizate non sint, memorie earum festive et sollemniter recoluntur'. The cults in question were those of B. Joan of Orvieto and Margaret of Città di Castello.

[33] There are many signs of this. Clearest is the evidence of contemporaries: see Sacchetti, *Lettere*, pp. 1113–15: the author (a secular clerk) of the first legend of B. Margaret of Città di Castello (d. 1320) wrote, *c.*1348, in his prologue: 'Fratres quandoque et maxime mendicantes consueverunt a quodam proprietatis affectu in suorum sanctorum laudibus superati, recedere ab omni tramite rationis, uti sub sancti vel sancte velamine in eorum sordibus et maculis coperti humanis sucrescentibus oblationibus et subsidiis foveantur':

Paradoxically, it was just when a clear distincton was beginning to be made, in law and terminology, between the (canonized) 'saints' and the (uncanonized) 'blesseds', that is, in the second half of the fourteenth century, that the boundaries between the two categories became least clear at the level of external manifestations of devotion. In fact, the only difference in practice between *sancti* and *beati* was that the latter could not enjoy a public cult.[34] But this rule was interpreted in very different ways; in many regions and in the churches of the Mendicant orders, it meant only that they did not possess their own office. Even this was not always the case, since several offices of *beati* have survived, and there may well have been others.[35] These texts were usually provided with a preamble specifying

M. H. Laurent, 'La plus ancienne légende de la B. Marguerite de Città di Castello', *AFP*, 10 (1940), p. 119. In Mendicant hagiography, well into the fourteenth century, uncanonized saints from the order are often described as *sanctus*: see the *Vita* of B. Gerard Cagnoli (d. 1342) written in 1351 by the Franciscan Bartolomeo Albizzi, ed. F. Rotolo, *Miscellanea Francescana*, 57 (1957), pp. 397–446. Lastly, the process of Charles of Blois (Angers 1371) reveals how differently laity and clergy might behave at this period: a noblewoman said she had not dared to build a chapel dedicated to the deceased duke, since the fact that he had not been canonized prohibited this (see note 8 above); in contrast, two Friars Minor recounted how, in Perigueux at the same period, the Franciscans constructed a chapel in his honour within their church (*ibid.*, pp. 277–80). The canonists themselves were struck by the indiscipline of the Mendicants in matters concerning the cult of the saints: Guy Pape, *Super decretales: In eadem glosa in fine dicatur quod per hanc glosam damnatur consuetudo istorum mendicantium atque aliorum religiosorum qui sollemnia faciunt officia pro aliquibus beatis, non solum pro sanctificatis a Sede Apostolica*, I (Venice edn of 1588), p. 245 (commenting on the decretal *Venerabilis*).

[34] Though the rule had been clearly spelt out by the thirteenth-century canonists: 'Non negamus quoniam cuilibet liceat alicui defuncto quem credebat bonum virum porrigere preces ut pro eo intercedat ad Deum, quia Deus fidem eorum attendit; non tamen pro eis licet facere officium sollemne vel preces sollemnes': Innocent IV, *In quinque libros decretalium . . . commentaria* (Venice, 1588), p. 188. The Mendicants were well aware of these rules, as shown by this passage from Angelo Clareno, who, in 1317, sought to exonerate the Spirituals accused by their enemies of abusively rendering to Peter John Olivi honours reserved to canonized saints: 'nec enim facte sunt nec fiunt nec recitantur sollempnes orationes et officcia in honorem eius, nec in kalendario nec (in) letania ponitur nomen eius nec similia fiunt que ecclesia facere pro sanctis canonizatis consuevit': ed. F. Ehrle, 'Olivis Leben und Schriften' in *Archiv für Literatur und Kirchengeschichte des Mittelalters*, III (1887), p. 443.

[35] The texts of several personal offices of uncanonized saints survive: for Franco of Assergi (d. *c.*1250 in the Abruzzi), a rhythmical office in six lessons: *Francus confessor caelicus* (end thirteenth–beginning fourteenth century), ed. *PC*, Paris, BN, H. 929, *Summarium*, fols. A 2v–A 3v; for Clare of Montefalco (d. 1380), office and mass, ed. A. Semenza, 'Vita S. Clarae de Cruce ex codice monte falconensi saeculi XIV desumpta', *Analecta Augustiniana*, 18 (1941), pp. 1–8. In England, John of Dalderby (d. 1320), Thomas of Lancaster (d. 1322) and Richard Rolle of Hampole (d. 1349) all had their own office: R. Wickendon, 'John de Dalderby, Bishop of Lincoln, 1300–1320', *Archaeological Journal*, 40 (1883), pp. 218–24 (Office *Forma morum, doctor veri*); R. M. Woolley, *The officium and miracula of Richard of Hampole* (London, 1919); J. C. Purvis, *Saint John of Bridlington* (Bridlington, 1924), p. 30.

that they should not be used until the person whose virtues they celebrated had been canonized. But there is good reason to think that this was a purely formal clause or pious falsehood.[36] Further, on the liturgical plane, the characteristic of canonized saints was not possession of a personal office, but inclusion in a category of saints with a special office (martyrs, confessors, virgins etc.).[37] We know, for example, from several depositions made at the process of St Thomas Aquinas, that the monks of Fossanova celebrated in his honour, from the day after his death, the mass *Os justi*, which was that of the confessors, although it was another fifty years before he was canonized.[38] Similarly, in 1411, the general chapter of the Carmelite order, on its own initiative, introduced into the liturgy of the order the feast of the Sicilian Carmelite, Albert of Trapani (d. 1307), given the office of a confessor, even though his canonization had been sought without success since 1375.[39] In some parts of Christendom, greater caution or moderation was shown, and only a *missa de reliquiis* or *missa de omnibus sanctis* was celebrated on the anniversary of the death of a saint who had not been canonized.[40]

[36] We may wonder whether these offices were actually used, when we read at the beginning of that of Richard Rolle: 'Officium de sancto Ricardo heremita, postquam fuerit ab ecclesia canonizatus, quia interim non licet publice in ecclesia cantare de eo horas canonicas vel solempnizare festum de ipso' (Woolley, *Officium and miracula*, p. 12). Such statements seem to me to reveal both awareness of the rules in force and every intention of ignoring them.

[37] We should remember Innocent IV's definition of canonization: 'Canonizare est sanctos canonice et regulariter statuere quod aliquis honoretur pro sancto, puta solemne officium pro eo facere sicut fit pro aliis sanctis qui sunt eiusdem conditionis, ut si canonizatur confessor, fiat pro eo officium confessorum et si martyr, fiat pro eo officium martyrum, et sic de aliis': *In quinque libros*, p. 188.

[38] *PC Thomas Aquinas*, ed. A. Ferrua, *S. Thomae Aquinatis vitae fontes praecipuae* (Alba, 1968), pp. 224–5: 'Interrogatus si in translatione ipsius corporis fuit aliqua missa celebrata, dixit quod sic in mane sequenti post ipsam translationem Interrogatus quam missam cantaverunt, dixit quod missam de uno confessore in qua cantatur Os justi et cetera.' Another witness defended the Cistercian monks of Fossanova as follows: 'considerando non esse congruum cantare pre eo missam pro defunctis cum haberent eum pro sancto viro' (*ibid.*, p. 215).

[39] Acts of the General Chapter of the Carmelites, 1411: 'Item de beato Alberto de Trapano fiat festum duplex die sancti Donati et fiat de eo ut unius confessoris non episcopi, donec officium proprium de eo fuerit divulgatum, quod quidem iam habetur': ed. G. Wessels, *Acta capitulorum generalium ordinis Fratrum B. V. Marie de Monte Carmelo* (Rome, 1914), p. 145.

[40] Contrary to the claims of Innocent IV (see note 37 above), it was generally believed in the fourteenth and fifteenth centuries that it was possession of a personal office and mass which characterized canonized saints. See, with regard to B. Dorothea of Montau, the commentary preceding the text of her mass in the *Annales capituli Pomesianensis* (early fifteenth century): 'Haec missa cantari debet de omnibus sanctis usque mater nostra supradicta felix Dorothea fuerit canonizata. Postquam autem fuerit canonizata, tunc primo

It seems that, thanks to the Schism and subsequent crisis of authority within the Church, the clergy tended to become increasingly less scrupulous in this sphere, as we see from the proliferation in the late fourteenth and early fifteenth centuries of personal offices of saints who had not been recognized by the papacy.[41] But this relative indiscipline never amounted to complete neglect of the rules in force; in 1411, an action was brought against the Dominicans of San Zanipolo in Venice by some of the congregation, who complained to the bishop of Castello that the brethren were publicly worshipping, in their church, St Catherine of Siena, who had not been canonized.[42] The Preachers defended themselves by insisting that they were not alone in celebrating *memoriae* or *commemorationes* in honour of their *beati*, and that many other regulars and even seculars did the same for other persons; they also emphasized that these ceremonies did not include either mass or recitation of an office specific to the saint, but consisted of a sermon on her life and virtues, announced by the ringing of bells and followed by a banquet. They prudently avoided using the word *festum*, which risked suggesting a liturgical act.[43]

Should we believe these claims, which imply scrupulous respect for the canonical norms? And what is the precise significance of the word *officium*,

---

missa de omnibus sanctis debebit obmitti et missa de ipsa B. Dorothea sub nota ad eius tumulum cotidie decantari': *AA.SS.* Oct. XIII, p. 489. See also note 39 above.

[41] One fifteenth-century example: the feasts of three local uncanonized saints, with their own offices and masses, were celebrated in San Gimignano in Tuscany: Fina (d. 1253), Bartolo (d. 1300) and Nanni (?): G. Garosi, *Inventario dei manoscritti delle Biblioteche d'Italia*, 88: *San Gimignano, Biblioteca Communale* (Florence, 1972), p. 183.

[42] After a sermon by the Dominican Bartholomew of Ferrara on St Catherine in this church in Venice on 5 May 1411, seven people went to the bishop, Francesco Bembo, to express their unease because she was a saint about whom the Church had not yet pronounced (she was canonized only in 1461): Laurent, *Il processo Castellano*, Introduction. According to R. Fawtier (*Sainte Catherine de Sienne: éssai de critique des sources: sources hagiographiques* (Paris, 1921), pp. 26–44), the Venice trial was 'in name only', since the accusers, judges and 'accused' all wished to promote the cult of St Catherine of Siena. This does not detract from the interest for us of the incident – true or false – which started the affair.

[43] See the evidence of the Dominican Thomas of Siena: 'Item dico quod tam in Ianua quam in Pisis, Senis, Urbeveteri et in pluribus aliis locis Ytaliae me vidisse ac audivisse celebrari huiusmodi memorias de multis appellatis beatis et nondum canonizatis et hoc tam in ecclesiis secularium sacerdotum quam religiosorum ordinum diversorum': *PC Catherine of Siena*, p. 30. There is a similar statement in the letter sent by the abbot of Saint-Victor of Marseilles in 1414 to the Council of Constance concerning the cult accorded in his abbey to B. Urban V: ed. J. B. Magnan, *Histoire d'Urbain V* (Paris, 1862), pp. 480–4. At the process of Catherine of Siena, the Franciscan Bartholomew of Ferrara was even more precise, stating that the ceremonies in no way contravened the rules fixed by the Roman Church for control of the cult of saints, since they were not celebrating the personal office of the *beatus*, but that of the Sunday or saint whose calendar festival it was (*ibid.*, pp. 8–9).

often employed in Italian communal statutes of the period to indicate celebrations organized by the clergy in honour of local saints who had not been canonized?[44] It is difficult to give a clear answer to these questions and the very imprecision of the notion allowed many possibilities for transgression. We are, in any case, very far from what was authorized by canon law, since a famous Italian jurist of the late fifteenth century, Troilo Malvezzi, defined the *beati* as persons venerated by the faithful but 'whose anniversary is not celebrated, in whose memory no office is said, and to whom no church is dedicated'.[45] There is an air of unreality about this text, so far does it depart from the reality revealed by the documents. The same author is closer to the truth when, a little further on, he says that the best proof that a distinction exists between the saints and the blessed is that painters represent the former with a halo round the head, whereas the latter have only rays.[46] At the end of the Middle Ages, the difference between the two categories was clearly perceived by all, and no-one contested, in principle, the superiority of canonized over non-canonized saints. This did not prevent a certain confusion at the level of local worship, since more or less equal honour was paid to both. 'Beatification' was not yet a clearly defined juridical status, as it became under Urban VIII (1634). It was simply a fact of life, product of a consensus between a local church and a civic community. Clergy and faithful tried to legitimize the worship accorded to saints not recognized by the Roman Church by presenting it as the first stage in a canonization process which would one day receive papal approval.[47] Admittedly, this pious anticipation implies awareness of the law in force, but it was also a way of circumventing its provisions.

---

[44] In 1307, the commune of Orvieto instituted an offering of candles in favour of the church of the Augustines 'die quo celebratur officium corporis beati fratris Clementis': Orvieto, *Archivio di Stato, Liber reformationum et consiliorum, ad an. 1306–1307* (Reformation of 7 May 1307). This was B. Clement of Osimo, OHSA (d. 1291). The same day, a similar decision was made concerning the offering to be made to the Dominicans 'in die in quo celebratur officium pro sorore Vanna', that is B. Joan of Orvieto (d. 1306).

[45] 'Sed dicitur beatus cuius nec dies mortis nec officium in eius memoriam celebratur, nec etiam ecclesia sibi dedicatur': Troilo Malvezzi (d. 1496), *De sanctorum canonizatione opusculum* (Bologna, 1487), c. 32.

[46] *Ibid.*: 'pingunt imaginem beati cum radiis, sancti vero cum diademate circum caput ut inter eos appareat differentia'.

[47] The papacy itself long encouraged this attitude by presenting canonization as the ratification by the Church militant of a judgement already made by the Church triumphant. Thus Honorius III, in the bull ordering the opening of canonization proceedings for Abbot Maurice of Carnoët (d. 1191): 'quia cum populus devota presumptione, ut sic diximus, nunc usurpat, seu forsan divino instinctu anticipat, illum appellando sanctum absque auctoritate Sedis Apostolicae venerando': *Etsi frigescente*, 4.XII.1224 (Pressutti, 5197). The severity of the reproaches addressed to the faithful, we see, relative.

It could hardly be otherwise, since the attitude of medieval Christians towards the saints was unhampered by juridical considerations. The medieval Church and even the simple faithful believed they were authorized to pronounce on people's posthumous fate; in 1300, Boniface VIII did not hesitate to grant the Jubilee indulgence to pilgrims who died on their way to Rome, thereby demonstrating his conviction that his jurisdictional powers were not confined to the world of the living.[48] Similarly, clergy and laity alike were firmly convinced that a Christian who had led on earth a life according to the will of God could not but be welcomed by Him after death. From this perspective, pontifical canonization was no more than official confirmation of an evident reality. The popes themselves, in bulls ordering enquiries, were the first to assert that 'one should not hide a light under a bushel'.[49] In this context, canonization processes were regarded by the faithful as dilatory and largely superfluous procedures, since, in their eyes, the result was known in advance. They therefore saw nothing wrong in taking the initiative in giving a certain splendour to the cult of a servant of God, even if the Roman Church had not pronounced on their sanctity.

With regard to control of the cult of the saints, the situation at the beginning of the fifteenth century was highly paradoxical. On the one hand, the canonization procedure had reached maximum complexity; the long and varied enquiries were generally conducted with extreme care by the commissioners *in partibus*, and the material they assembled was scrutinized in the Curia with meticulous attention to detail by commissions composed of eminent and learned men. However, at the very time when this juridical perfection was achieved, the canonization process seemed to play only a subsidiary role in the evaluation of sanctity. If the enquiry revealed technical irregularities, the pope could substitute his own authority, clear evidence of the subsidiary nature of the procedure.[50] Further, failures outnumbered successes, and contemporaries, when they saw their hopes frustrated, were not slow to complain and criticize the arbitrary nature of

---

[48] A. Frugoni, 'Il Giubileo di Bonifacio VIII', *Bullettino dell'istituto storico Italiano per il Medio Evo e Archivo Muratoriano*, 62 (1950), pp. 1–103.

[49] See the texts quoted by Reber, *Die Gestaltung des Kultes weiblicher Heiliger im Spätmittelalter*, p. 112, note 5.

[50] Thus Gregory XI compensated for five major formal errors drawn to his attention by the *ad hoc* commission of cardinals at the process of Charles of Blois; see the bull *Provida sedis apostolica* 13.II.1376, ed. B. A. Pocquet du Haut-Jussé, 'La sainteté de Charles de Blois', *Revue des questions historiques*, 54 (1926), pp. 108–15.

the proceedings. Their recriminations are understandable when we remember the huge effort and expenditure involved in sustaining a process. But there was, in the last analysis, a misunderstanding as to the role and function of canonization. The faithful still saw it as the ratification, after verification, of a cult already instituted by a local group, ecclesiastical or lay. But, by the end of the thirteenth century, the popes were striving to make canonization what it remains to this day, an exceptional favour accorded to a small number of saints, whose glorification was judged opportune *hic et nunc* by the Roman Church, *caput et cardo* of the universal Church.

This rigorous selectivity, which coexisted, in practice, with a certain leniency towards reigning families and countries with most influence with the Holy See, had enormous consequences for a western Christendom which was increasingly sensitized to sanctity, in both its 'modern' (mysticism) and traditional (for example, the holy hermit or pilgrim) forms. The crucial fact was the gradual establishment of two sectors in the sphere of the cult of the saints: on the one hand, a tiny band of the privileged, who had been lucky enough to emerge unscathed from the pitfalls of the canonization processes; on the other, a throng of the obscure and the failed, who continued nevertheless to be venerated. The existence of a juridical distinction between the canonized *sancti* and the uncanonized *beati* was now more or less understood, even if it was little respected. It shows that, in the end, in the fourteenth century, a gulf had opened up between official sainthood and local devotions which blossomed subject only to the very lax control exercised by bishops and heads of religious houses.[51] One of the most popular saints in the late medieval West was, after all, St Rock, a plague-ridden pilgrim, a mysterious person whose cult grew without benefit of any recognition by the Roman Church; it was only at the end of the sixteenth century that his situation was regularized canonically.[52]

---

[51] There was some criticism of the anarchic proliferation of local cults and saints' feasts in the late fourteenth and early fifteenth centuries; see the critical comments of Henry of Langenstein 'de nimia sanctorum multitudine' in chapter 18 of his *Consilium pacis de Unione Ecclesiae*, ed. H. von der Hardt, *Magnum oecumenicum Constantiense concilium*, II (Frankfurt and Leipzig, 1697), p. 56, and Gerson's efforts at the Council of Constance to introduce stricter discipline (*ibid.*, IV (1699), p. 39). In 1413, Nicolas of Clamanges wrote a treatise with the eloquent title 'Contre l'institution de fêtes nouvelles' (ed. P. Glorieux, 'Mœurs de chrétienté au temps de Jeanne d'Arc: le traité "Contre l'institution de fêtes nouvelles" ', *Mélanges de science religieuse*, 23 (1966), pp. 5–29).

[52] For the origins and vicissitudes of the cult of St Rock, see A. Vauchez, sv Rocco, in *Bibliotheca sanctorum*, XI (Rome, 1968), cc. 264–73.

It is not enough to note the dichotomy which emerged, from the end of the thirteenth century, between an official sainthood, consecrated by canonization, and the local cults which proliferated in an increasingly anarchic fashion. We still need to explain it, and, at the same time, account for the incoherence which seems to characterize papal policy in this sphere. The institution of the reservation of the right of canonization, and the development of a new procedure with regard to the enquiries, had, in fact, enabled the Holy See to establish a flexible but real control over manifestations of sanctity during the first decades of the thirteenth century. Under Honorius III and Innocent IV, Rome ruled with an equally heavy hand over the cults which emerged in Italy in the wake of the hermits and the Mendicants and those which continued to be promoted by bishops, princes and monks elsewhere in Christendom. Admittedly, the popes of this period were far from pronouncing on all new devotions, but it was rare for the latter to spread very far without being the subject of an enquiry which allowed their soundness to be evaluated by the papacy. It can be argued that the canonization processes were, by and large, representative of sanctity as it was effectively perceived by the faithful up to the 1260s. After that, however, and especially in the fourteenth century, it was as if the papacy had renounced intervention, except in rare cases, in the cult of the saints, while at the same time increasing the rigidity of the system of verification which it had itself put into place from the late twelfth century on. The blockage which ensued was to some extent due to the chance causes discussed above, that is, a succession of very short papacies, the crisis experienced by the Roman Church under Boniface VIII, and the itinerant nature of the papacy until it settled at Avignon under John XXII. But none of these reasons was decisive in itself; at the height of the conflict between the papacy and Frederick II, Gregory IX and Innocent IV had found time to keep a very close eye on the new devotions, as the many bulls despatched all over Christendom by their chancery show. The problem, therefore, is why their successors then lost interest.

The first possible explanation is theological. From the end of the thirteenth century, the popes and their entourage tended to make the canonization of saints a sphere in which the doctrine of papal infallibility, then much favoured within ruling Church circles, applied. This idea received the authoritative support of St Thomas Aquinas, and was then strengthened by convinced hard-liners such as Augustine of Ancona (Agostino

Trionfo, 1243–1328).[53] One can understand why, in these circumstances, the Holy See was increasingly slow to canonize saints, since, each time, its responsibility was engaged to almost the same degree as for a dogmatic definition in a matter of faith. The necessity of only pronouncing advisedly and in full knowledge of the cause also explains the increasing length of the procedure, the desire to interrogate a large number of witnesses, and the meticulous scrutiny of their depositions by the Curia. From the same perspective, one appreciates the huge importance attached to the evidence of one or more of the saints' confessors, released, on such occasions, from the secrecy of the confessional, so as to enable the enquiry to go beyond appearances, the confessor being, in the words of St Thomas, he who 'knew like God'.[54]

Another factor which tended to restrict the use made by the papacy of its prerogatives was the development of ecclesiology. As Y. Congar has shown, the end of the thirteenth century saw the triumph of the hierocratic trend and the strengthening of papal monarchy within the Church.[55] From Bartholomew of Lucca to Alvaro Pelayo, by way of Giles of Rome and James of Viterbo, theologians endlessly reiterated that the Church was a hierarchized body whose head was Christ, visibly represented on earth by the pope, his vicar. In their view, the latter was not simply the first of the bishops and their leader, but a person apart, exercising a sort of universal episcopacy, as if the whole of the Church was his diocese and the ordinar-

---

[53] The great thirteenth-century canonists (Innocent IV, *Hostiensis*), and even more Joannes Andreae in the early fourteenth, did not exclude the possibility that the pope might err in canonizing a saint; see, for example, *Johannis Andreae Glossa ordinaria in L*, VI, III, 20: 'Et si Ecclesia in canonizatione errarit, quod non est credendum, licet accidere possit . . . nihilominus preces in honorem talis acceptae et gratae sunt. Per fidem enim Christi, omnia purgantur . . . et esto quod veritas canonizationis deficiat, non deficit fides.' But St Thomas, in his *Quodlibet*, q. 8, no. 10, argued that 'since the canonization of the saints is a certain profession of faith by which we believe in their glory, we must have the piety to believe that even on their subject the Church cannot err'. And *Augustinus Triumphus, Summa de potestate ecclesiastica*, q. 14, no. 4 (Rome edn of 1584) unhesitatingly asserts that 'papam secundum praesentem iustitiam canonizando habentem pro teste exteriorem evidentiam errare non posse': M. Schenk, *Die Unfehlbarkeit des Papstes in der Heiligsprechung* (Freiburg, 1965). It is surprising that there is nothing on this subject in the otherwise excellent study by B. Tierney, *Origins of papal infallibility 1150–1350* (Leiden, 1972).

[54] V. Martinez-Garcia, 'El testimonio del confessor en los processos de beatification de los servos de Dios y canonizacion de los bienaventurados', unpublished thesis, Gregorian University of Rome, 1954. Instances of the confessor giving evidence at canonization processes were already common in the thirteenth century, but they become more explicit in the fourteenth, and John XXII mentions the evidence of Thomas Aquinas' confessor in his bull of canonization (*AA.SS.* Mar. I, p. 668).

[55] Y. Congar, *L'Eglise de saint Augustin à l'époque moderne* (Paris, 1970), especially pp. 268–81.

ies his 'lieutenants'.[56] In practice, the suggestions the latter made to the Supreme Pontiff had little chance of gaining attention unless they had the support of temporal sovereigns influential with and loyal to the papacy. The Avignon popes, for example, rarely acted on requests for canonization from diocesan prelates, especially if they came from an episcopate, such as that of England, seen as hostile to Rome and the Curia.

One final observation may point us in the direction of the solution to the puzzle of the changing attitude of the papacy to canonization at the end of the thirteenth century. We have already noted that it was just when requests were becoming more numerous, especially between 1270 and 1330, that the Holy See began to intervene less frequently and often bluntly to refuse the requests with which it was besieged. The coincidence of these two contrary phenomena was hardly fortuitous. Since the second half of the twelfth century, there had been significant changes in the West in the sphere of the cult of the saints. They need to be examined with care inasmuch as they explain the increasingly negative response, and sometimes outright rejection, which characterized the attitude of the Roman Church towards local devotions at the end of the Middle Ages.

---

[56] *Ibid.*, p. 279. On the administrative centralization resulting from this ecclesiology, see G. Mollat, *Les papes d'Avignon, 1305–1378*, pp. 553–65 of Paris edn of 1975, with full bibliography, trans. J. Love, *The popes at Avignon, 1305–1378* (London, 1963).

PART III

THE RISE OF THE CULT OF THE SAINTS AND THE ASSERTION OF 'MODERN' SAINTHOOD

ᲔᎧᎧᎧᎧᎧ

Between 1150 and 1350, the cult of the saints in the West was transformed in two ways, which, beneath an apparent continuity, profoundly modified its nature and role in religious life. First, the number of individuals recognized as saints by the faithful greatly increased, reaching a very high figure. A quantitative approach to this phenomenon is extremely difficult, and those who have attempted it have produced very different results. The number of saints venerated in the Latin Church who lived in the thirteenth century is 188 according to the American sociologist P. Sorokin, 312 according to another sociologist, the Belgian P. Delooz, and 518 according to M. Goodich.[1] Whilst such variations present problems for the historian,[2] the trend, however uncertain the documentary basis for the statistics, is clear. If we confine ourselves to the material in Sorokin and Delooz, who alone provide figures for the whole period, the distribution by century of saints who died between 1000 and 1400 is as follows:

---

[1] P. Sorokin, *Altruistic love: a study of American 'good neighbour' and Christian saints* (Boston, 1950), p. 179; Delooz, *Sociologie et canonisations*, p. 244; M. Goodich, 'A profile of thirteenth century sainthood', *Comparative Studies in Society and History*, 17 (1976), p. 430.

[2] The differences are in fact due to the different material used. Sorokin's figures are based on the saints listed in the twelve volumes of the 1926–8 edition of A. Butler, H. Thurston and D. Attwater's *Lives of the saints*, which is essentially based on material collected in the eighteenth century; Delooz has added the saints listed by the Benedictines of Paris in their *Vies des saints et des bienheureux selon l'ordre du calendrier*, 13 vols. (Paris, 1935–59); Goodich seems to have quarried systematically the *Acta sanctorum* and *Analecta Bollandiana*, which explains the greater length of his list.

	Sorokin	Delooz
Eleventh century	120	226
Twelfth century	152	291
Thirteenth century	188	312
Fourteenth century	144	195
Fifteenth century	119	147

Given that all the figures for the development of the cult of the saints in the West point in the same direction, we may confidently conclude that the twelfth and thirteenth centuries were a period of significant quantitative growth, and that it became, between 1150 and 1350, one of the principal expressions of popular devotion.[3] These estimates are still very far from enabling us to appreciate the full scale of the phenomenon, given that they include only those servants of God who lived in the Middle Ages, and take no account of the cult accorded to older intercessors.

The corollary of this growth is the success of 'modern' sainthood. Up to the twelfth century, clergy and faithful primarily venerated saints dating from the first centuries of the Church.[4] Later, these devotions lost none of their prestige, and the vitality of the pilgrimages to the main traditional sanctuaries testifies to their permanence.[5] But, after 1150, in many regions, cults accorded to persons who had only recently died proliferated and they often, in the space of a few decades, became as famous and as highly regarded as the Apostles and the martyrs. This development was linked to a change of perspective which is visible in the Church from the time of the Gregorian Reform. Under the influence of a papacy which now aimed to realize *hic et nunc* an ideal Christianity, there was, from the end of the eleventh century, a break with the Christianity of the first millennium.[6] Admittedly, the period of reference remained the apostolic age, and the success of dynamic myths such as the ideal of the *Ecclesie primitive forma* or the *vita apostolica* at this period is well known. But, in the religious as in the cultural sphere, the people of the twelfth century saw themselves, to borrow the famous expression of Bernard of Chartres, as 'dwarfs perched on the shoulders of giants'. Free of any complex with

---

[3] This is clear from the table of uncanonized saints arranged by fifty-year period in Delooz, *Sociologie et canonisations*, p. 233.

[4] See above, p. 20.

[5] There is a useful synthesis (and bibliography) of medieval pilgrimages in P. A. Sigal, *Les marcheurs de Dieu* (Paris, 1974).

[6] I have discussed this turning-point in my *La spiritualité du Moyen Age occidental* (Paris, 1975), especially pp. 67–8.

regard to a past which they felt they were reviving, the contemporaries of Alexander III and Innocent III were conscious of seeing further than their predecessors. As a result, they were inclined to appreciate the religious experiences they witnessed, and see their age as on a par with the great epochs in the history of the Church.

CHAPTER 6

THE ROLE OF THE PAPACY

ⓔⓢⓔⓢⓔⓢ

The papacy gave a decisive impetus to this development by according the honour of canonization to persons who had only recently died, such as SS Thomas Becket (1173) and Bernard (1174). For the first time since the age of SS Martin and Benedict, the cult of servants of God who were neither Apostles nor Doctors of the Church extended, within the space of a few decades, to the whole of western Christendom, where it aroused universal enthusiasm.[1]

This was, of course, a sign of the success of the centralizing policy which the papacy had pursued for more than a century, and of the efficiency of the networks created by Rome to communicate its wishes to the whole ecclesial body. But the canonization and rapid diffusion throughout the West of the cult of St Thomas Becket had another significance. The feast of the murdered prelate, which had been announced to the whole Christian world in five solemn bulls, was quickly inscribed by the basilicas of the Lateran and Vatican in their calendars, which from then on were constantly enriched by the addition of names of recently deceased saints.[2]

---

[1] For the canonization of St Bernard, see Bredero, *Etudes sur la Vita prima de S. Bernard*; Bredero, 'The canonization of Saint Bernard', pp. 63–99. For the exceptional importance and immense repercussions for Christendom in the late twelfth and thirteenth centuries of Alexander III's canonization of St Thomas Becket, see *Thomas Becket. Actes du colloque international de Sédières (19–24 août 1973)*, ed. R. Foreville (Paris, 1975). One indication of the popularity of this saint is the success of the legends composed in his honour in several countries; see E. Walberg, *La tradition hagiographique de S. Thomas Becket avant la fin du XIIe siècle* (Paris, 1925); P. A. Brown, *The development of the legend of Thomas Becket* (Philadelphia, 1930); R. Foreville, 'Mort et survie de S. Thomas Becket', *Cahiers de civilisation médiévale*, 19 (1971), pp. 21–38.

[2] Jounel, *Le culte des saints*, pp. 11–12, shows how, at St John Lateran and St Peter's, the name of the new martyr was added to the liturgical calendars soon after his canonization. Jounel's conclusions regarding the great Roman basilicas are equally valid for less prestigious churches, as has been shown for the Four Crowned Martyrs, by T. Klauser, 'Ein Kirchenkalender aus der römischen Titelkirche der heiligen Vier Gekrönten', in *Festgabe Kardinal Schulte* (Cologne, 1935), pp. 11–40. This thirteenth-century liturgical calendar,

Table 5 *Distribution of canonization processes according to the time between the death of the saint and the beginning of the procedure (based on the seventy-one processes ordered by the papacy between 1198 and 1431)*

Lapse of time between the death of the saint and the canonization process	Process of canonization	
	1198–1304 %	1305–1431 %
Over 100 years	20.4	4.5
Between 100 and 60 years	8.2	9.1
Fewer than 60 years	71.4	86.4

This choice was a decisive turning-point in the history of Christianity. When most eastern Churches, that of Russia apart, allotted only a small place to 'modern' saints in their liturgical books, the Roman Church, without in any way downgrading the ancient devotions, opened up its sanctoral to persons more recent in time.[3] By instituting the process of canonization, it sought also to strengthen a control which was intended to offer models of unimpeachable orthodoxy for the imitation of the faithful.[4]

The way in which the canonization procedure developed between the late twelfth and early fifteenth centuries confirmed this initial choice, made at the time of Alexander III and Gregory IX, in favour of 'modern' sanctity. For proof, we need only consider the proportions of old and recent saints among those who were the subject of an enquiry decreed by the papacy between 1198 and 1431, as shown in table 5.

If we consider as 'recent' those saints who died fewer than sixty years before an enquiry was held, we see that the latter were proportionately much more numerous in the fourteenth than in the thirteenth century, and that, after 1304, the category of very old saints (that is, dead for over a hundred years at the time of their process) practically disappeared, although it had still accounted for a fifth of cases in the preceding century.[5] To be even more precise, we may note that fourteen of the sixteen processes of old saints took place between 1198 and 1250. Subsequently, popes usually bluntly refused requests to canonize persons remote in time, confining themselves to granting, if need be, simple authorizations of

---

still partly visible today, includes the names of SS Gilbert of Sempringham, William of York, Lawrence O'Toole and Elizabeth of Hungary, all recently canonized.

[3] Jounel, *Le culte des saints*, p. 12.

[4] For a fuller discussion, see below pp. 516–17.

[5] Sixty years is the upper limit for it to be possible for witnesses who had known the saint personally or directly to testify at the process.

THE ROLE OF THE PAPACY

translation, which amounted to approval of a local cult.[6] On the other hand, from the years 1225–30, they tended to reserve their favour for modern saints, either people they had known personally, as when Gregory IX canonized his contemporaries and friends SS Francis of Assisi and Dominic, or people whose form of sainthood they judged to be particularly appropriate to the needs of the Church, as in the case of the canonizations of SS Peter Martyr by Innocent IV and Louis IX by Boniface VIII.[7]

Papal action on behalf of the cult of recent saints would not, however, have been so successful had it not struck a chord in people's hearts and in the way, in the thirteenth and fourteenth centuries, they saw their own history. Indeed, there were many clerics at the time of Innocent III and Gregory IX who believed they were witnessing both an upsurge of violence on the part of the forces of evil and an outpouring of grace within the Church to combat it. The apocalyptic vocabulary some of them, not least the popes, employed may induce scepticism and incline us to see only rhetorical exaggeration. But Frederick II really was, in their eyes, Antichrist, and the proliferation of heresies a sign that the end of the world was near. It is hardly necessary to refer to the scholarly speculations of a Joachim of Fiore to explain this very special climate, without which the influence of eschatological beliefs cannot be understood.[8] Everyone, at their own level and in their own sphere, felt they were witnessing the emergence of 'new times'. It is symptomatic that this epithet was often added to the name of contemporary saints. The papacy strove to promote everywhere the cult of the 'new martyrs', SS Thomas Becket (d. 1170) and Peter Martyr (d. 1252); St Francis was called a 'new apostle' by his first biographer.[9]

Even the English Benedictine Matthew Paris, referring to the abundance of saints and miracles in the British Isles between 1230 and 1250, linked it to the advent of an age of sanctity, prefigured in the prologue to

---

[6] For example, in the case of Bertrand of Comminges (d. 1125), also Robert of La Chaise-Dieu (d. 1067). See above, p. 69.

[7] See above, pp. 71–4.

[8] For the success of eschatological themes in the thirteenth century, see L. Salvatorelli, 'Movimento francescano e Gioachimismo', in *Relazioni del Xe congresso internazionale di scienze storiche*, III (Florence, 1955), pp. 403–48; C. Baraut, sv Joachim de Fiore, in *Dictionnaire de spiritualité*, VIII (Paris, 1974), cc. 1179–1201, with good bibliography.

[9] Thomas of Celano, *Tractatus de miraculis S. Francisci*, in *Analecta Franciscana*, X (Quaracchi, 1926–41), I, p. 271. In his Chronicle, written *c.*1335, the Franciscan Fra Elemosina devoted a whole section entitled *de novis sanctis* to SS Francis and Dominic (Paris, BN, MS lat. 5006, fol. 154v, §4). In this context, the word *novus* also has an eschatological significance which should not be forgotten.

the Rule of St Benedict.[10] His example is important, because historians have tended to confine the impact of eschatological themes to Franciscan circles. But this monastic author devoted a whole section in his chronicle to the fact that, around 1240, *novi sancti clarent in Anglia*.[11] Returning to the theme for the year 1250, he widened his panorama of 'modern' saint-hood to the whole of Christendom and mentioned four contemporary saints: St Edmund Abingdon, archbishop of Canterbury, the hermit Robert of Knaresborough, St Elizabeth of Hungary and the prophetess St Hildegard, all 'distinguished by amazing miracles'.[12] Even the most sober theologians and canonists shared this collective exaltation. We find traces in bulls of canonization, where popes celebrated, with much recourse to biblical imagery, the assistance of the saints in the battle against heresy.[13] Here, too, the rhetorical formula is not entirely remote from reality, since the majority of those who were recognized as saints by Rome at this period, from St Homobonus to St Peter Martyr, were fierce opponents of the Cathars, and many towns and regions had been recovered for Catholicism by their action and miracles: SS Dominic in Languedoc and Antony of Padua in Venetia, John Bonus in Romagna and, lastly, St Francis himself, indirectly but no less effectively.[14] To combat dualistic doctrines and demonstrate to the masses the superiority of orthodoxy, the Church was in dire need, in the first two-thirds of the thirteenth century, of Christian perfection. It appealed to the witness of recent saints to coun-ter the influence of the *boni homines*, whose simple life and austere morals had won them great popular prestige.[15]

[10] Matthew Paris, *Chronica maiora*, ed. H. V. Luard, V (London, 1880), p. 195: 'videbatur igitur tempus innovari de quo plenus spiritu omnium sanctorum factus, in principio regulae suae commemorat Benedictus'.
[11] *Ibid.*, IV (London, 1877), p. 378. The saints he mentions are Roger, bishop of London (d. 1244), Master John *de Foxtuna*, St Edmund, Robert of Abingdon and the hermit Robert of Knaresborough. Only St Edmund was canonized; John *de Foxtuna* is completely unknown.
[12] *Ibid.*, V, p. 195.
[13] See, for example, the bulls of canonization of SS Homobonus, Francis, Dominic and Peter Martyr, ed. Fontanini, pp. 34–6, 60–4, 70–2, 82–8.
[14] K. Esser, 'Franziskus von Assisi und die Katharer seiner Zeit', *AFH*, 51 (1958), pp. 225–64.
[15] This direct involvement of thirteenth-century saints in the battle against heresy can be seen in the acts of some contemporary canonization processes: at that of John Bonus (d. 1249), for example, one witness, the master carpenter Jacob declared that he had aban-doned Catharism under the hermit's influence (*AA.SS.* Oct. IX, pp. 828–9). For the prestige of the Cathar Perfecti among the laity, see Le Roy Ladurie, *Montaillou*, pp. 540–2.

CHAPTER 7

THE ROLE OF THE REGULARS

એઝ એઝ એઝ

The move to 'modernize' the sanctoral was particularly successful among the regulars, who were often its principal architects. As might be expected, it was within the new orders that the feeling of reviving the sanctity of the early Church was strongest.

THE FRIARS MINOR

Contrary to some traditional ecclesiastical circles, for whom the world was growing old and in decline,[1] the Mendicants, and especially the Minors, held that the apostolic age had returned and that the flowering of sanctity within their ranks was its surest sign. Even those who could not be suspected of Joachimism, such as St Bonaventure, distinguished three great periods in the history of the Christian people: that of the Apostles and martyrs, characterized by the frequency of prodigies and miracles; that of the Doctors, notable for their learning and doctrine; and a final age, when God, having created the champions of voluntary poverty and begging – SS Francis and Dominic and their disciples – would restore evangelical perfection within the church and destroy the greed which had possessed the world.[2] At the end of the century, Olivi, much influenced by the arguments of the abbot of Fiore, was even more precise, distinguishing

---

[1] This attitude is clearly visible in the reaction of some monastic or regular canonical chroniclers towards the Mendicant orders in their early days. For example, in the *Chronicon Montis Sereni* (a Praemonstratensian abbey in the diocese of Magdeburg) *ad annum 1224*, in *MGH.SS.*, XXIII, p. 220: 'Non facile credi potest quod quisquam vel ex ordine sanctorum Praedicatorum vel Minorum Fratrum Augustino vel Benedicto sanctior sit futurus.'

[2] St Bonaventure, *De perfectione evangelica*, q.2, a.2, no. 20, in M. Bierbaum, *Bettelorden und Weltgeistlichkeit an der Universität Paris* (Münster, 1920), p. 269: 'Sic ultimo tempore [Deus] introduxit viros voluntarie mendicantes et pauperes rebus mundanis ut destruere- tur . . . per tertios avaritia quae in fine saeculi maxime regnat.'

no fewer than seven successive phases in history: the ages of the Apostles, the martyrs and the councils had been succeeded by the age of monasticism. This having degenerated, the fifth age was that of wealth and evil in the Church. This had ended with the foundation of the Franciscan order, charged by God to prepare the seventh and final stage, when the Church, freed from all stain, would at last rediscover purity and peace.[3]

From this perspective, to live in the thirteenth century was both an opportunity and a privilege. The sixth age, which had opened with the preaching of the Poverello, enjoyed a *superheminentia* over preceding ages thanks to the providential appearance of St Francis.[4] For the Minors, to whatever tendency they belonged, St Francis was not just another saint but an exceptional being to whom God had granted, by placing on him the stigmata, at La Verna, a prerogative of love which made him a new Christ: *alter Christus*.[5] Brother Elias, at the time of his death, wrote that 'no-one had seen his like, if not in the person of the son of God'.[6] St Bonaventure, in the *Legenda major*, developed for the first time in unequivocal fashion the theme of the similarity of Francis to Christ, which gave his sainthood a special significance. For St Bonaventure, the founder of the Minors was the angel of the sixth seal, thanks to whom a new age in the history of salvation had begun.[7] Later texts in the Franciscan hagiographical tradition emphasized even more strongly the fact that the life of St Francis was indeed a 'copy' of that of the Saviour, and that, in the words of the author of the *Miracula sancti Francisci*, composed in the second half of the fourteenth century, 'God renewed his Passion in the

---

[3] *Petrus Iohannis Olivi, Lectura super Apocalypsum*, c.6, quoted in R. Manselli, *La 'Lectura super Apocalypsim' di Pietro di Giovanni Olivi: ricerche sull'escatologismo medievale* (Rome, 1955), pp. 149–52.

[4] *Petrus Iohannis Olivi, Questiones de perfectione evangelica*, q.8, quoted in Manselli, *La 'Lectura super Apocalypsim'*, p. 154: 'Inter omnes sanctos claruit in eo [= St Francis] vita singularis et divinissima in omni genere et opere. Et cum hoc facta sunt per eum singularia et multiplicia miracula quorum omnium consummatio fuit impressio stigmatum et plagarum Christi.'

[5] For this central theme in Franciscan hagiography and preaching, see the texts collected and discussed in Stanislao da Campagnola, *L'Angelo del sesto sigillo e l'alter Christus* (Rome, 1971).

[6] Brother Elias, *Epistola encyclica de transitu S. Francisci*, ed. in *Analecta Franciscana*, X (Quaracchi, 1926–41), pp. 525–8: 'A saeculo non est auditum tale signum praeterquam in filio Dei qui est Christus Deus: non diu ante mortem frater et pater noster apparuit crucifixus, quinque plagas que vere sunt stigmata Christi portans in corpore suo.'

[7] St Bonaventure, *Legenda major*, ed. in *Analecta Franciscana*, X (Quaracchi, 1926–41), p. 620. See also M. Bihl, 'Franciscus fuitne Angelus sexti sigilli?', *Antonianum*, 2 (1927), pp. 59–70.

person of St Francis.'[8] The latter's superiority over the saints who had preceded him led naturally to the conclusion that his order was pre-eminent. This claim was repeated and developed during the quarrel with the seculars.[9] For the Minors and the Preachers, those who adopted their rule, in whatever fashion, were destined for perfection or at least well-placed to achieve it.

However, the founders of the Mendicant orders had been guarded, if not hostile, towards external manifestations of sainthood. If we are to believe the *Chronica XXIV generalium*, St Francis had strongly deplored the miracles occurring at the tomb of one of his first companions, Peter of Catania, and instructed him, in the name of holy obedience, to cease, so as not to give the laity cause to disrupt the life of the brethren.[10] Even if the episode is legendary, it expresses the ideas of the founder as they appear in the *Admonitiones*: 'We ought to be ashamed', he wrote, 'we servants of God. For it was the saints who acted. We, in our stories and sermons, are content to exploit their deeds, in order to derive honour and glory for ourselves.'[11] The Poverello's mistrust of hagiography was made plain after the death of the brethren who had been martyred in Morocco. The immediate reaction of the companions of St Francis was to compile a 'Legend' exalting their noble deeds. But when St Francis learned of this and observed, in the words of Jordan of Giano, 'that the brethren gained glory from their passion', he forbade anyone to read it and pushed it away, saying, 'let everyone gain glory with his own passion and not that of others'.[12] This attitude persisted among some of his disciples, such as Nicholas of Montefeltre, who implored God not to work miracles after his death,[13] and Salimbene, who was sceptical about the *miracula truffatoria* of the Dominican John of Vicenza and the lay saints of his time.[14]

The reticence of the Friars Minor towards the cult of the saints was,

---

[8] *Miracula sancti Francisci*, ed. L. Oliger, *AFH*, 12 (1919), p. 362. See also the collection of documents in Vauchez, 'Les stigmates de saint François', pp. 622–3.

[9] I. Ratzinger, 'Der Einfluss des Bettelordensstreites', in *Festschrift M. Schmaus* (Munich, 1957), pp. 697–724.

[10] *Chronica XXIV generalium*, *Analecta Franciscana*, III (Quaracchi and Florence, 1897), p. 34.

[11] St Francis of Assisi, *Admonitiones*, ed. and trans. T. Desbonnets and D. Vorreux, in *Saint François d'Assise: documents* (Paris, 1968), p. 44. See also Thomas of Celano, *Vita secunda*, c. 103, p. 463.

[12] Jordan of Giano, *Chronica*, in *Analecta Franciscana*, I (Quaracchi, 1885), pp. 3–4.

[13] Salimbene, *Cronica*, II, pp. 809–12.

[14] *Ibid.*, I, pp. 109–10, II, pp. 733–5.

however, shortlived. Their intense veneration of St Francis was expressed, soon after his death, by the appearance of the *Vita prima* of Thomas of Celano, followed, in 1244, by a *Vita secunda*, and, around 1253, by a *Tractatus de miraculis*. Further, the construction of the basilica at Assisi, through the impetus of brother Elias, must surely be seen as the most visible sign that the hagiographical mentality had triumphed within the order. The polemic which developed around the stigmata of their founder only impelled the brothers to redouble their zeal. They were all the readier in that, for them, as we have seen, St Francis was no ordinary saint.[15] In 1244, the general chapter decided to collect as much information as possible about the prodigies attributed to his intercession. This decision provoked some protests, in particular from the few companions of the Poverello who were still alive. They objected to the importance attached to the miracles, 'which do not make, but only reveal, sanctity', and demanded a greater emphasis on the life of the saint.[16] These recriminations came only shortly before the generalship of St Bonaventure, whose *Legenda major*, written in 1263, replaced all the earlier *Vitae* of St Francis.[17]

Up to the mid-thirteenth century, the zeal of the Franciscans was almost entirely directed towards the glorification of their founder and, after his canonization in 1228, the diffusion of his cult. Apart from St Antony of Padua, who was canonized in 1232, they showed no interest in any other figure. It was only with reluctance, and under papal pressure, that they agreed to venerate St Clare. In 1260, Alexander IV was obliged to condemn the attitude of a Friar Minor from Vienna, who had criticized this devotion in a sermon,[18] and it was only in 1340, at the general chapter in Assisi, that her cult was put on a par with those of the order's other saints.[19] Further, it does not appear that the order intervened on behalf

[15] Thus, according to Brother Leo, 'Omnes sancti sunt perfecti sed non est de minoribus sanctus pater noster Franciscus': *Vita fratris Leonis*, in *Analecta Franciscana*, III (1897), p. 66. Olivi went even further by speaking of some saints who were more perfect than others, 'sicut fuit Beata Virgo principaliter, postea Apostoli omnes, beatus Franciscus et beata Clara': *Informatio Petri Johannis*, ed. R. Manselli, in *Spirituali e beghini in Provenza* (Rome, 1959), App. 1, p. 279.
[16] *Testimonium trium sociorum sancti Francisci de vita et sanctitate ipsius*, AFH, 10 (1917), pp. 81–2.
[17] St Bonaventure, *Legenda major*, pp. 579–722.
[18] Her office was introduced into the order's liturgy in 1260. The rite of major double was accorded her in 1263, but the general chapter forbade the celebration of the octave of her feast: A. Van Dijk, 'Il culto di Santa Chiara nel Medio Evo', in *Santa Chiara d'Assisi: studi e cronaca del VIIo centenario* (Assisi, 1953), pp. 155–205. For the Vienna incident, see Alexander IV, *Profundi doloris*, 3.VI.1260, in *Bull. Franc.*, II, p. 398.
[19] 'Item statutum fuit commemoratio sanctae Clarae fiat per totum ordinem sicut de aliis sanctis nostris': Van Dijk, 'Il culto di Santa Chiara'.

of those of its members who enjoyed a reputation for sanctity in Italy: Benvenuto of Gubbio (d. 1232) at Corneto, Ambrose of Massa (d. 1240) at Orvieto and Simon of Collazzone (d. 1250) in and around Spoleto. The enquiries concerning them were initiated by the papacy at the request of the local civil powers, and none of these causes succeeded.[20] At this period, the Franciscans did not dissipate their energies, as we see from the accusations levelled by Giles of Assisi at the general ministers who made little effort to promote the cult of some brethren martyred on Islamic territory.[21]

At this same period, however, there appeared among the sons of St Francis a tendency to exalt the memory of all the members of the 'triple militia' who had shown signs of sanctity during their lifetime. During the polemics in which they engaged with both the secular clergy and the Dominicans, the perfection of their way of life was often questioned. What better argument could be deployed against their detractors and rivals than the number of saints from their ranks, clear sign, in the words of Brother Giles, that 'since the beginning of the world, there has never been a better or more effective religious order than that of the Friars Minor'?[22] As early as 1244–6, Thomas of Pavia had adopted this position when compiling his *Dialogus de gestis sanctorum Fratrum Minorum*, which found room for other figures alongside the great saints like SS Francis and Antony.[23]

But this shift was primarily characterized by the production of *Vitae* written to preserve the memory and diffuse the cult of some of their followers, as, for example, in 1248–9 by Brothers Guy of Cortona and Hippolytus of Florence on behalf of B. Umiliana dei Cerchi (d. 1246), by Giunta Bevignate for St Margaret of Cortona (d. 1297), and by Arnold of Foligno for St Angela (d. 1309). Beginning in Italy, the movement steadily spread beyond. At the general chapter in Padua in 1276, it was decided that the Minors should collect evidence about the lives and miracles of their founder 'and other saintly brethren'.[24] This call was heeded. In every country of Christendom, the Franciscans began, if they had not already done so, to write the life of and record the prodigies accomplished by

---

[20] For these cults, see pp. 41–3 above and 339–44 below.

[21] *Dicta B. Fratris Aegidii*, c. XXV: *de negligentia praelatorum in canonizatione aliquorum fratrum* (Quaracchi and Florence, 1905), p. 75.

[22] *Ibid.*, c. XIX, p. 64.

[23] *Dialogus de gestis sanctorum Fratrum Minorum auctore fr. Thoma de Pavia*, ed. F. M. Delorme (Quaracchi, 1923).

[24] See *AFH*, 7 (1914), p. 681. For examples of miracles publicized on the occasion of general chapters, see L. Lemmens, *Testimonia minora saeculi XIII de sancto Francisco* (Quaracchi, 1926), pp. 87–91.

their brethren who had died in an odour of sanctity.[25] Many collections of miracles were compiled, and then read publicly at meetings of provincial or general chapters, which assured the persons in question a fame extending beyond their monastery or town.

Further, the first half of the fourteenth century saw the appearance of hagiographical compilations concerning all the saints claimed by the order. It was at this period that the *Dialogus de vitis sanctorum Fratrum Minorum* was completed, and works such as the *Catalogus sanctorum Fratrum Minorem* (*c*.1335) and *Provinciale ordinis Fratrum Minorum* composed.[26] This hagiographical policy culminated at the end of the century in huge compilations such as the *Chronica XXIV generalium* and, above all, the extraordinary 'Book of Conformities' of Bartholomew of Pisa (1399).[27] Not content with honouring their own 'saints', who were counted by the hundred in the fourteenth century alone in Italy, the Friars Minor propagated far and wide the names of many tertiaries, both men and women, and even persons who had no other claim to their support than having expressed sympathy for the order. This was the case, for example, with St Louis, whose cult was promoted by the Franciscans in the Germanic countries and even as far afield as Scandinavia,[28] and with Charles of Blois, who was amply repaid after his death for the favour he had shown in his lifetime, since the convents of Blois, Angers, Guingamp, Dinan and Périgueux were among the principal centres from which his devotion spread.[29] However they viewed this phenomenon, contemporary witnesses were all in agree-

---

[25] See, for example, the collection of miracles compiled at Borgo San Sepolcro in 1305, immediately after the death of B. Rainerius, ed. Kern, 'Le Bienheureux Rainier de Borgo San Sepolcro', p. 238.

[26] *Dialogus de vitis sanctorum Fratrum Minorum*, ed. L. Lemmens (Rome, 1902). The compilation includes *Dialogus de gestis sanctorum Fratrum Minorum*, ed. Delorme; *Catalogus sanctorum Fratrum Minorum*, ed. L. Lemmens (Rome, 1903); *Provinciale ordinis Fratrum Minorum*, ed. L. Eubel (Quaracchi. 1892). Also from this period (1314–22) is *Memorabilia de sanctis Fratribus Minoribus*, ed. D. M. Faloci Pulignani, *Miscellanea Francescana*, 15 (1915), pp. 65–9. Iconography was also important in this process; see plate 14.

[27] *Chronica XXIV generalium*; Bartholomew de Renonico (or 'of Pisa'), *De conformitate vite beati Francisci ad vitam Domini Iesu*, ed. in *Analecta Franciscana*, IV and V (Quaracchi, 1906, 1912). For the latter, highly controversial in the fifteenth century and during the Reformation, see C. Erickson, 'Bartholomew of Pisa, Francis exalted: *De conformitate*', *Medieval Studies*, 34 (1972), pp. 252–74.

[28] M. Barth, 'Zum Kult des Hl. Königs Ludwig im deutschen Sprachgebiet und in Skandinavien', in *Festschrift J. Vincke, Frieburger Diözesan Archiv*, 3rd ser., 14 and 15 (1962–3), pp. 127–226.

[29] A. de Sérent, 'Charles de Blois duc de Bretagne (1319–1364) et l'ordre des Frères mineurs', *Etudes Franciscaines*, 8 (1957), pp. 59–75; Martin, *Les Ordres Mendiants en Bretagne*, pp. 366–71, 409–11.

ment in recognising the fundamental role of the Minors in the diffusion of the new cults.

In this, preaching played an important part. It was through the sermons of Raymond of Gilhac and his companions that the people of Marseilles learned of the sainthood of Louis of Anjou, and news of his miracles spread throughout Provence.[30] The chapels built by the Franciscans in their convents and the paintings they placed there familiarized the faithful with new figures. Well placed in general to obtain indulgences, the brethren used and abused this convenient procedure to stimulate new devotions.[31] Not only were their saints more numerous, but, thanks to a network of houses which covered the whole of the West, and the mobility and influence of the brethren, they enjoyed more favourable conditions for diffusion than had ever previously existed in the Middle Ages. The Franciscan order was both highly organized and, in most regions, solidly rooted. This enabled it to adapt to the evolution of popular religiosity, but also to influence it by means of the lay groups which flourished in its wake. There can be no doubt that the cult of the saints was one of the areas in which it achieved greatest success.

THE FRIARS PREACHER AND OTHER MENDICANT ORDERS

The history of the attitude of the Dominicans towards the cult of the saints has many similarities with that of the Franciscans. To begin with, the Preachers attached little importance to it. The body of St Dominic lay in the ground for twelve years without receiving any special honours and it was not until 1233, at the instigation of Gregory IX, that the brethren proceeded to its solemn translation into a tomb of stone.[32] But the policy

---

[30] See the statements of witnesses at his canonization process: *Processus canonizationis et legendae variae sancti Ludovici O.F.M. episcopi Tolosani*, in *Analecta Franciscana*, VII (Quaracchi, 1951), p. 176.

[31] For the cult accorded throughout Christendom to SS Francis and Dominic in the thirteenth century, see Stanislao da Campagnola, *Francesco d'Assisi nei suoi scritti e nelle sue biografie dei secoli XIII–XIV* (Assisi, 1977), especially pp. 203–18; M. H. Vicaire, ' "Vesperus" (l'étoile du soir) ou l'image de Saint Dominique pour ses frères au XIIIe siècle', in *Dominique et ses prêcheurs* (Freiburg and Paris, 1977), pp. 280–304. Papal favour was undiminished in the fourteenth century; in the bull *Ante thronum*, 26.II.1343 (ed. *Bull. Franc.*, VI, p. 105), Clement VI extended the indulgences granted to all Franciscan convents for the feasts of SS Francis and Antony of Padua to the feast of St Louis of Anjou (d. 1297).

[32] Salimbene, *Cronica*, p. 110.

of the order soon changed, especially after the canonization of St Peter Martyr in 1253. Though reservations persisted within the order, the Holy See brushed them aside to intervene frequently and insistently with various national episcopates to persuade them to celebrate the new feast. Another series of bulls urged the secular clergy, too, to adopt the cult of St Dominic, which seems to have met with resistance in certain regions. At the outset, then, the two saints of the order of the Friars Preacher were ideally placed to be venerated throughout Christendom as a result of the quite exceptional favour shown them by the papacy.[33]

To the extent that the personality of St Dominic seems to have been less striking than that of St Francis, the attention of his spiritual sons was less concentrated on his person and soon turned towards all the manifestations of sanctity which might exist within the order. In 1256, the general chapter in Paris asked the priors to inform the Master General of 'any miracle or edifying deed occurring within the order or because of the order, which comes to their knowledge'.[34] This was, in fact, in preparation for a series of hagiographical compilations, the most remarkable of which were the *Vitae fratrum* of Gerard of Frachet, publication of which was announced by Humbert of Romans in a letter of 1260, and the *Bonum universale de apibus* of Thomas of Cantimpré.[35] A few years earlier, a provincial chapter meeting at Montpellier had enjoined convents to send to the provincial prior accounts 'of the miraculous deaths of brethren'.[36] Engaged in polemics with the secular clergy on the subject of poverty and evangelical perfection, the Dominicans were keen to demonstrate that sainthood flourished within their ranks. They differed from the Minors, however, by also showing interest in old saints who had no connection with their order. On the literary plane, we need only mention the Golden Legend of James *de Voragine*, whose work was continued in the fourteenth century by Peter Calo.[37] But the Preachers were equally active in the domain of the cult strictly speaking. For this, the chronicle of Bernard Gui on the Dominican convents of the French Midi contains valuable

---

[33] See above, p. 111. For opposition to the cult of St Dominic, see Thierry d'Appolda, *AA.SS*. Aug. I, pp. 618–25.

[34] *Acta capitulorum generalium ordinis Praedicatorum*, I, p. 83.

[35] *Acta capitulorum provincialium ordinis Praedicatorum*, ed. C. Douais (Toulouse, 1894), p. 49.

[36] *Ibid.*

[37] *Legenda aurea*, ed. T. Graesse (Leipzig, 1879); A. Poncelet, 'Le légendier de Pierre Calo', *Anal. Boll.*, 29 (1910), pp. 41–116. The precursor in this domain was Jean de Mailly, who, *c*.1250, wrote an *Abrégé des gestes et miracles des saints*, ed. and trans. A. Dondaine (Paris, 1947).

evidence.[38] In many other places, they helped to breathe new life into devotions which had faded and gave them a new audience.

From the fourteenth century, however, they mostly concentrated on the cult of recent saints. The cause of St Thomas Aquinas gave the Preachers an opportunity to demonstrate their cohesion. The stakes were high, since it was the value of the doctrine of the 'universal teacher', and even the place of the Preachers within the Church, which was at issue. The favour shown them by John XXII and their influence at the Curia enabled them to triumph over the opposition which seems to have surfaced on this occasion.[39] Alongside this great figure, there were others, of lesser stature, who were either regulars, like Brother Donadieu of Carcassonne (d. 1295) and the famous popular preacher Venturino of Bergamo (d. 1346), or lay people, usually tertiaries who had gravitated in the orbit of the Dominican convents, such as Villana dei Botti in Florence (d. 1361) and Benvenuta Bojani in Cividale del Friuli (d. 1295).[40] The trend to favour the order's saints was particularly strong in Italy at the end of the fourteenth century. This is apparent in the visions of St Catherine of Siena, which related principally, if we are to believe certain witnesses at the process in Venice, to SS Dominic, Peter Martyr, Thomas Aquinas and Margaret of Hungary and Agnes of Montepulciano.[41] Elsewhere, proud of their missionary martyrs, the Preachers cultivated their memory in hagiographical texts and iconography.[42] This attitude only grew stronger with time. For the Preachers, the diffusion in their churches of iconographical representations of the stigmata of St Catherine of Siena in the fifteenth century was a way

[38] Bernard Gui, *De fundatione et prioribus conventuum provinciarum Tolosanae et provinciae ordinis Praedicatorum*, ed. P. Amargier (Rome, 1961). In Castres in 1259, for example, the Friars exhumed and solemnly translated the relics of St Vincent, to whom the church they had inherited there was dedicated (pp. 143–8).

[39] M. Grabmann, 'Die Kanonization des Hl. Thomas von Aquin in ihrer Bedeutung für die Verbreitung seiner Lehre im 14.Jahrhundert' in *Divus Thomas* (1923), pp. 233–49; also his 'Hagiographische Texte in einer Hs. des Kirchenhist. Seminars der Universität München', *AFP*, 19 (1949), pp. 379–82, which includes a fourteenth-century text revealing Franciscan attempts to prevent the canonization of Aquinas right up to the last moment.

[40] Kaeppeli, 'Vie du frère Martin Donadieu de Carcassonne', pp. 276–90. For Venturino of Bergamo, leader of the popular crusade of 1335, see the '*Legenda beati fratris Venturini ordinis Praedicatorum*', ed. A Grion, *Bergomum*, 30 (1956), pp. 38–110.

[41] *PC Catherine of Siena*, 2nd and 24th witnesses, pp. 138, 455.

[42] See the catalogues of Dominican martyrs published by R. J. Loenertz in *AFP*, 12 (1942), pp. 281–303, 19 (1949), pp. 275–9. Many were venerated within the order in the fourteenth century. An ideal conception of the sanctity of the order is often expressed in the prologues of Dominican legendries, such as that of Cividale (1402) (ed. M. H. Laurent, *Anal. Boll.*, 58 (1940), p. 38): 'Ordo Predicatorum plurimos a sui principio in diversis mundi partibus sanctos protulit multis notos, martires siquidem et gloriosissimos confessores.'

of retaliating against the claims of the Friars Minor as to the unique and exceptional nature of the stigmata of St Francis, and of placing themselves on an equal footing in the increasingly bitter rivalry which was developing between them.[43] But, from our perspective, the result counts more than the motives, and, on this level, it is clear that the name and likeness of a saint whose reputation might never have spread beyond the frontiers of Italy without Dominican support were disseminated throughout Christendom.

To complete our survey of the ways in which cults were propagated by the Mendicant orders, we need to emphasize the role of bishops from their ranks, of whom there were many by the second half of the thirteenth century, and the appearance of trade-offs between the orders in the liturgical sphere. In fact, when a Friar Minor or Preacher was appointed to a bishopric, his first concern was generally to introduce into his diocese the feasts of his order's saints, above all those of its founders. We have an excellent example in the Franciscan Walter of Bruges, bishop of Poitiers in the early fourteenth century, who intervened on several occasions to persuade the Benedictine abbeys in his diocese to celebrate the feast of St Francis. Each time, this took the form of the institution, for a sum of money, of a perpetual mass.[44] Elsewhere, the great centralized religious orders negotiated agreements with each other designed to increase the fame of their saints. In 1255, for example, the Cistercians decided to include in their liturgical calendar, as feasts with a dozen lessons, those of SS Dominic and Peter Martyr; in return, the Dominicans adopted that of St Bernard. A similar agreement was concluded in 1259 between St Bonaventure and the Cistercians. In future, the latter solemnly commemorated the feast of St Francis, the Friars Minor that of St Bernard.[45]

An extension of our enquiry to the other Mendicant orders would only lead to similar conclusions. The Hermits of St Augustine and the Carmelites were slow to join the other religious orders in adding to the number of saints from their ranks and spreading the new devotions. But the Augustinians did not lag behind for long, as we see from their promotion of the

[43] Vauchez, 'Les stigmates de S. François', p. 611.
[44] P. Caillebaut, 'Autour du bienheureux Gautier de Bruges', La France franciscaine, 2 (1923), pp. 186–90.
[45] J. M. Canivez, Statuta capitulorum generalium ordinis Cisterciensis, II (Louvain, 1933), p. 410, n. 4, p. 450, n. 9; A. Van Dijk, 'The Calendar in the Breviary of S. Francis', Franciscan Studies, 9 (1948), p. 27; W. R. Bonniwell, A History of the Dominican Liturgy (New York, 1945).

cult of St Nicholas of Tolentino in Italy.[46] The Carmelites initially showed a clear preference for the traditional devotions, but they did not remain immune to the general trend. After 1350, at the instigation of the general chapter, they tried to obtain the canonization of two of their members, Albert of Trapani (d. 1307) and Peter Thomas (d. 1366). A special commission was even set up in 1375 to ask the prelates and civil authorities of all the countries where they were represented to petition the pope on behalf of these causes.[47] We see here the same process of diffusion and institutionalization of cults of recent saints which characterizes the Mendicant Orders in the later Middle Ages.[48]

THE MONKS AND THE REGULAR CANONS

The religious orders of the old type had less cause than the Mendicants to interest themselves in the cult of the saints. Their vocation was not essentially pastoral and the development of a devotion towards a monk or nun posed problems for their community which it was preferable to avoid, such as how to receive visitors and provide for pilgrims. Further, the monastic mentality was, in general, backward-looking. For the sons of St Benedict, the more the Church distanced itself from the time of its origins and of the founding father, the more the signs of corruption and decadence within it increased: *Mundus senescit*. Accordingly, the world of the cloisters was for long untouched by the impulse to seek out the signs of sanctity which might be concealed in the present. The example of the Cistercian order, the most recent of the various branches of the Benedictine obedience, is interesting in this regard. To begin with, the white monks even lacked interest in their own celebrities – with the exception of their leader, St Bernard, canon-

---

[46] At the 1325 canonization process, many witnesses said that the saint's fame had immediately been propagated 'a fratribus sui ordinis et a personis aliis secularibus': *PC Nicholas of Tolentino*, Siena, Archivio di Stato, Legato Bichi, MS Y. 111, fol. 208v. One witness even named two brothers, Giacomo and Gentile, as official propagators of the *fama* (*ibid.*, fol. 190v). For the cult of hermit saints, see R. Arbesmann, 'A legendary of early Augustinian saints', *Analecta Augustiniana*, 29 (1966), pp. 5–58; *Jordani de Saxonia Liber Vitas fratrum*, ed. R. Arbesmann and G. Hümpfner (New York, 1943).

[47] See the acts of the general chapters of the Carmelite order, ed. G. Wessels (Rome, 1912), pp. 145ff.

[48] The situation was similar in the case of the order of the Servites of Mary; see B. de Gaiffier, 'Notes bibliographiques sur l'histoire de l'ordre des Servites de Marie', *Anal. Boll.*, 93 (1975), pp. 167–76; F. A. Dal Pino, *I Frati Servi di Maria dalle origini all'approvazione (1233 ca–1304)* (Louvain, 1972), especially pp. 33–8.

ized in 1174 – and made no attempt to obtain official recognition of their merits.[49] In the late twelfth and early thirteenth centuries, this provoked mockery among the laity and acerbic comments on the part of their enemies.[50] Until about 1200, the general chapter of Cîteaux kept to the traditional line: it refrained from according special honours to monks who had died in an odour of sanctity, so that the regular life was undisturbed by an influx of lay visitors to their tombs. On occasion, sanctions were taken against abbots who allowed such abuses within their monastery.[51] Under pressure from the faithful, however, and perhaps also as a result of rivalry with the Mendicants, this rigour was soon relaxed. Especially from about 1210, the Cistercians began to pursue an active policy on behalf of saints drawn from their ranks, or even simply at one time members. In 1220, the abbot of Cîteaux was instructed by the general chapter to write to the pope seeking the canonization of Abbot Hugh of Bonnevaux, though admittedly at the request of the archbishop of Vienne and his suffragans.[52] The same year, he asked for the canonization of Robert of Molesme (d. 1111) and the general chapter decreed, in 1222, that his feast should be celebrated on 17 April, with an office of twelve lessons and one mass, *sicut de beato Benedicto*.[53] At the same period, Cîteaux actively supported the causes of the Breton abbot, Maurice of Carnoët (d. 1191) and, above all, of Archbishop William of Bourges (d. 1209), a former Grandmontine who had been at Pontigny, and who was canonized in

---

[49] In this, they remained true to the thinking of St Bernard: 'patriae est, non exilii, frequentia haec gaudiorum, et numerositas festivitatum cives decet, non exules' (*Ep.* 174, in *PL*. 182, c. 335). Twelfth-century hagiographical texts frequently show Cistercian abbeys prohibiting saints whose bodies lay in their abbeys from performing miracles. See, for example, *Vita Gerardi*, ed. G. Morin, '*De Vita et cultu B. Gerardi de Orcimonte*', *Studien und Mitteilungen aus dem Bened. und dem Cist. Orden*, 6 (1886), p. 295, also the texts cited by S. Lenssen, 'Aperçu historique sur la vénération des saints cisterciens', *Collectanea ordinis Cisterciensium Reformatorum*, 6 (1939), pp. 7–31, 167–95, 10 (1948), p. 15.

[50] In the *Dialogus miraculorum*, Caesar of Heisterbach reports a nobleman exclaiming: 'The grey monks! Have you ever seen any saints there? On Sundays, when the priest reads his calendar, I've yet to hear him name a single grey monk': A. Hilka, *Die Wundergeschichten des Caesarius von Heisterbach* (Bonn, 1937), I, p. 116. See also Matthew Paris, *Vita S. Edmundi*, c. 48, p. 276.

[51] See, for example, ed. Canivez, *Statuta capitulorum generalium ordinis Cisterciensis*, I, p. 176, no. 33 (1194): 'Abbas Bonaevallis [B. Hugh of Bonnevaux] qui sepultus est in oratorio pro religionis suae opinione ibi sic remaneat. De iis vero qui contra ordinis formam hoc facere praesumpserunt, dominus abbas Cistercii inquirat et digne corrigat.' The rule forbade the burial of abbots inside the church; see also *Monasticon Cisterciense*, ed. J. Paris and H. Ségalon (Solesmes, 1892), p. 433.

[52] Canivez, *Statuta*, I, p. 526, no. 48.

[53] *Ibid.*, I, p. 527, no. 53, II, pp. 15–16.

1218. His feast was soon extended to the whole order and, in 1261, his name was even included in the litanies.[54]

In parallel with this development, the first half of the thirteenth century saw an explosion of Cistercian hagiography, which exalted the merits of many monks, nuns and lay brothers who had belonged to the order, and of recluses who had lived under its aegis.[55] Over time, this interest in the cult of the saints only increased. In 1236, the Cistercians obtained from Gregory IX an enquiry into the life and miracles of John of Montmirail, a monk at Longpont (d. 1217), who enjoyed a great reputation for sanctity.[56] His body had already, in 1233, been moved from the abbey cemetery into the cloister. The enquiry having foundered, in 1253 the general chapter authorized a new translation of the body from the cloister to the church at Longpont and the erection of a mausoleum in his honour.[57] But the white monks also supported the cause of persons less close to them, such as the archbishop of Canterbury, St Edmund Abingdon, who died in 1240 after having spent some time at Pontigny, where his body was buried. In 1241, the general chapter, at the request of Pontigny, instructed Abbot Bruno of La Ferté to send the pope a letter of postulation.[58] Throughout the process, the English Cistercian cardinal John Tolet played an important role in promoting the cause, as did Stephen of Lexington, a former associate of the saint and abbot of Clairvaux from 1243.[59] When St Edmund was finally canonized, the faithful flocked to the abbey of Pontigny, which seems to have had little difficulty accepting, if it had not actually sought them, the many dispensations granted by Innocent IV and Alexander IV which were necessary to contravene the prohibitions of their rule. In fact, it was not long before the monks were authorized to place the saint's relics in a casket decorated with gold, silver and precious stones, and allow into the abbey the women who had travelled from England to take advantage of the indulgences granted to pilgrims.[60]

The attitude of the Cistercians towards the cult of the saints was there-

---

[54] *Ibid.*, I, pp. 367, 485, II, pp. 477–8. See also S. Steffen, 'Der hl. Wilhelm Erzbischof von Bourges', *Cistercienser Chronik*, 19 (1907), pp. 78–9; S. Lenssen, *Hagiologium Cisterciense*, I (Tilburg, 1948), pp. 41–4.

[55] S. Roisin, *L'hagiographie cistercienne dans le diocèse de Liège au XIIIe siècle* (Louvain, 1947); but not all the *Vitae* discussed by Roisin were written by Cistercians.

[56] M. A. Dimier, 'Le bienheureux Jean de Montmirail, moine de Longpont', *Mémoires de la fédération des sociétés savantes de l'Aisne*, 7 (1960–1), pp. 1–12.

[57] Canivez, *Statuta*, II, p. 394.

[58] *Ibid.*, II, p. 223.

[59] Lawrence, *St Edmund of Abingdon*, pp. 17–18, 118–19.

[60] Martène and Durand, *Thesaurus*, I, cc. 1922–4.

fore reversed. In the space of a few decades, indifference and even negligence gave way to an active positive policy. Their efforts did not, however, overall, meet with great success. Apart from the two bishops, SS William of Bourges and Edmund, who had other supporters, not one of the saints they promoted was canonized in the thirteenth or fourteenth centuries. These failures were probably due in part to chance causes, in particular financial difficulties. The crisis which was beginning to affect monastic temporalities was hardly favourable to sustaining increasingly lengthy and expensive proceedings.[61] But this can hardly explain why, among the cults the white monks sought to promote, some never achieved popularity. We should perhaps see this relative failure as a reflection of the loss of fervour visible in their ranks in the thirteenth century, and the consequent decline of their 'brand image' among the public. Further, unlike the Mendicants, they did not have the benefit of the institutional network provided by the confraternities, which made it possible to reach the laity. In fact, they were hardly able to extend their influence beyond the cloister, which restricted the diffusion of their spirituality and their models.[62] In spite of their strong organization and centralized structures, their role in the growth of the cult of recent saints was only secondary in the thirteenth century and negligible in the fourteenth.

The black monks and the other monastic congregations played an even less significant role in the renewal of the sanctoral visible in the thirteenth and fourteenth centuries throughout much of Christendom. Isolated communities or small congregations had less weight than the Cistercian order and could hardly constitute effective pressure groups. Also, many abbeys experienced severe crises at this period and the prestige of the traditional Benedictines seems to have been fairly low, which hardly encouraged the faithful to seek intercessors from their ranks. An exception must be made, however, for Italy, where groups with eremitical tendencies such as the

[61] Such problems were emphasized by Stephen of Lexington, abbot of Clairvaux, in a letter of c.1245 to Cardinal John Tolet: 'Sunt apud nos tria sanctorum corpora multis miraculis coruscantia qui adscribi sanctorum catalogo meruerint; sed visa difficultate quae incumbit negotio tam praeclaro . . . petitionem nostram quamcumque favorabilem proponere non audemus et suademus in casu simili alios abstinere' (ed. in Martène and Durand, *Thesaurus*, III, c. 1849).
[62] There were exceptions, in particular in central and eastern Europe, for example St Hedwig, duchess of Silesia (d. 1243), canonized in 1267, who was much influenced by Cistercian spirituality and ended her days in the abbey at Trzebnica. But the success of her cause was not primarily due to Cistercian pressure: J. Gottschalk, 'Die Förderer der Heiligsprechung Hedwigs', *Archiv für Schlesische Kirchengeschichte*, 21 (1963), pp. 73–133; Gottschalk, *St Hedwig Herzogin von Schlesien* (Cologne, 1964).

Camaldolese and Vallombrosans, or reformed orders like the Silvestrins and Olivetins, sought to promote the cult of their most eminent members. But this is an exceptional case, to a large degree explicable by the sensibility of local populations to the modern forms of sainthood. Also, the devotion to the great Italian abbeys of the thirteenth and fourteenth centuries remained essentially regional.[63]

The same is true of the regular canons of all obediences, who, having obtained the canonization of some of their members at the beginning of the thirteenth century, hardly referred to them again.[64] It was as if the monastic and canonical religious orders had decided not to compete with the Mendicants on the terrain of the cult of the saints. There could be no better illustration of the change in the significance of this devotion, which, in the space of a few decades, had become a pastoral issue of the first order, as a result of its success among the laity.

[63] Among the cults of the monk saints, only that of B. Silvester Guzzolini (d. 1267), founder of the Silvestrins, achieved widespread popularity, shown by the many episcopal indulgences granted to those who visited his tomb at Monte Fano, and by the fact that he became the co-patron of the town of Fabriano in the fourteenth century: Bolzonette, *Il Monte Fano e un grande anachoreta*, pp. 74–5, 110; *Atti del convegno di studi storici per l'VIII centenario della nascita di S. Silvestro, 1177–1977*, Studia Picena, 44, 1977 (Fano, 1978). For the cult of B. Bernard Tolomei, founder of the abbey of Monte Oliveto, near Siena, see *Saggi e ricerche nel VII centenario del Beato Bernardo Tolomei, 1272–1972* (Monte Oliveto, 1972).

[64] For the crisis of monastic and canonical sainthood in the thirteenth and fourteenth centuries, see below, pp. 327–9.

CHAPTER 8

THE SECULAR CLERGY AND THE LAITY

ಐಐಐಐ

To put it all down to the Mendicant orders, as is so often the case with any innovation in the religious sphere in the thirteenth century, would be, however, to exaggerate. The Friars Minor and Preachers no more invented the cult of the 'modern' saints than they originated the penitential movement among the laity. In both cases, they only developed and disseminated throughout Christendom formulas which had been tried out by others before their foundation. The tendency of historians to exaggerate the specific contribution of the Mendicants owes much to the nature of the documentation. We have access to the acts of a number of general and provincial chapters of the different orders. Not all have survived, but we have enough to be able to note their decisions and trace their application in the various regions of Christendom. Nothing comparable survives, unfortunately, for the secular clergy, and anyone with even a nodding acquaintance with synodal statutes, in any case few for the thirteenth century in many countries, knows that they generally say very little about the cult of the saints. Nevertheless, I have often come across entries, when reading a chronicle or canonization process, which suggest that bishops and parish priests were less indifferent than is often claimed to recent manifestations of sainthood.[1] In the current state of research, it is difficult to go beyond this general impression, which only studies of a number of dioceses could confirm.

Even when there is evidence of the involvement of the secular clergy,

---

[1] We learn from the deposition of one witness at the canonization process of Philip of Bourges that the saint's mother, Mathea, was the object of a cult in her native village: 'et quaesivit a capellano dicte capelle que erat cause quare dipictum erat diadema in capite ipsius et dixit dictus capellanus testi qui loquitur, quod ipse et alii boni viri de terra illa reputabant dictam Matheam esse sanctam' (*PC Philip of Bourges*, fol. 35v). This devotion would have been totally unknown had it not been mentioned by this witness.

128

it is difficult to establish the precise nature of their role. Did they take the initiative in devotions or follow in the wake of a spontaneous surge of popular piety? To this fundamental question, we can offer only a partial reply, varying according to region. In north-west Europe, sensibility to the new forms of sanctity seems to have remained essentially a clerical phenomenon. We see this in the thirteenth century in the Low Countries (Flanders, Brabant, around Liège), which produced many *Vitae* of lay saints and recluses of both sexes, beguines and lay brothers. They were written, according to circumstances, by prelates like James of Vitry, who wrote the Life of Mary of Oignies (d. 1213) in 1215–16, by Cistercians such as the authors of the Lives of the Blesseds from the abbey of Villers, or by Dominicans such as Thomas of Cantimpré.[2] But the cult accorded these people hardly extended beyond restricted devout circles, and none was the subject of a canonization process in the Middle Ages.

In Italy, on the other hand, the faithful seem to have behaved in a much more independent fashion. Admittedly, the cult of St Homobonus (d. 1197), canonized in 1199 at the request of Bishop Sicard, seems still to have been clerically controlled, only becoming popular in Cremona in the late thirteenth and early fourteenth centuries.[3] But a change can be detected around 1230, when the urban masses of central and northern Italy developed great enthusiasm for the founders of the Mendicant orders, as we see from the huge popularity of St Francis (d. 1226), the disturbances which followed the death in Padua in 1231 of St Antony, and the rapid growth of the cult of St Dominic in Bologna, after the great religious movement of the Alleluia and the preaching of the Dominican friar John of Vicenza.[4] From 1250, manifestations of devotion proliferated in these

---

[2] James of Vitry, *Vita B. Mariae Oignaciensis*, *AA.SS.* Iun. V, pp. 547–72; for the Cistercian *Vitae*, see Roisin, *L'hagiographie cistercienne*, pp. 173–4; for Dominican hagiography in these regions, see G. G. Meersseman, 'Frères prêcheurs et mouvement dévot en Flandre au XIIIe siècle', *AFP*, 18 (1948), pp. 69–130 (with an edition of the *Vita Margarete de Ypris*).

[3] The body of St Homobonus, canonized by Innocent III on 12 January 1199, was solemnly translated to the church of St Giles in Cremona in 1202. But it was not until 1292 that the diocesan synod disseminated the cult throughout the diocese, and only in 1356 that his remains were deposited in the cathedral crypt. That same year, Bishop Ugolino Ardengherio founded the 'Consortium sancti Homoboni', an association of pious lay people wishing to engage in charitable works. The celebration of the merchant saint's feast as a holiday appeared in the communal statutes of Cremona c.1339. A few years earlier, his likeness had begun to appear on the town's coinage. The history of the cult of St Homobonus remains to be written; meanwhile see D. Bergamaschi, *S. Omobono e il suo tempo* (Cremona, 1899); G. Varischi, *Sant'Omobono* (Cremona, 1937).

[4] For these religious movements and their political context, see A. Vauchez, 'Une campagne de pacification en Lombardie autour de 1233. L'action politique des Ordres Mendiants

same regions round the bodies of certain pious and recently deceased hermits and penitents. This surge of popular piety, oriented towards the new saints, most of whom came from the laity, has to be related to the success of the processions of flagellants in Perugia in 1260, where they were accompanied by the revival of the cult of 'saint' Bevignate, a mysterious person about whom nothing is known, beyond his residence in Perugia between the late twelfth and early thirteenth centuries.[5] These two concomitant movements reveal the aspirations of the faithful to appropriate an ideal of perfection and religious practices previously reserved to the clergy: first, sainthood and second, the meritorious practice of flagellation, which the *battuti* of 1260 had not invented, but which they had borrowed from the regulars and made into a devotion which was public and accessible to all.

A few years later, the great towns of the Po plain experienced explosions of religious fervour, which sometimes turned into collective delirium, after the death of certain persons regarded as saints by the laity and secular clergy but dismissed as imposters by the Mendicants: Antony Peregrinus in Padua in 1267, the hermit Parisio in Treviso in the same year, Armanno Pungilupo in Ferrara in 1269, Facio in Cremona in 1271, Albert of Villa d'Ogna in 1279 in Parma and Reggio Emilia.[6] To the horror of the Franciscan Salimbene, in whom the spectacle inspired only disgust and disapproval, the people became in their turn creators of saints, whom they chose from their own ranks.[7]

This situation was not unique to Italy, though it was here that it assumed its most spectacular forms. Throughout most of Christendom, from the last third of the thirteenth century, the 'saint factory' ran at top speed, and a steady stream of new names was added to the old sanctoral. In England, too, the number of saints grew between the last decades of the thirteenth and the mid-fourteenth centuries, as we see from the demands for canonization presented to the papacy by the English episcopate and the increase in devotions noted by contemporary chroniclers.[8]

Unfortunately, we know little about most of these cults, which remained for the most part purely local. A collection of miracles, a legend or a

---

d'après la réforme des statuts communaux et les accords de paix', *MEFR*, 78 (1966), pp. 503–49.
[5] *Il Movimento dei Disciplinati nel settimo centenario del suo inizio (Perugia, 1260)* (Perugia, 1962); Kern, 'Saint Bevignate de Pérouse'.
[6] See above, pp. 85–6.
[7] Salimbene, *Cronica*, II, pp. 733–6.
[8] See above, pp. 72–3.

few iconographical representations are often the only evidence for their existence. As a result, it is impossible to paint a full picture or appreciate the intensity or duration of the veneration they received. However, the way witnesses spoke of the new saints at processes of canonization makes it possible to observe an interesting development between the early thirteenth and mid-fourteenth centuries. The new intercessors seem, at first, to have had some difficulty in gaining acceptance.[9] Alongside the late arrivals, the old saints continued for a long time to appear more reliable, and the faithful abandoned them with some unease, as if in so doing they committed a sort of sacrilege. This explains the dreams and visions in which, witnesses claimed, well-known intercessors like SS Martin and John the Baptist opportunely appeared in order to recommend their juniors and guarantee their sanctity. Besides, the faithful were often tempted to hedge their bets by devoting themselves to saints of different periods, usually one old and one new.[10] The clergy themselves sometimes did the same. At the canonization process of St Thomas Aquinas, some regulars claimed to have seen visions of St Augustine, in which he had vouched for the orthodoxy of the doctrine of the *Doctor communis*.[11]

During the course of the fourteenth century, and even earlier in some regions, this trend was reversed, and when the faithful had to choose

---

[9] This 'prejudice' was fiercely attacked (1202–5) by the author of the prologue to the *Livre de S. Gilbert* (= of Sempringham, ed. Foreville, p. 3): 'Mira tamen et miserabili cecitate quidam obvoluti sunt, cum dictis et gestis veterum sanctorum que vel quos numquam viderunt, ut decet, habeant fidem et deferant honorem, huius sancti quem in carne viderunt vitam sanctissimam conspexerunt, facta mirifice contuentur, tot et tantorum testium voces audiunt, summi Pontificis et Sanctae Romanae ecclesiae auctoritatem susceperunt, operibus derogant, laudatoribus contradicunt, venerationi resistunt.'

[10] In the thirteenth century, many people only sought the aid of a new saint in association with a traditional intercessor. For example, a woman who went to the tomb of St Elizabeth of Thuringia in Marburg said that, on the way, she met an old man who said to her: 'non sis immemor Beati Nicolae quando mittis manum sub lapidem, qui in omnibus cooperabatur beate Elyzabet': A. Huyskens, *Quellenstudien zur Geschichte der Hl. Elisabeth Landgräfin von Thüringen* (Marburg, 1908), p. 254. Indeed, for a long time, recourse to recent saints seems to have been only a last resort, when habitual protectors had proved unhelpful; in the process of Philip of Bourges in 1265–6, witnesses admitted that they had only invoked the archbishop after having vainly invoked SS Giles of Rocamadour and Veran of Jargeau, the Virgin, SS Stephen and Radegund and Philip's uncle, St William of Bourges (*PC Philip of Bourges*, fols. 56, 57v, 62–63v, 74, 81v); as late as the early fourteenth century in Italy, some Adriatic fishermen were saved from a storm thanks to the protection of St Nicholas of Tolentino, after they had vainly implored the assistance of SS Thomas of Ortona, Cyriac of Ancona and Marcellin and Julian of Rimini (*PC Nicholas of Tolentino*, fol. 234).

[11] At the process in Naples in 1319, the Dominican Antony of Brescia referred to an apparition of St Augustine during which the latter declared, of St Thomas: 'mihi in gloria est aequalis, excepto quod ipse in virginitatis aureola me excedit': *PC Thomas Aquinas*, pp. 298–9; see also the statement of a Benedictine monk (*ibid.*, p. 300).

between two intercessors, it was often the more recent saint who won the day.[12] The result was a relative decline in the old devotions. In fourteenth-century Italy, some absolutely new saints surpassed in efficacy, and hence popularity, servants of God who had been venerated for decades. If we are to believe certain depositions at the canonization processes, St Clare of Montefalco supplanted St Clare of Assisi in the hearts of some of the Umbrian faithful in the years 1310–19, while there appeared, at the same period, not only a *sanctus Augustinus novellus* (Agostino Novello, Hermit of St Augustine, d. 1309), whose cult was very popular in fourteenth-century Siena, but a *sanctus Franciscus novus* (Francesco de Fabriano, OFM, d. 1322) in the Marches.[13] The success of a new devotion eclipsed, at least for a while, those which had previously prevailed, and, in a given town or region, it was the name of the latest intercessor that was on everyone's lips.[14]

The constant enrichment and renewal of the sanctoral which marked

---

[12] At the process of St Thomas Cantilupe, one witness, William of Lonsdale, said that, after dedicating his hemiplegic daughter to the bishop of Hereford: 'iterum vovit eam ad sanctum Aloy sub conditione si sanctus Thomas non sanaret eam': *PC Thomas of Hereford*, fol. 65. In Sweden, in the late fourteenth and early fifteenth centuries, people chose their intercessor by drawing lots from three names. At the process of St Bridget, we see chance favouring her in preference to SS Olav and Thibald (*PC*, p. 70); a few decades later, the inhabitants of the same region made their choice from amongst three recent saints: Bridget (d. 1373), Ingrid of Skänninge (d. 1282) and Nicholas of Linköping (d. 1391): *Vita sancti Nicolai*, ed. H. Schück, *Tva svenska Biografier från Medeltiden* (Stockholm, 1895), pp. 313–32. The same was true of hagiography, in that the faithful, from the thirteenth century, seem to have been more susceptible to the example of saints near in time; see the *Vita beatae Iulianae Corneliensis* (Juliana of Mont-Cornillon, d. 1258), ed. *AA.SS.* Apr. I, p. 442: 'sed licet sanctorum sanctarumque temporis antiqui gesta auribus inculcata fidelium virtutum semper esse debeant incentiva, scio tamen quod exempla sanctorum nostri temporis quanto recentiora tanto magis sunt motiva'.

[13] At the process of St Clare of Montefalco, a woman told how she had heard a voice telling her to dedicate herself to St Clare, at which she thought of St Clare of Assisi, but the voice corrected her, saying: 'Sancta Clara de qua loquor habuit magistrum spiritualem et non terrenum . . . et ejus humanitas est pura sicut sancti Iohannis, et ipsa vocatur S. Clara de cruce': *PC Clare of Montefalco*, fol. 641. For the origins of the cult of B. Augustine (d. 1309), see the *Cronaca Senese* of Agnolo di Turra, ed. A. Lisini and F. Iacometti, *RIS*[2], 15, 6 (Bologna, 1939), p. 36: 'e mostrò Idio per lui molti miracoli, e cominciosi per lui fare in Siena una granda festa per le compagnie di Siena, e chiamavasi beato Agostino Novello'. B. Francis of Fabriano was already venerated under the title of *sanctus Franciscus novus* in 1346: *PC Francis of Fabriano* (Fabriano, 1773), *ASV, Ritti*, Proc. 699, fol. 119.

[14] At canonization processes, witnesses often emphasized the success of the devotion to the saint in question. For example, in the case of Charles of Blois (*PC*, p. 219): 'in partibus in quibus iste nunc moratur, magis requiritus dictus Dominus Carolus quam aliquis alius sanctus'. The expressions of enthusiasm sometimes verged on heresy; a devotee of Clare of Montefalco declared that the saint 'fuit de excellentioribus sanctis qui fuerunt ab apostolis citra' (*PC*, fol. 904), whilst a nun from San Ginesio said, at the process of Nicholas of Tolentino, 'nullus est praeter deum sanctior ipso' (*PC*, fol. 51v).

the fourteenth and fifteenth centuries was accompanied by a change in the significance of the cult of the saints. From the thirteenth century, as G. Duby has shown, Christianity, long the religion of the elite and the dominant classes, eventually penetrated the masses. The people made it their own and, while accepting its dogmas and beliefs, moulded it to suit their own aspirations.[15] Like religion in general, the cult of the saints descended from heaven to earth and, as it became more popular, it became, in a sense, more accessible. In the later Middle Ages, the laity preferred intercessors who were closer in space and time, that is, modern and local, to the traditional saints, those of the beginnings and early centuries of the Church, who remained overwhelmingly preponderant in the liturgical books and ecclesiastical legendries. In the eyes of the faithful, the most effective protectors were now those one knew and by whom one was known, as contemporary and compatriot;[16] those one had seen in their lifetime, or heard spoken of by those close to them, were the subject of a *specialis affectio*, since they were infinitely closer than the great names officially worshipped.[17] Further, it was popularly believed that the new

[15] G. Duby, *Le temps des cathédrales: l'art et la société, 980–1420* (Paris, 1976), p. 261, trans. E. Levieux and B. Thompson, *The age of the cathedrals: art and society 980–1420* (London, 1981): 'after 1200 . . . the Christian religion had at last ceased being a matter of rites and priests. In the fourteenth century it slowly enlisted the masses. That period, as already said, became declericalized. Which did not mean that it was less Christian. If anything, it was more Christian, in a more private and certainly far deeper way, owing to the dissemination of the Gospel and its impact on the popular mind' (p. 221 of English translation).

[16] There is no shortage of examples to support this statement. To quote only the most eloquent: at the process of Philip of Bourges, one witness said he had invoked him as follows: 'Ha, sancte Philippe, ego nutrivi nepotes vestros et erudivi . . . succuratis michi in angustiis quae patior' (*PC*, fol. 86); another exclaimed: 'Beate Philippe, ego vidi vos in ossibus et carne in partibus istis et alibi . . . impetretis michi a Domino sanitatem' (*ibid.*, fol. 88v). A similar feeling of solidarity, based on proximity in time and space, was successfully exploited by the prior of the Dominicans of Siena to persuade the Commune in 1329 formally to adopt the feast of the Sienese Preacher Ambrose of Sansedoni (d. 1287): 'quem cognovistis, quem audistis, quem puro corde et reverentia dilexistis, quem manus vestrae contrectaverunt, per quem verba vitae aeternae civitati istae generosissimae manifestata et exposita sunt' (*AA.SS.* Mar. III, p. 242). There are many similar expressions in the canonization processes of St Yves and Charles of Blois, whose cult was much more enthusiastically supported by the Bretons in the fourteenth century because they were compatriots: *PC Yves*, p. 127; *PC Charles of Blois*, pp. 247, 340. In some cases, the feeling of a privileged relationship between a saint and the inhabitants of the town where the body lay led the faithful to entertain strange ideas. A sick man of Orvieto, when he heard that B. Ambrose of Massa, a local saint, had healed a young girl at Montepulciano, sarcastically attacked him as follows: 'Sancte Ambrosi! Alienos liberas et domesticos derelinquis?': *Dialogus de gestis sanctorum Fratrum Minorum*, p. 66.

[17] In some regions of Italy, this relationship became almost exclusive, as we see from a prayer of the Sienese chronicler Bindino da Travale (d. 1417), which mentions only Sienese saints: 'A schritto, o santo Ambrogio Sansedoni, frate di santo Domenico, dottore,

saints lent a more sympathetic ear to requests, inasmuch as they, in a sense, needed to create a clientele of devotees to put their prestige on a sound footing.[18] Was it not the case that the first manifestations of the servants of God after their death were requests for a cult, in the form of visions and apparitions? In responding to their wishes, one performed a pious duty, certainly, but one also acquired merit in the eyes of a celestial protector.

It would be going too far, however, to claim that the cult of the saints developed in the same way in all the countries of western Christendom. This change, well attested in Italy and England, where it was particularly precocious, is also visible in France, Aragon, southern Germany and the Rhineland. In the late fourteenth century, it spread to the Scandinavian countries and eastern Prussia.[19] But some regions, such as eastern Europe (from Bohemia in the north to Yugoslavia), Scotland, Castile and Portugal, seem hardly to have been affected, at least to my knowledge. To explain these differences, one can argue that a greater or lesser sensibility to the recent forms of sainthood distinguishes zones of modernity and zones of archaism.[20] The countries where the clergy and faithful remained most

dammi grazia che tale dire io possa disporre. O santo Andrea Ghallerani, che cho le vergine Maria parlasti cho lei palese, di chiedere grazia mi sia chortese. Beato santo Pietro pettinaio, chiede grazia a Di che io dispongha l'archa de lo intelletto mio. O san Pietro Martoro, i cuagli fuste tutti sanesi e rignaste al mondo con virtu di valore, atiatemi a disponare l'archa chol vostro chalore. O Chaterina santa de Fontebranda, figliola di mona L'apa, che in voi fu virtu tanta a gli occhi miei, ne la chiesa di santo Domenicho ti vidi adorare Giesu con tanto disio, ora al mondo se'morta e se' a' piedi di Dio. Ora chonciede a me tanto valore ch'io dispongi l'archa ed il suo valore': Bindino da Travale, *Cronaca*, ed. V. Lusini (Siena, 1900), pp. 172–3. The saints in question were Ambrose Sansedoni (d. 1287), Peter Pettinaio (d. 1289), Andrew Gallerani (d. 1251), Peter of Siena (a Dominican martyred in 1295) and St Catherine of Siena (d. 1380). See plate 15.

[18] See, for example, *PC Clare of Montefalco*, p. 829: 'Ego rogo te per virtutes tuas quos debeas me liberare ab isto dolore et ego promitto tibi, si hoc feceris, notificare centum personis.'

[19] As far away as Iceland, in the fifteenth century, there appeared hagiographical works in the vernacular devoted to saints relatively close in time like SS Dominic, Nicholas of Tolentino and Rock; see O. Widding and H. Bekker-Nielson, 'Low German influence on late Icelandic hagiography', *The Germanic Review*, 37 (1962), pp. 237–62.

[20] In his *Sociologie et canonizations* (pp. 178–82), P. Delooz asks why certain peoples, especially in Italy, were more 'programmed' than others to perceive sanctity. He claims, following the American sociologist R. K. Merton, that perception is a function of social structure, which is hardly in doubt. But this very general explanation cannot satisfy the historian, since in many cases countries with very similar social structures, for example the Low Countries and communal Italy in the thirteenth century, did not react in the same way with respect to the cult of the saints, whilst contemporary England, though much less developed than the Mediterranean regions, is the country which most resembles them as regards the new devotions. The functionalist hypothesis, which Delooz refers to only to reject, is more interesting. I will show below the importance of the cult of the saints in the functioning of medieval Italian society. For these methodological problems,

attached to the traditional devotions were, above all, almost exclusively rural. As Van Gennep has shown, the cult of the Franciscan saints never became popular in Savoy, because the mountain peoples already had specialized intercessors to whom they appealed in case of need. With the exception of St Antony of Padua, who was unrivalled at finding lost objects, the Franciscan saints never achieved a position in the peasant 'pantheon'.[21] The argument is probably valid for other more urbanized countries which remained apart from the main trade routes, such as the Spanish interior, where the Mendicant orders, great disseminators of the new cults, were poorly represented.[22] But this explanation is not wholly adequate, since the cult of the 'modern' saints was very successful in England and, later, Scandinavia, where towns were relatively unimportant and the influence of the Friars was overshadowed by that of a secular clergy and episcopate which retained power and prestige.[23] Only detailed regional studies, taking account not only of economic and social structures but of the history of ecclesiastical institutions and the power relations between the various elements among the clergy, would make it possible to explain the map of the cult of the medieval saints. Alongside zones of high density lay vast 'blanks', which do not wholly coincide with gaps in our knowledge.[24] The discussion below will be confined to the devotions

---

see H. Desroche, J. Maître and A. Vauchez, 'Sociologie de la sainteté canonizée', *Archives de sociologie des religions*, 30 (1970), pp. 109–15.

[21] A. Van Gennep, 'Essai sur le culte populaire des saints franciscains en Savoie', *Revue d'histoire franciscaine*, 3 (1927), pp. 113–221, repr. in his *Le culte populaire des saints en Savoie* (Paris, 1973).

[22] According to Delooz (*Sociologie et canonisations*, p. 27), there were, in the second Franciscan order, 965 persons who died in an odour of sanctity, most of them Italian, between 1209 and 1500. Even though we should treat these figures with caution, given that some of these 'saints' were only venerated as such within their convent or province, the number remains impressive.

[23] The differences between the two countries in this respect are discussed by Brentano, *Two Churches*. Scandinavia is a special case, since, given its relatively late conversion to Christianity, its local saints could only be modern.

[24] No such map, of course, exists, and it is by no means certain that one could be compiled. The only existing attempts are based on 'patrozinienforschung', that is, the study of dedications of churches and places of worship. This discipline has been brilliantly developed in Germany, especially in M. Zender, *Räume und Schichten mittelalterlicher Heiligenverehrung in ihrer Bedeutung für die Volkskunde* (Düsseldorf, 1959), and Zender, 'Entwicklung und Gestalt der Heiligenverehrung zwischen Rhein und Elbe im Mittelalter', in *Ostwestfälischweserländische Forschungen zur geschichtlichen Landeskunde* (Münster, 1970), pp. 280–303. But, despite his efforts to reach popular cults, Zender's work tells us about official worship, even though the saints to whom the churches in a given region were dedicated often eventually became popular. For the poor showing of the names of recent saints in the naming of ships, see G. and H. Bresc, 'Les saints protecteurs de bateaux, 1200–1460', *Ethnologie française*, 9 (1979), pp. 161–78.

directed to the recent saints. But we should not, for all that, forget the existence of those regions which clung to their traditions and where no pressure was exerted on behalf of the new cults.[25] Less interesting to the historian, more concerned with change than continuity, they nevertheless played an important role at the level of Christendom as a whole, acting as counterbalance, through their loyalty to the old intercessors, to the trend which, elsewhere, swept the faithful into a sort of stampede in pursuit of sainthood.

[25] See below, pp. 270–8, and maps 1–3.

THE CULT OF THE SAINTS BETWEEN UNIVERSALIST AIMS AND THE RISE OF PARTICULARISMS

ↃↃↃↃↃↃↃↃↃↃↃↃↃↃↃↃↃↃↃↃↃↃↃↃↃↃↃↃↃↃↃↃↃↃↃↃ

If the whole of Christendom did not march in step in the sphere of the cult of the saints, it was the 'developed' regions which set the tone, not the rest. In Italy, England, France and, to a lesser degree, the Germanic and Scandinavian countries, the exhortations to venerate recent saints by the papacy itself, as well as by the regular and secular clergy, were only too enthusiastically received. The subsequent boom in local devotions was soon causing concern to a hierarchy alarmed to see the faithful neglect the traditional devotions and create new ones for themselves.[1] These circumstances help to explain the U-turn executed by the Holy See, which, having been generous with canonizations, or at least enquiries, during the first two-thirds of the thirteenth century, subsequently acted with extreme rigour for fear of being overwhelmed by the rising tide of local cults. This change of attitude was altogether consistent with the overall development which characterizes the history of the western Church between the last decades of the thirteenth century and the beginning of the Avignon papacy. In fact, this half century was marked by a rupture, sometimes imperceptible, sometimes abrupt, with the popular ideas which Innocent III and his immediate successors had been able to tame and reintegrate

---

[1] For example, in 1293, the diocesan synod of Angers was worried about the decline of the cult traditionally accorded to St Maurice, patron of the cathedral: 'cum inter ceteras huius provinciae cathedrales ecclesia ista beati Mauritii apud populares et diocesanos in minori reverentia, ut patet ad oculum, habeatur, cum nullus eorum concursus appareat ad eamdem sicut habetur in aliis evidentius, quamvis ibidem plurium corpora beatorum requiescant': Bouchel, *Decretorum*, p. 614. The Franciscans, though largely responsible for the proliferation of devotions to modern saints, were not slow to react when they met competition from the seculars or the laity. Thus Salimbene, an indignant observer of the demonstrations of popular enthusiasm for the bodies of certain lay saints in many towns of the Po plain between 1267 and 1279, opposed to them the cult of the founders of the Mendicant orders: 'revera Dominus venit non solum personaliter in se ipso, verum etiam in Beato Francisco et Beato Antonio et sancto Dominico et in istorum filiis quibus credere peccatores debebant ut salutem consequi mererentur': *Cronica*, p. 735.

137

into orthodoxy. At the same time, there was an increasing clericalization of the monastic world. The decision of the Council of Lyons II in 1274 to suppress the lesser Mendicant orders is highly significant in this regard, as are the diatribes of Salimbene, a few years later, against the *Apostoli* of Gerard Segalelli, and the impassioned invective of the Dominican visionary Robert of Uzès against the Brothers of the Sack, accused of fomenting subversion in society and the Church.[2] This was a decisive turning-point on the social and the cultural plane. Over and above the conflicts which occupied the front of the stage, between Mendicants and seculars or between partisans and adversaries of pontifical monarchy, a Holy Alliance was forged, of clergy who were unanimous in their desire to allow the laity only a marginal role and reject the faith of the masses, who were for the most part uneducated. Western Christianity began to be defined as a scholarly religion, a doctrine formulated and defended by university men, who used their power to eliminate the popular elements it contained. This is a process which can also be traced in the sphere of attitudes towards voluntary poverty and in the history of the movements of penitents and beguines, and in which the cult of the saints had only a minor role. Unable to regulate it, the upper echelons of the clergy were content to ignore what was happening below. The time, not so far distant, when the papacy had canonized a lay penitent within a few years of his death, or investigated the sanctity of any hermit who drew crowds to his cave, was well and truly in the past by 1260. The welcoming attitude of Honorius III or Gregory IX to requests from communities and local churches gave way to a rigorous elitism, which eventually privileged almost exclusively scholars and princes. Even then, there were still some clerics who, at the end of the fourteenth century, criticized the Holy See for being too liberal and for devaluing canonization by granting it too freely![3]

[2] For the importance of the Council of Lyons as a turning-point in religious life, see the proceedings of the conference entitled *1274, année charnière* (Paris, 1977). For Salimbene and the *Apostoli*, see Cronica, pp. 903–4. For the suppression of the order of the Brothers of the Sack, see M. de Fontette, 'Les Mendiants supprimès au 2e Concile de Lyon (1274). Frères Sachets et Frères Pies', in *Les Mendiants en pays d'Oc au XIIIe siècle* (Toulouse, 1973), pp. 193–216. It was those who had survived the dissolution that Robert of Uzès encountered at Avignon *c.*1290 and attacked in his *Livre des Visions*, ed. J. Bignami-Odier, 'Les visions de Robert d'Uzès, O. P.', *AFP*, 25 (1955), pp. 282–3.
[3] For example, Henry of Langenstein, in his *Concilium pacis de unione ac reformatione ecclesiae in concilio universali quaerenda* (Paris, 1381–2), asked the participants of a hypothetical council, assembled to heal the Church of its ills, to discuss 'si conveniat Urbanum Vum, Brigidam de Svecia, ducem Britanniae Carolum, non obstante sanctorum multitudine, canonizari' and 'si deceat quorumdam novorum sanctorum festa solemnis peragi quam praecipuorum apostolorum': ed. von der Hardt, *Magnum oecumenicum Constantiense concil-*

To appreciate the real significance of this turning-point at the end of the thirteenth century, we need to see it in the wider context of the relations between clergy and laity within the Church. Under the influence of the former, the faithful acquired a taste for the cult of the saints and made it, in a sense, their own. They preferred the saints close to them in space and time, the number of whom increased accordingly.[4] In the fourteenth and fifteenth centuries, this trend gathered pace and spread to every community; the smallest town, soon even the tiniest village, wanted a patron saint of its own. This sentiment was particularly strong in Italy, where it was encouraged by local particularism and urban patriotism. But the demand was no less fervent in the peripheral countries, which saw themselves as the outcasts of Christendom. The Swedish author of the Life of Nicholas of Linköping, written in 1414, wrote, significantly, a few years before the opening of the canonization process:

> Although we cannot solemnize the feast of all the saints, it is nevertheless right that each region or even each city or parish should venerate with special honours its own patron, as was ordered by God in Mosaic Law: honour your father and your mother, which means: you honour your father, I will honour mine. France accords a cult to Denis, England to Thomas, Sweden to Siegfried. And we, too, in our diocese of Linköping, ought to venerate our father Nicholas and redouble our efforts to have him canonized, he whom we know to be triumphant in heaven, where, together with St Bridget, he sings a new song.[5]

This universal aspiration for a *sanctus proprius* reveals the paradoxical fate of the cult of the saints in the Middle Ages. A victim of its own success, it ended by exacerbating particularisms, and, to the despair of the more far-sighted clergy, it helped to make Christianity into a fragmented Church.

The remarks above clearly illustrate the failure of the efforts of the Roman Church to control and channel the manifestations of the cult of the saints. In the twelfth and thirteenth centuries, this policy had led to the institution of papal reservation and the creation and development of the process of

---

ium, II, c. 56. See also Franco Sacchetti, *Opere*, ed. A. Borlenghi (Milan, 1957), pp. 1113, 1119: 'all these new saints make people lose faith in the old ones'.

[4] 'We should be ashamed of the custom whereby, in almost all the canonical churches, new feasts are instituted every day at the request of any old lay person', wrote, in the early fifteenth century, Nicholas of Clamanges, in his treatise *Contre l'institution de fêtes nouvelles*, ed. and trans. P. Glorieux, in *Mélanges de science religieuse*, 23 (1966), p. 27.

[5] *Vita sancti Nicolai* (= *BHL* 6101), ed. H. Schück, *Tva Svenska biografier*, p. 315.

canonization, and led the papacy to intervene on behalf of a few persons whose virtues it deemed worthy of veneration by the faithful as a whole: SS Thomas Becket, Francis, Dominic, Peter Martyr etc. To make these great figures known, it had not hesitated to intercede with national episcopates and make generous grants of indulgences. But the results did not match up to its expectations. The adoption of a new intercessor was within the province of local communities, both civil and religious, and the pressure exerted by external powers, however prestigious, was often in vain. Further, the West in the thirteenth century experienced a quantitative 'explosion' of the cult of the saints which meant the rise of new devotions, under pressure from the laity, but also from the Mendicant orders, who wished to provide accessible models of behaviour for the latter to imitate. Aghast at this anarchic proliferation, the Holy See chose to dissociate itself and confirm the rupture between the two categories of saints – the canonized and the rest – by, in the fourteenth century, establishing a distinction between *sancti* and *beati*. The history of the control of the cult of the saints at the end of the Middle Ages reveals, therefore, the inability of the hierarchical Church to encompass within a single model the diverse conceptions of sainthood existing in a popular mind now only too sensitized to this dimension of the religious life.

BOOK II

TYPOLOGY OF MEDIEVAL
SAINTHOOD

ღღღ

One is a saint only to and through other people, according to contemporary sociologists who have studied canonizations.[1] In their view, a saint is a person whom others have seen as such and who has fulfilled this role for them. Studying medieval sanctity from a scientific perspective, we can only accept this definition, which, over and above distinctions of a liturgical or juridical order laid down by the Church, makes it possible for us to appreciate the whole of the process by which, at every period, the Christian people chooses from among its ranks an elite of intercessors and models. But the historian, here more demanding than the sociologist, has to investigate the identity of those 'others' who were the originators of reputations for sanctity.

Was it the papacy, which, after rigorous examination, accorded a few rare and privileged persons the honours of official recognition and endeavoured to disseminate their cult throughout Christendom? We have seen that, in general, in the Middle Ages, the papacy did no more than pronounce on requests made to it by local churches and religious orders. In all cases, canonization was granted only if the promoters of the cause were able to demonstrate to the Holy See a widespread *fama sanctitatis*, attested by petitions from the civil and religious authorities of the town or country where the body of a servant of God lay. Should we therefore conclude that it was the clergy, secular or regular, who played a decisive role in the birth and development of the new cults, as we have seen in the case of those propagated by certain religious orders, in particular the Mendicants? But popular devotion often preceded that of the clergy, who were content to follow lay initiatives. In practice, it is difficult to establish which

---

[1] See, in particular, P. Delooz, 'Pour une étude sociologique de la sainteté canonisée dans l'Eglise catholique', *Archives de sociologie des religions*, 13 (1962), pp. 17–43.

141

persons or groups originated a devotion. This is to some extent due to the gaps in our documentation which, with few exceptions, only allows us to observe the existence of a devotion once it was institutionalized. In fact, two conditions had to be met before the cult of a saint could develop: popular acclaim and clerical approval.[2] If the former was lacking, the most worthy cause foundered, if only because of the absence of miracles.[3] But a devotion which aroused, for a while, great popular enthusiasm could only last if it was welcomed by and could entrench itself within the framework of an ecclesiastical institution such as a confraternity, parish or abbey. In so far as collaboration between clergy and laity was inevitable, we may say that, in all the manifestations of the cult of the saints for which evidence has survived, elements of popular origin and ecclesiastical influence are inextricably interwoven. The respective role of each varied according to period and place, as we will show below, but local sanctity always retained a dual aspect.

This broad definition excludes only two categories of saints: first, those whose fame did not extend beyond the gates of their abbey or convent, and who are known to us only through obituaries or hagiographical texts for the use of the clergy. They were fairly numerous in monastic communities and nunneries, especially of orders which did not seek contact with external society.[4] Second, there were those who may be called popular, despite the ambiguities surrounding the word.[5] I use it here to indicate

---

[2] The well-known formula *vox populi, vox Dei* is certainly very old. It is already present in the *Vita sancti Thome* (= Becket), Anonymous of Lambeth, written *c*.1172–3; see Walberg, *La tradition hagiographique de S. Thomas Becket* (1929), p. 143. But the phrase itself is ambiguous, since the whole problem is to know which *populus* is meant!

[3] As, for example, in the case of the Dominican saint, Martin Donadieu of Carcassonne, whose cult was promoted by his order, but in vain, according to his biographers, because of the impiety of the people of Carcassonne 'qui a divinis beneficiis patrandis meritis sancti viri pro illis diebus reddiderat se indignum': Kaeppeli, 'Vie de frère Martin Donadieu de Carcassonne', pp. 276–90.

[4] These cults are best known when, thanks to some important event, they emerged from the narrow circles to which they have previously been confined and were adopted by the faithful. Particularly interesting is the case of B. Antony of Amendola, in the Marches (d. 1435), a Hermit of St Augustine whose saintly reputation was confined to the local convent until 1455, when the region escaped an outbreak of plague; the miracle was attributed to his intercession and in due course (*c*.1470) he became patron of the town, with all the honours of a public cult: *PC Antony of Amendola* (Fermo, 1755), *ASV, Ritti*, Proc. 744, fols. 231–67.

[5] They have been the subject of a number of recent complementary studies. Of the many recent works on popular religion in the Middle Ages, I refer only to those explicitly discussing this problem: F. Rapp, 'Réflexions sur la religion populaire au Moyen Age', in *La religion populaire, approches historiques*, ed. B. Plongeron (Paris, 1976), pp. 51–98; J. C. Schmitt, ' "Religion populaire" et culture folklorique', *Annales ESC*, 31 (1976), pp. 931–53 (with recent bibliography). See also the collective volume *La religion populaire en*

persons whose cult was born and developed at the lowest levels of society, even if it later found support elsewhere among the laity and the clergy. In fact, the latter, in the Middle Ages, were far from constituting a socially and culturally homogeneous group, and some of those in close contact with the faithful, such as village and parish priests or hermits, were inclined to tolerate more or less lawful religious practices, either because they shared their beliefs or because they wished to avoid conflict with their flock.[6] Without their active or passive complicity, these devotions could not have survived. But we should not, therefore, lose sight of the fact that they were essentially lay creations, which explains why they were so often doomed to moulder in obscurity.

The distinctions I have made above between different levels of sanctity, that is, official, local and popular, will orient my discussion in the following chapters. My aim is to trace, starting this time from the bottom and not the top, the path which led from the elementary perception of sanctity to the most subtle theological elaborations. However, these successive stages will be of very uneven length, by reason of the unevenness of the documentation, which risks seriously distorting our perspectives. Official sainthood, that which, in the Middle Ages, was approved by the papacy or simply subject to its evaluation, is well known thanks to bulls and processes of canonization, which I will draw on extensively. Local sanctity, too, is easy of access. The existence of *Vitae* and sometimes even of liturgical offices, iconographical representations and references to the cult in texts of ecclesiastical or lay origin add up to a range of sources which, when compared and collated, make it possible to obtain a fairly precise idea of the forms and content of these devotions. The same is not true of the popular cults, about which we have only the most fragmentary evidence; at best, the Bollandists have devoted to these saints a few pages in the *Acta sanctorum*, where the evidence is mostly late, that is if they have not classed them among the *praetermissi* by the very fact of the obscurity in which they are shrouded. Our only reliable sources are references, usually very brief, in chronicles or collections of *exempla*.[7] More interest-

---

Languedoc du XIIIe siècle à la moitié du XIVe siècle (Toulouse, 1976), including my own contribution, the Conclusion, pp. 429–44.

[6] The attitude of the parish clergy, sympathetic to the faithful but obliged to keep a prudent distance, is particularly clearly shown by the passage from the informative process of Werner of Bacharach quoted in note 31, p. 94 above.

[7] The only contemporary text for the cult of William of Rochester, a pilgrim murdered in England c.1201, is the *Flores historiarum*, a monastic chronicle composed at Westminster in the early fourteenth century, ed. R. H. Luard (London, 1890) (Rolls Series, 95), pp.

ing are the documents drawn up when the clergy sought to bring these cults into the open, either to condemn them, or, conversely, get them recognized by the ecclesiastical hierarchy.[8] An enquiry sheds a ray of light allowing us to glimpse realities which are usually concealed. Such cases remain, however, exceptional and it would be unrealistic to hope for many new discoveries. The very nature of these devotions and their marginal character are enough to explain the silence of the sources. It is difficult, as a result, to appreciate the true scale of popular sanctity. Nevertheless, it is essential to know whether it was simply a residual phenomenon or, conversely, the tip of an iceberg. I have no wish to dodge this difficult question, as my later discussion will show. But it is prudent to signal at the outset that the distortions at the level of documentation, independently of any methodological *a priori*, make the task of the historian in this sphere particularly difficult.

Between the end of the twelfth and the beginning of the fifteenth centuries, in the West, a large number of men and women were regarded as saints and venerated as such. By using the evidence it has been possible to assemble on this subject, I will try to identify if not the laws, at least the criteria determining the selective perception which conferred on them the prerogatives and powers generally recognized to the servants of God. Why did a particular monk or friar, hermit or penitent, bishop or king appear as a supernatural person in the eyes of contemporaries? We can only answer this huge question by first examining, at the different levels I have distinguished, what conception and what typology of sainthood pre-existed in people's minds.

124, 414; the cult of Margaret of Louvain (d. 1255) is known thanks to Caesar of Heisterbach, who devoted a long section to her in his *Dialogus miraculorum*, ed. J. Strange (Cologne, 1851), pp. 386–7; that of Margaret of Roskilde is known through Heribert of Clairvaux, *De miraculis*, ed. L. Weibull, *Scandia*, 4 (1931), pp. 270–90 (preferable to the edition in *PL*, 235. cc. 1379–81). For the cult of Robert le Busere, killed between London and Canterbury, see below, p. 581.

[8] Hardly surprisingly, the only one of these cults to be well documented is that of Werner of Bacharach, whose canonization was sought by the local clergy between 1426 and 1429 with the support of the Count Palatine of the Rhine, Lewis III. Many documents were produced at the enquiry which make it possible to reconstruct the history of the devotion from its origins. The text is MS Palat. lat. 858 and MS 1139 of the municipal library of Trier, partly edited by the Bollandists in *AA.SS*. Apr. II, pp. 714–34. Condemnations issued by the papacy or inquisitors allow us to glimpse cults accorded to persons regarded by the hierarchy as heretics. See below, pp. 425–6.

PART I

POPULAR SAINTHOOD AND LOCAL SAINTHOOD

cɔeɔeɔ

CHAPTER 9

POPULAR SAINTHOOD

ℭ𝔰ℭ𝔰ℭ𝔰

During the course of my research, I have been struck by the similarities which are apparent in the histories of several saints whose medieval cult developed in very different countries. These were almost always little-known persons, whose fame hardly extended beyond their village or its immediate surroundings. Further, the external manifestations of their cult seem usually to have been restricted to the building of an oratory or a chapel, or the establishment of a pilgrimage and popular festivals.[1] *Vitae* written in honour of such saints are extremely rare, and they are known primarily through chronicles or iconographical evidence.[2] In the few cases where they found a biographer, the hagiographic compositions are late, dating from a period when the devotion was already firmly entrenched, and only a very small number of manuscripts survive.[3] Further, many of

---

[1] For example: construction of a chapel in the Middle Ages for Panacea (d. 1383), buried at Ghemme, diocese of Novara (*AA.SS.* Aug. I, pp. 167–8) and for Radegund of Wellenberg (d. *c.*1330) (*AA.SS.* Aug. III, pp. 93–6); dedication of a chapel within an existing church for Peter Parenzo at Orvieto (Natalini, *S. Pietro Parenzo*, pp. 118ff). In the case of Werner, the cult developed in a chapel officially dedicated to St Cunibert, which took the name *capella sancti Wernheri* in the fifteenth century (*AA.SS.* Apr. II, pp. 707ff). Pilgrimages are attested in almost all cases. One of the best known is that to Pontefract, where the memory of Thomas of Lancaster was venerated (H. Tait, 'Pilgrim signs and Thomas Earl of Lancaster', *British Museum Quarterly*, 20 (1955), pp. 39–46). For festivals, information is rare; that of Margaret of Roskilde was marked by a collect within the twelve bailiwicks of the island of Själland, where she had lived (G. D. Gordini, sv Margherita di Roskilde, in *BS*, VIII, cc. 780–1).
[2] For the chronicles, see note 7, p. 143 above. Medieval iconographical documentation is known in the case of Buonmercato of Ferrara (a fourteenth-century fresco is reproduced in *AA.SS.* Iun. II, p. 786), and, above all, William of Norwich, thirteenth- and fourteenth-century representations of whom survive in several English churches: A. Jessop and M. R. James, *The life and miracles of St William of Norwich by Thomas of Monmouth* (Cambridge, 1896), especially pp. 85–8.
[3] It was not until the second half of the fourteenth century that Werner (d. 1287) acquired a legend in German (ed. K. Christ, 'Werner von Bacharach. Eine mittelrheinische Legende', in *Festschrift Otto Glauning*, II (Leipzig, 1928), pp. 1–28), followed, a little later, by

147

these cults were prohibited by the ecclesiastical hierarchy, both in the Middle Ages and later, which did not prevent them from surviving up to the nineteenth, or even into the twentieth, centuries.[4] Last and, in my view, most important, they all, men and women, suffered death in peculiarly horrible circumstances. All this is to be seen in the list below, which I have compiled on the basis of the documentation known to me, but which makes no claims to be exhaustive:

1   Murdered women

Margaret of Oelishoeve or of Roskilde (d. 1176), killed by her husband (Denmark).[5]

Panacea (or Panasia) (d. 1383), a young girl killed by her mother-in-law at Quarona, a little village in the Valsesia (northern Italy).[6]

Margaret of Louvain (d. 1225), a servant killed by brigands along with her parents (Belgium).[7]

Radegund (or Radiana) of Wellenberg, near Augsburg (d. *c.*1330), a farm servant eaten by wolves (southern Germany).[8]

2   Murdered men

(a)   While working:

---

a *Passio sancti Werner* (= *BHL* 8860). Another 'martyr' of the Jews, Conrad of Weissensee (d. 1303), is commemorated in a fourteenth-century *Passio*, of which only one copy survives, MS 423 of the University Library of Erlangen; see also *Anal. Boll.*, 47 (1929), p. 390.

[4] The most interesting example is Werner, whose cult was forbidden by the emperor Rudolph and the archbishop of Mainz in 1288 (*Chronicon Colmariense, MGH.SS.*, XVII, p. 255). In 1289 and 1293, some German bishops granted indulgences to the chapel of St Cunibert at Bacharach which held his body (*AA.SS.* Apr. II, p. 715). In 1337–40, Archbishop Baldwin of Trier seized the treasure contained in the chapel, which effectively put a stop to the external manifestations of the cult and the construction of a new chapel. The devotion only really emerged from clandestinity after the recognition of the remains of the 'saint' by Cardinal-legate Giordano Orsini in 1426 (E. Iserloh, 'Werner von Oberwesel. Zur Tilgung seines Festes im Trierer Kalendar', *Trierer theologische Zeitschrift*, 72 (1963), pp. 270–85). Similarly, the cult of Buonmercato, which had some success at Ferrara in the late fourteenth century, was twice forbidden in the seventeenth century by the bishops of Ferrara, but restored in the eighteenth century: Frizzi, *Memorie per la storia di Ferrara*, III, pp. 358–62.

[5] For her life and death, see *AA.SS.* Oct. XI, pp. 713-20, with account of the translation (= *BHL* 5324); for her cult, see *Vetus chronica Sialandie*, ed. M. C. Gertz, *Scriptores minores historicae Danicae Medii Aevi*, II (Copenhagen, 1922), p. 56; *Anal. Boll.*, 52 (1934), pp. 121–3. Her case evokes that of St Godeleva of Ghistelles (d. 1070), also killed by her husband, whose Life was written before 1084 by the monk Drogo of Saint-Winoc: M. Coens, 'La vie ancienne de Ste Godelive de Ghistelles', *Anal. Boll.*, 44 (1926), pp. 102–37; also the collective volume *Stola S. Godelevae* (Bruges, 1971).

[6] *AA.SS.* Maii I, pp. 167–8.

[7] *AA.SS.* Sept. I, pp. 582–95; Caesar of Heisterbach, *Dialogus*, pp. 386–7.

[8] *AA.SS.* Aug. III, pp. 93–6.

Renald (or Reinold), eldest of the four sons of Aymon, or of a monk of Cologne according to other traditions, killed by jealous workmen in Cologne (thirteenth century) (German Rhineland).[9]

Honorius of Thénezay or of Buzançais (thirteenth century), a cattle-dealer murdered by two servants whom he had reproached for their dishonesty (France).[10]

Buonmercato of Ferrara (d. 1378), cleric accused of killing the rector of the church of Santa Maria del Pino and lynched by the crowd (Italy).[11]

(b) During political conflicts:

Pietro Parenzo, podesta of Orvieto (d. 1199), murdered by the Ghibellines (Italy).[12]

Simon de Montfort (d. 1265), earl of Leicester, leader of the baronial opposition to Henry III, killed at the battle of Evesham (England).[13]

Cabrit and Bassa (d. 1285), executed in horrible circumstances by the troops of Alfonso III, after leading the resistence of Alaro, on the island of Majorca, in favour of James III (Aragon).[14]

Thomas of Lancaster (d. 1322), leader of the opposition to Edward II, executed at Pontefract after his capture by the king (England).[15]

(c) Pilgrims:

William of Rochester (d. 1202?), pilgrim murdered by a foundling he had taken in (England).[16]

[9] *AA.SS.* Ian. I, pp. 585–7; P. Fiebig, *St. Reinoldus in Kult, Liturgie und Kunst* (Dortmund, 1956).

[10] P. Vigué, *Saint Honoré de Thénezay ou de Buzançais* (Poitiers, 1908); *Anal. Boll.*, 27 (1908), pp. 498–9. The two servants who killed him had included a stolen cow in a flock to be sold in Poitou, which the saint made them return to its owner.

[11] *AA.SS.* Iun. III, pp. 784–8.

[12] For the history and cult, see the fine study by Natalini, *S. Pietro Parenzo*, which prints the complete dossier. This 'martyr', whom Innocent III refused to recognize as a saint, was celebrated from 1200 in Orvieto cathedral and in 1347 became patron and protector of the city.

[13] A collection of miracles was compiled between 1265 and 1277, ed. J. O. Halliwell, *The chronicle of William de Rishanger of the Barons' Wars: the miracles of Simon de Montfort* (London, 1840), pp. 67–109 (Camden Society, Old Series, 15). A better manuscript than the one used by Halliwell is BL, MS Cotton Vespas, A. VI, fols. 162–83. A liturgical office was even composed in his honour: C. Bémont, *Simon de Montfort, comte de Leicester* (Paris, 1884), p. xv (trans. E. Jacob, *Simon de Montfort, Earl of Leicester* (Oxford, 1930), but without appendices of documents).

[14] A brief *Passio* of these two exists (= *BHL* 1557); see also *BS*, III (Rome, 1963), cc. 623–4.

[15] L. Boyle, sv Tommaso di Lancaster, in *BS*, XII (Rome, 1969), cc. 582–4, with bibliography.

[16] *AA.SS.* Maii V, pp. 270–1. In the *Flores historiarum*, ed. Luard, William is mentioned twice: 'In illo tempore sanctus Willelmus de Pert martyrizatur extra civitatem Roffensem et in ecclesia cathedrali Roffensi spelitur miraculis choruscando' (p. 124) and p. 414,

Gerald of Cologne (d. 1241), a German pilgrim killed by bandits near Cremona (Italy).[17]

Nantvin (d. 1286), a German pilgrim travelling to Rome. Unjustly accused of pederasty by the peasants of Wolfratshausen, near Munich, he was burned alive.[18]

3   Child or adolescent victims of the Jews

William of Norwich (d. 1144) (England).[19]

Richard of Pontoise or of Paris (d. 1179) (France).[20]

Herbert of Huntingdon (d. c.1180) (England).[21]

Dominic of Val (d. 1250) (Aragon).[22]

Hugh of Lincoln (d. 1255) (England).[23]

Werner of Oberwesel (d. 1287) (German Rhineland).[24]

Rudolph of Berne (d. 1294) (Switzerland).[25]

Conrad of Weissensee, near Erfurt (d. 1303) (central Germany).[26]

Lewis of Ravensburg (d. 1429) (southern Germany).[27]

---

referring to his canonization by Alexander IV in 1256, for which there is no other documentary evidence.

[17] *AA.SS.* Oct. III, pp. 955–64; R. Borgo, *Vita, morte e miracoli del Beato Geroldo* (Cremona, 1581).

[18] *AA.SS.* Aug. II, pp. 214–15; he was sometimes called Conrad: M. Rader, *Bavaria sancta*, II (Munich, 1628), p. 308.

[19] *AA.SS.* Mar. III, p. 558; Jessop and James, *Life and miracles of St William of Norwich*. Of recent works devoted to this cult, see D. Anderson, *A saint at stake: the strange death of William of Norwich* (London, 1964); J. Van der Straeten, *Anal. Boll.*, 84 (1966), pp. 296–7.

[20] *AA.SS.* Mar. III, pp. 593–4, which includes a fifteenth-century *Passio auctore Roberto Gaguino* (= *BHL* 7213).

[21] *BHL* 3833 b.

[22] *AA.SS.* Aug. VI, pp. 777–83; *PC Dominic of Val* (Saragossa, 1805), Paris, BN, H. 850. This dossier contains a fourteenth-century *Passio*, documents on a confraternity which already existed at Saragossa in 1403 and the transcription of an inscription in the cathedral of St Saviour, composed c.1340–50: 'Hic infans jacet pro Christi nomine martir/Beatus Dominicus de Val'. The day of his feast, 31 August, was also that of the choir children (Sanctus Dominiculus).

[23] *AA.SS.* Iul. VI, pp. 494–5; Matthew Paris, *Chronica majora*, pp. 516–19.

[24] See above pp. 143–4, 148. In addition to the books already cited, see F. Pauly, 'Zur Vita des Werner von Oberwesel. Legende und Wirklichkeit', in *Archiv für Mittelrheinische Kirchengeschichte*, 16 (1964), pp. 94–109. For the spread of the cult, which was also popular from the sixteenth century in many parts of France, see H. de Grèzes, *Saint Vernier (Verny, Werner, Garnier) patron des vignerons en Auvergne, en Bourgogne et en Franche-Comté* (Clermont-Ferrand, 1889).

[25] *AA.SS.* Apr. II, pp. 500–2; G. Studer, ed., *Berner chronik* (Berne, 1871), p. 29.

[26] See above, pp. 147–8. Reference to the 'martyr' and the first miracles appears in *Monumenta Erpherfurtensia*, ed. O. Holder-Egger, in *MGH. SRG.*, XLII, p. 29.

[27] For this boy of fourteen, said to have been killed by Jews in 1429 on the shore of Lake Constance, see *AA.SS.* Apr. III, pp. 978–9.

Andrew of Rinn (d. 1462) (Austria).[28]
Simon of Trent (d. 1475) (northern Italy).[29]
Lorenzino Sossio (d. 1485) (northern Italy).[30]

All these persons had in common the fact of having been killed or assassinated in a wholly unmerited way. The wives slain by their husbands were all young, beautiful and virtuous; the maidservants slaughtered by wolves or brigands had been remarkable in their lifetime for their charity to the poor and the sick. The men, on the other hand, were defenders of just causes – as with the 'political martyrs' – or had been accused of crimes they had not committed, like the cleric Buonmercato of Ferrara, found guilty of theft and murder, or the pilgrim Nantvin, falsely accused of pederasty. In every case, their innocence was inevitably recognized after the event. However diverse the circumstances, two fundamental elements are found in every story: the shedding of blood and the glaring injustice of their death. As today, when a condemned person is shown to have been the victim of a grave judicial error, the spectacle of innocent suffering is deeply shocking to the popular mind. The contrast between the severity of the punishment inflicted and its iniquitous character gives rise to an emotion which, immediately transposed onto the religious register, develops into a devotion. By virtue of a process which we may see as a law of popular affectivity, pity provokes piety. Victims become martyrs, hence saints, since, in the popular mind, these two notions overlap and there are no other saints than those who died a violent death on behalf of justice.[31]

---

[28] A child of three, said to have been killed by Jews in the Tyrol (*AA.SS.* Iul. III, pp. 462–70).

[29] This case is one of the best known, thanks to the *processus de nece pueri* ordered and conducted by the bishop of Trent, John Hinderbach, ed. E. Oreglia in *La Civiltà Cattolica*, 11th ser., 8 (1881), pp. 225–31, 344–52, 476–83, 598–606, 730–8; 9 (1882), pp. 107–13, 219–25, 353–62, 472–9, 605–13; 10 (1882), pp. 727–38. See also W. P. Eckert, 'Aus den Akten des Trienter Judenprozesses', in *Judentum im Mittelalter*, ed. P. Wilpert (Berlin, 1966), pp. 281–336. The extensive hagiographical dossier is listed in *BHL*, nos. 7762–72. There is a good summary in I. Rogger, sv Simone di Trento, in *BS*, XI (Rome, 1968), cc. 1184–8.

[30] M. Nardelli, 'Il presunto martirio del Beato Lorenzino Sossio da Marostica', *Archivio Veneto*, 130 (1972), pp. 25–45.

[31] One need only think of the importance of martyrdom in popular religious movements from the eleventh to the thirteenth centuries. For the heretics who were discovered at Monforte, near Milan, in 1028, martyrdom was the only means to salvation, whilst the twelfth-century Cathars proclaimed that all who were burnt for remaining true to their faith were 'martyrs of God'. For the significance attached by the Cathars to *endura*, see

Should we see this popular reaction as evidence of a loyalty to the old ideal of primitive Christianity, for which the only saints were the martyrs, or do we need to seek other explanations? It may here be helpful to make some comparisons with a case studied some years ago by H.-I. Marrou which bears some resemblance to those we have just considered.[32] I refer to the cult accorded in Milan from the fourth century to the 'Innocents', a term which indicated three officials of the Imperial administration put to death on the orders of the Emperor Valentinian for having ventured to remind him of his duties in judicial matters. After their execution, they were venerated by the Christians of Milan at the place called *Ad innocentes*, and, although the Church never pronounced regarding them, the memory of their horrible death survived locally up to the modern period. As Marrou observed, the hagiographic texts and narratives of clerical origin present these victims of late imperial totalitarianism as martyrs for having carried to the supreme sacrifice their imitation of the Saviour. But this is surely a *pia interpretatio*, which reveals ecclesiastical embarrassment in the face of a spontaneous surge of popular feeling.[33] Certainly, it is under cover of the word martyr and thanks to its ambiguity that the cult was able to survive and develop on the liturgical plane. But the large number of popular 'martyrs' we encounter in the Middle Ages suggests that the word encompassed very different realities. The death of a Margaret of Roskilde or an Honoré of Buzançais had nothing to do with the profession of Christian faith taken as far as the gift of oneself. Although the vocabulary employed in the texts to describe these violent episodes may be borrowed from the language of religion (*sanctus*, *martyr* etc.), we may still suspect that what we see is in reality a 'salvage operation' on the part of the clergy with regard to representations and attitudes the specific Christian content of which seemed to them to be dubious.[34]

R. Manselli, 'Un'abiura del XIIo secolo e l'eresia catara', *Studi sulle eresie del secolo XII* (2nd edn, Rome, 1975), pp. 173–90.

[32] H.-I. Marrou, 'Ammien Marcellin et les "Innocents" de Milan', *Recherches de science religieuse*, 39–40 (1951–2), pp. 179–90. The point of departure for this remarkable study is a passage from Marcellin, *Rerum gestarum libri XXXI*, L. XXVII, 7, 5–6.

[33] Marrou, 'Ammien Marcellin', pp. 187–8.

[34] This emerges very clearly from the commentary by the Cistercian Caesar of Heisterbach on the history of Margaret of Louvain in his *Dialogus miraculorum*. The parents of the saint, who had been killed with her, appeared to a monk of the abbey of Villers to tell him that, unlike their daughter, they had not yet achieved glory. When his disciple and interlocuter expressed surprise at this differential treatment, Caesar replied: 'Omnes quidem occisi sunt sed non omnes miraculis clarescunt. Unde patet quod non poena facit martyrium sed cause.' This failed to convince the disciple, who persisted: 'Quaenam exstitit causa martyrii in puella ista?' To which the monk replied: 'Ut iam fatus sum, simplicitas et vita innocua.' Later, he excluded from the glory of martyrdom those who killed themselves 'ex nimia simplicitate' (*Dialogus miraculorum*, pp. 386–7). We know,

This is surely also how we should interpret the success of the theme of the murdered pilgrim. The reality of the fact is not in doubt, given the large number of the faithful tramping the roads of the West, staff in hand. But we should not exclude the possibility of an *a posteriori* embellishment, designed to increase the religious charge in the emotion provoked by the discovery of the bleeding body of an anonymous traveller.[35]

The attitude of some clergy – always foreigners, since locally, the consensus was complete – towards these cults supports the impression of a large autonomy in popular representations of sanctity. The Dominican Stephen of Bourbon, in his treatise *On the seven gifts of the Holy Spirit*, tells how, at Villars-les-Dombes, which he happened to visit, the peasantry venerated, under the name of St Guinefort, a dog which had suffered an unjust death. Left alone by its masters with their child, the dog had killed a snake which threatened the child's life. On their return, the parents found the baby bathed in blood and, thinking it had been attacked by the dog, threw the latter into a well where it died. But the beast's innocence was soon revealed and a devotion rapidly developed around its tomb, which became a much frequented place of pilgrimage, and scene of a large number of miracles.[36] As in the cases noted above, the spectacle of blood unjustly shed – even that of an animal – and of the defeat of Good by Evil provoked among the faithful a reaction of emotion and veneration which developed into a cult. The Dominican did not conceal his indignation at this abuse of the notion of martyrdom and described his various efforts to root out this impious cult;[37] in vain, it appears, since pastoral visits in

---

also from Caesar, that the quality of martyr was refused by certain Parisian masters to St Thomas Becket: 'Thomas episcopus Cantuariensis qui nostris temporibus pro Ecclesiae libertate usque ad mortem dimicavit, nullis miraculis in suis persecutionibus corruscavit, satisque de illo post occisionem disputatum est' (*ibid.*, p. 357).

[35] The account written *c.*1242 and entitled *Vita, obitus et miracula beati Geroldi martyris Coloniensis* (ed. *AA.SS.* Oct. III, pp. 955–64) describes the clergy of Cremona taking over the cult of Gerald, whose body, found by fishermen after he had been killed by robbers, was placed in the church of St Vital, in the town. It was recognized as that of a pilgrim because he carried a song book. The detail is authentic; how else would it have been known that he was a citizen of Cologne by the name of Gerald?

[36] Stephen of Bourbon, *Anecdotes historiques*, ed. A. Lecoy de la Marche (Paris, 1877), pp. 325–8. See also P. Saintyves, *En marge de la Légende Dorée: songes, miracles et survivances* (Paris, 1930), especially pp. 411–44; J.-C. Schmitt, *Le saint lévrier. Guinefort, guérisseur d'enfants depuis le XIIIe siècle* (Paris, 1979), trans. M. Thom, *The holy greyhound: Guinefort, healer of children since the thirteenth century* (Cambridge, 1983).

[37] Stephen of Bourbon, *Anecdotes*, p. 326: 'Homines rusticani videntes nobile factum canis et quomodo innocenter mortuus est pro eo de quo debuit reportare bonum, locum visitaverunt et canem tamquam martyrem honoraverunt et pro suis infirmitatibus et necessitatibus rogaverunt.'

the nineteenth century revealed that several centuries later, devotion to 'saint' Guinefort remained highly popular in the countryside of Ain.

It is difficult to get a precise idea of the content of the mental representations which originated what is sometimes called 'popular canonization'.[38] We really only know about it through works written by clerics who used words from their language to indicate realities which probably had a different connotation. We can therefore only formulate an opinion on the basis of the raw and unquestionable facts provided by the typology of the individuals venerated as saints among the ordinary people. We need to note the existence of certain differences between the various parts of Christendom and periods under discussion. It is in England, the Germanic countries and the alpine regions, for example, that the cult of 'child martyrs', all presented as victims of the Jews, enjoyed its greatest success.[39] These devotions brought together two aspects of the popular mentality with no apparent connection: a high valuation of childhood, regarded as the age of innocence and perfection; and a virulent anti-Semitism, which found its justification in the accusations of ritual murder and profanation of the Host levelled against the Jews.[40] In this sphere, popular sensibility developed autonomously. The medieval Church never canonized a child, or even a *iuvenis*; at the level of local cult, young saints, whether male or female, were few, so strong remained the clerical prejudice which linked the *gravitas morum* with *senectus*.[41] Similarly, the papacy and the upper clergy refused for a long time to ratify the opinion of the masses regarding the so-called 'martyrs' fallen victim to the Jews. This is shown most

---

[38] The expression is German in origin, and it is in Germany that study of these questions is most advanced; see, for example, N. Kyll, 'Volkskanonisation im Raum des alten Trierer Bistums', *Rheinisches Jahrbuch für Volkskunde*, 11 (1960), pp. 7–61; also the useful survey in H. Schauerte, *Die Wolkstümliche Heiligenverehrung* (Münster, 1948) and Schauerte, 'Entwicklung und gegenwärtiger Stand der religiösen Volkskundeforschung', *Historisches Jahrbuch*, 72 (1953), pp. 516–34.

[39] In the absence of a general study of this collective mental phenomenon and its context, see the useful synthesis of K. H. Rengstorf and S. von Kortzfleisch, *Kirche und Synagoge*, I (Stuttgart, 1968), especially chapters 2 (B. Blumkranz) and 3 (W. Eckert); also Wilpert, ed., *Judentum im Mittelalter*.

[40] For the accusations of ritual murder periodically levelled against the Jews in the Middle Ages, see K. Hruby, sv Ritualmord, *LThK*, VIII, cc. 1330–1; also the articles *Blutbeschuldigung* and *Blutmärchen* in *Jüdisches Lexikon*, I (Berlin, 1927), cc. 1084ff.

[41] P. Toubert, *Croisades d'enfants et mouvements de pauvreté au XIIIe siècle*, in *Faculté des Lettres et des Sciences Humaines de l'Université de Paris. Centre de recherches d'histoire du Moyen Age. Recherches sur les pauvres et la pauvreté*, no. 4 (1965–6); J. De Ghellinck, 'Iuventus, gravitas, senectus', in *Studia mediaevalia in honorem . . . R. J. Martin* (Bruges, 1948), pp. 39–59; also *Enfant et sociétés: annales de démographie historique* (Paris and The Hague, 1973).

notably by the long-delayed approval by the Holy See of the cult of Werner
of Oberwesel, who had been venerated since his death in 1287 at Bacharach, in the Rhineland. In fact, it was only in 1426 that his remains were
recognized by the cardinal-legate Giordano Orsini, and the enquiry *in
partibus* carried out in 1428–9 by the priest Winand of Steeg, on the
initiative of Lewis III, count palatine of the Rhine, was never followed
up.[42]

England also produced a number of political martyrs. Between the end
of the twelfth and the fifteenth centuries, English public opinion spontaneously canonized all the great leaders of opposition to the monarchy
who died as a result of royal action in tragic circumstances, without the
Roman Church ratifying these choices.[43] The crux of the problem was
once again the authenticity of the martyrdom which, in the eyes of the
masses, was attested by the mere shedding of innocent blood, whilst the
more demanding clergy wished to reserve this title to those who had
exposed their life for the faith in a conscious and voluntary manner.[44]

One last observation springs to mind when we look at the geographical
origin of these popular martyr saints: numerous in England and the Germanic countries, they were, in contrast, rare in the Mediterranean world,
especially in Italy. With the exception of Pietro Parenzo and Buonmercato
of Ferrara, the other persons of this type of whom we are aware were
venerated in the peripheral regions in the north of the peninsula, whilst
communal Italy, which produced many new cults at this period, seems to
have been largely unresponsive to this form of sainthood.[45] It is tempting
to conclude that the representations we have been discussing were linked
to a rural, or at least weakly urbanized, milieu. This is confirmed by an
examination of the location of a number of these devotions which sprang

[42] See note 24, p. 150 above. In the sixteenth century, the cult of Werner spread beyond
his native Rhineland, but he was then venerated as patron of *vignerons*, not as a martyr
to the Jews. The ecclesiastical hierarchy eventually succumbed to popular pressure, but
managed to change completely the significance of the devotion (Grèzes, *Saint Vernier*, pp.
160–200).

[43] J. C. Russell, 'The canonization of opposition to the King in Angevin England', in *Haskins
anniversary essays* (New York, 1929), pp. 280–98.

[44] The cult of the 'child martyrs' was fiercely attacked by a Dominican theologian close to
Pope Sixtus IV, Jean-Baptiste de Giudici, bishop of Ventimiglia 1471–84, in his treatise
'De canonizatione beati Bonaventurae', ed. E. Baluze, *Miscellanea*, IV (Lucca, 1764), pp.
471–87. He denied in particular that children could be saints because, by definition, they
could perform no act of will. They therefore had no personal merit, even if they were
killed, because 'non voluntas sed necessitas [eos] facit martyres' (p. 486). It was not until
the twentieth century – and the triumph of ultramontane and populist Catholicism – that
a child of twelve was honoured, that is, Maria Goretti, canonized by Pius XII in 1950.

[45] See below, pp. 190ff.

up in villages or little market towns. It is clear that the peasant world did not remain immune to the trend to renew the sanctoral found in the West in the later Middle Ages. Indifferent to the figures proposed by the urban clergy, in particular the Mendicants, it was well able to express, in some countries, an original creative dynamism. But it seems that these popular cults, based on a conception of sanctity which was fast becoming archaic, if not heretical, as a result of its unilateral insistence on the shedding of blood assimilated to martyrdom, were relegated to a marginal existence.[46] Their survival, when this is revealed by the documents, is all the more remarkable and attests to the deep roots and permanence of conceptions which were not those that the more advanced and dynamic of the clergy were then trying to impose.

[46] It is interesting to note that when popular cults found clerical supporters, it was from among secular priests or black or white monks, as in the case of William of Norwich, whose remains were transferred in 1171 to the choir of Norwich cathedral. When they were attacked, it was by Mendicants, as in the case of the dog Guinefort and Werner of Bacharach. A German Dominican, probably the inquisitor Henry Kalteisen, wrote *c.*1428 a little treatise called *De sancto Wernhero in Bacheraco* (ed. in part in Iserloh, 'Werner von Oberwesel', p. 284), in which he questions the sainthood of this person, who had died without receiving the sacraments at an age (18) when, he said, mortal sins were frequently committed, and who, in any case, had hardly behaved in a Christian fashion when he had worked for Jews during Holy Week!

CHAPTER 10

LOCAL SAINTHOOD

Popular cults of the type discussed in the previous chapter are of great interest to the historian, who is given an insight into primary representations of sainthood. But, as we observed at the outset, statistically speaking, they are not significant in the documentation currently at our disposal. By definition, if it is to last, the cult of a saint needs the support of the clergy and the approval of an ecclesiastical authority. The majority of well-documented devotions were, therefore, located at the level of local sainthood, that is, where the religious conceptions of the faithful and the requirements of the clergy intersected. The dialectical relationship between the two groups took very different forms according to region and period. The Church, in the person of its representatives, was sometimes tolerant of the saints to whom the laity were attached, content to eliminate aspects of their history or cult which it saw as incompatible with the Christian faith; sometimes it sought to impose its own models, in the hope that they would replace those which had previously prevailed, which seemed inadequate or ambiguous. Mostly, we find a range of less clear-cut attitudes, falling somewhere between passive tolerance and exclusion.

The power relations between clergy and laity are not, however, the only factor we need to consider. The typology of sainthood was also influenced by the social and political structures of the country or region where it developed. We have seen that, in most cases, popular cults were accorded to persons of modest origins: maidservants, apprentices, poor pilgrims, craftsmen and small merchants.[1] In the local cult, in contrast, the influence of the ruling classes was much stronger. Even when the basic representations of sainthood remained those of popular sensibility, the persons

---

[1] There are, admittedly, exceptions to this rule, but almost all concern political martyrs such as Peter Parenzo, Simon de Montfort and Thomas of Lancaster, seen, at the time, as defenders of the people.

around whom the *aura sanctitatis* developed came mostly from the elites, who sought to appropriate for their own ends the supernatural prestige popularly attributed to the servants of God.

The conditions in which the perception of sainthood at the local level was formed varied significantly from one region to another. We cannot, at this level, consider Christendom as a homogeneous unit. With regard to the recruitment of saints, we can distinguish, within the late medieval West, two zones of unequal extent, each with pronounced characteristics: on the one hand, the countries extending from north-western to eastern Europe, including France and the Low Countries; on the other, the Mediterranean regions, especially Italy. Each of these socio-cultural areas had different types of saints. It is difficult to see this as fortuitous. Consequently, after examining this diversity, I will seek to explain it, without concealing the difficulties of the enterprise.

THE NON-MEDITERRANEAN WEST: THE SUFFERING LEADER

In countries remote from the shores of the Mediterranean, the majority of the saints who were the object of a local cult between the twelfth and the fifteenth centuries were persons who had in common their high birth and membership of the world of power and wealth. It would, of course, be quite wrong to imagine a sort of automatic transposition into the next world of earthly hierarchies. Of the great of this world, popular opinion canonized only those who had suffered persecution for justice, and the persons and lords who were remembered with horror by their subjects were legion. But when the conditions in which a *fama sanctitatis* could develop were present, it is striking how often, in this part of Christendom, it was a temporal or spiritual leader who was the beneficiary.

Martyrdom and sainthood

Kings and princes: the 'holy sufferers'

Throughout the Middle Ages, a large number of the saints venerated in the West were kings or princes. This should not surprise us, since we know that, in the eyes of their subjects, medieval sovereigns enjoyed special graces – beauty, strength, serenity – and supernatural powers, as attested by belief in the thaumaturgical virtue of the royal touch in France

and England, and by the aura of sacrality surrounding the emperor in the
Germanic world.[2] The question of royal sainthood remains, however, very
obscure, since an immutable terminology – *rex sanctus, sanctitas regis* –
covered, in practice, very different realities according to country and
period. I have no wish to enter the debate between F. Graus and K. Bosl
and F. Prinz regarding the sacred character of the monarchy among the
Germanic peoples and the survival of this notion during the early Middle
Ages.[3] But the insistence with which Graus set out to deny the charismatic
aspects of the institution of monarchy in the barbarian kingdoms, and
emphasize, in contrast, the decisive role played by the church in the
sacralization of power during the early Middle Ages, has given rise to
reservations which I fully share.[4] One cannot fail to note that the majority
of kings who were considered as saints before the ninth century died a
violent death, whether on the battlefield or struck down by their enemies,
and were subsequently venerated as martyrs. Though the clergy sometimes shared these devotions, they seem not to have taken the initiative,
given that the persons in question were far from having led an edifying
life. The oldest example of 'holy king' in the medieval period, after all,
was St Sigismund (d. 523), king of Burgundy, who had strangled his son
Sigeric with his own hands. But his miserable end – he perished in a well
into which he had been thrown by his adversary Clodomir – provoked a

---

[2] The classic texts are M. Bloch, *Les rois thaumaturges: étude sur le caractère surnaturel attribué
à la puissance royale, particulièrement en France et en Angleterre* (2nd edn, Paris, 1961); P.
E. Schramm, *Der König von Frankreich* (Weimar, 1939), especially pp. 152–5. See also,
for England, J. M. Wallace-Hadrill, *Early Germanic kingship in England and on the Continent* (Oxford, 1971), and, for the empire, H. Wolfram, 'Splendor Imperii. Die Epiphanie
von Tugend und Heil in Herrschaft und Reich', *MIOG, Ergänzungsbände*, 20, 3 (1963);
D. Hiltbrunner, 'Die Heiligkeit des Kaisers. Zur Geschichte des Begriffs "Sacer" ',
Frühmittelalterliche Studien, 2 (1968), pp. 1–30. These ideas had lost none of their power
at the end of the Middle Ages, as we see from Adam of Murimuth's portrait of Edward
III: 'corpore elegans, vultum habens Deo similem quia tanta gratia in eo mirifice relucebat
ut si quis in eius faciem palam respexisset vel nocte de illo somniasset, illo die indubie
speravit sibi jocunda et prospera evenire': *Continuatio chronicarum*, ed. T. Hog (London,
1846), p. 226. Philippe de Commynes reports Louis XI as saying: 'It seemed to him that
a king had more power and virtue in his kingdom where he was annointed and consecrated
than elsewhere': *Mémoires*, VI, 2, ed. A. Pauphilet and E. Pognon, in *Historiens et
chroniqueurs du Moyen Age* (Paris, 1958), p. 1250.

[3] On the problem of sacred royalty among the Germans, see O. Höffler, 'Der Sakralcharakter des germanischen Königtums', in *La Regalita sacra. Atti dell'VIII congresso internazionale di storia delle religioni (Roma, 1955)* (Leiden, 1959), pp. 664–701; for Graus'
views, see his *Volk, Herrscher und Heiliger*; for the debate in general, see S. Boesch-Gajano,
Studi Medievali, 3rd ser., 8 (1967), pp. 901–9; Boesch-Gajano, *Agiografia altomedioevale*,
pp. 29–33; for England, see W. A. Chaney, *The cult of kingship in Anglo-Saxon England:
the transition from paganism to Christianity* (Manchester, 1970).

[4] See the review by R. Folz, *Revue historique*, 238 (1967), pp. 154–6.

strong popular reaction and a devotion which the clergy did not disavow, since Sigismund had been the first barbarian leader of Gaul to convert to orthodox Catholicism. Thanks to popular emotion and clerical recognition, a cult could emerge and grow, based on the abbey of Saint-Maurice of Agaune which Sigismund had founded in 515, in the lands which had belonged to the Burgundian kingdom.[5] After him, other sovereigns similarly enjoyed a reputation for sainthood as a result of the sufferings they had endured. This was the case with Dagobert II, assassinated in 680 by a member of his household, and with Charles the Simple, who died in captivity in the tower at Péronne in 929.[6] Relating this event, the author of the Chronicle of Saint Benignus of Dijon could write: 'During his lifetime, he was called the simple because of his benevolence. Now, he can with reason be called the saint, because he has been summoned to a better life, having been unjustly condemned to a long captivity by those who became disloyal and traitorous towards him.'[7] A few centuries later, in England, the same feeling of pity turning into a popular 'beatification' explains the cult of Edward II, who had been less than popular in his lifetime. But when he was struck down by his wife and a coalition of his enemies, a surge of emotion swept through the country and miracles occurred at his tomb, which soon became a popular place of pilgrimage, to the displeasure of contemporary ecclesiastical chroniclers.[8]

---

[5] R. Folz, 'Zur Frage der heiligen Könige. Heiligkeit und Nachleben in der Geschichte des burgundischen Königtums', *Deutches Archiv für Erforschung des Mittelalters*, 14 (1958), pp. 317–44; Folz, 'La légende liturgique de S. Sigismond d'après un manuscrit d'Agaune', in *Speculum historiale, Festschrift J. Spörl* (Freiburg and Munich, 1965), pp. 152–66.

[6] *Vita S. Dagoberti regis Francorum*, ed. B. Krusch, in *MGH. SRM.*, II, pp. 509ff. As R. Folz has shown, the author of the *Vita*, written in the late eleventh century in Lotharingia (Stenay, Gorze), confused Dagobert II, who was murdered, with Dagobert III (711–15), making him into a ruler devoted to the reformihg clergy and a prince of peace: 'Tradition hagiographique et culte de S. Dagobert, roi des Francs', *Le Moyen Age*, 69 (1963), pp. 14–63.

[7] *Chronicon S. Benigni Divionensis*, ed. E. Garnier and J. Bougaud, in *Analecta Divionensia* (1875), p. 126.

[8] E. Perroy, *La guerre de Cent Ans* (Paris, 1945), pp. 39–40, trans. W. B. Wells, *The Hundred Years' War* (London, 1959). Clerical hostility is visible in several chronicles; see, in particular, *Monachi cuiusdam Malmesberiensis Vita Edwardi II*, in *Chronicles of the reigns of Edward I and Edward II*, ed. W. Stubbs (London, 1883), p. 290 (Rolls Series, 76): 'De cuius meritis an inter sanctos numerandus sit frequens in vulgo, sicut quondam de Thoma comite Lancastriae, adhuc disceptatio est, sed revera nec carceris inclusio nec etiam oblationum frequentia aut miraculorum simulacra, cum talia sint indifferentia, quemquam sanctum probant nisi correspondeat sanctimonia vite precedentis. Sed presumptio flagitiosorum impunitatem sibi et suis similibus inaniter sperantium ambitioque matronarum circumgirare affectantium rumorem talis venerationis multum amplificat et dilatat.' This kind of reaction was exceptional before the thirteenth century. As a general rule, the lower clergy shared the views of the people while the local ecclesiastical hierarchy, usually with close ties to the monarchy, left well alone.

It was not only kings who benefited from this tendency to sanctify the powerful. With the rise of feudalism and the concomitant weakening of monarchies in the tenth and eleventh centuries, the dukes and counts who ruled the territorial principalities also sought to appropriate the sacred prerogatives of kingship.[9] With the assistance of their entourage and the clergy they had showered with gifts, this was not difficult, and those who died in tragic circumstances, such as William Longespée in Normandy in 943 and Charles the Good in Flanders in 1127, were popularly regarded as martyrs and saints.[10] Alongside the suffering king, the West now placed the image of the murdered prince, soon to be joined by the knightly vassal venerated as a martyr for having remained faithful unto death to his lord.[11] The descent of the royal model of sainthood to the lower levels of the aristocracy occurred in parallel with the changes to political structures at the same period which resulted in the triumph of feudalism.

There are many possible explanations for the success and survival of this sacralization of the suffering leader, whether king, prince or lord. Some historians of religion, from Frazer to Murray, have emphasized the significance attached to the death of the king from an ethnological perspective. The king was, in effect, an exceptional person, inasmuch as the Spirit of God, that is, essentially, the power through which fertility was given to all human beings, resided in him, and remained there as long as he retained his physical and mental strength. When he began to show signs of decline, the Spirit must leave him to pass into a young and vigorous body, which necessitated the murder of the old king.[12] Admittedly, in the popular mind, the fertility of the soil and material prosperity

---

[9] G. Duby, 'L'image du prince en France au début du XIIe siècle', *Cahiers d'histoire*, 17 (1972), pp. 211–16.

[10] In the 'Complainte sur la mort de Guillaume Longue Epée', which has the chorus 'Cuncti flete pro Willelmo innocente interfecto', the dead duke is presented as a saint 'iam conjunctus celo'. The text is ed. P. Lauer, *Le règne de Louis IV d'Outre-mer* (Paris, 1900), pp. 319–23. Charles the Good, Count of Flanders, was the object of a cult which started soon after his assassination in the church of St Donatien in Bruges: A. D'Haenens, sv Carlo il buono, in *BS*, III (Rome, 1963), cc. 794–7. He is explicitly given the title of martyr by the author of the *Anonymi Passio Caroli* (*MGH.SS.*, XII, pp. 619–23) and by Galbert of Bruges in his *Vita Karoli comitis Flandrensis* (ed. *AA.SS.* Mar. I, pp. 163–79).

[11] This religious exaltation of vassalic loyalty is emphasized by M. Bloch, *La société féodale* (2nd edn, Paris, 1968), pp. 325–8, trans. L. A. Manyon, *Feudal Society* (London, 1961). Bloch quotes the words of a bishop at the council of Limoges in 1031, spoken to a knight who, under threat, had killed his lord (*PL*, 142, c. 400): 'Thou shouldst have accepted death for his sake; thy fidelity would have made thee a martyr of God' (p. 232 of English edn).

[12] See, in particular, J. G. Frazer, *The golden bough* (London, 1900); M. Murray, *The divine king in England: a study in anthropology* (London, 1954).

were associated, in the Middle Ages, with the person of the king, as
many stories contained within hagiographical texts reveal.[13] But there is
no evidence, at least for this period, that his death was a sort of rite, which
must be accomplished to ensure the normal functioning of society, by
facilitating the transmission of power to a younger successor. We may
retain, however, the notion that the king or, more generally, the leader
performed for his subjects the role of mediator between the heavenly world
and the world below. The emotion provoked by his death was so intense
because of the fear of an interruption to the functions he fulfilled while
alive. This is confirmed by study of the cult of the saint kings in orthodox
Russia, where it survived longer than in the West.[14] There, many members of royal or princely families were venerated as martyrs as a result of
the suffering they had unjustly endured. In medieval and modern Russia,
the most popular saints were the 'holy sufferers' (*strastoterptsy*), tsars or
princes such as Boris and Gleb, who let themselves be killed without
putting up any resistance.[15] This archetypal form of sainthood, later found
in Andrew Bogoljubski, Michael of Tver and Alexander Newski, and on
the basis of which, over time, a whole theology of royalty was constructed,
was often incarnated by persons who had led a far from virtuous, even a
frankly sinful, existence.[16] But considerations of an ethical order counted
for little in the eyes of the people. What mattered for the moujiks was not
so much that the sovereign had lived well according to the moral criteria
defined by the Church, but that he had assured, right to the end, the
safety of his people, in particular by accepting the death inflicted on him.
The clergy themselves seem not to have been repelled by this model; by

---

[13] In the *Vita S. Dagoberti regis*, written in late eleventh-century Lotharingia, the beneficial
action of the sovereign is described in detail; he sowed fields at the request of peasants who
came running to see him: 'tantam frugum habundanciam tribuit omnipotens Dominus
illis hominibus ut nullus ambigeret quos pro meritis Dagoberti hanc incolis terrae illius
concessisset' (p. 515). Similarly, after the death of the emperor Henry IV at Liège in
1106, a crowd rushed to his tomb: 'tantus exarserant in eius immoderatum favorem ut
quotquot illius tetigessent feretrum, se sanctificatos ab eo crederent, nonnullis etiam
terram sepulchri eius ungulis propriis scalpentibus et per agros suos domosque quasi pro
benedictione spargentibus; alii frumenta vetera feretro ipsius superiacebant ut, una cum
novis immixta illa sererent; sperabant enim taliter fertilem sibi messem profuturam':
Sigeberti chronica, ed. *MGH.SS.*, VI, p. 372.

[14] P. Fedotov, *Sviatie drevniei rusi* (tenth to seventeenth centuries) (Paris, 1931), pp. 19–33;
Fedotov, *The Russian religious mind* (Cambridge, Mass., 1946), pp. 94–110; L. Kologrivof,
La sainteté en Russie (Bruges, 1953); A. Besançon, *Le Tsarevitch immolé* (Paris, 1967).

[15] Besançon, *Tsarevitch immolé*, pp. 61, 80–5; T. Cherniavsky, *Tsar and people* (Yale, 1961),
p. 17.

[16] W. Philip, 'Heiligkeit und Herrschaft in der Vita Aleksandr Nevskijs', *Forschungen zur
Osteuropäischen Geschichte*, 18 (1973), pp. 55–72.

sacrificing himself, was the tsarevitch not, after all, reliving the Passion of Christ, innocent and consenting victim?

At first sight, these ideas may appear alien to the political and religious traditions of the West, where, in my view, 'sacred royalty', in the sense given to the term by ethnologists and historians of religion, did not exist in the Middle Ages.[17] But in the very depths of the popular mind, there long survived a system of representations which is not without analogies with that of the Russian empire. The crowds who flocked to the tomb of certain emperors or kings did not see sainthood as primarily a collection of qualities and virtues. For them, it was identified with the halo of sacrality surrounding those in power, who assured to their subjects all the benefits they had a right to expect from the *bonitas regis*: prosperity, fertility of the soil and animals etc.[18] This process did not happen automatically and the emotional shock provoked by the violent death of a prince was not enough in itself to give rise to a reputation for sainthood. For public opinion to be mobilized in favour of the dead person, and for miracles to be attributed to him, it was also necessary for there to be a generally favourable judgement of him, or for the events which followed his death to cause him to be regretted. The association of the tragic or ignominious end of a prince and the favourable memory – real or mythical – left by his reign in the collective memory produced the spark from which the devotion could catch fire and spread.[19] If the judgement of the people coincided with that of the clergy, the cult might enjoy great success, including on the liturgical plane. If they diverged, the wave of enthusiasm soon subsided, only to

[17] But as R. W. Southern has justly remarked, 'the union of supernatural powers in a temporal ruler, so contrary to the political temper of Europe as we know it, is one of the might-have-beens of history': *The making of the Middle Ages* (London, 1959), p. 99.

[18] The effects of the *bonitas regis* are precisely recorded by Alcuin in a letter of 793 (*ep*. 18, *MGH. Ep*., IV, p. 51): 'regis bonitas est gentis prosperitas, victoria exercitus, aeris temperies, terrae habundantia, filiorum benedictio, sanitas plebis'.

[19] This was still the case with Charles of Blois, duke of Brittany (d. 1364); regarded as a bigot and even ridiculed by the lords in his entourage, he was nevertheless remembered fondly by the people, whom he had refrained from taxing too heavily. His tragic death at the battle of Auray and the faults of his successor, John IV de Monfort, unpopular for his close collaboration with the English and harsh fiscal exactions, combined to create fertile ground for the emergence of a cult. At the enquiry held in 1371 by Franciscans near Guingamp, a number of peasants were assembled and interrogated, in Breton, by a friar, who asked them what they thought about the deceased duke. They replied: 'tempore dicti domini Caroli, tam nobiles quam bassi in his partibus ad beneplacitum habuimus victualia, vestes, et alia necessaria, licet guerrae viguissent penitus, et post decessum ipsius strages, paupertas, miserie et penuria invaserunt nos et in frugibus fetibusque per guerras et oppressiones inimicorum': *ASV, Collectorie* 434 A, fol. 11v. It is interesting to compare this with Alcuin's definition of *bonitas regis*, quoted in note 18 above.

be reborn, at a later date, with another subject. However conditioned, in
its initiatives and expressions, by the ruling classes, the popular mind
retained a margin of autonomy which allowed it to choose from within
the privileged group constituted by those in power.[20]

Alongside these martyr saints or princes, whose sufferings provoked
such a strong popular response, the Church endeavoured to promote
the cult of a few sovereigns who, in its eyes, incarnated the ideal of
the *rex bonus* or *rex justus*, as it had been defined since the early Middle
Ages by various authors, from Isidore of Seville to Alcuin.[21] These
were, in general, men distinguished by their close collaboration with
the clergy and their munificence in the sphere of church and abbey
building. The first king in this line, which was to continue up to St
Louis and beyond, was probably Gontran (561–93), who, according to
Gregory of Tours, governed *ac si bonus sacerdos*.[22] After him, came St
Sigisbert, king of Austrasia (d. 656), whose cult developed in the
eleventh and twelfth centuries.[23] But it was above all under the Carolingians, when the Church set out to moralize the exercise of power by
the laity and Christianize the royal function, by means of the unction

[20] This is apparent in the contradictory reactions recorded after the death of the king of
Denmark, Knut Lavard (d. 1131), canonized by Alexander III in 1169. According to the
author of the *Compendium Saxonis gestorum Danorum* (ed. M. C. Gertz in *Scriptores minores
historiae Danicae Medii Aevi*, I (Copenhagen, 1918), p. 384): 'rege perempto, populus
gaudebat, cum lacrimari deberet. Sed deus regis innocentiam et occultam vite ipsius
bonitatem per aperta miracula ostendere dignabatur, quibus prophanus populus reluc-
tando dicebat eum iniuste interfectum et ideo illa miracula deceptiones esse.' The discrep-
ancy persisted, since, returning to the theme, he later said: 'sic nequam populus induci
poterat ut sanctitatem coleret integre cuius tamen in celis gloriam divina potencia ostendebat quam postea Romanus Pontifex canonice honorandam etiam in terris mandavit' (p.
429). It was only at the very end of the Middle Ages that St Knut became the 'holy king'
of Denmark, like SS Olav for Norway and Eric for Sweden (E. Jörgensen, *Helgendyrkelse
i Danmark* (Copenhagen, 1909).
[21] Graus, *Volk, Herrscher und Heiliger*, pp. 390–433; E. Ewig, 'Zum christlichen Königsged-
anken im Frühmittelalter', in *Das Königtum, seine geistigen und rechtlichen Grundlagen*
(Lindau and Constance, 1956), pp. 45ff. In practice, the two types of holy king we have
distinguished, the martyr king and the *rex bonus*, rarely existed in a pure form. St Edward
the Confessor (d. 1066) presents all the features of the 'holy sufferer', but was also highly
esteemed by the English clergy, as his canonization by Alexander III in 1161 reveals; see
B. W. Scholtz, 'The canonization of Edward the Confessor', *Speculum*, 36 (1961), pp.
78ff. The same could be said of St Wenceslas, Duke of Bohemia, murdered between 929
and 935, who favoured the Church: R. Turek, sv Venceslao, in *BS*, XII (Rome, 1969),
cc. 991–7.
[22] Gregory of Tours, *Historia Francorum*, VII, 7; IX, 21. For Gontran, see Bloch, *Société
féodale*, pp. 34–5; Graus, *Volk, Herrscher und Heiliger*, pp. 394–5.
[23] R. Folz, 'Vie posthume et culte de S. Sigisbert, roi d'Austrasie, in *Festschrift P. E.
Schramm*, I (Wiesbaden, 1964), pp. 7–26.

of consecration, that this policy became significant.[24] In France and England, the trend to sacralize the institution of monarchy reached its apogee just when the latter had become weak and appeared to be threatened in its very foundations by the rise of feudalism, that is, during the first decades of the eleventh century.[25] At the same time, in the recently converted countries, the clergy encouraged the cult of the sovereigns who had promoted the Catholic religion among their people or defended it against an aggressive revival of paganism.[26] In all cases, in exalting the king, it was his piety, sense of justice and generosity to the poor that were emphasized. At the same time, the Church tried to strengthen the sense of national unity against particularist tendencies and feudal fragmentation by making sovereigns the 'lieutenants' or standard-bearers of a saint, symbol of the kingdom of which he became the official protector.[27] But the endeavour was ambiguous and could result in confusion between *regnum* and *sacerdotium*, by conferring on emperors or certain royal dynasties prestige of a supernatural order, which it was by no means certain would always be used for the good of the Church. Accordingly, the papacy, once it had recovered a degree of autonomy and consolidated its power base in Rome, embarked on a vast operation to 'demythologize' lay power. Gregory VII, in particular, did not hesitate to attack head-on the belief in royal sainthood. In his famous letter of 1081 to Bishop Hermann of Metz, he stressed that only a tiny number of sovereigns enjoyed a

---

[24] Of the many works on this subject, see, in particular, H. H. Anton, *Fürstenspiegel und Herrscherethos in der Karolingerzeit* (Bonn, 1968); W. Ullmann, *The Carolingian Renaissance and the idea of kingship* (London, 1969).

[25] J. T. Rosenthal, 'Edward the Confessor and Robert the Pious. Eleventh century kingship and biography', *Medieval Studies*, 33 (1971), pp. 7–20; H. Günther, *Kaiser Heinrich II, der Heilige* (Kempten, 1904).

[26] Particularly in Scandinavia and Hungary. For the latter, see G. Schreiber, *Stephan I der Heilige, König von Ungarn: eine hagiographische Studie* (Paderborn, 1938); E. Pasztor, sv Stefano, primo re d'Ungheria, in *BS*, XII (Rome, 1969), cc. 19–22.

[27] For the function of cults such as those of SS Stephen in Hungary and Eric in Sweden, see K. Gorski, 'Le roi saint. Un problème d'idéologie féodale', *Annales ESC*, 24 (1969), pp. 370–6; also R. Folz' review of P. E. Schramm, *Herrschaftszeichen und Staatssymbolik*, 3 vols. (Stuttgart, 1954–6), in *Revue historique*, 218 (1957), p. 125; K. H. Krüger, 'Dionysius und Vitus als frühottonische Königsheilige (Zu Widukind, I, 33), *Frühmittelalterliche Studien*, 8 (1974), pp. 131–54. The Capetians are presented in the historiography of the period as standard-bearers of St Denis; the king of Castile as *vexillifer sancti Jacobi*; the king of Norway as vicar of St Olav, *rex perpetuus* of the kingdom, etc. See Helgaud of Fleury, *Vie de Robert le pieux*, ed. R. H. Bautier (Paris, 1963), p. 63: 'et quorum (= the saints) vicem ad horam gerebat in terris . . . eorum quoque perpetuo consortio letatur in celis'.

reputation for sainthood within the Church, whereas the prelates, clerics and monks who had been accorded a cult were legion.[28]

The Gregorian campaign to desacralize the empire and, in consequence, royal power had very different results according to country. In Scandinavia, saints continued, well into the thirteenth century, to be recruited from among the kings and princes murdered or killed in battle, such as Eric in Sweden (d. 1160), and Eric Plovpenning (d. 1258) and Nicholas of Aarhus (d. 1180), son of King Knut Magnusson, in Denmark.[29] In the Germanic world, the revival of imperial ideology and the conflicts between the papacy and the sovereigns were accompanied by an attempt to give an unquestionable canonical base to the cult of Charlemagne, which enjoyed great success in the twelfth century, in particular in the liturgical sphere.[30] In England, royalty lost much of its popular prestige as a result of its battles, from the late twelfth century, with the clergy and ruling classes, from landowning nobility to urban bourgeoisie. But among ordinary people, the image of the suffering king remained vivid, as is shown by the outbursts of piety which followed the tragic deaths of Edward II in 1327 and Henry VI in 1471.[31] In France, lastly, belief in royal sainthood

[28] Gregory VII, letter to Hermann of Metz, 15.III.1081, ed. C. Caspar, in *MGH. Ep. sel. ad usum scholarum*, II, p. 558: 'In tota autentica scriptura, non invenimus septem imperatores vel reges quorum vita adeo fieret religione precipua et virtute signorum decorata.' The problem is what was meant by *autentica scriptura*, since in eleventh-century England alone, more than twenty kings and queens were venerated as saints by clergy and faithful, and the cult of some, such as Oswald (d. 642), Ethelred and Ethelbert (d. *c*.670) and Edmund (d. 870) remained very popular to the end of the Middle Ages.

[29] For the cult of St Eric, see K. Kumlien, 'Sveriges kristnande i slutskedet spörsmal om vittnessbord och verklighet', in *Historisk Tidskrift* (Stockholm, 1962), pp. 288–94. This cult was still very much alive in mid-fourteenth-century Sweden, as the hostility of St Bridget reveals: *Liber revelationum*, II, c. 29. For Eric Plovpenning, see A. L. Sibilia, sv Erico IV, re di Danimarca, in *BS*, IV (Rome 1964), cc. 1321–2; for Nicholas, see idem, in *BS*, IX (Rome, 1967), c. 913.

[30] Charlemagne was canonized in 1165 by the anti-pope Paschal III, supported by Frederick Barbarossa (P. A. Becker, 'Die Heiligsprechung Karls des Grossen', in *Berichte über die Verhandlung des Sächsichen Akademie der Wissenschaften zu Leipzig*, Phil. Hist. Klasse, 84, 3 (Berlin, 1947). See also R. Folz, 'Essai sur le culte liturgique de Charlemagne dans les églises de l'Empire', thèse complémentaire (Paris, 1951); Folz, 'Aspects du culte liturgique de Saint Charlemagne en France', in *Karl der Grosse. Lebenswerk und Nachleben*, IV (Düsseldorf, 1967), pp. 77–99. It is in this context that we should see the translation of the relics of the Magi from Milan to Cologne, on the initiative of Rainald of Dassel and Frederick Barbarossa, and the spread of their cult in imperial territory (H. Hofmann, *Die Heilige Drei Könige: zur Heiligenverehrung im kirchlichen, gesellschaftlichen und politischen Leben des Mittelalters* (Bonn, 1975).

[31] For popular devotion to Edward II, see note 8 above. Richard II tried hard to have him canonized between 1385 and 1398: E. Perroy, *The diplomatic correspondence of Richard II*, *Camden Society*, 3rd ser., 48 (1933), pp. 62, 210; Ralph Higden, *Polychronicon*, IX, pp. 79, 237. For the cult of Henry VI after his murder in the Tower of London, see. P. Grosjean, *Henrici VI Angliae regis miracula postuma* (Brussels, 1935).

survived among the people and could even give rise to a devotion each time that the image of the suffering king – St Louis dying of plague before Tunis, Charles of Blois killed at the battle of Auray – was superimposed on that of the *rex justus*, the just and pious king, that the Church had tried to make prevail since the Carolingian period. But by the end of the thirteenth century, kings approved by the clergy themselves became rare, as the monarchy, by becoming laicized, came into frequent conflict with the Church or the papacy. After the two French princes, both 'martyrs' and 'beguins', no king in the West would again be accorded the honours of a public cult until the end of the fifteenth century.[32]

Bishops: murder in the cathedral

The clergy were not content to reject requests from the laity concerning a particular king with a reputation for sanctity in his own country. They proposed new models of saints drawn from their own ranks and endeavoured to turn to the advantage of spiritual leaders the popular belief in the redeeming virtues of undeserved suffering which had so far benefited almost exclusively temporal rulers. Admittedly, the cult of the holy bishops had enjoyed considerable success in the West before the end of the twelfth century. But the bishops whose cult the Church now sought to promote were not simply good prelates. They were men who had been persecuted for justice and sometimes killed while performing their duties; the 'murder in the cathedral' came just at the right time to take over from that of the royal victim.

It was not by chance that this model of sainthood enjoyed its greatest success between the late twelfth and early fourteenth centuries, that is, at a time when, in a number of countries, the conflict between Church and monarchy was at its height. The tragic death (1170) and canonization

---

[32] Nor should we forget the importance of the holy queens and princesses. This phenomenon dates back to the seventh century (Graus, *Volk, Herrscher und Heiliger*, pp. 411–12; R. Folz, 'Tradition hagiographique et culte de sainte Bathilde, reine des Francs', *CRAI* (1975), pp. 369–84, but it really took off later, especially in central and eastern Europe, with the cults of SS Hedwig (d. 1241), duchess of Silesia and Margaret of Hungary (d. 1270), whilst the Franciscans wrote lives of Queen Salome (d. 1268), Kinga or Cunegund, duchess of Cracow (d. 1292) and Hedwig of Anjou, queen of Poland (d. 1399), all ed. in *Monumenta Poloniae historica*, IV (Cracow, 1884), pp. 770–96, 662–744, 763–9. However, the saintly queens and princesses are very different from the kings and princes, because, in most cases, they exercised no political power. It was not, therefore, a sanctification through the exercise of power but of merits associated with the exercise of a discreet influence in favour of the Church and the practice of virtues during a life at court.

(1173) of St Thomas Becket were here decisive events. The cult of the murdered archbishop was quickly adopted throughout Christendom, as the rapid inclusion of his feast in the calendars and liturgical books of the Roman, and many other, churches shows.[33] But it also created a model which was duplicated right up to the end of the Middle Ages. A few years after the death of the archbishop of Canterbury, the bishop of Vicenza, John Cacciafronte (1183) was murdered by a local lord whose encroachments on episcopal revenues he had condemned.[34] If his canonization process failed, it is not because his cause was less good than that of the English archbishop, but, more likely, because, in the very different political and religious context of Italy, social pressure did not favour prelates, however zealous or meritorious. In north-western and eastern Europe, however, the 'Becket model' struck a chord.[35] One unlikely consequence was the canonization in 1253 of St Stanislas, a former bishop of Cracow (d. 1079), who had been struck down by the men of King Boleslas II.[36] But it was in the British Isles and Scandinavia that the holy bishop-martyr enjoyed the most enduring success. These were countries with a powerful episcopate, a public strongly attached to the defence of local liberties and a monarchy whose prestige had suffered at the hands of a turbulent aristocracy. Most of the English saints who were the object of a major local cult at this period were bishops. As well as two regulars, eight bishops were canonized between the end of the twelfth and the mid-fifteenth centuries.[37] Their preponderance is hardly less if we consider the

---

[33] See above, pp. 109–10; R. Foreville, *Le jubilé de saint Thomas Becket, du XIIIe au XVe siècle (1220–1470): études et documents* (Paris 1958); see also plate 16.

[34] Asked why the bishop of Vicenza had been killed, several witnesses replied: 'pro manutenendis et salvandis racionibus episcopatus et ecclesie unice fuit mortuus'; *PC John Cacciafronte*. pp. 244–5. There are similarities in the cult of B. Adelprato (d. 1173 or 1177), bishop of Trent, killed by a local lord, and buried in his cathedral, where he was venerated as a martyr: *AA. SS.* Mar. III, 707–8; I. Roger, sv Adelprato, in *BS*, I (Rome, 1961), cc. 247–8.

[35] For example, St William Pinchon, bishop of Saint-Brieuc (d. 1234), canonized in 1247 by Innocent IV, who had defended the liberties of the Church against the duke of Brittany and the laity: *AA.SS.* Iul. VI, pp. 122–7.

[36] For St Stanislas, see D. Borawska, *W sprawie genezy Kultu sw. Stanislawa bpa* (Warsaw, 1950); C. Labuda, 'Tworcrosc hagiograficzna i historiograficzna Wincentego z Kielce' (with summary in French), *Studia Zrodloznawcze*, 16 (1971), pp. 103–37, which shows how the Polish Dominican Vincent of Kielce, after the canonization, revised an earlier legend which put too much emphasis on the merits of King Boleslas (d. 1080), Stanislas' murderer. See also W. Vrusczak, 'Les répercussions de la mort de S. Thomas Becket en Pologne', in *Thomas Becket. Actes du colloque international de Sédières (19–24 août 1973)* (Paris, 1975), pp. 115–25; J. Lisowski, *Kanonizacia Sw. Stanislawa* (Rome, 1953).

[37] They are, with date of canonization: SS Wulfstan of Worcester (1202), Hugh of Lincoln (1219), William of York (1223), Lawrence O'Toole of Dublin (1226), Edmund of Canter-

requests for canonization submitted to the papacy by the English clergy at this period that were unsuccessful: of the eight known, five concerned bishops, two were laymen of royal blood and one was a monk.[38]

Many factors contributed to this selective perception of sainthood to the almost exclusive benefit of prelates. The first is probably the strong impression made on the faithful by their aristocratic birth and ability to govern. In their vast dioceses, whose borders often coincided with those of the old Anglo-Saxon kingdoms, the English bishops seemed like the successors of the ancient kings. Richly endowed with land and property, they behaved like great magnates, exercising over their flocks an authority which was not only spiritual.[39] To quote one example among many, the chief virtues attributed to St Thomas Cantilupe, bishop of Hereford (d. 1282), by the witnesses at his canonization process were those of a leader and lord. A fierce and pugnacious defender of the rights of his church against all external powers, he was distinguished also by his generosity. Like St Edmund of Canterbury, who died deep in debt, for which he was honoured by his biographer, the bishop of Hereford spent lavishly and never gave the impression of being hard up.[40]

However appreciated they were by contemporaries, these qualities alone would probably not have been enough to give the bishops a reputation for sainthood, if there had not also been the halo of martyrdom, or at least persecution. As J. C. Russell showed, very nearly all the English saints between the thirteenth and fifteenth centuries were persons of aristocratic rank – prelates and great laymen – who had opposed royal power. Their

---

bury (1246), Richard of Chichester (1256), Thomas of Hereford (1320) and Osmund of Salisbury (1457). The two regulars were Gilbert of Sempringham (1202) and John of Bridlington (1401).

[38] In chronological order of request: Robert Grosseteste, bishop of Lincoln (1254), Robert Winchelsea, archbishop of Canterbury (1318), William March, bishop of Wells (1325), John of Dalderby, bishop of Lincoln (1327) and Richard Fitzralph, archbishop of Armagh (1385). There were also some prelates with a local cult, but whose canonization seems never to have been requested: Roger Niger, bishop of London (d. 1241), Walter of Suffeld, bishop of Norwich (d. 1257) and William Button II, bishop of Wells (d. 1247): Kemp, *Canonization and authority*, pp. 117–27. The other English saints whose canonization was requested from the Holy See were Thomas of Lancaster (1327), Edward II (1386) and Thomas de la Hale, a monk of Dover (1390).

[39] J. Godfrey, *The English parish, 600–1300* (London, 1969), p. 14: 'It is the essentially "royal" character of the English conversion, with Germanic kings adopting the Faith on behalf of their peoples, which accounts for the large English dioceses.'

[40] See the deposition of Walter of Kinlle at the canonization process of St Thomas Cantilupe: 'Dictus dominus Thomas, qui plura expendebat et in duobus adventibus regis ad civitatem Herefordensem dicebatur expendisse mille libras sterlingorum, semper habundabatur in vita et in morte': MS Vat. lat. 4015, fol. 78v.

posthumous popularity is explained, according to Russell, by the prestige they acquired among the people through their fight in defence of their privileges and those of their flocks.[41] In this resistance to arbitrary kings, the English bishops, from SS Hugh of Lincoln to Edmund of Canterbury and from Robert Grosseteste to Robert Winchelsea, played an important role. And though, with the exception of Richard Scrope, the archbishop of York beheaded in 1405, none paid with his life for his participation in rebellion, many had to suffer exile or, at some stage, royal hostility.[42] This was all that was necessary for them to be identified with the man who had become the prototype and obligatory reference for all sainthood in England, St Thomas Becket.[43] On occasion, the desire to conform to the ideal model led to actual fabrications. Matthew Paris, for example, in his biography of St Edmund (d. 1240), did not hesitate to transform the archbishop of Canterbury's last visit *ad limina* into exile as a result of his disputes with Henry III.[44]

The fascination of the 'Becket model' was such that it was popularly applied even to laymen, such as Thomas of Lancaster (d. 1322), as we see from a passage in the office composed around 1330 in honour of the martyred duke:

> Gaude Thoma, ducum decens, lucerna Lancastrie,
> Quia per necem imitaris Thomam Canturie
> Cuius caput conculcatur pacem ob ecclesiae
> Atque tuum obtruncatur causa pacis Angliae.
> Esto nobis tutor in omni discrimine.[45]

Such a text enables us to appreciate all the ambiguity of the cult of the holy bishops in England. In them, the Church celebrated intrepid defenders of its liberty, as well as pastors concerned scrupulously to perform all the duties of their office.[46] For the laity, they were above all innocent victims of royal arbitrary power.[47]

---

[41] Russell, 'The canonization of opposition', pp. 280ff.

[42] Scrope was regarded as a martyr at York, and a chapel was built on the site of his execution: J. W. McKenna, 'Popular canonization as political propaganda: the cult of Archbishop Scrope', *Speculum*, 45 (1970), pp. 608–23.

[43] Matthew Paris, *Vita S. Edmundi*, ed. in Lawrence, *St Edmund of Abingdon*, pp. 222–89, especially p. 260: 'Archiepiscopus conabatur ex tunc beati Thome martiris sequi vestigia pedetentim.' Another biographer of St Edmund, Eustace of Faversham, reproduced whole passages from the *Vita sancti Thomae* of John of Salisbury, applied to his subject.

[44] Lawrence, *St Edmund of Abingdon*, pp. 168–82.

[45] T. Wright, ed., *Political songs* (Cambridge, 1996), p. 270.

[46] See the discussion of episcopal sanctity below, pp. 285ff.

[47] The emergence, well into the fourteenth century, of devotions to certain kings killed in cruel circumstances (Edward II, Henry VI etc.) is partly explicable in this mental context. To weep for and venerate the dead king, even if he had been hated in his lifetime, was

The clergy, at all events, were careful not to react against a confusion which assured the success of the cult of the great prelates. Better, if the political dimension was not central to the biography of a particular holy bishop, the notion of martyrdom was reintroduced by means of other 'persecutions'. At the canonization process of St Thomas Cantilupe (d. 1282), several witnesses, mostly clerics, went so far as to describe the bishop as a 'martyr', because of the difficulties he had experienced, at the end of his life, through his dispute with his metropolitan, Archbishop John Peckham.[48] Admittedly, this was a serious matter, since the illustrious Franciscan had not hesitated to excommunicate his suffragan, who had been obliged to go to the Curia, where he died, to defend himself. But from this to talk of martyrdom was a very big step, which some witnesses were prepared to take, as they told how, when the bishop's remains were being brought back from Italy, they bled whenever the journey took them through the lands of his principal enemies, in particular the see of Canterbury.[49] The clergy who supported his cause were well aware that the cult of this prelate, who had earlier enjoyed a successful university career, and been Henry III's chancellor at the time of the Baronial Revolt, stood no chance of becoming popular unless they could graft onto this relatively untroubled existence a pathetic element which would turn him into a suffering leader and an innocent man persecuted for justice.

The situation was comparable in the Scandinavian countries, where, in the thirteenth and fourteenth centuries, kings and bishops not only frequently confronted each other over political issues, but also vied with each other in the sphere of sainthood. In the 1250s, the kings of Norway prevented a successful conclusion to the canonization process of the former archbishop of Nidaros, Eystein Erlendsson (d. 1188), who had been forced to seek exile in England after a dispute with King Sverre.[50] In the fourteenth century, St Bridget of Sweden and

perhaps, for many people, the only way they could protest against the violence and bad government of his successor.

[48] In his deposition, Bishop Richard Swinfield of Hereford said that his predecessor had ended his life 'martyrizatus laboribus, angustiis et expensis' (AA.SS. Oct. I, p. 603); another witness, Robert of Gloucester, chancellor of Hereford cathedral, said he had seen an apparition of Thomas in white vestments 'quasi dictus beatus Thomas premium martyris recepisset' (MS Vat. lat. 4015, fol. 98v).

[49] PC Thomas of Hereford, fol. 17.

[50] See above, n. 29, p. 70. The failure of his process did not prevent him being venerated as a saint by the Norwegians, as appears from a passage in Matthew Paris, Chronica majora, III, p. 521 (ad an. 1250): 'Sanctus Augustinus in Norvegia claris, probatis et approbatis miraculis illustratur.' The popularity of the cult of the Icelandic saints in their country is revealed in iconography; see plate 17.

the devout circles which gravitated around her attacked the cult of St Eric, who, or so she remarked, might be in purgatory or in hell, but was certainly not in heaven.[51] They wanted to substitute, for the holy kings traditionally venerated in Sweden, figures who were regarded as more authentically Christian, such as St Botwid, the apostle of Södermanland (d. 1317), and, above all, Brynulph Algotsson, bishop of Skara (d. 1317), who was beginning to be venerated in his diocese early in the fifteenth century, when his memory had long faded. The other great Swedish saint of the late Middle Ages, Nicholas Hermansson, bishop of Linköping (d. 1387), was from the same devout circles. Significantly, at his canonization process in 1417, this prelate was presented as a defender of law and justice, victim of the persecutions inflicted on him by several 'tyrants', above all King Albert. The witnesses insisted that his life had frequently been in danger, in particular when the sovereign came to Linköping and threatened him with death.[52] A similar episode was mentioned at the process of Brynulph of Skara, where one witness claimed that King Magnus had considered murdering him, before finally humiliating himself before him.[53]

The conclusions which emerge from our examination of the 'modern' forms of sainthood in northern and north-western Europe are equally valid for other non-Mediterranean regions, for which the documentation is less abundant or revealing. We see, first, that right to the end of the Middle Ages, the saints of these countries continued largely to come from the ruling classes – kings, princes or bishops. Even St Bridget of Sweden, who waged war on the cult of the 'holy king' St Eric, was described in contemporary texts as *principessa Nericie*. But among these 'great men', bishops were increasingly preponderant with the passage of time, if only thanks to the continuity assured to their liturgical cult by the support of the cathedral clergy. Though lay rulers were never wholly eliminated, the prelates gradually replaced them, by

---

[51] St Bridget, *Liber revelationum*, II, c. 29: 'utrum ipse est in inferno vel in purgatorio nondum est tibi licitum scire, sed cum tempus fuerit loquendi'.

[52] *PC Nicholas of Linköping*, p. 134. The 21st article (p. 60) reads as follows: 'Item fortis iste zelotes velud alter Helyas qui principem non temuit contra quemdam regem Swecie illustrem Albertum . . . vehementer se erexit . . . mortem subire non metuens quam idem rex sibi inferre realiter bis attemptavit.'

[53] Canonization process of Brynulph of Skara (Skara, 1417), ed. C. Annerstedt, in *Scriptores rerum suecicarum medii aevi*, III, 2 (Uppsala, 1876), p. 164.

being assimilated to the model of the 'holy sufferers', which remained the archetype of sainthood in the popular mind.[54]

Nobility and sainthood

Aristocratic prestige and sainthood

The changes occurring over time between the various categories (kings, princes and bishops) best represented in local sainthood in no way detract from the statement made at the beginning of this chapter: during the final centuries of the Middle Ages, in the non-Mediterranean West, the majority of recent saints were of aristocratic origin. This situation was not new. It perpetuated a phenomenon which dated back to the early Middle Ages, a period when saints began to be recruited almost exclusively from families distinguished by both birth and power. The association between nobility and sainthood, before it became a hagiographical commonplace, had long been a sociological reality, as we see, for example, from the osmosis visible in Merovingian Gaul between the world of the high laity and that of the bishops.[55] Sanctity, power and aristocratic distinction were so closely associated that it has been possible to speak, in this connection, of a veritable 'hagiocracy'.[56] In the Carolingian world, despite a slight lowering of the social level of saints owing to the increase in the number of monks and hermits among the servants of God, hagiographical literature continued to propagate the idea that moral and spiritual perfection could only with diffi-

---

[54] One of the rare holy monks venerated in England at this period was Thomas de la Hale, a Benedictine of Dover, killed by French soldiers during a raid in 1295. Indulgences were granted between 1296 and 1302 by the bishop of Winchester to pilgrims who visited his tomb. New indulgences were granted in 1370 by the archbishop of Canterbury; in 1380, at the request of Richard II and the English clergy, Urban VI agreed to a canonization process, but nothing came of it: P. Grosjean, 'Thomas de La Hale, moine et martyr à Douvres en 1295', *Anal. Boll.*, 72 (1954), pp. 167–91.

[55] For seventh- and eighth-century Bavaria, see K. Bosl, 'Der Adelheilige, Idealtypus und Wirklichkeit, Gesellschaft und Kultur im Merowingerzeitlichen Bayern des VII, und VIII, Jahrhunderts', in *Speculum historiale: Festscrift J. Spörl* (Freiburg, 1965), pp. 167–87; F. Prinz, 'Heiligenkult und Adelherrschaft im Spiegel Merowingischer Hagiographie', *Historische Zeitschrift*, 204 (1967), pp. 529–44. Both emphasize the continuity of the Germanic notion of 'nobility of blood'. Their views are disputed by F. Graus, 'Sozialgeschichtliche Aspekte der Hagiographie der Merowinger- und Karolingerzeit. Die Viten des südalemannischen Raumes und die sogenannten Adelsheiligen', in *Mönchtum, Episkopat und Adel in der Gründungszeit des Klosters Reichenau*, ed. A. Borst (Sigmaringen, 1974), pp. 131–76.

[56] Chelini, *Histoire religieuse de l'Occident médiéval*, p. 71.

culty be attained outside an illustrious lineage.[57] Far from attacking this conception, the Church encouraged it, and this eventually left an indelible impression on people's minds. But the very success of this topos implies a minimum of receptivity on the part of the public for whom these *Vitae* were intended, that is, the existence of a correspondence between the scale of values they conveyed and the representations of sainthood in the common mind.

The clergy, however, had very early seen the danger presented by too great an emphasis on the privileges of the nobility with regard to sanctity. The more astute among them, therefore, sought to deny the almost automatic nature of this relationship, by emphasizing the superiority of nobility of character over nobility of blood. This is the real significance of the formula *nobilis origine . . . sed nobiliter virtute*, so common in medieval hagiographical literature, especially from the eleventh century.[58] But we should not overestimate its impact. Those who employed it certainly intended to react by this means against a 'magic' conception of sainthood; but they were neither able nor willing to attack it head on, and the adage *nobilis . . . nobilior* continued for centuries to convey an ambiguous message. Though it stressed the moral dimension of Christian perfection, it surely also consecrated the link occasionally established between aristocratic birth and sainthood, so blocking for a long time to come any shift in the recruitment of saints in a less elitist direction.[59]

---

[57] J. J. Mak, 'Middeleuwse Heiligenverering', *Nederlandsch Archief voor Kerkgeschiednis*, 38 (1951), pp. 142–63. See also E. Spaey, 'De Opvatting der Heiligheid in Vlaanderen en Lotharingen in de tweede helft der 9e eeuw', *Ons Geestelijk Erf*, 1 (1927), pp. 255–77, 346–69; J.-C. Poulin, *L'idéal de sainteté dans l'Aquitaine carolingienne d'après les sources hagiographiques (750–950)* (Quebec, 1975), pp. 47–8.

[58] The formula *nobilis genere sed multo nobilior sanctitate* appears in St Jerome (*Ep. 108*, 1). It became very popular during the early Middle Ages when nobility and sanctity usually went together. See, for example, Alcuin, *Ep. 241* (letter to Gondrad, 801); 'Sint nobiles in moribus sicut sunt nobiles ex parentibus.' It survived at the level of stereotype to the end of the Middle Ages and into the early modern period. References for the thirteenth and fourteenth centuries are too many to quote, but see *Vita beate Brigide prioris Petri et magistri Petri*, compiled in 1373 by the saint's two confessors: 'Sicut legimus de beato Johanne Baptista et de sancto Nicolao, multociens cooperantur merita parentum ut filiis gracia maior accrescat et perseveret in finem, sic sancte memorie domina Brigida . . . de parentibus justis et devotis processit qui nobiles fuerunt secundum carnem, quia de nobili genere regum Gottorum, sed nobiliores secundum Deum': I. Collijn, *Acta et processus canonizationis beate Birgitte* (Stockholm, 1930), p. 74.

[59] See, for example, how Odo of Cluny presents St Gerald of Aurillac in the *Vita Geraldi* (I, *PL*, 133, c. 639): 'potens et dives et utique sanctus'; also the discussion in A. Frugoni, 'Incontro con Cluny' in *Spiritualità Cluniacense* (Todi, 1960), pp. 11–29; M. Heinzelmann, 'Sanctitas und Tugendadel, Zu Konzeptionem von "Heiligkeit" im 5, und 10, Jahrhundert', *Francia* 5 (1977), pp. 741–52.

To explain this profound complicity between clergy and nobles, it is not enough to refer to their common membership of the ruling classes, or the solidarity promoted between them by the fact of living in idleness on the income from landed rents and the labour of others. We need also to remember that the acculturation of Christianity in western societies was achieved by the combined efforts of the ecclesiastical and lay powers. Despite the conflicts which later divided them, the medieval Church never ceased to honour the temporal leaders – kings and *potentes* – to whom, in a sense, it owed a debt of gratitude.[60] Further, the clergy's own conception of sainthood helps to explain why they mostly chose persons of high rank to propose for the veneration of the faithful. In practice, to achieve the norms of Christian perfection, as they were defined by the Church in the eleventh and twelfth centuries, was hardly conceivable outside the sphere of the ruling classes. In a society where wealth and power were regarded as signs of divine favour and election, the great of this world were *a priori* best placed to achieve salvation and distinction in the eyes of the world at large. Their eminent social position and the means at their disposal enabled them to construct places of worship and distribute alms, defend and propagate the Christian faith and support the clergy. The aristocracy was even in an advantageous position with regard to renunciation, since only those with possessions were in a position to dispossess themselves; paradoxically, their temporal power only rendered their spiritual success more striking.[61]

One might expect this prerogative of the nobility not to have survived the changes which, between the mid-twelfth and the mid-thirteenth centuries, transformed the ideal of Christian perfection. Among the values extolled by the clergy, evangelical virtues such as humility, poverty and asceticism were now to the fore. Their exaltation ought to have allowed members of the lower ranks of society to accede in their turn to the honours of the local cult. In non-Mediterranean Europe, this happened in the case of a few hermits and recluses who enjoyed great local prestige

---

[60] Interesting remarks in V. Fumagalli, *Terra e società nell'Italia padana: i secoli IX–X* (Bologna, 1974), pp. 138–42.

[61] For the preponderance of the social elites in Catholic sanctity, see K. and C. George, 'Roman Catholic sainthood and social status', *Journal of Religion*, 35 (1955), pp. 95–8 (based on some 250 saints in Butler, Thurston and Attwater, *Lives of the saints*). At the canonization process of St Margaret of Hungary in 1276, a Hungarian peasant, asked why he believed the daughter of Bela IV was a saint, replied: 'Scio quod fuit filia regis et audivi quod humiliavit se et paupertatem diligebat': *PC Margaret of Hungary*, p. 334.

and were venerated after their death.[62] But the devotion they aroused rarely lasted very long, once the initial wave of enthusiasm had worn itself out. The content and forms of sanctity might have changed, but the new saints still mostly came from the high nobility. The most illustrious representatives of the penitential movement, which in Italy at that period was very successful among the urban bourgeoisie, were, in central and eastern Europe, all princesses: SS Elizabeth of Hungary (d. 1231), Hedwig (d. 1243) and Margaret of Hungary (d. 1270), and Agnes of Bohemia (d. 1282) etc. The chief figures in the flowering of sainthood in the wake of the Mendicant orders in the thirteenth and fourteenth centuries were members of the aristocracy, whether lay or in orders: SS Louis of France (d. 1270), Louis of Anjou (d. 1297) and Elzear (d. 1323), and Delphine of Sabran (d. 1360), Charles of Blois (d. 1364) and Joan-Marie of Maillé (d. 1414) etc. North of the Alps, it was not until the beginning of the fifteenth century that the clergy set out to promote the cult of saints of popular or bourgeois origin, such as the mystic Dorothy of Montau (d. 1395), wife of a craftsman of Gdansk, or the enigmatic St Sebald, an eleventh-century hermit canonized in 1429 by Martin V.[63] With very few exceptions, it was as if the perception of sainthood could only operate to the benefit of the social elites. All nobles were certainly not seen as saints, but almost all saints came from the nobility. For a long time to come, the celestial court only opened its doors to people who already occupied high positions on earth.

---

[62] The cult of the holy hermits seems to have flourished in Germany and England. In the Germanic countries, the tradition dates back to the eleventh century and its success was initially bound up with the conflict between supporters and opponents of Church Reform. See H. Keller, ' "Adelsheiliger" und Pauper Christi in Ekkeberts Vita sancti Haimeradi', in *Adel und Kirche: Gerd Tellenback zum 65. Geburtstag dargebracht von Freunden und Schülern*, ed. J. Fleckenstein and K. Schmid (Frieburg, 1968), pp. 307–24; H. Grundmann, 'Zur Vita S. Gerlaci eremitae', *Deutsches Archiv*, 18 (1962), pp. 539–54 (a thirteenth-century Life of the hermit d. 1166). In England, the Yorkshire hermit Robert of Knaresborough (d. 1218) was one of the greatest saints of his day according to Matthew Paris: 'eodem anno [= 1238], claruit fama sancti Roberti heremitae apud Knaresburc, cujus tumba oleum medicinale fertur abundanter emisisse': *Chronica major*, III, p. 521, see also IV, p. 378 (= 1244). For Robert, see J. Bazire, *The metrical Life of St Robert of Knaresborough* (London, 1953); H. Farmer, sv Roberto di Knaresborough, in *BS*, XI (Rome, 1968), cc. 234–5. Mention might also be made of the cult of the mystical hermit Richard Rolle of Hampole (d. 1349), though it seems to have been fairly localized: Woolley, *Officium and miracula*.

[63] St Sebald, whose origins are obscure, was presented in late medieval hagiographical and liturgical texts as the son of a king. In the fourteenth century, a hymn in his honour called him *stirpe de regali natus*. About 1380, a Nuremberg canon composed a biography in German ('Er was ein kunek') which made him the son of a king of Denmark (Borst, 'Die Sebaldlegenden', pp. 19–175).

That the latter were so prominent and so overwhelmingly preponderant at the level of local sainthood owes something to the barrier opposed by the ruling classes to devotions concerning saints of modest extraction.[64] But it must also be recognized that the poor had, to a degree, adopted the scale of values which the Church and the lay aristocracy had taught them, by common accord, through innumerable channels, not least legends and works of art. Initially imposed, this world view dominated by the idea of a correspondence between the earthly and celestial hierarchies had eventually been universally assimilated. The fate of the 'great' of this world still, after all, fascinates the man in the street today, especially if it assumes a tragic dimension. Why, then, should we be surprised if it was the same in the Middle Ages? The popular success of the aristocratic models is explained both by the social pressure which was strongly exerted in this direction and by the supernatural prestige which the nobility retained in the popular mind. The importance attached to the origins of the servants of God, and the favourable prejudice created if they belonged to an illustrious lineage, was, in the last analysis, based on the assumption of a magical quality in the mere fact of high birth.[65]

'Beata stirps': the sainthood of lineage

When we are able to go beyond this simple observation, and discover the precise reasons for a particular person being regarded as a saint by his or her contemporaries, we see that it was not so much the nobility of the individual which counted as the membership of a family group which enjoyed particular popular prestige. The deep roots of this belief in the hereditary transmission of a charisma within certain families go back to the early Middle Ages, if not beyond. In fact, the Germanic invasions had

[64] This 'block' is all the more difficult to discern in that it is generally found at the level of the perception of sanctity. For example, in a country like Castile, whose royal family produced four *beati* in the Middle Ages (*AA.SS.* Mar. I, p. 748, Maii I, p. 763, Maii VII, pp. 280–414), the conviction that sainthood could only exist within the aristocracy was so widespread that it was extremely difficult for the cult of saints of popular origin to develop. There is an echo of this attitude in the words of a noble from the entourage of King Ferdinand (d. 1250) regarding St Isidore the Farm-servant (d. *c.*1130): 'Ego bene crederem quod qui esset filius principis vel alicuius magnatis bene posset fieri sanctus, sed virum laboricii seu ruricolam non credo ullatenus fore sanctum': *Legenda de S. Isidoro por Juan Diacono* (pre 1275), ed. F. Fita, *Buletin de la real academia de la historia*, 9 (1886), p. 118. His cult grew rapidly in the late Middle Ages and early modern period, especially in the Spanish colonies in South America.

[65] Interesting remarks in R. Bolgar, *The classical heritage and its beneficiaries* (Cambridge, 1961), p. 135.

given new vigour to conceptions already in favour among the Romans, according to which membership of a *gens* or a renowned *genus* implied sharing in a collection of gifts and powers transmitted by blood.[66] With the demarcation of coherent lineages which took place in the eleventh and twelfth centuries within the upper ranks of feudal society in most parts of the West, this belief was only strengthened. The making – or remaking – of genealogical trees in noble families, and the adoption of a more or less mythical prestigious ancestor, attest to the need felt by the aristocracy to equip itself with a glorious past in order to legitimize its present situation.[67] In this socio-cultural context, it is hardly surprising that certain particularly well-placed families tried, often successfully, to encourage the idea of a hereditary transmission of sainthood in their case.

One might expect the clergy to have felt some misgivings about these claims, which called into question the gratuitous nature of spiritual gifts

[66] See, for example, the letter from Theoderic to Theodehad in Cassiodorus, *Variae*, IV, 39 (vv. 507–11), ed. in *MGH.AA.*, XII, p. 131: 'Quid enim faciunt sordes animorum in splenore natalium . . . Hamoli sanguis virum non decet vulgare desiderium, quia genus suum conspicit esse purpuratum.' See also Venence Fortunat, *Carmina. Lib. IX. ad Chilpericum regem*, in *MGH.AA.*, IV, p. 201, vv. 10–14:

> Tu genus ornasti, te genus ornat avi,
> Excepisti eternum fulgorem ab origine gentis
> sed per te proavis splendor honore redit.

[67] For the theme of the hereditary transmission of sainthood in certain noble lineages in the Middle Ages, see K. Hauck, 'Geblütsheiligkeit', in *Liber Floridus Paul Lehmann* (St Ottilien, 1950), pp. 187–240. The theme also appears in eleventh-century French historiography, for example Helgaud of Fleury's *Vie de Robert le Pieux*, ed. Bautier, p. 98: 'O felix participatione Dei pietas et misericordia que sic floruerunt in tanto et tali viro [= Hugh Capet] quas et iste Robertus noster quasi hereditario dote a patre relictas possedit.' Having long disappeared from the Christian world, the conception survives to this day in some parts of the Islamic world; see E. Gellner, *Saints of the Atlas* (London, 1969); Gellner 'Pouvoir politique et fonction religieuse dans l'Islam marocain', *Annales ESC*, 25 (1970), pp. 699–713. Gellner shows the role played among the Berber tribes of the High Atlas by the 'igguramen', members of famous families regarded as holy who settle near the tombs of their ancestors and enjoy great prestige. For lineages in the eleventh and twelfth centuries in the West, see G. Duby, 'Remarques sur la littérature généalogique en France aux XIe et XIIe siècles', *CRAI* (1967), pp. 333–45, repr. in Duby, *Hommes et structures du Moyen Age* (Paris and The Hague, 1973), pp. 287–98; also the acts of the conference *Famille et parenté dans l'Occident médiéval*, ed. G. Duby and J. Le Goff (Rome, 1977). For the importance of the familial model in mentalities, see M. Sot, 'Historiographie épiscopale et modèle familial en Occident au XIe siècle', *Annales ESC*, 33 (1978), pp. 433–49. William of Malmesbury says that, according to some of his contemporaries, the healing power possessed by St Edward the Confessor derived 'non ex sanctitate sed ex regalis prosapiae hereditate' (*Historia regum*, ed. W. Stubbs, II (London, 1887), p. 273 (Rolls Series, 90)). See also J. Nelson, 'Royal saints and early medieval kingship', in *Sanctity and secularity*, ed. D. Baker (Oxford, 1973), pp. 39–44; E. Hoffmann, *Die heilige Könige bei den Angelsachsen und den Skandinavischen Völkern: Königsheiliger und Königshaus* (Neumünster, 1975).

and divine liberty. This was far from the case, because, in their mental universe, there was no shortage of models capable of providing a religious justification for these conceptions. Here, biblical references played a decisive role; the Tree of Jesse, after all, so often portrayed in the twelfth and thirteenth centuries on the windows and doorways of churches, offered a perfect example of a predestined lineage within which grace was transmitted from one generation to the next. All its members had not been saints, but perfection had blossomed there with rare intensity and frequency.[68] In the medieval West, outside the Mediterranean, there was a widespread belief that certain persons from noble families enjoyed a sort of 'capital' of sanctity, which had been theirs from the beginning, by reason of the accumulated merits of their ancestors and parents. They might, of course, reveal themselves unworthy of this inheritance. But if they made the effort to make it bear fruit, they achieved perfection more easily than others. The clergy endeavoured to 'Christianize' these beliefs by emphasizing not the sacred character of the lineage as such, but the presence within it of individuals whose virtues and miracles had been recognized by the Church.[69] The solidarity existing between the members of the group was revealed in two ways: the saint received from his or her parents and ancestors a collection of graces;[70] but the saint's own merits in turn brought reflected glory on his or her family, which was associated, as a result, with the veneration which the saint attracted. The reputation for sanctity of St Edmund Rich, archbishop of Canterbury (d. 1243), for example, was such that his brother Robert and his two sisters, Alice and Margaret, were regarded in their time as saints. Similarly, in the second

---

[68] For the iconographical theme of the tree of Jesse in twelfth- and thirteenth-century art, see G. Duby, *L'Europe des cathédrales, 1140–1280* (Geneva, 1966), pp. 30–3.

[69] Odo of Cluny, having explained that St Gerald of Aurillac had received from his parents numerous virtues *veluti quadam hereditaria dote*, emphasized that he came from a *stirps* which had already produced St Caesar of Arles and the holy abbot Aredius: *Vita Geraldi*, I, 1; see also II, 5: 'isdem pater ejus religiosus fuit, qui de prosapia religiosorum descenderat'. A similar claim is made in the fourteenth-century Life of St Thomas Aquinas by the Dominican William of Tocco, c. 38, '*de naturali propagine dicti doctoris*', ed. Ferrua, p. 83. The hagiography mentions several ancestors of the illustrious doctor who had died in an odour of sanctity, from which he concluded that his hero 'se ostendit sanctae generationis heredem'.

[70] At thirteenth- and fourteenth-century canonization processes, witnesses endeavoured to attach their subject to a 'family of saints'. For example, Philip Berruyer, archbishop of Bourges (d. 1261), was the nephew of William of Donjeon, also archbishop of Bourges, who had been canonized by Honorius III in 1218; his maternal grandmother and an aunt were also venerated locally: *PC Philip of Bourges*, fol. 28v. St Thomas Cantilupe, bishop of Hereford (d. 1282) was the nephew of William, bishop of Worcester, at whose tomb numerous miracles had occurred: *PC Thomas of Hereford*, fol. 40v.

half of the thirteenth century, a devotion grew up around the tomb of the landgrave Lewis IV (d. 1227), in the wake of that already enjoyed by his wife, St Elizabeth of Thuringia.[71] These phenomena of 'canonization by participation' may surprise. But we should remember that this was, after all, the period when the cult of St Anne, mother of the Virgin Mary and grandmother of Christ, developed throughout the West.[72]

For the historian, this conception of sainthood of family or lineage at once raises the question of whether it was a residual phenomenon, survival of a mentality which was dying out, or a belief deeply entrenched in the minds of the people of the time. The fact that most of the cases known to us concern central or eastern Europe might suggest archaism. Between 1150 and 1500, thirty-two persons from the family of the counts of Andechs were regarded as saints, the most illustrious of whom was St Hedwig (d. 1243), daughter of Berthold IV of Andechs-Meran and duchess of Silesia, canonized in 1267.[73] Similarly in thirteenth- and early fourteenth-century Hungary, many members of the Arpad dynasty were the object of a cult. This continued a tradition, since the first kings of Hungary were regarded as saints, even by the Roman Church.[74] There is some evidence, however, that these devotions were not a survival from the past. In practice, far from dying out with the Arpads, Hungarian dynastic sainthood was given a new lease of life when, in 1307, the Angevins of Naples seized the crown of St Stephen. This family, of French origin,

---

[71] For St Edmund's brother and sisters, see Matthew Paris, *Chronica major*, IV, pp. 102–3, 342, 378 (*ad an. 1244*), V, pp. 621, 642; for Lewis IV, whose cult started at the abbey of Reinhardsbrunn, where his body lay, see K. Kunze, sv Ludovico IV, in *BS*, VIII (Rome, 1966), cc. 312–14. Another example is Catherine of Sweden, daughter of St Bridget (d. 1381), venerated as a saint in northern Europe.

[72] P. V. Charland, *Le culte de sainte Anne en Occident* (Quebec, 1921); B. Kleinschmidt, *Die Heilige Anna: ihre Verehrung in Geschichte, Kunst und Volksglaube* (Düsseldorf, 1934); J. Galbert and M. Parent, 'La légende des trois mariages de Ste Anne. Un texte nouveau', in *Etudes d'histoire littéraire et doctrinale du XIIIe siècle* (Paris and Ottawa, 1932), pp. 165–84. It would be interesting to look more closely at the passage from holy lineage to the 'Holy Family' in fifteenth-century iconography and art, by means of the 'sacra conversazione'.

[73] Gottschalk, *St Hedwig Herzogin von Schlesien*, pp. 52–60. For more detail, see the *Tractatus sive speculum genealogiae sanctae Hedwigis*, written in the last third of the thirteenth century by an anonymous cleric, ed. in *AA.SS*. Oct. VIII, pp. 265–7.

[74] SS Stephen (d. 1030), Emeric or Henry (d. 1031) and Ladislas (d. 1095) were joined in the thirteenth and fourteenth centuries by St Elizabeth of Hungary (or of Thuringia) (d. 1231) and her nieces: St Margaret, daughter of Bela IV (d. 1270), and BB Cunegund of Kinga (d. 1292) and Iolenta (or Iolanda) (d. 1298), both of whom married Polish princes. Also venerated at this period were BB Elizabeth of Hungary, daughter of Andrew II (d. 1336), a Dominican nun at Töss, and Agnes of Bohemia (d. *c*.1280), daughter of Constance of Hungary and Ottakar I. For royal sanctity in Hungary, see T. von Bogyay, J. Bak and G. Silagi, *Die heiligen Könige* (Graz, 1976).

also included two recent saints in its ranks, SS Louis of France (d. 1270, canonized 1297) and Louis of Anjou (d. 1297, canonized 1317), son of Charles II. There is hagiographical and iconographical evidence that the cult of St Margaret of Hungary (d. 1270) flourished at the beginning of the fourteenth century in Naples and southern Italy.[75] We also have tangible proof of the desire of the new sovereigns to associate the two sacred traditions, that of Hungary and that of France: an altar hanging presented to St Peter's in Rome by Queen Elizabeth, wife of the king of Hungary, Lewis the Great (1342–82), which is described in an inventory of the Basilica's Treasure drawn up in 1361, portrayed, in addition to the Virgin and SS Peter and Paul, only members of the dynasty: St Stephen, his son St Emeric or Henry, SS Ladislas and Louis of Anjou.[76] Similarly, in the Legendry produced in 1331 on the orders of the Angevins of Hungary, the manuscript of which is partially conserved in the Vatican Library, we find among other Lives, those of SS Stephen, Emeric, Ladislas, Elizabeth, Louis of France and Louis of Anjou.[77] This seems to me to confirm that the Angevins of Naples and Hungary made a systematic effort to exploit the belief in the sanctity of their dynasty in order to enhance their prestige and give a religious basis to their political domination.[78]

Nor was this an isolated case; even sovereigns whose power was assured, like Frederick II, sought to turn to their advantage the prestige surrounding the saints of their line.[79] The same was true of the Capetians in

[75] E. Koltay-Kastner, 'La leggenda della B. Marguerita d'Ungheria alla Corte angioina di Napoli', in *Studi e documenti italo-ungheresi*, III (Rome, 1938–9), pp. 174–80; F. Banfi, 'Specchio delle anime semplici dalla B. Margarita scritto', *Memorie Domenicane*, 15 (1940), pp. 3–16, 131–40. In fact, this was a false attribution, the work of an Italian Franciscan sympathizer of the 'Free Spirit', to give an air of orthodoxy to the Italian translation of the mystical treatise of Margaret Porète (*Gli Angioini di Napoli e di Ungheria* (Rome, 1974)).

[76] E. Muntz and A. L. Frottingham, 'Il tesoro della Basilica di S. Pietro in Vaticano dal XIIo al XVo secolo', *Archivio della R. società di storia patria*, 6 (1883), p. 14.

[77] F. Levardy, 'Il Leggendario ungherese degli Angio conservato nella Biblioteca Vaticana, nel Morgan Library e nell'Ermitage', *Acta historiae artium academiae scientiarum Hungariae*, 9 (1963), pp. 75–108.

[78] This is particularly clear in the case of Robert of Naples (d. 1343), who had himself painted by Simone Martini, 1317–20, at the feet of his brother St Louis of Anjou, who is placing the royal crown on his head (see plate 18). M. Toynbee has shown the political purpose of this picture, designed to legitimize Robert's exclusive rights to the throne of Sicily (*S. Louis of Toulouse*, pp. 221–2).

[79] The most significant text here is the extraordinary letter – possibly written by Peter de la Vigne – sent in 1236 by Frederick to Brother Elias, in which he describes the translation of the remains of St Elizabeth of Thuringia, which he had just attended. He emphasized the ties of lineage uniting him with the saint and the common nobility of his own blood and that of the recently canonized princess, a nobility which he did not hesitate to call 'sacerdotal'. The text is in E. Winkelmann, *Acta imperii inedita*, I (Innsbruck, 1880), pp.

France.[80] The deposition of Charles of Anjou at the canonization process of his brother Louis IX sheds light on one of the clearest attempts to do this. In it, the king of Naples presented his family as a *beata stirps*, in which sainthood flourished in every generation. He discoursed at length on the memory of their mother Blanche of Castile, who, he claimed, had died a saint, having donned the habit of a nun, and whose sons were themselves saints.[81] Not content with emphasizing the merits of St Louis, about whom he was being questioned, he took advantage of the occasion to claim that Robert of Artois, struck down by the Saracens at Mansourah, should be seen as a martyr to the faith and that Alphonse of Poitiers had been inspired by the desire for martyrdom when, after the debacle of Tunis, he had tried to go to the Holy Land instead of returning to France.[82] Admittedly, this demonstration failed, and, other than St Louis, no Capetian was accorded the honours of a liturgical cult. But membership of this dynasty remained, in the fourteenth century, a sign, if not a criterion, of sainthood, since the first of the articles taken from the canonization process of Charles of Blois, between 1372 and 1376, emphasized his family ties with 'the House of the kings of France, of which so many members distinguished themselves by the brilliance of their miracles and are venerated as saints by the Church'.[83]

These examples show that, far from constituting a marginal phenomenon, essentially concerning countries on the periphery of Christendom,

---

299–300. For the circumstances of its composition, see G. Barone, *Frate Elia*, *BISIME*, 85 (1974–5), pp. 89–144.

[80] The Capetians were only perpetuating a tradition started by the Carolingians, since Angilram and Paul the Deacon set out the genealogy of Charlemagne on the episcopal list for the city of Metz through the intermediary of Bishop Arnulph, ancestor of the Frankish king; see N. Sot, 'Historiographie épiscopale et modèle familial', pp. 433–49, especially pp. 439–41.

[81] This is one of the few fragments of the canonization process to have survived: ed. P. Riant, 'Déposition de Charles d'Anjou pour la canonisation de S. Louis', in *Notices et documents publiés par la Société de l'histoire de France, à l'occasion de son 50e anniversaire* (Paris, 1889), pp. 155–80.

[82] *Ibid.*: 'sancta illa anima soluta est, unde sancta radix sanctos ramos protulit, non solum regem sanctum [= St Louis] et comitem Atrebatensem, martirem gloriosum et comitem Pictaviensem affectu'.

[83] *PC Charles of Blois*, ASV. *Collectorie*, 434, fol. 1: 'In primis ponit et probare intendit quod dictus dominus Karolus ex utroque parente nobilissimam traxit originem, utpote de illustrissima domo regum Francie in qua multi fuerunt refulgentes miraculis et qui sancti in ecclesia venerantur, quorum dictus Karolus pius extitit venerator et devotissimus imitator.' It is clear from the evidence presented at the process of 1371 that Charles of Blois was devoted to St Louis of Anjou. At the end of the Middle Ages, a cult of 'St Clovis' appeared in France: see C. Beaune, 'Saint Clovis', in *Le métier d'historien au Moyen Age: études sur l'historiographie médiévale*, ed. B. Guenée (Paris, 1977), pp. 139–56.

the familial and aristocratic conception of sainthood was alive and well in the late Middle Ages. But we should recognize that it had changed significantly with the passage of time. The charisma associated with the fact of high birth had lost ground, in favour of the sacred character of certain dynasties which were able to count among their ranks saints recognized by the Church and had the means to develop their cult.

IN THE MEDITERRANEAN COUNTRIES: THE SUFFERING OF THE POOR

A less aristocratic sainthood

In the sphere of local sainthood, the Mediterranean countries differed sharply from the rest of western Christendom, displaying their own distinctive features. The exact boundaries of this zone are difficult to define precisely. Italy was the centre, in particular communal Italy, that is, the Po plain, Tuscany, Umbria, the Marches and Latium. It is here that the specific characteristics of this socio-cultural zone appear in what one might call their purest form. The model loses some of its coherence in proportion as one moves away from these regions. In Provence, Languedoc and Catalonia, as indeed in southern Italy and Sicily, it diverged in different directions under the influence of other representations. But even in an impure state, the Mediterranean model of sainthood retained its originality compared with those which prevailed elsewhere in the West.

Sainthood and society in medieval Italy: a statistical approach

To identify the basic features of local sainthood in the Mediterranean regions, it is to Italy, therefore, that we should turn. For the country as a whole, with its modern boundaries, we may draw on the work of D. Weinstein and R. M. Bell on the social origin of the saints who lived between 1200 and 1500. On the basis of the names in Butler, Thurston and Attwater's *Lives of the saints*, they provide figures which I have used for table 6.[84]

---

[84] D. Weinstein and R. M. Bell, 'Saints and society: Italian saints of the late Middle Age and Renaissance', *Memorie Domenicane*, n.s., 4 (1973), pp. 180–94. It would have been possible to achieve more accurate and safer results by using the names of saints in the *Bibliotheca sanctorum*, 12 vols. (Rome, 1961–9), which is more complete, especially for Italy, than the older collection. For the merits of this enterprise, see A. D'Haenens, 'Erudition et vulgarisation: une conciliation possible. A propos d'une encyclopédie hagiog-

Table 6 *Social origin of saints in the West (1150–1500)*

Social category	Italians %	Non-Italians %	Number of cases
Reigning families or high nobility	15	47	111
Middle and lesser aristocracy	35	27	101
Commercial and craft bourgeoisie	31	16	74
Peasants and workers	19	10	47
Unknown	30	32	150

The most striking fact to emerge from table 6 is the relatively modest social origin of the majority of Italian saints, as compared with the other saints venerated elsewhere in Christendom at this period. Admittedly, it was not unknown, south of the Alps, for princesses and nobles to acquire a reputation for sanctity after entering a monastery or Mendicant house. But they remained striking exceptions, who only prove the rule; in Italy, the majority of saints in the late Middle Ages came from the lower levels of the aristocracy or from the 'Popolo', that is, the commercial and craft bourgeoisie.[85] In its social recruitment, Italian sanctity was not strictly speaking 'democratic', even though the proportion of saints belonging to the peasantry or the urban working class was significantly higher than elsewhere (19 as compared with 10 per cent), but it nevertheless had a generally less elitist character than that of the rest of Christendom. A more detailed study than the global statistical approach of Weinstein and Bell would probably show that the majority of saints of modest origins were anchorites or recluses; it was the strength of the eremitical tradition that allowed local sainthood to retain a significant popular base. In the towns, the saints were more 'bourgeois'; it was above all penitents and Mendicant brethren, who, between 1220 and 1500, formed the big battalions of Italian sainthood, and they were mostly from well-off families.

It is also clear from the work of Weinstein and Bell that the links

raphique récente', *RHE*, 63 (1968), pp. 826–34, and, above all, S. Boesch Gajano, 'La "Bibliotheca sanctorum". Problemi di agiografia medievale', *RSCI*, 26 (1972), pp. 139–53.

[85] I will mention only the two St Beatrices of Este, d. 1226 and 1262, Benedictine nuns; Simon of Collazzone (d. 1250), a Franciscan, son of a countess; Benignus of Medici (d. 1472), a hermit. But persons of high rank were few. The desire to place their subjects in the 'happy medium' of the 'Popolo' is clear in the hagiographies; see, for example, the beginning of the *Vita* of B. Raymond 'Palmerio' of Piacenza (d. 1200), ed. *AA.SS.* Iul. VI, p. 640: 'parentes habuit nec illustris originis nec viles admodum sed cives privatos . . . nec pauperes nec opulentos'.

Table 7 *Political influence of the saints (1200–1500) as a function of their family background*

Degree of influence of the saints	Italian %	Non-Italian %	Number of cases
Important	10	20	78
Considerable	6	11	43
Not negligible	5	21	69
None	79	48	295

between Italian saints and those in power were much less close than elsewhere, which would tend to suggest that specifically religious factors played a larger role in the perception of sainthood.[86]

We should not, however, conclude from table 7 that Italian sainthood was 'apolitical' or removed from the realities of this world. On the contrary, many of those venerated in Italy at this period exercised some influence on political structures and endeavoured to use it to change contemporary society. But the fact that, in Italy, barely one fifth of saints were involved through their family background in the exercise of power, compared with over half in the rest of Christendom, confirms that the recruitment of the medieval Italian 'pantheon' was much less dependent than elsewhere on membership of elevated and influential social circles.

Lastly, if we divide the saints according to the main activity they engaged in during their lifetime, we also find interesting results, though the accuracy of the figures leaves much to be desired, given the difficulty, in some cases, of distinguishing social origin (nobility) from function (clergy or peasants).[87]

Table 8 brings out the essentially lay character of Italian sainthood (only 35 per cent of the saints were clerics, compared with 45 per cent in the rest of Christendom). However, we cannot distinguish seculars from regulars, as both are included in the category 'lower clergy'; a more precise distribution would probably reveal the preponderance of the Mendicant orders among Italian ecclesiastical saints.

Debatable though the conclusions based on these statistics may be, in detail, they nevertheless enable us to confirm, at the global level, certain impressions which strike anyone who embarks on a study of local Italian

[86] Weinstein and Bell, 'Saints and society', p. 187.
[87] *Ibid.*, p. 185.

Table 8 *Occupations of the saints in early life (1200–1500)*

Activity of the saints in early life	Italian %	Non-Italian %	Number of cases
Royalty	1	9	27
Nobility	10	7	39
Prelates	10	16	65
Lower clergy	25	29	131
Skilled workers	17	14	74
Peasants	21	10	71
Too young or unknown	16	15	78

sainthood. While in most of Christendom, the distribution of saints between the different social groups is in inverse relation to their numerical importance, bringing to mind an inverted pyramid, in Italy, the imbalance between the actual size of the different classes and their position in local sainthood is much less pronounced. Admittedly, the bourgeoisie and, above all, the 'upper middle class' are significantly over-represented, whilst the lower classes account for a smaller proportion of saints than one would expect if the two scales were exactly to coincide. But the distortions are slight compared with those found at the same period in the rest of the West, where kings and members of the high aristocracy took the lion's share, leaving only a tiny place to the lower classes, from bourgeoisie to peasantry. We may therefore describe local sanctity in Italy as popular, in the sense that the choice of saints was made in a way which was approximately in line with the composition of society, whilst in the rest of Christendom it favoured the ruling classes to the detriment of all others.

There is one last characteristic distinguishing Mediterranean sainthood. Whereas elsewhere in Christendom the saints often came from families of saints and their biographers tried to show, sometimes against all the odds, that they belonged to illustrious lineages, the Italian saint appears always as a *homo novus*, who owes his sainthood only to God and his own merits. Far from concealing the obscurity of their birth, many hagiographers made a virtue of it, as if the better to emphasize both the efficacy of grace and the perfection of their subject.[88] At all events, there was no mention

---

[88] Thus, in the Life of the B. Oringa Menabuoi (d. 1310): 'hanc enim Dominus infimam iuxta seculi conditionem elegit ut summam suae potentie indicaret': I. Lami, 'Vita della B. Oringa Cristiana', in *Deliciae eruditorum*, XVIII (Florence, 1769), p. 191.

of the hereditary transmission of any charisma. Further, in the thirteenth century especially, access to sainthood seemed to involve a rupture with the earthly family, in particular the father. We see here the influence of the Franciscan model, strikingly illustrated by the Poverello, St Clare of Assisi, John Pelingotto of Urbino etc. But if these conflictual episodes quickly became a hagiographical commonplace, they nevertheless still corresponded to a lived reality, as shown, for example, by the experience of Salimbene and Thomas Aquinas, both of whom had to flee the paternal roof before they could embark on the religious life they wished for within the Mendicant orders.[89] Admittedly, many Italian saints felt the need to become part of an order or spiritual family, whether as monks or tertiaries. But this attachment, which went with imitation of the model offered by the sanctity of the founder (*sanctus Franciscus forma Minorum*), was the result of an engagement freely entered into, not ties of blood or the press-ure of family solidarity. The medieval Italian saint was not an heir but a 'self-made man'.

A hierarchy without prestige

If we accept the hypothesis of a more or less close correlation between the political and social structures of a given country and the forms of sainthood which emerged there, it will come as no surprise to observe that late medieval Italy produced no cult of a king or queen. This is not to say that no sovereign or princess was ever venerated in the peninsula between the late twelfth and the early fifteenth centuries. The large body of icono-graphical evidence illustrating devotion to St Louis of Anjou shows that it would be wrong to see the compatriots of Dante as insensible to the prestige of the monarchical model, even if, in this particular case, the son of the king was concealed under a Franciscan habit and episcopal trap-pings.[90] But his cult was imported, and among the native saints, those who possessed temporal power played no role as such.

It is more surprising to observe how few bishops figured among the recent saints venerated in the Mediterranean countries at this period, whilst elsewhere in Christendom they formed the largest group. The only

---

[89] M. Goodich, 'Childhood and adolescence among the thirteenth-century saints', *History of Childhood Quarterly*, 1 (1973), pp. 285–309.

[90] Bertaux, 'Les Saints Louis dans l'art italien', pp. 616–44; B. Kleinschmidt, 'St Ludwig von Toulouse in der Kunst', *AFH*, 2 (1909), pp. 197–215. The paintings and iconograph-ical cycles are described in Kaftal 1, cc. 634–8.

188 TYPOLOGY OF MEDIEVAL SAINTHOOD

Italian prelate to have been the subject of a process of canonization was the bishop of Vicenza, John Cacciafronte (d. 1183), whose cult developed after 1223, once several miracles had occurred at his tomb. But popular pressure on behalf of the cause of this doughty defender of the rights of the Church, struck down by a rebellious vassal, cannot have been very strong, since the enquiry, held at Cremona and Vicenza in 1223–4 on the orders of Honorius III, came to nothing and it seems that his fame had not spread beyond the boundaries of the diocese.[91] Another enquiry was instituted by the same pope into the life and miracles of a former bishop of Furcona (= L'Aquila), Rainerius (d. 1077), but with no more success.[92] From other evidence, in particular hagiographical literature, we know that some prelates enjoyed a well-established local *fama sanctitatis*. They include Hugh of Volterra (d. 1184), whose cult was immediate and enjoyed official recognition from 1197 in the form of a grant of indulgences to those who visited his tomb.[93] But these three cases all concern men who lived before the thirteenth century. After 1200, the attribution of sainthood to diocesan prelates became even less common, to disappear completely in the fourteenth century. Among the rare bishops whose cult is still attested at the local level at this period, we may note Rinaldo of Nocera Umbra (d. 1222),[94] Albert Prandoni of Ferrara (d. 1279), to whom miracles were attributed after his death, but who was vilified by Salimbene in his Chronicle,[95] Benvenuto Scotivoli of Osimo (d. 1282),[96] and Raynaldus of Concorezzo, archbishop of Ravenna (d. 1321).[97] This is not many, even if we add the names of a few obscure prelates, compared with the hundreds of lay saints and 'frati' who began to be accorded a cult at this

---

[91] *AA.SS.* Mar. II, pp. 943–4; Schiavo, *B. Giovanni Cacciafronte.*

[92] Honorius III, *Mirificans misericordias*, I.10.1225, Pressutti, 5672.

[93] *AA.SS.* Sept. III, pp. 296–309; M. Bocci, sv Ugo, vescovo di Volterra, in *BS*, XII (Rome, 1969), cc. 780–2.

[94] G. Sigismondi, 'La Legenda beati Raynaldi e il suo valore storico', *Bollettino della deputazione di storia patria per l'Umbria*, 56 (1960), pp. 1–111. Written in the fourteenth century, the legend is a plagiarism of the *Vita Martini* and other hagiographical texts. See also *AA.SS.* Feb. II, pp. 372ff; G. Sigismondi, sv Rinaldo, vescovo di Nocera Umbra, in *BS*, XI (Rome, 1968), cc. 199–204.

[95] Salimbene, *Cronica*, I, p. 462. There is no contemporary biography of this bishop, whose local cult was never strong; see *AA.SS.* Aug. III, pp. 160–3; A. Balboni, sv Prandoni, Alberto, in *BS*, X (Rome 1968), cc. 1089–92.

[96] *AA.SS.* Mar. III, pp. 390–3. There is no Life of this saint, whose canonization was requested in vain in 1284 by the commune of Osimo: G. Odoardi. sv Benvenuto Scotivali, in *BS*, II (Rome, 1962), cc. 1252–3; Kaftal 2, cc. 189–90.

[97] Raynaldus of Concorezzo seems to have enjoyed real popularity after his death, and his cult is well attested in Romagna: *AA.SS.* Aug. III, pp. 668ff; L. Samarati, sv Rinaldo da Concorezzo, in *BS*, XI (Rome, 1968), cc. 192–8.

period in the peninsula. This situation is all the more remarkable in that it contrasts with the great popularity which holy bishops had enjoyed in the same regions in the eleventh and twelfth centuries, as we see from the canonizations of Peter of Anagni (d. 1109) by Paschal II in 1110, Gerard of Potenza (d. 1119) by Calixtus II in 1123 or 1124, and Ubald of Gubbio (d. 1191) by Celestine III in 1192. It is as if the model of episcopal sainthood, having shone brightly at the period of Church Reform and the battles between Church and Empire, then lost its appeal.[98] This phenomenon is probably related to the contemporary political and social context. Communal autonomy was, after all, in many cases, acquired at the expense of the bishops. To exalt the merits of some of them would have been to enhance the prestige of what was often, for the mass of the faithful, the enemy. Further, most Italian towns were already under the patronage of illustrious holy bishops, whose cult often went back to the first centuries of the Church: Ambrose at Milan, Cyr (Siro) at Pavia, Petronius at Bologna, Constant and Herculien (Ercolano) at Perugia, Juvenal at Narni etc. The cities, and soon the communes, were therefore amply provided with protectors of episcopal rank, which reduced the need to add to these intercessors, who were still deeply venerated, new patron saints belonging to the same category.[99]

The often difficult relations between the episcopate and the Mendicant orders, principal creators of new cults in the thirteenth and fourteenth centuries, and the latter's growing popular influence, reduced even further the instances where the conduct of the bishops won the general admiration without which it was difficult for a cult to develop after their death. It has recently been shown that, of the sixty-one contemporary bishops mentioned by the Italian Franciscan Salimbene in his Chronicle, only sixteen are presented in a favourable light (*honestus*, *magnificus*, *bonus*), and six described as *sanctus*. Yet this judgement applied to their morals and, in two cases, those of the French Franciscan Eudes Rigaud and the English Robert Grosseteste, to bishops from outside the Mediterranean world. The majority of Italian prelates, in contrast, were criticized for their weakness on the doctrinal plane and their inability to preach, when their faults

---

[98] For the prestige of the model of episcopal sanctity in Latium between 1050 and 1150, see Toubert, *Latium médiéval*, II, pp. 806–40.

[99] H. C. Peyer, *Stadt und Stadtpatron im mittelalterlichen Italien* (Zurich, 1955); *La coscienza cittadina nei comuni italiani del Duecento (XI convegno del centro di studi sulla spiritualità medievale, Todi 1970)* (Todi, 1972), especially A. M. Orselli, 'Spirito cittadino e temi politico-culturali nel culto di San Petronio', pp. 283–343.

were not more serious, such as *avaritia* or their liking for the *gula*.[100] Though Salimbene cannot be regarded as an objective witness, his anti-establishment and critical attitude probably echoed that of many of his compatriots who, far from letting themselves be impressed by the dignity of the office, showed themselves very alive to the inadequacies of the persons. Caught between a papacy which was too close, communal authorities which distrusted him and regulars who wielded greater influence, the Italian bishop of the thirteenth and fourteenth centuries was usually lacking in prestige and excluded from the group from which the people chose its heroes and intercessors.[101]

The way of renunciation

In the Mediterranean countries, in the later Middle Ages, the *vox populi*, source of reputations for sanctity, chose not sovereigns or the great of this world, or even good bishops, but preferred men or women of modest, if not obscure, origins, who impressed their contemporaries by the sufferings they endured during their lifetime for the love of God and their neighbour. The link between suffering and sainthood, the importance of which we have already noted elsewhere in Christendom, was no less close, but it took different forms: in the first case, the perception of sanctity was based on violent death and bloodshed, that is a fate suffered, even if accepted in faith; in the latter, what counted were the ordeals the servants of God voluntarily inflicted on themselves throughout their earthly existence.

Asceticism and sainthood

Saints were primarily distinguished by a series of denials which were popularly regarded as both the signs and the conditions of perfection: indifference to worldly goods, renunciation of the pleasures of the senses, relinquishment of all personal will in a profound desire for humility. From

---

[100] Mariano d'Alatri, 'Il vescovo nella Cronaca di Salimbene di Parma', *Collectanea Franciscana*, 42 (1972), pp. 5–38. For relations between bishops and the Mendicant orders in thirteenth-century Italy, see R. Manselli, 'I vescovi italiani, gli ordini religiosi e i movimenti popolari', in *Vescovi e diocesi in Italia nel Medio Evo* (Padua, 1975), pp. 315–35.

[101] See the remarks of R. Brentano, *Two Churches*, pp. 180–210. Also, the Italian bishops of the thirteenth and fourteenth centuries were hardly persecuted by the civil authorities and could not be seen as martyrs.

this perspective, the touchstone of sanctity was neither birth nor function fulfilled in the Church or society, but the degree of penitence attained in practice. The witnesses at processes of canonization in these regions resorted to formulas such as 'fuit homo bone vite' or 'fuit homo sancte conversationis'. When these very vague phrases were explained, it emerges that they generally referred to voluntary mortification or renunciation.[102] There was a universal conviction that the more a life was ascetic, that is, unlike that of ordinary mortals, the more pleasing it was to God. Even if he lived in this world, the saint ought to behave as, in effect, a 'spiritual' man, whose actions were a perpetual source of wonder and soon awe to those around him. Perfection was first measured by the degree of austerity with regard to food; the length of fasts and intensity of privations were its most obvious signs. This explains why hagiographers and witnesses at processes of canonization put so much emphasis on the exploits accomplished by their subjects in this sphere.[103] But mortification did not have the same significance for those who inflicted it on themselves and those who looked on. The former wished to chastise their body in order to make it expiate for past faults and to master it; the latter were more alive to the result brought about by such practices, almost automatically in their eyes. Humiliated and mortified in his flesh, the saint restored in himself, here below, his original innocence; asceticism erased the marks of sin and conferred on his body the power to perform miracles, in his lifetime as well as after death. This was the experience described, precisely and soberly, by a witness at the canonization process of Peter of Morrone, when he told how he had first met the hermit of Maiella: 'each time he showed himself to the people, at the mere sight of his face, no-one present could refrain from devotion from weeping tears of contrition and being racked with sobs'. He himself, seeing his emaciated and torn face, had 'felt the hairs on his head stand on end . . . and if he had not been

---

[102] At the canonization process of the hermit John Bonus (d. 1249), ed. *AA.SS.* Oct. IX, p. 825, a witness declared: 'propter vitam asperam quam ducebat in heremo suo, dictus frater Iohannes Bonus reputabatur ab omnibus gentibus de Cesena et confinibus eius sanctus'. For a history of medieval asceticism, see L. Gougaud, *Dévotions et pratiques ascétiques au Moyen Age* (Maredsous, 1929).

[103] From this standpoint, a man who ate and drank normally could not be a saint, whatever his other virtues. St Francis of Assisi, exasperated by the saintly reputation he had acquired, was confident he could destroy it by declaring to the crowd which came to his hermitage at Poggio Bustone, near Rieti: 'You come to me with great devotion, believing me to be a holy man, but I confess to God and to you that, during this last Lent, I ate food prepared with pork fat': Desbonnets and Vorreux, *Saint François d'Assise*, p. 1069.

prevented by the tie of marriage, he would there and then have donned the habit of his religious order'.[104] Another witness added that 'those who saw him were filled with a spiritual joy, as if they had seen God'.[105] The meaning of this last remark is clarified when it is compared with another statement concerning Peter of Morrone: 'He led a life of such strict abstinence and privations that he seemed to be kept alive by a special effect of divine grace.'[106] This phrase is particularly significant because it shows how the mental transition was made from the natural to the supernatural, and from the human to the divine. Beyond a certain level of asceticism, survival was only possible, it was believed, thanks to a direct intervention by God, compensating, in some mysterious way, for the absence of food, and thereby according a sign of election to whoever enjoyed such a favour.[107]

But asceticism was not restricted to privations. It consisted also of voluntarily inflicting suffering on oneself, the least of which was that caused by wearing a hair shirt. The saints of these regions usually slept on the bare ground, making do with a stone for pillow. Some went further and invented additional refinements. This was the case with the hermits, as we see from the example of Lawrence of Subiaco (d. 1243), called Lawrence Loricatus because of the iron breastplate he always wore, which dug into his chest, as well as metal hoops lined with points which pierced his head when he dozed off.[108] Admittedly, St Lawrence came from Apulia and so was part of a tradition marked by eastern influences, well attested by the eleventh century in the person of St Dominic Loricatus (d. 1060),

---

[104] *PC Peter of Morrone*, ed. F. X. Seppelt, 'Die Akten des Kanonisationsprozesses in dem Codex zu Sulmona', in *Monumenta Coelestiniana* (Paderborn, 1921), p. 211.

[105] *PC Peter of Morrone*, p. 230.

[106] *Ibid.*, p. 329.

[107] At the process of the hermit John Bonus of Mantua, a witness said: 'nisi Spiritus Sanctus et gratia Dei nutrissent et sustentassent dictum fratrem Iohannem Bonum, numquam vixisset': *PC John Bonus*, ed. *AA.SS.* Oct. IX, p. 830. A similar claim was made with regard to St Clare of Montefalco: see the *articuli interrogatorii*, 77 and 79 of the process of 1319 in *ASV, Ritti*, Proc. 2929, fol. 606.

[108] *PC Lawrence Loricatus*, ed. W. Gnandt, *Vita S. Cleridoniae virginis, B. Laurentii anachoretae necnon et servi Dei Hippolyti Pugnetti monachi* (Innsbruck, 1902), pp. 67–99, especially pp. 68–9: 'utebatur lorica sub tunica et . . . circulos ferreos gestabat ad nudum duos quolibet bracchio et in cruribus et tibiis similiter quatuor; et circa ventrem unum habebat. In capite vero unum circulum gestabat habentem in superiore parte duas virgas ferreas transversas in modum crucis quarum una pendebat ab occipite usque ad frontem, altera ab aure usque ad aurem pertingebat in quibus pendebant duae laminae ferreae ab utraque parte utramque tangentes mandibulam, in quarum qualibet quinque clavi affixi erant ab intus habentes aculeos ut, quando caput deponere volebat ad dormiendum penitus ab iisdem citius expergiscerentur, quare coactus erat, appodiatus rupi, stando somnum capere.'

which persisted to the end of the Middle Ages and even beyond in southern and central Italy.[109] Though not all the saints of the Mediterranean regions went to such extremes, there were few who were not distinguished in the eyes of their contemporaries by an exceptional practice of mortification. It was usually on the basis of such acts that a saintly reputation was built. If they were absent, or if there were no witnesses, public opinion remained passive and indifferent, even if it was assured by the ecclesiastical hierarchy that a particular person was an authentic saint. It might, on the other hand, be fired by someone held in low regard by the clergy, but who had led a 'holy life' in the eyes of the faithful.[110]

A whole stratum of local Italian sainthood, and that which was most deeply entrenched, consisted of hermits, recluses and, more generally, people distinguished by the practice of extreme asceticism. Among monks and nuns, the only ones to be venerated at this period in Italy were members of semi-eremitical congregations like the Camaldolese and Vallombrosans, or monks who had left their monastery in order to lead a solitary life.[111] But however great the prestige of clerical eremitism in some

---

[109] See the *Vita* written by St Peter Damien (= *BHL* 239), ed. *AA.SS.* Oct. VI, pp. 621–7. For the survival of this ascetic tendency into the eighteenth century, see G. De Rosa, 'Sainteté, clergé et peuple dans le Mezzogiorno italien', *Revue d'histoire de la spiritualité*, 52 (1976), pp. 245–64.

[110] See, for example, the conflict between the inhabitants and the Dominicans of Forlì concerning the sanctity of the (Dominican) B. Marcolino (d. 1397), discussed below, pp. 405–6.

[111] Many Camaldolese monks were regarded as saints: see the collection of documents in G. B. Mitarelli and A. Costadoni, *Annales Camaldulenses*, 9 vols. (Venice, 1755–73). This work needs to be used with care, as its authors have annexed to their congregation a number of lay hermits and recluses who probably had no connection with it. Among authentic Camaldolese saints, the most famous for our period are Parisio of Treviso (d. 1267), whose canonization was sought in vain by the commune of Treviso between 1268 and 1346 (G. B. Mitarelli, *Memorie della vita de S. Parisio* (Venice, 1748)) and B. Pellegrino of Camaldoli (d. 1291), whose visions were transcribed by Brother Simon (*AA.SS.* Iun. I, p. 370; *Annales Camaldulenses*, IV, pp. 184ff). For Vallombrosan hagiography, see S. Boesch Gajano, 'Storia e tradizione vallombrosana', *BISIME*, 76 (1964), pp. 99–215. We should not forget the importance of female Vallombrosan monasticism, one of whose glories was B. Umiltà of Faenza (d. 1310), who, after a period as a recluse, became a nun and founder of the monastery of St John the Evangelist in Florence (*AA.SS.* Maii V, pp. 205–12; Kaftal 1, cc. 487–96). The few Benedictines who were the subject of a cult at this period were, in fact, hermits, such as B. Franco of Assergi (d. early thirteenth century), who lived as a solitary on the slopes of the Gran Sasso (*AA.SS.* Iun. I, pp. 544–7; *PC*, Paris, BN, H.929), or recluses such as Justin Francucci-Bezzoli (d. 1319), venerated at Arezzo (*AA.SS.* Mar. II, pp. 242–5). The reformed – in the sense of more ascetic – congregations such as the Silvestrins also produced a few saints. Note, in addition to their founder, Silvester Guzzolini (d. 1267), whose cult was very popular in the Marches (Bolzonetti, *Il Monte Fano e un grande anacoreta*), Hugh of Sassoferrato (d. 1250) (*PC* (Sassoferrato, 1756), Paris, BN, H.964, *Summarium*, pp. 17–22, 56–60) and John of the Staff (d. 1290) (*PC* (Fabriano, 1758) ASV, *Riti*, Proc. 698, fols. 112–44v).

regions, the majority of the ascetic saints who were the object of a cult in the later Middle Ages were from the laity. The whole period was a sort of Golden Age of eremitical sainthood, but we need to distinguish between the anchorites of the late twelfth and thirteenth centuries and those who lived after 1348. The former came mostly from very modest backgrounds, since the life-style and spirituality of the hermit was particularly well suited to the religious needs of the inhabitants of the countryside and mountains.[112] The latter came from more elevated circles; they were often men from the bourgeoisie, even sometimes the aristocracy, who had fled the large towns to find in the fields or forest a remedy for the ills then afflicting society and the Church.[113] Another distinction, which does not necessarily tally with the first, needs to be made between a 'wild' eremitism, independent of any religious community, and that which developed in more or less close association with a monastery or convent. We may confidently include in the first category local saints of central Italy such as Gerard of Villamagna (d. 1242), near Florence,[114] Torello of Poppi (d. 1282), in the mountains of Casentino,[115] Marzio of Gualdo Tadino (d. 1301), who, with a few disciples, occupied the *locus* situated on the wooded hills dominating the town which had been abandoned by the Friars Minor,[116] Giolo (Iolus) of Sellano, near Spoleto (d. *c*.1315)[117] and Martin

---

[112] E. Delaruelle, 'Les ermites et la spiritualité populaire', in *L'Eremitisme in Occidente nei secoli XI e XII, Atti della seconda settimana di studio, La Mendola, 1962* (Milan, 1965), pp. 212–47, repr. in Delaruelle, *La piété populaire au Moyen Age* (Turin, 1975), pp. 125–54; thirteenth-century eremitism has, unfortunately, been little studied.

[113] For the renewed popularity of eremitism, especially in the upper ranks of society, see the early chapters of F. Antal, *Florentine painting and its social background* (London, 1947); M. Meiss, *Painting in Florence and Siena after the Black Death: the arts, religion and society in the mid-fourteenth century* (New York, 1964).

[114] The only *Vita* is sixteenth century (ed. *AA.SS.* Maii III, pp. 247–50), but there is medieval evidence of the success of his cult in Tuscany, and we know that a whole cycle of frescoes was devoted to his life and miracles in the parish church of San Donnino in Villamagna: *AA.SS.* Maii III, p. 245; *Posito super cultu B. Gerardi de Villamagna* (Rome, 1832); Kaftal 1, cc. 447–9. He was long, wrongly, believed to be a Franciscan tertiary; M. Bertagna ('Sul terz'ordine francescano in Toscana nel sec. XIII, note storiche e considerazioni', in *L'ordine della penitenza di San Francesco d'Assisi (Assisi, 1972)*, ed. O. Schmucki (Rome, 1973), p. 268) confirms that he was only later attached to the Third Order of Minors.

[115] For a contemporary Latin Life, see *AA.SS.* Mar. II, pp. 499–505 (= *BHL* 8305); also documents collected in G. G. Goretti-Ministi, *Vita di San Torello da Poppi* (Rome, 1926), especially pp. 48ff. For his iconography, see Kaftal 1, c. 992.

[116] His story is known from an unpublished *Vita* in the Legendry of San Francesco of Gualdo (author unknown), of which I have prepared an edition. See F. Dolbeau, 'Le Légendier de San Francesco de Gualdo: tentative de reconstitution', *Bollettino della deputazione di storia patria per l'Umbria*, 72 (1976), pp. 157–75, especially p. 173.

[117] *AA.SS.* Iun. II, pp. 252–5. In the same area, we may note the existence of Hugolino of Bevagna (d. 1350), founder of a hermitage which later became an abbey: M. Sensi, sv Ugolino, in *BS*, XII (Rome, 1969), cc. 784–7.

of Genoa (d. 1343), who sought solitude on a reef of the Riviera di
Ponente.[118] There were also many solitaries in southern Italy and Sicily,
such as Nicholas of Santa Maria a Circolo (d. 1310), near Naples,[119] and
William of Scicli (d. 1404) near Noto,[120] and also in Lombardy, for
example Miro de Canzo (d. *c.*1380).[121] There were even female hermits,
such as Ugolina of Biliemme, near Verceil (d. 1300), though she remained
an exception.[122] The second group included men such as Lawrence Loricatus (d. 1243), who had close ties with the monks of Subiaco,[123] and
John Bonus (d. 1249), founder of the 'Zambonini', who, by amalgamating
with other communities of eremitical origin, gave birth to the order of the
Hermits of St Augustine.[124] It is striking that these two saints were the
subject of a process of canonization, whereas no 'wild' hermit was deemed
worthy of this honour in the late Middle Ages.

For women, the normal form of solitary religious life was not eremitism
but reclusion, which was particularly common in Italy in the towns. Many
virgins and widows in search of perfection took refuge in cells adjoining
churches or monasteries, or built along the city walls.[125] We can get some
idea of the way of life of these *mulieres incarcerate* from contemporary
documents such as the *Vita sanctae Viridianae*, written in the thirteenth
century by a Florentine cleric in honour of the recluse Verdiana of Castelfiorentino (d. 1241).[126] Her history is, in fact, typical: born of poor parents
in a small town in the Florentine *contado*, she first looked after flocks then
worked as a domestic servant in the house of a rich relative and made a
pilgrimage to Santiago and Rome with other women. On her return, she
built a little cell near a church dedicated to St Antony, which had recently

---

[118] *AA.SS.* Apr. I, pp. 102–5.
[119] *AA.SS.* Maii II, pp. 705ff; G. A. Galante, *Memorie del B. Nicola eremita di Santa Maria
a Circolo in Napoli* (Naples, 1877).
[120] E. Sigona, sv Guglielmo di Noto, in *BS*, VII (Rome, 1966), cc. 477–8.
[121] Miro lived near Lake Como: *AA.SS.* Maii II, pp. 601–9.
[122] *AA.SS.* Aug. II, pp. 395–8; Lodovico della Croce, *La Vita di S. Ugolina vergine di
Vercelli* (Milan, 1665), which includes passages from a lost fourteenth-century Life.
[123] R. Grégoire, sv Laurent l'encuirassé, in *Dictionnaire de spiritualité*, IX (Paris, 1976), cc.
392–3; *PC*, ed. Gnandt.
[124] B. Van Luijk, *Gli eremiti neri nel Dugento . . . Origine, sviluppo e unione* (Pisa, 1968),
especially pp. 67–84; *PC*.
[125] In the absence of a general study, see A. Bartoli Langeli, 'I penitenti a Spoleto nel
Duecento', in *L'ordine della penitenza*, ed. Schmucki, pp. 303–30, which is mostly concerned with the *religiosae mulieres* of Montefalco and Monteluco.
[126] O. Pogni, ed., *Vita di S. Verdiana d'incognito autore . . . compilata dal fiorentino monac
Biagio* (Empoli, 1936), reviewed in *Anal. Boll.*, 54 (1936), p. 464; Pogni, *La gloriosa
vergine romita di Castelfiorentino: vita, chiesa, spedale di S. Verdiana* (Castelfiorentino,
1934), reviewed in *Anal. Boll.*, 54 (1936), pp. 261–2. A second Life, written *c.*1420 by
the Dominican Lorenzo Giacomini, based on the first, is in *AA.SS.* Feb. I, pp. 257–61.

been built *extra castrum*. She soon acquired a reputation for sanctity, because she was regularly attacked in her cell by snakes which the local people eventually killed. Her ascetic exploits and ardour in prayer earned her a visit from Archbishop Ardingo of Florence. She died having spent thirty-four years in her cell, and was soon venerated locally as a saint. An altar was dedicated to her, where her remains were laid, and the church soon bore her name. She was invoked in particular against snake-bites, which explains why her tomb became a place of pilgrimage.[127] Very close to Verdiana in space and time was the recluse Joan of Signa (d. 1307), who has also incorrectly been enrolled in the Franciscan Third Order by the order's hagiographers.[128] To us, these beguines may seem obscure, but they were the object of an intense and enduring local cult, as we can see today from the fifteenth-century cycle of frescoes entirely devoted to the life and miracles of B. Joan in the parish church of Signa, near Florence.[129] We know, too, that a confraternity in this small town was placed under her patronage, an honour rarely accorded to recent and uncanonized saints.[130]

In the fourteenth century, female 'reclusive' sainthood continued, as we see from the Life and cult of B. Clare of Rimini (d. 1326), well known thanks to a rich hagiographical tradition and the works devoted to her by her compatriot Garampi, who assembled and studied all the documents concerning her which still survived in the mid-eighteenth century.[131] B. Joan, too, was claimed by the Franciscan order, but there can be no doubt that she was an 'independent' recluse, who at first lived alone, then with a small community in cells built along the walls of Rimini.[132] A fourteenth-century *Vita* presents her as a beguine who worked for a living and begged

[127] I. Moretti and R. Stopani, 'Santa Verdiana a Castelfiorentino', *Antichità viva*, 11 (1972), pp. 29–34; N. Del Re, sv Verdiana, in *BS*, XII (Rome, 1969), cc. 1023–7.
[128] The fourteenth-century *Vita* (ed. S. Mencherini, *AFH*, 10 (1917), pp. 378–86) makes no mention of her membership of the Franciscan third order. Most of these fictional attachments are the work of Brother Mariano of Florence (1474–1523), whose *Compendium chronicarum ordinis Fratrum Minorum*, published 1909–11 in *AFH*, has long exercised a baleful influence over hagiographers and historians.
[129] See Kaftal 1, cc. 539–49. Tuscan churches have preserved the memory of many saints of this type in their iconographical decoration, such as Fina in San Gimignano (d. 1253), Julia in Certaldo (d. 1367) etc.
[130] There was a *Societas beate Johanne de Signa* at Signa in 1385, and a *Societas Sancti Spiritus de sancta Viridiana* at Castelfiorentino in 1350: C. M. de La Roncière, 'La place des confréries dans l'encadrement religieux du contado florentin au XIVe siècle, II, Appendices', *MEFR*, 85 (1973), pp. 639, 659.
[131] Garampi, *Beata Chiara di Rimini*; her canonization process (Rimini, 1694–7, 1782–3) is in *ASV*, Riti, Proc. 88 and Paris, BN, H.820–1.
[132] Garampi, *Beata Chiara di Rimini*, pp. 79–150.

9 Dominican saints and blesseds (Master of the Dominican
Effigies, sacristy, Santa Maria Novella, Florence)

10 Canonized saints with halo: on the left, St Thomas Aquinas, on the right, St Dominic (Master of the Dominican Effigies, detail, sacristy, Santa Maria Novella, Florence)

11 B. John of Schio (= John of Vicenza, OP, d. 1256 or 1260) (Tommaso
da Modena, c.1352, Saint Nicholas of Treviso)

12 Dominican saints and blesseds: Peter de Palude, Albert the Great and Raymond of Peñafort (Fra Angelico, chapter house of St Mark's, Florence)

13 Iconographical glorification of a local uncanonized saint: B. Fina of San Gimignano: St Gregory the Great appears to B. Fina (Domenico Ghirlandaio, *c.*1473, Collegiate church, San Gimignano)

14 The Mendicant orders and the exaltation of their saints: triptych with Crucifixion and six Franciscan saints, from left to right, SS Elizabeth, Clare, Francis, Louis of Anjou and Antony of Padua and B. Gerard of Villamagna (Zannono di Pietro, early fifteenth century, Palazzo communale, Rieti)

15 Four Sienese saints: B. Ambrose Sansedoni, SS Bernardino and Catherine of Siena
and B. Peter Pettinaio (Vecchietta, reliquary lid, 1445, Pinacoteca, Siena)

16 The murder of St Thomas Becket (1170) (embroidered mitre, English, c.1200, Bayerisches Nationalmuseum, Munich)

when necessary; she wore a striped gown of coarse cloth and, like the
hermits, fasted and severely mortified herself, for example wearing a hair
shirt and bands of iron next to her skin. Her spirituality seems to have
been explicitly and constantly focussed on meditation on the Passion of
Christ, whose sufferings and humiliations she tried to relive, for example
by having herself tied to a pillar and whipped by her companions on Good
Friday.[133]

Since it is not my purpose to compile an exhaustive inventory of all the
cults, but to identify the types of sanctity in favour at the local level, I
will content myself with these few examples. It would be wrong to see
them as isolated or exceptional figures.[134] In the Mediterranean region,
the level of sanctity I earlier called 'popular' was weak and the emotion
aroused by the shedding of innocent blood was not enough to give rise to
a popular 'canonization'.[135] In contrast, the devotion of the faithful was
spontaneously aroused by men and women who endeavoured to reproduce
in their life and their body the sufferings of Christ.

What some saints sought in solitude and reclusion, others found in the
peregrinatio religiosa. Pilgrims played an important role in the local sainthood of the Mediterranean regions. Journeys made for God constituted
an almost indispensable element in the sanctification of the laity and
played an important role in the life of saints like the hermits and the
penitents; both Verdiana of Castelfiorentino and Facio of Cremona, before
dedicating themselves entirely to mortification or works of charity, were
first pilgrims who travelled the roads to Santiago de Compostella and
Rome.[136] But, in town and country, persons whose sole merit was to have
led a travelling life for a more or less protracted period were also venerated. Schematically, one can distinguish two types of pilgrim saints: some
were pious persons who attracted the attention of their compatriots by

[133] The Life, translated into Italian, is *ibid.*, pp. 1–76; see also pp. 234ff.
[134] Of other saints of this type, we may quote, in Italy, B. Fina of San Gimignano (d. 1253),
whose fourteenth-century Life by the Dominican Giovanni del Coppo is in *AA.SS.* Mar.
II, pp. 236–41 (see also A. Dondaine, 'La vie et les oeuvres de Jean de San Gimignano',
AFP, 9 (1939), pp. 165–8), and B. Julia of Certaldo (d. 1367) (A. M. Giacomini, sv
Rena, Giulia della, in *BS*, XI (Rome, 1968), cc. 115–16); in Provence, B. Douceline (d.
1274), who lived among Franciscans and founded a community of reclusive beguines
near Marseilles: R. Gout, *La Vie de Sainte Douceline, texte provençal du XIVe siècle* (Paris,
1927); B. de Gaiffier, sv Douceline (sainte), in *Dictionnaire de spiritualité*, III (Paris, 1957),
cc. 1672–3; for her spirituality, see C. Carozzi, 'Une béguine joachimite: Douceline, soeur
d'Hugues de Digne', in *Franciscains d'Oc: les Spirituels, ca. 1280–1324* (Toulouse, 1975),
pp. 169–201.
[135] See above, p. 151.
[136] See above, p. 195 and below, p. 201.

their repeated visits to the principal Christian sanctuaries, such as Bona of Pisa (d. 1207), who had been nine times to Compostella, if we are to believe her biographer.[137]

Most prestigous, however, were those who had made a pilgrimage to the Holy Land, who, in Italy, were given the surname 'Palmerio'.[138] The second and larger category consisted of foreigners who died during the course of their travels. Though the murdered pilgrim remained an exception, the pilgrim from England or Germany or Languedoc who died of disease or exhaustion in an Italian town was, in contrast, very common.[139] An aura of mystery surrounded such people, which made it possible to graft on to the single incontrovertible fact – their death on the road – all sorts of more or less fictitious stories or traditions. To ennoble these obscure saints, about whom by definition nothing was known, their hagiographers liked to make them important persons travelling incognito: St Pellegrino (d. twelfth century), according to the biography written in the fourteenth century by the clergy of the sanctuary which bore his name, was the son of a king of Scotland who had renounced the throne to go to the Holy Land.[140] A similar legend developed in the fifteenth century around a Scandinavian pilgrim, called Henry or Eric, who died in Perugia in 1415. It was rumoured that he was the son of the king of Denmark, and he was soon accorded a cult in the parish church of St Andrew.[141]

[137] See the thirteenth-century Life ed. *AA.SS.* Maii VI, pp. 142–60; G. Sainati, *Vita dei santi, beati e servi di Dio nati nella diocesi di Pisa* (Pisa, 1894), pp. 132–50. Another illustrious hermit was B. Antony 'the pilgrim' of Padua (d. 1267); his feast was solemnly celebrated by the commune of Padua from 1269, and miracles occurred at his tomb up to the fourteenth century: *Anal. Boll.*, 14 (1895), pp. 108–14. The Life written in 1436 by Sicco Pollentone (ed. *Anal. Boll.*, 13 (1894), pp. 417–25) is superior to that in *AA.SS.* Feb. I, pp. 264–5, as it was based on an unpublished biography composed *c.*1270 with a view to his canonization.

[138] For example, B. Raymond 'Palmerio' of Piacenza (d. 1200), who travelled to Jerusalem before devoting himself to charitable works in his native town. See below, p. 201.

[139] Apart from the special case of B. Gerald (d. 1241), a pilgrim murdered near Cremona and venerated in the town (see above, p. 150), the principal saints in this category venerated in Italy were: Contardo, d. at Broni, between Pavia and Piacenza, in 1242, whose fourteenth-century Life is in *AA.SS.* Apr. II, pp. 448–52, and Gerius (Gerio), a pilgrim of Lunel, d. Montesanto, in the Marches, *c.*1270: *AA.SS.* Maii VI, pp. 159–61; *PC* (Fermo, 1738), *ASV, Riti*, Proc. 743 and Paris, BN, H.934. Some English pilgrims who died *en route* to the Holy Land were celebrated in southern Italy: Gerard (twelfth century), d. Gallinaro in Campania (*AA.SS.* Aug. II, pp. 693–8; V. Fenicchia, sv Gerardo, in *BS*, VI (Rome, 1965), cc. 186–7), and Bernard (twelfth century) d. Rocca d'Arce, in southern Latium (*AA.SS.* Oct. VI, pp. 628–32; V. Fenicchia, sv Bernardo il Pellegrino, in *BS*, III (Rome, 1963), cc. 61–3).

[140] *Vita* (= *BHL* 6630) in *AA.SS.* Aug. I, pp. 77–80.

[141] The *Vita* (= *BHL* 3817) begins as follows: 'Beatus Henricus, rex trium regnorum, exivit de partibus suis.' See also *AA.SS.* Mar. II, pp. 338–40; P. Burchi, sv Enrico, in *BS*, IV (Rome, 1964), cc. 1231–2.

This, however, was a later clerical interpretation, since, initially, the devotion to the pilgrim saints seems to have paid no regard to their social extraction. As a general rule, these cults remained purely local; the pilgrim saints were hardly venerated outside their native town, or, in the case of foreigners, the country where their bodies were found. Occasionally, their fame extended to neighbouring regions, as in the case of St Pellegrino, whose cult spread from the sanctuary and hospice of San Pellegrino in the Alps throughout the Tuscan Apennines, reaching as far as Lucca and Pistoia.[142] His name is in itself significant and it seems likely he was an unknown pilgrim who was endowed with a generic title. The most extraordinary case, however, is that of St Rock, probably a native of Montpellier, who died, probably in the late fourteenth century, somewhere in northern Italy.[143] The astonishing success of the devotion to this intercessor, first in Italy and then throughout the whole of Christendom in the modern period, illustrates the enduring prestige of the holy pilgrim in the popular mind.

Saints of charity and labour

In northern and central Italy, the late twelfth century saw the appearance of a new category of saint, which was extremely successful in these regions until the end of the thirteenth century: saints of charity and labour, of whom at least one, if not several, were found in every city in the peninsula. They were lay people and citizens, in every sense of the term, inasmuch as their cult did not usually go beyond the boundaries of their native town and its *contado*. The most famous of these saints is Homobonus (d. 1198), the merchant of Cremona canonized in 1199, but he is neither the oldest nor the most representative.[144] The first manifestations of this form of sainthood appeared in Pisa in the person of St Rainerius (Ranieri, d. 1160). His history, as told by his biographer Benincasa, who wrote a Life a few years after his death, is typical: the son of a rich merchant of modest origins, who gave him a good education, Rainerius preferred to make a pilgrimage to the Holy Land rather than succeed his father and only

---

[142] A. Mercati, *S. Pellegrino delle Alpi in Garfagnana: note agiografiche e storiche* (Rome, 1926), repr. in Mercati, *Saggi di storia e letteratura*, I (Rome 1951), pp. 145–206, 430–1; R. Volpini, sv Pellegrino, eremita santo, in *BS*, X (Rome, 1968), cc. 452–9.

[143] For the difficult problems posed by the biography and dating of St Rock, see A. Vauchez, sv Rocco, santo, in *BS*, XI (Rome, 1968), cc. 264–73.

[144] For St Homobonus, see n. 3, p. 129 above; also plate 19.

returned to Pisa thirteen years later. Here, he led a life devoted to charitable works and preaching. His death aroused great emotion in the town and he was soon venerated as a saint. An uncorroborated tradition claims that he was canonized by Alexander III. However that may be, his feast, 17 June, was soon celebrated with solemnity and major ceremonies were organized on this occasion by the commune.[145] Several saints of the same type soon emerged in Pisa: Dominic Vernagalli (d. 1218), founder of an orphanage for foundlings,[146] and, above all, Ubaldesca (d. 1206), the only woman in this category. A country girl, she became a lay sister at the Hospital of St John of Jerusalem in Pisa, where she was notable for her charity to the sick and her practice of begging.[147] Her cult was adopted by the hospital and rapidly became popular, and she is one of the Pisan saints mentioned by name in a sermon delivered by Archbishop Frederick Visconti in 1250.[148]

However precocious the appearance of these forms of lay sanctity in Pisa, it was in northern Italy that they seem to have been most successful. Here, popular veneration was primarily focussed on founders of hospitals or institutions of welfare, such as Gerard Tintori of Monza (d. 1207),[149] Walter of Lodi (d. 1224),[150] and Amato Ronconi of Saludeccio, near Rimini (d. 1256 or 1265),[151] to whom should be added, in

---

[145] The *Vita* (= *BHL* 7084) is ed. *AA.SS.* Iun. III, pp. 421–69; see also N. Caturegli, sv Ranieri, in *BS*, XI (Rome, 1968), cc. 37–44, and plate 20.

[146] *AA.SS.* Apr. II, p. 791. According to *Annales Camaldulenses*, IV, pp. 254–6, he became a priest and oblate of the Camaldoli of San Michele in Borgo.

[147] *AA.SS.* Maii VI, pp. 199–202; Sainati, *Vita dei santi*, pp. 122–31; N. Caturegli, sv Ubaldesca, in *BS*, XII (Rome, 1969), cc. 731–2. Another woman famed for her charity to the sick was the object of a cult in the fourteenth century: St Flora, a nun at the hospital of Beaulieu, near Cahors (d. 1347); see C. Brunel, 'Vita e miracoli de Sancta Flor', *Anal. Boll.*, 64 (1946), pp. 5–49.

[148] Frederico Visconti, *Sermones*, in *Cod. Laurent. Plut.*, XXXIII, 1: 'sanctos nostros, quos prediximus, non curaverunt facere per Romanam Ecclesiam canonizari, id est sanctorum cathalogo ascribi, ut sic possent a nobis publice venerari'. The saints in question were Rainerius, Ubaldesca, Bona and Dominic Vernagalli.

[149] See the *Chronicon Modoetense* of Bonincontro Morigia, ed. in *RIS*, XII, cc. 1085–8; G. Riva, 'Due documenti di S. Gerardo nell'archivio della Congregazione di Carità di Monza (1174 e 1198)', *Archivio storico Lombardo*, 4th ser., 6 (1906), pp. 181–94; *AA.SS.* Iun. I, pp. 754–63; L. Modorati, *Vita di S. Gerardo. Cenni storico* (Monza, 1925).

[150] L. Salamina, 'S. Gualtero (Lodi, 1184–1224)', *Archivio storico Lodigiano*, 61 (1942), pp. 96–134; the thirteenth-century Life is in A. Caretta, 'La Vita di S. Gualtero di Lodi', *ibid.*, 88 (1968), pp. 3–27, which makes it unnecessary to consult the very brief note in *AA.SS.* Iul. V, p. 323.

[151] *PC* (Rimini, 1733–4), in *ASV*, *Riti*, Proc. 89; L. Tonini, *Rimini nel sec. XIII* (Rimini, 1866), pp. 356–60, 672–5.

Tuscany, Andrew Gallerani.[152] In the same tradition, significantly, are those pilgrims who, after going several times to Rome, Santiago de Compostella and even Jerusalem, then, if we are to believe their biographers, saw an apparition of Christ, who asked them to devote themselves in future exclusively to the service of the poor.[153] Even if the episode is fictitious, it probably expresses the realization in devout circles of the superiority of action towards one's neighbour over the solitary ascetic effort. This is apparent in the Life of Raymond 'Palmerio' of Piacenza who, after many journeys to the Holy Land, turned to healing the ills of contemporary urban society: prostitution and growing poverty, but also faction fights, the injustice of the courts which oppressed the poor and the interminable conflicts between neighbouring cities. One of the most original aspects of this sanctity, in fact, was its active character and involvement in the political and social conflicts of the age, in particular the strife between rich and poor. To establish an 'identikit' picture of such persons would be largely arbitrary, since each one faced specific problems and resolved them in his or her own way. There were big differences between the attitude of Raymond 'Palmerio' who, at Piacenza, in the years 1185–1200, was prepared to attack the bishop, whom he accused of caring more for the defence of his own interests than the search for peace, and that of Facio of Cremona, who, in the years 1250–70, appears as a driving force within the Guelph party in eastern Lombardy, ever ready to go into battle against the enemies of the Church. The *partialitas* of vice became virtue, in proportion to the hardening of the conflicts in each town which pitted good Catholics against the supporters of Frederick II and the heretics.[154] But, beyond the differences, all these saints are

[152] For Gallerani, founder of the hospital of the confraternity of Mercy in Siena, see the thirteenth-century *Vita* ed. in *AA.SS.* Mar. III, pp. 49–57; E. Carli, 'Considerazione sul B. Andrea Gallerani', *Economica e storia*, 11 (1964), pp. 253–62. See also plate 21.
[153] For example, in the Life of Raymond 'Palmerio' (d. 1200), written 1212 by a certain *Magister Rufinus* of Piacenza, ed. *AA.SS.* Iul. VI, pp. 646–57. See also *ibid.*, p. 650: 'ibis tu eroque tecum ego et gratiam dabo qua possis ad eleemosynam divites, dissidentes ad pacem, aberrantes denique et vagas praesertim mulierculas ad rectam vivendi normam adducere'. See also the Life of B. Facio of Cremona, ed. A. Vauchez, 'Sainteté laïque au XIIIe siècle: la Vie du B. Facio de Crémone (v. 1196–1272)', *MEFR*, 84 (1972), pp. 13–53, esp. pp. 25ff. For the importance of charitable works in the religious life of thirteenth-century Christians, see M. Mollat, ed., *Assistance et charité* (Toulouse, 1978).
[154] For the attitude of Raymond 'Palmerio', see *AA.SS.* Iul. VI, pp. 654–5; for B. Facio, see Vauchez, 'B. Facio de Crémone', pp. 26–8. The activities of St Homobonus in Cremona *super pace reformanda* are described in detail in the Italian fourteenth-century

presented by their biographers as 'committed' militants, which is all the more remarkable in that the traditions and weight of hagiographical convention worked in the opposite direction.

The other interesting aspect of the life of these men is their attitude to work. All were from the 'Popolo', that is, from the small and middling craft and commercial bourgeoisie, and had worked with their hands: Raymond 'Palmerio' was a shoemaker, Facio a goldsmith and Albert of Villa d'Ogna (d. 1279) a wine porter;[155] the same was true of the Tuscan saints in this category: Luchesio of Poggibonsi (d. *c*.1240) sold foodstuffs and Peter 'Pettinaio' (d. 1289) was a comb merchant in Siena.[156] It would have been difficult for their hagiographers, who usually wrote their *Vitae* soon after their death, to conceal the fact that these men had acquired a reputation for sanctity whilst practising a manual trade or even a commercial career. But in the whole medieval clerical tradition, these forms of work found no favour and even appeared incompatible with perfection. Accordingly, we see the saints, after a period of time, abandon their occupation to devote themselves entirely to charitable works and contemplation. In the case of St Homobonus, this turning-point occurred immediately after his conversion, while it seems to have been later in the case of Raymond 'Palmerio'.[157] However, we can detect a trend to attach greater value to work during the course of the thirteenth century; according to his biographer, Facio of Cremona did not give up his trade as a goldsmith, but specialized in the manufacture of chalices and crucifixes, which he

Life, which begins: *Della cipta di Cremona*, ed. G. Bertoni, 'Di una Vita di S. Omobono del sec. XIV', *Bollettino storico Cremonese*, 3 (1938), pp. 161–76. For the political context, see U. Gualazzini, 'Dalle prime affermazioni del "Populus" di Cremona agli statuti della "Societas Populi" del 1229', *Archivio storico Lombardo*, n.s., 2 (1937), pp. 3–66, esp. pp. 44–5.

[155] The *Chronicon Parmense* (*RIS*, IX, cc. 791–2) and the *Memoriale potestatum Regiensium* (*RIS*, VIII, c. 1145) both describe B. Albert as *portator vini sive brentifer*, which allowed the Franciscan Salimbene to mock him as *vini portator et potator necnon et peccator* (*Cronica*, II, p. 733). The trades of the other saints are mentioned in their *Vitae*.

[156] In Tuscany, the saints in this category were Franciscan tertiaries, which was not the case in the plain of the Po, where they had links with the secular clergy. The early fourteenth-century Life of B. Luchesio is 'Nota e documenti intorno a S. Lucchese', ed. M. Bertagna, *AFH*, 62 (1969), pp. 452–7; for Peter Pettinaio, see the Life written *c*.1330 by the Sienese Franciscan Pietro da Monterone, trans. into Italian by S. Ferri, *Vita del Beato Pietro Pettinaio* (Siena, 1529); also A. Vauchez, sv Pietro Pettinaio in *BS*, X (Rome, 1968), cc. 719–22; R. Manselli, sv, in *Enciclopedia Dantesca*, IV (Rome, 1973), pp. 492–3.

[157] According to the bull of canonization of St Homobonus of 1199, ed. O. Hageneder and A. Haidacher, *Die register Innocenz III* (Graz and Cologne, 1964), pp. 761–4, and the fourteenth-century *Vitae*. The oldest Life, written *c*.1200 by Bishop Sicard of Cremona, has disappeared without trace.

then offered to churches which were without.[158] The Franciscan author
of the Life of Peter 'Pettinaio', the latest of all, since written c.1330,
shows his subject endeavouring to apply the just price in the Siena
market, where he sold his combs cheaply but paid high prices for the
horn from which they were made.[159] But we should remember that
this text is the only one to reveal a desire to define a Christian ethic
of professional and commercial activity. Nor was this episode in the
saint's life the most important, since he eventually abandoned his
labours to devote himself, during his last years, to purely religious
tasks.[160] We here come up against the limitations of the hagiographical
documentation and the difficult problems posed by its use as a historical
source. These ends to pious lives, distanced from labour, are perhaps
simply a means employed by the authors to bring within a conventional
context people who did not conform to the canons of traditional hagiography. But we must also recognize the possibility that these lay
saints, under the influence of the clergy who guided them in spiritual
matters, eventually themselves came to believe that, in order to deepen
their religious life, they had to abandon all work.

We find the same ambiguity in the attitude of these saints to marriage
and family life. Their behaviour in this sphere was very different from
that which the hagiographical tradition conventionally attributed to saints.
Though the wife of St Homobonus, in the *Vitae* devoted to her husband,[161]
appears as a mean-minded and quarrelsome spouse, we find, in contrast,
positive appreciations of conjugal life in the biographies of Raymond 'Palmerio' and Peter 'Pettinaio'. Both seem to have felt respect and tenderness
for their partners, seeking to take account, as far as possible, of their
needs and tastes.[162] These are interesting observations, certainly, but fleet-

---

[158] In the treasury of Cremona cathedral, there are processional crosses still said to have
been made by B. Facio. But A. Puerari has shown that the crosses in question cannot
be earlier than the fourteenth century: *Il duomo di Cremona* (Milan, 1971). The gold-
smithing trade was a *labor spiritualis* in clerical eyes, as shown by the legend of St Eligius.

[159] Ferri, *Beato Pietro Pettinaio*, pp. 5ff.

[160] *Ibid.*, pp. 84ff. He advised the celebrated Dominican preacher Ambrose Sansedoni not
to accept the bishopric of Siena, to which he had just been elected, and he maintained
a spiritual correspondence with a group of pious lay people in Florence.

[161] See, for example, the unflattering portrait in *Labentibus annis*, ed. F. S. Gatta, 'Un
antico codice reggiano su Omobono, "il santo popolare" di Cremona', *Bollettino storico
Cremonese*, 7 (1942), pp. 96–115, esp. p. 112.

[162] According to the *Vita* of 1212 (*AA.SS.* Iul. VI, p. 648), Raymond 'Palmerio' 'conjugem
arguebat docebatque ut filiam, amabat ut sororem, venerabatur ut matrem'; Peter Pettinaio 'did not call his wife spouse but rather mother or boss' and tried to get home in
time for meals to please her (Ferri, *Beato Pietro Pettinaio*, p. 6).

ing. The other lay saints of this type were unmarried; in the case of the two who were not, progress towards sainthood went hand in hand with moderation within marriage, then complete abandonment of conjugal relations. In the last analysis, it is as if, for the married men, women and children were little more than obstacles to their desire for perfection, the truly saintly period of their existence only beginning after the death of their wives and children.[163] Here again, it is difficult to know how much was hagiographical convention and how much reality. There are some signs which suggest to me that, in the real life of these saints, their spouses did not represent only an obstacle to their spiritual advancement. Public opinion seems to have agreed, since Bonadonna, the wife of B. Luchesio, was considered a saint and venerated locally, although hagiography sought only to exalt her husband.[164]

However, we risk giving a false idea of the lay saints of communal Italy if, to satisfy a contemporary curiosity, we put too much emphasis on their attitude to the problems of work and family life, or try to suggest that it was their conduct in this sphere which most impressed their contemporaries. As far as we can tell from the reactions not only of the hagiographers but of the chroniclers who mention them in passing, these people were distinguished above all by an ascetic life-style (frequent and prolonged fasts, periodic continence or total chastity within marriage) and their piety and charity.[165] They were, in the fullest sense of the term, penitents.[166] The days they passed in prayer

---

[163] Raymond 'Palmerio', who had six children, could only go on a pilgrimage after the death of the five oldest, all of the same disease in the same year, and of his wife (*AA.SS.* Iul. VI, p. 649). The same could be said of the women saints of the period, most of whom were not considered as such until after the death of their husbands (see below, pp. 381–3).
[164] Kaftal 1, cc. 211–12.
[165] The author of the *Chronica pontificum et imperatorum Mantuana* (ed. *MGH.SS.*, XXIV, p. 216), says, for the year 1256, of Facio of Cremona (d. 1272): 'fuit quidam homo Cremonae, qui Faciolus vocabatur, qui per LXXVII dies in domo Praedicatorum stetit, qui non comedit neque bibit aliquid preter corpus Christi, quod bis suscepit intra predictum tempus'. Of the death of B. Albert of Villa d'Ogna (1279), the author of the *Chronicon Placentinum* (ed. *MGH.SS.*, XVIII, pp. 571–2), wrote: 'in civitate Cremonae mortuus est quidam homo qui fuit portator vini et blavae, bonus homo, timens Deum et visitans saepe et saepius limina Sancti Petri, faciens eleemosynas, perseverans in orationibus . . . in ecclesia'. For the reactions of other local chroniclers, see *Annales Parmenses maiores*, *MGH.SS.*, XVIII, p. 687; *Alberti Millioli, Liber de temporibus*, in *MGH.SS.*, XXI, pp. 369, 553; and the documents collected for the canonization process: *PC Albert of Villa d'Ogna* (Cremona, 1644), in *ASV*, Riti, Proc. 661.
[166] For the success of the penitential ideal and life-style in Italy and in the Mediterranean in the late twelfth and thirteenth centuries, see G. G. Meersseman, *Dossier de l'ordre de la pénitence au XIIIe siècle* (Freiburg, 1961); Meersseman, 'Disciplinati e penitenti nel Duecento', in *Il movimento dei Disciplinati*, pp. 43–72.

in churches and the foundation of charitable institutions attributed to them made a greater impression on those who observed them live than other aspects of their existence which seem to us more original.[167] On one point, however, we share the judgement of the thirteenth century. I refer to the ascendancy these pious lay people exercised over the clergy, both locally and regionally. Their biographers show them reforming monasteries, like Facio of Cremona, who got the better of a 'demon' which was tormenting the nuns of St Catherine de Quarto in Bologna.[168] Dante and Ubertin of Casale reveal the profound influence exercised on devout circles in Tuscany by the simple comb merchant, Peter 'Pettinaio' of Siena.[169] This was an important development which toppled the traditional hierarchy of the states of perfection within the Church. To recognize in lay saints a sort of moral and spiritual authority, based on their merits alone, was, in a sense, to put them on a par with the clergy. However that may be, what we glimpse of the life of these people in the hagiographical texts and other contemporary documents is sufficiently novel for it to be possible to say that this strand in lay sainthood probably constituted what was most advanced and 'modern' in medieval spirituality.

From the late thirteenth century, saintly men engaging in charitable works and a professional career, so characteristic of the years 1180–1280, became rarer. The last representatives of this type are Nevolone of Faenza (d. 1280) and Henry, or Rigo, of Treviso (d. 1315).[170] They give the impression of having been more contemplative and less involved in

[167] Raymond 'Palmerio' founded a hospice for abandoned children and a shelter for destitute women in Piacenza: AA.SS. Iul. VI; A. Vauchez, sv Raimondo Zanfogni, in BS, XI (Rome, 1968), cc. 26–9. In Cremona, B. Facio established a charitable congregation, the Fratres de Consortio Sancti Spiritus, which spread to many other Lombard towns: Vauchez, 'B. Facio de Crémone', pp. 25–9.

[168] Ibid., pp. 34, 42.

[169] He is mentioned by Dante in Purgatory, c. XIII, vv. 124–9, and by Ubertin of Casale in the prologue to the Arbor Vitae Crucifixae Iesu. See also Bartholomew of Pisa, 'De conformitate', in Analecta Franciscana, IV (Quaracchi, 1907), p. 351.

[170] For Nevolone (or Novellone), see AA.SS. Iul. VI, pp. 495–9; F. Lanzoni, 'Una Vita del Beato Nevolone Faentino, terziario francescano (m. 1280) composta nel secolo XV', AFH, 6 (1913), pp. 645–53. It has never been proved that Nevolone, who has also been claimed by the Camaldolese, belonged to the Franciscan third order (A. Vauchez, sv Nevolone, in BS, IX (Rome, 1967), cc. 839–40). For Henry 'of Bolzano' (where he was born) or 'of Treviso', see the Life written by Pier Domenico di Baone, later bishop of Treviso (= BHL 3807) in AA.SS. Iun. II, pp. 368–92; also Azzoni Avogari, De B. Henrico qui Tarvisii decessit anno Christi MCCCXV commentarius (Venice, 1760). For the fortunes of the cult, see PC (Treviso, 1746–7), ASV, Riti, Proc. 3021, and Paris, BN, H. 951.

internal city conflicts.[171] We no longer see them acting as arbiters between parties or families. Perhaps this diminution of their social role is connected with the relative pacification which accompanied the triumph of the Guelphs throughout Italy after 1270, and the beginnings of the decline of the communal regime in favour of the 'Signoria', which meant fewer faction fights. But we cannot fail to note that the fading of this line of saints, linked for the most part, at least in northern Italy, to the secular clergy, went together with a strengthening of the influence of the Mendicant orders, who, after 1270, waged war on the popular religious movements and the saints from the 'Popolo'. It was at this period that Salimbene attacked both the movement of the 'Apostles' of Gerard Segalelli and the cult of the wine porter Albert of Villa d'Ogna (d. 1279), whilst the Mendicant inquisitors made one enquiry after another in order to prove that Armanno Pungilupo (d. 1269), venerated in Ferrara cathedral, was, in fact, a supporter of Catharism.[172] It is not part of my purpose to establish right and wrong in these conflicts. But their very existence attests to an attempt, eventually successful, on the part of the regulars to regain control over the lay sanctity, highly questionable in their eyes, which had developed, with the support of the seculars, in the communal context. From now on, with very few exceptions, the simple faithful only acceded to the honours of a local cult with the assistance of the Mendicant orders and their third orders. It is significant that the only two men to continue this trend in the fourteenth century, Peter Crisci of Foligno (d. 1323) and Tommasuccio of Nocera (d. 1377), himself a Franciscan tertiary, initially had brushes with the Inquisition, and that the latter was very badly treated

---

[171] For Nevolone, P. Cantinelli, *Chronicum Faentium*, ed. in *RIS*, 2, XXVIII, 2, p. 42; for Henry of Treviso, see the prologue of the *Vita* in *AA.SS.* Iun. II, p. 366: 'de his quae lucrabatur ex laboribus suis partem suam erogabet et continuo mentem devotam gerebat et operibus divinis secretim intendebat'.

[172] Salimbene, *Cronica*, II, pp. 729–33; For Armanno Pungilupo, see Benati, 'Armanno Pungilupo'. It is worth quoting the eulogy for Armanno prepared by the canons of Ferrara Cathedral between 1270 and 1280 to defend his reputation for sanctity, already under attack by the Mendicants: 'Vir Dei beatus Armannus, natione Ferrariensis, peracto lungi temporis spatio, coram Deo et hominibus poenitentia laude digna, vigiliis, jejuniis et orationibus vacans, fidelis et castus, humilis, patiens, misericors, benignus et simplex, vera simplicitate columbae, Deo devotus et Virgini gloriosae, sicut Domino placuit, Christi crucem bajulans miraculose ab ipso vocatus, diem clausit extremum': *Inquisitio miraculorum*, ed. L. A. Muratori, in *Antiquitates Italicae Medii Aevi*. V (1742), c. 97. After many enquiries and processes, his body was exhumed and burned in 1301 by the Dominican inquisitor in Ferrara, who also destroyed his tomb in the cathedral. The furious populace rushed to the Dominican convent to attack him and he was saved only by the intervention of the soldiers of the marquis Azzo d'Este, who restored order (Benati, 'Armanno Pungilupo', p. 114).

in Siena by the Friars Minor, who did not appreciate his prophetic denunciations.[173] This was a sign of the times; the lay sanctity which had flourished spontaneously and unimpeded in the thirteenth century had become both suspect and marginal.

The Mendicant orders and local sainthood

In the late thirteenth and, even more, in the fourteenth centuries, the Mendicant orders, apparently worried by the proliferation of devotions over which they had no control, abandoned their initial attitude of hostility to local saints, and set out instead to dominate their cults with a view to using them to impose their own models of sainthood. This policy was first tried in regions such as Umbria and Tuscany, where the Friars Minor and the Preachers enjoyed great influence from an early date. It was then adopted throughout Italy and Provence and, to a lesser degree, Languedoc and Catalonia. It was by no means wholly successful, especially in rural areas and small towns, where people continued in the fourteenth century to venerate hermits and recluses who for the most part had no Mendicant connections. In larger towns, however, where Mendicant influence was much stronger, their activities bore fruit and considerably modified the nature of local sanctity.

Feminization

As the model of sainthood most honoured in the towns was lay, the Franciscans and Dominicans first set out to promote the cult of devout persons, especially women, who had gravitated in their orbit on the spiritual plane or were actually members of associations of penitents linked to the two great orders.[174] The process made a tentative beginning in mid-thirteenth-

---

[173] Peter Crisci of Foligno had contacts with Angela of Foligno and Clare of Montefalco. Suspected of sympathizing with the 'Spirituals', he was summoned to Spoleto by the inquisitor, but exonerated, according to his Life, written c.1365 by the Dominican John Gorini, ed. M. Faloci Pulignani, *Anal. Boll.*, 8 (1889), pp. 358–69 (= *BHL* 6709); see also M. Sensi, sv Pietro Crisci in *BS*, X (Rome, 1968), cc. 821–3. The revelations of Tommasuccio of Nocera or of Foligno appear in his *Légenda*, ed. Faloci Pulignani. His incarceration in Siena is described in chapter 24.

[174] The complex world of the devout laity and the confraternities of penitents in the thirteenth century remains obscure. Meersseman, in the works cited in note 166 above, has convincingly shown that there was no Franciscan or Dominican third order in central Italy before the 1280s, only groups of lay penitents who enjoyed considerable autonomy and attached

century Florence, where two Franciscans, Guy of Cortona and Hippolytus of Florence, wrote up the Life and miracles of B. Umiliana dei Cerchi (d. 1246), a tertiary linked to the convent of Santa Croce,[175] who, after the death of her husband, had lived as a recluse in her own home, the 'Torre dei Cerchi', devoting herself to the harshest of penitences and contemplation.

This biography played an important role in the history of Italian lay sainthood, as it was the first of a whole series of *Vitae* on the same model, which continued up to the beginning of the fifteenth century. For reasons to which we will return, the Mendicant orders preferred to promote forms and examples of female sanctity. The Franciscan hagiography of the Mediterranean regions did not, of course, entirely ignore men. In addition to Luchesio of Poggibonsi (d. 1250) and Peter 'Pettinaio' of Siena (d. 1258), whom we have already discussed, we should note tertiaries such as John Pelingotto of Urbino (d. 1304),[176] St Elzear of Sabran in Provence (d. 1323),[177] and B. Cecco (d. 1350), a disciple of Peter Crisci of Foligno, who restored churches in the Marches and, with B. Michelina of Pesaro, founded the brotherhood of the Annunziata in that town.[178] However, with the exception of St Elzear, who was canonized in 1369, these were essentially second-class saints. The greatest lay saints exalted by the Mendicant orders were women, such as Margaret of Cortona (d. 1297), whose Life was written soon after her death by the Franciscan Giunta Bevignate,[179] Angela of

themselves freely to a particular convent to receive spiritual assistance. Though initially hostilely received by some Franciscan historians, since the foundation of the 'triple militia' (monks, nuns and tertiaries) has traditionally been attributed to St Francis, his arguments have eventually been widely accepted. Nevertheless, there already existed in the thirteenth century an *ordo penitencie beati Francisci*, as several articles published in *L'Ordine della penitenza di San Francesco d'Assisi* have shown.

[175] See the Life in *AA.SS.* Maii IV, pp. 385–418. For the historic person, see R. Davidsohn, *Storia di Firenze*, II (Florence, 1956), pp. 180–8; for the cult, see R. Sciammanini, sv Cerchi, Umiliana dei, in *BS*, III (Rome, 1963), cc. 1132–5; R. Franco, *La Beata Umiliana de' Cerchi Francescana del terz'Ordine in Firenze* (Rome, 1977).

[176] His life bears many resemblances to that of St Francis of Assisi: son of a cloth merchant, he dramatically renounced his trade and paternal fortune to devote himself, after his conversion, to devout practices and charitable works: see the contemporary *Vita* (= *BHL* 6850) in *AA.SS.* Iun. I, pp. 145–51.

[177] The *Vita* (= *BHL* 2523) is in *AA.SS.* Sept. VII, pp. 576–93.

[178] For Cecco de Pesaro, see the Life in *AA.SS.* Aug. I, pp. 660–2 (= *BHL* 3138); S. Ortolani, *Vita del B. Cecco di Pesaro* (Fano, 1859).

[179] Giunta Bevignate, *Legenda de vita et miraculis beate Margarite de Cortona*, ed. *AA.SS.* Feb. III, pp. 298–357. The Bollandists' edition lacks chapter 12 (= the miracles) of the Life, which was published in da Pelago, *Antica Legenda di S. Margherita di Cortona*, pp. 316–39. See also *PC* (Cortona, 1640), *ASV, Riti*, Proc. 552 and Paris, BN, H. 1187–92.

Foligno (d. 1309), celebrated by her confessor Brother Arnold,[180] and Michelina of Pesaro (d. 1356).[181]

This trend was even more marked among the Dominicans, who, having long lagged behind the Franciscans in this sphere, began to take an active interest in local cults from 1300. There were no men among the tertiaries and penitents whose cult they promoted, only recluses and 'Mantellate', such as Vanna (Joan) of Orvieto (d. 1306), who had been closely connected with the celebrated Dominican James Bianconi of Bevagna, himself regarded and venerated as a saint. Her Life was written in 1323 by the Dominican James Scalza of Orvieto (d. 1337), and translated into Italian in 1400 by Thomas Caffarini, then in the convent in Venice.[182] Over the following decades, the Preachers tried to establish the sanctity of several other women who had gravitated in their orbit, including Benvenuta Bojani (d. 1295) at Cividale del Friuli,[183] Margaret of Città di Castello (d. 1320),[184] and Villana dei Botti (d. 1361) in Florence.[185] This trend was even more marked in the late fourteenth and early fifteenth centuries, when the Dominican Observance, around John Dominici and Raymond of Capua, developed the cult of lay penitents associated with the order; one sign of this was Thomas Caffarini's *Tractatus de ordine fratrum de poenitentia S. Dominici*, which gives pride of place to the saints listed above together with Agnes of Montepulciano (d. 1317), Catherine of Siena (d. 1380) and Mary of Venice (d. 1399).[186]

---

[180] The *Vita* (= *BHL* 455) is *AA.SS.* Ian. I, pp. 186–234.

[181] *Legenda Vitae* (= *BHL* 5957) is *AA.SS.* Iun. III, pp. 925–8. See also *PC Michelina of Pesaro* (Pesaro, 1733), *ASV, Riti*, Proc. 2263 and Paris, BN, H. 1263; A. degli Abbati Olivieri, *Della patria della B. Michelina e del B. Cecco del Terz'Ordine di San Francesco* (Pesaro, 1774).

[182] *Legenda B. Virginis vannae seu Ioannae de Urbeveteri sororis de poenitenita S. Dominici* (= *BHL* 4289), ed. V. Mareddu, *Leggenda latina della B. Giovanna detta Vanna* (Orvieto, 1853); see also T. Kaeppeli, in *RSCI*, 6 (1952), p. 95. The Italian translation of Thomas Caffarini, OP, is ed. L. Fiumi, *Leggenda della B. Vanna* (Città di Castello, 1885). See also *PC Joan of Orvieto* (Orvieto, 1753), *ASV, Riti*, Proc. 3327 and Paris, BN, H. 1018.

[183] The Life by Conrad of Castellario (= *BHL* 1149) is ed. *AA.SS.* Oct. XIII, pp. 145–85; see also *PC Benvenuta Bojani* (Cividale, 1759–60), *ASV, Riti*, Proc. 3324 and Paris, BN, H. 740.

[184] For the oldest (*c*.1348) Life, written by a secular, see Laurent, 'La plus ancienne légende de la B. Marguerite de Città di Castello'; there is another Life, by a Dominican, ed. A. Poncelet, '*Vita beatae Margaritae virginis de Civitate Castelli*', *Anal. Boll.*, 19 (1900), pp. 21–36.

[185] Her Life was written by the Dominican Girolamo de Giovanni, *c*.1420, and is ed. S. Orlandi, 'La Beata Villana, terziaria domenicana fiorentina nel sec. XIV', *Memorie Domenicane*, 88 (1961), pp. 218–27.

[186] *Tractatus de ordine fratrum de poenitentia di Fr. Tommaso da Siena*, ed. M. H. Laurent and F. Valli (Milan, 1938). At the same period Raymond of Capua produced a Life of Agnes of Montepulciano (= *BHL* 155), ed. *AA.SS.* Apr. II, pp. 792–812 and the *Legenda*

To appreciate the degree of interest shown by the Mendicant orders in local sanctity in the fourteenth century, we should also note that a number of regulars from their own ranks – some known, others anonymous – wrote the Life and disseminated the cult of female saints who had never belonged to their third orders, but who were likely to find favour with the laity. One such was Zita of Lucca (d. 1272), a pious and charitable servant whose cult was established in 1278 by the commune of Lucca and propagated throughout Italy by the Friars Minor and the Preachers; another was Fina of San Gimignano (d. 1253), whose Life was written by the Dominican John del Coppo.[187] Sometimes they even produced a new legend to add lustre to saints whose Life had already been written some decades earlier by seculars or monks.[188] Even when they did not expressly annexe these saints, they tried to update their image and make them conform to their own models.

A comparison of these biographies makes it possible to see how lay female sainthood was conceived by their authors. These saints were usually young girls of modest origins or, at least, deprived of wealth, often after losing their father.[189] Having worked with their hands during childhood, they abandoned the active life with the advent of adolescence in order to escape masculine attentions. They were, in fact, fiercely deter-

---

maior of St Catherine of Siena, ed. *AA.SS*. Apr. III, pp. 853–959 (= *BHL* 1702). Thomas Caffarini is the author of the *Legenda minor* of St Catherine of Siena, ed. E. Franceschini (Milan, 1942), the *Supplementum legendae prolixae*, ed. G. Tinagli (Siena, 1938) and the Life of Mary of Venice (= *BHL* 5522), ed. F. Corner, *Ecclesiae Venetae*, D. IX, 1 (Venice, 1742), pp. 363–420. See Fawtier, *Sainte Catherine de Sienne*.

[187] The Life of St Zita (= *BHL* 9091) is *AA.SS*. Apr. III, pp. 497–527. For the local cult, see F. P. Luiso, 'L'Anziano di S. Zita', in *Miscellanea lucchese di studi storici e letterari in memoria di Salvatore Bongi* (Lucca, 1931), pp. 61–91; *PC Zita* (Lucca 1694–5), *ASV, Riti*, Proc. 1315 and Paris, BN, H. 1390. For Dominican propagation of the cult, see the deposition of Brother Thomas of Siena, 24 May 1411, at the process of St Catherine of Siena, ed. Laurent, *Il processo Castellano*, pp. 30–1: 'et in Venetiis quampluries predicavi in ecclesia S. Crisostomi de vita et virtutibus B. Zitae de Lucca in certo die commemorationis sive celebritatis dicte beate que ibidem fit die XXVIIIa mensis aprilis'. For the Life of B. Fina, see Dondaine, 'La vie et les œuvres de Jean de San Gimignano', pp. 128–83.

[188] For example, in 1420 the Dominican bishop L. Giacomini wrote a new Life of B. Verdiana de Castelfiorentino (ed. *AA.SS*. Feb. I, pp. 257–66), on the basis of one added in the late thirteenth century by the monk Blaise to a collection of Lives of saints of Florence and the vicinity; this *vita antiquior* (= *BHL* 8540) is ed. O. Pogni, *Vita di S. Verdiana* (Empoli, 1936).

[189] Vanna of Orvieto was the daughter of a rich landowner of Carnaiola (diocese of Orvieto), who was ruined in the wars. She lost her father at the age of three, her mother at five. Margaret of Città di Castello was born to a minor aristocratic family at Metola in the Metauro valley, but as she was blind, her parents abandoned her at the age of five in Città di Castello, where she was taken in by a couple in modest circumstances.

mined to preserve their virginity, preferring to flee the paternal home or workshop rather than consent to the marriage plans hatched by their family. It was usually at this stage – or with widowhood in the case of the few married women in this group – that they entered communities of tertiaries – *sorores indutae, vestitae, mantellate* – linked to one or other of the great Mendicant orders. They were then able to devote themselves in complete tranquillity to an exclusively religious life. Prayer and meditation sometimes led on to mystical states, during which they relived with greater or lesser intensity the various stages of Christ's Passion. These exceptional graces, which were accompanied by the phenomena of levitation or ecstasies, aroused the curiosity of the local population, who rushed to see the saint 'in all her states' and touch her insensible body.[190] Their death was greeted by a surge of popular enthusiasm and accompanied by prodigies – bells ringing of their own accord, sweet celestial music – and miracles.[191] This ideal type does not allow for certain characteristics specific to each of these women, who did not lack personality. But the common features outnumber the differences, especially with regard to their spirituality, which was focussed on flight from the world and refusal of marriage, extreme asceticism and devotion to the sufferings of Christ. Some of them believed they were charged by God to deliver to the world and the Church prophetic warnings and 'revelations', which made them ideal mouthpieces for the reform movements of rigorist inspiration, whether the Franciscans of 'spiritual' tendency or the Dominican Observance.[192]

Between the end of the thirteenth and the beginning of the fifteenth centuries, the Mendicant orders, in particular the two greatest, attempted to enrich the content of sainthood by orienting the devotion of the faithful towards specific lay saints who had been under their influence on the religious plane. Thanks to their intervention in local cults, the models

[190] There is an excellent study of these paramystical phenomena, found in most *Vitae* of saints connected to the Mendicant orders, and of reactions to them, in the case of Provence, by C. Carozzi, 'Douceline et les autres', in *La religion populaire en Languedoc*, pp. 251–67.

[191] These figure in almost all the Lives in question, and also in the canonization processes of saints of this type; that of Delphine of Sabran, for example, a Franciscan beguine (d. 1363), says that celestial music resounded throughout Apt at the moment of her death: *PC Delphine*, fol. 22v.

[192] This is probably why, apart from Delphine of Sabran and St Catherine of Siena, no such saint was the subject of a medieval canonization process. The link with the Observance is clear in the Legend of B. Vanna of Orvieto (d. 1306); written in Latin in 1323 by a local Dominican, it was sent to Venice at the request of Thomas Caffarini, who translated it into Italian (see note 182 above). For the latter's hagiographical activities, see M. H. Laurent's preface to G. Tinagli, *Vita di Santa Caterina da Siena scritta da Fr. Tommaso Caffarini* (Siena, 1938), pp. 7–61.

began to change. The almost exclusive emphasis on female sanctity – when men had previously been more numerous – was a sign of these new orientations. Through the example of these female saints, the regulars sought to impose their own conception of sanctity, based on contemplation and the mystical life. Among the lay saints of the thirteenth century, such concerns had been accompanied by a deep feeling for suffering humanity and a pronounced interest in temporal activities; the spirit of prayer went hand in hand with good works and the desire to pacify and moralize the society in which they lived. The values now proposed for the imitation of the faithful were purely spiritual. What mattered most was the search for union with God through solitary meditation on the mysteries of salvation.

Clericalization

At the same time as, and in parallel with, the feminization discussed above, there was, especially in Italy, a clericalization of male sainthood; in the late Middle Ages, the saints whose cults were propagated by the Mendicants were either women from the laity or men who had lived a conventual life.[193] The latter were so numerous that it would be tedious to list them. The rivalry which developed between the various orders from the end of the thirteenth century encouraged an ill-advised proliferation of brethren honoured with the title *sanctus* or *beatus* by the Minors, the Preachers, the Hermits of St Augustine, the Carmelites or the Servites. Literally hundreds of these servants of God are named in conventual necrologies, provincial martyrologies and legendries.[194] Not all these reputations for sanctity reached beyond the walls of the convent where they had blossomed. But, even if we confine ourselves to the Mendicant saints whose local cult and popularity are well established, the number remains impressive.

In the thirteenth century, as we have seen, the Mendicant orders were content to disseminate the cult of their founders and their heroes: SS Francis and Dominic, SS Antony of Padua and Peter Martyr. This little group of saints was added to in the early fourteenth century by the canoni-

---

[193] This process went hand in hand with the increasing clericalization of the Mendicant orders, well analysed for the Friars Minor by R. Manselli, 'La clericalizzazione dei minori e San Bonaventura', in *S. Bonaventura Francescano* (Todi, 1974), pp. 181–208.

[194] See, for example, the impressive list of Tuscan Franciscan 'saints' compiled in the eighteenth century by L. Nuti ('Santi e Beati della Toscana', *Miscellanea Francescana*, 32 (1932), pp. 89–118) and, for Lombardy, the *Martyrologium Fratrum Minorum provinciae Mediolanensis*, ed. P. Sevesi (Milan, 1927).

zations of SS Louis of Anjou (d. 1297) and Thomas Aquinas (d. 1274). By iconography and by preaching, their spiritual sons endeavoured to make them known and venerated throughout Christendom.[195] But at the same time, especially in the Mediterranean region, the Mendicants promoted the cult of certain individuals who were less illustrious but who enjoyed great local fame. In the case of the Dominicans, we may note, without any claim to exhaustivity, the Sienese preacher Ambrose Sansedoni (d. 1287),[196] James of Bevagna (d. 1301) in Umbria,[197] and James Salomon in Venice (d. 1314).[198] Famous Franciscans were even more numerous, and the movement started earlier, especially in central Italy. Among the first generations of Friars Minor, we know of at least three whose *fama sanctitatis* is attested by documents external to the order: Benvenuto of Gubbio (d. *c.*1232) in Corneto, in Apulia, Ambrose of Massa (d. 1240) in Orvieto, and Simon of Collazzone (d. 1250) in the Spoleto region.[199] Once this first, and apparently short-lived, wave of enthusiasm had died down, it was not until the years 1280–1310 that the local cult of 'frati' saints revived on any scale, under the combined pressure of the brethren and of communes who wanted to acquire a 'modern' patron. This was the case, for example, with Andrew de' Conti of Anagni (d. 1302)[200] in southern Latium, Benvenuto of Recanati (d. 1289)[201] and Francis 'the New' (d. 1322) in the Marches,[202] Rainerius of Borgo San Sepolcro (d. 1304)[203] and John of La Verna (d. 1322), who had a vision

[195] See below, pp. 449–51.
[196] See the *Legenda antiqua* composed by four contemporary Dominicans in *AA.SS.* Mar. III, pp. 180–209; also the *Vita* by Brother Recupero, *ibid.*, pp. 210–39; for his preaching, see T. Kaeppeli, 'Le prediche del B. Ambrogio Sansedoni', *AFP*, 38 (1968), pp. 5–19.
[197] James Bianconi of Bevagna, prior of the Dominican convent in Orvieto, and B. Vanna's director of conscience, seems to have been the subject of a fourteenth-century canonization process now lost; see *AA.SS.* Aug. IV, pp. 728–34; also F. Alberti, *Notizie antiche e moderni riguardanti Bevagna, città dell'Umbria* (Venice, 1792), pp. 82–106, 174–8.
[198] The Life is *AA.SS.* Maii VII, pp. 460–74 (= *BHL* 4110); see also *Supplementum ad Vitam beati Iacobi Veneti*, ed. *Anal. Boll.*, 12 (1893), pp. 369–70.
[199] All three were the subject of canonization processes in the thirteenth century (see above pp. 47, 52, 68–9). We may add B. Andrew Caccioli of Spello (d. 1254) in Umbria, who became the patron of his native town in 1360: *AA.SS.* Iun. I, pp. 364–70; *PC* (Spoleto, 1730–4), *ASV, Riti,* Proc. 2912; G. Odoardi, sv Andrea Caccioli, in *BS*, I (Rome, 1961), cc. 1155–6.
[200] *PC* (Piglio and Anagni, 1721–3), *ASV, Riti,* Proc. 37–8; G. Odoardi, sv Andrea Conti, in *BS*, I (Rome, 1961), cc. 1156–7.
[201] *PC Benvenuto* (Recanati, 1796), Paris, BN, H. 741; G. Odoardi, sv Benvenuto da Recanati, in *BS*, II (Rome, 1962), c. 1252.
[202] For Francis Venimbeni, see *PC* (Fabriano, 1773), *ASV, Riti,* Proc. 699; also the *Vita* in *AA.SS.* Apr. III, pp. 984–90.
[203] See *AA.SS.* Nov. I, pp. 391–5; Kern, 'Le B. Rainier de San Sepolcro'.

of the stigmata of St Francis,[204] in Umbria, and the missionary Orderic of Pordenone (d. 1331) near Udine.[205] The last wave of Franciscan sanctity was more southern; its chief representatives are Gandulph of Binasco (d. c.1260), venerated in Polizzi, Sicily, after 1320,[206] Gerard Cagnoli of Palermo (d. 1342), whose cult eventually spread throughout central Italy and Corsica from the Franciscan convent of Pisa,[207] and Philip of Aix (d. 1369), who spent most of his life in Naples, where his death sparked off a veritable popular demonstration.[208]

It was not only the saints of the two principal Mendicant orders who attracted the attention of the faithful; those of the Augustinians, the Carmelites and the Servites offered serious competition, especially in the fourteenth century. The Augustinians promoted the cult of some of the great men of their order, such as Clement of Osimo (d. 1291), particularly venerated in Orvieto, site of his tomb,[209] James of Viterbo (d. 1308) in his native town,[210] and Augustine 'the New' (Agostino Novello), who was to become one of the patron saints of Siena.[211] The Augustinian saints also included some simple regulars of often extreme ascetic tendencies, who enjoyed great popular favour in certain regions; examples are St Nicholas of Tolentino (d. 1305),[212] Simon of Todi (d. 1322), who was very popular in Bologna,[213] and Simon Fidati of Casci (d. 1348).[214] The increase in their

---

[204] The *Vita* is *AA.SS*. Aug. II, pp. 389–99; see also *PC* (Arezzo, 1877), *ASV, Riti*, Proc. 3854.

[205] *PC*, Paris, BN, H. 1275; H. Cordier, *Les voyages en Asie au XIVe siècle du B. Frère Orderic de Pordenone* (Paris, 1891), especially pp. LX–LXIII on the origins of the local cult in Italy.

[206] For his cult, see *Dialogus de vita*, written by James of Narni, bishop of Cefalu, c.1320, ed. *AA.SS*. Sept. V, pp. 704–6; also other contemporary documents, *ibid.*, pp. 707–19.

[207] F. Rotolo, ed., 'La leggenda del B. Gerardo Cagnoli O.M. (1276–1342)', *Miscellanea Francescana*, 57 (1957), pp. 397–446; R. Toso d'Arenzano, sv Cagnoli, Gerardo, in *BS*, III (Rome, 1963), cc. 641–2.

[208] *AA.SS*. Maii IV, p. 135; *Vita* (= *BHL* 6820), ed. G. B. Tondini, *Della memorie istoriche concernenti la vita del cardinale Tommaso da Frignano* (Macerata, 1782).

[209] *PC* (Orvieto, 1757), *ASV, Riti*, Proc. 3228; P. Burchi, sv Clemente da Osimo, in *BS*, IV (Rome, 1964), cc. 35–6.

[210] *PC* (Naples and Viterbo, 1888–92), *ASV, Riti*, Proc. 4016; N. Del Re, sv Giacomo da Viterbo, in *BS*, VI (Rome, 1965), cc. 425–7.

[211] The *Vita* (= *BHL* 804) is in *AA.SS*. Maii IV, pp. 616–21; see also A. Giacomini, sv Agostino Novello, in *BS*, I (Rome, 1961), cc. 601–8.

[212] See *PC Nicholas of Tolentino*; below, pp. 335–6.

[213] *AA.SS*. Apr. II, pp. 816–28; F. Caraffa, sv Simone da Todi, in *BS*, XI (Rome, 1968), c. 1184.

[214] The Life by his disciple John of Salerno (= *BHL* 7756) is ed. N. Mattioli, *Il B. Simone Fidati da Cascia* (Rome, 1898), pp. 16–26; see also M. Salsano, sv Fidati, Simone, da Cascia, in *BS*, V (Rome, 1964), cc. 674–5. Other Augustinian saints venerated in Italy included: B. Philip of Piacenza (d. 1306) (*PC* (Piacenza, 1760–1), Paris, BN, H. 719; *AA.SS*. Maii V, pp. 434ff), Hugolino of Cortona (d. 1370) (*PC* (Florence, 1804), Paris,

number, especially in central Italy, should probably be related to the significant fall in the number of new Franciscan saints after 1330. In fact the Augustinians seem to have been the principal beneficiaries of the diminished prestige of the Friars Minor which followed the quarrels rending the order at this period and the decadence which ensued.[215] The Servites and the Carmelites benefited in their turn and managed, at a more modest level, to make themselves felt in the domain of local sanctity, where their role had previously been modest.[216]

It is difficult to reduce to one single model persons so diverse. Grossly oversimplifying, however, we may distinguish two main types: in the thirteenth century, the Mendicant saints, almost all Franciscans and Dominicans, were prestigious preachers (such as Ambrose Sansedoni) or founders of a convent (like James Bianconi) or an order (like Philip Benizzi, d. 1285, one of the creators of the Servites of Mary); in the fourteenth century, it seems rather to have been brethren who remained faithful to the original ideal or who were remarkable for their asceticism or their charity who received popular 'canonization', such as the Dominican Marcolino of Forli (d. 1397), the Hermit of St Augustine, Simon of Cascia (d. 1348) and the Servite Pellegrino Laziosi (d. 1345). Behind the religious habit, we find once more the characteristic features of ascetic and penitential sanctity, temporarily eclipsed by the apolistic zeal of the first generations.

Under the influence of the Mendicants, therefore, the Italian 'pantheon' changed perceptibly between the end of the thirteenth and the beginning of the fifteenth centuries. It evolved in two ways: there was a feminization

---

BN, H. 1373) and Antony of Amendola (d. 1435), venerated in the Marches (*PC* (Fermo, 1755), *ASV, Riti*, Proc. 744).

[215] For the decline of Franciscan influence in the Florentine contado, see C. M. de La Roncière, 'L'influence des Franciscains dans la campagne de Florence au XIVe siècle (1280–1360)', *MEFR*, 87 (1975), pp. 27–103, especially pp. 95–100.

[216] The principal Servite saints with a local cult were: Philip Benizzi (d. 1285) (see *Processus de miraculis* = *BHL* 6821); Joachim of Siena (d. 1306) (P. M. Suarez, sv Gioacchino da Siena, in *BS*, VI (Rome, 1965), cc. 476–8); Francis Patrizzi of Siena (d. 1328) (a *Vita* by Christopher of Parma (= *BHL* 3139) is ed. P. Soulier, *Anal. Boll.*, 14 (1895), pp. 174–95); and Pellegrino Laziosi of Forli (d. 1345) (*PC* (Forli, 1697–8), *ASV, Riti*, Proc. 828; a *Vita* (= *BHL* 6628) by Vital de Avantiis is ed. B. Canali, *Vita del B. Pellegrino Laziosi da Forli* (Lucca, 1725), pp. 165–70). Carmelite saints include: Albert of Trapani or of Messina (d. 1307) (*Vita* and miracles in *AA.SS.* Aug. II, pp. 226–35 (= *BHL* 228, 229)) and Andrea Corsini, bishop of Fiesole (d. 1373) (*PC* (Fiesole, 1602–3), *ASV, Riti*, Proc. 759). The town of Florence asked Pope Paul II to canonize the latter: see the documents published by *Daniel a Virgine Maria, Speculum Carmelitanum*, II (Antwerp, 1680), pp. 264–8; also *AA.SS.* Ian. II, pp. 1061–72; F. Caraffa, sv Andrea Corsini, in *BS*, I (Rome, 1961), cc. 1158–68.

of lay sanctity, and also a clericalization evident in the growing importance, from 1300, of regulars from the new orders. The success of these
cults, linked to the increasing influence exercised by the 'frati' over urban
institutions and populations, was general and longlasting. The very diversity of the orders contributed to their success; hardly had the popularity
of the oldest orders – the Minors and the Preachers – begun to wane, in
the second third of the fourteenth century, when the newer orders took
up the torch and maintained the prestige of the model.

At the end of the Middle Ages, there was hardly an Italian town of any
size which was without, for patron, or among its patrons, a saint from the
Mendicant orders. Once having seized the initiative, the Mendicants carried all before them, as they were able to offer saints of every type to a
public which was always on the lookout for some new object of veneration.
Their activities contributed to the total eclipse of the episcopal model,
which was already in decline, and which only survived where it was
adopted by the regulars themselves. This is shown by the extraordinary
diffusion throughout fourteenth-century Italy and Provence of iconographical representations of the cult of St Louis of Anjou, who combined
the mitre of the prelate with the Franciscan habit of frieze.[217] The Mendicants were equally successful in eclipsing the lay saints of charity and
work, replacing them with their own tertiaries. Lastly, being themselves
pastors and preachers, they monopolized the prestige of priesthood,
thereby preventing secular priests from winning the honours of a cult.[218]
They even rivalled the hermits, as we see from the popularity of the
Augustinian St Nicholas of Tolentino. It was only in the domain of the
sainthood of pilgrimage and reclusion that they had nothing to offer. It
was therefore at this level that there survived a margin of liberty and
initiative sufficient to allow the people to continue, from time to time, to
play the role of creators of cults, otherwise lost to the Mendicants.[219]

Our study of local cults in the West between the end of the twelfth and
the beginning of the fifteenth centuries has shown the existence of an
invisible but real frontier running through medieval Christendom, separat-
ing two groups of countries, each characterized by a different conception

---

[217] Kaftal 1, cc. 633–8; Kaftal 2, cc. 698–702.
[218] See below, pp. 310–15.
[219] Even St Rock, a lay pilgrim whose cult spread throughout Christendom in the fifteenth
century was claimed, quite incorrectly, by the Franciscans, who retrospectively enlisted
him in their third order: Vauchez, sv Rocco, in *BS*, XI (Rome, 1968), cc. 264–73.

of sainthood. In the regions outside the Mediterranean world, a saint was first of all a dead person, or more precisely a dead body, that performed miracles. This designation was awarded to a man or a woman less as a function of the life they had led than of the martyrdom, often bloody, they had suffered. Reputations for sanctity also attached almost exclusively to persons of high rank, who came to the attention of their contemporaries both through their exercise of power, political or religious, and their membership of an illustrious lineage: kings, princes and bishops. Even when the criteria of Christian perfection began to change, particularly under the influence of the Mendicant orders, saints continued largely to be recruited from these milieux. Lastly, this local sainthood stifled and marginalized a popular sainthood whose heroes were hermits or innocent victims of murder, for the most part from the people themselves.

In the Mediterranean countries, and especially in Italy, it was the emotion experienced by the faithful at the spectacle of an existence renounced which played the decisive role in the genesis of reputations for sainthood. It was a way of life, before it revealed itself, as elsewhere, by miracles. The link with suffering was no less close than elsewhere in Christendom, but it held less fascination when it had been endured than when it was voluntarily assumed for love of God and one's neighbour; asceticism, poverty and chastity were intended both to liberate the body from sin and allow the saint to assimilate to a humble and suffering Christ. The *viri Dei* who enjoyed the greatest prestige were therefore not martyrs but those who reproduced, and in a sense actualized, the Passion in their own flesh. Furthermore, their social recruitment was more varied, even though saints from the urban bourgeoisie continued to outnumber by far those who were workers or peasants. In fact what differentiated these regions from the rest of Christendom was rather the absence of a privileged relationship between birth, power and sainthood. The latter was above all the fruit of a religious experience and in the eyes of the people, social origin counted for little as long as the signs of a life renounced were present. One last point differentiated the two geographical areas: in the Mediterranean countries, it seems that the people assimilated the conception of sanctity we have just described. As a general rule, we do not find, at the level of local cult, either open or concealed conflict between the devotions dear to the laity and those promoted by the clergy. This is not to say that perfect harmony reigned in this sphere; difficulties emerged in Italy in the fourteenth century, following the efforts of the Mendicant orders to orient the models of sainthood proposed for the imitation of the laity in a more contemplative direction, whereas most people were still more susceptible to the prestige of asceticism, pilgrimage and charitable works. But however sharp these antagonisms, they were nevertheless located within the same mental universe.

Comparable forms of sainthood existed in northern France, the Low Countries, the Anglo-Saxon and Germanic worlds and the Slav and Scandinavian countries. Female lay mysticism was, after all, born and produced its finest flowers by the end of the twelfth century in the regions stretching from Brabant and Liège to Thuringia, by way of the Rhine valley. But this flowering of sainthood did not here lead to public cults, much less canonization processes, as it did in Mediterranean Europe. It is true that these beguines led discreet and retired lives hidden away in their reclusoria, but this was equally the case in Italy and Provence, where they were nevertheless venerated during their lifetime. The difference between the two geographical areas I have defined is less, it seems to me, at the level of lived sainthood than at that of sainthood as it was actually perceived by the circles in which the devotion originated. To understand this dimorphism, therefore, we need to examine the way in which reputations for sainthood were born and became entrenched in the medieval West.

THE ORIGINS OF THE DIMORPHISM: THE RISE OF THE CULTS AND SOCIO-POLITICAL STRUCTURES

A study of the forms of sainthood favoured at a given period in the various parts of Christendom, if it is to be more than just an inventory, has to be accompanied by an attempt to relate the ideal models to the society which produced them. This link is difficult to discern once the cult of a saint has already achieved a degree of fame; to say that it was popular is simply to recognize that it was widespread among the population, which tells us nothing about its real origin. It is necessary, therefore, whenever possible, to go back to the origin of the devotion and ask why, in a given country or group of countries, the perception of sanctity and the development of the new cults happened selectively, if not exclusively, to the advantage of certain categories of people.

Aristocratic models

As we have seen, outside the Mediterranean countries, the intercessors who enriched local sainthood between the late twelfth and early fifteenth centuries were almost all from the nobility, and often the very highest. But when we seek to reconstruct in detail the genesis of these devotions, we soon realize that, within the socio-cultural area in which the aristocratic models prevailed, there were significant differences from one country to another.

The clerical construct

In the British Isles and Scandinavia, it was the model of the holy bishop which enjoyed the greatest success in the later Middle Ages. This observation leads the historian to ask why, in these regions, the secular prelates attracted the attention of their contemporaries more than other categories of saints. An exceptionally well-documented case, that of St Thomas Cantilupe, bishop of Hereford, will allow us to reconstruct, at least in broad outline, the process from the birth of a devotion to its general diffusion, and to study the social aspects of the dynamics of the cult in action.[220] The bishop died in 1282 at San Severo, near Orvieto, on his way to the Roman Curia to defend himself against the accusations of the archbishop of Canterbury, John Peckham, and to try to get the pope to lift the excommunication pronounced by his metropolitan. His eventual successor, Canon Richard Swinfield, carried his remains back to England. His heart, which he had promised in his will to Edmund, Earl of Cornwall, was deposited at Ashridge and his bones were laid in a tomb in the north transept of Hereford Cathedral. A campaign then began, orchestrated by the majority of the cathedral chapter, to have the sanctity of their dead bishop recognized.[221] Miracles were recorded as early as 1283. This provoked the wrath of the archbishop of Canterbury, who was all the angrier in that the conflict over the autonomy of jurisdiction of the diocesan official which had led to the bishop's excommunication was still unresolved. The procurator of the Hereford chapter was, in fact, suspended from his functions by the official of Canterbury for having made public a cure which

---

[220] *PC Thomas of Hereford*, MS Vat. lat., 4015; large sections are ed. in *AA.SS.* Oct. I, pp. 584–696.

[221] For the vicissitudes of the cult before his canonization, see *A roll of household expenses of Richard de Swinfield, Bishop of Hereford during part of the years 1289 and 1290*, ed. J. Webb, 2 vols. (Camden Society, 59, 62, London, 1854), esp. I, pp. clxxxiiff; Bannister, *The cathedral church of Hereford*, pp. 68–72, 165–75. My book was completed before I became aware of R. C. Finucane's *Miracles and pilgrims*; the chapter dealing with the miracles of St Thomas and the pilgrimage to Hereford (pp. 173–98) largely confirms my own conclusions.

had occurred within the cathedral and attributed it to the intercession of the holy bishop.[222] But the opposition of the primate could not prevent the spread of the *fama sanctitatis*, because the majority of the English prelates sided with the bishop and demonstrated their support by, one after the other, granting forty days' indulgence to those of their flock who made a pilgrimage to his tomb.[223] Richard Swinfield, once elected to the see of Hereford, did everything in his power to rehabilitate the memory of his predecessor and promote his cult. He asked his procurators at the Curia to carry out an investigation at San Severo to discover whether any miracles had occurred at the spot where Thomas had initially been buried.[224] At Hereford, meanwhile, they came thick and fast, so much so that, in the week 28 March–3 April 1287, it was possible to proceed to the solemn translation of the prelate's remains into a new tomb, still in the cathedral, in the presence of Edward I and many bishops. An obit was then instituted in his memory.[225] The devotion soon spread beyond the boundaries of the diocese to the whole of England.[226]

At the process of canonization in 1307, all the witnesses questioned about the general diffusion of the *fama sanctitatis* of St Thomas dated it to sixteen or twenty years before, that is between 1287 and 1291.[227] It was, in fact, in 1288 that the cathedral clergy had organized the first celebration of the feast of the saint. It is difficult to say what exactly this liturgical ceremony consisted of: probably a mass *de reliquiis*, with a special commemoration of the new servant of God, as we know happened at Lincoln

---

[222] The cure was of a 'frenetic' called Edith. Unable to deny the reality of the miracle, which had occurred before several witnesses, the official of Canterbury, Thomas of Saint-Omer, attributed it to Thomas Cantilupe's immediate predecessor, Robert le Breton (1268–75), who had also died in an odour of sanctity. But Edith was adamant that 'se fuisse curatam meritis dicti sancti Thomas qui apparuerat ei et quem viderat quando erat episcopus Herefordensis, et non meritis domini Roberti': *AA.SS.* Oct. I, p. 696. The manuscript of the first collection of miracles, recorded in 1283–4, is described by T. D. Hardy, *Descriptive catalogue of material*, III (London, 1871), pp. 217–20.

[223] For example, in 1284, by the bishop of Worcester: *Charters and records of Hereford Cathedral*, ed. W. Capes (Hereford, 1908), p. 153. For the activities of the English episcopate, see above, p. 40.

[224] *Registrum Ricardi de Swinfield episcopi Herefordensis*, ed. W. Capes (London, 1909), p. 68.

[225] J. Britton, *The history and antiquities of the cathedral church of Hereford* (London, 1836), pp. 56–8.

[226] The best evidence is perhaps the statement of one witness at the process of 1307 (*PC Thomas of Hereford*, fol. 79v): 'Pene commune iuramentum multorum de Anglia volencium aliquid asserere iuramento est quia iurant per sanctum Thomam de Hereford.' Similarly, when two Englishmen met in France and exchanged news, the first thing mentioned was the proliferation of miracles obtained through his intercession: *AA.SS.* Oct. I, p. 698.

[227] *PC Thomas of Hereford*, fol. 79v (over twenty years), fol. 87 (eighteen years).

on the anniversary of the death of Robert Grosseteste (d. 1253).[228] That the pilgrimage was enjoying increasing success at the same period is suggested by a conflict which arose within the chapter in 1288, and flared up again in 1293 and 1295, over the question of the distribution of the wax offered at the tomb of St Thomas.[229] It was now not only his feast which attracted visitors; they filed through the cathedral all year round, but in particular at Easter, Whitsuntide and in the autumn.[230] According to some witnesses at the process, there were distinct stages in the growth of the devotion: for two years, from 1287 to 1289, rumours (*rumores*) circulated concerning the miraculous power of his remains; then, around 1290, the throng of people (*concursus*) reached such proportions that churches situated on the roads leading to Hereford grew rich in their turn from the offerings left as they passed by.[231] So widespread was his popularity among the English people that it became possible to contemplate embarking on the canonization procedure.[232] In 1290, the bishop and chapter of Hereford wrote to Pope Nicholas IV to this effect. Their overtures were tirelessly repeated until Clement V, in 1307, granted a bull appointing three commissioners to investigate the life and miracles of Thomas Cantilupe.[233] The pressure by the English bishops and king on the Holy See was stepped up once the *informatio in partibus*, held in London and Hereford in 1307, had been completed. Their insistence eventually overcame the hesitations of the Sacred College and the bishop of Hereford was canonized by John XXII at Avignon on 17 April 1320.[234]

This example allows us to see the extent to which, in thirteenth- and fourteenth-century England, the initiative in the cult of the saints was taken by the clergy. The process by which the devotion developed and spread had, from start to finish, a specifically ecclesiastical character. Admittedly, the laity played a by no means negligible role, and without

---

[228] Britton, *Cathedral church of Hereford*, p. 57; Kemp, 'Robert Grosseteste'.

[229] *Registrum Ricardi de Swinfield*, pp. 230, 287–9.

[230] 'Quia tunc homines vacantes ab operibus suis possunt liberius peregrinari': *PC Thomas of Hereford*, fol. 87.

[231] *Ibid.*, fol. 121v.

[232] *Ibid.*, fol. 31v: 'ita est publicum ut de Sancto Thoma Cantuariensi vel plus, quia plures confluunt ibi. Et ad quamcumque villam Anglie homo veniat, gentes communiter dicunt predicta.' The popularity of the Hereford pilgrimage further increased when several English bishops added it to the list of penitential pilgrimages recommended to expiate sins. See, for example, *Registrum Hamonis Hethe episopi Roffensis, A.D. 1319–1352*, ed. C. Johnson, I (Oxford, 1948), p. 200.

[233] See above, p. 78.

[234] John XXII, *Unigenitus filius*, 17.IV.1320, ed. in Fontanini, *Codex constitutionem*, pp. 131–4.

the favourable reception they gave to the new saint and their faith in the efficacy of his intercession, the best efforts of Bishop Swinfield (1283–1317) and his successor, Orleton (1317–27), would probably have been in vain. But though they contributed to the success of the cult, they were not its creators, nor, at least to begin with, its propagators. Their acceptance of the clerical model remained passive; their devotion was externalized only in pilgrimages, provoked in large measure by the promise of indulgences. The feasts were above all liturgical celebrations (obit, anniversary mass etc.) and in no surviving document is there any evidence of popular rejoicing. The regular clergy, lastly, observed these activities with a certain reserve; the Mendicant orders had been the last to join the campaign in favour of the canonization of Robert Grosseteste in 1289.[235] At the process of canonization of Thomas Cantilupe, the only statements which reveal a degree of scepticism with regard to the bishop's sainthood were those of a few London Franciscans. Not content with reporting the words of an old friend of St Thomas, now himself a Minor, to the effect that he was a good man but no more, they denounced the deceptions which had accompanied the proliferation of miracles attributed to him, letting it be known that they had been orchestrated in a suspect manner by the Hereford chapter.[236] Lastly, though the episcopate gained the cooperation of the lay authorities, the latter only participated in the birth of the cult to the extent of attending ceremonies organized by the clergy, such as the translation of 1287, and by providing diplomatic support for the manœuvres which preceded the canonization. From start to finish, the creation of a reputation for sainthood remained essentially a clerical construct.

The action of the Hereford cathedral clergy had been all the more effective in that it received a degree of popular support. Some of the depositions of witnesses at the process in 1307 allow us to trace the progress of the popularity of the new saint, and to some extent explain it. One of the alleged miracles concerned a hanged man who was miraculously saved by the intercession of St Thomas.[237] The man was a thief called William Craig, who had been seized and hanged from a gallows by

---

[235] Cole, 'Proceedings relative to the canonization of Robert Grosseteste', pp. 29–30.
[236] The four Franciscans were Hugh of London, Henry of Sinton, John of Westwood and Walter of Canterbury (witnesses 25–28, *PC Thomas of Hereford*, fols. 45v–48v). Henry went as far as to say 'quod ipse et alii fratres ordinis non facile credunt miracula que audiunt interdum a populo enarrari, quia constat eis multas fraudes super operacione miraculorum intervenisse in Anglia' (fol. 47v; see Appendix 2 below, p. 583).
[237] *Ibid.*, fols. 8–14 (witnesses 2–4).

the judicial authorities in 1292. He appeared already to be dead when the median beam of the gibbet broke. According to the witnesses, Earl William de Braose and his wife Mary, who were present at the execution, the robber was hanged a second time, but the rope broke. As his body showed all the signs of death, the priest William 'de Codimeston' had it carried into the chapel of the nearest village. Mary of Braose then dedicated it to St Thomas, and soon, against all expectations, the corpse showed signs of life.[238] A few weeks later, William Craig was restored to health and able to make a pilgrimage to Hereford in gratitude. Picturesque though the story may be, it is mainly interesting to us in that it permits us to see the relationship which was established between the miracle – however real – and the intercession of St Thomas Cantilupe. In the absence of William Craig himself, who had died two years earlier, the baron, his wife and the priest all stated that the thief had said that he had seen a bishop supporting his feet while he was swinging at the end of the rope, without being able to recognize him.[239] The identification between the bishop of the vision and St Thomas only became clear when Mary of Braose explicitly dedicated the dead man to him.

The vision of the hanged man – even if a later forgery – reveals the model of sainthood which prevailed in late thirteenth-century England in the popular mind, under the influence of the secular clergy. The lay aristocracy, recognizing the prelate as one of them, contributed to the success of the cult by spreading his name. In another miracle of St Thomas Cantilupe described at the process of canonization, some knights, arriving at the very moment when a group of peasants had pulled a drowned child from the water, suggested that they should dedicate the child to the bishop of Hereford, which they did with predictable success.[240] Whether clergy or laity, it was always the ruling classes who suggested the name of the intercessor and assured the growth of the devotion. This did not prevent it from becoming popular once the masses had adopted the new intercessor, whose thaumaturgical powers seem to have been remarkable. It is a striking fact that the cult of St Thomas had no connection with the

---

[238] The words are given in French, the language originally used (*ibid.*, fol. 11): 'Prions Deu et seint Thomas de Cantelup que luy donne vie et si il luy donne vie, nous le emmenerons a lavant dit seint Thomas.' As she made the vow, Mary of Braose bent a penny on William Craig's head, as was the custom in England.

[239] *Ibid.*, fol. 12: 'non tamen exprimebat dictus Willelmus Craigh predictum episcopum fuisse dictum Dominum Thomam de Cantilupo' (witness 3, Henry of Braose). William of Codimeston was even clearer on this point (fol. 14).

[240] See MS BN lat. 5373 A, fol. 67.

urban community of Hereford, where he had been bishop for many years. Among the witnesses at the 1307 process, inhabitants of the surrounding countryside or further afield were far more numerous than those from the town where the dead saint was buried. This situation is only apparently paradoxical; the thirteenth-century English bishop was not primarily an urban person, and Thomas Cantilupe had been, in his lifetime, one of those 'manor bishops' who spent more time on their rural estates than in their episcopal town. In fact, his reputation for sanctity was the work not of the inhabitants of Hereford but of the cathedral chapter with the support of the country 'gentry'.[241]

Sometimes, the cult seems to have been wholly a clerical 'construct', as in the case of the holy bishop Brynulph of Skara (1240–1317), in early fifteenth-century Sweden. Brynulph had been remembered after his death as a good bishop but the negligence of his contemporaries, followed by the Black Death, which removed the last persons who had known him, had not allowed his *fama sanctitatis* to develop into a devotion. Or so at least it was claimed at the process of canonization in 1417 in order to explain the total absence of a cult prior to 1404.[242] At the end of the fourteenth century, however, he was once again talked about and St Bridget, in one of her Revelations, learned from the mouth of the Virgin Mary that Brynulph had been one of the chosen and that she regretted that he had never been honoured. The divine message was confirmed by a sweet perfume emanating from his tomb in the cathedral at Skara.[243] In 1404, wishing to endow his diocese with an authentic saint, Bishop Brynulph II proceeded to the exhumation and translation of the relics of his predecessor. Miracles were immediately performed with the water used to wash his body; people began to flock to his tomb, where cures proliferated. They were carefully recorded and published from 1413. In 1414, the bishop of Skara started to investigate the life of St Brynulph and assembled all the written documents concerning him he could find. He himself and his clergy had good reason to glorify the memory of this

---

[241] R. Brentano (*Two Churches*, p. 219) has stressed the difference between English 'manor bishops' and Italian 'city bishops'. As we will see, the thirteenth-century English bishop was also a 'scholar bishop', which further emphasized his aristocratic character.

[242] *PC Brynulph of Skara*, ed. C. Annerstedt, in *Scriptores rerum suecicarum Medii Aevi*, III, 2 (Uppsala, 1876), pp. 163, 181. According to one witness, only thirty-four out of 500 priests survived the Black Death in the diocese.

[243] *PC Bridget*, p. 531. This vision must be seen in the context of the struggle in devout Scandinavian circles to replace the cult of the holy kings with that of the holy bishops.

prelate, who had stood up to the lay authorities, like the other contemporary bishop whose canonization was sought by the Swedish episcopate at this period, Nicholas of Linköping (d. 1391).[244] The regulars lent their support; witnesses at the process in 1417 remembered having heard the Franciscan preacher Johannes Helgonis describe Brynulph in glowing terms in a sermon preached in the vernacular, and another Franciscan, Brother Mathias, advised penitents to dedicate themselves to the saint.[245] The faithful soon adopted the new devotion. At the same process, a lay witness called Ambernus told how, having heard a voice tell him to 'make a vow to a holy man, the idea came to him in a flash to address his vow to St Brynulph of Skara', at which he was cured of his ills.[246] Another reliable sign is that, around 1410, mothers in the diocese began to invoke the new saint when their children's lives were in danger; those who were saved by his intercession then became *viri beati Brynolphi*.[247] In the space of a few years, Brynulph became a popular saint. A request for his canonization was presented at the council of Constance in 1416, and a year later, during the enquiry into his life and miracles, Brynulph II could point to the diffusion throughout the diocese and even beyond of his predecessor's reputation for sainthood.[248] Like Nicholas of Linköping in the next diocese, but more so since he had long mouldered in obscurity, the cult of Brynulph of Skara was a pure construct of the diocesan clergy, where the laity's only role, as in England, was to accept the model offered to them.

This is not to say, of course, that, in the British Isles and the Scandinavian countries, all the recent cults followed a similar pattern. Devotion to a hermit or monk could emerge and grow more spontaneously, with the support of elements external to the secular clergy. But the saints who were most prominent, and who won admirers from beyond the monastery or village where they had lived, were persons on whose behalf the episcopate had mobilized and whose cult they had promoted with the assistance of the ruling classes. It is hardly surprising, in these circumstances, that they were all, if not bishops, at least members of the aristocracy.

---

[244] *PC Brynulph*, p. 166: the second witness, the Franciscan Hermann Nilsson, reported the words of an old canon: 'Heu nobis! heu, quia nemo est qui se opponat murum pro domo Domini, sicut fecit beatus pater noster Brynolphus.' For relations between Church and State in late fourteenth- and early fifteenth-century Sweden, see Y. Brilioth, *Kungadöme och Pävemakt, 1363–1414* (Uppsala, 1925).

[245] *PC Brynulph*, pp. 165, 174.

[246] *Ibid.*, p. 173.

[247] *Ibid.*, p. 169.

[248] Gallen, 'Les causes de Ste Ingrid et les saints suédois'.

The dynastic initiative

In France, or, to be more precise, the area of modern France, that is including Brittany and Provence, there was not the same homogeneity as in England at the level of local sanctity. Prelates like St William and Philip of Bourges, a king like St Louis and a priest like St Yves, the greatest saints produced by thirteenth-century France, appear, at first sight, to have little in common. When we look more closely, however, we cannot but be struck by the decisive role played by the monarchy in this sphere. We know that St Louis was present at many translations of relics and that he encouraged the cults introduced by the Mendicant orders, such as that of St Peter Martyr.[249] He was also the first to request the canonization of the archbishop of Bourges, Philip Berruyer, from Pope Urban IV.[250] One might interpret this as simply a sign of his personal piety, but the attitude of his successors shows this to be an insufficient explanation. They first set out to glorify the memory of the son of Blanche of Castile.[251] Several Mendicants who had known him during his lifetime were invited by the royal family to commit their memories to writing in *Vitae*, which, as is well known, was done by the Dominicans Geoffrey of Beaulieu, William of Chartres and William of Saint-Pathus.[252] A few years later, the Mendicants and the Capetian dynasty again colluded after the death at Brignoles in 1297 of the young St Louis of Anjou, a Friar Minor and bishop of Toulouse. His body was conveyed to Marseilles and deposited with the Cordeliers. They made themselves the propagators of the cult, at least locally, since the authorities of the Franciscan order seem at first to have shown little enthusiasm for the cause of the young prince, who had been

---

[249] Carolus-Barré, 'Saint Louis et la translation des corps saints', pp. 1087–112. For the introduction into France of the cult of St Peter Martyr, see D. M. Chapotin, *Histoire des Dominicains de la province de France: le siècle des fondations* (Rouen, 1898).

[250] Urban IV, *Ut corda fidelium*, 30.VII.1262, in unpublished MS Vat. lat. 4019, fol. 3v, decreeing the canonization process of Philip of Bourges, at the request of Louis IX and the French bishops.

[251] The attitude of Charles of Anjou is made very clear in his deposition at the canonization process of 1282–3 ('Déposition de Charles d'Anjou', ed. Riant, pp. 155–80); see above, p. 182.

[252] The first two are ed. F. Du Chesne, *Historiae Francorum scriptores*, V (Paris, 1649), pp. 444–65, 466–77; the third is published in *Recueil des historiens des Gaules et de la France*, XX (Paris, 1840), pp. 116ff. There is no good general study of the cult of St Louis in medieval France, though the material for such a study in the field of art has been assembled; see E. Mâle, 'La vie de Saint Louis dans l'art français au commencement du XIVe siècle', in *Mélanges E. Bertaux* (Paris, 1924), pp. 193–204; P. M. Auzas, 'Essai d'un répertoire iconographique de Saint Louis', in *Septième centenaire de la mort de Saint Louis. Actes des colloques de Royaumont et Paris (21–27 mai 1970)* (Paris, 1976), pp. 3–56.

much influenced by Peter Olivi and whose sympathies had clearly lain with the 'spiritual' tendency.[253] But miracles soon occurred at his tomb and within a few years his reputation for sainthood had spread throughout Provence.[254] This sudden celebrity was exploited by the opportunist Charles II, who used the popularity of his younger son – despite having thwarted his vocation – to further his dynastic ambitions.[255] In so doing, he was seeking to imitate the House of France, whose prestige had benefited a few years earlier from the canonization of Louis IX. Accordingly, in 1300, Charles began to work for the canonization of his son. His efforts succeeded during the pontificate of John XXII, who was well disposed towards the Angevin dynasty and had known the young saint personally. The enquiry was held in 1307 in Marseilles.[256] But already, in 1306, Robert of Anjou, vicar of Charles II in Provence, in the name of his father, had instituted an annual rent of 25 livres to celebrate his brother's anniversary.[257] And it is clear from the process of 1307 that a confraternity dedicated to St Louis of Anjou was already in existence in Aix.[258] After the canonization, King Robert established a free fair to be held at Marseilles on the day of the saint's feast and the two following days;[259] on 8 November 1319 he attended the solemn translation of the remains, which was an occasion for much popular rejoicing.[260] He went on to make many foundations in honour of his brother, writing, for example, to the Dominican prior and brothers of Saint-Maximin in 1337 to ask them to dedicate

[253] E. Pasztor, *Per la storia di S. Ludovico d'Angio (1274–1297)* (Rome, 1955).
[254] If the seventy miracles recorded at the enquiry of 1307 are classified by diocese (on the basis of place of origin of the beneficiary), the results are: Marseilles 24; Aix 8; Sisteron 5; Fréjus 5; Arles 4; Carpentras 4; Avignon 3; Toulon 3; Gap 3; Nîmes 2; Valence 2; Narbonne 1; Nice 1; Limoges 1; Cahors 1; Riez 2; unknown 1. As these figures show, his reputation was essentially confined to Provence, and diminished in proportion as one left the Aix–Marseilles region.
[255] Another clever use of the cult of saints by Charles II was his success in persuading Boniface VIII to accept that the true relics of Mary Magdalene were at Saint-Maximin, not Vézelay, as had previously been believed, which spelled doom for the Burgundian sanctuary: V. Saxer, *Le dossier vézelien de Marie Madeleine: invention et translation des reliques en 1265–1267* (Brussels, 1975).
[256] *PC Louis of Anjou*, ed. in *Processus canonizationis et Legendae variae sancti Ludovici O.F.M. episcopi Tolosani, Analecta Franciscana*, VII (Quaracchi, 1951), pp. 1–154.
[257] Laurent, *Le culte de S. Louis d'Anjou*, p. 38, note 27.
[258] *PC Louis of Anjou*, p. 93 (deposition of Durandus Curaterii of Aix): 'et dixit quod Aquis cives eiusdem loci colunt et faciunt festum de ipso quolibet anno sicut de uno sancto, et in honore Dei et ipsius domini Ludovici fecerunt et constituerunt cives predicti confratriam et anno quolibet augmentatur et crescit in numero personarum'. One would very much like to know the social status of the members of this precocious confraternity.
[259] Laurent, *Le culte de S. Louis d'Anjou*, pp. 43–4.
[260] *Ibid.*, pp. 47–52.

228 TYPOLOGY OF MEDIEVAL SAINTHOOD

the first chapel to be built in their church to the new saint.[261] In 1362 the abbey of Saint-Victor of Marseilles decided to make his feast a holiday in gratitude for the House of Anjou, from which it had received many gifts.[262]

Devotion to St Louis of Anjou was not confined to Provence or even southern France, but spread in the northern part of the kingdom thanks to the activities of the monarchy. Philip VI of Valois, nephew of the saint, settled rents on the *frairies* in his kingdom, which were dedicated to him, such as that established in 1329 in the church of the Friars Minor in Le Mans, which received a royal endowment of 200 livres.[263] The following year, the king went in person to Marseilles to venerate the relics of his uncle and, on this occasion, instituted an annual alms of 50 *livres parisis* on behalf of the town's Franciscan convent.[264] Later, another scion of the French royal family, Charles of Blois, duke of Brittany, a devotee of the young saint, raised an altar in his honour in the church of the Cordeliers of Guingamp.[265]

The cult of St Louis of Anjou, about which we are better informed than about that of St Louis, owed much of its success, at least in France, to the close collaboration between various branches of a dynasty, that is, the Capetians, and a Mendicant order, that is, the Friars Minor. In fact, it is very difficult to distinguish their respective roles in the spread of the devotion. The Franciscans of Marseilles were probably the originators of the *fama sanctitatis* of the young prince. But, as we have seen, the Angevins of Naples, followed by the Valois, very soon realized how it could be used to their advantage. The political aspect of the cult persisted up to the end of the Middle Ages: in 1423 the Aragonese, who had seized Marseilles, transferred the relics of St Louis of Anjou to Valencia. All subsequent efforts to recover them proved vain; in the bitter struggle for the succession to Joan II, who had recognized him as heir presumptive to the throne of Sicily, Alfonso V had seized one of the most precious symbols of dynastic legitimacy. Transplanted to Spain, the cult vegetated, cut

---

[261] *Ibid.*, p. 59.

[262] *Ibid.*, p. 66.

[263] L. Guilloreau, 'Une fondation royale en l'honneur de S. Louis d'Anjou chez les Cordeliers du Mans', *Revue historique et archéologique du Maine*, 49 (1901), pp. 46–9.

[264] Laurent, *Le culte de S. Louis d'Anjou*, pp. 55–6.

[265] *PC Charles of Blois*, ed. de Sérent, p. 54: 'dum erat comes Penthevri, fecit fieri in dicta ecclesia fratrum minorum de Guingampo . . . unum altare in honorem beati Ludovici de Marsilia, de cuius genere erat, videlicet in parte sinistra dicte ecclesie, prope cornu maioris altaris eiusdem'.

off from its familial roots.[266] But it remained alive in France, despite the loss of the precious remains.[267]

As we see from this particular case, the intervention of the kings of France and related princely families in the diffusion of new cults took a quite specific form. It was not simply diplomatic support, of the type given by the kings of England at this period to the efforts of the English episcopate to persuade the pope to start canonization proceedings on behalf of a particular English saint.[268] In fourteenth-century France, it seems to have been the monarchy itself, with the support of the Mendicant orders, which created the devotion towards certain servants of God, with a clearly political purpose.[269]

The best example of a cult which was both political and dynastic is that of Charles of Blois himself. This prince, husband of Marie of Penthièvre, was killed on 29 November 1364, at the battle of Auray, and his body buried in the church of the Cordeliers of Guingamp. Throughout his reign, the pious duke had defended the French cause in Brittany and been close to the Mendicant orders, on whom he had showered gifts.[270] But his entourage – the great Breton lords of his party – seem not to have held him in high regard during his lifetime and had been critical of his excessive generosity to the Church.[271] No miracle was attributed to him in the years immediately after his death. However, from 1366, groups of children began to arrive at Guingamp on pilgrimage 'from the regions of Blois and from France', that is from those regions held by Louis of Anjou, son-in-law of Charles through his wife Marie of Brittany and opponent of John

[266] Laurent, *Le culte de S. Louis d'Anjou*, pp. 97–102.

[267] *Ibid.*, pp. 103–8.

[268] Though this did, of course, happen. We know from the bull of canonization and other contemporary documents that, some time between 1342 and 1347, Charles of Blois, Duke of Brittany, scion of the Valois, went in person to Avignon to ask Clement VI, in consistory, to canonize St Yves (de la Borderie, *Monument originaux de l'histoire de S. Yves*, pp. xxvii–xxix). After the Schism, Charles VI imperiously demanded of Clement VII the canonization of the young cardinal Peter of Luxembourg (d. 1387) (*AA.SS.*, Iul. I, pp. 535–6, letter of 16.VI.1389).

[269] Nowhere is the link between Mendicants and state in the domain of the cult of the saints clearer than in their iconographical schemas. Thus, Charles of Blois was represented in the Dominican church at Guingamp alongside several Dominican saints: 'ymagines sanctorum de Britannia qui fuerunt de genere regum, ducum et comitum' (*PC Charles of Blois*, p. 53).

[270] de Sérent, 'Charles de Blois, duc de Bretagne'; H. Martin, *Les Ordres Mendiants*, pp. 366–71, 409–11.

[271] At the canonization process of 1371, many witnesses told how Charles of Blois had made himself unpopular by his 'clericalism' (*PC*, pp. 38, 49, 128, 168 etc.).

IV, the new duke, who had English support. The statements recorded at the process in 1371 on the subject of the origins of the devotion repay close scrutiny. According to a clerk of Guingamp, Yves Bégut, these little ones (*parvuli*) 'said they were going to see St Charles and that they lived off alms'. He and others who had seen them also told how 'God had revealed to men the sanctity of the dead duke; subsequently the people of the region thronged to his tomb.' Bégut also emphasized that the children had shown the way to pilgrims who came after them 'by erecting at crossroads piles of stones which bore in French the name of Montjoies, to indicate the route to those who went there'.[272] Another witness, Alain Maréchal, was even more specific in his deposition, declaring that 'people realized that God was working miracles thanks to the children who came from the region of Blois to visit the said tomb'.[273] After the children had been there, cures proliferated at Guingamp. The first to be officially recognized was made public in 1367 by the bishop of Tréguier, who granted forty days' indulgence 'to those who prayed for Charles of Blois and for the revelation and multiplication of his miracles'.[274] Events at Dinan brought the excitement to a climax: John IV, the ally of the English and conqueror of Charles of Blois, had ordered the effigy of his predecessor on the wall of the church of the Cordeliers in Dinan to be whitewashed. In February 1368, when the duke was staying in the town, the brethren noticed that the image had begun to bleed, and popular uproar followed.[275] News of the prodigy spread throughout Brittany and sparked off a wave of enthusiasm. 'Saint' Charles became, with St Yves, the official protector of the Bretons. The Breton companies who left for Italy in the service of Urban V in 1368 invoked both of them together.[276] That same

---

[272] *Ibid.*, pp. 324, 337. For children's pilgrimages in the late Middle Ages, see J. Delalande, *Les extraordinaires croisades d'enfants et de pastoureaux au Moyen Âge* (Paris, 1961); U. Gabler, 'Die Kinderwallfahrten aus Deutschland und der Schweiz zum Mont Saint-Michel', *Zeitschrift für Schweizerische Kirchengeschichte*, 63 (1969), pp. 221–331.
[273] *PC Charles of Blois*, p. 283.
[274] For the birth of the cult, see F. Plaine, *Essai historique sur le culte du Bienheureux Charles de Blois* (Nantes, 1872). The text of the letter of indulgence is in *ASV, Collectorie* 434 A, fol. 15.
[275] Martin, *Les Ordres Mendiants*, p. 409.
[276] See the expedition song in the *Geste des Bretons en Italie* of William de la Penne, ed. in Martène and Durand, *Thesaurus*, III, col. 1474:

> Les Bretons crient: Vive l'Eglise
> en appelant tous à voix vive
> voustre merci, Charles et Yves
> qu'aux dits Bretons furent amis.

See also *PC Charles of Blois*, p. 387.

year, images of the saint were offered for the veneration of the faithful in the Franciscan convents of Angers and Blois, and even Périgueux.[277] Wood-carvers reproduced his features and sold their works to the people although this was forbidden by the authorities.[278] The time was ripe for the opening of a process of canonization, which was requested in 1369 by Charles' widow, Joan of Penthièvre, and soon granted by Urban V.[279] Owing to the opposition of John IV, the commissioners had to stay in Angers, but many Bretons travelled there to affirm their faith in the saint-hood of their former duke. The costs of the process were borne in their entirety by Louis of Anjou.[280]

There can be little doubt that the whole process originated in a political will, that of Louis of Anjou, in view of the fact that the cult was initially imported from the territories controlled by the Valois. The discontent felt by the local population at the government of John IV, together with the activities of the Friars Minor of Guingamp and other local convents caused a U-turn in public opinion in favour of the dead sovereign. Subsequently, from 1367, the devotion assumed a specifically Breton character, with the support of the Breton bishops, and soon became very popular. But it seems doubtful whether, without the intervention of the French royal family, with Franciscan support, the reputation for sanctity of Charles of Blois would ever have found such a response.

To argue that, in late medieval France, only members of the ruling dynasty could accede to the honours of the cult would be to distort the truth. It is clear, however, that to achieve fame, the cause of a saint had to have the approval, if not support, of the government. Unlike their English equivalents, the French secular clergy seem to have felt little desire, in the fourteenth century, to promote new devotions. The natural allies of the monarchy were, therefore, the Mendicants, whose spirituality

---

[277] The convent at Angers was a great centre for the propagation of the cult of Charles of Blois and where the canonization process of 1371 was held. A collection of miracles recorded by the Friars Minor of Périgueux is in *ASV, Collectorie* 434 A, fols. 242–5.

[278] *PC Charles of Blois*, p. 396.

[279] Pocquet du Haut-Jussé, *Les papes et les ducs de Bretagne*, I, pp. 357–60; A. Vauchez, 'Canonisation et politique au XIVe siècle'.

[280] For the letters from Louis of Anjou telling his 'money men' in Angers to hurry up and pay the commissioners, who were threatening to decamp, see above p. 65, note 11. The political importance of the event is also shown by the sermon of the bishop of Saint-Brieuc, Hugh of Montelais, on 22 October 1372, when he rallied to Louis of Anjou: 'Item jurons et promettons comme dessus que la canonization de Monsieur Charles de sainte mémoire, duc de Bretagne, de laquelle le procès est commencé en cours de Rome, ne empescherons ne ceux qui voudront empescher ne conseillerons' (Hay du Chastelet, *Histoire de Bertrand du Guesclin*, p. 309).

and pastoral zeal made them, in contrast, always keen to encourage them. But they did not, as in Italy, seek to orient the piety of the faithful towards humble lay people or regulars from their own ranks. Putting their influence at the service of the royal and princely families, they chose rather to encourage veneration of eminent members of the aristocracy.[281] Had they tried to do other, they would probably have failed; in France, the rise of the new devotions, which would condemn popular cults to obscurity, could only succeed with the support of the ruling classes and monarchy.

Bourgeois and popular models

Popular emotion and panic pilgrimages

In the Mediterranean countries, and especially in Italy, the circumstances in which the new cults emerged and developed were very far from uniform. Devotion was kindled, as we have seen, by the spectacle of the life of renunciation led by certain persons who were already called saints during their lifetime and who were known to all. News of their death spread like wildfire through the village or town where they had lived. Immediately, the faithful left their houses and rushed to wherever the still-warm body lay in order to touch it and be 'sanctified'.[282] There followed the disorderly, even violent, scenes so often described by hagiographers and chroniclers; amidst general tumult, some tore the clothes of the deceased to pieces, whilst others pulled out their hair and nails. Those who were unable to get close enough in the crush tried at least to touch the corpse with objects which they then carried home as talismans.[283] The

---

[281] This was still the case in 1414–15, when the cult of Joan-Marie of Maillé (d. 1414) started in the middle Loire. The informative process carried out at Tours by the Friars Minor and the biography composed by the warden of the convent were sent to Avignon by the count of Bourbon, James de la Marche. The saint belonged to the Bourbon family and had been close to the countess of Alençon, and the 'queens of Cyprus', Charlotte and Yolande. See the *epistola nuncupatoria* of the warden of the Friars Minor of Tours, ed. *AA.SS.* Mar. III, pp. 173–4.

[282] For how news of the death of the Franciscan Philip of Aix was received in Naples in 1369, see *Chronica XXIV generalium, Analecta Franciscana*, III (Quaracchi/Florence, 1897), p. 570: 'Cum autem adhuc ejus mors, paucis demptis fratribus, non esset nota, rumor a deo immissus totam Neapolitanam lustravit civitatem, omnibus fere acclamantibus: mortuus est quidam sanctissimus frater Minorum in monasterio Sanctae Clarae. Et subito factus est tantus concursus hominum utriusque aetatis et sexus ut propter pressuram per pluries dies non posset tradi ecclesiasticae sepulturae.'

[283] On news of the death of Douceline in Marseilles in 1275, 'as soon as people knew she was dead, they all rushed eagerly to see and touch the holy body, so great was the devotion felt for her. Everyone who could find something which had belonged to her

disposal of the body was often a cause of conflict between laity and clergy; the former suspected the latter of seeking to deprive them of their devotion by taking the body elsewhere. They frequently took the initiative, therefore, and carried it into a church of their choice or the cathedral.[284] This was what happened at Assisi on 25 May 1230, when the communal authorities, afraid they might lose the body of St Francis, performed the translation on their own authority, having forbidden the commissioners sent for this purpose by Gregory IX to act.[285] At Padua, in the days following the death of St Antony, the whole Caudalunga quarter teetered on the verge of insurrection because the Franciscans were proposing to take the saint's remains from the convent of the Clares of Arcella, where, on 13 June 1231, he had died, to their own church of Santa Maria Materdomini in the town centre. It needed an order from the bishop and the threat of armed intervention by the forces of the podesta before the body of the illustrious preacher could reach the site earmarked by the Brethren for his tomb.[286]

In general, the faithful were inclined to accuse the clergy of halfheartedness. The latter, though usually willing, wanted to take their time and do things according to the rules. As a result, the faithful often took the law into their own hands in order to accord the saint the honours they

carried it off to make into relics and everyone touched her with their rosaries or their rings or even their hoods. People even brought knives to cut her gown into pieces to divide between them. It was greatly feared that they might pull to pieces the holy body itself': *Vie de Sainte Douceline (1315)*, ed. and trans. J. H. Albenès (Marseilles, 1879), p. 155. For a psychological interpretaton of such scenes, see Carozzi, 'Douceline et les autres', pp. 259–61. There were similar violent scenes in 1387 in Avignon after the death of Peter of Luxemburg; see *AA.SS.* Iul. I, p. 495; *Annales avignonnaises de 1382 à 1410, extraites des Archives Datini*, ed. R. Brun, in *Mémoires de l'institut historique de Provence*, 12 (1935), p. 100, especially the letter written July 1387: 'Just imagine that since the day he was buried till now there have been so many people that you would think it was the coronation. They must bring at least a hundred kilos of candles every day and there are already more than a thousand wax images of one sort or another. It is the greatest event and the greatest devotion seen for a century.'

[284] After the death of the Franciscan Benvenuto of Gubbio (1232), the inhabitants of Corneto, Apulia, 'rushed to the Brothers' convent and despite their objections seized the body to carry it into the church of St Peter and give it an honourable burial' (*Dialogus de vitis sanctorum Fratrum Minorum*, ed. L. Lemmens (Rome, 1902), p. 34). See also Pietro Cantinelli on the beginnings of the cult of B. Nevolone of Faenza (d. 1280) in his *Chronicon (A. 1228–1306)*, ed. F. Torraca, in *RIS²*, XXVIII, 2 (Città di Castello, 1902), p. 402.

[285] Gregory IX condemned the attitude of the civil authorities and inhabitants of Assisi in the bull *Speravimus hactenus*, 16.VI.1230 (ed. in *Bull. Franc.*, I, pp. 66–7), which includes a fascinating account of events.

[286] There is a detailed, even picturesque, account in *S. Antonii Legenda prima*, pp. 64–5. See also J. Toussaert, *Antonius von Padua* (Cologne, 1967), pp. 450ff.

believed were deserved.[287] The first decision to be taken concerned the funeral: to allow the body of a servant of God to share the common lot would have been a sign of impiety. Rich devotees or the communal authorities accordingly purchased spices to embalm it. This operation was performed by doctors who removed the viscera, which were then placed in a vase and deposited in a cloister or the sacristy of a church.[288] The rest of the body, which must on no account be buried, was put into a wooden reliquary until a specially designed little mausoleum (*archa*) could be built to hold it. Only stone – often marble or porphyry – would assure the saint a worthy sepulchre. These tombs, built at great cost to the local population, were soon surrounded by railings so that the precious remains were still visible and accessible to pilgrims but could not be stolen.[289]

While the problems posed by the saint's funeral were being sorted out, usually very quickly, the town where the saint had died went into a state of shock. For many weeks, even months, an extraordinary atmosphere of collective devotion and festivity peculiar to the Mediterranean regions prevailed. Thus, at Padua, throughout June and July 1231, night and day, long processions spontaneously formed near the church which contained the body of St Antony and filed through the town. The barefoot crowd took over the city streets, carrying lighted candles and enormous trees of wax, born aloft by several men or carried on floats drawn by oxen. Some were in the form of candelabra, others of vines or fruits. The whole town was lit up and the population spent the night in prayer in the squares, confessing to the monks or priests who were in attendance.[290] There were similar scenes in Bologna in 1233, at the time of the 'Alleluia', which was marked by the exhumation and translation of the remains of St Dominic (d. 1221), and at Mantua, where the hermit John Bonus had gone to die,

---

[287] This was the case at Tagliacozzo in 1239 on the occasion of the translation of the remains of B. Odo of Novara (d. 1200): 'dum autem clerus ad debitas ceremonias pergendas se prepararet, plebs morae compatiens variis instrumentis ligneis ac fereis tumulum ex quo corpus transferendum erat aprire tentavit': *Anal. Boll.*, 1 (1882), p. 323.

[288] See the detailed description in the *Vie de Ste Marguerite de Città di Castello*, ed. M. H. Laurent, *AFP*, 10 (1940), p. 127.

[289] For a stone tomb offered by a private person (a rich Marseilles merchant, William of la Fonc) see *Vie de Sainte Douceline*, p. 201. In Italy the cost of making the *archa* was usually borne by the commune. See, for example, the deliberations of the council of Rieti, 5 November 1447, 'super sepulchrum faciendum faciendo et modo collocandi sacratissimum corpus B. Thomae ordinis pauperum de Observantia sancti Francisci', in *PC Thomas Bellacci* (d. 1447), Paris, BN, H. 1359, pp. 46–7.

[290] See the chapter entitled *De processionibus et devotione populi* in *S. Antonii Legenda prima*, pp. 71–4.

during the last months of 1249.[291] As soon as the first miracles were recorded – which usually happened without delay – the throng of towns-people was swollen by crowds of pilgrims from the contado, and soon from further afield. As prodigies proliferated, a veritable collective psychosis developed, which the Italian chroniclers called a *devotio*.[292] Salimbene described in some detail the 'folly' which, in his own words, gripped, one after the other, most of the large towns of the Po plain between 1267 and 1279 after the deaths of various lay saints, whose merits he also questioned: Antony the Pilgrim at Padua in 1267, Armanno Pungilupo at Ferrara in the same year, and above all Albert of Villa d'Ogna at Cremona, Parma and Reggio Emilia in 1279.[293] Dwelling at some length on the demonstrations of popular enthusiasm which followed Albert of Villa d'Ogna's death, he offered as explanations the desire of the sick and the infirm to be cured, the love of novelty on the part of the curious, the lure of pecuniary gain for the upper clergy, the jealousy felt by secular priests for the Mendicants and, lastly, the wish of citizens banned for political reasons to return, thanks to the amnesty which was common practice on such occasions.[294] The analysis is interesting, and all the factors he mentions certainly played a part at some stage. It does not, however, go to the heart of the matter, since it fails to explain how the movement began. On this point, the urban chronicles are more explicit. The author of the *Chronicon Parmense*, when he, like Salimbene, described the success of the *devotio* in honour of Albert of Villa d'Ogna in 1279, emphasized that it had been introduced into Parma by the *brentatores*, that is, the wine-porters, who were themselves influenced by their fellows in Cremona. The 'saint', during his lifetime, had practised this trade. At Parma, the success of the cult was immediate. Processions were organized by the

---

[291] For the Alleluia movement, see A. Vauchez, 'Une campagne de pacification en Lombardie autour de 1233'. For events in Mantua, see *PC John Bonus, AA.SS.* Oct. IX, p. 850: 'tempore mortis dicti fratris Johannis Boni, gentes Mantuae ibant et de partibus circum-stantibus catervatim cum magnis cereis et muneribus multis et pane et vino ad ecclesiam S. Agnetis, ubi est et erat corpus ejus, propter publicam famam sanctitatis et mirabilia quae Deus faciebat pro ipso'. The same witness stressed the spontaneity of the movement: 'dixit quod nec potestas Mantuae nex aliquis nisi Deus facere posset gentes Mantuae ad tantam reverentiam commoveri ad quantum propter publicam famam sanctitatis dicti viri et miraculorum eius gentes Mantuae tunc temporis sunt commotae'.

[292] The author of the *Chronicon Parmense* called the Alleluia movement *devocio fratrum predicatorum* (*RIS*[2], IX, 9, p. 10).

[293] Salimbene, *Cronica*, pp. 733–6.

[294] *Ibid.*, p. 736: 'de multiplici causa devocionis istius Alberti'. For Albert, see above, p. 204.

various district and professional *societates*. The parish clergy joined in and had Albert's likeness depicted in the churches. Miracles occurred in front of the images, and the devotion of the faithful was redoubled.[295] With the offerings of pilgrims, the commune and the *arti* arranged the purchase of a house to found a hospice which was named after the saint. The fact that Albert had been a layman was clearly crucial to the success of the cult. But the same thing might happen when the servant of God was a monk.[296]

This phenomenon was not confined either to Lombardy or to the period described by Salimbene, and religious manifestations of a similar type happened throughout the Mediterranean world during the thirteenth and fourteenth centuries.[297] In one case, the course of events can be traced on an almost daily basis thanks to a documentation which is both abundant and objective. The Book of the Reformations of the commune of Treviso has preserved the decisions taken by the town's civil authorities, with a summary of the deliberations which preceded them, on the occasion of the death of 'St' Henry and the great *devotio* which followed.[298] B. 'Rigo' or 'Arrigo', as he is called in contemporary texts, was a poor penitent from Bolzano who was renowned throughout the town of Treviso for his piety. When he died on 10 June 1315, a crowd flocked into the quarter called Panceria to see and touch his body. His funeral took place in an atmosphere of general exaltation which, when miracles were performed and the faithful saw blood running from his corpse, turned into collective delirium.[299] By 11 June, the authorities were besieged by demands and proposals regarding the saint's tomb, and the Council unanimously passed

[295] *Chronicon Parmense*, pp. 34–5: 'et certi brentatores de Parma qui Cremonam iverunt praeterea cum fuerunt Parmae fecerunt depingi figuram eius ad trofinam ecclesiae Sancti Patri in platea communis Parmae, ad quam figuram magna miracula dicta sunt fieri . . . et haec miracula inter alia fuerunt quia omnes misterii de Parma a majore usque ad minorem iverunt ad dictam figuram cum paliis et candellis'.

[296] As in Naples, on the death of the Franciscan Philip of Aix in 1369 (see above, p. 232, note 282).

[297] For the anthropological significance of these manifestations, which are by no means confined to the Middle Ages, see A. Dupront, 'Formes de la culture de masse: de la doléance au pèlerinage panique', in *Niveaux de culture et groupes sociaux* (Paris and The Hague, 1971), pp. 149–67.

[298] *Libri reformationum communis Tervisii*, quoted in *PC Henry of Treviso ASV, Riti*, Proc. 3021. Some documents concerning this case were edited by R. degli Azzoni Avogari, *De B. Henrico*.

[299] There is an excellent description of events in the *Vita* written after 1359 by the bishop of Treviso, Pier Domenico da Baone, who, as a young man, had been present at the disturbances when he was a clerk in the cathedral (*AA.SS.* Iun. II, pp. 370–86). Boccacio also gives a colourful version of events in Treviso in the *Decameron*, with a humorous account of the misfortunes of three Florentines who had infiltrated the crowd to see the miracles.

a Reformation ordering a tomb to be built at the expense of the commune. Altogether, it cost them over 1,000 livres.[300] The same day, as a sign of joy, all those imprisoned for debt who were able to obtain the 'peace' of their creditors – twenty-four – were released. Finally, the order was given for Henry's likeness to be painted on the walls of the communal palace.[301] The decisions taken over the following days and weeks enable us to trace the progress of the 'devotion': on 16 June, the commune had to take extraordinary measures to assure food for the multitudes who were flooding in to Treviso; on 17 June, the podesta was empowered to oblige those who were in possession of corn to sell it 'so that there should be no dearness either at present or in future'.[302] A month later it was necessary to compensate the collectors of the tax on bread, as the collection of farmed taxes had been suspended for fourteen days. This period of time probably roughly corresponds to the 'panic' phase of the movement. But it had not entirely died down, as on 6 October the guards who had been employed to protect the provisional tomb asked the authorities to hand over three months' unpaid wages.[303] Furthermore, on 7 January 1316, that is some six months after the saint's death, the bishop of Treviso defended his intention to leave the body where it was in the cathedral on the grounds that 'a multitude of people throng from all over to see it'.[304] That this was far from idle boasting is suggested by the statement of the chronicler Mica Madii de Barbazanis of Split in Dalmatia, in the History he produced around 1320, that 'the very holy body lies in the city of Treviso in the episcopal church, working miracles on the sick who flock to his tomb with devotion'.[305] Taking advantage of the festive atmosphere then prevailing in the town, those who had been banished sought permission to return, which was granted on 10 September 1316 by a vote of 171 for to 32 against. Lastly, on the first Sunday in May 1316 the remains of the saint were solemnly translated by the bishop in the presence of the clergy, the

---

[300] 'Cum dominus Potestas et Anciani et consules communis Tervisii per homines huius civitatis pluries et pluries sint rogati et requisiti ut providere debeant quid sit agendum de corpore beati Rigi qui nuper de hoc seculo a Deo sumptus est' (Azzoni Avogari, *De B. Henrico*, p. 1). See also the meeting on 13 June 1315 'super sepultura et honorificatione beati Rigi pro quo dominus noster Jesus Christus multa mirabilia hostendere dignatus est' (*PC*, fol. 56).

[301] Azzoni Avogari, *De B. Henrico*, p. 35; *PC*, fol. 58.

[302] Azzoni Avogari, *De B. Henrico*, pp. 11, 38.

[303] *Ibid.*, p. 33.

[304] *Ibid.*, p. 45.

[305] *Historia edita per Micam Madii de Barbazanis de Spalato de gestis Romanorum imperatorum et summorum pontificum*, part 2, c. VIII, ed. in *Archivio storico per la Dalmazia*, I, 3 (1926), p. 10.

civil authorities and the entire population; meanwhile, a tomb of stone
had been completed and a start made on the construction of a chapel in
the cathedral.[306]

So for more than a year the municipal life of Treviso was marked by
the death of Henry of Bolzano and the displays of piety which followed.
But the commune did more than police the cult and finance the buildings
associated with its growth. It intervened in domains which seem, *a priori*,
to come less within its competence than within that of the clergy. It was the
Council which, on 14 June 1315, appointed the members of a commission
entrusted with the task of writing a Life of 'St' Henry and of another local
saint, B. Parisio (1267); the commission consisted of four councillors: the
bishop, the priors of the Dominicans and the Augustinians and the warden
of the Friars Minor.[307] It was also the Council that decided that two copies
of a register of miracles should be kept, one to remain in the sacristy of
the cathedral, the other intended for the communal chancery.[308] The
Council also instructed the podesta to open negotiations with the Curia to
obtain the canonization of the two saints and voted a Reformation making
it obligatory on members to discuss this matter annually, a text which was
to be inserted in the book of statutes of Treviso.[309] Lastly, from 1316, 'St'
Henry is referred to in official texts as the patron of the city, on the same
level as St Liberal, who had watched over its destiny since the twelfth
century.[310] The bishop was clearly associated with all these decisions and
his advice prevailed when, contrary to a commission appointed by the
commune, he recommended that the tomb be built at the spot where the
body already lay. But he did nothing without consulting the Council and
he was careful to point out, in the memoranda he presented to the civil
authorities, that 'on this point as on others he was entirely willing to follow
the wishes and advice of the citizens of Treviso'.[311]

In thirteenth- and fourteenth-century communal Italy the formation of
a reputation for sanctity was primarily the work of the laity. Of course,
the clergy got involved in these pious movements. In hagiographic
accounts which deal with the origin of the cults, references to bells starting
to ring of their own accord at the moment of a saint's death are too

---

[306] Azzoni Avogari, *De B. Henrico*, p. 56.
[307] *Ibid.*, pp. 51–2.
[308] *Ibid.*, p. 9.
[309] PC, fol. 58.
[310] Azzoni Avogari, *De B. Henrico*, p. 61.
[311] *Ibid.*, p. 45.

frequent not to put us on our guard and induce a little scepticism as to the spontaneity of some manifestations of religious enthusiasm. It remains the case that it was groups of faithful lay people or trade associations which made the name of the new servant of God known and triggered off the rise of the devotion; the civil powers took over the growing cult; the clergy were associated with the ceremonies which followed, but remained in a subordinate position compared with the commune. Furthermore, the very rhythm of the city's religious life was marked by the phenomenon of the devotions; the death of the saints, and their funerals and translations were, for the people, opportunities to make direct contact with the super-natural and rejoice, within the context of an explosion of collective fervour, during which the quarrels between parties and clans momentarily sub-sided. This was an important aspect of the piety of the faithful during the later Middle Ages, too often viewed exclusively from the angle of a routine conformism.

Communities as intermediaries

Not all the new cults which appeared in the Mediterranean countries during the later Middle Ages were born in an atmosphere of religious enthusiasm such as I have just described. Even in Italy, where collective 'devotions' were quite common, there were many servants of God who were accorded the honours of a cult less rapidly and in less exceptional circumstances. Some of these saints, especially in the towns, only became popular as a result of the efforts made by groups or institutions to have the sanctity of their founder or official protector recognized. For these groups, the fact of counting a saint among their ranks was not only a matter of pride. The permanence of the cult strengthened their cohesion and its success enabled them to measure their influence in the locality.

   Chief among the institutions which ensured the new saints a good chance of success was the family. This is clear in the case of B. Umiliana dei Cerchi, a penitent of Franciscan obedience who died at Florence in 1246.[312] Her body was buried in Santa Croce. But Umiliana belonged to the rich and powerful Cerchi family, and when they built a family chapel in the great Franciscan church, they were able to arrange for her remains to be transferred to it. From this point on, popular devotion, which remained strong at least into the fourteenth century, was shared between

---

[312] See above, p. 208, note 175.

the chapel of the Cerchi and the sacristy of the Friars, where the latter continued to venerate her memory. The wills of members of the Cerchi family and, after its disappearance at the end of the fourteenth century, those of the Riccardi, who were related, included legacies designed to safeguard the cult of their official protectress. These were often quite large; in 1361, Francesco di Simone dei Cerchi provided for half the income from a house he left to his heirs to be devoted 'to celebrating a feast of saint Umiliana, of the house of Cerchi, in the church of Santa Croce, in the month of May', the other half to serve 'to celebrate an office in the same church in September, every year, in perpetuity'. He also left to the Friars Minor of Santa Croce 20 gold florins to embellish the relics of B. Umiliana, which were kept in the family chapel, and 5 livres to celebrate her feast in the Franciscan convent.[313]

This type of association between clergy and laity to maintain and promote a cult was also found at Lucca, in the case of B. Zita (d. 1278).[314] Here the saint was adopted; she had been a maidservant with one of the great dynasties of the Lucca patriciate, the Fatinelli. They took charge of the devotion and in 1321 built a chapel with an altar dedicated to 'saint' Zita in the church of San Frediano, which belonged to regular canons.[315] Here, too, wills enable us to trace the loyalty of the family towards its protégée, now turned protectress; in 1373, John Fatinelli set aside part of his fortune for the embellishment of the chapel, on the occasion of the expected translation of the saint's relics; he provided for the construction of an altar and a reliquary, also setting aside 60 livres for the celebration of a mass on the new altar.[316] In 1382, he also commissioned a painting depicting Zita and instituted a bequest intended to finance the celebration of a daily mass in the chapel. Inevitably, the Fatinelli all wanted to be buried before the tomb of the saint, as we see from wills of 1383, 1388, 1389 and 1401.[317] The family character of the cult was so generally accepted that it was to a member of the family, Antony Fatinelli, that in 1519 Leo X addressed a bull authorizing the celebration of the feast of B. Zita on 27 April with the rite of major double.[318] This fact is all the more remarkable in that the saint had long been venerated beyond the town

---

[313] *PC Umiliana dei Cerchi*, ASV, *Riti*, Proc. 775, fols. 514v–515.
[314] For 'Saint' Zita, see above, p. 210, note 187.
[315] *PC Zita* (Lucca, 1696), Paris, BN, H. 1390, *Informatio super dubio*, pp. 2–6.
[316] *PC Zita* (Lucca, 1624–5), ASV, *Riti*, Proc. 1315, fols. 61r–63v.
[317] *Ibid.*, fols. 43v–44r.
[318] *Ibid.*, fols. 68v–70r.

and territory of Lucca.[319] Although this was a city officially ruled by a communal government, the devotion to B. Zita took the form of a dynastic cult, even if the dynasty was bourgeois.[320]

This *condominium* exercised by laity and regulars over the cult of local saints was not without its problems. In Lucca, at the beginning of the fifteenth century, a row broke out between the Fatinelli family and the canons of San Frediano, who were claiming the right to oversee family chapels, which their patrons tended to regard as autonomous entities, by virtue of the privilege of foundation. The agreement reached between the Fatinelli and the chapter in 1410 was a compromise: the family's right of *jurispatronatus* over the chapel was recognized, but they had to agree to choose its 'rector' from among the canons, and the prior of the chapter reserved the right to confirm the appointment.[321] The zeal of families might also falter, with inevitable repercussions for the fortunes of the cult. At the end of the fourteenth century, the Riccardi ceased to hand over to the Brethren of Santa Croce the sums provided, as a perpetual legacy, to assure the annual celebration of the feast of B. Umiliana dei Cerchi. This negligence may have been due to the financial difficulties the family were then experiencing, or it may be that a relationship which was, after all, remote had eventually, over time, lost its importance in their eyes. However that may be, the Franciscans saw it differently. In 1404 they brought an action against the defaulting heirs which they eventually won. A compromise was reached between the two parties in 1409, and from 1410 the cult continued undisturbed, the payments by the family having been resumed.[322]

In other cases, the ties of blood enabled certain devotions to survive in spite of fluctuations in the piety of the faithful. This was so in the case of B. Villana dei Botti (d. 1361), a Dominican tertiary from a good Florentine merchant family.[323] Already during her lifetime, her popularity was extraordinary, and a huge crowd gathered at news of her death. The body had to be left exposed to the veneration of the faithful; this went on for thirty-

---

[319] See above, p. 210, note 187.

[320] This was the case in many fourteenth-century Italian towns where certain families exercised a hegemony of 'seigneurial' or princely type. In Pesaro, the Malatesta maintained the cult of B. Michelina (d. 1356), a Franciscan tertiary who had married a Malatesta. Pandolfo Malatesta built a marble tomb for her, 1356–9, and the *Fraternitas Schorzatorum sub nomine Annunciationis sanctae Mariae* she had founded developed the devotion (*PC Michelina of Pesaro, ASV, Riti,* Proc. 2264, fols. 482ff).

[321] The full text is in *PC Zita, ASV, Riti,* Proc. 1315, fols. 85–94.

[322] *PC Umiliana, ASV, Riti,* Proc. 775, fols. 511r–513r.

[323] See above, p. 209, note 185.

seven days without it displaying the least sign of corruption. The cult was
promoted by a Dominican of Santa Maria Novella, Tommaso di Cionelli
dei Cavalcanti, who had organized the celebration of the anniversary feast
by 1362, with the recitation of the office of the Virgin and procession to
the tomb.[324] In the late fourteenth and early fifteenth centuries, however,
the devotion declined after being criticized by Franco Sacchetti.[325] It was
relaunched around 1420 by B. Villana's grandson, the Dominican Jacopo,
who arranged for a *Vita* to be written by his fellow Dominican Girolamo
di Giovanni, and for her relics to be re-covered with silver.[326] The cult
revived; Fra Angelico painted a picture of B. Villana in 1436.[327] In 1441–
5 a number of confraternities who had put themselves under her protection
built a new tomb of marble in her honour, evidence of continued fervour.
In this case, the combined efforts of the family and of the religious bodies
(the Dominicans of Florence and the confraternities) enabled the cult to
become entrenched and to last.

The spiritual families were no less anxious to obtain recognition of the
sainthood of those of their members who could aspire to this honour. In
many convents, the memory of monks and nuns who had led an edifying
life was preserved. The evidence for this is abundant.[328] But most of these
people were forgotten by a new generation, once those who had known
them personally were dead and only a funerary inscription or reference
in a necrology testified to the prestige they had once enjoyed, unless confraternities linked to the community or order gave one of these cults a
greater chance of success by placing themselves under their protection.
By invoking the name of the 'saint', and by gathering before the altar
dedicated to them or the reliquary containing their remains, these lay
people helped to spread the saints fame beyond the restricted circle of the
clergy. The role played in this sphere by devout groups who gravitated
in the orbit of the Mendicants is well known.[329] But there were other

[324] S. Orlandi, *La Beata Villana dei Botti*, p. 39.
[325] 'E Predicatori hanno . . . Beata Villanà che fu mia vicina e fu giovanna fiorentina; pur
andava vestita come d'altre e fannonne gia festa': F. Sacchetti, *Opere*, ed. Borlenghi, p.
1116.
[326] S. Orlandi, *La Beata Villana dei Botti*, pp. 76–90.
[327] It is still in Santa Maria Novella: Kaftal 1, cc. 1017–18.
[328] See, for example, S. Orlandi, *'Necrologio' di Santa Maria Novella*, 2 vols. (Florence,
1955).
[329] At Verruchio, near Forli, in 1387, the rules of a confraternity of flagellants stipulated
that the brothers should meet once a month at the Hermits of St Augustine 'e li stare ad
une messa all'altare del Beato Gregorio'. The latter was a figure of the second rank, B.
Gregory of Verruchio (d. 1343), OHSA, whose reputation only spread beyond the walls of
his convent thanks to this particular brotherhood. More generally, see G. G. Meersseman,

confraternities founded by seculars in honour of their own saints, about which we are less well informed.[330] In any case, it is remarkable that in the Mediterranean countries the diffusion of a new cult, even that of a regular, had to be mediated by the laity, who enjoyed considerable autonomy in the choice of their intercessors.

In many ways similar to the confraternities were those charitable institutions which piously preserved the memory of their founders, some of whom, in the end, became the object of a true cult. This was quite common in Italy, where many hospitals had been created in the twelfth and thirteenth centuries, and there can be no doubt that names such as those of BB. Raymond Palmerio in Piacenza, Facio in Cremona, Gerardo dei Tintori in Monza and Amato Ronconi in Saludecio survived only because the charitable institutions born on their initiative were later placed under their patronage.[331] The phenomenon can be analysed in some detail in the case of B. Gerardo dei Tintori. When this pious layman, who had founded a hospital in Monza, died in 1207, he was buried with no particular ceremony in a cemetery attached to the old church of St Ambrose, and his remains were placed in a simple urn of stone. A text of 1208 calls his foundation the *Domus fratris Gerardi* or *domini Gerardi*. In 1230 the description *beatus* appears, and in 1247, *sanctus*. This evolution is linked to that of the *Hospitale sancti Gerardi*, which long remained the only centre of the devotion.[332] In the late fifteenth century a church was built in his honour near the hospital, and one of the town gates took his name. From this period, the celebration of his feast by the municipal authorities and townspeople is mentioned in the statutes of Monza, and the scale of the devotion locally led St Charles Borromeo, in the sixteenth century, to ask that a canonization process be started.[333]

In the light of these few examples, it seems clear that the role played by the small communities – family or convent, confraternity or hospital – in the cult of the saints was fundamental, but also limited. They made

---

'Etudes sur les anciennes confréries dominicaines, I, Les confréries de S. Dominique', *AFP*, 20 (1950), pp. 5–113 and 'II, Les confréries de S. Pierre Martyr', *AFP*, 21 (1951), pp. 51–196, repr. in Meersseman, *Ordo fraternitas: confraternite e pietà dei laici nel medioevo*, II (Rome, 1977), pp. 577–1117.

[330] For example, that founded by a curé of Biville, Normandy, in 1317, in his parish in honour of his holy predecessor Thomas Hélye (d. 1257). Its statutes, translated into Latin, are ed. in *AA.SS.* Oct. VIII, p. 598.

[331] See above, pp. 199ff.

[332] Documents cited by L. Modorati, *Memorie intorno alla chiesa ed al culto di S. Gerardo di Monza* (Monza, 1918), pp. 30–55.

[333] A. Frisi, *Memorie storiche di Monza*, I, pp. 236–8, 263–72; *AA.SS.* Iun. I, pp. 766ff.

possible the survival of a recollection which, without them, would soon have faded in the collective memory. But they were not, in general, sufficiently important to assure their patron saint great renown, even at the level of the city. Their principal aim, sometimes tenaciously pursued for decades, even centuries, was to persuade a larger and more influential group, if possible the town itself through the communal institutions, to adopt their cult. This quest took many different forms; we see it clearly in the case of B. Andrew Gallerani (d. 1251), founder of the hospital and confraternity of the Misericord in Siena. In 1274 the Brethren of the hospital won from the bishop of Siena an indulgence of forty days on behalf of those who visited his tomb on Easter Monday. In 1347, the brotherhood finally got the Council of the commune to vote a Reformation laying down that the feast of its founder should in future be solemnly celebrated by the authorities and people of Siena.[334] Nearly a century after the saint's death, the perseverance of the group who supported his cult succeeded in elevating it onto a superior plane.

Thus, the diffusion of cults in the Mediterranean countries, especially in communal Italy, happened not from the top down but starting from communities of every type, the true basic cells of social life.[335] The saints who were their standard-bearers and representatives did not all come from the people, although this was often the case, since even an aristocratic family like the Fatinelli in Lucca deigned to place themselves under the patronage of a humble maidservant like B. Zita. But the most original feature of this sainthood was that it was based on a wide consensus which the civil or religious authorities only ratified by according to the servant of God the honours of a local cult. The large number of 'modern' saints found in these regions and their relatively popular recruitment were an expression of the dynamism of communal structures and the associative impulse within a society which can be defined as a number of autonomous collectivities, not as a hierarchised organisation. Further, the faithful of these regions dealt with the clergy on an equal footing and were no less ardent in promoting the new devotions. Admittedly, the collaboration of priests and regulars was essential, but in the eyes of the laity, the cult of

[334] The indulgence is in *AA.SS.* Mar. III, p. 51; for the meeting in 1347: Siena, State Archives, *Deliberazioni del Consiglio Generale*, 140, fols. 42–3.
[335] In Provence, which was a transitional zone, both types are found, as is clear from the 'contradictory' examples of SS Douceline (d. 1279) and Louis of Anjou (d. 1297) in Marseilles; the former developed in the 'Italian' manner, the latter in the 'French'.

the saints was a sphere in which their initiative could be freely exercised and where their role remained, in effect, preponderant.

Although the perception of sainthood and the growth of a devotion did not follow the same path in every country of non-Mediterranean Europe, they all belonged nevertheless to the same social and mental universe, as is shown by the essentially receptive attitude of the people in the choice of its privileged intercessors. In France, England, the Scandinavian countries and eastern Europe, those in power endeavoured to orient the piety of the faithful towards models which conformed to the tastes and interests of the ruling classes. If it so happened that the common people took the initiative in this sphere, they were usually thwarted by the ecclesiastical hierarchy or government; at best, devotions of popular origin languished in semi-clandestinity, overshadowed by those favoured by the clergy and encouraged by the great. In the Mediterranean regions, in contrast, the new saints were freely chosen by the laity, who adhered to their cult either directly and spontaneously, through the manifestations of collective enthusiasm of the *devotio*, or through the intermediary of groups or institutions which were firmly entrenched in the city. The religious dimorphism of Christendom, the existence of which we have shown through our study of the birth and rise of the cult of the saints, echoes another cleavage: that which separated the essentially vertical and hierarchized social structures which characterized most of the West in the later Middle Ages, from the much less rigid social structures of the Mediterranean world, which reached their apogee in communal Italy.

PART II

OFFICIAL SAINTHOOD: FORMS AND CRITERIA OF CHRISTIAN PERFECTION ACCORDING TO PROCESSES OF CANONIZATION

෮෮෮෮

CHAPTER 11

TYPOLOGY OF OFFICIAL SAINTHOOD: QUANTITATIVE ASPECTS

ᏬᎦᏬᎦᏬᎦ

We come now to the next stage in our enquiry, which will consist of comparing the typology of popular and local sainthood with that of official sainthood, in order to show the similarities and differences between them. To this end, the logical first step would be a comparison between the list of medieval saints who were the object of a cult in their day and that of canonized saints. In practice, this is hardly possible since, whilst it is easy enough to list the servants of God inscribed in the catalogue of saints, the same is far from the case with those about whom the papacy made no pronouncement. Admittedly, hagiographical dictionaries and encyclopedias record hundreds, even thousands, of names, which it is tempting simply to add one to the other. But these lists are of only relative value since they are for the most part based on the Roman Martyrology or those of the great religious orders. Anyone who has worked even superficially on the saints of a particular region, especially in Italy, knows how easy it would be to add to the list many 'blesseds' who are mentioned in local legendries or conventual necrologies.[1] On the other hand, a number of people who were venerated in their day in the churches of the secular clergy have remained in obscurity and been omitted from lists drawn up in the modern period.[2] Chance and a misplaced loyalty have played too large a role in the compilation of these inventories for them to be seen as

---

[1] See above, p. 212, note 194. Every Italian town has collections made between the sixteenth and nineteenth centuries which record dozens of names of people who enjoyed a local reputation for sanctity in the Middle Ages; see, for example, R. Magnani, *Vita de' santi e venerabili e servi di Dio della città di Faenza* (Faenza, 1741); J.-B. Melloni, *Atti o memorie degli Uomini illustri in santità o nati o morti in Bologna* (Bologna, 1713–18), ed. A. Benati and M. Fanti (Rome, 1971).

[2] John of 'Foxtuna', one of the 'great' English saints of the 1250s according to Matthew Paris, does not appear in any hagiographical collection (see above, p. 112, note 84). Philip Berruyer, archbishop of Bourges (d. 1261), is among the *praetermissi* in the *Acta sanctorum*: *AA.SS.* Ian. I, p. 565.

more than a very partial reflection of sainthood as it was actually perceived by medieval people.

The statistical study of sainthood is a fascinating project which has already attracted many scholars.[3] But the results remain disappointing, thanks to the shifting nature of a documentary base which is often unreliable. Should we, therefore, resign ourselves to using as point of reference only the list of saints duly canonized by the papacy? This list is of exceptional interest and will receive particular attention, if only because of the importance for Christendom as a whole of decisions taken by the supreme magisterium. But to take account in this study only of the thirty-three persons inscribed in the catalogue of saints between 1198 and 1431 would be carrying caution to extremes. The historian can hardly draw general conclusions from such a restricted sample, and, in any case, we know of a number of causes which, in the fourteenth or early fifteenth century, were the subject of a favourable judgement by the cardinals after a properly conducted process, but which never resulted in formal canonization for reasons of chance. The dossier of the archbishop of Bourges, Philip Berruyer (d. 1261), got bogged down on at least six occasions between 1266 and 1364, as a result of the death of the popes who had started proceedings and the vicissitudes of the Holy See,[4] and the canonization of Charles of Blois, postponed owing to the departure of Gregory XI for Rome on 13 September 1376, never took place.[5] During our period, however, these two persons were regarded as authentic saints by the highest authorities in the Church. It seems to me, therefore, that alongside canonization, so rarely granted, the opening by the papacy of an enquiry concerning a person locally regarded as holy represents a valid indicator. In effect, it constituted a sort of tacit recognition of the sainthood and cult accorded to them. This was particularly the case after 1260, when the Holy See began to be much less receptive to new requests and established a real barrier at the stage of postulation. I have in the end, therefore, used the names of all the saints concerning whom a pope ordered an enquiry

[3] See above, pp. 105, 183, note 84. The most interesting attempt is that of Delooz, *Sociologie et canonisations*.

[4] See above, p. 63, note 6.

[5] M. H. Laurent, 'Charles de Blois fut-il canonisé en 1376?', *RHE*, 46 (1951), pp. 182–6. Laurent convincingly demonstrates that the answer is no, but previously the situation was very unclear, including to contemporaries, as is shown by the evidence presented for the opposing view by N. Denis-Boulet, 'La canonisation de Charles de Blois', *RHEF*, 28 (1942), pp. 216–24. Laurent's conclusions have been accepted by B. Pocquet du Haut-Jussé (*Annales de Bretagne*, 59 (1952)) and the Bollandists (*Anal. Boll.*, 71 (1953), pp. 249–51).

de vita, miraculis et fama between 1198 and 1431.[6] From our standpoint, it is hardly relevant whether the enquiry succeeded or not. What is significant is the opening of a process of canonization, since we know that this normally happened only after a prior enquiry, conducted by the local episcopate or pontifical legates, which guaranteed that the cause was serious and that devotion towards the new saint was widespread.[7] I will in future use the general term 'recognized saints' for the persons who were the object of an enquiry ordered by the Holy See, whether or not they were canonized. They numbered seventy-one for the period between 1198 and 1431, as will be seen from table 9.[8]

Table 9 gives us two figures which it is interesting to compare: of seventy-one enquiries *in partibus* decreed by the Holy See between 1198 and 1431, thirty-three, that is, just under half, resulted in canonizations.[9] The proportion is fairly high, which confirms the impression that when a process was officially opened by the papacy, it was because the papacy looked on the cause favourably.

It would be interesting to be able to compare this table of partial or complete successes with one recording failures. But compiling the latter poses much more complex problems. We know that the Curia did not act on many of the requests for canonization it received, and I tried in table 4 to compile a list of the petitions which were rejected. It remains, however, very incomplete and can provide only a very questionable statistical base.[10] It would be equally vain to compare the list of requests and that of processes decreed, since only the latter can be more or less complete. On the other hand, we are able to calculate, for a particular type of saint, for example bishops or laity, the percentage of canonizations obtained compared with the total number of processes ordered by the papacy on behalf of people in that category. This figure, which I will call the success

[6] No such list previously existed for the medieval period, though there are more or less accurate lists of beatified saints, for example that of G. Löw, sv Beatificazione, in *Enciclopedia Cattolica*, II (Rome, 1949), pp. 1098–100, and of canonized saints, for example those of Klauser, 'Die Liturgie der Heiligsprechung', pp. 212–33 and Delooz, *Sociologie et canonisation*, pp. 440–6; both are generally satisfactory despite errors of detail.

[7] See above, pp. 42–3.

[8] In fact, there are seventy-two names in table 9. But as the enquiry held in 1411–16 in Venice into the merits of St Catherine of Siena was ordered by a bishop, not a pope, I have omitted her from my calculations.

[9] Table 9 in fact includes thirty-seven canonizations, since two saints of our period were canonized after 1431, but so soon after that we may consider them as medieval canonizations, namely Nicholas of Tolentino, can. 1446 by Eugenius IV and Catherine of Siena, can. by Pius II in 1461.

[10] See table 4, pp. 72–3.

Table 9 Processes of canonization and canonizations (1198–1431)

The saints are listed in chronological order, based on the date of the pontifical bull decreeing the opening of the process of canonization (the first, where there were several).

The absence of a date in column 4 means that the process did not take place. A question mark means there is no document to attest that it was held. The absence of a date in column 5 means that the canonization was not pronounced. In column 4, dates separated by 'and' (for example, 1223 and 1233) mean that the process was recommenced on the orders of the papacy, which had either requested a new enquiry or further information. Two years given in succession (for example, 1223–4) mean that one enquiry extended over two calendar years. Two dates separated by 'between' (for example, between 1251 and 1254) mean an enquiry whose exact date is unknown, but which can be pinned down to a period between the two dates given.

Saints	Categories	Opening of the process (1st bull)		Date(s) of enquiry in partibus	Date of canonization	Pope pronouncing canonization
		Year	Pope			
Homobonus (d. 1197)	L	1198	Innocent III (1198–1216)	1199	1199	Innocent III
Cunegund (d. 1040)	L	1199	,,	1200	1200	,,
Caradoc (d. 1124)	L	1200	,,	a	—	—
Gilbert of Sempringham (d. 1189)	RC	1200	,,	1201[b]	1202	Innocent III
Wulfstan (d. 1095)	B	1201	,,	1202	1203	,,
Procopius (d. 1053)	M	?1203	,,	1203–4	1204	,,
William of Donjeon or of Bourges (d. 1203)	B	1217	Honorius III (1216–27)	1217	1218	Honorius III
William of Aebelholt or of Eskill (d. 1203)	RC	1218	,,	after 1218	1224	,,
John of Gualdo (d. 1170)	M	1218	,,	1221	—	—
Bertrand of Comminges (d. 1125)	B	1218	,,	?	?	—
Hugh of Lincoln (d. 1200)	B	1219	,,	1219	1220	Honorius III
Robert of Molesme (d. 1111)	M	1221	,,	1221	c	—
Hugh of Bonnevaux (d. 1194)	M	1221	,,	?1222	—	—
Stephen of Die (d. 1208)	B	1222	,,	1223 and 1233	—	—
William of York (d. 1154)	B	1223	,,	1223 and 1224	1226	Honorius III
John Cacciafronte (d. 1183)	B	1223	,,	1223–4	—	—
Maurice of Carnoët (d. 1191)	M	1224	,,	1225 and 1226	—	—

Saints	Categories	Opening of the process (1st bull) Year	Opening of the process (1st bull) Pope	Date(s) of enquiry *in partibus*	Date of canonization	Pope pronouncing canonization
Lawrence O'Toole (d. 1181)	B	1224	"	1225	1226	Honorius III
Rainerius of Furcona (d. 1077)	B	1225	"	?	—	—
Hildegard of Bingen (d. 1179)	N	1228	Gregory IX (1227–41)	1233 and 1237	—	Gregory IX
Francis of Assisi (d. 1226)	OM	1228	"	1228	1228	?
Osmund of Salisbury (d. 1099)	B	1228	"	1228	1457	Calixtus III
Virgil of Salzburg (d. 784)	B	1230	"	1231 or 1232	1233	Gregory IX
Luke Banfiy (d. 1179)	B	1231	"	1232 and 1233	—	—
Antony of Padua (d. 1231)	OM	1231	"	1231 or 1232	1232	Gregory IX
Elizabeth of Thuringia (d. 1231)	L	1232	"	1233 and 1235	1235	?
Dominic (d. 1221)	OM	1233	"	1234	1234	?
Benvenuto of Gubbio (d. c.1232)	OM	1236	"	1236	—	—
John of Montmirail (d. 1217)	M	1236	"	?	—	—
Bruno of Wurzburg (d. 1045)	B	1238	"	after 1238 and after 1247	—	—
Odo of Novara (d. 1200)	M	1239	"	1240	—	—
Ambrose of Massa (d. 1240)	OM	1240	"	1240–1 and after 1251–2	—	—
Eystein (Augustine) Erlendsson (d. 1188)	B	1241	"	between 1251 and 1254	—	—
Lawrence Loricatus of Subiaco (d. 1242)	L	1243	Innocent IV (1243–54)	1244	—	—
Edmund of Abingdon or of Canterbury (d. 1240)	B	1244	"	1244 and 1245	1247	Innocent IV
William Pinchon (d. 1234)	B	?	"	between 1240 and 1247	1247	?
Margaret of Scotland (d. 1093)	L	1245	"	1245 and between 1247 and 1249	1250	?
Stanislas (d. 1079)	B	1250	"	1250 and 1252	1253	?

Table 9 (*cont.*)

Saints	Categories	Opening of the process (1st bull) Year	Opening of the process (1st bull) Pope	Date(s) of enquiry *in partibus*	Date of canonization	Pope pronouncing canonization
John Bonus of Mantua (d. 1249)	OM	1251	,,	1251 and 1253, 1254	—	—
Simon of Collazzone (d. 1250)	OM	1252	,,	1252	—	—
Peter of Verona or Martyr (d. 1252)	OM	1252	,,	1252	1253	Innocent IV
Rose of Viterbo (d. 1251)	L	1252	,,	?	—	—
Clare of Assisi (d. 1253)	OM	1253	,,	1253	1255	Alexander IV
Nicholas of Aarhus or of Denmark (d. 1180)	L	1254	Alexander IV (1254–61)	1255	—	—
Richard of Chichester (d. 1253)	B	1256	,,	1256	1262	Urban IV
Hedwig of Silesia (d. 1243)	L	1262	Urban IV (1261–4)	1262 and 1263	1267	Clement IV
Philip Berruyer of Bourges (d. 1261)	B	1262	,,	1265–6	—	—
Margaret of Hungary (d. 1270)	OM	1271	Gregory X (1271–6)	1271 and 1276	d	—
Louis IX (d. 1270)	L	1281	Martin IV (1281–5)	1282–3	1297	Boniface VIII
Peter of Morrone (Celestine V) (d. 1296)	P	1305	Clement V (1305–14)	1306	1313	Clement V
Thomas Cantilupe or of Hereford (d. 1282)	B	1306	,,	1307	1320	John XXII
Louis of Anjou or of Marseilles or of Toulouse (d. 1297)	OM	1307	,,	1308	1317	,,
Clare of Montefalco (d. 1308)	OM[e]	1317	John XXII (1316–34)	1318–19	—	—
Thomas Aquinas (d. 1274)	OM	1318	,,	1319 and 1321	1323	John XXII
Gregory X (d. 1272)	P	1325	,,	?	—	,,
Nicholas of Tolentino (d. 1305)	OM	1325	,,	1325 and 1357	1446	Eugenius IV
Yves Hélory (d. 1303)	Pr	1330	,,	1330	1347	Clement VI
Elzear of Sabran (d. 1323)	L	1351	Clement VI (1342–52)	1351–2	1369	Urban V
Delphine of Sabran or of Puimichel (d. 1360)	L	1363	Urban V (1362–70)	1363	—	—

Saints	Categories	Opening of the process (1st bull)		Date(s) of enquiry in partibus	Date of canonization	Pope pronouncing canonization
		Year	Pope			
Charles of Blois (d. 1364)	L	1369	,,	1371	–	Urban V
Bridget of Sweden (d. 1373)	L	1375	Urban VI (1378–89)	1376–80	1391–1415 1419	Boniface IX, John XXIII, Martin V
Thomas de la Hale (d. 1295)	M	1380	,,	?	–	–
Urban V (d. 1370)	P	1381	Clement VII (1378–94)	after 1381	–	–
Peter of Luxembourg (d. 1387)	C	1389	,,	1390 and 1418	–	–
John of Bridlington (d. 1379)	RC	1391	Boniface IX (1389–1404)	after 1391	1401	Boniface IX
Richard Fitzralph (d. 1360)	B	1399	,,	after 1399	–	–
Dorothy of Montau (d. 1394)	L	1404	,,	1404–6	–	–
Catherine of Siena (d. 1379)	L	ⸯ	Gregory XII (1406–15)	1411–16	1461	Pius II
Ingrid of Skänninge (d. 1282)	L	1416	Council of Constance (1414–17)	1417	–	–
Brynulph of Skara (d. 1317)	B	1416	,,	1417	–	–
Nicholas Hermannsson of Linköping (d. 1391)	B	1416	,,	1417	–	–
Sebald of Nuremburg (eleventh century)	L	1418	Martin V (1417–31)	–	1425	Martin V

Abbreviations: B = bishop; C = cardinal; L = lay; M = monk; N = nun; OM = mendicant order; P = pope; Pr = priest; RC = regular canon.

Notes:

a The enquiry, decreed by Innocent III, was never held by the commissioners.

b There were, in fact, two enquiries in the same year, the first having been rejected by the pope for technical errors.

c Simple authorization of local cult in 1221.

d Canonized in 1943 by Pius XII.

e She belonged to a community of recluses under the rule of St Augustine, but in fact directed by Franciscans. Canonized in 1881 by Leo XIII.

f The enquiry held in Venice in 1411–16 concerning the sanctity of St Catherine was a diocesan process, ordered by the bishop of Castello. But it was used as a process of canonization in 1461, when Pius II was asked to canonize her.

Table 10 *Distribution of the saints recognized by the Roman Church (1198–1431) as a function of canonical status*

	Regulars %	Secular clergy %	Laity %
Processes (71)	35.2	40.8 (bishops 39.4, priests 1.4)	24
Canonizations (35)	31.4	42.9 (bishops 40, priests 2.9)	25.7

Note:
Regulars include monks and nuns, regular canons and members of the Mendicant orders, both male and female.

rate, will provide useful information about the trends within official sainthood.

STATISTICAL APPROACHES

At the statistical level, the point of departure for a typology of sainthood has to be the canonical status of the saints. The latter had in their lifetime been regulars, secular clergy (bishops and priests) or members of the laity. These distinctions are not purely juridical. In fact, they relate back to the list of states of life in the Church, traditional since the early centuries, and enable us to trace the evolution of this schema which monasticism, from the tenth century on, had made more rigid and hierarchical by turning it into a scale of perfection based on the greater or lesser degree of distance of each of these states from the carnal life.[11]

When we look at the relative importance of the types of sainthood according to the processes of canonization ordered by the papacy and canonizations pronounced between 1198 and 1431, we find fairly similar results, as we see from table 10. One fact at once stands out: of the saints recognized by the Roman Church between 1198 and 1431, three out of four were clergy or regulars. Within this clerical group, the bishops alone accounted for more than half, whilst the lower clergy were insignificant.

---

[11] Vauchez, *La spiritualité du Moyen Age occidental*, pp. 53–5.

Table 11 *Bishops and popes who were the object of a process of canonization (1198–1431)*

Name	Year of death	Year of process	Country	Date of canonization
Wulfstan of Worcester	1095	1202	England	1203
William of Bourges	1209	1217	France	1218
Bertrand of Comminges	1125	?	France	?
Hugh of Lincoln	1200	1219	England	1220
William of York	1154	1223	England	1226
John of Vicenza	1183	1223/4	Italy	
Lawrence O'Toole of Dublin	1180	1225	Ireland	1226
Rainerius of Furcona	1077	after 1225	Italy	
Osmund of Salisbury	1099	1228	England	1457
Virgil of Salzburg	784	1231 or 1232	Germanic countries	1233
Luke Banffy of Esztergom	1179	1231 or 1232	Hungary	
Stephen of Die	1208	1223/33	France	
Bruno of Würzburg	1045	between 1238 and 1247	Germanic countries	
Eystein of Nidaros	1188	between 1251 and 1254	Norway	
Edmund of Canterbury	1240	1244/5	England	1247
William Pinchon of Saint-Brieuc	1234	c.1246	France	1247
Stanislas of Cracow	1079	1250	Poland	1253
Richard of Chichester	1253	1256	England	1262
Philip of Bourges	1261	1265/6	France	
Peter of Morrone (Celestine V)	1296	1306	Italy	1313
Thomas of Hereford	1287	1307	England	1320
Gregory X	1276	?	Italy	
Urban V	1370	after 1381	France	
Peter of Luxembourg	1390	1390	France	
Richard Fitzralph	1360	1399	Ireland	
Brynulph of Skara	1317	1417	Sweden	
Nicholas of Linköping	1391	1417	Sweden	
Priest				
Yves	1303	1330	France	1347

The holy bishops: a preponderance under threat

Of the seventy-one saints now under consideration, twenty-seven were bishops or popes. Of the thirty-five saints canonized between 1198 and 1431, thirteen belonged to this category, as we see from table 11.[12]

[12] I have included among the bishops popes who were the subject of a process of canonization, including Cardinal Peter of Luxembourg (d. 1387), briefly the 'Clementist' bishop of Metz. On the other hand, St Louis of Anjou, who was bishop of Toulouse for a short

Table 12 *Proportion of saint-bishops in relation to all the saints recognized by the Roman Church (1198–1431)*

% of processes			% of canonizations		
1198–1431	1198–1304	1305–1431	1198–1431	1198–1304	1305–1431
38	38.8	36.5	37.1	41.7	27.3

The relative importance of bishops as a proportion of the total number of saints recognized by the Roman Church is shown in table 12.

Here, again, the global results are in harmony: for the period as a whole, about 40 per cent of the saints who were the object of a process of canonization and of those who were actually canonized were bishops. The success rate, that is the relation between processes held and those which succeeded, is fairly high within this category: of twenty-seven processes concerning holy bishops, thirteen, that is, nearly half (48.1 per cent), resulted in a canonization.

We should, however, note that the relative importance of the group of holy bishops tended to diminish in the fourteenth century. This trend is particularly marked at the level of canonizations (fewer than 30 per cent of bishops canonized between 1305 and 1431, compared with over 40 per cent in the thirteenth century).

Between 1266 and 1378, the papacy opened no enquiry concerning a bishop, with the exception of St Louis of Anjou, who is better seen as a Franciscan saint, and two popes, Celestine V and Gregory X. It is also significant that the category of the holy bishops, which included no pope in the thirteenth century, included three, plus one cardinal, out of the eight processes of canonization concerning prelates between 1305 and 1431, that is half. It is as if, from the last third of the thirteenth century, the episcopal model lost favour at the upper levels of the Roman Church. A glance at requests for canonization refused by the Holy See at this period (see table 4) confirms this impression: between 1280 and 1330 in particular, the papacy refused to ʻexamine the causes of at least nine bishops, who were regarded as saints within their diocese.[13] On the other hand, after the Great Schism, the processes of canonization concerning

time early in 1297 before resigning, appears among the regulars. His sanctity and cult were closely linked with the Franciscan order.
[13] See above, pp. 72–3.

Table 13 *Distribution of saint-bishops by country according to the processes of canonization (in percentages)*

	England & Ireland	France[a]	Italy	Scandinavia	Germanic countries	Eastern Europe[b]
1198–1431	32.2	25	14.3	14.3	7.1	7.1
1198–1304	35	25	10	10	10	10
1305–1431	25	25	25[c]	25	—	—

Notes:
[a] Including Brittany.
[b] Poland, Bohemia, Hungary.
[c] These were popes Celestine V and Gregory X; no diocesan bishop was the object of a process of canonization in Italy in the fourteenth century.

bishops recovered for a while, as if the crisis and the Council had unblocked a mechanism which had jammed.

Further, it is interesting to note that the bishops who were the object of a process of canonization were very unevenly distributed between countries, as we see from table 13.

Table 14 shows the distribution of the bishops who were actually canonized.

Episcopal sainthood emerges as the preponderant type of sainthood in England: nine processes of canonization, out of the fourteen held there between 1198 and 1431, concerned bishops and eight of the eleven English saints canonized at this period belonged to this category.[14] It was also important throughout north-west Europe (Scandinavia: four out of seven processes, but no canonization), in France (seven out of sixteen processes, two out of six canonizations) and in eastern Europe (two out of four

Table 14 *Distribution by country of the saint-bishops actually canonized (in percentages)*

England and Ireland	France	Italy	Scandinavia	Germanic countries	Eastern Europe
61.5	15.4	7.7	0	7.7	7.7

[14] The English and Irish account for 32.2 per cent of bishops who were the object of a process of canonization, but 61.5 per cent of canonized prelates; the situation in France was the opposite: with 25 per cent of processes, the French episcopate obtained only 15.4 per cent of canonizations.

processes, one out of two canonizations). It was much less well represented in the Germanic countries (two out of eight processes, one out of five canonizations) and above all in Italy (four out of twenty-two processes – but two concerning popes – and one canonization, that of Celestine V, pope for a few months in 1294 without having previously been a bishop). These disparities between countries, already apparent in the preceding chapters, should not make us lose sight of the crucial fact, that is, the numerical preponderance of episcopal sainthood over all the other forms of sainthood, at the global level, especially in the thirteenth century.

A very rare phenomenon: the saint-priest

Only a few lines are needed to deal with sacerdotal sainthood. Between 1198 and 1431, one single secular priest was the object of a process and eventually canonized: St Yves (d. 1303, process 1330). Clement VI's decision to honour the rector of Louannec is certainly of some importance, since it was without precedent. But the fact that St Yves was the only saint of his type is striking evidence of the scant regard felt by the ecclesiastical hierarchy for the secular priests engaged in the parish ministry. What with bishops whose prestige was rooted in their aristocratic origins and regulars who held crowds spellbound with their apostolic zeal, the simple priest, in the Middle Ages, was hard put to it to find a place.[15]

The differing fortunes of the regulars

In the Middle Ages, the regulars formed a very diverse group. In fact, this label indicates persons who had no more in common than having pronounced perpetual vows and led a conventual life. Until the early thirteenth century, despite differences between rules and observances, they fell into two main categories: the monks and the regular canons. Between them, these two provided not only the majority of new saints of western Christendom in the eleventh and twelfth centuries, but the most prestigious: St Hugh at Cluny, St Bernard at Cîteaux, St Bruno with the Carthusians, St Stephen of Muret at Grandmont etc. Subsequently, they were rivalled by the Mendicant orders: Friars Minor and Preachers, Her-

---

[15] See below, pp. 310–15.

Table 15 *Proportion of regulars among the saints recognized by the Roman Church (1198–1431)*

% of processes			% of canonizations		
1198–1431	1198–1304	1305–1431	1198–1431	1198–1304	1305–1431
36.6	40.8	27.4	34.3	33.3	36.4

mits of St Augustine, Carmelites and Servites of Mary, who swelled the ranks of this far from homogeneous group.

In the thirteenth century, the majority of saints who were the object of a process of canonization still came from the regulars, as we see from table 15. About one third of the saints recognized by the Church between 1189 and 1431 were monks or Mendicant 'brothers', that is a substantial proportion. But these impressive figures risk concealing certain less favourable trends. The processes decreed in favour of regulars represented only 27.4 per cent of new causes between 1305 and 1431, as against 40.8 in the preceding century, a sign of their declining popularity. At the level of canonizations, on the other hand, the proportion of regulars increased slightly between the thirteenth and the fourteenth centuries, from 33.3 to 36.4 per cent. However, these global observations have only limited significance since the category is far from homogeneous, monks and regular canons being lumped together with the new orders under this generic title.

As far as recognized sainthood is concerned, the two groups developed in different directions. Between 1198 and 1431, the number of saints belonging to the old orders steadily decreased (except for the regular canons, who stagnated at a low level: two saints in the thirteenth century, one in the fourteenth), whilst the Mendicants were extremely successful from the beginning, and never faltered. Table 17 brings out these changes.

Of enquiries ordered on behalf of regular saints, half in the thirteenth century and nearly two-thirds in the fourteenth concerned Mendicants. Among regulars actually canonized, two-thirds were Mendicants in the thirteenth century, three-quarters in the fourteenth. Further, their success rate was much higher than that of saints from the old orders – 70 per cent, compared with 30 per cent. The former figure is exceptional, and

Table 16 *Regulars who were the object of a process of canonization (1198–1431)*

Name	Year of death	Year of process	Country	Category	Date of canonization
Gilbert of Sempringham	1189	1201	England	RC	1202
Procopius of Sazawa	1053	1203/4	Moravia	OSB	1204
William of Eskill	1203	1218	Denmark and France	RC	1224
John of Gualdo	1170	1221	Italy	OSB	
Robert of Molesme	1111	1221	France	OSB	
Hugh of Bonnevaux	1194	1222	France	Cist	
Maurice of Carnoët	1191	1225	France	Cist	
Hildegard of Bingen	1179	1233	Rhineland	OSB	
Francis of Assisi	1226	1228	Italy	OFM	1228
Antony of Padua	1231	1231/2	Italy	OFM	1232
Dominic	1221	1234	Spain[a]	OP	1234
Benvenuto of Gubbio	1232	1236	Italy	OFM	
John of Montmirail	1217	1236	France	Cist	
Odo of Novara	1200	1240	Italy	Carth then recluse	
Ambrose of Massa	1240	1240/1	Italy	OFM	
John Bonus	1249	1251/4	Italy	OHSA	
Simon of Collazzone	1250	1252	Italy	OFM	
Peter of Verona	1252	1252	Italy	OP	1253
Clare of Assisi	1253	1253	Italy	Clare	1255
Margaret of Hungary	1270	1271/6	Hungary	OP	
Louis of Anjou	1297	1308	France	OFM	1317
Clare of Montefalco	1308	1318/19	Italy	recluse then N OFM[b]	
Thomas Aquinas	1274	1319/21	Italy	OP	1323
Nicholas of Tolentino	1305	1325	Italy	OHSA	1446
Thomas de la Hale	1295	after 1380	England	OSB	?
John of Bridlington	1379	after 1391	England	RC	1401

Abbreviations: RC = regular canon; N = nun; OFM = Order of Friars Minor; OP = Order of Preachers; OHSA = Hermits of St Augustine; Cist = Cistercian; Carth = Carthusian; OSB = Benedictine
Notes:
[a] St Dominic has, nevertheless, been counted as an Italian saint, since his cult developed from Bologna. Dominic was Spanish only by birth, his active life led entirely in France and Italy.
[b] Clare of Montefalco and her companions formed a community of recluses living according to the rule of St Augustine. But their entourage (confessors etc.) were all Friars Minor. She is therefore difficult to classifiy, but it is not unreasonable to class her among the nuns who gravitated in the orbit of the Mendicants.

far surpasses that reached by any other category (lay saints, holy bishops etc.); the latter is lowest of all. If the two are combined, we get a very modest success rate (46.1 per cent), but one which is in itself meaningless as it results from two contradictory trends.

Table 17 *Respective importance of monks and Mendicants, in relation to the total number of saints from the regulars recognized by the Roman Church (1198–1431)*

| Type of regular | % in relation to all regulars | | | |
| | processes | | canonizations | |
	thirteenth century	fourteenth century	thirteenth century	fourteenth century
Mendicants	50	66.7	62.5	75
Religious orders	50	33.3	37.5	25

Similar contrasts appear when we look at the distribution by country of saints from the religious orders: among the Mendicants, 85.7 per cent were Italian by origin; only SS Margaret of Hungary and Louis of Anjou (that is two out of fourteen) lived outside the peninsula.[16] Saints from the old orders, in contrast, were recruited much more widely: 41.7 per cent were French, 23 per cent English, 16.7 per cent Italian, 8.3 per cent German and a similar percentage Slav. We are therefore justified in contrasting a Mendicant sainthood which flourished almost exclusively in Italy with a monastic and canonical sainthood which was at its strongest in France and England. In the last analysis, whilst the Roman Church continued to recruit a significant proportion of its saints from religious houses throughout the Middle Ages, from the second third of the thirteenth century there was a tendency to favour the Mendicant orders far more than the monks or regular canons.

The increasing success of the laity

Among the types of saints honoured by the Church in the thirteenth and fourteenth centuries, the laity occupied a by no means negligible place. This phenomenon is all the more striking in that it was new. When we look at canonizations made by the papacy in the twelfth century, we see that the laity were rarely accorded this honour. At most, we find the names of a few sovereigns such as Henry II (canonized in 1146), Edward the Confessor (1161) and Knut Lavard (1169). The situation was very different after 1198, as we see from table 19, when, on average, one out

---

[16] Though St Louis had spent part of his youth in Naples.

Table 18 *Lay men and women who were the object of a process of canonization (1198–1431)*

Name	Year of death	Year of process	Country	Date of canonization
Homobonus	1197	1198	Italy	1199
Caradoc	1124	1200	England	–
Cunegund	1040	1200	Germanic countries	1200
Elizabeth of Thuringia	1231	1233/5	Germanic countries	1235
Lawrence of Subiaco	1242	1244	Italy	–
Margaret of Scotland	1044	1245/9	Scotland	1250
Rose of Viterbo	1251	1252/3	Italy	–
Nicholas of Denmark	1180	1254 or 5	Denmark	–
Hedwig of Silesia	1243	1262	Germanic countries	1267
Louis IX	1270	1282/3	France	1297
Elzear	1323	1351/2	Provence	1369
Delphine	1360	1363	Provence	–
Charles of Blois	1364	1371	France	–
Bridget	1373	1376/80	Sweden	1391
Dorothy of Montau	1394	1404/6	Germanic countries	–
Catherine of Siena	1380	1411/16	Italy	1461[a]
Ingrid[b]	1282	1417	Sweden	–
Sebald	eleventh century	none[c]	Germanic countries	1429

Notes:
[a] In juridical terms, the enquiry made in Venice 1411–16 was not, strictly speaking a process of canonization but a diocesan informative process. However, we are justified in putting it on the same level as the others since it was carried out with particular care; furthermore, when Pius II wished to promote the canonization in 1460, rather than order a new enquiry, he instructed three cardinals to scrutinize the acts of the Venice process.
[b] Ingrid of Skänninge ended her life as a Dominican nun, but she only entered a religious order in 1281, shortly before her death.
[c] There was no process, strictly speaking. On the basis of the documents provided by the town of Nuremberg, Martin V decided to proceed to canonization. See above, pp. 83–4.

of four saints was from the laity; in the fourteenth century, the figure rises to nearly one in three.

Further, if we compare the number of processes concerning lay saints with the number of canonizations made within this category, we find a

Table 19 *Relative importance of lay sainthood (1198–1431)*

% of processes			% of canonizations		
1198–1431	1198–1304	1305–1431	1198–1431	1198–1304	1305–1431
24	20.4	30.4	25.7	24	30
(17/71)	(10/49)	(7/22)	(9/35)	(6/25)	(3/10)

Table 20 *Distribution of lay saints by country (1198–1431) (in percentages)*

	Germanic countries	France[a]	Italy	Scandinavia	England
1198–1431	23.5	23.5	23.5	17.7	11.8
1198–1304	27.2	9.2	27.2	18.2	18.2
1305–1431	16.5	50	16.5	17	0

Note:
[a] Including Provence and Brittany.

success rate of 53 per cent, which is reasonable. We may say, therefore, that generally speaking, lay sainthood was honoured between 1198 and 1431, and that its relative importance only increased with the passage of time.

A study of the distribution of lay saints by country produces equally interesting results, as we see from table 20. Lay sanctity is most strongly represented in France, Italy and the Germanic countries. But this was a model which had little success in the British Isles, especially when we note that the only two British lay saints whose cult was recognized by the Roman Church between 1198 and 1431 were a Welsh hermit of the early twelfth century and a queen of Scotland of the eleventh.[17] This impression is confirmed by an analysis of the requests sent to the papacy by the English episcopate and monarchy seeking the opening of a process of canonization: only two concerned lay men (Thomas of Lancaster in 1327–31 and Edward II in 1386) and neither was successful. A study of the list of lay men and women canonized produces similar results: four were from the Germanic countries (Cunegund, Elizabeth of Thuringia, Hedwig and Sebald), two from France (Louis IX and Elzear of Sabran), one each from Scotland, Sweden and Italy (Margaret of Scotland, Bridget and Homobonus). This last figure is all the more remarkable when we remember that, in the thirteenth and fourteenth centuries, Italy was the land *par excellence* of lay saints at the level of local cults.[18]

In France, on the other hand, the late Middle Ages was marked by a significant increase in lay sainthood, thanks largely to peripheral regions such as Brittany (Charles of Blois) and, above all, Provence (Elzear and Delphine). We should note, lastly, that the countries of eastern Europe

---

[17] Namely, St Caradoc (d. 1124) and Margaret of Scotland (d. 1093); only the latter was canonized.
[18] See above, pp. 190ff.

Table 21 *Distribution by category and period of saints recognized by the Roman Church (1198–1431) (in percentages)*

		1198–1304		
	Bishops	Secular priests	Regulars	Laity
Processes	38.8	—	40.8	20.4
Canonizations	41.7	—	33.3	25
		1305–1431		
	Bishops	Secular priests	Regulars	Laity
Processes	36.5	4.3	27.4	31.8
Canonizations	27.3	9	36.4	27.3[a]

Note:
[a] 33.3 per cent if we include St Catherine of Siena, canonized in 1461.

(with the exception of Prussia) are absent from table 18; this probably owes more to their greater remoteness from the Roman Curia than to a lack of representatives in this category, since hagiography has preserved a large number of *Vitae* of Polish princesses who were regarded as saints in the late fourteenth and early fifteenth centuries.[19]

Overall, we derive from this study of the lay sainthood recognized by the Church an impression of a far greater distortion than in the case of other groups between official sainthood and sainthood as it was actually perceived and venerated by the Christian people. Whilst holy kings and princes continued, especially in the thirteenth century, to accede to the honours of canonization in significant numbers, the new forms of religious life were far less successful when they were incarnated by persons of modest origins: neither the cult of Margaret of Cortona nor that of Angela of Foligno was recognized by the Holy See at this period, and the cause of Dorothy of Mantau is still pending today. It appears that, from the great penitential and mystical trend which transformed the religious life of the laity in the thirteenth and fourteenth centuries, the papacy chose only persons whose purely religious merits were enhanced by their distinguished origins.

To summarize the evolution of the attitude of the Roman Church in the choice of saints during the later Middle Ages, it will be helpful to bring together in one table (table 21) the results obtained.

What most stands out is certainly the significant decline of episcopal sainthood within canonized sainthood as a whole. This phenomenon, which we may relate to the rejection by the Avignon papacy of many requests for canonization concerning bishops, confirms that, in ruling

[19] See above, p. 167, note 32.

circles within the Roman Church, the prestige of the episcopal model had lost ground. Nevertheless, in certain Christian countries, popular pressure continued to be exercised in favour of holy prelates, as we see from the relative stability of the proportion of processes concerning them.

This contrast is hardly surprising. It is well known that the fourteenth century was characterized on the ecclesiological and canonical plane by the success of arguments exalting the primacy of the Roman Church and tending to reduce the powers of the ordinary to the benefit of the pontifical monarchy.[20] But by increasingly refusing to accord the honours of a public cult to prelates regarded as saints within their dioceses, the fourteenth-century papacy increased the distance between official sainthood and local sainthood as it was perceived in north-western Europe, in particular in England and the Scandinavian countries.

On the other hand, the regulars, who, after 1305, seem no longer to have aroused quite so much enthusiasm among the faithful (27.4 per cent of processes ordered as opposed to 40.8 per cent), were increasingly favourably regarded in high places within the Church, and their import-ance among canonized saints rose slightly (from 33.3 per cent in the thir-teenth century to 36.4 per cent after). This figure is all the more remark-able in that it conceals the profound changes which had affected the monastic world: the old orders were systematically excluded from canoniz-ation between 1224 and 1401, whilst the Mendicant orders replaced them in the favour of the papacy, which supported them in every way it could.

The laity, lastly, progressed significantly from one century to the next, overtaking the regulars in the fourteenth century at the level of processes and catching up with the bishops at that of canonizations. With a success rate higher than that of the other categories (with the exception of clerical Mendicants), they now formed an important group, whose emergence constituted one of the major innovations of our period.

THE RECRUITMENT OF SAINTS: SOCIOLOGICAL APPROACHES

Men, women and sainthood

The respective position of men and women among the saints recognized by the Church between 1198 and 1431 is shown in table 22. These general figures show very clearly the disparity in the recruitment of the saints: at

[20] See above, pp. 102–3.

Table 22 *Distribution by sex of the saints recognized by the Church (1198–1431) (in percentages)*

Sex	Processes	Canonizations
Men	81.7	85.7
Women	18.3	14.3

the level of processes and, even more, at that of canonizations, men were in an overwhelming majority.[21] This is easily explicable, given the preponderance of bishops among the saints of this period. But this *a priori* inferiority of female sainthood is not compensated for by the proportion of women among the saints from the religious orders. In fact, in this category, 84 per cent of the processes held concerned men, and only 16 per cent women. When we look at the canonizations pronounced, the disproportion is even greater. The eleven regulars canonized included only one woman, Clare of Assisi. Admittedly, this figure is an average between an almost exclusively male monastic sainthood (except for St Hildegard) and a 'mendicant' sainthood within which women had a not insignificant role (21.4 per cent of the processes in this category concerned women, though the percentage falls to 12.5 for canonizations). The greater openness of the new orders to female forms of religious life was thus not enough to modify to any great degree the essentially masculine connotation of sainthood as recognized by the Church.

The situation as regards lay saints was very different, as, between 1198 and 1431, it experienced a high degree of feminization, as we see from table 23. Globally, women were more numerous than men, in the case of

Table 23 *Lay saints (1198–1431): distribution by sex (in percentages)*

Sex	Processes	Canonizations
Women	58.8	55.5
Men	41.2	44.5

[21] A total of thirteen female saints were the object of a process of canonization during our period; they were, in chronological order of process, Cunegund, Elizabeth of Thuringia, Hildegard, Margaret of Scotland, Rose of Viterbo, Clare of Assisi, Margaret of Hungary, Clare of Montefalco, Delphine of Sabran, Bridget of Sweden, Dorothy of Montau, Catherine of Siena and Ingrid of Skänninge. Five were canonized in the Middle Ages (Cunegund,

both processes and canonizations. If we break these results down by century, we see a very clear trend; among the processes of canonization of lay saints, 50 per cent in the thirteenth century concerned women, compared with 71.4 per cent during the later period. After 1305, two out of three of the lay persons whose sainthood was recognized by the Church were women.

This trend coincides with that noted above for the Mediterranean countries at the level of local sainthood during the last centuries of the Middle Ages. The papacy encouraged this process by welcoming requests concerning women most of whom were linked to the Mendicant orders. Male lay sainthood – still represented in the twelfth century by St Homobonus and numerous hermits and pilgrims – disappeared completely from curial horizons.

This increasing feminization of lay sainthood is visible in the global figures, and the percentage of processes of canonization decreed on behalf of holy women passed from 16.3 in the thirteenth century to 27.3 in the years 1305–1431. We see a pale reflection of the movement of the beguines and mystics which gave many lay people, but especially women, access to an intense religious life and the prestige of sainthood. But at the level of canonizations actually pronounced by the papacy, women saints continued to be much less 'successful' than their male homologues, which can only be explained by a certain reticence towards them on the part of the ecclesiastical hierarchy. Thanks to the crises which shook the Church after 1378, inspired prophetesses and visionaries increased in number. But only saints like Bridget of Sweden and Catherine of Siena, whose glorification could strengthen the position of one of the rival obediences – in this case the 'Urbanist' camp – succeeded, not without difficulty, and the breakthrough was short-lived.[22] At the end of the Middle Ages, canonization remained essentially a male prerogative.

Elizabeth of Thuringia, Margaret of Scotland, Clare of Assisi and Bridget) to whom we may add Catherine of Siena, canonized in 1461. The percentage of women saints, small though it is, was higher in the thirteenth and fourteenth centuries than earlier, according to an analysis of the names in the *Bibliotheca sanctorum*; see J. Tibbetts-Schulenburg, 'Sexism and the Celestial Gynaecum from 500 to 1200', *Journal of Medieval History*, 4 (1978), pp. 117–33.

[22] St Bridget had to be canonized three times (by Boniface IX in 1391, John XXIII in 1415 and Martin V in 1419) before the authenticity of her sanctity was finally accepted. Even then her canonization seemed inappropriate to many clerics, as we see from the complaints of Gerson in *De probatione spirituum*; see Kemp, *Canonization and authority*, pp. 128–31.

Table 24 *Distribution of processes of canonization by country (1198–1431)*
(in percentages)

	England Scotland Ireland	France (with Brittany and Provence)	Italy	Germanic countries	Scandinavian countries	Eastern Europe[a]
1198–1431	19.7	23.9	31	9.5	9.9	5.6
1198–1304	20.4	20.4	32.7	12.2	6.1	8.2
1305–1431	18.2	31.8	27.3	4.5	18.2	—

Note:
[a] That is, Poland, Hungary and Bohemia.

The geographical disparities in sainthood

The results of a first analysis of the respective position of the various countries of western Christendom, at the level of processes of canonization decreed by the papacy, appear in table 24. This table, together with map 1, reveals the inequality which existed between two groups of countries: on the one hand, Italy, France and England, which accounted for three-quarters of the processes of canonization held at this period; on the other, the Germanic, Scandinavian and Slav countries, much less favoured, since they together accounted for only a quarter of the causes. We need to add a third group, those which had no saint recognized by the Roman Church in our period; these were essentially the states of the Iberian peninsula, that is Aragon, Castile and Portugal, together with the Low Countries (the modern Belgium and Holland) and northern Germany.

How are we to explain these disparities? They relate in part to the greater or lesser proximity of the countries in question to the Roman Curia; Italy in the thirteenth century, like southern France in the fourteenth, benefited from its advantageous geographical position, close to the pontifical court where decisions regarding the cult of the saints were made. But this was not the only factor involved; we need also to recognize what P. Delooz has called the 'social distance' within the Church, that is, the intensity and nature of the relations which existed between the papacy and the various states. The success of England at the level of sainthood recognized by the Church, despite its distance from Rome, may be explained by the number of permanent procurators and special envoys maintained at the Curia, at great expense, by the monarchy and episcopate.[23] Conversely, the total absence of Catalan saints was the result not so much of the remoteness of Barcelona from Rome or Avignon as of the frequently strained, even conflictual, relations existing between the papacy and the Crown of Aragon after the conquest of southern Italy by the Angevins until the fall of the latter in the fifteenth century.[24]

The poor representation of the countries of central and eastern Europe in officially recognized sainthood is probably due to the fact that these countries, especially the most remote, were peripheral to the preoccupations of the Holy See, apart from a few exceptional periods, such as the reign of Frederick II in the thirteenth century. But here, too, it would be mistaken to attribute everything to political or administrative factors. In the case of northern Germany and the Slav countries, it seems likely that the 'modern' saints were less popular than in western and Mediterranean Europe, both people and clergy remaining largely faithful to the old cults and the traditional intercessors. The creative ferment which characterized England and Italy, and produced a steady stream of new saints, was not present there to the same degree. This is even more true of countries like Castile and Portugal, which were largely content with the existing cults.[25] Stranger is the case of the Low Countries, where no process of canonization was held in the later Middle Ages, even though the most modern forms of beguine and mystical sanctity were immensely successful there.

The disparity between countries emerges even more clearly when we separate the two main chronological periods I have defined. In the thirteenth century, there was a marked preponderance of Italian saints (32.7 per cent of all processes), which must relate both to the presence in that country of the Roman Curia and to the birth of the Mendicant orders, which were, at least to begin with, a specifically Italian phenomenon. France and England came next (both 20.4 per cent); the Germanic and Slav countries occupied a lesser, but not negligible place; Scandinavia was poorly represented. Between 1305 and 1431, Italy lost ground (only 27.3 per cent of all processes). France, on the other hand, forged ahead, thanks to Provence, particularly favoured in the fourteenth century, and Brittany. We observe here an aspect of the nepotism of the Avignon popes, who

[23] See above, p. 65, note 13.
[24] The success of the causes supported by the Neapolitan sovereigns during the fourteenth century only proves the point. See above, pp. 78–81.
[25] St Dominic belonged to Spain only through his birth and early years. His cult developed from Bologna, and it is not unreasonable to see him as an Italian saint; the same is true of the Portuguese Antony of Padua.

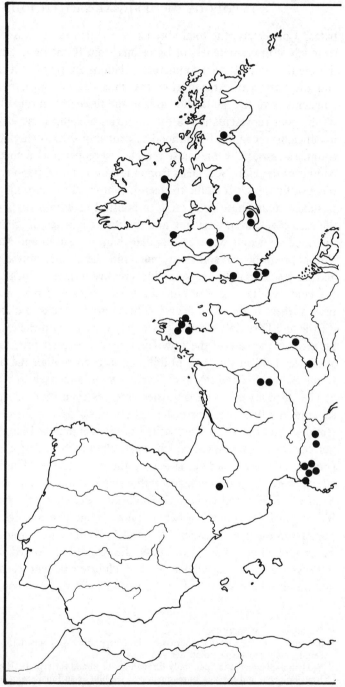

Map 1 Geographical distribution of the processes of canonization
ordered by the papacy between 1198 and 1431.

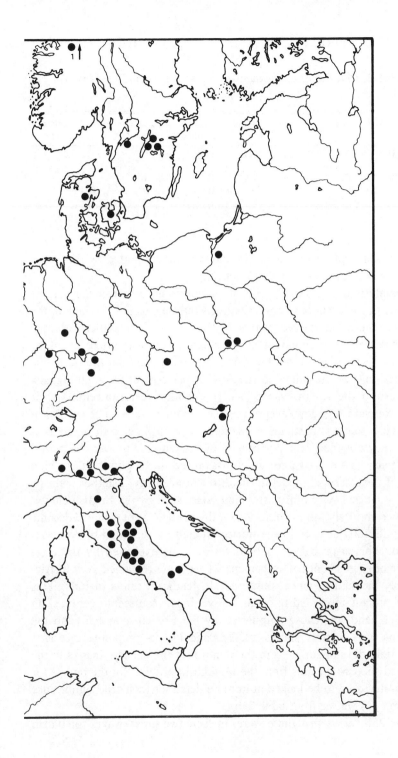

Table 25a *Distribution of canonizations by country (1198–1431) (in percentages)*

	England	Italy	France	German countries	Scandinavian countries	Eastern Europe
1198–1431	31.4	25.7	17.1	14.4	5.7	5.7
1198–1304	36	24	12	16	4	8
1305–1431	20	30	30	10	10	—

favoured saints who were either close to them or supported by the sovereigns to whom they were closest politically.

An analysis of the distribution of canonizations between the various countries of Christendom largely confirms the conclusions reached on the basis of processes, as we see from table 25a. This table, together with map 2, again reveals the preponderance of England, France and Italy. It will be noted, however, that, in the thirteenth century, saints from the Germanic countries enjoyed considerable success (16 per cent of the total, against 12 per cent in the case of France), whereas in the fourteenth century their share dropped to the low level of the Scandinavian states. The success of the English saints is particularly marked: with 19.7 per cent of the processes, they obtained 31.4 per cent of the canonizations over the period as a whole. This remarkable success was owed to the popularity in high places of the episcopal model in the thirteenth century, together with the highly organized system of postulation established by the English clergy. In France and Italy, on the other hand, the percentage of canonized saints was significantly smaller in the thirteenth century than that of processes decreed. This is probably, in both cases, to be explained by the large number of causes concerning persons whose fame remained very restricted: holy monks in France, purely local Mendicant saints in Italy. This type of process rarely led to canonization. In the fourteenth century, on the other hand, the causes supported by the French monarchy and the Angevins were notably successful. England lost its preponderance as a result. Italy did not suffer from the removal of the papacy, thanks to the sustained success of saints from the Mendicant orders. But the figures for this country need to be looked at in more detail for their true significance to emerge, as we see from table 25b.

Table 25b shows that there were, in fact, two great 'waves' of Italian

Table 25b *Proportion of Italian saints in
relation to all processes (in percentages)*

1198–1253	30.2
1254–1304	0
1305–1355	55.6
1356–1431	7.1

sainthood between 1198 and 1431. One was contemporary with the birth of the Mendicant orders, and essentially concerned the generation of the founders, that is, between 1228 and 1253. There followed a period of fifty years during which no Italian cause was considered by the papacy. This was the time of conflict between the new orders and the seculars and the Joachimite crisis. Between 1305 and 1325, Italian saints again achieved prominence; there were five, comprising two popes (Celestine V and Gregory X), two regulars (Thomas Aquinas and Nicholas of Tolentino) and a nun (Clare of Montefalco). One could even include in this group St Louis of Anjou (process in 1308), who was as Neapolitan as he was Provençal. Subsequently, the proportion of Italian saints steadily fell until the mid-fifteenth century. It is difficult to see this as simply a consequence of the establishment of the popes in Avignon. It is more likely to result from the violent crises which shook the Franciscan order, from the pontificate of John XXII on, and, more generally, from the decadence of the Mendicant orders, that great source of saints in the period 1330–80.

At a deeper level, these figures bring out the gulf which separated the sainthood approved by the Roman Church and that which was recognized and venerated at the local level.

On the basis of all the saints listed for the whole of western Christendom in the latest edition of Butler's *Lives of the saints*, Weinstein and Bell have pointed out that whilst fewer than half (70 out of 177) were Italian in the thirteenth century, the proportion rises to nearly two-thirds (103 out of 159) in the period 1300–1425.[26] The statistical basis of these figures is admittedly open to doubt in particular cases, and it is likely that the type of secondary source used by Butler to compile his list to some extent favoured saints from south of the Alps, whose memory was rapidly recorded and transmitted by the Mendicant orders. But these cavils do not detract from the general conclusion: whilst the servants of God born

---

[26] Weinstein and Bell, 'Saints and society'.

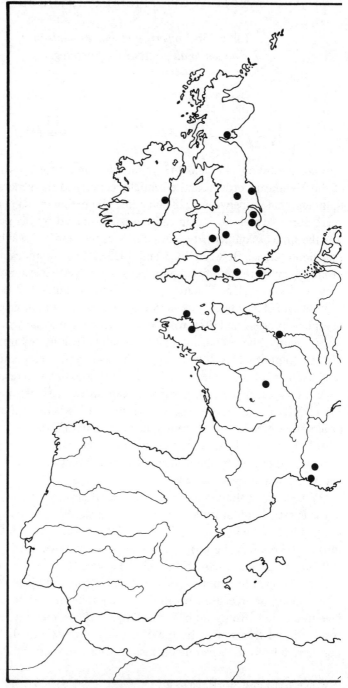

Map 2 Geographical distribution of the canonizations made by the papacy between 1198 and 1431.

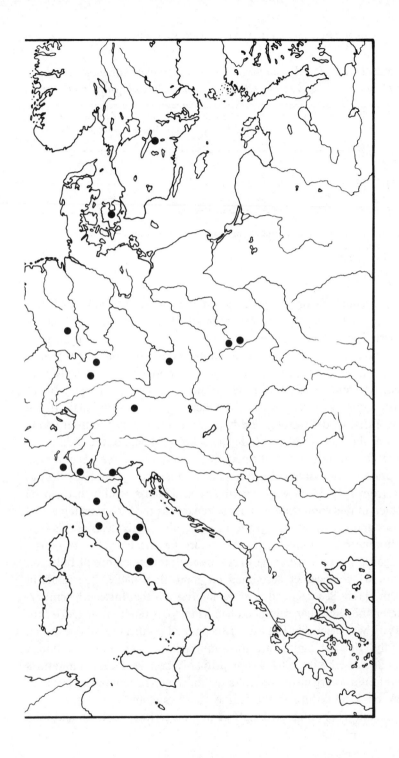

Table 26 *Distribution by country of requests for canonization addressed to the Holy See between 1198 and 1431 but not acted on (in percentages)*[a]

	Italy	England	Aragon and Sicily (after 1282)	France	Germanic countries	Eastern Europe[b]	Latin East[c]
1198–1431	35	18	17	11	10	6	3
1198–1304	52	8	16	16	8	—	—
1305–1431	18	28	18	6	12	12	6

Notes:
[a] For details of the sources for this table and map 3, see table 4 above.
[b] Poland, Bohemia, Hungary and Croatia.
[c] In practice, Cyprus.

in Italy accounted for just over a quarter of those whose cult was recognized by the papacy between 1198 and 1431, they made up, at the same period, over half of the recent saints who were venerated at the local level. In no other country was there a comparable situation, characterized by the existence of innumerable devotions that were ignored by the Roman Church. At a simple statistical level, we see the contrast between a 'modern' sainthood favoured by the Mendicants and a traditional, if not archaic, curial model, whose rigidity prevented the Holy See from taking account of the most brilliant products of the apostolate of the 'frati'.

These conclusions are confirmed by an analysis of the geographical distribution of the requests for canonization rejected by the Holy See, as we see from map 3. As we have already said, the statistics that can be assembled in this connection are not as reliable as those concerning actual processes and canonizations, given that a number of requests of this type have disappeared without trace (it was rare for the Holy See to reply). Once again, one cannot but be struck by the preponderance of Italy and England, which together accounted for more than half of the saints in whom the Holy See declined to show interest. In the thirteenth century, lay and eremitical Italian sainthood had a low 'pass rate'; in the fourteenth century, it was primarily English episcopal and political sainthood which did badly. But the figures are misleading; if the percentage of Italian failures decreased after 1304, it was primarily because local communities now preferred to organize new cults within the civic context, rather than embark on a procedure at the Curia whose outcome they knew to be unpredictable. The other striking fact to emerge from table 26 and map

Table 27 *Distribution of the saints recognized by the Roman Church between 1198 and 1431 according to social origin (in percentages)*

Saints	Noble	Middle class	Popular	Social origin unknown
Subject of a canonization process (71)	62	15.5	8.4	14.1
Actually canonized by a medieval pope (35)	60	17.1	8.6	14.3

3 is the failure of the Aragonese monarchy to persuade the Roman Church to recognize the sainthood of a number of persons who seemed, nevertheless, likely to find favour. We have already discussed the essentially political factors which explain this situation, which is in marked contrast to the exceptionally high success rate of the saints from Provence.[27]

The social origins of the saints

It is not without interest, lastly, to examine the social origin of the saints, given that the 'celestial society' created by the Church between 1198 and 1431 was only a very inexact copy of the composition of earthly society, as we see from table 27.

One cannot but be struck by the overwhelming preponderance of the aristocracy among the saints recognized by the Roman Church in the last centuries of the Middle Ages, at the level both of processes ordered and canonizations pronounced. Despite the inadequacies of the statistics, given that the social origins of a significant proportion (about 14 per cent) of the saints are unknown or imperfectly known, there can be no doubt that the recruitment of the new intercessors was hardly democratic. Like the kings of the period, God surrounded himself mainly with princes and nobles, plus a few members of the bourgeoisie and a tiny handful of sons of peasants, who had usually managed to overcome the obstacles associated with their obscure birth by entering the clergy; of the three saints of modest origins canonized, one was a pope (Celestine V), another a regular Mendicant (St Nicholas of Tolentino) and the third an eleventh-century hermit (St Sebald), who was in any case presented by his fourteenth-century hagiographers as the son of a king of Denmark.[28]

When we come to look more closely at the modalities of this massive

[27] See above, pp. 75–81.
[28] See above, p. 84, note 77.

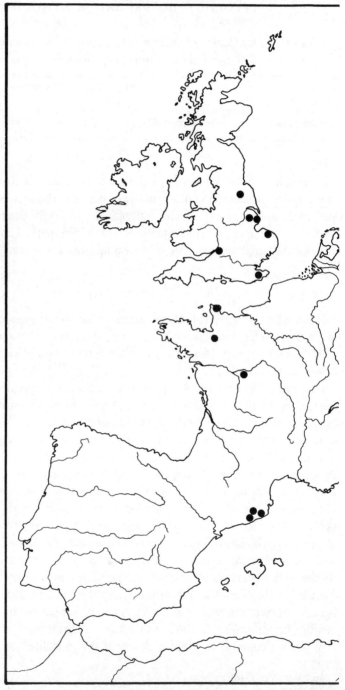

Map 3 Geographical distribution of the requests for canonization submitted to the Holy See between 1198 and 1431 but not acted on.

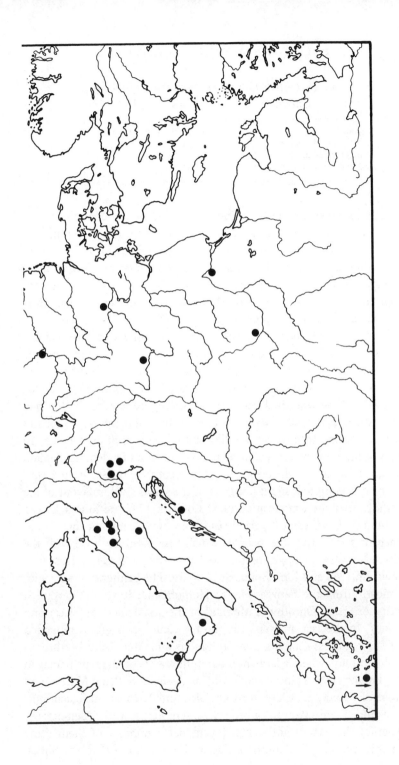

Table 28 *Distribution by social category of the lay saints recognized by the Roman Church (1198–1431)*

Social groups	% of all the lay saints
Reigning dynasties	41.1
Seigneurial aristocracy	17.8
Middle and lower classes	41.1

aristocratic presence among the saints recognized by the Church, we see that it relates to the importance, especially in the thirteenth century, of the saint-bishops, who, in almost all cases, came from royal families or illustrious lineages. One might expect the category of lay saints to be more open in its recruitment. But an analysis of the distribution of this category between the various social groups shows that there was, in fact, little difference, as we see from table 28.

If we add the percentage of saints from reigning dynasties (kings, princes and dukes) to that from the nobility, we reach a result which is almost identical to the average figure calculated earlier for all the saints of the period (58.9 per cent, against 62 per cent). If we remove from the list the names of those who died before 1200, the figure is even higher than the general average, that is, 63.6 per cent of the 'contemporary' saints in this category came from royal families or the seigneurial aristocracy. In the light of these figures, it would be wrong to speak of a democratization of lay sainthood in the thirteenth and fourteenth centuries. At the very most, one can point to a slight lowering of the social level in favour of the aristocracy; after the canonization of St Louis in 1297, no king achieved this honour in the medieval period. But there was a simultaneous disappearance of saints from the people, which was often the case with the hermits, who were no longer represented after the processes of Lawrence of Subiaco in 1243 and John Bonus in 1249–51. The penitents and mystics came mostly from the bourgeoisie (St Homobonus, Rose of Viterbo, St Catherine of Siena, Dorothy of Montau) or the aristocracy (St Elzear and Delphine). In the last analysis, the most socially open group remained that of the regulars – monks, regular canons and Mendicant brethren – especially in Italy, where a large number of the saints of this type belonged to the 'Popolo' (SS Francis and Clare of Assisi, SS Peter Martyr and Ambrose of Massa, SS Clare of Montefalco and Nicholas of Tolentino). But it would be mistaken to put too much emphasis on the 'democratic' character of the Mendicant saints, given that a number of them came from noble lineages (St Antony of Padua, Benvenuto of Gubbio, Simon of Collazzone, St Thomas Aquinas) or royal families (SS Margaret of Hungary and Louis of Anjou). With a few striking exceptions, those enjoying the prestige of blood and power remained best placed to achieve sainthood up to the end of the Middle Ages.

Our quantitative analysis has demonstrated the principal features of the sainthood recognized by the Roman Church, and its evolution. At the beginning of the thirteenth century, the saints came mostly from among the bishops and regulars, in particular the monks. Lay saints were few, and with almost only one exception (St Homobonus), all belonged to royal families. There were few women among them, and even fewer among the regulars. Lastly, these saints were fairly evenly distributed over the various parts of Christendom, with the exception of a few 'cold' regions, where the new cults had little appeal. Over the following decades, the situation changed perceptibly; the old religious orders lost their prestige and ceased to be considered – by the faithful or by the hierarchy – as the natural home of sanctity. They were overtaken in this role by the Mendicant orders, whose saints were extremely successful, especially in Italy. From the end of the thirteenth century, the number of processes and canonizations fell and it becomes harder to identify trends. However, it is clear that local and official sainthood increasingly diverged. The Roman Church lost interest in the holy hermits, recluses and penitents, though devotion to them grew enormously at this period in the Mediterranean countries. Further, the Avignon papacy turned a cold shoulder to the requests it received from the countries of north-west Europe on behalf of holy bishops, and tried to substitute the model of the holy pope or cardinal for that of the diocesan bishop. It also favoured servants of God from the Mendicant orders or close to them spiritually. The saints were still almost exclusively persons of high rank, whose fame owed as much to their birth as to their religious fervour. After the Schism, the distance between recognized sainthood and the local cults diminished a little; the proportion of lay saints increased, and within this category, women eventually became preponderant during the last decades of the fourteenth and the early fifteenth centuries. But this tendency was short-lived, and once they had restored their authority within the Church, the fifteenth-century popes canonized only Mendicant regulars or pious lay persons associated with these orders.[29]

We cannot rely solely on statistics to reach conclusions in a field such

[29] See above, p. 76, note 44.

as the history of sainthood, which is a reality difficult to reduce to figures. A typology which is confined to this level risks superficiality since it ignores realities which lend themselves less easily to a quantitative approach than the canonical status of persons. Whilst it is important for us to know, for example, the proportion of bishops among the saints of the thirteenth and fourteenth centuries, it is no less important to ask what, for the Church, which controlled canonization, was the 'ideal-type' of episcopal sainthood during the period under consideration. The apparent continuity implied by the distribution of saints between given categories (bishops and priests, regulars, laity) risks concealing changes which may have occurred in the traditional models of sainthood. Lastly, the appearance of new forms of perfection helped to challenge the distinctions based on states of life. We must next, therefore, seek to establish typologies with criteria which are less formal and closer to lived realities.

CHAPTER 12

FORMS OF SAINTHOOD AND WAYS OF LIFE

ოოო

THE SAINTHOOD OF THE CLERGY

The saint-bishop

As our statistical study has shown, most of the saints recognized by the Roman Church between 1198 and 1431 were bishops.[1] This is hardly surprising, given that episcopal sanctity had always, since the end of Antiquity, been of prime importance within the Church.[2] After an apogee lasting from about 500 to 800, the episcopal ideal lost its pre-eminence in favour of an eremitical and monastic model.[3] It enjoyed renewed success, however, in the tenth and eleventh centuries, especially in the Anglo-Saxon and Germanic countries, and remained important throughout western Christendom until the beginning of the thirteenth century. This experience of Christian perfection achieved through the exercise of episcopal office was expressed in a number of canonical, spiritual and hagiographical texts which had a profound influence on the clerical mentality. We need, therefore, to look, if only briefly, at this heritage in order to appreciate the extent of the influence it continued to exercise in the last centuries of the Middle Ages.

The Good Shepherd in texts prior to the thirteenth century: an ambivalent tradition

The key text defining the norms which made it possible to assess the life and works of a bishop remained, until the end of the Middle Ages, the

---

[1] See above, p. 258.
[2] See above, p. 17.
[3] Poulain, *L'idéal de sainteté*, p. 67.

Liber regulae pastoralis of Gregory the Great, which was influential throughout the medieval West and even in the Byzantine world.[4] In practice, this treatise, which takes the form of a long letter addressed by the pope, about 590, to Archbishop John of Ravenna, was as much a code of sacerdotal sanctity as a manual of pastoral theology for the benefit of the bishops. But it was often used and quoted in the Carolingian period at the time of the reconstruction of the Frankish Church on the basis of the territorial episcopate. Alcuin was much influenced by it, and the reforms which were adopted by the Councils of Aachen (816 and 836) and Rome (826) bore its mark. It was at this period that, in view of the gulf existing between the ideal proposed by Gregory the Great and the reality of the sacerdotal condition, a text which had originally been written for the priestly body as a whole began to be applied exclusively to bishops. In the twelfth century, the influence of the *Liber regulae pastoralis* is still clear in the *Decretum* of Gratian.[5] *Distinctiones* 21–101, that 'mirror of the bishop', owes much to it. The picture of episcopal sainthood, as it emerges from this normative text, which was to form the basis of medieval canon law in this area, is effectively a summary of the *Regula pastoralis*, with the addition of a number of scriptural references, mostly taken from the Epistles of St Paul (Timothy III, 2, 6 and Titus I, 6), and the Fathers of the Church, in particular SS Jerome and Ambrose.[6]

According to Gratian, the good bishop ought to be:

Irreproachable in his morals,
sober and level-headed,
shrewd, courteous and hospitable,
moderate in food and dress, discreet,
neither a drinker nor a fighter but benevolent,
an enemy of violence and quarrelling,
neither a neophyte nor a usurer.[7]

---

[4] *Liber regulae pastoralis*, ed. *PL*, 77, cc. 13–128; for the contents, see G. Hocquard, 'L'idéal du Pasteur des âmes selon S. Grégoire le Grand', in *La tradition sacerdotale: études sur le sacerdoce* (Le Puy, 1959), pp. 143–67; for its influence in the East, see A. Guillou, 'L'évêque dans la société méditerranéenne des VI–VIIe siècles: un modèle', *BECh*, 131 (1973), pp. 5–19.

[5] J. Gaudemet, 'Patristique et pastorale. La contribution de Grégoire le Grand au "Miroir de l'évêque" dans le Décret de Gratien', in *Etudes d'histoire du droit canonique dédiées à Gabriel Le Bras*, I (Paris, 1965), pp. 129–39.

[6] Pauline influence is emphasized by G. Le Bras, 'Les Ecritures dans le Décret de Gratien', *Zeitschrift der Savigny Stiftung für Rechtsgeschichte, Kan. Abteilung*, 58 (1938), pp. 47–80.

[7] A detailed analysis in J. Rambaud-Buhot, 'Le Décret de Gratien legs du passé, avènement de l'âge classique', in *Entretiens sur la renaissance du XIIe siècle*, ed. M. de Gandillac and E. Jeauneau (Paris and The Hague, 1968), pp. 493–506, especially p. 500.

As we see, Gregory the Great – and Gratian, who followed him closely –
did not make exceptional demands of the bishop. He was not expected to
perform ascetic exploits or shine as a scholar, but be sober and temperate.
What was crucial was that he should be of good morals and, above all,
demonstrate the qualities of a leader and good administrator. The chief
virtues required of him were benevolence and discretion, moderation and
balance.

In view of the circumstances (Investitures Struggle and the battle
between Church and Empire), the author of the *Decretum* dwelt at length
on the question of access to the episcopate. He gave a long list of candidates who ought to be excluded: penitents, soldiers, civil servants, serfs,
the infirm, sons of priests, monks without the permission of their abbot
etc. These passages reflect the preoccupations of ecclesiastical milieux
close to the papacy, which had sought, since the eleventh century, to
rescue the episcopate from the double temptation of simony and nichola-
ism, and make it into an instrument for the reform of the Church.[8] We
find an echo of these requirements in the processes of canonization of the
thirteenth and fourteenth centuries; the clergy who gave evidence seized
every opportunity to emphasize that the holy bishop they had known had
been *concorditer electus*.[9] And the biographer of St Hugh of Avalon, bishop
of Lincoln (d. 1200), took pains to stress that the holy prelate, before
leaving the Grande Chartreuse at the request of Henry II Plantagenet, had
sought guarantees that he had been freely elected by the chapter.[10] Even
if the reality was sometimes rather different, or at any rate more complex,
it was important that access to the episcopate should appear to be the result
of a choice made by the canons of a cathedral church, representatives of
the diocesan clergy.[11]

In the texts of the twelfth-century moralists, especially St Bernard,
author of the *De moribus et officiis episcoporum*, the emphasis is on the
virtues of chastity, charity and humility, deemed essential for bishops by
the abbot of Clairvaux.[12] These new demands followed from the drive to

---

[8] C. Capitani, 'La figura del Vescovo in alcune collezioni canoniche della seconda metà del
secolo XI', in *Vescovi e diocesi in Italia nel Medio Evo (sec. IX–XIII)* (Padua, 1964), pp.
161–91.
[9] *PC Thomas of Hereford*, fol. 95; *PC Brynulph*, p. 141; *PC Nicholas of Linköping*, p. 56.
[10] Adam of Eynsham, *Magna Vita sancti Hugonis*, ed. D. Douie and H. Farmer, I (London,
1961), pp. 71, 100.
[11] As we see from the process of Nicholas of Linköping, free election was no longer sufficient
in the fourteenth century; the election must also be confirmed by the pope, hence the
Swedish prelate's journey to Avignon; *PC Nicholas of Linköping*, p. 56.
[12] St Bernard, *De moribus et officiis episcoporum*, in *PL*, 182, cc. 806–34. In the *De institutione
episcoporum* (ed. in *PL*, 207, cc. 1097–1112), Peter of Blois (d. 1200) suggests the example

'monasticize' the episcopate initiated by Gregory VII and continued by his successors. It met with considerable resistance, on the part both of those concerned and the faithful themselves, but was nevertheless highly influential in the thirteenth century. It changed the image of the bishop by adding to the qualities traditionally required of the leader and man of action requirements of an ascetic and moral order which had previously been more characteristic of the regulars.

Remarkably, the same ambivalence is evident in the hagiographical sources concerning saint-bishops. This tradition dates back to the first centuries in the life of the Church and can boast an output as large as it is varied. The image of the bishop was profoundly influenced by one particularly famous text, the *Vita Martini* of Sulpitius Severus, which exercised great influence to the end of the Middle Ages.[13] This is not the place for a lengthy discussion of the circumstances surrounding the composition of this celebrated work or the politico-religious context within which it was written. What is important from our perspective is that this text, copied and read for centuries, conveyed and transmitted, in the person of the bishop of Tours, a lived synthesis of monastic perfection and pastoral action. From then on, no author of a *Vita* of a saint-bishop failed to refer – even when his subject was very remote from it – to the Martinian model, which was, as is well known, notably more monastic than episcopal. As a result, we find in these bishops, to varying degrees, both the qualities of the leader who rules firmly over his Church, fighting evil in all its forms, and the virtues of the man of religion who seeks in prayer, fasting and ascetic practices the elements of a spiritual life capable of counterbalancing the demands of action and government. Merovingian hagiography added new features to this model: aristocratic origins – the bishop was invariably from a rich and powerful family – and the role of defender of the people against royal power and the arbitrary violence inflicted by the lay aristocracy on the people.[14] In the Carolingian period, the Lives of holy bishops returned to a more authentically Martinian tradition at the spiritual level, their pastoral activity usually being limited to attending councils and synods and occasional preaching.[15]

In the tenth and eleventh centuries, in particular in the Empire,

of the Good Shepherd to prelates. Nor should we forget that St Bernard wrote a Life of St Malachy, Archbishop of Armagh (d. 1148) (= *BHL* 5188).
[13] Sulpitius Severus, *Vie de Saint Martin*, ed. J. Fontaine, 3 vols. (Paris, 1966–9).
[14] Graus, *Volk, Herrscher und Heiliger*, pp. 115–20 and bibliography, pp. 495–513.
[15] Poulain, *L'idéal de sainteté*, pp. 34–41, 64–7.

there developed a whole body of literature devoted to exalting the virtues and actions of holy prelates. This was the period of the *Gesta episcoporum* which appeared more or less all over the West, whilst the great religious metropolises carefully enriched their *Liber pontificalis*, that of the Roman Church being only the most famous.[16] This is not the place to discuss this historiographical and hagiographical output, as abundant as it was varied. We need note only its most characteristic features, given that they had a lasting impact on the clerical conception of episcopal sainthood. The purpose, avowed or not, of the authors of these Lives was to show how their subjects had been able to achieve a balance between the public and political duties they assumed in the context of the 'Reichskirche' (*cura exteriorum*) and moral and spiritual preoccupations, strictly speaking (*cura interiorum*). The goal these saints had set out to achieve during their lifetime was the establishment or restoration of the *pax*, that is the order without which the religious life could not flourish. In the *Vitae*, therefore, we see them lavishing good advice and entreaties but also, when necessary, resorting to arms if the recipients of their exhortations failed to see reason. Mild and gentle towards the good and the weak, they could be harsh and severe towards the wicked and the proud. The main problem for the hagiographers was to explain how they had managed harmoniously to reconcile in their existence the two complementary but seemingly contradictory aspects of their power – *dux et pastor* – and conduct – *timor et amor*.[17] The political dimension was ever-present in their actions, which could only be closely related to that of the monarchy; for them, the establishment of *justitia* was the result of close collaboration between the *sacerdotalis religio* and the *regia fortitudo*.[18] The good bishop, lastly, was concerned to develop his temporalities and expand the possessions of his bishopric in the name of the interests of the local church. His power and wealth were praised as long as he used them wisely, for example by building churches, and gave lavishly, especially to the

[16] O. Köhler, *Das Bild des geistlichen Fürsten in den Viten des 10, 11, 12. Jahrhunderts* (Berlin, 1935); G. Arnaldi, 'Intorno al Liber Pontificalis', in *Monseigneur Duchesne et son temps* (Rome, 1975), pp. 120–36.

[17] *Ibid.*, pp. 5–29. The principal texts on which these analyses are based are *Vita Adalberonis II episcopi Mettensis* (d. 1005), ed. in *MGH.SS.*, IV, pp. 659–72; *Vita Hartwici episcopi Salisburgensis* (d. 1023), ed. in *MGH.SS.*, XI, pp. 95–7; *Vita Brunonis episcopi Coloniensis* (d. 965), ed. in *MGH.SS.*, IV, pp. 254–75.

[18] Köhler, *Das Bild des geistlichen Fürsten*, pp. 27–8, 65–6; interesting remarks in H. Kallfelz, *Vitae quorumdam episcoporum saeculorum X, XI, XII. Lebensbeschreibung einiger Bischöfe des 10–12. Jahrhunderts* (Darmstadt, 1973).

poor.[19] The influence of the monastic ideal was also unobtrusively evident: the holy bishop behaved humbly, but only towards his inferiors. He rejected ostentation and popularity and the more illustrious his birth, the more modest his behaviour.[20] In fact, all these bishops were nobles, if not related to the royal family, and, in the eyes of their hagiographers, their high birth created a predisposition to sanctity. They were also cultivated men, admired for their wisdom and competence.

After the Gregorian Reform, which, by prohibiting simonaic practices, effectively challenged or at least cast doubt on the validity of the authority of many bishops, the model transmitted by this great hagiographical tradition suffered a crisis. The rise of the new religious orders and the exaltation of the ideal of the *vita apostolica* favoured the triumph of ascetic ideas; the result was a wave of saints from the ranks of the white and black monks, regular canons and hermits. The prestige of the bishop seemed to decline in some countries, such as northern France and Germany, where the number of *Vitae* devoted to saints of this type between 1150 and 1200 was much smaller than in the preceding half-century. This was particularly true, admittedly, of the prelates from the secular clergy, who were increasingly rivalled by bishops from the regulars.[21] It was mainly the latter who enjoyed a reputation for sanctity at a period when the episcopate as a whole was held in low esteem.[22] There was, as a result, a revival of the Martinian model among hagiographers as among the

---

[19] Köhler, *Das Bild des geistlichen Fürsten*, chapter 2, gives many references, taken primarily from *Vita Meinwerci episcopi Patherbrunnensis* (d. 1036), ed. in *MGH.SS.*, XI, pp. 106–61 and *Vita Bernwardi episcopi Hildeshemensis* (d. 1022), ed. in *MGH.SS.*, IV, pp. 757–82.

[20] Evidence of asceticism is relatively unimportant in all these Lives. See, for example, the prologue to the *Vita maior Bardonis episcopi Moguntini* (d. 1051), ed. in *MGH.SS.*, XI, cc. 318–21: 'quae de ceteris sanctis scripta sunt, quia aut jejunaverunt, aut homines fugerunt aut cetera similia, nisi alio ordine, nulla in eo inveniri possunt'.

[21] P. Oliger, *Les évêques réguliers: recherches sur leur condition juridique depuis les origines du monachisme jusqu'à la fin du Moyen Age* (Paris and Louvain, 1958), pp. 105–13.

[22] Adam of Eynsham (*Magna Vita sancti Hugonis*, II, p. 53) records the comments of an English Carthusian to St Hugh of Lincoln (d. 1200) on the subject of the bishops of his day: 'In these times he is worthy of honour, who is not utterly depraved, and a man is called good who does not injure his neighbour to the utmost of his ability. Also, it is reckoned an act of the highest virtue on the part of the mighty, if they ever assist anyone, and do not tyrannize over everybody. These are now highly praised and spoken of as saints!' But the bishop of Lincoln could quote two holy prelates in reply: Hugh of Grenoble (d. 1137) and Anthelm of Belley (d. 1178). The former had been influenced by the Grande Chartreuse; the latter was a Carthusian who became a bishop. See also J. Picard, *Vie de S. Antelme, évêque de Belley, par son chapelain Guillaume, chartreux de Portes* (Laignieu, Ain, 1978).

authors of spiritual and moralizing works.[23] In the majority of Lives, the image of the ascetic now took precedence over that of the hierarch.[24] In fact, many of the saint-bishops of the early thirteenth century were regulars who, after a longer or shorter period in a monastery, left, at the request of a pope or sovereign – reluctantly, if we are to believe their followers – to become a bishop. This was the case with John Cacciafronte of Vicenza (d. 1183), a Benedictine prior, with Hugh of Avalon (d. 1200) and Stephen of Châtillon (d. 1208), both Carthusians, respectively at Lincoln and Die, and William of Donjeon (d. 1209), successively a Grandmontine and a Cistercian before becoming archbishop of Bourges.[25] During the course of the thirteenth century, the monastic connotation of the episcopate diminished, in favour of the Mendicant orders. There were soon many bishops from the latter's ranks, distinguished primarily by their pastoral zeal. According to Salimbene, they were almost alone in the practice of preaching in Italy in the 1260s.[26] Nevertheless, in spite of a few sporadic devotions, their cult had little success.[27] The reputation for sanctity of a prelate, in the thirteenth century, was first and foremost the work of his close collaborators and especially the canons of his chapter. In the atmosphere of rivalry and sometimes conflict which soon developed

---

[23] In the *Magna Vita*, written in the early thirteenth century, Adam of Eynsham presents St Hugh of Lincoln as a disciple and imitator of Christ and St Martin (I, p. 24): 'Hic vero Christi tyro et Martini Beatissimi familiaris cultor et devotus imitator.' St Hugh had been a monk at the Grande Chartreuse before becoming a bishop (II, p. 43). In Italy, the early fourteenth-century Life of the holy bishop Rinaldo of Nocera Umbra (d. 1222) is a plagiarism of that of St Martin, with the addition of a few episodes drawn from other sources: Sigismondi, 'Legenda beati Raynaldi'.

[24] See, for example, the letter from Bishop Hato of Troyes, 1145–6, to the Cistercian Peter of St John: 'The Letters from Peter of St. John to Hato of Troyes', ed. G. Constable and J. Kritzeck, in *Petrus Venerabilis, 1156–1956* (Rome, 1956), p. 49: 'crucient qui volunt corpora sua et pellitiis vestibus ac femoralibus carere gratulentur. Ego quod ad salutem sufficit mutari debere non estimo neque, si salvus esse possum, magis salvus esse desidero.'

[25] John Cacciafronte was prior of St Victor, then abbot of St Lawrence at Cremona (*PC*, p. 243); for St Hugh, see above, p. 287; for Stephen of Die, see the acts of the enquiry made in 1231, ed. *AA.SS*. Sept. III, pp. 175–201; for William of Bourges, see J. Becquet, 'La première crise de l'ordre de Grandmont', *Bulletin de la société archéologique et historique du Limousin*, 87 (1960), pp. 284–324, especially pp. 296–7.

[26] Mariano d'Alatri, 'Il vescovo nella Cronaca di Salimbene di Parma', *Collectanea Franciscana*, 42 (1972), pp. 5–38. For Franciscan bishops in the thirteenth century, see R. W. Thomson, *Friars in the cathedral: the first Franciscan bishops, 1226–1261* (Toronto, 1975).

[27] Almost the only examples are the Dominican Bartholomew of Breganza (d. 1270), with a local cult at Vicenza, where he had been bishop (*PC Bartholomew of Breganza* (Vicenza, 1701–82), *ASV, Riti*, Proc. 3623), and the Carmelite Andrew Corsini, bishop of Fiesole 1350–73 (*AA.SS*. Ian. II, pp. 1061–72).

between the secular clergy and the new orders, it is hardly surprising that the former showed little enthusiasm for exalting the memory of Franciscans or Dominicans who had distinguished themselves as bishops.

The sainthood of the bishop according to processes of canonization (1198–1431)

The acts of processes of canonization reveal the image of the bishop prevailing during the late Middle Ages. In the statements of witnesses, we observe both the continuity of a model defined in broad outline since the early Middle Ages by a whole ecclesiastical tradition, and the changes affecting it between the thirteenth and the fifteenth centuries. An in-depth study of episcopal sainthood becomes a real possibility in the 1250s, when we have both the *articuli* proposed by the promoters of the cause with a view to defining the 'profile' of the prelate whose sainthood they hoped to persuade the Roman Church to recognize, and a faithful transcription of the depositions, which sometimes altered or remodelled this idealized image.

'Viriliter': the bishop as leader and defender of his church

The holy bishops, as they emerge from processes of canonization between 1198 and 1431, were all nobles. Most of them came from great aristocratic lineages, or were even connected to ruling dynasties.[28] The families to which they belonged produced, as a general rule, only knights and clerics who occupied high positions within the Church. The 'vocation' of the future bishop, inasmuch as we can perceive it, appears as a choice made in boyhood between the *militia mundi* and the *militia Christi*.[29] Influenced by a relative – often an uncle already embarked on an ecclesiastical career – the future saint decided to *militare* in the service of God and the Church.[30]

---

[28] *PC John Cacciafronte*, p. 241: 'ex nobili genere'; *PC Hugh of Lincoln*, p. 95: 'nobilitate generis satis clarus et originem ducens a parentibus ordinis militaris'; for the family of Philip of Bourges and its role in the Crusades, see *PC*, fol. 28; For Thomas of Hereford, see *PC*, fol. 5: 'dictus dominus Thomas traxit originem a nobilibus parentibus regni Anglie'; Peter of Luxembourg was related to the emperor and the kings of France: *PC*, art. 2, p. 468.
[29] At the approach of death, Philip Berruyer's father summoned his children 'et quaesivit ab eis qualem vitam eligerent, clericatum aut militiam, et dictus archiepiscopus clericatum elegit': *PC Philip of Bourges*, fol. 33v.
[30] When St Thomas Cantilupe's uncle, Bishop William of Worcester, asked his nephew what he wanted to be when he grew up, and Thomas replied that he wanted to be a *miles*, the bishop said 'quod esset miles Christi et quod Deo et sancto Thome martiri Cantuariensi episcopo in clericali ordine militaret': *PC Thomas of Hereford*, fol. 56.

He grew up in a chivalric ethos and throughout his life had access to a capital of resources and relations he was later able to draw on in order fully to perform his role as bishop (*sui status decentiam manutenere*).[31]

For these bishops, the prestige of culture was added to the prestige of birth and office. This was an important innovation, as the holy monk-bishops of the late twelfth century were not in general remarkable for their interest in knowledge or their learning. After 1240, all the bishops who were the object of a process of canonization had behind them a distinguished scholarly and university career. Admittedly, not all were 'scholar bishops', but all – French, English and Swedish – had at least been *scholaris Parisius*.[32] This was particularly true of the English saints; from Edmund of Abingdon to Thomas Cantilupe, they had all held teaching positions at the highest level before being given charge of a diocese.[33] Thanks to all these advantages, the saint-bishops of this period rose rapidly to positions of power within the Church, without having exercised a parish ministry. Once their studies were complete, sometimes even before, they received one or more canonical prebends. The most 'pastoral' of thirteenth-century bishops, Philip Berruyer, archbishop of Bourges (d. 1261), was first a canon at Saint-Martin and the cathedral of Tours; he then became archdeacon at Beaugency, then at Tours. Elected archbishop of Tours, he rejected the appeals of the chapter, but accepted the see of Orléans and, eventually, that of Bourges. A few years later, St Thomas Cantilupe accumulated canonries at Hereford, York, London and Lich-field before becoming archdeacon of Stamford and bishop of Hereford.[34] The same was largely true of the holy Swedish bishops of the fourteenth century, as we see from the processes of Brynulph of Skara (d. 1317) and Nicholas of Linköping (d. 1391). None of these bishops, at any rate, had experienced the humble servitudes of the *cura animarum* or shared the life of the priests they were later called on to direct.

---

[31] The income of St Thomas Cantilupe's father was estimated by witnesses at between £1,000 and £2,000 a year; his mother, Margaret of Evreux, daughter of Geoffrey of Gournay, was also wealthy: *PC Thomas of Hereford*, fols. 5, 33v.

[32] *PC Philip of Bourges* fol. 28v; *PC Brynulph*, art. 2, p. 141; Nicholas of Linköping studied law and theology at Paris and Orléans: *PC*, art. 5, p. 52.

[33] For the relationship between sanctity and culture in the late Middle Ages, see below, pp. 397–407.

[34] The change was marked: St Edmund of Canterbury 'beneficium unicum tantum . . . nunquam nisi cum residentia voluit accipere': *Quodrilogus*, ed. Lawrence, *S. Edmund of Abingdon*, p. 198; similarly, Philip Berruyer 'in tota vita sua noluit habere duo beneficia': *PC Philip of Bourges*, fol. 29. Some years later, St Thomas of Hereford got a dispensation from Innocent IV authorizing him to accumulate several benefices: *PC*, fol. 56v. Peter

Describing the actions of the holy prelates, the witnesses, whoever they were, usually referred first to the firmness with which they had performed their role as leader of the diocese. Doughty defender of the rights of his church, the good bishop fiercely opposed any encroachment, whether by kings, princes or lay lords. One word recurs repeatedly in their statements to define this courageous stand: *viriliter*.[35] It was applied primarily to those who had impressed their contemporaries by the zeal with which they had maintained ecclesiastical franchises and prerogatives.[36] With St Thomas Cantilupe (d. 1282), we see episcopal power go on the offensive; the bishop of Hereford was determined to recover the landed possessions his predecessors had let slip and he fiercely reclaimed rights which had fallen into disuse. To this end, he embarked on a series of lawsuits and conflicts in which he was eventually victorious, notwithstanding the power of his opponents, who included some of the most important names from the lay English aristocracy. The clergy and faithful of his diocese appear to have admired him greatly for this, which probably lies behind his reputation for sanctity.[37] Similarly, in fourteenth-century Sweden, Nicholas of Link-öping risked his life on numerous occasions by opposing certain magnates.[38] This was a constant theme; throughout Christendom during the period of interest to us here, the good bishop was inspired by a 'zeal for justice' (*zelus justitiae*).[39] He defended the oppressed and vigorously opposed violence against the clergy.[40] In the Anglo-Saxon and Scandinavian countries, he was ready even to attack the sovereign, reproaching him for his abuses of power, dissolute life or excessive tolerance of Jews and usurers.[41] This freedom of expression brought persecution in its wake for

---

of Luxembourg was appointed a canon of Notre Dame in Paris at the age of eight: *PC*, art. 15, p. 468.

[35] *PC Philip of Bourges*: 'bene et viriliter se habuit, tamquam bonus prelatus' (fol. 45).

[36] *PC John Cacciafronte*: 'fama erat quod pro manutenendis et salvandis racionibus episcopatus et ecclesie unice fuit mortuus' (p. 245).

[37] Many witnesses gave vivid accounts of his disputes with the Earl of Gloucester, the Welsh prince Llewellyn and numerous bishops (*PC Thomas of Hereford*, fols. 7, 21v, 22r, 35r–v, 58v etc.). They emphasized his amazing audacity in defending his rights. According to one witness, the people said and thought that his tenacity in defence of the rights of the Church 'esse potissimum quare Deus operabat miracula pro dicto domino Thoma' (fol. 78).

[38] *PC Brynulph*, art. 13, p. 142; *PC Nicholas of Linköping*, art. 20, p. 60.

[39] See, for example, *PC Thomas of Hereford*, fol. 79.

[40] The defence of the property of the Church was indistinguishable from that of the poor; see *PC John Cacciafronte*, p. 245: the bishop was murdered 'pro manutendis pauperibus de villa Maladii, qui destruebantur per divites et nobiles et magnates'.

[41] For the case of Hugh of Lincoln, see *Magna Vita*, I, pp. 71, 114–20; Edmund of Canterbury made himself *odiosus regi et curialibus* by his remonstrances (*Quadrilogus*, p. 199); for the conflict between Thomas of Hereford and Henry III concerning the Jews, see *PC*, fol. 105.

the holy bishops, who sometimes risked their lives in a violent clash which might lead to martyrdom.[42] Even when the reality was rather different, the clergy attempted at the processes of canonization to make the bishops whose cult they wished to promote match up to this ideal model. We have seen how successful they were at the level of local cults.[43] Up to the beginning of the fourteenth century, they were equally successful in the sphere of recognized sainthood. Subsequently, the 'Becket model' seems to have lost prestige in the eyes of a papacy which, after the attack at Anagni, preferred compromise to confrontation in its dealings with national monarchies. This was probably one reason why, after 1320, the Holy See firmly rejected the requests for the canonization of 'martyr' bishops which continued to flow in from the countries of north-west Europe.[44]

'In salutem populi': pastoral zeal and reforming activity

The holy bishop does not only appear, in the processes of canonization, as a strong leader and vigilant defender of the property and rights of his church. He fought also in another battle, that of the faith he was charged with defending and transmitting.[45] It was the clergy who were most consistent in emphasizing this aspect, lauding prelates for having, at their own cost, sent knights on crusade, persecuted heretics and encouraged missionaries.[46] But the laity seem not to have remained indifferent when they saw a bishop exercise in salutem populi the powers he had received at his consecration.[47]

---

[42] PC Brynulph, p. 166; PC Nicholas of Linköping, pp. 126–8, 218–19, 229–230, 264 etc.

[43] See above, pp. 162–72.

[44] See table 4, p. 72 above. The high proportion of bishops 1320–30 is very striking. Apart from the English prelates, we should note the case of Archbishop Burchard III of Magdeburg, murdered by the townspeople in 1325. A request for canonization was sent to John XXII by his successor, Otto (W. Schum, 'Miracula Burchardi III archiepiscopi Magdeburgensis', Neues Archiv, 12 (1886–7), pp. 586–90); the pope expressed his indignation at the crime, but did not act on the request (G. Schmidt, Geschichtsquellen der Provinz Sachsen, 21 (1886), pp. 180–4).

[45] A curé who had spent five years in the entourage of Philip Berruyer summed up his sanctity as follows: 'fidem predicavit, in fide mansit et in fide decessit': PC Philip of Bourges, fol. 41.

[46] Philip of Bourges sent two knights at his own cost to the 1248 crusade (PC, fol. 31). John Cacciafronte, at Vicenza, fought against the very influential heretics in the region (PC, p. 244). Nicholas of Linköping gave a large sum of money to a Franciscan in his diocese to organize a mission to Russia (PC, pp. 176–7).

[47] The process of Philip of Bourges refers to the displays of popular enthusiasm which occurred during the pastoral visits of this exemplary prelate, who 'quando non predicabat nec celebrabat, dicebat sociis suis: hodie comedimus panem sine fructu' (PC, fols. 41r–v).

The good bishop, in accord with the tradition we have already described, should be a model of piety and devotion. Thus the saint-prelates of the thirteenth and fourteenth centuries impressed their contemporaries by their regular recitation of the canonical hours and by frequently, if not daily, celebrating – or hearing – mass. If they said mass themselves, they did not fail to weep copious tears at the moment of the consecration.[48] Prayer, reading and meditation occupied their evenings and part of their nights. Some were even 'rapt' in contemplation.[49] Finally, the drawing up of a will and, above all, an edifying death were evidence for all to see of the depth of the faith which inspired them.[50]

The *Regula pastoralis* and the *Decretum* of Gratian also emphasized, as we have seen, that the bishop ought to be chaste and of irreproachable morals. Not content with themselves conforming to these requirements, late medieval prelates attached an ever-increasing importance to purity. If we are to believe his biographer, St Hugh of Lincoln (d. 1200) behaved in a simple and affectionate manner towards women.[51] A few decades later, a St Thomas Cantilupe (d. 1282) was remarkable for a veritable misogyny and for his prudery; according to witnesses at his process of canonization, he never took a bath and refused to embrace even his own sisters once he became bishop.[52] This could have been an individual trait of character, but this does not seem to have been the case, since holy bishops are lauded in other late thirteenth- and early fourteenth-century texts for having inspired in all around them a love of virginity. According to an office composed at this period in honour of John of Dalderby (d. 1320), a bishop ought to set the clergy of his diocese an example of chastity.[53] We therefore see bishops taking measures to combat the immorality

---

[48] Thomas of Hereford recited matins on rising with his chaplain and the other canonical hours during the course of the day; on feast days and Sundays, the hours were sung and he celebrated mass (*PC*, fol. 19). For the tears he shed during the office, *ibid.*, fols. 37, 60. Nicholas of Linköping communicated every day (*PC*, p. 194).

[49] *PC Thomas of Hereford*, fol. 37v.

[50] PC Philip of Bourges, fol. 30v.

[51] His benevolent and open-minded attitude towards women is described at length in the *Magna Vita*, II, p. 48: 'satis a sexu femineo Deus omnipotens diligi promeruit qui nasci de femina non refugit. Magnificum quoque ac vere dignum ex hoc feminis privilegium contulit. Nam, cum viro concessum non sit ut dicatur pater Dei, hoc tamen prestitum est mulieri.' For the positive attitude of many twelfth-century clerics to women and marriage, see J. Leclercq, *Love in marriage in twelfth century Europe* (Hobart, 1978).

[52] *PC Thomas of Hereford*, fols. 31v–32r, 43v, 96r–v.

[53] The words are: 'Ave presul inclite, Gemma puritatis, Cultor innocentie, Norma castitatis': *Istoria de sancto Joanne de Dalderby quondam epi [sic] Lincoln*, ed. M. Wickenden, 'John de Dalderby, Bishop of Lincoln, 1300–1320', *The Archaeological Journal*, 40 (1883), pp. 215–24, especially p. 219.

of their servants, in line with the decisions of the great thirteenth-century councils, in particular the Fourth Lateran Council. Thomas Cantilupe warned and reprimanded offenders, removing from office those who refused to mend their ways.[54] Philip Berruyer did the same in the diocese of Bourges, but rather more gently, it seems. Many witnesses emphasized at the process of 1265–6 that when 'sinister rumours' began to circulate about certain prelates, he transferred the suspects or sent them on a course of study; he also showed some concern for the fate of those he had been obliged to dismiss when they proved incorrigible.[55]

In general, the holy prelate was concerned for both the material and spiritual welfare of his clergy. They showed their gratitude by seeking to promote his cult after his death: *dulcis amor cleri*, as was said of the bishop in the office *Iste confessor*, very frequently used in the Middle Ages for papal confessors.[56] We know, in fact, that in fourteenth-century Sweden, Brynulph of Skara and Nicholas of Linköping were fondly remembered in their respective dioceses for having improved the lot of the canons of their chapters.[57] In other cases, we see bishops praised for taking measures on behalf of poor clerks, in particular by giving them grants to enable them to go the 'the schools'.[58] Another criterion which seems to have had great importance in the eyes of contemporaries was the way in which they chose their collaborators. Philip Berruyer was praised for having an honest entourage, recruited without nepotism, and for having exercised strict control over his *familia*. He was also praised for having conferred the benefices at his disposal on competent and worthy persons, except in one particular case when he entrusted an archdeaconry to a member of his family who turned out to be a bad lot. But the saint had the humility to recognize his error and bitterly regretted his appointment.[59] The good prelate, lastly, was the friend and protector of regulars. Philip Berruyer helped the Friars Preacher to settle in Bourges, despite the opposition of his chapter;[60] Thomas of Hereford favoured all the Mendicant orders, who, by and large, repaid him well, since four Dominicans, four Francis-

---

[54] *PC Nicholas of Linköping*, p. 198; *PC Thomas of Hereford*, fols. 95–7.

[55] *PC Philip of Bourges*, fols. 39, 40.

[56] 'Ave pastor ovium, dulcis amor cleri', antiphon of the office of John of Dalderby ('John de Dalderby', ed. Wickenden, p. 223).

[57] Brynulph drew on his patrimony to create five additional canonical prebends (*PC*, art. 4, p. 142); Nicholas of Linköping improved the lot of the resident canons by a levy on the income of the bishopric (*PC*, pp. 116, 130).

[58] *PC Edmund*, p. 188; *PC Thomas of Hereford*, fol. 18v.

[59] *PC Philip of Bourges*, fols. 30r–v.

[60] *Ibid.*, fol. 30r.

cans, four Carmelites and two Hermits of St Augustine testified in his
favour at the process of canonization in 1307.[61] This sympathy for pious
regulars, which went hand in hand with great severity towards slack
monks, was motivated by a desire to raise the level of the diocesan clergy,
another sign of which was the promulgation of synodal statutes. In 1417,
at the process of canonization of Brynulph, his successor Brynulph II
presented the enquiry with the text of those composed by the holy bishop
of Skara in the early years of the fourteenth century.[62]

The clergy were neither the only nor even the principal beneficiaries of
the pastoral concern of bishops. The *officium pastoris*, as it is defined in
late medieval processes of canonization, was directed primarily at the
laity.[63] The holy prelate lived first and foremost for the people entrusted to
him by God, praying for them even on his deathbed and taking whatever
measures were necessary for their salvation.[64] This activity took three
different forms: *gubernatio*, *visitatio* and *correctio*. The first concerned the
exercise by the bishop of his functions in the domain of worship and the
sacraments. Not content with personally celebrating mass in his cathedral,
he often preached, even if, in some countries, such as England, he needed
an interpreter to make him intelligible to the faithful whose language he
could not speak.[65] He also conferred the sacrament of confirmation, either
during pastoral visits or on chance encounters, which meant he had to get
down from his horse.[66] Nor did he refuse to hear confessions when asked

---

[61] St Thomas of Hereford had been a student and friend of the Dominican Robert Kilwardby, later archbishop of Canterbury. Four Friars Minor from the London convent
cast doubt on his sanctity and the reality of the miracles attributed to him, but their
attitude was probably influenced by the conflict between Thomas and his metropolitan
John Peckham.

[62] For measures against monks: *PC Thomas of Hereford*, fol. 36; for synodal statutes, *PC
Brynulph*, p. 148.

[63] To this end, St Thomas: 'in ecclesiis suis . . . volebat quod essent presbiteri scientes
predicare qui essent bone et honeste conversationis': *PC*, fol. 60v. The three aspects of
the *officium pastoris* are defined in fol. 78v.

[64] Philip of Bourges died saying: 'Domine, populum quem michi commisisti, ex nunc in
tua custodia relinquo': *PC*, fol. 35.

[65] *PC Thomas of Hereford*, fol. 78v. John Cacciafronte was described as 'predicator bonus
et benignus' and one witness said he had seen him 'in publica concione concionari pro
libertate Ecclesiae et pro parte domni Alexandri [Alexander III], praesentibus adversariis
et contradictoribus': *PC*, p. 240. Philip of Bourges travelled through his diocese 'sepe et
sepius predicando': *PC*, fol. 30.

[66] There can have been few bishops who conferred the sacrament of confirmation in the
proper conditions, since Adam of Eynsham praises St Hugh of Lincoln for having always
dismounted to lay his hands on children (*Magna Vita*, I, p. 127). A witness at the process
of St Thomas said that the bishop of Hereford 'quando equitabat, portabat semper stolam
ad collum subtus capam vel rodeundellum suum et erat circumcinctus dicta stola ad
modum crucis ex parte interiori, et portabat dictam stolam ut esset paratus ad crismandum

to do so.[67] Lastly, he also promoted the cult of the saints; Philip of Bourges proceeded to the translation of the relics of St Severia, and the Swedish bishops of the fourteenth century composed verse offices and hymns in honour of the saints venerated in their diocese and the Virgin Mary.[68]

In general, the depositions of witnesses convey the impression that the regular performance by prelates of their liturgical functions was in many cases an important element in the birth of their reputation for sanctity. A bishop who lived in his diocese, sang mass, at least on great occasions, and himself confirmed children, made an impression on his contemporaries, because he was an exception. To be regarded as a saint, he needed also to have built and restored the churches for which he was responsible, evidence of both his pastoral zeal and generosity. The witnesses at the process of Hugh of Lincoln emphasized that he went to great lengths to finance work on his new cathedral.[69] Thomas Cantilupe was praised for having built not only churches but barns and farmhouses in the parishes where he possessed the living, since the cost of these works fell entirely on him and did not involve tithes or exceptional taxes on the diocesan clergy.[70]

However, it was on the pastoral visits that the qualities of the holy prelate were best displayed. The importance accorded to the performance of the *officium visitationis* in the statements of witnesses makes plain that it constituted a sort of test for the bishop, especially in the eyes of the clergy, who were extremely sensitive to the way in which the bishop and his entourage conducted themselves on this occasion. The best example here is that of Philip of Bourges, who seems to have been particularly conscientious about visiting his diocese and the province of which he was the metropolitan. Questioned on this subject, one cleric reported that the archbishop of Bourges always used to ask what it was customary to collect during such visits, but that he ceased to do so after the Council of Lyons I.[71] When he observed grave deficiencies, he imposed fines on the offenders but never insisted that they be paid in cash.[72] The travels of the prelate were also the occasion for what were often friendly meetings with

---

pueros occurentes eidem, quorum confirmatio petebatur': *PC*, fol. 59. See also *PC Philip of Bourges*, fols. 30, 36v.

[67] Thomas of Hereford confessed in the churches whose patron he was: *PC*, fol. 58.

[68] *PC Philip of Bourges*, fols. 36, 96; *PC Brynulph*, pp. 142, 150; *PC Nicholas of Linköping*, p. 202.

[69] *PC Hugh of Lincoln*, p. 97.

[70] Contemporaries seem to have appreciated 'quod de redditibus unius loci non fierent hedificia alio loco': *PC Thomas of Hereford*, fol. 121; see also fol. 36.

[71] *PC Philip of Bourges*, fol. 30.

[72] *Ibid.*, fol. 40v.

his flock, who appealed to his thaumaturgical powers to obtain cures for the sick or the possessed, or rain in time of drought.[73] In the Scandinavian countries in the fourteenth century, the pastor took advantage of such occasions to attack popular belief in the casting of spells.[74]

Lastly, the practice of *correctio*, that is the attack on abuses of every type, often appears among the meritorious acts performed by saint-bishops. It was incumbent on them, first, to intervene in the moral sphere by fighting vice and denouncing public sinners, in particular concubines and adulterers, on whom they imposed penances if they repented and abjured.[75] They also attacked 'bad customs' and did not hesitate, if necessary, to repress revolts, as did Philip Berruyer when bishop of Orléans.[76] In general, however, this function was exercised above all against the 'great' – kings or powerful lords – who encroached on the rights of the Church or oppressed the poor. The pastoral role of the bishop here overlapped with his function as protector, the paramount importance of which we have already emphasized.[77]

The saint-bishop between asceticism and abundance

In the *articuli* submitted by the promoters of processes of canonization, the holy bishops of the thirteenth and fourteenth centuries were invariably presented as ascetics. The claims concerning this aspect of their perfection were corroborated by witnesses – especially clerics – who claimed that the prelate in question had yearned, in his heart of hearts, to return to his monastery, if he was a monk, or to become a hermit, if he was a secular.[78] Only pastoral zeal kept him in a world whose futile bustle he deplored;

---

[73] According to the Cistercian Peter of Aubigné, 'quando visitabat dictus archiepiscopus in partibus Lemoviciensibus . . . a populo cum magna devotione recipiebatur et gentes deosculabantur pedes ipsius archiepiscopi, et quando non poterant ad ipsum attingere, osculabantur passus equi sui': *PC Philip of Bourges*, fol. 41.

[74] *PC Nicholas of Linköping*, p. 132. Hugh of Lincoln had silenced a 'prophetess' popular among the peasantry, and healed many who were 'possessed' during his pastoral tours: *Magna Vita*, II, pp. 118–25.

[75] For this repressive aspect, see in particular *PC Thomas of Hereford*, fols. 36, 90, 104; *PC Nicholas of Linköping*, pp. 172–4, 276.

[76] *PC Philip of Bourges*, fol. 30: 'si sciebat aliquas pravas consuetudines inducebat barones ut eas revocarent'. For the affair at Orléans and the way in which Philip Berruyer repressed the revolt of the townspeople who had killed some clergy, *ibid.*, fols. 28v, 46v.

[77] See above, pp. 292ff.

[78] Of St Hugh, Adam of Eynsham wrote (*Magna Vita*, I, p. 43): 'erat ei sicut et patrono suo Martino semper gloria in ordine monastico'. Nicholas of Linköping would have become a monk but for the resistance of his entourage; in any case, he lived like a hermit: *PC*, art. 13, pp. 56–8.

to compensate for the concessions he was obliged to make to temporal preoccupations, he privately engaged in rigorous penances on the model of the monks, wearing a hair shirt next to his skin, or a belt or chain of iron round his waist etc.[79] He scourged himself or was scourged and often slept at the foot of his bed.[80] But the austerity of his life was measured above all by what he ate; on this point, details abound, so that we are well-informed about the pattern of fasts observed by holy bishops and the rigour of their abstinence. Philip of Bourges fasted for forty days before Christmas as well as every Friday, contenting himself with a little bread dipped in wine, and ate meat only on Wednesdays. During Lent, he refused even fish, at least until Innocent IV, alarmed by his asceticism, entreated him to eat better.[81] The description given by St Thomas Cantilupe's barber of his master's meals is very similar and he tells us that the bishop of Hereford 'ate very little and drank even less'.[82] Other members of his entourage also recalled with emotion how they had heard the prelate say that 'for twenty years, he had never eaten his fill'.[83]

There is no *a priori* reason to question the accuracy of this information. But, as certain statements at the same processes of canonization contradict it, at least in part, we may reasonably ask whether what we are seeing is an attempt, conscious or not, to apply to the bishops the Martinian ascetic schema whose presence in the hagiographic tradition we noted above.[84] Thus, in the process of Philip of Bourges, which is full of references to his self-inflicted privations, we find also the statement of a diocesan priest who refused to believe in his sanctity 'because he ate and drank normally'.[85] The contradictions are even sharper in the case of St Thomas Cantilupe. Many witnesses stressed that the bishop of Hereford was not a hypocrite (*papelardus*) and that he fully accepted the obligations of his position with regard to dress and ceremonial, though not seeking to appear better than others.[86] Some even cast doubt on the rigour of his ascetic

---

[79] Philip of Bourges 'frequenter recipiebat disciplinas, aliquando cum virgis, aliquando cum corrigiis, aliquando de pugno': *PC*, fol. 43. For the ascetic practices of Thomas of Hereford, see *PC*, fols. 34v, 107 etc.

[80] *Ibid.*, fol. 103.

[81] *PC Philip of Bourges*, fols. 31v, 32v, 43.

[82] *PC Thomas of Hereford*, fols. 19v, 24.

[83] The phrase is repeated by several witnesses (*ibid.*, fols. 15v, 16, 108, 121 etc).

[84] See above, pp. 290–1.

[85] *PC Philip of Bourges*, fol. 72: 'non credo quod deus pro ipso miracula faciat qui bene commedebat et bibebat'.

[86] 'Nec ostendebat se esse aliis meliorem vel excellentioris vitae sed conformabat se in vestibus extrinsecis et in apparatu lecti et in aliis comparibus suis, et portabat mantellum intra domum': *PC Thomas of Hereford*, fol. 21; see also fol. 36v.

practices. His own nephew, who had lived with him for many years, said that he had never seen his hairshirt, although he helped him to dress every day, and that his bed was made up with fine sheets and a pillow. He also declared that his uncle owned the best horses in England, though quickly adding that he preferred to ride one which was less outstanding and that he always rode with his face turned towards the ground 'as if he despised himself'.[87] On the subject of his food, the witnesses are equally contradictory, and some imply that he led without apparent unease the luxurious life-style of a great lord.[88] In the last analysis, it is difficult to gain a clear picture of the way of life of St Thomas Cantilupe; even if he was accustomed to a certain degree of luxury as a result of his family background and office, it is perfectly possible that he privately felt only contempt for the external trappings of power. But the promoters of his cause emphasized certain features of his personality in order to make this man of learning and government into a martyr to asceticism.

Similar observations may be made with regard to St Thomas' poverty and humility. In the thirteenth century, these two virtues became the basic criteria of official sainthood. Accordingly, a number of witnesses declared that Thomas Cantilupe was simple with the simple and benevolent towards the poor.[89] But as soon as we try to go beyond these general assertions, facts are elusive. The only precise statement contained in the process regarding his 'poverty' is that he was no richer at the end of his episcopate than at the beginning! We know, in any case, that, before he became bishop of Hereford, St Thomas had accumulated numerous ecclesiastical benefices by virtue of a dispensation granted by Pope Innocent IV, and that he enjoyed an annual income of 1,000 marks.[90] It then becomes clear why, in the bull of canonization, John XXII should laud this prelate as one who was, in the pontiff's own words, *pauper spiritu, dives rebus*.[91] As regards his humility, it is enough to quote the words of one Franciscan who was very favourably disposed towards him. Questioned on this subject during the process, he said that 'he saw no circumstance in which he could or should have shown great humility'.[92] The

---

[87] *Ibid.*, fols. 57v–59v.

[88] *Ibid.*, fol. 49v: 'et reputabatur bonus homo et bene literatus, bonus conviva et nobilis, et nullus erat similis in ecclesia Londiniensi in valore, et dicebatur quod in domo sua bibebat aquam et alii bonum vinum'.

[89] *Ibid.*, fol. 120v.

[90] *Ibid.*, fol. 93v.

[91] John XXII, *Unigenitus filius*, 17.VI.1320, ed. Fontanini, *Codex constitutionum*, p. 133.

[92] *PC Thomas of Hereford*, fol. 79: 'item respondit quod credebat dictum dominum Thomam habuisse humilitatis virtutem. Interrogatus in quo magis notaverit dictam humilitatem,

laity did not, in any case, expect a bishop to be poor or to behave like someone of modest rank. On the contrary, he needed to have ample resources at his disposal, since one of his duties was to give alms. The charity dispensed by the holy prelates, according to the processes of canonization, seems to have followed a regular pattern and taken the form of institutional assistance rather than generous acts. John Cacciafronte at Vicenza gave clothes to the poor every Thursday;[93] Thomas of Hereford fed every day as many poor as there were years in his episcopate. Distributions were also made on fixed days in favour of poor clerics or scholars.[94] Direct contact with the poor seems to have become less frequent with the passage of time. Hugh of Lincoln visited lepers and himself buried abandoned corpses;[95] Philip of Bourges still often ate with the poor,[96] but Thomas Cantilupe, while periodically reminding his entourage that 'the poor are our brothers', was himself content to wash the feet of thirteen of them every Maundy Thursday and distribute money at the end of the ceremony.[97] The true test of a bishop's charity was his behaviour in time of famine. If he then drew on his own reserves to provide the corn necessary to the survival of the hungry, in the form of a gift or loan, he was remembered for his generosity. The treasure he had stored up, far from appearing as the fruit of his 'avarice', rather revealed his remarkable foresight and concern for the common good.[98]

In general, clergy and faithful alike seem to have approved of their pastors being both rich and lavish. This quality, described by the words

---

respondit quod non vidit magnam materiam in qua debuit vel potuit exercere magnam humilitatem.'
[93] PC John Cacciafronte, pp. 242, 245.
[94] PC Thomas of Hereford, fols. 16v, 40.
[95] PC Hugh of Lincoln, p. 96; Magna Vita, I, p. 131.
[96] PC Philip of Bourges, fols. 29r–v. One witness added: 'maiores expensas faciebat in elemosina quam in coquina': fol. 37v.
[97] 'Pauperes vocabat fratres et frequenter redarguebat ipsum testem et alios familiares suos quando non vocabant dictos pauperes fratres, asserens dictus dominus Thomas pauperes dumtaxat esse quos Deus odiebat et quos vos vocatis pauperes nobis esse ditiores': PC Thomas of Hereford, fol. 23. But another witness said: 'non tamen recordatur quod tunc pauperes comederunt cum eo': fol. 121.
[98] PC John Cacciafronte, p. 245: 'tempore caristiae fecit congregare totam suam segetem episcopatus apud ipsam episcopatum et dividi inter pauperes et infirmos'. See also PC Philip of Bourges, fol. 38. Thomas of Hereford 'quando indigebant blado, faciebat eis tradi de blado suo mutuo ut redderent bladum pro blado in sequenti anno et quando tunc solvere non poterant propter paupertatem, remittebat eis': PC, fol. 104v. According to the process of Brynulph of Skara, when the saint took no action in one year of famine, his own father led a body of the poor to the island where his son then lived in order to make him feel ashamed of his conduct: PC, p. 149. The generosity of a bishop was sometimes the occasion for 'miracles', when the stocks of grain increased instead of diminishing: PC Nicholas of Linköping, p. 282.

habundantia or *magnanimitas*, assumed the practice of charity towards the poor and the sick, as well as a strongly developed sense of hospitality.[99] But it implied above all a spirit of largess and a casual attitude towards economic realities, based on a profound contempt for money. St Edmund of Canterbury was praised by his biographer for having left debts, and one of the *articuli* of the process of St Nicholas of Linköping emphasized that when his purse was opened after his death, it was quite empty.[100] But it is in the process of St Thomas Cantilupe that this emerges most clearly. Witnesses remarked that, unlike his predecessor, who always gave the impression of being hard up, the holy bishop of Hereford 'seemed always to be well off, in life as in death'.[101] The bishop's largess, revealed in his taste for luxury and spending, continued after his death. The beneficial radiance which emanated from his remains and the effective protection he afforded his diocese appeared to the witnesses as the direct prolongation of this virtue, which can be defined as a Christianized form of evergetism.[102]

Thus, in the sadly very few cases where the statements of witnesses are sufficiently full and detailed to enable us to go beyond general assertions, we see that the sainthood of prelates was read in two ways, which was reflected, at the level of the witnesses, in some contradictory statements. The image of a monk engaging secretly in the harshest penitential practices and remarkable for his humility and poverty was superimposed, more or less harmoniously, on that of the temporal and religious leader and wealthy aristocrat. The latter, which associated sainthood with the exercise of power and the wise use of authority and wealth, predominated among the majority of witnesses, especially those from the laity. The former, which is found in the 'articles' which orient the statements and in the evidence of a few 'great minds', corresponds rather to the model then in favour in

[99] This is nicely shown by the statement of one witness at the process of Nicholas of Linköping: 'firmiter credit eum in terra corporaliter vixisse tamquam sanctissimum virum et bonis omnibus habundantem': *PC*, p. 230.
[100] *PC Edmund of Canterbury, Quadrilogus*, p. 188: 'plus expendit quam habuit, unde et debitis semper obligatus fuit. Hospitalitatis gratiam nullo denegavit. Pauperibus et egenis elemosinas largiter erogavit.' See also *PC Nicholas of Linköping*, art. 31, p. 64.
[101] *PC Thomas of Hereford*, fols. 78v–79: 'dominus Iohannes le Bretun predecessor immediatus dicti domini Thome, cuius noticiam dictus testis dixit se habuisse, non faciebat tot sumptus sicut dictus dominus Thomas et videbatur semper egere. Dictus autem dominus Thomas, qui plura expendebat et in duobus adventibus regis ad civitatem Herefordensem dicebatur expendisse mille libras sterlingorum, semper habundabatur in vita et in morte.'
[102] When some peasants from his diocese came to Nicholas of Linköping in search of a cure for their ills, he 'consuluit ut ad propria festinarent et agros suos colerent. Unde factum est ut illo anno sua dyocesis in maximis frugibus habundaret' (*PC*, p. 160).

elevated circles of the Roman Church, whose approval was necessary if the canonization was to be obtained.

To this end, the organizers of the processes sought to make the bishops whose causes they supported into men who were essentially religious. Accordingly, certain aspects of their activities, such as their relations with the monarchy, which had loomed so large in the Germanic hagiography of the eleventh and twelfth centuries, were mentioned only when they were a source of conflict, as was the case in the British Isles and the Scandinavian countries. None of the witnesses at his process in 1265–6 so much as mentioned the good relations which existed between Philip Berruyer and Louis IX, as if this was something too profane and a purely temporal issue. Similarly, the role of the prelates as administrators and lords was only fleetingly referred to, whilst witnesses dwelled at length on their pastoral zeal, which made it possible to confer on their daily acts the character of an apostolate. At the level of official sainthood, therefore, it was a spiritual image of the bishop which prevailed, and candidates for canonization were as far as possible made to conform. The Martinian model superseded the Ottonian model. But this was very far from being one of those periodic oscillations between the two faces of the pastor which are visible throughout the history of the Church. In the late Middle Ages, the episcopal office itself was affected by a crisis which challenged one of the oldest and most traditional forms of Christian sainthood.

The crisis of episcopal sainthood

The contradictions discussed above help to explain the loss of prestige suffered by the episcopate in many Christian countries from the end of the thirteenth century. The heroic period of church reform, by provoking violent confrontations between good bishops and the lay powers, had given the former the chance to demonstrate their pastoral zeal; with its passing, they became – or reverted to being – primarily administrators of temporal property and lords concerned to defend their rights. As preachers of the Gospel, they were supplanted by the Mendicant orders, even by simple priests. Their position within the ecclesiastical hierarchy suffered, especially in the fourteenth century, when the majority of prelates lost all autonomy in relation to the Holy See.[103] This crisis of authority inevitably

---

[103] Among the factors which militated against episcopal sanctity, by making it more difficult for a devotion to a prelate to emerge, was the papal policy of transferring bishops from one see to another; this was increasingly common from the fourteenth century and such

had repercussions for the model of episcopal sainthood, which seemed less attractive than in the past, except in countries like England and Sweden, where the more energetic pastors continued to enjoy great popularity in their capacity as defenders of local liberties under threat from central government.[104]

The decline of the episcopal office in most of Christendom probably explains why, just at this period, the end of the thirteenth century, people ceased to attribute thaumaturgical powers to saint-bishops in their lifetime. Previously, they had been credited with many cures, especially of people possessed, as we see from the canonization processes of St Hugh of Lincoln and Philip of Bourges. When the latter was making his pastoral visits, the sick were brought to him to be touched and the clergy were as ready as anyone to seek cures for the illnesses which tormented them.[105] Later, in contrast, the majority of the miracles *in vita* attested in the processes were prodigies, which were classed as supernatural phenomena only to satisfy the requirements of the process of canonization, which said that the saints must have performed miracles in their lifetime as well as after their death.[106] Among the feats claimed by the promoters of these causes, whether of St Thomas Aquinas or Brynulph of Skara, there were no cures which had aroused great popular enthusiasm. The bishop was now perceived as a saint only by the elite of the cathedral clergy who promoted and organized the devotion.[107]

Cut off from their popular roots, the bishops of the fourteenth century were no better off with regard to official sainthood, as is shown by the significant reduction in the proportion of those who were canonized after

bishops, imposed on the local clergy by the centre, were less likely to become popular than elected bishops from the region.

[104] For the decline of the episcopal model at the level of local sanctity in the Mediterranean countries, see above, pp. 187–90; for the specific circumstances explaining its continued prestige in north-western Europe, see above, pp. 222–4.

[105] As shown by the large number of miracles *in vita* recorded at his process of canonization in 1265–6: *PC*, fols. 51–2, 89, 93 etc.

[106] The only miracle *in vita* attributed to St Thomas of Hereford was to have silenced some birds whose singing disturbed a church service: *Summarium*, Paris, BN, lat. 5373 A, fol. 69v.

[107] One wonders about the attitude of the lower clergy to saint-bishops when one finds, in the statements of two priests at the process of Philip of Bourges, the following: 'quod melius vellet facere urinam super sepulturam eius quam super ipsius capitergium' and 'non credam quod sanctus sit donec restituerit michi dampna que tulerunt michi garciones sui quando capiebat procurationes suas in domo': *PC Philip of Bourges*, fols. 70v, 71. Even if they later repented these blasphemous words, doubts linger as to their feelings about their former leader!

1304.[108] Without going over again the ecclesiological and political motives which made the posthumous glorification of diocesan prelates unpopular with the Avignon popes, we may note that the mental climate was unfavourable to the episcopal model. Under the influence of the spiritual ideas which had developed in the wake of the Mendicant orders, increasing importance was attached to exceptional charismas and mystical phenomena. Neither of these was particularly characteristic of bishops, in spite of the efforts made at processes to emphasize their contemplative tendencies.[109] This contradiction between the new ideal and traditional representations is already visible in the process of St Thomas Cantilupe, at which some Franciscans from the London convent expressed their doubts about his reputation for sanctity and quoted the words of another Friar Minor who had known him well: 'Truly he was a good man and led a good life. But I do not know what miracles he performed.'[110] One could hardly have a clearer statement that the qualities so admired by the majority of witnesses, in particular the bishop of Hereford's vigorous defence of the rights of his church, were not obvious evidence of sanctity. The same was true of other fourteenth-century bishops, requests for whose canonization were almost all rejected by the Holy See, or whose processes came to nothing; to be recognized as a saint by the Roman Church, it was not enough to have been honest and conscientious. There must also be some exceptional quality of the sort which was usually absent from the episcopal career.

The impression of crisis in the episcopal model of sainthood is confirmed when we look at the processes of canonization of St Louis of Anjou and Peter of Luxembourg.[111] Both were young men who were made bishops at an early age thanks to their family connections. The former was appointed to the see of Toulouse in 1296 by Boniface VIII, at the age of twenty-two; he died at Brignoles the year after when on his way to see the pope to resign his office. The latter was made bishop of Metz by Clement VII in 1383, at the age of fourteen, and became a cardinal the

---

[108] See above, pp. 257–60.
[109] The clergy stressed that the holy bishop was often lost in contemplation, to the extent of appearing *raptus*; see, for example, *PC Thomas of Hereford*, fol. 121.
[110] *Ibid.*, fol. 46v. See below, pp. 580–3.
[111] The first took place in Marseilles in 1308: see '*Processus canonizationis et legendae variae sancti Ludovici OFM episcopi Tolosani*', in *Analecta Franciscana*, VII (Quaracchi and Florence, 1951), pp. 1–254; the second in Avignon in 1387: see *AA.SS.* Iul. I, pp. 486–628.

same year. But in 1385, he resigned his pastoral office and retired to Paris, then Avignon, where he died in 1387. The very careers of these saints are evidence of the decadence of the episcopal office in the late Middle Ages, in the way they contravened the rules laid down by canon law with regard to age and eligibility. These were appointments motivated by political considerations and imposed on the local churches. But what is most interesting, from our perspective, is that elevation to the episcopate produced a major crisis of conscience in both these young men. Hardly had they taken possession of their sees when they realized that the exercise of pastoral authority was incompatible with their quest for moral and spiritual perfection.

St Louis of Anjou, who had been influenced by the Friars Minor during his captivity in Catalonia and who was in regular contact with Peter Olivi, was profoundly marked by Franciscan spirituality.[112] On the day of his consecration, which took place in the church of Ara Coeli in Rome on 5 February 1297, he removed his episcopal mitre and vestments at the end of the ceremony to resume the frieze habit of the sons of St Francis.[113] Immediately he arrived in Toulouse, according to William of Cornillon, he reduced the size of his *familia* and investigated the revenues of the bishopric with a view to increasing his distributions of alms to the poor. The same witness, and others after him, also referred to the young prelate's desire for austerity in his dress, household and life-style as a whole.[114] He refused to ride in a cart or on horseback, regarding such a practice as incompatible with his ideal of humility.[115] He seems soon, however, to have become convinced of the futility of his efforts to remain faithful to his rule of life in such unpropitious circumstances. From this point on, he longed only to resign his office to become a simple monk, and he was on his way to the pope to rid himself of his burden when death intervened. Paradoxically, it is almost always as a bishop that he is represented in the substantial surviving iconography devoted to him, since the juxtaposition of the chasuble and the Franciscan habit gave painters a theme which lent itself to chromatic experimentation.[116] At his process of canonization, in

[112] I will return to the question of his spirituality when discussing the Mendicants (see below, pp. 344–6). For the education of and influences on the young prince, see *L'Epître de Pierre Jean-Olieu aux fils de Charles II de Naples en l'an 1295*, ed. M. H. Vicaire, in *Franciscains d'Oc: Les Spirituels*, pp. 127–38.

[113] He accepted the bishopric of Toulouse only on the express condition that he was first permitted to make his profession as a Friar Minor: *PC Louis of Anjou*, art. 31, pp. 15–16.

[114] *Ibid.*, pp. 25–8, 75–6.

[115] *Ibid.*, art. 43, p. 17.

[116] Kleinschmidt, 'St Ludwig von Toulouse'; Kaftal 2, cc. 697–701.

Marseilles in 1308, much was made of episcopal sanctity since the brethren from the 'spiritual' tendency who gave evidence presented him as the model of the Franciscan prelate as defined by Olivi, according to which prelates from the Mendicant orders 'ad usus pauperis observantiam . . . aliquo modo amplius quam antea tenebatur'. The evidence of William of Cornillon, for example, is all designed to demonstrate that this ideal had truly been realized in St Louis of Anjou during his brief episcopate and that his elevation to a bishopric had not prevented him from remaining faithful to evangelical poverty.[117] However interesting this debate, it nevertheless appears, with hindsight, somewhat misplaced. What is important, in my view, is not so much the way in which the young Friar Minor behaved when a bishop as the haste with which he sought to be freed from his office. In this, he was only following an older Franciscan tradition, illustrated by, for example, Brother Rainaldo of Arezzo, who, having been appointed bishop of Rieti, resigned dramatically soon after and, in front of a stunned pope and cardinals, delivered a scathing sermon on the necessity of despising and rejecting all honours in order to save one's soul.[118] Those who venerated in St Louis of Anjou the prince who had renounced his estate for love of poverty and humility, rather than the good bishop, were not mistaken.[119] In fact, his example provides an excellent illustration of the crisis of the episcopacy, which appears less as an office offering possibilities of sanctification than as an obstacle on the road towards Christian perfection.

Nearly a century later, we find a similar dramatic tension between aspirations and reality in the even briefer life of Peter of Luxembourg.[120] Made bishop of Metz, a town in the hands of the Urbanist camp, he was first obliged, with his brother Valeran of Ligny, to fight to recover his diocese from the 'schismatics'. During the military operations, he tried to limit the damage and urged mercy for the vanquished enemies.[121] He also insisted that his supporters did not compensate themselves for the costs of the war at the expense of the property of his church.[122] This brought him into conflict with his brother, who felt he had been penalized financi-

---

[117] Pasztor, *Per la storia*.
[118] Salimbene, *Cronica*, I, pp. 468–9, 473–7.
[119] For reverberations in the Irish literature, see the texts quoted by Toynbee, *Saint Louis of Toulouse*, pp. 245–6.
[120] I know of no good study of Peter of Luxembourg; see K. Kunze, sv Pietro di Lussemburgo, in *BS*, X (Rome, 1968), cc. 705–9. See also plate 22.
[121] *PC Peter of Luxembourg*, arts. 36–9, p. 470.
[122] *Ibid.*, art. 40, p. 470.

ally and refused to spare his opponents. Compelled to inflict suffering and privations on his flock, quarrelling with his family, who could not understand his scruples, he preferred to resign an office which put him in an intolerable position. A few months later, he was summoned to Avignon by Clement VII, who made him a cardinal.[123] But his malaise returned and, in the words of an article of the process of 1387, 'he began to fear he would lose his peace of mind and see the fervour of his inner devotion dimmed'.[124] At the sight of curial life, he trembled for the salvation of his soul and redoubled his austerity. His dream was to traverse Christendom as a pilgrim and ambassador to bring the Schism to an end, but he had to abandon the idea under pressure from his entourage.[125] In any case, disease soon removed him from the scene.

Gloomy young men (Peter of Luxembourg brusquely reminded his entourage that 'Christ never laughed'),[126] disappointed by reality, lacking all faith in ecclesiastical institutions – these were the saint-bishops of late medieval France.[127] Their reputation for sanctity, which was considerable in both cases, owed little to their brief spell at the head of a diocese. It derived rather from their flight towards pure spirituality once they had realized the vanity, even fundamentally corrupting nature, of all exercise of power. By this stage, the holy bishop was no longer he who succeeded but he who failed, or at least renounced, when his rejection of power was the expression of unsatisfied religious needs.

The saint-priest

The crisis of the episcopal model allowed new types of clerical sainthood to appear in the West: the saint-priest and the saint-pope. Admittedly, the number of servants of God from these categories was small, at the level of local cult or, even more, of canonizations.[128] But it is not without

---

[123] *Ibid.*, arts. 41–2, p. 470.

[124] *Ibid.*, art. 43, p. 470.

[125] *Ibid.*, arts. 64–72, pp. 471, 486.

[126] *Ibid.*, p. 467.

[127] *Ibid.*, p. 486: 'dicebat ipse cardinalis quod papa, cardinales, et prelati deberent saepe processiones, nudis pedibus, facere et aliis laicis bonum exemplum per bonas predicationes et vitae sanctitatem ostendere, et quod ita faciendo Deus provideret statui Ecclesiae'. He dreamed of becoming a hermit (*ibid.*, p. 483). A similar attitude towards the exercise of power within the Church is visible almost a century earlier in Peter of Morrone (Celestine V), who renounced the pontifical throne after hearing the biblical verse: 'For what shall it profit a man, if he shall gain the whole world, and lose his own soul?': *PC Peter of Morrone*, p. 213.

[128] See the figures quoted above, pp. 259–60.

interest, nevertheless, to observe that, alongside the diocesan bishop who had previously monopolized attention, other forms of priestly life found favour among the faithful in the later Middle Ages.

This is particularly remarkable in the case of the priest, since, until the thirteenth century, the parish clergy were entirely lacking in prestige. As is well known, there was a whole satirical literature of lay origin devoted to denouncing the vices of the rural clergy and mocking their short-comings.[129] The image of the priest as it is transmitted by the fabliaux is that of someone ignorant and coarse, often grasping and almost always ridiculous. But texts of ecclesiastical origin treat them no better. Synodal statutes bear witness to a great distrust of the parish clergy and the pastoral visits which have survived from before the thirteenth century reveal the often fruitless efforts of prelates to get them to observe conciliar norms with regard to chastity, and a minimum of dignity in the exercise of their liturgical and sacramental duties.[130] There was nothing here likely to give rise to a reputation for sanctity.

However, from the second half of the thirteenth century, in certain regions, such as western France and Tuscany, there appeared cults in favour of simple priests,[131] evidence that attitudes to the priestly state were

---

[129] J. Bédier, *Les Fabliaux: étude de littérature populaire et d'histoire littéraire au Moyen Age* (2nd edn, Paris, 1895); P. Nykrog, *Les Fabliaux: étude d'histoire littéraire et de stylistique médiévale* (Geneva, 1973).

[130] See, for example, O. Pontal, *Les statuts de Paris et le synodal de l'Ouest (XIIIe s.)* (Paris, 1971); P. Andrieu-Guitrancourt, *L'archevêque Eudes Rigaud* (Paris, 1938). The thirteenth-century canonization processes of the saint-bishops do not reveal how effective their efforts to reform the clergy were. An early thirteenth-century text, the *Magna Vita* of St Hugh of Lincoln (II, pp. 96–7), suggests they were largely ineffective.

[131] In addition to Thomas of Biville and St Yves, who are discussed below, we may note, for France, B. John 'the Discalced' (unshod) (1280–1349), rector of the parish of Saint-Grégoire in Rennes, before becoming a Friar Minor (Martin, *Les Ordres Mendiants*, pp. 356–7); his *Vita*, written between 1356 and 1364, is ed. L. Paolini, in *Acta ordinis Fratrum Minorum*, 29 (1910), pp. 16–28; see also W. Lampen, 'B. Iohannes discalceatus', *Collectanea Franciscana*, 26 (1956), pp. 421–6 and *AFH*, 4 (1911), pp. 765–7. For Tuscany, note B. Bartolo of San Gimignano (d. 1300) (E. Castaldo, *Santo Bartolo, il Giob della Toscana* (Florence, 1928); also *Anal. Boll.*, 47 (1929), pp. 218–19). B. Bartolo was famous less for his priestly activities than for his patience when, struck down by leprosy, he had to retire to a leper-house. Another priest, Giacomo Villa, was venerated at Città della Pieve, where he ran a hospital, in connection with which he was murdered in 1284 or 1304 (E. Canuti, *Documenti per la vita e per il culto del B. Giacomo Villa* (Perugia, 1952), especially pp. 13–17, which prints a fourteenth-century *Vita*). Other Tuscan saint-priests include Gerardo Bonamici, priest at San Martino, near Castelfranco, diocese of Lucca (d. 1292 or 1300) (V. Checchi, *Il B. Gherardo Bonamici, terziario francescano* (Florence, 1939)) and Davanzato of Poggibonsi (d. 1295), priest of Santa Lucia a Casciano, near Barberino Val d'Elsa (*AA.SS.* Iul. II, pp. 525–6; F. Vandelli, *Un parocco santo nella Valdelsa, il B. Davanzato* (Florence, 1972)). Though these priests were claimed by the Mendicant orders, in no case is their membership of a third order proved.

beginning to change. The earliest case is that of Thomas Hélye, *curé* of Biville in Normandy (d. 1257), whose canonization was requested several times between 1260 and 1274.[132] His cause failed, but the devotion persisted in the diocese of Coutances.[133] Yves Hélory of Kermartin (d. 1310) was made a priest in 1284 and, having been official of Rennes and of Tréguier, became *curé* of Trédrez, then, in 1292, of Louannec, where he died.[134] His name was soon famous throughout Brittany and Duke John III requested his canonization from Clement V and John XXII. In 1329, the latter opened an enquiry into his life and miracles, which took place at Tréguier in 1330. After repeated approaches by Charles of Blois, supported by John the Good, king of France, St Yves was canonized by Clement VI in 1347.[135]

These holy priests were unusual in their high educational level. Both Thomas Hélye and Yves Hélory had studied at university; the former had been a student in Paris around 1236, so had known Hugh of Saint-Cher and Eudes of Châteauroux; Yves had studied at Paris and Orléans between 1261 and 1279. For them, the parish ministry was a choice freely made. Their social origin and titles promised a brilliant ecclesiastical career, free from pastoral duties. It was as a result of a veritable conversion, due, in the case of St Yves, to Franciscan influence, that they assumed responsibility for a parish and devoted themselves to preaching the Gospel by word and deed.[136] The aura of sanctity which surrounded them, therefore,

---

[132] A vicar from Coutances cathedral was sent to the Curia in 1260 by Bishop John of Essais to seek his canonization. Cardinal Hugh of Saint-Cher, who had been Thomas' confessor and his master at the University of Paris, supported the request. A diocesan enquiry was ordered by Urban IV, and took place in 1264. A summary of the saint's life and a list of fourteen miracles were presented to the new pope, Clement IV, but he considered the dossier to be inadequate and asked for further information about the miracles, probably through Cardinal Eudes of Châteauroux, who had also known Thomas Hélye when Chancellor of the University of Paris. Things went no further (*Notae Constantienses*, in *Recueil des historiens des Gaules et de la France*, XXIII, p. 545; *AA.SS.* Oct. VIII, pp. 606–16).

[133] As is shown by the production in the fourteenth century of a *Vita auctore Clemente* (= *BHL* 8252–3), ed. L. Delise, in L. de Pontaumont, *Vie du B. Thomas Hélie de Biville* (Cherbourg, 1868), pp. 27–57, and the founding of a confraternity under his patronage, whose statutes are ed. in *AA.SS.* Oct. VIII, pp. 614–16. See also B. Jacqueline, 'Le bienheureux Thomas Hélye', *Revue du département de la Manche*, 4 (1962), pp. 5–14.

[134] The acts of the process of 1330 are in de La Borderie, *Monuments originaux de l'histoire de S. Yves*. The principal stages in the biography of St Yves are discussed in L. Duval-Arnould, 'Note chronologique sur S. Yves de Tréguier', *Anal. Boll.*, 92 (1974), pp. 409–24.

[135] For the political aspects of this canonization, see above, pp. 79–80.

[136] A Friar Minor of Guingamp, Guidomarus Morelli, said at the process of canonization: 'ipse quesivit in secreto ab eodem domino Yvone qualiter incepit vitam ita arctam et sanctam. Qui cum magna difficultate respondit eidem cum esset officialis archidiaconi

originated in an act of voluntary abasement, which was not available to everyone. They were neither of them ordinary country parsons. They were intellectuals who went back to the countryside, 'Oxbridge types' who chose to live among the peasantry.

Humility, consequently, was prominent among the virtues attributed to them by their contemporaries.[137] St Yves, about whom we are better informed than about his Norman predecessor, was remarkable for the austerity of his way of life; his clothes were of coarse cloth, usually frieze, and he went about in sandals.[138] He wore a hairshirt of tow and slept on the ground, on a little straw, with a stone for pillow. His shirt was crawling with lice, and he must have been filthy in the extreme to have shocked the Breton peasantry of his day.[139] He was equally austere with regard to food; though his ecclesiastical and patrimonial income was more than adequate, he ate only one meal a day, practised total abstinence throughout Lent and dined on bread and water on Wednesdays and Fridays.[140] But this extreme asceticism was accompanied in St Yves by great generosity towards the poor, in whom he recognized the presence of Christ.[141] He showed a marked preference for the lowly and his actions on their behalf, in his capacity as ecclesiastical judge and advocate, made a profound and lasting impression on the collective Breton memory.[142] The legend here corresponds to reality; witnesses at the process of 1330 were unanimous in presenting his sanctity as the result of praiseworthy efforts by someone of high rank to share the existence of the most deprived and serve the people.[143]

The other aspect of the life of these saint-priests which seems to have made a strong impression on contemporaries was their tireless pastoral

---

Redonensis et audiebat ibidem Quartum Sententiarum et de Biblia in domo fratrum minorum, propter verba divina que audiebat, ex tunc incepit spernere mundum et appetere celestia': *PC Yves*, p. 54.

[137] *Ibid.*, p. 56: 'erat homo magne humilitatis, interius in corde et exterius in habitu et in gestu'.

[138] *Ibid.*, pp. 9–10: 'habitu vili et humili, videlicet epitogio et tunica longis usque ad talos panni albi modici precii et valoris vocati cordet sue burel induebatur, et sotularibus altis corrigiatis ad instar Cisterciencium utebatur per XII annos'.

[139] *Ibid.*, p. 39.

[140] *Ibid.*, pp. 10, 13.

[141] *Ibid.*, p. 106: 'numquam vidit quod ipse alicui pauperi petenti elemosinam denegaret': distributions of bread (pp. 30, 33), cloth (pp. 3, 33), beans (p. 92) and wood (p. 32).

[142] *Ibid.*, p. 90: 'magis gaudebat esse cum pauperibus quam cum divitibus'; also pp. 32-3: 'libentius pauperem quam divitem audiebat'. Note also the famous rhyme: 'Sanctus Yvo erat Brito, advocatus et non latro, res miranda populo.'

[143] In his day, thanks to his excessive sympathy for the poor, he was also called *rusticus*, *coquinus*, *trucanus*, *pannosus* etc.: *Ibid.*, p. 33.

zeal. 'He was never idle', said several witnesses at the process of St Yves, whilst the Life of Thomas Hélye of Biville, based on the enquiry made with a view to his canonization, dwells at length on his apostolate in the parishes of the Cotentin.[144] That a secular priest had the desire and the ability to preach the Word of God was a source of amazement to the faithful, who flocked to hear him.[145] St Yves, too, was highly successful both in his own parish and as an itinerant preacher in the diocese of Tréguier.[146] It is hard for us to imagine the impact of his sermons, but, in the eyes of the witnesses, they were of unarguable and almost measurable efficacy. As one of them said, 'after he had begun to preach to the local people, they became twice as good as they had been before, as everybody said in the area'.[147] It seems likely that he emphasized the connection between religion and morality, since one of his former parishioners said that, before he was rector of Louannec, 'people were much more inclined to immorality and sin than they are now'. We know that he tackled very concrete issues in his sermons, explaining to the laity why they ought to do penance and practise the Christian virtues.[148] We observe here the influence of the Mendicant orders, with whom St Yves had studied, and of whom he regarded himself as the unworthy imitator, though his parishioners much preferred his sermons to theirs.[149] A gifted orator, the holy priest was also a great reader. His contemporaries remarked on the time he spent every day reading the Bible and the Lives of saints.[150] Indeed, he carried a Bible about with him.[151] His reputation as a man of learning was by no means irrelevant to the prestige he enjoyed in the countryside around Tréguier. But, far from profiting from this cultural superiority, he used it to the benefit of the poor and promoted the schooling of children from modest homes.[152]

---

[144] *Ibid.*, pp. 40, 56; *Vita* (of Thomas of Biville), *passim*.
[145] *Ibid.*, p. 47: 'cum beatus vir predicaret in coemeterio Sancti Georgii juxta Sanctam Laudum nec poterat ecclesia populum continere'.
[146] *PC Yves*, pp. 13, 20, 32 etc.
[147] *Ibid.*, pp. 104–5.
[148] *Ibid.*, pp. 110, 87.
[149] St Yves led his flock to hear the Dominicans 'even though they didn't want to' (*ibid.*, p. 72). He was in close contact with the Cordeliers of Guingamp and sent some of his penitents to them (*ibid.*, p. 45).
[150] *Ibid.*, p. 23: 'post missam vero lectionem biblie eis legebat'; see also p. 57: 'qualibet die celebrabat, legebat et studiebat in libro Sancte Scripture. Scribebat etiam flores sanctorum.'
[151] *Ibid.*, p. 66: 'continue deferebat unum librum secum vocatum bibliam, ut dicebatur' (a lay witness); a clerical witness said he 'portabat suam Bibliam et breviarium' (p. 74).
[152] *Ibid.*, p. 94: 'pauperes et orphanos nutribat et ipse ut litteras addiscerent informabat et ad scolas ponebat, et salarium magistri de suo proprio persolvebat'.

The evidence concerning these holy priests suggests a double image: in their social origins and especially in their education, they were atypical. Unlike most of their fellows, they belonged to the world of the powerful and the educated, even if they had chosen to leave it to keep faith with the Gospel. But it was their austere and ascetic life and their strict practice of humility and poverty which impressed their contemporaries. Closer to the people and less absorbed in the tasks of government than the bishops, priests were, in theory, in the late Middle Ages, well placed to accede in their turn to the honours of a public cult. The small number of parish priests whose sainthood was effectively recognized by the papacy is evidence that psychological obstacles continued to impede the success of this model. There are hints of this in the iconography of St Yves, which conveyed the image of good judge and advocate of the poor, but glossed over the very pastoral ministry and life amongst the peasantry which loomed so large in the depositions gathered during his canonization process.[153] We need, therefore, to keep the canonization of the rector of Louannec in proportion; it would be wrong to see it as evidence of the entry of the good priest into the group of spiritual leaders capable of arousing the admiration and enthusiasm of the faithful. But what happened in 1347 had, nevertheless, a greater significance than its numerical insignificance might suggest. Familiar as we are, under the influence of a tradition which dates back to the seventeenth century, with the notion of priesthood and sanctity as linked, it is hard for us to appreciate the novelty of the designation 'saint-priest' which occurs so frequently in the acts of the process of canonization of St Yves.[154] It was, however, the first time for centuries that the Roman Church had accorded this prestigious title to a secular cleric who had exercised a parish ministry at the lowest level.

The saint-pope

It might seem strange to draw a distinction between the sainthood of the bishops and that of the popes, given that the latter were bishops of Rome.

---

[153] Indeed, it was as a lawyer that St Yves was venerated outside Brittany (K. H. Burmeister, 'Der hl. Ivo und seine Verehrung an den deutschen Rechtsfakultäten', *Zeitschrift der Savigny-Stiftung für Rechtsgeschichte, germ. Abteilung*, 92 (1975), pp. 60–88). See also plate 23.

[154] *PC Yves*, p. 67: 'plures vocabant ipsum dominum Yvonem presbyterum sanctum'. In general, in a process like that of St Yves, no false note was struck; peasants, priests, monks and Mendicant brethren were unanimous in praising him in extravagant terms, saying, in the words of one witness, 'that he had not his like under the sun, since his life and his conduct were a mirror and an example to others' (*ibid.*, p. 91).

In the fourteenth century, however, it is reasonable to do so, since the pontiffs who were regarded as saints lived only very briefly, if at all, in that city. Furthermore, their prestige was linked less to their activities within their diocese than to the way in which they led and directed the Church as a whole. This is not to say, of course, that it was not until the end of the Middle Ages that the honours of a cult were accorded to successors of St Peter. In Rome itself, a dozen of them appear as early as the eighth century in the papal sacramentary.[155] They were mostly martyrs from before the peace of Constantine, with a few confessors whose pontificate had been particularly important for the capital of Christendom, such as SS Silvester, Leo and Gregory the Great. In the eleventh century, this list was greatly expanded and the Aventine Calendar contains the names of no fewer than thirty-five popes, including some very recent ones such as Leo IX (d. 1054). Other lists of popes regarded as saints appeared at the same period in Rome and in other parts of Christendom, such as those contained in the sacramentary of Ratisbon (MS Vat. lat. 3806) and the Lateran Calendar (twelfth century). In all, by 1200, 'about sixty Roman popes were commemorated in one or other Roman, or even trans-alpine, liturgical calendar'.[156]

But this development, favoured by Gregorian reform, was at odds with the policy that the Holy See was seeking to impose elsewhere in the sphere of the cult of the saints, by subjecting the life and miracles of the servants of God to a critical examination in the context of a formal enquiry. Consequently, no pope was proclaimed a saint by the Roman Church in the twelfth or thirteenth century. The study of the pontifical historiography of the period confirms, besides, that the popes did not enjoy a systematically favourable treatment at the hands of their biographers.[157] With the Investitures Struggle, the idealized portraits and stereotypical eulogies are replaced, in the *Vitae*, by descriptions which are more realistic, even sometimes slightly critical.[158] Admittedly, these texts, like the references

---

[155] Jounel, *Le culte des saints*, p. 169.

[156] *Ibid.*, p. 172.

[157] I. M. Watterich, ed., *Pontificium Romanorum qui fuerunt ab exeunte saeculo IX usque ad finem saeculi XIII vitae ab aequalibus conscriptae*, 2 vols. (Leipzig, 1862); for the thirteenth century, see the sources discussed by Toubert, *Latium médiéval*, I, pp. 48–9, and A. Paravicini Bagliani, 'La storiografia pontifica del sec. XIII. Prospettive di ricerca', *Römische historische Mitteilungen*, 18 (1976), pp. 45–54.

[158] H. Schmidinger, 'Das Papstbild in der Geschichtsschreibung des späteren Mittelalters', *Römische historische Mitteilungen*, I (1956–7), pp. 106–29. For similar trends in the iconography, see G. B. Ladner, *Die Papstbildnisse des Altertums und des Mittelalters, II: Von Innocenz II zu Benedikt XI* (Rome, 1970).

to saint-popes in the liturgical calendars, were essentially of local significance. They were a demonstration of the Church of Rome's veneration
for some of its leaders, comparable to those found in the eleventh and
twelfth centuries in all the great ecclesiastical metropolises where the *Gesta
episcoporum* preserve and transmit the memory of certain exemplary prelates, who were often the object of a cult in the cathedral church of their
diocese.

It was not until the last quarter of the thirteenth century that a cult was
accorded to a pope as such. This development was clearly linked to that
of the role of the Holy See within the Church and the victory of pontifical
monarchy, which entailed the decline of the prestige and prerogatives of
the episcopate. But it also owed much to the longing for a temporal and
spiritual reform of the Church which was so ardently desired by large
sectors of opinion convinced that it could only come from the top, that
is, from the papacy.[159] This all helps to explain why, in the years 1270–
1304, a reputation for sanctity was attached to several popes who seemed
both desirous and capable of making the hoped-for changes: Gregory X
(d. 1276), elected at the conclave of Viterbo and organizer of the Council
of Lyons II;[160] Innocent V – the Dominican Peter of Tarentaise – who
reigned for a few months in 1276;[161] and, above all, Celestine V (d. 1296) –
the hermit, Peter of Morrone – who catalysed the aspirations of the 'spirituals' for a renewal of the Church in a more evangelical direction.[162] His

---

[159] For these aspirations and the importance of eschatological trends in the second half of
the thirteenth century, see R. Manselli, 'L'attesa dell'età nuova e il Gioachimismo', in
*L'attesa dell'età nuova nella spiritualità della fine del Medioevo, IIIo convegno del centro di
studi sulla spiritualità medievale, Todi, 16–19 octobre 1960* (Todi, 1962), pp. 145–70.

[160] The cult of B. Gregory X (d. 1276) developed at Piacenza and, above all, Arezzo, where
he died and where his body lay in a magnificent tomb in the cathedral. Large numbers
of miracles were attributed to him, as we see from the collection in MS Vat. lat., 3457,
fols. 43–6, and those published by Benedict XIV, *De servorum Dei beatificatione*, II, pp.
554–93. A process of canonization was ordered by John XXII: *Fons sapientiae*, 10.V.1325;
see also Mollat, *Lettres communes de Jean XXII*, no. 22302, ed. P. M. Campi, *Historia
ecclesiastica di Piacenza* (Piacenza, 1651), pp. 284–5. The enquiry was to have been held
at Arezzo, Piacenza and Liège, where Tedaldo Visconti had been archdeacon, but it is
not known whether it took place. No acts have survived. In 1435, a new request for
canonization was presented, with no more success, by the commune of Arezzo, which
had in 1327 ordered the feast of the holy pope to be celebrated annually in the new
cathedral which was jointly dedicated to St Donatus: Campi, *Historia ecclesiastica*, III,
pp. 92–5; *PC Gregory X* (Piacenza and Arezzo, 1643), *ASV, Riti*, Proc. 2150, fols. 57ff.

[161] For this cult, which seems to have been restricted to the order of Friars Preacher, see
M. H. Laurent, *Le Bienheureux Innocent V (Pierre de Tarentaise) et son temps* (Vatican
City, 1947); N. del Re, sv Innocenzo V, in *BS*. VII (Rome, 1966), cc. 844–6.

[162] For Celestine V and contemporary recognition of the significance of his papacy, see F.
Baethgen, *Der Engelpapst: Idee und Wirklichkeit* (Leipzig, 1943); A. Frugoni, *Celestiniana*

pontificate was very brief (from July to December 1294) and, unfortunately, the enquiry carried out in 1306, on the orders of Clement V, with
a view to his canonization dealt almost exclusively with his period as a
hermit, that is with the fifty or so years he spent, first alone and then with
disciples, in the remote reaches of the Abruzzi.[163] It gives us, therefore,
very little direct information as to how contemporaries saw the 'angelic
pope'.

Between the pontificate of Boniface VIII, a controversial and hated
figure, and the Great Schism, two other popes were regarded as saints.
The first was Benedict XI – the Dominican Nicolò Boccasino – who
reigned from October 1303 to July 1304; his cult grew primarily in Perugia
and within the order of Preachers.[164] The second was Urban V, well documented thanks to what survives of the enquiry decreed in 1381 by Clement
VII into his life and miracles.[165] It consists of a highly developed schema
for the interrogation, which makes it possible to observe both how the
pontiff was remembered by the clergy and how they wished him to be

(Rome, 1954); also the bibliography in G. Marchetti Longhi, sv Celestino V, in *BS*. III
(Rome, 1963), cc. 1100–7.

[163] Of the some 324 depositions collected in the Abruzzi by the archbishop of Naples, James
Capocci, OHSA, in 1306, fewer than half survive (witnesses 8–130, 138, 161, 162, 172).
They have been edited by F. X. Seppelt, 'Die Akten des Kanonisationprozesses in dem
Kodex zu Sulmona', in *Monumenta Coelestiniana: Quellen zur Geschichte des Papstes Coeles-
tin V* (Paderborn, 1921), pp. 209–334. The content of the missing statements can partly
be reconstructed thanks to L. Marini, *Vita e Miracoli di S. Pietro di Morrone. già Celestino
papa V* (Milan, 1637), who had access to a manuscript from Collemaggio (L'Aquila)
containing the Summary of the process, and to the *Summarium* in MS Paris, Bibl. Arsenal,
1071. See also Anon., 'S. Pierre Célestin et ses premiers biographes', *Anal. Boll.*, 16
(1897), pp. 364–487; and the story of the canonization processes in *AA.SS.* Maii IV, pp.
530–1. It was no doubt deliberate that the process failed to deal with his pontificate. The
question of the relations between Celestine and his succesor was a delicate one, best
avoided in 1306, when Philip the Fair was demanding that Peter of Morrone be canonized
as a martyr, and spreading rumours that he had been assassinated on the orders of
Boniface VIII. The only references to the events of 1294 are in the depositions of the
eighth witness (*PC Peter of Morrone*, p. 213) and of Brother Bartholomew of Trasacco
(*ibid.*, p. 334): 'vita sua quasi semper fuit uniformis et indefectibilis, quam eciam in
papatu non dimisit nisi quantum ad aliqua pauca et levia'.

[164] A Life was written by the Dominican hagiographer and chronicler, Bernard Gui (= *BHL*
1091); three others followed during the fourteenth century (= *BHL* 1090, 1093, 1094).
See E. Martène and E. Durand, *Veterum scriptorum . . . amplissima collectio*, VI (Paris,
1729), cc. 371–5. Many miracles were recorded at Perugia, where his body lay: *ibid.*,
pp. 375–6; *Anal. Boll.*, 19 (1900), pp. 14–20.

[165] The canonization was requested as early as 1375 by King Waldemar of Denmark in a
letter to Gregory XI, who took his time replying: Raynaldi, *Ann. eccl., ad an. 1370*, VII,
p. 194. After the Schism, further requests were made to Clement VII by Queen Joan of
Naples, Louis of Anjou, Charles V and Charles VI. The Avignon pope ordered an enquiry
in the bull *Prides in consistorio*, 17.IV.1381, *ibid.*, p. 445.

seen.[166] For a study of official sainthood, these *articuli* are extremely valuable and, in the absence of comparable documents for the other popes who were the subject of a canonization process, I will concentrate on them.

At first sight, the model of the saint-pope looks very like that of the holy bishop. Like the thirteenth- and fourteenth-century prelates whose processes we have discussed, William of Grimoard was of noble birth.[167] Having entered the Benedictine monastery of Chirac at a very early age, he remained, for the rest of his life, even after he became pope, loyal to the monastic rule and life-style,[168] but his activities soon became secular in nature. The future Urban V had a brilliant university career and, while abbot of Saint-Germain of Auxerre, then of Saint-Victor of Marseilles, he was entrusted by the Holy See with delicate diplomatic missions, at which he excelled.[169] Other articles refer to his activities as bishop of Rome, to which he returned in 1367.[170] The process shows him striving to restore the city's religious life which had been disrupted by the prolonged absence of the papacy. It was emphasized, in particular, that he gave new life to the cult of SS Peter and Paul, by showing very great honour to their relics.[171] Lastly, he set out to improve the morals of the laity and, to this end, embarked on a veritable familial pastoral mission which seems to have deeply impressed contemporaries.[172] The result, according to Bishop Guy of Arezzo, *vicarius Urbis* in 1368–9, was that 'in less than three years, twenty thousand people confessed and communicated in Rome, all people who had never confessed or communicated before, even though they had passed the age when they were required to do so. And among all the

---

[166] The documents are ed. J. H. Albanès and V. Chevalier 'Information sur la vie et les miracles du B. Urbain V', in *Actes anciens et documents concernant le Bienheureux Urbain V pape*, I (Paris and Marseilles, 1897), pp. 375–88, which also contains the fifteen medieval Lives of Urban V (pp. 1–113). See also E. Hocedez, 'Vita prima Urbani V auctore anonymo synchrono', *Anal. Boll.*, 26 (1907), pp. 305–16.

[167] *PC Urban V*, arts. 5–8, pp. 378–80.

[168] *Ibid.*, arts. 12, 13, 24, pp. 380–1, 385.

[169] *Ibid.*, arts. 10, 11, 20, pp. 380, 383.

[170] Mollat, *Les papes d'Avignon* (with full bibliography).

[171] *PC Urban V*, arts. 92–8, pp. 402–3.

[172] *Ibid.*, art. 42, p. 417: 'plurimos de ipsis Romanis, majoribus, mediocribus et infimis diversimodo ad se traxit, nunc per secreta particularia coloquia, nunc per publica parlamenta, nunc invitando eos ad prandia et ipsos alloquendo, in tantum quod propter ista et propter predicationes quas eis fieri faciebat per solempnes personas et propter justiciam quam faciebat observari, ipsos plurimum ad bonos mores convertit, ita quod plures ex ipsis inceperunt cum propriis uxoribus comedere, quod antea non faciebant'.

Romans and the people of the surroundings, morality began to improve, as did conduct.'[173]

Among the 179 articles *de vita* which retrace the life and virtues of Urban V, only a tiny number concern his role as leader of a local church. Most of them describe the qualities and meritorious deeds of the Holy Pontiff who, from Avignon and, at the end of his reign, from Rome, presided over the destinies of Christendom as a whole. The attitude of Urban V to the moral and ascetic life seems to have been characterized by the search for the happy medium: neither laxity nor excessive austerity; he wished to be poor, but not to live in poverty.[174] His jovial nature gave him a pleasant manner and his natural affability endeared him to all he met.[175] Many articles also celebrate his sense of justice. A professor of canon law, he had, before his election to the pontifical throne, frequently been employed as arbiter of conflicts and his efforts in this sphere had won him an excellent reputation.[176] Once he became pope, he encouraged juridical studies in order, he explained, to have good institutions and good magistrates.[177] He did not hesitate to reproach kings and prelates for their injustices and intervened personally to ensure that each of his subjects was judged as was his right, whether in Rome or in Avignon.[178] His spirit of justice seems to have inspired his reforming activity, which, to a very large extent, explains his popularity. He himself set an example by being content with a modest entourage, avoiding undue favouritism to members of his family, and refusing the presents and favours pressed on him by the great of this world.[179] Further, he fought unceasingly against the abuses which were rife in the Curia and the Church, chastising dishonest collectors and corrupt courtiers.[180] He was credited with having rid Avignon of the bands of brigands and robbers who had exercised a veritable reign of terror there, and with restoring order to Rome and the Church

---

[173] *Ibid.*, art. 142, p. 417.

[174] *Ibid.*, art. 65, p. 396: 'predictus dominus Urbanus mundanalibus rebus sic usus est parce quod illas inordinate amare refutavit: unde sepius dixit quod volebat esse pauper sed propter reverentiam Ecclesie et quietem subditorum non penuriosus'.

[175] *Ibid.*, art. 23, p. 385: 'non tristiciam, non exterminationem seu extenuationem corporis pertendens . . . se sempler affabilem et propitium exhibebat potentibus et pauperibus, notis et incognitis'.

[176] *Ibid.*, art. 19, p. 383: 'reputabatur quasi per omnes ejus noticiam habentes unus de probioribus et melioribus canonistis mundi'.

[177] *Ibid.*, arts. 104, 125–6, pp. 407–13.

[178] *Ibid.*, art. 143, p. 418.

[179] *Ibid.*, arts. 22, 71–3, pp. 384, 399.

[180] *Ibid.*, arts. 74–5, pp. 399–400.

States.[181] In the ecclesiastical sphere strictly speaking, the authors of the
articles laud Urban V for having taken measures to prevent simonaic
practices and the accumulation of benefices, though he recognized that he
could not stop them altogether.[182]

From the description of the activities of Pope Grimoard in the *articuli
interrogatorii* we get the impression of sanctification through the assiduous
exercise of power. The pope's working day, from his morning audiences
to his afternoon walks, by way of the signing of petitions and the reception
of cardinals, was recorded at length and in detail.[183] Urban V is presented
as a wise sovereign, concerned to be fair, conscientiously and thoroughly
performing the tasks which fell to him.[184] Like all the monarchs of his
day, he disposed of large financial resources. Many articles emphasize his
generosity towards the poor, to whom he sent the leftovers from his table
and on whose behalf he organized frequent distributions of food and
alms.[185] On numerous occasions, he acted to combat famine, especially in
Rome, where he sold corn at half the market price, in Provence and in
the region of Mende, where grain imports made at an opportune moment
succeeded in ending the crisis. Thus he appeared to his contemporaries
as a guarantee and symbol of prosperity.[186] A large number of articles
were devoted to the initiatives he took, in a range of spheres, to put into
circulation the riches which lay unused in the Treasury of the Roman
Church. He wished to distribute to churches, for the clergy to employ in
worship, all the precious objects he found in the coffers on his accession
or that he later received as gifts.[187] He also spent lavishly to build and
rebuild churches and palaces in both Rome and southern France, and
gave many relics to religious communities.[188]

But the most innovatory aspect of his activities was probably his cultural
and social policy. William of Grimoard founded many scholarships for
poor students and established, at his own cost, new teaching chairs and
colleges. At Montpellier, he founded a veritable public library, 'where all

[181] *Ibid.*, arts. 79, 144–5, 152–4, pp. 400, 418–22.
[182] *Ibid.*, arts. 77–8, p. 400.
[183] *Ibid.*, arts. 34–7, pp. 380–9.
[184] He arranged to be treated by his doctors outside normal working hours so as not to lose
any time: *ibid.*, art. 61, p. 395.
[185] *Ibid.*, arts. 59, 132–4, pp. 395, 414–15.
[186] *Ibid.*, arts. 135–7, p. 415: 'quamdiu fuit papa, ubicumque fuerit, nonfuit caristia nec
iuxta loca in quibus Curia residebat'; art. 136, p. 415.
[187] *Ibid.*, arts. 66–9, pp. 397–8. See also art. 397 for the unused wealth: 'omnia illa erant
quasi inutilia, mortua; et omnia precepit de facto et fecit distribui et donari'.
[188] *Ibid.*, arts. 91, 99, 102–3, 111, 114, pp. 403, 406, 409–10.

the poor and others without books could come to enjoy the consolation they sought'.[189] In fact, he saw the raising of the cultural level not only as a way of improving the training of the clergy but, more generally, as a factor for the moral and human improvement of the faithful as a whole.[190] On the social plane, though he did not neglect the traditional forms of charity and welfare, he understood that the best way to counteract economic hardship and poverty was to create employment. Accordingly, on his return to Rome in 1367, he hired between eight hundred and a thousand unemployed persons to work in the vineyards located near the Apostolic Palace and spent some 28,000 florins on this project in one single winter. To those of his retinue who criticized these costly works, he said: 'I can see no more useful or fruitful way of being charitable to the poor of Rome, because the Romans were without work and, for this reason, slipped into wrongdoing and committed many crimes. They are now occupied by this work; they earn money. This is, for them, a chance to realize how agreeable it is to earn money and to accustom them to flee idleness and despondency.'[191]

In the last analysis, the image of the pope which emerges from the 'capitulations' presented by the procurator Peter Olivier of Falgar is more that of a temporal sovereign than of a religious leader. Admittedly, several articles emphasize his piety and the devotion with which he followed or celebrated mass;[192] others show him as the defender of the faith, suppressing heresies, organizing crusades and striving to make Jews and schismatics return to the Church.[193] But it could hardly be claimed that these are the aspects which are most in evidence. Concerned for peace and justice, feeling himself responsible for the prosperity of the Church and his subjects, Urban V was remembered as a balanced and benevolent man, generous and cultivated.[194] His election had been followed by prodigies;[195] during his reign, he was honoured by all the earthly kings and the

---

[189] *Ibid.*, arts. 104, 121–6, 128–9, pp. 407, 412–14.
[190] For his cultural policy and its role in the appreciation of his sanctity, see below, pp. 404–5.
[191] *PC Urban V*, art. 141, pp. 416–17.
[192] *Ibid.*, arts. 32, 53, 80, 90, pp. 388, 392, 400–1, 403.
[193] *Ibid.*, arts. 47–51, pp. 391–2.
[194] Petrarch, who did not much like him, wrote immediately after his death: 'per piacere agli uomini, dispiacque a Cristo, a Pietro e a tutti i buoni': *De rebus senilibus*, XIII, 13. But this severe judgement, explained by Urban V's return to Avignon in 1370, reveals that the pope was very popular and we should remember that, only a few years earlier, Petrarch had written an eloquent eulogy of the pope as 'Vicar of the Sun of Justice': *ibid.*, 1, VII, ep. 1.
[195] *PC Urban V*, arts. 30–1, pp. 387–8.

emperor Charles IV held the bridle of his horse in the streets of Rome.[196] Many miracles were attributed to him after his death, especially after the translation of his body to Saint-Victor of Marseilles.[197] In him, public opinion seems to have canonized a man who had tried honestly to realize in society and in the Church the ideal of 'good government'.

In the evolution of the forms of sanctity peculiar to the clergy during the last centuries of the Middle Ages, the most striking feature is the diversification of the models capable of gaining the approval of the laity and attracting the attention of the Roman Church. Alongside the saint-bishops who, until the thirteenth century, had been overwhelmingly pre-ponderant, there appeared the saint-priests and saint-popes, types hitherto unknown, but which became fairly common after 1300. It was as if the two aspects hitherto closely linked within the episcopal function – pastoral activity and the exercise of power – had become more difficult to reconcile in the late Middle Ages. The papacy itself did not escape these tensions, spectacularly illustrated by the 'great renunciation' of St Peter of Morrone, who could find no other way out of the contradictions into which his accession to the Holy See had plunged him than to resign his office. During the Avignon papacy, in a number of regions of Christendom, the place previously occupied by the diocesan prelates was taken either by popes regarded primarily as sovereigns and admired as such, or by Mendi-cant monks, in a better position to lead a life both oriented towards the world and conforming to evangelical requirements.

THE SAINTHOOD OF THE REGULARS

As our statistical study has shown, the regulars were an important group among the servants of God whose merits were recognized by the Roman Church between 1198 and 1431,[198] accounting for 40 per cent of the total in the thirteenth century, and nearly a third in the subsequent period. Within this group, however, if we are to progress beyond the level of generality which effectively prevents a historical approach, we need to

---

[196] *Ibid.*, art. 81, p. 401.
[197] *Ibid.*, arts. 168–790, pp. 426–30, and *secunda pars. de miraculis*, pp. 430–80 (89 articles). The miracles recorded at Marseilles between 1374 and 1378 are ed. Albanès and Cheva-lier, *Information sur la vie*, pp. 124–365. There is iconographical evidence of the diffusion of Urban's cult in Italy: Kaftal 2, cc. 1107–8.
[198] See above, pp. 260–3.

distinguish between the various forms of consecrated life existing at the period.

Monastic and canonical sainthood

Documents which throw light on the attitude of the Church towards the sainthood of the monks and regular canons are far from plentiful. The majority of the canonization processes concerning them took place during the first half of the thirteenth century, that is, at a period when the enquiries were still conducted in a fairly summary fashion. When the acts have survived, which is by no means always the case, they usually give us only a conventional biographical schema, followed by a list of miracles.[199] It is difficult to get from this a clear idea of the image of a saint-monk or saint-canon present in the minds of those who sought to promote their cult. This is all the more unfortunate in that, up to the 1230s, both the Benedictine ideal and the canonical life according to the rule of St Augustine seem still to have enjoyed great prestige. The wave of sanctity which, in the twelfth century, had spread from the cloisters throughout Christendom continued until the beginning of the thirteenth century at the level of official sainthood, since most of the regulars canonized by the papacy between 1202 and 1223 had lived before 1200; this was the case with St Gilbert of Sempringham (d. 1189), founder of the order which took his name,[200] the Moravian monk Procopius of Sazava (d. 1053),[201] Robert of Molesme (d. 1111), founder of Cîteaux,[202] and William of Aebelholt (d.

---

[199] The report sent in 1222 to Pope Honorius III by the commissioners responsible for the enquiry into the merits of the Cistercian abbot, Hugh of Bonnevaux (d. 1194) consisted only of the following: 'Beatus Hugo, de nobilibus et catholicis Valentinae diocesis ortus parentibus, nobilitatem sanguinis animi nobilitate venustans, a primaevo iuventutis flore in castris Domini militaturus, habitum religionis assumpsit, in quo quam strenue, quam viriliter et perfecte perstiterit subjecta satis miracula demonstrant': *PC Hugh of Bonnevaux*, ed. Martène and Durand, *Thesaurus*, I, c. 888. The gaps in the process can to some extent be filled in from the *Vitae*, but the material in the hagiographical texts is less reliable.

[200] R. Foreville, 'L'Eglise et la royauté en Angleterre sous Henri II Plantagenet (1154–1189)', thesis, University of Paris (1943), especially pp. 209–11; Foreville, 'Un procès de canonisation'.

[201] There is a complete edition of the sources for the history and cult of St Procopius in V. Chaloupecky and B. Ryba, *Stredovèké legendy prokopské* (Prague, 1953); see also J. Kadlec, sv Procopio, in *BS*, X (Rome, 1968), cc. 1167–73.

[202] His canonization was requested by many Burgundian abbeys supported by the Cistercian order. Honorius III ordered an enquiry (*Gloriosus Deus*, 25.I.1221, Pressutti, no. 3031) by the bishops of Langres and Valence and the abbot of Cluny, who visited Molesme and sent their report to the pope within a year. Honorius III found it inadequate and

17 Medieval Icelandic saint-bishops: Gudmundr Arason (d. 1237), John of Holar (d. 1121) and Thorlak Thorhallsson (d. 1193) (altar frontal from Holar cathedral, fifteenth century, now in the National Museum of Iceland, Reykjavik)

18 St Louis of Anjou crowning his brother, King Robert (Simone Martini, *c.*1320, Galleria Nazionale di Capodimonte, Naples)

19 A citizen saint: Homobonus of Cremona (d. 1197) (statue on the front of the church of St Homobonus, early thirteenth century, Cremona)

20 B. Rainier of Pisa (d. 1160) surrounded by members of a confraternity of flagellants
(Pisan school, fourteenth century, Museo Civico, Pisa)

19 A citizen saint: Homobonus of Cremona (d. 1197) (statue on the front of the church of St Homobonus, early thirteenth century, Cremona)

20 B. Rainier of Pisa (d. 1160) surrounded by members of a confraternity of flagellants
(Pisan school, fourteenth century, Museo Civico, Pisa)

21 A charitable saint: B. Andrew Gallerani (d. 1251): *below*, the saint distributes
alms to the poor and prays before the Crucifix; *top left*, the stigmatization of St Francis;
top right, episodes from the life of St Dominic (early fourteenth-century painting,
San Domenico, now in the Pinacoteca, Siena)

22 B. Peter of Luxembourg at prayer (fifteenth-century painting, Avignon school, Musée Calvet, Avignon)

23 St Yves, the honest judge, listens to the impecunious widow rather than to her adversary, who tries to corrupt him (Domenico di Michelino, painting, early fifteenth-century, Museo dell'Opera di Duomo, Florence)

24 The dream of Innocent III: St Dominic supports the collapsing church (polyptych of St Dominic, church of St Catherine, Pisa)

1203).[203] The same is true of those who were the subject of an enquiry *de vita et miraculis*, but never canonized in the Middle Ages: John (d. 1170), founder and first prior of the abbey of Santa Maria de Gualdo Mazocca, in the diocese of Benevento,[204] Hugh, Cistercian abbot of Bonnevaux in Dauphiné,[205] Maurice of Carnoët (d. 1191), a Breton Cistercian abbot,[206] Hildegard of Bingen (d. 1179), a Benedictine nun from Rupertsberg,[207] and Odo of Novara (d. 1200), a Carthusian who ended his days as a recluse at Tagliacozzo.[208] The only really contemporary saint-monks who

---

authorized only a local cult: 'concedimus vobis ut ipsum tamquam sanctum in vestra ecclesia venerantes, ejus apud Dominum suffragia fiducialiter imploretis: *Cum olim nobis*, 8.I.1222, Presutti, 3701. The complete dossier is ed. P. Labbé, *Novae bibliothecae manuscriptorum librorum*, I (Paris, 1657), pp. 647–50.

[203] William of Aebelholt or of Eskill was a French regular canon of the congregation of Saint-Victor, who reformed the collegials and monasteries of Denmark in the late twelfth century. The enquiry into his life and miracles was ordered by Honorius III at the request of the Danish episcopate (*Licet angelus Sathanae*, 28.V.1218, Presutti, no. 1386, ed. *Bull. Rom.*, III, p. 199). The process, conducted by the archbishop of Lund, the bishop of Roskilde and the Cistercian abbot of Hervad, has been lost. See C. Boillon, sv Guglielmo, abbate di Eskill, santo, in *BS*, VII (Rome, 1966), cc. 464–5.

[204] Honorius III ordered an enquiry (*Ineffabilis sapientia*, 3.VI.1218, Pressutti, 1405, ed. *Bull. Rom.*, III, p. 344) by the bishops of Dragonara and Lucera and the prior of San Fortunato, diocese of Benevento. It took place but there was no further action: Casamassa, 'Per una nota marginale del Cod. Vat. Lat. 5949'.

[205] The enquiry was ordered by Honorius III at the request of the archbishop of Vienne and his suffragans, supported by the Cistercian order (*Quia sua incommutabili*, 3.XII.1221, Pressutti, 3592) and conducted by the archbishop of Vienne and the bishop of Grenoble. The complete dossier is in Martène and Durand, *Thesaurus*, I, cc. 887–8.

[206] The enquiry was ordered by Honorius III at the request of several Breton bishops and the abbey of Carnoët, supported by the general chapter of the Cistercian order (*Etsi frigescente caritate*, 4.XII.1224, Pressutti, 5197, ed. *AA.SS.* Oct. VI, p. 382), and conducted by the bishop of Saint-Pol de Léon and the abbot of Saint-Gingaloe of Landevenec; the results were deemed insufficient by the pope (*Venerabili fratre nostro*, 5.IX.1225, Pressutti, 5622, ed. *AA.SS.* Oct. VI, pp. 382–3) on a technicality.

[207] An enquiry was ordered by Gregory IX (*Mirabilis Deus*, 27.I.1228, Auvray, 3648, ed. *Anal. Boll.*, 2 (1883), pp. 118–19). The process took place at Bingen in 1233; its acts were published by P. Bruder, '*Acta inquisitionis de virtutibus et miraculis S. Hildegardis*', *Anal. Boll.*, 2 (1883), pp. 119–29. In 1237, Gregory IX asked for the enquiry to be completed (*Supplicantibus nobis*, 6.V.1237, ed. S. A. Wurdtwein, *Nova subsidia diplomatica*, IX (Heidelberg, 1788), p. 12) and Innocent IV for the dossier to be sent to him (*Supplicantibus olim*, 24.XI.1243, ed. Wurdtwein, *Nova subsidia*, XI, pp. 34–6). Things went no further until the pontificate of John XXII, when new approaches were made to the Holy See. They resulted only in the grant of collective letters of indulgence sent from Avignon by twelve bishops on 5 December 1324: *Anal. Boll.*, 2 (1883), p. 129.

[208] An enquiry was ordered by Gregory IX, by the abbot of Saint-Martin of Turano and Brother Peter, warden of the Friars Minor of the diocese of Marses (*Ad audientiam nostram*, 10.XII.1239, ed. *Bull. Franc.*, 1, p. 277). The process took place at Tagliacozzo in 1240 and is ed. *Anal. Boll.*, 1 (1882), pp. 323–54. There was no further action: R. Amedo, 'Il B. Oddone di Novara, monaco certosino', *Novarien*, 3 (1969), pp. 5–45; *AA.SS.* Ian. II, pp. 259–61.

attracted the attention of the Holy See were the Cistercian John of Montmirail (d. 1217), a monk at the abbey of Longpont,[209] and an English Benedictine, Thomas de la Hale (d. 1295), killed by soldiers during a French raid on Dover.[210] He was the last.[211] One regular canon, John of Bridlington, or of Thweng (d. 1379), was canonized by Boniface IX in 1401.[212] There were still, well into the fourteenth century, Benedictines such as Urban V who enjoyed a reputation for sanctity, but it is clear from their processes of canonization that the practice of monasticism played only a subsidiary role in the appreciation of their sanctity.[213]

We need to ask why it was that the states and types of life which had been so highly esteemed by the Holy See at the end of the twelfth century – St Bernard was canonized in 1174, St Bruno in 1181, St Stephen of Muret in 1189 and St John Gualbert in 1193 – went out of favour a few decades later. There are many possible explanations for this sudden fall from grace. The first is that, at the end of the twelfth century, the papacy had accorded the honours of canonization almost exclusively to the founders of orders or congregations. Few new orders were created in the thirteenth century and, when the movement for monastic reform revived on a significant scale in the first half of the fifteenth century, those who took the initiative – such as Louis Barbo (d. 1443) in Italy and Martin of Vargas in Spain (d.

[209] The enquiry was entrusted by Gregory IX to the bishop of Paris and the prior of Saint-Victor (*Mirabilis Deus*, 25.IX.1236, Auvray, 3165, ed. in Manrique, *Ann. Cist.*, 4, p. 519). It probably took place, but nothing survives. At the time of the Council of Lyons I, the issue was raised again: Albert of Armagh, *Historia canonizationis S. Edmundi Cantuarensis archiepiscopi*, ed. Martène and Durand, *Thesaurus*, III, c. 1849: 'eadem consideratione ducti (the difficulty of obtaining a canonization), abbas et conventus Longiponti de fratre Johanne canonizando, sicut probata miracula persuedebant, causam ipsius reassumere formidabant'. See also Dimier, 'Le bienheureux Jean de Montmirail'.

[210] An enquiry was ordered by Urban VI at the request of Richard II, to be conducted by the archbishop of Canterbury and the bishops of London and Rochester (*Grandis nobis adest*, 20.XII.1380, ed. D. Wilkins, *Concilia Magnae Britanniae et Hiberniae*, III (London, 1737), p. 174). They delegated the task to bishops of lesser rank (*ibid.*, p. 175); no trace of the process survives. See also Grosjean, 'Thomas de la Hale'.

[211] J. Van der Straeten, 'Robert de la Chaise-Dieu, sa canonisation', *Anal. Boll.*, 82 (1964), pp. 37–56, shows that the founder of the abbey of Chaise-Dieu was not canonized by Clement VI; his letter to the bishop of Le Puy (*Lettres closes, patentes et curiales se rapportant à la France*, III, ed. E. Déprez, G. Mollat and J. Glénisson (Paris, 1961), no. 5064) is simply a bull inaugurating the new, recently rebuilt, church of Chaise-Dieu.

[212] Boniface IX ordered an enquiry by three cardinals (*Quia saepe*, 16.II.1391), ed. in part in Bliss, *Papal Letters*, IV, pp. 378–9, of which nothing survives, but which apparently satisfied the pope since he pronounced the canonization (*De summis caelorum*, 24.IX.1401, ed. J. S. Purvis, *St John of Bridlington* (Bridlington, 1924), pp. 31–7). See also Grosjean, 'S. Ioanne Bridlingtoniensi'; J. A. Twemlow, 'The liturgical credentials of a forgotten English saint', in *Mélanges Bémont* (Paris, 1913).

[213] See above, pp. 320–3.

1446) – met so much resistance and were embroiled in such fierce conflicts in their efforts to impose their ideas that there was never any question of their later being venerated as saints.[214]

With the exception of St Gilbert of Sempringham, the monks and canons whose canonization was requested from the Holy See after 1200 were persons of the second rank whose reputation for sanctity was confined to one region, such as Hugh of Bonnevaux and John of Montmirail. It is hardly surprising, therefore, that their cause ultimately failed, given the increasingly strict demands of the papacy in respect of the *fama*. After 1230, for someone to be recognized as a saint by the Church, it was no longer enough for them to have been admired by their entourage or spiritual children. It was necessary for the devotion to have spread further afield and to have reached the laity, whose faith in the new intercessor was demonstrated by the appearance of miracles. In this context, the regulars who led a cloistered life were at a disadvantage in relation to the other clergy. The rule prohibited them from rendering special funerary honours to members of the community. Further, it was difficult for the monks to attract crowds into abbeys or encourage the growth of pilgrimages to the tomb of their saints without disrupting the conventual life.[215] Only the regular canons, more open to the world and often engaged in preaching, were able to make a mark in this sphere.[216]

But the principal reason for this change, in the last analysis, was the decline experienced by most religious orders of the old type between 1200 and 1300. If we except a few small Italian congregations such as the

[214] See the interesting remarks of R. Girard in his unpublished *mémoire de maîtrise*, 'Les saints bénédictins des XIVe et XVe siècles d'après les documents contemporains', Bordeaux, 1974 (which he and his supervisor, M. Bernard Guillemain, have kindly allowed me to consult). The only monastic congregation created in the thirteenth century, that of the Silvestrins, in the Marches, was the subject of a considerable hagiographical literature, but this is, in a sense, the exception that proves the rule. See J. Leclercq, 'La "Vita di S. Silvestro", l'irragiamento del santo e dei suoi primi discepoli', in *Atti del congresso di studi storici per l'VIIIo centenario della nascita di S. Silvestro, 1177–1977* (Fano, 1978), pp. 1–21; and above, n. 63, p. 127.

[215] There is an interesting indication of this in the canonization process of St Hildegard (p. 127): 'Quaerentibus etiam nobis (= the commissioners) a conventu quare beata Hildegardis modo non faceret signa, dixerunt quod, cum post ejus mortem Dominus tot miracula ostenderet et con cursus populorum tantus fieret ad sepulcrum ejus, religio et divinum officium per tumultum populi turbabantur tantum quod domino archiepiscopo illud retulerunt. Unde ipse accedens personaliter ad locum, praecepit ut a signis cessaret.'

[216] For example, St Gilbert of Sempringham, described by Archbishop Hubert Walter of Canterbury as 'actionis et contemplacionis vices alternabat' (Foreville, 'Un procès de canonisation', p. 31). Similarly, the bull of canonization of St John of Bridlington said he was 'in spiritualibus providus, in temporalibus circumspectus' (Purvis, *St John of Bridlington*, p. 34).

Table 29 *Benedictines who died in an odour of sanctity (1100–1500)*

Saints	Century of death			
	twelfth	thirteenth	fourteenth	fifteenth
Benedictine – all branches[a]	362	257	49	62
'Black' Benedictines[b]	102	26	11	9

Notes:
[a] Based on R. Rios, *Corona sanctorum anni Benedictini* (Ramsgate, 1958), who uses very broad criteria.
[b] Based on P. Schmitz, *Histoire de l'ordre de Saint Benoît*, III (Maredsous, 1957), pp. 426–47, who uses stricter criteria.

Camaldoli and the Vallombrosans, the number of saint-monks and saint-canons is small, even at the level of local sanctity.[217] The figures to support this statement are debatable, since, as soon as one starts to count the *beati*, about whom the Church did not usually pronounce, and whose names are transmitted to us by menologies compiled according to rather shifting criteria, there is a risk of conflicting estimates. Remarkably, however, these heterogeneous lists suggest similar trends.

Table 29 confirms the impression that the thirteenth and fourteenth centuries were unfavourable for monastic sainthood and especially for the Benedictine black monks. A handful of cults, usually small in size and enjoying limited backing, had little chance of coming to the attention of the Holy See. When, exceptionally, an enquiry was opened concerning a monk or nun in this category, it is clear that their canonical status counted for little in their reputation. The process of canonization of Hildegard, held at Bingen in 1233,[218] makes plain that what had most impressed the witnesses who had known her in her lifetime was the fact that many of her predictions had proved correct, in particular her prior announcement of the day of her death.[219] She was also credited with having recorded her revelations in a number of books which had then been approved by Parisian theologians.[220] Great importance was also attached to her thaumaturgical powers, which she had exercised well before her death to the benefit of those possessed by devils and epileptics, who had recovered their reason after receiving her blessing.[221] There is nothing here, it will be seen, that

[217] See above, pp. 123–4.
[218] See above, n. 207, p. 325.
[219] *PC Hildegard*, pp. 120, 124.
[220] *Ibid.*, pp. 124, 126, 128.
[221] *Ibid.*, pp. 120, 122, 124 etc.

is specifically monastic. Rather, the sainthood of Hildegard heralded that of the great lay visionaries and prophetesses of the fourteenth century, such as Bridget of Sweden and Catherine of Siena, since she did not hesitate to pass on to the ecclesiastical hierarchy and great men of this world warnings and messages she had received from God.[222] Similarly, Odo of Novara (d. 1200), a former Carthusian venerated at Tagliacozzo, appears in the acts of the enquiry as a sort of hermit. He had been expelled from his monastery and taken refuge in a little cell near this small town in the Abruzzi. Nuns and lay people from the area came to him seeking spiritual assistance and, above all, a cure for their illnesses.[223] We may therefore conclude that, in the few cases where saints from within monasticism succeeded in gaining the sympathy of the faithful and attracting the attention of the Holy See, this owed less to their faithful observance of the rule than to personal charismas which were in no way typical of the form of religious life they had chosen.

Eremitical sainthood

Unlike monasticism, eremitism did not, strictly speaking, constitute a canonical status, and it may seem odd to lump together under this rubric saints who remained laymen to the end of their life, such as Galgano (d. 1181) and John Bonus (d. 1249), and others who were monks or priests, such as Lawrence Loricatus (d. 1243), St Peter of Morrone (d. 1296) and St Nicholas of Tolentino (d. 1305).[224] In the eyes of contemporaries, however, these distinctions counted for little; the hermit was defined by

---

[222] *Ibid.*, p. 125: she corresponded with popes Eugenius III, Adrian VI and Anastasius IV and the emperors Conrad and Frederick Barbarossa, 'et sic ad meliora eos reduxit'.

[223] See above, n. 208. At the enquiry of 1240 (ed. *Anal. Boll.*, 1 (1882), p. 328), it was said: 'et omnes euntes ad eum monebat et animabat in bono, quia homo valde litteratus erat'.

[224] The hermits who were the subject of a process of canonization between the late twelfth and early fifteenth centuries were: Galgano of Chiusdino (d. 1181), whose process (1185) is published in Schneider, 'Der Einsiedler Galgan von Chiusdino', pp. 69–77; Caradoc (d. 1124), a Welsh hermit whose Life was written by Giraldus Cambrensis, who also obtained an enquiry from Innocent III (*Multa jamdudum*, 8.V.1200, ed. J. S. Brewer, *Geraldi Cambrensis opera*, III (London, 1863), pp. 64–5), which cannot have gone ahead as the two abbots appointed destroyed the pontifical documents (*ibid.*, p. 83). The process of Lawrence Loricatus (Subiaco, 1244) is ed. Gnandt, *Vita S. Claridoniae*, pp. 67–103; that of John Bonus (Cesena and Mantua, 1251–4) is *AA.SS.* Oct. IX, pp. 771–885; that of Peter of Morrone (Sulmona in the Abruzzi, 1306) is ed. Seppelt, 'Die Akten des Kanonisationsprozesses in dem Codex zu Sulmona'. Lastly, for St Nicholas of Tolentino and his cult in the fourteenth century, see the acts of the 1325 canonization process, ed. N. Occhioni, *Il processo per la canonizzazione di S. Nicola da Tolentino* (Rome, 1984). For eremiticism in local sanctity, see above, pp. 193–5.

his style of life, not by his membership of a particular juridical category.

The image of the saint-hermit in the processes of canonization is that of an ascetic who carried to extremes all forms of rejection of the world. This choice sometimes followed a conversion; Lawrence Loricatus retreated to the forests and caves of the Subiaco region after having killed a man and made a pilgrimage to Santiago de Compostela in expiation.[225] It was also sometimes the culmination of a spiritual journey, in particular among the regulars, for whom the practice of solitude or reclusion was a way of transcending the communal life.[226] In all cases, the hermit revealed himself first and foremost by the choice of a secluded spot, which enabled him to lead the *vita asperga* to which he aspired, usually deep in the woods or in some inaccessible mountain.[227] In his retreat, he devoted himself to prayer. St Peter of Morrone is presented by those who knew him as a man of prayer; every day he recited the whole of the Psalter and the canonical hours, and made five hundred genuflections (a thousand during Lent!).[228] He kept silent for weeks on end and systematically avoided the company of women.[229] Once he had become famous throughout the Abruzzi, he repeatedly changed his home, but the crowds followed him wherever he went.[230] The depositions suggest that extreme austerity was the principal characteristic of eremitical sainthood: St Galgano ate only raw potherbs washed down with a little water and fasted every day but Sunday;[231] Lawrence Loricatus also confined himself to vegetables and a little bread given him by shepherds.[232] But it is in the process of St Peter of Morrone that we find the fullest account of the dietary and vestimentary asceticism of the hermit. The witnesses were all agreed that he wore only cheap, coarse clothes, and hair shirts of horsehair full of knots. He ordinarily went barefoot, except in winter, when he wore wooden clogs; he ate no meat, even when he was ill, nor eggs nor dairy produce nor oil,

---

[225] *PC Lawrence of Subiaco*, p. 68.

[226] For the history and status of the monastic hermits, see J. Leclercq, *Aux sources de la spiritualité occidentale* (Paris, 1964), pp. 225–37.

[227] *PC Peter of Morrone*, p. 328–9: 'vidit dictum fratrem Petrum commorantem in heremis et locis aridis et asperis, scilicet in montibus et in carcere seu cella, de quibus non exibat nisi causa mutandi locum'. Similarly, Lawrence of Subiaco 'non solum solitariam sed montanam, silvosam et asperam elegit sibi et incoluit in heremis mansionem': *PC*, p. 68.

[228] *PC Peter of Morrone*, pp. 333–4.

[229] *Ibid.*, p. 233.

[230] The people of Sulmona and the surrounding area, anxious not to lose track of him, organized veritable manhunts and made a path through the snow to give access to his refuge: *ibid.*, p. 324.

[231] *PC Galgano*, p. 75.

[232] *PC Lawrence of Subiaco*, pp. 68–9.

but only cabbage leaves, turnips, chestnuts and beans. During Lent, he ate nothing at all on Wednesdays and Fridays, and sometimes ate only twice a week.[233] Lastly, the saint-hermits deliberately inflicted great suffering on themselves, as when John Bonus pushed little pieces of wood into the flesh of his feet, which made it extremely painful to walk.[234] These privations and mortifications were presented in the processes as the stages in a spiritual battle against the flesh and the forces of evil, which ended only with death.[235] This was not a metaphor, since the holy hermits were constantly attacked and beaten in their cells by demons.[236] But the Church questioned the meaning of this combat and sought to know whether its violence was the sign of an imperfectly mastered sinful nature or of an authentic sanctity.[237] The anchorite fighting a lonely battle in the front line was, in fact, particularly exposed to falls and deviations.

The strange and extreme nature of this way of life provoked great popular enthusiasm. Of all the saints we meet in the medieval processes of canonization, it is the hermits who performed most miracles during their lifetime. They were credited, first, with a mastery over nature, which was revealed in many different ways; Lawrence Loricatus and Nicholas of Tolentino caused springs to gush beside their cells;[238] John Bonus walked through fire without getting burnt, stopped a downpour which threatened the huts of his companions and even caused a stick of dead wood to burst into flower.[239] The same saint turned water into wine in order to dispel the doubts of his disciplines regarding the real presence of Christ in the sacrament at the altar.[240] But it was above all the successful healers who were appealed to by the faithful who were in search of cures for their ills. Far from discouraging these activities, the hermits forbade those who

---

[233] *PC Peter of Morrone*, pp. 308, 328–30.

[234] *PC John Bonus*, pp. 774, 777–8.

[235] John Bonus exhorted his companions to be 'boni bellatores contra vitia carnis': *PC*, p. 774.

[236] John Bonus was attacked by a malign demon on several occasions: *PC*, p. 774. Nicholas of Tolentino was beaten up by the Devil at least five times: *PC*, art. 20, fol. 6v.

[237] As shown, for example, by the question put to a witness at the process of St Nicholas of Tolentino concerning his asceticism: 'interrogatus si ipse frater Nicolaus fecisset ea intentione ut gastigaret [*sic*] corpus suum ut malis temptacionibus et voluptatibus carnalibus resisteret, dixit quod secundum judicium dicti testis quod ipsa faciebat ut integraliter et mere posset servire Domino nostro Iesu Christo': *PC Nicholas of Tolentino*, fol. 253v.

[238] *PC Lawrence of Subiaco*, 30, p. 79; 92, p. 93; *PC Nicholas of Tolentino*, 221, fol. 82. This was a traditional attribute of hermits; see L. Gnädinger, *Eremitica: Studien zur altfranzösischen Heiligenvita des 12. und 13. Jahrhunderts* (Tübingen, 1972).

[239] *PC John Bonus*, pp. 774, 792–4.

[240] *Ibid.*, pp. 73, 774, 777.

sought their help from simultaneously undergoing medical treatment, opposing Christ to the expensive and ineffectual doctors of this world.[241] They cured by placing their hands on people or, in the case of women or those too ill to travel, by sending them an object they had blessed.[242] In the processes of canonization, it was emphasized that these frequent encounters with the faithful were also the occasion for pastoral activity. The saints did not hesitate to ask the most intimate questions about people's morals, even making the cure conditional on fulfilling exacting conditions, such as reconciliation with enemies or renunciation of adultery.[243] They were the first to emphasize that the miracles which were performed through their intermediary were owed to God alone and that they themselves were only the unworthy instruments of His grace.[244] Sometimes we see them preaching veritable sermons, as when John Bonus 'exhorted all those who came to him to do good, mend their ways and do penance. And many were those who, inspired by his exhortations and his example, were inspired to lead a better life and renounce their evil deeds.'[245]

This aspect became increasingly important with the passage of time. It was linked to a change in the very nature of eremitical sainthood during the course of the thirteenth century. The hermits described in the earliest processes of canonization were true solitaries. The disciples who eventually joined Galgano or Lawrence Loricatus were mentioned at the enquiry only incidentally and seem, in any case, to have been few.[246] In contrast, John Bonus, Peter of Morrone and Nicholas of Tolentino lived their religious experience in a communal context. In the case of the two former, eremitism emerges as a sort of very free

[241] *PC Lawrence of Subiaco*, 57, p. 86: 'vovit Deo beatoque fratri Laurentio se numquam de cetero adhibiturum aliquod medicamentum si mereretur resanari. Et emisso voto plena fide, mox coepit meliorari.'
[242] Peter of Morrone made the sign of the cross over the injured organ or part of the body, or gave husbands small wooden crosses he had blessed to take to their wives: *PC*, p. 234. Nicholas of Tolentino proved a remarkable healer during his lifetime: *PC*, art. 1, fol. 5v.
[243] *PC Lawrence of Subiaco*, p. 70; *PC John Bonus*, p. 784; *PC Peter of Morrone*, pp. 244–6.
[244] Peter of Morrone said to the sick he had healed, 'fili mi, ista sunt dei et non mei', or 'fili mi, recede cum benedictione et nemimi dicas quod fecerim quia non sum homo pro talibus, immo quod Deus vult facere, facit propter graciam suam': *PC*, pp. 234, 272.
[245] *PC John Bonus*, p. 817. See also p. 843. The effectiveness of his preaching and example in the fight against the Cathars, who were very influential in the towns of Romagna, was much stressed: *PC*, p. 783.
[246] *PC Galgano*, p. 76: one witness spoke of a man possessed who had been cured and had subsequently become a hermit under his influence. *PC Lawrence of Subiaco*, p. 98; deposition of a disciple of thirty-four years, Amato of Cantorano.

and mobile cenobitism,[247] and St Nicholas of Tolentino was a regular with close ties to a monastery.[248]

Eremitical sainthood was probably the form of sainthood which, in the Middle Ages, aroused the greatest spontaneous enthusiasm amongst the faithful. The anchorite enjoyed enormous prestige as a result of his ascetic exploits. His very survival, despite the privations and mortifications he voluntarily endured, amounted to a permanent miracle, which could only be explained by divine intervention in his favour. His power over nature and animals and his thaumaturgical gifts made him, during his lifetime, someone out of the ordinary, whom people wanted to meet and whom they regarded with veneration. The ecclesiastical hierarchy, however, did not share their enthusiasm. Between 1198 and 1431, the only hermit to be canonized was Peter of Morrone, Celestine V. We may well suspect that, if he had never left his hermitage of Maiella to become pope, his reputation for sanctity would have remained purely local. The other medieval hermit to be canonized, St Nicholas of Tolentino (d. 1305), had to wait nearly a hundred and fifty years for this honour, even though the enquiries into his life and miracles held in 1325 and 1357 confirmed that his cult enjoyed extraordinary success throughout central and southern Italy.[249] All the other causes remained in limbo for unexplained reasons. This unusually high failure rate contrasts with the lasting popularity of the saint-hermits at the level of the local cult. The Roman Church seems to have feared that the solitary religious life and the quest for ascetic achievements led only to lack of proportion. In the processes concerning anchorites, we see the commissioners asking whether they had not been *fantastici*, and the witnesses insisting that they had not.[250] Further, their excessive austerity might lead ultimately to forms of self-destruction close to *endura*, which was highly ambiguous from a Christian point of view. It comes as no surprise to learn from a witness at the process of Lawrence Loricatus that Cardinal Ugolino had tried to persuade him to relax the

---

[247] John Bonus was harassed by Franciscans who wanted to impose their rule on him: *PC*, p. 846. For communal eremitism in Italy, see K. Elm, 'Italienische Eremitengemeinschaften des 12. und 13. Jahrhunderts', in *L'Eremitismo in Occidente nei secoli XI et XII* (Milan, 1965), pp. 503–29.

[248] *PC Nicholas of Tolentino*, art. 10, fol. 6.

[249] See the many miracles published in *AA.SS.* Sept. III, pp. 636–743. From the fifteenth century, the cult of St Nicholas of Tolentino spread throughout the whole of the Christian world under the influence of the Hermits of St Augustine.

[250] *PC Nicholas of Tolentino*, 1, fol. 25: 'fuit homo boni sensus et non fantasticus'; *ibid.*, p. 173, fol. 153: 'non erat fantasticus, immo sapiens et discretus'.

rigour of his penitential observances.[251] Lastly, the mobility of the anchorite could be interpreted as a sign of instability and detract from his reputation for sanctity. This is the impression given by the prologue of the Office of an English mystical hermit, Richard Rolle, who died at Hampole in 1349,[252] in which the author said, as if to defend his subject for his frequent moves: 'There can be no doubt that it was under divine inspiration that he lived in many places, in order to promote the salvation of many people and also to avoid anything which impeded contemplation, as many very holy Fathers whose Lives we read have done in solitude. Canon law and the decrees of the Church give many reasons why one should leave a place.'[253] In the fourteenth century, when vagabondage was becoming a social plague, the hermit risked being associated with the world of the marginals, and the hagiographers felt obliged to justify their frequent moves by pastoral concerns.

Lastly, the orthodoxy of the solitaries could always be questioned, even in the most seemingly favourable cases. Thus, after a first enquiry into the life and miracles of John Bonus, founder of the 'Zamboniti', held in Mantua in 1251, Innocent IV ordered a second, in 1253, which took place the following year, dealing primarily with the faith of this saint and the miracles he had worked after his death. The witnesses, beginning with the bishop of Cesena, set out to show that the former jongleur had been a *fidelissimus catholicus*, and that he had devoted his energies to fighting the enemies of the Roman Church, whether heretics or supporters of Frederick II.[254] Their lack of culture also made theologians uneasy. In the thirteenth-century processes, the witnesses were at pains to point out that the saints in whose favour they testified, though they lacked formal education, were less ignorant than might be supposed. Lawrence Loricatus, for example, had learned his alphabet and Psalter so well with the monks of Subiaco that, towards the end of his life, he composed prayers in Latin which the regulars then wrote

[251] *PC Lawrence of Subiaco*, 1, p. 69: 'consuluit [Hugolinus] ut discretiorem vitam ageret, quandoquidem propter nimium vitae rigorem poterat potius demereri apud Deum quam mereri. Cui frater Laurentius obediens de predicta austeritate paululum relaxavit.'
[252] Author of the *Melos amoris*, who became a hermit after studying at Oxford (D. Knowles, *La tradition mystique en Angleterre* (Paris, 1961), pp. 58–80). After his death, he was venerated locally as a saint and an office was composed in his honour, in the expectation of a canonization that never materialized.
[253] Woolley, *Richard Rolle*, p. 39.
[254] *PC John Bonus*, pp. 814–55. Significantly, the author of the office of Richard Rolle chose as antiphon the following words: 'Quicumque vult salvus esse, ante omnia opus est ut teneat catholicam fidem' (Woolley, *Richard Rolle*, p. 56).

down.[255] From the end of the thirteenth century, the hermits who were
the subject of an enquiry seem to have been better educated: Peter of
Morrone spent much of his time reading the Bible and writing;[256]
Nicholas of Tolentino had been to school as a child in Sant'Angelo,
and witnesses recalled that he had been an apt pupil.[257] It may be that
the cultural level of the hermits had improved, but it is more likely
that an educated and clerical eremitism stood a greater chance of
winning the favour of the Roman Church than a 'primitive' eremitism.[258]

In the last centuries of the Middle Ages, the Roman Church seems to
have been increasingly suspicious of a sanctity like that of the hermits,
acquired, in a sense, by dint of sheer hard work. It preferred religious
experience pursued within a communal context and attaching greater
importance to the sacramental and liturgical life. It is hardly surprising,
therefore, that the last hermit whose sanctity was consecrated by the medieval papacy was a regular who belonged to the order of the Hermits of St
Augustine, St Nicholas of Tolentino. He synthesized the eremitical
vocation and the apostolic ideal of the Mendicant orders. This zealous and
pious regular 'did everything that true and faithful Christians and Catholics do', in the words of a witness at the process of 1325.[259] He belonged
to the monastery of Tolentino, but lived apart from the other monks, in
a little cell, where he devoted himself to penance and prayer, night and
day.[260] Those who had known him emphasized the twofold nature of his
sanctity: on the one hand, an exceptional degree of asceticism, attested by
the constant war waged against him by demons; on the other, a tireless

[255] PC Lawrence of Subiaco, 98, p. 96. The Liber orationum of B. Lawrence has survived
and is ed. W. Gnandt, Liber orationum beati Laurentii Loricati monachi sublacensis
(Paderborn, 1902). At the process of John Bonus, an illiteratus layman, the story was
told of how he had confounded a canon of Cesena on a question of canon law on the
basis of a passage in the Decretals, 'cum ipse frater Johannes Bonus sit idiota ita quod
aliquam litteram non cognoscebat et ipsum librum numquam viderit nec tetigerit': PC,
p. 774.
[256] PC Peter of Morrone, 62, p. 333. An autobiography is ed. AA.SS. Maii IV, pp. 421–5;
for this text and its authenticity, see Anal. Boll., 16 (1897), pp. 365–70; J. Hollnsteiner,
Römische Quartalschrift, 31 (1923), pp. 29–40.
[257] PC Nicholas of Tolentino, 88, fol. 85: 'libenter ibat ad ecclesiam . . . et ad scholas ad
discendum, ac si esset magnus'.
[258] In his report to Sixtus IV on the canonization of St Bonaventure, the Dominican bishop
of Ventimiglia, John Baptist de' Giudici, referred to a hermit of the time of Eugenius
IV, Francis of Pietrasanta, who was regarded as a saint by the general public, and even
by the pope and cardinals, 'quem postea finis docuit ex ignorantia per omnem vitam
illusiones diaboli fuisse secutum praemiumque durae amisisse penitentiae': ed. in Baluze,
Miscellanea, IV, p. 478.
[259] PC Nicholas of Tolentino, fol. 34.
[260] Ibid., fol. 35.

pastoral zeal and a charity attentive to each person's needs.[261] St Nicholas
was a priest; he was an excellent preacher and a highly regarded confessor;
he celebrated mass with such devotion that all who saw him went away
consoled.[262] Lastly, he visited the sick, intervened with the powerful on
behalf of the poor, and played, whenever he could, the role of peacemaker
and arbiter.[263] His contemporaries seem to have admired this harmonious
balance between asceticism and apostleship and, at his process, were
unstinting in his praise; one phrase recurs: 'he was a scrupulous observer
of the rule'.[264] There could be no clearer indication that, with St Nicholas
of Tolentino, we are already much closer to the ideal of sainthood of the
Mendicant orders than to that of the hermits.

The sainthood of the Mendicants

The men

The appearance of the Mendicant orders, especially the first two, the
Friars Minor and the Preachers, was one of the major events in the history
of the thirteenth-century Church.[265] Their birth and expansion brought
about a profound renewal of the forms of religious life and spirituality.
Central to this change were SS Francis and Dominic, soon represented in
iconography as pillars supporting with their bare hands a church in the
process of collapsing before a somnolent pope.[266] Strange though it may
seem, I will spend little time on St Francis, though his influence was

[261] *Ibid.*, 7, fol. 29v: 'erat homo bone et sancte conversationis et multum fundatus in caritate
et abstinentia, et in oratione erat semper intentus'.
[262] *Ibid.*, 81, fol. 83v; 83, fol. 86: 'et in tantum erat humilis et benignus in audiendo confes-
siones quod videbatur sibi quod esset quidam angelus'; witness 139 (fol. 130) explained
the saint's success as a confessor by the fact that 'ipse frater . . . promittebat facere
penitentiam pro ipso peccatore et faciebat'.
[263] *Ibid.*, 14, fol. 38; 77, fol. 78; 266, fol. 208.
[264] *Ibid.* Another witness was more specific: 'fuit homo mirabilis honestatis, et maxime
orationis ac etiam maxime patientie, magne etiam abstinencie et magne misericordie et
magne observancie regularis': 148, fol. 134.
[265] The two principal histories of the Franciscan order in the Middle Ages are: P. Gratien,
Histoire de la fondation et de l'évolution de l'ordre des Frères Mineurs au XIIIe siècle (Paris
and Gembloux, 1928); J. Moorman, *A history of the Franciscan order, from its origins to
the year 1517* (Oxford, 1968). Sadly, there is no equivalent work for the Dominican order,
but the eight volumes of P. Mortier, *Historie des maîtres généraux de l'ordre des Frères
Prêcheurs* (Paris, 1903–20) are still useful.
[266] The success of the iconographical theme of the 'dream of Innocent III' is well known,
related sometimes to St Francis, sometimes to St Dominic. The most famous illustrations
are those of Giotto at Assisi and Taddeo Gaddi at Florence. See Kaftal 1, c. 314, fig.
360; Kaftal 2, c. 474, fig. 535. See also plate 24.

profound and left its mark not only on the order he founded but on the whole society of his day.[267] This is partly a consequence of the nature of the available documentation. His sanctity was so self-evident and so universally acknowledged that Gregory IX saw no point in submitting it to the test of the process of canonization.[268] Further, apart from a few narrative texts which provide precious but brief indications, we know St Francis only from his own writings, which are few, and through hagiographical sources which were very early used to orient the destiny of the Franciscan order in one direction or another, as a function of the problems posed by its growth.[269] Neither of these is of much help for an objective appreciation of his existence or of the way he was remembered by those who knew him.[270] Further, the personality of the Poverello was on such a grand scale that it to a degree escapes historical determinations. Admittedly, recent specialists have been able to show how much his experience and message owed to the spiritual trends of the twelfth century.[271] But, in the eyes of his contemporaries, the religious synthesis he developed from the moment he renounced his paternal fortune until the stigmatization at La Verna was so radically innovative that many of them did not hesitate to see in him another Christ, *alter Christus*, opening up a new stage in the history of salvation.[272]

Instead, therefore, of trying to define the true nature of the sainthood of the founder of the Minors, I will seek to show what was made of it by

[267] E. Delaruelle, 'Saint François d'Assise et la piété populaire', in *La piété populaire au Moyen Age* (Turion, 1975), pp. 247–75. His influence was particularly strong in the Mediterranean countries, especially Italy; see H. Hefele, *Die Bettelorden und das religiöse Volksleben Ober- und Mittelitaliens im 13. Jahrhundert* (Leipzig, 1910); F. Glaser, *Die Franziskanische Bewegung: Ein Beitrag zur Geschichte sozialer Reformideen im Mittelalter* (Stuttgart and Berlin, 1903).

[268] Bihl, 'De canonizatione S. Francisci'.

[269] Contemporary accounts of St Francis, apart from the hagiographical texts, have been collected by L. Lemmens, *Testimonia minora saeculi XIII de Sancto Francisco* (Quaracchi and Florence, 1926).

[270] It is easy to show the extent to which the two successive interpretations of the personality of St Francis by Thomas of Celano in the *Vita prima* and the *Vita secunda* are linked to stages in the life of the order. See F. de Beer, *La conversion de S. François selon Thomas de Celano: étude comparative des traités relatifs à la conversion en Vita I et Vita II* (Paris, 1963). The same could be said of the *Legenda major* of St Bonaventure. This does not mean that the historian should therefore stop trying to know the 'true' St Francis, as has justly been said by G. Miccoli, 'La conversione di San Francesco secondo Tommaso da Celano', *Studi Medievali*, 5 (1964), pp. 775–92, who proposes a renewal of the 'Francis question' employing new methodologies.

[271] E. d'Ascoli, 'La vita spirituale anteriore a S. Francesco d'Assisi', *Collectanea Franciscana*, 2 (1932), pp. 5–34, 153–78; I. da Milano, 'La spiritualità evangelica anteriore a S. Francesco', *Quaderni di spiritualità francescana*, 4 (1963), pp. 34–70.

[272] Stanislao da Campagnola, *L'Angelo del sesto sigillo*.

his followers. The merits attributed to the saints of his order will reveal, not, of course, the real face of the historical St Francis, but the *novum* of Franciscan sanctity and what distinguished it from the ideas of Christian perfection which had previously prevailed. This approach is all the more justified in that the main problem for the disciples of St Francis, during the later Middle Ages, was how to remain faithful to the rule he left and conform to the ideal model constituted by his person: *Franciscus forma Minorum*. The formula is even truer than it seems: all the religious experiences lived within the order and all the conflicts which rent it from the last decades of the thirteenth century had their origin in this desire to conform to the absolute norm constituted by the sainthood of St Francis.[273]

The situation is significantly different for the other Mendicant orders, whose founders never loomed so large in their history. St Dominic, great man though he was, had nothing like the same influence on the Preachers and his image remains rather unclear.[274] Is this difference attributable to his personality, which was less striking, or to the less charismatic and more structured nature of the order he founded? Both factors were present to a degree it is difficult to establish.[275] But it is undeniable that Dominican sainthood, in the last centuries of the Middle Ages, resulted less from imitation of a person than from fidelity to a rule.[276] In the context of our

---

[273] The expression appears for the first time in the hymn *Salve sancte Pater*, written by Cardinal Thomas of Capua (d. 1243), ed. in *Legendae sancti Francisci Assisiensis s. XIII et XIV conscriptae, Analectae Franciscana*, X (Quaracchi and Florence, 1941), p. 387. The theme is already present in the lives of St Francis by Thomas of Celano, ed. and trans. Desbonnets and Vorreux, *S. François d'Assise: documents*, pp. 237–8, 295 (= *I Celano*, cc. 24, 90). See plates 25, 26.

[274] K. Elm, 'Franziskus und Dominikus. Wirkungen und Antriebskräfte zweier Ordensstifter', *Saeculum*, 22 (1971), pp. 127–47. See also plate 27.

[275] The personality of St Dominic remains elusive, despite the survival of the acts of the canonization processes held in Bologna and the county of Toulouse in 1233 (*Acta canonizationis*, ed. A. Walz, in *Monumenta ordinis Fratrum Praedicatorum historica*, 16 (Rome, 1935), pp. 88–134); there is some interesting biographical material in *Miracula beati Dominici*, collected by Sister Cecilia, ed. A. Walz in *Miscellanea Pio Pashini*, I (Rome, 1948), pp. 293–328. My references are to the acts of the process ed. Vicaire, *Saint Dominique*.

[276] B. Altaner, 'Zur Beurteilung der Persönlichkeit und der Entwicklung der Ordensidee des hl. Dominikus', *Zeitschrift für Kirchengeschichte*, 46 (1927), pp. 396–407. The discretion of Jordan of Saxony, in *Libellus de principiis*, with regard to the founder is emphasized in C. N. L. Brooke, 'St Dominic and his first biographer', *Transactions of the Royal Historical Society*, 5th ser., 17 (1967), pp. 23–40. References to the personality of St Dominic seem to have become important in Dominican hagiography only in the fourteenth century, probaby as a result of the desire for parallelism, in this and other areas, between Minors and Preachers. Thus, in the Legend of B. Venturino of Bergamo, OP (d. 1346) (ed. Grion, 'Legenda beati fratris Venturini', p. 41), the father of the future preacher exhorts him as follows: 'et volo te scire quod sanctus Dominicus cuius habitum induisti fuit unus homo. Et si volueris, potes et tu esse alter Dominicus.'

discussion of the sanctity of the Mendicants, therefore, we are justified in lumping together a person of the first rank like St Dominic and other, lesser figures, such as the Franciscans Benvenuto of Gubbio (d. 1232), Ambrose of Massa (d. 1240) and Simon of Collazzone (d. 1250). All four belonged to the first generations of the new orders and many common features emerge from the evidence collected for their processes of canonization.[277]

They were, first, 'converts', like St Francis himself, that is, men who in their youth or as adults had renounced a life not so much of sin as of relative worldliness, in order to embark on a more demanding religious experience. St Dominic had been a canon of Osma before devoting himself to evangelical preaching in Languedoc;[278] Ambrose of Massa was a priest when he met Brother Morico, one of the first companions of the Poverello, under whose influence he abandoned all his possessions to enter the order of the Friars Minor.[279] Both Simon of Collazzone and Benvenuto of Gubbio belonged to rich and influential families and left noble homes, the former to devote himself to preaching, the latter to care for lepers.[280] They were, to varying degrees, rich, or at least comfortably off, but, at a particular point in their lives, chose voluntarily to follow the path of humility. Among the virtues attributed to them by witnesses at the processes of canonization, it was this which was most frequently mentioned, followed by poverty, with which it was closely connected. In St Dominic, it was revealed by refusal of the episcopal dignity, which he was several times offered.[281] In the Franciscan saints, it went even further: Ambrose of

[277] The first Mendicants to be canonized were SS Francis of Assisi (d. 1226) and Antony of Padua (d. 1231). As we have seen, there is no canonization process for the former. When Gregory IX went to Assisi in 1228, he was satisfied with a rapid enquiry into the miracles performed since the saint's death (*I Celano*, 124). The same was true of St Antony, whom the pope had known and admired. But proper processes were carried out for all the other Mendicant saints. For that of St Dominic, see n. 275 above. The enquiry into the life and miracles of Benvenuto of Gubbio took place at Corneto (Apulia) in 1236; a summary survives, ed. F. M. Delorme in *Dialogus de gestis sanctorum Fratrum Minorum* (Quaracchi and Florence, 1923), pp. 77–132. The process of B. Ambrose of Massa (d. 1240) (Orvieto, 1236) is ed. *AA.SS.* Nov. IV, pp. 571–608. That of B. Simon (d. 1250) was held at Spoleto in 1252; see M. Faloci Pulignani, 'Il Beato Simone de Collazzone e il processo nel 1252', *Miscellanea Francescana*, 12 (1920), pp. 117–32. We may compare with them St Peter Martyr (d. 1252), whose process has not survived, but who was canonized in 1253 by Innocent IV; for the murdered inquisitor and the sources for his life and cult, see A. Dondaine, 'Saint Pierre martyr. Etudes', *AFP*, 23 (1953), pp. 66–162.
[278] *PC Dominic*, p. 61.
[279] *PC Ambrose of Massa*, p. 573.
[280] *PC Simon of Collazzone*, arts. 19, 46, pp. 118, 120; *Dialogus de gestis*, pp. 75ff.
[281] *PC Dominic*, pp. 54–5. I refer above (pp. 309–10) to the importance of the theme of refusing bishoprics, as a demonstration of humility, among the Friars Minor. The same

Massa cooked for the brethren, washed dishes and volunteered for the dirtiest jobs;[282] Simon of Collazzone, the 'son of the contessa', as he is called in some contemporary texts, neglected his person and wore the dirtiest clothes he could find, 'despising himself because of God'.[283] But perhaps the most remarkable aspect of this desire for humility is that it incorporated the traditional demonstrations of asceticism, by conferring on them an evangelical significance: like the hermits, St Dominic scourged himself, abstained from all meat and never slept in a bed, but always on the bare ground.[284] We do not see, however, in him or in the other early Mendicant saints, any tendency to destroy the body by inflicting excessive penances on it. Asceticism and mortification figured in their life as instruments of renunciation and expressions of the desire to imitate the suffering Christ.[285] Besides, the witnesses were very alive to the fact that these saints

was true of the Preachers, at least to begin with. As well as St Dominic (see *Saint Dominique*, ed. Vicaire, pp. 54–5), the Dominican preacher Ambrose Sansedoni (d. 1287) refused a mitre 'magis volens Deo cum fratribus sui ordinis in subjectione servire quam temporalis honoris cathedra sublimari' (*Vita*, ed. M. H. Laurent, *Anal. Boll.*, 58 (1940), p. 380). But it was considered meritorious to accept hierarchical office within the order itself and perform such duties worthily, as we see from the process of Simon of Collazzone, who was provincial minister in the Marches: *PC Simon of Collazzone*, art. 44, p. 120. Responsibilities of this type were seen as duties perfectly compatible with the practice of humility.

[282] *PC Ambrose of Massa*, p. 573.
[283] *PC Simon of Collazzone*, art. 38, p. 119.
[284] *PC Dominic*, p. 81.
[285] *PC Dominic*, pp. 65, 69. This point is, in my opinion, of fundamental importance, given that, during the thirteenth century, in the quarrel between them and the seculars, the Mendicants – and especially the Franciscans – made themselves apologists for the most epic abstinence and asceticism. But the teaching of St Francis on this point is quite clear; on many occasions, he stressed the necessity of discretion in the practice of penance: 'if, in eating and drinking, we are required to deny ourselves the superfluity which is damaging to body and soul, how much more should we deny ourselves excessive mortification, since God desires mercy not sacrifice' (*Légende de Pérouse*, ed. Desbonnets and Vorreux, *S. François d'Assise*, pp. 874–5). He also forbade the Friars to wear next to the skin the iron bands, breastplates and excessively coarse hair shirts favoured by hermits (*ibid.*, pp. 875, 971). He also suppressed a regulation, issued in his absence by Gregory of Naples, prohibiting the brethren from eating meat on certain days, asking 'whether it was possible to impose rules contrary to gospel liberty on those who observed the Holy Gospel' (*Chronica XXIV generalium*, pp. 31, 39). This was also the attitude of Bernard of Quintavalle (*ibid.*, p. 43). Nothing would be more false, of course, than to present St Francis and his first companions as 'bon viveurs', but it is undeniable that, for them, asceticism was simply a means, as it was for St Dominic. These moderate positions were abandoned by St Bonaventure who, in the *Apologia pauperum*, saw abstinence as an essential element in Christian perfection (*Opera omnia*, VIII (Quaracchi, 1898), pp. 233ff). This was also the position of the anonymous Franciscan author of the treatise *Manus quae contra*, directed against William of Saint-Amour. His work provoked a fierce riposte from Gerard of Abbeville who, in 1269, produced the *Contra adversarium perfectionis christianae*, ed. S. Clasen, *AFH*, 31 (1938), pp. 276–329; 32 (1939), pp. 89–200; the Parisian master argued in particular, against the Mendicants, that 'the fact of eating and drinking wine,

performed the harshest tasks joyfully and without visible distress.[286] Love of poverty, lastly, played an important role in their life: St Dominic, according to John Hispannus, 'was so good that he led the brethren of his order to abandon and despise all temporal property, live in poverty, no longer ride on horseback, live off alms and carry nothing with them on their travels'.[287] The Franciscan saints were no less zealous: Ambrose of Massa went out to beg on behalf of the other brethren, as result of which his feet got badly chapped, while Simon of Collazzone, who had been 'noble, powerful and wealthy', renounced his possessions to follow Christ.[288]

None of these virtues, however, seems to have been of paramount importance in the appreciation of the sanctity of the Mendicants. Its originality lay in the fact that the search for merit was always subordinated to love of one's neighbour. All their activities were organized round the apostolate and the desire to win souls for God which was central to their vocation. This orientation towards others and towards the world was referred to in the thirteenth-century processes by the term *zelus animarum* or *zelus spiritualis*.[289] St Dominic proposed going to preach the Christian faith to the 'Cumans', whose ravages he had observed during his travels in Germany. He also considered 'giving his life and soul to convert the Saracens', before finally devoting his energies to the battle against heresy in Languedoc and the county of Toulouse.[290] One witness at the process in Bologna, attempting to summarize the activities of the founder of the Preachers, said that 'he appeared to have more zeal than anyone else, to his knowledge, for the salvation of the human race'.[291] Poverty and humility, from this perspective, were above all necessary conditions for the apostolic message to be heard. If it was rejected, the saints bore the

---

as did our Lord, in no way detracted from Christian perfection' (p. 304) and that to break a fast in case of need was not a fault (pp. 318–29). He was returning, perhaps without realizing it, to the original position of the founders. See J. J. Sullivan, *Fast and abstinence in the first order of Saint Francis* (Washington, 1957).

[286] There are frequent references to joy in the process of St Dominic: *PC*, pp. 54, 65, 73 etc. For the place of joy in primitive Franciscan spirituality, see *Dicta beati Aegidii Assisiensis*, ed. L. Lemmens (Quaracchi and Florence, 1903), p. 99: 'ex sancta devotione, gaudio et letitia meretur homo lucrari meritum et coronam martyrii'.

[287] *PC Dominic*, p. 53; see also pp. 46, 68.

[288] *PC Ambrose of Massa*, p. 573; *PC Simon of Collazzone*, arts. 7, 35, pp. 117, 119.

[289] *PC Dominic*, pp. 47, 69. *PC Ambrose of Massa*, pp. 574–5: 'erat sollicitus peccatoribus penitentie medelam adhibere'.

[290] *PC Dominic*, p. 43–4, 53–4, 69, 72, 73. C. Thouzellier, 'La pauvreté, arme contre l'Albigéisme en 1206', *Revue de l'histoire des religions*, 151 (1957), pp. 79–92.

[291] *Ibid.*, p. 43: another witness added that 'his charity and compassion extended not only to the faithful, but even to the infidel, pagans and as far as the damned in hell'.

ordeal bravely, ready even, if need be, for martyrdom.[292] But their love of their neighbour excluded all spiritualism. The first generations of Mendicants were distinguished by a great capacity for compassion towards all who suffered and an active charity, especially towards the poor and the sick.[293]

This faith oriented towards others could not be communicated if it did not itself have firm roots. Bible reading, prayer and contemplation were, accordingly, important in the life of the saints.[294] They gladly followed the offices, celebrated mass and found time, even in the most difficult circumstances, to engage in personal prayer.[295] They were also irreproachable and inflexible with regard to chastity.[296] Total obedience towards their superiors and loyalty to the rule was central to their life and guaranteed the effectiveness of their pastoral ministry. The description of demonstrations of this submissive spirit accounts for many of the articles: St Dominic was described as 'a zealot for regular observance';[297] among the Franciscan saints, the relationship between sanctity and fulfilment of the requirements of the rule was also very close. This was not just an ideal which was recommended as a model. It truly constituted the norm of all perfection and only those who followed it to the letter could hope one day to share the glory of the Founder.[298] On this point, the Mendicants seem

---

[292] *Ibid.*, p. 55: 'he had heard him expressing the wish to be scourged, cut to pieces and die for his faith in Jesus Christ'; see also p. 68.

[293] St Dominic often went out of his way to console his brethren and even strangers he met: *PC*, pp. 62–3, 73. So did Simon of Collazzone (*PC*, arts. 19, 32, pp. 118–19), who also paid special attention to lepers (art. 43, p. 120). Ambrose of Massa sought medicines for the poor (*PC*, pp. 573, 574) and sometimes abandoned mass in order to tend the sick (p. 575).

[294] *PC Dominic*, p. 55: 'he always carried the Gospel of St Matthew and the epistles of St Paul, and read them frequently, till he almost knew them by heart'. For the new balance established by St Dominic between theology and missionary activity, see J. W. Krank, 'Die Spannung zwischen Ordensleben und wissenschaftlicher Arbiet im frühen Domenikanerorden', *Archiv für Kulturgeschichte*, 49 (1967), pp. 164–207.

[295] *PC Simon of Collazzone*, art. 20, p. 118: 'lectiones Domini libenter audiebat et divina officia cum summa diligentia celebrabat'. *PC Ambrose of Massa*, p. 574: 'et libenter cantabat missam et in officiis divinis morabatur'.

[296] *PC Dominic, passim. PC Ambrose of Massa*, p. 573: 'castitate praecipuus, substinere non valens in vitio luxuriae devolutos, quorum mala sibi quantum poterat disciplicebant'.

[297] *PC Dominic*, p. 46. Another witness said that he had seen him 'observe the rule and observance of the Friars Preacher very strictly, readily granting dispensations to the brethren, but never to himself': *ibid.*, p. 44.

[298] *PC Ambrose of Massa*, p. 573: 'tanta fuit obedientia ut nunquam praecepta sua in aliquo praetermiserit sed die et nocte per aquas et nives, in fame et siti, in frigore et nuditate, se ipsum ad obedientiam interius et exterius colligebat'. Simon of Collazzone is presented as 'zelator ordinis' (art. 8) and 'observator ordinis' (art. 12), who 'diligebat ordinem S. Francisci' (art. 13): *PC*, pp. 117–18. Benvenuto of Gubbio appears in his process as a faithful imitator of St Francis: *Dialogus*, pp. 73–6.

close to the old religious orders, especially the monks, but their ethos was very different in that their principal objective was apostolic.

The fact that the ministry of the Word was central to Franciscan and Dominican sainthood was absolutely new and important in a way it is difficult for us to appreciate after centuries of post-Tridentine Catholicism. But at the beginning of the thirteenth century, with very rare exceptions, no-one spoke to the faithful about God in simple, clear language. Bishops had other concerns; even when they took the trouble to preach, they were not always understood by their flock.[299] Priests were generally incapable of it and monks and hermits only exceptionally addressed the laity, since this was not their vocation. The Mendicant saints, on the other hand, owed their prestige to the fact that they were in the service of the Gospel and dedicated their life to propagating it. According to a Languedocian witness, Abbot William Peyrac, St Dominic 'devoted himself to preaching with such fervour that he exhorted and obliged the Brethren to preach the Word of God day and night, in churches and private houses, in the fields and on the roads, in a word, everywhere, and to speak only of God'.[300] An Italian witness declared that 'when he preached, he found words so disturbing that he was very often himself moved to tears and made his listeners weep, so much so that he had never heard a man whose words were so effective at moving people to contrition and tears'.[301] With minor variations, we find the same admiring expressions with regard to the Franciscan saints, who were also indefatigable preachers.[302] There was, however, one difference between the Preachers and the Minors in this regard; while in St Dominic and his spiritual sons, preaching was backed up by study and intellectual labour, there was nothing comparable among the Franciscans, whose 'simplicity' was universally praised.[303] Unlike the

---

[299] See n. 66, p. 298 above.

[300] *PC Dominic*, p. 82. See also plate 28.

[301] *Ibid.*, p. 63.

[302] *PC Simon of Collazzone*, art. 10, p. 118: 'tantum zelum animarum habebat idem frater Symon quod nec propter frigus nec propter nives dimittebat quominus iret ad castella et villas, cause predicationis'.

[303] *PC Dominic*, p. 55: 'orally and in correspondence, Brother Dominic exhorted the brethren of the order constantly to study the Old and the New Testament'. For the simplicity of the Friars Minor hostile to the 'learning that puffs up', see *PC Benvenuto of Gubbio*, in *Dialogus*, p. 95, and the examples quoted by L. Izzo, *La semplicità evangelica nella spiritualità di S. Francesco d'Assisi* (Rome, 1971). Caution is needed here, however, as, in practice, the Franciscans soon began to incline towards learning, as shown by D. Berg, *Armut und Wissenschaft: Beiträge sur Gechichte des Studienwesens der Bettelorden in 13. Jahrhundert* (Düsseldorf, 1977). See also the volume of essays ed. G. Arnaldi, *Le scuole degli Ordini Mendicanti* (Todi, 1978).

hagiographical texts, the acts of the enquiries which have survived make no mention of the 'holy folly' which characterized some companions of the Poverello.[304] But we do find a faint echo of the words of St Francis, who boasted of being *illiteratus et idiota* and declared to the chapter of The Mats, 'the Lord told me that he wanted to make me a new fool (*paçcus*) in the world, and God did not wish to lead us by any other science than that'.[305]

Despite these differences, which in any case diminished after 1250, the sainthood of the Mendicants constituted from the beginning a coherent and profoundly original reality, which combined the ascetic rigour of the hermits, monastic fidelity to the rule, and the apostolic spirit, demonstrated by preaching the Gospel. Living in the world without leading a worldly life, obliged to recite divine office but not cloistered, the new orders offered a model with a very high moral and spiritual charge. This did not prevent some of them from having been, in their lifetime and even more after their death, great healers.[306] But it seems to have been their charity and their tireless pastoral zeal, rather than their miracles or ascetic exploits, which appealed to the faithful. It is this aspect of their sanctity that the papacy chose to exalt, by canonizing, between 1228 and 1253, SS Francis of Assisi, Antony of Padua, Dominic and Peter Martyr.

When we try to establish what had become of this ideal by the end of the thirteenth and early fourteenth centuries, through the processes of SS Louis of Anjou (d. 1297) and Thomas Aquinas (d. 1274), we find both the persistence of certain features characteristic of the age of the founders and a perceptible change which is not entirely due to the complexity of the enquiries of 1306 and 1319.[307] The young Angevin prince, who had renounced the crown of Sicily, then the bishopric of Toulouse urged on

[304] The Life of Brother Ginepro (d. 1258) shows him entering, naked, towns such as Assisi and Viterbo: see *Vita fratris Juniperi*, in *Chronica XXIV generalium*, cc. IX, XI; G. Petrocchi, ed., *La Vita di frate Ginepro, vilgarizzamento* (Bologna, 1960), pp. 52–8, 68–70. For 'holy folly' in the Middle Ages, see S. Hilpisch, 'Die Torheit um Christi Willen', *Zeitschrift für Aszese und Mystik*, 6 (1931), pp. 21ff; E. Benz, 'Heilige Narrheit', *Kyrios*, 3 (1938), pp. 1ff.

[305] *Légende de Pérouse*, para. 114, p. 987.

[306] The regulars interrogated about St Dominic at the Bologna process did not credit him with any miracles. But many of the Languedocian witnesses declared they had seen him delivering those possessed by devils and healing the sick (*PC Dominic*, pp. 79, 84). At the process of Ambrose of Massa, seventy-six miracles were attested by 130 witnesses.

[307] For St Louis of Anjou, see *Processus canonizationis et legendae variae*, pp. 1–274. The acts of the process of St Thomas Aquinas (Naples, 1319) were ed. M. H. Laurent, in *Fontes vitae S. Thomas Aquinatis*, IV (Saint-Maximin, 1937), pp. 272–518, and later by A. Ferrua, *S. Thomas Aquinatis vitae fontes praecipuae* (Alba, 1968), pp. 203–350. My references are to the more recent edition.

him by Boniface VIII, was Franciscan in his rejection of power and wealth.[308] At the Marseilles process, witnesses emphasized his love of poverty and his charity to the disinherited.[309] His humility and his desire to convert pagans to the Christian faith were also firmly in the tradition of the Poverello, to whom certain depositions seem to have tried, sometimes in a rather forced and clumsy way, to liken him.[310] But the austerity of life required by the Rule seems to become, in him, moralism. Both articles and witnesses stress at every possible opportunity that he went to great lengths to avoid the company of women, refusing even to embrace his mother and sisters.[311] Similarly, he had as little contact as possible with the laity, preferring the company of the clergy, particularly the Friars Minor, who flocked round him during his captivity in Catalonia and in Naples and Toulouse.[312] In some ways, this mistrust of profane realities seems far removed from the original Franciscan ethos. We observe at the process – but probably also in the real life of St Louis of Anjou, since the witnesses were unanimous on this point – a return in force of the spirituality of the *contemptus mundi*: flight from the world, abstinence and penance, an 'angelic life'.[313] The Devil himself made an appearance at this enquiry, in the form of a terrible cat which vanished when the young prince made the sign of the cross.[314] Further, the sanctity of Louis of Anjou did not follow from a conversion. On the contrary, Brother William of Cornillon praised him for having 'preserved throughout his life his baptismal innocence'.[315] In St Louis of Anjou, Christian perfection appears less the result of a transformation of the carnal man into a being inspired

---

[308] See above, pp. 355–8; J. Paul, 'Evangélisme et Franciscanisme chez Louis d'Anjou', in *Les Mendiants en pays d'Oc au XIIIe siècle* (Toulouse, 1973), pp. 375–401; Paul, 'S. Louis d'Anjou, franciscain et évêque de Toulouse', in *Les évêques, les clercs et le roi (1250–1300)* (Toulouse, 1972), pp. 59–90.

[309] *PC Louis of Anjou*, art. 15, p. 12 (he met and embraced a leper); art. 17, p. 13: 'reputans esse perditum nisi quod esset amore Christi pauperibus distributum'. See also arts. 34–6, 14–42, pp. 16, 17.

[310] The articles refer to St Louis' efforts to convert Jews and Saracens to Christianity (*PC*, art. 16, p. 13), but the witnesses interrogated on this point spoke only of Jews and some even cast doubt on the reality of the second point. It would appear that, as in art. 15 (kissing the leper), there was an attempt to liken him to St Francis (Paul, 'Evangélisme', p. 388).

[311] *PC Louis of Anjou*, arts. 4, 9, pp. 11, 12.

[312] *Ibid.*, art. 12, p. 12.

[313] The expression *vita angelica* was used by the Benedictine abbot of Saint-Victor of Marseilles, William of Sabran (*PC*, p. 79); but it was also used by a Franciscan like William of Saint-Marcel (*ibid.*, p. 81).

[314] *PC Louis of Anjou*, art. 21, p. 13 (referring to a story by his brother, Raymund Berenger).

[315] *Ibid.*, p. 31: 'credit . . . quod innocentia baptismalis duravit in eo sine macula quamdiu vixit'.

by the Holy Spirit than the defence of a miraculously transmitted inheritance. At the same time, there was a narrowing of apostolic perspectives.
His renunciation of a bishopric, presented as a sign of his humility, seems
primarily motivated by the fear of not being able to find salvation through
devoting himself to the *cura animorum*.[316] In all these ways, St Louis of
Anjou is nearer to the monastic ideal than to that of the enthusiastic
apostles of the Franciscan springtime.

Even more striking is the change in the attitude of the saints to study.
It is hardly surprising that the son of Charles II should have received a
sound scholarly education in his youth. What is more surprising, however,
is the importance attached to learning in the appreciation of his sanctity.
A lay witness respectfully described him as a *magnus clericus* and referred
to the six or seven pack animals needed to transport his books.[317] Other
depositions reveal his liking for *disputatio* of intellectual and doctrinal
questions, and the time he spent reading the works of St Bernard.[318] When
he went to Paris in 1297, there was talk of awarding him the title of master
of theology, but he declined this offer.[319] The young prince-bishop who
had developed a taste for intellectual labour and devoted most of his time
to it thus appears as a scholar. The regulars, mostly Friars Minor, who
gave evidence in his favour, in order to emphasize his supernatural dimension, claimed that such great learning in a man so young could not but
be a gift of God.[320]

There was similar praise of intellectual activity, though to a greater
degree, in the process of St Thomas Aquinas. The image which emerges
from the enquiry into his life and merits held in Naples in 1319 is, admittedly, primarily that of someone humble, chaste and sober, indifferent to
food and clothes, assiduous in prayer and divine office.[321] The witnesses
offer little detail about these virtues or the way in which the saint lived
them, except in regard to an episode which occurred in his youth, when

---

[316] The Franciscan William of Saint-Marcel reports him as saying: 'sufficit michi si possum reddere racionem Deo anima mea': *PC*, p. 80.

[317] See the deposition of the 'domicellus Bermundus de Rocca', *ibid.*, pp. 31–42, especially p. 35; see also p. 82.

[318] *Ibid.*, arts. 2, 23 (learned discussions with Richard de Mediavilla, in Naples), 26, pp. 11, 14, 15.

[319] *Ibid.*, art. 44, p. 17.

[320] *Ibid.*, p. 51: 'dicebatur . . . quod magis sciebat dominus Ludovicus quam magister et istud dicebatur provenisse ex infusione gracie Dei'. See also p. 72.

[321] *PC Thomas Aquinas*, p. 204: 'ipse frater Thomas fuit homo magne honestatis, munditie et sanctitatis, et cotidie, dum erat sanus, celebrabat et continue vacabat studio et orationibus. Audivit etiam quod fuit virgo dum vixit, sicut ab utero matris sue.'

his family, wishing to distract him from his religious vocation, arranged
for a charming young woman to meet and seduce him. The unflinching
resistance he offered to this temptation gave him a lifelong immunity to
the promptings of the flesh.[322] To those who had known him, St Thomas
appeared to be 'entirely spiritual and wholly cut off from earthly things'.[323]
He struck people by his absent-mindedness, which revealed his indifference to material things and, above all, by the tireless zeal with which he
laboured, allowing himself only the minimum of leisure in which to eat
and sleep.[324] But, at the process of 1319, the man is obscured by the work.
His personal merits would not have been sufficient if he not been the
author of several dozen theological treatises, carefully listed by the logothete Bartholomew of Capua. That they were inspired was not in doubt
and their growing success attested to their permanence.[325]

The sainthood of the *Doctor communis* was primarily intellectual and
doctrinal: prayer, meditation and writing were the three principal aspects
of a life devoted to contemplation and the elucidation of the divine mysteries. In the face of this form of perfection, which distinguished him from
the other saints of his day, it is tempting to see St Thomas as an exception.
He belongs, however, to the Mendicants, not only because he was a
member of the order of Preachers, but in the spirit which inspired his
labours. Many witnesses emphasized how much his works had helped
Christians, and even the laity, to deepen their understanding of the verities
of the faith.[326] We rediscover here the pastoral dimension which was central to the Mendicant ideal: *Contemplata aliis tradere*. The motto of the
Dominicans found its finest illustration in St Thomas Aquinas. But times
had changed since the generations of the founders. In the fourteenth cen-

---

[322] This episode, described at the process by William of Tocco (*ibid.*, p. 291) gave rise to
the legend of the *cingulum castitatis* brought to St Thomas from heaven by two angels.

[323] *Ibid.*, pp. 315, 336.

[324] *Ibid.*, p. 210: 'numquam preter quietis naturalis horas horam habebat aliquam otiosam,
sed aut legebat aut scribebat aut scribi faciebat'.

[325] *Ibid.*, pp. 328–31; see also p. 327: 'scripta ipsius fratris Thome, licet post eius mortem
a multis et magnis impugnata fuerunt et reprehentionum morsibus attemptata, tamen
nunquam decrevit eius auctoritas sed semper invaluit et diffusa sunt ubique terrarum
cum cultu et reverentia, et sicut idem testis audivit a multis et multis, etiam ad barbaras
nationes'. For relations between Bartholomew of Capua and Thomas Aquinas, see I.
Taurisano, 'Discepoli e biografi di S. Tommaso', in *S. Tommaso d'Aquino: miscellanea
storica-artistica* (Rome, 1924), pp. 155–8; A. Nitschke, 'Die Reden des Logothetes Bartholomaeus von Capua', *QFIAB*, 35 (1955), pp. 226–74. See also plate 29.

[326] *PC Thomas Aquinas*, p. 327: 'viam aperuit intelligentibus ad sciendum . . . quilibet
secundum modulum sue cogitationis seu capacitatis potest facile capere fructum ex
scriptis eiusdem, et propterea etiam layci et parum intelligentes querunt et appetunt ipsa
scripta habere'.

tury, the Roman Church preferred the defence of Catholic doctrine and orthodoxy to preaching the Gospel to the infidel, or even the battle, in the field, against heresy. While the many martyrs that the Mendicant orders asked the papacy to canonize did not find favour, the magisterial theological synthesis of Aquinas earned him the highest honour.[327]

The women

We should not allow the great stature of the male Mendicant saints who were canonized in the medieval period, from St Francis of Assisi to St Thomas Aquinas, to make us forget that many women from the same movement were accorded sainthood and the honour of a public cult. This is hardly surprising given that the preaching of the new orders had, as is well known, exercised a profound influence on women, to the point where a whole satirical literature soon accused the brethren of being rather too eager to ingratiate themselves in the hope of increasing their power within lay society.[328] At this point, I will discuss only the saints whose religious experience was lived within the context of the conventual life. But we should remember that they were in a minority in relation to those who sought to realize the ideal of the founders while remaining in the world and the lay state.[329]

The position of women in thirteenth-century society prevented them from putting into practice, without major modifications, the rules of either St Francis or St Dominic, neither of whom, in any case, had intended to found an order for women. The way of life of the nuns was inevitably very different from that of the Minors or Preachers, which was chiefly characterized by the importance of preaching and intellectual labour, and mobility in the service of apostleship. Consequently, the Franciscan and Dominican women saints appear, at first sight, to be very similar to the traditional nuns whose way of life they shared, since they, too, were strictly enclosed.[330] However, a closer examination of the canonization processes of SS Clare of Assisi, Margaret of Hungary and Clare of Montefalco reveals that, in spite of the constraints imposed by their condition

---

[327] See below, pp. 418–19.

[328] For example, in fabliaux such as 'The Cordelier's Breeches' or 'Brother Denis', where the virulence is equalled only by the frankness.

[329] For the influence of Franciscan spirituality on lay sanctity, see above, pp. 207ff.

[330] For the lifestyle of the first Clares, see E. Grau, 'Die Kluasur im Kloster S. Damiano zu Lebzeiten der Heiligen Klara', in *Studia historico-ecclesiastica: Festgabe für Prof. Luchesius G. Spätling* (Rome, 1977), pp. 311–46.

and canonical status, these women developed within their convents an original spirituality, which was very different from that of the Benedictine nuns.[331] What relates these three figures to the Mendicant ideal is, first, the great importance they attached in their life to humility and poverty. The witnesses at the process of St Clare of Assisi emphasized her desire for abasement, which found expression in washing the sisters' feet; they also recalled her efforts to persuade the papacy to recognize and confirm the 'privilege of poverty' which was central to her religious experience.[332] St Margaret of Hungary is known to have lived in great poverty and distributed to the poor the money she was given by her brother, King Stephen. Under the influence of her director of conscience, a Hungarian Dominican by the name of Marcel, who considered humility to be 'the mother and guardian of the virtues', she systematically sought out the roughest tasks.[333] But it is probably Clare of Montefalco who travelled

---

[331] The enquiry into the life and miracles of St Clare of Assisi (d. 1253) took place in the year of her death, and she was canonized in 1255 by Alexander IV. The text has survived in a version in fifteenth-century Umbrian dialect, ed. Lazzeri, 'Il processo di canonizzazione de S. Chiara d'Assisi'. For the value of this source and the other contemporary hagiographical material concerning her, see M. Fassebinder, 'Untersuchungen über die Quellen zum Leben der Hl. Klara von Assisi', *Franziskanische Studien*, 23 (1936), pp. 296–335; Reber, *Die Gestaltung des Kultes weiblicher Heiliger*, pp. 47–52. The process of Margaret of Hungary (d. 1270), a Dominican nun, took place in 1276, but she was canonized only in 1943 by Pius XII. The acts of the enquiry have survived in part, but the lost sections seem to have dealt exclusively with her miracles. They are ed. G. Fraknoi, *Monumenta Romana Episcopatus Vespriniensis*, I (Budapest, 1896), pp. 163–383. There is a useful bibliography in E. Pasztor, sv Margherita d'Ungheria, santa, in *BS*, VIII (Rome, 1968), cc. 796–800. The process of Clare of Montefalco (d. 1308), canonized in 1881 by Leo XIII, took place in 1318–19. The full text does not survive, but large parts of it are currently being edited by E. Menesto and C. Leonardi: see E. Menesto, *Il processo di canonizzazione di Chiara da Montefalco* (Florence and Perugia, 1984). Her precise canonical status poses problems: she spent her childhood and adolescence in a reclusorium directed by her sister, Joan. It was so successful that, in 1290, the little community adopted the rule of St Augustine in order to be attached to a *religio* approved by the hierarchy. This does not mean, as has sometimes been assumed, that St Clare joined the order of the Hermits of St Augustine. Up to her death, she and her community were in close contact with the Franciscans and much influenced by their spirituality, as shown by S. Nessi, 'S. Chiara da Montefalco e il Francescanesimo', *Miscellanea Francescana*, 69 (1969), pp. 369–408. Also, St Francis of Assisi is constantly referred to in the process of canonization; at the moment of her death, the saint cried out: 'ecce vita eterna, sanctus Franciscus meus': *PC*, fol. 423; though one witness said: 'soror Clara predicta tenuerat vitam sancti Francisci et ivit post vitam Iesu Christi': fols. 925–6.

[332] For the 'privilege of poverty' and its importance to St Clare, see P. Sabatier, 'Le privilège de la pauvreté', *Revue d'histoire franciscaine*, 1 (1924), pp. 1–54, 469–82; E. Grau, 'Das "Privilegium pauperitas" der Hl. Klara, Geschichte und Bedeutung', *Wissenschaft und Weisheit*, 38 (1975), pp. 17–25.

[333] See, for example, the *Vita beate Margarete de Ungaria*, written between 1274 and 1276 by a Hungarian Dominican, ed. in *Inquisitio de vita b. Margaritae ab Ungaria* (Vatican City, 1943), pp. 166ff. At the process, her charitable activities were described by one of

furthest down this road; ready to perform any service, she busied herself cooking, washing up, cleaning and caring for the old and sick sisters.[334] Once she had become Superior of the community, she continued to do dirty jobs and, refusing any hierarchical title, continued to be called by her Christian name.[335] In her exhortations to her companions, she emphasized selflessness above all.[336] In the early years of her life of reclusion, before the anchorage she directed adopted the rule of St Augustine, she did not hesitate to go out and beg to assure the survival of her little community; thirty-four years later, witnesses still spoke of this episode with emotion and stressed the joy – very Franciscan – with which she had accepted suffering, ordeals and death itself.[337] The behaviour of these women was rooted in a profound devotion to the suffering Christ, which impelled them to accept serenely, and even search out, opportunities to identify with the holy victim.

However, their sanctity differed from that of the founders of the Mendicant orders and their spiritual sons in the importance in it of asceticism. To SS Francis and Dominic, this was only a means to attain a certain inner freedom, which precluded any search for suffering for its own sake or to excess.[338] Among the female saints, in contrast, this *discretio* was lacking and mortification appears as the fundamental aspect of perfection. Clare of Assisi astonished the nuns among whom she lived by her amazing abstinence; she was content, each year, with bread and water during two Lents and slept on a bed of vine shoots with a little straw for pillow.[339] One might suspect the witnesses at the canonization process in 1254, most of whom were sisters in the nunnery she had founded and which she

---

her companions as follows: 'interrogata de quo fuit de tanta bonitate vite, respondit in serviendo infirmos, lavando capita eis et servientibus illud faciebat, et dabat eis comedere et faciebat eis lectos et balnea et radebat eis capita quando oportebat et scopabat infirmariam et alia servitia quae facere poterat': *PC*, p. 76.

[334] *PC Clare of Montefalco*, fols. 22–3.

[335] *Ibid.*, fols. 55, 177.

[336] She longed 'quod domine haberent humilitatem et fundarentur in humilitate, tamquam in fundamento virtutis et dicebat quod precipue de hac virtute humilitatis sepe sepius loquebatur et docebat et instruebat sorores dicti monasterii': *ibid.*, fol. 54; see also fol. 201.

[337] The community had, in fact, at one time been extremely poor, depending entirely on alms (*ibid.*, fols. 42–5; 166). Spiritual joy is also mentioned in the process of St Clare of Assisi (*PC*, p. 453): 'sempre era allegra nel Signore e mai se vedeva turbata'.

[338] See above, pp. 340–1.

[339] One nun said that the life of St Clare had been amazing 'per la molta abstinentia, la quale non pareva se dovesse potere fare da uomo': *PC Clare of Assisi*, p. 469. In the same vein, another sister claimed that she had sanctified herself 'in molta maceratione della carne et molta asperita della vita': *ibid.*, p. 470; see also pp. 448, 475.

directed till her death, of having exaggerated the rigour of her penitential practices with an edifying intent. But we know, from other evidence, that it was real, since St Francis himself had to ask her to relax her fasts, which she did only from a spirit of obedience.[340] The harshness of St Clare with regard to her body, however, pales into insignificance when compared with the passion for self-destruction which inspired the other two women saints. Margaret of Hungary, in her Dominican convent on the Isle of the Danube, assaulted her flesh in every conceivable fashion, not out of faithfulness to the rule, which did not demand it, but of her own volition, as one witness at her process in 1276 declared.[341] She also scourged herself frequently, using three different types of switch; she had iron rings round her limbs and cords next to her skin so tight that they caused sores.[342] Clare of Montefalco engaged in prolonged fasts, scourged herself and often plunged her feet into ice, keeping them there for the time it took to say a *Pater noster* with her arms outstretched. In her exhortations to the sisters about her, she ceaselessly preached penitence, seen as a preparation for the encounter with the celestial Husband.[343]

All three, lastly, fervently longed for a bloody martyrdom. Clare of Assisi would like to have gone to Morocco and given her life for the faith, like the first companions sent there by St Francis.[344] Margaret of Hungary joyfully anticipated the arrival of the Tartars, which would allow her to die for Christ. But in her, the longing for death, the fear of sin and the horror of men seem closely connected. On many occasions, she considered cutting off her nose to make herself hideous and sure of preserving her virginity.[345] We find the same preoccupation in Clare of Montefalco, who claimed she would rather spend the rest of her days in hell than allow a man to approach her![346] Admittedly, the male saints, too, cultivated the

[340] *Ibid.*, p. 460.
[341] *PC Margaret of Hungary*, p. 460.
[342] *Ibid.*, pp. 182, 204, 251. According to one sister who had lived with her 'ista sancta sic taliter destruxerat corpus suum et faciem quod quasi deformata erat in facie': *ibid.*, p. 254.
[343] *PC Clare of Montefalco*, fols. 56, 78, 153, 159, 162, 342.
[344] *PC Clare of Assisi*, p. 465: 'voleva sostenare el martiro per amore del Signore'.
[345] *PC Margaret of Hungary*, pp. 184, 193 and especially p. 264: 'Rogo Deum pro Christianis quod ipsi [Tartari] non veniant, sed quantum est pro me, vellem quod iam ipsi venissent, quia libenter sustinerem pro fide Christi mortem'. She had threatened her family that she would mutilate her face every time her father tried to make her marry. See also *ibid.*, p. 202: 'michi est melius esse sine labris in paradiso quam ire in infernum cum labris et naso'.
[346] *PC Clare of Montefalco*, fol. 146; p. 184; see also fols. 2, 5, 91 and the deposition of her brother, Francis, a Friar Minor, on the subject of her love of purity: 'ipsa decebat quod hec virtus est virtus celestis et divina, quam virtutem Christus prae aliis diligebat'. In

love of chastity and showed themselves inflexible in this area. But we do not find in them the same insistence or, above all, the same atmosphere of exaltation which often gave female sanctity a paroxysmal aspect. It is as if the nuns linked to the Mendicant orders were struggling to transcend by an excess of heroism the strict limits within which their daily lives were led.

It would be quite erroneous to present the various forms assumed by the experience of sanctification in the nunneries from a purely static perspective. Though, in Margaret of Hungary, the search for suffering seems hardly to have had any other purpose than the acquisition of merit, this was not the case in Franciscan circles.[347] For the disciplines of St Francis, meditation on the sufferings of the Passion was an effective way of establishing a direct relationship with God.[348] By dint of meditating on the mystery of Redemption, viewed in its most painful aspects, St Clare of Assisi, if we are to believe her companions, became unconscious for a day

contrast, her well-known emotional attachment to St Francis was expressed with considerable realism in the dream reported by Sister Philippa at the canonization process. Clare, having seen him appear, rushed to join him: 'et essendo pervenuta ad sancto Francesco, epso sancto trasse del suo seno una mammilla et disse ad essa vergine Chiara: Viene, receve et sugge. Et avendo lei succhato, epso sancto la admoniva che suggesse un'altra volta; et epsa suggendo, quello che de li suggeva era tando dolce et delectevole che per nesuno modo lo porterai explicare. Et havendo succhato, quella rotondita overo boccha de la poppa dondo escie lo lacte remase intra li labri de epsa beata Chiara; et pigliando epsa con le mane quelle che li era remaso nella boccha, li pareva che fusse oro cosi chiaro et lucido, che ce se vedeva tucta, come quasi in uno specchio': *PC Clare of Assisi*, p. 458. For the significance of this vision, see M. Bartoli, *AFH*, 73 (1980), pp. 449–72.

[347] With regard to the canonization of Margaret of Hungary, when consulted, as a historian of spirituality, by Pius XII, Father F. Callaey wrote in 1941: 'in her, sanctity was measured by the degree of external austerity and she never got past this first stage'. He also noted her lack of balance in ascetic effort and said that the young Dominican nun did penance 'not to master her body but to expiate her failings': 'Studio critico sulla vita e le virtu della B. Margherita d'Ungheria', in *Inquisitio*, pp. 25–7. This harsh judgement is challenged by E. Pasztor in the *Bibliotheca sanctorum*. It is clear, at all events, that the young Hungarian princess was ardently devoted to Christ. We know from witnesses at the process that she had the story of the Passion read to her as often as possible, that she listened to it standing up and weeping, and that from Maundy Thursday to Easter morning she neither slept nor ate so as not to be distracted from her meditation: *PC Margaret of Hungary*, p. 177.

[348] O. von Rieden, 'Das Leiden Christi im Leben des Hl. Franziskus von Assisi. Eine quellenvergleichende Untersuchung im Lichte der zeitgenössischen Passionsfrömmigkeit', *Collectanea Franciscana*, 30 (1960), pp. 5–30, 129–45, 241–63, 353–97. The possibility of a physiological 'transcription' of spiritual realities was claimed by St Bonaventure, who played an important role in the spread of this belief: 'Mens in carne patuit', he wrote in the *Itinerarium* (Prol. 3) with regard to the stigmata of the Poverello: E. Gilson, 'S. Bonaventure et l'iconographie de la Passion', *Revue d'histoire franciscaine*, 1 (1924), pp. 405–24. It is significant that the *Meditationes de Passione Christi* (ed. M. J. Stalling (Washington, 1965)), not, in fact, written till the fourteenth century, was attributed to St Bonaventure.

and a night, and some witnesses declared that they had seen the Christ Child in her arms.[349] In St Clare of Montefalco – also called Clare of the Cross – the search for mystical union through an ever closer identification with the Man of Sorrows, reached its greatest intensity. Constantly focussing her thoughts on the torments endured by Christ during his last hours, she relived and sought to reproduce in her body the principal stages in his agony, from the Garden of Olives to Golgotha.[350] Eventually, she came to believe, and made those around her believe, that Christ had planted his cross in her heart.[351] This explains the terrible scenes which followed her death; she had hardly breathed her last when the sisters of her nunnery flung themselves on her body to retrieve the precious heart, and found, when they cut her open, the *insignia* of the Passion: first the cross, then the scourge, the lance, the sponge, the crown of thorns etc.[352] This discovery, which won the saint instant fame and was the basis of her cult, seemed quite normal to those who had known her; everybody knew, as one witness said at the process in 1318–19, that 'the heart of Sister Clare found its delight in God and God in her heart'.[353] Her life had been marked by extraordinary phenomena – visions, apparitions and revelations.[354] She also possessed the ability to look into people's consciences, divining evil thoughts and hidden faults.[355] She was, lastly, credited with the gift of prophecy and the ability to resolve the most difficult theological problems.[356] More than half a century before the great women mystics and

[349] *PC Clare of Assisi*, pp. 457–8, 476, 477.
[350] The 'gratia consolationis Passionis Christi', that is, a direct vision of the Passion and its beneficial effects, was frequently mentioned during the process: *PC Clare of Montefalco*, fols. 139, 323. The saint's wish to identify herself with Christ is attested by such expressions as: 'O quantus fuit dolor quam Deus meus Jesus Christus sustinuit pro me! ego sum digna si plus possem doloribus et infirmitatibus majoribus omnia habere': *ibid.*, fol. 171; see also fols. 196, 323.
[351] After an apparition of Christ with his cross, 'ex tunc in corde suo semper sensibilem crucem sensit' (*ibid.*, fol. 523). At the moment of her death, she said: 'Io non ajo paura neuna, che io aggio Jesu Cristo mio crocifisso entro el cor mio' (*ibid.*, fol. 275). See plates 30, 31.
[352] *Ibid.*, arts. 159–89, fols. 631–8.
[353] *Ibid.*, fol. 323.
[354] The visions of St Clare of Montefalco largely concerned the Last Judgement, hell and paradise (*ibid.*, fols. 74–5, 140, 219, 336, 492). The apparitions enabled her to see a sun brighter than in reality, emanating from a Christ whose feet touched the ground and whose head touched heaven (*ibid.*, fol. 945); or Jesus carrying his cross on his shoulders (p. 523). Witnesses also described strange luminous manifestations around her (fols. 63–4, 507).
[355] This gift is frequently mentioned: *ibid.*, arts. 86–104, 125 130, fols. 608–22.
[356] 'Habebat intelligentiam virtutis et gratiae atque divinae sapientiae': *ibid.*, fol. 487. Many clerics and even some cardinals came to consult her about tricky problems: *ibid.*, fols. 105–6.

visionaries of the fourteenth century, Clare of Montefalco was already regarded as the mouthpiece of the Holy Spirit.[357]

The rise of mysticism was not a phenomenon restricted to the world of the nuns, or even to the devout circles which gravitated round the Mendicant orders. But one cannot fail to note the parallelism between the flowering of this form of sanctity among women and the increased emphasis on scholarship which occurred simultaneously among the male Minors and Preachers, as our discussion of the canonization processes of SS Louis of Anjou and Thomas Aquinas showed.[358] From the end of the thirteenth century, there was a growing gulf between an essentially male model, which attached great importance to intellectual and doctrinal activity, and an ascetic and mystical trend, which encompassed all the female saints of the period, much more attracted by the 'magic of extremes' than by scholarship or theology. This meant some of the latter had their orthodoxy questioned. Clare of Montefalco was suspected of having been too close to supporters of the heresy of the Free Spirit.[359] Contemporaries wondered which of these two trends remained faithful to the ideal and wishes of the founders. The Avignon papacy ruled in favour of the former by canonizing the Universal Teacher and allowing no woman to accede to this status.[360] The historian merely notes how quickly the synthesis achieved at the highest level by SS Francis and Dominic began to unravel. By the end of the thirteenth century, tensions had emerged between the contemplative life and apostleship, the love of poverty and obedience to the hierarchical Church, faithfulness to doctrine and the freedom of the spirit, which no-one, not even a saint, was able to resolve.

THE SAINTHOOD OF THE LAITY

Our statistical study revealed a significant increase in the number of lay men and women whose cult was recognized by the papacy in the last

---

[357] Her learning, according to the witnesses, resulted either from a direct vision of God (*ibid.*, fol. 401: 'videbat Deum in se et se in Deum'), or from an infusion of the Holy Spirit: *ibid.*, fol. 490: 'recte Spiritus Sanctus loquebatur in ea'; see also fol. 900.

[358] See above, pp. 346–8.

[359] Oliger, *De secta Spiritus libertatis*, pp. 9–27, 91–126.

[360] The most interesting evidence of the opposition in 'spiritual' circles to the canonization of St Thomas Aquinas is probably the confession of Prous Boneta, a Montpellier beguine condemned by the Inquisition of Carcassonne in March 1325, who, in her deposition, contrasted the 'old religion' of SS Dominic and Francis with that of the *ecclesia moderna*, incarnated by Aquinas: N. H. May, ed., 'The confession of Prous Boneta', in *Essays in honour of J. Evans* (New York, 1955), pp. 3–30.

centuries of the Middle Ages.[361] This development is all the more remarkable in that, during the feudal period, under the influence of monastic spirituality, the fact of living in the world seemed incompatible with Christian perfection; those who, though baptized, were neither regulars nor secular clergy, could hardly avoid the triple defilement that 'carnal' existence implied to the upholders of *contemptus mundi*: the profession of arms, sexual relations – even within legitimate marriage – and the use of money inevitably exposed them to the seductions of sin. Though not *a priori* excluded from salvation, the simple faithful were less well placed than others to achieve it. Convinced themselves of the sinful character of their condition, they tried to reduce this handicap by attaching themselves – often *in articulo mortis* – to a religious order whose habit they wore, or by placing themselves in the service of the monks or regular canons as *conversi*.[362]

During the second half of the twelfth century, the inferiority of the laity in the domain of sainthood began slowly to diminish. Under the influence of the 'apostolic' movements and of heresies, an increasing number of men and women claimed the possibility of leading an authentic Christian life without having to renounce their condition. Their requests were initially coolly received by the clergy, who saw them only as signs of insubordination. But shrewd popes such as Alexander III and, above all, Innocent III, were able to impose changes which made it possible to surmount certain canonical obstacles.[363] The former opened up a breach

---

[361] See above, pp. 263–6.

[362] Vauchez, *La spiritualité du Moyen Age*, pp. 53–8. For the position of the laity in the medieval Church, see Y. M. Congar, sv Laïc et laïcat, in *Dictionnaire de spiritualité*, IX (Paris, 1976), cc. 79–93, especially c. 84 (with full bibliography); *I laici nella 'societas christiana' dei secoli XI e XII. Atti della 3a settimana di studio (La Mendola, 21–27 agosto 1965)* (Milan, 1968). In his *L'idéal de sainteté*, J.-C. Poulain claims that a new model of lay sanctity, lived in the world, appeared, incarnated by St Gerald of Aurillac (d. 909), whose Life was written *c.*925–30 by Odo of Cluny (pp. 81–98). Interesting and in some ways original though the *Vita Geraldi* is, especially in its long version, it is in my view going too far to see it as the point of departure for a development which led to a sanctification of the lay estate through the exercise of seigneurial power. One swallow does not make a summer, as B. de Gaiffier justly observed in his review of this book (*Anal. Boll.*, 95 (1977), pp. 195–6), and it is premature to see in the hagiography of the eleventh century a transition from 'sanctity outside the world to sanctity through the world', as Poulain claims (pp. 119–44). At most, we see a sanctity lived in the world, which is a very different matter. See the interesting remarks of D. Baker, 'Vir Dei: secular sanctity in the early tenth century', in *Popular belief and practice* (Cambridge, 1972), pp. 41–53; also the methodological observations of W. Pohlkamp, 'Hagiographische Texte als Zeugnisse einer "histoire de la sainteté". Bericht über ein Buch zum Heiligkeitsideal im karolingischen Aquitanien', *Frühmittelalterliche Studien*, 11 (1977), pp. 229–40.

[363] Vauchez, *La spiritualité du Moyen Age*, pp. 105–45.

in the sexual prohibitions weighing on the laity by stipulating that the old canons which said that the married faithful ought to observe continence on fast days should be regarded simply as advice, not precepts. He went even further by recognizing, in a letter sent in 1173 to the Master of the Militia of St James, a military order recently founded in Spain, that being in a state of perfection was not absolutely linked to virginity and that the vow of obedience to the service of the faith was sufficient to confer on the knights the status of *religiosi*.[364] In adopting this new attitude, the Church was only adapting – not without difficulty, as the continuing condemnations of many popular religious movements between 1179 and 1200 show – to a situation which was the work of the laity themselves. The latter had already, in large numbers, voluntarily embraced the penitential state, which allowed them to lead an intense spiritual life while remaining in the world and among people.[365] Innocent III in a way ratified this spontaneous evolution by canonizing St Homobonus (d. 1197) in 1199.

Men

The canonization of the merchant of Cremona is all the more noteworthy in that he was the only medieval lay saint officially recognized by the Church who did not belong to a princely or royal family. Unfortunately, the surviving documentation concerning him is scanty and mostly dates from over a century after his death, which makes it difficult to use.[366]

---

[364] *PL*, 200, 1029. For this and similar orders created at this period, see J. Leclercq, 'La vie et la prière des chevaliers de Santiago d'après leur règle primitive', in *Liturgica*, 2 (Montserrat, 1958), pp. 347–57; J. O'Callaghan, 'Hermandades between the Military Orders of Calatrava and Santiago during the Castillan Reconquest (1158–1162)', *Speculum*, 44 (1969), pp. 609–18; E. C. Blanco, *The Rule of the Spanish Military Order of St James, 1170–1493* (Leiden, 1971).

[365] The pioneering work of G. G. Meersseman on the historical importance and significance of the penitential state has been republished as *Ordo fraternitatis: confraternite e pietà dei laici nel Medioevo*. For the movement's origins, see his 'I penitenti nei secoli XI e XII', in *I laici nella 'societas christiana'*, pp. 306–39, and for its importance in the West, especially in Italy, after 1200, his *Dossier de l'ordre de la Pénitence* and 'Disciplinati e penitenti'. For an anthropological interpretation of the penitential phenomenon, see the somewhat confused but suggestive essay of I. Magli, *Vomini della Penitenza: lineamenti antropologici del Medio Evo italiano* (1968).

[366] The main source of contemporary information is the bull *Quieta pietas*, 12.I.1199, based on material provided for Innocent III by Bishop Sicard of Cremona and the deposition of the priest Osbert. The best edition is that of O. Hageneder and A. Haidacher, *Die Register Innocenz' III*, I (Graz and Cologne, 1964), pp. 761–4. Many Lives of the holy merchant were written in the fourteenth century, listed by B. de Gaiffier in *Le Moyen Age*, 65 (1959), pp. 364–6. The oldest seems to be a choral office (*Cum orbita solis*) written in the thirteenth century and published by F. Zanoni, 'Vita metrica dei SS. Imerio e

However, by confining ourselves to the oldest texts, in particular the bull of canonization promulgated in 1199 by Innocent III, we can distinguish the principal features of his sanctity. Homobonus is presented as above all a man of great piety, who devoted most of his time to reciting prayers and attending church services. We learn that he had a special veneration for the Holy Cross and that he died during a mass, prostrated before the crucifix.[367] The pope also lauded the new saint's obedience to the priest Osbert, his patron and confessor, who had appeared in person before him and guaranteed his penitent's perfection.[368] But the features which are most characteristic of his lay status were his great charity, which won him the titles 'father of the poor' and 'comforter of the afflicted', and the determined efforts he made to restore peace within the town of Cremona, rent by conflicts between parties and clans.[369] His politico-religious engagement also took the form of a battle against the heretics who were prominent in several Lombard towns at the end of the twelfth century.[370]

Interesting though these details are, the bull *Quia pietas* is silent on many aspects of the life of Homobonus about which we would like to be better informed. Neither the text of Innocent III nor the thirteenth-century choral office make any reference to his family. Yet we know from other documents, whose reliability on this point there seems no reason to doubt, that Homobonus was married and had two sons.[371] The married state might no longer present an insuperable obstacle to sainthood, but it had hardly become a condition favourable to its emergence. It is the same with professional activities: the bull does not even mention that the saint had been in trade, while the choral office praises him for having given it up.[372] It was not, therefore, as a worker, husband or father that Homobonus earned the plaudits of the Roman Church, but rather as a penitent

---

Omobonu', *Annali della Biblioteca e Libreria civica di Cremona*, 9 (1956), pp. 29–32. See also Sicard of Cremona, *Cronica*, ed. O. Holder-Egger, in *MGH.SS.*, XXXI, pp. 176, 187.

[367] *Quia pietas*, p. 763.

[368] *Ibid.*, p. 764.

[369] *Ibid.*, p. 763. *Vita metrica*, p. 30. He sheltered the poor in his house and buried the dead.

[370] *Quia pietas*, p. 763: 'hereticorum, quorum pernities partes illas infecit, austerus exstitit aspernator'.

[371] See, in particular, the Life *Labentibus annis*, ed. A. C. Maini, *Sancti Homoboni . . . Vita antiquior* (Modena, 1857), 7–14 (= *BHL* 3971); also the Italian *Vita 'Della cipta di Cremona'*, ed. Bertoni. See also above, pp. 129 and 203.

[372] 'Segregans eum a contubernio perverse negotiationis, vocavit ad officium beate contemplationis': *Vita metrica*, p. 20; see also *ibid.*, p. 30: 'deserens comercia temporalium, mercator efficitur regni celorum'.

who remained faithful to orthodoxy and subject to the authority of the clergy.[373] His canonization shows, admittedly, that it was no longer necessary to withdraw from the world to achieve salvation and set an example of a saintly life. But it would be wrong to conclude from it that the Church acknowledged positive value in the temporal realities which formed the context within which the laity led their lives.[374]

The other saints in this category whose merits were recognized by the Holy See in the later Middle Ages all belonged to ruling or aristocratic families.[375] None of them came from Italy, where there were many men like St Homobonus, without the popes deigning to show interest in their cult.[376] Certain dynasties, like the Capetians, received particularly favourable treatment.[377] Their most illustrious representative was, of course, Louis IX. The almost complete disappearance of the acts of the process of canonization held at Saint-Denis in 1282–3 has deprived us of a document which would have been extremely useful to an appreciation of the

---

[373] *Quia pietas*, p. 764: 'In orationibus, vigiliis et aliis penitencie fructibus . . . plus injuncto satisfaciens exhibebat'.

[374] For a lay man or woman, to adopt the penitential state meant to assume voluntarily the life-style prescribed by the Church for repentant public sinners. Entry into the *ordo penitentium* did not imply membership of a religious order, or even of a community of tertiaries. All that was needed was a *professio in signis*: the fact of wearing a rough hair shirt and a special robe in one piece and of a certain colour was generally accepted as evidence of the 'conversion' of penitents. As such, they were forbidden to attend public performances, banquets etc. They also practised a degree of bodily asceticism: abstinence and more frequent fasts than for the rest of the population, periodic continence for those who were married, perpetual chastity for the others. They were often called *continentes* in thirteenth-century documents. They were required to live simply and in poverty, be charitable and attend religious offices in addition to those which were obligatory. Lastly, they refused to bear arms or swear oaths, which frequently got them into trouble with the civil authorities in Italy. The Mendicant orders gave a great boost to the fraternities of penitents, which, though often gravitating in their wake, remained autonomous until 1280–90. See, in addition to the works of Meersseman quoted above, *L'Ordine della Penitenza di San Francesco d'Assisi nel secolo XIII. Atti del convegno di studi Francescani (Assisi, 3–5 lglio 1972)*, ed. O. Schmucki (Rome, 1973).

[375] They were: Nicholas of Denmark, son of King Knut Magnusson (d. 1180, process 1254); St Louis (d. 1270, can. 1297); Elzear of Sabran, Count of Ariano (d. 1323, can. 1369); Charles of Blois, Duke of Brittany (d. 1364, process 1371). The situation was slightly less clear-cut in the case of the women: Cunegund, wife of Emperor Henry II (d. 1040, can. 1200), Elizabeth of Hungary or of Thuringia (d. 1231, can. 1235), Queen Margaret of Scotland (d. 1093, can. 1249), Hedwig of Silesia (d. 1243, can. 1267), Delphine of Sabran (d. 1360, process 1363) and Bridget of Sweden (d. 1373, can. 1391) all belonged to royal families or the high nobility; Rose of Viterbo (d. 1251, process 1253), Dorothy of Montau (d. 1394, process 1404–6), Catherine of Siena (d. 1380, process 1411–16) and Ingrid of Skänninge (d. 1282, process 1417) did not; but none of the latter was canonized in the Middle Ages.

[376] See above, pp. 265–6.

[377] See above, pp. 279–83.

idea of the saint-king held by the Church and the faithful in the second half of the thirteenth century. The fragments which survive and the hagiographical and liturgical texts based on it, give us, nevertheless, some indications.[378] The impression to emerge most clearly is that, in the eyes of the clergy of his day, the pious king of France incarnated the ideal of the *rex justus*. In describing how St Louis exercised royal power, the clergy were at pains to emphasize the way his actions conformed to Christian doctrine and the beneficial effects of his collaboration with the bishops, heirs to the Old Testament prophets and mouthpieces of the divine will.[379] There is no reason to doubt the legitimacy of these claims. We know how closely the views of sovereign and Church coincided and no-one deserved the title 'Most Christian King' more, both for his sense of justice and his constant concern not to do wrong to anyone in performing his duties as head of state.[380] But it is noticeable that, in practice, the praise of the 'good government' of Louis IX played only a minor role in the clerical eulogies. In the major speech delivered on the occasion of his canonization, in 1297, Boniface VIII lauded him for having despised the world to subject it to God, while remaining among men; he also praised his humility and his 'virginal' purity, which had enabled him to resist the

---

[378] L. Carolus-Barré, 'Les enquêtes pour la canonization de saint Louis – de Grégoire X à Boniface VIII – et la bulle Gloria laus du 11 août 1297', *RHEF*, 57 (1971), pp. 19–29. The acts of the process must have been voluminous, since, in the words of Boniface VIII, 'de hoc plus facta est scriptura quam unus asinus posset portare' (1st sermon on the canonization of St Louis, ed. F. Du Chesne, *Historiae Francorum scriptores*, V (Paris, 1649), pp. 483–4). The surviving fragments of the 1282 enquiry are ed. H. F. Delaborde, 'Fragments de l'enquête faite à Saint-Denis en 1282 en vue de la canonisation de saint Louis', *Mémoires de la Société de l'histoire de Paris et de l'Ile-de-France*, 23 (1896), pp. 1–71; Riant, 'Déposition de Charles d'Anjou'. Queen Margaret's confessor, William of Saint-Pathus, used the process for his *Vie de S. Louis*, ed. H. F. Delaborde (Paris, 1899); in his *Histoire de Saint Louis*, ed. N. de Wailly (Paris, 1874), Joinville expanded on the evidence he gave at Saint-Denis in 1282. There is also much useful information on the attitude of the papacy and the clergy to Louis IX in the two sermons delivered by Boniface VIII on the occasion of his canonization (ed. Du Chesne, *Historiae Francorum scriptores*, V, pp. 481–6) as well as in the liturgical texts composed in his honour between 1297 and *c*.1310; see R. Folz, 'La sainteté de Louis IX d'après les textes liturgiques de sa fête', *RHEF*, 57 (1971), pp. 31–45.

[379] Emphasized by Boniface VIII in his first sermon on St Louis (ed. Du Chesne, p. 482): 'concordes sunt enim pax et iusticia. Et ideo sicut sedit in iusticia, ita regnum eius quievit in pace.' In the happy phrase of R. Folz ('La sainteté de Louis IX', p. 420), 'the tranquility of the kingdom was only, in the eyes of the pope, an external projection of the peace which reigned in the heart of the king'. For the conception of order in the age of Louis IX, see D. M. Bell, *L'idéal éthique de la royauté en France au Moyen Age d'après quelques moralistes du temps* (Geneva, 1972). A. Grabois, 'L'idéal de la royauté biblique dans la pensée de Thomas Becket', in *Thomas Becket. Actes du Colloque*, pp. 103–10.

[380] Folz, 'La sainteté de Louis IX', pp. 38, 44.

temptations of the Devil and submit his flesh to the spirit.[381] The emphasis
was very firmly on the 'beguin king' of the later years, steeped in devotion
and wholly detached from earthly considerations, the sight of whom made
Joinville weep.[382] These are themes we have already encountered in the
texts concerning St Homobonus. They define a conception of sanctity
based on renunciation and penitence. We look in vain for the notion of
sanctification possible through the performance of the duties and tasks
specific to his condition.[383] Of the secular life, the Church sanctified only
the use of arms, justified by the need to keep order and to defend Christendom against its principal adversaries, the Saracens in the Holy Land and
the heretics within. One aspect of the sanctity of St Louis shows that he
was of a generation later than St Homobonus and therefore influenced by
the Mendicant orders.[384] This was his zeal for the propagation of the
Christian faith. The king's deep piety filled him with the desire to make
the rule of God's law universal, which explains both the measures he took
against blasphemers and his two crusades.[385] In him, belonging to the
Church excluded all ritualism and legalism. It took the form of a sustained
desire to translate into action the teachings and advice of the Gospel and
a love of souls which made him desire their salvation.[386] The burning
apostolic zeal of St Louis, and his tragic death before Tunis, explain why
he was sometimes called a martyr,[387] and why Boniface VIII could say of
him, before his canonization, 'his life was not only human but super-

---

[381] 2nd sermon, ed. Du Chesne, p. 489: 'Vicit enim mundum quia stans in mundo mundum
prostravit et calcavit contemnendo, et Deo subdidit terrena quae mundi sunt.'

[382] 1st sermon, ed. Du Chesne, p. 482: 'Vestes enim quas postea habuit non erant regiae
sed religiosae, non erant militis sed viri simplicis.'

[383] The only reference to St Louis in his role as husband appears in the 2nd sermon of
Boniface VIII: 'iste numquam carnem suam divisit in plures nec cum aliqua peccatum
commisit, ita quod excepta uxore propria virgo ab aliis permansit': ed. Du Chesnue, p.
483. His wife, Margaret of Provence, was not called as a witness at the process, though
his brother, Charles of Anjou, made a lengthy statement.

[384] As is well known, St Louis had close links with both the Friars Minor and the Preachers,
who disseminated the penitential ideal among the laity; see L. K. Little, 'Saint Louis'
involvement with the Friars', Church History, 33 (1964), pp. 125–48; L. Carolus-Barré,
'Les Franciscains et le procès de canonisation de saint Louis', Les amis de S. François,
n.s. 12 (1971), pp. 3–6.

[385] Boniface VIII, 2nd sermon, ed. Du Chesne, p. 486: 'non est memoria apud homines,
ut credimus, quod inventus fuit isti similis nostris temporibus, qui tantum zelaret pro
salute aliorum'.

[386] Boniface VIII, 1st sermon, ed. Du Chesne, p. 481: '[Vita eius] non fuit interrupta sed
ab infantia continuata et de bono in melius semper procedens, semper augmentata.'

[387] See the antiphon quoted by Folz, 'La sainteté de Louis IX', p. 43: 'O martyr par le
désir, toi qui par le zèle ardent de ta piété compatis au Crucifié dont tu as porté à deux
reprises la croix, la Passion t'a manqué mais ta ferveur et ta recherche du Christ font de
toi un martyr.'

human'.[388] The spread of the cult of St Louis was due, as we have seen, to the effective measures taken by the French monarchy, supported by the Mendicant orders, who carried it beyond the frontiers of France.[389] But it would not have been so successful if he had not combined the different images of the king which impregnated the medieval mentality: the suffering leader, the just sovereign and the austere penitent.

In the fourteenth century, the union of high birth and the penitential ideal, so characteristic of official sainthood, is illustrated by two lay figures who are less well known than Louis IX but still of great interest: St Elzear of Sabran (d. 1323), count of Ariano, canonized by Urban V in 1369, and Charles of Blois, duke of Brittany (d. 1364), almost canonized in 1376 during the pontificate of Gregory XI. Both, as their titles make plain, were, like St Louis, men of power. However, St Elzear differed from the king of France in more ways than one, even though barely half a century separated them.[390] The way in which this great Provençal lord exercised power both over his own patrimonial estates and in southern Italy in the service of the Angevins of Naples seems to have played only a minor role in his reputation for sanctity.[391] The texts of clerical origin which describe him emphasize, in particular, his virginal marriage, which quickly became famous. Husband of Delphine of Puimichel, he agreed, at her pressing request, to observe continence and eventually to make a vow of chastity with her.[392] In the *Libellus supplex* presented to John XXII in 1327 and probably written by Francis of Meyronnes, Elzear is presented, with much bombast, as the equal of SS Joseph, John the Evangelist (who, according to St Jerome, *de nuptiis a Christo fuit vocatus*), Valerian, husband of St Cecilia, and Alexis.[393] He was even superior to these great men in that,

---

[388] Boniface VIII, 1st sermon, ed. Du Chesne, p. 481: 'Vita eius non fuit solum vita hominis sed supra hominem.'

[389] See above, p. 118.

[390] The acts of the canonization process of St Elzear (Apt, 1351–2) have been lost; there exists only a *Summarium* written between 1362 and 1364, ed. J. Cambell, 'Le sommaire de l'enquête pour la canonisation de S. Elzéar de Sabran, TOF (d. 1323)', *Miscellanea Francescana*, 73 (1973), pp. 438–73. But the principal features of his sanctity are fairly well known thanks to the *Libellus supplex* presented to John XXII in 1327 by the bishop of Apt with a view to the canonization, ed. *AA.SS.* Sept. VII, pp. 521–2; also the Latin *Vita* (= *BHL* 2523) written 1369, probably by a Franciscan with access to the acts of the process, ed. *ibid.*, pp. 539–54. See also Cambell, *Les Vies occitanes*; F. Baron, 'Le mausolée de saint Elzéar de Sabran à Apt', *Bulletin Monumental*, 136 (1978), pp. 267–83.

[391] Though Elzear's response to the revolt of Ariano against the Angevins is referred to in the Latin *Vita*, pp. 549–50.

[392] *Vita*, pp. 541, 550–1.

[393] The attribution of the *Libellus supplex* to Francis of Meyronnes is disputed. Against the Bollandists and tradition, C.-V. Langlois, 'François de Meyronnes, frère mineur', in

far from breaking the union contracted by sacrament, he had been able to preserve his virginal innocence within a long shared life.[394] He also displayed the Franciscan virtues of humility and poverty, which he practised to a high degree. At the château of Puimichel, where he spent much of his life with his young wife, he created a devout little community which divided its time, according to a strict timetable, between worship, works of charity and spiritual discussion dealing with the most difficult problems.[395] In fact, unlike St Louis, who thought that it was not for the laity to discuss matters of faith, which were best left to the clergy, St Elzear, according to his biographer, was a spiritual and even a theologian. The *Vita* refers on many occasions to the visions and ecstasies during which the goodness and love of God were revealed to him.[396] When he meditated, he was seized by a sort of internal inflammation and experienced sensations similar to those that contemporary hagiographical texts attribute to the women saints.[397]

The specifically lay character of the sainthood of St Elzear is even less obvious than in his thirteenth-century predecessors, and his way of life seemed to his contemporaries to resemble that of the monks.[398] Admittedly, he remained in the world, though having been tempted to abandon it completely to become a hermit,[399] but the reasons for his choice are not spelled out. It was probably his Franciscan entourage who pointed out the beneficial role he could play with regard to the people among whom he lived. St Elzear retained only the appearance of the lay condition;

Histoire littéraire de la France, XXXIII (Paris, 1927), p. 338, argued that the Provençal Franciscan could not be the author since he died in 1325 or 1326. His death is now usually put as late as 1328 or 1329, which would make it possible for him to have written the *Libellus* after being present at St Elzear's death in Paris in 1323: E. Longpré, sv François de Meyronnes, in *Catholicisme, hier, aujourd'hui, demain*, IV (Paris, 1956), cc. 1555–7.

[394] 'Iste autem per viginti septem annos [in fact 25] in eodem domo et in eodem thalamo et in eodem thoro cum conjuge intacte servatus': *Libellus supplex*, pp. 521–2.

[395] *Vita*, pp. 546–7. The biographer tells us that Elzear and Delphine spoke together 'de finalibus temporibus ex malitia Antichristi' (*ibid.*, p. 553). Their conduct and style of life can only really be understood in the context of a spiritual climate strongly influenced by eschatological preoccupations.

[396] *Vita*, pp. 542–3. His visions were highly theological, dealing with, for example, the procession of the Holy Spirit and the structure *ad intra* of the Trinity. For him, Christ was defined above all as *excessus amoris* or *excessivus amor*: *Vita*, p. 543.

[397] Elzear was the only male saint of this period to have enjoyed truly mystical gifts.

[398] 'Magis apparebat ibi vera religio et vita monachalis quam domus comitis seu vita secularis': *Vita*, p. 546.

[399] He changed his mind after a vision (*ibid.*, p. 546). But towards the end of his life he was thinking about abandoning 'omnia ista negotia destructiva' (*ibid.*, p. 554) when death intervened.

behaving externally like a great lord, in fact he lived like a monk.[400] One can no longer even talk, in his case, of the penitential ideal, since the goal he set himself was not the expiation of his faults at the cost of some renunciations but the preservation of his impeccability. For him, God had so loved men that he had placed them in a state of innocence. He who succeeded in preserving this by avoiding all forms of sin was assured of salvation. From this perspective, it was desirable to renounce not only 'luxury' but even the union of the flesh.[401] It is impossible for us to distinguish St Elzear's own contribution to this spirituality from that of his biographer. But it is significant that the only layman whose sanctity was ratified by the papacy in the fourteenth century was someone so extraordinary that he seems to spring straight from the Golden Legend.[402]

Whilst for these three saints – SS Homobonus, Louis IX and Elzear – the surviving documentation is fragmentary, the personality and conduct of Charles of Blois (d. 1364) can be studied in greater depth. The statements collected first in Brittany and then at the process held in Angers in 1371 have survived and enable us to form a clear impression of how the dead duke of Brittany was regarded by the two hundred or so clergy and lay people heard on this occasion.[403] The depositions are largely in accord:

[400] Here, his behaviour may be compared to that of St Gerald of Aurillac, as it was described, c.925, by Odo of Cluny in the *Vita Geraldi*: V. Fumagalli, 'Note sulla Vita Geraldi di Odone di Cluny', *BISIME*, 76 (1964), pp. 217–40; Poulain, *L'idéal de sainteté*, pp. 81–116.

[401] *Vita*, pp. 543ff. For this conception of divine love and grace, see C. Campros, 'A perpaus de la perfection d'Alzeas et de Delfina', *Annales de l'Institut d'études occitanes*, 4th ser., 1 (1965), pp. 88–105, emphasizing the probable influence on this strange couple of Arnold of Villeneuve and the 'spiritual' circles which gravitated around him.

[402] If there was a change in lay sanctity between the thirteenth and fourteenth centuries, it has to be accepted that it was in a restrictive direction, since the clergy who celebrated the merits of St Elzear were not content to pass over in silence the fact that he was married (St Homobonus) or refer to his chastity within marriage (St Louis), but exalted his refusal to consummate his marriage, which restored in all its rigour the link between virginity and Christian perfection which had been somewhat relaxed in the late twelfth and thirteenth centuries.

[403] The acts of the process (Angers, 1371) are in Sérent, ed., *Monuments du procès de canonisation du Bienheureux Charles de Blois*; see also Vauchez, 'Canonisation et politique au XIVe siècle'. The enquiry of 1371 contained several technical faults which were raised by the cardinals responsible for scrutinizing it: Pocquet du Haut-Jussé, 'La sainteté de Charles de Blois', pp. 110–15. In particular, the promoters of the cause had failed to draw up *articuli interrogatorii*; to regularize the situation, they provided a set after the event, which are in MS *ASV, Collectorie* 434, fols. 1–35v. Gregory XI's departure from Avignon for Rome prevented the canonization, which seemed likely during the summer of 1376. See the definitive conclusions of Laurent, 'Charles de Blois fut-il canonisé', approved by the Bollandists (*Anal. Boll.*, 71 (1955), pp. 249–51). For the personality of Charles of Blois, see F. Baix, *DHGE*, IX, cc. 223–8; H. Claude, sv Carlo di Blois, in *BS*, III (Rome, 1963), cc. 793–4.

if Charles of Blois was regarded as a saint, it was primarily because of his extreme devoutness. Indeed, this pious lord multiplied prayers and religious practices to the point where they took up a large part of his time. We can see this from the daily timetable which can be reconstructed from the statements of witnesses:

> On rising, recitation of the *Credo* and the *Confiteor*, all the canonical hours, from matins to compline, and at least fifteen psalms.
> Before meals, reading a passage from the Gospel.
> During meals, reading and commentary of the Lives of the saints, in particular the Golden Legend.
> After meals, recitation of grace and the psalm *Miserere*.
> At bedtime, suffrages in honour of the saints; reading of the Gospel *In principio*, the hymn *Veni Sancte Spiritus* and a prayer; singing of *Salve Regina*.

In addition, on Mondays, Wednesdays and Fridays, he recited the office and matins for the dead and, on Marian feasts, that of the matins of the Virgin with nine readings and nine responses. During the course of the day, he often said three *Pater Nosters* and three *Aves* in honour of the Holy Trinity, five *Paters* and five *Aves* in honour of the five wounds of Christ, seven *Paters* and *Aves* against mortal sins, thirteen others in honour of the Apostles etc.[404] His piety was no less remarkable in the matter of the sacraments: he confessed every evening, sometimes even to a layman if there was no priest to hand, and as often as three times a day, so that, in the words of one witness, 'he never went to bed in a state of mortal sin'.[405] He attended mass at least once and sometimes three or four times a day, as he had obtained a papal privilege to celebrate the holy mysteries anywhere and at any time. He communicated at the major feasts and received the eucharist kneeling, weeping and violently beating his breast.[406] Every time he passed a church, he went in to say a prayer and when he saw a cross by the roadside, he never failed to cry: 'Hail, Precious Cross on which Christ, the saviour of the world, was hanged.'[407]

His austerity made an equally deep impression; the duke of Brittany always ate moderately and fasted on the vigils of feast days; his dress was very simple and he wore a hair shirt next to the skin, under his shirt. But

---

[404] *PC Charles of Blois*, witnesses 1, 9, 17, 50, 51, etc., pp. 12ff, 3–30, 48, 175, 176 etc.
[405] *Ibid.*, witness 9, p. 30.
[406] *Ibid.*, witness 11, pp. 35ff.
[407] *Ibid.*, witness 21, p. 72.

he inflicted many other sufferings on his body; his chest was constantly squeezed by knotted cords which dug into the flesh and caused sores which harboured vermin.[408] He often put sand or pebbles in his shoes. On Fridays, he scourged himself till the blood ran, whilst reciting the seven psalms of penitence.[409] Lastly, he slept on a simple palliasse, except for the rare nights when he joined his wife, Joan of Penthièvre, in the matrimonial bed.[410] As she was not invited to testify at the process of canonization in 1371, we know very little about his family life. The deposition of a valet suggests that his wife did not altogether share his penitential zeal.[411] Further, when he lost his two children, he showed no signs of grief, simply saying 'Blessed be God.'[412] But such revelations are rare and meagre. It is obvious that this was an area which was of no interest either to the witnesses or, even more, to the commissioners who interrogated them, since relations between spouses or within the family were part of the earthly attachments which a Christian of that time was required to transcend to achieve perfection.[413]

Most elements in the sanctity of Charles of Blois could equally well appear – marriage apart – in the life of a saint-monk. Indeed, contemporaries were sometimes uneasy in the face of a person whose devotion and asceticism were unaccustomed, even weird, in a layman. The most favourably inclined were content to observe that their former leader 'recited more prayers than a priest' or that 'you never saw a regular – Preacher, Minor or Hermit – who was as humble or devout'.[414] Others allowed a little criticism of his behaviour to creep in; one remembered having said to him, 'that he would be a better bishop, abbot or man of the church than prince', whilst a noble said that people had mocked him openly at his court and that 'it was a great pity that he hadn't become a monk'.[415]

[408] *Ibid.*, witnesses 1 and 10, pp. 14, 34–5.
[409] *Ibid.*, witnesses 9 and 11, pp. 31, 35.
[410] *Ibid.*, witnesses 5 and 10, pp. 22, 34.
[411] *Ibid.*, witness 10, p. 34: 'Dum autem cum dicta uxore sua iacebat, lectus erat partitus, videlicet pars in qua uxor iacebat cum culcitra cervicali plumeis, et pars in qua dictus dominus Carolus cum straminibus et matha et cervicali sine pluma.'
[412] *Ibid.*, witness 11, p. 39.
[413] Among the *articuli interrogatori* written retrospectively by the promoters of his cause, one (no. 28) is devoted to his purity; it notes his continence and faithfulness to his wife (*castitas conjugalis*): ASV, *Collectorie*, 434, fol. 24. The duke seems to have shown little enthusiasm for the marriage, if we are to believe one witness: 'confitebatur quod nisi esset juramentum et fides quibus erat astrictus uxori, numquam ipsam carnaliter cognovisset', *PC*, p. 157.
[414] *Ibid.*, witnesses 51, 11 and 17, pp. 176, 42, 62.
[415] *Ibid.*, witness 36, p. 128.

In any case, Charles of Blois freely admitted, in private, that he had missed his vocation: 'I think that it would have been better for me to have become a Friar Minor than a duke.'[416] One servant even declared at the process that he had said: 'If I hadn't had a wife and children, I would gladly have entered the Carthusian Order.'[417] His fascination for the monastic ideal and the religious life probably explains his humble and deferential behaviour towards men of the Church, seculars as well as regulars. At meetings and banquets, he always gave precedence to the bishops and begged them not to get up when he entered a room; when he met a bishop, even from a poor diocese, he got down from his horse to greet him.[418] He felt such respect for the priesthood that he believed priests and regulars were worthy of the highest honours; so when one of them requested his hospitality, he made him sit at his own table.[419] His generosity to the clergy, particularly to the Franciscans and Dominicans he favoured, was thought excessive by his entourage. At Rennes, Nantes and Guingamp, he rebuilt parish and conventual churches and decorated them richly with mouldings and paintings 'in the Lombard style', and he also distributed precious ecclesiastical ornaments.[420] Not content with embellishing places of worship and enriching their treasuries, which was, after all, one of the duties of a prince, the duke defended the liberties and privileges of the clergy against the encroachments of his own officers and whenever there was a dispute between one of them and an abbot or a bishop, he supported the clergy.[421] We are a long way here from the balance of St Louis, who, while always supporting the Church in matters of faith or morals, stood up to the bishops and even the pope when they trespassed on the prerogatives of the monarchy or made excessive demands. A profound sense of *honestas*, that is, the conduct required by royal majesty and proper to his rank in society, counterbalanced in St Louis the desire to conform in all things to the demands of the Gospel.[422] In contrast, Charles of Blois

---

[416] *Ibid.*, witness 31, pp. 104–5.

[417] *Ibid.*, witness 47, p. 162.

[418] *Ibid.*, witnesses 9, 32 and 34, pp. 27, 109, 112.

[419] *Ibid.*, witness 21, p. 65.

[420] *Ibid.*, witnesses 9, 10, 17, 20 and 28, pp. 28–9, 33, 52–3, 68, 91. For his generosity to the Mendicants, see de Sérent, 'Charles de Blois, duc de Bretagne': Martin, *Les Ordres Mendiants*, pp. 366–71, 409–11.

[421] *PC*, witness 11, p. 41: 'dum erat discordia inter prelatos ducatus sui et officiales dicti domini Caroli, ipse semper partem ecclesie sustinebat'.

[422] Y. M. Congar, 'L'Eglise et l'Etat sous S. Louis', in *Septième centenaire de la mort de Saint Louis. Actes des colloques de Royaumont et Paris* (Paris, 1975), pp. 265–71; Folz, 'La sainteté de Louis IX', p. 37.

inclined to the most extreme clericalism, expressed by a policy of abasement and concessions to the Church.[423] To the lords of his party, the French duke seemed a bigot verging on the ridiculous. Even the wave of devotion which followed his death and the tendency, very marked in the processes of canonization, to idealize retrospectively candidates for sanctity, cannot wholly conceal the scorn felt by the Breton aristocracy for the way of life of this layman who did so little honour to the values of his estate.[424]

One may well ask how, in these circumstances, Charles of Blois acquired a reputation for sanctity. I will not repeat here my earlier discussion of the origins of the cult, when I emphasized its political and even dynastic dimension.[425] However, it is clear that the concerted action of the French royal house, represented by his son-in-law, Louis of Anjou, and the Friars Minor would not alone have been enough to cause the surge of devotion and miracles which occurred throughout the duchy after 1369, had the Breton people not remembered him as a prince who cared for the well-being of his subjects. In fact, the depositions recorded during the 1371 process show that his charity was renowned. Like that of St Louis, it revealed Franciscan influence; Charles of Blois was not only generous but 'compassionate and merciful towards the poor'. Not content with personally distributing alms to the hundreds of poor who flocked to the gates of his palace, he sent doctors to visit pregnant women in their homes, built hospices, in particular at Nantes and Guingamp, and sometimes himself visited the sick.[426] This zeal for the disinherited did not preclude the wish to distinguish the true poor from the false, which was very typical of the fourteenth century, a period when begging began to provoke hostile reactions.[427] Lastly, he showed great interest in the plight

[423] *PC*, witness 11, p. 38: 'deridebatur per assistentes dicentes ei quod damnum erat ipse non fuerat religiosus'; see also witnesses 17 and 38, pp. 52, 142, and above all, witness 56, p. 189: 'tanta suffragia et orationes dicebat quod valde longum et tediosum erat adstantibus et in tantum quod iste [first witness] et alii astantes de ipso deridebant'.

[424] The reproaches of his brother on this point are significant: *PC*, witness 1, p. 13; see also witness 11, p. 41. His decision to have part of the forest of Huelgoat felled to allow the Dominicans of Morlaix to rebuild their convent was very unpopular: *ibid.*, witness 47, p. 168.

[425] See above, pp. 229–31.

[426] *Ibid.*, witnesses 5, 34, and 48, pp. 20–1, 112, 165.

[427] *Ibid.*, witness 30, p. 101: 'vidit et audivit pluries, dum ipse dominus Carolus erat in dicta villa Brugensi, quando ipse dominus Carolus incedebat et videbat pauperes debiles et impotentes, ipse se arreptabat et dicebat secum adstantibus: "ecce pauperem impotentem" vel "pauperes impotentes", quando plures essent, "isti sunt digni habendi elemosinam" '. See also witness 28, p. 97.

of unfortunate children, giving dowries to orphan girls so that they could marry and educating at his own expense the more gifted boys, whom he sent to 'the schools'.[428]

As with St Louis and St Yves, his favourite saint, he saw charity as inseparable from justice. 'He was just and loved justice', according to the majority of witnesses.[429] This concern was shown first in his choice of advisors and officials and in the way he supervised them.[430] At the 1371 process, he was praised for ensuring speedy judgements, even if it meant upsetting a bureaucracy which tended to take liberties with his subjects. In an age when states were developing their administrative structures, one of the qualities most appreciated in princes was a readiness to see that cases were dealt with promptly and at minimum cost.[431] His concern for the public good made him deeply regret the ruinous war between him and his rival, John IV de Montfort, who had English support.[432] Unable to end the conflict, he did everything he could to reduce its impact on the people; refusing to increase their fiscal burden, he preferred to borrow money from the king of France and the pope, as a result of which he accumulated huge debts.[433] The hard times which followed his death and the incompetence of his successor did the rest. It therefore came as no surprise to find a witness – a modest barber – declaring that in Brittany, 'everybody regretted the good times of Monseigneur Charles, when, though war raged, plenty and prosperity prevailed'.[434]

Our study of the processes of canonization has brought out all the ambiguity of the notion of lay sainthood at the end of the Middle Ages. For the clergy, it was essentially defined by an austere and devout life, the practice of charity and total submission to the Church. Neither temporal

---

[428] *Ibid.*, witnesses 21 and 38, pp. 79, 132.

[429] *Ibid.*, witnesses 9 and 31, pp. 30, 108.

[430] *Ibid.*, witness 11, p. 35: 'habebat bonos senescallos et officiarios et sapientes ac bone vite, qui consuetudines dicti ducatus bene sciebant et precipiebat eis quod facerent justiciam'. See also witness 21, p. 67.

[431] *Ibid.*, witness 31, p. 108; witness 34, p. 113: 'quando videbat pauperes supplicantes de foris expectantes, increpabat gentes consilii sui dicendo quod erat malefactum et quod si essent divites, cicius fuissent per eos expediti'.

[432] *Ibid.*, witnesses 13 and 27, pp. 42, 190.

[433] *Ibid.*, witnesses 49 and 56, pp. 170, 190.

[434] *Ibid.*, witness 47, p. 169: 'communiter dicitur per populum quod gentes ducatus Britannie, vivente dicto domino Carolus, maiorem abundantiam segetum et omnium aliorum bonorum habebant et diciores erant in bonis temporalibus, quamvis guerris oppressi fuissent, quam post mortem suam fuerunt'. This statement should be compared with the declaration made by the Breton peasants assembled by the Friars Minor at the time of the preliminary enquiry at Guingamp; see above, p. 163, n. 19.

duties, apart from the exercise of power, nor married or family life were routes to sanctification for the simple faithful. On the contrary, the demands of the penitential ideal, pushed sometimes as far as mysticism, led lay people who yearned for perfection to withdraw from the world or live in it like monks. In this new climate, the royal or princely model itself eventually lost its consistency. From St Louis to Charles of Blois, we can trace the diminution in the already limited role of the specifically lay elements present in the ideal image of the Christian king as conceived by the clergy. In an age when, on the political and cultural level, the faithful were behaving with increasing independence, the only response of the Church seems to have been to offer them a form of sainthood which lost credibility in proportion as it resembled that of the regulars.

Women

Of the forms of sainthood honoured in the last centuries of the Middle Ages, female lay sainthood is the best documented. Ten women were the subject of a process of canonization between 1198 and 1431, four of whom were canonized. They are, in chronological order: St Cunegund (d. 1033, canonized 1200), St Elizabeth of Thuringia (d. 1231, canonized 1234), St Margaret of Scotland (d. 1093, canonized 1249), Rose of Viterbo (d. 1251, enquiry 1252/3), St Hedwig (d. 1243, canonized 1267), Delphine of Sabran (d. 1360, enquiry 1363), St Bridget of Sweden (d. 1373, canonized 1391), Dorothy of Montau (d. 1394, enquiry 1404–6), St Catherine of Siena (d. 1380, enquiry 1411–16, canonized 1460) and Ingrid of Skän-ninge (d. 1282, enquiry 1417).[435] I will pass briefly over SS Cunegund and Margaret of Scotland, both of whom lived in the twelfth century. Their canonization was only a consecration and ratification by the papacy of the immemorial cult accorded them in their respective countries.[436] It

[435] I will also refer to the informative diocesan process held at Tours in 1415 on behalf of Joan-Marie of Maillé (1331–1414), ed. in part in *AA.SS.* Mar. III, pp. 744–62.
[436] For St Cunegund, we have only the bull of canonization promulgated by Innocent III (ed. Fontanini, *Codex constitutionum*, pp. 37–9). For the cult accorded to her jointly with her husband, Henry II (= St Henry), see Klauser, *Der Heinrichs- und Kunegundenkult im mittelalterlichen Bistum Bamberg*, and critical review by M. Coens in *Anal. Boll.*, 76 (1958), pp. 262–4; F. Pelzer, 'Ein Elogium Joachims von Flore auf Kaiser Heinrich II und sein Gemählin die Hl. Kunegunde', in *Liber Floridus Paul Lehmann* (Saint Ottilien, 1950), pp. 329–54. The enquiry ordered by Innocent IV in 1245 into the life and miracles of Margaret of Scotland was held in 1246, and begun again in 1247 or 1248 because of technical errors. Nothing of it survives. The pope authorized the translation of her relics

is interesting, however, to note that both fitted the model of the holy queen or empress, which was very popular in western Europe between the eleventh and the thirteenth centuries and in eastern Europe at the end of the Middle Ages.[437] For all the others, we have either the complete acts of the processes of canonization (St Elizabeth, Delphine, St Bridget, Dorothy of Montau and St Catherine of Siena) or contemporary documents based closely on them (St Hedwig).[438] Thanks to this rich documentation, the historian can hope to explain the reasons for the emergence of female lay sainthood, the statistical importance of which was stressed above.[439] We need now to put it in the context of the ideas of the period and the development of spirituality, so as to understand its significance and its limitations.[440]

The image of women in the clerical mind was not *a priori* a favourable starting-point for any member of their sex to acquire the title of saint. The monastic tradition, going one step further than the misogynous St Jerome, whose works were widely read and discussed in the Middle Ages, constantly emphasized the close connection between women and sin.[441] In the many eleventh- and twelfth-century treatises devoted to *contemptus mundi*, the daughters of Eve were generally presented as creatures incapable of rising to an understanding of things of the spirit. Frivolous, fickle and inconstant, they inspired only distrust and disapproval in writers of the feudal period.[442] Only a few rare individuals – mostly queens or great aristocratic ladies – managed, by strength of will, to rise above the failings of their sex and escape this harsh criticism.[443] Women laboured

---

in 1249, which was done in 1251. The complete dossier is ed. C. Innes, *Registrum de Dunfermelyne* (Edinburgh, 1842), pp. 181–6; the story of the translation is in *AA.SS.* Iun. II, pp. 338–9; good bibliography in D. McRoberts, sv Margherita di Scozia, in *BS*, 8 (Rome, 1966), cc. 781–6.

[437] See above, p. 167, n. 32.

[438] For details of these canonization processes, see the list of sources below, pp. 540ff.

[439] See above, pp. 268–9.

[440] There are useful observations in the otherwise disappointing book by Reber, *Die Gestaltung des Kultes weiblicher Heiliger*.

[441] P. Delhaye, 'Le dossier antimatrimonial de l'Adversus Jovinianum et son influence sur quelques écrits latins du XIIe siècle', *Medieval Studies*, 13 (1951), pp. 65–86; M. L. Portmann, *Die Darstellung der Frau in der Geschichtschreibung des früheren Mittelalters* (Basle and Stuttgart, 1958). For the debate on the condition of women in the Middle Ages provoked by this book, see the reviews by S. Roisin, *Revue belge de philologie et d'histoire*, 38 (1960) and B. Gaiffier, *Anal. Boll.*, 78 (1960), pp. 206–7.

[442] See the texts quoted by R. Bultot, *Christianisme et valeurs humaines: la doctrine du mépris du monde en Occident de S. Ambroise à Innocent III*, IV: *Le XIe siècle*, 2 vols. (Louvain and Paris, 1963–4).

[443] For example, Empress Adelaide (d. 999), canonized 1097; Countess Mathilda of Canossa, who was close to Gregory VII; Ermengard, countess of Maine, for whom Robert of

under a dual handicap which, in general, denied them access to sainthood: their physical and moral weakness, which, in the minds of their male contemporaries, was not in doubt; and their status within the Church, which condemned them to a passive role, except in a few rare cases where birth or marriage gave them powers which could be used to the advantage of the clergy. Even when they aspired to an intense religious life, they could satisfy this desire only by entering a nunnery,[444] in which case their mute and hidden lives were effectively hidden from the *vox populi*.[445]

In the twelfth century, things began slowly to change.[446] Under the influence of Marian spirituality, then in full flood, their role in the history of salvation was seen in a less negative light. 'If our Lord wished to be born of a woman, it was not only for men but also for women', wrote Pope Alexander III in 1173, in the letter to the Master of the Order of St James already quoted. He explicitly stated that the wives and widows of the knights might legitimately be regarded as members of a religious order, by the same title as their husbands.[447] We may also suspect an element of opportunism in the more open attitude of the Church, at a time when the heretical movements were enjoying particular success among women, who found in them a way of escaping the disabilities they had previously suffered.[448] Consequently, between 1180 and 1230, new forms of religious life developed, adapted to the needs of lay women. In the Low Countries, in the wide sense of the term, there appeared reclusoria of beguines combining work and prayer in the context of a communal, but not enclosed, life.[449] Groups of a similar type soon proliferated in the

---

Arbrissel was a sort of 'spiritual director'. For Adelaide, see Odilo of Cluny's *Epitaphium Adelheidae imperatricis*, followed by a *Liber miraculorum Adelhaidis imperatricis*, in *PL*, 142, cc. 963–91; Paulhart, 'Zur heiligsprechung der Kaiserin Adelheid'.

[444] M. de Fontette, *Les religieuses à l'âge classique du droit canon: recherches sur les structures juridiques des branches féminines des ordres* (Paris, 1967). In the early thirteenth century, a religious experience as original as that of St Clare of Assisi still led on to an enclosed life of the most traditional type.

[445] The exception who proves the rule is St Hildegard (d. 1179); see above, pp. 325–6.

[446] M. Bernards, *Speculum Virginium: Geistigkeit und Seelenleben der Frau im Hochmittelalter* (Cologne, 1955); J. Ancelet-Hustache, 'A propos du "Speculum Virginum"'. Ascétique et mystique féminine du Haut Moyen Age', *Etudes germaniques*, 15 (1960), pp. 152–60.

[447] *PL*, 200, 1024; for the Order of Santiago, see above, p. 356.

[448] E. Werner, 'Zur Frauenfrage und zum Frauenkult im Mittelalter: Robert von Arbrissel und Fontevrault', *Forschungen und Fortschritte*, 29 (1955), pp. 269–76; Werner, 'Die Stellung des Katharismus zur Frau', *Studi Medievali*, n.s., 2 (1961), pp. 295–301. G. Koch's *Frauenfrage und Ketzertum im Mittelalter* (East Berlin, 1962) is strongly criticized by E. Delaruelle, *RHE*, 60 (1965), pp. 159–61, and R. Morghen, *Cahiers de civilisation médiévale*, 9 (1966), pp. 239–43.

[449] A. Mens, *Oorsprong en betekenis van de Nederlandse Begijnen* (Brussels, 1947); E. McDonnell, *The beguines and beghards in medieval culture, with special emphasis on the Belgian scene*

Rhineland.[450] In Italy, devout women seem to have preferred to seek salvation *in domibus propriis*, as shown by the success of the third order of the Humiliati and the *ordo paenitentium beati Francisci* in towns from Lombardy to Latium.[451] Unmarried women who joined these orders continued to live at home with their parents, where they led a life devoted to prayer and penitential practices.[452] Sometimes, they left home to shut themselves away in cells or *reclusoria* where, with the permission of the local bishop, they lived by the labour of their own hands and alms donated by private persons or the commune.[453] Married women could, like their husbands, join communities of penitents or, later, tertiaries, who ordered their lives according to a *propositium*, an ideal of life rather than a rule, since it did not involve permanent vows and the fact of transgressing did not constitute a sin strictly speaking.[454]

It is within this developing spiritual and institutional context that we should see the forms of female lay sainthood found from the thirteenth century on. The women who were the subject of a process of canonization at this period belonged to the penitential trend, and I have emphasized its importance in the religious advancement of the faithful. But the complexity of their personalities and situations means we cannot make these women conform to one single model.

Penitence and charity

In many ways, St Hedwig, duchess of Silesia (d. 1243), seems to continue into the thirteenth century a tradition well represented in the

---

(New Brunswick, 1954). The Cistercians and, later, the Dominicans greatly influenced lay female movements here: S. Roisin, 'L'efflorescence cistercienne et le courant féminin de piété a XIIIe siècle', *RHE*, 39 (1943), pp. 342–78.

[450] H. Grundmann's *Religiöse Bewegungen im Mittelalter* (2nd edn, Darmstadt, 1961), pp. 170–355, 394–475, 524–44, remains fundamental. See also M. Bolton, 'Mulieres sanctae', in *Sanctity and secularity: the Church and the world*, ed. D. Baker (Oxford, 1973), pp. 77–95; J.-C. Schmitt, *Mort d'une hérésie: l'Eglise et les clercs face aux béguines et aux béghards du Rhin Supérieur, du XIVe au XVe siècle* (Paris and The Hague, 1978).

[451] A. Mens, sv Humiliés, in *Dictionnaire de spiritualité*, VII (Paris, 1969), cc. 1129–36. The existence of an *Ordo Poenitentium beati Francisci* before 1280 in Italy, questioned by Meersseman (*Dossier de l'Ordre de la Pénitence*), is convincingly reasserted in Schmucki, ed., *L'Ordine della Penitenza di San Francesco d'Assisi*; see also Mariano d'Alatri, ed., *I Frati Penitenti di San Francesco nella società del due e trecento* (Rome, 1977).

[452] As with Rose of Viterbo, Umiliana dei Cerchi in Florence and Vanna in Orvieto; see above, pp. 207–9.

[453] Their way of life is described in great detail in Garampi, *Beata Chiara da Rimini*, pp. 79–150; see also M. Sensi, 'Incarcerate e Penitenti a Foligno nella prima metà del trecento', in *I Frati Penitenti di San Francesco*, pp. 291–308.

[454] G. G. Meersseman, 'La loi purement pénale d'après les statuts des confréries médiévales', in *Mélanges Joseph De Ghellinck* (Gembloux, 1951), pp. 975–1002. In the words of

hagiography of the preceding centuries: that of the princess or queen who achieved sainthood through the wise use of the influence she wielded as a result of her high birth and prominent social position.[455] She was praised for having founded a Cistercian abbey – Trebnitz (Trzebnica) – which attracted nuns from the best families of the Silesian nobility and was directed by her own daughter.[456] Fascinated by the cloistered life, Hedwig tended to see as sacred everything that emanated from the regulars and could conceive of salvation only in close association with monasticism. In general, she felt for the clergy an intense veneration, linked to her eucharistic piety.[457] Other aspects of her personality also call to mind the saintly women of the early Middle Ages. Her biographer celebrated the firmness and insensibility she demonstrated in difficult circumstances, praising her for not having shed a single tear on the death of her husband and son, Henry, struck down by the Tartars.[458] But in other ways, the sanctity of this great lady was marked by the concerns of her time. Though she remained a widow, she refused to become a nun at Trebnitz, despite the appeals of her family. Her choice was motivated by the desire to live in the world so that she could continue to engage in the works of charity she believed to be more important and more meritorious.[459] She felt a great love for the poor and devoted herself to alleviating all forms of misery; she maintained a squad of indigents on a permanent basis and distrib-

Henricus de Segusio (*Hostiensis*), 'Broadly speaking, we call religious those who live a holy and religious life at home, not because they accept a specific rule but because they lead a harder and simpler life than do the rest of the laity who live in a purely worldly manner': *Summa aurea*, III (Venice, 1570), p. 193.

[455] Her process has not survived, but the *Legenda maior* (= *BHL* 3766), written *c*.1300 by a German cleric, is closely based on it: ed. *AA.SS.* Oct. VIII, pp. 224–64. There is also a late thirteenth-century genealogy demonstrating her noble origins and lineage (= *BHL* 3768), ed. *AA.SS.* Oct. VIII, pp. 265–7. See also Gottschalk, *Die Hl. Hedwige Herzogin von Schlesian*: T. Wasowicz, *Legenda Slaska* (Warsaw, 1967).

[456] T. Kruszynski, 'Swieta Jadwiga i jet sanktuarium w Trzebnicy', *Collectanea theologica*, 28 (1957), pp. 598–705.

[457] *Legenda maior*, p. 228. Indeed, she felt a veritable 'Eucharistic starvation', as a result of which she attended as many masses as possible. One of the clerics in her entourage composed the following verse on this subject, quoted in the *Legenda maior* (p. 235): 'In sola missa non est contenta ducissa. Quot sunt presbyteri, missas tot oportet haberi.' St Hedwig attached great importance to holy water and piously collected the crumbs from the table of clergy and regulars, which she regarded 'ut angelorum escam sanctorum': *ibid.*, p. 228.

[458] *Legenda maior*, p. 229.

[459] When her daughter, a Cistercian nun, asked why she would not join her in the nunnery, St Hedwig replied: 'non ignoras, filia, quantun sit meriti eleemosynas elargiri': *ibid.*, p. 229.

uted alms to those who sought her aid.[460] Her solicitude for the *pauperes Christi* was rooted in an ardent devotion to the humanity of Christ, and especially his Passion.[461] Meditation on the sufferings of the man-God drove her to increase the number of her penitential practices; she wore a coarse hair shirt and even a belt which cut into her flesh (and which her Franciscan confessor eventually made her remove), scourged herself, fasted etc. As she wore no stockings inside her sandals, she soon developed bloody sores which some of the witnesses at the canonization process tried to liken to stigmata. But, in her case, these mortifications were not accompanied by any desire for glory and were tempered by a sense of *discretio* which enabled her to avoid the excess which provoked unease.[462] In the last analysis, the sanctity of Hedwig was characterized by a mixture of archaic and modern features, which we should probably see as a consequence of the dual influence she had experienced on the spiritual plane: that of the Cistercians, first, whose rigour had marked her deeply; then that of the Mendicant orders, especially the Franciscans, from whom she chose her confessors during the last years of her life.

The life of St Elizabeth, daughter of King Andrew II of Hungary and wife of Landgrave Lewis of Thuringia, shows a similar dual influence.[463] From her marriage until her death, her director of conscience was the terrible inquisitor, Conrad of Marburg, who probably belonged to the Praemonstratensian order, whilst also being very alive to the message which the Friars Minor were then beginning to preach throughout the Germanic world with dazzling success.[464] But the new elements clearly predominate. The essence of the sanctity of St Elizabeth was charity, seen as an active engagement on behalf of the poor, whose

[460] *Ibid.*, pp. 237–9. See also p. 229: 'pauperes omnes et precipue religiosos reputabat dominos suos, non quidem divitiis sed sanctitate sibi prelatos'.
[461] *Ibid.*, p. 236: 'ubicumque in terra videbat stipulas crucem figurantes, genibus flexis adorans tollensque et deosculans, eas in loco tali reposuit ubi non poterant conculcari'.
[462] *Ibid.*, pp. 231–2. The author quotes, in particular, the evidence of Sister Juliana of Trebnitz, who calls these wounds 'signacula sanctitatis'. For her *discretio*, see *ibid.*, p. 230.
[463] W. Maurer, 'Zum Verständnis der heiligen Elisabeth von Thüringen', *Zeitschrift für Kirchengeschichte*, 65 (1953–4), pp. 16–64; Maurer, 'Die heilige Elisabeth im Lichte der Frömmigkeit ihrer Zeit', *Theologische Literaturzeitung*, 79 (1954), pp. 401–10; J. Ancelet-Hustache, *Sainte Elisabeth de Hongrie* (Paris, 1947).
[464] The acts of her process have survived; they comprise the *Dicta IV ancillarum*, the evidence of Conrad of Marburg, and the miracles recorded in 1233, all ed. Huyskens, *Quellenstudien zur Geschichte der hl. Elisabeth. Landgräfin von Thüringen*.

life and sufferings she attempted to share.[465] Refusing to enter a nunnery after the death of her husband, in 1227, she assumed the habit of a penitent to put herself entirely at their service.[466] As with the Mendicant saints, love of the disinherited was for her inseparable from a striving for humility. We know from her maidservants that she refused to be called *domina* and insisted on being addressed informally.[467] Her deepest desire was to be able to beg, but Conrad of Marburg formally prohibited this, which caused her much soul-searching.[468]

There was more to the sanctity of St Elizabeth, however, than generous alms-giving and love of the poor seen as Christ-like figures. She also possessed a strong sense of justice and injustice. While her husband was alive, this obsession led her to abstain from 'impure' dishes, that is, any food which she suspected of resulting from exactions from the poor or the Church, to use which would have offended her conscience.[469] The refusal of all compromise with evil, including in its economic form, which characterized her life as a great lady later culminated in a veritable mysticism of asceticism. After the death of her husband, she renounced all her possessions in order to bring a little happiness and joy into the lives of the sick and the lepers.[470] Even more than St Clare, whose desire for poverty was frustrated by the constraints of the cloistered religious life, it was St Elizabeth who, of the women of her time, best realized the ideal of St Francis in this sphere.[471] This is hardly surprising, given the extent to

---

[465] This point is made by Gregory IX in the bull of canonization, which is ed. L. Santifaller, 'Zur originalüberlieferung der Heiligsprechungsurkunde der Landgräfin Elisabeth von Thüringen vom Jahre 1235', in *Acht Jahrhunderte Deutscher Orden in Einzeldatstellungen*, ed. K. Weiser (Bad Godesburg, 1967), pp. 73–88.

[466] See the depositions of the witnesses at the 1233 process, ed. Huyskens, *Quellenstudien*, pp. 135, 148; W. Maruer, 'Die hl. Elisabeth und ihr Marburger Hospital', *Jahrbuch d. Heissischen Kirchengeschichtevereinigung*, 7 (1956), pp. 36–9.

[467] Guyskens, *Quellenstudien*, p. 136.

[468] In the face of the dogged refusal of her confessor, she eventually cried: 'hoc faciam quod me non potestis prohibere!': Huyskens, *Quellenstudien*, p. 157; see also pp. 120, 125.

[469] *Dicta IV ancillarum*, pp. 115, 116, 129 etc. For the precise significance of this behaviour, which seems to have made a deep impression on contemporaries, see A. Vauchez, 'Charité et pauvreté chez Ste Elisabeth de Thuringe', in *Etudes sur l'histoire de la pauvreté (Moyen Age–XVIe siècle)*, ed. M. Mollat, I (Paris, 1974), pp. 163–73.

[470] Joy was a very important element in the spiritual life of St Elizabeth – something she felt both when giving alms and performing the dirtiest jobs (*PC*, p. 119) and tried to procure for others: (after a distribution of alms) 'ceperunt cantare pauperes et bene se habere, quo audito dicebat beata Elisabeth, "ecce dixi vobis quod letos deberemus facere homines" . . . et ipsa gaudens erat cum gaudentibus' (p. 133).

[471] Contrary to the views of several French historians, in particular M. Bihl, 'Die heilige Elisabeth von Thüringen als Terziarin', *Franziskanische Studien*, 18 (1931), pp. 259–93,

which early Franciscanism was a lay religious movement, whose spiritual requirements could more easily be lived in their entirety by the simple faithful, strangers to both the limitations and the privileges implied by the canonical status of the regulars.[472] The fact that SS Elizabeth and Hedwig were canonized respectively in 1231 and 1267 is evidence that the Roman Church approved this development. Sanctification through the practice of charity and the search for poverty now constituted the 'royal way' of lay sainthood, especially for women. It was not, however, the only way, and the prestige of the model incarnated by the two great German women saints was soon to be eclipsed by other forms of perfection.

From contemplation to mysticism

In parallel with this charitable trend, there emerged another dimension of sainthood: the contemplative life. This was central to the religious experience of the other two lay women who were the object of a process of canonization in the thirteenth century: Rose of Viterbo (d. 1251) and Ingrid of Skänninge (d. 1282).[473] Despite the fragmentary nature of the documentation, we can see that, with them, the penitential movement had evolved in an increasingly 'spiritual' direction. There was, in Rose of Viterbo, none of the evangelical realism or concern to share in a concrete way the life of the people which characterized the first Franciscan generation.[474] Although she renounced her possessions and the pleasures of the world, the essence of her sanctity, for contemporaries, seems to have lain primarily in her visionary gifts; she had apparitions of the Virgin Mary,

St Elisabeth never belonged to the third Franciscan order, as was, in fact, noted in his Chronicle by an Italian Friar Minor, Fra Elemosina (d. 1339); see S. Gieben, 'Bruder Elemosinas Doppelbericht zum Leben der hl. Elisabeth von Thüringen', *Collectanea Franciscana*, 35 (1965), pp. 166–76. But her spirituality was influenced by the Poverello and his disciples.

[472] K. Esser, *Origini e valori autentici dell'ordine dei Frati Minori* (Milan, 1972).

[473] For Rose of Viterbo, the only contemporary document is the *Vita prima*, written in the second half of the thirteenth century, of which only the first ten chapters survive, ed. G. Abate, *S. Rosa di Viterbo terziaria Francescana: fonti storiche della vita e loro revisione critica* (Rome, 1952). The acts of the process ordered by Calixtus III in 1456 and held in 1457, still preserved in the archives of the monastery of St Rose at Viterbo, are ed. *AA.SS.* Sept. II, pp. 442–79. Only a few fragments of St Ingrid's canonization process survive; they are ed. H. Schuck, 'Tva svenska biografer fran Medeltiden', *Antiqvarisk Tidskrift*, 5 (1895), pp. 463–6; also Gallen, 'Les causes de Ste Ingrid et des saints suédois au temps de la Réforme', pp. 32–7.

[474] It has never been proved that the community of penitents to which St Rose was attached belonged to the Franciscans; see S. da Campagnola, 'L' "ordo poenitentium" di San Francesco nelle cronache del Duecento', in *L'Ordine dell Penitenza*, pp. 157–8.

also of Christ on the cross, at the sight of which, she cried out and groaned.[475] When she went out, she carried a diptych painted with the face of the Saviour. The only specifically lay feature of her life was her activity on behalf of the Roman Church in a town which was dominated by the Ghibellines and where heretics and supporters of Frederick II held sway. As a result, she and her family were expelled from Viterbo, in December 1250, by the podesta, Mainetto di Bovolo. The death of the emperor, a few weeks later, made it possible for her to return and enjoy the reputation of prophetess, since some remarks she had made before her expulsion could be interpreted as a premonition of this important event. She then tried to join the Clares, but they refused to accept her.[476] The life of Ingrid of Skänninge has some features in common with that of Rose of Viterbo, although it was lived in a different context. The daughter of an important Swedish noble family, she placed herself, after the death of her husband, under the direction of the Dominican Peter of Dacia, and formed a small community of beguines, before making a pilgrimage to Jerusalem and Rome. Her principal objective then became to obtain permission from the pope to found a convent of Dominican nuns at Skänninge. Martin IV eventually agreed and the new foundation was opened in 1281. Ingrid, who had meanwhile become a Dominican nun, died there the following year.[477]

The fact that these two women aspired to lead a life of the monastic type is an illustration of the growing importance of contemplation in the Church's conception of female sainthood, and even of sainthood itself.[478]

---

[475] *Vita prima*, p. 227. Before the women who surrounded her, St Rose cried: 'Andate quia ego video sponsam Christi speciosissimam, quam nemo vestrum vidit.' Before Christ on the Cross, she asked: 'Pater, quis te crucifixit?'

[476] F. Casolini, sv Rosa di Viterbo, in *BS*, XI (Rome, 1968), cc. 413–25.

[477] A. L. Sibilia, sv Ingrid Elofsdotter, in *BS*, VII (Rome, 1966), cc. 816–17; J. Gallen, *La province de Dacie de l'ordre des Frères Prêcheurs* (Rome and Helsinki, 1946), pp. 124–9. Her life, Dominican influence apart, seems to anticipate that of St Bridget, and it was under the influence of spiritual circles linked to Bridget and at the abbey of Vadstena that her canonization process started in 1417, nothing of the sort having, apparently, been considered in the thirteenth century.

[478] For this shift at the level of local sanctity, see above, pp. 210–12. The shift from active to contemplative sanctity can be traced in the life of B. Jutta of Sangerhausen (d. *c.*1260), for whom an enquiry *de vita et miraculis* was held in 1275 on the initiative of the clergy of the diocese of Kulmsee (East Prussia). This diocesan process has been reconstructed on the basis of original documents and later copies by H. Westpfahl, 'Untersuchungen über Jutta von Sangerhausen', *Zeitschrift für Geschichte und Altertumskunde Ermlands*, 26 (1938), pp. 515–96. Left a widow with several children, Jutta first adopted the practice of voluntary poverty, 'exemplo sanctae Elisabeth Thuringiae lantgraviae, quibus ex finibus erat': *PC*, p. 580. When her children grew up, she began to serve lepers; Christ, in an apparition, made her touch the wound in his side (pp. 584–6); finally, she opted

In fact, during the course of the thirteenth century, female spirituality increasingly evolved in a mystical direction. This was first visible in Germany, where Mechtilde of Magdeburg (d. 1282 or 1298), Mechtilde of Hackeborn (d. 1295) and Gertrude the Great (d. 1302) carried on the visionary tradition started by Elizabeth of Schönau (d. 1165) and Hildegard of Bingen (d. 1179).[479] In the Low Countries, after 1200, centres of intense religious life blossomed, both in certain Cistercian houses and among the laity. From Mary of Oignies (d. 1213) to Margaret of Ypres (d. 1237) and Hadewijch of Antwerp (mid-thirteenth century), many beguines and penitents scaled the highest peaks of contemplation.[480] In the Mediterranean countries, these trends seem to have developed later and in close association with the Mendicant orders. The first generation of mystics appeared there between 1260 and 1310. Its most celebrated representatives in Provence were Douceline (d. 1274), sister of Hugh of Digne, and in Italy Margaret of Cortona (d. 1297) and Angela of Foligno (d. 1309).[481] But it was only in the fourteenth century that the Roman Church began to pay attention to the sanctity of these ecstatic women, who enjoyed extraordinary gifts ranging from the power to see into people's hearts to levitation.[482]

for the way of contemplation and went to Prussia, where she settled in a hermitage deep in the forests which stretched from Kulmsee to Torun, where she stayed till her death and was soon renowned for the mystical graces and revelations she received (pp. 589–91). See also AA.SS. Maii II, pp. 604–13; J. Westpfahl, sv Jutta de Sangerhausen (bienheureuse), in Dictionnaire de spiritualité, VIII (Paris, 1974), cc. 1648–9.

[479] M. Grabmann, 'Die deutsche Frauenmystik des Mittelalters. Ein Uberblick', in Mittelalterliches Geistesleben (Munich, 1926), pp. 469–88; of the many works devoted to these mystics, I quote only two: K. Koster, 'Das visionäre Werk Elisabeths von Schönau', Archiv für Mittelrheinische Kirchengeschichte, 4 (1952), pp. 79–119; P. Doyère, sv Gertrude d'Helfta (sainte), in Dictionnaire de spiritualité, VI (Paris, 1967), cc. 331–9.

[480] For an overall view, see Roisin, L'hagiographie cistercienne; for the lay element, A. Mens, L'Ombrie italienne et l'Ombrie brabançonne: deux courants religieux parallèles d'inspiration commune (Paris, 1967); see also Meersseman, 'Les frères prêcheurs'; J. Leclercq, F. Vandenbroucke and L. Bouyer, La spiritualité du Moyen Age (Paris, 1957), pp. 430–8.

[481] Mystical states are described in detail in the Life of St Douceline, which first appeared in 1297, La Vie de Sainte Douceline, ed. Gout. See also A. Sisto, Figure del primo Francescanesimo in Provenza: Ugo e Douceline di Digne (Florence, 1971); Carozzi, 'Une béguine joachimite'. Mystical trends in central Italy in the late thirteenth century are discussed in G. Petrocchi's excellent 'Correnti e linee della spiritualità umbra ed italiana del Duecento', in Atti del IVe convegno di studi Umbri (Gubbio 1966) (Perugia, 1967), pp. 133–76, with full bibliography.

[482] Apart from St Clare of Montefalco, discussed above with the nuns, the mystics who were the subject of a process of canonization in the fourteenth century were: Delphine of Puimichel (or of Sabran) (d. 1360); the acts of the process held in 1363 in Apt are in MS 355, Bibliothèque Méjanes, Aix-en-Provence; St Bridget (d. 1373); the acts of the enquiry held in Sweden and Italy into her life and miracles, between 1376 and 1380, are ed. Collijn, Acta et processus canonizacionis Beate Birgitte; Dorothy of Montau (d. 1394);

With the exception of Clare of Montefalco, all these saints were lay women whose spiritual experience was lived outside the cloister.[483] This paradoxical situation is probably in part explained by the laxity which had affected many nunneries by the late thirteenth century, making them unattractive to high-minded souls in search of perfection. But it is also a result of changed ideas, the religious life increasingly tending to be identified with a solitary search for union with God, which was difficult to reconcile with the requirements of a collective life.[484]

The ratification by the Church of mystical sainthood was an important event in the history of spirituality. Previously, with rare exceptions, women had only been able to realize their religious vocation in association with a community of men and in their wake. At the beginning of the thirteenth century, Elizabeth of Thuringia was still, as we have seen, strictly subjected to her director of conscience, who on occasion imposed his own conceptions on her and even struck her.[485] A few decades later, the relations between the saints and their male entourages had begun to change. Admittedly, from Margaret of Cortona to Dorothy of Montau, pious lay women continued, as in the past, to be surrounded by clergy, but, in many cases, the latter appear more as disciples than spiritual masters.[486] The best known and most spectacular example is that of St Catherine of Siena, whose 'brigade' united in mutual admiration of the 'mama' ecclesiastics from very different backgrounds, though the Dominicans pre-

---

the enquiry carried out at Marienwerder (Eastern Prussia) between 1404 and 1406 is in MS 1241, Staatliche Archivlager, Göttingen; St Catherine of Siena (d. 1380); the diocesan process held in Venice between 1411 and 1416 on the orders of the bishop of Castello, which served as canonization process in 1461, is ed. Laurent, *Il processo Castellano*.

[483] Delphine of Puimichel, Bridget of Sweden, Dorothy of Montau and Joan-Marie of Maillé were married and subsequently widowed; Catherine of Siena lived at home with her family.

[484] Many of the lay women who were the subject of a canonization process in the fourteenth century lived in a reclusorium. The best justification of reclusion is in the process of Delphine of Sabran (*PC*, fol. 93v), where it is said that she shut herself up 'ut sic sola cum solo sponso Christo liberius Deo servire et contemplare posset'. A similar attitude is visible in Dorothy of Montau, who ended her days in a cell adjoining the cathedral of Marienwerder (*PC*, arts. 17, 18), and Joan-Marie of Maillé, a recluse at Tours and Angers: *PC* in *AA.SS*. Oct. VIII, p. 747; also *Vita* (*BHL* 5515), *ibid.*, pp. 735–8.

[485] See above, p. 375, n. 468.

[486] The phenomenon is more marked in the Mediterranean regions, where the laity enjoyed great autonomy in relation to the clergy in religious affairs, than in northern Europe. Dorothy of Montau seems to have been very much under the control of her director and future biographer, the theologian John of Marienwerder: *PC Dorothy*, fol. 203: 'Adiunxit ei Dominus dicens: tu et confessor tuus unam debetis habere voluntatem; et illam debet habere non tu sed ille.' See also R. Stachnik and A. Triller, *Dorothea von Montau: eine preussische Heilige des 14. Jahrhunderts* (Münster, 1976).

dominated.[487] But this was not exceptional, being equally present in the cases of Delphine and St Bridget. The former, from her reclusorium in Cabrières and her *oustau* in Apt, exercised a profound influence on many clerics, both seculars and regulars, from Provence and the Comtat, who came to her in search of 'spiritual consolations'.[488] St Bridget was surrounded by regulars, such as *Petrus Olavi* and Alfonso of Jaen, anxious to collect and commit to writing the revelations dictated by her divine Husband.[489] So, through the mystical experience, women were able, at the end of the Middle Ages, to break the tie of dependence which bound them to men and invert it to their own advantage. Previously excluded from the ministry of the Word, they were now the organ chosen by the Spirit to transmit its messages to the Christian people.

The mystical saints of the fourteenth century did not hesitate to make representations to the pope and prelates, sometimes in the strongest terms, in order to acquaint them with the will of God. We know from the acts of her canonization process that Delphine of Sabran had a meeting with Clement VI in Avignon, which must have had some importance though we do not know what was said. She received several visits from Urban V's brother, Cardinal Anglic Grimoard, who testified at length concerning her.[490] We are better informed about the virulent criticisms of the state of the Church and the suggestions for reform made to Gregory XI by St Bridget, who saw the pontiff's return to Rome as only paving the way for a profound transformation within the hierarchy and the clergy. These pressing warnings to princes and the great of this world were accompanied by accusations and threats.[491] The precise role of Catherine of Siena in the

---

[487] R. Fawtier and L. Canet, *La double expérience de Catherine Benincasa (Saint Catherine de Sienne)* (Paris, 1948); G. G. Meersseman, 'Gli amici spirituali di S. Caterina a Roma nel 1378, alla luce del primo manifesto urbanista', *Bollettino senese di storia patria*, 69 (1962), pp. 82–123.

[488] We know from depositions at her canonization process in 1363 that she 'converted' Bertrand, bishop of Apt, and many canons to a better life and that she brought back into the fold Franciscans with heretical ideas about poverty and the Roman Church: *PC Delphine*, fols. 54v, 188v.

[489] Of course, St Bridget, like the other mystics of her day, was herself influenced by her advisors, and they may have modified the message they were entrusted with writing down, if only in the course of translating it from the vernacular into Latin. But the fact remains that it was she who took the initiative, her entourage acting simply as instrument and mouthpiece, even if their role was larger than appears. See plate 32.

[490] *PC Delphine*, fols. 83r–v.

[491] *PC Bridget*, p. 519: 'quod statim postquam veniret [the pope to Rome], inciperet reformare sanctam Dei ecclesiam et omnes status ecclesiasticos et reducere eos pristinum statum sanctitatis primevorum patrum sanctorum et quod extirparet certa vicia de Curia Romana et mutaret consiliarios et mores suos'. See also *ibid.*, pp. 525–6.

events of 1376–8 has been much discussed by historians in recent decades.[492] At the very least, the witnesses who testified at the process in Venice (1406–11) were convinced that it had been considerable,[493] and, from our perspective, their conviction matters more than the objective historical reality. It shows that, for some ecclesiastical circles and the papacy itself, the intervention of a woman in the affairs of the Church was something that was, if not normal, at least admissible, when the authenticity of her message was attested by extraordinary gifts and unquestionable orthodoxy.[494]

In spite of the new role it allowed women to play within the Church, the success of the mystical model was not without ambiguity. With the single exception of St Catherine of Siena, all the prophetesses and visionaries of the late Middle Ages were wives, and some were mothers. But their reputation for sanctity owed nothing to this aspect of their lives. The processes of canonization portray the marriage as simply an accident in their life or, at most, a stage soon put behind them, whose importance the promoters of the cause and the witnesses sought to minimize. I have already made the same point with regard to the male lay saints.[495] But the question was trickier in the case of women, since, in their case, a centuries-old hagiographical tradition linked perfection and virginity.[496] The persistence of these ideas in the fourteenth century is shown by the example of Delphine of Puimichel, who imposed, then persuaded her husband, Elzear of Sabran, to accept, a total renunciation of carnal relations.[497]

[492] In particular by Fawtier, *La double expérience*, pp. 150ff (who plays it down).
[493] *PC Catherine of Siena*, ed. Laurent, pp. 430ff.
[494] This type of direct appeal to sovereigns is characteristic of female sainthood between the mid-fourteenth and mid-fifteenth centuries. In addition to the obvious example of Joan of Arc, we may note B. Joan-Marie of Maillé, who went to Tours in 1395 and Paris in 1398 to convey to Charles VI the warnings given her by God: *Vita* (= *BHL* 5515), ed. *AA.SS.* Oct. VIII, pp. 740–1; B. Ursuline of Parma (1375–1408), who travelled to Rome and Avignon to ask Boniface IX and Clement VII to bring the Schism to an end: *Vita* (= *BHL* 8452), ed. *AA.SS.* Apr. I, pp. 723–39.
[495] See above, pp. 357–8.
[496] P. Browe, *Beiträge zur Sexualethik des Mittelalters* (Breslau, 1932) remains a useful synthesis; see also S. Pinckaers, 'Ce que le Moyen Age pensait du mariage', *La vie spirituelle, Supplément*, 20 (1968), pp. 413–40. For the formation of Christian doctrine in this area, see C. H. Nodet, 'Position de S. Jérome en face des problèmes sexuels', in *Mystique et continence* (Paris, 1952), pp. 308–56; M. Meslin, 'Sainteté et mariage au cours de la seconde querelle pélagienne', *ibid.*, pp. 293–307. Despite its promising title, J. Bugge's *Virginitas: an essay in the history of medieval idea* (The Hague, 1975) adds little new.
[497] *PC Delphine*, art. 1, fol. 11; witness 5 on art. 1, fol. 68: 'delectabatur loqui de conservacione virginitatis et propterea tenebat semper religiosas personas secum'. The theme of virginal marriage is very common in medieval hagiography, as shown by B. de Gaiffier, 'Intactam sponsam relinquens', *Anal. Boll.*, 65 (1947), pp. 157–97. The problem was

Admittedly, the history of this couple is exceptional, but, in the texts concerning the other women saints, marriage is rarely mentioned in a favourable light. Usually, it appears purely as a social obligation, to which they had to conform to avoid incurring the wrath of their family.[498] It was also emphasized that the union of the spouses was consummated only some time after the ceremony and, most of all, that the saint never took pleasure in her relations with her husband, when he insisted on his *debitum conjugale*.[499] The sexual act, even performed within Christian marriage and with procreation as its purpose, remained fundamentally sinful, since it might be a source of pleasure.[500] The married women saints, therefore, practised periodic continence – increasingly frequently as they grew older – and endeavoured to persuade their husbands to abstain from all sexual activity after the birth of a number of children.[501] A few texts do refer to the triple purpose of marriage (*bonum prolis*, *bonum fidei*, *bonum*

also discussed by theologians and canonists. Peter Lombard made a collection of texts in support of its validity (*Sentences*, IV, 26 6) and his position was supported by Thomas Aquinas, who said in his *Summa (II a II ae*, 152, fol. 4): 'As his [Lombard's] text shows, a marriage without carnal relations is holier.' See also G. Le Bras, 'Le mariage dans la théologie et le droit de l'Eglise du XIe au XIIIe siècle', *Cahiers de civilisation médiévale*, 11 (1968), pp. 191–202.

[498] See, for example, the justification in the bull of canonization of St Bridget issued by Boniface IX in 1391: 'eadem, licet in statu virginali servire Deo totis desideriis affectaret, tandem per parentes compulsa quondam Ulfoni desponsatur': *AA.SS*. Oct. IV, p. 459.

[499] St Bridget remained a virgin for two years after her marriage (*PC*, art. 23, p. 20), Dorothy of Montau for a fortnight (*PC*, witness 74, fol. 139).

[500] J. T. Noonan, *Contraception et mariage: evolution ou contradiction de la pensée chrétienne?* (Paris, 1969), especially part 1, discussing the views of various medieval authors who wrote on this question; for the attitude of theologians and clergy to marriage and sexual pleasure, see J. C. Ziegler, *Die Ehelehre der Pönitentialsummen von 1200–1300: eine Untersuchung zur Geschichte der Moral- und Pastoral-Theologie* (Ratisbon, 1956). The depositions recorded at the processes are in accord with such ideas, for example in the case of Dorothy of Montau. Her spiritual director, John of Marienwerder, says that she 'necque in actu matrimonii unquam illecebrosam temptationem sensibiliter percepit', adding 'hoc licet videatur mirabile, attamen reputo non incredibile et verum credo'. According to another witness, she took steps to make the sexual act painful: 'in actu matrimonii quando debitum reddebat marito suo, testas nucum infra lumbos ligaverat et in vulnere posuerit ut in tali actu affligeretur in tantum quod non sentiret aliquam delectationem': *PC Dorothy*, fols. 197, 238.

[501] Even for the ordinary faithful, conjugal relations were forbidden during pregnancy (see *PC Dorothy*, fol. 139: 'audivit ab ipsa Dorothea quod non solebat se facere cognosci quando fuit impreagnata') and lactation; also at certain times prescribed by the Church (Noonan, *Contraception et mariage*, pp. 364ff), but from the end of the twelfth century this was no longer purely advisory. The saints clearly observed the rules strictly, as we see, for example, from the *Legenda maior* of St Hedwig, closely based on the process: 'hunc modum in matrimonio continendi [from Advent to Epiphany, from Septuagesima to the Octave of Easter and from Rogations to the Octave of Whitsuntide, that is about twenty weeks in all] sancitum a sancta matre Ecclesia quousque poterat instruebat'. Hedwig eventually persuaded her husband to make a vow of perpetual chastity before a bishop: *AA.SS*. Oct. VIII, pp. 225–6.

sacramenti), emphasizing in passing that the couple had achieved all these aims.[502] In practice, it was the wife who took responsibility for the husband on the spiritual plane; under the benign influence of his pious companion, the husband, presented as a gross creature, filled with evil desires, attained a spiritual and moral life worthy of praise and sometimes eventually himself became a sort of monk, even a saint.[503] Whether this happened or not, the death of the husband – since almost all these women spent longer as widows than wives – appears in the processes as a veritable liberation. Far from contemplating a second marriage or devoting themselves to the education of their children, they welcomed with open arms the opportunity to renounce temporal preoccupations and earthly possessions, a necessary precondition for sanctification.[504] At the end of a life of prayer and contemplation, the female soul, escaping this mortal coil, achieved a mystical union with Christ which rendered void all earthly unions.[505]

Far from lessening with time, the disparagement of married life, seen only as a concession to human weakness and the necessities of social life, continued to grow during the later Middle Ages, under the influence of mystical spirituality. Whilst in the process of Elizabeth of Thuringia, in 1234, there were still a few references to the love existing between the saint and her young husband, after 1330 we find only unions contracted unwillingly, which seem to have given satisfaction to neither party.[506] The

---

[502] *PC Dorothy*, art. 12, fol. 9: 'inter quos conjuges fuit honestum et honorabile connubium et torus immaculus, triplicique bono matrimonio decoratus'. The depositions of many witnesses flatly contradicted this claim. See below, n. 506.

[503] See, for example, the processes of St Hedwig ('jam quasi monachus factus est': *Legenda maior*, p. 226) and, above all, Delphine, whose husband, St Elzear of Sabran, canonized in 1369, is presented by his biographers as a new Joseph. See plate 33.

[504] St Elizabeth, after the death of her husband, sent away her youngest child, then eighteen months old, 'ne minis diligeret eum et ne per illum impediretur in servition Dei': *PC*, p. 137. St Bridget shed no tears when told of the death of her sons: *PC*, p. 314. These signs of savage virtue may reveal not so much the mental cruelty of the saints as the desire of the promoters of the cause and the witnesses to illustrate dramatically the triumph of grace over nature.

[505] The theme of celestial marriage is already present in the bull of canonization of St Elizabeth, promulgated by Gregory IX in 1235 (Fontanini, *Codex constitutionum*, pp. 73–4). But it remained a colourful metaphor, whereas, in the fourteenth century, the notion of mystical marriage assumed a much more concrete form. This is very clear in the case of Dorothy of Montau, who, during the course of her ecstasies, experienced physiological sensations similar to those which accompany orgasm: *PC*, fol. 156. The conclusions of L. Beirnaert, 'La signification du symbolisme conjugal dans la vie mystique', in *Mystique et continence*, pp. 380–9, seem to me much too cautious when compared with several medieval mystical texts where the theme is not treated only symbolically.

[506] Dorothy of Montau's husband seems to have beaten her because of her frigidity: *PC*, fol. 141. The biographer of Joan-Marie of Maillé, the Friar Minor Martin of Boisgaultier, refers in sombre terms to her married life: *Vita*, p. 735. The extreme case, not much later than our period, is that of St Francesca Romana (1394–1440), who, when she slept with her husband, Lorenzo dei Ponziani, vomited profusely immediately after; see the

fact that a woman had been married did not prevent her from achieving
sainthood, but the notion of conjugal chastity lost ground, whilst virginity
once again became the ideal norm of Christian perfection.[507] Joan of Arc
dressing as a man to accomplish her mission is more representative of the
religious conceptions of the age than the many female saints with a husband and children.[508] Virgins and wives were firmly persuaded that carnal
attachments constituted an obstacle that must at all costs be overcome in
their quest for God.

With this complete reversal of perspectives, those who incarnated, in
the eyes of the spiritual writers of the feudal period, physical and moral
weakness, were, from the end of the fourteenth century, best placed to
achieve salvation. This change in the Church's attitude was closely linked
to the spiritualization of the religious ideal.[509] More detached than men
from temporal contingencies, since they lacked culture, power and wealth
of their own, and not even their bodies belonged to them, they escaped
most of the temptations which threatened men.[510] It might even be said
that they acceded all the more easily to sainthood because they were mere
nothings. Their perfection was defined by a total abandonment to divine
will, rewarded by the grant of exceptional graces: the gift of clairvoyance,
the prophetic spirit, visions, revelations etc. Their ignorance allowed them
to possess innate knowledge, their fervent devotion to the body of Christ
to do without material food, their ready association with his sufferings to
achieve physical insensibility, in the rapture of the perfect union.[511] It is
not enough to note the increasing importance of women among the lay
saints. We need also to consider which aspects of femininity attracted the
attention of the clergy. The latter were fascinated not by their qualities as

acts of the process of canonization, ed. P. Lugano, *I processi inediti per Francesca Bussa
di Ponziani (S. Francesca Romana) 1440–1453* (Vatican City, 1945).

[507] At the process of St Catherine of Siena, the Dominican Thomas Caffarini claimed that
her cause was superior to that of St Bridget of Sweden because the latter had been
married: *PC Catherine of Siena*, p. 97.

[508] For the significance of the way in which some women saints, from Christian Antiquity
to the end of the Middle Ages, disguised themselves as men, see M. Delcourt, 'Le
complexe de Diane dans l'hagiographie chrétienne', *Revue de l'histoire des religions*, 153
(1959), pp. 1–33 (who sees it as a sign of a break with the feminine past and a renunciation
of sexual life); E. Patlagean, 'L'histoire de la femme déguisée en moine et l'évolution de
la sainteté féminine à Byzance', *Studi Medievali*, 3rd ser., 17 (1976), pp. 597–623.

[509] See above, pp. 210–12 for this trend at the level of local sanctity.

[510] This, at least, is what the saints themselves believed. See, for example, *PC Delphine*, fol.
65: 'dicebat [Delphine] quod homo qui est in mundo et habet divicias non potest se
abstinere a peccato. Sed si dimittit omnia et dat se ad serviendum Deo, Deus habet
misericordiam ipsius et talis homo potest esse in tuto salutis anime sue.'

[511] Meister Eckhart, *Traité des sermons*, ed. P. André (Paris, 1953), p. 114. See also plate 34.

wives and mothers, but by the affective, irrational, even pathological, aspects of their personality. Thanks to the crisis which undermined theological systems and institutions, the female saints became for the Church the last resort. Their prestige was accordingly enhanced. But the lay condition was in the end diminished by this trend towards a conception of Christian perfection which was increasingly alienated from temporal realities and social life.

At the conclusion of this analysis of the processes of canonization concerning men and women who had lived in the world, we need to ask whether the Church, in the last centuries of the Middle Ages, defined a model of sainthood adapted to the conditions of life and aspirations of the Christian people. If we look only at the statistics, the answer would be largely positive, since the ordinary faithful were more numerous among the recent saints the papacy canonized or contemplated canonizing. But if we seek to go beyond this quantitative approach, the reality is more ambiguous. One cannot but be struck by the fact that the lay saints who attracted the attention of the Holy See from the end of the thirteenth century were not 'popular', at least to begin with, and that they owed their fame to the activities of the clergy in their entourage and the lay or ecclesiastical authorities, rather than to popular enthusiasm. It is not without significance that the cult of St Catherine of Siena (d. 1380) spread from Venice, under the influence of the Dominican observance, and not from her native city, where it only developed later. The same was true of the other mystics of this period, whose fame was originally confined to very restricted devout circles.[512] More remarkable still is the fact that, after St Louis, the specifically temporal dimension of the life of the saints, both male and female, was increasingly rarely referred to or lauded in the processes of canonization. To speak of the 'advancement of the laity' seems, in these circumstances, rash. Whilst it is true that a growing number of lay people were canonized, it does not follow that the Church encouraged a spirituality appropriate to their estate. This had very nearly emerged between the end of the twelfth and the mid-thirteenth centuries, as is shown by some aspects of local sainthood and the canonization of persons as involved in the struggles of their age as SS Homobonus and Elizabeth of Thuringia.[513]

---

[512] This is not, of course, to say that they never became popular later, when pride in having a regional or national saint recognized by the papacy operated in their favour, as in the case of Charles of Blois in Brittany and, above all, of St Bridget in Sweden.

[513] See above, pp. 199ff, 356–8.

But this springtime of lay sainthood had no tomorrow. Under the influence of the regulars and especially the Mendicant orders, there followed a veritable 'monasticization of the laity', which culminated in the mystical movement.[514] In fact, the majority of the male and female lay saints recognized by the Church from the second half of the thirteenth century were mouthpieces for a typically clerical religion. While they were distinguished from the priests and regulars by their way of life, they nevertheless spoke the same language and relayed their message. If it was now accepted that a religious experience lived in the world might, in certain cases, lead to Christian perfection, the idea of sanctification through the world remained as alien as in the past to the clerical mentality. The exceptional role played by certain lay people in the Church at the time of the Avignon papacy and the Schism should not mislead us; at a period when the hierarchies, bogged down in temporal problems and political conflicts, proved incapable of overcoming their contradictions, it was useful for the Church that the simple faithful affirmed, by their testimony, the primacy of the spiritual. Once the institutional crisis was over, order was restored. It was not by chance that, apart from St Catherine of Siena and one eleventh-century English bishop, all the saints canonized by the papacy between 1431 and 1482 belonged to the Mendicant orders, from Nicholas of Tolentino to Bernardino of Siena and from Albert of Messina to Bonaventure. Now and for centuries to come, monks and nuns, apostles and witnesses of a religion regarded as purer, occupied the forefront of the stage, offering, with the support of the Holy See, a model of sainthood valid for all the other categories of Christian. This was a decisive turning-point in the history of Roman Catholicism, which we need to look at in greater detail.

---

[514] A. von Harnack, *Lehrbuch der Dogmengeschichte*, III (Leipzig, 1897), p. 385, referring to the Mendicant orders, used the expression 'Monachisierung des Laientums'. It may be extended to all the lay people who, closely or at a distance, were influenced by the Friars. In the case of the Minors, the conviction, however alien to the order's founder, that life in the world was dangerous for the soul, emerged very early. See the *Dicta beati Aegidii Assisiensis*, ed. F. Delorme (Florence and Quaracchi, 1905), pp. 105–6: 'Gratia autem quam quis habet in saeculo facile perditur et difficile conservatur. Nam saecularium negotiorum sollicitudo mater turbationis et amaritudinis dulcedinem gratiae impedit et perturbat nec cohabitare pacifice possunt simul.'

CHAPTER 13

THE EVOLUTION OF THE CRITERIA OF SAINTHOOD FROM THE LATE TWELFTH TO THE EARLY FIFTEENTH CENTURIES

* cacaca*

In our attempt to establish the content of the notion of sainthood within the Church during the last three centuries of the Middle Ages, we have so far concentrated on the ideal of perfection specific to each category of the faithful. But the canonical status of the servants of God, important though it might be at this period, is not the only factor which needs to be taken into account. It is all the more important that we look beyond these categories because, between the thirteenth and the fifteenth centuries, the differences between the various conditions of life tended to diminish, new divisions being superimposed on the old, rendering them increasingly obsolete. The distinction between lay and religious women saints, for example, had little importance after 1300, since both attracted clerical attention primarily through their mystical states, which were similar in both cases.[1] A study of forms of sainthood which pays too much respect to juridical distinctions risks, therefore, missing the essence. For its proper significance to be appreciated, the evolution of the models approved by the Church has to be analysed as a function of changes in spirituality. We may then be surprised to discover, over and beyond the peculiarities inherent to different modes of presence in the world, unexpected affinities between persons apparently remote from each other. On the basis of the common features which can be established for each period, we will try to understand the most characteristic 'moments' of official sainthood between the end of the twelfth and the beginning of the fifteenth centuries.

We need always to keep in mind, however, that any chronological division in a field such as this must be treated with caution. Even if a period presents a certain unity, the historian will always find within it figures who are, or appear to be, atypical. Forms of devotion do not follow one

---

[1] See above, pp. 210–11, 377–85.

after the other like clockwork. We need rather to think in terms of dominant tendencies which alternate and sometimes combine, in a variety of
ways, at the level of individuals and of groups. In the thirteenth century,
for example, when Franciscan ideas were at their most influential, there
were men and women saints who remained faithful to the Cistercian ideal,
or belonged to even older spiritual trends. Further, all the countries of
medieval Christendom did not march in step in religious matters at this
period. A holy bishop who would have been an old-fashioned, even anach-
ronistic, figure in fourteenth-century Italy, might be perfectly in tune with
the social and political structures of fourteenth-century Sweden. We need,
therefore, both to avoid oversimplification in periodization and to recognize the degree of arbitrariness inseparable from an attempt to correlate
changes in sanctity with changes in ecclesiastical institutions and
sensibility.

ASCETICISM, POVERTY AND PASTORAL ZEAL: THE 'EVANGELICAL' MODEL (LATE TWELFTH TO LATE THIRTEENTH CENTURIES)

If we stand back a little from the individual figures who were recognized
as saints by the papacy between 1198 and about 1280, we are at once
struck by the major role played in their lives by devotion to the humanity
of Christ and the desire to follow and imitate him (*sequela Christi*).[2] Some
of them sought to get closer to and even identify with the Victim of Calvary
through voluntary suffering. This burning zeal to resemble, based on
meditation on the Passion, was particularly characteristic of hermits and
recluses such as Lawrence Loricatus and John Bonus. But it was also
present in many lay saints, especially women, and even in a Dominican
nun like St Margaret of Hungary. To these saints, the proliferation of
exhausting fasts, a more or less permanent abstinence, even the pursuit
of self-destruction, were favoured routes to perfection. Punishing their
body with ferocious energy, as if it was the domain *par excellence* of evil,
they struggled to protect themselves from the anguish inspired by their
salvation through the performance of meritorious deeds, as if, in a sense,
to compel God to show them consideration. We find here an echo of the
penitential ideal which was so powerful among the laity in the thirteenth

---

[2] See the references in R. Grégoire 'L'adage ascétique "Nudus nudum Christum sequi" ',
in *Studi storici in onore di O. Bertolini*, I (Pisa, 1972), pp. 395–409.

century. What, after all, were the penitents but men and women who, by renouncing the purely worldly aspects of life and abstaining together, hoped to restore the communication with God which had been broken by sin and lead him to reveal himself to his creatures in his true nature as Father?[3]

The majority of the saints canonized by the papacy in the thirteenth century expressed their devotion to Christ in a less external manner. To SS Francis and Clare, for example, though they belonged to the penitential trend and though their imitation of the Son of God involved mortification, the point was to renounce sin, not oneself. The best way to do this was not to exhaust one's body but to triumph over the world by imitating, as faithfully as possible, the actual life of Jesus: 'For us, God made himself poor on earth. That is why we have chosen, after his example and that of his most holy Mother, the way of authentic poverty', as the founder of the Friars Minor never tired of repeating to his disciples.[4] He, and those who adopted his spirituality, both regulars and laity, went beyond and internalized asceticism. It was not a relaxation, as they were all reputed to have led a very austere life and there is no reason to doubt this. But to them, deprivation and suffering were only a stage. Rather than the pursuit of physical pain, it was the experience of abasement and renunciation that constituted the supreme way towards Christian perfection, since they put the individual in an 'evangelical' situation. The ideal reference was the 'Son of man who hath not where to lay his head' and the spiritual programme was that of the Beatitudes.[5]

At the level of theoretical formulations, the approach of the thirteenth-century saints was not substantially different from that described in numerous twelfth-century treatises whose authors, from St Bernard to William of Saint-Thierry and Richard of Saint-Victor, set out to trace the itinerary of the 'return' to God.[6] The originality of the ideal of sanctity lived and propagated by SS Francis and Dominic lay in the means pro-

[3] For the anthropological basis of the penitential ideal, see Magli, *Gli uomini della penitenza*.
[4] *Légende de Pérouse*, III, p. 875. See also *Il Celano*, cc. 83, 85, 200, also *2 Reg.*, 6, 3.
[5] A. M. Landgraf, 'Das Armutsideal des 13. Jahrhunderts', *Franziskanische Studien*, 32 (1950), pp. 219–41, 346–60; T. Manteuffel, *Naissance d'une hérésie: les adeptes de la pauvreté volontaire au Moyen Age* (Paris and The Hague, 1970). The link between Mendicant spirituality and social change is emphasized by L. K. Little, 'L'utilité sociale de la pauvreté volontaire', in Mollat, *Etudes sur l'histoire de la pauvreté*, I, pp. 447–59; Little, *Religious poverty and the profit economy in medieval Europe* (London, 1978). See also H. Roggen, *Die Lebensform des Hl. Franziskus von Assisi in ihrem Verhältnis zur feudalen und bürgerlichen Gesellschaft Italiens* (Malines, 1965).
[6] E. Gilson, *Saint Bernard: un itinéraire de retour à Dieu* (Paris, 1964).

posed to achieve this end. For the great spirituals of the twelfth century, the fact that man was in the image of God, inferior, admittedly, and degraded, but participating nevertheless in divine greatness, made it possible in his case alone for the soul to rise towards its creator. It was enough for whoever aspired to perfection to raise himself by ascetic effort above the carnal life to restore this resemblance obscured by sin. It was a matter for the individual and his interiority, in the context of a dialogue between the conscience and his God, which was at the heart of what has justly been called a 'Christian Socratism'.[7] In the thirteenth century, on the other hand, the saints who belonged to the 'evangelical' tendency put the emphasis on the necessity of mediation through one's neighbour. To the Poverello, the love of God was indissociable from the love of men. It was not enough to imitate Jesus in gestures and conduct; it was also necessary to seek out and love him in the most wretched of his creatures. In the words of Thomas of Celano, Francis 'saw Christ suffer in every wretch he encountered' and 'recognized in all the poor the son of Our Lady, who was poor'.[8] From this perspective, poverty and charity went hand in hand and were more important than all the rest. We see this in St Elizabeth of Thuringia, careful never to weaken herself by excessive asceticism to the point where she was unable to serve God and the poor, and in Ambrose of Massa, who abandoned mass to go and tend the sick who had need of him.[9] Even St Clare of Assisi, buried in her cloister, continued to take a close interest in the needs of those who lived in the world and show them active sympathy. At her process of canonization, many witnesses referred to the protection enjoyed, thanks to her prayers, by the town of Assisi during the assault by Vital of Aversa and the Ghibellines, and to the special graces that, in her lifetime, she bestowed on her fellow citizens.[10]

Among the diverse aspects of this intense charity, the one most highly esteemed by the Roman Church in the thirteenth century was the desire to save souls (*zelus animarum*). As the century progressed, the papacy showed increasing interest in the saints who were primarily distinguished by their apostolic and pastoral zeal. The religious dimension of charity

---

[7] P. Courcelle, *Connais-toi toi-même: de Socrate à Saint Bernard* (Paris, 1974–5).

[8] *Il Celano*, c. 83, p. 418.

[9] *PC Elizabeth of Thuringia*, p. 136: 'Adeo circumspecta fuit quod medicum ad hoc querebat ut eam sic dietaret, ne forsan sibi nimis subtraherit et de substractione indebita infirmitatem incurrerit per quam divino obsequio se substraheret et sic de nimia abstinentia Domino rationem redderet.' For the attitude of Ambrose of Massa to the poor, see above, pp. 341–2.

[10] *PC Clare of Assisi*, p. 456.

became the essential criterion of sainthood. This change concerned primarily the bishops; those who were the subject of a process of canonization at this period were pastoral prelates anxious to implement, at the level of their diocese, the programme of the great reforming councils from Lateran III to Lyons II, such as St Hugh of Lincoln and Philip of Bourges.[11] The glorification of St Yves, admired by his contemporaries for his total devotion to the *cura animarum* and his efforts to improve, by preaching and example, the moral conduct of his flock, should also be seen in this light.[12]

The best representatives of this trend were, however, the Mendicants. St Francis himself had been ready to brave the sultan of 'Babylon' in the hope of converting him to Christianity and had sent some of his earliest companions to Morocco, where they met their deaths.[13] But his personal charisma and canonical status oriented him rather towards penitential exhortation and evangelical witness. St Dominic, on the other hand, having considered setting out to convert the Cumans and having devoted himself to the spiritual reconquest of Albigensian Languedoc, urged his first companions in the direction of theological studies and a type of preaching based rather on the proclamation of the Word of God and its doctrinal exposition. In essence, between the papacy of Innocent III and that of Boniface VIII, official sainthood evolved from contempt for the world to contempt for oneself and then to the winning of souls.

The papal decision to favour forms of sainthood increasingly closely linked to apostleship is hardly surprising. It was consistent with its basic preoccupations, which were, at this period, to strengthen the Church's hold over society and to Christianize in depth the masses who, in many regions, were distracted by heretical movements. This twofold aim found its clearest expression in the canonization of saints such as Louis IX, the pious sovereign who tried to build Gospel demands into legislation and the exercise of power, and the two great Mendicant preachers, SS Antony of Padua and Peter Martyr, the latter an indefatigable inquisitor murdered by heretics near Milan in 1252. Further proof of the real nature of this choice is provided by the Holy See's firm rejection of all demands for the canonization of saints of the purely ascetic or charitable type, who were

---

[11] See above, pp. 295–300.
[12] See above, pp. 310–15.
[13] *Il Celano*, 57, p. 266. See also B. Sderci, *L'apostolato di S. Francesco e dei Francescani* (Quaracchi, 1909); H. De Roeck, *De normis regulae ordinis Fratrum Minorum circa missiones inter infideles* (Rome, 1961).

much admired by the faithful.[14] However great his reputation throughout Romagna and within his order, the hermit John Bonus was never canonized, and the canonization of Peter of Morrone owed more to the pressing insistence of Philip the Fair than to the length of his fasts or his unbounded generosity. The virtues of temperance, sobriety and chastity, like concern for the poor and their needs, continued to be extolled by the Church and required of the servants of God. But it would not be going too far to say that, in the end, of the evangelical spirituality which inspired the best Christians of their day, all that the thirteenth-century popes retained was its apostolic dimension, in the specifically religious sense of the word.

THE CRISIS OF EVANGELISM AND THE PROMOTION OF LEARNING (*c*.1300–*c*.1370)

It is much less easy to establish the principal trends in the evolution of sainthood for the period between the death of St Louis and that of Urban V than for the preceding century. This is partly a matter of the documentation; processes of canonization, especially after 1330, are few and many causes got lost in the procedural maze. But the main reason why historians find it so difficult to characterize the saints of this period is that the latter were complex, if not ambivalent, characters. Should St Louis of Anjou, for example, be regarded as a bishop or as a Franciscan, or Charles of Blois as a model sovereign or a monk manqué? The external signs themselves are less revealing than before; in the thirteenth century, a saint was defined in the popular mind by a number of concrete gestures and attitudes: renunciation of worldly possessions and adoption of penitential status, demonstrated by the wearing of a characteristic robe, among the laity, active charity and pastoral zeal among the clergy. This was no longer the case in the fourteenth century, when the criteria of Christian perfection were internalized, whilst new elements entered into the Church's evaluation of candidates for canonization. The personal merits of St Thomas Aquinas, however great, probably had less importance in the eyes of the pope who canonized him than his theological achievements. There was, between the end of the thirteenth and the beginning of the fourteenth centuries, if not actually a rupture, a profound modification in the content of sainthood as it was defined by the Church.

---

[14] See above, pp. 72–3.

The crisis of the 'evangelical' model

Reading the processes of canonization from the first two-thirds of the fourteenth century and the bulls promulgated by the papacy on this occasion, one soon becomes aware of certain differences of emphasis compared with the preceding period. In general, concern for one's neighbour and his material and spiritual welfare played a much smaller role in the life of the servants of God and in the appreciation of their perfection. In the documents concerning bishops, pastoral activity and their efforts to raise the moral and religious level of the clergy and faithful were no longer emphasized so strongly. The bishops who caught the attention of the Holy See were primarily distinguished by the vigour with which they battled against lay encroachment in defence of the rights and privileges of their Church, or by the effective exercise of an authority which was asserted through increasingly frequent sanctions and excommunications.[15] In England, in 1307, St Thomas Cantilupe, bishop of Hereford, was lauded for having hated the Jews and extracted from Henry III measures to expel them.[16] People marvelled at the stubborn determination which enabled him to emerge victorious from a series of lawsuits and disputes in which he was pitted against local lords who had failed to respect his privileges.[17] The same was true in the fifteenth century in the case of the Swedish bishops, in particular Brynulph of Skara (d. 1317), who resisted 'like a wall' the attempts of the local aristocracy and the monarchy to appropriate ecclesiastical property.[18] The image of the saint-bishop after 1300 was that of a belligerent and litigious lord, a good administrator, certainly, but preoccupied by the effort put into defending his rights and the temporal bases of his power. The papacy itself was not immune to this development. Urban V, for example, tried to improve the morals of the Romans, and wished to employ in worship the objects of precious metal which had accumulated in the pontifical treasury. But most of the praiseworthy acts attributed to him in the *articuli* of his process of canonization could just as well have appeared in the biography of a lay sovereign: the restoration of order and justice to his Court and states, the adequate victualling of his capital, the battle against unemployment by means of a programme of

[15] See above, pp. 305–8.
[16] *PC Thomas Cantilupe*, fols. 104v–105.
[17] See above, pp. 294–5.
[18] *PC Brynulph*, p. 142.

building works etc.[19] His most striking virtues in the eyes of his entourage
were his concern for the common good, his generosity and his sense of
proportion. If we add his natural *curialitas*, frequently referred to, we have
a collection of human qualities which were no doubt very remarkable but
which were closer to the ideal of perfection of the aristocracy of the day
than to evangelical requirements.[20]

The other sign of the emergence of a new atmosphere in the early
fourteenth century is the change in the attitude of the Church to poverty.
In the thirteenth century, the papacy, not without hesitation, had ratified
the requirement to renounce possessions which was central to Mendicant
spirituality, and made it its own. For proof, we need only quote some
passages from the bull of canonization of St Clare of Assisi, promulgated
in 1255 by Alexander IV.[21] In it, the friend of St Francis is presented as
a woman 'who loved and served poverty with zeal . . . she subscribed to
it so ardently, she was so attached to it and so desired it that she found
in it always a profound joy . . . she therefore resisted the influence of
some sisters who wanted her to agree to their nunnery becoming a property owner'.[22] After 1310, in contrast, poverty ceased to be presented as
'the queen of virtues' in pontifical documents, which, when they listed
the merits of saints, celebrated in preference their piety, their obedience
to the Church and their orthodoxy. This development is probably connected to the conflicts which broke out at this period within the Franciscan
order on the subject of the poverty of Christ. The pontificate of John
XXII is here of particular importance, as it was during his reign that the
question was settled on the theoretical level by the bull *Cum inter nonullos*
(12.XI.1323), which condemned as false and dangerous the claim that
neither Christ nor the Apostles had ever owned anything *iure proprietatis,
dominii seu iuris proprii*.[23] That same year, John XXII canonized Thomas
Aquinas, who asserted, basing himself on the example of Abraham, in

---

[19] *PC Urban V*, arts. 72, 79, pp. 399–400, arts. 91–159, pp. 403–24.

[20] For the importance of *curialitas* in the value system of medieval society, see J. Paul,
'L'éloge des personnes et l'idéal humain au XIIIe siècle, d'après la chronique de Fra
Salimbene', *Le Moyen Age*, 73 (1967), pp. 403–30.

[21] Alexander IV, *Clara claris*, 19.X.1255. The best edition is ed. Z. Lazzeri, 'Un antico
esemplare della Bolla di canonizzazione di S. Chiara', *AFH*, 13 (1920), pp. 499–507.

[22] Alexander IV, *Clara claris*, ed. Lazzeri, p. 505.

[23] F. Tocco, *La quistione della povertà nel secolo XIV* (Naples, 1910); M. D. Lambert,
*Franciscan poverty: the doctrine of the absolute poverty of Christ and the Apostles in the
Franciscan order, 1260–1323* (London, 1961); C. Schmitt, sv Povertà, in *Dizionario degli
Istituti di Perfezione*, VII (Rome, 1983), cc. 323–8; L. Duval-Arnould, 'La constitution
"Cum inter nonnullos" de Jean XXII sur la pauvreté du Christ et des apôtres: rédaction
préparatoire et rédaction définitive', *AFH*, 77 (1984), pp. 406–20.

whom perfection went together with great wealth, that 'poverty is not valuable for itself but by reason of the end to which it leads'.[24] Many Friars Minor and devout lay people, refusing to accept the pope's decisions, went so far as to accuse the Roman Church of having become the 'great Whore of Babylon' referred to in the Apocalypse. The conflict is not in itself of interest to us here, and its vicissitudes have been thoroughly discussed by historians. But its repercussions for the content of the notion of sainthood were profound; under the influence of the revolt of the Spirituals and the Fraticelli, poverty became a suspect notion in the Church. We see this in the answers given by thirteen theologians consulted on the issue by John XXII before he pronounced *ex cathedra*. The tone is conveyed by the memorandum he received from the general master of the Dominicans, Harvey Nédellec, which reads as follows: 'the poor are called saints (*beati*) not because poverty is in itself (*essentialiter*) sanctity, but because it predisposes to sanctity inasmuch as temporal possessions constitute obstacles to the love of God'. Furthermore, he goes on, 'poverty can coexist with feelings contrary to love. In fact, many poor wretches live in poverty and are without love.'[25] Lastly, the eminent theologian wondered whether it was not improper for a cleric to beg, since begging, by creating a permanent preoccupation with subsistence, distracted from contemplation. Privation then simply risked increasing the desire for temporal goods and finally turning him away from Good: 'to trust to chance for the necessities of life when one can do otherwise, seems dangerous. And inasmuch as those who indulge in it say that they put their trust not in chance but in Providence, the danger is doubled, since it is in a sense to tempt God to expect from divine Providence things she is free to give or refuse, especially when one can procure them by human labour'.[26]

I have quoted from this text at such length because it seems to me to illustrate very clearly the change of opinion with regard to poverty which occurred in the ruling circles of the Church during the first decades of the fourteenth century. It is, therefore, hardly surprising that, in pontifical documents concerning the cult of the saints, the realistic nature of evangelical poverty tends to disappear in favour of the much vaguer concept

[24] See above, p. 79.
[25] J. G. Sikes, ed., 'Hervaeus Natalis, Liber de paupertate Christi et apostolorum', *Archives d'histoire littéraire et doctrinale du Moyen Age*, 11 (1937), pp. 209–97. For Dominican conceptions of poverty, see H. C. Lambermond, *Der Armutsgedanke des hl. Dominikus und seines Ordens* (Zwolle, 1926); W. A. Hinnebusch, 'Poverty in the Order of Preachers', *Catholic Historical Review*, 45 (1960), pp. 436–53.
[26] 'Hervaeus Natalis', p. 292.

of spiritual poverty. Thus, in the bull of canonization of Thomas Cantil-upe, in 1320, John XXII praised the bishop of Hereford for having been, in his lifetime, *verus pauper spiritu, dives rebus*.[27] A few years earlier, in 1317, having been obliged, for essentially political reasons, to canonize St Louis of Anjou, he mentioned among the young prince's virtues only his learning, piety, chastity and compassion for the poor.[28] This conventional eulogy is all the more surprising in that the majority of depositions gath-ered during the process had emphasized his desire to live in complete poverty and that Clement V himself, in the bull ordering the enquiry into his life and miracles, had stressed that 'despising the pomp and vanity of the world, he followed in the footsteps of the poor Christ and entered the order of the Friars Minor who professed poverty'.[29] Between the two documents, a decisive turning-point had been passed: poverty in all its concrete and ostentatious aspects – the rejection of possessions, begging, wearing clothes of a certain type – was no longer an accepted test of the sainthood of a servant of God.

This change within ruling Church circles should certainly be related to that within the surrounding society, where the propertied classes seem to have felt a diminished enthusiasm for the poor and for pov-erty.[30] Some fourteenth-century saints themselves drew a distinction between the poor who were worthy to receive alms, for example the infirm, and those who were unworthy, because they were able to work.[31] This type of discrimination does not appear in any process of canonization or hagiographical text before 1300. Its appearance probably reveals a greater awareness of the economic aspects of poverty and the social complexity of the problem. It also shows that, to the men of the age, the pauper was no longer seen as the human face of Christ, or even as a privileged intercessor with God.

---

[27] John XXII, *Unigenitus filius*, 17.IV.1320, ed. Fontanini, p. 132. At the canonization process, some witnesses praised the former bishop for not having greatly enriched himself during his episcopate: *PC Thomas Cantilupe*, fol. 93v: 'dictus dominus Thomas ante episcopatum fuerat fere ita locuplex sicut quando fuit episcopus'. It is known that his income had risen to approximately 1,000 marks a year by 1275.

[28] John XXII, *Sol oriens mundo*, 7.IV.1317, ed. in *Processus canonizationis et legendae variae sancti Ludovici O.F.M.* (Quaracchi and Florence, 1951), pp. 395–9.

[29] Clement V, *Ineffabilis providentia*, 1.VIII.1307, ed. in *Processus canonizationis*, pp. 1–3. The contrast between the two bulls is emphasized in Pasztor, *Per la storia*.

[30] M. Mollat, *Les pauvres au Moyen Age: étude sociale* (Paris, 1978), trans. A. Goldhammer, *The poor in the Middle Ages: a social history* (London, 1986).

[31] See, for example, *PC Charles of Blois*, p. 101, quoted in n. 427, p. 367 above.

The promotion of learning

The decline of the evangelical ideal is also linked to the enhanced prestige of cultural values, such as learning and doctrine, within the Church. This was a radical innovation, since, in hagiographical literature prior to the thirteenth century and in the early processes of canonization, intellectual activites did not rate highly. Indeed, they were often ignored, either because the saints in question had effectively received no formal education or because their biographers or the witnesses testifying on their behalf saw no point in drawing attention to it. The criteria of sainthood prevailing around 1200 were, in fact, strongly influenced by monasticism, and in particular the ascetic monasticism of the Cistercians. The attitude of St Bernard, canonized in 1174, is highly revealing. The abbot of Clairvaux was by no means uncultivated and his fluent and harmonious prose bears witness to the excellent classical education he had received in his youth. Nevertheless, he did not view the scholarly world with favour. In his writings, he liked to oppose to human schools the one true School – that is, the cloister – where Christ himself taught those who knew how to seek him in meditation and prayer.[32] Nor would he allow monks to engage in teaching: *Monachi non est docere sed lugere*. When he preached to the students in Paris, it was to advise them to flee that 'new Babylon' in favour of places of refuge where they might expect, by doing penance, the glory of eternal life. 'Believe me', he wrote to Master Henry Murdach, 'you will find more in forests than in books. The woods and rocks will teach you things no master will tell you.'[33]

After St Bernard, the opposition between school and cloister became a frequent hagiographical commonplace. In the saints' Lives of the late twelfth century, it is routinely assumed that knowledge, as soon as it went beyond the basic level necessary to understand the Scriptures, constituted a useless screen between the soul and Christ. The school was presented as a secular or worldly institution where one risked losing one's soul.[34] This monkish attitude to culture was not, of course, universal within the Church, as we shall see. But the majority of saints were then recruited from among anchorites and regulars of whatever order, and the spirituality

[32] P. Delhaye, 'L'organisation scolaire du XIIe siècle', *Traditio*, 5 (1947), pp. 211–68, especially pp. 226–8; St Bernard, *Eps.* 88, 89, in *PL*, 182, cc. 218, 221.
[33] *Ep.* 104, *PL*, 182, c. 238.
[34] Delhaye, 'L'organisation scolaire', p. 228.

of the latter served as point of reference for bishops, priests and even the laity, so that the influence of this attitude extended far beyond the monastic world.

At the same time, alongside this tendency to devalue scholarship, we see many clergy aspire to a more developed intellectual life. The regular canons, in particular the Victorins, were in the forefront of this trend, which encouraged the ecclesiastical world towards the study of the liberal arts and theology.[35] They received the support of the papacy, which, from the reign of Alexander III, frequently enjoined bishops and cathedral chapters to open schools and endeavoured to ensure that the *licentia docendi* was awarded freely to all who merited it. At the Third Lateran Council, in 1179, these recommendations were given the force of law.[36]

The appeals of the papacy for the promotion of scholarly learning among the clergy and for an increase in the number of schools with a pastoral aim found favour with some bishops, and it was through their intermediary that schooling and culture appeared in the list of positive values which, in the eyes of the Church, contributed to the creation of a reputation for sanctity. At the process of canonization of the bishop of Vicenza, John Cacciafronte (d. 1184), held at Cremona and Vicenza in 1223–4, priests who had known him lauded him for having, at his own expense, brought a theologian from Lombardy to start a school in Vicenza.[37] A few years earlier, St Hugh, bishop of Lincoln (d. 1200), was praised by his biographer for having acquired a large number of books and for persuading the king to provide money to buy parchment and a Bible.[38] But these remain rare references which are far from prominent in the list of their virtues and deeds. In the late twelfth and early thirteenth centuries, it was regarded as desirable for a prelate to be a cultivated man who promoted the development of sacred culture, from which his personal qualities and the training of his clergy could only benefit. But the principal merits of the saint-bishop were of an ascetic and, increasingly, a pastoral order.

With the passage of time, the commitment of the saint-bishops to cultural life and schools increased. This trend is particularly marked in England, which provided, admittedly, most of the bishops who were the subject of a process of canonization in the thirteenth century. The

---

[35] *Ibid.*, p. 239.
[36] *Ibid.*, pp. 259–60.
[37] *PC John Cacciafronte*, p. 244. One witness said he had been a student there in 1184 (p. 245).
[38] *Magna vita sancti Hugonis*, p. 85.

English episcopate was distinguished by remarkable intellectual qualities
and a pronounced taste for study, even research. We need only mention
names such as Robert Grosseteste, regarded in his day as a saint and
venerated as one within England, and John Peckham.[39] Those bishops
who were well-regarded in their day were all, to a greater or lesser
degree, university men, and this was mentioned in the depositions of
witnesses at the processes of canonization. In the *Quadrilogus*, a treatise
consisting of four statements attesting to the sanctity of Edmund of
Abingdon, archbishop of Canterbury (d. 1240), canonized by Innocent
IV in 1246, the merits attributed to the holy bishop include tenure of
a *cathedra magistralis* at Oxford, devoting his life to study and sending
many young clerics to the schools.[40] Also included among the virtues
lauded in him and in other cultivated bishops was the habit of falling
asleep fully dressed at the foot of his bed, after working late into the
night at his books.[41]

The trend for sainthood in bishops to coincide with a high degree of
culture, even tenure of university office, culminated in the process of
canonization of St Thomas Cantilupe (d. 1282). Before becoming a bishop
in 1275, Thomas had studied the arts, canon law and theology in Paris
and civil law at Orléans. On his return to England, he taught law and
then theology at the University of Oxford, where he was twice chancellor
(1261–3 and 1273–4).[42] From several depositions made at the process in
1307, we know that he was connected with the Friars Minor and Preachers, and that Robert Kilwardby, his confessor, described him as 'a credit

[39] D. A. Callus, *Robert Grosseteste, scholar and bishop* (Oxford, 1955). Despite repeated
attempts, the English episcopate failed to get a process of canonization started. However,
this probably had more to do with his well-known hostility towards the Roman Curia
than his intellectual boldness: Kemp, 'The attempted canonization of Robert Grosseteste'.
[40] *Quadrilogus*, ed. Lawrence, *St Edmund of Abingdon*, pp. 187–202, especially p. 168. He
had enjoyed a successful career at Oxford before his election to Canterbury in 1233 (*ibid.*,
pp. 110–24). His canonization was requested by the University where he had been Regent
of Arts for six years and then, after a period in Paris, taught theology.
[41] *Vita sancti Edmundi auctore Eustachio de Faversham*, ed. Lawrence, *St Edmund of Abingdon*, p. 205. The same biography reports that he refused the archbishop of York's offer
to copy a glossed Bible, 'quod formidabat ne forte oneraret abbatias et prioratus scriptoribus sic reputatis': *ibid.*, p. 252.
[42] For his university career, see A. B. Emden, *A biographical register of the University of
Oxford*, II (Oxford, 1958). In the *relatio* presented to John XXII by the cardinals appointed
to examine the dossier, this phase of his life is summarized as follows: 'in minori et maiori
aetate multum studuit et fuit magister in artibus, doctor in theologia et rexit actu in
artibus Parisius, Oxonii in decretis et post in theologia, et eiusdem universitatis Oxoniensis
cancellarius fuit et ipsum studium tempore sui officii bene rexit. Apocalipsim in studio
Parisensi legit': MA BN, lat. 5373 A, fol. 66r. See also *PC Thomas Cantilupe*, fol. 24v
(witness 12).

to the University of Oxford'.[43] We also learn that, as chancellor, he was able to maintain order and discipline within the university, which, by the end of the thirteenth century, could be seen as a sign of sanctity![44] The lesser servants in his household seem chiefly to have been impressed by how hard he worked at his intellectual labours, going late to bed and rising earlier than other people in order to read and meditate.[45] In the bull of canonization promulgated on 17 April 1320, John XXII emphasized in his eulogy the great culture and passion for intellectual labour which characterized the new saint, who, after a few years as a bishop (1275–82), had passed from his university career to eternal life. Remarkably, the pope referred in this text to his competence not only in theology but *in humanis scientiis*.[46] From this point on, the university cursus was almost invariably to figure in the career of saint-bishops, and in the list of their merits.[47]

However interesting this change in the Church's attitude to culture, its significance would have been limited if it had been confined to a category of saints which, though important in the thirteenth century, was very far from representing the totality of saints recognized by the Church. The greatest names of the age, in this sphere, those whose cult was most widespread, were not SS Edmund and Thomas Cantilupe – though they were very popular in England – but SS Francis of Assisi, Antony of Padua, Dominic etc. In the popular mind, in the thirteenth century, especially in the Mediterranean countries, the Friars Minor and Preachers – the best of them at least – were the true saints. The Roman Church ratified this judgement of the *vox populi* by canonizing many of their most eminent members. We need to look, therefore, at the attitude of the saints from the

---

[43] *Ibid.*, fol. 26 (witness 6); *AA.SS.* Oct. I, p. 601 (witness 67).

[44] He confiscated weapons belonging to a seditious student and managed to damp down disputes between the *Australes* and the *Boreales*: *PC Thomas Cantilupe*, fol. 40 (witness 17).

[45] *Ibid.*, fols. 19v (witness 6), 108 (witness 60).

[46] 'Studiis litterarum sic se dedicavit totaliter, sic in ipsis solicite studiis et profecit quod tam in humanis scientiis quam etiam in divina honorem magisterii est adeptus': *Unigenitus filius*, ed. Fontanini, *Codex constitutionum*, pp. 131–4, especially p. 132.

[47] Philip Berruyer, archbishop of Bourges (d. 1261) had been *scholaris Parisius*: *PC*, fol. 28v; Brynulph of Skara (d. 1317) had studied successfully at Paris: *PC*, art. 2, p. 142; Nicholas of Linköping (d. 1391) had studied both types of law in Paris and Orléans: *PC*, art. 5, p. 52. The rhymed office composed in the fourteenth century in honour of John of Dalderby, bishop of Lincoln (d. 1320), who enjoyed a great reputation for sanctity in England, ends as follows: 'Johannes est Christo datus puericie/ Studio fuit occupatus non vacans stultitie/ Gradum scandit magistratus gemine scientie/ Docet mores ut vir/ gratus non actus nequicie': Wickenden, 'John of Dalderby', p. 222.

Mendicant orders to culture and at the role it played in the appreciation of their sainthood.

We know that the position of St Francis in this sphere was not without ambiguity; on the one hand, he welcomed into his order educated clerics with degrees alongside simple and untaught brethren, believing that a collaboration between the two must be beneficial.[48] On the other hand, he was obsessed by the fear that the brethren might neglect virtue in favour of the pursuit of knowledge, a subtle, and so all the more dangerous, form of power and possession.[49] This dual attitude emerges clearly in the note he sent to St Antony of Padua in 1223 or 1224: 'It pleases me that you are teaching the brethren holy theology, as long as those who engage in this study do not extinguish in themselves the spirit of holy prayer and devotion, as it is written in the Rule.'[50]

After the death of its founder, the Franciscan order, as is well known, turned increasingly in the direction of clericalization, and therefore of study, establishing many *studia* throughout Christendom. To what extent was this a betrayal of the wishes of the Poverello? It is not clear, and one may be inclined to doubt it on seeing the importance of the education received in the schools of the Friars Minor in the life of a cleric like St Yves.[51] His was not an isolated case, since the Franciscan *studia* seem to have played an equally important role in the life of other saints of the period belonging to the secular clergy.[52]

In the case of St Dominic, and the order of the Friars Preacher, we find no trace of the tensions and unease which characterized the Franciscan position with regard to scholarly culture. The witnesses at the process of canonization in 1233 spoke admiringly of the decision of the founder to withdraw his first companions from Languedoc in order to send them to Paris and Bologna to study.[53] He himself had a deep love of intellectual labour and studied unceasingly, conscious that the effectiveness of the pastoral activity in which he and his companions were engaged was depen-

---

[48] *Il Celano*, 20, p. 149; 144, pp. 501–3. Theologians should be honoured: *ibid.*, 122, p. 480.

[49] *Ibid.*, 146, p. 505.

[50] Letter 8 (to St Antony), p. 149; *Reg.*, 5, 2. For St Francis, the problem was striking a balance between wisdom and simplicity: *Il Celano*, 142, p. 499.

[51] See above, p. 313. The witnesses said he had been 'multum sapiens et litteratus': *ibid.*, p. 54, witness 17.

[52] Thomas Cantilupe 'audivit theologiam in scholis fratrum minorum [= the Cordeliers in Paris]': *PC Thomas Cantilupe*, fol. 107, witness 60.

[53] *PC Dominic*, in Vicaire, *S. Dominique*, p. 52 (witness 5, brother John Hispanus).

402 TYPOLOGY OF MEDIEVAL SAINTHOOD

dent on a deeper doctrinal knowledge.[54] The only consideration which could make him deviate from this overriding objective was charity; he had, after all, sold books annotated in his own hand when studying in Palencia in order to succour victims of a famine. 'I have no wish', he said, 'to pore over dried up parchments while people are dying of hunger.'[55] We should not, however, confuse the rule and objectives of the religious orders with the criteria which prevailed in the estimation of sanctity by the Church. Even if, objectively, St Dominic's love of study and wish to give the Friars Preacher a university education was important in his life and activities, little of this emerges in his process of canonization; it was other aspects of his personality (his apostolic zeal, devotion, austerity etc.) that had most impressed witnesses and commissioners. The love of culture as such was rarely cited among the virtues attributed to him, and when it was mentioned, it is made clear that it was solely his sacred culture which was at issue: knowledge of the Scriptures and theology.

In the fourteenth century, intellectual activity and scholarly culture were taken into account by the Church when it passed judgement on the life of the saints from the regulars. We see this for the first time in the process of St Louis of Anjou, which took place in Marseilles in 1308. Among the *articuli interrogatorii* prepared by the promoters of the cause, those devoted to his education and his taste for the discussion of ideas loom large, to the point where we may reasonably see him as the first intellectual to be canonized by the medieval Church.[56] We may note in passing that his education was entirely the work of the Franciscans in his entourage, who were his teachers during the years he spent as hostage, first in Catalonia and then in Naples, at Castel dell'Ovo. Some witnesses, for the most part from the 'spiritual' tendency within the order, seem even to have been a little alarmed by the intellectual curiosity of the young

---

[54] 'Orally and by letter, Brother Dominic urged the brethren of the order to study constantly the New and the Old Testaments': *ibid.*, p. 55.

[55] The episode is reported by both John Hispanus and brother Stephen, provincial of Lombardy: *ibid.*, cc. 29, 35, pp. 55, 61.

[56] 'Studio litteratum sic ferventer inhesit ut infra septennium ipsum in grammaticalibus, philosophicis, moralibus et theologicis sufficienter instructus verbum Dei clero et populo eleganter et fructuose proponeret': *PC Louis of Anjou*, art. 2, p. 11; see also art. 23, p. 14: 'post prandium se vaniloquiis non immisciens comuniter intendebat collacioni alicui super materia theologica vel philosophica seu morali, maxime post adventum fr. Riccardi de Mediavilla in theologia magistri sibi in magistrum ac socium deputati'. Article 25 is devoted to his reading (in particular the works of St Bernard) (p. 15); see also art. 27: 'sic erat devocioni et studiis deditus ut interdum de mensa surgeret nesciens an in illa bibisset'. Also, we know that it needed six or seven pack animals to transport his books, and that he got so worked up in debate that he went red in the face: p. 35, witness 2.

prince who had become a Friar Minor and a bishop. They repeatedly emphasized that his learning was so great that it could not be human in origin.[57] The theme of innate – as opposed to acquired – learning was very popular in the fourteenth century in processes of canonization; it made it possible to reconcile the learning which was increasingly common among the saints, as a result of the spread of education, with the conventions of traditional hagiography.

Whatever his intellectual qualities, to the witnesses trying to describe his sanctity St Louis of Anjou was primarily remarkable for his love of poverty and renunciation of all forms of power, in society and in the Church. It was some years later before an authentic Doctor, in the person of St Thomas Aquinas, was canonized, in 1323 by John XXII. In his process, held in Naples in 1319, the man is overshadowed by the *œuvre*.[58] Admittedly, the witnesses provide a certain amount of information about his chastity, his modesty and his indifference to worldly goods. But this was to some extent beside the point, and it is significant that the fullest and most detailed deposition, that of the logothete Bartholomew of Capua, ended with a list of the saint's works.[59] Perhaps conscious of the novelty of this form of sainthood, many witnesses seem to have felt some unease. It is in this context that we should see the stories of visions during which St Augustine informed various people of his high regard for the Thomist doctrine and gave him his support.[60] Others emphasized the spiritual experience which happened to St Thomas in Naples during the last months of his life, after which he said, according to his *socius*, brother Reginald, 'Everything I have written now seems to me trivial compared with that of which I have had a vision and a revelation.'[61] Whether St

---

[57] *PC Louis of Anjou*, p. 60: 'magis videbatur divini doni infusio quam humani ingenii et studii exquisicio' (witness 5). The same witness, Brother Fortis, developed this theme later, emphasizing the mediocre cultural level of the regulars around him, which made incomprehensible, without divine intervention, the young prince's progress. See also p. 98 (witness 19).

[58] Confirmed by the anecdote recounted by Gerson: 'cum in canonizatione sancti Thome de Aquino opponeretur a quibusdam quod non fecerat miracula vel non multa, dictum fuit per Papam non esse curandum et adieecit: quoniam tot miracula fecit quod determinavit quaestiones': *Opera omnia*, ed. Du Pin, II (Antwerp, 1709), c. 712.

[59] *PC Thomas Aquinas*, pp. 328–31. He also produced the following argument in favour of St Thomas' sanctity: 'Numquam decrevit eius auctoritas sed semper invaluit.' See plate 35.

[60] *Ibid.*, p. 298: 'Ego sum Augustinus doctor Ecclesiae, qui missus sum ad te ut indicarem tibi doctrinam et gloriam frati Thome de Aquino qui mecum est.' See also pp. 300, 325. The bishop of Hippo's interventions were clearly intended to confer on Thomas Aquinas a certificate of orthodoxy which his Aristotelianism put at risk.

[61] *Ibid.*, p. 319. Bartholomew of Capua also emphasized that, after this vision, experienced during a mass, 'numquam scripsit neque dictavit aliquid, immo suspendit organa scrip-

Thomas ever spoke these words, we will, of course, never know. But even if some accounts of the great theologian tried to present him as a mystic, it remains the case that, in canonizing St Thomas Aquinas, the Roman Church awarded its highest accolade to a university teacher and his work, the fruit of half a century of toil.[62]

In fact, it was during the Avignon papacy that *studium* came closest to *sanctitas*, to the point of becoming one of its constituent elements. The surviving documentation suggests that this convergence reached its apogee in the process of canonization of Pope Urban V (d. 1370). Sadly, all that survives are the *articuli*, that is the capitulations which the promoters of the cause aimed to have approved and demonstrated by the witnesses during the course of the enquiry.[63] These, however, are enough to illustrate my point. In them, Urban V is presented above all as a man of culture. Although he was a monk, he liked to read and write, and had a particular interest in theology and law.[64] Once pope, one of his main aims was to improve the cultural level of the clergy. To this end, he founded a monastery in Montpellier which was intended to receive and train specialists in canon law.[65] As a general rule, he aimed to promote to positions of responsibility clerics who had been through the schools and universities, and to provide a formal education for those who had not.[66] Accordingly, at his own expense, he founded new teaching chairs and increased the number of scholars, both in the *studia particularia*, where they studied the arts, and in the *studia generalia*, where they specialized in law and medicine.[67] Not content with trying to raise the cultural level

tionis in tertia parte Summe, in tractatu de Penitentia'. He also reported some words of St Albert the Great: 'idem frater Thomas in scripturis suis finem imposuit omnibus laborantibus usque ad finem saeculi et quod omnes deinceps frustra laborarent' (p. 325). True or false, the story tended to discourage those who wanted to continue doctrinal reflection by the rational method dear to St Thomas, making his work into a 'monument' rather than an example to follow.

[62] Bull of canonization *Redemptionis misit* 17.VII.1323: 'perfecto vacans studio intendebat Deo, praetermittebat terrena ut assequeretur eterna, praemittebat divina ut roboraretur in schola': Fontanini, *Codex*, p. 136.

[63] Ed. J. Albanès and U. Chevalier, *Actes anciens et documents concernant le B. Urbain V*, II (Paris and Marseilles, 1897), pp. 375–480.

[64] 'Fuit ingeniosus et intentus litterarum scientiis et artes liberales didiscit in diversis studiis particularibus et generalibus': PC Urban V, art. 10, p. 380; see also arts. 11, 14, p. 381, art. 19, p. 383, art. 40, p. 390, art. 47, p. 391.

[65] *Ibid.*, art. 104, p. 407.

[66] *Ibid.*, art. 121, p. 412: 'demonstravit se bonas personas et licteratas diligere, illis multipliciter proficiendo et illos promovendo . . . multi illeterati et alii licterati non graduati et etiam alii male morigerati ad licteraturum et gradus et bonos mores sunt reducti'.

[67] *Ibid.*, arts. 122–6, 128–9: Urban V supported more than 1,400 scholars, recruited from among the 'subtiliores et doctibiliores pauperes studentes': *ibid.*, pp. 413–14.

of the clergy, Urban V also tried to make books accessible to the laity.[68] His interest was clearly far from purely utilitarian or restricted to the study of theology. To his contemporaries, he was remarkable for an authentic policy of cultural development, based on a deep conviction that raising the intellectual level of the clergy and the faithful could only be beneficial for their morality and for society as a whole.[69] At the time, he was much criticized for this open attitude. When he was attacked for creating far too many students, he apparently said: 'It is highly desirable and I personally desire that there should be many educated people within the Church of God. Certainly, all those I have enabled to study will not become beneficed clergy. Many, however, will be regulars or secular priests; others will marry. But whatever their future state, even if they later become manual workers, it will always be useful to them to have studied, as they will be apter pupils and more competent.'[70] This text has a very modern ring to the reader of today: the need for an education policy, the long-term benefits of education and even the utility of the general availability of access to continuing education.

With Urban V, who was not canonized but who was, in his day, immensely popular throughout Christendom, as the many miracles attributed to his intercession and the wide diffusion of his cult reveal, the trend to equate sainthood and culture, visible since the beginning of the thirteenth century, reached its highest point. In future, it was accepted that knowledge in general and doctrinal knowledge in particular were factors which elevated and enhanced the Christian man. This development mirrors that taking place at the same period within the Mendicant orders. This is illustrated by a picturesque episode of which a very detailed account has survived.[71] It concerns the events which followed the death of the Dominican Marcolino of Forli, which took place in Forli in 1397. A conflict developed between a large crowd, consisting mostly of artisans and shopkeepers, and the Friars Preacher of the local convent. The latter wanted to bury their brother without further ado. Alerted by a child who ran through the streets proclaiming Marcolino's death, the people rushed to the monastery and prevented the brethren from proceeding. There

---

[68] See n. 189, p. 322 above.
[69] *PC Urban V*, art. 127, p. 413: 'studia suo tempore multum fuerunt dilatata et in personis clericorum viguerunt plurimum boni mores'.
[70] *Ibid.*, art. 131, p. 414.
[71] The episode is well known thanks to the long report sent by John Dominici to Raymond of Capua, Master-General of the Dominican order, ed. Corner, *Ecclesiae Venetae*, VII, pp. 186–92.

followed a strange dialogue, punctuated by threats, inside the convent church and over the dead body. The Dominicans claimed that he was a *homo simplex*, so eccentric as to verge on the ridiculous, who deserved no special consideration. Only the convent cook thought differently, because, when washing the corpse, he had discovered large calluses on the knees, evidence of long hours spent kneeling in prayer. After lengthy but fruitless discussion, the crowd withdrew and the brethren went ahead with the burial the following night. But when they heard, the people returned next days in large numbers to try to have the body exhumed.

For them, Marcolino was a saint; did he not, every day, even though he was a priest, recite 100 *Pater noster* and 100 *Ave* like the lay brothers, and did he not scourge himself? Furthermore, he was generous to the poor, kind to children and possessed the gift of reading men's minds and hearts. A carpenter added that the pious monk had once healed a wound in his hand by an application of herbs, which, he said, was how, out of humility, he concealed his great thaumaturgical powers. To these arguments, the Dominicans replied that it was not permitted to institute the cult of new saints without authorization from the hierarchy and emphasized, above all, that Marcolino, an ignorant man, had been a poor preacher. Treacherously, they even added that their former brother often dozed off at table or when celebrating mass, to which the people replied that he was not asleep but 'rapt' and lost in contemplation. This lively debate reveals two different conceptions of sainthood: that of the laity was ascetic, caring and thaumaturgical, whereas for the Dominicans a saint was first of all a dignified and cultured person, brilliant and effective on the pastoral plane. This dialogue between the deaf could end only in violence. Exasperated by the quibbles of the Dominicans, the crowd eventually opened the tomb and removed Brother Marcolino's remains.[72] At once, a delightful smell pervaded the church and many miracles occurred. Nothing now could halt the progress of the cult, which was soon approved by the bishop of Forli and adopted by the Dominicans themselves, whose church became a busy place of pilgrimage.[73]

Though the Roman Church played no part in this incident, it shows how ideas within the Church, and especially among the regulars, had changed. Admittedly, we cannot, in this case, speak of the clergy as a

---

[72] *Ibid.*, p. 191: 'violentia revolvitur lapis sepulturae, exhibetur corpus sancti, odoris fragrantia repletur ecclesia'.

[73] See the documents collected for the process of canonization of B. Marcolino (Forli, 1624–5), in *ASV, Riti*, Proc. 773.

homogeneous block, since one of the principal defenders of the devotion to Marcolino was John Dominici, inspirer of the Dominican observance, and author of the account which enables us to follow the dispute and understand the positions of the opposing parties.[74] But the reaction of the Preachers of Forli is probably more representative of the trends then prevailing in ecclesiastical circles than that of the famous reformer, still in a minority within his order. The promotion of the cultural and doctrinal aspects of sainthood widened the gulf between the official conceptions and those of the laity, who, in the Mediterranean countries, remained deeply attached to the penitential ideal and evangelical spirituality.

THE 'MYSTICAL INVASION' (c.1370–c.1430)

Just when the Church was moving towards an 'acculturation' of sainthood, a wave of visionary and prophetic mysticism swept through Christendom, blocking this trend for several decades. The humanist tendencies so influential under the Avignon popes gave way, in the last decades of the fourteenth century, to a conception of Christian perfection which was both fideist and pietist, characterized by a great distrust of intellectual activities and the *scientia quae inflat*. Despite appearances, this was not so much a new form of spirituality as the emergence of a current which had originated in the mid-thirteenth century. There were already, at that period, many within the Franciscan order who deplored what they saw as the excessive importance attached to study in the training and life of the clergy. The revealing exclamation of Giles of Assisi, one of the companions of the Poverello who lived long enough to see the changes which transformed the original fraternity, is well known: 'Paris, Paris, why are you destroying the order of St Francis?'[75] After him, the opposition between Paris and Assisi, that is between the conventual or eremitic life in poverty and the university, became commonplace among the Friars Minor of spiritual tendency and those under their influence. There is an echo in the first Italian mystics, who were very close to them: Margaret of Cortona (d. 1297), Angela of Foligno (d. 1309) and, above all, Clare of Montefalco

---

[74] The conclusion of John Dominici's letter is very revealing: 'Regnare volumus in terra, vel terram, sicut decet, non contempnimus. Ecce, quod indocti rapiunt caelum, humiles ad ipsum accedunt, simplices ipsum mercantur, acquirunt pauperes, paenitentes assequuntur': ed. Corner, *Ecclesiae Venetae*, p. 192. For John Dominici, see G. Cracco, sv Banchiri, Giovanni di Domenico, in *Dizionario bibliografico degli Italiani*, V (Rome, 1963), pp. 657–64.

[75] *Vita fratris Aegidii*, in *Chronica XXIV generalium*, p. 86.

(d. 1308). We know from the latter's process of canonization, held in
1318–19, that she opposed the mystical experience of God, based on
humility, penitence and meditation on the sufferings of Christ, to intellectual knowledge, which she believed to be greatly inferior and full of dangers for the soul.[76] The attitude of these women is understandable, inasmuch as they themselves, with few exceptions, had received no scholarly
education and were unable to live their religious experience at the doctrinal
level which prevailed among the clergy. Admittedly, we should not push
this antithesis too far, since there were many ignorant and uneducated
mystics who tried to acquire the minimum education necessary to make
direct contact with the Word of God.[77] But even if they did not escape the
trend to attach greater value to scholarship, they challenged it indirectly by
their personal ideal of sanctity, based on the conviction that the more they
recognized themselves as unworthy to know God and devoid of all merit,
the more his creatures were capable of loving him.

Long kept in obscurity by the ecclesiastical hierarchy and the educated
clergy, the mystical trend eventually made its break-through in the late
fourteenth and early fifteenth centuries, thanks to the crises then threatening ecclesiastical institutions and the papacy itself. The 'Avignon
Captivity', the Great Schism and the resulting conflicts between rival
obediences called into question the scale of values which lauded learning
within the Church. The malaise then affecting Christendom affected every
category of saint. We see it at its most acute in Peter of Luxembourg (d.
1387), a cardinal at the age of eighteen, who, in his palace at Avignon,
dreamed of abandoning his studies in order to make a pilgrimage across

[76] According to her brother Francis, then a young Friar Minor, she had once said: 'Nollem
quod tu curares semper de ista scientia et de ista extollentia semper disceptares. Et dico
tibi pro parte mea quod maiorem consolationem haberem si tu esse laicus et coquinarius
fratrum cum bono spiritu et fervore devotionis quam si esses de quibuscumque lectoribus
unus maior': PC Clare of Montefalco, ASV, Riti, Proc. 2929, fol. 481; see also fol. 488.
Her position on this point should not be confused with that of the Franciscan Spirituals,
who were hostile not to scholarly culture as such, but rather to the power and wealth it
could confer, as we see from the example of St Louis of Anjou.
[77] There was a change between the late thirteenth and the fourteenth century. B. Oringa
(d. 1310), founder and superior of a community of enclosed Franciscan tertiaries in Tuscany, could never learn to read, even though the Virgin Mary appeared to her in a vision
to give her a book. But she was careful to recruit young sisters who were able to read
and teach others: Vita, ed. Lami, Deliciae eruditorum, pp. 208–10. The same was true of
Clare of Montefalco. But the mystics of the second half of the fourteenth century (Bridget
of Sweden, Catherine of Siena and Dorothy of Montau) seem rapidly to have learned to
read Latin texts, which only went to show, at their processes of canonization, that they
had received innate knowledge from God: PC Bridget, art. 38, p. 24; PC Dorothy, fol.
154, witness 79.

Europe, and stressed the need for the Church, if it wished to regain its unity, to renounce the means to power – which, in his eyes, included learning – and base itself on piety alone.[78] His was not a lone voice; between 1370 and 1430, popular religious movements such as that of the Flagellants and reforming trends like the Franciscan and Dominican observance strove to relegate culture to the domain of purely profane realities. University clerics like John Gerson and Henry of Langenstein might sound the alarm, oppose the canonization of St Bridget of Sweden and emphasize the danger to sound doctrine of the proliferation of private revelations, whose authenticity was difficult to control.[79] Their efforts could not prevent the papacy from giving a favourable reception to requests to approve the cult of these strange women who exercised an extraordinary ascendancy over their followers.[80]

There are some grounds for seeing the mystical tendency which emerged at the end of the fourteenth century as a resurgence of the penitential trend of the previous century, eclipsed during the Avignon papacy. Indeed, the processes of canonization of these saints point strongly to a return in force of certain virtues and behaviour traditionally associated with the most rigorous ascetic spirituality.[81] The sufferings voluntarily endured by these women are emphasized, as if in mute protest against the laxity of the clergy and the secularizing trends then apparent within the ecclesiastical hierarchy.[82] Further, most of them demonstrated a deep

---

[78] To a friend who said to him: 'debetis circa studium vacare et alia agibilia. Nam si habeatis scientiam et nobilitatem poteritis Ecclesiam relevare', Peter of Luxembourg replied: 'Credatis pro certo quos nos in Curia Romana existentes, non facimus quod debemus, Quia pro expedito habeatis quod propter scientiam, nobilitatem, potentiam et arma, Ecclesia sancta Dei non reparabitur, sed per devotionem, orationes et alia bona opera': *PC Peter of Luxembourg, AA.SS.* Iul. I, p. 477.

[79] See, for example, Gerson's *De probatione spirituum*, and his mistrust of the mystics, beginning with Ruysbroek. His contemporaries, Henry of Langenstein and Peter of Ailly, revealed similar attitudes.

[80] This fascination is recorded in the very early fourteenth century. We learn from the canonization process of Clare of Montefalco that Cardinal Pietro Colonna visited her on several occasions. He also showed interest in the revelations of Angela of Foligno, whose content he approved in 1309. Another cardinal, Napolean Orsini, loomed large at St Clare's process, and made a highly favourable report in consistory: *PC Clare of Montefalco*, p. 566; *Relatio cardinalium in consistorio*, MS Bibl. Angers 821, fols. 357–80.

[81] Pilgrimage played an important role in the religious experience of the fourteenth-century mystical saints: St Bridget went to Rome, Santiago de Compostella, Cologne (The Three Kings and the 11,000 Virgins), Saint Michael of Gargano, Saint-Maximin (St Mary Magdalen), Ortona (St Thomas), Assisi and Jerusalem: *PC Bridget*, art. 13, p. 14. Dorothy of Montau went to Rome for the Jubilee of 1390: *PC Dorothy of Montau*, fol. 152.

[82] Delphine searched for 'new ways of doing penance' in the *Vitae Patrum*, and scourged herself every time she felt she had offended God: *PC Delphine*, witnesses 8 and 14, fols. 96v, 121v. St Catherine of Siena punished herself with iron hooks and sometimes went

attachment to poverty; Clare of Montefalco, Delphine of Sabran and Dorothy of Montau even begged, less from necessity than to experience the
humiliation, which they welcomed with joy.[83] Given that these women
also claimed to be under the direct influence of the Holy Spirit and to be
accountable only to Christ, one understands why they were persecuted by
some of the clergy before their sainthood was recognized by the Church.[84]

However, it would be a mistake to attach too much importance to these
aspects of the sanctity of the mystics, which were not those which most
impressed contemporaries or the papacy when it had to pronounce concerning them. Further, although their religious ideal resembled that of
the thirteenth century, the emphasis was different than in a St Francis or
a St Elizabeth. Admittedly, they all saw Christian perfection as an imitation of Christ. But there was no longer any question – except in the case
of Delphine of Sabran (d. 1360), who belonged to the Franciscan tendency – of 'following, naked, the naked Christ' by assisting the disinherited
or sharing the life of the poor. 'It is more perfect to imitate Christ in his
sufferings than in his actions', declared, significantly, John of Marienwerder, apropos his protégée, Dorothy of Montau.[85] This scepticism
concerning the virtues of action not only challenged the importance of
works of charity as compared with contemplation of the sorrowful mysteries. It also led to a new conception of sainthood defined as 'a perfect
knowledge of God resulting from a direct vision'.[86] The only way to

---

for fifty days without food: PC Catherine of Siena, pp. 33, 267. Dorothy of Montau
plunged her limbs into icy water and left them to freeze, before putting salt on the wounds
to make them even more painful: PC Dorothy of Montau, fol. 189.

[83] Delphine 'wanted to be poor and not to be called countess or honoured by people': PC
Delphine, fol. 64v; for her experiences of begging, see fols. 93, 119. At the process of
Dorothy of Montau, her confessor declared: 'in tantum diligebat paupertatem quod cupie-
bat esse pauper toto spiritu et nonnumquam in despecto et simulato habitu sedit inter
mendicos': PC Dorothy, fols. 149v–150.

[84] The orthodoxy of the mystics was a priori dubious and the clergy were often hostile to
them during their lifetime. Thus, Delphine of Sabran was obliged, at the insistence of
her confessor, to make a public profession of faith on her death-bed, for reasons which
seem to have escaped her: PC Delphine, fol. 99. Catherine of Siena was subjected to a
severe examination by three prelates, one of whom, a Franciscan archbishop, remained
hostile: PC Catherine of Siena, pp. 269–70. She was also persecuted in Siena by a theologian and popular preacher, the Franciscan Lazzarino of Pisa, though he eventually
admitted he had wronged her and placed himself under her direction (ibid., p. 330). It
is hardly surprising that some of these saints' claims provoked clerical suspicion; Dorothy
of Montau, for example, said: 'Ego non erro nec possum errare quia habeo unum doctorem
et magistrum qui me et omnes homines diligenter informat': PC Dorothy, fol. 71.

[85] Ibid., fol. 190: 'ut esset perfecta Christi imitatrix in passionibus arduis, cum perfectius
esset Christum imitari in passionibus quam in actibus'.

[86] This is the definition given by a witness questioned about the sanctity of Catherine of
Siena: 'perfecta Dei dilectio ex clara visione precedens': PC, p. 152.

achieve this was to travel the *Via crucis* to the end, through thought and suffering. This approach was diametrically opposed to the voluntarist search for perfection which characterized, for example, St Margaret of Hungary in the thirteenth century. St Bridget, in her Revelations and in her sayings as reported by witnesses, never missed an opportunity to stress that the prophetic function she performed was independent of her own merits. Neither birth nor condition of life nor cultural level weighed with God, who sent his Spirit and his message to those who showed themselves obedient to his call.[87] The mystical current went well beyond the penitential ideal in that it totally spiritualized the religious life, by confining it to the inner life and defining its purpose as identification of the human soul with God, in the loving fusion of wills.[88] It constituted the high point and culmination of the evolution which, since the thirteenth century, had tended to make the religious into an autonomous world.

Far from being popular, late medieval mystical sanctity was, on the contrary, profoundly elitist. It claimed the high ground and gloried in doing so. It flourished within restricted devout circles, groups of 'friends of God' to which clergy and laity who longed for perfection came to seek the 'spiritual consolations' which their parish or conventual communities could not provide.[89] The mystics were not uninterested in the salvation of the people, but they addressed themselves exclusively to political and religious leaders: kings, popes, at a pinch bishops and superiors of orders. For the people, with whom they had little contact, they felt only distrust:

---

[87] This attitude was so novel that it was not always understood by contemporaries. Bishop Heming of Abo, when he visited St Bridget in Rome, was shocked when he saw her eat heartily 'de cibis delicatis sibi appositis': *PC Bridget*, p. 521. She indirectly challenged the hierarchy of states of life, what is more, by playing down the importance of traditional distinctions. She said to her entourage, after a vision: 'audivi nunc in spiritu vocem dicentem michi quod virginitas meretur cononam, viduitas appropinquat Deo et coniugium non excluditur a celo, sed obedientia omnes introducit ad gloriam': *ibid.*, p. 491.

[88] This notion was clearly formulated by Clare of Montefalco, in words reported at her process of canonization (*PC*, fol. 484): 'tanta est amicitia Dei ad animam et anime ad Deum quod quicquid Deus vult, vult anima et quicquid vult talis anima, vult etiam Deus ipse'.

[89] Clare of Montefalco was in contact with a whole network of spiritual friends extending from Spoleto to Perugia and Rome: *PC*, fols. 206, 363–4. She converted many who came to see her: *ibid.*, fols. 783, 884–93. For the reactions of those who met her, see *ibid.*, fols. 523–4: 'Numquam audivit (testis) aliquam personam quae tam alte et tam excellenter et profunde loqueretur de Deo sicut faciebat ipsa, et vere credit quod ex magna infusione divina loquebatur quae dicebat. Et dixit quod ipse semper habuit maximam et inestimabilem delectationem in audiendo eam.' For similar comments, see *PC Delphine*, fol. 104v. For devout circles where mysticism flourished in the Germanic countries, see F. Rapp, 'Les groupes informels à la fin du Moyen Age: types rhénans', in *Les groupes informels dans l'Eglise* (Strasbourg, 1971), pp. 180–93.

did they not demand prodigies and miracles, when all that mattered to these women was the conversion of the heart?[90] This refined conception of the religious life was long restricted to a minority, if not suspect. But the Great Schism and the conciliar crisis, by undermining the certainties of the clergy and the confidence of the people in ecclesiastical institutions, brought to the fore the ideal of reforming circles. For the latter, the Church and society were so corrupted by sin that grace and salvation could no longer be communicated through the usual channels, but only by a few exceptional persons marked out by extraordinary gifts. From this perspective, prophetic denunciation, visions and revelations were an extension to a sinful world which had lost its faith of the fervent and intimate dialogue which these sanctified souls enjoyed with their Creator. This was not only a new language; the capacity to proclaim the divine will to men soon became the chief criterion of perfection.[91] The mystical discourse, coming to the aid of imperilled hierarchies, was rewarded by a legitimacy and a consideration which it had long been denied.

[90] Delphine of Sabran, for example, refused to receive pilgrims who came to see her in the hope of being cured: *PC*, fols. 100v–101v. As a general rule, the mystics were hostile to popular religion, which they saw as no more than a mass of superstitions. The process of canonization of St Bridget records some of her diatribes against the magical practices of the Swedish peasantry: *PC Bridget*, p. 387.

[91] At the end of the fourteenth century, attempts were made to transform into mystics saints who seem not to have been mystics at all. Thus, in the process of canonization of Peter of Luxembourg, who was contemplative and anxious, but never an ecstatic or a prophet, one article claimed that 'it is likely that he had many and important communications and consolations from God, though this remained unknown to men'. To corroborate this claim, designed to make the young saint conform to the model of sainthood then in vogue, one witness (only) claimed that Christ on the cross appeared to him when he was praying at Châteauneuf-du-Pape: *PC Peter of Luxembourg*, art. 74, p. 489. In 1417, a bishop like Nicholas of Linköping was presented, in the depositions of witnesses at his process of canonization, as a great prophet, whose predictions later came true: *PC Nicholas of Linköping*, witnesses 2, 9, 12 and 20, pp. 137–8, 230, 268, 299.

THE ROMAN CHURCH IN THE FACE OF POPULAR AND LOCAL SAINTHOOD: A SILENT REJECTION

❧❧❧

In the preceding chapters, we have surveyed the whole field of sainthood, from popular perceptions to official consecration, defining each time the significance of the word *sanctus* and the corresponding typology. To insist too much on these distinctions, however, would risk giving a false impression, since the various levels of representations we have noted did not constitute autonomous entities. We need now, therefore, to shift the emphasis to the relations between them. This is no easy task, since each of the categories we have distinguished related to the others in complex ways which, though undeniably real, are often difficult to define. The documentation at our disposal is not particularly helpful to an attempt to unravel the threads of this tangled web, since the interconnections rarely took the form of open conflict, which would have thrown light on the opposing positions. During the last centuries of the Middle Ages, with only rare exceptions, the ecclesiastical authorities did not seek violent confrontation with popular beliefs and practices in the sphere of the cult of the saints. Even when they disapproved of them, they preferred to act flexibly, both orienting established devotions in a more orthodox direction and offering new models they thought preferable on the spiritual plane. This process of religious acculturation left traces which we have noted in passing, but they are difficult to interpret in the absence of texts explaining clerical intentions. In other words, it is as important to study the omissions and silences of the institution as its explicit rejections and condemnations, if we are to understand what was really at issue in the dialogue conducted over the centuries between the mass of Christians, local communities and the Roman Church.

In most countries of Christendom, the people, as we have seen, spontaneously regarded as saints men, women and children who had

413

died a violent but undeserved death.[1] A number of such persons were accorded a local cult, like the young Werner (d. 1287), venerated in the little region between Oberwesel and Bacharach, with the agreement of the local priests and some prelates, who even granted indulgences to the chapel where he was buried.[2] The Roman Church, in the late Middle Ages, firmly rejected all requests for the canonization of lay people whose main, if not only, claim to fame was to have died in a just cause. More precisely, we should distinguish two successive phases in the attitude of the Holy See. During the first two-thirds of the thirteenth century, the popes showed little enthusiasm for the 'martyrs' whose cult the people wanted them to approve, though without wholly denying official recognition to this form of sanctity. For example, Innocent III refused to open a process of canonization on behalf of Peter Parenzo, a Roman noble he had sent as podesta to Orvieto, where he was murdered by the 'Patarins'.[3] He probably saw this as primarily a political crime, which may well have been the case, given that this over-zealous collaborator of the Holy See had repressed not only heretics strictly speaking but the local Ghibelline nobility, who were suspected of sympathizing with them.[4] On the other hand, the same pope reacted very strongly to news of the murder of Peter of Castelnau, his legate in Languedoc, killed in 1208 by the henchmen of the count of Toulouse, and it appears that he would willingly have canonized him, if the total absence of a local devotion had not made it difficult to embark on a procedure which assumed the prior existence of a *fama sanctitatis*.[5] The distinction between the martyrs who performed miracles without being recognized by Rome and those exalted

---

[1] See above, pp. 147–56.

[2] See above, p. 94, note 31, pp. 148–51. The first indulgences date from the late thirteenth century.

[3] When Innocent III stopped at Orvieto in 1216, a delegation of notables *bone opinionis et fame* asked to see him to describe the miracles performed at the tomb of Peter Parenzo, but the pontiff refused: Natalini, *S. Pietro Parenzo*, pp. 118ff; M. Maccarrone, *Studi su Innocenzo III* (Padua, 1972).

[4] A *Vita* of the 'saint-martyr' was written in the thirteenth century by a canon from Orvieto cathedral. The version published by Natalini is more complete than that of the Bollandists (= *BHL* 6763; *AA.SS.* Maii V, pp. 86–97). The author, greatly though he admired his subject, did not conceal the fact that, on his death, there were many who cried: 'Thanks be to God for the death of this execrable man who unjustly persecuted so many people.'

[5] See above, p. 37; also A. Villemagne, *Bullaire du Bienheureux Pierre de Castelnau* (Montpellier, 1917). Contrary to the claims of several hagiographical encyclopedias, Peter of Castelnau was never canonized. In 1209, on the orders of the pope, there was a simple translation of his remains, which were placed in a stone tomb in the crypt of Saint-Gilles (*AA.SS.* Mar. V, p. 416).

by the papacy but without popular acclaim only increased over the following decades.[6]

The only people who had died a violent death whose sainthood was accepted by the Roman Church at this period were two clerics killed for defending the Church, SS Stanislas and Peter Martyr, both canonized in 1253.[7] The former, an archbishop of Cracow, murdered in 1079, was the object of a well-established cult within Poland which the papacy simply ratified.[8] The latter was canonized with unusual speed and the papacy then did everything in its power to make his cult spread throughout Christendom. The glorification of this regular by Innocent IV was an act of homage to the Mendicant orders, many of whose members had lost their lives at the hands of heretics or supporters of Frederick II. Each time, the pope sent the brethren a bull proclaiming his certainty that the victims had been 'enrolled in the college of martyrs for having shed their blood in the name of Christ', but took no further action.[9] After the murder of Peter of Verona, the Holy See cast aside its caution and hastened to accord him the supreme honour; an indefatigable preacher and zealous inquisitor, he could justifiably be presented as an authentic martyr.[10]

[6] This remark applies not only to the popular martyrs, but also to the prelates murdered as they performed their duties, such as the bishop of Vicenza, John Cacciafronte (d. 1179), whose process of canonization (in 1222–3) failed, and Archbishop Engelbert of Cologne (d. 1225), whose life was written by Caesar of Heisterbach soon after his death (= *BHL* 2546), and who was credited with several miracles (*BHL* 2547, 2548; N. Del Re, sv Engelberto, in *BS*, IV (Rome, 1964), cc. 1209–10).
[7] For St Peter Martyr, see Innocent IV, *Magnis et crebris*, 29.IV.1253 (though the canonization was pronounced on 24 March), ed. Fontanini, *Codex*, pp. 82–6. For St Stanislas, Innocent IV, *Olim a gentilium*, 17.X.1253, *ibid.*, pp. 89–91. See plate 36.
[8] The enquiry into his miracles is ed. W. Ketrzynski, *Monumenta Poloniae historica*, IV (Lvov, 1884), pp. 285–315; see also above, p. 168.
[9] Bull of Innocent IV (20.VII.1243) regarding the massacre of the 'martyrs' of Avignonnet (the inquisitors and their notaries), ed. *Bull. Franc.*, I pp. 305–6. In 1248, the same pope deplored the murder of the Franciscan inquisitor, Peter of Arcagnano (*ibid.*, p. 720). For the violent death of the Dominican Conrad of Germany (d. 1230), and attempts to obtain his canonization, see the *Chronica ordinis fratrum* of Galvano Fiamma, ed. G. Odetto, *AFP*, 10 (1940), pp. 352–3.
[10] The canonization of St Peter Martyr provoked many protests, which are reflected in inquisition records; see, in particular, the texts published by E. Dupré Theseider, 'L'eresia a Bologna nei tempi di Dante', in *Studi storici in onore di G. Volpe* (Florence, 1961), pp. 417–18; also L. Paolini, *L'Eresia a Bologna far XIII e XIV secolo* (Rome, 1975), pp. 35–7. A Bologna artisan declared to his judges that the Mendicants 'fecerunt unum Petrum martyrem sanctum, cum non sit sanctus nec est et deridet dictum sanctum Petrum martyrem et multum detrahit sibi'. The *Vita* of St Peter Martyr written by the Dominican Thomas Lentini (= *BHL* 6723) contains many references to punishments miraculously inflicted on the saint's detractors (*AA.SS.* Apr. III, pp. 705ff.) This is more than just a hagiographical commonplace, since many signs of hostility to the new cult are recorded also by Gerard of Frachet in his *Vitae fratrum*, ed. B. M. Reichert, *MOPH*, I (Louvain, 1896), pp. 240ff.

Nevertheless, this canonization remained an exception and, between 1254 and 1481, the Roman Church did not recognize as a saint a single servant of God who had died a violent death. This fact cannot be attributed to a shortage of candidates murdered 'out of hatred for the faith', as it was put in contemporary documents. Never, perhaps, were so many princes, pilgrims and children venerated for having shed their blood as in the late thirteenth and early fourteenth centuries.[11] But even more than in the past, the papacy showed a deep aversion for these individuals, whose cult often presented obvious political aspects. It is harder to understand why the many inquisitors and missionaries who perished at this period, in both West and East, were similarly ignored by the Holy See, whereas the hagiographical collections and martyrologies of the Mendicant orders exalted their memory.[12] John XXII, for

---

[11] See above, pp. 148–51, 166–7.

[12] They were many of them, and their death did not go unremarked. One of the best known is Pagan of Lecco, Dominican inquisitor in Lombardy, murdered 26 December 1277 at Colorina, in the Valtellina, by the men of a local lord sympathetic to the heretics. The general chapter of the Preachers, meeting in Milan in 1278, asked the brethren to make his martyrdom known and record miracles performed through his intercession (*Acta capitulorum generalium ordinis Praedicatorum*, ed. B. M. Reichert, III, p. 198). Nicholas III reacted with the bull *Ut orthodoxae fidei* (ed. J. Gay, *Registres de Nicolas III (1277–1280)*, no. 585 (Paris, 1898), p. 250), in which he deplored his death. The martyr's memory was kept alive in Dominican hagiography: see Stephen of Salagnac, *De quatuor in quibus*, ed. Kaeppeli, in *MOPH*, pp. 29–30; Johannes Meyer, *Liber de viris illustribus ordinis Praedicatorum*, ed. P. Van Loe (Leipzig, 1918), p. 41. For the history of the cult, see V. M. Folli, *Il Beato Pagano da Lecco, martire domenicano (1205–1277)* (Lecce, 1932). Other inquisitors were also regarded within their order as martyrs in the late thirteenth and fourteenth centuries: Peter of Cadiretta, a Dominican murdered by the Cathars near Seo de Urgel in 1277 or 1279 (*BS*, X (Rome, 1968), c. 675); Catalan Faure and Peter Pascal, Franciscans killed near Chabeuil, diocese of Valence (France), in 1321 by the Waldenses, for whom John XXII ordered a diocesan enquiry which came to nothing (*Vox sanguinis innocentis*, 30.XI.1321, ed. *Bull. Franc.*, V, p. 217); Antony Pavoni, Dominican inquisitor of Savigliano, killed by the Waldenses near Pignerol in 1374, whose 'martyrdom' was announced to Christendom in three bulls of Gregory XI in 1375, which were without follow-up (*AA.SS.* Apr. I, pp. 853–5). The list of martyrs killed on missions to the East is too long to be given in full. For the Dominicans, see R. Loenertz, 'Un catalogue d'écrivains et deux catalogues de martyrs dominicains', *AFP*, 12 (1942), pp. 279–303; Loenertz, 'Un catalogue de martyrs dominicains: note complémentaire', *AFP*, 19 (1949), pp. 275–9; J. Richard, *La papauté et les missions d'Orient au Moyen Age (XIIIe–XIVe siècles)* (Rome, 1978). Only the forty-nine Dominicans killed by the Tartars at Sandomierz in 1259 received special favour, when pilgrims to their tombs were granted an indulgence by Boniface VIII (*Bull. OP*, II, p. 45; *Monumenta Poloniae historica*, III (Cracow, 1878), p. 374). It is difficult to compile an accurate list of medieval Franciscan martyrs; least incomplete is that in Bartholomew of Pisa's *Liber de conformitate* (1399), ed. in *Analecta Franciscana*, III (1897), pp. 417–18. Among the best known are: the martyrs of Ceuta, that is, Daniel and his six companions, executed at Ceuta in 1227 (*BHL*, 2092–4; *BS*, IV (Rome, 1964), cc. 469–70); John of Perugia and Peter of Sassoferrato, martyred at

example, failed to act on a request from James II of Aragon concerning the Franciscan martyrs of Morocco (d. 1216), and the cult accorded to the Dominicans killed in the fourteenth century, in Armenia, Persia and on the northern fringes of Christendom, never spread beyond the order itself.[13]

By the end of the Middle Ages, the identification of sainthood with martyrdom was only a memory. Increasingly hostile to popular religiosity, the Roman Church set its face against this conception of Christian perfection, however traditional, and as a result ignored the phenomenon of the missionary martyr. Popes such as Urban V and Gregory XI even intervened firmly to condemn the cult accorded locally to 'false martyrs'.[14] This hardening of attitude coincided with the success among the upper ranks of the clergy of a new conception of sainthood which attached greater value to scholarship and doctrinal orthodoxy. It was not by chance that the first treatise in which a high-ranking prelate explicitly attacked certain aspects of popular devotion – that of the Dominican John Baptist de' Giudici, bishop of Ventimiglia – was written on the occasion of the canonization of St Bonaventure, the 'Seraphic Teacher'. In it, the author deplored the fact that the Church tolerated in some places the cult accorded to murdered children, 'who lacked proper merit since it was not their will but necessity which had made them martyrs', and at the same time openly asserted that 'the saints it was right to canonize were those who had shown proof of an

---

Valence in 1230 (*BS*, VI (Rome, 1966), cc. 1052–3); Monald of Ancona and his companions, killed in Armenia in 1314 (*BHL*, 5991–2, *AA.SS.* Mar. II, pp. 407–9; *BS*, IX (Rome, 1967), c. 543); Peter of Siena and his companions, whose death in Tana in 1322 was portrayed in St Francis' Basilica, Siena, before 1348 (G. H. Edgell, 'Le martyre du frère Pierre de Sienne et de ses compagnons à Tana, fresques d'Ambrogio Lorenzetti', *La Gazette des Beaux-Arts*, 71 (1929), pp. 307–8). For this group of Franciscan saints, see *AA.SS.* Apr. I, pp. 51–6; *BS*, XI (Rome, 1968), cc. 587–9.

[13] James II's petition is in H. Finke, *Acta Aragonensia*, I (Berlin, 1908), p. 754. For the cult of these martyrs, executed at Marrakesh in 1216, see R. Menth, 'Zur Verehrung der Protomärtyrer des Franziskanischen Ordens Sankt Berard und Genossen', *Franziskanische Studien*, 26 (1939), pp. 101–20. They were finally canonized by Sixtus IV in 1481 (*AA.SS.* Ian. II, pp. 62–71). For the Dominican order, see R. Loenertz, 'Les missions dominicains en Orient au XIVe siècle et la Société des Frères Pérégrinants dans le Christ', *AFP*, 2 (1932), pp. 1–83.

[14] See above, p. 90, notes 17–18. Urban V's bull is particularly significant, as he condemns, with unusual severity in such matters, the cult accorded in Romagna to a Dominican called James and a Hermit of Saint Augustine called Franceschino *percussum ictu fulminis et extinctum*. He criticized not only the title *beati* which they were wrongly given, but the pilgrimages which drew large numbers of the faithful to their tombs: Urban V, *Molesta significatio*, 1.IX.1368, ed. Benedict XIV, *De servorum Dei beatificatione*, II, p. 463.

eminent sanctity, above all if they were distinguished for the excellence of their doctrine'.[15] Late though it is, this text, written in 1480 at the request of Pope Sixtus IV, is still of great interest, since it gives clear expression to the thinking behind the actions of the ecclesiastical hierarchy in this sphere since the fourteenth century.

The Roman Church set its face equally, in the fourteenth century, against a model which enjoyed great prestige in most countries in the West, with the exception of Italy, that is, charismatic sanctity, linked to the exercise of office among and in the service of the people of God. The saint-kings and, above all, the saint-bishops who had fascinated the faithful for centuries ceased to impress popes and the 'great minds' in their entourage as models worthy of being offered to the universal Church. Few processes were decreed after 1310 on behalf of saints in this category and none of them succeeded. It is all the more difficult to see this as chance in that we know that requests concerning such people continued to flood into the Curia right to the end of the Middle Ages, though to no avail.[16]

One might have expected the late medieval papacy, with its strong geographical links with Italy and Provence, to be more sympathetic to the religious ideas which prevailed in the Mediterranean world. In these regions, as we have seen, the devotion of the faithful was given in preference to the poor or to the rich who had voluntarily made themselves poor, who were remarkable for their asceticism, piety and charity.[17] According to place and period, they might be lay penitents, hermits, recluses or Mendicants. This ideal gained official recognition at the end of the twelfth and in the first half of the thirteenth centuries with the canonizations of SS Homobonus and Francis of Assisi. But subsequently the papacy recognized only the clerical products of the penitential trend; the only hermit canonized after 1200, St Nicholas of Tolentino, belonged to a Mendicant order. Further, the popes tended to reserve their favour for persons of high rank like SS Louis of Anjou, Thomas Aquinas and Elzear,

---

[15] *Baptistae Vintimilliensis ex ordine Praedicatorum ad Xistum quartum pontificem maximum de canonizatione beati Bonaventurae*, ed. E. Baluze, *Miscellanea*, IV (Lucca, 1764), pp. 473, 486; the same author also observes, revealingly (p. 474): 'quod autem arguitur quod Ecclesia tales venerationes [= the cult of child martyrs] tolerando probare videtur, dicitur quod aliud est tolerare, aliud approbare. Multa Ecclesia tolerat quae non probat, sicut in civitatibus lupanaria et Iudaeos.'

[16] See above, pp. 72–3.

[17] At certain periods, the hierarchical Church had already made use of these 'men of God' (G. Cracco, 'Uomini di Dio e uomini di Chiesa', *Ricerche di storia sociale e religiosa*, n.s., 12 (1977), pp. 163–202) in connection with the Dialogues of Gregory the Great.

who demonstrated, during their lifetime, their attachment to evangelical values, but who were primarily distinguished by their high birth and the intensity of their intellectual and spiritual life. In contrast, none of the many Italian saints of modest extraction, whose reputation was based on the desire to share the sufferings of Christ in a concrete fashion and on the practice of humility, was then canonized. The religious model which inspired official sainthood and which was expressed in the questions put to the witnesses at the processes of canonization was certainly marked by the spirituality then favoured in the Latin world. But it was not identical to it, but rather turned it in a direction which was both clerical and socially elitist.

The contrast between more or less spontaneous forms of local sainthood and those which found favour in ruling Church circles can probably in part be explained by the increasing rarity of canonizations between the late thirteenth and early fifteenth centuries. The causes presented to the Holy See by bishops and civil powers usually met with indifference on the part of the Curia. In the most favourable cases, the will to succeed was lacking.[18] On the other hand, some of the canonizations pronounced by the papacy at this period seem to have been received with reserve, even hostility, by the faithful, as in the case of St Thomas Aquinas.[19] Mostly, they made little impact on public opinion, which was unmoved by St Elzear, canonized by Urban V in 1369, or by St John of Bridlington, canonized in 1401 by Boniface IX. In both cases, in spite of the pontifical sentence which should have made the cult universal, it remained very restricted.[20] The glorification of St Bridget was so controversial at the time that the decision taken in 1391 by Boniface IX had to be reiterated by John XXIII and the

---

[18] It is not enough, with P. Delooz (*Sociologie et canonisations*, p. 229), to assert 'a sort of parallelism between the visible prosperity of the Church and the number of canonizations', so that the small number of canonizations in the fourteenth century simply illustrates the 'decline' of the Church at this period. The complex causes of this reduction need closer analysis; see the useful comments of S. Spanò in his review of Delooz in *Rivista di storia e litteratura religiosa*, 6 (1970), pp. 133–8.

[19] See, in particular, the statements made 6 August 1325 by the Montpellier beguine Prous Boneta before the tribunal of the Inquisition at Carcassonne (May, 'Confession of Prous Boneta', p. 24); see above, p. 354, note 360.

[20] Elzear of Sabran was canonized by his godson, Urban V, on 14 April 1369, but the bull of canonization was promulgated by his successor, Gregory XI, 5 January 1371 (*Gloriosos Christi*, ed. *Bull. Franc.*, VI, p. 430). His cult seems to have remained confined to the Comtat Venaissin and northern Provence, and even here, to have been limited. The cult of John of Thweng, or of Bridlington, hardly existed outside Yorkshire (Purvis, *St John of Bridlington*).

Council of Constance in 1415, and then again by Martin V in 1419. The controversy she provoked was related to the conflict between rival obediences resulting from the Schism. But its significance went wider. The receptiveness of the papacy at the end of the fourteenth century to the mystical trend caused turmoil in the upper reaches of the Church, because it questioned the value system centred on culture which had prevailed during the Avignon papacy; between 1375 and 1430, official sainthood was influenced by the pietist milieux which had struggled for decades to reform the Church, by favouring, in all areas, a return to its roots and by emphasizing the essentially religious nature of its mission. But this development did little to narrow the gap between the official and popular conceptions since the cult of the visionaries and ecstatic prophetesses was not at all popular, at least to begin with. The reputation and canonization of St Bridget owed more to the influence and pressure of her Italian friends than to the enthusiasm of the Swedish people, just as the devotion to St Catherine of Siena owed more to the Dominican observance than to her fellow-citizens. The ideal of perfection incarnated by these women was too internalized to be generally understood; it was also too ambiguous and paroxysmal to gain the wholehearted approval of the clergy. Its success was, as a result, both ephemeral and fragile. The processes of canonization concerning the mystics were by no means guaranteed immediate success: St Catherine of Siena (d. 1380) was canonized only in 1461, during the pontificate of her compatriot, Pius II, and the reality of her stigmata was still the subject of fierce debate at the end of the fifteenth century.[21] The sanctity of Clare of Montefalco was not officially recognized by the Church until 1881. The causes of Delphine of Sabran and Dorothy of Montau are still under consideration by the competent Roman Congregation!

At the beginning of the fifteenth century, the gulf between the sainthood defined by the hierarchical magisterium and that perceived by the local communities was greater than at the time of Innocent III and Gregory IX. Since the last third of the thirteenth century, the

---

[21] The Franciscans believed that only St Francis of Assisi had received the stigmata, whereas the Dominicans claimed they had also been received by St Catherine of Siena. The dispute became very bitter in 1472–8, when the Franciscan pope Sixtus IV forbade, in a series of bulls, the depiction of St Catherine with stigmata on the walls of churches and talking about them to the faithful: L. Wadding, *Annales minorem*, XV, cc. 70–4; *Acta capitulorum generalium ordinis Praedicatorum*, ed. B. M. Reichert, *MOPH*, VIII, p. 432; *AFH*, 36 (1943), pp. 212–14.

Roman Church had adopted a model whose constituent elements were largely drawn from the spirituality of the Mediterranean regions, in particular that of the Mendicant Orders; the martyr was excluded because of his ambiguity and possible association with popular religiosity. Even charismatic and functional sainthood, that of the kings and bishops who were so prestigious north and east of the Alps, was relegated to the second rank.[22] On the other hand, an ideal of perfection based more on demands of an ascetic, moral, doctrinal and even, in some cases, mystical order was asserted in canonizations. This was one aspect of the process of spiritualization which characterized the evolution of western Christianity in the later Middle Ages. But in extending and imposing on the whole of Christendom a definition of the conduct regarded as saintly derived largely from the religious experience of the Latin world, the papacy strengthened the suspicion with which it was viewed by many of the faithful and even the clergy in other parts of the West. In England, the Scandinavian countries and much of the Germanic world, there was a chasm between the models of sainthood advocated by the papacy and those which were favoured by local populations. This situation lasted until the Reformation resolved the problem in radical fashion by abolishing the cult of the saints.[23]

In the Latin countries, the Roman Church was obliged, in the modern period, to ratify most of the cults which had freely developed since the end of the twelfth century and which it had previously ignored. The tenacity of the faithful, and their attachment to these devotions, deeply entrenched in social life, compelled the papacy to act to prevent their developing outside the institution.[24] But it took

---

[22] See above, pp. 158–72.

[23] For the popularity of local cults in England in the fifteenth and sixteenth centuries, of both canonized and uncanonized saints, see Finucane, *Miracles and pilgrims*, pp. 189–216.

[24] One reason why the Roman Church felt obliged to give local cults official consecration was the contrast between the gaiety of the festivals organized in their honour by local communities and the absence of liturgical solemnity. This was noted in 1515 by Pope Leo X, when he authorized the public cult of Margaret of Cortona, even though she had not been canonized: 'cum solemne et publicum festum, cum caeremoniis quae aliquando communitates in ipsarum festivitatibus facere consueverint, celebratum fuerat et ad celebrationem tanti festi non solum populus Cortonensis sed etiam vicinarum civitatum, terrarum et castrorum pro magna parte confluunt, nihilominus quia in missis et officiis illius diei nulla de ipsa beata Margarita, pro eo quod canonizata seu in sanctorum catalogo non existit, mentio seu commemoratio fit aut habetur, plures ibidem confluentes admirantur': ed. L. Da Pelago, *Antica leggenda della vita e dei miracoli di S. Margherita di Cortona* (Lucca, 1793), p. 183. Similar statements appear in the same pope's bull of 1519 authorizing the cult of B. Zita of Lucca (d. 1272) (*PC Zita, ASV, Riti,* Proc. 1315, fols. 68v–

centuries – from the mid-fifteenth to the early nineteenth – to stem the tumultuous flow of local sanctity and give a juridical status, by means of canonization *per viam cultus*, to innumerable individuals to whose memory the masses have remained faithful to this day.[25]

---

70), and that of Julius II (1509) in favour of the cult of B. Amato Ronconi de Saludeccio (d. 1256 or 1265) (*PC Amato Ronconi*, *ASV*, *Riti*, Proc. 89, fols. 220–6v).

[25] The process of regularizing these local cults began with the pontificates of Eugenius IV and Calixtus III, in the mid-fifteenth century. It speeded up in the early sixteenth century under Julius II and Leo X, reaching its peak in the 150 years following the decrees of Urban VIII regarding the institution of beatification in 1625 and 1634. For the juridical aspects of this lengthy operation, see J. Brosch, *Der Heiligsprechungsprozess 'per viam cultus'* (Rome, 1938); Brosch, 'Die aequipollente Kanonisation', *Theologie und Glaube*, 51 (1961), pp. 47–51. Some of these processes of canonization are preserved in the Bibliothèque Nationale in Paris, where they remained after the return to Rome of the Vatican Archives in 1817. There is a good inventory of this series (H) in C. De Clercq, 'Les causes des serviteurs de Dieu; le fond dit des canonisations à la Bibliothèque Nationale de Paris', *Revue de droit canon*, 4 (1954), pp. 76–100, which improves on A. de Bourmont, 'Index processum authenticorum beatificationis et canonisationis qui conservantur in Bibliotheca Nationali Parisiensi', *Anal. Boll.*, 5 (1886), pp. 147–61. But the essential source remains the Rites (*Riti*, processi) in the Vatican Archives, which contain the hundreds of dossiers which I have used for this book.

BOOK III

THE SIGNS AND SIGNIFICATIONS
OF SAINTHOOD

ᏮᏮᏮᏮ

As a historical subject, Christian sainthood can be approached in three
ways. The first, both juridical and sociological, consists of examining the
canonical situation of the servants of God and, more generally, their way
of life. It is then possible to distinguish, as we have done above, many
types of saint who, in a given country or period, enjoyed high esteem,
and trace the fluctuations in their popularity. A study of medieval sainthood which was restricted to a list of the *status vitae* then in favour would,
however, risk superficiality unless it was accompanied by a study of the
ideal models which determined the choice of new intercessors. It is important to know that, in a particular region or social group, people set more
or less store by, for example, martyrdom, asceticism or the mystical
experience. By combining these two approaches, I have tried to sketch in
broad outline a sociology of western spirituality in the later Middle Ages,
showing the more or less harmonious coexistence of various conceptions
of Christian perfection. We need now to embark on the third and final
stage of my regressive approach. This involves going back to the criteria
for the selective perception which determined when the title of *beatus* or
sanctus was attributed to a person, dead or alive. At the period of interest
to us here, an individual was canonized not primarily by public opinion,
or even by the Holy See, because of being a pious lay man or woman, a
good bishop, or an exemplary regular, but because people recognized in
that individual the presence of the characteristic signs of sainthood, as
they were inscribed in the collective memory. A series of representations,
which preceded the devotion, determined the judgement passed on the
servants of God. I will seek to establish what these were, without concealing the difficulties of such an enterprise, or claiming to solve all the
problems which await anyone who ventures onto the unknown territory

which the study of the mental structures of medieval people still constitutes.

In what follows, I shall largely be relying on the records of the enquiries *in partibus*. On the basis of hundreds of depositions concerning the life and miracles of the saints, I will try to establish what were the signs and the effects of sainthood in the eyes of most people. Next, an analysis of the documents arising from the curial stage of the process will allow us to see to what extent the 'great minds' in the pontifical entourage shared the ways of seeing of the simple faithful.

PART I

THE MANIFESTATIONS AND EFFECTS OF SAINTHOOD IN THE POPULAR MIND

∾∾∾

According to Christian tradition, the saints, in compensation for their merits and the sufferings they endured, were rewarded by God with a force (*virtus*) which remained present and continued to act in their remains after death.[1] This conception of sainthood and its reward was universally accepted in the later Middle Ages. It is found even among the 'spiritual' groups and the heretical sects, whose members were as keen as anyone to venerate the relics of their heroes.[2] With the exception

---

[1] For the different meanings of the word *virtus* in the literature of Christian Antiquity and the early Middle Ages, see A. M. Van Omme, *Virtus, een semantiese studie* (Utrecht, 1947); S. Axters, 'Over "Virtus" en heiligheidscomplex onder de Merowingers', in *Miscellanea historica in honorem A. De Meyer* (Louvain, 1946), pp. 266–85. Axters shows that, in Merovingian hagiographical texts, the word usually (two out of three uses) meant force, power or capacity to perform miracles.

[2] In principle, the Cathars and the Waldenses were hostile to the cult of the saints and the notion of intercession, since they believed there could be no difference between those who were saved; see the doctrinal texts ed. I. von Döllinger in *Beiträge zur Sektengeschichte des Mittelalters*, II (Munich, 1890), pp. 66, 320, 325. But in practice, in the thirteenth and fourteenth centuries, they were generally content to deny the sainthood of some of those venerated by the Roman Church, whose historical role they saw as particularly calamitous, such as St Silvester, who had endowed the Church with property and linked it to the civil powers, and, above all, SS Dominic and Peter Martyr, patrons of the regulars who persecuted them; see Stephen of Bourbon, *Traité sur les sept dons du Saint-Esprit*, ed. Lecoy de la Marche, p. 297. Moreover, contaminated by prevailing modes of thought, they even, in some cases, accorded a veritable cult to the relics of their own victims of the Inquisition; see Mariano d'Alatri, 'Culto dei santi ed eretici in Italia nei secoli XII e XIII', *Collectanea Franciscana*, 45 (1975), pp. 85–104. The same phenomenon is found outside Italy, as shown by the detailed report by the Spanish bishop Lucas of Tuy on the cult accorded by the Cathars of Leon to the heretic Arnold (*Lucae Tudensis . . . adversus Albigensium errores*, ed. J. de Matiana, III (Ingoldstadt, 1612), pp. 169–71). During the persecutions unleashed by John XXII against the 'spiritual' Franciscans and their supporters in Languedoc, beguins came at night to collect the ashes of those who had been

of a few forward-looking theologians, whose writings on this matter seem to have made little impact in their day, very few people before the fifteenth century seriously questioned the supernatural powers of the servants of God.[3]

executed, and venerated them. Questioned in 1323 at Lodève about this spontaneous form of cult, one of them said to the inquisitors 'that he thought the said beguins had been unjustly condemned, that they were saved . . . and that the day would come when it would emerge that they were saints'. Another added that he had 'carried in his purse, for a year and a half, pieces of the flesh of those who had been burned, as relics of martyrs of Christ and saints in Paradise': Manselli, *Spirituali e beghini in Provenza*, pp. 313–16. The author of the story in Italian entitled *Il supplizzio di Fra' Michele da Calci (1389)*, which includes an emotional description of the execution of a Fraticelli at Florence in 1388, also regarded his hero as a martyr: *Prosatori minori del Trecento*, I: *Scrittori di religione*, ed. G. De Luca (Milan, 1954), pp. 213–36.

[3] One of the rare dissenting voices was that of John Wyclif, in his *Trialogus* (ed. G. V. Lechler (Oxford, 1869), p. 236). Wyclif did not expressly condemn the cult of the saints, but regarded it as useless and dangerous, because it deflected popular piety, and he urged people rather to appeal directly to Christ 'quia ipse est mediator et intercessor optimus'. A similar attitude was found among some fourteenth-century dissidents and heretics, who particularly attacked the cult of images, which they regarded as idolatrous, and pilgrimages; see the texts ed. Merlo, *Eretici e inquisitori*, especially pp. 24–5.

CHAPTER 14

'VIRTUS': THE LANGUAGE OF THE BODY

ఴఴఴ

HOLY BODIES AND THEIR ATTRIBUTES

Before being a quality of the soul or a spiritual state, sainthood, in the popular mind, was first an energy (*virtus*) which expressed itself through a body. Its presence was revealed by a number of signs of a physiological order. The first was incorruptibility. It was believed that the mortal remains of the saints could not experience the same lot as those of ordinary mortals. Once life had gone out of their body, it became 'soft as the flesh of a child', which was a first sign of their divine election.[1] Before being laid in the ground, the body remained in this state for many days, so that the dead person seemed to be sleeping rather than dead. Once buried, the body was supposed not to decompose. The phenomenon of well-preserved remains played a key role in the birth of a *fama sanctitatis*, especially in the case of remains 'found' after a long spell underground or transferred from one tomb to another.[2] It would be wrong to see this as a feature of popular superstition. The most cultivated regulars shared the same conviction, as we see from Bernard Gui's detailed account of the elevation of the remains of the Dominican inquisitor, Bernard of Caux, which took place in Agen in 1281. Bernard had been buried twenty-eight years earlier in the Dominican church, with his two companions, Bertrand of Belcastel and Arnold Bélenger. When their tombs were opened, all that survived of the last two were bones, whereas the body of Bernard of Caux had remained intact and there was no unpleasant smell. The Friars, along with the people who came running as soon as they heard, saw this as a sure

---

[1] See, for example, Thomas of Celano's account of the death of St Francis of Assisi (*Vita prima*, c. 9, ed. Desbonnets and Vorreux, p. 314): 'his limbs became supple and flexible once again; the nerves were not at all contracted'.

[2] For these phenomena and beliefs well before our period, see Saintyves, *En marge de la Légende Dorée*, pp. 282–324.

427

sign of sanctity and rendered the very greatest honours to his corpse, before burying it in the middle of their church.[3]

Just as important as the state of preservation of the body was the smell it gave off. The odour which emanated from saints, though sometimes already perceptible in their lifetime, was primarily apparent after their death.[4] Public opinion was very exacting on this point, and if the corpse of a servant of God did not emit 'the odour of sanctity', the veneration might stop as quickly as it had begun. Salimbene gives an interesting example of this when he describes the collapse of the devotion to Albert of Villa d'Ogna (d. 1279) at Parma, where the new cult had been enthusiastically received. According to Salimbene, a canon who was carrying the reliquary which was supposed to contain his remains noticed a suspicious smell. When the receptacle was opened, it was discovered that a clove of garlic had been placed there in the guise of a relic, which put a stop to the fraud.[5] The importance of this criterion of sainthood was so great that the clergy sometimes hesitated for a very long time before proceeding with the translation of the body of someone they held in high esteem, for fear of a nasty smell emanating from his remains.[6]

Belief in the privileges of holy bodies was, at the period of interest to us here, universal. On this point, St Thomas Aquinas thought no differ-

---

[3] Bernard Gui, *De fundatione et prioribus conventuum provinciarum Tolosanae et provinciae ordinis Praedicatorum*, ed. P. Amargier (Rome, 1961), pp. 109–12.

[4] E. Lohmeyer, 'Vom göttlichen Wohlgeruch', *Sitzungsberichte der Heidelberger Akademie, Phil.-Hist. Klasse*, 10 (1919), pp. 1–52, shows that, for the Greeks and Romans, a pleasant smell was always regarded as an attribute of divinity. For the Middle Ages, E. Stückelberg, 'Der Geruch der Heilgkeit', *Schweizersches Archiv für Volkskunde*, 22 (1919), pp. 203–5, explains the odour of sanctity by the custom of burying the bodies of important persons in spices. A miracle attributed to B. Rainerius of Borgo San Sepolcro, a lay Franciscan brother who died in an odour of sanctity in 1304, seems to support this interpretation: a cardinal, miraculously forewarned by a vision of the saint, gave the brethren of the convent of Borgo San Sepolcro all the products they needed to embalm his body (Kern, 'Le Bienheureux Rainier de Borgo San Sepolcro', p. 282). When the reputation for sanctity was confirmed and the body exhumed, it was still impregnated with the smell of the spices. See also W. Deonna, 'Εὐωδία: croyances antiques et modernes, l'odeur suave des dieux et des élus', *Genava*, 17 (1939), pp. 167–263.

[5] Salimbene, *Cronica*, p. 734: 'cumque sensisset, viderunt et ipsi et cognoverunt se esse deceptos pariter et confusos, quia non nisi unum spicum alii invenerunt'.

[6] As the precautions taken by the Preachers of Bologna when the body of St Dominic was exhumed, in 1233, show. At the process of canonization, later that year, one of the witnesses, Brother Rudolph, said that 'the moment he lifted this stone [over the remains] . . . a strong, even a very strong, odour, pleasing and delightful, that he did not recognize, was emitted'. He vigorously rejected any 'positivist' explanation, claiming that 'neither oil nor perfume was put in the reliquary or the tomb, and this could not have happened without his knowing because, as procurator of the house, nothing was done except on his orders': *PC Dominic*, pp. 60–1. Shortly before her death, St Margaret of Hungary said to her companions: 'Ne timeatis quod ullus fetor exibit de corpore meo': *PC*, p. 184.

ently from the most ignorant peasant, even if he justified the popular belief by theological arguments which the latter would have found totally incomprehensible.[7] Similarly, it was generally accepted that the relics continued to live and intervene in events; had not some of them been seen to bleed when crossing the lands of a persecutor, or refuse to let themselves be transferred to another place or another reliquary?[8] Sometimes the radiation emanating from the precious remains took the concrete form of oil seeping out from the sides of the stone under which a saint had been buried. This phenomenon seems to have been less common in the West than in the East, but it is still mentioned several times in the thirteenth and fourteenth centuries, as, for example, in a letter sent to Innocent IV in 1261 by the bishop of Lincoln, Oliver Sutton, seeking the canonization of his predecessor, Robert Grosseteste.[9] The liquid which seeped out from tombs was seen as a sign of the divine election and supernatural power of a servant of God, and was, accordingly, piously collected by the faithful.[10] They also attached great importance to the earth, even the dust, that could be collected from near where the bodies of saints had been buried.[11] Pilgrims scratched at the soil roundabout with their nails so as to benefit

---

[7] *Summa theologica*, IIIa, q. XXV, a. 6: 'it is obvious that we ought to venerate the saints of Christ as limbs of Christ and friends of God and our intercessors. That is why, in celebrating their memory, we ought to venerate their relics, whatever they are, in a dignified and worthy manner, and particularly their bodies which were, here below, temples and organs of the Holy Spirit living and working in them and which, come the glorious Resurrection, will help to give its form to the body of Christ.'

[8] The body of St Thomas Cantilupe bled when his remains were being brought back from Italy, where he had died, as they passed through the diocese of Canterbury, where his opponent, the Franciscan John Peckham, was archbishop: *PC*, fols. 17, 32v. For the stubborn refusal of some remains to be translated, see *PC Mary of Cervellon* (d. 1290), Paris, BN, H. 1246, p. 43 (account of the ceremony at Barcelona in 1380); see also n. 29, p. 93 above.

[9] The tomb of St Nicholas at Bari was famous for its abundant flow of oil, still mentioned in the fourteenth century by the Franciscan Servasanto of Faenza: *Liber de virtutibus et vitiis*, ed. L. Oliger, in *Miscellanea F. Ehrle*, I (Rome, 1924), p. 188. Oliver Sutton's letter is in Cole, 'Proceedings relative to the canonization of Robert Grosseteste', p. 15. In his *Martyrologium* of 1324, John of Schalby described the prodigy as follows: 'Inter que tumba marmorea eiusdem viri Dei oleum purissimum repetitis vicibus pluribus in ecclesia emanavit': Appendix to *Giraldi Cambrensis opera*, VII, pp. 205–6. Similar claims were made about the tomb of St Elizabeth of Thuringia at Marburg, according to the Cistercian Caesar of Heisterbach (ed. A. Huyskens, *Die Schriften des Caesarius von Heisterbach über die hl. Elisabeth von Thüringen* (Bonn, 1937), pp. 386–9).

[10] John Damascene suggested a symbolic interpretation of this phenomenon as early as the eighth century: *De fide orthodoxa*, ed. H. Etienne, *Theologica* (Lyons, 1519), fol. 168: 'ex martyrum reliquiis unguentum suave olens emanare incredibile est nullo pacto, profecto iis qui sciunt dei virtutem et ab ipso sanctorum honorem'.

[11] At the tomb of St Elizabeth, a pilgrim seeking a cure for a bad arm, 'primo manum eamdem terra sepulchri linivit quam dedit Crafto sacerdos loci, unde ipsa nocte aliquantulum mitius habuit': *PC Elizabeth of Thuringia*, p. 254.

from the mysterious irradiation, which also spread to water. Most eagerly sought after was the liquid which had been used to wash the bones of a saint on the occasion of a translation, a few drops of which were worth their weight in gold. Mostly, however, pilgrims made do with pouring the contents of a jug over the tomb, so that it became impregnated with the beneficial *virtus*, then drinking the precious liquid.[12]

However varied these outward signs, they combined to make the body the locus of sanctification, and physical phenomena its most telling signs.[13] It is therefore hardly surprising that the desire to own fragments of the remains of saints was felt as strongly by the clergy, at this period, as by the laity. This is well-known in the case of the old relics, often disputed between churches and religious communities.[14] But the canonization processes of the thirteenth and fourteenth centuries show that the attention paid to the servants of God during their lifetime, by their contemporaries, was no less, especially in the Mediterranean countries. People waited with unconcealed impatience for the moment of death to take possession of the remains, as we see from accounts of the last moments of SS Francis and Antony of Padua.[15] Everybody knew that the beneficial radiation which

[12] A witness at the enquiry into the miracles of St Peter Thomas (Famagusta, 1366) said he had seen 'aliquas mulieres patientes, ut sibi videbatur, quae cum devotione fundebant aquam super tumulum dicti domini patriarchae, quam ipsae bibebant': Smet, *Life of St Peter Thomas*, p. 168. By the end of Antiquity, the custom of pouring wine mixed with spices over the tombs of martyrs was already widespread throughout the West (Herrmann-Mascard, *Les reliques des saints*, p. 48). Far from discouraging such practices, the clergy urged them on the faithful. At the process of canonization of Peter of Luxembourg (Avignon, 1390), a lay witness claimed to have been miraculously cured by a small quantity of earth from the tomb mixed with wine, a mixture administered to him by a Dominican bishop: *AA.SS.* Iul. I, p. 515.

[13] The hierarchical Church fully ratified these beliefs, as the frequent use of the expression *canonizare corpus* in the fourteenth century to indicate the official ceremony of canonization shows. When the devotees of a servant of God addressed him, they often expressly referred to his body: 'O corpus sanctum, adiuva me', cried a salt merchant who had fallen into the Rhone, imploring the protection of Peter of Luxembourg (*PC, AA.SS.* Iul. I, p. 502); similarly, 'oravit ad corpus sanctum, vovens eum [a drowned child] corpori sancto pro salvatione dicti pueri' (*ibid.*).

[14] P. I. Geary, *Furta sacra: thefts of relics in the central Middle Ages* (Princeton, 1978). To quote only one latish example (1275), Innocent V had to instruct the bishop of Minervino to investigate the theft of the relics of St Roger from the church of Cannae, Apulia, by the clergy and faithful of Barletta, who were threatened with the gravest canonical penalties if they failed to return them to their rightful owners: *AA.SS.* Oct. VII, p. 73. For this complex affair, see also G. Lucchesi, sv Ruggero, in *BS*, XI (Rome, 1968), cc. 491–3. The enquiry revealed a degree of connivance between the 'thieves' and an element among the Cannae clergy who wanted to breath new life into a declining devotion. A small part of the relics eventually returned to Cannae, the major part remaining in Barletta, in the nunnery of St Stephen, which took the name of St Roger in the fourteenth century.

[15] When the inhabitants of Assisi heard that the 'Poverello' was seriously ill, they despatched an armed escort to Bagnara, near Nocera, where he then was, with orders to bring him back, dead or alive, to his native town. When this had been done, the commune posted

was already apparent around them in this world would gain in intensity when their soul, having cast off its bodily shell, returned to its celestial home.[16] Hardly had a servant of God breathed their last than a series of macabre operations began: the opening up of the corpse, removal of the viscera to be placed in an urn, deposition of the remains in a temporary reliquary, often of wood, while awaiting the construction of a tomb of stone or mausoleum.[17] Additional precautions were sometimes taken to ensure that the remains were well preserved. The monks of Fossanova, jealous guardians of the body of St Thomas Aquinas, who had died in their abbey in 1274, boiled it a few months later to separate the bones from the flesh, then removed the head which was deposited at Priverno, the nearest town, where it was watched day and night by an armed guard.[18] Even in less extreme cases, transfers of relics or fragments of relics from one tomb to another, deemed worthier, or from one place to another, were frequent. The clergy encouraged these ceremonies, often marked by miracles which gave a new impetus to languishing cults. The details of these transfers of bones and bodies are obscure, and the historian can usually do no more than record them, without knowing what precise purpose they served, or what influenced them. This is most unfortunate because the translations which punctuated the life of religious communities and faithful suggest a whole strategy on the part of different ecclesiastical groups and political powers, which would, if we could understand it, tell us much about medieval society.[19]

The general consensus concerning the physiological aspects of sainthood did not exclude the possibility of differences between clergy and laity. The latter tended to see the external signs discussed above as infallible indicators. As a result, it was by no means unknown, in the thirteenth and fourteenth centuries, for the chance discovery of a corpse in a good state of preservation to give rise to a devotion. This was sometimes a

---

guards in front of the episcopal palace until his death, for fear the Franciscans would seize the body secretly and take it away: *Legenda antiqua Perusiana*, c. LXIV, ed. Desbonnets and Vorreux, p. 937.

[16] Processes of canonization recorded and consecrated this belief since there were usually more miracles *post mortem* than *in vita*.

[17] See, for example, the *Vita* of B. Margaret of Città di Castello (d. 1320), ed. Laurent, *AFP*, 10 (1940), p. 127. It was as they were removing the entrails that the sisters of her nunnery found the signs of Christ's Passion in the heart of St Clare of Montefalco, which was when they decided to cut into all the other organs: *PC Clare of Montefalco*, fols. 691ff.

[18] There is a detailed account of these operations in *Translatio corporis S. Thome de Aquino*, ed. M. H. Laurent, 'Un légendier dominicain peu connu', *Anal. Boll.*, 58 (1940), p. 43.

[19] When the documents make such an analysis possible, the results can be of very great interest; see, for example, Saxer, *Le dossier Vézelien de Marie-Madeleine*.

source of conflict, but this seems to have been rare.[20] Far from seeking confrontation, the clergy tried instead to endow the newly 'found' body with a conventional identity and biography which, by making it that of an edifying person, established a connection between their assumed perfection and the supernatural phenomena which surrounded the corpse.[21]

The Church also tried to take advantage of the universal belief in the 'virtues' of saints' bodies to further its pastoral objectives. According to a tradition dating back to the beginnings of Christianity, the place where, after their death, the power of the servants of God was most strongly manifested was wherever they had left their mortal remains.[22] Consequently, in the thirteenth century, some saints chose to die not where they had lived, but where their posthumous reputation would have the most beneficial effects. In 1249, the hermit John Bonus unobtrusively left the place near Cesena where he had lived for many years, in order to end his days in Mantua, his native city, in the hope of contributing to the destruction of the Cathar heresy which had many followers there.[23] Three years later, at his process of canonization, the inhabitants of Cesena made it clear that they were not yet reconciled to the loss of his relics, which they

---

[20] This, at least, is suggested by the scanty and, sadly, rarely explicit documentation. We know, for example, that, in 1387, the provincial synod of Poitiers, presided over by Bishop Simon of Caraman, took measures against 'the simple people who, at the instigation of some infidels, had adopted the habit of adoring the bodies of dead persons which had been found [intact] and venerating them as if they were saints': L. Bouchel, *Decreta ecclesiae Gallicanae*, 1, IV (Paris, 1621), pp. 572–3. But no more is known about this incident. Things were very different when it was the clergy who had originated a devotion. In 1388, the canons of Santa-Colomba of Rimini, seeking a tomb for the body of Nicolo da Prato, vicar-general of Carlo Malatesta, found, under the paving of the choir, an intact body with priestly ornaments. Convinced that they must be the remains of a saint, they accorded them honour, attracting visitors and then miracles. The canons then decided that the body must be that of John Gueruli, a canon of the cathedral who had died in an odour of sanctity in 1320. The cult prospered and no fewer than 160 miraculous cures were attested by ex-votos for 1388 and 1389 alone; see A. Turchini, 'Legenda, culto, iconografia del beato Giovanni Gueruli da Verrucchio', *Studi Romagnoli*, 21 (1970), pp. 425–53; L. Tonini, *Storia civile e sacra Riminese*, IV (Rimini, 1880), pp. 376–9, 479ff. At Polizzi (Sicily), in 1320, it was the inhabitants who obliged the bishop of Cefalu to translate the relics of a Franciscan, Gandulph of Binasco (d. 1260), who was buried in the local church. Their interest had been aroused by the pleasant smell emanating from his tomb, which gave rise to a local cult. As he was a highly praiseworthy regular, the prelate deferred to their wishes and drew up a *Vita* celebrating his merits: *AA.SS.* Sept. V, pp. 707ff.
[21] See the examples discussed above, p. 153.
[22] H. Delehaye, '*Loca sanctorum*', *Anal. Boll.*, 48 (1930), pp. 1–64.
[23] At the approach of death, he said to his disciples: 'Istud corpus morietur ubi natum est, scilicet in civitate Mantuae, et ibi fiet sibi magnus honor, et mors mea erit ad destructionem hereticorum multorum ibidem existentium . . . et ad corroborationem fidei christianae': *PC John Bonus*, p. 783.

believed ought to be returned to them, even offering the citizens of Mantua an advantageous financial deal.[24] In the fourteenth century, the papacy intervened on a number of occasions to try to get the remains of a recently deceased saint taken to wherever they would be best placed to edify the largest number and benefit the Church, rather than where chance – called Providence by those in possession – had placed them. It took nearly a century, and many vicissitudes, before Urban V, as part of his policy towards the university, managed to reassemble and deposit in Toulouse, in 1369, the relics of St Thomas Aquinas, which had previously been in the possession of the monks of Fossanova and several Campanian churches.[25] This and other similar interventions show that the hierarchy was trying to alter and integrate popular conceptions, from an apologetic perspective. By refusing to accord a special – it is tempting to say 'magic' – significance to the particular place where the saint had died, it helped imperceptibly to break the close link which had previously existed between sainthood and the place where it was revealed.

FROM RELICS TO 'GLORIOUS BODIES'

Most of the attributes of sainthood discussed above are already present in early medieval texts relating to the cult of the saints. Is this to say that nothing had changed in this sphere between the sixth and the thirteenth centuries? Admittedly, belief in the *virtus* emanating from the bodies of saints can justifiably be seen as a permanent feature; most of the prodigies mentioned in our processes of canonization differ little from those described by Gregory of Tours. But we should not allow the apparent

---

[24] They offered no less than 1,000 silver marks: *PC John Bonus*, pp. 824, 836. There was a similar, but opposite, situation in the case of St Louis of Anjou: in 1319, the inhabitants of Toulouse asked King Robert for part of the body of his brother, who had been their bishop; the royal chamberlain, Augier de Mer, replied on his behalf that this was quite impossible since the Marseillais would never agree, as 'the holy body had remained in Marseilles by virtue of a decision of the saint himself and divine will': C. Vielle, *Saint-Louis d'Anjou, évêque de Toulouse* (Vanves, 1930), pp. 489–90. The argument is all the more specious in that the saint actually died in Brignoles.

[25] In the thirteenth century, the bishop and municipal authorities of Padua compelled the inhabitants of the Caudalunga quarter to surrender the body of St Antony, who had died at the convent of the Clares of Arcella, so that it could be taken to the conventual church of the Friars Minor: *S. Antonii legenda prima*, ed. L. de Kerval, pp. 64–5; Toussaert, *Antonius von Padua*, pp. 450ff. For the circumstances and motives behind the transfer of the relics of St Thomas Aquinas to Toulouse, see E. Delaruelle, 'La translation des reliques de S. Thomas d'Aquin à Toulouse (1369) et la politique universitaire d'Urban V', *Bulletin de littérature ecclésiastique*, 56 (1955), pp. 129–46; C. Douais, *Les reliques de Saint Thomas d'Aquin* (Paris, 1903).

stability of the representations associated with sainthood to obscure the fact that there had been changes, however difficult they are to identify or date. In Merovingian times, the common conception of *virtus* was that of 'an immanent force whose efficacy is apparent but whose laws are obscure'.[26] It was the Sacred in its raw state, the Christian reference being provided only by the clergy, who alone could establish a connection between the miracles which occurred around the tombs of the saints and the merits, real or assumed, of their author.[27] Under the influence of the spiritual currents emerging in the West after the year 1000, things changed, as the growing popularity of hagiographical literature among an increasingly wide public reveals.[28] It would be mistaken, however, to jump to the conclusion that the saints, from being the amulets and therapists they had been in the past, suddenly became models of moral and religious perfection for the faithful. The idea that the principal role of the servants of God was to provide examples of virtues for the latter to copy only became general at a later date, under the influence of the Mendicant orders, who tried to channel and orient towards more elevated ends the unbounded faith of the masses in the power of relics. But between the eleventh and the fourteenth centuries, people were less interested in the virtues of the saints than in the spectacular intervention of God in their life.[29] The aura of supernatural phenomena which in earlier periods attached primarily to their remains extended to their earthly existence. From this perspective, *virtus* was no longer only a mysterious impulse emanating from tombs. It became a collection of extraordinary powers and gifts with which God had rewarded his servants in this world. Everything that distinguished them from ordinary mortals – from their extreme

---

[26] This is the definition of E. Delaruelle, 'La spiritualité des pèlerinages à Saint-Martin de Tours', in *Pelegrinaggi e culto dei santi in Europa fino alla prima crociata, IVo convegno del centro di studi sulla spiritualità medievale (Todi, 1961)* (Todi, 1963), p. 219, repr. in Delaruelle, *La piété populaire au Moyen Age* (Turin, 1975), p. 495.

[27] Marignan, *Le culte des saints sous les Mérovingiens*; Boesch Gajano, *Agiografia altomedioevale*. Jacques Le Goff, 'Culture cléricale et traditions folkloriques', *Annales ESC*, 22 (1967), pp. 106–26, has shown that early medieval hagiography cannot be seen simply as a reflection of popular mentality, even though it transmitted some representations drawn from lower-class culture.

[28] There is no thorough study of this phenomenon; see, however, B. de Gaiffier, 'L'hagiographie et son public', in *Mélanges Van der Essen* (Louvain, 1947), pp. 135–66; de Gaiffier, 'L'hagiographie dans le Marquisat de Flandre et le Duché de Basse Lotharingie au XIe siècle', in *Etudes critiques d'hagiographie et d'iconologie* (Brussels, 1967), pp. 415–507.

[29] W. Von den Steinen, *Der Kosmos des Mittelalters, von Karl dem Grossen zu Bernhard von Clairvaux* (Berne and Munich, 1959), pp. 105–6.

asceticism to their theological prowess – was then interpreted as a demonstration of divine power.

Among the signs which revealed the existence of a *virtus* in a saint in his or her lifetime, the most obvious were those relating to physical appearance. The impression produced by the sight of certain people seems to have played a major role in the birth of their *fama sanctitatis*. In general, the face was regarded as the reflection of the soul; you could read there the virtues of the saints, and merely to contemplate it was often enough to convert the hardest of hearts. When the young – and handsome – Louis of Anjou made his entry into Toulouse, where he had just been made bishop by Boniface VIII, 'everyone made haste to the scene to welcome a pastor so noble and perfect, and many, seeing this young man of royal blood, illustrious and pious, were convinced he was filled with the grace of the Holy Spirit . . . a carnal and sinful man cried out in front of everybody "That man is a saint" '.[30]

Admittedly, this passage appears in a hagiographical text, the documentary value and real significance of which are open to doubt, but the statements of witnesses at processes of canonization confirm this impression; in them, the servants of God appear as creatures of resplendent beauty, which was interpreted as a sign of supreme perfection.[31]

The radiation of divine power in a human being also materialized in a series of luminous phenomena, which eventually became essential attributes of sainthood.[32] In this field, it is extremely difficult to tell at exactly what point one passes from concrete fact to its allegorical expression, given the way the medieval mentality was inclined to express in terms of perceptible realities what, to us, belongs rather in the realm of interiority. In the end, however, it hardly matters where objective perception ceases and symbolic interpretation begins. What is of interest to the historian is

---

[30] *Chronicon XXIV generalium*, p. 435. In other texts, the beauty of the saints is presented as a sort of permanent miracle; see, for example, *Miracula beati Dominici*, ed. A. Walz, in *Miscellanea Pio Paschini*, I (Rome, 1948), pp. 306–26, where the fifteenth miracle (p. 325) is the attractive physical appearance of the founder of the Preachers.

[31] This belief is in line with biblical tradition, in particular a passage in *Ecclesiasticus* (XXIX, 29), often quoted in the Middle Ages: 'ex visu cognoscitur vir et ab occursu faciei cognoscitur sanctus'. At the process of canonization of St Catherine of Siena (p. 145), a witness declared: 'tanta etiam alacritas et iocunditas eius resplendebat in facie ut veluti tota refulgens dos claritatis aliqualiter relucerit in ea'.

[32] Raymond of Capua wrote of St Catherine of Siena: 'Vidi faciem eius sicut faciem angeli emittentem radios et splendorem, habentemque figuram quodam modo aliam, ita ut in mente dicerem: ista non est facies Catherinae': *Legenda maior*, p. 940.

that, whatever their cultural level, thirteenth- and fourteenth-century people believed saints to be creatures of light.[33] On this point, theologian and simple faithful were at one; basing himself on a tradition dating back to Isidore of Seville and Pseudo-Denis, St Thomas Aquinas declared that the spiritual illumination that took place in the soul which enjoyed the beatific vision was also reflected in the body.[34] God is light. To the extent that they lived in union with Christ, 'eternal splendour of the Father', the saints captured on their faces something of his brilliance; dead or alive, they radiated.[35] In another text, the Universal Teacher claimed that there was no visible difference between the 'light of glory' which would clothe the bodies of the elect after the Resurrection and natural light; they were distinguished only by a difference in intensity.[36] His teaching on this point accords with the popular conception of the servants of God as potential 'glorious bodies', largely escaping the laws of human nature. As a general rule, the link between sainthood and light was revealed with particular clarity at the moment of death, which was accompanied by extraordinary signs, such as the appearance of a ball of fire above the house where a servant of God lay dying; at the precise moment of death, a great light pierced the darkness, sign of the entry of the soul into its celestial home.[37]

[33] Questioned about the sanctity of Clare of Montefalco (d. 1308), one of her confessors said: 'erat in ea tantum lumen quod . . . non intelligebat eam sed habebat magnam fidem in ea': *PC*, fol. 140. For the growing importance of luminous phenomena in German monastic hagiography in the fourteenth century, see W. Blank, *Die Nonnenviten des 14. Jahrhunderts: eine Studie zur hagiographischen Literatur des Mittelalters unter besonderer Berücksichtigung der Visionem und ihrer Lichtphänomene* (Freiburg im Breisgau, 1962).

[34] Isidore of Seville, *De natura rerum*, c. XXIV, 2: 'Stellae autem secundum mysticum sensum sancti viri intelliguntur . . . sicut enim omnes stellae a sole illuminantur, ita sancti a Christo gloria coelestis regni glorificantur.' St Thomas Aquinas was probably drawing on this text when he wrote (*Contra gentes*, IV, c. 86): 'sicut igitur anima divina visione fruens quadam spirituali claritate replebitur, ita per quamdam redundantiam ex anima in ipsum corpus suo modo claritatis gloria induetur'.

[35] That God was essentially perceived as light in the Middle Ages is shown, for example, in the *Tractatus de luce* of the Franciscan Bartholomew of Bologna, ed. I. Squadrani, *Antonianum*, 7 (1932), pp. 201–493. The Word being the light of the world, everything to do with it is *splendor, radium* etc.: E. Longpré, 'Bartolomeo di Bologna, un maestro francescano del sec. XIII', *Studi Francescani*, 20 (1923), pp. 365–84. It had already been said several centuries earlier by the author of the hymn in honour of St Ursmer (d. 713), ed. K. Strecker, *MGH. Poetae Latini Medii Aevi*, IV, 2 (Berlin, 1923), p. 210: 'Christe, sanctorum corona omnium splendiflua.' It is also what painters were seeking to express when they represented saints with their head surrounded by a nimbus, halo or rays: M. Collinet-Guérin, *Histoire du nimbe* (Paris, 1961).

[36] Thomas Aquinas, *In IVum Sent.*, dist. 44, q. 2, a. 4: 'Claritas gloriae erit alterius generis quam claritas naturae quantum ad causam, sed non quantum ad speciem; unde si claritas naturae ratione suae speciei est proportionata visui, ita claritas gloriosa.'

[37] See Bernard Gui's account of the death of the saintly Hugua of Castres, *De fundatione et prioribus*, ed. Amargier, p. 163: 'in cuius transitu, globus igneus et claritas luminis appa-

The body itself changed in appearance and seemed to come to life; the features of the dead person lit up and assumed a joyful expression.[38] When the body was reduced to the state of relics, the miracles which occurred around it were frequently accompanied by a flash of light.[39]

These visible signs of sainthood, which were universally accepted, were not, however, without ambiguity, as we see in the case of beauty, the sight of which was often enough to provoke in the laity an admiration which could turn into veneration. According to a fourteenth-century Dominican legendry, the popularity of St Thomas in Campania owed much to his appearance and his corpulence: 'He was so big', noted the author, 'that because of his imposing physique, he was called the Sicilian ox . . . when he took a walk in the country, the people working in the fields abandoned their labours and rushed to see him, admiring the imposing stature of his body and the beauty of his human features.' This episode led the hagiographer to a conclusion which is no less interesting than his story: 'They went to see him much more on account of his beauty than by reason of his sanctity or noble origins.'[40] The late medieval clergy, conscious of the ambivalence of the sacred, eventually challenged the link between grace and supernatural power, which is evident in many texts concerning sovereigns.[41] They set out to establish, whenever possible,

---

ruit supra domum illam in qua jacebat . . . sicque anima eius de presenti vita egreditur . . . ad patriam claritatis eterne progrediens'. A similar idea was expressed at the canonization process of St Clare of Montefalco (fol. 434): 'in ipsa hora migrationis sororis Clarae, apparuit quaedam lux clarissima et incepit in fronte et clarificavit totam faciem et in apparitione istius lucis clarissime dicta soror Clara migravit'.

[38] At the death of St Edmund of Canterbury (d. 1240): 'quasi subito circumfulsit eum lux de caelo, ita subito perfudit eum quedam luculenta rubedo et facies quam prius cinereus pallor obtexerat, mox erumpente caritatis eius fervore, velut rosei coloris decorem induebat': *Quadrilogus*, ed. Lawrence, *St Edmund of Abingdon*, p. 201.

[39] At the enquiry into the miracles of St Peter Thomas (d. 1366), a witness admitted having thought that 'si dominus Petrus sanctus esset, descenderet lumen de caelo super eius tumulum . . . in testimonium sanctitatis': Smet, *Life of St Peter Thomas*, p. 168. For shafts of light accompanying miracles, see *PC Thomas Cantilupe* (fol. 69): 'tunc apparuerat in dicta ecclesia quadam magna choruscatio sive lux, qua existente in dicta ecclesia ossa dicte Alicie fecerunt aliqualem fragorem seu strepitum et nervi fuerunt extensi et tota fuerat curata'.

[40] *Translatione corporis S. Thomas de Aquino*, ed. Laurent, p. 43.

[41] For the links between beauty and perfection, see G. Van der Leeuw, *Sacred and profane beauty: the Holy in art* (London, 1963). For the beauty of the king and its effects, see Adam Murimuth on the subject of Edward III: 'Corpore elegans, vultum habens deo similem, quia tanta gratia in eo mirifice relucebat ut si quis in eius faciem respexisset, illo die indubie speravit sibi jocunda solatia et prospera evenire': *Continuatio chronicarum*, ed. T. Hog (London, 1849), p. 226. Interestingly, in the fourteenth century, some clergy reacted against such ideas; the Dominican inquisitor Nicholas Eymerich, in his *Elucidarius elicidarii*, declared 'rash and false' the claim by the author of the *Elucidarium* (twelfth

a relationship between the luminous phenomena which surrounded the servants of God and specific theological concepts.[42] The physiological aspects of sanctification were not denied, certainly, but the Church only recognized them to the extent that they testified to an intense inner life. In the Mediterranean countries, where the ascetic ideal prevailed, ugliness became a criterion of sainthood, as a sign of an existence composed of suffering and privation.[43] Elsewhere in Christendom, the change was less marked, but, alongside the old, there emerged new signs, whose spiritual content seemed more authentic. Chief among them was the gift of tears (*gratia lacrimarum*), referred to in thirteenth- and fourteenth-century processes of canonization. This charisma was fairly rare in the West after the time of Gregory the Great, whereas in the Byzantine East it is frequently mentioned in hagiographical texts from before the year 1000.[44] The evolution of religious sensibility restored it to favour in the Latin Church from the twelfth century. St Bernard and the Cistercian school saw the tears of compunction a monk ought to shed as proof of the love of God.[45] They were provoked by meditation on the *memoria* of Christ, that is his palpable memory, and gave a foretaste of the beatific vision to be enjoyed by the sanctified soul in the future life. For spiritual writers, they were both a condition and a sign of the visitation of the soul by the Word in this world.[46] These mystical reflections on the value of the gift of tears were long accessible only to very restricted, and above all monastic, circles. But when meditation on the sorrowful mysteries, in particular the Passion, assumed a central place in western spirituality, the gift of tears played an increasingly important role in the life of the saints and in the appreciation

century) that the good and the wicked could be recognized by their appearance: Y. Lefèbvre, *L'Elucidarium et les lucidaires* (Paris, 1954), p. 508.

[42] In the case of St Margaret of Hungary (d. 1270), whose face had brightened after her death, the archbishop of Esztergom explained to the sisters of her nunnery that this was evidence that she had in her 'the principle of her resurrection': *PC*, p. 279.

[43] One witness said of St Peter of Morrone: 'in solo aspectu faciei illius, quociens ostendebat se populo, nullus fere de astantibus abstinere poterat ex devocione concepta a compunctionis lacrimis cum singultu'; at the sight of this emaciated face, 'subito tanta orripillatio capillorum facta est ei, quod videbatur illi quod omnes capilli sui avolarent': *PC Peter of Morrone*, p. 211. In the Golden Legend, there are traces of two different notions: the external aspect of certain saints is in accord with their interior and they have an 'angelic' appearance; others have repulsive or pitiful appearances: M.-C. Pouchelle, 'Représentations du corps dans la Légende Dorée', *Ethnologie française*, 6 (1976), pp. 293–308.

[44] P. Adnès, sv Larmes, in *Dictionnaire de spiritualité*, IX (Paris, 1976), cc. 287–303; M. Lot-Borodine, 'Les mystères du "don des larmes" dans l'Orient chrétien', *La vie spirituelle, Supplement*, 48 (1935–6), pp. 65ff.

[45] 'Let me cry throughout my life', asked Aelred of Rievaulx in a prayer (*PL*, 158, c. 894).

[46] See the texts quoted by P. Régamey, 'La componction du cœur', *La vie spirituelle*, 45 (1935), pp. 86–99.

of their degree of perfection.[47] Some penitents and recluses interpreted
the absence of tears as a sign of remoteness from God and inflicted appal-
ling torments on themselves in order to recover this grace; Umiliana dei
Cerchi, in mid-thirteenth-century Florence, put quicklime on her eyes to
make herself weep, while in mid-fourteenth-century Provence, Delphine
of Puimichel declared that she would rather lose her sight than refrain
from the tears 'through which the eye of the spirit is refined and purified
and the Creator better known'.[48] This was not a phenomenon specific to
saints of the mystical or penitential type. By the second half of the thirteenth century, the reputation for sanctity of a servant of God could not
flourish if the gift of tears was lacking. Processes of canonization describe
bishops and monks who burst into tears at the moment of consecration,
sign of a soul free of that 'inner dryness' which, in the eyes of the spiritual
writers of the day, was the first step on the road to sin.[49] The perception of
sanctity remained closely linked to a sensory code (smell, touch, luminous
phenomena etc.), but it was enriched and spiritualized with the passage
of time.

HUMAN BODY AND BODY OF CHRIST

The trend which, from the twelfth century, led to an internalization of
the manifestations of sainthood crossed a new threshold, in the thirteenth
century, with the appearance of stigmatization. The significance of the
events at La Verna, where a seraphim inflicted on St Francis in ecstasy
the five wounds of Christ, went far beyond the person of the Poverello
and the role played by this extraordinary event in the history of the order
of the Friars Minor.[50] By solemnly attesting and frequently reaffirming its
reality, the Roman Church helped to introduce into the domain of auth-

---

[47] Initially confined to monastic circles, the gift of tears is subsequently mentioned in a wide
range of literary and hagiographical texts; see B. Steidle, 'Die Tränen. Ein mystisches
Problem im alten Mönchtum', *Benediktinische Monatschrift*, 20 (1938), pp. 181–7; H. G.
Weinand, 'Tränan. Untersuchung über das Weinen in der deutschen Sprache und Literatur des Mittelalters', unpublished thesis (Bonn, 1958), pp. 171–7.

[48] For B. Umiliana, see *Vita auctore Vito de Cortona* (= *BHL* 4041), *AA.SS.* Maii IV, p.
389. For B. Delphine, see Cambell, *Vies occitanes*, p. 203.

[49] See, for example, *PC Thomas of Hereford*, fol. 60: 'multum plorabat in missa quando
celebrabat'. See also S. Wenzel, *The sin of sloth: 'Acedia' in medieval thought and literature*
(Chapel Hill, 1967), pp. 205–51; Vicaire, *Dominique et ses Prêcheurs*, pp. 426–30.

[50] For the importance of the stigmatization of St Francis (14 September 1224), attested
by contemporary witnesses, see O. von Rieden, 'De S. Francisci Assiensis stigmatum
susceptione dissertatio historico-critica luce testimoniorum saec. XIII', *Collectanea Franciscana*, 33 (1963), pp. 210–66, 392–422 (with full bibliography). For reactions to this
unprecedented event, see Vauchez, 'Les stigmates de S. François'.

entic religious experience and normality physiological signs which had previously been ignored by the clergy or seen as sacrilegious deceptions.[51] After 1230, the idea that a human being could identify themself with Christ in the flesh rapidly gained ground, despite the efforts of the Franciscans to reserve this prerogative for their founder. Perhaps surprisingly, the faithful seem to have accepted this innovation more readily than the majority of churchmen, always inclined to see as offensive to divine majesty any form of 'divinization' of the human body.[52] But under the influence of the regulars, in particular the Mendicants, hagiography was, by the end of the thirteenth century, beginning to devote more attention to these and other, even more astonishing, signs.[53] In the process of canonization of Clare of Montefalco (d. 1308), which took place in 1318–19, we first encounter extraordinary paramystical phenomena, attested by hun-

[51] The first known cases of stigmatization appear about 1220, in what was hardly, from the point of view of orthodoxy, a favourable context: in England, a man was condemned to life imprisonment for having called himself Jesus, after inflicting the stigmata on himself and publicly exhibiting the five wounds of Christ on his body: Powicke and Cheney, *Councils and Synods*, II pp. 105–6. Other contemporary documents allude to persons inflicting the wounds on themselves out of devotion to Christ's Passion: Stephen of Bourbon, *Tractatus de diversis materiis predicabilis*, ed. A. Lecoy de la Marche (Paris, 1877), p. 277; Caesar of Heisterbach, *Dialogus miraculorum*, ed. Strange, II, p. 100.

[52] Between 1237 and 1291, no fewer than nine pontifical bulls asserted the reality of the stigmata against detractors. One (Gregory IX, *Usque ad terminos*, 11.IV.1237, ed. *Bull. Franc.*, I, pp. 211–12) denounced the attitude of the bishop of Olomouc, Bohemia, who had forbidden the iconographical representation and veneration of the stigmata of St Francis 'because only the son of the eternal Father had been crucified for the salvation of mankind and the Christian religion ought to accord a supplicatory devotion only to his wounds'. See also Vauchez, 'Les stigmates de S. François', p. 514.

[53] See the list of medieval stigmatics in the (hypercritical) article by E. Debongnie, 'Essai critique sur l'histoire des stigmatisations au Moyen Age', *Etudes Carmélitaines*, 21 (1936), pp. 36–42; also in J. M. Höcht, *Träger der Wundmale Christi: eine Geschichte der bedeutendsten Stigmatisierten von Franziskus bis zur Gegenwart*, I (Weisbaden, 1951). The theme enjoyed great success among beguines, as shown by the biography of Elizabeth of Spalbeeck or of Herkenrode (d. 1270). See also Thomas of Cantimpré, OP, *Bonum universale de apibus* (c. 1266), L. I, c. 25, fol. 7 (Douai, 1627); Philip of Clairvaux, OCist, *Vita Elizabeth sanctimonialis in Erkenrode*, ed. in *Catalogus codicum hagiographicorum bibliothecae regiae Bruxellensis*, I (Brussels, 1886), pp. 362–79; A. Stroick, 'Wer ist die Stigmatisierte in einer Reformschrift für das zweite Lyoner Reformkonzil', *Historisches Jahrbuch*, 50 (1930), pp. 342–9. But it was primarily in the late fourteenth and early fifteenth centuries that the theme of stigmatization flourished, attested by, for example, part 2 of the Dominican Thomas Caffarini's *Libellus de supplemento*, ed. G. Cavallini and I. Foralosso (Rome, 1974). Phenomena of levitation are recorded in the Life of B. Margaret of Ypres (d. 1237) (ed. G. G. Meersseman, *AFP*, 18 (1948), p. 117) and the *Vita maior* of St Hedwig (d. 1243) (= *BHL* 3766), written, admittedly, c.1300. For all these signs and the saints in whom they were found, see H. Thurston, *Physical phenomena of mysticism: a collection of studies on praeternatural phenomena in the Lives of the saints and others* (London, 1952). One of the most extraordinary medieval hagiographical texts in this connection is the Life of the Cistercian nun Lukarda of Oberweimar (d. 1309), ed. *Anal. Boll.*, 18 (1899), pp. 305–67.

dreds of witnesses, both clerical and lay, who were unanimous in seeing
them as incontestable indicators of sainthood. In some depositions, in
addition to the luminous prodigies which surrounded the saint, a series
of psychosomatic states were described and analysed in some detail. We
are therefore able to differentiate, among the different forms of ecstasies
experienced by Clare, the *elevatio mentis*, a simple 'absence' resulting from
intense contemplation, from the *raptus*, characterized by the loss of bodily
sensibility, which marked the end of the mystical ascent and expressed
the fullness of the loving union of the soul with God;[54] the saint was then
totally immobile, her hands joined and her eyes closed; her face became
more luminous and highly coloured than normal. At such moments, she
could be touched and even pricked with needles – which frequently happened – without showing the slightest reaction. Her body seemed even to
float, miraculously defying the laws of gravity.[55] These privileged
moments, which lasted anything from a few minutes to a half-day, were
accompanied by physiological changes described by the witnesses in
minute detail. Not content with enjoying in this world the prerogatives of
the 'glorious bodies' as defined by theologians (*impassibilitas*, *claritas*, *agil-
itas* and *subtilitas*), the great fourteenth-century mystics felt in their flesh
the effects of the spiritual consolations with which they had been blessed.[56]
Clare of Montefalco, by dint of meditating on the Passion and trying to

---

[54] 'Elevatio est quedam meditatio sive contemplatio per amorem ad deum': *PC Clare of
Montefalco*, fol. 190; the elevation could be *minor* or *major* (*ibid.*, fol. 402). The *raptus* is
described as 'intensa et fortis elevatio mentis ad Deum', after which the saint 'surgit
consolata et gaudiosa corporaliter et spiritualiter' (*ibid.*, fol. 46). The ecstasy was
accompanied by intense joy, as already signalled by St Thomas Aquinas: 'non modo ex
ratione contemplationis vita contemplativa est hominibus delectabilis sed ex divini amoris
radice est omnibus aliis delectabilibus longe jucundior': *Summa theologica*, *IIa IIae*, q.
CLXXX, art. 7. But the Universal Teacher elsewhere emphasized that mystical rapture
had its limits: 'non potest Deus ab homine puro in hac mortali vita per essentiam videri'
(*ibid.*, Ia p., q. XII, art. 11). The sole exception to this rule was St Paul, who saw God
face to face with his body (*ibid.*, *IIa IIae*, q. CLXXX). Among thirteenth-century mystics,
it was less a question of a direct vision than the sensation of a presence.

[55] 'Et videbatur ipsa Clara tota demissa et dissoluta, et manus eius videbantur quasi cera
mollis et ossa non sentiebantur et videbantur tota distemperata': *PC Clare of Montefalco*,
fol. 400. Phenomena of levitation are especially common in the life of B. Douceline (d.
1274), written early in the fourteenth century: R. Gout, ed., *La Vie de Sainte Douceline,
texte provençal du XIVe siècle* (Paris, 1927), pp. 108–15. They appear also in the process
of canonization of St Bridget: *PC*, p. 24; P. Debongnie ('Les levitations de Ste Brigitte
de Suède', *RHE*, 34 (1938), pp. 70–83), questions the reality of the phenomenon in her
case; but his conclusions do not alter the fact that, in the fourteenth century, levitation
had become an attribute of sainthood.

[56] *PC Catherine of Siena*, p. 144. During one ecstasy, Dorothy of Montau 'sensit siquidem
quoddam vividum quasi foetum . . . et nunc Dominus ex ea se ipsum voluit parere vel
gignere': *PC*, fol. 156.

relive it in thought and deed, eventually had an apparition of Christ carrying his cross and, from then on, according to one witness, 'she always felt a perceptible cross in her heart'. It is therefore hardly surprising that, immediately after her death, the sisters of her monastery proceeded to a veritable dissection of her body, discovering inside it first a cross, then, one after the other, all the *insignia* of the Passion, from the crown of thorns to the sponge of Calvary, not forgetting the column of flagellation.[57]

With Dorothy of Montau, a few decades later, we encounter both the stigmata and an exchange of hearts between God and his servant. Many witnesses claimed to have seen, beneath her tunic, bloody wounds which were reflections of injuries inflicted on her by God in his love.[58] The *extractio cordis* is mentioned both by very simple people and by theologians in her entourage, who insisted on the physiological reality of the phenomenon.[59] It was the subject of a special article (no. 21), about which the majority of those who had known her were interrogated.[60] A few years later, in the process of St Catherine of Siena, the same gifts appear. According to the Dominicans who had been members of her 'brigade', the 'mama', too, had received the stigmata and been given a new heart by God during the course of her relations with her divine spouse.[61]

This testimony suggests very strongly that, in the later Middle Ages, the bodily repercussions of mystical states were not seen as symbols or allegories, but as palpable realities, speaking for themselves. A new criterion of the authenticity of sainthood appeared: physiological similarity to the person of Christ, incontestable sign of the union of hearts and the

---

[57] *PC Clare of Montefalco*, fols. 274, 523.

[58] *PC Dorothy of Montau*, fol. 147v: 'plura accepit exterius in corpore vulnera et hoc sepius et sepissime Dominus in sopore et etiam vigilando impressisset eidem'; see also *ibid.*, fols. 96, 168.

[59] The 43rd witness, Metza Hugische of Danzig, declared 'se audivisse a pluribus fide dignis quod cor vetus ipsius matris Dorotheae sibi fuit extractum et in locum illius cor novum et fervidum intrusum': *PC*, fol. 71. The theologian John of Marienwerder was more precise: 'illa cordis extractio et alterius intrusio suo judicio non fuit solum alteratio naturae sed etiam mutatio substantiae, quia non solum fuit renovatio sui cordis spiritualis sed etiam corporalis': *ibid.*, fol. 204.

[60] Text in *Gedanen. beatificationis . . . Dorotheae Montoviensis*, p. 241. On the exchange of hearts, see A. Cabassus, sv Coeurs (échange des), in *Dictionnaire de spiritualité*, II (Paris, 1953), cc. 1046–51 (disappointing for the Middle Ages).

[61] According to Thomas Caffarini, she received 'in manu dextra certum indicium per modum cuiusdam stigmatis in apice impressi': *PC Catherine of Siena*, p. 45; further on, he attributes the five stigmata to her (*ibid.*, pp. 144–5) to make her resemble her divine spouse. For the violent controversies between the Dominicans and the Franciscans and Pope Sixtus IV with regard to the stigmata of St Catherine, see Vauchez, 'Les stigmates de S. François', p. 611. The exchange of heart with Christ was described at the Venice process (p. 144).

effusion of the Spirit of God into his creature. We should note, nevertheless, that the saints displaying these extraordinary manifestations were only a tiny elite. However important its repercussions, the 'mystical invasion' of the fourteenth century was very far from eclipsing or even less abolishing the other forms of sainthood on which the process of spiritualization had less impact. For reasons which I have tried to explain above, women were the principal beneficiaries of this development, even though it started with a man, St Francis of Assisi. It was women who pushed to extremes the tendency, apparent in hagiography since the eleventh century, to extend to the living saints the prerogatives of the elect, since they, to express their religious experience, had at their disposal only the language of the body. This shift helped to increase further the extraordinary aspect of sainthood. The identification of the human body with the glorious body, even the body of Christ, led, paradoxically, to a new form of marvel: physiological marvellousness. This had a fine future ahead of it, as we see from the curiosity still provoked in our day by instances of stigmatization or transverberation, from Thérèse Neumann to Father Pio.

CHAPTER 15

THE STRUCTURES AND EXPANSION OF THE FIELD OF THE MIRACULOUS

ഗ~ഗ~ഗ~

The belief in the omnipresence of the supernatural and in the constant intervention of the inhabitants of the hereafter in the world of the living was a basic feature of the medieval mentality. In medieval eyes, the miracles of the saints constituted one of the principal ways in which this close relationship between heaven and earth took concrete form. A consideration of the action and effects of the radiation emanating from the bodies of the saints will help to reveal the fundamental representations of sainthood and their evolution.

THE RULES OF INTERCESSION

From the tomb to the image: the locus of the invocation

The historian embarking on a study of the miracles of the thirteenth and fourteenth centuries must first ask whether the way in which the faithful sought to capture and profit from this beneficial energy had remained the same throughout the Middle Ages. In the collections of miracles from the Merovingian and Carolingian periods, the *virtus* of a saint is a force which acts in a given place: it was enough to visit and touch the tomb of a servant of God to be healed. At the beginning of the thirteenth century, these ideas had lost none of their potency. In the first processes of canonization, we find more or less all the modes and rites of healing attested for the early Middle Ages, which usually date back to pre-Christian, if not prehistoric, times. Most of those cured had recovered their health after travelling to the place where the remains of a saint lay and sleeping nearby, since it was believed that their therapeutic power acted most effectively during sleep.[1] Ideally, the incubation culminated in a vision or apparition of the intercessor whose help had been sought, soon followed by the cure. The church was flooded with light and, if the beneficiaries of the miracle were *contracti* (paralytics, hemiplegics etc.), who accounted for the majority of those frequenting the sanctuaries, there was a loud noise as bones and nerves went back into place.[2] The departure of the malady was sometimes preceded by profuse night sweats, after which the invalid woke with the dawn, fresh as a daisy.[3] It was rare, however, for the miracle to happen on the first day. Pilgrims usually had to spend some time at the sanctuary – at least nine days (a novena), sometimes two or three weeks – before their wishes were granted.[4]

The 'magical' character of these healing rites is confirmed by the attitude of the faithful to the thaumaturgical saints when they revealed their gifts in their lifetime. In the process of canonization of St Peter of Morrone (Celestine V, d. 1296), it is several times mentioned that his disciples had to discourage people who asked him to recite incantations over their wounds or diseased limbs. The hermit of Maiella, not wishing to be thought a sorcerer, was only prepared to bless the damaged organs with

[1] At the enquiry into the miracles of St Elizabeth of Thuringia, a man miraculously cured reported an old man as saying to him: 'sine dubio curaberis, si meo consilio manum debilem ad caput sepulchri sub lapide miseris, et quanto profundis tanto cicius curaberis': *PC Elizabeth*, p. 254. For the practice of incubation in the Middle Ages, see D. Mallardo, 'L'incubazione nella cristianità medievale napoletana', *Anal. Boll.*, 57 (1949), pp. 465–98; H. Silvestre, 'Note complémentaire sur l'incubation et ses survivances', *Revue du Moyen Age latin*, 5 (1949), pp. 141–8. There is fourteenth-century evidence both of its survival and of attacks on it: when a doctor who had gone blind was content to beg St Louis of Anjou to cure him, his wife, 'videns quod omnes febre languidi quacumque detinerentur infirmitate, solum quod dormirent super sepulchrum predicti sancti Ludovici sani et incolumes redierant, sic aggressa est virum suum: quare stat hic ad solem et non vadit ad dormiendum super tumulum sancti Ludovici? . . . si dicit quod non potest dormire ibi, bibat tantum de vino puro ut postmodum dormiat velit nolit': *Liber miraculorum S. Ludovici episcopi, Analecta Franciscana*, VII (Quaracchi, 1954), pp. 309–10.
[2] For example, *PC Thomas of Hereford*, fol. 69: 'tunc apparuerat in dicta ecclesia quaedam magna choruscatio sive lux, qua apparente et existente in dicta ecclesia, ossa dicte Alice fecerant fragorem sue strepitum et nervi fuerant extensi et tota fuerat curata'. For the exact meaning of the word *contractus*, see P. A. Sigal, 'Comment on concevait et on traitait la paralysie en Occident dans le Haut Moyen Age (Ve–XIIIe siècles)', *Revue d'histoire des sciences*, 197 (1971), pp. 153–211.
[3] *PC John Cacciafronte*, p. 248: 'duxerunt eum ad sanctum et parum stetit; ipse coepit sudare et versatus est in aqua . . . et tunc per misericordiam Dei liberatus est'. See also *PC Hugh of Lincoln*, p. 100.
[4] *PC Elizabeth*, p. 254: 'adiecit etiam stultos esse illos esse qui, proiectis oblationibus recedunt, cum in hoc complacitum sit sanctis ut cum expectatione et perseverantia eorum suffragia petantur'. See plates 37–8.

the sign of the cross.[5] If they could not see him, as in the case of women, who were not allowed to approach his cell, the faithful were content to touch objects which he had touched. They refused to leave without having received a sign or a favour in proportion to the often considerable effort they had expended to reach his cell deep in the Abruzzi.[6] Things were no different elsewhere in Europe; the sick and the mad were brought to St Hugh of Lincoln for him to make the sign of the cross over their head with his saliva.[7] When Philip Berruyer, archbishop of Bourges, visited the parishes in his diocese in the mid-thirteenth century, peasants rushed up to him to touch and kiss his feet; those unable to manage this kissed the hoof marks left by his horse; the monks were no different and, at the abbeys where he stopped, sick monks were brought to him to be cured of their ills.[8] This universal faith in the thaumaturgical virtue of bishops is probably related to the fact that they possessed full sacerdotal power, and, like the Apostles whose successors they were, laid hands on those who sought the sacrament of confirmation as well as on the sick. This is suggested by the reaction of the hermit John Bonus – a layman – who began by declaring to those who came to him seeking a cure that he was 'neither doctor nor priest', before, out of charity, giving in to their demands.[9]

It would be wrong to conclude, however, from these few examples, that the attitude of the masses to miracles had remained unchanged since the time of St Martin. On the contrary, a new and important phenomenon revealed a significant change in the relations between human beings and heavenly intercessors, that is, the increase in the proportion of miracles performed by saints some distance from the place where their remains lay. In many regions, after 1200, the promise to travel to the tomb of a servant of God to obtain a favour became conditional and the supplicant only made this journey if the favour requested was granted. The act persisted, but it was now only a rite of satisfaction, not something indispens-

---

[5] An archpriest of Sulmona, hardly uneducated since he was called *magister Gentilis*, said to one of the saint's companions: 'Quomodo possum facere quod pater sanctus . . . incantet michi in gula propter scrofulas istas quas habeo?' It is hardly surprising if the laity did the same: *PC Peter of Morrone*, p. 272.

[6] Turned away by Peter of Morrone, some peasants who had brought a sick man to him to be cured declared firmly: 'nec redire intendimus sine gratia aliquali': *ibid.*, p. 254. Similarly, a woman suffering from gout settled near the tomb of St Louis of Anjou 'nolens inde recedere donec fuisset curata': *PC Louis of Anjou*, p. 188.

[7] *PC Hugh of Lincoln*, pp. 97–8.

[8] *PC Philip of Bourges*, fols. 36v, 41, 50, 51, 93v.

[9] *PC John Bonus, AA.SS.* Oct. IX, p. 825.

Table 30 *Distribution of* post mortem *miracles attested in processes of canonization (1201–1417) as a function of the place where they occurred*[a]

Saints	Date of process	At the tomb	At a distance (= without direct contact with the relics)
Gilbert of Sempringham	1201	———————	—
Hugh of Lincoln	1219	——————	—
Hugh of Bonnevaux	1222	————	
John Cacciafronte	1223/4	——————	
Odo of Novara	1240	————	
Ambrose of Massa	1240/1		———————
Philip of Bourges	1265/6	—	——————
Thomas Cantilupe	1307	——————	
Louis of Anjou	1307		———————
Yves	1330		———————
Delphine	1363		——————
Charles of Blois	1371		———————
Urban V	1381		———————
Peter of Luxembourg	1390		———————
Nicholas of Linköping	1417		——————

Note:
[a] In the processes of SS Hildegard (1233–43) and Margaret of Hungary (1276), most of the miracles recorded seem to have occurred at the tomb, but the confused nature of the depositions makes it difficult to count them with any confidence. In the other processes not mentioned here, the information about the circumstances of the miracles is not sufficiently detailed for reliable statistics to be based on them.

able to the performance of the miracle.[10] These cures at a distance became increasingly frequent after 1300, as the processes of canonization of SS Louis of Anjou and Yves and of Charles of Blois reveal.[11] Table 30 shows that the change happened earlier in Italy and France than in England and Sweden, where the link between the performance of prodigies and contact with the holy body remained close.[12] As a general rule, however, in the

[10] An example of a conditional vow: 'convertit se cum multo dolore et devocione ad beatum Ludovicum de Marsilia . . . vovens quod si dictus filius suus de sua ydropisi curaretur, dicta mater cum uno sudario et una libra cere dictum filium suum duceret Marsiliam ad sepulchrum beati Ludovici': *PC Louis of Anjou*, p. 184.
[11] This is not, of course, related to how near or far from the tomb witnesses were when they invoked the saint; most of those cured by the intercession of St Louis of Anjou between 1298 and 1307 came from and still lived in Marseilles; but they did not go to the church of the Friars Minor to touch his relics, which they could easily have done.
[12] This was also the case in the Slav countries, according to an episode in the *Miracula beati Wenceslai* concerning the vicissitudes of a prisoner several times freed by the intercession

later Middle Ages, devotion to the saints tended to be distanced from the cult of relics, even though, in the conditional vows, a concrete topographical reference always persisted.[13] The powers of the saints gained in universality, since they were less closely linked than in the past to a single place, that is, where their remains lay.[14] Above all, the spiritual charge of the cults accorded to them grew, inasmuch as their beneficial action was not exercised automatically, but through intermediaries – the image and the word – which were capable of conveying a specifically Christian religious message.

Among the factors which helped to dissociate the cult of the servants of God from the pilgrimage to their tombs, the spread of the image was crucial.[15] Admittedly, the iconographical representation of the saints was as old as Christianity itself. They are, after all, portrayed on the triumphal arch of the old Roman basilicas, on either side of Christ in majesty, whose light shines over them. Some are individualized and their names are indicated on the mosaics; others belong to groups distinguished by their specific attributes (martyrs, virgins etc.). They are all there, fixed in a hieratic pose, inseparable from the Saviour who awaits them in the celestial Jerusalem, to associate them in his victory. From the eleventh century, on the walls of some urban churches, cycles of more narrative frescoes illustrated various episodes from the legend of a particular confessor whose relics – or memory – were venerated by the faithful. But they usually

---

of St Wenceslas and eventually sold into slavery abroad by his gaolers, 'putantes beatum martirem longe a se petitorum preces exaudire non posse': P. Devos, 'Le dossier de S. Wenceslas dans un manuscrit du XIIIe siècle (Cod. Bollandianus 433)', *Anal. Boll.*, 82 (1964), p. 124.

[13] Even in countries where the link between the *virtus* of a saint and the place where it was most powerful remained close, a degree of uncertainty was apparent in the fourteenth century as to precisely where this privileged place was. A witness at the canonization process of St Thomas Cantilupe told how, having gone blind, he first had some eyes of wax taken to the birthplace of the prelate, which produced only a slight improvement; he then sent someone to Hereford to pray for him on the saint's tomb, and his sight improved further; but it was only when he went there in person that he was completely cured: *PC Thomas of Hereford*, fol. 27.

[14] When his wife told him to sleep on the tomb of St Louis of Anjou, the blind merchant of Marseilles (see n. 1 above) replied: 'Nonne scis tu quia virtus sancti ita bene potest me iuvare hic sicut ibi, et in vigilia sicut in sompno? Nescis quid dicis et ideo manifeste apparet quod non habes fidem in sanctis.' Real or fictitious, this dialogue reveals two different conceptions of the intercession of the saints. This divergence only grew more marked over the following centuries, with the proliferation of Marian sanctuaries which people visited to thank the Virgin for an act attributed to her, not to touch her relics, by definition rare (though some were claimed).

[15] For the replacement of the relic by the image in the Mediterranean region, see A. Dupront, 'Pèlerinages et lieux sacrés', *Mélanges F. Braudel*, II (Paris, 1973), pp. 189–206.

concerned saints remote in time, such as SS Clement and Alexis, portrayed on the walls of the lower basilica of St Clement in Rome.[16] In the thirteenth century, images of recent saints became common, as for example at Anagni, where the effigy of St Thomas Becket was painted within a few decades of his death, in a chapel in the cathedral crypt.[17] In Rome itself, it was in the 1280s that the new saints – SS Francis of Assisi and Antony of Padua – appeared for the first time alongside those customarily included in the traditional groups (the Virgin and the Apostles, St John Baptist, SS Peter and Paul, St Lawrence and St Agnes) in the absidal mosaics of St Mary Major and St John Lateran,[18] and in the Aracoeli (Capocci and Colonna chapels). More important still were the consequences of the spread of altarpieces and polyptychs which had saints as their central figures (their miracles being portrayed on the sides and predella). St Francis of Assisi was the first to benefit from this fashion, as is shown by the innumerable paintings of his likeness – some made very soon after his death – still preserved today in the churches and museums of central Italy.[19] The fact that an entire cycle of frescoes covering the walls of the upper basilica at Assisi was devoted to him by Giotto, after some experiments in the lower basilica, had immense consequences on the artistic plane. Previously, the great decorative cycles in the churches had usually had as their theme the history of salvation – from the creation of the world to the Resurrection of Christ and the announcement of the end of the world. By preferring the life and miracles of a recent saint to stories from the Old and New Testaments, the Friars Minor demonstrated their conviction that St Francis of Assisi was, indeed, a second Christ.[20]

[16] H. Toubert, 'Rome et le Mont-Cassin: nouvelles remarques sur les fresques de l'église inférieure de Saint-Clément de Rome', *Dumbarton Oaks Papers*, 30 (1976), pp. 1–33.

[17] Today much damaged, but described in A. Prosperi, *Anagni e suoi monumenti* (Anagni, 1970), pp. 46–9; see also Kaftal 2, cc. 1095–8, where they are dated to the first decades of the thirteenth century.

[18] B. Kleinschmidt, 'Die künstlerische Kanonisation des hl. Vaters Franziskus', *AFH*, 3 (1910), pp. 615–25; L. Oliger, 'Due mosaici con S. Francesco della Chiesa d'Aracoeli di Roma', *AFH*, 4 (1911), pp. 213–51.

[19] Some are even earlier; the fresco in Subiaco depicting St Francis must have been painted while he was still alive: B. Ladner, 'Das älteste Bild des hl. Franz von Assisi. Ein Betrag zur mittelalterlichen Porträtsikonographie', in *Festschrift E. P. Schramm*, I (Wiesbaden, 1964), pp. 449–60. For the iconography of St Francis in Italy in the thirteenth century, see G. Kaftal, *St Francis in Italian painting* (London, 1950). The *Tractatus de miraculis B. Francisci*, ed. *Analecta Franciscana*, 10 (1926–41), pp. 275–6, reveals the early diffusion of images of St Francis in the homes of the faithful when it mentions a Roman matron (probably pre-1250) who venerated him deeply, 'cuius imaginem depictam habebat in secreto cubiculo, ubi patrem in abscondito orabat'. See also plate 39.

[20] H. W. Van Os, 'St. Francis as a Second Christ in early Italian painting', *Simiolus, Netherland's Quarterly for the History of Art*, 7 (1975), pp. 11ff.

Despite all their efforts, the Mendicants could not reserve these prerogatives to their founders and heroes for long; in the fourteenth century, especially in Italy, more and more chapels and even churches were covered with paintings portraying the life and miracles not only of recent saints but of simple uncanonized *beati*.[21]

At the same time, the images of saints began to acquire an autonomy and a mobility which made them prime instruments in the diffusion of their cults. There was no disciplinary rule to check this iconographical flowering, since the Church regarded it as an expression of private devotion, perfectly acceptable as long as it was not accompanied by unseemly signs of devotion.[22] Even in the case of representations of servants of God not officially recognized by the papacy, there was little likelihood of the ecclesiastical authorities intervening. This great freedom encouraged a proliferation of images of every sort devoted to the saints. It was not a purely Italian phenomenon, even if it is in Italy that traces of this abundant artistic output have best survived, and there are many indications that the situation was similar in France and England.[23] In the Mediterranean countries, the representation of the saints nearly always took the form of a painting: fresco, altarpiece or painted picture.[24] Elsewhere in Christendom, statues of stone or wood were equally common.[25] But in the fourteenth century, Italian fashions

---

[21] We should remember Salimbene's diatribes against the inhabitants of the towns of Lombardy, Emilia and Romagna, who covered the walls of their churches and cities with portraits of popular but uncanonized saints, with the approval of the secular clergy (*Cronica*, II, p. 733). The initiative came from the communal authorities, as shown by article 43 of the statutes of Osimo, in the Marches ('de faciendo depingi picturas . . . in quaslibet portas'), providing for likenesses of the Virgin and SS Christopher and Benvenuto to be painted on the gates of the town: Vecchetti, *Memorie istorico-critiche di Osimo*, pp. 471–2. We know that there were many cycles of frescoes devoted to uncanonized saints in Italy; the most important was at Cortona, in the church of St Basil, mid-fourteenth-century, in honour of St Margaret (d. 1297). It had disappeared by the seventeenth century, but several copies survive, in particular in the canonization process of 1640, *ASV*, *Riti*, Proc. 552, pp. 1003–39. There was also a cycle dedicated to B. Gerard of Villamagna (d. 1242) in the parish church of San Donnino, his native region, in Tuscany: *AA.SS.* Maii III, p. 145. The principal series still visible today is that in honour of B. Joan of Signa (d. 1307) in the parish church of Signa, near Florence (Kaftal 1, cc. 539–49) dating from 1441.
[22] See above, p. 86.
[23] For France, see above, p. 128. For England, iconographical survivals are rare, as a result of the destruction following the Reformation. But there still survive in churches and collections of paintings numerous images of the child martyr, William of Norwich (d. 1144), who was never canonized. Many are reproduced in Jessop and James, *Life and Miracles of St William of Norwich*.
[24] See the catalogue of the exhibition *Retables italiens du XIIIe au XVe siècle*, organized by C. Ressort (Paris, 1978), with bibliography.
[25] See, for example, *PC Charles of Blois* (Angers, 1371), p. 242.

spread north of the Alps. Charles of Blois, according to his process of canonization in 1371, had pictures of St Yves painted *ad modum Lombardie*, which he presented to the Mendicant churches in his duchy.[26] At the beginning of the fifteenth century, a further stage in the diffusion and popularization of the portraits of the saints arrived with the appearance of pious images. We first hear of them – without knowing whether they are the first – at the process of canonization of St Catherine of Siena. In his lengthy deposition, the Dominican Thomas Caffarini, chief organizer of the cult of the 'mama', said that 'very recently' (this was in 1410) 'strips' representing the principal episodes in her life had been painted on paper and thousands of copies made to be put up in churches on the day of the celebration of her feast. They could be taken away, he added, which made it possible for people to venerate the saint privately in their own homes.[27]

The wider diffusion of representations of the saints inevitably had repercussions for their function. The image was first an ex-voto. People offered the servants of God little pictures depicting the miracles obtained through their intercession.[28] In the case of a new saint, whose cult was not yet established, the act of the donor was also a piece of propaganda; what

---

[26] *Ibid.*, pp. 74, 101.

[27] *PC Catherine of Siena*, p. 93: 'ordinatum fuit per quemdam devotum eiusdem precipuum ut ymago ipsius virginis etiam ystorialiter [= conforming to the legend] de facili multiplicabilis depingeretur in cartis, de quibus in die commemorationis prefate plurime inter ramos seu florum manipulos ponerentur . . . ut sic possent iuxta debitam licentiam non solum in publico sed etiam in propriis stationibus sive domibus venerari. Et certus sum quod ex quo coeperunt dicte ymagines virginis fieri, plura millia facta sunt et quotidie fiunt.' For the use of the images of saints in the modern period, see A. Vecchi, *Il culto delle immagini nelle stampe popolari* (Florence, 1968). There is no satisfactory study of this phenomenon for the Middle Ages; we need, first, more studies of the representation of individual saints in manuscripts, as attempted by some art historians, for example, Mâle, 'La vie de S. Louis'; C. Nordenfalk, 'St. Bridget of Sweden as represented in Illuminated Ms.', in *Essays in honour of Erwin Panofsky*, I (New York, 1961), pp. 371–93; W. Braunfels, *Der Hedwigscodex von 1353 (Sammlung Ludwig)* (Berlin, 1972), pp. 204, 232.

[28] See the general study by L. Kriss-Retenbeck, *Ex voto: Zeichen, Bild und Abbild im christlichen Votivbrauchtum* (Zurich, 1972); interesting remarks in W. Brückner, 'Volkstümliche Denkstrukturen und hochschichtliches Weltbild im Votivwesen. Zur Forschungssituation und Theorie des bildlichen Opferkults', *Schweizerisches Archiv für Volkskunde*, 59 (1963), pp. 189–203. Their existence is attested in Siena in the late thirteenth century, near the tomb of Ambrose Sansedoni, OP (d. 1287), according to the *Vita*, by Recupero of Arezzo (= *BHL* 383), ed. *AA.SS.* Mar. III, p. 219. An offering of a painted image of the saint the length of the person miraculously cured is mentioned in the process of St Nicholas of Tolentino: *PC*, fol. 113. In the legend of the Franciscan St Gerardo Cagnoli (d. 1342), a woman offered the convent of the Friars Minor of Pisa 'tabulam parvulam cum hostiolis pictam coram sancto Gerardo': F. Rotolo, 'La Leggenda del B. Gerardo Cagnoli O.M. (1261–1342) di Fra' Bartolomeo Albizzi, O.M.', in *Miscellanea Francescana*, 57 (1957), p. 407.

better way to show one's gratitude to a saint than to make his or her name
and power known?[29] The image – painting or sculpture – also helped to
familiarize the faithful with new faces. It made it possible to identify
intercessors when they appeared in a dream or vision.[30] This gave great
importance to the first representation, generally executed at the request
of the small community which had originated the devotion. In fact, it
determined the conventional features of the saint, a decisive element in
the propagation of the cult; in extreme cases, the success of an iconographical model in itself eventually became proof of the sanctity of that individual.[31] But the images of the saints were not only expressions of gratitude
on the part of the donors. In the last centuries of the Middle Ages, they
tended to become intermediaries which greatly extended the influence of
those they portrayed. From the thirteenth century in Italy, the fourteenth
in France and England, the faithful increasingly often dedicated themselves to a heavenly protector before a painting or statue seen as substitutes
for their tomb.[32] Eventually, the image came to play the same role as the
relics; one placed it on the diseased or damaged part of the body, after
invoking the name of the saint.[33] It came to acquire an autonomous
thaumaturgical power and became the seat of the power of the servants

[29] A merchant of Lucca, cured by the intermediary of B. Gerard Cagnoli, 'misit ad expensas
suas Pisas duos pictores qui, forma accepta de figura sancti Gerardi et de ipsius informati
miraculis, reversi Lucam ipsum in ecclesia Fratrum Minorum pinxerunt solemniter, ipsam
imaginem sexdecim miraculis de patratis per eum accingentes': *ibid.*, p. 440; see also p.
421. A merchant of Genoa, cured at Naples, spread the image of St Bridget in his native
town: *PC*, p. 166.

[30] At the canonization process of Dorothy of Montau, a witness said that the saint had
appeared to him in a vision 'in tali habitu sicut depicta est in ecclesia Pomesianensi': *PC*,
fol. 273. There are many similar incidents in fourteenth-century Italian canonization
processes.

[31] The point is made in the articles presented for the canonization of Urban V (p. 377): 'in
diversis et plurimis ecclesiis, eius ymago et ymagina seu effigies fuerunt et sunt picte et
de die in diem pinguuntur et sic picte honorifice et patenter honorantur cum devocione
et reverencia sicut alie ymagines sanctorum, et fiunt oblaciones diverse et diversimode'.

[32] *PC Yves*, p. 472: 'fecit se portari coram ymagine ipsius sancti Yvonis quam idem testis
fieri fecerat in ecclesia de Capella Alneti . . . cuius tunc rector erat'. At the process of
Charles of Blois, a witness said that his daughter had been cured after a novena spent in
front of an image of the saint: *PC*, p. 235. But some witnesses reveal how the link with
the tomb lingered in the popular mind; a woman of Macerata, in the Marches, whose
son had been healed by the intercession of St Nicholas, 'obtulit quamdam camisiam dicti
eius filii supra quamdam figuram depictam in ecclesia ad similitudinem dicti fratris Nico-
ley, quod Tholentinum propter deformitatem viarum ire non poterat': *PC*, fol. 153v.

[33] In 1389, the duchess of Bourbon, in the middle of a difficult birth, asked her confessor
to dedicate her to Peter of Luxembourg, which he did: 'Dicta vero domina interim
imaginem dicti Domini Cardinalis super ventrem suum fecit apponi.' The baby soon
arrived, and the birth was easy: *PC*, art. 202; *AA.SS.* Apr. I, p. 509.

26 A Franciscan saint: B. Jacopono of Todi (Paolo Uccello, painting, c.1430, Cathedral, Prato)

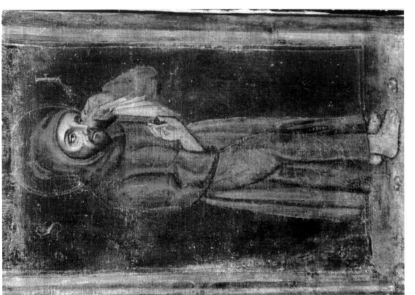

25 Portrait of St Francis of Assisi (?fifteenth-century fresco, Franciscan monastery of Greccio)

27 St Dominic (artist unknown, thirteenth century, Dominican monastery of Bologna)

28 Mendicant preaching: St Peter Martyr preaches at Florence (Andrea da Firenze, *c.*1355, fresco, Santa Maria Novella, Spaniards' Chapel, Florence)

29 St Thomas Aquinas and his pupils (The Story of St Thomas Aquinas, late
fourteenth-century fresco, Santa Maria del Piano, Loreto Aprutino, Abruzzi)

28 Mendicant preaching: St Peter Martyr preaches at Florence (Andrea da Firenze, c.1355, fresco, Santa Maria Novella, Spaniards' Chapel, Florence)

29 St Thomas Aquinas and his pupils (The Story of St Thomas Aquinas, late fourteenth-century fresco, Santa Maria del Piano, Loreto Aprutino, Abruzzi)

30 St Clare of Montefalco's vision of Christ carrying his cross (Umbrian school, *c.*1330, church of St Clare, Montefalco)

31 The death of St Clare of Montefalco (1308) (Umbrian school, *c.*1330, church of
St Clare, Montefalco)

32 St Bridget has a vision of Christ crucified (Swedish, fifteenth-century painting, Stockholm Museum)

33 A saint converts her husband: 1 she instructs her husband, Ugolotto Caccianemici of Faenza; 2 husband and wife put on the habit and enter religion (Pietro Lorenzetti, Polyptych of B. Umiliana of Faenza (d. 1310), Uffizi Museum, Florence)

THE FIELD OF THE MIRACULOUS 453

of God.[34] Through iconography, a new conception of piety emerged, less focussed on the remains of the saints than on their earthly existence. By popularizing the idea that the latter were living creatures possessing, here on earth, the attributes and prerogatives of the 'glorious bodies', and by introducing their representations into the daily life of the faithful, the products of the craftsmen and artists helped to 'delocalize' the devotion accorded to them.

Contract and devotion: the changes in the vow

In the miracles described in medieval sources, the intercession of a saint on someone's behalf was conditional on the making of a vow, whether the favour was requested on the occasion of a pilgrimage to the tomb or before an image. However brief, this spoken formula was the constituent element in the relationship established between a man or woman and his or her heavenly protector. It always contained both an invocation of the saint addressed by name (*sancte* or *beate X, adiuva me*, for example) and a precise commitment or series of commitments, the performance of which constituted either the prior condition or the price paid for the miracle. This moral contract was not entered into lightly; before dedication to an intercessor, a monk or nun had to get permission from his or her superior, since, by making the contract, some liberty was surrendered.[35] We may, without exaggeration, compare the vow to homage; it seems likely that the rites of 'devotion' were influenced by feudo-vassalic ritual, or, at the very least, originated in the same outlook. In dedicating themselves to a saint, in the thirteenth and fourteenth centuries, individuals placed themselves under the saint's exclusive protection and promised, often before witnesses, to do something they believed would please him or her. Admittedly, the majority of these commitments were made *ad experimentum*; if they did not get what they wanted after a certain period of time, the

---

[34] *Ibid.*, art. 201: a Provençal nobleman dedicated his wife to Peter of Luxembourg before she gave birth, after bringing an image of the saint into the house. At the birth, the baby bore a resemblance to the young cardinal as he appeared in the image. The icon lived; it could even bleed, like that of Charles of Blois in the church of the Cordeliers of Dinan, when it was removed by the English and the supporters of John IV de Montfort: *PC*, p. 283.

[35] See, for example, *PC Clare of Montefalco*, fol. 137: 'Domina Isaia recommandavit se et devovit sorori Clarae ad suggestionem sororis Ioannae abbatissae concedentis sibi licentiam de voto.' In the process of St Elizabeth, a Cistercian abbot expressed unease at the vow made by one of his monks: 'ob institutione regulae, scilicet Benedicti, qui vetat fratres sine permissione spiritualis patris speciale aliquid facere vel vovere': *PC*, p. 244.

supplicants recovered their freedom.[36] But if the request was successful, they must remain faithful to their 'patron' as long as they lived.[37]

It is obviously impossible to know how often the expectations of the faithful were met since, by definition, processes of canonization and collections of miracles only record the evidence of those who were satisfied. The latter felt obliged to carry out their commitments under pain of incurring the vengeance of the saint, in the form of a return or aggravation of the illness from which they had been delivered. Recourse to doctors, when the saint had already started a cure, had the same result. These relapses were popularly attributed to a lack of faith, which amounted to a sort of unilateral breaking of the contract.[38] On the other hand, if the vow addressed to a saint or the pilgrimage made to the tomb did not produce the desired outcome, the individual was justified in seeking a more effective intercessor. This seems to have happened quite frequently, to judge from the statements made at the enquiries by those who had been miraculously cured. They went out of their way to emphasize the efficacy of whoever had healed them, in contrast to the impotence of the intercessors they had previously appealed to in vain.[39]

What was the precise nature of the vow? In principle, it consisted of making a gift of one's own person or of the person on whose behalf the saint's intervention was sought, usually a child or relative. The formulas known to us are so many and varied that it seems unlikely there was ever a single model. But the basic ideas expressed are always essentially the same. First, there was the notion of restitution, implied in the Latin texts by the use of the verb *reddere*: one 'gave back' to the saint and to God the person dedicated to that saint, that is, one surrendered responsibility for the person and he or she became the saint's property. But at the same

[36] For example, the vow made by the *curé* of Saint-Julien, diocese of Gap, to St Louis of Anjou: 'devovit se per hunc modem quod si beatus Ludovicus apud Deum sanitatis graciam impetraret ita quod dominica sequenti posset missam et divinum officium celebrare et populum sibi commissum regere, ipse tempore paschali veniret ad sepulchrum ipsius Massilia causa peregrinacionis et devocionis': *PC*, p. 194.

[37] 'Ego ero tibi semper fidelis', declared one woman, in her vow (*PC Clare of Montefalco*, fol. 875), stating the obvious.

[38] For the return of the sickness in more acute form after a broken vow, see *PC Clare of Montefalco*, fol. 800; for the same after resorting to a doctor after making a vow, see *PC Lawrence of Subiaco*, p. 86; in this case, a new vow was necessary because the first had been broken: 'vivit Deo beatoque fratri Laurentio se numquam de cetero adhibiturum aliquod medicamentum si mereretur resanari'. See also plate 40.

[39] At the process of Nicholas of Tolentino (d. 1305), some merchants said they had been saved from a shipwreck by his intervention after they had appealed in vain to SS Thomas of Ortona, Cyriac of Ancona and Marcellin and Julian of Rimini: *PC*, fol. 234.

time, the saint was asked to restore the person alive or well to the family, and a series of commitments were made, to be performed if the wish was granted.[40] The content of these promises varied enormously, but they developed in the same direction though more or less rapidly according to country. In the late twelfth and up to the middle of the thirteenth centuries, the gift of oneself was still common, especially in the Germanic world.[41] If the saint in question belonged to a religious order, the promise was sometimes to enter a convent or serve it as a lay brother. Children for whom a cure was sought were often made to take a vow of chastity, or the supplicant took it on their behalf. If a miracle occurred, the parents left the child at the monastery or church which housed the tomb of the saint as an oblate.[42] The vow still retained all its power and was accompanied by a renunciation of liberty, more or less complete, but real.

By the end of the twelfth century, less restrictive forms of commitment were appearing. At the enquiry into the miracles of St Galgano, held at Montesiepi, near Siena, in 1185, only one woman had become a nun after a miraculous cure, whereas two men declared that they had promised to labour for a year in the service of the saint, that is, of the abbey he had founded and where he was buried.[43] We should probably compare the status of these temporary oblates to that of the *cerecensuales* common in the Germanic world, who came every year to place a rent in recognition of their servitude before the tomb of the patron saint of the church or abbey to which they were answerable.[44] These were, however, survivals,

---

[40] *PC Philip of Bourges*, fol. 68: 'Domine, reddo vobis et beato Philippo filiam meam et si redditis eam mihi, requiram vos, beatum Philippum, nudis pedibus sine camisia.' At the process of St Yves, the bishop of Saint-Pol de Léon, William Villesauxe, advised dedicating a mad woman as follows (1329): 'Consulo et laudo quod voveatur et reddatur ipsa infirma S. Yvoni et confido quos curabitur. Et ego nunc ipsam voveo et reddo Jhesu Christo et S. Yvoni et adducatur ea ad sepulchrum S. Yvonis': *PC*, p. 178.

[41] The process of St Elizabeth records the words of a girl of eighteen who travelled to Marburg to beg to be cured: 'Mater, quia homines libere conditionis sumus, si placet tibi, ponam caput meum supra sepulchrum domine Elizabeth, dum illuc pervenerimus, et offeram ei me perpetue servituram': *PC*, p. 178.

[42] At the canonization process of St Margaret of Hungary (p. 297), a mother is reported as saying to her blind daughter: 'Vove castitatem et promittas beate Margarethe quod in perpetuum servies ei.' There are similar statements in the miracles of Urban V (p. 290).

[43] *PC Galgano*, pp. 75, 77. The practice of dedicating oneself to the service of a church for a year persisted in fourteenth-century Sweden: *PC Bridget*, pp. 116–17, 280. For the gift of oneself to the saints, see Hermann-Masquard, *Les reliques des saints*, pp. 285–7.

[44] For categories of dependants, see R. Boutruche, *Seigneurie et féodalité*, I (Paris, 1968), pp. 141–2. Such gifts to a saint were still frequent in the thirteenth century; see, for example, the diploma of Archbishop Engelbert of Cologne, confirming in 1222 the *traditio* of five persons to the altar of St Adelaide of Vilich: *Adelaidis . . . positio, sancta rituum congregatio, sectio historica*, CX (Vatican City, 1959), pp. 59–60.

since, in the vast majority of cases, especially after 1250, there was no clause of this type in the vows made to saints.[45] The gift of oneself seems often to have been commuted by those who made the vow into a lifelong financial commitment; they promised, in return for a miracle, to pay a money rent to the church which contained the relics of the intercessor they invoked.[46] Increasingly, however, offerings in kind became the norm. In England, where the change seems to have happened very early, specific rites were associated with the vow; as they recited the formula of invocation, those requesting a miracle bent a penny in honour of the saint whose intervention they sought; they were then measured against a length of string and, with its aid, a candle of the same length as their body was made. These customs were still practised at the end of the fourteenth century and were not objected to. Even better, the priest was often persuaded to do the measuring himself.[47]

It is hardly possible here to describe in detail the many rites of substitution and thanksgiving revealed by the wording of vows from the thirteenth and fourteenth centuries. However, we may note in passing the important role played by wax, in the form of candles of the same length and weight as the person dedicating themselves or the ex-voto representing the diseased and healed part of the body, the ship saved from the storm

---

[45] D. Gontier and C. Le Bas, 'Analyse socio-économique de quelques recueils de miracles dans la Normandie du XIe au XIIIe siècle', *Annales de Normandie*, 24 (1974), pp. 72ff., have shown that the wording and content of vows changed significantly in Norman collections of miracles between the early twelfth and the late thirteenth centuries. In the earliest cases, the most common personal commitment was either to put oneself in the service of a certain saint (*se tradere alicui sancto in servicio*) or to promise to pay a perpetual recognitary tax (*se alligare pro census capitis*); later, that is in miracles performed by the founders of Savigny and by Thomas Hélye of Biville (d. 1275), the formulas *se vovere* or *vovere aliquem* almost entirely replaced them, and involved lighter obligations.

[46] A merchant of Berry, in 1265, became the 'man of St Stephen for 12d' to obtain his cure; this sum was to be paid annually at Bourges Cathedral on the saint's feast day: *PC Philip of Bourges*, fols. 73v–74. In thirteenth-century Germany, the annual rent paid to saints varied from 2d to 4d: *PC Elizabeth*, pp. 179, 182, 252. The word 'man' was still used in fourteenth-century Brittany of someone who dedicated themself to a saint: 'Ego voveo me dicto sancto Yvoni et promitto me esse hominem suum et sibi dare annuatim sex denarios pro curatione mea': *PC Yves*, p. 151.

[47] For this practice, also found on the Continent, see *PC Hugh of Lincoln*, p. 99: 'acceptoque filo candelis idoneo, cepit puerum mensurare'. The role of the penny bent as rite of substitution is emphasized in a miracle of Richard Rolle of Hampole (ed. Woolley, *Richard Rolle*, p. 82), where those present said to a priest who had come to assist a dying man: 'plica denarium super mortuum offerendum in honorem beati Ricardi'. If a cure followed, the coin was given to the saint. In Normandy, the vow was often accompanied by a gift of tow: Gontier and Le Bas, 'Recueils de miracles', p. 32. In fourteenth-century Italy, the clothes of children healed through their intercession were left on the tombs of saints: *PC Nicholas of Tolentino*, fol. 110v.

etc.[48] Sometimes, silver was used. When the commission instructed by Clement V to investigate the miracles of St Thomas Cantilupe listed the offerings found at his tomb in Hereford Cathedral, they came up with the following:

170 silver ships
41 wax ships
129 silver images of a person or of human limbs
1,424 wax images of a person or of human limbs
77 animal figures
108 crutches
3 wooden vehicles.[49]

As the subjects of the canonization processes were usually recent saints, the *devotio* often entailed a promise to propagate their cult, for example to celebrate a mass or recite prayers in honour of the intercessor or, more often, to abstain from work on the day of their feast, or fast the day before, or name a child after them.[50] In the fourteenth century, this militant action also often took the form of having their likeness portrayed on the walls of a church or in a painting to be hung there.[51] All these forms of vow imply that people felt under an obligation to promote the reputation of their protector. This may well have contributed to the success of the new cults which were established from the end of the thirteenth century. In fact,

[48] *PC Yves*, p. 212: 'promitto vobis unam candelam in longitudine de longitudine mei et grossitudine, ut liberetis me et detis mihi sanitatem'. See also M. Hélin, 'Une fière chandelle', in *Hommage à Marie Delcourt* (Brussels, 1970), pp. 406–17, and the documents collected by A.-M. Bautier, 'Typologies des ex-voto mentionnés dans des textes antérieurs à 1200', in *Actes du 99e congrès des sociétés savantes (Besançon, 1974)*, I (Paris, 1977), pp. 237–82. For the protective role of wax, and in particular of wax-coated threads, sometimes put round churches or towns threatened with epidemics, see L. Kretzenbascher, *Ketternkirchen in Bayern und in Osterreich* (Munich, 1973).

[49] *PC Thomas of Hereford*, fol. 74. At Tréguier, near the tomb of St Yves, in 1331, there were twenty-seven ships of silver and ninety of wax: *PC Yves*, p. 5; the 145th witness at this process was a manufacturer of wax ships, Alan le Cervisier of Tréguier, who said that business was good. The process of Charles of Blois (*PC*, p. 301) contains a detailed description of the objects found at his tomb at Guingamp: 'naves, ymagines, pedes cum tibiis, manus, brachia, capita, castra, domus, animalia, aves, ciphi, forme seu figure pecuniarum, doliorum vini, et figure oculorum, mamillarum, genitalium cere, ferracula, pedum et manuum ac eciam camisie pro insignis resuscitatorum, baculi seu potentie, torchie et cerei magni', etc. For maritime ex-votos, see *Ex-voto marins du Ponant, Catalogue de l'exposition*, arranged by M. Mollat (Paris, 1975).

[50] Of many possible examples, I quote only one which is typical: 'Domine Yvo . . . peto a vobis filium meum et si restituatis michi eum, omnibus diebus vite mee jejunabo quinta et sexta feria, videlicet sexta feria in pane et aqua, et numquam utar vestibus lineis nec lingiis': *PC Yves*, p. 119.

[51] See above, pp. 548–53.

the faithful felt themselves to be in a strong, or at least less weak, position
with regard to the saints who did not yet enjoy great fame. Consequently,
they did not hesitate to provoke, even defy, them to get them to act on
their behalf.[52]

Another new element in the vows of this period was the promise to
perform charitable works. The practice of commutation, already visible
in the transition from the actual gift of the person to that of the same
weight in wax or payment of a money rent, continued to advance in the
fourteenth century. In some cases, the rite of substitution persisted, as,
for example, when a father promised to give the saint who saved his child
its weight in corn, flour or oil.[53] In other cases, it disappeared and the
content of the vow changed. The offering in kind was increasingly frequently accompanied by the promise of a personal ascetic feat or charitable
deed. The commitment to fast on the day of the saint's feast in his or her
honour, or to visit the sanctuary barefoot and dressed only in a shirt,
reveals the influence of the penitential spirituality dear to the laity.[54] The
recognitary rent turned, especially in Italy, into alms, and references to
gifts of cash for the use of the poor are increasingly common in vows.[55]
But the new formulas did not replace the old. In general, promises of this
type, far from supplanting the traditional commitments, were added to
and combined with them in a variety of ways. This produced some compli-
cated commitments, of which I will quote just two examples: at the process
of Clare of Montefalco, in 1318, a witness by the name of Pucpus, son of
Ser Gentile of Spoleto, said that he had vowed to make a pilgrimage to
the saint's tomb, barefoot, at least once a year, to offer there a wax image
the weight of his brother (on whose behalf he was seeking a cure) and a
twisted candle weighing two pounds, and to provide 50 livres in Cortona
pennies for the marriage of a young girl or the construction of a fine tomb
to St Clare, whichever the nuns wished;[56] at the enquiry into the miracles

[52] For example, in the miracles of Gandulph of Binasco, OFM (d. 1260): 'conditionaliter votum vovit quod si suis miraculis beatus Gandolphus eum sanaret, ad ejus honorem missam faceret celebrari, alioquin de cetero non adoraret pro sancto': *AA.SS.* Sept. V, p. 707. This attitude to the saints was not new; for its importance in the life and even liturgy of monasteries in the eleventh and twelfth centuries, see P. Geary, 'L'humiliation des saints', *Annales ESC*, 1 (1979), pp. 27–42.
[53] For compensation in corn, see *PC Nicholas of Tolentino*, fol. 89v: in other goods, *PC Elizabeth*, p. 169.
[54] *PC Urban V*, p. 430: 'vovit quod veniret visitatum sepulcrum ipsius domini Urbani in camisia et femoralibus cum una tibia cere cum duobus candelis grossis'.
[55] *PC Clare of Montefalco*, fol. 799: 'si me liberaveris, prometto in die tui festi dare commedere uni pauperi'.
[56] *Ibid.*, fol. 793.

of St Nicholas of Tolentino in 1325, the notary Francesco Audrioli of Macerata, whose thumb had been cut off by his brother, promised to travel to Tolentino if the wound healed, taking with him a hand of wax, to fast every year on the eve of the new saint's feast, and put his pen at his service. He explained that he had fulfilled this last promise by writing to the pope and cardinals, and by drawing up petitions in the name of the commune of Macerata requesting the canonization of his benefactor.[57]

An analysis of the forms of devotion in the last centuries of the Middle Ages produces, in the last analysis, a very mixed picture, in which practices that one might be tempted, at first sight, to call magical or superstitious coexisted, apparently without difficulty, with acts which expressed a spirituality of the evangelical type. But it is perhaps our vocabulary which is largely responsible for this seeming contradiction. The word 'magic', in particular, is highly equivocal, in that it seems to imply that the only authentic Christianity is that expressed in a moral or doctrinal discourse. Admittedly, by the fourteenth century, the process of dissociation which led to the eventual rejection of large areas of popular religion as superstition, even sorcery, had already begun, as we see from the writings of the great inquisitors of this period, from Bernard Gui to Nicholas Eymerich. But its effects were not yet visible in the sphere of the cult of the saints, where the most archaic expressions of veneration caused the majority of the clergy no concern, as long as the orthodoxy of those who were its object was not in doubt.

The evolution in the form and content of the vows between the twelfth and the fourteenth centuries reflects, however, changes in the relationships between the faithful and the intercessors they invoked when in need. Increasingly frequently with the passage of time, people demanded satisfaction before fulfilling the promises they had made to the servants of God. These, in any case, tended to become lighter and, after a complex process of commutation, restrictive commitments were replaced by promises of personal asceticism or charity. These changes were a sign of a new attitude towards the saints, now fully integrated into the religious universe of the faithful; reverential fear had given way to a feeling of confidence, which was expressed in an affectionate familiarity.[58] The idea of a commit-

---

[57] *PC Nicholas of Tolentino*, fol. 89v.

[58] The growing importance of affection between the faithful and the intercessors they invoked is visible in the vocabulary; in the fourteenth-century, the *affectio* between the person making the vow and their patron saint is often mentioned. At the process of Charles of Blois, a witness who had miraculously escaped hanging thanks to the duke's assistance said that the idea of dedicating himself to the latter had come to him when a woman had

ment to be performed under pain of punishment persisted. But the self-confident or dramatic dialogue which became common between the faithful and their heavenly protectors reveals a shift in the direction of the modern meaning of the word devotion, which implies free choice and following one's inclinations.[59]

In the later Middle Ages, the laity seem to have fully assimilated the rules of intercession as they were defined by the Church. Remarkably, by 1250 in Italy and from 1300 elsewhere in Christendom, references to Christ or to God were common in the formulas employed to request the intervention of the saints.[60] On occasion, these even achieved a degree of theological sophistication. For example, in the process of canonization of Charles of Blois, witnesses asked what words they had used in their prayer of invocation (*quibus verbis interpositis?*) said they had spoken as follows:

> Saint Charles, if it is true that you are a saint in Paradise and that, through the intercession of your merits, Our Saviour Jesus Christ has deigned to perform miracles for you, obtain health for my daughter from Our Saviour Jesus Christ and the Blessed Virgin Mary, or that she soon dies, and for this I dedicate her to you.

or, from the same document:

> Lord saint Charles, I request God and your blessed body that, if you once did something which pleased him, by reason of which he ought to act for you, that it please you to pray him to restore my daughter.[61]

In a few rare, but not exceptional, cases, the faithful even excused themselves to the intercessor for having requested their cure and accepted in advance that they might be refused. Some particularly devout lay people hesitated between a natural desire to be delivered from their ills and an awareness of the redemptive value of suffering.[62] Admittedly, those who

---

said, when he was condemned to death, 'quod si aliquam specialem affectionem habebat ad aliquem sanctum, ipsum affectuose requireret', at which point he remembered 'quod habebat specialem affectionem ad sanctum Dominum Carolum quondam ducem Brittannie, quem credebat firmiter esse sanctum': *PC*, p. 205.

[59] Many early-fourteenth-century Provençal vows contained phrases along the following lines: 'ipse devote convertens se ad Beatum Ludovicum' or 'devotens se eidem et promittens', etc.: *PC Louis of Anjou*, p. 172.

[60] *PC John Bonus* (1251–4), p. 875: 'Domine Jesu Christe, rogo te ut meritis fratris Johannis Boni qui jacet in hoc sepulchro, digneris me illuminare ut ego possim laborare et facere facta mea.' See also *PC Clare of Montefalco*, fol. 561: 'invocavit Christum et rogavit eum quod meritis Beate Clare . . . liberaret puerum'.

[61] *PC Charles of Blois*, pp. 231, 235.

[62] *PC Clare of Montefalco*, fol. 568: 'Beata Clara, ego rogo te quod per tuam sanctitatem et tua bona opera tu debeas me liberare, si pro meliori est et esse debet anime mee; alioquin misereris mei et intercede pro me ad Dominum, ut faciat mihi misericordiam.' Similarly,

pondered such problems were in a minority and, for the majority, the saints remained above all an effective recourse in adversity. But the general conception of their role was no longer quite what it had been at the time of Gregory of Tours. Some words of St Louis, reported by William of Saint-Pathus, perfectly encapsulate the way in which late thirteenth-century Christians saw the intercession of the saints:

> It is the same with the saints in Paradise as with the counsellors of kings . . . whoever has business with an earthly king seeks, in effect, to know who he holds in high regard and who, having his ear, is able to approach him successfully. He then seeks out this favoured person and begs him to convey his request. It is the same with the saints in Paradise who, being the friends of Our Lord and his intimates, can invoke him in all confidence, since he cannot fail to listen to them.[63]

The theme of the 'heavenly court' or the 'court of Paradise' which is so common in thirteenth- and fourteenth-century texts concerning the saints was not simply a stylistic convention. It seems to express how many of the faithful then saw the relations between God and his servants, likening them to those between kings and their great vassals and officials. In medieval processes of canonization, however, there was a certain hesitation when the inquisitors put precise questions to witnesses in order to draw them out on their belief in the efficacy of the power of the saints. For the vast majority, God performed miracles *for* the saints, that is, in consideration of their own merits. From this perspective, it was as if the servants of God had acquired, through the sufferings they had endured during their lifetime, a means of putting pressure on God, in a sense obliging him to intervene on behalf of whoever had put themselves under their protection.[64] Some clergy and devout lay people, on the other hand, believed

in the process of St Louis of Anjou (p. 189), a woman: 'devovit se beato Ludovico . . . non ad istum finem quod vellet a dicta infirmitate curari, quia enim eam multum libenter et pacienter sustinebat quando recordabatur quod Christus in manibus suis fuerat perforatus et passus longe magis vehementum dolorem quam ipsa haberet vel posset sustinere, sed ut Deus manifestaret in ea miracula que debebat facere propter bonam et sanctam vitam quam duxerat et tenuerat beatus Ludovicus quando vivebat'.

[63] *Vie de Saint Louis*, ed. Delaborde, p. 73.

[64] Canonization processes contain many examples; see, for example, *PC Louis of Anjou*, p. 32: 'tenet pro firmo quod sit sanctus et quod propter sanctam et perfectam vitam quam ipse habuit et tenuit quamdiu superfuit in hoc mundo, Deus debeat facere miracula pro eo'; or (*ibid.*, p. 82): 'Interrogatus si credit quod merita beati Ludovici requirunt quod Deus debeat facere miracule pro eo et tanta sic facit, dixit quod quando ipse cogitat vitam suam et excellentiam perfectionis quam habuit et tenuit beatus Ludovicus, ipse credit quod merita sua requirunt quod Deus faciat miracula pro eo. Immo miratur quod non plura faciat, quia numquam vidit hominem magis perfectum.' See also *PC Philip of Bourges*, fol. 52v.

that God acted *through* his saints, who were effectively reduced to the role of intermediaries of divine grace.[65] An extreme instance of this is the definition of intercession given by B. Delphine of Puimichel (d. 1360), in a harangue addressed to a group of pilgrims who had asked her to cure them:

> The saints are only powerful to the extent that God gives them the grace to pray for us. Consequently, repent and confess your sins. The latter impede the prayers of the saints. Avoid evil and do good; in which case, the saints are obliged to pray for you and beg what you request.[66]

From this perspective, God's action was dependent on the practice of the moral virtues, of penitence and prayer on the part of the supplicants, the saints being content to encourage by their prayers the action of Grace in the heart of man. At a pinch, their assistance was almost superfluous. Admittedly, this was an isolated opinion, representative only of a very specific milieu, that of the Provençal beguines and their Franciscan confessors. But the mere fact that it could be expressed and recorded in a process of canonization is evidence of the existence, in the fourteenth century, of a pietist tendency inclined to integrate the cult of the saints into a purely spiritual conception of the religious life, within which it eventually lost its specificity.

THE RESULTS OF INTERCESSION

What was it that the crowds who flocked to wherever a saint's relics were to be found, or rushed to see one, expected? What did they ask for when they implored the aid of their regular intercessor or tried out a new one? It is difficult to give precise answers to these questions, so varied, though also in some ways similar, were the results expected from the intervention of the servants of God. Historians have been discouraged by the abundance of the documentation and its relatively stereotyped character and there has long been a tendency to dismiss as trivial and unusable the thousands of prodigies recorded in the hagiographical texts and other sources concerning the cult of the saints. This neglect seems to me unjustified and I believe that, subject to some methodological precautions,

---

[65] For the hesitation between the two conceptions, see the deposition of Brother Roger of Hunnedon, sub-prior of the London Augustinians, at the process of Thomas Cantilupe (*PC*, fol. 38): 'credit tamen idem testis . . . quod si sanctus et quod Deus pro eo sive per eum sicut pro sancto vel per sanctum miracula operatur'.

[66] *PC Delphine*, fol. 101. See also below, pp. 475–6.

the stories of miracles can provide valuable information in the most diverse fields. I will try below to analyse the requests made by the faithful to their protectors, with the emphasis on their content rather than on the way they were expressed.

Fertility and prosperity

To most people, the saints were first and foremost beings who possessed power over nature and the elements. Did they not make rain or fine weather, in the most concrete meaning of the words?[67] More generally, the presence of a saint or his or her relics in a given place or region could stimulate the productive forces of nature. This confidence in the economic efficacy of sainthood is already apparent in some early medieval hagiographical texts, such as the Life of St Didier, Bishop of Cahors (d. 655), of whom his biographer wrote:

> During his lifetime, the harvests were abundant, the vines and the crops were so fruitful that neither before nor since had anyone seen anything like it. In the town, hardly anyone was poor, no-one found it difficult to get what he wanted and people lacked neither food nor clothing. All needs were satisfied and there was more than enough of everything.[68]

Given what is known about the role played by the bishops in the towns of Merovingian Gaul and their evergetism, such a text is susceptible of a positivist explanation; holder of local power and master of a part of the soil and its resources, his initiatives compensating for the failure of the public authority, in particular with regard to subsistence, a prelate who conscientiously performed the duties of his office could make a strong

[67] This is already visible in stories told by the author of the *Gesta Hammaburgensis ecclesiae pontificum*, ed. W. Trillmich, IV, pp. 344–5, about one of the first bishops of Scania: 'claruit autem virtutem miraculis, ita ut poscentibus in necessitate barbaris, imbrem faceret descendere vel denuo serenitatem venire et alia quae hactenus queruntur a doctoribus'. As the last phrase shows, this power was thought to be a prerogative of bishops (*doctores*) and, more generally, the clergy. Gregory VII complained to King Haakon of Denmark about the violent attacks made by his subjects on priests when they failed to get the weather they wanted: *Gregorii VII registrum*, ed. E. Caspar (*MGH. Ep. selectae*, II), VII, 21, p. 498; R. Manselli, 'Gregorio VII di fronte al paganesimo nordico: la lettera a Haakon, re di Danimarca', *Rivista di Storia della Chiesa in Italia*, 28 (1974), pp. 127–32. References to episcopal charismas in the meteorological field also appear in fifteenth-century Scandinavian processes of canonization, for example, *PC Nicholas of Linköping*, p. 70; *PC Franco d'Assergi*, Paris, BN, H. 929, *Summarium*, fol. 15v (Franco was a hermit who died in the Abruzzi *c*.1300).

[68] *Vita Desiderii Cadurcae urbis episcopi*, ed. B. Krusch and W. Levison, in *MGH.SRM.*, IV, p. 581. For the saint-bishops of Gaul, see M. Heinzelmann, *Bischofherrschaft in Gallien* (Munich, 1976).

impression on his flock and be remembered as a benefactor whose
efficiency and largess had allowed them to live, for a while, in prosperity.
It is more surprising to see, several centuries later, the same powers attributed to relics, whether of a bishop or a hermit. But this is to forget that,
in the popular mind, the *virtus* of the servants of God, far from evaporating
with their physical death, only redoubled in intensity when they cast off
this mortal coil. Furthermore, as we have shown above, the Church had
tried since the eleventh century to attribute to the saints the prerogatives
of the *rex justus*, as they had been defined by the early medieval clergy.[69]
Like the sovereigns whom they gradually supplanted as mediators between
the Divine and humankind, they assured, in the widest sense of the word,
the safety and prosperity of the peoples placed under their protection.
Sanctity created the conditions for abundance, dream of societies of scar-
city. This is demonstrated, at the beginning of the fourteenth century,
by the deposition of an English Carmelite, who declared to the commissioners entrusted with the enquiry into the life and miracles of St
Thomas Cantilupe (d. 1282):

> it is generally believed that, since the bones of Monseigneur Thomas were
> brought to Hereford Cathedral, the harvests have been more plentiful, the
> waters have borne more fish and the animals have produced more young.[70]

There is an almost identical claim in the reply made by the Breton peasants
to the Franciscans who questioned them about the sanctity of Charles of
Blois at the enquiry held in Guingamp in 1371:

> During his lifetime, we, the inhabitants of this region, both ordinary people
> and nobles, had plenty of food, clothes and all the necessities of life, even
> though war never ceased to rage. In contrast, since his death, massacre and
> poverty, misery and penury have descended upon us, and the harvests and
> cattle have suffered greatly as a result of the wars and oppression inflicted
> on us by our enemies.[71]

The conviction that the saints – dead or alive – constituted an effective
shield against natural catastrophes and that their presence increased the

---

[69] See above, p. 163. For the results of the king's justice, according to the author of *De XII abusivis saeculi*, ed. G. Hartel, III (Vienna, 1871), p. 167: 'Ecce quantum iustitia regis saeculo valeat intuentibus perspicere patet: pax populorum est, tutamentum patriae, immunitas plebis, munimentum gentis, cura languorum, gaudium hominum, temperies aeris, serenitas maris, terrae fecunditas, solacium pauperum, hereditas filiorum et sibimet ipsi spes futurae beatitudinis.'
[70] *PC Thomas of Hereford*, fol. 40v.
[71] *ASV, Collectorie* 434 A, fol. 11r. There is an echo of these claims in the process at Angers in 1371 (*PC Charles of Blois*, p. 169).

available resources was widely held throughout western Christendom in the later Middle Ages; the pastors of Sabarthès who, in 1320, before the inquisitors of the bishop of Pamiers, claimed that 'since the Bonshommes had to flee the region, the soil was less productive . . . to the point where it no longer produces anything worthwhile', thought like the Swedish peasants who, a few decades later, attributed to the arrival of the relics of St Bridget in her native country all the happy events which had occurred since.[72] This way of appreciating the efficiency of sainthood, seen as a supernatural force which dispelled evil in all its forms and restored order to a world troubled by sin, was not unique to the lower social orders or the rural masses, as one might at first be tempted to assume. It seems clear that, on this point, the most cultivated clergy thought no differently from the peasantry. At the process of canonization of Dorothy of Montau (1404–6), her former confessor, John of Marienwerder, who had taught theology at the University of Prague, dwelled at length on the efficacy of the saint's tears in combatting the effects of drought in the countryside of eastern Prussia.[73] Ignorant of the distinctions later made between the biological and the inner life, the most intellectually rigorous were in accord with the simple-minded in endowing the servants of God with a collection of powers which contributed to the material prosperity of society and the well-being of individuals. Thanks to them, there was, for a while, in a particular place, a sort of Golden Age, at once land of Cockaigne and anticipation of Paradise.[74]

---

[72] *Le Registre d'inquisition de Jacques Fournier, évêque de Pamiers (1318–1325)*, ed. J. Duvernoy, III (Toulouse, 1965), p. 307. At the process of St Bridget, her daughter described the general feeling in Sweden as follows: 'credimus quod virtus corporis sui et reliquiarum, postquam venit ad regnum, portavit nobis pacem . . . quia antea semper fuimus in tribulacionibus et angustiis sed venerunt nobis pax et omnia bona': *PC Bridget*, pp. 313–14. At the end of the Middle Ages, people became very conscious of the saints' ability to protect against epidemics; see, for example, *PC Joan-Marie of Maillé, AA.SS.* Mar. III, p. 758: 'creditur firmiter quod si dicta sancta adhuc vitam gessisset in humanis, pestis mortalitatis in dicta villa Andegavensi tamdiu non durasset'.

[73] *PC Dorothy*, fol. 316: 'Multoties fuit iussa a Domino, praesertim in tempore siccitatis, ut terram in spiritu gyraret et suis lacrimis irrigaret. Et ita lacrimando in spiritu cognovit satis seu segetibus ex his speciales profectus provenire. Unde vidit nunnumquam in spiritu quod ad effusionem suarum lacrimarum, sulci camporum usquequaque aquarum abundantia, scilicet pluvia, replebantur, quod rei eventus de gratia Dei comprobavit.'

[74] It is tempting to compare these texts with the idyllic picture of the primitive Church – that of the saints – painted at this period by Nicholas of Clamanges, who described a world where, thanks to the saints, towns and villages were populous, stables were full of powerful draught animals, the trees were weighed down with fruit, the fields were covered with corn, men lived long lives, and peace and prosperity reigned: quoted by E. Delaruelle, *L'Eglise au temps du Grand Schisme et de la crise conciliaire, 1378–1449* (Paris, 1962), pp. 894–5.

Healing, protection and salvation

In the majority of accounts of miracles linked to the cult of the saints, however, the latter appear primarily as miracle-workers, to whom one appealed to recover one's health. Some witnesses admitted that they had only considered resorting to a celestial intercessor when all treatments had failed and they had been abandoned by the doctors to their unhappy fate. Others claimed they had dedicated themselves as soon as pain or illness had struck and were in good health as a result.[75] Alongside this therapeutic function, which was central to most requests, the servants of God, always disposed to come to the rescue of those who sought their help, also assumed the role of protectors against natural catastrophes and all forms of adversity.

Can we go beyond these general statements, valid for all periods, and try to define more precisely the respective importance of the different types of miracles in the later Middle Ages? The attempt is worth making, but, if our results are to be significant, we need to be aware from the outset of the limitations imposed by the nature of the documentation. In effect, we never see the miracles in their raw state, by which I mean all the acts regarded as miraculous by the faithful, but only those that the clergy deemed worthy of writing down, whether in the *Libri miraculorum* of the sanctuaries of pilgrimage or in the acts of the processes of canonization. There may well have been a gap between the two forms of perception of the miraculous, but this is no more than conjecture, unverifiable in the absence of sources which are not of ecclesiastical origin. In the processes of canonization, as in the Lives of saints, a choice has been made from among the many prodigies available to the promoters of the cult; we see this in the very few cases where both the official enquiry and an earlier collection, in which the miracles were recorded on a daily basis, survive.[76] When this comparison is possible, it reveals that the organizers of the processes tended to prefer the miracles which appear in the Bible,

---

[75] Both attitudes were present at the same period. For the former, see *PC Clare of Montefalco*, fol. 1023: 'Libera me de hac infirmitate, quia non invenio medicum qui me iuvet de hac infirmitate'; whereas a witness at the process of St Nicholas of Tolentino (*PC*, fol. 90) said: 'cum fuit passa aliquam infirmitatem, recurrit ad dictum Beatum Nicolaum et non vult alium medicum'. Some promises are revealing: 'promisit dare ei in pecunia quantum daretur uni medico qui sanaret eum': *ibid.*, fol. 230.

[76] For the relationship between the miracles in the *Libri miraculorum* and the canonization processes, see J. Paul, 'Miracles et mentalité religieuse populaire à Marseille au début du XIVe siècle', in *Religion populaire en Languedoc*, pp. 61–89; Paul, 'Le "liber miraculorum" de saint Louis d'Anjou', *AFH*, 69 (1976), pp. 209–19.

and especially those which the New Testament attributes to Christ and his Apostles, from the healing of paralytics to the multiplication of the loaves and the fishes.[77] Similarly, there is a marked increase in the number of resurrections from the dead: very rare, if not non-existent, in the processes of the first half of the thirteenth century, they accounted for 10 per cent of miracles in the fourteenth century. This should probably be seen as a consequence of the development of the canonization procedure rather than of a change of attitude on the part of the faithful towards the saints. Aware that it was difficult to get a favourable decision out of the papacy and that the Curia was very demanding with regard to miracles, the promoters of a cause were tempted to raise the threshold of the miraculous to prove the sanctity of their candidate. They accordingly preferred to retain the spectacular cures and resurrections at the expense of other, more dubious, prodigies such as the finding of lost objects or deliverance from toothache through the intercession of a servant of God.[78]

In spite of these reservations, and as long as we keep them always in mind, an analysis of the typology of the miracles in processes of canonization between the early thirteenth and the fifteenth centuries suggests a number of significant conclusions. However dense the filter, it still let through a certain amount of information which sheds light on the attitude of the people of that period to the supernatural. Table 31 enables us to formulate several hypotheses on the basis of a fairly large statistical base. At first sight, there appear to be no dramatic changes to the structure of the field of the miraculous; in almost all the enquiries, cures are overwhelmingly predominant, as in the past. But the relationship between the two categories becomes less unequal with the passage of time: nine to one in the thirteenth century, it falls to less than eight to one on average in the fourteenth century. The relative fall in the percentage of cures is primarily visible in the processes concerning saints who performed many

---

[77] B. de Gaiffier, 'Miracles bibliques et Vies de saints', *Nouvelle revue théologique*, 88 (1966), pp. 376–85, repr. in de Gaiffier, *Etudes critiques d'hagiographie et d'iconologie* (Brussels, 1976), pp. 50–61; J. Leclercq, 'L'écriture sainte dans l'hagiographie monastique du Haut Moyen Age', *La Bibbia nell'Alto Medioevo* (Spoleto, 1963), pp. 67–101; and, for the East, E. Patlagean, 'Ancienne hagiographie et histoire sociale', *Annales ESC*, 23 (1968), p. 119. Particularly influential for hagiography was the description of the thaumaturgical powers of the Apostles as described in Acts (III, 1–10; IV, 15–16 etc.). Under the title *virtus apostolica*, medieval hagiographers included the following charisms: *fugare demones, sanare infirmitates, resuscitare mortuos, predicare futura*. See, for example, *Vita B. Margaritae virginis de Civitate Castelli*, ed. *Anal. Boll.*, 19 (1900), pp. 21–36, especially chapter 9.

[78] The miracles of this type (lost objects found etc.) which appear in the *Liber miraculorum S. Ludovici episcopi*, ed. *Analacta Franciscana*, VII (Quaracchi, 1951), pp. 275–331, are missing from the saint's canonization process: Paul, 'Liber miraculorum', pp. 64–5.

Table 31 *Development of the typology of the miracles recorded in processes of canonization (1201–1417)*

Types of miracles	% of total number of miracles (= average)	
	1201–1300[a]	1301–1417[b]
1. Resurrections	2.2	10.2
2. Contagious and organic illnesses	28.6	31.2
3. Paralysis, motor problems (*contracti*)	28.8	12.5
4. Wounds, fractures, non-fatal accidents	5.2	5.6
5. Blind, deaf, mute	12.4	11.7
6. Mental illnesses (possessed by demons, epileptics, mad)	10.7	5.1
7. Difficult births, sterility	1.2	3.3
8. Deliverance and protection	3.2	11.8
9. Religious miracles[c]	3.8	5
10. Miscellaneous	3.9	3.6
Therapeutic miracles (categories 1–7)	90.2	79.3
Other miracles (categories 8–10)	9.8	20.7

Notes:
[a] Percentages based on the following eight processes of canonization: St Gilbert of Sempringham (1201), St Hugh of Lincoln (1219), Hugh of Bonnevaux (*c.*1221), John Cacciafronte of Vicenza (1223–4), Ambrose of Massa (1240), Lawrence Loricatus (1240), Simon of Collazzone (1252), Philip of Bourges (1265–6). In the process of St Hildegard (1233–43), the recording of the statements is too confused for precise figures to be based on it, though it is clear that the majority of miracles consisted of cures of people possessed by devils, epileptics, the blind and the feverish.
[b] Percentages based on the following ten processes of canonization: St Peter of Morrone (1306), St Louis of Anjou (1307), St Nicholas of Tolentino (1323), St Yves (1330), Delphine of Puimichel (1363), Charles of Blois (1371), Urban V (1381), Peter of Luxembourg (1389–90), Dorothy of Montau (1404–6), Nicholas of Linköping (1417).
[c] That is, punishments for blasphemy or broken vows, visions and apparitions, sacramental miracles etc.

miracles in their lifetime, in which case the thaumaturgical function, though remaining fundamental, lost ground to the protective function. Miracles of this type accounted for over a third of the total in the processes of St Yves and Charles of Blois, over a quarter in that of Delphine, even though the latter was unquestionably endowed with a highly effective healing power. Admittedly, it would be risky to draw general conclusions from these figures, and in the latest processes, those of Peter of Luxembourg (Avignon 1390) and Nicholas of Linköping (Sweden 1417), the percentage of cures again reached a very high level. At least one can point to a tendency for the tutelary role of the saints to increase, though people never stopped asking them to restore health to those ill in mind or body.

Another change worthy of note is the perceptible reduction in the percentage of miraculous cures of the mentally ill (possession, epilepsy, various forms of madness etc.). Up to the beginning of the fourteenth century, this category still accounted for an average of 10 per cent of miracles; later, this figure fell to about 5 per cent of the total. We should probably relate this change to the efforts made by the Church, from the thirteenth century onwards, to establish a clearer frontier between the sacramental and the miraculous. The healing of those possessed, at the end of the Middle Ages, seems to be more a matter of exorcism, an intervention independent of the dignity of whoever performed it, than of an individual charisma.[79] But it may also reflect a decision to put less emphasis on this type of prodigy in the processes, given that the results obtained by the intervention of the saints in the field of mental illness remained generally fragile (there are many references in the texts to relapses involving a new miraculous cure) and thus hardly conclusive.

In the last analysis, the most striking feature in the evolution of the typology of the miracles is probably the marked reduction in the number of *contracti*, that is, people afflicted with various motor and nervous problems revealed by partial or total hemiplegia or paraplegia.[80] Patients of this type accounted for at least 40 per cent of the clientele of sanctuaries in the early thirteenth century (64.2 per cent at Orvieto in 1240, in the enquiry into the miracles of the Franciscan Ambrose of Massa), compared with an average of only 12 per cent in the processes after 1300, and often considerably less. There are several possible explanations for this change, which is also apparent in other hagiographical documents. In his study of the miracles worked by the relics of St Gibrien, at Saint-Rémi of Reims, P. Sigal suggested that, at the end of the Middle Ages, the word *contracti* was used only for clear cases of paralysis, in the modern meaning of the word, confirmed by the presence of numerous doctors in fourteenth-century enquiries.[81] But this is surely to exaggerate the achievements of medical science between 1100 and 1400 and mistake the role of doctors in the processes of canonization. If their evidence after 1300 acquired greater importance, it was less because they were expected to produce a precise diagnosis, which was usually lacking, than for the 'scientific backing' they brought to claims of the incurable nature of an illness, which

---

[79] For medieval attitudes to madness, see, in the absence of weightier studies, T. F. Graham, *Medieval minds: mental health in the Middle Ages* (London, 1967); H. H. Beek, *Waanzin in de Middleleuwen Beeld van de gestoorde en bemoienis met de zieke* (Nykerk, 1969). See also R. M. Woolley, *Exorcism and the healing of the sick* (London, 1932).

[80] For the *contracti*, see Sigal, 'La paralysie en Occident'; also plate 41.

[81] P. A. Sigal, 'Maladie, pèlerinage et guérison au XIIe siècle. Les miracles de Saint Gibrien à Reims', *Annales ESC*, 24 (1969), pp. 1522–39, especially p. 1527.

gave additional lustre to the results obtained by the saints.[82] There is another explanation, which is in my view more plausible. This change in the typology of miracles perhaps primarily reflects the changes in the vow discussed above. In the thirteenth century, as in previous periods, the people taken to the tombs of the saints were those most seriously afflicted, that is essentially the paralytics and other *contracti*, as well as the raving mad and epileptics. To the extent that, in the fourteenth century, the effects of the intercession were increasingly experienced at a distance, since it was no longer necessary to touch the relics to achieve a result, the field of the miraculous spread to other types of sickness and other needs, which correspondingly reduced the relative importance of the traditional sectors.

This explanation also accounts for the considerable increase in the number of children cured. As soon as it was no longer necessary to go in person to the tomb of a saint to be cured, there was an explosion of stories of miracles concerning children who were stillborn, smothered in their beds or drowned in the moats of castles or millponds, which had hitherto been rare.[83] The same is true of women who carried a difficult pregnancy to full term. In the thirteenth century, this type of miracle was very infrequent, future mothers being, by definition, in no condition to travel at the very moment when the saint's assistance was needed; later, it became common, which is understandable since it was only necessary to make a vow to be delivered of an illness or suffering. In general, in the later Middle Ages, the saints were invoked more than in the past in all life's difficulties: imprisonment, a sentence of hanging, threats by bandits, one's enemies etc.[84] It was to the saints that one turned when lost in a wood or

[82] D'Antonelli, *De inquisitione medico-legali super miraculis*. One of the most interesting pieces of medical evidence found in canonization processes is that of John of Tournemire, Clement VII's doctor, concerning his daughter, miraculously cured of a breast tumour by the intercession of Peter of Luxembourg in 1390: *AA.SS.* Iul. I, pp. 577, 598–9; his deposition is translated into French and discussed by E. Wickersheimer, 'Les guérisons miraculeuses du cardinal Pierre de Luxembourg (1387–1390)', in *Comptes-rendus du 2e congrès international d'histoire de la médecine* (Paris, 1922), pp. 372–81. It is significant that this leading expert of his day used, to describe his daughter's illness, the popular expression *noli me tangere*.

[83] The proportion of children among those cured became very high with the canonization process of St Thomas Cantilupe, 1306–7. It is tempting to see this as reflecting a greater concern with childhood; my own explanation, whilst not contradicting this, seems to me more convincing. See plate 42.

[84] This sort of intervention by saints was not new, but is more frequently mentioned in the later Middle Ages. See the texts discussed by B. de Gaiffier, 'Un thème hagiographique; le pendu miraculeusement sauvé', *Etudes critiques d'hagiographie*, pp. 194–226; de Gaiffier, 'Liberatus a suspendio', ibid., pp. 227–32.

at sea, if one's house caught fire or an epidemic raged. Far from shrinking, the field of their interventions continued to expand, without faith in their thaumaturgical powers diminishing.

To assess the precise significance of these conclusions, based solely on an analysis of canonization processes, it is useful to compare them with those based on an analysis of collections of miracles, whose compilers were less obsessed with the desired end, that is to demonstrate the sainthood of a servant of God to the Holy See, than were the promoters of official enquiries. When we look at Sigal's study of the miracles of St Gibrien (Reims 1145) and D. Gontier and C. Le Bas' work on the *Libri miraculorum* of twelve Norman sanctuaries (end of the eleventh to end of the thirteenth centuries) we find a striking similarity between the two types of source at the level of general trends.[85] In the twelfth- and thirteenth-century collections, the miracle *par excellence* is the cure of a sickness or accident suffered by a person or, less frequently, an animal; among the prodigies attributed to the relics of St Gibrien, at Saint-Rémi of Reims, such interventions accounted for 96 per cent of the total. This figure is exceptionally high, but the proportion of sick or accident victims was still higher than 80 per cent in the Norman sanctuaries.[86] Among those miraculously cured, the *contracti* were by far the most numerous: nearly 50 per cent at Reims in 1145, just under 40 per cent on average in Normandy in the twelfth and thirteenth centuries. There were also many mad or other 'lunatic' and 'possessed' people (about 8 per cent at Reims, 10 per cent in Normandy) and a significant number of people who were blind, deaf or dumb (about 20 per cent). The number of resurrections, lastly, was tiny: less than 2 per cent of the total in Champagne, about 3 per cent in Normandy. All these figures are close to those based on the thirteenth-century canonization processes.[87]

---

[85] Sigal, 'Maladie, pèlerinage et guérison'; Gontier and Le Bas, 'Recueils de miracles'. The latter is based on the miracles attributed to SS Catherine (Rouen), Austreberte (Pavilly), Ouen (Rouen), Wulfrun (Saint-Wandrille), Valentine (Jumièges), Nicholas (various places), Paul, Clare and Cyriac, the founders of Savigny, and Thomas Hélye (Biville), the 'precious blood' of Fécamp and the Virgin Mary (Coutances Cathedral and Saint-Pierre sur Dives).

[86] Sigal, 'Maladie, pèlerinage et guérison', p. 1527, gives two other figures: 43 per cent of cures in the miracles of St Faith (which is small) and 75 per cent in those of St Wulfrun at Saint-Wandrille (second half of twelfth century).

[87] A similar conclusion emerges from an analysis of the sixty-five miracles of St Louis, before his canonization, recorded by William of Saint-Pathus: see M. A. Dollfuss, 'Etude clinique de quelques miracles de Saint Louis', *Bulletin de la Société des Antiquaires de France* (1971), pp. 23–35; Dollfuss, 'Les affections oculaires dans les miracles de S. Louis', *Bulletin de la Société française d'histoire des hôpitaux*, 24 (1970), pp. 3–9.

There is a similar resemblance between the miracles in the collections and those in the official enquiries of the end of the Middle Ages. In the 'Book of Miracles' of Saint-Catherine of Fierbois in Poitou, compiled between 1375 and 1470, cures accounted for only 54 per cent of the prodigies recorded.[88] The *contracti* and the various types of mental or nervous illness constituted respectively only 3.8 and 2 per cent, whilst the proportion of women saved in a difficult pregnancy rose to 3.1 per cent. The saint's interventions to protect the faithful from various dangers accounted for 46 per cent of the total, an even larger proportion than that found in the fourteenth-century processes. The main difference between the two types of document is in resurrections, which were less numerous at Fierbois (6.5 per cent) than in the enquiries concerning St Yves and Charles of Blois (over 15 per cent). I discussed above the significance of this characteristic distortion of the canonization processes. This peculiarity apart, we see at Saint-Catherine of Fierbois the same changes in the miraculous that we noted in the case of the fourteenth- and fifteenth-century enquiries, that is an increase in the protective and liberating role of the saints and the extension of their power of intercession to all areas of human life. It would be interesting to make further comparisons to give a broader base to these conclusions, but it is highly likely that the results would be, in essence, comparable, if not identical, as concerns the typology of miracles and its evolution.

There are signs, lastly, that the miraculous power of the saints was now believed to extend to the religious life strictly speaking. In the thirteenth century, when one approached a servant of God, it was essentially to ask for a cure, and people objected when the saint took advantage of their presence to question them about their behaviour. 'Let us stick to the business in hand', was the curt reply of a notary who had taken his sick daughter to St Peter of Morrone, when the latter, who knew he was dealing with a notorious lecher, began to question him about his private life.[89] The role of the saints was to heal, not to convert. They were well aware of this, and generally quite prepared to perform the prodigy requested of them. They stressed, however, in passing, that the thaumaturgical power attributed to them was a gift from God,[90] and endeavoured

---

[88] Y. Chauvin, ed., *Livre des miracles de sainte-Catherine-de-Fierbois (1375–1470)* (Poitiers, 1976).

[89] *PC Peter of Morrone*, p. 226.

[90] The greatest miracle-workers among the saints, in particular the hermits, had a hard struggle to combat the tendency of the faithful to attribute cures to their merits. At the process of Peter of Morrone (*PC*, p. 238), a *contractus* he healed is reported as crying:

to make granting the request conditional on the renunciation of certain morally reprehensible types of behaviour.[91] In the fourteenth century, this changed. Among the requests made to the saints there were some which concerned neither the restoration of health nor protection against the various calamities which could threaten material life: for example, appeals to resuscitate stillborn children long enough for them to be baptised,[92] or requests from blind people for their sight to be restored for a few moments so that they could see the consecrated host.[93] But the most important change was probably an appreciation of the potential moral and spiritual impact of sanctity. Asked, in 1330, why they venerated St Yves, some of his peasant parishioners began by saying that 'when he started to preach to the local people, they became twice as good as they had been before, by the common consent of the neighbourhood'.[94] This was not an isolated case; the processes of St Clare of Montefalco (1318) and Delphine of Puimichel (1363) include frequent observations of a similar nature, by no means all made by the clergy or regulars. The miracles performed by Delphine included several conversions owed to her influence.[95] Nor was

'Liberatus sum, liberatus sum, quia frater Petrus me liberavit.' John Bonus told a man who asked him to perform miracles that he was not God, to which came the reply: 'Vos non estis Deus sed scio quod estis ille qui potest me sanare': *PC*, p. 825.

[91] John Bonus would only cure a woman's daughter if she promised to settle her differences with a relative she disliked (*PC*, p. 788). In the process of Lawrence of Subiaco, there are miraculous cures of adulterers on condition they renounced their scandalous liaison.

[92] The 'respite' is a type of miracle which became common in the modern period; it consisted of the momentary resurrection of a child that had died unbaptized, which, by allowing a valid baptism, assured the child's salvation and enabled it to be buried in consecrated ground: see M. Bernos, 'Réflexions sur un miracle à l'Annonciade d'Aix en Provence. Contribution à l'étude des sanctuaires "à répit" ', *Annales du Midi*, 82 (1970), pp. 5–20; Bernos, 'Miracles chez les Servites en Provence à l'époque moderne', *Revue d'histoire de la spiritualité*, 49 (1973), pp. 243–56. The earliest known cases date from the fourteenth century. Some fifteenth-century examples are noted by P. Paravy, 'Angoisse collective et miracles au seuil de la mort: résurrection et baptêmes d'enfants morts-nés en Dauphiné au XVe siècle', in *La mort au Moyen Age. Colloque de la Société des historiens médiévistes de l'Enseignement Supérieur public (Strasbourg, 1975)* (Strasbourg, 1977), pp. 87–102.

[93] *PC Nicholas of Linköping*, p. 358. The blind man cried: 'adiuva me tuis meritis preciosis ut videre possim creatorem quem toto corde videre desidero'. For belief in the salutary virtue of contemplation of the host, see A. L. Mayer, 'Die heilbringende Schau', in *Heilige Uberlieferung, Festschrift I. Herwegen* (Münster, 1938), pp. 234–62.

[94] *PC Yves*, p. 105; see also p. 87. There is a comparable claim in the office published under the title *In translatione S. Ludovici episcopo Tolosani* in *Analecta Franciscana*, VII, p. 260: 'Hoc autem praetermittendum non est de huius sancti virtutibus quod accedentes ad sacrum sepulchrum non sine stupore . . . in quadam insolita et mira immutatione hactenus inexperta sepe inveniuntur divinitus immutati, quasi ipsa ossa felicia sanctatate redolencia vim divinam haberent sibi animos modo quodam mirabili in melius alterandi.' There could hardly be a better example of the spiritualizing effect of *virtus*!

[95] At the process of Clare of Montefalco (*PC*, fol. 885), Blaise of Spoleto declared that, under her influence, 'mutatus fuit in alium hominem'. At that of Delphine (*PC*, fols.

this confined to prodigies accomplished by the saints during their lifetime; the faithful sometimes attributed their resistance to temptation to the intercession of saints dead for several years.[96] Statistically, these miracles are insignificant, and it would be going too far to speak of a general change in the representations of sainthood. We should, however, note their appearance, as there is nothing comparable in the earlier texts.[97]

More significant, perhaps, is the change of attitude towards the saints revealed by some fourteenth-century processes. Their depositions suggest that some witnesses visited a given servant of God not to ask for a cure but to verify and, if possible, experience personally the reality of the miraculous gifts attributed to them. The chief of these was spiritual clairvoyance, that gift of 'clear sight' which made it possible to see into people's hearts and divine their hidden secrets.[98] Another was the prophetic charisma, which was a direct extension of it; at the end of the Middle Ages, men and women who foretold the arrival of collective catastrophes or threatened their contemporaries with the wrath of God if they did not convert were regarded as saints, especially if their predictions came true in their lifetime or immediately after their death.[99] In this context, the saints were more than ever exceptional beings. But the prodigies expected of them were not only therapeutic or apotropaic. In the popular mind, they were beginning to be seen also as clairvoyants who shared the divine privilege of omniscience.

This change is confirmed by the attitude of the saints to their own charismas; after about 1330, those who were the object of a process of

---

122r–v), the fourteenth witness listed all the people, who, to his knowledge, had been converted by the saint; it included clergy as well as laity, not least the bishop of Apt.

[96] At the process of St Thomas Aquinas, a canon of Salerno claimed to have been delivered from carnal desires through his intercession: *PC Thomas Aquinas*, p. 266; for a similar miracle see *PC Delphine*, fols. 25v–26 (article 61).

[97] There are many miracles which can be categorized as religious in twelfth-century books of miracles and thirteenth-century processes, but these include the prodigies by which saints took vengeance on those who refused to believe in their *virtus* and who blasphemed against them. This type of miracle persisted up to the end of the Middle Ages, but became numerically insignificant. At the process of St Yves (Tréguier, 1330), only two of the hundred miracles recorded by the inquisitors were of this type (*PC Yves*, pp. 385, 421).

[98] A witness at the process of Clare of Montefalco (*PC*, fol. 712) described his motives for visiting the saint as follows: 'Eamus ad Montemfalcum et loquamur cuidam sanctae quae vocatur soror Clara, de qua est fama quod dicat multa occulta hominum et precipue eorum quos nunquam vidit et experiemur utrum si [*sic*] haec vera sunt.' For the gift of clear sight, see P. Pourrat, sv Clairvoyance spirituelle, in *Dictionnaire de spiritualité*, II (Paris, 1953), cc. 922–9.

[99] This was as common in the Nordic countries (process of St Bridget, Dorothy of Montau and Nicholas of Linköping) as in Italy from the second half of the fourteenth century; see below, pp. 523–4.

canonization seem not to have been, in their lifetime, great miracle-workers. Even more, when cures followed their touch, they seem to have been, if anything, embarrassed by manifestations of a power which was beyond their control and risked making them appear as sorcerers or magicians. Many witnesses at the process of Delphine of Puimichel (d. 1360) told how a sick woman had one day been cured after touching the hem of her gown without the saint being aware of what was happening. Soon after, the woman began to proclaim far and wide the news of this prodigy, which filled the saint with shame and despair. 'If God does not come to my aid', she is supposed to have said, 'I will soon be cast into hell for this.'[100] She agreed, however, to lay her hands on certain sick people, when she could see that they had faith and on condition that they behaved discreetly. But if we are to believe Canon Durand André of Apt, her doctor and confessor, she refused to see a band of blind, epileptic and sick people from the dioceses of Uzès, Maguelonne and Avignon, who came 'to see the saintly countess, in the hope of obtaining health through her sanctity and merits'. They spent four days before her cell begging her to appear, while she bemoaned the situation:

> See how silly, stupid and senseless are these people who want to see me! Why do they come to me? I am neither Peter nor Paul, but a putrid body promised to the worms and a heap of iniquities. They ask for signs, they ask for prodigies, they ask for miracles. I am afraid rather that they and I are given as signs Dathan and Abyron who were buried alive.[101]

This was, admittedly, an extreme, and therefore atypical, reaction. But since, at the same process of canonization (Apt, 1363), two Franciscans who had known the saint well in her lifetime claimed that she performed no miracles, either before or after her death, we may conclude that this was a religious milieu that was impervious or indifferent to miracles, where sainthood was an exclusively spiritual phenomenon.[102] Though numerically insignificant, it is nevertheless, by its very existence, evidence of a change in attitudes which extended to a religious elite of lay women.

Our analysis of the depositions of witnesses at medieval processes of

---

[100] *PC Delphine*, fol. 101.

[101] *Ibid.*, fol. 100v.

[102] *Ibid.*, fols. 69, 73v. The two men were Isnard Risi and Bertrand Joubert. In the thirteenth century, the companions of St Clare of Assisi, asked about the nature of her spirituality, defined it as an unspeakable reality, of a spiritual order: 'Ancho disse che non credava che né lei né nessuna de le Sore potesse pienamente dire la santità e la grandessa de la

canonization produces what may, at first sight, appear contradictory impressions. First, it seems that no-one questioned the existence of visible signs and concrete manifestations of sanctity. Even in the case of prodigies that we might be inclined to describe as spiritual, like the 'exchange of hearts' among the mystics, the most rigorous theologians concurred with public opinion in regarding them as an objective reality, of a physiological order. The same was true of the benefits expected of the celestial intercessors; at the end of the fourteenth century, a bishop dedicated himself to a saint in exactly the same way as his manservant, and the favours they requested were often not very much different. This similarity confirms the validity of the concept of the popular mind, that I have used for convenience. However, the semiotic field of sainthood perceptibly changed between the end of the twelfth and the beginning of the fifteenth centuries. The change took place at different speeds according to region and social circle. It was far advanced by the first third of the fourteenth century in the Mediterranean countries, especially among the aristocracy and the urban bourgeoisie; it seems to have been less marked elsewhere in Christendom, above all in the Germanic and Scandinavian countries and among the peasantry. To begin with, in effect, the signs of sainthood recorded by our documents derived from a sacred that was relatively undifferentiated. From the 1300s, the relationship between the faithful and the saints began to lose its 'mechanistic' and automatic character. The *virtus* of the servants of God was no longer seen only as a collection of mysterious forces acting in a privileged place; the contract between the faithful and their heavenly protector continued to be based on the principle of 'a fair exchange', but became more personalized in devotion, and sometimes acquired a new affective, moral or religious dimension. The miracles requested were essentially cures, but other sides of life came within the sphere of influence of sanctity, the effectiveness of which was more often defined in terms of protection and even salvation.

As far as we can tell, these changes seem to have taken place without conflict and relatively spontaneously. It is hardly likely that the depositions recorded by the commissioners *in partibus* were amended at a later stage, or that the promoters of the causes of canonization told the lay witnesses what to say, prompting them to conceal what might offend ecclesiastical ears. There is therefore no reason to question them, even if the circum-

---

vita de la sancta memoria di madonna Chiara, exceptio che non havesse lo Spirito Santo che glie lo facerse dire': *PC*, p. 451.

stances in which the statements were recorded, almost always in translation, may have given a clerical gloss to the views actually held by the faithful. The evolution visible in this sphere is not the result of pressure intended to eliminate forms of religiosity which were deemed impure. It proceeded by additions, not rejections, and the new forms of devotion coexisted without difficulty alongside others which began to appear archaic. The clergy – or at least most of them – do not seem to have tried to persuade the faithful to renounce traditional practices. Their interventions were rather designed to ensure that the signs, whatever they were, did not in themselves play a decisive role in the appreciation of sainthood, and to emphasize that they were the results not the cause. If there was disagreement between the masses and the religious elite (which included some lay people, as we have seen), it was at this level that it existed. We will find confirmation of this below, when we discuss the way in which the Roman Church scrutinized the reports of the enquiries in which the beliefs and convictions of the majority were expressed.

PART II

THE ROMAN CHURCH AND SAINTHOOD

✺✺✺✺

CHAPTER 16

THE HOLY SEE AND THE CRITIQUE OF
MIRACLES

comoco

Our study of the enquiry procedure established by the Roman Church during the first two-thirds of the thirteenth century has shown that it intervened in the causes of saints at two different levels:[1] first, when the pope decided to embark on a process of a servant of God who enjoyed a *fama sanctitatis*, then, after the commissioners entrusted with the *informatio in partibus* had made their report to the Curia. In the first case, a reputation attested by a number of miracles was often all that was needed for the pope to grant the favour requested by the postulators. The second, in contrast, consisted of a proper trial conducted by cardinals. The role of the latter, of whom there were usually three (a bishop, a priest and a deacon), was, with their colleagues, to produce summaries of the voluminous dossiers with which they were presented, and to act as devil's advocates before the fact, since they were required to highlight any weak points.[2] The promoters of causes of canonization dreaded their decisions and the scepticism of the members of the Sacred College was notorious throughout Christendom.[3] We will see below how far this was justified.

---

[1] See above, pp. 35–7.
[2] The role of the cardinals, which was, our documentation suggests, considerable, has been little studied. For the thirteenth century, see J. B. Sägmuller, *Die Thätigkeit und Stellung der Kardinäle bis Bonifaz VIII* (Freiburg im Breisgau, 1896), pp. 49–51.
[3] See n. 10, p. 35 above. In the mid-thirteenth century, Albert of Armagh described the reaction of a cardinal to whom he had sent the report of the enquiry into the miracles of St Edmund of Canterbury (d. 1240) as follows: 'We do not believe in your miracles and we refuse to give them the approval of the Apostolic See because the signs have disappeared and the voices are stilled. There is only one thing to do: look at the works, which must be examined in future. I expect, however, that had the universal church not accepted the cult and legend of St Martin . . . personally, I would go so far as to say that St Martin did not resuscitate three people. For our Lord Jesus Christ would never have granted such a privilege, since even he, when he was in this world, did not resuscitate three dead persons, according to the Scriptures': Albert of Armagh, *Historia canonizationis et translationis S. Edmundi*, ed. Martène and Durand, *Thesaurus*, III, cc. 1847–8. We should, of course, take such claims, found in other contemporary documents, with a pinch of

481

Thanks to the survival of a number of late thirteenth- and fourteenth-century documents, we are able to reconstruct the working methods of the cardinals.[4] First the chaplains of their *familia* examined the record of the enquiry. This was the *rubricatio*, which was designed to disentangle from the jumble of depositions the various elements of the sanctity of the candidate, and present them in the form of general propositions (*rubricae*). These chapter headings were written in red letters, and references to the statements of witnesses which corroborated them were entered in the margins in small print. This tedious task, which sometimes took several years, was followed by the compilation of a document called the *abbrevatio* or, more often, the *recollectio*, which enabled the three cardinals responsible for the enquiry to form a clear idea of the merits and miracles of a servant of God. At this level, the critical dimension was as yet little developed, since it was primarily a matter of reordering round certain themes the claims of witnesses scattered throughout the acts.

The intervention of the princes of the Church was more effective at the next stage, which consisted of compiling, on the basis of the *recollectio*, a document designed to be read and examined in consistory; this was called sometimes the *recollectio minor*, more often the *summarium*. In the process of Clare of Montefalco, for example, Cardinal Napoleon Orsini (d. 1342) and his two colleagues first compiled a voluminous review, in triplicate, of the statements concerning the saint's life and miracles, then produced, around 1328, an abbreviated version which contained what they considered to be the principal aspects of her life along with a selection of thirty-five particularly convincing miracles (out of the 330 which appeared in the *recollectio maior*).[5] But the most interesting documents from our

---

salt. It was in the interests of those who had successfully engineered a canonization to exaggerate after the event the degree of resistance they had overcome. But the repetition of many enquiries on the orders of the Holy See and the many failures show that these fears were not wholly groundless. See above pp. 51–5.

[4] See the list of documents dealing with the curial phase of the process in the list of sources, pp. 546–8 below. The procedure, perfected by the last third of the thirteenth century, was described *c*.1330 by the canonist Joannes Andreae in his Commentary on the Decretals. The process of St Bridget of Sweden suggests that the procedure he described was meticulously followed: *PC Bridget*, pp. 571–607.

[5] The acts of her canonization process passed through the hands of at least nine cardinals between 1319 and 1329, due to deaths and promotions. Only one, Napoleon Orsini, was there from start to finish, and it was he who presented the final *relatio* to John XXII, without gaining his approval. For his role in the canonization processes of the first third of the fourteenth century, see A. Willemsen, *Kardinal Napoleon Orsini (1273–1342)* (Berlin, 1927), pp. 143, 196. Fourteenth-century *summaria* almost invariably contained an assessment of or interesting value judgements on the miracles. That drawn up *c*.1330 on the basis of the enquiry of 1265–6 concerning the sanctity of Philip of Bourges, includes

point of view are the observations of the cardinals, both those entrusted by the pope with the examination and preparation of the dossier and the other members of the Sacred College, who were all consulted at one or more consistories held specially to decide whether it was appropriate to proceed to a canonization. On the basis of these texts, we will attempt to establish the attitude of the 'great minds' of the Roman Curia faced with the conceptions of sainthood which emerged from the enquiries: to what extent did they share the popular view, to what extent did they differ?

OBSERVATIONS ON THE MIRACLES OF SS LOUIS AND PETER OF MORRONE (CELESTINE V)

Among the surviving fragments of the canonization process of St Louis are several miracles accompanied by the comments of Cardinal Giordano Orsini (d. 1287) who examined them in 1284 or 1285.[6] His remarks concerning the fifth miracle attributed to the saint-king – the healing of a deformed beggar-woman called Amelot of Chambly – are significant. He began by eliminating hearsay evidence by noting in the margin: 'non probat miraculum quia non deposuit se fuisse presentem in loco et hora curationis'. He then indicated the contradictions between the various witnesses: the first had said that Amelot had been cured after six or seven days spent in prayer near the tomb, the fourth that it was after eight days; one said that the miracle had happened before High Mass, another that it was after breakfast. The cardinal emphasized the special value which should be attached to the evidence of the sixth witness, who had given Amelot shelter; he claimed she had been cured after three or four days, at breakfast-time. Although he contradicted the others with regard to the exact number of days, it was he who most deserved to be believed. There was no conclusion; the prelate implicitly accepted the authenticity of the miracle. The pope ratified his judgement, as we see from the later note:

the following: 'Item in isto opere sunt quadraginta tria miracula quorum quedam sunt probata ad plenum, quedam autem, licet non sint probata ad plenum, tamen adminiculantur.' The anonymous author then listed seventeen miracles which seemed to him well established, which reveals his conception of a 'good miracle': *PC Philip of Bourges*, fol. 3v. See also the beginning of the *relatio* on the miracles of Charles of Blois (d. 1364), presented in consistory to Gregory XI between 1374 and 1376, which retains only thirty-four of the 187 miracles described by witnesses: 'Sequitur extractus de miraculis perpetratis vivente recolende memorie domino Karolo et de hiis dumtaxat qui melius et clarius probata videntur': MS *ASV, Collectorie* 434, fol. 84.
[6] Delaborde, 'L'enquête faite à Saint-Denis'.

'De hoc miraculo scripsit Dominus noster; videtur probatum in omni sui parte.'[7]

More detailed and interesting is the opinion of Cardinal Pietro Colonna regarding the second miracle of St Louis, the healing of Amelot of Chaumont, a poor cripple healed on the king's tomb at Saint-Denis.[8] This text was drawn up between January 1295 and March 1297, when Boniface VIII asked all the cardinals present at the Curia to give him a written report concerning the king of France's sanctity, before the meeting of the consistory at which the decision to canonize him was taken. The cardinal's very detailed analysis gives us a clear picture of his method. He argued according to the scholastic procedure of *pro et contra*. But the criteria he used to approach supernatural phenomena were purely juridical. He supported his argument with numerous quotations not only from the *Decretum* of Gratian and the *Decretals* but also the *Digest* and *Code* of Justinian. Seneca is cited twice. Here too, the prelate began by noting the contradictions regarding the circumstances of the cure, but he was always careful to state whether they concerned essentials or points of detail. Certain objections were dismissed at the outset; there was no reason to think that Amelot of Chaumont's infirmity was faked, since one could hardly presume to be false facts reported in a similar fashion by several sworn witnesses. Furthermore, one should respect the opinion of the judges, that is, the inquisitors, who had been in direct contact with the witnesses and able to observe the degree of confidence they inspired. If they had accepted these statements, there was no reason to cast doubt on them. With the same robust good sense, he rejected the objection that the depositions were suspect on the grounds that the witnesses were not only poor but Normans![9] He concluded by stating that if there was no other objection, one could have faith in this miracle, especially since the reality of the infirmity in question had been proved by the woman's restoration to health and since, at the moment of the cure, everybody had heard the sound of her bones cracking. What is striking in this particular case is the contrast between the weighty proof, supported by many juridical refer-

---

[7] *Ibid.*, pp. 35–9.

[8] L. Carolus-Barré, 'Consultation du Cardinal Pietro Colonna sur le IIe miracle de S. Louis', *BECh*, 117 (1959), pp. 57–72.

[9] *Ibid.*, p. 77: 'Quod dicitur quod testes deponentes fuerunt pauperes similiter non videtur attendendum, quia divites non iacent ad sepulcrum nec per albergatias ubi dicta Amelota hospitabatur . . . quod dicitur quod que curata fuit nacione fuit Normanda et testes Normandi, qui consueverunt esse mali, non est curandum quia in qualibet nacione consueverunt esse boni et mali.'

ences, and the highly questionable nature of the conclusions the cardinal reached, since his whole proof was tautological: the reality of the miracle proved that of the illness, which itself proved that there really had been a cure.

A few years later, during the pontificate of Clement V, many members of the Curia were consulted about the miracles attributed to St Peter of Morrone. They are probably responsible for some comments in the margins of a manuscript in the cathedral of Sulmona which contains the acts of the enquiry held in the Abruzzi in 1306, since they frequently refer to the *auditores*.[10] It is impossible to say precisely to which stage of the procedure these notes belong, but their content suggests that the report of the enquiry had already been the subject of a preliminary examination by the pope, and that he had sent the dossier to the cardinals for further information and consideration. It is known that the process of Celestine V was conducted with particular care, given the delicate nature of the case and the unremitting pressure put on the Holy See by Philip the Fair, who, not content with having transferred some of his relics to Bourges, wanted the Church to recognize that he had died a martyr, in order to blacken further the reputation of Boniface VIII.[11] Clement V, having instructed four cardinals to examine the document, then appointed a new commission consisting of eight others; at the Council of Vienne, he instituted a third, composed entirely of bishops from outside the Curia. It was probably during one of the exchanges between the pope and these *ad hoc* commissions, which went on from 1310 to 1313, that the marginal remarks in question were made. They reveal that the cardinals could not agree among themselves about certain miracles and left the pope with the task of reaching a decision. In other cases, it was the pontiff himself who questioned their reality, especially when they depended on hearsay evidence.[12] More detailed are the objections reported in chapter XIII of the

[10] For this manuscript, see Seppelt, *Monumenta Coelestiniana*, pp. l–liii. Almost all the many marginal notes end with the phrase 'secundum auditores' (*ibid.*, pp. 211–334). See also *Anal. Boll.*, 16 (1897), pp. 391–2.

[11] See above, p. 77. The *Summarium*, Paris (Bibliothèque de l'Arsenal, MS 1071, fol. 31) contains the following observation: 'et non multo post beatus Petrus mortuus est in dicto carcere de uno clavo qui in cerebro eius infixus est et hac de causa quando canonizatus fuit, rex Francie qui expensis suis eum canonizari fecit . . . volebat quod sanctus Petrus martir diceretur'.

[12] See the detailed account by Cardinal James Caetani Stefaneschi, ed. Labande, 'Le cérémonial romain de Jacques Cajétan', pp. 64–5. The constant toing and froing between the apostolic officials, the cardinals and the pope is revealed in phrases such as: 'quia auditores non fuerunt concordes, videatur iterum et referatur ad examen domini nostri secundum auditores': *PC Peter of Morrone*, p. 259; see also pp. 271, 294, 306, 360. The

Ordo Romanus XIV, entitled: *Examinationes testium super canonisatione fratris Petri*.[13] Here, Clement V first cast doubt on the miraculous nature of the cure of a man with scrofula after he had touched a chain which had belonged to the holy hermit, on the grounds that the cure had not been instantaneous and that this type of disease could easily be treated by a doctor or natural means. The pope was equally sceptical in the case of a paralysed woman who had been cured after touching a chain worn by St Peter of Morrone. He noted contradictions between the principal witnesses to this miracle, one of whom said that the woman herself had put the metal chain round her body, whereas another claimed that it was her brother who had done so.[14] We may wonder whether the pope's hostility to this 'miracle' was primarily because it involved touching an object, in this case, the metal chain, which might have magical connotations.

However, the Ceremonial only recorded the discussions concerning these two prodigies and we would know nothing of the others but for the lucky survival of the report of a secret preparatory consistory held in 1313 and devoted to a last examination of the dossier of Celestine V.[15] Each of the miracles which had been retained by the commissions referred to above was examined in turn and all the cardinals present were asked to answer two questions: 'Is this a miracle?'; 'Is it sufficiently proved?' In this instance, certain members of the Sacred College answered every question in the affirmative, for example the Colonna, which is hardly surprising on the part of bitter enemies of Boniface VIII, whilst others, such as Richard Petroni of Siena, who had defended his memory at the Council of Vienne, gave negative replies. Some refused to decide one way or the other (*dubitat*) or said that, in such and such a case, there had indeed been a miracle but it had not been proved.[16] When everyone had expressed

miraculous cure of a blind woman provoked the following comment: 'iste testis probat quod caruit visu et postea illuminata est, non tamen probat ipsum miraculum nisi de auditu secundum papam'. In general, the pope referred doubtful cases back to the cardinals for further scrutiny; see, for example, *ibid.*, pp. 228, 229: 'videatur iterum ista depositio per cardinales et iudicent eam sicut eis videbitur secundum papam'.
[13] The best edition is B. Schimmelpfennig, *Die Zeremonienbücher der Römischen Kurie im Mittelalter* (Rome, 1973), p. 174.
[14] *Ibid.*
[15] 'Procès-verbal du dernier consistoire secret préparatoire à la canonisation de Pierre Célestin', ed. *Anal Boll.*, 16 (1897), pp. 389–92, 475–87.
[16] The discussion must have been heated, as the two Colonna cardinals, James and Peter, dismissed five preliminary objections before pronouncing on the validity of the miracles. The first was to the effect that the canonization process had not been preceded by an enquiry *de fama et miraculis in genere*, that is, a diocesan process; they replied that Peter

his opinion, the pope gave his own and, if it was positive, the scribe noted: 'Dominus diffinivit istud miraculum esse et esse probatum sufficienter.' In general, the pope followed the majority view. In the case of the second miracle, for example, nine out of eighteen cardinals recorded their opposition, and Clement V rejected it. On the other hand, he ratified another, which all the cardinals had accepted was real, but which only four of them had said was insufficiently proved. Overall, at least fourteen of the nineteen miracles discussed at the consistory were retained.[17]

Many impressions emerge from the various documents concerning the miracles of Peter of Morrone; first, the checking of supernatural phenomena by the Curia was not as strict as the complaints of postulators whose hopes had been dashed might give one to believe. The cardinals and their colleagues seem to have been primarily interested in irregularities in the recording of the statements (excessively brief summaries, depositions not repeated when their content resembled that of earlier statements etc.). Further, we observe at this level a tendency, already visible in fourteenth-century enquiries, to take account only of prodigies it was difficult to challenge, like the resurrections of dead children or the cures of sick people regarded as incurable by doctors. Lastly, the report of the secret consistory reveals that the judgement passed on miracles was often inspired by external considerations; in the absence of objective criteria, the cardinals and probably the pope himself were, after all, more likely to reach a decision on the basis of their impression of the author than of the facts revealed by the enquiry.

of Morrone's reputation for sanctity was universally accepted, so no enquiry was necessary. They then refused to accept that the enquiry *in partibus* should be repeated because there had only been one commissioner; this irregularity (due to the death of one of the two prelates appointed) did not seem to them sufficiently grave. They argued, third, that only the rubrics established during the previous consistories ought to be examined: 'cum enim post multas discussiones et collationes diversas conscriptae fuerunt, nullatenus debent in dubium revocari'. Last, they said that the sanctity of Celestine V's life had been sufficiently proved by the depositions of the witnesses and that there was no need to waste time demonstrating it before discussing the miracles: 'nam in hac vita qui nunc sanctus est, potest postmodum sanctus non esse. Miracula vero post mortem facta sunt finalis bonae et sanctae vitae propria argumenta.' James Colonna even added that, 'cum vitam dicti domini Caelestini bonam et sanctam fuisse firmiter teneat, non curat attestaciones quascumque videre super hoc nec in legendis huiusmodi fatigari': *ibid.*, pp. 475–6. Cardinal Richard Petroni of Siena (d. 1314), on the other hand, who had been appointed by Boniface VIII in 1298, said that the enquiry had not been properly conducted and that it ought to be begun again: *ibid.*, p. 476.

[17] In two cases, we have the text of the deliberations of the cardinals but without the pope's decision; in two other cases, we have the pontifical sentence without the opinions of the cardinals: *ibid.*, pp. 479, 483.

OBSERVATIONS ON THE MIRACLES OF
ST THOMAS CANTILUPE

The results of this survey of curial documentation would be disappointing if it were not for the survival of a text of exceptional interest which has not hitherto attracted the attention of historians. This is a very detailed report compiled by an unidentified person at the Curia, at the time when Pope John XXII was considering whether to canonize the former bishop of Hereford, Thomas Cantilupe (d. 1282).[18] The enquiry *in partibus* had been held in 1307 in Hereford and London and had been conducted with particular care.[19] Between the despatch of the acts to Avignon and the promulgation of the sentence of canonization, on 17 April 1320, there was a series of examinations and consultations whose progress we can follow thanks to this document. The first stage, as usual, consisted of the rubrication which culminated in the compilation of a *recollectio*.[20] A curialist of high rank (perhaps a cardinal) then composed a *summarium* which is printed in full in Appendix 1.[21] It contained, after a brief summary of the life and merits of St Thomas Cantilupe, a detailed critical study of twenty-six miracles chosen from the thirty-eight recorded in the reports of the enquiry of 1307. It seems highly likely that this was a working document intended either for the cardinals who would be asked in consistory to make a decision as to the bishop of Hereford's sainthood or for the pope himself. Its author set out to examine all the possible objections (*dubia*) and prepare replies in advance. Unlike the other texts discussed here, this report has little to say on the subject of the form or degree of validity of the statements. These matters had probably already been dealt with at an earlier stage of the proceedings.[22] Our author

---

[18] For Thomas Cantilupe, see above, pp. 292–307; for the circumstances of the process and the pressure brought to bear by the king of England, see above, p. 78 and below, n. 24, p. 489.

[19] The enquiry *in partibus* took place between 13 July and 13 November 1307 under three commissioners appointed by Clement V: William Durand, bishop of Mende, Ralph Baldock, bishop of London, and William of Festa, papal chaplain. They collected the depositions of 320 witnesses. We know from MS Ottob. lat. 2516, fols. 44–46v, that the dossier was examined by a commission of six cardinals in May 1313. The bull of canonization, *Unigenitus filius* (ed. *AA.SS.* Oct. I, pp. 597–8) was promulgated on the day of the canonization (17 April 1320) by Pope John XXII.

[20] MS BN, lat., 5373 A, fols. 70–119v.

[21] *Ibid.*, fols. 66–9v. See appendix 1.

[22] The author of the *summarium* refers to an already complex documentation he had in front of him as he prepared his text (*ibid.*, fol. 66): 'ut patet in sexterno continente quedam excerpta de processu inquisicionis originalis ad Sedem predictam transmisse'. There is one problem I have not been able to resolve; the *summarium* examines more miracles (twenty-six) than were retained by the authors of the rubrics (nineteen), and they are not

gave his verdict on the essentials, that is, on the reality and credibility of the prodigies attributed to St Thomas Cantilupe. This is, to my knowledge, the only medieval document which allows us to observe in detail how the clergy reacted in the face of the supernatural. Though its author remains unknown, the date of the document can be established with some precision. The text refers to a master of theology who had been present at a serious accident 'in the house of James Colonna of happy memory, once cardinal-deacon of the Holy Roman Church'.[23] As Colonna died on 14 August 1318 and since our document must antedate April 1320, it seems reasonable to assume that it was produced at Avignon in 1319 or early in 1320, in preparation for the preparatory consistory where the final decision was to be taken.[24]

The remarkable labours of the author of this text resulted in unqualified approval for most of the miracles he examined, including the most unlikely. Of the twenty-six he studied, only one (no. 27) was rejected without explanation; three (nos. 31, 33 and 34) were pronounced dubious; all the others were ratified. The method adopted to study the prodigies was that of *sic et non*: after a brief summary of the facts and the content of the depositions concerning a miracle, the curialist then imagined the objections which might be suggested either by the evidence or, above all, by the circumstances or nature of the miracle. Then he sought – and almost always found – a solution which made it possible to overcome these contradictions and prove, on the basis of learned arguments, that it was truly a miracle as defined by the Church.

The author of the *summarium* reveals a remarkable knowledge of popular beliefs. After justifying the existence of miracles in the Christian religion in

---

always the same. A possible explanation is that, when it was written, probably in 1319, the decision to canonize St Thomas Cantilupe had already virtually been taken by the pope, which would explain why the author of the *summarium* was less critical, contrary to custom, than the chaplains who had prepared the rubricated *recollectio*; but this is simply a hypothesis.

[23] *Ibid.*, fol. 68. The author of the *summarium* was probably English, since he was familar with the measuring rites which were common in England and often quotes Bede and the Lives of English saints.

[24] We know that Edward II pressed John XXII and certain cardinals very hard for the examination of the enquiry into the life and miracles of Thomas Cantilupe to be resumed and concluded in May 1318 and January 1319 (Rymer, *Foedera*, II, pp. 151–2, 168). The composition of the commission of cardinals was changed several times between 1312 and 1319, as a result of deaths and promotions. The decision to canonize the bishop of Hereford must have been taken in 1319, since on 17 January 1320, four months before the official canonization, his successor, Adam of Orleton, granted annual pensions to two cardinals who had presumably worked particularly hard in favour of his cause: A. T. Bannister, *Registrum Ade de Orleton episcopi Herefordensis, A.D. MCCCXVII–MCCCXXVII* (London, 1908), pp. 120–1.

general terms by the powers given to Christ and the Apostles, he defended certain rites which might strike his readers as tainted by superstition, such as the practice of measuring the person dedicated to a saint and then making candles of the same length that were carried to the tomb after the cure.[25] He compared this practice to the behaviour of Elias and Elisha, who, according to the Book of Kings, stretched themselves out over children to restore them to life, and interpreted it as 'an external expression of inner devotion'.[26] Even if this analogy strikes us as a little strained, the intellectual approach on which it was based deserves our attention: a parallel was drawn between the miracles of St Thomas Cantilupe and those of the Old and New Testaments, which served as a sort of ideal reference. Much use was also made of hagiographical texts, from the *Itinerarium Clementis* (no. 19) to the Lives of SS Hippolytus (no. 1), Nicholas of Myra (no. 25) and Francis (no. 26). The author of the *summarium* had a relaxed attitude to gradual or incomplete miracles and devoted much time to explaining that cures which were gradual, partial or left visible traces of the disease or wound were no less extraordinary than the others.[27]

The most original aspect of his proof was the use of medical and 'scientific' arguments. In the case of the fifth miracle (a child who had fallen from the top of a tower and been found with only a few minor fractures, instead of dead, as might have been expected), he developed a long theory of the fall of bodies and quoted, in support of his claims, examples designed to demonstrate that the fact in itself was not impossible.[28] In the case of the third miracle, in contrast, he tried to prove that a child who had fallen into water wrapped in a sheet could not survive for more than a few minutes.[29] In spite of these references to the 'laws of nature', the frontier between the normal and the extraordinary was, for him, purely empirical. This is apparent when he faced the problems posed by the many infant resurrections attributed to the bishop of Hereford. He accepted them unhesitatingly and listed, in

---

[25] For these rites, see above, pp. 456–7.

[26] MS BN, lat., 5373 A, fol. 66v: first miracle of the *summarium* (= no. 1).

[27] Though this was inconsistent with the attitude often adopted by the papacy; see the letter of the commissioners entrusted with the enquiry into the miracles of St Edmund of Canterbury to Innocent IV (November 1245): 'Porro, quanquam multa et famosa miracula nobis oblata fuissent, nos tamen illos potissime examinare curavimus quae iuxta tenorem authentici nobis directi negotio videbantur congruere, utpote super quibus pluralitas testium habebatur et in quibus naturae beneficia nihil valebant, sed subita morborum curatio opus divine miserationis evidenter ostendebat': Martène and Durand, *Thesaurus*, III, c. 1914; see also above, pp. 485–6.

[28] MS BN, lat., 5373 A, fols. 67v–68: fifth miracle of the *summarium* (= no. 10).

[29] *Ibid.*, fol. 67v: third miracle of the *summarium* (= no. 4).

support, the five physical signs of true death that he found in every case, none of which strike us as convincing.[30] This provided him with an opportunity to formulate his conception of the relations between the soul and the body, according to which the former was joined to the latter as both form and motor. The absence of movement and breath was therefore sufficient, in his eyes, to prove that the soul was no longer active in the victim as *virtus motiva in interioribus*. Death being defined as a separation of the body from the soul, when the former became cold and stiff, unequivocal signs, there could no longer be life in it, which meant one could speak of a miracle when the subject was observed to come to himself after a period of time. Far from encouraging a critical attitude, the science of this 'great mind' provided a scholarly justification for facts which, at first sight, offended common sense. Among the prodigies he examined, the only ones he did not approve were those attested by hearsay alone or in a contradictory fashion. Even then, he was content to declare them doubtful.[31] In the last analysis, the religious connotation of the miracle was a decisive criterion in its assessment; if it had been preceded by a prayer, a gesture of devotion or a pious act, it stood a good chance of being authentic, even if the evidence for it was not wholly convincing;[32] similarly, the partial or incomplete nature of some cures was explained by the lukewarmness of those who had made the vow, sign of an absence of deep faith in the power of God and the saints.[33] From this perspective, the most amazing facts were acceptable and it was justifiable to regard them as miraculous. The curialist wondered whether the cure of two paralytic women (nos. 6 and 7) could have been achieved *per artem*, and not *per miraculum*, but then evaded the question by resorting to a quotation from the Gospel. Similarly, he got round the difficulty presented by relapses in those miraculously cured by asserting that they should be seen as a conse-

---

[30] *Ibid.*, fol. 68v: tenth miracle of the *summarium* (= no. 38). These signs are: 'corporis et membrorum immobilitas, inflexibilitas iuncturarum, frigiditas in omni tempore, privatio anhelitus, carencia usus sensuum'.

[31] The seventh, eighth and ninth miracles of the *summarium* (= nos. 33, 36 and 37) are declared only possible and not proved, as is the fifteenth (*ibid.*, fol. 68v).

[32] See, for example, the seventeenth miracle of the *summarium* (= no. 35): 'Miraculum de Guinelda Gydihorn videtur probatum per tres testes et visionibus subsequentibus dicetur. Facit pro miraculo quod fuit confessa peccata sua et docto sancto Thome mensurata' (*ibid.*, fol. 69).

[33] *Ibid.*, fol. 67: second miracle of the *summarium* (= no. 2): 'que aliquotiens eveniunt propter teporem devocionis orantium. Unde et parentes huius pueri non leguntur in attestationibus divinum implorasse auxilium nisi ab aliis excitati nec etiam in oratione diutius perstitisse.'

Table 32 *The miracles of St Thomas Cantilupe*

1 2		3	4	5	6
1.	Joan, daughter of Adam le Schirreve, aged 5, drowned in a fishpond	x	x	yes	x
2.	John, son of William Drake, aged 1½, drowned	x	x	yes	
3.	William, son of John de Lorimer, aged 2½, drowned in a fishpond				x
4.	Nicholas, son of John Piscatoris, aged 9, drowned in a river		x	yes	x
5.	Geoffrey, son of Robert Russel, aged 1½, crushed by a cart wheel		x	yes	x
6.	Juliana Kock, adult, paralysed	x	x	yes	x
7.	Margaret, adult, paralysed		x	yes	
8.	John of Holaurton, adult, humpback	x	x	yes	x
9.	John of Burton, a child without a tongue (it grew and he talked)	x	x	yes	
10.	Robert, son of Gervase, aged 2 years 3 months, dead and resuscitated	x	x	yes	
11.	Ship and sailors saved from shipwreck	x	x	yes	
12.	Edith, adult, raging mad				
13.	William Craig, adult, hanged but miraculously saved				
14.	Agnes de La Broke, adult gone blind	x	x	yes	x
15.	Christine, adult, hanged				
16 and 17.	Adam and Roger, blind children	xx	xx	yes	x(16)
18.	Agnes de La Hulle, adult, paralysed				
19.	Brother Richard de Insula, OFM, many and huge warts				
20.	Hugh le Barber, adult, blind	x	x	yes	
21.	Gilbert, son of Richard, drowned				
22.	Alicia, daughter of William of Lonsdale, paralysed child with decomposing foot	x			x
23.	John, son of Hugh the Chandler, blind child				
24.	Miracle of the tombstone over the bones of St Thomas at Hereford				
25.	Miraculous dream of Bishop Richard Swinfield the night before the translation				
26.	Miracle of the birds while Thomas sang the *Veni Creator*	x	x	yes	
27.	Milo Pichard, adult, paralysed	x	x	no	
28.	Hugh of Stoklon, dumb (tongue cut out)				

Table 32 *(cont.)*

1 2	3	4	5	6
29. John of Creddle, paralysed for 7 years		x	yes	
30. Juliana of Creddle, paralysed		x	yes	
31. Philip Paniot (or Paynort), adult paralytic	x	x	doubtful	
32. John, son of Adam de La Hulle, child who died a natural death	x	x	yes	
33. Lucy of Asperton, child drowned in a pond	x	x	doubtful	x
34. Anicia de La Putte, adult, paralysed for 7 years		x	doubtful	
35. Quenelta (or Guenelda) Gydehorn (or Gudihorn), adult, paralysed	x	x	yes	
36. Margaret, daughter of Richard Pinke, cot-death at 16 weeks	x	x	yes	
37. John, son of Robert of Bokland, stillborn		x	yes	
38. Agnes, daughter of William and Leticia, smothered by her mother in her sleep		x	yes	

Column 1: Number of the miracle.
Column 2: In the Acts of the canonization process (enquiry of 1307 = MS Vat. lat. 4015, fols. 123–245, ed. *AA.SS* Oct. I, pp. 609–40, 697–703.
Column 3: In the rubrics (= MS BN, lat. 5373 A, fols. 70–119 v).
Column 4: Examined. ⎫ In the *Summarium* (= MS BN, lat. 5373 A, fols. 66–69v).
Column 5: Conclusion. ⎭
Column 6: In the Bull of canonization (17.IV. 1320), ed. *AA.SS* Oct. I, pp. 597–8.

quence of sin or an opportunity for spiritual improvement.[34] Against all expectations, he accepted without difficulty the miraculous character of the cure of a paralysed woman who had recovered the use of her legs after taking a bath. Since she had declared that she had acted after a vision of Thomas Cantilupe, our author concluded that the natural properties of the water were irrelevant to this prodigy.[35] If he could find precedents or a basis for comparison in the biblical or hagiographical texts, he was ready to believe in the most unlikely miracles, even that supposed to have happened to John of Burton (no. 9), a child born without a tongue who began to speak after a

[34] *Ibid.*, fol. 68v: eleventh and twelfth miracles of the *summarium* (= nos. 6 and 7); fol. 69: nineteenth miracle of the *summarium* (= no. 14).
[35] *Ibid.*, fol. 69: 'per visum in sompnis hominem miraculose sanitatem posse recipere numus catholicus debet in dubium revocare, cum de hoc etiam sint in scriptis sanctorum exempla'.

pilgrimage to the tomb of St Thomas at Hereford, and displayed a tongue apparently well formed.[36] At the enquiry *in partibus*, his authenticity had been much debated and certain witnesses, namely four Franciscans from London, had not hesitated to declare it a hoax.[37] It is clear from their depositions that the clergy were far from constituting a homogeneous block. Indeed, the other ecclesiastical witnesses who appeared before the enquiry of 1307 all declared their faith in the reality of the prodigies attributed to the intercession of the bishop of Hereford, including the Hereford Franciscans.[38] The critical attitude of the London Minors may in part be explained by their loyalty to the memory of the former archbishop of Canterbury, John Peckham, who had been in dispute with his suffragan and had eventually excommunicated him, in 1281.

But irrespective of the local context, this incident shows that the alleged 'credulity of medieval people' faced with a miracle is a myth. If ordinary people were easily deceived and inclined to detect the hand of God in every apparently inexplicable fact, churchmen, especially the 'great minds', were not as naïve as is sometimes assumed. It would be equally incorrect to see them as free thinkers or sceptics. The truth is that they really only believed in 'their' miracles, that is, those performed by members of the group to which they belonged (religious order, local community etc.) or by persons in whom they recognized themselves. Thus Salimbene, in his *Chronicle*, referred with sarcastic irony to the 'prodigies' performed in 1233 by the Dominican John of Vicenza, but set great store by those of his brethren who enjoyed a reputation for sanctity.[39] In the process of canonization of St Thomas Cantilupe, the Mendicants cast doubt on the authenticity of some of the cures attributed to the bishop of Hereford, using as argument the existence of organizations to provide 'miracles on request' and imposters like John of Burton, who had fooled the cathedral canons, unless, of course, they had been in cahoots . . . The author of the *summarium*, on the other hand, accepted this miracle without batting an eyelid, thanks to a comparison, to say the least acrobatic, with the Gospel story of the cure of the deaf-mute and a hagiographic *exemplum*. He probably already knew that John XXII had decided 'in petto' to canonize the prelate, or hoped to dispel his last reservations.

For a better appreciation of our anonymous curialist's attitude, we need, lastly, to look at the miracles he eliminated from the thirty-eight that

---

[36] *Ibid.*, fol. 69v: 'et sine hesitatone credi potest quod in aliis meritis sanctorum legitur esse factum'.
[37] *PC Thomas of Hereford*, fols. 45v–48v; see appendix 2.
[38] *Ibid.*, fols. 72, 81–6.
[39] Salimbene, *Cronica*, I, p. 102.

appeared in the report of the 1307 enquiry (see table 32). First, he rejected acts which, in the fourteenth century, were no longer seen as miraculous in clerical circles, such as curing a mad woman (no. 12), or which did not seem sufficiently extraordinary, such as the disappearance of the warts from the hands of Brother Richard de Insula (no. 19) and the mysterious dream of Bishop Richard Swinfield (no. 25). Similarly, he omitted the prodigies which were common in the hagiographical texts of the period, such as the hanging not followed by death (nos. 13 and 15), or the affair of St Thomas Cantilupe's tombstone, which weighed heavy and light in turn (no. 24), and those which repeated miracles of the same type for which the evidence was better (nos. 3, 21, 22, 23 and 28). Overall, he was less strict than the authors of the rubricated *recollectio*, who had retained only nineteen miracles, omitting, for example, that of the paralysed woman healed after a bath (no. 30) and the last two infant resurrections (nos. 37 and 18), with which the author of the *summarium* found no fault.[40] In the bull of canonization of St Thomas Cantilupe, John XXII was even more rigorous, mentioning only ten miracles which seemed to him well established: three resurrections, three cures of paralytics, three of blind people and the disappearance of a hump.[41] In the absence of detailed information about the preparatory consistory, we have no way of knowing how the pope and the cardinals received the *summarium*, assuming that the text in question (Appendix 1) really is the one that the members of the Sacred College had before them at the meetings which preceded the final decision.[42] However that may be, the differences between these various documents concern only matters of detail and we are justified in arguing that the report analysed above was representative of the attitude of the clergy of the Roman Curia to supernatural phenomena.

---

[40] MS, BN, lat., 5373 A, fols. 70–119v; see also table 32.

[41] *AA.SS.* Oct. I, pp. 597–8; see also table 32.

[42] We know only, from the *Ordo Romanus XIV*, that the pope questioned all the cardinals present at the Curia about each miracle (but those of the *recollectio* or those of the *summarium*?), after they had read the supporting statements. Their validity was discussed first. If it was judged satisfactory, a scribe noted in the margin: 'plenarie probat iste testis'. The objections were then examined, particularly those resulting from contradictions between the witnesses. Where these applied only to secondary aspects, the scribe noted opposite the text: 'non obstat contrarietas'. A few days later, at a new consistory, the pope and cardinals pronounced on the essentials and decided to approve the life and miracles of St Thomas Cantilupe. The pope then gave his sentence: 'Ad honorem sancte Trinitatis et beate Marie et beatorum Apostolorum Petri et Pauli et omnium sanctorum et exaltationem fidei, diffinimus tot et tanta probata esse de vita et miraculis sancti Thome de Cantalupo episcopi Effordensis quod sufficiunt ad eius canonizationem. Item diffinimus eadem auctoritate procedendum esse ad eius canonizationem': Schimmelpfennig, *Die Zeremonienbücher*, p. 164.

When he tried to distinguish true miracles from false, the anonymous curialist based himself on quotations from St Augustine and, above all, Gregory
the Great and Bede, that is, on the authorities already quoted by Guibert of
Nogent in the twelfth century.[43] His learning seems very traditional; his
proofs reveal an excellent knowledge of the Bible and he made frequent use
of the hagiographical literature of the early Middle Ages; in contrast, there
is no sign of the work of the philosophers and theologians who had discussed
this question during the preceding decades.[44] But it is by no means certain
that he would have argued differently if he had been familar with them.
From Alexander of Hales to St Bonaventure, the great doctors of Scholasti-
cism were in accord in defining the miracle both by its 'supranatural' nature
and its utility. In the absence of a precise or coherent conception of Nature,
the second criterion inevitably played the key role: the true miracles, for
these theologians, were those which were performed by good agents and
which were ordained for the glory of God.[45] According to Albert the Great,
three conditions must be fulfilled before one could assert the miraculous
nature of a prodigy: its utility, the fact that it served to strengthen faith, and
invocation of the name of God before it occurred.[46] These were indeed the
perspectives from which the cardinals and their colleagues approached their
examination of the enquiries *in partibus* with which they were presented by

---

[43] The works quoted are: St Augustine, *De civitate Dei*, 1, XXII; Gregory the Great, *Dialogi*,
and, above all, Bede, *De gestis Anglorum*, 1, III and 1, V, 3, *Super Marcum* and *Super
Lucam*. The principal statements of St Augustine on the question of miracles are in *De
utilitate credendi*, I, 16, 34 (= *PL*, 42, c. 90) and *Contra Faustum*, 26, 3 (= *PL*, 42, c.
481). For the Augustinian conception of the miracle, see J. De Vooght, 'La théologie du
miracle chez S. Augustin', *Recherches de théologie ancienne et médiévale*, 9 (1939), pp. 197–
222; P. Courcelle, *Recherches sur les Confessions de S. Augustin* (Paris, 1950), pp. 141–8.
Gregory the Great's attitude to miracles is well analysed by P. Boglioni, 'Miracle et
merveilleux religieux chez Grégoire le Grand', in *Cahiers d'études médiévales* (Montreal),
I (1974), pp. 11–102. Gregory believed that all facts of nature were equally *mira et stupenda*,
but that man, under the influence of habit, had ceased to regard them as such; consequently, God had reserved certain works *non maiora sed insolita* to astonish the human
spirit and make it recognize the divine reality. Hence, there was little difference between
the natural and the miraculous, the latter being defined simply by the *admiratio* it could
provoke. Gregory was not concerned with the ontological structure of the miracle, but
only with the concrete function it could have for the life of an individual or a community.
His views on this subject had great influence on the medieval clergy.

[44] The Old Testament was frequently quoted, especially the Book of Kings. But the stories
of the miracles of Christ narrated in the Gospels were also often cited. Thus the healing
of the centurian's servant enabled the author to claim the possibility of a miraculous cure
(thirteenth miracle) occurring when the sick person was travelling to the sanctuary at
Hereford.

[45] Alexander of Hales, *Summa*, part 2, q. 43; St Bonaventure, *II. Sentent.*, *dist.*, VIII, p.
II, a. 2, q. 2.

[46] A. Van Hove, *La doctrine du miracle chez S. Thomas d'Aquin* (Paris, 1927), especially pp.
314ff.

the pope. Only St Thomas went beyond this highly empirical definition which was already present in Gregory the Great. In the *Summa*, he emphasized the transcendent and, in a sense, metaphysical nature of the miracle, claiming that its essence was to be performed directly by God without the active involvement of second causes, which made it easier to distinguish the truly miraculous acts from the mass of *mirabilia* and other prodigies.[47] Further, he was the first to have established a distinction between miracles *supra naturam* (like the Transfiguration and the Resurrection), those which were *contra naturam* (for example, the Virgin Conception of Mary and the temporary drying up of the Red Sea) and those he called *praeter naturam* (changing water into wine, various cures etc.).[48] Intellectually satisfying though these categories may be, they would not have been, we have to accept, particularly helpful to the curialists confronted with the statements of witnesses who claimed to have benefited from a cure or a supernatural favour. In fact, they always came up against the same obstacle: to establish concretely what was *supra*, *contra* or *praeter naturam*, the clergy of the early fourteenth century would have to have been able to refer to a rigorous

---

[47] S. Thomas Aquinas, *Summa theologica*, *Ia* p., q. 105, a. 7: 'Miraculum dicitur quasi admiratione plenum, quod scilicet habet causam simpliciter et omnibus occultam. Haec autem est Deus. Unde illa quae a Deo fiunt praeter causas nobis notas miracula dicuntur.' See also *ibid.*, q. 110, a. 4, also *De potentia*, q. 6, a. 2ff. The opinions of theologians seem however to have had less influence in this sphere than those of the canonists. According to Henricus de Segusio (*Hostiensis*), four conditions had to exist before miraculous facts were regarded as authentic by the Church: that they derived from God not magic, that they were contrary to nature, that they resulted not from the recitation of a formula (*non ex vi verborum*) but the merits of the saint, and that they served to strengthen faith: Henricus de Segusio, *Summa aurea* (Lyons, 1568), 1. III, pp. 276–7. These requirements were not a dead letter, and there are echoes of them in enquiries *in partibus* after 1260; one of the questions put to witnesses ('quibus verbis interpositis?') was designed to show whether there had been a recitation of incantations or spells, and the commissioners often asked people if their cure had helped to increase their faith and devotion. The reply, obviously, was always positive. See *PC Thomas of Hereford*, fol. 52v and above all fol. 68: 'Interrogata in quo est ipsa [a woman miraculously cured] ratione dicti miraculi facta devotior, respondit quod dicit in mane cum surgit Credo in Deum et quinquies orationem dominicam et Ave Maria, quod ante dictam curationem non faciebat.'

[48] St Thomas Aquinas, I. *Sent.*, d. 16, q. 1a ad 2 et 3; in q. 43a. 7 ad 6; in *IIae* q. 106a. 4; *Com. in I. Cor.*, c. 13 lect. 1; *In Eph.* c. 2 lect. 2. For the originality of his attitude to miracles, see J. A. Hardon, 'The concept of miracle from Augustine to modern apologetics', *Theological Studies*, 15 (1954), pp. 229–57. The influence of his definitions is visible in the fourteenth-century canonists. See, for example, *Johannes Andreae, In tertium Decretalium librum novella commentaria, De reliquiis et veneracione sanctorum*, cap. *Gloriosus*, quoted in Collijn, pp. 605–6: 'Nec est praetermittemdum quod miraculum non potest directe probari, sive constat in modo sive in facto, utputa qualitudo febricitantis vel suscitatio mortui, cum testes habeant deponere secundum naturam et naturales sensus . . . sed in tali casu nulla causa naturalis potest assignari nec potest sensu percipi. Et ideo non potest probari sed probatur indirecte. Nam cognito quod hoc non fit secundum naturam, cognoscitur quod fit ultra, preter et supra naturam. Et sic indirecte potest probari.'

definition of Nature which was beyond their reach. One then understands why, like the authors of the early Middle Ages who provided them with more useful models, they appreciated the reality and the value of miracles from an apologetic perspective.

When, in certain thirteenth- and fourteenth-century texts, one sees the pro- moters of the cause of a saint express their resentment against the Roman Curia, accused of erecting a barrier against the legitimate requests of local churches in the form of unreasonable demands, one is initially inclined to believe that these accusations contain at least a grain of truth. I long believed myself that this clerical elite, products of the schools and universities, constituted a world apart, whose reactions to the supernatural were different from those found at the same period in the popular mind. Having carefully studied the working documents drawn up by the curialists on the basis of the enquiries *in partibus*, I have come to believe that this is not the case, and that the attitude of the popes and the cardinals was very much the same as that of the ordinary faithful. They were sceptical inasmuch as, for them, miracles could not be objectively proved. But, far from concluding that they should therefore question the reality of those sub- mitted to them, they were ready to accept them as long as they were corrobor- ated by witnesses who were in agreement, bore a resemblance to those described in the scriptural texts, and contributed to the edification of the Chris- tian people. In the last centuries of the Middle Ages, the Roman Church did not attempt to restrict the field of the miraculous. At most, it preferred prodigies which, in the current state of knowledge, it was difficult to attribute to second causes, like resurrections. More than appreciating the authenticity of the super- natural signs, its attitude tended to minimize their importance in the evaluation of sanctity and make them strictly subordinate to the merits of the servants of God. In the fourteenth century, miracles served simply to confirm the validity of a reputation ratified by the hierarchy on the basis of other criteria. This is revealed by some words of John XXII reported by Gerson. During the course of the discussions which preceded the canonization of St Thomas Aquinas (1323), a member of his entourage remarked that the Universal Doctor had performed only a small number of cures. The pontiff dismissed this objection, saying that he 'had performed as many miracles as he had solved problems'.[49] We cannot be sure of the authenticity of these words, but everything we know about the attitude of the Holy See to miracles makes it possible to claim that it expresses very well the deep beliefs of the pontiff and his colleagues.

[49] Gerson, *Opera omnia*, ed. Du Pin, II, c. 712.

CHAPTER 17

THE LIFE AND VIRTUES OF SAINTS IN THE PROCESSES OF CANONIZATION

☙☙☙

THE PROMOTION OF THE BIOGRAPHICAL ASPECTS OF SAINTHOOD

Whilst, in the popular mind, the various manifestations of sainthood all derived from a single principal, the *virtus* residing in the body of the servants of God, the Roman Church had, by the end of the twelfth century, begun to break away from this conception by requiring, in the words of Innocent III, 'virtue of morals and virtue of signs'. Not content with giving the force of law to this distinction, the pope subordinated the second aspect to the first, asserting that 'where true merits preceded and where amazing miracles followed, there is sure evidence of sainthood, leading us to venerate he whom God thus indicates for our veneration'.[1] Lastly, by emphasizing the ambiguity of the supernatural phenomena, which might just as well be the work of the Devil as of God, he reduced their value as proof: even recognized miracles were no longer themselves alone sufficient proofs of sainthood. The result was the process of canonization, the juridical and institutional beginnings of which I discussed above.[2] The difficulty experienced by the postulators in adapting to the new procedure shows that the Holy See was, on this point, ahead of its time. Its demands ran counter to the convictions of the laity and the majority of the clergy, for whom the multiplication of prodigies performed by relics was conclusive proof.[3] There are traces of this mental gulf in

---

[1] Innocent III, *Cum secundum*, 3.IV.1200 (= bull of canonization of St Cunegund), ed. J. Petersohn, 'Die litterae Papst Innocenz III zur Heiligsprechung der Kaiserin Kunigunde (1200)', *Jahrbuch für fränkische Landesforschung*, 37 (1977), pp. 21–5.

[2] See above, pp. 33–57.

[3] It is significant that a contemporary chronicler could attribute Gregory IX's canonization of St Francis of Assisi to the fact that he had worked miracles: 'Gregorius papa mensi Iulii de Perusio vadit Assisium, ubi fratrem Franciscum Minorum fratrum ordinis inventorem propter duo que fecit miracula in aperto, in ceco videlicet uno et claudo, quibus visum

Table 33 *Depositions at processes of canonization distinguished according to their content (1185–1417)*

Saints	Date of process	Total number of witnesses	Depositions (%) on the life	on the miracles
Galgano (d. 1181)	1185	20	11	89
Gilbert of Sempringham (d. 1189)	1201	79		100
Hugh of Lincoln (d. 1200)	1219	36		100
Hugh of Bonnevaux (d. 1194)	1221	28		100
John Cacciafronte (d. 1183)	1223/4	55	38.2	61.8
Dominic (d. 1221)	1233	36	90	10
Odo of Novara (d. 1200)	1240	105	4	96
Ambrose of Massa (d. 1240)	1240	148	6.1	93.9
Simon of Collazzone (d. 1250)	1252	226	19.5	80.5
Clare of Assisi (d. 1253)	1253	20	90	10
Philip of Bourges (d. 1261)	1265/6	166	12.7	87.3
Thomas Cantilupe (d. 1282)	1307	221	28.1	71.9
Louis of Anjou (d. 1297)	1307	228	14.5	85.5
Yves (d. 1303)	1330	243	21.6	78.4
Charles of Blois (d. 1364)	1371	163	34.4	65.6
Peter of Luxembourg (d. 1387)	1390	92	21.8	78.2
Brynulph of Skara (d. 1317)	1417	17	70.6	29.4
Nicholas of Linköping (d. 1391)	1417	104	20	80

some texts from the first half of the thirteenth century, for example the prologue to the *Libellus de dictis IV ancillarum*, a collection of statements concerning the life and virtues of St Elizabeth of Thuringia, whose author justified his decision not to compile a simple *Liber miraculorum* on the grounds that 'at the Curia, they pay more attention to excellence of life and beauty of behaviour than to miracles, which sometimes the trickery of men and sometimes the deception of the devil render deceptive'.[4]

In the long run, these requirements were accepted by the postulators, as an analysis of the distribution of depositions between the late eleventh and the early fifteenth centuries shows; if we distinguish, within each process, those which concern the life and those concerning the miracles of a servant of God, a certain change is visible (see table 33).[5]

Table 33 shows that the number of depositions concerning the life of

et gressum reddiderat, canonizavit': *Rycardi de Sancto Germano notarii chronica*, ed. G. H. Pertz, *MGH.SS.*, XIX (Hanover, 1866), p. 350.
[4] *Libellus de dictis IV ancillarum*, ed. Huyskens, p. 2.
[5] Table 33 omits some enquiries, where the distinction between depositions concerning the life and the miracles was not always respected, the witnesses speaking of both together; this is particularly marked in the processes of SS Margaret of Hungary, Clare of Montefalco and Nicholas of Tolentino and Delphine of Puimichel.

the saints was usually relatively insignificant in the thirteenth century. This is not only because some of the enquiries held at that period concerned persons who had been dead for some time, and about whose lives little was known. Even when the saints had died recently, as with Galgano and Ambrose of Massa, the commissioners were primarily interested in their miracles. Conversely, in the only enquiry after 1300 which concerned a servant of God who had died some time before (Brynulph of Skara), over 70 per cent of the depositions related to his life. This contrast reveals different conceptions of sainthood, which, from beneficial emanations from relics, became, at the end of the Middle Ages, a collection of extraordinary virtues. It is clear that the clergy and regulars were here ahead of the laity; in the thirteenth century, when the ordinary faithful were strongly represented among the witnesses, the vast majority of the depositions concerned the miracles, as in the cases of Odo of Novara and Ambrose of Massa. When, in contrast, the majority of witnesses were ecclesiastics, the depositions about the life of the saint concerned primarily their virtues and merits, as in the processes of SS Dominic and Clare, and, to a lesser extent, John Cacciafronte of Vicenza. Such contrasts are no longer found in the following centuries; with the exception of the process of St Brynulph, the ratio between depositions concerning the virtues and those concerning the miracles is more or less stable (one to four, on average).

Further, a close study of table 33 suggests another change; in the thirteenth century, the processes of canonization concerned two quite different types of saints. The first were primarily perceived as such by the faithful, on account of the miracles they performed (*in vita* or *post mortem*), and the ecclesiastical enquiry then served to show that a virtuous existence had preceded and made them possible; this was the case with Odo of Novara, Ambrose of Massa and Simon of Collazzone. The second group owed their fame to the activities of their entourage, composed mainly of clerics. At a pinch, they could have done without miracles, but, to meet the demands of the papacy, the promoters of the devotion credited them with the necessary minimum. From the last third of the thirteenth century, saints of the former type became rarer, whilst there was an increase in the number of processes in which information about the miracles simply made it possible to gauge the degree of popular devotion to a cult 'constructed' by the clergy. After 1300, in fact, the programme defined by Innocent III at the end of the twelfth century had been achieved.

Table 34 confirms and clarifies the conclusions drawn from table 33.

Among the miracles attributed to the saints by the witnesses at processes of canonization, it is useful to distinguish those they performed in their lifetime and those which occurred after their death. If we exclude the aberrant cases, that is, those of servants of God dead for more than forty years, who were almost always credited with *post mortem* miracles (John Cacciafronte at Cremona and Vicenza, Odo of Novara at Tagliacozzo), we see that the number of saints who revealed their powers while in this world perceptibly diminished between the end of the twelfth and the beginning of the fifteenth centuries; five out of seven processes held between 1185 and 1300 concerned persons credited with at least 10 per cent of miracles of this type; between 1301 and 1417, the figure was only four out of twelve. The proportion of those who performed over 90 per cent of their miracles posthumously rose perceptibly at the end of the Middle Ages. These were saints who were not necessarily less 'popular' than the others, but whose reputation originated in the favourable judgement of their merits by a clerical group, not their ability to heal the sick and the mad.

This change may seem to be at variance with the requirements of the Holy See, which, by the thirteenth century, instructed the inquisitors to look not only at the posthumous miracles but also at those performed during the lifetime of the saints.[6] The order was intended to ensure that men and women who appeared to demonstrate the highest virtues did not, in secret, lead a life of laxity. The majority of fourteenth-century processes, accordingly, contain at least a few miracles *in vita*, sometimes many. But when we look more closely at these prodigies, we see that they bore little resemblance to those customarily attributed to the *viri Dei* of earlier periods. For example, the twenty-one miracles credited to St Yves before his death, out of a total of one hundred, according to the acts of the enquiry of 1331, are composed as follows:

> he spent seven days without food or drink
> by his prayer, bread was miraculously provided to a pauper
> a multiplication of loaves (twice) and wheat (once)
> thanks to him, a poor man found an object he had lost
> transfiguration of a pauper to whom the saint had made a gift
> a prophecy made by St Yves came true
> the saint was surprised in conversation with St Tugdual
> a brilliant dove illumined the village church when he was there

[6] Henricus de Segusio (*Hostiensis*), *Super secundo Decretalium* (Venice edn, 1581), p. 105: 'et non solum de miraculis factis post mortem sed etiam in vita . . . fiat inquisicio'.

Table 34 *Distribution of the miracles attested in processes of canonization according to whether they were performed in the saint's lifetime (*in vita) *or after death (*post mortem)

Saints	Date of process	Number of miracles attested	Miracles *in vita* (%)	Miracles *post mortem* (%)
Galgano (d. 1181)	1185	19	21.1	78.9
Gilbert of Sempringham (d. 1189)	1201	30[a]	3.3	96.7
Hugh of Lincoln (d. 1200)	1219	36	13.9	86.1
Hugh of Bonnevaux (d. 1194)	1221	28	75	25
Ambrose of Massa (d. 1240)	1240/1	81	5	95
Lawrence Loricatus (d. 1243)	1244	58	63.8	36.2
Philip of Bourges (d. 1261)	1265/6	43	16.3	83.7
Peter of Morrone (d. 1296)	1306	62	65	35
Thomas Cantilupe (d. 1282)	1307	29	0.5	99.5
Louis of Anjou (d. 1297)	1307	75	0	100
Nicholas of Tolentino (d. 1305)	1325	301	8	92
Yves (d. 1303)	1330	100	21	79
Elzear (d. 1323)	1351	98[b]	6.1	93.9
Delphine (d. 1360)	1363	40	47.5	52.5
Charles of Blois (d. 1364)	1371	192	2.6	97.4
Urban V (d. 1370)	1381	89	0	100
Peter of Luxembourg (d. 1387)	1390	180	0	100
Dorothy of Montau (d. 1394)	1404/6	225	2.2	97.8
Nicholas of Linköping (d. 1391)	1417	57	15.8	84.2

Notes:
[a] In the first collection.
[b] Approximate figure, deduced from the *Summarium*.

a flash of light illumined the saint when he raised the host
a bird perched on him
water receded to let him pass
he miraculously lengthened beams which had been cut too short
he liberated a woman possessed by demons
he healed a cripple
he restored peace between enemies
he successfully defended the rights of the church of Tréguier against royal officials
he put out a fire
his sanctity was miraculously revealed to a certain Maurille
a layman who refused to listen to his preaching was paralysed.[7]

Overall, these miracles include only two cures, one of which concerned a woman possessed. The case of St Yves is not exceptional; of the eight

[7] *PC Yves*, pp. 378–86.

miracles *in vita* attributed to Nicholas of Linköping in 1417, only one involved healing the sick, and again, it was a woman possessed.[8] The others were all either *exempla* designed to edify the faithful and illustrate virtues of the servant of God, or what one late fourteenth-century curialist rather oddly called *miracula miraculosa*, that is, a number of extraordinary deeds intended to demonstrate his mastery over the elements.[9] We see here the influence of the hagiographical literature which also, at the same period, emphasized the supernatural signs which revealed, already in this world, the divine election of the saints.[10] We may conclude that, from the pontificate of John XXII, the Roman Church eliminated, or at least marginalized, the thaumaturgical aspects of sainthood. Bishops and popes now rarely performed miracles of this type. The same was true of the regulars after Nicholas of Tolentino. The women mystics, with the exception of Delphine, who suffered all her life from her reputation as a healer, made very sparing use of their gifts in this sphere, if we are to believe their processes of canonization; at the enquiry held in Rome in 1380, only two out of fifty articles refer to the cures performed by St Bridget during her stay in Italy, whilst St Catherine of Siena had been content to restore the sight of one blind man and deliver two possessed women.[11] Lastly, though it was said in one of the capitulations of the process of Dorothy of Montau that she performed miracles 'both while she was alive and after her death', it seems that the phrase was more of a convention than the reality, since a lay woman who had known her well declared 'that it was true, with only this reservation that she never noticed miracles that God performed by virtue of the merits and prayers of the saint, during her lifetime'.[12]

The thaumaturgical function of the servants of God was not challenged directly, therefore, but downgraded among their posthumous attributes. Even the changes in the structure and content of the enquiries between the beginning of the thirteenth and the end of the fourteenth centuries

---

[8] *PC Nicholas of Linköping*, p. 66.
[9] Namely the anonymous author of the *recollectio* compiled in the Curia *c*.1374–6 on the basis of the acts of the enquiry concerning Charles of Blois (*ASV, Collectorie*, 434, fol. 84). The five miracles *in vita* attributed to the duke of Brittany were: a miraculous stoppage of the tide during the siege of Saint-Brieuc, the abundant harvests reaped by the peasants from lands trampled by his troops and three cures of blind persons. In the process of Dorothy of Montau (d. 1394), the five miracles *in vita* attested were two protective and three religious miracles: *PC Dorothy*, fols. 317–19.
[10] See the interesting remarks in Reber, *Die Gestaltung des Kultes*, pp. 136–42.
[11] *PC Bridget*, arts. 24–5, p. 23; *PC Catherine of Siena*, pp. 321, 393–4, 428.
[12] *PC Dorothy of Montau*, fol. 88 (the fiftieth witness, Elizabeth Schrope, on article 143).

reveal a marked trend to promote the life of the saints at the expense of their miracles; the number of articles devoted to their virtues, that of witnesses called to testify on this point and the increasingly spiritual nature of the *miracula in vita* all contributed to make their earthly existence crucial to their perfection.

THE 'SAINTLY LIFE'

What was a saintly life in the opinion of the late medieval Church? There are several types of source which can help us to answer this question; the most interesting are the *articuli interrogatorii* which appear in the majority of processes of canonization from the end of the thirteenth century. In these schemas, the postulators laid out, in the form of propositions to be demonstrated, the aspects of the perfection of their subject which seemed to them essential. The portraits which emerge are as edifying as possible and therefore, to a large degree, conventional. However, it is not without interest to examine these models and the way they changed. Idealized though they are, they express the idea of sainthood then prevailing in ecclesiastical circles. I will also make use of the *recollectiones* and *summaria* which were drawn up in the Curia on the basis of the records of the enquiries *in partibus*. The documents of this type, which we may describe as 'secondary', are perhaps less significant, since they reflect the conceptions of a numerically restricted group, but as the latter were colleagues of the pope, who had the exclusive privilege of inscribing a servant of God in the catalogue of saints, their views have considerable significance.

For the period before 1233, our documentary base is fairly small and not very helpful. The use of articles was not yet widespread and, above all, the enquiry *de vita* remained embryonic. When it has survived, we see that it consisted of little more than a list of virtues, focussed on asceticism and devotion.[13] Gilbert of Sempringham, for example, in the report sent to Innocent III in 1202 by Archbishop Hubert Walter, is presented as a champion of abstinence and chastity. These very general eulogies are accompanied by a few less timeless observations on the balance between action and contemplation achieved

---

[13] These lists of virtues, which appear in the majority of hagiographical texts, remained more or less the same from the sixth to the twelfth centuries. They have been studied by L. von Hertling, 'Der mittelalterliche Heiligentypus nach den Tugendkatalogen', *Zeitschrift für Aszese und Mystik*, 8 (1933), pp. 260–8.

by the founder of Sempringham in his life and on his decision in favour of voluntary poverty.[14] During the following decades, the space accorded to the biographical elements steadily increased, in line with the wishes of Innocent III and his successors, and references to virtues alternate with edifying anecdotes clearly located in their times.[15] But the change was slow, and the process of St Dominic, in 1233, the first where the use of *articuli interrogatorii* is clearly attested, contains only a list of the principal qualities and meritorious deeds of the founder of the Preachers, listed without any historical perspective. According to the capitulations drawn up in Bologna by Brother Philip of Verceil for the use of the Languedoc inquisitors, the saint had been:

1. zealous for souls
2. fervent in prayer
3. and in preaching
4. a persecutor of heretics
5. a lover of poverty
6. mean to himself
7. but generous to others
8. chaste
9. humble
10. patient
11. an intrepid persecutor
12. joyous in tribulation
13. religious
14. disregarded himself
15. consoled sick brethren
16. and the troubled
17. a lover of regularity
18. an example to the brethren
19. fled glory in this world
20. generous
21. hospitable
22. a friend to the regulars
23. had no other bed than the church

---

[14] 'Un procès de canonisation', ed. Foreville, p. 31.
[15] In, for example, the canonization process of St Hugh of Lincoln (1291): *PC*, pp. 95–7.

24. wore coarse clothing
25. zealous in matters of faith and peace.[16]

From the second half of the thirteenth century, the characteristics of the enquiry *de vita* became clearer and more fixed. It now contained, in addition to a catalogue of virtues, a recapitulation of the principal stages in the life of the saints and their career, presented in chronological order. A new element appeared: the *conversatio*, that is, the way in which the servants of God had behaved in the different states or offices they had occupied.[17] In the fourteenth century, a final chapter was added in some processes: evidence about visions, revelations and prophecies, which acquired great importance with the rise of mystical sanctity.[18] By the end of this process, there was hardly any aspect of the life of the candidates which was not subject to close scrutiny.

'Vita et conversatio'

The origins and childhood of the saints

One cannot but be struck by the importance the late medieval clergy attached to the ancestry of the saints, especially if they belonged to illustrious families.[19] It is clear that aristocratic birth and sainthood remained closely connected in their minds.[20] If the modest origins of the parents could not be concealed, a prodigy conveniently emphasized the divine election of the servants of God: the promoters of the process of St Nicholas of Tolentino, for example, claimed that his birth had followed a vision. His parents, childless and already old, were told in a dream to make a pilgrimage to St Nicholas of Bari, thanks to whose intercession they conceived a son, who took the name of his celestial protector. This scenario,

[16] *PC Dominic*, ed. Vicaire, p. 24.
[17] In official documents, enquiries ordered by the papacy were now called *inquisitio* (or *informatio*) *de vita et conversatione*.
[18] The first process in which this new category appears is that of St Clare of Montefalco (d. 1308). Many articles were devoted to her visions and revelations in the enquiry of 1318–19, and part of the *relatio* prepared between 1328 and 1331 by Cardinal Napoleon Orsini was exclusively devoted to analysing and evaluating them: *PC Clare of Montefalco*, fols. 598–630; *ASV, Riti*, Proc. 2927, fols. 105–41.
[19] See above, pp. 177–83.
[20] *PC Charles of Blois*, art. 1 (*ASV, Collectorie* 434, fol. 1): 'in primis ponit et probare intendit quod dictus dominus Karolus ex utroque parente nobilissimam traxit originem, utpote de illustrissima domo regum Francie in qua multi fuerunt refulgentes miraculis et qui ut sancti in ecclesia venerantur'.

inspired by the story of John the Baptist, perhaps simply concealed adoption, as the evidence of one witness suggests, and was intended to divert attention from the extreme obscurity of his family.[21] The authors of the *summaria* always began by devoting a chapter entitled *De genealogia* to the ancestors of the saints, emphasizing that the latter had been good Catholics, united in legitimate marriage and reasonably well-off.[22] In general, these genealogies were primarily matrilineal; it was the mother, presented in a highly favourable light, who took pride of place; she was praised for having encouraged the child's religious vocation, whilst the father was simply mentioned.[23]

These selective researches into the family backgrounds of saints expressed the notion that they were not only the physical children of their parents but that they drew from them and their more distant ancestors their spiritual substance; only a good tree could bear good fruit. During the course of the fourteenth century, however, this ancestral conception of sainthood seems to have lost ground in processes and, after 1350, the genealogical information rarely went further back than the parents; whether they belonged to the very highest nobility, like St Bridget of Sweden, or to the petty bourgeoisie, like Dorothy of Montau, the servants of God were now indebted for their merits only to those who had given them life.[24]

This development coincided with a greater interest in childhood in the processes, and the two are probably related. The hagiographical literature traditionally attached little importance to the early years of the saints, which constituted what one might call the profane period of their existence, least interesting from the perspective of edification. The authors of *Vitae* preferred to pass rapidly over this unrewarding age, when their subjects were no more than small impulsive beings, given over to vanity and play. This silence also corresponded to an objective reality; the childhood, properly speaking, of the saints, as of all people of their time, was brief and they soon began to behave as small adults; after all, St Margaret

---

[21] *PC Nicholas of Tolentino*, art. 5, fols. 5v–6.

[22] *PC Philip of Bourges*, fols. 28, 43v.

[23] Dorothy of Montau was a saint *ob meritum matris* (*PC*, fol. 187v). So was Peter of Luxembourg, even though his father was mentioned in positive terms (*PC*, p. 468, arts. 4–6 on his father, 7–11 on his mother). In the process of Philip of Bourges, the sanctity of his mother and maternal aunt was stressed (*PC*, fol. 28, witness 1).

[24] See, for example, the prologue to *Vita B. Brigidae prioris Petri et magistri Petri*, ed. Collijn, *Acta et processus canonizationis beate Birgitte*, p. 614: 'sicut legimus de beato Iohanne Baptista et de sancto Nicolao, multociens cooperantur merita parentum ut filiis accrescat gracia maior et perseveret usque in finem'.

of Hungary entered a nunnery at the age of four and Delphine was engaged to St Elzear when she was not yet thirteen. The subsequent change is not always easy to discern since the authors of the *articuli* and the *summaria* continued to employ, with regard to childhood, the old hagiographical *topoi*, seeking to demonstrate that the behaviour of their subjects distinguished them at a very early age from that of other children;[25] but this traditional evocation of the *puer cor senile gerens* should not cause us to forget the original contribution of the fourteenth century, that is, the promotion of the years of childhood as a time of cultural apprenticeship and Christian training. In the process of Charles of Blois (d. 1364), for example, seven articles are devoted to the education that the *infans sanctus* – the expression has no precedent in an official document – received during the first fifteen years of his life, and to his gradual initiation into the sacraments.[26] In the enquiry concerning Peter of Luxembourg (d. 1387), no fewer than twenty-four articles (nos. 12–35) describe how this anxious adolescent very early revealed his taste for the religious life and moral perfection. In this way, we learn that before being appointed bishop of Metz at the age of fifteen by Clement VII, he had acquired a good scholarly (art. 13) and even theological (arts. 26–7) education in Paris with masters such as Francis of Saint-Michel and Michael of Vervins.[27] On the other hand, there is no trace in these late medieval processes of canonization of those 'bad parents' who opposed the religious vocation of their children, who are so common in the hagiographical texts of the thirteenth century. After 1323, there are no more earthly fathers seeking to thwart

[25] St Elizabeth of Thuringia, at the age of five, frequently genuflected and entered churches rather than play with her friends (*PC*, p. 112). St Clare of Montefalco revealed a taste for the most austere religious life at the age of four. For the hagiographical theme of the *puer senex*, see A. Festugière, 'Lieux communs littéraires et thèmes de folklore dans l'hagiographie primitive', *Weiner Studien*, 73 (1960), pp. 123–52, especially pp. 137–9.

[26] *PC Charles of Blois*, art. 4 (*ASV, Collectorie* 434, fol. 4v): 'Item ponit et probare intendit quod cum procedente etate traditus discipline Credo in Deum et Confiteor didicisset, dum intrabat in lectum et surgebat, devotione magna quantum patiebatur etas predicta dicebat. Et ex post cum scivit legere septem psalmos penitentiales cum letania et horas beate Virginis cum tribus lectionibus premissis addidit.' The first process to treat childhood as the time of scholarly and religious education is that of St Nicholas of Tolentino in 1323: *PC*, arts. 6–9, fol. 6; see also fol. 95, witness 88: 'libenter ibat ad ecclesiam, ad divina et ad predicationes, et ad scholas ad discendum, ac si esset magnus'. The two concepts are similarly associated in the process of St Yves: *Relatio processus*, p. 309. For the promotion of childhood and, even more, adolescence in the religious sphere in the late Middle Ages, see R. Trexler, 'Ritual in Florence. Adolescence and salvation in the Renaissance', in *The pursuit of holiness in late medieval and Renaissance religion* (Leiden, 1974), pp. 200–64.

[27] *PC Peter of Luxembourg*, pp. 469, 470.

the designs of the Heavenly father. The villain was now usually the husband, often accused of putting obstacles in the way of the spiritual development of his wife.[28]

As adults: piety and devotions

Important though childhood and adolescence became, they were never
more than a prelude to the affirmation of a sanctity which usually blossomed with adulthood. At this level, the differences are greater than the
common features; it is difficult to compare the behaviour of a bishop with
that of a hermit or recluse, so different were their specific vocations. But
without making artificial comparisons between irreducible destinies, one
can point to certain features which are present in all the processes of the
period and which tell us what sort of life should, according to the Church,
be led by the servants of God during the years of their maturity.

In the articles and the *summaria*, the saints are presented first and foremost as men and women of prayer. This took different forms according
to their estate: in the case of the clergy and the regulars, it was primarily
a matter of the divine office and liturgy, whereas the mystics plunged into
contemplation of the mysteries of the life of Christ and endeavoured to
engage in an intimate dialogue with him.[29] In all cases, prayer was central
to their existence and took up much of their time. This was a traditional
feature of hagiographical literature. More novel is the importance attached
to the sacraments as a sign of piety. In the thirteenth-century processes,
they are mentioned only occasionally, in connection with the saint-bishops
who consecrated the host while weeping copious tears.[30] In the fourteenth
century, the sacraments attracted more attention; Charles of Blois confessed every evening and as many as three times a day. In the words of
one witness, 'he never went to bed in a state of mortal sin'.[31] The eucharist

---

[28] See above, pp. 381–5.
[29] Lawrence Loricatus, the hermit of Subiaco, composed a *Liber orationum* which was written
down by monks at his dictation (*PC*, p. 96, witness 98). St Margaret of Hungary damaged
her face by spending all day praying with her head pressed into the ground (*PC*, p. 254,
witness 28). St Clare of Montefalco relived the drama of Calvary with such intensity that
all food and drink seemed to her bitter, in memory of the liquid Christ drank on the
Cross (*PC*, fol. 195, witness 2). St Nicholas of Tolentino is presented as a monk who
engaged in perpetual prayer (*PC*, fol. 6v, article 18).
[30] See, for example, *PC Philip of Bourges*, fol. 30; *PC Thomas of Hereford*, fol. 60, witness 37.
[31] *PC Charles of Blois*, p. 30, witness 9. He communicated at every feast, with unusual
demonstrations of devotion (p. 161, witness 39): 'recipiebat corpus Domini cum magna
devocione quia capucium et cingulum amovebat et coram sacerdote tenente corpus
Domini, antequam communicaret, diu stabat flexis genibus lacrimando et nonnulla suspi-

was no less highly regarded; luminous prodigies occurred in the church where St Yves officiated, at the moment of elevation, and Delphine received communion with transports of joy. Among the mystics, devotion to the body and blood of Christ often assumed a paroxysmal dimension; St Catherine of Siena, it was said at her process, only survived thanks to the sacrament of the altar and refused all other forms of food.[32] Dorothy of Montau was physically ill on the rare days when she was not brought the consecrated host, and when the priest finally raised the chalice to her lips, she sometimes bit the metal so hard that it retained the marks of her teeth.[33]

The search for a close union with God through the sacraments did not exclude other manifestations of devotion or other, apparently more down-to-earth, religious practices. Even in the case of the mystics, it was emphasized that they engaged in all sorts of *opera meritoria*, ranging from manual labour to the harshest ascetic practices, not forgetting vigils and fasts. In so doing, they sought to afflict and bruise their bodies, so as to deny a foothold to the 'Old Enemy', who was only waiting for one sign of laxity to seize his opportunity.[34]

Pilgrimages were also emphasized. The schemas employed to investigate the life of the saints reveal no trace of the criticisms made, especially from the fourteenth century, by various spiritual and moral authors with regard to these journeys, which they saw as offering opportunities for sin rather more than for religious improvement.[35] The importance to St Bridget of Sweden of her arrival in Rome on the occasion of the Jubilee of 1350 is well known; though given less prominence, similar travels marked the life of Dorothy of Montau, who went to both Aix-la-Chapelle and Rome in 1390, and received many favours during this journey.[36] The

---

ria et gemitus emittendo, adeo et taliter quod iste et alii astantes ad devocienem quamplurimum excitabantur'.

[32] *PC Catherine of Siena*, pp. 50, 267, witnesses 1 and 3.

[33] *PC Dorothy of Montau*, fols. 116, 146v, 196, witnesses 66, 79 and 107.

[34] *Ibid.*, fol. 96v, witness 55: 'valde operosa fuit in operibus meritoriis'.

[35] E. Delaruelle, 'Le pèlerinage intérieur au XVe siècle', *Eleona*, 42 (1962), pp. 6–12, repr. in Delaruelle, *La piéte populaire au Moyen Age* (Turin, 1975), pp. 555–61; G. Constable, 'Opposition to pilgrimage in the Middle Ages', in *Studia Gratiana* (Rome, 1976), pp. 123–46. For the continuing importance of pilgrimage in lay religious life in the late Middle Ages, see F. Rapp, 'Les pèlerinages dans la vie religieuse de l'Occident médiéval aux XIVe et XVe siècles', in *Les pèlerinages de l'Antiquité biblique et classique à l'Occident médiéval*, ed. M. Philonenko and M. Simon (Paris, 1973), pp. 119–60.

[36] The formidable list of places of pilgrimage visited by St Bridget appears in articles 13 and 14 of her process; it includes Santiago de Compostella, Rome, Bethlehem and Jerusalem: *PC Bridget*, p. 14. For Dorothy of Montau, see *PC*, fol. 9, art. 16 and fol. 152, witness 79.

importance in these cases of the *peregrinatio religiosa* may perhaps owe something to the fact that these were lay saints, both from northern Europe, and fascinated by the holy places of the Church. But the same passion for pilgrimages appears among the aspirations of a 'great mind' like Peter of Luxembourg, who, in his palace at Avignon, dreamed of making a tour of all the principal sanctuaries of Christendom, from Notre-Dame of Le Puy by way of Saint Thomas of Canterbury to the monastery of the Eleven Thousand Virgins in Cologne.[37] It is as if the accentuation of spiritual and mystical tendencies, a new element which disrupted the traditional hagiographical schemas, was accompanied by an increased interest in the most concrete forms of devotion.

The saint in death

But the most original aspect of the biographical schemas which oriented late medieval canonization processes is the role played by the saint's death. Up to the mid-thirteenth century, the last moments of the servants of God seem not to have attracted particular attention. At most, it was noted that, after death, the body was well preserved and gave off a pleasant smell. As late as 1265, at the enquiry into the merits of Philip of Bourges, the commissioners were content to ask the witnesses who had been present at his death if the prelate had made a will before leaving this world and how he had disposed of his property.[38] After 1300, in contrast, one has the impression that the quality of a life was judged by the manner of death. In the process of Clare of Montefalco, in 1318–19, no fewer than twenty-three articles were devoted solely to describing her death throes and demise.[39] These detailed descriptions reveal the influence of the representations of sanctity in the *Ars moriendi*, which reached a high degree of refinement in the late Middle Ages.[40] In describing in such detail the last moments

---

[37] *PC Peter of Luxembourg*, arts. 64–71, pp. 472–3.

[38] *PC Philip of Bourges*, fol. 30.

[39] *PC Clare of Montefalco*, arts. 132–55, fols. 622–30. In the process of Peter of Luxembourg, sixteen articles (nos. 78–93) deal with his fatal illness and death (*PC*, p. 490). The importance of the last moments is strongly emphasized in the *Vita* of St Nicholas of Linköping, written in 1414, before the canonization process (ed. Schück, *Tva svenska Biografier*, p. 313): 'post mortem secure eorum merita extollere possumus maxime quorum finis optimus vitam precedentem commendat'. The death of the saint is also treated at length in the *summaria*; see, for example, the *relatio* of the process of St Yves, *PC*, pp. 374–8.

[40] See A. Tenenti, *La vie et la mort à travers l'art du XVe siècle* (Paris, 1952), and, above all, A. Rudolf, *Von der Kunst des heilsamen Lebens und Sterbens* (Cologne, 1959); also *La mort au Moyen Age. Actes du colloque de la Société des historiens médiévistes de l'Enseignement Supérieur public (Strasbourg 1975)*, (Strasbourg, 1977).

of the saints, the clergy seem to have had two principal aims. The first was to make the death of the saint resemble as closely as possible that of Christ.[41] After his example, the servants of God controlled their death, whose date and time they announced in advance to their followers.[42] Far from succumbing to rebellion or bitterness, they accepted suffering with humility, addressing many edifying words to their entourage and confidently receiving the last sacraments, an act which gave visible expression to their faith and their attachment to the Church.[43] But, perhaps more importantly, in the spirit of the age, one of the principal criteria of sainthood was perseverance to the end; nothing was decided till the last moment, and as long as life remained, the whole meaning of the life of a servant of God might be called into question by one equivocal word or attitude. The emphasis was put, therefore, on the joy they manifested at the approach of death, a sign of their certainty of soon sharing in the glory of Paradise.[44] Once dead, the physical signs of election described above made their appearance: serene beauty of face, a pleasant smell, supple body which seemed still to be alive and remained in this state for many days, quite naturally etc.[45] Far from adopting the hagiographical theme of saints dying in obscurity, their death only revealed to the local population by the ringing of bells, the postulators emphasized, in the processes, the public and spectacular nature of their end; from the celestial music which everybody heard to the luminous phenomena which marked their entry into eternity, nothing was missing that might confer on these last decisive moments the character of funeral rites.[46]

The virtues: nature and degrees

The second part of the enquiry into the life of the saints consisted of the *informatio de virtutibus*. The information appearing under this heading in

---

[41] A witness at the process of Philip of Bourges insisted that the death throes of the archbishop had been as painful as the Passion of Christ but that he had borne this ordeal with patience, in expiation for his sins: *PC*, fol. 30.

[42] This was an old hagiographical *topos*, found in the *Vita Martini* of Sulpicius Severus: D. Antin, 'La mort de Saint Martin', *Revue des études anciennes*, 66 (1964), pp. 108–20.

[43] See, for example, the profession of faith by Delphine: *PC*, fol. 30.

[44] *PC Nicholas of Tolentino*, fol. 183, witness 221. Before passing away, Clare of Montefalco cried out: 'O fraternitas vite eterne!': *PC*, fol. 108, witness 1.

[45] See above, pp. 427–8.

[46] Article 49 of Delphine's process (1363) refers to the mysterious music heard in the streets of Apt at the moment of her death, which was attested by many witnesses (nos. 9, 10, 11, 28, 49, 50, 51 and 52): *PC*, fol. 22. See also M. Dulong, 'Les derniers moments de

514   THE SIGNS AND SIGNIFICATIONS OF SAINTHOOD

the *articuli* or in the documents drawn up in the Curia on the basis of the acts of the process does not, at first sight, appear very helpful to the historian. The clergy tended to credit the servants of God with every perfection in order to make their sainthood incontrovertible. In these circumstances, it is difficult to tell which qualities really distinguished the latter in the eyes of their contemporaries. The image suggested by the articles produced by the postulators conforms to the most traditional hagiographical canons; the saints are presented as beings providentially destined to sainthood, as others to damnation, and possessing, by this title, every virtue.[47] Far from increasing with time, their margin of liberty was being restricted during our period. In the late twelfth and early thirteenth centuries, those who were the subject of a canonization process still included many converts who had begun by living, to varying degrees, in sin: not only St Francis of Assisi but Lawrence Loricatus (d. 1243), who had killed a man before retiring to a cave near Subiaco, and John Bonus (d. 1249), who had been a jongleur before becoming a hermit, etc. The theme of redemption, which had been so popular in the West at the apogee of penitential spirituality, seems to have lost ground, at least at the level of official sanctity, from the last third of the thirteenth century.[48] After 1270, no saint who was the subject of an enquiry belonged to the category of repentant sinners. Further, the hagiographical texts describing those

Ste Dauphine à Apt d'après le procès de canonisation', *Provence historique*, 6 (1956), pp. 132–8.

[47] The traditional conception of sainthood appears, for example, in Honorius *Augustodunensis*, for whom 'one is born a saint, one does not become one': see Lefèbvre, *L'Elucidarium et les lucidaires*, p. 338. But the hagiographical tradition is not univocal, and some authors of *Vitae*, by the first half of the thirteenth century, present sainthood as, in the happy phrase of S. Roisin, 'a spiritual art deriving from a science of asceticism': *L'hagiographie cistercienne*, p. 103; see also Roisin, 'La méthode hagiographique de Thomas de Cantimpré', in *Miscellanea historica in honorem Alberti De Meyer* (Louvain, 1947), pp. 546–57. Depositions at canonization processes often make contradictory claims regarding the virtues of the saints, some witnesses insisting on their gradual acquisition (*crescebat de virtute in virtutem*), others that all the perfections had been there from the start. See, for example, *PC Clare of Assisi*, pp. 433, 489, 490, 492, witnesses 3, 17, 18 and 20; *PC Clare of Montefalco*, fols, 2, 475ff, witnesses 1 and 43.

[48] For the theme of the sinner converted and its success in hagiographical literature, see E. Dorn, *Der sündige Heilige in der Legende des Mittelalters* (Munich, 1967) and the many studies of the legend and cult of Mary Magdalene in the West. For recent saints, see F. De Beer, *La conversion de S. François selon Thomas de Celano: étude comparative des textes relatifs à la conversion en Vita I et Vita II* (Paris, 1968). Sinner saints did not altogether disappear from the Franciscan tradition after 1270, as is shown by the cases of Raymond Lull (d. 1315), who led a fairly dissolute life before entering the third order (*Vita beati Raimundi Lulli*, ed. B. de Gaiffier, in *Anal. Boll.*, 43 (1930), pp. 129–75), and St Margaret of Cortona, who was the mistress of a knight for many years; but none was honoured by the Roman Church at the time.

who had already been canonized began to be amended to eliminate any-thing that might give too vivid a picture of their imperfections. Around 1263, for example, St Bonaventure, then general minister of the Friars Minor, altered the rhythmic office written in 1235 in honour of St Francis by Julian of Speyer. The verse which had originally read:

> Hic vir in vanitatibus
> nutritus indecenter
> plus suis nutritoribus
> se gessit insolenter,

had its last two lines altered to:

> divinis charismatibus
> preventus est clementer.[49]

St Dominic had suffered a similar fate some years earlier, in 1242, when his legend was expurgated on orders from the very top of the order of Preachers.[50] These efforts, which in retrospect appear naïve, to delete from the existence of the saints the aspects regarded as too human, cannot be explained solely in terms of excessive clerical zeal on behalf of their patrons. They were in response to directives from the Holy See which asserted, at this period, through the mouth of Innocent IV, that sainthood consisted not of the occasional practice of a few virtues, but of a life marked by an uninterrupted succession of virtuous deeds.[51] These requirements had two consequences. First, they drove the postulators to adhere even more closely to the current hagiographical schemas and apply them at all costs to the life of their candidate, even if the reality was at odds with the ideal model.[52]

---

[49] L. Oliger, 'De ultima mutatione officii sancti Francisci', AFH, 1 (1908), pp. 45–8.

[50] In 1242, the Dominican general chapter took the following decision: 'monemus et volumus quod abradatur de legenda beati Dominici ubi semetipsum asserit, licet in carnis integrit-ate divina gratia conservatum, nondum illam imperfectionem evadere posse quin magis afficeretur juvencularum colloquiis quam affatibus vetularum': MOPH, III, 1, ed. B. M. Reichert (Louvain, 1898), p. 24.

[51] Innocent IV, In quinque libros decretalium, p. 188: 'non sufficit quod in uno fuerit gloriosus vel semel tantum, sed quod in multis et multotiens, imo quod continue eius vita fuerit gloriosa'.

[52] It is clear that some of the clergy were conscious of the contradictions involved when, the postulators having claimed that their candidate possessed all the virtues, it became clear from the depositions that the latter was primarily known for a few eminent qualities which are frequently mentioned. In the process of St Thomas Cantilupe, a Friar Minor neatly resolved the problem by asserting that whilst it was certainly the case that the bishop of Hereford possessed in habitu all the perfections attributed to him, he had been particularly remarkable for the practice of some of them in operacione et actu: PC Thomas of Hereford, fol. 81, witness 48.

Second, they encouraged an identification of sanctity with impeccability, which was vouched for by the confessor.[53]

A choice had, nevertheless, to be made from among these saints, all more perfect than the rest in the eyes of their supporters. The papacy soon found it necessary to define criteria for examining the merits, as it had done in the case of the miracles. Innocent IV had already emphasized that no-one could be canonized who did not have faith.[54] Around 1270, Henricus de Segusio went further, claiming, in his glosses on the decretal *Venerabili*, that the enquiry *de vita* ought to demonstrate three fundamental features in the life of a saint: intensity of penitential practices (fasting and abstinence, wearing a hair shirt, austerity in dress and conduct, mortification), purity of morals and courageous acts performed. Cardinal *Hostiensis* also emphasized two virtues whose presence seemed to him essential before one could talk of sainthood: simplicity and humility. He asked, lastly, for an investigation of the persecutions suffered by the saints, so as to specify their nature and be assured that they had been confronted *ex caritate*.[55] Later commentators on the decretals *Audivimus* and *Venerabili* added little to this schema. Joannes Andreae adopted it and stressed that one could only speak of sainthood when both faith and works were present; if not, he said, one ought to venerate as saints infants who had died after being baptized, which would be absurd.[56]

These requirements were no dead letter and, in the fourteenth century, influenced both the commissioners entrusted with enquiries by the Holy

---

[53] For the growing importance of the evidence of the confessor in canonization processes, see Martinez Garcia, 'El testimonio del confessor'; also n. 54, p. 102 above. In the process of St Louis of Anjou, there were numerous references to his impeccability (*PC*, p. 30): 'et tantum habuit Deum in reverentia et timore quod numquam credit eum peccasse mortaliter'; also: 'credit simpliciter quod innocentia baptismalis duravit in eo sine macule quamdiu vixit'. There is a similar conception of sanctity, with an even greater insistence on the preservation of the state of innocence in the *Vita* of St Elzear (d. 1323), ed. *AA.SS.* Sept. VII, pp. 543ff.

[54] Innocent IV, *In quinque libros decretalium*, p. 188.

[55] Henricus de Segusio (*Hostiensis*), *Super secundo decretalium*, p. 105: 'pro laboribus multis . . . moribus castis . . . actibus strenuis'; also: 'maxime quaeri debet de simplicitate et humilitate . . . nam superbis Deus resistit, humilibus autem Deus dat gratiam'. Further on, he opposed humility to *presumptio ex studiis*. It is tempting to see this as evidence of the influence of the Mendicant orders and their spirituality, but we should not forget that the Rule of Saint Benedict defined the twelve degrees of humility as the supreme way to Christian perfection, and that the theme had been taken up and developed by the Cistercians: *Rule of St Benedict*, c. VII: image of Jacob's ladder. Its success in Cistercian circles is attested, among other things, by the *Tractatus de gradibus humilitatis*, ed. *PL*, 182, cc. 941–72, which shows the influence of St Bernard's sermons on this theme.

[56] Joannes Andreae, *In tertium decretalium librum novella commentaria* (*c*.1330) (Venice edn of 1581, p. 230).

See and the curialists assigned to examine their reports.[57] Not all aspects, of course, received equal attention. In the case of a bishop, for example, it was hardly necessary to deliberate at length on his faith and enough to be assured of his loyalty to the Roman Church.[58] But in the case of the laity or nuns, who might have been exposed to heterodox influences, extreme care was necessary. In 1253, Innocent IV ordered a supplementary enquiry *de fide* in addition to those made in 1251 into the life and miracles of John Bonus (d. 1249). The pontiff probably felt some perplexity faced with this founder of an order, very popular in Romagna, who had remained a layman all his life and been in contact with Cathars and supporters of Frederick II.[59] In the fourteenth century, there are signs of similar unease at processes concerning women who had been, or were suspected of having been, close to the 'spiritual' Franciscan tendency. Delphine, for example, when her death seemed imminent, was required to make a profession of Catholic faith before her confessor, the point of which clearly escaped her, so fully did she feel to be in harmony with the Church, but which her entourage emphasized at the enquiry of 1363.[60] The case which caused most anxiety was that of Clare of Montefalco, who had undeniably been in contact with Franciscans infected by the heresy of the Free Spirit. The majority of witnesses went out of their way to allay suspicions about her orthodoxy, but one Friar Minor sent the commissioners a very hostile deposition, which must have made a bad impression in her dossier.[61] One senses, also, from the questions put to the nuns of her convent, that the commissioners were anxious to know what exactly she had thought and said on the subject of freedom of choice, free will and other equally delicate topics.

[57] See, for example, the plan of the *relatio* of the process of St Yves (*PC*, pp. 301–78), and the constant reference to Joannes Andreae in the *Rubricatio* of that of St Bridget (*PC*, pp. 571–609).

[58] *PC Thomas of Hereford*, fol. 94. The articles of this process are also interesting because they were drawn up by the commissioners, not the postulators, and show the influence of *Hostiensis*: *AA.SS*. Oct. I, pp. 589–90.

[59] *AA.SS*. Oct. IX, pp. 814–55.

[60] *PC Delphine*, fols. 99r–v, witness 8 on article 45. To convince her, her confessor said: 'Domina, credo et scio vos fore christianissimam sed propter multa sinistra que possent in futuro et emulis et invidis suboriri, videtur michi fore dicendum.' She declared before the bishop of Apt: 'semper hereticos, scismaticos et oppinantes et suspectos in fide evitati'.

[61] *PC Clare of Montefalco*, fols. 877–81, ed. in *Summarium (quod incipit: in festo B. Clarae)* (Rome, 1734), pp. 23–4. The hostile witness was Brother Thomas Bono of Foligno, who criticized her for having had as chaplains two Brethren later accused of heresy and also implied that she was epileptic. For the religious context of the process of 1318–19, see L. Oliger, *De secta Spiritus libertatis in Umbria saec. XIV* (Rome, 1943), pp. 9–27, 91–126.

In general, however, these problems rarely surfaced, as the Holy See made preliminary enquiries about candidates for canonization and, if their doctrine and conduct appeared suspect, stopped the procedure in its tracks. It was, consequently, mainly the ascetic and moral virtues which occupied the commissioners and the curialists. The question of chastity was central to their preoccupations. In the process of Delphine, nine out of fifty articles were devoted to her love of virginity and the fact that she had retained it throughout her married life. The same theme had already been developed in the *Libellus supplex* written in support of a request to John XXII for the canonization of her husband, St Elzear.[62] The aim was to demonstrate that the saints had endured a lengthy martyrdom out of love of God. In some fourteenth-century processes, certain witnesses – all clerics – went beyond these general claims and tried to analyse the component parts of sainthood by using classifications of virtues taken from the best authors. An English Dominican, for example, to explain the perfection of St Thomas Cantilupe, referred to the following schema, which he attributed to St Augustine:

> purity of the flesh
> repentance for sins
> humility of spirit
> fervour in charity
> practice of good works
> patience in trials
> curbing every pleasure and turning his mind towards Christ.[63]

According to another witness at the same process, this time a Franciscan, the bishop of Hereford possessed all the qualities of the good shepherd, as they had been listed by St Paul in the Epistle to Timothy.[64] Others applied to his life the formula in the Epistle to the Galatians, *fides per dilectionem operans*, and showed that it was justified.[65] A few years earlier, in the process of Clare of Montefalco, her brother, a Friar Minor, had interpreted her behaviour in the light of the four cardinal and three theo-

---

[62] *PC Delphine*, arts. 1, 7–14, fols. 10v, 12–14; *Libellus supplex*, ed. in *AA.SS.* Sept. VII, p. 522.

[63] *PC Thomas of Hereford*, fol. 43, witness 23.

[64] *Ibid.*, fol. 78v, witness 47.

[65] *Epistle to the Galatians*, V, 6. According to Bishop Richard Swinfield, Thomas had 'rectam fidem, spem certam, perfectam caritatem': *AA.SS.* Oct. I, p. 599.

logical virtues.[66] These ecclesiastical approaches are interesting in the way they reveal the desire of the educated clergy to give a global and coherent vision of sainthood, defined with the aid of precise theological concepts, but they do not appear in the articles or documents drawn up in the Curia, which remained faithful to models directly inspired by the most traditional hagiographical literature.

The presence of all these merits was not enough in itself to demonstrate sainthood. The Roman Church did not appreciate the life of the servants of God only in terms of their virtues. It was also necessary for them to have been possessed to an exceptional degree and for the divine power which caused them to have been revealed, in certain spheres, by a type of behaviour which was superhuman. The expression appears for the first time in the sermon delivered by Boniface VIII on the occasion of the canonization of St Louis.[67] It subsequently enjoyed great success and played a key role in some processes, including that of St Thomas Cantilupe.[68] Contrary to what has been claimed, even recently, by historians of spirituality, the notion of heroic virtue does not date from the Renaissance or Counter-Reformation, even if it was only then that it became common. It had influenced the attitude of the Holy See to the saints since the end of the thirteenth century and the word appears in 1347 in a pontifical document promulgated on the occasion of the canonization of St Yves.[69]

---

[66] *PC Clare of Montefalco*, fols. 475–85, witness 45. For the origins of the concept of the cardinal virtue and its role in the history of Christian ethics, see J. Mähl, *Quadriga virtutum: die Kardinaltugenden in der Geistesgeschichte der Karolingerzeit* (Cologne, 1969); R. Baron, 'A propos des ramifications des vertus au XIIe siècle', *Revue de théologie ancienne et médiévale*, 23 (1956), pp. 19–39.

[67] Innocent IV had defined sainthood as 'multiplex excellentia vite' (*Apparatus in V libros decretalium* (Lyons, 1525), fol. 174v), but the expression is imprecise. Boniface VIII, in his first sermon on the canonization of St Louis, said of the saint: 'Vita eius non fuit solum vita hominis ed supra hominem': ed. F. Du Chesne, *Historiae Francorum scriptores*, V (Paris, 1649), p. 481.

[68] In the articles presented by the commissioners, the purpose of the enquiry *de vita* is defined as to discover 'si aliquas virtutes sive operationes virtutum habuit in excellentia praecipuas et quanto tempore in eis perseveraverit et si dictas excellentias et operationes virtutum habebat singulariter sive notabiliter ultra modum, conditionem seu conversationem aliorum qui erant in consimili statu vel gradu cum eo': *PC Thomas of Hereford*, *AA.SS.* Oct. I, p. 589.

[69] Clement VI stated: 'non omnes qui habent meritoria opera venerari debent ut sancti, sed qui habent opera excellentie, opera quedam supererogationis et virtutes quasdam heroicas': E. Baluze, *Miscellanea*, IV (Lucca, 1764), p. 484. For the origins and history of the concept of heroic virtue, see R. Hofmann, *Die heroische Tugend: Geschichte und Inhalt eines theologischen Begriffs* (Munich, 1933), pp. 148–54; A. de Bonhome, sv Héroïcité des vertus, in *Dictionnaire de spiritualité*, VII (Paris, 1969), cc. 337–43. Ignoring medieval processes of canonization, these authors barely go back beyond the sixteenth century.

It reappears in the process of St Catherine of Siena and, above all, in a treatise I have already cited, written around 1480 by the bishop of Ventimigla, John Baptist de' Giudici, OP, in connection with the canonization of St Bonaventure.[70] For this prelate, who made explicit what had been the tacit doctrine of the Curia for nearly two centuries, it was essential to distinguish *sanctitas communis*, that is, the state achieved by those who died without mortal sin, from *sanctitas eminens et excellens*, by virtue of which those who were distinguished by the excellence of their merits and the singularity of their actions were called saints by the Church. Significantly, he likened the first term to the sanctity of the people of God in the Old Testament (*sanctitas popularis*) and the second to that of the Levites and high priests (*sanctitas sacerdotalis*). This comparison is less unreal than it might appear, since it specified that only those distinguished by the brilliance of their doctrine were worthy to become saints. It was thus not forcing the point to contrast a popular sainthood, excluded from canonization, with a clerical and scholarly sainthood which could justly aspire to it.[71]

These distinctions, which may appear rather abstract, enable us to appreciate an important stage in the religious history of the West. By defining sainthood, in the last analysis, by the excellence and soon the heroism of the virtues, the Roman Church, in the late Middle Ages, made a choice with immense consequences. By emphasizing the extraordinary, the singular and the superhuman, it oriented Christian piety in a direction it would follow for centuries: that of 'against nature'.[72] It made the saint a being *mirabilis in vita et in miraculis*, whose behaviour was beyond what

---

The same is true of R. De Maio, 'L'ideale eroico nei processo di canonizzazione della Controriforma', *Ricerche di storia sociale e religiosa*, 2 (1972), pp. 139–60.

[70] *PC Catherine of Siena*, p. 99, witness 2: 'nec non tam supradicte quam ceterarum virtutum et heroicarum perfectionem attigendo'; see also *PC Peter of Luxembourg*, article 1, p. 446: 'hic mitem et benignum et mansuetum ultra quos humanitas pateretur se exhibuit'. Jean-Baptiste de' Giudici, bishop of Ventimiglia (1471–84), *De canonizatione S. Bonaventurae*, ed. E. Baluze, *Miscellanea*, IV, pp. 471–84.

[71] *Ibid.*, pp. 472–3.

[72] It is really only with Benedict XV that pontifical documents recognize another conception of sainthood, that can be called modern in the sense that it breaks with the heroic interpretation which had prevailed since the fourteenth century. According to Benedict XV, 'sainthood consists only in conformity to the divine will, in a constant and true performance of the duties of one's own estate': *Décret d'héroïcité des vertus de Jean-Baptiste de Bourgogne*, *OFM* (Vatican City, 1916), quoted by G. de Sainte Marie-Madeleine, 'Normes actuelles de la sainteté', in *Trouble et lumière* (Paris, 1949), pp. 175–88. For current requirements by the Roman Church with regard to canonization, see S. Indelicato, 'De sanctitate quae pro beatificatione et canonizatione servorum Dei requiritur probanda', *Monitor Ecclesiasticus*, 75 (1950), pp. 109–23.

was normally allowed by human nature. The biographical marvel – the life as a permanent miracle – replaced the other marvels, but we are still within the sphere of the miraculous. It is by no means obvious that this was the only possible evolution, given the ideas then current. Many contemporary clergy had a very different idea of Christian perfection. For Salimbene, for example, representative of both his age and his order, sainthood was, in the happy phrase of J. Paul, 'not the product of a few extraordinary actions or striking merits, but the description of a life without misdeeds or wrong acts, regular for the regulars, moral for all'.[73] Excluding the sanctity of office, which had allowed so many bishops and abbots to be accorded a public cult in the past, indifferent to popular sainthood, which it regarded as vulgar if not suspect, the papacy, at the end of the Middle Ages, used the process of canonization as a dense filter, on the basis of prior assumptions of a theological order that I will now discuss.

The gifts of the Holy Spirit

A new element had entered into the definition and appreciation of sanctity by the Church: the Holy Spirit. It had never, of course, been wholly absent, but its gifts were seen primarily as antidotes to the seven deadly sins.[74] Many hagiographical texts were constructed on the basis of this classic opposition:

Gifts of the Holy Spirit	Deadly sins
Fear	Pride
Piety	Envy
Knowledge	Anger
Strength	Sloth
Counsel	Vanity
Intelligence	Greed
Wisdom	Lust

In the thirteenth century, explicit references to the charismas possessed by the saints and attributed to the intervention of the Holy Spirit began to appear in the *Vitae*, in particular the power to see into hearts (gift of

[73] Paul, 'L'éloge des personnes'.
[74] M. Bloomfield, *The seven deadly sins: an introduction to the history of a religious concept, with special reference to medieval literature* (East Lansing, Michigan, 1952); S. Wenzel, 'The seven deadly sins. Some problems of research', *Speculum*, 43 (1968), pp. 1–22.

clairvoyance) and predict the future, which was presented as a form of participation in divine omniscience.[75] These notions appear for the first time in a canonization process in 1233–43, at the enquiry into St Hildegard (d. 1179). Not content with predicting the day of her death, the visionary of Bingen had announced the reign of a bad bishop and passed on to two emperors, Conrad and Frederick Barbarossa, the warnings she had received for them from heaven.[76] But her case remained exceptional, and the Holy Spirit is rarely mentioned in the other processes of this period.

The change which occurred between 1260 and 1300 has to be related to developments in theology. The work of St Thomas Aquinas helped to change decisively the question of relations between nature and grace. In this regard, his classic definition of sainthood has less importance than the conclusions he reached after reflecting on the virtues and gifts.[77] In his Commentary on the Sentences, Aquinas distinguished and, to a certain degree, contrasted a human way of behaving, based on the virtues, and a superhuman way, characterized by the use of the gifts. The latter, which were direct impulses of the Spirit, that is of divine grace, were obviously far superior. Even if, in the *Summa*, he subsequently slightly softened this antithesis, it remains the case that, in his eyes, it was better to act under the direct impulse of the Holy Spirit than that of reason, even illumined by faith.[78] The gifts corresponded to a higher degree of perfection than the moral virtues. They were, properly speaking, a participation in God's manner of acting.

The name of St Thomas Aquinas does not appear in the processes of canonization. But there is a striking coincidence between his theological conceptions and the way in which sainthood was defined by the 'great

---

[75] See, for example, *Vita fratris Simonis de Alna* (a lay brother of the Cistercian abbey of Villers, d. 1229), Bibl. royale Belgium, MS 8965, fols. 213v, 215, 219; also Roisin, *L'hagiographie cistercienne*, p. 187.

[76] *PC Hildegard*, pp. 124, 125, witnesses 15 and 19.

[77] In the *Summa theologica*, IIa IIae, q. 81, a. 8, Aquinas defined sanctity as follows: 'sanctitas dicitur per quam mens hominis se ipsam et suos actus applicat Deo'. For the way in which twelfth- and thirteenth-century theologians saw the question of the relations between nature and grace, see M. Landgraf, 'Die Erkenntnis der heiligmachende Gnade in der Frühscholastik', *Scholastik*, 3 (1928), pp. 28–64; O. Lottin, *Psychologie et morale aux XIIe et XIIIe siècles*, III (Louvain, 1949), especially pp. 459–535.

[78] St Thomas Aquinas, *In III. Sententiarum*, dist. 34, q. 1, a. 1: 'Dona a virtutibus distiguuntur in hoc quod virtutes proficiunt ad actus modo humano, sed dona ultra humanum modum.' In the *Summa*, he further stressed the continuity between virtues and gifts, in which he saw two forms of obedience to the action of the Holy Spirit, one active (the virtues), the other passive (the gifts): see J. de Guibert, 'Dons du Saint-Esprit et mode d'agir ultra-humain', *Revue d'ascétique et de mystique*, 3 (1922), pp. 394–411; M. P. Binyon, *The virtues: a methodological study in the Thomistic Ethics* (Chicago, 1947).

minds' from the end of the thirteenth century. Not only was the Holy Spirit much more frequently mentioned but it began to be connected with certain aspects of the life of the saints, in particular their learning, profane as well as sacred. In the principal processes of the early fourteenth century, those of SS Louis of Anjou and Thomas, intellectual capacities and culture are presented as the consequence of a divine gift. It was stressed, for example, that Aquinas could not have written so many sublime works on his own.[79] In this as in other domains, sanctity was revealed through the extraordinary, and theological reflections on the infusion of the Spirit ultimately minimized the role of man in his own sanctification.

The late thirteenth- and fourteenth-century popes attempted to limit this direct intervention of the Spirit to the sphere of learning and doctrine. In the *Liber Sextus* of the Decretals, Boniface VIII made obligatory the celebration of the feast of the four great Doctors of the Western Church.[80] His successors, from John XXII to Sixtus IV, emphasized the links between culture, orthodoxy and sanctity, gradually equating ignorance with error.[81] But it was not only the theologians who attached greater importance to the third person in the Trinity. From the last third of the thirteenth century, the idea that every baptized person, whoever they were, could act directly under the impulse of the Spirit seems to have been widespread in circles which included many lay people. This is clear from the canonization process of St Clare of Montefalco, in 1318–19, the first to include a systematic enquiry into the authenticity of the visions and revelations of a servant of God.[82] The Curia was extremely suspicious of the charismas whose anarchic proliferation risked, in the long term, challenging the authority of the magisterium.[83] The Avignon papacy pre-

---

[79] Thus the learning of St Louis of Anjou 'magis videbatur divini infusio quam humani ingenii et studii exquisitio': *PC*, p. 60; see also *PC Thomas Aquinas*, p. 326. In the process of Delphine (1363), article 36 reports some words of Clement VI, who, impressed by the saint's theological knowledge, said, 'quod, cum ipsa domina non fuisset litteris imbuta, non poterat tanta nec talia nec tam profunda scire nisi ab infusione Spiritus Sancti hoc processisset': *PC*, fol. 19. But the artificiality of this presentation is made plain by the depositions of witnesses revealing that this 'untutored' woman had read the *Liber de vitiis et virtutibus* of St Bernard, the Soliloquies of St Augustine and the Homilies of Gregory the Great!

[80] Boniface VIII, *Liber sextus*, 1. III, tit. 22 (Rome edn of 1582), p. 580.

[81] See above, pp. 397–407. In his treatise on the canonization of St Bonaventure, J. B. de' Giudici said it was better to canonize a scholar than an ignoramus, 'quia nihil ignorantia periculosius est, quae errorum mater a sapientibus diffinitur'.

[82] *Summarium* of the process of canonization of St Clare of Montefalco, in *ASV*, *Riti*, proc. 2927, fols. 48–112.

[83] See, for example, the reply of Agostino Trionfo, *c*.1325, to the question 'Utrum papa debeat aliquem canonizare in sanctum propter donum prophetiae?' in his *Summa de potest-*

ferred to ignore these manifestations of religious enthusiasm, which fascinated the faithful and even many of the clergy. Excluded from official
sainthood, the visionary and prophetic current nevertheless continued,
throughout the fourteenth century, to put pressure on the institution.[84]
After 1350, the saints were no longer content to read hearts to discover
hidden faults; they intervened directly in the problems of the Church
and society, announcing to their contemporaries the imminence of major
catastrophes and divine punishment if they did not mend their ways.[85] At
this level, the distinction between revelations and prophecies disappeared;
the servants of God communicated to their followers and the hierarchy
diachronic visions which encompassed both the incarnation of Christ and
the destinies of the local and universal Church.[86] After the Schism, which
threw into crisis and weakened the pontifical monarchy, the Holy See
eventually took note of what had happened. In the processes concerning
visionaries held between 1380 and 1416, the gift of prophecy played a
decisive role in the appreciation of sainthood, which was now defined by
obedience to the Holy Spirit which inspired fiery images in those it had
chosen.[87]

---

ate ecclesiastica, q. XIV, a. 5 (Rome edn of 1582), p. 103: 'Quia ergo donum prophetiae
convenit malis hominibus interdum magis quam bonis propter aliquam dispositionem
quam requisivit prophetica revelatio, ideo propter tale donum non debet aliquis pro sancto
venerari vel canonizari, nisi sunt alia signa testificantia eius sanctitatem et bonitatem.' For
the attitude of the medieval Church to prophetic charisma, see P. Alphandéry, 'Prophètes
et ministères prophétiques dans le Moyen Age latin', *Revue d'histoire et de philosophie
religieuse*, 12 (1932), pp. 334–59; Lottin, 'La théorie des dons du Saint-Esprit'.

[84] See above, p. 474.

[85] This also applies to hagiographical literature, which pays more attention to prophetism,
for example, in the case of B. Tommasuccio (d. 1377), who roved the towns of Umbria
and Tuscany denouncing the misdeeds of the clergy and the sins of the faithful: *Leggenda
del Beato Tommasuccio*, ed. Faloci Pulignani.

[86] The content of the visions recorded in canonization processes changes significantly: those
of Clare of Montefalco, according to the enquiry of 1318–19, concerned psychomachy,
the Last Judgement, Hell, Paradise (*PC*, fols. 75, 140, 119, 336, 492, witnesses 1, 2, 3
and 4) and, above all, Christ's Passion (fols. 140, 197, witnesses 1 and 2); St Bridget's
revelations also concerned the principal mysteries of salvation and points of doctrine (*PC*,
art. 32, p. 23), but most of them referred to the papacy and Sweden (pp. 88, 97–8, 379,
384, 498, 519, 525). A few years later, the premonitions attributed to Dorothy of Montau
concerned the Schism, the vicissitudes of the Teutonic order and the conversion of the
Lithuanians (*PC*, art. 30, fol. 312 and fols. 193–4, 238). For the visions of the medieval
mystics, see E. Benz, 'Vision und führung in der christlichen Mystik', *Eranos Jahrbuch*,
3 (1962), pp. 117–69; Benz, *Die Vision: Erfahrungsformen und Bilderwelt* (Stuttgart, 1969).
The inspired discourse of these women who claimed to talk on behalf of God was often
ill received by the clergy who thought that the Revelation had been realized and that
there was nothing to be gained from particular revelations; this was the argument of a
Cyprus Dominican in 1371, who went so far as to call St Bridget mad: *PC Bridget*, pp.
429–31.

[87] This is, in some ways, a wholly traditional approach to sainthood. In Christian hagiography from the *Vita Antonii* of Athanasius, as in the Old Testament, the powers recognized

This conception triumphed at the beginning of the fifteenth century, with Dorothy of Montau, St Catherine of Siena, Joan-Marie of Maillé etc.[88] The trend to deify the saints, which we have traced from the end of the thirteenth century, then reached its apogee. As in the most traditional hagiography, the saints were credited with all the perfections and endowed with all the powers and, more than ever, they appeared as exceptions. But the marvellous in which their existence was steeped was wholly spiritualized; their behaviour and virtues counted for less than the message which the Holy Spirit had instructed them to deliver to the Church. They were no longer active or contemplative but those who could see, who, having had the privilege of meeting and speaking to God, had retained some reflected glory and sought to love him perfectly.[89] This was a definition which did not contradict those which had previously prevailed in ecclesiastical circles, but which implied a new hierarchy in the signs of Christian perfection. In his long deposition at the process of Catherine of Siena, the Dominican Thomas Caffarini, her biographer and propagator of her cult, claimed she had possessed the five following prerogatives:

the prerogatives of the body (stigmata, exchange of hearts etc.)
perfection of virtues and gifts of the Spirit
the particular excellence of her way of life (= the heroic virtues)
the dignity of the three haloes (of the preachers, the virgins and the martyrs)
the particular graces granted her by God.[90]

With the exception of miracle-working, an absence which is hardly surprising, the list includes various elements we have encountered at one or other stage of our study. But the progression Caffarini established is

to the *viri Dei* are the capacity to see things hidden or distant, prediction of future events and thaumaturgic power: see B. Steidle, ' "Homo Dei Antonius". Zum Bild des "Mannes Gottes" im alten Mönchtum', in *Antonius Magnus Eremita, 356–1956* (Rome, 1956), pp. 148–200; G. Penco, 'Le figure bibliche del "vir Dei" nell'agiografia monastica', *Benedictina*, 15 (1963), pp. 1–13. What was new at the end of the Middle Ages was the Roman Church taking the first two of these gifts into account in the evaluation and definition of sainthood. This was perhaps a result of the growing influence of the hagiographical schemas, in particular those which transmitted the *Vitae Patrum*.

[88] John of Marienwerder, confessor and director of conscience of Dorothy of Montau, credited her directly with the seven gifts of the Holy Spirit: *PC Dorothy*, fol. 203, witness 107. At the end of the Middle Ages, the bishops themselves were distinguished for their prophecies: *PC Nicholas of Linköping*, pp. 138, 202, 226, 228.

[89] Catherine's sanctity was defined as 'perfecta Dei dilectio ex clara visone procedens': *PC Catherine of Siena*, p. 152.

[90] *Ibid.*, pp. 144, 150. For Thomas Caffarini and his hagiographical activities, see O. Visani, 'Note su Tommaso Nacci Caffarini', *Rivista di storia e letteratura religiosa*, 9 (1973), pp. 277–97.

significant; under the last heading, he included the gift of seeing into hearts, that of converting sinners and her prophetic activity on behalf of the reform of the Church and the return of the papacy to Rome.[91] Fully accepted by the institution, since they served and helped to strengthen it, the charismatic aspects of sainthood had now moved to the head of the list, in accord with the dominant tendencies of the age.

[91] *PC Catherine of Siena*, p. 147.

THE HAGIOGRAPHICAL MENTALITY AND THE POPULAR MIND

രാരാ

Our study of late medieval canonization processes has revealed two parallel trends: a growing emphasis on the life of the saints and the increasingly strong influence of hagiographical conventions, which eventually made saints into extraordinary beings. To appreciate the significance of this evolution, we need to ask whether it was specific to the documents we have used – the *articuli interrogatorii* and the texts drawn up within the Curia – or was also present in the popular mind. In brief, was it a phenomenon restricted to an ecclesiastical elite or a profound change in religious sensibility?

On the first point, the answer is clear. From the years 1300–50, even in the non-Mediterranean countries, the saints began to be regarded as living beings who had acquired by their merits a power of intercession with God. There is ample evidence that these conceptions were shared by the most diverse circles, which included the common people. Even the role of providing assistance, once attributed to the saints' relics, now tended to be associated with their physical presence. When, for example, in 1371, at an informal preliminary enquiry, the Franciscans of Guingamp asked the Breton peasants why they believed that Charles of Blois was a saint, they replied that, *while he was alive*, prosperity had reigned, whereas, since his death, everything had gone wrong in Brittany.[1] A few years later, in 1414, at the diocesan process of Joan-Marie of Maillé in Touraine, a woman of the people claimed that *'if [she] had still been alive, the plague would not have taken such a terrible toll in the town of Angers'*.[2] In Sweden in the late fourteenth and early fifteenth centuries, the lay witnesses put most emphasis on the prophetic messages delivered by

[1] See note 71 above, p. 464.
[2] See note 72 above, p. 465.

527

the servants of God when they were still in this world and presented this gift as the chief source of their *fama sanctitatis*.[3] In Italy and Provence, the perfection attributed to a man or a woman had long been closely linked to the influence they exercised on the moral and spiritual plane.[4] These similar evaluations attest to the success of the Church's efforts to put consideration of the merits and virtues of servants of God before that of the prodigies performed by their remains. Of course, attitudes did not all change at the same pace, and there were regional differences of emphasis; the mystical phenomena which so delighted the inhabitants of Montefalco and Apt would probably have astounded the Breton or Swedish peasants referred to above. But all were agreed that sainthood was the fruit of a devout, ascetic and virtuous life, assuring to those who led it the power to work miracles.

Logically, this change of perspective ought to have made sainthood more commonplace. In practice, the opposite happened; the late medieval saints, as they are presented in the processes of canonization, are far more extraordinary persons than those of the twelfth and thirteenth centuries. The change is visible in the sphere of the miraculous, since, after 1330, the saints were credited with a great many resurrections which the clergy of the thirteenth century had not dared to attribute to their predecessors; it is even more marked in the ways of evaluating their earthly existence, which, in the fourteenth century, was generally presented as an uninterrupted succession of prodigious events and deeds. This phenomenon, we should be clear at the outset, is not a product of the natural tendency of medieval authors to go always one step further in idealizing their subjects as their historical memory faded. L. de Kerval showed many years ago, with regard to St Antony of Padua, how 'the dosage of the marvellous was stepped up' in the successive versions of his Life, each biographer feeling himself justified in outdoing his predecessor in crediting the famous preacher with new miracles or some additional perfection.[5] In

---

[3] *PC Nicholas of Linköping*, pp. 226–30.

[4] This trend was particularly marked in the Mediterranean countries, as we see from the processes of St Clare of Montefalco and Delphine of Puimichel, but it is also visible in Brittany, *c.*1330, in the process of St Yves, who, according to a parishioner, had been 'quasi continuum documentum et per sua exempla, et opera que eis facto verbo et opere pretendebat', and who was described by a recluse as 'speculum et exemplum' (*PC Yves*, pp. 87, 61).

[5] L. de Kerval, *L'évolution et le développement du merveilleux dans les légendes de Saint Antoine de Padoue* (Paris, 1906). There is, to my knowledge, no worthwhile synthesis of the marvellous in the Middle Ages; there are only very abstract and general remarks in *Le merveilleux: 2e colloque sur les religions populaires (Québec, 1971)*, ed. F. Dumont, J. P. Montminy and M. Stein (Quebec, 1973).

the fourteenth-century processes of canonization, this phenomenon began immediately the saint died; the life of Delphine, as it was presented in the articles of the 1363 enquiry, three years after her death, was already legendary in the strict sense of the word, that is, characterized by a series of prodigies, not the least of which was the celestial music of angelic choirs which resounded through the sky at the moment of her death.[6] Indeed, the recluse of Apt and her husband, St Elzear, seem to be figures straight out of the Golden Legend. Reading documents of this type, the historian who seeks to distinguish fabrication from lived reality is at a loss how to proceed; are we to question the implicit premise which assumes, with regard to the history of medieval culture, a linear evolution leading from symbolism to realism and from the imaginary to the rational? Without going quite so far, we need to ask why, in the late Middle Ages, in a way that seems to us paradoxical, the image of the saints in processes of canonization came much closer to that transmitted by the hagiographical literature.

The first explanation which springs to mind relates to the significance of the canonization procedure itself. Since the thirteenth century, the Church had been anxious to provide only authentic saints whose merits were well established for the devotion of the faithful. But this requirement of veracity could hardly be applied in the sphere of the miraculous; as we have seen, the limited knowledge then available of the laws of nature did not allow much progress in the direction of a more precise demarcation of the field of the miraculous. Even among the 'great minds' of the Curia, it was generally assumed that supernatural facts could not be proved. On the other hand, the Holy See did everything in its power to promote the biographical aspects of sainthood at the expense of miracle-working. In the processes, the sensory code which underlay the popular perception of sainthood was enriched by new elements, such as the gift of tears, and changed significantly; the pleasant smell which had been an attribute of relics became, in the fourteenth century, a gift already possessed by the servants of God in their lifetime.[7] At the end of this process, all that

---

[6] *PC Delphine*, fols. 11–32v. Article 5 of the canonization process of St Nicholas of Tolentino (*PC*, fol. 6) refers to the appearance of an angel to instruct his parents to make a pilgrimage to St Nicholas of Bari if they wished to have a son and to call him Nicholas in honour of their benefactor.

[7] At the process of Delphine, Cardinal Anglic Grimoard claimed that: 'quadam vice, cum intraret cameram ipsius domine Delphine, senciit magnam redolenciam et mirabilem sibi, et quod nunquam simile senciit, et cito evanuit; et credit et videtur sibi quod non fuit naturalis sed celestis et divina' (*PC*, fol. 196v).

counted were outstanding merits, ardent devotion and extraordinary charismas, whereas the conceptions which associated sainthood with bloodshed, a proliferation of miracles and the wise exercise of high office within
the Church or society had lost their power.

The desire to distinguish a few great saints with universal application
from the mass of the *beati*, confined to the level of local cult, had a similar
effect. The elitist policy followed by the papacy in this respect, especially
from the last third of the thirteenth century, meant that the superiority of
the former over the latter had to be made abundantly clear. The clergy,
accordingly, credited them with all the attributes displayed by the saints
in the hagiographical texts. Another factor tended in the same direction:
after 1370, the majority of candidates belonged, more or less, to the mystical current which the hierarchical Church had long regarded with a degree
of suspicion. Some of them were of bourgeois, if not modest, origins. Did
the ecclesiastics who sought to have them canonized perhaps deliberately
present them as beings who were totally detached from reality and the
human condition so as to overcome the handicap of their socio-cultural
origins? The headlong rush towards the supernatural and the extraordinary (levitations, exchanges of hearts, various luminous phenomena) was
intended, from this perspective, to give status to a form of sainthood which
had difficulty in winning acceptance because it questioned the traditional
hierarchies.[8]

But, more importantly, it seems to me that we should seek the origins
of the growing convergence between the canonization processes and the
legends in the changed role assigned to the cult of the saints in the religious
life of the thirteenth and fourteenth centuries. Before 1200, it had primarily been popular with the clergy and the regulars, for whom to meditate
on the life of the servants of God was an occasion for recognizing their
own inadequacies.[9] The laity were really only interested in the miracles,
which aroused their admiration and awe and assured them an effective
protection against adversity.[10] Later, attitudes changed and, under the

---

[8] In the mid-thirteenth century, the Franciscan Lamprecht of Ratisbon asked what it was
that an old beguine could understand better than a learned and scholarly man: K. Weinhold, *Lamprecht von Regensburg, Sanct Francisken Leben und Tochter Syon* (Paderborn,
1880), p. 431.

[9] According to St Bernard, in the *Sermo in Vigilia sanctorum Apostolorum Petri et Pauli*
(quoted by Benedict XIV, *De beatificatione*, I, c. 993), what the monks expected from the
cult of the saints was: 'sic ergo in sanctorum festivitatibus et gaudere et confundi debemus:
gaudere quia patronos praemisimus, confundi quia eos imitari non possumus'.

[10] This generalization must obviously be qualified according to country and milieu. Though
the issue has not yet been systematically studied, it seems clear that in France, by the
twelfth century, there were legendries intended for the knightly aristocracy which concen-

influence of the Mendicant orders, the pastoral aspect of the cult of saints became predominant. Throughout Christendom, especially from the 1230s, preachers disseminated the idea that it was in the life of the saints and not in their miracles that their true greatness lay.[11] But the most impassioned speeches would not have been enough on their own to hold the attention of the faithful and cause them to consider the merits of the servants of God. The saints had to be presented in an attractive and racy way. As Jacques Le Goff has observed, 'what made medieval minds agree to believe in something was not what could be observed and proved by a natural law or by a regularly repeated mechanism; on the contrary, it was the extraordinary, the supernatural or at any rate the abnormal'.[12] As good teachers, the Friars and the clergy were generally careful not to reveal what they really believed, that is, that the greatest, if not the only, miracles of the saints were their works, whether in the form of the foundation of a religious order or the production of theological or spiritual treatises. They selected from their lives only *exempla*, that is, picturesque stories with an edifying intent, telling a lived history, some aspects of which were likely to catch the imagination.[13] With the *exempla*, we remain in the sphere of the *mirabilia*, that is, hagiography. To be effective, the preachers chose to employ publicly this festive language, which, as M. de Certeau has shown, indissolubly links the fantastic and the possible, the imaginary and the exemplary.[14] From this perspective, the evolution of the processes of canonization is only one aspect of a much wider transformation. The

---

trated on the military saints. But such collections seem to have been relatively rare before 1200.

[11] At the beginning of the fourteenth century, the Dominican preacher Giordano da Rivalto declared, without beating about the bush: 'Quando noi volemo conoscere uno santo, la sua grandezza, noi non porremo mente a' miracoli, ma alla vita, che vita egli menò; qui si conosce la grandezza de' santi.' This important text is quoted by C. Delcorno, *Giordano da Pisa e l'antica predicazione volgare* (Florence, 1975), p. 219. Many prologues to four-teenth- and fifteenth-century Lives of saints attest to the insistance of the clergy and regulars on the value of the example of the saints' lives. I quote only one typical example from the Life of Nicholas of Linköping (1414, = *BHL* 6101, p. 314): 'duplici enim de causa merita sanctorum celebramus et recolimus; primo ut deus laudetur et honoretur in sanctis suis qui eos non solum in celo glorificat sed eciam in terris eorum sanctitatem per crebra miracula manifestat, secundo ut populus per eorum sancta exempla excitetur ad bona opera, ut imitari non pigeat quos celebrare delectat atque ita non desperent homines eciam sibi, si voluerint, iustificacionis graciam posse prestari'. Note the difference of emphasis compared with the passage from St Bernard quoted in note 9 above.

[12] J. Le Goff, *La civilisation de l'Occident médiéval* (Paris, 1964), p. 402 (trans. Julia Barrow as *Medieval civilization 400–1500* (London, 1988), p. 329).

[13] J.-C. Schmitt, 'Recueils franciscains d' "exempla" et perfectionnement des techniques intellectuelles du XIIIe au Xve siècle', *BECh*, 135 (1977), pp. 5–21, with bibliography.

[14] M. de Certeau, sv Hagiographie, in *Encyclopaedia universalis*, 8 (Paris, 1968), pp. 207–9; Certeau, *L'écriture de l'histoire* (Paris, 1975), pp. 274–82.

emphasis on the most extraordinary aspects is less a product of a clerical reading of sainthood than of the desire of the Church to popularize a few 'stars' whose cult it wished to promote.[15]

One might be tempted to conclude that promotion of the biographical aspects of sainthood in the context of a hagiographical presentation was simply a device employed by the clergy to convey a moral and religious message. In fact, the problem is more complex; if, at the end of the Middle Ages, the saints were presented as exceptional beings, was it because the distance between lived sainthood and the sainthood constructed or reconstructed after the event by the clergy had increased?[16] Or had the concrete existence of the saints and the interpretation spontaneously given by those who had known them in their lifetime evolved in a more spiritual direction, to the point where it came spontaneously to conform to the models provided by the hagiographical tradition?

Paradoxical though it might seem, the latter thesis should not be rejected out of hand. In the thirteenth- and, above all, the fourteenth-century processes, the role played in the existence of the servants of God by meditation on the Lives of saints is often mentioned; witnesses testified that St Margaret of Hungary read the Passions of the martyrs and Clare of Montefalco the Lives of the virgins.[17] In the process of Charles of Blois, it was emphasized that he knew by heart the Golden Legend and the *Vitae Patrum*, and many other hagiographical texts which were read to him at mealtimes.[18] The same was true of St Bridget, according to the Swedish witnesses.[19] Lastly, the better Scandinavian bishops of this period were praised for having composed liturgical offices and *Vitae* in honour of the

---

[15] See, for example, the *exemplum* on St Elizabeth of Thuringia which appears in a sermon delivered by the Dominican Thomas of Chartres at the church of Saint-Germain of Auxerre in 1273 (MS BN, lat. 16481, fol. 214): 'Exemplum fuit quaedam bona virgo que vocatur Sancta Elizabet non mater beati Johannis, sed filia cuiusdam regis pagani qui vocabatur Landograndi, Landegrant. Et ista filia erat multum devota et humilis et circa opera caritatis et pietatis intenta, ita quod recipiebat in occulto pauperes in camera sua, et lavabat pedes eorum, et cubabat in pulcro lecto suo. Unde contigit quod dominus quodam die apparuit ei in specie unius leprosi horribilissimi. Ipsa tamen benigne eum recepit et lavit ei pedes. Quo requirente ut eum poneret, cubare in lectum suum, fecit, et de hoc accusata patri, pater accedens nichil invenit in lecto nisi rosas pulcerrimas et ita totum lectum odoriferum quod, cognita causa conversus fuit ad fidem. Rogabimus, etc.' (I would like to thank Nicole Bériou for having kindly supplied me with this text.)

[16] I prefer the expression 'constructed sainthood' to 'imagined sainthood', the phrase used by J. Poulain (*L'idéal de sainteté dans l'Aquitaine carolingienne*, p. 33). The word imagined seems to imply something fictitious lacking relation to reality, which is not the case here.

[17] *PC Margaret of Hungary*, pp. 213, 236, 254; *PC Clare of Montefalco*, fol. 165.

[18] *PC Charles of Blois*, p. 142; *PC Peter of Luxembourg*, art. 56, p. 484.

[19] *PC Bridget*, p. 66.

Virgin and their countries' principal saints.[20] It is not impossible that, by dint of poring over these texts, they were eventually permeated by them, and that they took from them, for example, their zeal for asceticism and virginity. We here encounter, in all their complexity, surprising interactions between the lived reality and the imaginary, in a society which, having a different conception of historical time than we do, regarded as current and still valid spiritual experiences which had occurred many centuries ago, in a very different social and historical context.

But the saints were not, after all, representative of average humanity and the fact that they were fascinated by hagiographical texts is not enough on its own to prove that this was a general phenomenon. There is other evidence to suggest that, after 1300, in the West, the religious climate became more favourable to the success of the themes conveyed by the legends. The spiritual literature of the fourteenth and fifteenth centuries has significant similarities with the trends we have noted in the processes of canonization and the *Vitae* of the same period. Chief among them is the disregard for the works and the emphasis on the gratuitous nature of divine election, independent of whatever merits the person might accumulate.[21] Charitable activity on behalf of the poor, militant action to bring about justice or peace, even work, which had, up to the end of the thirteenth century, been important elements in Christian perfection, were now hardly mentioned and seem even to have been held in disrepute. In contrast, we see the spread of a mystical conception of sainthood, defined as a state of inner asceticism so extreme that it allowed the soul to receive the Gift of God and the infusion of the Holy Spirit. Such a spirituality, precluding engagement with the world, reduced to an inner combat between the virtues and the vices, was perfectly in tune with the hagiographical schemas in which the promotion of the unequivocally supernatural emphasized the passive role of the creature in the face of the action of grace. The spectacle afforded by the saints in this world thus led contemporaries to see their life less as the history of an ever closer collaboration with God than as a spectacular demonstration of his power.

The increasing influence of the hagiographical conventions in late medieval processes of canonization is therefore the consequence of a twofold process: the clergy who sought to promote the cult of new saints submitted, for the approval of the witnesses, a model which was both in accord

---

[20] *PC Nicholas of Linköping*, art. 28, p. 64; *PC Brynulph of Skara*, art. 7, p. 142.
[21] Well brought out by F. Rapp, *L'Eglise et la vie religieuse en Occident à la fin du Moyen Age* (Paris, 1971), pp. 226–44.

with tradition and rich in marvels capable of arousing the enthusiasm of the faithful. But this transposition was easier to achieve to the extent that the life which the servants of God had actually led tended to resemble this ideal and purely spiritual conception of sainthood.

GENERAL CONCLUSION

CACACA

At the end of this study, it remains to account for the contradictory conclusions which have emerged. For, whereas in Books I and II I have emphasized the gulf between popular or local sainthood and official sainthood as regards cult and typology, in Book III I have laid stress on a 'popular mind', which seems to rule out profound divergences. A discussion of the content of mental attitudes and the problems analysing them poses for the historian will, I hope, make it possible to reconcile these apparently incompatible assertions.

A mentality, in the words of Jacques Le Goff, is first 'what an individual has in common with other people of his time' or again, 'the impersonal nature of thought'.[1] This definition applies very well to the signs and manifestations of sainthood which were the subject of a general consensus in the late Middle Ages. From the 'great minds' to the peasantry, no-one questioned the existence and the validity of the sensory code which made it possible to recognize a servant of God. Nor did anyone contest the importance of the physiological aspects of sanctification or the prerogatives of the bodies of saints, whether with regard to their incorruptibility or their indifference to the laws of gravity. Lastly, it was generally accepted that the radiance emanating from relics was particularly effective in the place where they lay, even if their beneficial effects were not always defined in the same terms. These ideas, generally accepted by the people of the age, were the criteria for the selective perception which led them to bestow on some of their contemporaries the title of *beatus* or *sanctus*. It is difficult to be precise about the origins of this mode of thought. It probably owed much to the influence of hagiography, mysterious and

---

[1] J. Le Goff, 'Les mentalités: une histoire ambiguë', in *Faire de l'histoire*, III: *Nouveaux objets* (Paris, 1974), pp. 76–94.

marvellous language which performed an essential function of communication in medieval society.[2] But the legends themselves conveyed a collection of representations and myths also found in the Greek and Roman
worlds and among the Germanic peoples. Christianity had eventually
assimilated them, either through certain cultic continuities or, above all,
the intermediary of the Bible, often used in the Middle Ages to provide
a scriptural justification for religious practices which were alien to the
spirit of the Gospels.[3] We may also note, in this connection, a near total
unanimity with regard to miracles and, more generally, the results which
could justifiably be expected from the intervention of the saints. When
they suffered from toothache or their life was threatened by a serious
illness, the most sober theologians invoked their heavenly protectors just
like the peasant worried about his crops or the fisherman in peril on the
sea. And when, in the fourteenth century, the field of intercession
extended to all aspects of existence, including the moral and religious life,
it was not only the laity who asked for more than cures. A minority of
critical minds apart – perhaps more numerous before 1250 than after –
people believed that everything was possible to God and his saints. We
have found, as a result, almost no significant disagreements in this sphere.

These nevertheless existed, as the different meanings of sainthood discussed above reveal. The disagreement concerned not the signs but their
interpretation. The people tended to accord them absolute value: some
cried saint at the sight of an angelic face or an imposing physique; for
others, the discovery of well-preserved human remains was enough to give
rise to a cult. For the clerical and lay elite, this purely anthropological
language made no sense. They did not doubt the reality of the signs, but
saw them as no more than the consequences of a moral behaviour and
spiritual life of which the Church was the only judge. The same was true,
as we have seen, with miracles. The papacy rarely denied the authenticity
of those submitted for its approval, content to verify that they were well
attested and useful to the faith. But in the eyes of the 'great minds',
convinced of the ambiguity of supernatural phenomena, their importance
was secondary. The presence of miracles continued to be necessary for

---

[2] B. de Gaiffier, 'La mentalité de l'hagiographie d'après quelques travaux récents', *Anal.
Boll.*, 86 (1968), pp. 391–9.
[3] A. Dupront, 'Anthropologie du sacré et cultes populaires. Histoire et vie du pèlerinage
en Europe Occidentale', *Miscellanea historiae ecclesiasticae*, 5 (1974), pp. 235–8. See also
the works of P. Saintyves, which are stimulating even if one cannot accept his view of
the saints as 'successors to the gods': *Essais de folklore biblique: magie, mythes et miracles
dans l'Ancien et le Nouveau Testament (Paris, 1922); En marge de la Légende Dorée.*

the Holy See to pronounce on the sanctity of a servant of God, but they now served only to assess the diffusion of a reputation which was based on other things; they were concessions to popular simplicity, not proofs of sainthood.[4]

The fact that a gulf developed between the various conceptions of saint-hood is also a feature of mentality, though it is inconsistent with the consensus I have claimed above. In the words of Jacques Le Goff, 'the existence of many mentalities at one period is one of the difficult but essential facts of the history of mentalities'.[5] We should perhaps be more precise and distinguish two orders of reality customarily confused within the concept of mentality, which makes it difficult for the historian to use. At one level, we may retain this term to indicate a group of representations and mental images common to all the people of a period. They are deter-mined by tradition, legacy of a sometimes distant past, but, above all, by the idea which, within the context of a given civilization, one could form of God, nature and the world order, given the level of technical and cultural development. These *a priori* schemas are not immutable, but they change very slowly, as long as the basic certainties on which they are based remain in place.[6] They are hardly affected by changed ideas. Thus, as we have seen, the highly original definition given by St Thomas Aquinas of the miracle or the questioning of traditional views of marriage, work and money under the influence of the pastoral thinking of the Mendicants had little impact on the way in which these realities were approached and evaluated in the canonization processes of the time.

One cannot, however, reduce the working of the human mind to a collection of spontaneous reactions setting in motion elementary mechan-isms. Just as, if not more, important is the way in which the mental field of individuals is constructed and organized in depth. To describe this second level, which is where the representations combine and organize in hierarchized systems, I propose the term mental structures, hackneyed though it may be. It is here that perceptible differences appear in the

---

[4] From the fourteenth century, in the prologues to the Lives of saints, the authors often explained that their works could be understood on three levels – the miracles, the example of the virtues of the saint, and his or her doctrine – only the first level, obviously, applying to most of them. See, for example, Laurent, 'Légende de la B. Marguerite de Città di Castello', *AFP*, 10 (1940), p. 110: 'ut quos doctrine fluenta non nutriunt, foveat exemplar sanctorum vel eos aliciant miracula vel prodigia quos non trahunt vite exempla seu vestigia beatorum'.

[5] J. Le Goff, 'Les mentalités', p. 88.

[6] See the remarks of G. Duby, 'L'histoire des systèmes de valeur', *History and Theory*, 11 (1972), pp. 15–25.

interpretation and definition of sainthood. Unlike mentalities, mental structures felt the influence of cultural trends. The spiritual experiences taking place within cloisters and convents, the theological debate, from the twelfth century on, about the importance of the virtues and the gifts of the Holy Spirit in Christian perfection, promoted, among an elite, an awareness of the importance of moral conduct and, more generally, the imitation of Christ in the appreciation of sanctity. Without contesting the traditional signs, a minority of the clergy and devout laity endeavoured, with the support of the Roman Church, to win acceptance for a purified conception of the religious life. This consigned to obscurity the popular 'martyrs', touching victims of the inexorable battle between Good and Evil, whose cult expressed the basic dualism of the masses more than their faithfulness to the spirit of the Gospels. Similarly, there was soon a loss of interest in the sanctity of function, of kings and princes, but also bishops, whose chief virtues, in the eyes of the people (*habundantia, curialitas, magnanimitas*), seemed too close to the criteria for human success. Sainthood eventually became a purely spiritual notion, unconnected to temporal realities and the values of the surrounding society. From a typically 'Gregorian' perspective, the takeover of the cult of the saints by the Roman Church, however late and partial, must result, in the end, in a complete distinction between the profane and the religious, now defined as an autonomous entity.

At the beginning of the fifteenth century, this point had not yet been reached. More precisely, the papacy, weakened by the Schism and the Hussite wars, was in no position to impose on the faithful conceptions that the majority of them did not share. The massive support of the laity, not least the temporal princes, for certain cults which were deplored by those committed to a purified and intellectualized Christianity, made it impossible for the latter openly to reveal their feelings. They had to resign themselves to tolerating what they could not suppress, even if they expressed their scepticism or hostility in private writings. In the face of these devotions, the Church adopted a dual attitude. Rather than seeking to uproot those which already existed, it preferred to give them official recognition in an attempt to eliminate the risks of deviation. This was shown, for example, in the case of Werner of Bacharach (d. 1287), whose cult was approved by pontifical legates in 1426–8 and who, from 'martyr' victim of the Jews, became, in the sixteenth century, an inoffensive patron of wine-makers, venerated from the Rhineland to the Jura and Auvergne. But what mattered most was to ensure that such abuses were not repeated.

I have chosen to end my study in 1431, which saw the end of the pontificate of Martin V. It was also the year of the process of Joan of Arc. That this was a political process hardly needs to be emphasized, but it was also the first process undertaken by the 'great minds' from the universities in order to prevent a popular cult from being born and developing. Sure that they knew what true Christianity was, the judges of Rouen aimed to brand with the mark of Satan the religion of Joan of Arc. The Fairy Tree, the fountain and the voices of SS Catherine and Margaret, the marks of veneration which had surrounded the Maid in the hour of her success, were all held against her as a result, essentially, of the same rejection: that of a sainthood lived and recognized by simple people.

REPORT OF A CURIALIST ON THE LIFE AND MIRACLES OF ST THOMAS CANTILUPE, BISHOP OF HEREFORD (D. 1282) (WRITTEN BETWEEN 1318 AND 1320)

*ഔ*ഔ*ഔ*

The words or phrases preceded by an asterisk which appear at the foot of the following pages are found in the margin of the manuscript, at the level of the line indicated by the asterisk.

The first figure in brackets which follows the word *miraculum* (or *miracula*) indicates the number of the miracle in the *Summarium*. The second figure, also in brackets, refers to the number of the miracle among the thirty-eight recorded at the enquiry of 1307; they are listed in detail in table 32.

(MS BN, lat. 5373 A, fols. 66r–69v)

In negocio canonizacionis pie memorie domini Thome quondam Herefordensis episcopi Sedes Apostolica de quinque principaliter mandavit inquiri, videlicet de fide, moribus, vita, fama et miraculis. De quatuor primis articulis multa laude digna videntur probari, ut patet in sexterno continente quedam excerpta de processu inquisicionis originalis ad Sedem predictam transmisse. Deponunt namque testes quod ipse a catholicis parentibus et multum nobilibus procreatus, de patre videlicet quondam domino Guillelmo de Cantalupo milite et barone, qui fuit senescallus quondam domini Henrici illustris regis Anglie, de matre quondam domina de Milecenta, comitissa Ebroycen, in Normannia, uxore dicti domini Guillelmi, que fuit filia quondam Godefridi de Gurnay, nupta prius comiti Ebroycensi et, eo mortuo, predicto domino Guillelmo. Natus fuit et baptizatus in villa de Hamelden, Lincolnensis diocesis, in quo loco nativitatis eius in honorem et reverentiam ipsius dicitur constructa esse capella per comitem Cornubie Edmundum filium Ricardi quondam regis Alemannie, in qua Deus pro ipso domino Thoma dicitur miracula operari. Fratres carnales habuit quatuor: magistrum Hugonem, magnum clericum, dominos Johannem, Guillelmum et Nicholaum milites, quorum patruus fuit

540

dominus Gualterius quondam episcopus Wygornensis reputatus sancte vite. In minori et maiori etate multum studuit et fuit magister in artibus, doctor in decretis, magister in theologia et rexit actu in artibus Parisius, Oxonii in decretis et post in theologia, et eiusdem universitatis Oxoniensis cancellarius fuit et ipsum studium tempore sui officii bene rexit. Apocalipsim in studio Parisiensi legit. Habebat ipse dominus Thomas in studio Parisiensi et aliis locis in familia sua continue de robis suis unum capellanum sibi missam valde mane antequam exiret ad scolas vel alia loca celebrantem. Beneficiatus fuit in diversis ecclesiis et bene se habuit in eis. Hinc ante episcopatum magnum et honorabilem statum et circa mille marcos redditus (habuit). In beneficiis et dignitatibus ecclesiasticis dispensationes habuit a felicis recordationis Innocentio papa quarto ut civili iure per quadriennium studere posset et super pluralitate beneficiorum et dignitatum. Capellanus domini pape factus fuit ab eodem Innocentio in exilio Lugduni. Cancellarius fuit et consiliarius clare memorie Henrici illustris regis Anglie patris domini Edwardi, postea eiusdem domini Edwardi consiliarius.

In statu episcopali episcopatum et ecclesiam Herefordensem bene rexit. Bone vite fuit, verax et fidelis, bene morigeratus, mitis, mansuetus, humilis et paciens misericors et benignus, elemosinarius magnus, pacificus, iustus et timens Deum, devotus in oracione et in contemplacione assiduus, pervigil et intentus; lacrimas in missa a canone usque ad finem multas effundebat, psalmos penitentiales cum letaniis et officium defunctorum cotidie recitabat, stolam ad collum subtus capam vel rodundellum quando equitabat ad modum crucis quasi semper portabat ut paratus esset ad confirmandum pueros occurentes. Predicator bonus, reprehensor maliloquorum, in comedendo et bibendo sobrius, ieiunator magnus et raro comedens nisi semel in die, carnes quarta feria et vinum ut plurimum sexta feria non sumebat. Camisiam cilicinam ad carnem vestiebat, zona eciam cilicina nodosa et aspera latitudinis duarum palmarum et quandoque ferrea carnem cingebat occulte. Ante episcopatum et in episcopatu pudicus fuit et castus, adeo quod de virginitate et puritate commendatus fuit a confessore suo fratre Roberto de Kylewardeby magistro in theologia, archiepiscopo Cantuarensi et postea cardinali, quando sub ipso archiepiscopo Oxonii incepit ipse Thomas in theologia. Discretus fuit et prudens, fortis et constans in recuperandis, tuendis et defendendis iuribus sui episcopatus, et multa propter hoc adversa sustinuit. Tempore felicis recordationis pape Martini quarti, accessit ad Curiam Romanam apud Urbem Veterem in vigilia beati Barnabe apostoli anno domini millesimo

CC LXXXII° causa prosequendarum appellationum que pro parte sua a bone memorie fratre I. archiepiscopo Cantuariensi et eius officiale propter diversa gravamina fuerant interiecta, et ibi a domino papa Martino et a cardinalibus cum osculo pacis benigne receptus et tandem in ipsa Curia infirmitate correptus, perceptis ecclesiasticis sacramentis, ad dominum feliciter transmigravit.

De quinto vero articulo, videlicet de miraculis, sciendum est quod XXVIII miracula de originali processu cum suis probacionibus excerpta in hoc opusculo continentur, super quibus potest de aliquibus dubitari. Ad quorum evidentiam notandum est quod operationem miraculorum fidei christicolarum debere attribui evangelico testimonio comprobatur, dum Salvator apostolis et discipulis (v°) in eum credentibus largitur potestatem infirmos curandi, mundandi leprosos, ejiciendi demones et mortuos suscitandi ac post resurrectionem suam eamdem potestatem ceteris in ipsum credentibus repromisit, que repromissio in antiquis sanctis adimpleta, testante Apostolo ad Hebreos: "Sancti per fidem vicerunt regna, operati sunt iusticiam, adepti sunt repromissiones", videtur in modernis temporibus fide et meritis dicti domini Thome in subscriptis casibus effectu mirifico comprobari. *

Miraculum (1) (= 1) Puella siquidem Iohanna nomine, liberis parentibus procreata, quinquennis, de parochia de Maurdyn dicte Herefordensis diocesis, per quemdam puerum sibi coetaneum in aquam cuiusdam stagni ludendo precipitata et in dicta aqua altitudinis XII pedum submersa ab hora diei decima usque post occasum solis, in mense Aprilis, et tandem ** de eodem stagno extracta mortua per patrem eiusdem beato Thome predicto cum magna devotione et lacrimis coram multis astantibus mensurata hoc ordine est vite et sanitati pristine restituta. Corpus siquidem ipsius *** puelle de aqua extractum et, ut premittitur, mensuratum, dum per pedes levaretur et aqua per os et nares et ceteras aperturas corporis habundantius proflueret et sonitus infra corpus ex impetu acque exeuntis audiretur, nullo signo vite in dicto corpore apparente, tandem delatum est ad domum parentum et accenso igne iuxta matrem tunc partu gravidam volente et agente dicta matre in lecto cum ea collocatam orantibusque patre matre ceterisque circumstantibus, circa auroram diei sequentis movit pedem dextrum, quam motionem in toto corpusculo est quidam tremor seu fremi-

---

* Mt. X, Mc. V, Luc. IX, Luc. X, Mc. ultimo, Ad He. XV.
** temporis spatium quo fuit mortus non probatur per omnes testes sed per aliquos.
*** Probantur per VI testes mors et resuscitatio miraculosa.

tus subsecutus et applicante matre os suum ad aurem puelle et petente: "quid in acqua facere voluisti?", respondit: "Iohannes me impulit", quo nomine puer qui ipsam impulerat vocabatur. Et sic dicta infantula dicto modo extincta et miraculose meritis dicti sancti vivificata pluribus orantibus et deum in sancto suo devote glorificantibus, viva omnium oculis est ostensa et coram multitudine ad altare parochialis ecclesie eiusdem ville in honore sancti Ethelberti regis et martiris dedicatum est portata et tandem ad tumulum dicti sancti Thome in Herefordensi ecclesia fuit

Dubio   sollempniter presentata.

Solutio   Dices mirandum videtur ad quem effectum per patrem dicte puelle fuerat corpusculum mensuratum. Responsio: consuetudinis est in plerisque partibus hoc fieri ut de eadem mensura ad reliquias sancti in Dei et

*   ipsius honorem fiat cerea facula vel candela; qui mos mensurandi ab Helya incepit et Heliseo. Helyas enim expandit se atque mensus est super puerum tribus vicibus clamavitque ad Dominum: "Domine Deus meus,

**   revertatur anima pueri huius in viscera eius". Heliseus autem posuit os suum super os pueri et oculos suos super oculis suis et manus super manus et incurvavit se super eum ad modum mensurantis. Ante legem etiam et in lege per sacrificia aut signa alia exteriora fiebat exterior protestatio devocionis interne, ex quibus omnibus sumpsit exordium quod fideles plerique in signum devocionis erga Deum et sanctum cuius meritis se sperant in tribulacione iuvari, mensurant mortuum aut languentem in signum sue devocionis et fidei, vel faciunt ymaginem vel quid aliud ut eo viso Deus honoretur in sanctis quorum merita in necessitatibus nostris suffragantur.

Dubio   Si mensuratio ex causis premissis fieri consuevit, mirum est quod sine precedenti motu pedis aut alterius membri dicta puella non fuit subito

***   resuscitata, si miraculo debeat ascribi. Dicit enim Beda super Marcum et est in omelia: sanitas que Domini confertur imperio tota simul redit tanto robore convertente ut eis continuo qui se adiuvarant ministrare sufficiat.

Solutio   Plura sunt scripture exempla quibus ostenditur quod quamvis vita vel sanitas que Domini confertur imperio tota simul redeat, signa tamen sanit-

****   atis aut vite aliquibus certis indiciis precedentibus ostenditur. De puero enim per Heliseum resuscitatum, legitur quod oscitavit septies et demum aperuit oculos ita quod plenam vivificationem signa vite aliqua pre-

---

* III Regum XVII.
** IV Regum.
*** Vide illud Marcum et Mattheum VIII, quo curata est socrus Petri.
**** IIII Regum IIII.

cedebant. Narrat etiam beatus Gregorius quod ingrediente anima in corpus pueri omne corpusculum contremuit et demum benedicens manum pueri tenuit et sic patri viventem dedit. Legitur etiam in vita sancti Ypoliti de quodam cui miraculose coxa nova loco vetuste divina ulcione prius consumpte fuerat restituta quod illa nova mollior quam vetusta ad sustinenciam corporis non potuit exequari vi [f° 67] unde ad publicationem miraculi per annum claudicavit et tunc beata Virgo precepit beato Ypolito ut quicquid curationi deesset suppleret. Plura alia in scripturis canonicis et sanctorum huius rei sunt exempla. Congruunt autem predicto miraculo fides et devotio parentum et aliorum in oratione usque ad resuscitationem puelle perseverantium, innocentia etiam puerorum, impellentis videlicet et impulsi, et cetera que legentibus deposiciones testium plene patent.

Miraculum (2) (= 2)   Ad laudem meritorum eiusdem sancti, accidit quod puer nondum biennis sed etatis unius anni et dimidii, Iohannis nomine, de villa que dicitur Parva Marche intra parochiam de Ledebury, Herefordensis diocesis, aqua submersus et mortuus de aqua extractus ad pie memorie dictum Thomam olim Herefordensem episcopum mensuratus, est miraculose ordine qui subsequitur vite pristine restitutus. Quadam die martis ante festum Ascensionis domini, absente patre dicti pueri et matre intra domum in necessario occupata ministerio, dictus puer domum in qua erat mater exiit quem expleto opere quod tunc agebat ipsa mater Editha nomine quesivit et circuens plateam domosque vicinorum et filium suum non inveniens, tandem circumspiciens presentibus duobus de vicinis, vidit filium suum iacentem submersum et mortuum in quadam aqua iuxta domum suam in qua solebant animalia adaquari habente profunditatem usque ad humeros humani corporis, facie autem dicti pueri versa versus fundum acque. Dicta mulier in aquam descendit ac filium extrahens coram dictis vicinis suis super terram posuit mortuum elevatoque corpore per unum eorum Gilbertum nomine capite dimisso ut aqua flueret nullo signo vite in eo apparente ipsoque aqua repleta, lamentantibus matre et vicinis ac patre superveniente, supervenerunt duo equites incogniti et descendentes de equis compatientes parentibus lugentibus et aliis qui astabant, monuerunt astantes ut flexis genibus rogarent Dominum quatenus meritis dicti domini Thome quondam Herefordensis episcopi vitam concederet dicto puero sic mortuo et submerso, unusque eorum extracto filo corpus ad dictum dominus Thomam mensuravit et post lapsum temporis, elevato

---

* libro dialogorum de sancto Benedicto.

dicto puero et aqua per meatus corporis exeunte, post ipso in terra reposito, apperuit primum unum oculum, secundo alium et sic per dies
sequentes pristine est sanitati restitutus, hoc excepto quod in oculis et
naso carnem habuit quasi viridem et croceo colore permixtam.

Dubio   Mirum videtur si miraculo pueri huius resuscitatio debet ascribi quoniam primo unum oculum aperuit, secundo alterum tertio os, ipso loqui
non valente usque ad diem tertium post resuscitationem antedictam nec
usque ad sequentem diem sabbati ambulare.

Solutio   Operationum vitalium in resuscitato aut curato apparitio successiva in
quibusdam antiquis miraculis invenimus preter illa enim que superius
*   expressa sunt teste Beda. Curatio miraculosa est aliquociens successiva.
Sanctus enim Iohannes Eboracensis archiepiscopus brachium virginis
tumore tanta inflatum ut nichil prorsus in cubito inflexionis haberet, benedicens primo sua benedictione sedavit dolorem, deinde fuga tumoris horrendi est secuta nec statim sed facto temporis non modico intervallo.
**   Demoniacus etiam curatus a domino, eiecto spiritu immundo, factus est
quasi mortuus et non statim viribus restitutus quousque dominus tenuit
manum eius. Que aliquotiens eveniunt propter teporem devotionis orantium. Unde et parentes huius pueri non leguntur in attestionibus divinum
implorasse auxilium nisi ab aliis excitati nec etiam in oratione diutius
perstitisse.

Dubio   Dubium oriri potest quin post resuscitationem non sint omnes partes
corporis colori pristino restitute apparentibus in quibusdam partibus coloribus dissuetis, cum potentie divine sit plenam restituere sanitatem.

Solutio   Respondetur quod sicut in corpore Christi apparuerunt cicacrices ad probationem veri corporis et victoriam ac gloriam resurgentis, sicut etiam in
corporibus martirum idem creditur esse futurum ad augmentum glorie et
signum sue victorie quam moriendo pro Christi nomine reportaverunt,
dicente Beda super Lucam de Christo: "non ex impotentia curandi cicatrices in Christo fuerunt sed ut in perpetuum victorie sue circumferat
***   triumphum", et Augustinus, De Civitate Dei: "fortassis in ille regno in
corporibus martyrum videbimus vulnerum cicatrices que pro Christi
nomine pertulerunt". Consimiliter in corpore suscitato reservantur vestigia generis mortis de qua est vite priori donatus ad monumentum talis
resuscitationis et edificationem illius in quo conversatur populi christiani,
quod in plerisque aliis legitur esse factum, ut patet ex dictis in precedenti

    *   Quinto libro de gestis Anglorum, III.
   **   Marcus, V.
  ***   Aug. De Civitate Dei, libro XXII.

miraculo. Hoc secundum miraculum quo ad substantiam facti probatur per quinque testes, sexto deponente de auditu tantum. Item presentes deponunt concorditer de morte pueri et resuscitatione eius sed de spacio temporis inter signa vite que apparuerunt pater a matre discordat, quod patris simplicitati imputandum (est), quia alii testes cum matre concordant.(v°).

Miraculum (3) (= 4) Tertium miraculum de filio cuiusdam piscatoris habente novem annos in etate vocato Nicolao submerso in Wayn quadam vigilia Penthecostes et mensurato ad dictum sanctum Thomam et eius meritis resuscitato. Videtur concorditer probari per quatuor testes quo ad omnia contingencia mortem et submersionem dicti Nicolai et eius miraculosam resuscitationem, licet in stato eiusdem pueri nunciantis submersionem dicta Nicolai aliqui testes discordent, que discordia non videtur eorum deposiciones de miraculo quod contingit vitiare. Sed hic possunt *Dubio* oriri duo dubia: primo an dictus Nicolaus lintheamine involutus potuit per naturam dicto tempore quo fuit in aqua habere vitam circa cor et membra vitalia sicut habuit oculos eo tempore apertos sub aqua.

Respondendum est quod non per naturam. De oculis siquidem, natur- *Solutio* ale est quod in eo statu quo cadens aut mergens se in aqua tenet oculos in prima submersione in eodem statu quamdiu est sub aqua habebit eosdem. Unde refertur quod aliquociens nauta portans in ore oleum descendens in aquam ad evellendam de fundo anchoram fixam descendit in eam oculis apertis et emisso oleo clare videns anchoram extrahit. Quando autem pulmo cessat ab attractu aeris et expellitur aer sine tractu alterius ita quod homo respirare non potest, necesse est hominem mori per naturam quantum ad refrigerationem fervoris circa cor et in corde attrahitur aer, quo attractu cessante et alio aere non attracto, necesse est hominem mori per naturam et morti attestatur habundancia aque replens vacuitates et receptacula aeris circa vitalia animalis. A puero autem iste exivit aqua ad mensuram duarum lagenarum.

Secundo dubitari potest quomodo si miraculose resucitatus extitit, non *Dubio* fuerat ei per longa aubsequentia spacia temporis sanitas restituta. Dicen- *Solutio* dum est quod si post resurectionem signum precedentis mortis eius retinuerit in corpore in coloris apparentia et aliis indiciis infirmatum, non est mirum. Hoc enim in plerisque antiquitus legitur esse factum et Beda * narrat de sancto Furseo quod anima eius a corpore educta et spiritu

* III libro de gestis Anglorum.

hominis mortui per demones indigne proiecto miro modo contacta post regressum eiusdem anime ad corpus eiusdem sancti omnibus diebus vite sue signum incendii quod in anima pertulit visibile cunctis in humero maxillaque portavit mirumque in modeum que anima in occulto passa sit caro palam premonstrabat. Si hoc in sancto gestum est, multo magis ad resuscitati hominis exercicium et mortis precedentis indicium color mortis et interpolate infirmitatis attractus aut parvitas in resuscitato corpore remanere poterit.

Miraculum (4) (= 5) Miraculum de resuscitatione Galfridi pueri etatis unius anni et dimidii cuius caput per plaustrum super eum transiens conquassatum probatur per duos testes, de quo miraculo dubium oriri non potest, nisi quod ex precedentibus est solutum.

Miraculum (5) (= 10) Miraculum de resuscitatione Rogeri pueri etatis duorum annorum et trium mensium. Cecidit in fossatum saxosum castri de Conewaye altitudinis XXVIII pedum. Probatur per sex testes.

Dubio Dubium autem esse potuit quomodo tenerum corpus pueri super fundum lapideum cadens de tanta profunditate non est totum conquassa-
Solutio tum. Dicendum quod licet fuit tenerum, tamen minoris ponderis quam corpus perfecti hominis et quanto minoris ponderis, tanto minor debebat apparere fractura minoremque ictum dare in descensu contingendo rupem vel terram et cum hoc modus casus fortuiti facit ad minorem corporis concussionem. Si enim in descensu membra et tibie quieta teneantur velud lapis fortiorem ictum dabit corpus cadens. Si vero in descensu membra predicta moveantur, minus corpus confrangetur. Unde corpus descendens a magna altitudine si in descendendo per aliquem interpellantem moveatur extra lineam descensus perpendicularem, minus sentiat de lesura, quod experimentaliter probatur in tantum quod si propre terram fiet dictus impulsus extra lineam sui descensus, vix fractura in corpore apparebit. Motus autem membrorum pueri ex hoc probatur quod inventum fuit corpus una tibia erecta et alia complicata. Item ex alia causa hoc evenire potuit, scilicet ex modo contingendi rupem in ipso casu si videlicet non de toto corpore eque plrimo sive equaliter cadebat super fundum, quod videtur evenisse ex tribus in dicto puero ex eo quod inventum fuit corpus eius super latus unum iacens, ex quo esse potuit quod manus sinistra primo terram tangebat in descensu. [f° 68r) Secundo ex livore sinistre vel
* dextre maxille, tertio ex livore coxe eiusdem partis ex quibus patet quod

---

* Mater deposuit de dextra parte, alii de sinistra sed aliis contingentibus substantiam facti plene concordat.

discordia quorumdam testium dicentium in loco casus dicti Rogerii fuisse modicam terram, aliis contrarium deponentibus non facit ad eventum illum de corporis integritate nec eciam vitiat miraculum quantum ad sub-stanciam facti quod evenit. Secundo quomodo non sine fractura corpus potuit mortuum inveniri. Et dicendum quod esse potuit ex interiorum membrorum et partium concussione quod necesse fuit ex casu predicto evenire mortique ipsius attestatur membrorum rigiditas frigidus et congel-atio roris supra corpus, carencia motus et usus sensuum, privatio anelitus et temporis spacium quo dicta mortis signa in ipse apparuerunt, de quibus omnibus sufficienter deposuerunt testes. Narravit quidam magister in theologia quod vidit puerum decem et octo annorum cadentem in domo bone memorie Iacobi de Columpna olim sacrosancte romane ecclesie dya-conus cardinalis ab altitudine quinquaginta pedum ita se moventem in descensu quod in casu super terram nulla apparebat conquassacio corporis exterior, in interioribus tamen ita confractum quod in perpetuo languet et dolet interius et languebit. Timor etiam in descensu et motus aeris una cum casu mortem facilime operantur. Ad miraculum vero tam de integrit-ate corporis quam miraculose resuscitationis eiusdem operatur oratio matris puerum in utero nondum natum gestientis auxilium dicti sancti Thome pro se et partu quem conceperat devotius implorantis ut, sicut de ceco nato, respondit Salvator: "neque hic peccavit neque parentes eius sed ut manifestentur opera dei in illo", ita poterant in puero ad manifesta-tionem divinorum operum dicta omnia evenisse.

Dubio
Solutio

Miraculum (6) (= 22)   Sextum miraculum de infante unius anni et dimi-dii mortui morte naturali resuscitati miraculose meritis dicti sancti nullum in se videtur dubium continere.

Miraculum (7) (= 33)   Septimum miraculum non probatur quo ad modum submersionis aut horam nec expresse quo ad determinationem aque in qua fuit aubmersa. Dubia autem alia in modum resuscitationis per premissa declarantur.

Miraculum (8) (= 36)   Miraculum de resuscitatione Margarite infantis XVI ebdomadarum probatur per tres testes, cuius possibilitas patet per predicta.

Miraculum (9) (= 37)   Idem est de miraculo pueri qui natus mortuus, post meritis sancti Thome est ressuscitatus, licet plures cause esse poterant

34 A saint dictates to her companions the revelations inspired by the Holy Spirit
(Pietro Lorenzetti, Polyptych of B. Umiliana of Faenza (d. 1310), 1341, Uffizzi
Museum, Florence)

35 The exaltation of culture and doctrine in the fourteenth century: the office of St Thomas Aquinas: *Salve Thomas, doctor Ecclesiae, lumen mundi, splendor Italiae* (Incipit of choral book, Italy, *c*.1340, Coll. Hoepli, Milan)

36 The murder of St Peter Martyr (d. 1252) (Andrea da Firenze, *c.*1355, fresco,
Santa Maria Novella, Spaniards' Chapel, Florence)

38 The first transfer of the body of St Thomas Aquinas by the monks of Fossanova (The Story of St Thomas Aquinas, late fourteenth-century fresco, Santa Maria del Piano, Loreto Aprutino, Abruzzi)

37 The death of St Clare, *c.*1410 (Master of Heiligenkreuz, Samuel H. Kress Collection, National Gallery of Art, Washington DC

641 - ROMA - MARGHERITONE D'AREZZO
S. FRANCESCO - (P. VATICANA)

39 A cultic image of St Francis of
Assisi (Margarito d'Arezzo,
thirteenth century, Vatican
Pinacoteca, Rome)

40 Fresco showing healing by touch (Monastero di
Tor de' Specchi, Rome)

43 St Francis drives out the devils from Arezzo (Bennozzo Gozzoli, Museo di S. Francesco, Montefalco)

ex quibus vita latere poterat in puero sic nato, nisi subtilius fuisset per obstetricem indagata.

Miraculum (10) (= 38) Item de puella oppressa quod mirandum per duos testes. Ex premissis dubitari solet an in corpore apparente mortuo, corporis et membrorum immobilitas et inflexibilitas iuncturarum, frigiditas in omni tempore, privatio anelitus, carencia usus sensuum sint sufficentia indicia vere mortis an corpus propter ista debeat vere mortuum iudicari. Dicendum est quod sic, quoniam anima unitur corpori ut forma et ut motor, et premissa arguunt carenciam omnium operationum vitalium; utroque modo carencia eius usus sensuum, frigiditas in omni tempore arguunt carenciam operationum anime ut est forma, quod de sensitiva est manifestum, de vegetativa etiam que est quasi fundamentum et radix aliorum, quia calor est instrumentum anime vegetative quo mediante corpus nutritur et viget, calore ergo sublato tollitur omnis operatio vegetative. Actus autem deficiens in corpore arguit animam non uniri corpori ut motorem et inflexibilitas iuncturarum virtutem motivam in interioribus ostendit deficere et idem arguit quando non perpenditur motus spirituum corporalium circa cor in temporibus et impulsibus brachiorum et circa nasum ad hoc facit etiam quando respiratio et expiracio non sentiuntur, tunc enim innotescit quod calor naturalis in corde et in membris aliis interioribus est extinctus. In corde enim animalis vivi vel recenter mortui pro aliqua parte est tantus calor quod, ut experimentum docet, hoc non posset sustinere digitus in illa parte cordis animalis propter vehemenciam caloris sicut nec in igne sine combustione et ad huius refrigeracionem etiam respirat animal, cum igitur anima non uniatur corpori pluribus modis et premissa arguunt animam nec uniri corpori ut formam nec motorem, separatio autem anime et corporis mors est. Sequitur quod premissa sunt vera indicia vere mortis.

Miracula (11 et 12) (= 6 et 7) Miraculum de Iuliana et Margarita per multos annos contractis ex infirmitate non ex natura, quia una post repetitam sportam in qua portabatur ad ecclesiam Herefordensem et obtentam habuit (v°.) recidivum sue infirmitatis, cui dixit sanctus Thomas quod surgeret et ambularet, et iterum est curata. Altera visum habuit vicibus repetitis quod quidam senex canonicus capa alba indutus porrigeret ei

---

* Hoc asserunt auctores medicine. (right margin)
** De contracta. (left margin)

0

manum cum anulo ad osculandum et extunc portata ad ecclesiam Herefordensem per dictum sanctum Thomam miraculose est curata. Probatur per
sex testes sed in aliquibus articulis deponunt tamen de auditu in substantia
facti, quo ad infirmitatem et sanitatem de visu. Hic diceret aliquis dubitando si ex infirmitate contracte fuerunt, par artem curari poterant et miraculo non debet ascribi. Infirmitatem curationis ex eventu habitam miraculose curare docet evangelium Lucae XIII, ubi dicitur: "Ecce mulier que
habebat speciem infirmitatis annis decem et octo, et erat inclinata nec
omnino poterat sursum respicere" et ibidem quod Christus ei imposuit
manus et continuo erecta est, cum ergo dicat Salvator, Iohannis XIV:
"Qui credit in me opera que ego facio et ipse faciet et maiora horum
faciet". Dubium esse non debet curationem miraculosam mulieris contracte et curate per infirmitatem posse fieri meritis cuiuscumque sancti.
Dubium esse potest quomodo una istarum contractarum repetita sporta
passa sit recidivum et post curata. Respondeo: recidivum pene ex peccato
accidere potest ex evangelio, dicente Christo, Iohannis quinto, languido
quem ad probaticam piscinam sanaverat: "Ecce sanus factus es, iam
amplius noli peccare ne deterius aliquid tibi contingat". Ex quo patet
quod propter peccatum recidivum gravius poterit evenire. Ad idem est
quod narrat beatus Gregorius, II Dialogorum, de clerico per beatum Benedictum a demonio liberato cui precepit idem Benedictus post curationem
ne carnes comederet nec ad sacros ordines ascenderet. Quo clerico post
multorum annorum curricula ad sacros ordines ascendente, rursum (sic)
a demonio gravius quam prius est vexatus. Consimile ingratitudinis peccatum videtur hec mulier commisisse dum sportam sue egritudinis testem
et miraculose curationis signum que ad excitandum mentes fidelium ad
devotionem sancti et laudem dei debuerit ad reliquias sancti dimisisse,
sicut est in illis partibus consuetum, ex avaritia repeterit nec mulieri a qua
ipsam mutuaverat satisfecit, a Deo correpta per sancti merita fuit iterum
miraculose curata.

II miracula (13 et 14) (= 29) Miraculum quod evenit de Iohanne de
Creddle qui habita visione quod veniret ad tumulum sancti Thome et
venit, non permissus tamen in ecclesiam intrare, in via revertendo est
curatus. Probatur per tres testes. Item de Iuliana de Creddele per multos
annos contracta; habuit in visione visionem sancti Thome dicentis ut se

*Marginal notes: Dubio, Solutio, *, ***

* Io, XIV, 12.
** Io. V, 14.

balnearet, ipsa post balneata curata est. Probatur per tres testes. Dubium Dubio
an curatio facta in via debeat miraculo deputari. Respondeo curationem Solutio
in via absque contactu corporali reliquiarum sancti debere meritis sancti
Thome deputari. Dicitur ex evangelio Matthei VIII et Luce VII per
servum centurionis qui credens Christum absentem corpore sanare posse
audivit a Christo: "Vade et sicut credidisti fiat tibi, et sanatus est puer in
illa hora". Item Iohannis quarto de filio Reguli cui cum diceret Christus
"Vade, filius tuus vivit" et sanatus est filius eius ante descensum suum
ad domum, ut habetur ibidem consimiliter curatio ipsius credentis post
apparicionem sancti sibi factam meritis eiusdem posse sanari absque contactu corporali reliquiarum eiusdem, cum per eum non steterit, est miraculo ascribendum. Dubitaret aliquis an curatio mulieris balneate miraculo Dubio
vel virtuti balnei sit ascribenda. Respondeo curationem post mandatum
factum pler visionem aut voce viva a sancto miraculo debere attribui, non
elemento adhibitio de mandato dicti sancti. Probatur auctoritate utriusque
Testmenti. Namaan enim Sirus descendit et lavit septies in Iordano iuxta
mandatum Helisei et mundatus est a lepra, ut habetur II Regum V., **
que mundatio meritis Helisei et miraculo ascribenda est, non virtuti aque
Iordanis. Consimiliter cecus curatus a Christo post lutum factum ex sputo
et linicione oculorum, ivit et lavit oculos a natatoria Siloe de mandato
Christi (Iohannis IX) et illuminatus est. Que illuminatio non virtuti aque
set Christi per operationem miraculosam est ascribenda. Eodem modo
curatio dicte mulieris se de mandato sancti sibi in visione facto balneantis
non virtuti balnei set divine et meritis sancti ac miraculo est deputandum.
Hec duo sub uno miraculo in attestionibus continentur.

Miraculum (15) (= 31) Philippus Paynert probatur contractus per
multos annos miraculose meritis sancti Thome curatus per quinque testes.
Sed nec modus curationis nec causa infirmitatis exprimuntur nec alia
indicia ex quibus substantia facti posset legentibus apparere. [f° 69r].

Miraculum (16) (= 34) Miraculum de quadam muliere Alisia nomine
habente confractionem ossium et amocionem partium de iunctura pedis
ex respiratione quadam habente etiam paraliticationem unius partis
corporis ex causa, ut videtur, quod iacuit inter duo ostia sic lesa. Que

* Mat. VIII, 13 et Lc. VII, 1–10.
** II. Reg., V. 14 sq.

postmodum apparente sibi in visu beato Thoma in parte est curata. Probatur per testes sed quia curata non invenitur in pede plene nec vulnera in toto clausa nec voluit morari usque ad plenam curationem, illi non est insistendum. Potius enim videtur quedam aleniatio quam curatio, licet in visione que ponitur multa mira dicat se vidisse et se a beato Thoma in diversis partibus corporis sollicite contractatam; sed licet visio possibilis fuerit, tamen non apparet effectus ex tam mirabili visione consecutus de talibus.

Miraculum (17) (= 35)   Miraculum de Guenelda Gydihorn videtur probatum per tres testes et visionibus subsequentibus dicetur. Facit pro miraculo quod fuit confessa peccata sua et dicto sancto Thome mensurata.

Miraculum (18) (= 27)   Miraculum de sanatione domini Milonis Pychard militis relinquatur.

Miraculum (19) (14)   Miraculum de Agnete de la Broke civitatis Herefordensis, ceca per V annos et illuminata meritis sancti Thome ipsa offerente oculos ibidem et post orante ut si utilius anime sue ipsam fore cecam quam videntem et ex hoc iterum ad preces suas obcecate, probatur quo ad (?) que possent esse de sanatione, eo quod dicitur fuisse mulier dives et *
devota. Dubium si miraculo debet ascribi recidivum cecitatis. Respondeo: idem legitur in itinerario Clementis de puella ad preces aliorum per beatum Petrum sanatam que finito ministerio in mensa iterum mandante beato Petro quod rediret ad locum infirma infirmata est eadem infirmitate qua prius, cumque quereret a beato Petro huius rei causam, respondit sic expedire anime sue. Erat enim pulcra valde.

Miraculum (20) (= 20)   Miraculum de Hugone le barbyr per infirmitatem obcecato et post mensurato ad sanctum Thomam et portata oblacione ad locum de quo dictus sanctus fuit oriundus et ad tumulum dicti sancti in ecclesia Herefordensi. Probatur quo ad illuminationem per quinque testes, ut patet ex deposicione testium quod sine arte vel remedio humano apposito fuit illuminatus post predictam cecitatem.

---

* Illuminationem per VI testes tractatam et quo ad obcecationem per aliquos eorum et excluduntur suspiciones.

(21–22) (= 16 et 17)   Probatur per VII testes XX. miraculum[1] de Adam et Rogerio fratribus illuminatis per merita dicti sancti Thome, de quibus Adam predictus perdidit visum per infirmitatem humoribus consistentibus ad oculos, sed portatus ad tumulum dicti sancti Thome, mensuratus prius ad eumdem, vidit dormiendo quemdam hominem indutum vestibus sacerdotalibus et tangentem cum dictis vestibus oculos suos. Quo facto expergefactus, vidit eum exeuntem cum lumine per quamdam fenestram vitream et extunc habuit visum clarum. Rogerius vero obcecatus uno oculo per quamdam incautam ligaturam circa capud ita quod quidam nodi albi reposito oculo prius per dictam ligaturam eruto in loco suo apparebant super pupillam oculi reposito et sic in eadem hora quo frater fuit illuminatus domi existens visum recuperavit. Dubium si dicta visio Ade potuit esse vera. Respondeo visiones veras esse posse. Legentium scripturam sanctam nemo est qui debet dubitare. Petro in extasi posito ostensa est visio, sicut docetur Actibus apostolorum: Iacob etiam visionem habuit in sompnis, ut habetur Genesi XXVIII., tertio etiam Regum; tertio Salomoni per visionem in sompnis data est a Deo sapientia; Iosep visionem habuit, Matthei I et II secundo; Magi visionem in sompnis habuerunt, Mat. II. Plures etiam alii de quibus longum esset enarrare, ita quod per visum in sompnis hominem miraculose sanitatem posse recipere nullus catholicus debet in dubium revocare, cum de hoc etiam quam plurima sint in scriptis sanctorum exempla.

(23) (= 9)   Probatur per IX testes quod Iohannes quidam natus sine lingua ad tumulum sancti Thome meritis eiusdem recepit finaliter linguam integram, humanam, Anglicum et Wallensem perfecte loquentem, licet per aliquos probetur quod primo receperat linguam imperfecte formatam qua corrupte, non plene et aperte loquebatur, secundo accedens ad tumulum dicti sancti perfectam linguam recepit. Si dubitet aliquis quomodo hoc fieri potuit, respondetur quod miraculum in lingua ut mutus loqueretur scimus ex Evangelio, Mt. IX. et Mc. VII. Item ut variis linguis loquerentur apostoli factum est miraculose, Actuum secundo, et quod apparuerunt eis dispartite lingue tamquam ignis seditque etc. Item tradidit beatus Gregorius Dialogorum libro III. de quibusdam affricanis episcopis qui a Wandalorum rege pro eo quod ad heresim Arrianam trahi non potuerant, puniti fuerunt in tantum ut lingue eorum amputarentur

---

[1] One of the earlier double miracles (11 and 12, or 13 and 14) has probably been counted as one only, which would explain the figure 20.

* Mt. IX, 32 et Mc. VII, 37.

radicitus et post miraculose pro defensione veritatis ita sine lingua loquendi usum habebant sicut loqui solebant dum linguas habebant. Cum [vᵒ] ergo sine lingua deus loquendi usum concesserat, etiam linguam qua loqueretur mutus meritis sancti concessisse potuit et sine hesitatione credi potest quod in aliis meritis sanctorum legitur esse factum.

(24) (= 8) Miraculum de quodam a gibbo in collo miraculose liberato et sanato meritis eiusdem sancti Thome probatur per duos testes.

(25) (= 11) Miraculum de navi et naute (sic) liberatis a periculo meritis sancti Thome, probatur per testes nominatos et visio duorum virorum qui fuerunt albis induti stantium in navi multum est possibilis et per consimilia miracula multorum sanctorum comprobata, ut in vita sancti Nicholai, Beda de gestis Anglorum, Gregorio et aliis.

(26) (= 26) Miraculum ultimum de avibus potest inter cetera miracula deputari propter officium quod tunc dictus sanctus intendebat. De aliis etiam sanctis est idem inventum, ut de beato Francisco quo ad mira que in avibus contingerunt, ut patet diversas historias prospicienti.

DEPOSITIONS OF THE LONDON FRANCISCANS AT THE PROCESS OF CANONIZATION OF ST THOMAS CANTILUPE (1307) (MS VAT. LAT 4015, FOLS. 45v–48v)

৩৩৩৩

XXV^{us} testis

(f° 45v)   Frater Hugonius de Londinio, de ordine Fratrum Minorum, conversus ex iudeis, testis supra iuratus et ex officio receptus, respondit interrogatus se esse in sexagesimo secundo anno etatis sue et quod non fuerat de parentela vel familia domini Thome predicti nec recolebat se unquam vidisse eumdem.

Interrogatus de fide, vita et conversatione dicti domini Thome, respondit se credere quod fuerit homo bone vite et bone conversacionis et quod numquam aliquid sinistri audivit da eo, nisi dumtaxat quod dicebatur fuisse excommunicatus a fratre Iohanne de Peccham tunc archiepiscopo Cantuariensi, et dicunt alii quod iuste et alii quod injuste. Item interrogatus si inter fratres ordinis ipsius testis cum quibus post obitum dicti domini Thome extitit conversatus et inter seculares et populares est fama publica et communis oppinio (sic) quod dicitur quod dictus dominus Thomas sit sanctus, et quod Deus pro eo sicut pro sancto miracula operatur [f° 46] dixit quod dicta fama et dicta communis oppinio, sicut audivit, est inter seculares et in populo, et hoc communiter dicunt. Omnes fratres autem sui ordinis et ipse testis bene credunt quod dictus dominus Thomas fuit bonus homo et honestus et bene sciunt quod fuit magister in theologia, sed difficiles sunt ad credendum quod Deus operetur pro eo miracula quia dicta miracula non viderunt fieri, licet ab aliis audiverint facta fuisse. Et dicta difficultas consurgit in eis quia quidam familiaris dicti domini Thome et senescallus et executor testamenti ipsius qui interfuit obitu suo et in vita sua fuerat cum eo XX annis et amplius, ut audivit referri, qui eciam ossa dicti domini Thome apportavit in Angliam et interfuit sepulture eorumdem, fuit post predicta factus frater minor et stetit in ordine eorum in Anglia viginti annis et ultra, qui fuit vocatus frater Iohannes de Clara et extitit magne reputacionis inter fratres ordinis

555

eorumdem predicti regni. Audito quod Deus operabatur miracula pro dicto domino Thoma, fuit semel ab ipso teste cum instancia rogatus et requisitus quod diceret ipsi testi, cum predictus frater Iohannes novisset vitam et conversationem dicti domini Thome, quod diceret ei si sciebat aliquod fuisse in eo propter quod Deus deberet pro eo miracula operari, et dictus frater Iohannes respondit in gallico: "Verrayement, il fut bon homo (sic) et de bone vie; mes ieo ne sey pas quey miracles dussent estre fet pur luy". Predicta fuit responsio in effectu dicti fratris Iohannis et dixit tam predictus testis se et fratres ordinis sui predictos difficiles esse ad credendum quod Deus pro dicto domino Thoma miracula operaretur. Contra constat eis super operacione miraculorum racione questus aliquo tempore et in aliis casibus multa fuisse conficta et specificavit de quibusdam fontibus et de quibusdam crucibus et de quodam interfecto inter inter Cantuarium et Londinium vocatum Robertum le Busere pro quibus Deus dicebatur miracula operari et de quadam domina de Crag iuxta Castrum Puellarum in Scotia ad duo milliaria que narraverat ipsi testi quod quidam mendicus intuitu pietatis cum videretur esse contractus ab ipsa in eius domo receptus, cum diceret quod nullo modo brachium poteret erigere ex eo quod pugnum subtus assellam tenebat, predicta domina palpato brachio dicti mendici et duro invento ac si nervus esset contractus, cum presumeret esse fucronneum, vocatis familiaribus suis per vim extracto pugno dicti pauperis de assella sua extendit brachium et confessus fuit quod in fraudem faciebat predicta, ratione questus, et ivit ad crucem de Publes in Scotia ad quam confluunt peregrini multi ut possit confingere se miraculose curatum ibidem. Dixit etiam quod mortuo fratre Galfrido de Sancto [v°] Edmundo ordinis eorum qui fuerat confessor regis Alemannie et qui reputabatur sanctus ab omnibus qui habuerant eius noticiam, venit quidam ad conventum dictorum fratrum de Oxonio in quo loco in ecclesia dictorum fratrum fuerat sepultus frater Gaufridus predictus, et dixit in secreto cuidam ex fratribus dicti conventus quod ipse faceret dictos fratres lucrari magnam pecuniam si vellent. Requisitus per quem modum, dixit quod cum dictus frater Gaufridus reputaretur sanctus ab omnibus, si fierent ibi aliqua miracula haberent inde magnum lucrum. Cum autem dictus frater peteret qualiter potuerint fieri miracula suprascripta nisi sic ordinaret altissimus, respondit quod habebat XXIIIIor in Anglia sibi obedientes qui facerent miracula quecumque ipse vellet et dixit quod ad diversa loca pro talibus miraculis faciendis in Anglia racione lucri mittebat eosdem et libenter recipiebatur. Dictus tamen frater minor tamquam ribaldum repulit eum. Interrogatus in quo loco, quo tempore et quibus presentibus predictus frater Iohannes de Clara narravit ipsi testi illa que supra deposuit de eodem, respondit quod in claustro conventus ordinis eorum Londiniensi et quod nullus fuit tunc presens nisi ipsi duo. De tempore dixit se non recordari.

XXVI testis

Frater Henricus de Sintone, guardianus fratrum minorum conventus Londinii, testis supra iuratus et ex officio receptus, respondit interrogatus se esse XLV annorum vel circa et quod non fuerat de parentela vel familia dicti domini Thome, et quod eum non viderat nisi semel et quod nichil sciebat de fide, vita, moribus et conversacione eiusdem nisi per relatum alienum audiverat narrari quod fuerat homo bonus, generosus et curialis, et numquam intellexerat aliquod sinistri de eo. [f° 47] Interrogatus si inter fratres ordinis sui cum quibus post obitum dicti domini Thome extitit conversatus et communiter inter seculares et populares homines est fama publica et communis quod dictus Thomas sit sanctus et quod Deus pro eo sicut pro sancto miracula operetur, respondit quod dicta fama et communis oppinio est in populo. Interrogatus quomodo hoc scit, dixit quod totum vulgus hoc clamat.

Interrogatus quod vocat famam publicam, dixit quod illud quod vulgus communiter clamat et dicit, et non credit multum differre inter famam publicam et communem oppinionem. Quoad fratres ordinis sui cum quibus predictus guardianus inquisivit si sciebant aliqua de sanctitate vite et de miraculis dicti domini Thome et quoad fratres dicti ordinis cum quibus habuit collationem de predictis, est fama publica et communis oppinio quod dictus dominus Thomas fuit bonus homo et bone vite sed tamen non viderunt quod Deus fuerit pro dicto domino Thomas aliquod miraculum operatus nec audiverunt multa miracula facta fuisse pro eo seu per eum. Verum tamen frater Iohannes de Clara qui fuerat per annos multos familiaris dicti domini Thome et in tempore obitus sui erat cum eo et eius senescallus et eius ossa tulit in Angliam et fuit executor testamenti eiusdem et postmodum intravit ordinem dictorum fratrum, requisitus ab ipso guardiano cum erat valde familiaris, fama miraculorum dicti domini Thome crebrescente, quod diceret ipsi testi si sciebat predicta et dictum dominum Thomam habuisse aliquam excellentiam vel eminenciam vite propter quam Deus deberet pro eo plus quam pro alio bono homine miracula operari, respondit dissimulando. Et tamen dictus frater Iohannes tenerrime diligebat dictum Thomam et promotus ad beneficia fuerat ab eodem. Dixit eciam predictus guardianus quod ipse et alii fratres ordinis sui non facile credunt miracula que audiunt interdum a populo enarrari quia constat eis multas fraudes hactennus super operacione miraculorum intervenisse in Anglia. Et idem guardianus, sicut dixit, audiverat a fratribus ordinis sui quod aliqui dixerunt eis quod si predicti fratres volebant, predicti operarentur diversa miracula in ecclesiis eorumdem pro quadam ymagine de novo posita in ecclesia eorumdem ita quod racione dictorum miraculorum predicti fratres possent lucrari et habere inde adiutorium pro eorum ecclesia construenda. (vº) Narravit dictus guardianus se semel audivisse a quibusdam canonicis Hereford. quod quidam puer quod (*sic*) dicebatur carere lingua et non posse fari receperat ad tumulum dicti domini Thome miraculose linguam integram et loquelam. Postmodum idem guardianus audivit a quibusdam fratribus sui ordinis quod ille puer erat trutannus et fuerat inventus post predicta in alio loco in quo fingebat se carere lingua et loquela, et cum aliquis ex astantibus cognovisset quod ille erat qui dicebatur miraculose in ecclesia Hereford. recepisse linguam et loquelam, dedit sibi de pugno super collum et tunc extraxit linguam quam retractaverat et quam se non habere fingebat et cepit loqui.

Interrogatus a quibus canonicis Hereford. et in quo loco et quibus presentibus et quo tempore audivit predictum miraculum de restauracione lingue et loquele dicti pueri enarrari, respondit se non recordari de nominibus dictorum canonicorum. Sed predicta fuerunt narrata fratri Galfrido de Schepeye, olim penitenciario domini pape de ordine eorum, et ipsi testi inter Oxonium et abbaciam de Eyvesham sunt viginti anni vel circa, et idem audivit postmodum narrari ab aliis, sicut dixit.

XXVII testis
Frater Iohannes de Westwode, OFM (*deposition* almost identical (fol. 48).

XXVIII testis
Frater Gualterius de Cantuario, OFM (*deposition* almost identical (fol. 48v).

LIST OF SOURCES

ოჳოჳოჳ

1. Processes of canonization

A. Diocesan informative processes and local enquiries (thirteenth to fifteenth centuries)

These are enquiries *de fama et sanctitate* carried out by the local ecclesiastical authorities in order to obtain from the Holy See a process of canonization or official recognition of a cult. They are in chronological order of process. The persons whose name is preceded by St have been canonized by the Roman Church.

1. Stephen of Die (d. 1208)
    Enquiry held at Die between 1222 and 1230: ed. in *AA.SS.* Sept. III, pp. 194–200.
2. St Elizabeth of Thuringia (or of Hungary) (d. 1231)
    Miracles recorded in August 1232, at Marburg: ed. A. Wyss, *Hessisches Urkundenbuch*, I (Leipzig, 1879), pp. 25–9.
    Conrad of Marburg, *Summa vitae*, ed. A. Huyskens, *Quellenstudien zur Geschichte der hl. Elisabeth Landgräfin von Thüringen* (Marburg, 1908), pp. 155–60.
    Forma de statu mortis Lantgraviae de Thuringia, with collection of miracles, *ibid.*, pp. 148–50.
3. Jutta of Sangerhausen (d. *c.*1260)
    Enquiry into the life and miracles, diocese of Kulmsee (East Prussia), 1275, ed. H. Westpfahl, 'Untersuchungen über Jutta von Sangerhausen', *Zeitschrift für Geschichte und Altertumskinde Ermlands*, 26 (1936), pp. 515–96.
4. St Raymond of Peñafort (d. 1279)
    First diocesan process (Barcelona, 1279), in MS Vat. lat. 6059, fols. 40–9.
    Second diocesan process (Barcelona, 1318), ed. J. Rius Serra, in *Sancti Raymundi de Penyafort opera omnia*, III: *Diplomatario* (Barcelona, 1954), pp. 207–63.
5. Peter Thomas (d. 1365)
    Enquiry carried out at Famagusta, Cyprus, in 1366, ed. J. Smet, *The Life of St Peter Thomas by Philippe de Mézières* (Rome, 1954), pp. 168–84 (Textus et studia historica Carmelitana, 2).

6. Urban V (d. 1370)
   Enquiry into the miracles, Avignon, 1376–9, ed. J. H. Albanès and U.
   Chevalier, *Actes anciens et documents concernant le Bienheureux pape Urbain
   V*, I (Paris, 1897), pp. 124–365.

7. Peter of Luxembourg (d. 1387)
   Depositions concerning the miracles (= 1102) recorded at Avignon between
   7 July and 23 December 1387, Archives départementales du Vaucluse, series
   H, Celestins of Avignon, reg. 62/1, 268 fols.

8. St Catherine of Siena (d. 1380)
   Process in Venice, 1411–16, ed. M. H. Laurent, *Il processo Castellano*
   (Milan, 1942) (Fontes vitae S. Catharinae Senensis historici, 9).

9. Joan-Marie of Maillé (d. 1414)
   Enquiry held in Tours, 1414/15, concerning her life and miracles, Bibliothèque Municipale de Tours, MS 1032 and Paris, BN, franc. 24445.
   Almost full edn in *AA.SS.* Mar. III, pp. 744–62, on the basis of another
   manuscript, now lost.

10. Werner of Oberwesel (or of Bacharach) (d. 1287)
    Enquiry concerning the miracles and cult, Bacharach (Rhineland), 1428/9.
    Complete text in MSS Palat. lat. 858 and Trier, Stadtbibliothek, Hs. 1139,
    ed. in part in *AA.SS.* Apr. II, pp. 714–34.

B. Processes of canonization ordered by the papacy (1185–1417)

The place and date of the *inquisitio in partibus* is given after the name and date of
death of the saint.

1. St Galgano (d. 1181): Monte Siepi (Tuscany), 1185
   Full text: ed. F. Schneider, 'Der Einsiedler Galgan von Chiusdino und die
   Anfänge von San Galgano', *Quellen und Forschungen aus italienischen
   Archiven und Bibliotheken*, 17 (1914–24), pp. 61–77.

2. St Gilbert of Sempringham (d. 1189): Sempringham, 1201 (England)
   Full text: ed. R. Foreville, and G. Keir, *The Book of St Gilbert* (Oxford,
   1987).

3. St Hugh of Lincoln (d. 1200): Lincoln, 1219
   Full text: ed. H. Farmer, 'The canonization of St Hugh of Lincoln',
   Lincolnshire Architectural and Archaeological Society Reports and Papers, 7
   (1956), pp. 86–117.

4. St Robert of Molesme (d. 1111): Molesme (Burgundy), 1221
   Full text: ed. P. Labbé, *Novae bibliothecae manuscriptorum librorum*, I (Paris,
   1657), cc. 647–50.

5. Hugh of Bonnevaux (d. 1194): Bonnevaux (Dauphiné), 1222
   Full text: ed. E. Martène and U. Durand, *Thesaurus novus anecdotorum*, I
   (Paris, 1717), cc. 888–93.

6. John Cacciafronte (d. 1183): Cremona and Vicenza, 1223–4
   Full text: ed. A. Schiavo, *Della vita e dei tempi del B. Giovanni Cacciafronte*
   (Vicenza, 1866), pp. 239–59 and G. Cracco, in *Studi Medievali*, 3rd ser.,

26 (1985), pp. 904–5, based on the Vicenza manuscript, Archivio Capitolare (Seminario vescovile di Vicenza), Perg. I, n. 46.

7. St Osmund (d. 1099): Salisbury, 1233
   Full text: ed. A. R. Malden, *The canonization of St Osmund* (Salisbury, 1901), pp. 32–54.

8. St Hildegard (d. 1179): Bingen (Rhineland), 1233 and 1243
   Full text: ed. P. Bruder, 'Acta inquisitionis de virtutibus et miraculis S. Hildegardis', *Anal. Boll.*, 2 (1883), pp. 118–29.

9. St Dominic (d. 1221): Bologna and various places in the county of Toulouse, 1233
   Full text of the Bologna enquiry; summary for the enquiry in the county of Toulouse: ed. A. Walz, 'Processus canonizationis S. Dominici', *MOPH*, 16 (1935), pp. 88–194. French translation based on this edition in M. H. Vicaire, *Saint Dominique: la vie apostolique* (Paris, 1965), pp. 31–85 (Chrétiens de tous les temps, 9). A number of fragments of the Toulouse enquiry not included in this edition have been published by V. J. Koudelka, 'Les dépositions des témoins au procès de canonisation de S. Dominique', *AFP*, 42 (1972), pp. 47–67, on the basis of another manuscript.

10. St Elizabeth of Thuringia (or of Hungary) (d. 1231): Marburg (Hesse), 1235
    The official text of the protocol of the enquiry carried out by the papal commissioners has been lost, but the substance of the depositions has been preserved in documents which are closely based on the original reports, and are ed. Huyskens, *Quellenstudien*, pp. 112–40, 155–239, 242–66. The statements of four of the saint's maidservants, which formed the core of the enquiry *de vita*, were recorded again, before 1241, in fuller form, in a treatise also ed. Huyskens, *Der sog. Libellus de dictis IV ancillarum* (Kempten and Munich, 1911). See also the fragments discovered and ed. by G. G. Meersseman, 'Le deposizioni delle compagne di S. Elisabetta di Turingia in un frammento conservato nell'Archivio di Stato a Friburgo', in *Miscellanea in onore di G. Battelli* (Rome, 1979), pp. 367–80.

11. Odo of Novara (d. 1200): Tagliacozzo (Abruzzi), 1240
    Full text: ed. in *Anal. Boll.*, 1 (1882), pp. 323–54 (Documenta de B. Odone Novariensi ordinis Carthusiani).

12. Ambrose of Massa (d. 1240): Orvieto, 1240–1
    Full text: ed. in *AA.SS.* Nov. IV, pp. 571–608.

13. Lawrence Loricatus (or of Subiaco) (d. 1243): Subiaco, 1244
    Full text. The original manuscript of the enquiry is MS *ASV, Archivum Arcis*, Arm. 1, XVIII, 3328. There are two editions, both imperfect: Benedict XIV (Prosper Lambertini), *De servorum Dei beatificatione et Beatorum canonizatione*, in his *Opera omnia*, III, app. IV (Prato, 1840), pp. 662–93; W. Gnandt, *Vita S. Cleridoniae virginis, B. Laurentii anachoretae necnon et servi Dei Hippolyti Pugnetti monachi* (Innsbruck, 1902), pp. 67–99.

14. St Edmund of Abingdon (Edmund Rich, Archbishop of Canterbury, d. 1240): Pontigny (Yonne) and Canterbury, 1244–5
    Fragments of the enquiry concerning the miracles held at Pontigny in July 1244 by the Archbishop of Armagh and the Dean of Paris: Sens Cathedral,

Trésor, doc. 22. Partial edition in E. Martène and U. Durand, *Thesaurus novus anecdotorum*, III (Paris, 1717), cc. 1881–98.

Accounts of the enquiries concerning the miracles held in England in 1244 and 1245: Sens Cathedral, Trésor, docs. 21, 25.

Account of the enquiry into the miracles held in Burgundy in 1245: Sens Cathedral, Trésor, doc. 23.

Fragments of the enquiry *de vita* held in England in 1244 are ed. C. H. Lawrence, *St Edmund of Abingdon: a study in hagiography and history* (Oxford, 1960), pp. 187–202 (*Quadrilogus*), 248–53 (*Breviloquium*). See also Oxford, Bodleian Library, MS 8690 (= MS Fell, 2), fols. 1–44.

15. St Stanislas (d. 1079): Cracow, 1250 and 1252

Enquiry concerning the miracles, ed. W. Ketrzynski, in *Monumenta Poloniae historica*, IV (Lvov, 1884), pp. 285–318.

16. John Bonus (d. 1249): Cesena and Mantua, 1251–4

Full text. The original manuscript is in Mantua, Archivio di Stato, fonds Gonzaga, busta 3305. Ed. in *AA.SS.* Oct. IX, pp. 771–885 (based on a good eighteenth-century copy). See C. Cipolla, 'Appunti ecceliniani: sul processo di canonizzazione el B. Giovanni Buono', *Atti del R. Istituto Veneto di Scienze, Lettere ed Arti*, 70 (1910), pp. 401–8.

17. Simon of Collazzone (d. 1250): Spoleto, 1252

Only the enquiry *de virtutibus* has survived. Original manuscript: Spoleto, Archivio di Stato, Perg. 26 (= rotulus). Ed. M. Faloci Pulignani, 'Il B. Simone da Collazzone e il suo processo', *Miscellanea Francescana*, 12 (1910), pp. 97–132 (based on a good eighteenth-century copy).

Summary of the miracles in Bartholomew of Renonico, *De conformitate*, ed. in *Analecta Franciscana*, IV (Quaracchi, 1906), pp. 240–1.

18. St Clare of Assisi (d. 1253): Assisi, 1253

Full text. The canonization process is known only through a fifteenth-century Italian translation, made in Umbria, and ed. Z. Lazzeri, 'Il processo di canonizzazione di S. Chiara d'Assisi', *AFH*, 13 (1920), pp. 439–93.

19. Philip Berruyer (or of Bourges) (d. 1261): Bourges, Beaugency and Orléans, 1265–6

Full text. The most complete manuscript is MS Vat. lat. 4019, fols. 28–100. See also Avignon, Archives départementales du Vaucluse, MS 1 G. 778, and Paris, BN, lat. 5373A, fols. 1–65.

20. St Margaret of Hungary (d. 1271): Dominican Monastery of the Isle of the Danube, near Budapest, 1276

Only part of the acts of the process has survived; it is ed. G. Fraknoi, *Monumenta Romana episcopatus Vesprimiensis*, I (Budapest, 1896), pp. 163–383.

21. St Louis (d. 1270): Saint-Denis, 1282

The acts of the enquiry held at Saint-Denis in 1282 concerning the life and miracles have largely been lost; there survive only fragments, published as follows: P. Riant, 'La déposition de Charles d'Anjou pour la canonisation de S. Louis', in *Notes et documents publiés par la Société de l'Histoire de France pour son 50e anniversaire* (Paris, 1884), pp. 155–76; H. F. Delaborde,

'Fragments de l'enquête faite à Saint-Denis en 1282, en vue de la canonisation de saint Louis', *Mémoires de la Société de l'histoire de Paris et de l'Ile-de-France*, 23 (1896), pp. 18–71.

22. St Peter of Morrone (Celestine V) (d. 1296): Sulmona (Abruzzi), 1306
    Only part of the process has survived (162 statements out of 322 in the original); they are published by F. X. Seppelt, 'Die Akten des Kanonisationsprozess in dem Codex zu Sulmona', in *Monumenta Coelestiniana: Quellen zur Geschichte des Papstes Coelestin V* (Paderborn, 1921), pp. 211–334.

23. St Thomas Cantilupe (or of Hereford) (d. 1282): London and Hereford, 13 July–13 November 1307
    Full text of the process: MS Vat. lat. 4015, fols. 1–121v. Extracts from the enquiry are published in *AA.SS.* Oct. I, pp. 585–696, but the edition is so faulty that I have generally preferred to refer to the original manuscript.

24. St Louis of Anjou (or of Toulouse, or of Marseilles) (d. 1297): Marseilles, 1308
    Full text: MS in Modena, Biblioteca Estense, Coll. Campori, 161. Ed. in *Processus canonizationis et legendae variae sancti Ludovici O.F.M. episcopi Tolosani* (Quaracchi amd Florence, 1951) (*Analecta Franciscana*, VII). For this edition and its imperfections, see the important review by M. H. Laurent, *RHE*, 46 (1951), pp. 786–91.

25. St Clare of Montefalco (d. 1308): Montefalco (Umbria), 1318–19
    Partial text (lacking the statements of witnesses 2 to 37), ed. E. Menesto, *Il processo di canonizzazione di Chiara da Montefalco* (Florence and Perugia, 1984), based on the manuscripts in *ASV, Riti*, Proc. 682–95.

26. St Thomas Aquinas (d. 1274): Naples (life and miracles), 1319, and Fossanova, 1321 (miracles only)
    Full text: the Naples process is ed. A. Ferrua, *Thomae Aquinatis vitae fontes praecipuae* (Alba, 1968), pp. 203–350. There are two editions of the Fossanova process: J. Rius Serra, 'Le procès de S. Thomas d'Aquin à Fossanova (1321)', *Analecta ordinis Praedicatorum*, 22 (1936), pp. 509–29, 576–631; M. H. Laurent, 'Processus Canonizationis S. Thomae Fossae Novae', in *Fontes vitae S. Thomae Aquinatis*, V (Saint-Maximin, 1941), pp. 409–532.

27. St Nicholas of Tolentino (d. 1305): Tolentino and various towns in the Marches, 1325
    Full text: ed. N. Occhioni, *Il processo per la canonizzazione di S. Nicola da Tolentino* (Rome, 1984).

28. St Yves (d. 1303): Tréguier (Brittany), 1330
    Full text: ed. A. de La Borderie, J. Daniel, R. P. Perquis and D. Tempier, in *Monuments originaux de l'histoire de S. Yves* (Saint-Brieuc, 1887), pp. 1–299.

29. Delphine of Sabran (d. 1361): Apt and Avignon, 1363
    Full text of the enquiry: Aix-en-Provence, Bibliothèque Méjanes, no. 335, 204 fols. See also Paris, Bibliothèque de l'Arsenal, MS 1075, fols. 75ff. The critical edition by J. Cambell, *Enquête pour le procès de canonisation de Dauphine de Puimichel, comtesse d'Ariano (m. 26.XI.1360)* (Turin, 1978), appeared too late for me to use in this book.

30. Charles of Blois (d. 1364): Angers, 1371
    Full text: ed. A. de Sérent, *Monuments du procès de canonisation du Bienheureux Charles de Blois, Duc de Bretagne, 1320–1364* (Saint-Brieuc, 1921).
    There are many versions of the Angers enquiry: a short one, known through the edition of D. Morice, in *Mémoires pour servir de preuves à l'histoire de Bretagne* (Paris, 1744), II, cc. 1–33, based on a manuscript of Saint-Aubin of Angers, now lost; a long one, of which the best example is MS Vat. lat. 4025. The edition of de Sérent, based on the Pau manuscript and MS BN, lat. 5381, has some gaps; it omits the statements of witnesses 57 to 60 about the life (fols. 79r–82r of MS Vat. lat. 4025) and the enquiry *de miraculis* held at Guingamp in 1371 by the Friars Minor (*ASV, Collectorie* 434 A, fols. 12–15v).

31. St Bridget (d. 1373): Sweden, Spoleto, Naples and Rome, 1376–80
    Full text: ed. I. Collijn, *Acta et processus canonizacionis beate Birgitte* (Stockholm, 1924–30), pp. 3–570.

32. Urban V (d. 1370): Avignon, between 1382 and 1390
    An enquiry concerning the life and miracles is ed. J. H. Albanès and U. Chevalier, *Actes anciens et documents concernant le Bienheureux Urbain V pape*, I (Paris, 1897), pp. 375–480. These are, in fact, the very full articles on the basis of which the witnesses were to be interrogated. It is not known whether the enquiry actually took place.

33. Peter of Luxembourg (d. 1387), Avignon, 1389–90
    Full text in many manuscripts in Avignon (copies of 1417–18): Musée Calvet (Bibliothèque municipale), no. 697, 374 fols., badly edited by the Bollandists in *AA.SS.* Iul. I, pp. 462–628; no. 698 is the same, but less complete at the end. Archives départementales du Vaucluse, Series H, Celestins of Avignon, reg. 62/2, 371 fols. See also Paris, BN, lat. 9747.

34. Dorothy of Montau (d. 1394): Marienwerder (East Prussia, now Poland), 1404–6
    Full text: Göttingen, Staatliches Archivlager, MS 1241, 359 fols. The critical edition of R. Stachnik, A. Triller and H. Westpfahl, *Die Akten des Kanonisationsprozess Dorotheas von Montau* (Cologne and Vienna, 1978), which will make reference to the manuscript unnecessary in future, appeared too late for me to use.

35. Brynulph of Skara (d. 1317): Skara (Sweden), 1417
    Full text: ed. C. Annerstedt, *Scriptores rerum Suecicarum Medii Aevi*, III, 2 (Uppsala, 1876), pp. 141–83.

36. Ingrid of Skänninge (d. 1281): Skänninge (Sweden), 1417
    Brief fragments are ed. J. Gallen, 'Les causes de Ste Ingrid et les saints suédois au temps de la Réforme', *AFP*, 7 (1937), pp. 32–6.

37. Nicholas Hermannsson (or of Linköping) (d. 1391): Linköping (Sweden), 1417
    Full text: ed. T. Lunden, *Sankt Nikolaus'av Linköping Kanonisationsprocess* (Stockholm, 1963), pp. 38–371.

C. Texts from the curial phase of the process (1202–1390)

1. St Gilbert of Sempringham (d. 1189, can. 1202)
   Ordo canonizationis, in *Vita B. Gilberti*, ed. W. Dugdale, *Monasticon Anglicanum*, VI, 2 (London, 1846), pp. xvi–xviii.
2. St Procopius of Sazava (Moravia) (d. 1053, can. 1204)
   De apericione canonizationis S. Procopii, ed. F. Krasl, *Sv. Prokop, jeho klaster a pamatka u lidu* (Prague, 1895), pp. 499–500.
3. St William of Bourges (d. 1209, can. 1218)
   Vita S. Guillelmi archiepiscopi Bituricensis, ed. *Anal. Boll.*, 3 (1884), pp. 350–61.
4. St Lawrence O'Toole (d. 1180, can. 1225)
   M. V. Ronan, 'St Laurentius, Archbishop of Dublin, original testimonies for canonization', *Irish Ecclesiastical Record*, n.s., 1 (1926), pp. 347–64; 2 (1926), pp. 246–56, 467–80.
   Account of the canonization by a contemporary, ed. G. Bessin, *Concilia Rothomagensis provinciae* (Rouen, 1717), II, pp. 47–59.
5. St Dominic (d. 1221, can. 1234)
   Jordan of Saxony, *Libellus de principiis ordinis*, ed. M. H. Laurent, in *Monumenta historica sancti patris nostri Dominici* (Rome, 1935), pp. 3–38 (= *MOPH*, 16, 2).
6. St Elizabeth of Thuringia (d. 1231, can. 1235)
   Processus et ordo canonizationis beate Elyzabet propter quorumdam detractiones et calumpnias, ed. in Huyskens, *Quellenstudien*, pp. 142–6.
   For the bull of canonization, see L. Santiffaler, 'Zur originalüberlieferung der Heiligsprechungsurkunde der Landgräfin Elisabeth von Thüringen vom Jahre 1235', in *Acht Jahrhunderte Deutscher Orden in Einzeldarstellung* (Bad Godesberg, 1967), pp. 73–88.
7. St Edmund of Abingdon (d. 1240, can. 1247)
   Albert, Archbishop of Armagh, *Historia canonizationis et translationis*, ed. Martène and Durand, *Thesaurus novus anecdotorum*, III, cc. 1835–58.
   Epistolae ad historiam B. Edmundi spectantes, ibid., cc. 1875–1926.
8. St Stanislas (d. 1079, can. 1253)
   Story of the canonization in *Vita major*, ed. in *Monumenta Poloniae historica*, IV (Lvov, 1884), pp. 399, 434–8.
9. St Clare of Assisi (d. 1253, can. 1255)
   Concilium Friderici Vicecomitis archiepiscopi Pisani, ed. Z. Lazzeri, *AFH*, 11 (1918), pp. 276–9.
10. St Hedwig (d. 1243, can. 1267)
    J. Gottschalk, 'Die Hedwigspredigt des Papstes Klemens IV', *Archiv für Schlesische Kirchengeschichte*, 15 (1957), pp. 17–35.
11. Philip of Bourges (d. 1261)
    Hand-over of the acts of the enquiry of 1265–6 to Cardinal Eudes of Châteauroux and instructions issued by him for them to be examined (between 1267 and 1270): MS Vat. lat. 4019, fols. 10–13.

12. St Louis (d. 1270, can. 1297)

L. Carolus-Barré, 'Consultation du cardinal Pietro Colonna sur le IIe miracle de S. Louis', *BECh*, 117 (1959), pp. 57–72 (= between 1295 and 1297).

Bonifacii VIII papae sermones duo de canonizatione regis Ludovici sanctissimi, ed. F. Du Chesne, *Historiae Francorum scriptores*, V (Paris, 1649), pp. 481–4.

13. St Louis of Anjou (d. 1270, can. 1317)

De canonisatione sancti Ludovici, ed. B. Schimmelpfennig, *Die Zeremonienbücher der römischen Kirche im Mittelalter* (Tübingen, 1973), p. 166.

14. St Peter of Morrone (Celestine V) (d. 1296, can. 1313)

Recollectio, Paris, Bibliothèque de l'Arsenal, MS 1071, fols. 1–33 (between 1307 and 1313)

'Procès-verbal du dernier consistoire secret préparatoire à la canonisation', ed. in *Anal. Boll.*, 16 (1897), pp. 389–92, 475–87.

De canonizatione sancti Petri de Morrone (description of the procedure followed in the process and account of the canonization by Cardinal James Caetani-Stefaneschi), in Schimmelpfennig, *Die Zeremonienbücher*, pp. 167–74.

15. St Thomas Cantilupe (or of Hereford) (d. 1282, can. 1320)

Recognitio facta anno 1313 processus canonizationis S. Thomae Herefordensis, in Vatican Library, Cod. Ottobon. 2516, fols. 44–6v.

Recollectio in MS Paris BN lat. 5373 A, fols. 66–126v (between 1318 and 1320).

Summarium (1319 or 1320): see appendix 1.

De canonizatione sancti Thome, ed. B. Schimmelpfennig, *Die Zeremonienbücher*, pp. 164–6.

16. St Clare of Montefalco (d. 1308, can. 1881)

Recollectio maior: only a few brief extracts survive, ed. in *Spoletana canonizationis S. Clarae positio super miraculis* (Rome, 1881), *Summarium novum*, pp. 50ff (between 1325 and 1329).

Recollectio minor (concerns 35 miracles retained from the 103 in the *Recollectio maior*), in *ASV, Riti*, Proc. 2927, fols. 143–569 (?1329).

Relatio cardinalium de vita et miraculis recitata in consistorio coram Iohanne XXII (between 1329 and 1331): *ASV, Riti*, Proc. 2927, fols. 48–142, and Angers, Bibliothèque municipale, MS 821, fols. 357–80. Partial edn in *Spoletana canonizationis, Summarium super dubio*, pp. 91–117, and *Summarium novum super dubio*, pp. 5–49. Italian translation of the whole *Relatio* in Agostino de Montefalco, *Vita, miracoli e revelazioni della Beata Chiara da Montefalco* (Venice, 1515).

17. St Thomas Aquinas (d. 1274, can. 1323)

Account of his canonization by a witness (probably Bernard Gui, in 1323), ed. P. Mandonnet, 'La canonisation de Saint Thomas d'Aquin, 1317–1323', in *Mélanges Thomistes* (Le Saulchoir, 1923), pp. 35–7 (Bibliothèque Thomiste, 3).

18. Philip Berruyer (d. 1261)

Repeat of the process in the Curia (1324): MS Vat. lat. 4019, fols. 13–27.

Relatio (1331): MS Vat. lat. 4020, 4021.

19. St Nicholas of Tolentino (d. 1305, can. 1446)

There are many manuscripts of the *Relatio* prepared by Cardinal William Godino for John XXII and presented by him to Benedict XII (between 1334 and 1335): MS K.I.15, Biblioteca Communale, Siena; MS Arch. Convento OESA, Tolentino; MS Vat. lat. 4027, 4028; MS *ASV, Riti*, Proc. 3000. Partial editions in *Il sesto centenario di San Nicola da Tolentino* (Tolentino, 1906), pp. 287ff.; D. Gandolfi, *Dissertatio historica de ducentis celeberrimis augustinianis scriptoribus* (Rome, 1704), pp. 350–5. See also *AA.SS.* Sept. III, pp. 664–6.

20. St Yves (d. 1303, can. 1347)

Recollectio, ed. de La Borderie *et al.*, *L'histoire de Saint Yves*, pp. 301–435. *Summarium vitae*, ed. *AA.SS.* Maii IV, pp. 539–42. Account of the canonization by a contemporary, ed. *ibid.*, pp. 578–80.

21. St Elzear (d. 1323, can. 1369)

Summarium vitae et miraculorum, MS Vat. lat. 4018 (between 1352 and 1369), ed. J. Cambell, 'Le sommaire de l'enquête pour la canonisation de S. Elzéar de Sabran, TOF (m. 1323)', *Miscellanea Francescana*, 73 (1973), pp. 438–73.

22. Delphine of Sabran (d. 1360)

Summarium, MS Archives paroissiales, Apt (Vaucluse).

23. Charles of Blois (d. 1364)

Processus super apericione libri habitus in Curia (= 1372), in MS *ASV, Collectorie*, 434 A, fols. 1–8v, ed. A. Vauchez, 'Canonisation et politique au XIVe siècle. Documents inédits des Archives du Vatican relatifs au procès de canonization de Charles de Blois, duc de Bretagne', in *Miscellanea in onore di Mgr M. Giusti*, II (Vatican City, 1978), pp. 381–404.

Recollectio, in MS *ASV, Collectorie* 434, fols. 43v–118v (1376).

Observations of the cardinals informing Gregory XI of the technical errors in the process, ed. B. Pocquet du Haut-Jussé, 'La "sainteté" de Charles de Blois', *Revue des questions historiques*, 54 (1926), pp. 104–5.

24. St Bridget (d. 1373, can. 1391, 1415, 1419)

Rubricatio seu summa tocius processus, in ed. Collijn, *Acta et processus canonizacionis beate Birgitte*, pp. 571–607 (between 1380 and 1390).

Contemporary account of the canonization, ed. K. H. Karlsson, *Lars Romares Berätelse om den Heiligi Birgittas Kanonisering* (Stockholm, 1901).

D. Processes of canonization after 1431

These were almost all processes *per viam cultus* performed, on papal instructions, between the seventeenth and the nineteenth centuries, to give juridical status to saints who enjoyed an immemorial cult. These enquiries, whose manuscripts are preserved in the Vatican Archives (*ASV, Riti*, Processi) and the printed Summaries, in part, in the Bibliothèque Nationale in Paris (canonization collections, series H), include many medieval documents copied for the occasion, the originals of which have often been lost. Consequently I have made much use of these sources despite their late date.

Amato Ronconi (d. 1256 or 1265) (lay)
PC (Rimini, 1733–4), in *ASV, Riti*, Proc. 89
Albert of Villa d'Ogna (d. 1279) (lay)
PC (Cremona, 1644 and 1746), in *ASV, Riti*, Proc. 661
Andrew Caccioli, of Spello (d. 1254) (OFM)
PC (Spoleto, 1730–4), in *ASV, Riti*, Proc. 2912
Andrew Corsini (d. 1373) (OCarm)
PC (Fiesole, 1602–3), in *ASV, Riti*, Proc. 759
Andrew Conti, of Anagni (d. 1302) (OFM)
PC (Piglio and Anagni, 1721–3) *ASV, Riti*, Proc. 37–8
Antony of Amendola (d. 1435) (OHSA)
PC (Fermo, 1755), in *ASV, Riti*, Proc. 744
Bartholomew of Breganza (d. 1270) (bishop OP)
PC (Vicenza, 1781–2), in *ASV, Riti*, Proc. 3623
Benvenuta Bojani (d. 1295) (lay)
PC (Cividale del Friuli, 1759–60), in *ASV, Riti*, Proc. 3324 and
Paris, BN, H. 740
Benvenuto of Recanati (d. 1289) (OFM)
PC (Recanati, 1796), Paris, BN, H. 741
Clare of Rimini (d. 1326) (lay)
PC (Rimini, 1694–7, 1782–3), in *ASV, Riti*, Proc. 88 and
Paris, BN, H. 820–1
Clement of Osimo (d. 1291) (OHSA)
PC (Orvieto, 1757), in *ASV, Riti*, Proc. 3228
Dominic of Val (d. 1250) (lay)
PC (Saragossa, 1805), Paris, BN, H. 850
Francesca Romana (d. 1450) (lay)
I processi inediti per Francesca Bussa di Ponziani (S. Francesca Romana) 1450–1453,
ed. P. Lugano (Rome, 1945) (Studi e Testi, 120)
Francis of Fabriano (d. 1322) (OFM)
PC (Fabriano, 1773), in *ASV, Riti*, Proc. 699
Franco of Assergi (d. mid-thirteenth century) (OSB)
PC (L'Aquila, 1756), Paris, BN, H. 929
Gerio of Montesanto (d. ?c.1270) (lay)
PC (Fermo, 1738), in *ASV, Riti*, Proc. 743 and Paris, BN, H. 934
Gregory X (d. 1274) (pope)
PC (Piacenza and Arezzo, 1643), in *ASV, Riti*, Proc. 2150
Henry of Bolzano or of Treviso (d. 1315) (lay)
PC (Treviso, 1746–7), in *ASV, Riti*, Proc. 3021 and Paris, BN, H. 951
Hugh of Sassoferrato (d. 1250) (OSB)
PC (Sassoferrato, 1756), Paris, BN, H. 964
Hugolino of Cortona (d. 1370) (OHSA)
PC (Florence, 1804), Paris, BN, H. 1373
Humiliana dei Cerchi (d. 1246) (lay)
PC (Florence, 1625, 1690), in *ASV, Riti*, Proc. 711–12 and Paris, BN, H. 3213–22
James of Viterbo (d. 1308) (OHSA)

PC (Naples and Viterbo, 1888–92), in *ASV, Riti*, Proc. 4016
  John of the Staff (d. 1290) (OSB)
PC (Fabriano, 1758) in *ASV, Riti*, Proc. 698
  John of La Verna (d. 1322) (OFM)
PC (Arezzo, 1877), in *ASV, Riti*, Proc. 3854
  Marcolino of Forli (d. 1397) (OP)
PC (Forli, 1624–5), in *ASV, Riti*, Proc. 722
  Margaret of Cortona (d. 1297) (lay)
PC (Cortona, 1640), in *ASV, Riti*, Proc. 552 and Paris, BN, H. 1187–92
  Mary of Cervellon (del Socos) (d. 1290) (Order of Mercy)
PC (Barcelona, 1690), Paris, BN, H. 1246
  Michelina of Pesaro (d. 1356) (lay)
PC (Pesaro, 1733), in *ASV, Riti*, Proc. 2263–4 and Paris, BN, H. 1263
  Orderic of Pordenone (d. 1331) (OFM)
PC (Pordenone, 1753), Paris, BN, H. 1275
  Pellegrino Laziosi (d. 1345) (OSM)
PC (Forli, 1697–8), in *ASV, Riti*, Proc. 828
  Philip of Piacenza (d. 1306) (OHSA)
PC (Piacenza, 1760–1), Paris, BN, H. 719
  Rose of Viterbo (d. 1252) (lay)
PC (Viterbo, 1457), in *AA.SS*. Sept. II, pp. 442–79
  Thomas Bellacci (d. 1447) (OFM)
PC (Rieti, 1770), Paris, BN, H. 1359
  Vanna of Orvieto (d. 1306) (lay)
PC (Orvieto, 1753), in *ASV, Riti*, Proc. 3327 and Paris, BN, H. 1018
  Zita of Lucca (d. 1272) (lay)
PC (Lucca, 1694–5), in *ASV, Riti*, Proc. 1315 and Paris, BN, H. 1390

II. The hagiographical documentation

A. Major and general collections

1. Modern

Acta sanctorum quotquot toto urbe coluntur, 67 vols., 1643–1940. (Unless otherwise stated, the pagination quoted is that of the third edn, Paris, 1863–70, for the first 60 vols.)

Baudot, J. and Chaussin, V., *Vies des Saints et des Bienheureux*, 13 vols. (Paris, 1935–59).

Daniel, *La Virgine Maria, Speculum Carmelitanum*, 2 vols., Antwerp, 1680.

Labbé, P., *Novae bibliothecae manuscriptorum librorum tomi II*, 2 vols. (Paris, 1657).

Manrique, A., *Cisterciensium seu verius ecclesiasticorum annalium a conditio Cistercio tomi III*, 4 vols. (Lyons, 1642–9).

Martène, E. and Durand, U., *Thesaurus novus anecdotorum*, 5 vols. (Paris, 1717).

Rios, R. *Corona sanctorum anni Benedictini* (Ramsgate, 1948).

Wadding, L., *Annales minorum*, 32 vols., 3rd edn, (Quaracchi and Rome, 1931–64).

2. Medieval

Bartholomew of Renonico, *De conformitate vite beati Francisci ad vitam Domini Iesu*, ed. in *Analecta Franciscana*, IV–V (Quaracchi, 1906–12).

Bernard Gui, *De fundatione et prioribus conventuum provinciarum Tolosanae et provinciae ordinis Praedicatorum*, ed. P. Amargier (Rome, 1961) (Monumenta ordinis Fratrum Praedicatorum historica, 24).

Catalogus sanctorum Fratrum Minorum, ed. L. Lemmens (Rome, 1903).

Caesar of Heisterbach, *Dialogus miraculorum*, ed. A. Hilka, *Die Wundergeschichten des Caesarius von Heisterbach* (Bonn, 1937) (Publikationem der Gesellschaft für rheinische Geschichtskunde, 43, 3).

Chronica XXIV generalium O.F.M., ed. in *Analecta Franciscana*, III (Quaracchi, 1897).

Dialogus de gestis sanctorum Fratrum Minorum, ed. F. Delorme (Quaracchi, 1923).

Dialogus de vitis sanctorum Fratrum Minorum, ed. L. Lemmens (Rome, 1902).

Gerard of Frachet, *Vitae fratrum O.P.*, ed. B. M. Reichert, in *Monumenta ordinis Praedicatorum historica*, I (Louvain, 1896).

Heribert of Clairvaux, *De miraculis*, ed. in *PL*, 235, cc. 1379–81.

James 'of Voragine', *Legenda aurea*, ed. T. Graesse (Leipzig, 1879).

John of Mailly, *Abrégé des gestes et miracles des saints*, ed. A. Dondaine (Paris, 1947).

Jordan of Saxony, *Liber vitas fratrum*, ed. R. Arbesmann and W. Humpfner (New York, 1943).

A Legendary of Early Augustinian Saints, ed. R. Arbesmann, *Analecta Augustiniana*, 29 (1966), pp. 5–58.

Le légendier de Pierre Calo, ed. A. Poncelet, *Anal. Boll.*, 29 (1910), pp. 41–116.

Memorabilia de sanctis Fratribus Minoribus, ed. M. Faloci Pulignani, *Miscellanea Francescana*, 15 (1915), pp. 65–9.

Meyer, Johannes, *Liber de viris illustribus ordinis Praedicatorum*, ed. P. Von Loë (Leipzig, 1918) (Quellen und Forschungen zur Geschichte des Dominikanerordens in Deutschland, 12).

Pontificum Romanorum qui fuerunt ab exeunte saeculo IX ad finem saeculi XIII vitae ab aequalibus conscriptae, ed. I. M. Watterich, 2 vols. (Leipzig, 1862).

Provinciale ordinis Fratrum Minorum, ed. L. Eubel (Quaracchi, 1892).

Stephen of Salagnac, OP, *De quatuor in quibus Deus Praedicatorum ordinem insignivit*, ed. T. Kaeppeli, in *Monumenta ordinis Praedicatorum historica*, XXII (Rome, 1949).

Thomas of Cantimpré, *Bonum universale de apibus*, Douai edn of 1627.

B. Vitae, *collections of miracles and various texts concerning a particular saint*

Agnes of Montepulciano, OP (d. 1317)
Vita auctore Raimundo de Capua (= *BHL* 155), ed. *AA.SS.* Apr. II, pp. 792–812.

Albert of Messina or of Trapani, OCarm (d. 1307)

Vita et miracula (= *BHL* 228), ed. *AA.SS*. Aug. II, pp. 226–35.

Ambrose Sansedoni, OP (d. 1287)

Vita S. Ambrogii auctoribus Gisberto, Recuperato, Aldobrandino, Oldrado (= *BHL* 382), ed. *AA.SS*. Mar. III, pp. 180–209.

Vita et miracula auctore Recupero Aretino (= *BHL* 383), ed. *AA.SS*. Mar. III, pp. 209–39.

Andrew Caccioli of Spello, OFM (d. 1254)

Vita auctore Thoma de Hispello (= *BHL* 451), ed. *AA.SS*. Iun. I, p. 365.

Andrew Gallerani (d. 1251) (lay)

Vita (= *BHL* 450), ed. *AA.SS*. Mar. III, pp. 49–57.

Angela of Foligno (d. 1309) (lay)

Vita auctore Arnaldo ordinis S. Francisci (= *BHL* 455), ed. *AA.SS*. Ian. I, pp. 186–234.

St Antony of Padua, OFM (d. 1231)

Sancti Antonii de Padua vitae duae, ed. L. de Kerval, Paris, 1904.

Antony 'the pilgrim' of Padua (d. 1267) (lay)

Vita by Sicco Pollentone (fifteenth century), ed. *Anal. Boll.*, 13 (1894), pp. 417–25.

Augustine of Siena, OHSA ('Agostino Novello') (d. 1309)

Vita (= *BHL* 804), ed. *AA.SS*. Maii IV, pp. 616–21.

Benedict XI, OP, pope (d. 1304)

Vitae (= *BHL* 1090–4), ed. E. Martène and U. Durand, *Veterum scriptorum . . . amplissima collectio*, VI (Paris, 1729), cc. 370–5.

Benvenuta Bojani (d. 1295) (lay)

Vita auctore Fr. Conrado de Castellario, O.P. (= *BHL* 1149), ed. *AA.SS*. Oct. XIII, pp. 145–85.

Bona of Pisa (d. 1207) (lay)

Vita (= *BHL* 1389), ed. *AA.SS*. Maii VII, pp. 142–60.

Bridget of Sweden (d. 1373) (lay)

Vita beate Brigide prioris Petri et magistri Petri (= *BHL* 1334), ed. Collijn, in *Acta et processus canonizationis beate Brigitte*, pp. 73–101.

Burchard, Archbishop of Magdeburg (d. 1325)

Epistula Iohannis XXII papae de caede Burchardis (8.VI.1326) (= *BHL* 1479), ed. G. Schmidt, *Geschichtsquellen der provinz Sachsen*, 21 (1886), pp. 180–4.

Miracula Burchardi III archiepiscopi Madgeburgensis (= *BHL* 1480–1), ed. W. Schum, *Neues Archiv.*, 12 (1886–7), pp. 588–90.

Capellus and Bassa (d. 1287) (lay)

Passio (= *BHL* 1557).

Catherine (?early fourth century) (lay)

Le Livre des miracles de Sainte Catherine de Fierbois (1375–1470), ed. Y. Chauvin, Poitiers, 1976 (Archives historiques du Poitou, 60)

Catherine of Siena (d. 1380) (lay)

Vita auctore Raimundo Capuano (= *BHL* 1702), ed. *AA.SS*. Apr. III, pp. 853–959.

Libellus de supplemento legende prolixe virginis beate Catherine de Senis (auct. Thomaso

Antonii de Senis 'Caffarini'), ed. G. Cavallini and I. Foralosso (Rome, 1974) (Testi Cateriniani, 3).

Legenda minor, by Thomas Caffarini, OP, ed. E. Franceschini (Milan, 1942) (Fontes vitae S. Catharinae Senensis historici, 10).

Supplementum legendae prolixae, ed. G. Tinagli (Siena, 1939).

Cecco of Pesaro (d. 1350) (lay)

Vita (= *BHL* 3138), ed. *AA.SS.* Aug. I, pp. 660–2.

Charles the Good (d. 1127) (lay)

Anonymi Passio Caroli, ed. R. Köpke, in *MGH.SS.*, XII (Hanover, 1856), pp. 619–23.

Vita Karoli comitis Flandrensis, by Galbert of Bruges, ed. *AA.SS.* Mar. I, pp. 163–79.

Clare of Montefalco (d. 1308) (nun)

Vita B. Clarae de Cruce ex codice montefalconensi saeculi XIV desumpta, ed. A. Semenza, *Analecta Augustiniana*, 18 (1941), pp. 1–8.

Conrad of Weissensee (d. 1303) (lay)

Passio beati Cunradi, Erlangen, University Library, MS 423 (fourteenth century).

Contardo (d. 1242) (lay)

Vita (fourteenth century), ed. *AA.SS.* Apr. II, pp. 448–52.

Cunegund (d. 1292) (lay)

Vita et miracula Sanctae Kyngae ducissae Cracoviensis (= *BHL* 4666), ed. X. Ketrzynski, in *Monumenta Poloniae historica*, IV (Cracow, 1884), pp. 622–744.

Dagobert (d. 680) (lay)

Vita S. Dagoberti regis Francorum, ed. B. Krusch, in *MGH.SRM.*, II, pp. 509ff.

Delphine (d. 1360) (lay)

Les vies occitanes de Saint Auzias et de Sainte Dauphine, ed. J. Cambell (Rome, 1963).

Didier of Cahors (d. 655) (bishop)

Vita Desiderii Cadurcae urbis episcopi (= *BHL* 2143), ed. B. Krusch and W. Levison, in *MGM.SRM.*, IV, pp. 581ff.

Dominic, OP (d. 1221)

Miracula beati Dominici, ed. A. Walz, in *Miscellanea Pio Paschini*, I (Rome, 1948), pp. 306–26 (*Lateranum*, n.s., 14).

Dominic Loricatus (Camald. monk) (d. 1060)

Vita auctore Pietro Damiani (= *BHL* 2239), ed. *AA.SS.* Oct. VI, pp. 621–7.

Douceline (d. 1274) (lay)

La vie de Sainte Douceline, texte provençal du XIVe siècle, ed. R. Gout (Paris, 1927).

Edmund of Canterbury (d. 1240) (bishop)

Vita S. Edmundi auctore Matthaeo Parisiensi, ed. C. H. Lawrence, in *St Edmund of Abingdon: a study in hagiography and history* (Oxford, 1960), pp. 222–89.

Elizabeth of Herkenrode (d. *c*.1270) (nun)

Vita Elizabeth sanctimonialis in Erkenrode, ed. in *Catalogus codicum hagiographicum Bibliothecae regiae Bruxellensis*, I (Brussels, 1886), pp. 362–79.

Elzear (d. 1323) (lay)

Vita (= *BHL* 2523), ed. *AA.SS.* Sept. VII, pp. 576–93.

Engelbert of Cologne (d. 1225) (bishop)

Vita by Caesar of Heisterbach (= *BHL* 2546)

Miracula (= *BHL* 2547–8), ed. A. Gelenius, *Vindex libertatis ecclesiasticae et martyr S. Engelbertus* (Cologne, 1633), pp. 1–280.

Facio of Cremona (d. 1272) (lay)

Vita (thirteenth century), ed. A. Vauchez, 'Sainteté laïque au XIIIe siècle: la Vie du B. Facio de Crémone (v.1196–1272)', *MEFR* (1972), pp. 13–55.

Fina of San Gimignano (d. 1253) (lay)

Vita by Giovanni del Coppo, OP (fourteenth century) (= *BHL* 2978), ed. *AA.SS.*, Mar. II, pp. 236–41.

Flora (d. 1347) (lay)

Vita e miracoli de sancta Flor, ed. C. Brunel, *Anal. Boll.*, 64 (1946), pp. 549ff.

Francis of Assisi, OFM (d. 1226)

Vita prima S. Francisci fr. Thomae de Celano (= *BHL* 3096), ed. in *Analecta Franciscana*, X (Quaracchi and Florence, 1926–41), pp. 1–115 (= *I Celano*).

Vita secunda S. Francisci fr. Thomae de Celano (= *BHL* 3105), ed. *ibid.*, pp. 127–268 (= *II Celano*).

Legenda maior S. Francisci auctore S. Bonaventura (= *BHL* 3107), ed. *ibid.*, pp. 555–652.

Tractatus de miraculis, ed. *ibid.*, pp. 269–331.

Legenda antiqua Perusina, ed. F. M. Delorme, *La 'Legenda antiqua S. Francisci', texte du MS 1046 (m. 69) de Pérouse* (Paris, 1926).

Miracula S. Francisci, ed. L. Oliger, *AFH*, 12 (1919), pp. 358–401.

Testimonium trium sociorum sancti Francisci de vita et sanctitate ipsius, *AFH*, 10 (1917), pp. 81–2.

Testimonia minora saeculi XIII de sanctis Franciso, ed. L. Lemmens (Quaracchi, 1926).

Desbonnets, T and Vorreux, D., *Saint François d'Assise: documents* (Paris, 1968).

Francis of Fabriano, OFM (d. 1322)

Vita et miracula auctore Dominico Bonaventura Fessis de Fabriano (= *BHL* 3137), ed. *AA.SS.* Apr. III, pp. 992–8.

Francis Patrizzi of Siena, OSM (d. 1328)

Vita auctore Christophoro de Parma (= *BHL* 3139), ed. P. Soulier, *Anal. Boll.*, 19 (1895), pp. 174–95.

Gandulph of Binasco, OFM (d. *c.*1260)

Dialogus de vita auctore Iacobo Narnia, ep. Cephaludensi (*c.*1320) (= *BHL* 3261), ed. in part in *AA.SS.* Sept. V, pp. 704–6.

Gerald of Aurillac (d. 909) (lay)

Vita Geraldi by Odo of Cluny (= *BHL* 3411), ed. in *PL*, 133, cc. 639–704.

Gerardo Cagnoli, OFM (d. 1342)

La leggenda del B. Gerardo Cagnoli, O. min. (1267–1342), di Fra' Bartolomeo Albizzi, O. min (d. 1351), ed. F. Rotolo, *Miscellanea Francescana*, 57 (1957), pp. 368–446.

Il trattato dei miracoli del B. Gerardo Cagnoli O. min. (1267–1342), di Fra' Bartolomeo Albizzi, O. min (d. 1351), *Miscellanea Francescana*, 66 (1966), pp. 134–90.

Gerio of Montesanto (d. *c*.1270) (lay)

Vita auctore Matthaeo Masio (= *BHL* 3448), ed. *AA.SS*. Maii VI, pp. 158–9.

Gerald of Cologne (d. 1240) (lay)

Vita, obitus et miracula beati Geroldi martyris Coloniensis, ed. *AA.SS*. Oct. III, pp. 955–64.

Giles of Assisi, OFM (d. 1262)

Vita fratris Aegidii (= *BHL* 87), in *Chronica XXIV Generalium* (= *Analecta Franciscana*, III) (Quaracchi, 1897), pp. 74–113.

Ginepro OFM (d. 1258)

Vita fratris Juniperi, ed. in *Chronica XXIV Generalium* (= *Analecta Franciscana*, III) (Quaracchi, 1897).

La vita di fratre Ginepro, volgarizzamento, ed. G. Petrocchi (Bologna, 1960).

Godeleva of Ghistelles (d. 1070) (lay)

La Vie ancienne de Sainte Godelive de Ghistelles, ed. M. Coens, *Anal. Boll.*, 44 (1926), pp. 102–37.

Hedwig of Anjou (d. 1339) (lay)

Miracula sanctae Hedwigis reginae Poloniae (= *BHL* 3769), ed. W. Ketrzynski, in *Monumenta Poloniae historica*, IV (Cracow, 1884), pp. 763–9.

Hedwig of Silesia (d. 1241) (lay)

Legenda maior (*c*.1300) (= *BHL* 3766), ed. *AA.SS*. Oct. VIII, pp. 224–64.

Tractatus sive speculum genealogiae sanctae Hedwigis (last third of thirteenth century) (= *BHL* 3768), ed. *AA.SS*. Oct. VIII, pp. 265–7.

Henry or Eric (d. Perugia, 1415) (lay)

Vita (= *BHL* 3817)

Henry of Bolzano or of Treviso (d. 1315) (lay)

Vita auctore Petro Dominico de Baone ep. Tarvisino (= *BHL* 3807), ed. *AA.SS*. Iun. II, pp. 365–9.

Henry VI (d. 1471) (lay)

Henrici VI Angliae regis miracula postuma, ed. P. Grosjean (Brussels, 1935) (Subsidia hagiographica, 22).

Homobonus (d. 1197) (lay)

Vita 'Labentibus annis' (= *BHL* 397), ed. F. S. Gatta, 'Un antica codice Reggiano su Omobono, il "santo popolare" di Cremona', *Bollettino storico Cremonese*, 7 (1942), pp. 95–115.

Vita 'della cipta di Cremona', ed. G. Bertoni, 'Di una Vita di S. Omobono del secolo XIV', *ibid.*, 3 (1938), pp. 161–78.

Hugh of Lincoln (d. 1200) (bishop)

Adam of Eynsham, *Magna vita sancti Hugonis*, ed. D. Douie and H. Farmer, 2 vols. (London, 1961).

Humiliana dei Cerchi (d. 1246) (lay)

Vita auctore Vito de Cortona (= *BHL* 4041), ed. *AA.SS*. Maii IV, pp. 385–418.

Isidore the farm-servant (d. ?eleventh century) (lay)

Legenda de S. Isidoro por Juan Diacono (= *BHL* 4494), ed. F. Fita, *Boletin de la Real Academia de la Historia*, 9 (1886), pp. 102–52.

James Salomon, OP (d. 1314)

Vita (= *BHL* 4110), ed. *AA.SS*. Maii VII, pp. 460–74.

Supplementum ad vitam beati Iacobi Veneti, ed. *Anal. Boll.*, 12 (1893), pp. 363–70.

James Villa (d. 1284 or 1304) (priest)

Vita (fourteenth century), ed. in E. Canuti, *Documenti per la vita e per il culto del B. Giacomo Villa* (Perugia, 1952), pp. 13–17.

John of La Verna, OFM (d. 1322)

Vita (= *BHL* 4393), ed. *AA.SS.* Aug. II, pp. 459–69.

John Discalceatus (d. 1349) (priest, then OFM)

Vita (fourteenth century), ed. L. Paolini, *Acta ordinis Fratrum Minorum*, 29 (1910), pp. 16–28.

John Pelingotto of Urbino (d. 1304) (lay)

Vita (= *BHL* 6850), ed. *AA.SS.* Iun. I, pp. 145–51.

Joan of Signa (d. 1307) (lay)

Vita (end fourteenth century) ed. S. Mencherini, *AFH*, 10 (1917), pp. 378–86.

Joan-Marie of Maillé (d. 1414) (lay)

Vita auctore Martino de Bosco Gualterii (= BHL 5514), ed. *AA.SS.* Mar. III, pp. 744–62.

Juliana of Mount Cornillon (d. 1258) (nun)

Vita beatae Iulianae Corneliensis (= *BHL* 4521), ed. *AA.SS.* Apr. I, pp. 442–75.

Leo, OFM (d. 1271)

Vita fratris Leonis (= *BHL* 4834), in *Analecta Franciscana*, III (Quaracchi, 1897), pp. 65–74.

Louis IX (d. 1270) (lay)

Vie de S. Louis by William of Saint-Pathus, ed. H. F. Delaborde (Paris, 1899).

Louis of Anjou (d. 1297) (bishop OFM)

Liber miraculorum S. Ludovici episcopi, ed. in *Analecta Franciscana*, VII (Quaracchi, 1951), pp. 275–331.

Luchesio (d. *c.*1240) (lay)

Vita, ed. M. Bertagna, 'Note e documenti intorno a S. Lucchese', *AFH*, 62 (1969), pp. 452–7.

Lukarda of Oberweimar (d. 1309) (nun)

Vita (= *BHL* 5064), ed. *Anal. Boll.*, 18 (1899), pp. 305–67.

Margaret of Città di Castello (d. 1320) (lay)

La plus ancienne légende de la B. Marguerite di Città di Castello (vers 1348), ed. M. H. Laurent, *AFP*, 10 (1940), pp. 109–31.

Vita (end fourteenth century) (= *BHL* 5313 b), ed. A. Poncelet, '*Vita beatae Margaritae virginis de civitate Castelli*', ed. *Anal. Boll.*, 19 (1900), pp. 21–36.

Margaret of Cortona (d. 1297) (lay)

Vita et miracula auctore Iuncta Bevignatis (= *BHL* 5314), ed. *AA.SS.* Feb. III, pp. 298–357.

Antica leggenda . . . di Margherita da Cortona, ed. L. da Pelago (Lucca, 1793), pp. 15–339 (contains chapter 12 of the *Vita*, which is missing in the *AA.SS.*)

Margaret of Hungary (d. 1270) (nun OP)

Vita beate Margarete de Ungaria (written *c.*1274–6 by a Hungarian Dominican), ed. in *Inquisitio de vita b. Margaritae ab Ungaria* (Vatican City, 1943), pp. 166ff (Sacra rituum congregatis, sectio historica, 50).

For the other *Vitae* of this saint, see. L. Mezey, 'A középkori Margit-Irodalom

Kerdései', in *Irodalmi anyanyelvuségünk keztedey* (Budapest, 1955), pp. 38–113.

Margaret of Oelishoeve or of Roskilde (d. 1176) (lay)

Translatio (= *BHL* 5324), ed. *AA.SS.* Oct. XI, pp. 717–18.

Margaret of Ypres (d. 1237) (lay)

Vita Margarete de Ypris, ed. G. G. Meersseman, *AFP*, 18 (1948), pp. 106–30.

Martin Donadieu OP (d. 1299)

Vita (fourteenth century), ed. T. Kaeppeli, 'Vie de frère Martin Donadieu de Carcassonne, O.P. (m. 1299) écrite par Bernard et Pierre Gui', *AFP*, 26 (1956), pp. 276–90.

Mary of Oignies (d. 1213) (lay)

Vita B. Mariae Oignaciensis (= *BHL* 5516), by James of Vitry, ed. *AA.SS.* Iun. V, pp. 547–72.

Mary of Venice (d. 1399) (lay)

Vita auctore Thoma de Senis (Thomas Caffarini) (= *BHL* 5522), ed. F. Corner, *Ecclesiae Venetae antiquis monumentis . . . illustratae* (Venice, 1742), d. XI, I, pp. 363–420.

Michelina of Pesaro (d. 1356)

Vita (= *BHL* 5957), ed. *AA.SS.* Iun. III, pp. 925–8.

Nevolone of Faenza (d. 1280) (lay)

Vita, ed. F. Lanzoni, 'Una Vita del Beato Nevolone faentino, terziario francescano', *AFH*, 6 (1913), pp. 645–53.

Nicholas of Linköping (d. 1391) (bishop)

Vita Sancti Nicolai, ed. H. Schük, 'Tva svenska Biografier fran Medeltilden', in *Antiquarisk Tidskrift*, V (Stockholm, 1895), pp. 313–32.

Oringa (d. 1310) (nun)

Vita della b. Oringa Cristiana (XIV s.) (= *BHL* 6350), ed. L. Lami, *Deliciae eruditorum*, XVIII (Florence, 1769), pp. 189–258.

Pellegrino (twelfth century) (lay)

Vita (= *BHL* 6630), ed. *AA.SS.* Aug. I, pp. 77–80.

Pellegrino Laziosi, OSM (d. 1345)

Vita by Vital 'de Avantiis' (= *BHL* 6628), ed. B. Canali, *La Vita del B. Pellegrino Laziosi da Forli* (Lucca, 1725), pp. 165–7.

Peter Crisci of Foligno (d. 1323) (lay)

Vita (= *BHL* 6709), by John Gorini, OP, ed. *AA.SS.* Iul. IV, pp. 665–8 and *Anal. Boll.*, 8 (1889), pp. 365–9.

Peter of Luxembourg (d. 1387) (bishop)

Vita antiquissima (= *BHL* 6718), ed. *AA.SS.* Iul. I, pp. 436–7.

St Peter Martyr, OP (d. 1252)

Vita auctore Thoma Agni de Lentino (= *BHL* 6723).

Peter Parenzo (d. 1199) (lay)

Vita (thirteenth century) (= *BHL* 6763), ed. P. Natalini, *San Pietro Parenzo* (Rome, 1936), pp. 118ff.

Peter Pettinaio (d. 1289) (lay)

Vita auctore Pietro de Monterone, OFM (c.1330), ed. S. Ferri, *Vita del beato Pietro Pettinaio* (Siena, 1529, Italian trans.).

Peter Thomas (d. 1366) (OCarm)

The Life of St Peter Thomas by Philippe de Mézières (= *BHL* 6778), ed. J. Smet, Rome, 1954, pp. 51–162.

Philip of Aix, OFM (d. 1369)

Vita et miracula (= *BHL* 6820), ed. G. B. Tondini, *Delle memorie istoriche concernenti la vita del cardinale Tommaso da Frignano* (Macerata, 1782), app. pp. V–X.

Philip Benizzi, OSM (d. 1285)

Processus de miraculis (= *BHL* 6821), ed. L. Gianius, *Annales sacri ordinis Fratrum Servorum B. Mariae Virginis*, 2nd edn (Florence, 1719), I, pp. 144–50.

Rainerius of Pisa (d. 1160) (lay)

Vita auctore Benincasa (= *BHL* 7084), ed. *AA.SS.* Iun. IV, pp. 345–81.

Raymund Lull (d. 1315) (lay)

Vita beati Raimundo Lulli, ed. B. de Gaiffier, *Anal. Boll.*, 43 (1930), pp. 129–75.

Raymond Palmerio (d. 1200) (lay)

Vita auctore Rufino canonico (= *BHL* 7068), ed. *AA.SS.* Iul. VI, pp. 644–57.

Raymond Peñafort, OP (d. 1275)

Sancti Raymundi de Penyafort opera omnia, ed. J. Rius Serra, III: *Diplomatario* (Barcelona, 1954).

Richard of Pontoise (d. 1179) (lay)

Passio auctore Roberto Gaguino (fifteenth century) (= *BHL* 7213), ed. *AA.SS.* Mar. III, pp. 590–2.

Robert of Knaresborough (d. 1235) (hermit)

The Metrical Life of St Robert of Knaresborough, ed. J. Bazire (London, 1953).

Rose of Viterbo (d. 1251) (lay)

Vita prima (thirteenth century), ed. G. Abate, *S. Rosa di Viterbo, terziaria francescana. Fonti storiche della vita e loro revisione critica* (Rome, 1952).

Salome (d. 1268) (lay)

Vita sanctae Salomeae reginae Haliciensis, auctore Stanislao Franciscano (= *BHL* 7466), ed. W. Ketrzynski, in *Monumenta Poloniae historica*, IV, Cracow, 1884, pp. 770–96.

Simon of Aulne (d. 1229) (Cist. lay bro.)

Vita fratris Simonis de Alna, Bibliothèque royale, Brussels, MS 8965, fols. 208–20.

Simon Fidati of Cascia (d. 1348) (OHSA)

Vita auctore Iohanne de Salerno ipsius discipulo (= *BHL* 7756), ed. N. Mattioli, *Il B. Simone Fidati da Cascia* (Rome, 1898), pp. 16–26.

Simon of Trente (d. 1475) (lay)

Processus de nece pueri, ed. E. Oreglia, in 'La Civiltà Cattolica', 11th ser., 8 (1881), pp. 225–31, 344–52, 476–83, 598–606, 730–8; 9 (1882), pp. 107–13, 219–25, 353–62, 472–9, 605–13; 10 (1883), pp. 727–38.

Stansilas (d. 1079) (bishop)

Vita maior (= *BHL* 7839), ed. *AA.SS.* Maii II, pp. 201–72.

Thomas Hélye of Biville (d. 1257) (priest)

Vita auctore Clemente (= *BHL* 8252–3), ed. L. Delisle, in L. de Pontaumont, *Vie du B. Thomas Hélie de Biville* (Cherbourg, 1848).

Tommasuccio of Nocera (d. 1377) (lay)

Vita, ed. M. Faloci Pulignani, *La leggenda del Beato Tommasuccio* (Gubbio, 1932).

Torello of Poppi (d. 1282) (lay)

Vita (= *BHL* 8305), ed. *AA.SS.* Mar. II, pp. 499–505.

   Thomas Aquinas (d. 1274) (OP)

Translatio corporis S. Thome de Aquino, ed. M. H. Laurent, 'Un légendier dominicain peu connu', *Anal. Boll.*, 58 (1940), p. 43.

   Urban V (d. 1370) (pope)

Vita prima auctore anonymo synchrono, ed. E. Hocedez, *Anal. Boll.*, 26 (1907), pp. 305–16.

   Ursuline of Parma (d. 1408) (lay)

Vita (= *BHL* 8452), ed. *AA.SS.* Apr. I, pp. 723–39.

   Vanna of Orvieto (d. 1306) (lay)

Legenda B. virginis Vannae seu Ioannae de Urbeveteri sororis de poenitentia S. Dominici (= *BHL* 4289), ed. V. Mareddu, *Leggenda latina della B. Giovanna detta Vanna* (Orvieto, 1853).

Vita by Thomas Caffarini, OP, ed. L. Fiumi, *Leggenda della B. Vanna* (Città di Castello, 1885).

   Venturino of Bergamo (d. 1346) (OP)

Legenda beati fratris Venturini ordinis Praedicatorum, ed. A. Grion, *Bergomum*, 30 (1956), pp. 38–110.

   Verdiana (or Viridiana) (d. 1242)

Vita (thirteenth century) (= *BHL* 8540), ed. O. Pogni, *Vita di S. Verdiana d'incognito autore . . . compilata dal fiorentino monaco Biagio* (Empoli, 1936), pp. 5–13.

Vita (= *BHL* 8539), by the Dominican bishop Giacomini (*c.*1420), ed. *AA.SS.* Feb. I, pp. 257–61.

   Villana de' Botti (d. 1361)

Vita by Girolamo di Giovanni, OP (*c.*1420), ed. S. Orlandi, 'La Beata Villana, terziaria domenicana fiorentina nel sec. XIV', *Memorie Domenicane*, 88 (1961), pp. 218–27.

   Walter of Lodi (d. 1224) (lay)

La Vita di S. Gualtero di Lodi, ed. A. Caretta, *Archivio Storico Lodigiano*, 88 (1968), pp. 3–27.

   Werner of Bacharach (d. 1287)

Passio sancti Werneri (= *BHL* 8860), ed. *AA.SS.* Apr. II, pp. 697–9.

   William of Norwich (d. 1144) (lay)

The Life and Miracles of St. William of Norwich (d. 1144) by Thomas of Monmouth, ed. A. Jessop and M. R. James (Cambridge, 1896) (= *BHL* 8926).

   Wulfstan (d. 1095) (bishop)

The Vita Wulfstani of William of Malmesbury (= *BHL* 8756), ed. R. R. Darlington (London, 1928) (Camden Society, 3rd ser., 40).

   Zita (d. 1272) (lay)

Vita (= *BHL* 9019), ed. *AA.SS.* Apr. III, pp. 497–527.

III. Miscellaneous sources

A. Diplomatic sources

1. For Christendom as a whole

Acta capitulorum generalium ordinis Fratrum B. Virginis de Monte Carmelo, I: 1318–1593, ed. G. Wessels, Rome, 1912.

Acta capitulorum generalium ordinis Praedicatorum (1220–1498), ed. B. M. Reichert, 3 vols. (Rome, 1898–1900) (Monumenta ordinis Fratrum Praedicatorum historica, vols III, IV and VIII).

Acta capitulorum provincialium ordinis Praedicatorum, ed. C. Douais (Toulouse, 1894).

Bullarium Franciscanum, ed. J. Sbaraglia and C. Eubel, 7 vols. (Rome, 1759–1904).

Bullarium ordinis FF. Praedicatorum, ed. T. Ripoll, 8 vols. (Rome, 1729–40).

Bullarium Romanum, ed. C. Coquelines, 14 vols., 1739–44.

Fontanini, G., *Codex constitutionum quas summi pontifices ediderunt in solemni canonizatione sanctorum a Johanne XV ad Benedictum XIII, 993–1729* (Rome, 1729).

Potthast, A., *Regesta Pontificum Romanorum inde ab a.1198 ad a.1304*, 2 vols. (Berlin, 1873–5).

Gregorii VII registrum, ed. E. Caspar, in *MGH. Ep. selectae*, 2 vols. (Berlin, 1920–3).

Das Register Innocenz' III, ed. O. Hageneder and A. Haidacher (Graz and Cologne, 1964).

Regesta Honorii papae III, ed. P. Pressutti, 2 vols. (Rome, 1888–95).

Les registres de Grégoire IX (1227–1241), ed. L. Auvray (Paris, 1890–1955) (BEFAR, 2nd ser., 9).

Les registres d'Innocent IV (1243–1254), ed. E. Berger (Paris, 1884–1921) (BEFAR, 2nd ser., 1).

Les registres de Nicolas III (1277–1280), ed. J. Gay (Paris, 1898) (BEFAR, 2nd ser., 14).

Registrum Clementis papae V, ed. L. Tosti, 8 vols. (Rome, 1885–92).

Jean XXII (1316–1334), Lettres communes, ed. G. Mollat, 16 vols., 1904–47 (BEFAR, 3rd ser., 1 bis).

Clément VI (1342–1352), Lettres closes, patentes et curiales se rapportant à la France, ed. E. Déprez, G. Mollat and J. Glénisson, 3 vols. (Paris, 1901–61) (BEFAR, 3rd ser., 3).

Urban V (1362–1370), Lettres communes, ed. M. Hayez and M. H. Laurent, 4 vols. (Rome, 1954–78) (BEFAR, 3rd ser., 5 bis).

Rinaldi, O., *Annales ecclesiastici ab anno MCXCVIII ubi desinit Baronius*, 15 vols. (Lucca, 1747–56).

Statuta capitulorum generalium ordinis Cisterciensis, ed. J. M. Canivez, I (Louvain, 1933).

2. By country or diocese

Bannister, A. T., ed., *Registrum Ade de Orleton (1317–1327)*, London, 1908 (Canterbury and York Society, Canterbury and York Series, 5)

Bliss, W. H., Johnson, C. and Twemlow, J. A., *Calendar of entries in the papal registers relating to Great Britain and Ireland*, II: *Papal letters*, 14 vols. (London, 1894–1960).

Bouchel, L., *Decretum ecclesiae Gallicanae . . . Libri VII* (Paris, 1609).

Brigstock-Sheffard, J. B., ed., *Literae Cantuarienses*, 3 vols. (London, 1887–9) (Rolls Series, 85).

Capes, W., ed., *Charters and records of Hereford Cathedral* (Hereford, 1908).

Capes, W., ed., *Registrum Ricardi de Swinfield episcopi Herefordensis A.D. MCCLXXXIII–MCCCXVII* (London, 1909) (Canterbury and York Society, Canterbury and York Series, 6)

Finke, H., ed., *Acta Aragonensia*, 2 vols. (Berlin, 1908).

Hauréau, G., ed., *Gallia Christiana*, XVI (Paris, 1865).

Hobhouse, E., ed., *Calendar of the Register of John de Drokensford, Bishop of Wells and Bath* (Bath, 1887).

Innes, C., ed., *Registrum de Dunfermelyne* (Edinburgh, 1842).

Johnson, C., ed., *Registrum Hamonis Hethe episcopi Roffensis, A.D. 1319–1352* (Oxford, 1948) (Canterbury and York Society, Canterbury and York Series, 40).

Lange, C., ed., *Diplomatarium Norvegicum*, 18 vols. (Oslo, 1849–1919).

Perroy, E., ed., *The diplomatic correspondence of Richard II* (London, 1933) (Camden Society, 3rd ser., 48).

Rymer, T., *Foedera*, 20 vols. (London, 1704–35).

Schannat, J. F. and Hartzheim, J., *Concilia Germaniae*, 11 vols. (Cologne, 1759–90).

Silverstolpe, C., ed., *Svenskt Diplomatarium*, 4 vols. (Stockholm, 1875–1920).

Webb, J., ed., *A roll of household expenses of Richard Swinfield, Bishop of Hereford, during part of the years 1289 and 1290*, 2 vols. (London, 1854) (Camden Society, 59 and 62).

Würdtwein S. A., *Nova subsidia diplomatica*, 14 vols. (Heidelberg, 1781–92).

B. Narrative sources

Adam of Murimuth, *Continuatio chronicarum*, ed. T. Hog (London, 1846).

Agnolo di Turra, *Cronaca Senese*, ed. A. Lisini and F. Iacometti, in *RIS*², 15, 6 (Bologna, 1936).

Annales Parmenses maiores, ed. P. Jaffé, in *MGH.SS.*, XVIII (Hanover, 1863), pp. 664–790.

Annales Placentini Gibellini, ed. G. Pertz, in *MGM.SS.*, XVIII (Hanover, 1863), pp. 457–581.

Die Berner Chronik von C. Justinger, ed. G. Studer (Berne, 1871).

Bindino di Cialli da Travale, *Cronaca (1315–1416)*, ed. V. Lusini (Siena, 1900).

Boccaccio, Giovanni, *Il Decameron*, ed. C. S. Singleton, 2 vols. (Bari, 1955) (Scrittori d'Italia, 97–8).

Chronicum Colmariense, ed. P. Jaffé, in *MGH.SS.*, XVII (Hanover, 1861), pp. 240–70.

Chronicon Faentinum (1228–1306) auctore Pietro Cantinelli, ed. F. Toracca, in *RIS²*, XXVIII, 2 (Città di Castello, 1902).

Chronicon Modoetense auctore Bonincontro Morigia, ed. L. A. Muratori, in *RIS²*, XII (Milan, 1728), cc. 1062–1184.

Chronicon Parmense, ed. L. A. Muratori, in *RIS²*, IX (Milan, 1726), cc. 766–880.

Chronica pontificum et imperatorum Mantuana, ed. G. Waitz, in *MGM.SS.*, XXIV (Hanover, 1879), pp. 214–20.

Chronicon S. Benigni Divionensis, ed. E. Garnier and J. Bougaud, in *Analecta Divionensia* (Dijon, 1875), pp. 1–228.

Commynes, Philippe de, *Mémoires*, ed. A. Pauphilet and E. Pognon, in *Historiens et chroniqueurs du Moyen Age* (Paris, 1958), pp. 951–1450.

Compendium Saxonis gestorum Danorum, ed. M. C. Gertz, in *Scriptores minores historiae Danicae medii aevi*, I (Copenhagen, 1918), pp. 216–439.

Dictum de Kenilworth, ed. W. Stubbs, in *Select Charters*, 2nd ed. (Oxford, 1874).

Flores historiarum, ed. H. E. Luard, 3 vols. (1890) (Rolls Series, 95).

La cronaca maggiore dell'ordine domenicano di Galvano Fiamma. Frammenti editi per cura di G. Odetto, *AFP*, 10 (1940), pp. 297–373.

Gesta Hammaburgensis ecclesiae pontificum, ed. W. Trillmich, 4 vols. (Hamburg, 1895).

The chronicle of William de Rishanger of the Barons' Wars: the miracles of Simon de Montfort, ed. J. O. Halliwell (London, 1840), pp. 67–109 (Camden Society, 15).

Joinville, *Histoire de S. Louis*, ed. N. de Wailly (Paris, 1874).

Jordan of Giano, *Chronica fratris Iordani a Iano ord. fratrum minorum*, ed. in *Analecta Franciscana*, I (Quaracchi, 1885), pp. 1–19.

Matthew Paris, *Chronica majora*, ed. H. R. Luard, 7 vols. (London, 1972–83) (Rolls Series, 57).

Memoriale potestatum Regiensium, ed. in *RIS*², VIII (Milan, 1726), cc. 1072–1176.

Mica Madio da Spalato, *Historia de gestis Romanorum imperatorum et summorum pontificum*, ed. in *Archivio storico per la Dalmazia*, I, 1926, pp. 9–33.

Monachi cuiusdam Malmesberiensis Vita Edwardi II, ed. W. Stubbs, in *Chronicles of the reigns of Edward I and Edward II*, 2 vols. (London, 1882–3) (Rolls Series, 76).

Monumenta Erpherfurtensia saec. XII, XIII, XIV, ed. O. Holder-Egger, in *MGH.SRG*. XLII.

Procès de condamnation de Jeanne d'Arc (1430), ed. P. Tisset and Y. Lanhers, 2 vols. (Paris, 1970).

Polychronicon Radulphi Higden monachi Cestrensis, ed. J. R. Lumby, 7 vols. (London, 1871–1906) (Rolls Series, 41).

Rycardi de Sancto Germano notarii Chronica, ed. G. H. Pertz, in *MGH.SS.*, XIX (Hanover, 1866), pp. 321–84.

Salimbene, *Cronica*, ed. G. Scalia, 2 vols. (Bari 1966) (Scrittori d'Italia, 232–3).

Sicard of Cremona, *Cronica*, ed. O. Holder-Egger, in *MGH.SS.*, XXXI, 1903, pp. 176–87.

Vetus Chronica Sialandie, ed. M. C. Gertz, in *Scriptores minores historiae danicae medii aevi*, II (Copenhagen, 1922), pp. 1–14.

C. Medieval ecclesiastical authors (Canonists, theologians, spirituals)

Antoninus, St, of Florence, *Curam illius habe* (Florence edn of 1565).

Augustinus Triumphus, Summa de potestate ecclesiastica (Rome edn of 1584).

Bartholomew of Bologna, OFM, *Tractatus de luce*, ed. I. Squadrani, *Antonianum*, 7 (1932), pp. 201–493.

Bernard, St, *De moribus et officiis episcoporum*, in *PL*, 182, cc. 80–834.

De XII abusivis saeculi, ed. G. Hartel (Vienna, 1871) (*Corpus scriptorum Ecclesiasticorum Latinorum*, 3, 3).

Dicta B. Aegidii Assisiensis (Quaracchi, 1905) (Bibliotheca Franciscana ascetica medii aevi, 3).

Elias of Cortona, OFM, *Epistola encyclica de transitu S. Francisci*, ed. in *Analecta Franciscana*, X (Quaracchi, 1926–41), pp. 523–8.

Frederick Visconti, *Sermones*, in Cod. Laurent, Plut. XXXIII, 1.

Gerson, John, *Opera omnia*, ed. E. Du Pin, 4 vols. (Antwerp, 1706).

Giraldi Cambrensis opera, ed. J. S. Brewer, 3 vols. (London, 1863).

Giudici, John-Baptist of, *De canonizatione beati Bonaventurae*, ed. E. Baluze, in *Miscellanea*, IV (Lucca, 1764), pp. 471–87.

Gregory the Great, *Liber regulae pastoralis*, in *PL*, 77, cc. 13–128.

Guibert of Nogent, *De pignoribus sanctorum*, in *PL*, 156, cc. 607–79.

Guido Papae, Super Decretales (Venice edn of 1588).

Helgaud of Fleury, *Vie de Robert le Pieux*, ed. R. H. Bautier (Paris, 1963) (Sources d'histoire médiévale publiées par l'IRHT, 1).

Henry of Langenstein, *Consilium pacis de Unione Ecclesiae*, ed. H. von der Hardt, in *Magnum Oecumenicum Constantiense concilium*, II (Frankfurt and Leipzig, 1697), cc. 56ff.

Henricus de Segusio (*Hostiensis*), *In quinque Decretalium libros commentaria* (Venice edn of 1581).

Summa aurea (Lyons edn of 1568).

Hervaeus Natalis, Liber de paupertate Christi et Apostolorum, ed. J. G. Sikes, *Archives d'histoire littéraire et doctrinale du Moyen Age*, 11 (1937), pp. 209–97.

Innocent IV (Sinibaldo Fieschi), *Apparatus in V libros decretalium* (Lyons edn of 1525).

In quinque libros Decretalium commentaria (Venice edn of 1578).

Le registre d'inquisition de Jacques Fournier, évêque de Pamiers (1318–1325), ed. J. Duvernoy, 3 vols. (Toulouse, 1965).

Joannes Andreae, *In tertium Decretalium librum novella commentaria* (Venice edn of 1581).

John Damascene, *De fide orthodoxa*, ed. H. Etienne, in *Theologica* (Lyons, 1519).

Lamprecht of Ratisbon, OFM, *Sanct Franzisken Leben und Tochter Syon*, ed. K. Weinhold, *Lamprecht von Regensburg* (Paderborn, 1880).

Lucae Tudensis . . . adversus Albigensium errores, ed. J. de Mariana, 3 vols. (Ingoldstadt, 1612).

Malvezzi (*Malvitius*) Troilo, *De sanctorum canonizatione opusculum* (Bologna, 1487).

Meditationes de Passione Christi (saec. XIV), ed. N. J. Stalling (Washington, 1965).

Odo of Cluny, *Sermo de sancto Benedicto*, in *PL*, 133, c. 722.

Ordo canonizationis sanctorum (*c.*1494), ed. in D. Wilkins, Concilia magna Britanniae et Hiberniae, III (London, 1737), p. 639.

Peter of Blois, *De institutione episcoporum*, ed. in *PL*, 207, cc. 1097–1112.

Epître de Pierre Jean Olieu aux fils de Charles II de Naples en l'an 1295, ed. and trans. M. H. Vicaire, in *Franciscains d'Oc: les Spirituels, ca. 1280–1324* (Toulouse 1975), pp. 127–38 (Cahiers de Fanjeaux, 10).

The letters from Peter of St John to Hato of Troyes, ed. G. Constable and J. Kritzeck, in *Petrus Venerabilis 1156–1956* (Rome, 1956), pp. 49ff (Studia Anselmiana, 40).

Il supplizio di Fra Michele da Calci (1389), ed. G. De Luca, in *Prosatori minori del Trecento*, I: *Scrittori di religione (Milan, 1954), pp. 213–36.*

Sachetti, Franco, *Opere*, ed. A. Borlenghi (Milan, 1957).

Stephen of Bourbon, OP, *Anecdotes historiques* or *Traité du sept dons du Saint Esprit*, ed. A. Lecoy de la Marche (Paris, 1877).

Thomas Aquinas, *In IVum librum Sententiarum* (Venice edn of 1586).

Summa theologiae, 5 vols. (Venice edn of 1588).

Thomas Caffarini, OP, *Tractatus de ordine fratrum de poenitentia di Fr. Tommaso da Siena*, ed. M. H. Laurent and F. Valli (Milan, 1938) (Fontes vitae S. Catharinae Senensis historici, 21).

William of Saint-Amour, *Contra adversarium perfectionis christianae*, ed. S. Clasen, *AFH*, 31 (1938), pp. 276–329, 32 (1939), pp. 89–200.

Wyclif, John, *Trialogus*, ed. G. V. Lechler (Oxford, 1869).

BIBLIOGRAPHY

* соесоесо*

Abate, G., *S. Rosa di Viterbo, terziaria francescana. Fonti storiche della vita e loro revisione critica* (Rome, 1952).

Abbati Olivieri, A. degli, *Della patria della B. Michelina e del B. Cecco del Terz'Ordine di S. Francesco* (Pesaro, 1762).

Adnès, P., sv Larmes, in *Dictionnaire de spiritualité*, IX (Paris, 1976), cc. 287–303.

Aigrain, R., *L'hagiographie, ses sources, ses méthodes, son histoire* (Paris, 1953).

Alberti, F., *Notizie antiche e moderne riguardanti Bevagna, città dell'Umbria* (Venice, 1792).

Alphandéry, P., 'Prophètes et ministères prophétiques dans le Moyen Age latin', *Revue d'histoire et de philosophie religieuse*, 12 (1932), pp. 334–59.

Altaner, B., 'Zur Beurteilung der Persönlichkeit und der Entwicklung der hl. Dominikus', *Zeitschrift für Kirchengeschichte*, 46 (1927), pp. 396–407.

Amedeo, R., 'Il B. Oddone di Novara, monaco certosino', *Novarien*, 3 (1969), pp. 5–45.

Amore, A., 'Culto e canonizzazione dei santi nell'antichità cristiana', *Antonianum*, 52 (1977), pp. 38–80.

'La canonizzazione vescovile', *Antonianum*, 52 (1977), pp. 231–66.

Ancelet-Hustache, J., 'Mechtilde de Magdebourg. Etude de psychologie religieuse', thesis, Paris, 1926.

Sainte Elisabeth de Hongrie (Paris, 1947).

'A propos du "Speculum virginum". Ascétique et mystique féminine du Haut Moyen Age', *Etudes germaniques*, 8 (1960), pp. 152–60.

Anderson, D., *A saint at stake: the strange death of William of Norwich* (London, 1964).

Andrieu-Guitrancourt, P., *L'archevêque Eudes Rigaud* (Paris, 1938).

Antal, F., *Florentine painting and its social background* (London, 1947).

Antin, D., 'La mort de Saint Martin', *Revue des études anciennes*, 66 (1964), pp. 108–20.

Anton, H. H., *Fürstenspiegel und Herrscherethos in der Karolingerzeit* (Bonn, 1968) (Bonner historische Forschungen, 32).

Antonelli, F., *De inquisitione medicolegali supra miraculis in causis beatificationis et canonizationis* (Rome, 1962) (Studia Antoniana, 18).

Arnaldi, G., 'Intorno al "Liber Pontificalis" ', in *Monseigneur Duchesne et son temps* (Rome, 1975), pp. 129–36 (Collection de l'Ecole française de Rome, 23).

Assistance et charité (Toulouse, 1978) (Cahiers de Fanjeaux, 13).

Auvry, C. and Laveille, A., *Histoire de la congrégation de Savigny*, 3 vols. (Paris, 1898).

Auzas, P. M., 'Essai d'un répertoire iconographique de Saint Louis', in *Septième centenaire de la mort de Saint Louis. Actes des colloques de Royaumont et Paris (21–27 mai 1970)* (Paris, 1976), pp. 3–56.

Axters, S., 'Over "Virtus" en heiligheidscomplex onder de Merowingers', in *Miscellanea historica in honorem A. De Meyer* (Louvain, 1946), pp. 266–85.

Azzoni Avogari, R. degli, *De B. Henrico qui Tarvisii decessit anno Christo MCCCXV commentarius* (Venice, 1760).

Baethgen, F., *Der Engelpapst: idee und wirklichkeit* (Leipzig, 1943).

Baix, R., 'Saint Hubert, sa mort, sa canonisation, ses reliques', in *Mélanges Fr. Rousseaux* (Brussels, 1958), pp. 71–80.

Baker, D., ' "Vir Dei": secular sanctity in the early tenth century', in *Popular belief and practice* (Cambridge, 1972), pp. 41–53 (Studies in Church History, 8).

Baker, D., ed., *Sanctity and secularity: the Church and the world* (Oxford, 1973) (Studies in Church history, 10).

Balboni, D., sv Prandoni, Alberto, in *BS*, X (Rome, 1968), cc. 1089–92.

Baldwin, J. W., 'The intellectual preparation for the canon of 1215 against the ordeals', *Speculum*, 36 (1961), pp. 613–36.

Banfi, F., 'Specchio delle anime semplici dalla B. Margarita scritto', *Memorie Domenicane*, 15 (1940), pp. 3–16, 131–40.

Bannister, A. T., *The cathedral church of Hereford* (London, 1924).

Baraut, C., sv Joachim de Flore, in *Dictionnaire de spiritualité*, VIII (Paris, 1974), cc. 1179–1201.

Baron, F., 'La mausolée de saint Elzéar de Sabran à Apt', *Bulletin monumental*, 136 (1978), pp. 267–83.

Baron, R., 'A propos des ramifications des vertus au XIIe siècle', *Revue de théologie ancienne et médiévale*, 23 (1956), pp. 19–39.

Barone, G., 'Frate Elia', *BISIME*, 85 (1974–5), pp. 89–144.

Barth, M., 'Zum Kult des hl. Königs Ludwig im deutschen Sprachgebiet und in Skandinavien', *Freiburger Diözesan Archiv*, 3rd ser., 14–15 (1962–3), pp. 127–226 (Festschrift J. Vincke).

Bartoli Langeli, A., 'I penitenti a Spoleto nel Duecento', in *L'Ordine della Penitenza di S. Francesco d'Assisi*, pp. 303–30.

Bautier, A. M., 'Typologie des ex voto mentionnés dans des textes antérieurs à 1200', in *La piété populaire. Actes du 99e congrès des sociétés savantes (Besançon 1974)*, I (Paris, 1977), pp. 237–82.

Beaune, C., 'Saint Clovis', in *Le métier d'historien au Moyen Age: études sur l'historiographie médiévale*, ed. B. Guenée, Paris, 1977, pp. 139–56 (Publications de la Sorbonne, Etudes, 13).

Becker, P. A., *Die Heiligsprechung Karls der Grossen* (Berlin, 1947) (Berichte über die Verhandlung der Sächsichen Akademie der Wissenschaften zu Leipzig, Phil.Hist. Klasse, 84, 3).

Becquet, J., 'La première crise de l'ordre de Grandmont', *Bulletin de la société archéologique et historique du Limousin*, 87 (1960), pp. 284–324.

Bédier, J., *Les Fabliaux: étude de littérature populaire et d'histoire littéraire au Moyen Age* (2nd edn, Paris, 1895) (Bibliothèque de l'Ecole pratique des Hautes Etudes, 98).

Beirnaert, L., 'La signification du symbolisme conjugal dans la vie mystique', in *Mystique et continence*, pp. 380–9.

Bekker-Nielson, H., 'A note on two Icelandic saints', *The Germanic Review*, 36 (1961), pp. 108–9.

Bell, D. M., *L'idéal éthique de la royauté en France au Moyen Age d'après quelques moralistes du temps* (Geneva, 1972).

Bémont, C., *Simon de Montfort, comte de Leicester* (Paris, 1884), ed. and trans. E. F. Jacob, *Simon de Montfort, Earl of Leicester* (Oxford, 1930).

Benati, A., 'Armanno Pungilupo nella storia ferrarese del 1200', *Analecta Pomposiana*, 2 (1966), pp. 85–123.

Benedict XIV (Prosper Lambertini), *De servorum Dei beatificatione et beatorum canonizatione*, 4 vols. (Bologna, 1734–8).

Benz, E., 'Heilige Narrheit', *Kyrios*, 3 (1938), pp. 1ff.
Die Vision: Erfahrungsformen und Bilderwelt (Stuttgart, 1969).

Berg, D., *Armut und Wissenschaft: Beiträge zur Geschichte des Studienwesens der Bettelorden im 13. Jahrhundert* (Dusseldorf, 1977) (Geschichte und Gesellschaft, 15).

Bergamaschi, D., *S. Omobono e il suo tempo* (Cremona, 1899).

Bernards, M., *Speculum virginum: Geistigkeit und Seelenleben der Frau im Hochmittelalter* (Cologne, 1955).

Bernos, M., 'Réflexions sur un miracle à l'Annonciade d'Aix-en-Provence. Contribution à l'étude des sanctuaires "à répit" ', *Annales du Midi*, 82 (1970), pp. 5–20.
'Miracles chez les Servites en Provence à l'époque moderne', *Revue d'histoire de la spiritualité*, 49 (1973), pp. 243–56.

Bertagna, M., 'Sul terz'ordine francescano in Toscana nel sec. XIII, note storiche e considerazione', in *L'Ordine della Penitenza di San Francesco d'Assisi*, pp. 263–77.

Bertaux, E., 'Les saints Louis dans l'art italien', *Revue des deux mondes*, 158 (1900), pp. 610–44.

Berthier, J.J., *Le chapitre de S. Nicolò de Trévise* (Rome, 1912).

Besançon, A., *Le Tsarevitch immolé* (Paris, 1967).

Bibliotheca sanctorum, under the dir. F. Caraffa, 12 vols. (Rome, 1961–9).

Bignami-Odier, J., 'Les visions de Robert d'Uzès', *AFP*, 25 (1955), pp. 258–310.

Bihel, E., 'De quodam elencho Assisiano testium oculatorum S. Francisci stigmatum', *AFH*, 19 (1926), pp. 931–6.

Bihl, M., 'Franciscus fuitne Angelus sexti sigilli?', *Antonianum*, 2 (1927), pp. 59–70.
'De canonizatione S. Francisci', *AFH*, 21 (1928), pp. 468–514.
'Die heilige Elizabeth von Thüringen als Terziärin', *Franziskanische Studien*, 18 (1931), pp. 259–93.

Binyon, M. P., *The virtues: a methodological study in the Thomistic ethics* (Chicago, 1947).

Blaher, D. J., *The ordinary processes in causes of beatification and canonization* (Washington, 1949) (The Catholic University of America, Canon Law Studies, 268).

Blanco, E. C., *The rule of the Spanish military order of St James, 1170–1493* (Leiden, 1971) (Medieval Iberian Peninsula Texts and Studies, 4).

Blank, W., *Die Nonnenviten des 14. Jahrhunderts: eine Studie zur hagiographischen Literatur des Mittelalters, unter besonderer Berücksichtigung der Visionen und ihrer Lichtphänomene* (Freiburg im Breisgau, 1962).

Bloch, M., review of Delehaye, H., *Sanctus: essai sur le culte des saints dans l'Antiquité*, *Revue de synthèse*, 47 (1929), pp. 88–90.

Les rois thaumaturges: études sur le caractère surnaturel attribué à la puissance royale, particulièrement en France et en Angleterre (2nd edn, Paris, 1961), trans. J. E. Anderson, *The royal touch: sacred monarchy and scrofula in England and France* (London, 1973).

La société féodale (2nd edn, Paris, 1968), trans. L. A. Manyon, *Feudal society* (London, 1961).

Bloomfield, M., *The seven deadly sins: an introduction to the history of a religious concept, with special reference to medieval literature* (East Lansing, Michigan, 1952).

Bock, F., 'Kaisertum, Kurie und Nationalstaat im Beginn des 14. Jahrhunderts', *Römische Quartalschrift*, 44 (1936), pp. 105–22, 169–220.

Boesch Gajano, S., 'Storia e tradizione vallombrosana', *BISIME*, 76 (1964), pp. 99–215.

Review of Graus, *Volk, Herrscher und Heiliger*, *Studi Medievali*, 3rd ser., 8 (1967), pp. 901–9.

'La "Biblioteca sanctorum". Problemi di agiografia medievale', *RSCI*, 26 (1972), pp. 139–53.

Agiografia altomedioevale (Bologna, 1976).

'Il santo nella visione storiografica di Gregorio di Tours', in *Gregorio di Tours (Todi, 1971)* (Todi, 1977), pp. 29–91 (Convegni del centro di studi sulla spiritualità medievale, 12).

Boglioni, P., 'Miracle et merveilleux religieux chez Grégoire le Grand', in *Cahiers d'études médiévales*, I (Montreal, 1974), pp. 11–102.

Bogyay, T. von, Bak, J. and Silagi, G., *Die heiligen Könige* (Graz, 1976) (Ungarns Geschichtsschrieber, 1).

Boillon, C., sv Guglielmo, abate di Eskil, in *BS*, VII (Rome, 1966), cc. 464–5.

Bolgar, R., *The classical heritage and its beneficiaries* (Cambridge, 1961).

Bolton, B. M., 'Mulieres sanctae', in *Sanctity and secularity*, ed. D. Baker, pp. 77–95.

Bolzonetti, A., *Il Monte Fano e un grande anacoreta* (Rome, 1906).

Bonhome, A. de, sv Héroïcité des vertus, in *Dictionnaire de spiritualité*, VII (Paris, 1969), cc. 337–43.

Bonnet, S., *Saint Rouin, histoire de l'ermitage et du pèlerinage* (Paris, 1956).

Borawaska, D., *W sprawie genezy kultu sw Stanislawa bpa* (Warsaw, 1950).

Borgo, R., *Vita, morte e miracoli del Beato Geroldo* (Cremona, 1581).

Borromeo, C., 'Avignone e la canonizzazione di Pier Celestino', in *Celestino V e il VII centenario della sua incoronazione* (L'Aquila, 1894), pp. 267–300.

Borst, A., 'Die Sebaldlegenden in der mittelalterlichen Geschichte Nürnbergs', *Jahrbuch für fränkische Landesforschung*, 26 (1966), pp. 19–178.

Bosl, K., 'Der Adelheilige. Idealtypus und Wirklichkeit, Gesellschaft und Kultur im merowingerzeitlichen Bayern des VII. und VIII. Jahrhunderts', in *Speculum historiale: festschrift J. Spörl* (Freiburg im Breisgau, 1965), pp. 167–87.

Botte, B., 'Confessor', *Archivum Latinitatis Medii Aevi*, 16 (1942), pp. 137–48.

Bourmont, A. de, 'Index processuum authenticorum beatificationis qui conservantur in Bibliotheca Nationali Parisiensi', *Anal. Boll.*, 5 (1886), pp. 147–61.

Boutruche, R., *Seigneurie et féodalité*, I (2nd edn, Paris, 1968).

Bouyer, L., *La vie de Saint Antoine: essai sur la spiritualité du monachisme primitif* (Saint-Wandrille, 1950).

Boyle, L., sv Tommaso di Lancaster, in *BS*, XII (Rome, 1968), cc. 582–4.

Brakel, C. H., 'Die vom Reformpapsttum geförderten Heiligenkulte', *Studi Gregoriani*, 9 (1972), pp. 240–311.

Braunfels, W., *Der Hedwigscodex von 1353 (Sammlung Ludwig)*, 2 vols. (Berlin, 1972).

Bredero, A., *Etudes sur la 'Vita prima' de Saint Bernard* (Rome, 1960).

'La canonisation de Saint Bernard et sa "Vita" sous un nouvel aspect', *Cîteaux, Commentaria Cisterciensia*, 25 (1974), pp. 185–98.

'The Canonization of Saint Bernard', in *Saint Bernard: studies commemorating the eighth century of his canonization* (Kalamazoo, 1977), pp. 63–99.

Brentano, R., *Two Churches: England and Italy in the thirteenth century* (Princeton, 1968).

Bresc, G. and H., 'Les Saints protecteurs de bateaux, 1200–1460', *Ethnologie française*, 9 (1979), pp. 161–78.

Brilioth, Y., *Kungadöme och Pavemakt, 1363–1414* (Uppsala, 1925).

Svenska Kyrkans Historia (Uppsala, 1941).

Britton, J., *The history and antiquities of the cathedral church of Hereford* (London, 1836).

Brocchini, E., *Sicardo di Cremona e la sua opera letteraria* (Cremona, 1958).

Brooke, C. N. L., 'St. Dominic and his first biographer', *Transactions of the Royal Historical Society*, 5th ser., 17 (1967), pp. 23–40.

Brosch, J., *Der Heiligsprechungsprozess 'per viam cultus'* (Rome, 1938).

'Die aequipollente Kanonisation', *Theologie und Glaube*, 51 (1961), pp. 47–51.

Browe, P., *Beiträge zur sexualethik des Mittelalters* (Breslau, 1932).

Brown, P. A., *The development of the legend of Thomas Becket* (Philadelphia, 1930).

Brückner, W., 'Volkstümliche Denkstrukturen und hochschichtlichen Weltbild in Votivweisen. Zur Forschungssituation und Theorie des bildlichen Opferkults', *Schweizerisches Archiv für Volkskunde*, 59 (1963), pp. 189–203.

Bugge, J., *Virginitas: an essay in the history of a medieval idea* (The Hague, 1975) (Archives internationales d'histoire des idées, series minor, 17).

Bugnini, A., 'Confessor', *Ephemerides liturgicae*, 60 (1946), pp. 169–70.

Bultot, R., *Christianisme et valeurs humaines: la doctrine du mépris du monde en*

Occident de S. Ambroise à Innocent III, IV: *Le XIe siècle*, 2 vols. (Paris, 1963–4).

Burchi, P., sv Clemente da Osimo, in *BS*, IV, Rome, 1964, cc. 35–6.

sv Enrico, in *BS*, IV (Rome, 1964), cc. 1231–2.

Burmeister, K. H., 'Der hl. Ivo und seine Verehrung an den deutsche Rechtsfakultäten', *Zeitschrift der Savigny-Stiftung für Rechtsgeschichte, Germ. Abteilung*, 92 (1975), pp. 60–88.

Butler, A., Thurston, H. and Attwater, D., *Lives of the saints*, 4 vols. (London, 1956).

Cabassut, A., sv Cœurs (échanges des), in *Dictionnaire de spiritualité*, II (Paris, 1953), cc. 1046–51.

Callaey, F., *L'idéalisme franciscain au XIVe siècle: étude sur Ubertin de Casale* (Louvain, 1911).

Callus, D. A., *Robert Grosseteste, scholar and bishop* (Oxford, 1955).

Cambell, J., *Les Vies occitanes de Saint Auzias et de Sainte Dauphine* (Rome, 1963).

Campi, P. M., *Historia ecclesiastica di Piacenza* (Piacenza, 1651).

Campros, P., 'A perpaus de la perfection d'Alzeas et de Delfina', *Annales de l'institut d'études occitanes*, 4th ser., 1 (1965), pp. 88–105.

Canuti, E., *Documenti per la vita e per il culto del B. Giacomo Villa* (Perugia, 1952).

Capitani, C., 'La figura del vescovo in alcune collezione canoniche della seconda metà del secolo XI', in *Vescovi e diocesi in Italia nel Medio Evo (sec. IX–XIII)* (Padua, 1964), pp. 161–91 (Italia sacra, 5).

Caraffa, F., sv Andrea Corsini, in *BS*, I, Rome, 1961, cc. 1158–68.

sv Pietro, eremita, in *BS*, X, Rome, 1968, cc. 735–7.

sv Simone da Todi, in *BS*, XI, Rome, 1968, c. 1184.

Carli, E., 'Considerazione sul B. Andrea Gallerani', *Economia e storia*, 11 (1964), pp. 253–62.

Carlsson, E., *Translacio archiepiscoporum: Eriklegends historicitet* (Uppsala, 1944).

Carolus-Barré, L., 'Consultation du cardinal Pietro Colonna sur le IIe miracle de S. Louis', *BECh*, 117 (1959), pp. 57–72.

'Saint Louis et la translation des corps saints', in *Etudes d'histoire du droit dédiées à G. Le Bras*, II (Paris, 1965), pp. 1087–662.

'Les Franciscains et le procès de canonisation de Saint Louis', *Les amis de S. François*, n.s., 12 (1971), pp. 3–6.

'Les enquêtes pour la canonisation de Saint Louis de Grégoire X à Boniface VIII et la bulle "Gloria Laus", du 11 août 1297', *RHEF*, 57 (1971), pp. 196–229.

Carozzi, C., 'Une béguine Joachimite: Douceline, soeur d'Hugues de Digne', in *Franciscains d'Oc: les Spirituels, ca. 1280–1324*, pp. 169–201.

'Douceline et les autres', in *La religion populaire en Languedoc* (Toulouse, 1976), pp. 251–67 (Cahiers de Fanjeaux, 11).

Casamassa, A., 'Per una nota marginale del Cod. Vat. lat. 5949', in *Miscellanea historica P. L. Oliger . . . oblata* (Rome, 1945), pp. 301–26 (Antonianum, 20).

Casolini, F., sv Rosa di Viterbo, in *BS*, XI, Rome, 1968, cc. 413–25.

Castaldo, E., *Santo Bartolo, il Giob della Toscana* (Florence, 1928).

Caturegli, N., sv Ranieri, in *BS*, XI, Rome, 1968, cc. 37–44.

sv Ubaldesca, in *BS*, XII, Rome, 1969, cc. 731–2.

Certeau, M. de, sv Hagiographie, in *Encyclopaedia universalis*, VIII (Paris, 1968), pp. 207–9.

L'écriture de l'histoire (Paris, 1975).

Chaloupecky, V. and Ryba, B., *Středověké legendy Prokopské* (Prague, 1953).

Chaney, W. A., *The cult of kingship in Anglo-Saxon England: the transition from paganism to Christianity* (Manchester, 1970).

Chapotin, M. D., *Histoire des Dominicains de la Province de France: le siècle des fondations* (Rouen, 1898).

Charland, P. V., *Le culte de Sainte Anne en Occident* (Quebec, 1921).

Checchi, V., *Il B. Gherardo Bonamici, terziario francescano* (Florence, 1939).

Chelini, J., *Histoire religieuse de l'Occident médiéval* (Paris, 1968).

Cherniavsky, T., *Tsar and people* (Yale, 1961).

Christ, K., 'Werner von Bacharach. Eine mittelrheinische Legende', in *Festschrift Otto Glaubing*, II (Leipzig, 1938), pp. 1–28.

Clasen, S., 'Das Heiligkeitsideal im Wandel der Zeiten. Ein Litteraturbericht über Heiligenleben des Altertums und des Mittelalters', in *Wissenschaft und Weisheit* (1970), pp. 40–64, 132–54.

Claude, H., sv Carlo di Blois, in *BS*, III, Rome, 1963, cc. 793–4.

Cole, E. G., 'Proceedings relative to the canonization of Robert Grosseteste, Bishop of Lincoln', *Associated Architectural Societies' Reports and Papers*, 33 (1915), pp. 1–34.

'Proceedings relative to the canonization of John of Dalderby, Bishop of Lincoln', *Associated Architectural Societies' Reports and Papers*, 34 (1916), pp. 243–76.

Collinet-Guérin, M., *Histoire du nimbe* (Paris, 1961).

Congar, Y., *L'Eglise de Saint Augustin à l'époque moderne* (Paris, 1970).

'L'Eglise et l'Etat sous S. Louis', in *Septième centenaire de la mort de Saint Louis. Actes des colloques de Royaumont et Paris (21–27 mai 1970)* (Paris, 1975), pp. 265–71.

sv Laïc et laïcat, in *Dictionnaire de spiritualité*, IX (Paris, 1976), cc. 79–93.

Constable, G., 'Opposition to pilgrimage in the Middle Ages', in *Studia Gratiana*, 19 *(Mélanges G. Fransen)* (Rome, 1976), pp. 123–46.

Cordier, H., *Les voyages en Asie au XIVe siècle du B. Frère Oderic de Pordenone* (Paris, 1891).

La coscienza cittadina nei comuni italiani del duecento (Todi, 1972) (Convegni del centro di studi sulla spiritualità medievale, 11).

Courcelle, P., *Recherches sur les Confessions de S. Augustin* (Paris, 1950).

Connais toi toi-même: de Socrate à Saint Bernard, 2 vols. (Paris, 1974–5).

Cracco, G., 'Uomini di Dio e uomini di Chiesa', *Ricerche di storia sociale e religiosa*, n.s., 12 (1977), pp. 163–202.

Dal Pino, F. A., *I Frati Servi di Maria dalle origini all'approvazione (1233 ca–1304)*, 3 vols. (Louvain, 1976).

Davidsohn, R., *Storia di Firenze*, 3 vols. (Florence, 1956).

Davis, C. T., 'Le pape Jean XXII et les Spirituels: Ubertin de Casale', in *Franciscains d'Oc: les Spirituels, ca. 1280–1324*, pp. 263–83.

De Beer, F., *La conversion de S. François selon Thomas de Celano: étude comparative des textes relatifs à la conversion en Vita I et Vita II* (Paris, 1968).

Debongnie, E., 'Essai critique sur l'histoire des stigmatisations au Moyen Age', *Etudes carmélitaines*, 21 (1936), pp. 36–42.

'Les lévitations de Sainte Brigitte de Suède', *RHE*, 34 (1938), pp. 70–83.

De Clercq, C., *La législation religieuse franque de Clovis à Charlemagne* (Louvain and Paris, 1936) (Université de Louvain, recueil de travaux, 2nd ser., fasc. 38).

'L'établissement progressif de la procédure de canonisation', *Revue de l'Université Laval*, 2 (1948), pp. 473–85.

'Les causes des serviteurs de Dieu: le fonds dit des canonisations à la Bibliothèque Nationale de Paris', *Revue de droit canon*, 4 (1954), pp. 76–100.

De Ghellinck, J., 'Iuventus, gravitas, senectus', in *Studia mediaevalia in honorem . . . R. J. Martin* (Bruges, 1948), pp. 39–59.

Delalande, J., *Les extraordinaires croisades d'enfants et de pastoureaux au Moyen Age* (Paris, 1961).

Delaruelle, E., 'Sainte Radegonde, son type de saintété et la chrétienté de son temps', in *Etudes mérovingiennes (Poitiers, 1952)* (Paris, 1953), pp. 65–74.

'La translation des reliques de S. Thomas d'Aquin à Toulouse et la politique universitaire d'Urbain V', *Bulletin de littérature ecclésiastique*, 56 (1955), pp. 129–46.

L'Eglise au temps du Grand Schisme et de la crise conciliaire, 1378–1449 (Paris, 1962) (Histoire de l'Eglise, XIV, 2).

'La spiritualité des pèlerinages à Saint-Martin de Tours', in *Pellegrinaggi e culto dei santi in Europa fino alla prima crociata* (Todi, 1963) (Convegni del centro di studi sulla spiritulità medievale, 4), repr. in *La piété populaire*, pp. 477–520.

'Les ermites et la spiritualité populaire', in *L'Eremitismo in Occidente nei secoli XI e XII* (Milan, 1965), pp. 212–47, repr. in *La piété populaire*, pp. 125–60.

'Saint François d'Assise et la piété populaire', in *S. Francesco nella ricerca storica degli ultimi ottanta anni* (Todi, 1971), pp. 125–55 (Convegni del centro di studi sulla spiritulità medievale, 9), repr. in *La piété populaire*, pp. 247–75.

La piété populaire au Moyen Age (Turin, 1975).

Delaruelle, E. and Higounet, C., 'Réformes prégrégoriennes en Comminges et canonisation de S. Bertrand', *Annales du Midi*, 61 (1948), pp. 152–7.

Delcorno, C., *Giordano da Pisa e l'antica predicazione volgare* (Florence, 1975).

Delcourt, M., 'Le complexe de Diane dans l'hagiographie chrétienne', *Revue de l'histoire des religions*, 153 (1958), pp. 1–33.

Delehaye, H., *Sanctus: essai sur le culte des saints dans l'Antiquité* (Brussels, 1927) (Subsidia hagiographica, 21).

'Loca sanctorum', *Anal. Boll.*, 48 (1930), pp. 1–64.

Les origines du culte des martyrs (2nd edn, Brussels, 1933) (Subsidia hagiographica, 20).

Etudes sur le légendier romain: les saints de novembre et décembre (2nd edn, Brussels, 1936) (Subsidia hagiographica, 23).

Les Passions des martyrs et les genres littéraires (2nd edn, Brussels, 1966) (Subsidia hagiographica, 13b).

Delhaye, P. 'L'organisation scolaire du XIIe siècle', *Traditio*, 5 (1947), pp. 211–68.
'Le dossier antimatrimonial de l' "Adversus Jovinianum" et son influence sur quelques écrits latins du XIIe siècle', *Mediaeval Studies*, 13 (1951), pp. 65–86.

Delooz, P., 'Pour une étude sociologique de la sainteté canonisée dans l'Eglise catholique', *Archives de sociologie des religions*, 13 (1962), pp. 17–43.
'Notes sur les canonisations occitanes à l'époque de la croisade des Albigeois', *Annales de l'institut d'études occitanes*, 4th ser., 1 (1965), pp. 106–112.
Sociologie et canonisations (Liège and The Hague, 1969).

Del Re, N., sv Giacomo da Viterbo, in *BS*, VI, Rome, 1965, cc. 425–7.
sv Engelberto, in *BS*, IV (Rome, 1964), cc. 1209–10.
sv Innocenzo V, in *BS*, VII (Rome, 1969), cc. 844–6.
sv Verdiana, in *BS*, XII (Rome, 1969) cc. 1023–7.

De Maio, R., 'L'ideale eroico nei processi di canonizzazione della controriforma', *Ricerche di storia sociale e religiosa*, 2 (1972), pp. 139–60.

Denis-Boulet, N., 'La canonisation de Charles de Blois', *RHEF*, 28 (1942), pp. 216–24.

Deonna, W., 'Εὐωδία: croyances antiques et modernes, l'odeur suave des dieux et des élus', *Genava*, 17 (1939), pp. 167–263.

De Roeck, H., *De normis regulae ordinis Fratrum Minorum circa missiones inter infideles* (Rome, 1961) (Studi e testi francescani, 19).

De Rosa, G., 'Sainteté, clergé et peuple dans le Mezzogiorno italien', *Revue d'histoire de la spiritualité*, 52 (1976), pp. 245–64.

Desroche, H., Maitre, J. and Vauchez, A., 'Sociologie de la sainteté canonisée', *Archives de sociologie des religions*, 30 (1970), pp. 109–15.

De Vooght, J., 'La théologie du miracle chez S. Augustin', *Recherches de théologie ancienne et médiévale*, 9 (1939), pp. 197–222.

Devos, P., 'Le dossier de S. Wenceslas dans un manuscrit du XIIIe siècle (Cod. Bollandianus 433)', *Anal. Boll.*, 82 (1964), pp. 87–131.

D'Haenens, A., sv Carlo il buono, in *BS*, III, Rome, 1963, cc. 794–7.
'Erudition et vulgarisation: une conciliation possible. A propos d'une encyclopédie hagiographique récente', *RHE*, 63 (1968), pp. 826–34.

Dimier, M. A., 'Le Bienheureux Jean de Montmirail, moine de Longpont', *Mémoires de la fédération des sociétés savantes de l'Aisne*, 7 (1960–1), pp. 182–91.

Dolbeau, F., 'Le légendier de S. François de Gualdo: tentative de reconstitution', *Bull. della dep. di storia patria per l'Umbria*, 72 (1976), pp. 157–75.

Dollfuss, M. A., 'Etude clinique de quelques miracles de Saint Louis', *Bulletin de la société des antiquaires de France* (1971), pp. 23–35.

Döllinger, I. von, *Beiträge zur Sektengeschichte des Mittelalters*, 2 vols. (Munich, 1890).

Dondaine, A., 'La vie et les œuvres de Jean de San Gimignano', *AFP*, 9 (1939), pp. 165–8.
'Saint Pierre martyr. Etudes', *AFP*, 23 (1953), pp. 66–162.

Dondi dell'Orologio, F., *Dissertazioni sopra l'istoria ecclesiastica di Padova*, 8 vols. (Padua, 1808).

Douais, C., *Les reliques de Saint Thomas d'Aquin* (Paris, 1903).

Dorn, E., *Der sündige Heilige in der Legende des Mittelalters* (Munich, 1967) (Medium Aevum, Philologische studien, 10).

1274, année charnière: mutations et continuités (Lyon–Paris, 1974) (Paris, 1977) (Colloques internationaux du CNRS, 558).

Doyère, P. sv Gertrude d'Helfta, in *Dictionnaire de spiritualité*, VI (Paris, 1967), cc. 331–9.

Duby, G., *L'Europe des cathédrales, 1140–1280* (Geneva, 1966).

'Remarques sur la littérature généalogique en France aux XIe et XIIe siècles', *CRAI* (1967), pp. 333–45, repr. in *Hommes et structures du Moyen Age* (Paris and The Hague, 1973), pp. 287–98.

'L'idéal du prince en France au début du XIe siècle', *Cahiers d'histoire*, 17 (1972), pp. 211–16.

'L'histoire des systèmes de valeur', *History and Theory*, 11 (1972), pp. 15–25.

'Histoire social et idéologie des sociétés', in *Faire de l'histoire*, I: *Nouveaux problèmes*, ed. J. Le Goff and P. Nora (Paris, 1974), pp. 147–68.

Le temps des cathédrales: l'art et la société, 980–1420 (Paris, 1976), trans. E. Levieux and B. Thompson, *The age of the cathedrals: art and society 980–1420* (London, 1981).

Du Cange, C., *L'histoire de S. Louis par Jean de Joinville* (Paris, 1668).

Dulong, M., 'Les derniers moments de Sainte Dauphine à Apt d'après le procès de canonisation', *Provence historique*, 6 (1956) (Mélanges Busquet), pp. 132–8.

Dumont, E., Montminy, J. P. and Stein, M., eds., *Le merveilleux. 2e Colloque sur les religions populaires (Québec, 1971)* (Quebec, 1973), p. 161 (Histoire et sociologie de la culture, 4).

Dupré Theseider, E., 'L'eresia a Bologna nei tempi di Dante', in *Studi storici in onore di Gioacchino Volpe*, I (Florence, 1957), pp. 381–444.

'La grande rapina dei corpi santi dall'Italia al tempo di Ottone I°', in *Festschrift P. E. Schramm*, I (Wiesbaden, 1964), pp. 420–32.

Dupront, A., 'Formes de la culture de masse: de la doléance au pèlerinage panique (18e–20e s.)', in *Niveaux de culture et groupes sociaux* (Paris and The Hague, 1967), pp. 149–67.

'Pèlerinages et lieux sacrés', in *Mélanges F. Braudel*, II (Paris, 1973), pp. 189–206.

'Anthropologie du sacré et cultes populaires. Histoire et vie du pèlerinage en Europe Occidentale', *Miscellanea historiae ecclesiasticae*, 5 (1974), pp. 235–8.

Duval-Arnould, L. 'Note chronologique sur S. Yves de Tréguier', *Anal. Boll.*, 92 (1974), pp. 409–24.

Eckert, W. P., 'Aus den Akten des Trienter Judenprozess', in *Judentum im Mittelalter*, ed. A. Wilpert (Berlin, 1966), pp. 281–336 (Miscellanea medievalia, 4).

Edgell, G. H., 'Le martyre du frère Pierre de Sienne et de ses compagnons à Tana. Fresques d'Ambrogio Lorenzetti', *La Gazette des Beaux-Arts*, 71 (1929), pp. 307–8.

Ehrle, F., 'Zur Vorgeschichte des Concils von Vienne', *Archiv für Literatur und Kirchengeschichte des Mittelalters*, 3 (1887), pp. 1–195.

'Olivis Leben und Schriften', *Archiv für Literatur und Kirchengeschichte des Mittelalters*, 3 (1887), pp. 409–533.

Elm, K., 'Italienische eremitengemeinschaften des 12. und 13. Jahrhunderts', in *L'Eremitismo in Occidente nei secoli XI e XII* (Milan, 1965), pp. 503–29.

'Franziskus und Dominikus. Wirkungen und Antriebskräfte zweier Ordensstifter', *Saeculum*, 22 (1971), pp. 127–47.

Emden, A. B., sv Canteloupe (Thomas de), in *Biographical register of the University of Oxford*, II (Oxford, 1958).

Emilio D'Ascoli, 'La vita spirituale anteriore a S. Francesco d'Assisi', *Collectanea franciscana*, 2 (1932), pp. 5–34, 153–78.

Enfant et sociétés (Paris and The Hague, 1973) (Annales de démographie historique).

Erickson, C., 'Bartholomew of Pisa, Francis exalted: "De conformitate" ', *Mediaeval Studies*, 34 (1972), pp. 252–74.

Esch, A., 'Die Zeugenaussagen im Heiligsprechungsverfahren für S. Francesca Romana als Quelle zur Sozialgeschichte Roms im frühen Quattrocento', *QFIAB*, 53 (1973), pp. 93–151.

Esser, K., 'Franziskus von Assisi und die Katharer seiner Zeit', *AFH*, 51 (1958), pp. 225–64.

Origini e valori autentici dell'ordine dei Frati Minori (Milan, 1972).

Ewig, E., 'Zum christlichen Königsdenken im Frühmittelalter', in *Das Königstum, seinegeistigen und rechtlichen Grundlagen* (Lindau and Constance, 1956) (Vorträge und Forschungen, 3).

'Der Martinskult im Frühmittelalter', *Archiv für Mittelrheinische Kirchengeschichte*, 14 (1962), pp. 11–26.

Ex voto marins du Ponant, catalogue of the exhibition directed by M. Mollat (Paris, 1975).

Faloci-Pulignani, M., 'Il Beato Simone da Collazzone e il suo processo nel 1252', *Miscellanea Francescana*, 12 (1910), pp. 117–32.

Famille et parenté dans l'Occident médiéval, Actes du colloque de Paris (1974), ed. G. Duby and J. Le Goff (Rome, 1977) (Collection de l'Ecole française de Rome, 22).

Fassebinder, M., 'Untersuchung über die Quellen zum Leben der hl. Klara von Assisi', *Franziskanische Studien*, 23 (1936), pp. 296–335.

Fawtier, R., *Sainte Catherine de Sienne: essai critique des sources: sources hagiographiques* (Paris, 1921) (= *BEFAR*, 121).

Fawtier, R. and Canet, L., *La double expérience de Catherine Benincasa (Sainte Catherine de Sienne)* (Paris, 1948).

Fedotov, P., *The Russian religious mind* (Cambridge, Mass., 1946).

Fenicchia, V., sv Bernardo il Pellegrino, in *BS*, III (Rome, 1963), cc. 61–3.

sv Gerardo (di Gallinaro), in *BS*, VI (Rome, 1965), cc. 186–7.

Ferré, J., 'Les principales dates de la vie d'Angèle de Foligno', *Revue d'histoire franciscaine*, 2 (1925), pp. 21–33.

Festugière, A. J., *La sainteté* (Paris, 1942).

'Lieux communs littéraires et thèmes de folklore dans l'hagiographie primitive', *Weiner Studien*, 73 (1960), pp. 123–52.

Fichtenau, H., 'Zum Reliquienwesen im früheren Mittelalter', *MIOG*, 60 (1952), pp. 60–89.

Fiebig, P., *St Reinoldus in Kult, Liturgie und Kunst* (Dortmund, 1956) (Beiträge zur Geschichte Dortmunds und der Graftschaft Mark, 53).

Finucane, R. C., *Miracles and pilgrims: popular beliefs in medieval England* (London, 1977).

Folz, R., 'Essai sur le culte liturgique de Charlemagne dans les églises de l'Empire', thèse complémentaire, Paris, 1951.

Review of Schramm, *Herrschaftszeichen und Staatssymbolik*, *Revue historique*, 218 (1957), pp. 125–7.

'Zur Frage der heiligen Könige. Heiligkeit und Nachleben in der Geschichte des burgundischen Königtums', *Deutsches archiv für Erforschung des Mittelalters*, 19 (1958), pp. 317–44.

'Tradition hagiographique et culte de S. Dagobert, roi des Francs', *Le Moyen Age*, 69 (1963), pp. 14–63.

'La chancellerie de Frédéric Ier et la canonisation de Charlemagne', *Le Moyen Age*, 70 (1964), pp. 13–31.

'Vie posthume et culte de S. Sigisbert, roi d'Austrasie', in *Festschrift P. E. Schramm*, I (Weisbaden, 1964), pp. 7–26.

'La légende liturgique de S. Sigismond d'après un manuscrit d'Agaune', *Speculum historiale, Festschrift J. Spörl* (Freiburg and Munich, 1965), pp. 152–66.

'Aspects du culte liturgique de Saint Charlemagne en France', in *Karl der Grosse: Lebenswerk und Nachleben*, IV (Dusseldorf, 1967), pp. 77–99.

Review of Graus, *Volk, Herrscher und Heiliger*, *Revue historique*, 91 (1967), pp. 154–5.

'La sainteté de Louis IX d'après les textes liturgiques de sa fête', *RHEF*, 57 (1971), pp. 31–45.

'Tradition hagiographique et culte de Sainte Bathilde, reine des Francs', *CRAI* (1975), pp. 369–84.

'Naissance et manifestation d'un culte royal: Saint Edmond roi d'Est-Anglie', in *Festschrift für Heinz Löwe zum 65. Geburtstag* (Cologne/Vienna, 1978), pp. 236–46.

Fontette, M. de, *Les religieuses à l'âge classique du droit canon: recherches sur les structures juridiques des branches féminines des ordres* (Paris, 1967).

'Les Mendiants supprimés au 2e Concile de Lyon (1274). Frères Sachets et Frères Pies', in *Les Mendiants en pays d'Oc au XIIIe siècle* (Toulouse, 1973), pp. 193–216 (Cahiers de Fanjeaux, 8).

Foreville, R., 'L'Eglise et la royauté en Angleterre sous Henri II Plantagenet (1154–1189)', thesis, Paris, 1943.

'Un procès de canonisation à l'aube du XIIIe au XVe siècle (1201–1202): le Livre de Saint Gilbert de Sempringham', thèse complémentaire, Paris, 1943.

Le jubilé de saint Thomas Becket, du XIIIe au XVe siècle (1220–1470). Etudes et documents (Paris, 1958) (Bibliothèque générale de l'EPHE, VIe section).

Latran I, II, III et Latran IV (Paris, 1965) (Histoire des conciles œcuméniques, 6)

'Mort et survie de S. Thomas Becket', *Cahiers de civilisation médiévale*, 19 (1971), pp. 21–38.

Forster, M., *Zur Geschichte des Reliquienkultus im Alten England* (Munich, 1943) (Sitzungberichte der Bayerischen Akademie der Wissenschaften, 8).

Franceschini, C. S., *Vita de S. Silvestro abbate* (Iesi, 1772).

Franciscains d'Oc: les Spirituels, ca. 1280–1324 (Toulouse, 1975) (Cahiers de Fanjeaux, 10).

Franco, M. R., *La Beata Umiliana de'Cerchi Francescana del Terz'Ordine in Firenze* (Rome, 1977).

Frank, J. W., 'Die Spannung zwischen Ordensleben und Wissenschaftlichen Arbeit im früher Dominikanerorden', *Archiv für Kulturgeschichte*, 49 (1967), pp. 164–207.

I frati penitenti di San Francesco nella società del due e trecento (Atti del secondo convegno di studi francescani, Roma, 12–14 ottobre 1976), ed. Mariano d'Alatri (Rome, 1977).

Frazer, J. G., *Les origines magiques de la royauté* (Paris, 1920).

Frizzi, A., *Memorie per la storia di Ferrara*, 3 vols. (Ferrara, 1850).

Frugoni, A., 'Il giubileo di Bonifacio VIII', *BISIME*, 62 (1950), pp. 1–103.

   'Incontro con Cluny', in *Spiritualità Cluniacense* (Todi, 1960), pp. 11–29 (Convegni del centro di studi sulla spiritualità medievale, 2).

   Celestiniana (Rome, 1954) (Studi storici, 6–7).

Frutaz, A. P., ' "Auctoritate . . . beatorum apostolorum Petri et Paul". Saggio sulle formule di canonizzazione', *Antonianum*, 42 (1967), pp. 435–501.

Fumagalli, V., 'Note sulla Vita Geraldi di Odone di Cluny', *BISIME*, 76 (1964), pp. 217–40.

   Terra e società nell'Italia padana: i secoli IX–X (Bologna, 1974).

Fumi, L., 'Processi della canonizzazione del B. Ambrogio da Massa, dei Minori', *Miscellanea Francescana*, I (1886), pp. 77–80, 129–36.

Gabler, U., 'Die Kinderwallfahrten aus Deutschland und der Schweiz zum Mont-Saint-Michel', *Zeitschrift für Schweizerische Kirchengeschichte*, 63 (1969), pp. 221–331.

Gagna, F., *De processu canonizationis a primis Ecclesiae saeculis usque ad Codicem Iuris canonici* (Rome, 1940).

Gaiffier, B. de, 'L'hagiographie et son public', in *Mélanges Van der Essen* (Louvain, 1947), pp. 135–66.

   sv Douceline (sainte), in *Dictionnaire de spiritualité*, III (Paris, 1957), cc. 1672–3.

   'Un thème hagiographique: le pendu miraculeusement sauvé', in *Etudes critiques d'hagiographie et d'iconologie* (Brussels, 1967), pp. 194–226 (Subsidia hagiographica, 43).

   'Miracles bibliques et Vies de saints', in *Etudes critiques d'hagiographie et d'iconologie*, pp. 50–61.

   'Liberatus a suspendio', in *Etudes critiques d'hagiographie et d'iconologie*, pp. 227–32.

   'L'hagiographie dans le marquisat de Flandre et le Duché de Basse Lotharingie au XIe siècle', in *Etudes critiques d'hagiographie et d'iconologie*, pp. 415–507.

   'Réflexions sur les origines du culte des martyrs', in *Etudes critiques d'hagiographie et d'iconologie*, pp. 7–30.

   'Mentalité de l'hagiographe médiéval d'après quelques travaux récents', *Anal. Boll.*, 86 (1968), pp. 391–9.

   'Notes bibliographiques sur l'histoire de l'ordre des Servites de Marie', *Anal. Boll.*, 93 (1975), pp. 167–76.

Galante, G. A., *Memorie del B. Nicola eremita di Santa Maria a Circolo in Napoli* (Naples, 1877).

Galbert, J. and Parent, M., 'La légende des trois mariages de Ste Anne', in *Etudes d'histoire littéraire et doctrinale du XIIIe siècle* (Paris and Ottawa, 1932), pp. 165–84.

Gallen, J., *La province de Dacie de l'ordre des Frères Prêcheurs* (Rome and Helsinki, 1946).

'Les causes de Ste Ingrid et des saints Suédois au temps de la Réforme', *AFP*, 7 (1937), pp. 5–40.

Garampi, G., *Memorie della Beata Chiara di Rimini* (Rome, 1755).

Garcia, V., 'El testimonio del confessor en los processos de beatification de los servos de Dios y canonazacion de los bienaventurados', thesis, Gregorian University of Rome, 1954.

Garcia Rodriguez, C., *El culto de los sanctos en la España romana y visigota* (Madrid, 1966).

Garosi, G., *Inventario dei manoscritti delle Biblioteche d'Italia*, LXXXVIII: *San Gimignano, Biblioteca comunale* (Florence, 1972).

Gaudemet, J., 'Patristique et pastorale. La contribution de Grégoire le Grand au "Miroir de l'évêque" dans le décret de Gratien', in *Etudes d'histoire du droit canonique dédiées à G. Le Bras*, I (Paris, 1965), pp. 129–39.

Geary, P. J., *Furta sacra: thefts of relics in the central Middle Ages* (Princeton, 1978).

'L'humiliation des saints', *Annales ESC*, I (1979), pp. 27–42.

Gellner, E., *Saints of the Atlas* (London, 1969).

'Pouvoir politique et fonction religieuse dans l'Islam marocain', *Annales ESC*, 25 (1970), pp. 699–713.

George, K. and C., 'Roman Catholic sainthood and social status', *Journal of Religion*, 35 (1955), pp. 85–98.

Giacomini, A., sv Agostino Novello, in *BS*, I (Rome, 1961), cc. 601–8.

Giacomini, A. M., sv Rena (Giulia della), in *BS*, XI (Rome, 1968), cc. 115–16.

Gieben, S., 'Bruder Elemosinas Doppelbericht zum Leben der hl. Elisabeth von Thüringen', *Collectanea Franciscana*, 35 (1965), pp. 166–76.

Gilson, E., 'S. Bonaventure et l'iconographie de la Passion', *Revue d'histoire franciscaine*, 1 (1924), pp. 405–24.

Saint Bernard: un itinéraire de retour à Dieu (Paris, 1964) (Chrétiens de tous les temps, 4).

Girard, R., 'Les saints bénédictins des XIVe et XVe siècles d'après les documents contemporains', mémoire de maîtrise, Bordeaux, 1974.

Glasser, F., *Die Franziskanische Bewegung: ein Betrag zur Geschichte sozialer Reformideen im Mittelalter* (Stuttgart and Berlin, 1903).

Glorieux, P., 'Mœurs de chrétienté au temps de Jeanne d'Arc: le traité "Contre l'institution de fêtes nouvelles" ', *Mélanges de science religieuse*, 23 (1966), pp. 5–29.

Gnädinger, L., *Eremitica: Studien zur altfranzösischen Heiligenvita des 12. und 13. Jahrhunderts* (Tübingen, 1972) (Beihefte zur Zeitschrift für romanische Philologie, 130).

Godfrey, J., *The English parish, 600–1300* (London, 1969).

Gontier, D. and Le Bas, C., 'Analyse socio-économique de quelques recueils de miracles dans la Normandie du XIe au XIIIe siècle', *Annales de Normandie*, 24 (1974), pp. 3–36.

Goodich, M., 'Childhood and adolescence among the thirteenth century saints', *History of Childhood Quarterly*, 1 (1973), pp. 285–309.

'The politics of canonization in the thirteenth century: lay and Mendicant saints', *Church History*, 44 (1975), pp. 294–307.

'A profile of thirteenth century sainthood', *Comparative Studies in Society and History*, 18 (1976), pp. 429–37.

Gordini, G. D., sv Margherita di Roskilde, in *BS*, VIII (Rome, 1967), cc. 780–1.

Goretti-Ministi, G. G., *Vita di San Torello da Poppi* (Rome, 1926).

Gorski, K., 'Le roi saint. Un problème d'idéologie féodale', *Annales ESC*, 24 (1969), pp. 370–6.

Gottschalk, J., 'Die Förderer der Heiligsprechung Hedwigs', *Archiv für Schlesische Kirchengeschichte*, 21 (1963), pp. 73–133.

Die Hl. Hedwig, Herzogin von Schlesien (Graz and Cologne, 1964).

Gougaud, L., *Dévotions et pratiques ascétiques au Moyen Age* (Maredsous, 1929).

Grabmann, M., 'Die kanonisation des hl. Thomas von Aquin in ihrer Bedeutung für die Verbreitung seiner Lehre im 14. Jahrhundert', *Divus Thomas* (1923), pp. 233–49.

'Die deutsche Frauenmystik des Mittelalters. Ein Uberblick', in *Mittelalterliches Geistesleben* (Munich, 1926), pp. 469–88.

'Hagiographische Texte in einer Hs. des Kirchenhist. Seminars der Universität München, *AFP*, 19 (1949), pp. 379–82.

Grabois, A., 'L'idéal de la royauté biblique dans la pensée de Thomas Becket', in *Thomas Becket, Actes du colloque international de Sédières* (Paris, 1975), pp. 103–10.

Graham, T., *Medieval minds: mental health in the Middle Ages* (London, 1967).

Gratien de Paris, *Histoire de la fondation et de l'évolution de l'ordre des Frères Mineurs au XIIIe siècle* (Paris and Gembloux, 1928).

Grau, E., 'Das "Privilegium paupertatis" der Hl. Klara. Geschichte und Bedeutung', *Wissenschaft und Weisheit*, 38 (1975), pp. 17–25.

'Die Klausur im Kloster S. Damiano zu Lebzeiten der Heiligen Klara', in *Studia historico-ecclesiastica: Festgabe für Prof. Luchesius G. Spätling O.F.M.* (Rome, 1977), pp. 311–46 (Bibliotheca pontificii Athenaei Antoniani, 19).

Graus, G., *Volk, Herrscher und Heiliger im Reich der Merowinger: Studien zur Hagiographie der Merowingerzeit* (Prague, 1965).

'Sozialgeschichtliche Aspekte der Hagiographie der Merowinger- und Karolingerzeit. Die Viten des südalemannischen Raumes und die sogennanten Adelsheiligen', in *Mönchtum, Episkopat und Adel im Gründungszeit des Klosters Reichenau* (Sigmaringen, 1974), pp. 131–76 (Vorträge und Forschungen, 20).

Grégoire, R., 'L'adage ascétique "Nudus nudum Christum sequi" ', in *Studi storici in onore di O. Bertolini*, I (Pisa, 1975), pp. 395–409.

sv Laurent l'Encuirassé, in *Dictionnaire de spiritualité*, IX (Paris, 1976), cc. 392–3.

Grèzes, H. de, *Saint Vernier (Verny, Werner, Garnier), patron des vignerons en Auvergne, en Bourgogne et en Franche-Comté* (Clermont-Ferrand, 1889).

Grosjean, P., 'De S. Iohanne Bridlingtoniensi collectanea', *Anal. Boll.*, 53 (1935), pp. 101–29.

'Thomas de la Hale, moine et martyr à Douvres en 1295', *Anal. Boll.*, 72 (1954), pp. 167–91.

Grundmann, H., *Religiöse Bewegungen im Mittelalter* (2nd edn, Darmstadt, 1961).

'Zur Vita S. Gerlaci eremitae', *Deutsches Archiv*, 18 (1962), pp. 539–54.

Gualazzini, U., 'Dalle prime affermazioni del "Populus" di Cremona agli statuti della "Societas Populi" del 1229', *Archivio storico Lombardo*, n.s., 2 (1937), pp. 3–66.

Guarnieri, R., 'Il movimento del Libero Spirito', *Archivio italiano per la storia della pietà*, 4, pp. 351–708.

Guenée, B., 'L'enquête historique ordonnée par Edouard Ier, roi d'Angleterre, en 1921', *CRAI* (1975), pp. 572–84.

Guibert, J. de, 'Dons du Saint-Esprit et mode d'agir ultrahumain', *Revue d'ascétique et de mystique*, 3 (1922), pp. 394–411.

Guilloreau, L., 'Une fondation royale en l'honneur de S. Louis d'Anjou chez les Cordeliers du Mans', *Revue historique et archéologique du Maine*, 49 (1901), pp. 46–9.

Guillou, A., 'L'évêque dans la société méditerranéenne des VIe–VIIe siècles: un modèle', *BECh*, 131 (1973), pp. 5–19.

Guiraud, J., 'Le commerce des reliques au commencement du IXe siècle', in *Mélanges G. B. De Rossi* (Rome, 1892), pp. 73–95 (Supplément aux MEFR).

Günther, H., *Kaiser Heinrich II, der Heilige* (Kempten, 1904).

Guth, K., *Guibert von Nogent und die hochmittelalterliche Kritik an der Reliquienverehrung* (Ottobeuren, 1970).

Guy, J. C., ed., *Paroles des anciens: apophtegmes des Pères du désert* (Paris, 1976).

Hardon, J. A., 'The concept of miracle from Augustine to modern apologetics', *Theological Studies*, 15 (1954), pp. 229–57.

Hauck, K., 'Geblütsheiligkeit', in *Liber Floridus P. Lehmann* (St Ottilien, 1950), pp. 187–240.

Hay du Chastelet, P., *Histoire de Bertrand du Guesclin* (Paris, 1666).

Hefele, H., *Die Bettelorden und das religiöse Volksleben Ober- und Mittelitaliens im 13. Jahrhundert* (Leipzig, 1910).

Heintz, A., 'Der heilige Simeon von Trier, seine kanonisation und seine Reliquien', in *Festschrift A. Thomas* (Trier, 1967), pp. 163–73.

Heinzelmann, M., *Bischofherrschaft in Gallien* (Munich, 1976) (*Francia*, Beiheft 5).

'Sanctitas und Tugendadel. Zu Konzeptionem von "Heiligkeit" im 5. und 10. Jahrhundert', *Francia*, 5 (1977), pp. 741–52.

Helin, M., 'Une fière chandelle', in *Hommage à Marie Delcourt* (Brussels, 1970), pp. 406–17 (Collection Latomus, 114).

Hermann-Masquard, N., *Les reliques des saints: formation coutumière d'un droit* (Paris, 1975).

Hertling, L., 'Der mittelalterliche Heiligentypus nach den Tugendkatalogen', *Zeitschrift für Aszese und Mystik*, 8 (1933), pp. 260–8.

'Materiali per la storia del processo di canonizzazione', *Gregorianum*, 16 (1935), pp. 170–95.

sv Canonisation, in *Dictionnaire de spiritualité*, XXII (Paris, 1953), cc. 79–81.

Hiltbrunner, D., 'Die Heiligkeit des Kaisers. Zur Geschichte des Begriffs "Sacer" ', *Frühmittelalterliche Studien*, 2 (1968), pp. 1–30.

Hilpisch, S., 'Die Torheit um Christi Willen', *Zeitschrift für Aszese und Mystik*, 6 (1931), pp. 21ff.

Hinnebusch, W. A., 'Poverty in the order of Preachers', *The Catholic Historical Review*, 45 (1960), pp. 436–53.

Höcht, J. M., *Träger der Wundmäle Christi: eine Geschichte der bedeutensten Stigmatisierten von Franziskus bis zum Gegenwart*, 2 vols. (Wiesbaden, 1951).

Hocquard, G., 'L'idéal du Pasteur des âmes selon S. Grégoire le Grand', in *La tradition sacerdotale* (Le Puy, 1959), pp. 143–67.

Höffler, O., 'Der Sakralcharakter des germanischen Königstums', in *La Regalità Sacra. Atti del VIIIo congresso internazionale di storia delle religioni (Roma, 1955)* (Leiden, 1959), pp. 644–701.

Hoffmann, E., *Die heilige Könige bei den Angelsachsen und den Skandinavischen Völkern: Königsheiliger und Königshaus* (Neumünster, 1975).

Hofmann, H., *Die heilige Drei Könige. Zur Heiligenverehrung im kirchlichen gesellschaftlichen und politischen Leben des Mittelalters* (Bonn, 1975) (Rheinisches Archiv, 94).

Hofmann, R., *Die heroische Tugend: Geschichte und Inhalt eines theologischen Begriffs* (Munich, 1933) (Münchener Studien zur historischen Theologie, 12).

Hotzelt, W., 'Translationen von Märtyrer-Reliquien aus Rom nach Bayern im 8. Jahrhundert', *Studien und Mitteilungen zur Geschichte des Benediktiner Orders*, 53 (1935), pp. 286ff.

Hruby, K., sv Ritualmord, in *LThK.*, VIII, cc. 1330–1.

Ilarino de Milano, 'La spiritualità evangelica anteriore a S. Francesco', *Quaderni di spiritualità francescana*, 4 (1963), pp. 34–70.

Indelicato, S., 'De sanctitate quae pro beatificatione et canonizatione servorum Dei requiritur probanda', *Monitor ecclesiasticus*, 75 (1950), pp. 109–23.

Iserloh, E., 'Werner von Oberwesel. Zur Tilgung seines Fests im Trierer Kalendar', *Trierer theologische Zeitschrift*, 72 (1963), pp. 270–85.

Izzo, L., *La semplicità evangelica nella spiritualità di S. Francesco d'Assisi* (Rome, 1971) (Studi e ricerche dell'istituto francescano di spiritualità, 2).

Jacob, E. F., 'St Richard of Chichester', *Journal of Ecclesiastical History*, 7 (1956), pp. 174–88.

Jacqueline, B., 'Le Bienheureux Thomas Hélye', *Revue départementale de la Manche*, 4 (1962), pp. 5–14.

Jörgensen, E., *Helgendyrkelse i Danmark* (Copenhagen, 1909).

Jounel, P. 'Le culte des saints', in A. Martimont, *L'Eglise en prière: introduction à la liturgie* (Paris, 1961), pp. 766–85.

    Le culte des saints dans les basiliques du Latran et du Vatican au XIIe siècle (Rome, 1977) (Collection de l'Ecole française de Rome, 26).

Kadlec, J., sv Procopio, in *BS*, X (Rome, 1968), cc. 1167–73.

Kaeppeli, T., 'Le prediche del B. Ambrogio Sansedoni', *AFP*, 38 (1968), pp. 5–19.

Kaftal, G., *St Francis in Italian painting* (London, 1950).

Saints in Italian art: iconography of the saints in Tuscan painting (Florence, 1952).

Saints in Italian art: iconography of the saints in central and south Italian schools of painting (Florence, 1965).

Iconography of the saints in the painting of north east Italy (Florence, 1978).

Kallfelz, H., *Vitae quorumdam episcoporum saeculorum X, XI, XII: Lebenschreibung einiger Bischöfe des 10–12 Jahrhunderts* (Darmstadt, 1973).

Keller, H. ' "Adelsheilige" und pauper Christi in Ekkeberts Vita sancti Haimeradi', in *Adel und Kirche: Gerd Tellenbach zum 65. Geburtstag dargebracht von Freunden und Schülern*, under the dir. of J. Fleckenstein and J. Schmid (Freiburg, 1968), pp. 307–24.

Kemp, E. W., 'Pope Alexander III and the canonization of the saints', *Transactions of the Royal Historical Society*, 4th ser., 27 (1945), pp. 13–28.

Canonization and authority in the Western Church (Oxford, 1948).

'The attempted canonization of Robert Grosseteste', in D. A. Callus, *Robert Grosseteste* (Oxford, 1955), Appendix 2, pp. 241–6.

Kern, L., 'Le Bienheureux Rainier de Borgo San Sepolcro, de l'ordre des Frères Mineurs', *Revue d'histoire franciscaine*, 7 (1930), pp. 233–83.

'Saint Bevignate de Pérouse', in *Studien aus dem Gebiete von Kirche und Kultur, Festschrift G. Schnürer* (Paderborn, 1930), pp. 39–53, repr. in his *Etudes d'histoire ecclésiastique et diplomatique* (Lausanne, 1973), pp. 1–15.

Kerval, L. de, *L'évolution et le développement du merveilleux dans les légendes de Saint Antoine de Padoue* (Paris, 1906).

Klaniczay, T., 'Attività letteraria dei Francescani e dei Domenicani nell'Ungheria Angioina', in *Gli Angioini di Napoli e di Ungheria. Atti del colloquio italoungherese* (Rome, 1974), pp. 27–40 (Acad. Naz. dei Lincei, Quad. no. 210).

Klauser, R., 'Zur Entwicklung des Heiligsprechungsverfahrens bis zum 13. Jahrhundert', *Zeitschrift der Savigny-Stiftung für Rechtgeschichte, Kan. Abteilung*, 40 (1954), pp. 85–101.

Der Heinrichs- und Kunegundenkult im Mittelalterlichen Bistum Bamberg (Bamberg, 1957).

Kleinschmidt, B., 'St Ludwig von Toulouse in der Kunst', *AFH*, 2 (1909), pp. 197–215.

'Die künstlerische Kanonisation des hl. Vaters Franziskus', *AFH*, 3 (1910), pp. 615–25.

Die heilige Anna: ihre Verehrung in Geschichte, Kunst und Volksglaube (Dusseldorf, 1934).

Knies, H., 'Miracula sanctae Elisabeth. Bemerkungen zu den canonisationsakten der heiligen Landgräfin', in *Universitas. Festschrift A. Stohr*, II (Mainz, 1960), pp. 78–88.

Knowles, D., *The English mystical tradition* (London, 1961).

Kohler, O., *Das Bild des geistlichen Fürsten in den Viten des 10, 11, 12. Jahrhunderts* (Berlin, 1935) (Abhandlungen zur Mittleren und Neueren Geschichte, 77).

Kologrivof, L., *La sainteté en Russie* (Bruges, 1953).

Koltay-Kastner, E., 'La leggenda della B. Margherita d'Ungheria alla Corte angioina di Napoli', *Studi e documenti italo-ungheresi*, 3 (1938–9), pp. 174–80.

Koster, K., 'Die visionären Werke Elisabeths von Schönau', *Archiv für Mittelrheinische Kirchengeschichte*, 4 (1952), pp. 19–119.

Kötting, B., *Der frühchristliche Reliquienkult und die Bestattung im Kirchengebaüde* (Cologne, 1965).

Koudela, V. J., 'Les dépositions des témoins au procès de canonisation de S. Dominique', *AFP*, 42 (1972), pp. 47–67.

Kretzenbascher, L., *Kettenkirchen in Bayern und in Osterreich* (Munich, 1973) (Bayerische Akademie der Wissenschaften, Phil.-Hist. Klasse, Abhandlungen, n.s., 76).

Kriss-Retenbeck, L., *Ex voto: Zeichen, Bild und Abbild im christlichen Votivbrauchtum* (Zurich, 1972).

Krüger, K. H., 'Dionysius und Vitus als frühottonische Königsheilige (Zu Widukind, I, 33)', *Frühmittelalterliche Studien*, 8 (1974), pp. 131–54.

Kruszynski, T., 'Swieta Jadwiga i jet Sanktuarium W Trzebnicy', *Collectanea theologica*, 28 (1957), pp. 598–705.

Kumlien, K., 'Sveriges Kristnande i slutskedet spörsmal om vittnessbord och verklighet', in *Historisk Tidskrift* (Stockholm, 1962), pp. 288–94.

Kunze, K., sv Ludovico IV di Turingia, in *BS*, VIII (Rome, 1968), cc. 312–4.

sv Pietro di Lussemburgo, in *BS*, X (Rome, 1968), cc. 705–9.

Kuttner, S., 'La réserve papale du droit de canonisation', *Revue historique de droit français et étranger*, 4th ser., 18 (1938), pp. 172–228.

'St Jón of Holar. Canon law and hagiography in medieval Iceland', *Analecta Cracoviensia*, 7 (1975), pp. 367–75.

Kyll, N., 'Volkskanonisation im Raum des alten Trierer Bistums', *Rheinisches Jahrbuch für Volskunde*, 11 (1960), pp. 7–61.

Labande, L. H., 'Le cérémonial romain de Jacques Cajétan', *BECh*, 54 (1893), pp. 45–74.

Labriolle, P. de, 'Martyr et confesseur', *Bulletin d'ancienne littérature et d'archéologie chrétienne*, 1 (1911), pp. 50–4.

Labuda, L., 'Tworcrosc hagiograficzna i historiograficzna Wincentiego z Kielce', *Studia Zrodloznawcze*, 16 (1971), pp. 103–37.

Ladner, B., 'Das älteste Bild des hl. Franz von Assisi. Eine Beitrag zur mittelalterlichen Portraitsikonographie', in *Festschrift P. E. Schramm*, I (Wiesbaden, 1964), pp. 449–60.

Ladner, G. B., *Die Papstbildnisse des Altertums und des Mittelalters*, II: *Von Innocenz II zu Benedikt XI* (Rome, 1970).

Lambermond, H. C., *Der Armutsgedanke des hl. Dominikus und seines Ordens* (Zwolle, 1926).

Lambert, M. D., *Franciscan poverty: the doctrines of the absolute poverty of Christ and the Apostles in the Franciscan order, 1210–1323* (London, 1961).

Lampen, W., 'B. Iohannes Discalceatus', *Collectanea Franciscana*, 26 (1956), pp. 421–6.

Landgraf, A. M., 'Das Armutsideal des 13. Jahrhunderts', *Franziskanische Studien*, 32 (1950), pp. 219–41, 346–60.

'Die Erkenntnis der heiligmachende Gnade in der Frühscholastik', *Scholastik*, 3 (1928), pp. 28–64.

Langlois, C.-V., 'François de Meyronnes, frère mineur', in *Histoire littéraire de la France*, XXXIII, Paris, 1927, pp. 388ff.

La Roncière, C. de, 'La place des confréries dans l'encadrement religieux du contado florentin. II, Appendices', *MEFR*, 85 (1973), pp. 633–71.

'L'influence des Franciscains dans la campagne de Florence au XIVe siècle', *MEFR*, 87 (1975), pp. 27–103.

Lauer, P., *Le règne de Louis IV d'Outre-mer* (Paris, 1900).

Laurent, M. H., *Le Bienheureux Innocent V (Pierre de Tarentaise) et son temps* (Vatican City, 1947).

'Charles de Blois fut-il canonisé en 1376?', *RHE*, 46 (1951), pp. 182–6.

Le culte de S. Louis d'Anjou à Marseille au XIVe siècle (Rome, 1954) (Temi e testi, 2).

Lawrence, C. H., *St Edmund of Abingdon: a study in hagiography and history* (Oxford, 1960).

Lazzeri, Z., 'Un antico esemplare della Bolla di canonizzazione di S. Chiara', *AFH*, 13 (1920), pp. 499–507.

Le Bras, G., 'Les Ecritures dans le Décret de Gratien', *Zeitschrift der Savigny-Stiftung für Rechtgeschichte, Kan. Abteilung*, 58 (1938), pp. 47–80.

'Le mariage dans la théologie et le droit de l'Eglise du XIe au XIIIe siècle', *Cahiers de civilisation médiévale*, 11 (1968), pp. 191–202.

Leclerq, H., sv Saint, in *Dictionnaire d'archéologie chrétienne et de liturgie*, XV (Paris, 1949), cc. 372–462.

Leclerq, J., 'La vie et la prière des chevaliers de Santiago d'après leur règle primitive', *Liturgica*, 2 (*Scripta et documenta*, 10) (1958), pp. 347–57.

'L'Ecriture Sainte dans l'hagiographie monastique du Haut Moyen Age', in *La Bibbia nell'alto Medio Evo* (Spoleto, 1963), pp. 67–101.

'La "Vita di S. Silvestro", l'irragiamento del santo e dei suoi primi discepoli', in *Atti del congresso di studi storici per l'VIIIo centenario della nascita di S. Silvestro, 1177–1977* (*Studia Picena*, 44, 1977) (Fano, 1978), pp. 1–21.

Review of de Gaiffier, *Etudes critiques d'hagiographie et d'iconologie*, *Studi Medievali*, n.s., 9 (1968), pp. 235–40.

Love in marriage in twelfth century Europe (Hobart, 1978) (University of Tasmania Occasional Papers, 13).

Leclerq, J., Vandenbroucke, F. and Bouyer, L., *La spiritualité du Moyen Age* (Paris, 1957) (Histoire de la spiritualité chrétienne, 2).

Lefèbvre, Y., *L' "Elucidarium" et les lucidaires* (Paris, 1954) (BEFAR, 185).

Le Goff, J., *La civilisation de l'Occident médiéval* (Paris, 1964), trans. J. Barrow, *Medieval civilization 400–1500* (Oxford, 1988).

'Culture cléricale et traditions folkloriques', *Annales ESC*, 22 (1967), pp. 106–26.

'Les mentalités: une histoire ambiguë', in *Faire de l'histoire*, III: *Nouveaux objets* (Paris, 1974), pp. 76–94.

Lenssen, S., 'Aperçu historique sur la vénération des saints cisterciens', *Collectanea ordinis Cisterciensum reformatorum*, 6 (1939), pp. 7–31, 167–95; 10 (1948), p. 15.

Hagiologium Cisterciense (Tilburg, 1948).

Lenzenweger, J., *Berthold, Abt von Garsten* (Graz, 1958).

Le Roy Ladurie, E., *Montaillou, village occitan de 1294 à 1324* (Paris, 1975), trans.

B. Bray, *Montaillou: Cathars and Catholics in a French village, 1294–1324* (London, 1978).

Levardy, F., 'Il leggendario ungherese degli Angio conservato nella Biblioteca Vaticana, nel Morgan Library e nell'Ermitage', *Acta Historiae Artium Academiae Scientiarum Hungariae*, 9 (1963), pp. 75–108.

Lindner, D., 'Die sogennante Erbheiligkeit des Papstes in der Kanonistik des Mittelalters', *Zeitschrift der Savigny-Stiftung für Rechtgeschichte, Kan. Abteilung*, 84 (1967), pp. 15–26.

Lisowski, J., *Kanonizacia Sw. Stanislawa* (Rome, 1953).

Little, L. K., 'Saint Louis' involvement with the Friars', *Church History*, 33 (1964), pp. 125–48.

'L'utilité social de la pauvreté volontaire', in *Etudes sur l'histoire de la pauvreté*, ed. M. Mollat, I (Paris, 1974), pp. 447–59.

Religious poverty and the profit economy in medieval Europe (London, 1978).

Lizerand, G., *Clément V et Philippe le Bel* (Paris, 1910).

Lodovico dalla Croce, *La vita di S. Ugolina vergine di Vercelli* (Milan, 1665).

Loenertz, R., 'Les missions dominicaines en Orient au XIVe siècle et la Société des Frères Pérégrinants dans le Christ', *AFP*, 2 (1932), pp. 1–83.

'Un catalogue d'écrivains et deux catalogues de martyrs dominicains', *AFP*, 12 (1942), pp. 279–303.

'Un catalogue de martyrs dominicains, note complémentaire', *AFP*, 19 (1949), pp. 275–9.

Lohmeyer, E., 'Von göttlichen Wohlgeruch', *Sitzungsberichte der Heidelberger Akademie, Phil.-Hist. Klasse*, 10 (1919), pp. 1–52.

Longpré, E., sv François de Meyronnes, in *Catholicisme hier, aujourd'hui, demain*, IV (Paris, 1956), cc. 1555–7.

Lot-Borodine, M., 'Le mystère du "don des larmes", dans l'Orient chrétien', *La vie spirituelle, Supplément*, 48 (1935), pp. 65–110.

Lottin, O., 'La théorie des dons du Saint-Esprit au début du XIVe siècle', in *Mélanges J. De Ghellinck* (Gembloux, 1951), pp. 849–75.

Psychologie et morale aux XIIe et XIIIe siècles, 3 vols. (Louvain, 1949).

Löw, J., 'Bemerkungen zu den Selig- und Heiligsprechungen', *Theologisch-praktische quartalschrift*, 103 (1955), pp. 89–102.

Lucchesi, G., sv Ruggero, in *BS*, XI (Rome, 1969), cc. 491–3.

Lucius, E., *Les origines du culte des saints dans l'Eglise chrétienne* (Paris, 1908).

Luiso, F. P., 'L'Anziano di S. Zita', in *Miscellanea Lucchese di studi storici e letterari in memoria di Salvatore Bongi* (Lucca, 1931), pp. 61–91.

Lunden, T., sv Kanonisering, in *Kulturhistorisk Lexicon für nordisk Middelalder*, VII (Copenhagen, 1963), cc. 213–21.

Maccarrone, M., 'Riforma e sviluppo della vita religiosa con Innocenzo III', *RSCI*, 16 (1962), pp. 29–62.

Studi su Innocenzo III (Padua, 1972) (Italia sacra, 17).

McCulloch, J., 'The cult of relics in the Letters and Dialogues of Pope Gregory the Great', *Traditio*, 22 (1976), pp. 145–84.

McDonnell, E., *The beghines and beghards in medieval culture, with special emphasis on the Belgian scene* (New Brunswick, 1954).

McKenna, J. W., 'Popular canonization as political propaganda', *Speculum*, 45 (1970), pp. 608–23.

McRoberts, D., sv Margherita di Scozia, in *BS*, VIII (Rome, 1966), cc. 781–6.

Magli, I., *Gli uomini della penitenza: lineamenti antropologici del Medio Evo italiano* (1968).

Magnan, J. B., *Histoire d'Urbain V* (Paris, 1862).

Magnani, R., *Vita de' santi e venerabili e servi di Dio della città di Faenza* (Faenza, 1741).

Mähl, J., *'Quadriga virtutum': die Kardinaltugenden in der Geistesgeschichte der Karolingerzeit* (Cologne, 1969).

Mak, J. J., 'Middeleuwse Heiligenverering', *Nederlandsch archief voor kerkgeschiednis*, 38 (1951), pp. 142–63.

Malden, A. R., *The canonization of St Osmund* (Salisbury, 1901).

Mâle, E., 'La vie de Saint Louis dans l'art français au commencement du XIVe siècle', in *Mélanges E. Bertaux* (Paris, 1924), pp. 193–204.

Mallardo, D., 'L'incubazione nella cristianità medievale napoletana', *Anal. Boll.*, 57 (1949), pp. 465–98.

Mancini, G., *Cortona nel Medio Evo* (Cortona, 1897).

Manselli, R., *La 'Lectura super Apocalypsim' di Pietro di Giovanni Olivi. Ricerche sull'escatologismo medievale* (Rome, 1955) (Studi storici, 19–21).

Spirituali e beghini in Provenza (Rome, 1959) (Studi storici, 31–4).

'L'Attesa dell'età nuova e il Gioachimismo', in *L'attesa dell'età nuova nella spiritualità della fine del medioevo* (Todi, 1962), pp. 145–70 (Convegni del centro di studi sulla spiritualità medievale, 3).

'I vescovi italiani, gli ordini religiosi e i movimenti popolari', in *Vescovi e diocesi in Italia nel Medio Evo* (Padua, 1964), pp. 315–55 (Italia sacra, 5).

sv Pietro Pettinaio, in *Enciclopedia Dantesca*, IV, Rome, 1973, pp. 492–3.

'Gregorio VII di fronte al paganesimo nordico: la lettera a Haakon, re di Danimarca', *RSCI*, 28 (1974), pp. 127–32.

'La clericalizzione dei Minori e San Bonaventura', in *S. Bonaventura francescano* (Todi, 1975), pp. 181–208 (Convegni del centro di studi sulla spiritualità medievale, 14).

'L'idéal du Spirituel selon Pierre Jean Olivi', in *Franciscains d'Oc: les Spirituels, ca. 1280–1324*, pp. 99–126.

Studi sulle eresie del secolo XII, 2nd edn (Rome, 1975) (Studi storici, 5).

Mantueffel, T., *Naissance d'une hérésie: les adeptes de la pauvreté volontaire au Moyen Age* (Paris and The Hague, 1970).

Marchetti Longhi, G., sv Celestino V, in *BS*, III (Rome, 1963), cc. 1100–7.

Mariano D'Alatri, 'Il vescovo nella Cronaca di Salimbene di Parma', *Collectanea Franciscana*, 42 (1972), pp. 5–38.

'Culto dei santi ed eretici in Italia nei secoli XII e XIII', *Collectanea Franciscana*, 45 (1975), pp. 85–104.

Marignan, A., *Etudes sur la civilisation française*, II: *Le culte des saints sous les Mérovingiens* (Paris, 1899).

Marini, L., *Vita e miracoli di S. Pietro di Morrone già Celestino papa V* (Milan, 1637).

Marrou, H. I., 'Ammien Marcellin et les "Innocents" de Milan', *Recherches de science religieuse*, 39–40 (1951–2) (Mélanges J. Lebreton), pp. 179–90.

Martin, H., *Les Ordres Mendiants en Bretagne (v.1230–v.1530)* (Paris and Rennes, 1975).

Martinez Garcia, V., 'El testimonio del confessor en los processos de beatification de los servos de Dios y canonizacion de los bienaventurados', thesis, Gregorian University, Rome, 1954.

Maurer, W., 'Zum Verständnis der heiligen Elisabeth von Thüringen', *Zeitschrift für Kirchengeschichte*, 65 (1953–4), pp. 16–64.

'Die heilige Elisabeth im Lichte der Frömmigkeit ihrer Zeit', *Theologische Literaturzeitung*, 79 (1954), pp. 401–10.

'Die hl. Elisabeth und ihr Marburger Hospital', *Jahrbuch d. Hessischen Kirchengeschichtevereinigung*, 7 (1956), pp. 36–69.

May, N. H., 'The Confession of Prous Boneta', in *Essays in Honour of John Evans* (New York, 1955), pp. 3–30.

Mayer, A. L., 'Die heilbringende Schau', in *Heiligen Uberlieferung, Festchrift I. Herwegen* (Münster, 1938), pp. 234–62.

Meersseman, G. G., 'Frères prêcheurs et mouvement dévot en Flandre au XIIIe siècle', *AFP*, 18 (1948), pp. 69–130.

'Etudes sur les anciennes confréries dominicaines, 1: Les confréries de S. Dominique', *AFP*, 20 (1950), pp. 5–113.

'Etudes sur les anciennes confréries dominicaines, 2: Les confréries de S. Pierre Martyr', *AFP*, 21 (1951), pp. 51–196.

'La loi purement pénale d'après les statuts des confréries médiévales', in *Mélanges J. De Ghellinck* (Gembloux, 1951), pp. 975–1002.

Dossier de l'ordre de la pénitence au XIIIe siècle (Freiburg, 1961) (Spicilegium Friburgense, 7).

'Gli amici spirituali di S. Caterina a Roma nel 1378', in *Symposium Catherinianum nel V° centenario della canonizzazione* (Siena, 1962), pp. 83–123 (Bollettino Senese di storia patria, 69).

'Disciplinati e penitenti nel Duecento', in *Il movimento dei Disciplinati nel settimo centenario dal suo inizio*, pp. 43–72.

Ordo Fraternitatis: confraternite e pietà dei laici nel medioevo, 3 vols. (Rome, 1977) (Italia sacra, 24–6).

Meiss, M., *Florentine painting after the Black Death: the arts, religion and society in the mid-fourteenth century* (New York, 1964).

Melloni, J. B., *Atti e memorie degli Uomini illustri in santità nati o morti in Bologna* (Bologna, 1773–1818), ed. posthumously by T. Benati and M. Fanti (Rome, 1971) (Monumenta Italiae ecclesiastica, hagiographica, 1).

Mens, A., *Oorsprong en Betekenis van de Nederlandse Begijnen* (Brussels, 1947).

L'Ombrie italienne et l'Ombrie brabançonne: deux courants religieux parallèles d'inspiration commune (Paris, 1967) (Etudes franciscaines, supplément, 17).

sv Humiliés, in *Dictionnaire de spiritualité*, VII (Paris, 1969), cc. 1129–33.

Menth, R., 'Zur Verehrung der Protomärtyrer des Franziskanischen Orden Sankt Berard und Genossen', *Franziskanische Studien*, 26 (1939), pp. 101–20.

Mercati, A., *S. Pellegrino delle Alpi in Garfagnana: note agiografiche e storiche* (Rome, 1926).

Merlo, G. G., *Eretici e inquisitori nella società piemontese del Trecento* (Turin, 1977).
Meslin, M., 'Sainteté et mariage au cours de la seconde querelle pélagienne', in *Mystique et continence*, pp. 293–307.
Mezey, L., 'A közepkori Margit-Irodalom Kérdései' (Problems of the medieval literature concerning St Margaret), in *Irodalmi anyanyelvusegünk kezdetei* (Budapest, 1955), pp. 38–113.
Miccoli, G., 'La conversione di S. Francesco secondo Tommaso di Celano', *Studi Medievali*, n.s., 5 (1964), pp. 775–92.
Mikoletsky, K. L., 'Sinn und Art der Heiligung im frähen Mittelalter', *MIOG*, 57 (1943), pp. 83–122.
Mitarelli, J. B., *Memorie della Vita di S. Parisio* (Venice, 1748).
Mitarelli, J. B. and Costadoni, A., *Annales Camaldulenses*, 9 vols. (Venice, 1755–73).
Mitri, A., *De figura iuridica postulatoris in causis beatificationis et canonizationis* (Rome, 1962).
Modorati, L., *Memorie intorno alla Chiesa ed al culto di S. Gerardo di Monza* (Monza, 1919).
Vita di S. Gerardo (Monza, 1925).
Mollat, G., *Les papes d'Avignon, 1305–1378*, 10th edn (Paris, 1964), trans. J. Love, *The popes at Avignon 1305–1378* (London, 1963).
Mollat, M., ed., *Etudes sur l'histoire de la pauvreté (Moyen Age, XVIe siècle)*, 2 vols. (Paris, 1974).
Les pauvres au Moyen Age: étude sociale (Paris, 1978), trans. A. Goldhammer, *The poor in the Middle Ages* (New Haven and London, 1986).
Monceaux, P., 'Les martyrs donatistes. Culte et relations', *Revue de l'histoire des religions*, 68 (1913), pp. 146–92, 310–44.
Moorman, J., *Church life in England in the thirteenth century* (Cambridge, 1945).
A history of the Franciscan order, from its origins to the year 1517 (Oxford, 1968).
Moretti, I. and Stopani, R., 'Santa Verdiana a Castelfiorentino', *Antichità viva*, 11 (1972), pp. 29–34.
Moretus H., 'De magno legendario Bodecensi', *Anal. Boll.*, 27 (1908), pp. 275ff.
Morin, G., 'De Vita et cultu B. Gerardi de Orcimonte (d. 1138)', *Studien und Mitteilungen aus dem Bened. und dem Cist. Orden*, 6 (1886), pp. 293–304.
Morris, C., 'A critique of popular religion: Guibert de Nogent on the miracles of the saints', in *Popular belief and practice* (Cambridge, 1972), pp. 55–60 (Studies in Church history, 8).
La mort au Moyen Age, Actes du colloque de la société des historiens médiévistes de l'enseignement supérieur public, Strasbourg, 1975 (Strasbourg, 1977).
Mortier, P., *Histoire des maîtres généraux de l'ordre des Frères Prêcheurs*, 8 vols. (Paris, 1903–20).
Il movimento dei Disciplinati nel settimo centenario dal suo inizio. Atti del convegno internazionale (25–28 settembre 1960) (Perugia, 1962).
Muller, H. F., *L'époque mérovingienne: essai de synthèse de philologie et d'histoire* (New York, 1945).
Muntz, E. and Frottingham, A. L., 'Il tesoro della Basilica di S. Pietro in Vaticano dal XII al XV secolo', *Archivio della r. società di storia patria*, 6 (1883), pp. 14ff.

Murray, M., *The divine king in England: a study in anthropology* (London, 1954).

Mystique et continence (Actes du 7e congrès international de psychologie religieuse, Avon 1950) (Bruges, 1952).

Nardelli, M., 'Il presunto martirio del Beato Lorenzino Sossio da Marostica', *Archivio Veneto*, 130 (1972), pp. 25–45.

Natalini, V., *S. Pietro Parenzo* (Rome, 1936) (Lateranum, n.s., II, 2).

Naz, R., sv Causes de béatification et de canonisation, in *Dictionnaire de droit canonique*, III (Paris, 1942), cc. 10–37.

Nelson, J., 'Royal saints and early medieval kingship', in *Sanctity and secularity: the Church and the world*, ed. D. Baker (Oxford, 1973), pp. 39–44.

Nessi, S., 'Inventario dei codici e delle pergamene esistenti nel ven. monastero di S. Chiara da Montefalco', *Archivi*, 28 (1961), pp. 232–51.

'I processi per la canonizzazione di Santa Chiara da Montefalco', *Bollettino della società Umbra di storia patria*, 65 (1968), pp. 103–60.

'S. Chiara da Montefalco e il Francescanesimo', *Miscellanea Francescana*, 69 (1969), pp. 369–408.

Nitschke, A., 'Die Reden des Logothetes Bartholomaeus von Capua', *QFIAB*, 35 (1955), pp. 226–74.

Nodet, C. H., 'Position de S. Jérôme en face des problèmes sexuels', in *Mystique et continence*, pp. 308–56.

Noonan, J. J., *Contraception et mariage: évolution ou contradiction de la pensée chrétienne?* (Paris, 1969).

Nordenfalk, C., 'S. Bridget of Sweden as represented in illuminated Ms.', in *Essays in honour of Erwin Panofsky*, I (1961), pp. 371–93.

Nuti, L., 'Santi e beati della Toscana', *Miscellanea Francescana*, 32 (1932), pp. 89–118.

Nykrog, P., *Les fabliaux: étude d'histoire littéraire et de stylistique médiévale* (Geneva, 1975).

O'Callaghan, J., 'Hermandades between the military orders of Calatrava and Santiago during the Castillan Reconquest (1158–1162)', *Speculum*, 44 (1969), pp. 609–18.

Odoardi, G., sv Andrea Caccioli, in *BS*, I (Rome, 1961), cc. 1155–6.

sv Andrea Conti, in *BS*, I (Rome, 1961), cc. 1156–7.

sv Benvenuto da Recanati, in *BS*, II (Rome, 1962), c. 1252.

sv Benvenuto Scotivoli, in *BS*, II (Rome, 1962), cc. 1252–3.

Oliger, L., 'De ultima mutatione officii sancti Francisci', *AFH*, 1 (1908), pp. 45–8.

'Due mosaici con S. Francesco della chiesa di Aracoeli di Roma', *AFH*, 4 (1911), pp. 213–51.

'Servasanto di Faenza O.F.M. e il suo "Liber de virtutibus et vitiis" ', in *Miscellanea F. Ehrle*, I (Rome, 1924), pp. 148–89 (Studi e testi, 37).

De secta Spiritus Libertatis in Umbria saec. XIV (Rome, 1943).

Oliger, P., *Les évêques réguliers: recherches sur leur condition juridique depuis les origines du monachisme jusqu'à la fin du Moyen Age* (Paris and Louvain, 1958).

L'Ordine della Penitenza de S. Francesco d'Assisi nel secolo XIII. Atti del convegno di studi francescani (Assisi, 3–5 luglio 1972), ed. O. Schmucki (Rome, 1973).

Orlandi, S., *La Beata Villana dei Botti, Terziaria domenicana fiorentina del sec. XIV* (Florence, 1955).

Beato Angelico, monografia storica della vite e delle opere (Florence, 1964).

Orlandi, S., ed., *'Necrologio' di Santa Maria Novella*, 2 vols. (Florence, 1955).

Orselli, A. M., *L'idea e il culto del santo patrono cittadino nella letteratura cristiana* (Bologna, 1965).

'Spirito cittadino e temi politico culturali nel culto di San Petronio', in *La coscienza cittadina* (Todi, 1972), pp. 283–343.

Ortolani, S., *Vita del B. Cecco di Pesaro* (Fano, 1859).

Ortolan, T., 'Canonisation des saints dans l'Eglise romaine', in *DTC*, II (Paris, 1932), cc. 1626–59.

Paolini, L., *L'eresia a Bologna fra XIII e XIV secolo*, I: *L'eresia catara alla fine del duecento* (Rome, 1975) (Studi storici, 93–6).

Paravicini Bagliani, A., 'La storiografia pontificia del secolo XIII. Prospettive di ricerca', *Römische historische Mitteilungen*, 18 (1976), pp. 45–54.

Paravy, P., 'Angoisse collective et miracles au seuil de la mort: résurrection et baptêmes d'enfants mort-nés en Dauphiné au XVe siècle', in *La mort au Moyen Age. Colloque de la société des historiens médiévistes de l'enseignement supérieur public (Strasbourg, 1975)* (Strasbourg, 1977), pp. 87–102.

Pasztor, E., *Per la storia di San Ludovico d'Angio (1274–1297)* (Rome, 1955) (Studi storici, 10).

sv Margherita d'Ungheria, in *BS*, VIII (Rome, 1968), cc. 796–800.

sv Stefano primo re d'Ungheria, in *BS*, XII (Rome, 1968), cc. 19–22.

Patlagean, E., 'A Byzance: ancienne hagiographie et histoire sociale', *Annales ESC*, 23 (1968), pp. 106–26.

'L'histoire de la femme déguisée en moine et l'évolution de la sainteté féminine à Byzance', *Studi Medievali*, 3rd ser. (1976), pp. 597–623.

Paul, J., 'L'éloge des personnes et l'idéal humain au XIIIe siècle, d'après la Chronique de Fra Salimbene', *Le Moyen Age*, 73 (1967), pp. 403–30.

'Saint Louis d'Anjou, Franciscain et évêque de Toulouse (1274–1297)', in *Les évêques, les clercs et le roi, 1250–1300* (Toulouse, 1972), pp. 59–90 (Cahiers de Fanjeaux, 7).

'Evangélisme et Franciscanisme chez Louis d'Anjou', in *Les Mendiants en pays d'Oc au XIIIe siècle* (Toulouse, 1973), pp. 375–401 (Cahiers de Fanjeaux, 8).

'Témoignage historique et hagiographie dans le procès de canonisation de Louis d'Anjou', *Provence historique*, 93–4 (1973), pp. 305–17.

'Le "Liber miraculorum" de Saint Louis d'Anjou', *AFH*, 69 (1976), pp. 209–19.

'Miracles et mentalité religieuse populaire à Marseille au début du XIVe siècle', in *La religion populaire en Languedoc* (Toulouse, 1976) (Cahiers de Fanjeaux, 11).

Paulhart, H., 'Zur Heiligsprechung der Kaiserin Adelheid', *MIOG*, 64 (1956), pp. 55–67.

Pauly, F., 'Zur Vita des Werner von Oberwesel. Legende und Wirklichkeit', *Archiv für mittelrheinische Kirchengeschichte*, 16 (1964), pp. 94–109.

Pelster, F., 'Ein Elogium Joachims von Flore auf Kaiser Heinrich II und seine Gemahlin die hl. Kunegunde', in *Liber Floridus Paul Lehmann* (Saint Ottilien, 1950), pp. 329–54.

Penco, G., 'Le figure bibliche del "vir Dei" nell'agiografia monastica', *Benedictana*, 15 (1963), pp. 1–13.

Perroy, G., *La guerre de Cent Ans* (Paris, 1945), trans. W. B. Wells, *The Hundred Years' War* (London, 1959).

Petersohn, J., 'Die päpstliche Kanonisationsdelegation des 11. und 12. Jahrhunderts und die Heiligsprechung Karls der Grossen', in *Proceedings of the fourth international congress of medieval canon law (Toronto, 1972)* (Vatican City, 1976), pp. 163–206 (Monumenta iuris canonici, series C: subsidia, 5).

'Die litterae Papst Innocenz III zur Heiligsprechung der Kaiserin Kunigunde (1200)', *Jahrbuch für fränkische Landesforschung*, 37 (1977), pp. 1–25.

Petrocchi, G., 'Correnti e linee della spiritualità umbra ed italiana del Duecento', in *Atti del IV convegno di studi Umbri (Gubbio, 1966)* (Perugia, 1967), pp. 133–76.

Peyer, H. C., *Stadt und Stadtpatron im mittelalterlichen Italien* (Zurich, 1955).

Pfister, R., sv Kultus, in *Paulus Realencyclopädie des classischen Altertumswissenschaft*, XI (Stuttgart, 1922), cc. 2106–92.

Philip, W., 'Heiligkeit und Herrschaft in der Vita Aleksandr Nevskijs', *Forschungen zur osteuropäischen Geschichte*, 18 (1973), pp. 55–72.

Picard, J., *Vie de S. Antelme, évêque de Belley, chartreux, par son chapelain Guillaume, chartreux de Portes* (Lagnieu (Ain), 1978) (Collections de recherches et d'études cartusiennes, 1).

Pietri, C., *Roma christiana: recherches sur l'Eglise de Rome, son organisation, sa politique, son idéologie de Miltiade à Sixte III (311–440)*, 2 vols. (Rome, 1976) (BEFAR, 224).

Pinckaers, S., 'Ce que le Moyen Age pensait du mariage', *La vie spirituelle, Supplément*, 20 (1968), pp. 413–40.

Plaine, F., *Essai historique sur le culte du Bienheureux Charles de Blois* (Nantes, 1872).

Pocquet du Haut-Jussé, B., 'La sainteté de Charles de Blois', *Revue des questions historiques*, 54 (1926), pp. 108–15.

Les papes et les ducs de Bretagne: essai sur les rapports du Saint-Siège avec un Etat, 2 vols. (Paris, 1928) (BEFAR, 133).

Pogni, O., *La gloriosa vergine romita di Castelfiorentino: vita, chiesa, spedale de S. Verdiana* (Castelfiorentino, 1934).

Pohlkamp, W., 'Hagiographische Texte als Zeugnisse einer "histoire de la sainteté". Bericht über ein Buch zum Heiligkeitsideal im karolingischen Aquitanien', *Frühmittelalterliche Studien*, 11 (1977), pp. 229–40.

Pontal, O., *Les statuts de Paris et le synodal de l'Ouest (XIIIe siècle)* (Paris, 1971) (Collection de documents inédits sur l'histoire de France, Section de philologie et d'histoire jusqu'en 1610, series in 8°, 9).

Portmann, M. L., *Die Darstellung der Frau in der Geschichtschreibung des früheren Mittelalters* (Basle and Stuttgart, 1958) (Basler Beiträge zur Geschichte, 69).

Positio super cultu B. Gerardi de Villemagna (Rome, 1832).

Pouchelle, M. C., 'Représentations du corps dans la Légende Dorée', *Ethnologie française*, 6 (1976), pp. 293–308.

Poulain, J. C., *L'idéal de sainteté dans l'Aquitaine carolingienne d'après les sources hagiographiques (750–950)* (Quebec, 1975).

Pourrat, P., sv Clairvoyance spirituelle, in *Dictionnaire de spiritualité*, II (Paris, 1953), cc. 922–9.

La povertà del secolo XII e Francesco d'Assisi (II convegno della società internazionale di studi francescani, Assisi, 1974) (Assisi, 1975).

Powicke, F. and Cheney, C., *Councils and synods relative to the English Church*, 2 vols. (Cambridge, 1964).

Prinz, F., 'Heiligenkult und Adelherrschaft im Spiegel merowingischer Hagiographie', *Historische Zeitschrift*, 204 (1967), pp. 529–44.

Prosperi, A., *Anagni e suoi monumenti* (Anagni, 1970).

Puerari, A., *Il duomo di Cremona* (Milan, 1971).

Purvis, J. C., *Saint John of Bridlington* (1924).

Rader, M., *Bavaria sancta*, 2 vols. (Munich, 1628).

Rambaud-Buhot, J., 'Le Décret de Gratien, legs du passé, avènement de l'âge classique', in *Entretiens sur la renaissance du XIIe siècle*, ed. M. de Gandillac and E. Jauneau (Paris and The Hague, 1969), pp. 493–506.

Rapp, F., 'Les groupes informels à la fin du Moyen Age: types rhénans', in *Les groupes informels dans l'Eglise* (Strasbourg, 1971), pp. 180–93 (Colloques du CERDIC, 2).

L'Eglise et la vie religieuse en Occident à la fin du Moyen Age (Paris, 1971) (Nouvelle Clio, 25).

'Les pèlerinages dans la vie religieuse de l'Occident médiéval aux XIVe et XVe siècles', in *Les pèlerinages de l'Antiquité biblique et classique à l'Occident médiéval*, ed. M. Philonenko and M. Simon (Paris, 1973), pp. 119–60 (Université de Strasbourg, Etudes d'histoire des religions, 1).

'Réflexions sur la religion populaire au Moyen Age', in *La religion populaire, approches historiques*, ed. B. Plongeron (Paris, 1976), pp. 51–98.

Ratzinger, I., 'Der Einfluss des Bettelordensstreites', in *Festschrift M. Schmaus* (Munich, 1957), pp. 697–724.

Reber, O., *Die Gestaltung des Kultes weiblicher Heiliger im Spättmittelalter* (Hersbruck, 1963).

Regamey, P., 'La componction du cœur', *La vie spirituelle*, 45 (1935), pp. 86–99.

Rengstorf, K. H. and Kortzfleisch, S., *Kirche und Synagoge*, 2 vols. (Stuttgart, 1968).

Retables italiens du XIIIe au XVe siècle. Catalogue of the exhibition arranged by C. Ressort (Paris, 1978).

Ricaud, Y., *VIe centenaire de la canonisation de Saint Yves (Avignon, 19 mai 1347–Tréguier, 19 mai 1947). Histoire de la canonisation* (n.p., 1947).

Richard, J., *La papauté et les missions d'Orient au Moyen Age (XIIIe–XVe siècles)* (Rome, 1977) (Collection de l'Ecole française de Rome, 33).

Riché, P., 'Translations de reliques à l'époque carolingienne. Histoire des reliques de Saint Malo', *Moyen Age*, 82 (1976), pp. 201–18.

Rieden, O. von, 'Das Leiden Christi im Leben des hl. Franziskus von Assisi. Eine quellenvergleichende Untersuchung im Lichte der zeitgenössischen Passionfrömmigkeit', *Collectanea Franciscana*, 30 (1960), pp. 5–30, 129–45, 241–63, 353–97.

'De S. Francisci Assisiensis stigmatum susceptione dissertatio historico-critica luce testimoniorum saec. XIII', *Collectanea Franciscana*, 33 (1963), pp. 210–66, 392–422.

Riva, G., 'Due documenti di S. Gerardo nell'archivio della Congregazione di Carità di Monza (1174 e 1198)', *Archivio storico Lombardo*, 4th ser., 6 (1906), pp. 181–94.

Roggen, H., *Die Lebensform des Hl. Franziskus von Assisi in ihrem Verhältnis zur feudalen und bürgerlichen Gesellschaft Italiens* (Malines, 1965).

Rogger, I., sv Adelprato, in *BS*, I (Rome, 1961), cc. 247–8.

sv Simone di Trento, in *BS*, XI (Rome, 1968), cc. 1184–8.

Roisin, S., 'L'efflorescence cistercienne et le courant féminin de piété au XIIIe siècle', *RHE*, 39 (1943), pp. 342–78.

L'hagiographie cistercienne dans le diocèse de Liège au XIIIe siècle (Louvain, 1947) (Université de Louvain, Recueil des travaux . . . d'histoire et de philologie, 3rd ser., 27).

'La méthode hagiographique de Thomas de Cantimpré', in *Miscellanea historica in honorem A. De Meyer* (Louvain, 1947), pp. 546–57.

Rordorf, W., 'Aux origines du culte des martyrs', *Irenikon*, 46 (1972), pp. 315–31.

Rosenthal, J. T., 'Edward the Confessor and Robert the Pious. Eleventh century kingship and biography', *Medieval Studies*, 33 (1971), pp. 7–20.

'The fifteenth-century episcopate: careers and bequests', in *Sanctity and secularity*, ed. Baker, pp. 117–27.

Rudolf, A., *Von der Kunst des heilsamen Lebens und Sterbens* (Cologne, 1959).

Russell, J. C., 'The canonization of opposition to the king in Angevin England', in *Haskins anniversary essays* (New York, 1929), pp. 280–98.

Sabatier, P., 'Le privilège de la pauvreté', *Revue d'histoire franciscaine*, 1 (1924), pp. 1–54, 469–82.

Sägmuller, J. B., *Die Thätigkeit und Stellung der Kardinäle bis Bonifaz VIII* (Freiburg im Breisgau, 1896).

Sainati, G., *Vita dei santi, beati e servi di Dio nati nella diocesi di Pisa* (Pisa, 1894).

Sainte Marie-Madeleine, G. de, 'Normes actuelles de la sainteté', in *Trouble et lumière* (Paris, 1949), pp. 175–88 (Etudes carmélitaines, 29).

Saintyves, P., *Essais de folklore biblique: magie, mythes et miracles dans l'Ancien et le Nouveau Testament* (Paris, 1922).

En marge de la Légende Dorée: songes, miracles et survivances. Essai sur la formation de quelques thèmes hagiographiques (Paris, 1930).

Salamina, L. 'S. Gualtero (Lodi, 1184–1224)', *Archivio storico Lodigiano*, 61 (1942), pp. 96–134.

Salsano, M., sv Fidati, Simone da Cescia, in *BS*, V (Rome, 1964), cc. 674–5.

Salvatorelli, L., 'Movimento francescano e gioachimismo', in *Relazioni del X congresso internazionale di scienze storiche*, III (Florence, 1955), pp. 403–48.

Samarati, L., sv Rinaldo da Concorezzo, in *BS*, XI (Rome, 1968), cc. 192–8.

Santifaller, L., 'Zur Originalüberlieferung der Heiligsprechungsurkunde der Landgräfin Elisabeth von Thüringen vom Jahre 1235', in *Acht Jahrhunderte Deutscher Orden in Einzeldarstellungen*, ed. K. Wieser (Bad Godesberg, 1967), pp. 73–88.

Saxer, V., *Le dossier vézelien de Marie-Madeleine: invention et translation des reliques en 1265–1267* (Brussels, 1975) (Subsidia hagiographica, 57).

Schauerte, H., *Die volkstümliche Heiligenverehrung* (Münster, 1948).

'Entwicklung und gegenwärtiger Stand der religiösen Volkskundeforschung', *Historisches Jahrbuch*, 72 (1953), pp. 516–34.

Schenk, M., *Die Unfehlbarkeicht des Papstes in der Heiligsprechung* (Freiburg, 1965) (Thomistische Studien, 9).

Schimmelpfennig, B., *Die Zeremonienbücher der römischen Kirche im Mittelalter* (Tübingen, 1973) (Bibliothek des deutschen historischen Instituts in Rom, 40).

Schlafke, J., 'Das Recht der Bischöfe in causis sanctorum', in *Kirche und ihre Amter und Stände: Festschrift Josef Kardinal Frings* (Cologne, 1860), pp. 417–33.

De competentia in causis sanctorum decernendi a primis post Christum natum saeculis usque ad annum 1234 (Rome, 1961).

Schmidinger, H., 'Das Papstbild in der Geschichtschreibung des späteren Mittelalters', *Römische historische Mitteilungen*, 1 (1956–7), pp. 106–29.

Schmitt, J.C., ' "Religion populaire" et culture folklorique', *Annales ESC*, 31 (1976), pp. 941–53.

'Recueils franciscains d' "exempla" et perfectionnement des techniques intellectuelles du XIIIe au XVe siècle', *BECh*, 135 (1977), pp. 5–21.

Mort d'une hérésie: l'Eglise et les clercs face aux béguines et aux béghards du Rhin supérieur du XIVe au XVe siècle (Paris and The Hague, 1978) (Civilisations et société, 56).

Le saint lévrier: Guinefort guérisseur d'enfants depuis le XIIIe siècle (Paris, 1979), trans. M. Thom, *The holy greyhound: Guinefort, healer of children since the thirteenth century* (Cambridge, 1983).

Schmitz, P., *Histoire de l'ordre de Saint Benoît*, 2 vols. (Maredsous, 1957).

Scholtz, B. W., 'The canonization of Edward the Confessor', *Speculum*, 36 (1961), pp. 38–60.

Schramm, P. E., *Der König von Frankreich*, 2 vols. (Weimar, 1939).

Schreiber, G., *Stephan I der Heilige, König von Ungarn: eine hagiographische Studie* (Paderborn, 1938).

Schuck, H., *Ecclesia Lincopensis* (Stockholm, 1959).

Schwartz, M., 'Die Heiligsprechung im 12. Jahrhundert', *Archiv für Kulturgeschichte*, 39 (1957), pp. 43–62.

Sciammanini, R., sv Cerchi (Umiliana dei), in *BS*, III (Rome, 1963), cc. 1132–5.

Le scuole degli Ordini Mendicanti (Todi, 1978) (Convegni del centro di studi sulla spiritualità medievale, 17).

Sderci, B., *L'apostolato di S. Francesco e dei Francescani* (Quaracchi, 1909).

Séjourné, P., sv Saints (culte des), in *Dictionnaire de théologie catholique*, XIV, 1 (Paris, 1939), cc. 870–979.

Sensi, M., sv Pietro Crisci, in *BS*, X (Rome, 1968), cc. 821–3.

sv Ugolino, in *BS*, XII (Rome, 1969), cc. 784–7.

'Incarcerate e Penitenti a Foligno nella prima metà del trecento', in *I Frati penitenti di San Francesco*, pp. 79–150.

Sérent, A. de, 'Charles de Blois, duc de Bretagne (1319–1364) et l'ordre des Frères Mineurs', *Etudes franciscaines*, 8 (1957), pp. 59–75.

Sevsi, P., *Martyrologium Fratrum Minorum provinciae Mediolanensis* (Milan, 1927).

Sibilia, A. L., sv Erico IV, re di Danimarca, in *BS*, IV (Rome, 1964), cc. 1321–2.

sv Ingrid Elofsdotter, in *BS*, VII (Rome, 1966), cc. 816–17.

Sigal, P. A., 'Maladie, pèlerinage et guérison au XIIe siècle. Les miracles de Saint Gibrien à Reims', *Annales ESC*, 24 (1969), pp. 1522–39.

'Comment on concevait et on traitait la paralysie en Occident dans le Haut Moyen Age (Ve–XIIIe siècles)', *Revue d'histoire des sciences*, 197 (1971), pp. 153–211.

Les marcheurs de Dieu (Paris, 1974).

Sigismondi, G., 'Le "Legenda" Beati Raynaldi e il suo valore storico', *Bollettino della deputazione di storia patria per l'Umbria*, 56 (1960), pp. 1–111.

sv Rinaldo, vescovo di Nocera Umbra, in *BS*, XI (Rome, 1968), cc. 199–204.

Sigona, E., sv Guglielmo di Noto, in *BS*, VII (Rome, 1966), cc. 477–8.

Silvestre H., 'Note complémentaire sur l'incubation et ses survivances', *Revue du Moyen Age latin*, 5 (1949), pp. 141–8.

Sisto, A., *Figure del primo Francescanesimo in Provenza: Ugo e Douceline di Digne* (Florence, 1971) (Biblioteca della rivista di storia e letteratura religiosa, Studi e testi, 3).

Sorokin, P., *Altruistic love: a study of American 'good neighbour' and Christian saints* (Boston, 1950).

Sot, M., 'Historiographie épiscopale et modèle familial en Occident au XIe siècle', *Annales ESC*, 33 (1978), pp. 433–49.

Southern, R. W., *The making of the Middle Ages* (London, 1959).

Spaey, E., 'De Opvatting der Heiligheit in Vlanderen en Lotharingen in de tweede helft der 9e eeuw', *Ons Geestelijkl Erf*, 1 (1957), pp. 255–77, 347–69.

Spano, S., review of P. Delooz, *Sociologie et canonisations*, *Rivista di storia e letteratura religiosa*, 6 (1970), pp. 133–8.

Stachnik, R. and Triller, A., *Dorothea von Montau: eine preussische Heilige des 14. Jahrhunderts* (Münster, 1976).

Stanislao da Campagnola, *L'Angello del sesto Sigillo e l' "alter Christus"* (Rome, 1971) (Studi e ricerche dell'istituto francescano di spiritualità, 1).

'L' "ordo poenitentium" di S. Francesco nelle cronache del Duecento', in *L'Ordine della Penitenza di S. Francesco d'Assisi*, pp. 145–79.

Francesco d'Assisi nei suoi scritti e nelle sue biografie dei secoli XIII–XIV (Assisi, 1977).

Steffen, S., 'Der heilige Wilhelm von Bourges', *Cistercienser Chronik*, 19 (1907), pp. 74–82.

Steidle B., 'Die Tränen. Eine mystiches problem im alten Mönchtum', *Benediktinische Monatschrift*, 20 (1938), pp. 181–7.

' "Homo Dei Antonius". Zum Bild des "Mannes Gottes" im alten Mönchtum', in *Antonius Magnus eremita (356–1956)* (Rome, 1956), pp. 148–200 (Studia Anselmiana, 38).

"Stola S. Godelevae", *Volume commémoratif* (Bruges, 1971) (Sacris erudiri, 20).

Stroick, A., 'Wer ist die Stigmatisierte in einer Reformschrift für des zweite Lyoner Reformkonzil?', *Historisches Jahrbuch*, 50 (1930), pp. 342–9.

Stuckelberg, E., 'Der Geruch der Heiligkeit', *Schweitzerischer Archiv für Volskunde*, 22 (1919), pp. 203–5.

Suarez, P. M., sv Gioacchino da Siena, in *BS*, VI (Rome, 1965), cc. 476–8.

Sullivan, J. J., *Fast and abstinence in the First Order of Saint Francis* (Washington, 1957) (The Catholic University of America Studies, 374).

Tabacco, G., *La casa di Francia nell'azione politica del papa Giovanni XXII* (Rome, 1953) (Studi storici, 1–4).

Tait, H., 'Pilgrim signs and Thomas Earl of Lancaster', *British Museum Quarterly*, 20 (1955), pp. 39–46.

Tenenti, A., *La vie et la mort à travers l'art du XVe siècle* (Paris, 1952) (Cahiers des annales, 8).

Thomas Becket. Actes du colloque international de Sédières (19–24 août 1973), ed. R. Foreville (Paris, 1975).

Thomson, R. W., *Friars in the cathedral: the first Franciscan bishops, 1226–1261* (Toronto, 1975).

Thouzellier, C., 'Un dépôt de l'archevêque de Nidaros à Sainte-Sabine', *AFP*, 21 (1951), pp. 294–300.

'La pauvreté, arme contre l'Albigéisme en 1206', *Revue de l'histoire des religions*, 151 (1957), pp. 79–92.

Thurston, H., *Physical phenomena of mysticism: a collection of studies on praeternatural phenomena in the lives of the saints and others* (London, 1952).

Tibbetts-Schulenburg, J., 'Sexism and the celestial gynaecum', *Journal of Medieval History*, 4 (1978), pp. 117–33.

Tierney, B., *Origins of papal infallibility, 1150–1350: a study on the concepts of infallibility, sovereignty and tradition in the Middle Ages* (London, 1972) (Studies in the history of Christian thought, 6).

Tocco, F., 'Guglielma Boema e i Guglielmiti', *Atti della r. accademia dei Lincei, Memorie*, 5th ser., VIII, (1900), pp. 3–22.

La quistione della povertà nel secolo XIV (Naples, 1910).

Tonini, L., *Storia civile e sacra Riminese*, 4 vols. (Rimini, 1880).

Rimini nel secolo XIII (Rimini, 1886).

Toso d'Arenzano, R., sv Cagnoli, Gerardo, in *BS*, III (Rome, 1963), cc. 641–4.

Toubert, H., 'Rome et le Mont Cassin: nouvelles remarques sur les fresques de l'église inférieure de Saint-Clément de Rome', *Dumbarton Oaks Papers*, 30 (1976), pp. 1–33.

Toubert, P., 'Techniques notariales et société aux XIIe–XIIIe siècles: les origines du minutier romain', in *Economies et sociétés au Moyen Age, Mélanges offerts à Edouard Perroy* (Paris, 1973), pp. 297–308.

Les structures du Latium médiéval: le Latium méridional et la Sabine du IXe à la fin du XIIe siècle, 2 vols. (Rome, 1975) (BEFAR, 221).

Toussaert, J., *Antonius von Padua* (Cologne, 1967).

Tout, T. F., sv Cantelupe (Thomas of), in *Dictionary of national biography*, III (London, 1908), pp. 900–4.

Toynbee, M., *S. Louis of Toulouse and the process of canonization in the fourteenth century* (Manchester, 1929).

Trexler, R. C., 'Ritual in Florence. Adolescence and salvation in the Renaissance', in *The pursuit of holiness in late medieval and renaissance religion*, ed. Trinkaus and Oberman, pp. 200–64.

Trinkaus, C. and Oberman, H. O., eds., *The pursuit of holiness in late medieval and renaissance religion* (Leiden, 1974) (Studies in medieval and Reformation thought, 10).

Tunberg, S., 'Erik den helige, Sveriges helgenkonung: Nagra Synpunkter', *Fornvännen*, 36 (1941), pp. 257–78.

Turchini, A., 'Leggenda, culto, iconographia del Beato Giovanni Gueruli da Ver-rucchio', *Studi Romagnoli*, 21 (1970), pp. 425–53.

Turek, R., sv Venceslao, in *BS*, I (Rome, 1961), cc. 991–7.

Twemlow, J. A., 'The liturgical credentials of a forgotten English saint', in *Mél-anges Bémont* (Paris, 1913), pp. 365–71.

Ullmann, W., ' "Romanus pontifex indubitanter efficitur sanctus". Dictatus papae 23, in retrospect and prospect', *Studi Gregoriani*, 6 (1961), pp. 229–64.

Urusczak, W., 'Les répercussions de la mort de S. Thomas Becket en Pologne', in *Thomas Becket. Actes du colloque . . . de Sédières*, pp. 115–25.

Vandelli, F., *Un parrocco santo nella Valdelsa, il B. Davanzato* (Florence, 1972).

Van den Bosch, J., *Capa, basilica, monasterium et le culte de Saint Martin de Tours: étude lexicologique et sémasiologique* (Nimwegen, 1959).

Van der Essen, L., *Etude critique et littérature des 'Vitae' des saints mérovingiens de l'ancienne Belgique* (Louvain and Paris, 1907).

Van der Leeuw, G., *Sacred and profane beauty: the holy in art* (London, 1963).

Van der Lof, J., 'Grégoire de Tours et la magie blanche', *Numen*, 21 (1974), pp. 228–37.

Van der Straeten, J., 'Robert de la Chaise-Dieu, sa canonisation', *Anal. Boll.*, 82 (1964), pp. 37–56.

Van Dijk, A., 'Il culto di Santa Chiara nel Medio Evo', in *Santa Chiara d'Assisi: studi e cronaca del VII° centenario* (Assisi, 1953), pp. 155–205.

Van Hove, A., *La doctrine du miracle chez S. Thomas d'Aquin* (Paris, 1927).

Van Luijk, B., *Gli eremiti neri nel Dugento: origine, sviluppo e unione* (Pisa, 1968) (Biblioteca del bollettino storico Pisano, Collana storica, 7).

Van Omme, A. M., *'Virtus', een semantiese studie* (Utrecht, 1947).

Van Os, H. W., 'St Francis as a second Christ in early Italian painting', *Simiolus, Netherland's Quarterly for the History of Art*, 7 (1975), pp. 11ff.

Varischi, G., *Sant'Omobon* (Cremona, 1937).

Vauchez, A., 'Une campagne de pacification en Lombardie autour de 1233. L'action politique des Ordres Mendiants d'après la réforme des statuts communaux et les accords de paix', *MEFR*, 78 (1966), pp. 503–49.

sv Nevelone, in *BS*, IX (Rome, 1967), cc. 839–40.

sv Pietro Pettinaio, in *BS*, X (Rome, 1968), cc. 719–22.

sv Raimundo Zanfogni, in *BS*, XI (Rome, 1968), cc. 26–9.

sv Rocco, in *BS*, XI (Rome, 1968), cc. 264–73.

'Les stigmates de S. François et leurs détracteurs aux derniers siècles du Moyen Age', *MEFR*, 80 (1968), pp. 595–625.

'Charité et pauvreté chez sainte Elisabeth de Thuringe d'après les Actes du procès de canonisation', in *Etudes sur l'histoire de la pauvreté*, ed. M. Mollat, I, pp. 163–73.

La spiritualité du Moyen Age occidental (Paris, 1975) (Coll. sup., l'historien, 19).

'Conclusion', in *La religion populaire en Languedoc du XIIIe siècle à la moitié du XIVe siècle* (Toulouse, 1976), pp. 429–44 (Cahiers de Fanjeaux, 11).

'Canonisation et politique au XIVe siècle. Documents inédits des Archives du Vatican relatifs au procès de canonisation de Charles de Blois, duc de Bretagne (d. 1364)', in *Miscellanea in onore di Mgr. M. Giusti*, II (Vatican City, 1978), pp. 381–404.

Vecchi, A., *Il culto delle immagini nelle stampe popolari* (Florence, 1968) (Biblioteca di Lares, 26).

Vecchietti, F. and Compagnoni, P., *Memorie istorico-critiche della chiesa e de' vescovi di Osimo*, 5 vols. (Rome, 1782–3).

Vicaire, M. H., *Histoire de Saint Dominique*, 2 vols. (Paris, 1957).

Saint Dominique, la vie apostolique (Paris, 1965) (Chrétiens de tous les temps, 10).

Dominique et ses Prêcheurs (Freiburg and Paris, 1977).

Vielle C., *Saint Louis d'Anjou, évêque de Toulouse* (Vanves, 1930).

Vigue, P., *Saint Honoré de Thénezay ou de Buzançais* (Poitiers, 1908).

Visani, O., 'Note su Tommaso Nacci Caffarini', *Rivista di storia e letteratura religiosa*, 9 (1973), pp. 277–97.

Von den Steinen, W., *Der Kosmos des Mittelalters, von Karl dem Grossen zu Bernhard von Clairvaux* (Berne and Munich, 1959).

Vorgrimler, H., sv Heiligenverehrung, in *Lexicon für Theologie und Kirche*, V (Freiburg im Breisgau, 1960), cc. 104–6.

Walberg, E., *La tradition hagiographique de S. Thomas Becket avant la fin du XIIe siècle* (Paris, 1925).

Wallace-Hadrill, J. M., *Early Germanic kingship in England and in the Continent* (Oxford, 1971).

Walsh, K., 'Archbishop Fitzralph and the Friars at the Papal Court in Avignon', *Traditio*, 31 (1975), pp. 223–45.

Wasowicz, T., *Legenda Slaska* (Warsaw, 1967).

Weigel, M., 'Dr Martin Konhofer. Ein beitrag zur kirchengeschichte Nürnbergs', *Mitteilungen des Vereins für Geschichte der Stadt Nürnberg*, 29 (1928), pp. 171–207.

Weinand, H. G., *Tränen: Untersuchung über das Weinen in der deutsche Sprache und literatur des Mittelalters* (Bonn, 1958).

Weinstein, D. and Bell, R. M., 'Saints and society: Italian saints of the late Middle Ages and Renaissance', *Memorie Domenicane*, n.s., 4 (1975), pp. 180–94.

Wenzel, S., *The sin of sloth: 'Acedia' in medieval thought and literature* (Chapel Hill, 1967).

'The seven deadly sins. Some problems of research', *Speculum*, 43 (1968), pp. 1–22.

Werner, E., 'Zur Frauenfrage und zum frauenkult im Mittelalter: Robert von Arbrissel und Fontevrault', *Forschungen und Fortschritte*, 29 (1955), pp. 269–76.

'Die stellung der Katharismus zur Frau', *Studi Medievali*, n.s., 2 (1961), pp. 295–301.

Westpfahl, H., 'Untersuchungen über Jutta von Sangerhausen', *Zeitschrift für Geschichte und Altertumskunde Ermlands*, 26 (1938), pp. 515–96.

Westpfahl, J., sv Jutta de Sangerhausen, in *Dictionnaire de spiritualité*, VIII (Paris, 1974), cc. 1648–9.

Wickenden, R., 'John of Dalderby, Bishop of Lincoln, 1300–1320', *The Archaeological Journal*, 40 (1883), pp. 218–25.

Wickersheimer, P., 'Les guérisons miraculeuses du cardinal Pierre de Luxembourg (1387–1390)', in *Comptes-rendus du 2e congrès international d'histoire de la médicine (Paris, 1921)* (Paris, 1922), pp. 372–81.

Widding, O. and Bekker-Nielson, H., 'Low German influence on late Icelandic hagiography', *The Germanic Review*, 37 (1962), pp. 237–62.

Willemsen, A., *Kardinal Napoleon Orsini (1273–1342)* (Berlin, 1927).

Wolfram, H., ' "Splendor imperii". Die epiphanie von Tugend und heil in herrschaft und Reich', *MIOG, Ergänzungsbande*, 20, 3 (1963).

Woolley, R. M., *The officium and miracula of Richard Rolle of Hampole* (London, 1929).

Exorcism and the healing of the sick (London, 1932).

Zanoni, F., 'Vita metrica dei SS. Imerio e Omobono', *Annali della biblioteca e libreria civica di Cremona*, 9 (1956), pp. 29–32.

Zender, M., *Räume und schichten mittelalterlichen Heiligenverehrung in ihrer Bedeutung für die Volkskunde* (Dusseldorf, 1959).

'Entwicklung und gestalt der heiligenverehrung zwischen Rhein und Elbe im Mittelalter', in *Ostwestfälischweserländische Forschungen zur geschichtlichen Landeskunde* (Münster, 1970), pp. 280–303 (Veröffentlichen des Provinzialinstituts fur Westfäl. Landes- und Volkskunde, I, 15).

Zerbi, P., *Papato, impero e 'Respublica christiana' dal 1187 al 1198* (Milan, 1955).

Ziegler, J. C., *Die Ehelehre der Pönitentialsummen von 1200–1300: eine Untersuchung zur Geschichte der Moral- und Pastoraltheologie* (Ratisbon, 1956).

BIBLIOGRAPHICAL UPDATE

*જ્ઞ*જ્ઞ*જ્ઞ*

Only books, conference proceedings and editions are included; articles in periodicals are omitted except where they have helped to renew the problematic of the subject.

Bekker-Nielson, H., ed., *Hagiography and Medieval Literature* (Odense, 1981).

Bell, R., *Holy anorexia* (Chicago, 1985).

Boesch-Gajano, S. and Sebastiani, L., eds., *Culto dei santi, istituzioni e classi sociali in età preindustriale* (L'Aquila, 1984).

Boureau, A., *La Légende Dorée: le système narratif de Jacques de Voragine (d. 1298)* (Paris, 1984).

Bronzini, G. B., 'Ex voto e cultura religiosa. Problemi d'interpretazione', *Rivista di storia e letteratura religiosa*, 15 (1979), pp. 3–27.

Brown, P., *Le culte des saints, son essor et san fonction dans la chrétienté latine* (Paris, 1984).

Cazelles, B., *Le corps de sainteté d'après Jehan Bouche d'Or, Jehan Paulus et quelques Vies des XIIe et XIIIe siècles* (Geneva, 1982).

Cerulli, E. and Morghen, R., eds., *Agriografia nell'Occidente cristiano, secoli XIII–XV* (Rome, 1981).

Christian, W. A., *Apparitions in late medieval and Renaissance Spain* (Princeton, 1981).

Corbet, P., *Les saints ottoniens* (Sigmaringen, 1986).

Dalarun, J., *L'impossible sainteté: la vie retrouvée de Robert d'Arbrissel (v.1045–1116), fondateur de Fontevraud* (Paris, 1985).

Dinzelbacher, P., *Vision und Visionliteratur im Mittelalter* (Stuttgart, 1981).

Dinzelbacher, P. and Bauer, D. R., *Frauenmystik im Mittelalter* (Ostfildern, 1985).

Dunn-Lardeau, B., ed., *Legenda aurea: sept siècles de diffusion* (Montreal and Paris, 1986).

Erba, A., 'Agiografia tardomedievale. A proposito di un'opera recente', *Rivista di storia e letteratura religiosa*, 21 (1985), pp. 430–55.

Farmer, H., *Saint Hugh of Lincoln* (London, 1985).

Folz, R., *Les saints rois du Moyen Age* (Brussels, 1984).

Gélis, J., 'De la mort à la vie: les sanctuaires à répit', *Ethnologie française*, 2 (1981), pp. 211–24.

619

Gélis, J. and Redon, O., eds., *Les miracles miroirs des corps* (Paris, 1983).

Golinelli, P., *Culti dei santi e vita cittadina a Reggio Emilia (sec. IX–XII)* (Modena, 1980).

Goodich, M., *Vita Perfecta: the ideal of sainthood in the thirteenth century* (Stuttgart, 1982).

Grégoire, R., *Manuale di agiologia: introduzione alla letteratura agiografica* (Fabriano, 1987).

Hackel, S., ed., *The Byzantine saint* (London, 1981).

Heinzelmann, M., *Translationsberichte und andere Quellen des Reliquienkultes* (Turnhout, 1979).

Jacopo da Varagine. Atti del Iº convegno di studi (Varazze, 1985) (Varrazze, 1987).

Jones, C. W., *St Nicholas of Myra, Bari and Manhattan* (Chicago, 1987).

Kieckhefer, R., *Unquiet souls: fourteenth century saints and their religious milieu* (Chicago, 1984).

Leonardi, C., 'Committenze agiografiche nel Trecento', in *Patronage and public in the Trecento*, ed. V. Moleta (Florence, 1986), pp. 37–58.

Manselli, R., *S. Francesco d'Assisi* (Rome, 1980).

Orselli, A. M., *La città altomedievale e il suo santo patrono: (ancora una volta) il 'campione pavese'* (Rome, 1979).

Passarelli, G., ed., *Il santo patrono nella città medievale: il culto di S. Valentino nella storia di Terni* (Rome, 1982).

Patlagean, E. and Riché, P., eds., *Hagiographie, cultures et sociétés, IVe–XIIe siècles* (Paris, 1981).

Philippart, G., *Les légendiers latins et autres manuscrits hagiographiques* (Turnhout, 1977).

Le peuple des saints: croyances et dévotions en Provence et Comtat Venaissin, des origines à la fin du Moyen Age (Actes du colloque d'Avignon, 1984), in *Mémoires de l'Académie de Vaucluse*, VI (1985).

Picasso, G., ed., *Una santa tutta Romana: saggi e ricerche nel VIo centenario di Francesca Bussi dei Ponziani (1384–1984)* (Monte Oliveto Maggiore, 1984).

Rezeau, *Les prières aux saints en français à la fin du Moyen Age*, 2 vols. (Geneva, 1982–3).

Rusconi, R., ed., *Il movimento religiosos femminile in Umbria nei secoli XIII–XIV* (Florence, 1984).

Schmitt, J.C., ed., *Les saints et les stars: le texte hagiographique dans la culture populaire* (Paris, 1983).

'La fabrique des saints', *Annales ESC*, 39 (1974), pp. 286–300.

Sigal, P. A., *L'homme et le miracle dans la France médiévale (XIe–XIIe siècle)* (Paris, 1985).

Sorelli, F., *La santità immitabile: 'Leggenda di Maria da Venezia' di Tommaso da Siena* (Venice, 1984).

Sumption, J., *Pilgrimage: an image of medieval religion* (London, 1975).

Temi e problemi nelle mistica femminile trecentesca (Todi, 1979) (Convegno del centro di studi sulla spiritualità medievale, XX) (Todi, 1983).

Thier, L. and Calufetti, A., *Il Libro della Beata Angela di Foligno. Edizione critica* (Grottaferrata, 1985).

Vauchez, A., *Religion et société dans l'Occident médiéval* (Turin, 1981).

sv Santità, in *Enciclopedia Einaudi*, XII (Turin, 1981), pp. 441–53.

Les laïcs au Moyen Age: pratiques et expériences religieuses (Paris, 1987), ed. Daniel Bornstein, trans. Margery Scheider, *The laity in the Middle Ages: religious beliefs and devotional practices* (Notre Dame and London, 1993).

'Il santo', in *L'uomo medievale*, ed. J. Le Goff (Rome and Bari, 1987), pp. 353–90.

Ward, B., *Miracles and the medieval mind: theory, record and event, 1100–1215* (Philadelphia, 1982).

Weinstein, D. and Bell, R., *Saints and society, 1000–1700* (Chicago, 1982).

Wilson, S., *Saints and their cults: studies in religious sociology, folklore and history* (Cambridge, 1983).

Zarri, G., 'Le sante vive. Per una tipologia della santità femminile nel primo Cinquecento', *Annali dell'istituto italogermanico in Trento*, 6 (1980), pp. 371–445.

INDEX OF PLACES

Molesme, abbey of, 53, 69, 324, 560
Monforte, 151
Montecorvino, 29
Montefalco, 66, 528, 563
Monte Fano, 92, 127
Monte Oliveto, 127
Montepulciano, 133
Montesanto, 198
Montesiepi, 35, 455, 560
Montpellier, 120, 321, 354, 404, 419
Monza, 243
Moravia, 262
Morlaix, 367
Morocco, 76, 115, 391, 417
Munich, 150

Nantes, 366–7
Naples, 5, 44, 54, 79, 131, 180–1, 195, 214, 232, 236, 262, 345, 346, 402–3, 452, 563, 564
Narbonne, 227
Narni, 189
Nevers, 63
Nice, 227
Nidarholm, 43
Nidaros, 30, 43, 70
Nîmes, 227
Nocera, 430–1
Normandy, 40, 161, 312, 456, 471, 484
Norway, 30, 43, 164–5, 171, 257
Norwich, 155
Noto, 195
Notre-Dame, church of, Paris, 294
Novara, 147
Nuremberg, 65, 66, 83, 176, 264

Oberwesel, 150, 414
Olomouc, 440
Orléans, 17, 63, 293, 300, 312, 399–400, 562
Ortona, 409
Orvieto, 41, 43, 47, 68, 69, 71, 98, 117, 133, 147, 149, 210, 213–14, 219, 372, 414, 469, 561
Osimo, 66, 71, 72, 450
Osma, 339
Oxford, 399–400

Padua, 41, 71, 72, 85, 117, 129–30, 198, 233–5, 433
Palermo, 214
Pamiers, 465
Paris, 80, 308, 312, 346, 362, 381, 399–401, 407
Parma, 86, 130, 235, 428
Passau, 30

Pavia, 189
Pavilly, 471
Penthièvre, 80
Périgueux, 95, 118, 231
Péronne, 160
Persia, 417
Perugia, 71, 72, 130, 189, 198, 318, 411
Pesaro, 92, 208, 241
Piacenza, 201, 243, 317
Piedmont, 3
Pignerol, 416
Pisa, 56, 87, 97, 199–200, 214, 451
Pistoia, 199
Po, plain of, 130, 137, 183, 235
Poggibonsi, 202
Poitiers, 92, 432
Poitou, 149, 472
Poland, 46, 69–70, 73, 167, 257, 259, 270, 278, 415, 564
Polizzi, 93, 214, 432
Pontefract, 147, 149
Pontigny, abbey of, 42, 44, 124, 125, 561
Poppi, 194
Porto, 42
Portugal, 134, 270–1
Prague, 27, 465
Priverno, 431
Provence, 67, 80, 90, 119, 183, 197, 207–8, 211, 216, 218, 226–8, 244, 264–5, 270–1, 321, 361, 378, 380, 418–19, 439, 453, 462, 528
Prussia, 62, 266, 377–8, 465, 564
Puimichel, 362

Quarona, 148

Ratisbon, 316
Ravenna, 89–90
Recanati, 93
Reggio Emilia, 86, 130, 235
Reims, 469
Rennes, 311–12, 366
Rhineland, 73, 92, 134, 149–50, 155, 218, 262, 372, 560, 561
Rieti, 90, 191, 309
Riez, 227
Rimini, 196, 200, 432
Rocamadour, 131
Rocca d'Arce, 198
Rochester, 149, 326
Romagna, 85, 89, 112, 188, 332, 392, 450, 517
Rome, 2, 14, 18, 20, 22, 23, 34, 35, 36, 44, 45, 50, 70, 99, 150, 195, 197, 201, 250, 319–23, 363, 377, 380, 409, 411, 448-9, 511, 564

INDEX OF PERSONS

෴෴෴

B. is used here for uncanonized saints who were the object of a cult, without this implying that they were beatified in the canonical sense.
St is used for saints canonized by the Roman Church since the twelfth century or by the competent ecclesiastical authorities before this date.

SUBJECT INDEX

❧❧❧❧

This index aims to highlight only certain topics and terms as a complement to the contents page. Many frequently used terms are omitted.

incorruptibility, 234, 241, 431, 535
incubation, 445
innocence, baptismal, 346, 362–3, 516

Jews, 92, 94, 147, 150–1, 154–6, 294, 345, 393, 538
Jubilee, 99, 409, 511

legendries, 121, 133, 212, 249, 530
leprosy, lepers, 303, 311, 339, 345, 375, 377
letters remissory, 42, 50, 68
levitation, 211, 378, 441, 530
Libellus de dictis IV ancillarum, 500
liberal arts, 398
light, luminous phenomena, 435–8
liturgical calendar, 18, 109–10, 122, 168, 316–17

madness, 468–72, 492, 494
marriage, 203–4, 211, 355, 361–2, 365–6, 369, 371, 372, 381–5, 508, 510, 518, 537
measuring ritual, 456, 490
mortification, 191–3, 197, 331, 333, 340, 388, 516
mystics, mysticism, 100, 211–12, 218, 269, 271, 282, 307, 334, 353, 362, 378, 380, 385, 387, 404, 407–12, 420–1, 438, 507, 524, 530, 533

noli me tangere (illness), 470

Observance
Dominican, 209, 211, 385, 407, 409, 420
Franciscan, 409
odour of sanctity, 34, 124, 224, 427–8, 432, 513, 529
office
divine, 342, 344, 510
liturgical, 49, 124, 143, 149, 362, 400, 533
personal (of a saint), 95, 97–8, 240, 242, 334, 357, 515
Ordo canonisationis sanctorum, 66
Ordo Romanus XIV, 486

paralysis, paralytics, 445, 468, 470, 492–3, 495, 503
pastoral visits, 153, 298–300, 306, 311
patrozinienforschung, 135
perfection, evangelical, 120
persecution, 516
plenitudo potestatis, 27

postulator, 28, 35, 36, 41–2, 45, 46, 48, 50, 51, 64, 67, 74, 500, 505, 514, 515
poverty, the poor, 76, 113, 120, 138, 165, 175, 201, 217, 300, 302–4, 308–9, 313–14, 320–2, 339–40, 345, 349, 354, 358, 362, 367, 373–6, 377, 389–90, 394–6, 407, 410, 502, 506, 533
procurators, 41, 44, 46, 49, 65, 76, 270
prophecy, prophetism, 34, 112, 211, 269, 328, 376, 381, 384, 407, 411–12, 420, 474, 502, 507, 523–4, 526
psychomachy, 524

raptus, 441
rays (round the head), 87, 98
recollectio, 482, 488, 495, 504, 505
Reform, Gregorian, 22, 290, 316
Regula pastoralis, 296
relatio, 55, 482, 512
relics, discovery of, 16, 19
reliquary, 91, 125, 234, 240, 242, 431
respite (miracle), 473
resurrections, 467–8, 471, 492, 495
rubrics, 482, 487, 489, 492–3
Rule
of St Augustine, 255, 324, 350
of St Benedict, 112, 516
of St Francis, 76, 338
of St Dominic, 342, 344–5, 465

St James, militia or order of, 356, 371
shipwreck, 135, 492
spirituals, 76, 79, 90, 207, 211, 227, 308–9, 395, 402, 407, 428, 517
stigmata, stigmatization, 73, 116, 122, 214, 337, 420, 439–43, 525
suffering leaders, 162, 166, 167
summarium, 55, 488–96, 505, 508, 512, 523

tears, 191, 296, 352, 364, 373, 438–9, 465, 510, 529
Third Order, 118–21, 194, 196, 205–9, 241, 311, 372, 375–6
toothache, 467
translation, 19–21, 24, 26–30, 32, 69, 91, 94, 125, 148, 166, 220, 222, 224, 227, 233, 234, 240, 299, 323, 369, 414, 428, 432
Tree of Jesse, 179

virgins, virginity, 96, 211, 296, 356, 359, 381–2, 384, 518, 525, 532
virtue, *virtus*, 36, 40, 48–9, 97, 163, 425, 427, 430, 433–4, 444, 448, 464, 467,